15 EDITION

Essentials of Marketing

A Marketing Strategy Planning Approach

William D. Perreault, Jr., Ph.D.
UNIVERSITY OF NORTH CAROLINA

Joseph P. Cannon, Ph.D.
COLORADO STATE UNIVERSITY

E. Jerome McCarthy, Ph.D.
MICHIGAN STATE UNIVERSITY

D1319377

Mc
Graw
Hill
Education

ESSENTIALS OF MARKETING: A MARKETING STRATEGY PLANNING APPROACH, FIFTEENTH EDITION

Published by McGraw-Hill Education, 2 Penn Plaza, New York, NY 10121. Copyright © 2017 by McGraw-Hill Education. All rights reserved. Printed in China. Previous edition © 2015, 2013, 2011 and 2009. No part of this publication may be reproduced or distributed in any form or by any means, or stored in a database or retrieval system, without the prior written consent of McGraw-Hill Education, including, but not limited to, in any network or other electronic storage or transmission, or broadcast for distance learning.

Some ancillaries, including electronic and print components, may not be available to customers outside the United States.

This book is printed on acid-free paper.

1 2 3 4 5 6 7 8 9 0 CTP/CTP 1 0 9 8 7 6

ISBN 978-1-259-92129-2
MHID 1-259-92129-8

mheducation.com/highered

Authors of Essentials of Marketing, 15/e

William D. Perreault, Jr.

William D. Perreault, Jr., is Kenan Professor of Business at the University of North Carolina. Dr. Perreault is the recipient of the two most prestigious awards in his field: the American Marketing Association Distinguished Educator Award and the Academy of Marketing Science Outstanding Educator Award. He also was selected for the Churchill Award, which honors career impact on marketing research. He was editor of the *Journal of Marketing Research* and has been on the review board of the *Journal of Marketing* and other journals.

The Decision Sciences Institute has recognized Dr. Perreault for innovations in marketing education, and at UNC he has received several awards for teaching excellence. His books include two other widely used texts: *Basic Marketing* and *The Marketing Game!*

Dr. Perreault is a past president of the American Marketing Association Academic Council and served as chair of an advisory committee to the U.S. Census Bureau and as a trustee of the Marketing Science Institute. He has also worked as a consultant to organizations that range from GE and IBM to the Federal Trade Commission and Venezuelan Ministry of Education.

Joseph P. Cannon

Joseph P. Cannon is professor of marketing at Colorado State University. He has also taught at the University of North Carolina at Chapel Hill, Emory University, Instituto de Empresa (Madrid, Spain), INSEAD (Fontainebleau, France), and Thammasat University (Bangkok, Thailand). He has received several teaching awards and the N. Preston Davis Award for Instructional Innovation.

Dr. Cannon's research has been published in the *Journal of Marketing, Journal of Marketing Research, Journal of the Academy of Marketing Science, Journal of Operations Management, Journal of Personal Selling and Sales Management, Journal of Public Policy and Marketing, Antitrust Bulletin,* and the *Academy of Management Review* among others. He is a two-time recipient of the Louis W. and Rhona L. Stern Award for high-impact research on interorganizational issues. He has also written many teaching cases. Dr. Cannon has served on the editorial review boards of the *Journal of Marketing, Journal of the Academy of Marketing Science, Journal of Personal Selling and Sales Management,* and *Journal of Marketing Education.* The *Journal of Marketing Education* has honored Dr. Cannon with several distinguished reviewer awards. He served as chair of the American Marketing Association's Interorganizational Special Interest Group (IOSIG). Before entering academics, Dr. Cannon worked in sales and marketing for Eastman Kodak Company.

E. Jerome McCarthy

E. Jerome McCarthy received his Ph.D. from the University of Minnesota and was a Ford Foundation Fellow at the Harvard Business School. He has taught at the Universities of Oregon, Notre Dame, and Michigan State. He was honored with the American Marketing Association's Trailblazer Award in 1987, and he was voted one of the "top five" leaders in marketing thought by marketing educators.

Besides publishing various articles, he is the author of books on data processing and social issues in marketing. He has been a frequent presenter at marketing conferences in the United States and internationally.

In addition to his academic interests, Dr. McCarthy has been involved in guiding the growth of organizations in the United States and overseas—both as a consultant and as a director. He has also been active in executive education. Throughout his career, his primary interests have been in (1) "converting" students to marketing and effective marketing strategy planning and (2) preparing teaching materials to help others do the same. This is why he has spent a large part of his career developing and improving marketing texts to reflect the most current thinking in the field.

Preface

Essentials of Marketing Is Designed to Satisfy Your Needs

This book is about marketing and marketing strategy planning. At its essence, marketing strategy planning is about figuring out how to do a superior job of satisfying customers. We take that point of view seriously and believe in practicing what we preach. So you can trust that this new edition of *Essentials of Marketing*—and all of the other teaching and learning materials that accompany it—will satisfy your needs. We're excited about this 15th edition of *Essentials of Marketing* and we hope that you will be as well.

In developing this edition, we've made hundreds of big and small additions, changes, and improvements in the text and all of the supporting materials that accompany it. We'll highlight some of those changes in this preface, but first some background on the evolution of *Essentials of Marketing*.

Building on Pioneering Strengths

Essentials of Marketing pioneered an innovative structure—using the "Four Ps" (Product, Price, Promotion, and Place) with a managerial approach—for the introductory marketing course. It quickly became one of the most widely used business textbooks ever published because it organized the best ideas about marketing so that readers could both understand and apply them. The unifying focus of these ideas is: how does a marketing manager decide which customers to target, and what is the best way to meet their needs?

Over many editions of *Essentials of Marketing,* there have been constant changes in marketing management and the market environment. As a result, we have made ongoing changes to the text to reflect marketing's best practices and ideas. Throughout all of these changes, *Essentials of Marketing* and the supporting materials that accompany it have been more widely used than any other teaching materials for introductory marketing. It is gratifying that the Four Ps framework has proved to be an organizing structure that has worked well for millions of students and teachers.

The success of *Essentials of Marketing* is not the result of a single strength—or one long-lasting innovation. Other textbooks have adopted our Four Ps framework, and we have continuously improved the book. And the text's Four Ps framework, managerial orientation, and strategy planning focus have proved to be foundation pillars that are remarkably robust for supporting new developments in the field and innovations in the text and package. Thus, with each new edition of *Essentials of Marketing* we have continued to innovate to better meet the needs of students and faculty. In fact, we have made ongoing changes in how we develop the logic of the Four Ps and the marketing strategy planning process. As always, though, our objective is to provide a flexible, high-quality text and choices from comprehensive and reliable support materials—so that instructors and students can accomplish their learning objectives.

What's Different about Essentials of Marketing?

The biggest distinguishing factor about *Essentials of Marketing* is our integrative approach to creating a teaching and learning package for the introductory marketing course. This integration makes it easier to learn about marketing, teach marketing, and apply it in the real world. For many students, the introductory marketing course will be the only marketing class they ever take. They need to come away with a strong understanding of the key concepts in marketing and how marketing operates in practice. So in *Essentials of Marketing:*

1. We examine *both* what marketing is and how to do it.
2. We integrate special topics such as services, international marketing, big data, social media, ethics, and more, across the text—with coverage in almost every chapter.
3. We deliver a supplements package completely developed or closely managed by the authors—so each part links closely with our content.

The supplements package is extensive—designed to allow you to *teach marketing your way* (see Exhibit P–1). The integration of these three elements delivers a proven product for instructors and students. Let us show you what we mean—and why and how instructors and students benefit from the *Essentials of Marketing* teaching and learning package.

Marketing operates in dynamic markets. Fast-changing global markets, environmental challenges and

Exhibit P-1
Essentials of Marketing Integrates Marketing

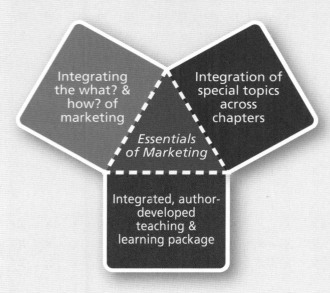

Integrating the what? & how? of marketing

Integration of special topics across chapters

Essentials of Marketing

Integrated, author-developed teaching & learning package

sustainability, and the blurring speed of technological advances—including an explosion in the use of digital tools by both consumers and businesses—are just a few of the current trends confronting today's marketing manager. Whereas some marketing texts merely attempt to describe this market environment, *Essentials of Marketing* teaches students *analytical abilities* and *how-to-do-it skills* that prepare them for success. To propel students in this direction, we deliberately include a variety of examples, explanations, frameworks, conceptual organizers, exercises, cases, and how-to-do-it techniques that relate to our overall framework for marketing strategy planning. Taken together, these different learning aids speed the development of "marketing sensibility" and enable students to analyze marketing situations and develop marketing plans in a confident and meaningful way. They are practical and they work. And because they are interesting and understandable, they motivate students to see marketing as the challenging and rewarding area it is. In the end, the *Essentials of Marketing* teaching and learning package prepares students to analyze marketing situations and develop exceptional marketing strategies—not just recite endless sets of lists.

In contrast to many other marketing textbooks, we emphasize careful *integration of special topics.* Some textbooks treat "special" topics—such as marketing relationships, international marketing, services marketing, the Internet, digital lifestyles, nonprofit organizations, marketing ethics, social issues, and business-to-business

marketing—in separate chapters (or parts of chapters). We deliberately avoid doing this because we are convinced that treating such topics separately leads to an unfortunate compartmentalization of ideas. For example, to simply tack on a new chapter covering e-commerce or Internet marketing applications completely ignores the reality that these are not isolated topics; rather, they must be considered broadly across the whole rubric of marketing decisions. Conversely, there is virtually no area of marketing decision making where it's safe to ignore the impact of e-commerce, the Internet, or information technology. The same is true with other topics.

Exhibit P–2 shows the coverage of some key topics across specific chapters.

The teaching and learning materials—designed and developed by the authors—are integrated to work effectively with *Essentials of Marketing.* We don't tack on extras that have been outsourced and therefore don't integrate well with our package. Because of this, you have flexible tools for *teaching and learning marketing your way.*

Marketing can be studied in many ways, and the *Essentials of Marketing* text material is only the central component of our *Professional Learning Units System* (*P.L.U.S.*) for students and for teachers. Instructors and students can select from our units to develop their own personalized teaching and learning systems. Our objective is to offer you a *P.L.U.S.* "menu" so that you can conveniently select units you want—and disregard what you do not want. Many combinations of units are possible depending on course and learning objectives. Later in this Preface, we highlight each *P.L.U.S.* element (full details can be found in the Instructor's Manual).

Students take the introductory marketing course only once. They deserve the benefits of a highly innovative yet *proven* set of integrated learning materials. Our teaching and learning materials—from the textbook to the iPod videos to the test question bank to the online materials—have been continually updated based on what has proven to work for generations of students.

What's New in This Edition of *Essentials of Marketing?*

Each revision of *Essentials of Marketing* has a few basic themes—areas we try to emphasize across the book. This edition could be boiled down to: 1) currency, 2) owned, earned, and social media, 3) marketing analytics, and 4) active learning. There are several big changes to this edition of *Essentials of Marketing* and hundreds of smaller ones. *Essentials of Marketing* is quick to recognize the many dramatic changes in the market environment and marketing strategy—we are also quick to jump on new pedagogical innovations. So here is a quick overview of what we changed for the 15th edition of *Essentials of Marketing.*

Exhibit P-2 Coverage of Special Topics Across Chapters*

Special Topic	Chapter																		
	1	2	3	4	5	6	7	8	9	10	11	12	13	14	15	16	17	18	19
Marketing relationships	X	X	X	X	X	X	X	X	X	X	X	X	X	X	X	X	X	X	X
International	X	X	X	X	X	X	X	X	X	X	X	X	X	X	X	X		X	X
Ethics	X	X	X	X	X	X	X	X	X	X	X	X	X	X	X	X	X	X	X
Services	X	X	X	X	X	X	X	X	X	X	X	X	X	X	X	X	X	X	X
B2B	X	X	X	X	X	X	X	X	X	X	X	X	X	X	X	X	X	X	X
Technology, Internet, "Big Data" & digital lifestyle	X	X	X	X	X	X	X	X	X	X	X	X	X	X	X	X	X	X	X
Environment & sustainability	X	X	X		X	X	X	X	X	X	X		X	X	X	X		X	X
Nonprofits	X	X	X	X		X	X	X			X		X		X	X		X	X
Quality	X	X	X	X	X	X	X	X	X		X		X	X	X	X	X	X	X
Customer value	X	X	X	X	X	X	X	X	X	X	X	X	X	X	X	X	X	X	X
Marketing's link with other functions	X	X	X	X	X	X	X	X	X	X	X	X	X	X	X	X	X	X	X

*"X" indicates coverage in the form of a section of the chapter, example, illustration, or discussion.

Currency. Every edition of *Essentials of Marketing* focuses on currency. Technology and consumer behavior are evolving in a fast-changing marketplace—and marketing practice is evolving as well. Instructors want current content and current examples. To prepare students to work in this new world, a textbook must be up-to-date and provide more than a passing nod to the future. In this edition:

- We add hundreds of new examples and images (ads and photos) that engage students.
- Our *What's Next?* boxes, embedded in each chapter, provide a forward-looking perspective.
- Our end-of-chapter *What's Now?* links connect students to content and examples that are updated every semester.
- We increase attention to marketing analytics chapter content and with end-of-chapter exercises ("Marketing Analytics: Data to Knowledge").
- And of course, we emphasize the fastest changing area of marketing—promotion; in particular, the use of different kinds of media, which leads to our second major update . . .

Owned, earned, and social media. These topics now get their own chapter. For the last decade, these media have been perhaps the hottest trend in marketing practice. Previous editions of *Essentials of Marketing* have carefully integrated these topics across the textbook. The prominence of these tools—and their nuance in the promotion blend—merits an entire chapter's coverage. With that comes a much greater focus on owned media (a company's own website, web pages, brochures, and blogs), earned media (press coverage and word-of-mouth), and social media (Facebook, Twitter, LinkedIn, and more). This new chapter (16) follows the *Essentials of Marketing* tradition by creating conceptual organizers that help students understand *why* and *how* these tools best fit in a contemporary promotion blend.

Marketing analytics. Our last edition of *Essentials of Marketing* significantly increased coverage of "big data." This edition builds on that with more "big data" examples and integration across chapters *and* increased attention to marketing analytics. Marketing strategy decisions are increasingly data-driven. Almost every chapter in this edition of *Essentials of Marketing* provides students with more exposure to analytics. In some chapters, it is with examples or topical coverage. Most chapters have added new end-of-chapter exercises (see "Marketing Analytics: Data to Knowledge"). These exercises are based on activities in previous editions; they're now integrated into the Connect model—making the exercises easier for instructors to assign and grade—and easier for students to complete. When students complete the exercises on Connect, they will be more prepared to discuss them in class.

Active learning exercises. Connect and Smartbook offer your students more opportunities to get grounded in the basic concepts of marketing. Many instructors count on these to prepare students for class and utilize more active learning activities inside or outside the classroom.

We have designed many new active learning exercises, so student can apply these concepts. This edition of *Essentials of Marketing* features:

- *What's Next?* Each chapter includes an active learning boxed element. These elements have all been updated to make them more forward-looking (as in, "what's next") and active learning focused. Each box offers an in-depth analysis of some trend or marketing future—and asks students about its implications.
- *Ethical Dilemma*—many of these exercises have been updated from previous editions, with a focus on students making decisions in gray areas, many introduced by the advancing technologies used in marketing.
- *Online Toolkit*—the Internet offers so many tools for today's marketing manager. Each chapter includes two "Online Toolkit" exercises, which expose students to something marketing-related online and provide discussion questions for class or homework assignment.
- *Questions and Problems*—in past editions, our chapter opening cases have primarily served to motivate a chapter's subject matter. In this edition, we have added two new end-of-chapter "Questions and Problems" (always questions 1 and 2) designed to have students reflect on the opening case studies. Students experience higher-order learning when they have to recognize concepts in a case study—so we ask them to do that in question 1. Question 2 turns the chapter opener into a discussion case. Both questions can be used for in-class discussion or homework assignments for instructors looking for higher-order learning objectives for their students.
- *Marketing Analytics*: *Data to Knowledge:* This end-of-chapter exercise—which can be done through Connect—shows students how data analysis is used by marketing managers. Using concepts and examples from each chapter, the exercises will build higher-order learning skills and demonstrate data-driven marketing decision making. Each practical question walks students through a real-life scenario, shows them how to use a spreadsheet for answers, and then asks (optional) discussion questions to build critical thinking skills.
- *Cases*—all of our cases have been updated—including some completely new ones.

Chapter-by-chapter. Besides the general updates mentioned here, let's walk through the chapter-by-chapter changes you will see in this edition of *Essentials of Marketing*. We updated each and every chapter opening case scenario. There are dozens of new examples and specific concepts spread throughout the book. Although we don't have space to list all of these changes, we can provide you with some highlights of the more significant changes with this edition of *Essentials of Marketing*:

Chapter 1. Refreshed with new and updated examples.

Chapter 2. An updated opener and refreshed examples throughout the chapter. Introduced the sample marketing plan (Appendix D). Updated and clarified coverage of *customer lifetime value* and *customer equity* in the text and in the new Online Toolkit exercise.

Chapter 3. This has traditionally been one of the longest chapters in the book—so we made an effort to streamline coverage of all topics. Enhanced discussion of the *mission statement,* major revision of competition—including the addition of an exhibit with a competitor matrix (Exhibit 3–3). Coverage of NAFTA has been cut back with a broader discussion of free trade in general and a new key term *free trade*. The technological environment was once again updated to reflect fast-moving changes here. There is also a new extended example on organic foods.

Chapter 4. The opener was updated to reflect continued success of LEGO and its growing emphasis on the girls' market. Introduced and provided some details on the idea of a *buyer persona*. Updated the *What's Next?* box on Target stores. A new section discusses location-based targeting through mobile phones.

Chapter 5. Updated the chapter opening case scenario on Apple to reflect its newest product (Apple Watch). Hierarchy of needs and selective processes were updated and clarified—and we explore whether customers learn needs from marketing. A new *What's Next?* box examines the sharing economy with a focus on automobiles and homes. Drawing on recent research we updated and revised the section on social media and social influence. New key term *purchase situation*.

Chapter 6. Updated throughout—mostly with new examples. Several changes reflect growing use of online search and social media in organizational buying. Reflecting reviewer feedback, we increased coverage of manufacturers in text and dropped a table with information on manufacturer size.

Chapter 7. Marketing research is heavily influenced by the technology revolution, so we included new material on how innovations in information technology refine the marketing research process. A new *What's Next?* box, "Big data predicts pop music hits," is informative and will be enjoyed by students. Major changes in our section on how to search the web. The sections on surveying, quantitative research, qualitative research, and Exhibit 7–6 were all updated—and a new Online Toolkit exercise was added.

Chapter 8. This chapter was updated throughout for currency. We reorganized the chapter a bit and added more coverage of "experiences" as a component of product. The battle of the brands is always evolving and our updated coverage reflects the latest. Updated coverage on service guarantees.

Chapter 9. Updated for currency. Added new section on patent law with new key term *patent*.

Chapter 10. Updated this chapter for currency. We added a new *What's Next?* box that examines distribution of virtual products (music, TV, movies, books). Clarified our coverage of direct versus indirect distribution and channel relationships.

Chapter 11. We revised our discussion of the trade-offs among physical distribution costs, customer service level, and sales with a longer, but clearer treatment. New examples throughout—including a discussion of drones as a form of distribution transportation.

Chapter 12. We always have a lot of revisions in our coverage of retailing—and this edition is no different. To remain current here, almost every edition requires significant rewriting of retailing and the Internet. We added the key terms *omnichannel* and *multichannel shoppers*. A new *What's Next?* box examines how leading retailers are using technology. We also added a new Online Toolkit exercise.

Chapter 13. This chapter always has a lot of new examples—students notice dated examples and we aim to eliminate them. We added a fun new Online Toolkit on the *AdFreak* blog. The chapter was made a bit shorter as some content was moved (more detail on opinion leaders and owned media) to the new chapter (Chapter 16).

Chapter 14. Updated for currency. New section on specializing salespeople by product lines.

Chapter 15. Reflecting evolutionary changes in advertising, this chapter always has major changes with each edition. This revision includes new Learning Objectives and a completely revised treatment of digital advertising that emphasizes advertising on mobile devices (which appears to finally be breaking through). Statistics have been updated throughout our Exhibits. We added new key terms including *advertising media, pay-per-click,* and *retargeting* that reflect the need to understand digital advertising. We also updated the "Advertising Everywhere" box (now called, *What's Next? Does advertising everywhere get us anywhere?*) and added a new Online Toolkit. We cover the controversial topic of native advertising—and add an Ethical Dilemma box to give your students a way to critically think about this. Chapter 15 is much shorter as we removed the "publicity" section— the topic is now covered (in a completely different and more thorough manner) in Chapter 16.

Chapter 16. This is an **entirely new** chapter. With the big changes going on in owned, earned, and social media, we found that most of what we had in other Promotion chapters was now dated. We needed to start almost from scratch. We maintain some of the organizing structure we had in previous editions around paid, owned, and earned media; but this chapter provides us the opportunity to delve more deeply into this important part of the promotion blend. Everything is new here—we expect you'll enjoy the whole chapter.

Chapter 17. The chapter opener was updated and revised—and we added a new learning objective. Our *What's Next?* box addresses a fascinating topic—the value of some very expensive medical treatments, which raises thought-provoking questions of values and ethics.

Chapter 18. Updated for currency. Revised learning objectives bring more coherence to the coverage.

Chapter 19. Updated for currency throughout—including the chapter-opening scenario on ethical marketing and the *What's Next?* box on big data.

Bonus Chapters. Now available to all adopters of *Essentials of Marketing 15e* are two chapters that previously resided only in our hard cover book *Basic Marketing*. These are now available through Connect and SmartBook and can be bound in a printed version of the text through McGraw-Hill's Create custom publishing. We are calling them "Bonus Chapters" because they are something extra and optional for instructors seeking this extended coverage. You will be able to access these optional chapters online within the Connect/SmartBook platform. Once you're logged into Connect, access your SmartBook and click on the Bonus Chapters Tab to access these additional chapters.

Bonus Chapter 1: Implementing and Controlling Marketing Plans: Evolution and Revolution. Previously Chapter 18 in *Basic Marketing 19e*, this chapter builds on implementation and control, two concepts introduced in Chapter 2. This chapter goes into more depth on these concepts and offers how-to approaches for making implementation and control more effective. The chapter discusses how new information technology tools facilitate these practices and demonstrates how firms use sales analysis, performance analysis, and cost analysis to control marketing strategies and plans.

Bonus Chapter 2: Managing Marketing's Link with Other Functional Areas. Previously Chapter 19 in *Basic Marketing 19e*, this revised chapter covers some of the important ways that marketing links to other functional areas. The emphasis is not on the technical details of these other functional areas, but rather on the most important ways that cross-functional links impact your ability to develop marketing strategies and plans that really work. The chapter includes separate sections that describe how finance, production and operations, accounting, information systems and human resources interact with marketing to create and implement successful marketing plans.

Nineteen Chapters—with an Emphasis on Marketing Strategy Planning

The emphasis of *Essentials of Marketing* is on marketing strategy planning. Nineteen chapters introduce the important concepts of marketing and help students see marketing through the eyes of the manager. The organization of the chapters and topics is carefully planned. We took special care in writing so that:

- It is possible to rearrange and use the chapters in many different sequences—to fit different needs.

Exhibit P-3 *Essentials of Marketing* and the Marketing Strategy Planning Process

Chapters 1, 2, & 7

Chapters 5 & 6

Chapters 8 & 9

Chapters 10, 11, & 12

Context: External Market Environment

Customers

Segmentation and Targeting

S. W. O. T.

Company

Differentiation and Positioning

Competitors

PRODUCT   PLACE

TARGET

PRICE   PROMOTION

Chapter 19

Chapters 13, 14, 15 & 16

Chapters 17 & 18

Chapter 4

Chapter 3

- All of the topics and chapters fit together into a clear, overall framework for the marketing strategy planning process.

Broadly speaking, the chapters fall into three groupings. The first seven chapters introduce marketing and a broad view of the marketing strategy planning process. We introduce the marketing strategy planning process in Chapter 2 and use this framework as a structure for our coverage of marketing. See Exhibit P–3. Chapters 3–7 cover topics such as the market environment, competition, segmentation, differentiation, and buyer behavior, as well as how marketing information systems and research provide information about these forces to improve marketing decisions. The second part of the text (Chapters 8–18) goes into the details of planning the Four Ps, with specific attention to the key strategy decisions in each area. Finally, we conclude with an integrative review (Chapter 19) and a critical assessment of marketing's challenges and opportunities.

The first chapter deals with the important role of marketing—focusing not only on how a marketing orientation guides a business or nonprofit organization in the process of providing superior value to customers but also on the role of macro-marketing and how a market-directed economy shapes choices and quality of life for consumers. Chapter 2 builds on these ideas with a focus on the marketing strategy planning process and why it involves narrowing down to the selection of a specific target market and blending the Four Ps into a marketing mix to meet the needs of those customers. With that foundation in place, Chapter 2 introduces an integrative model of the marketing strategy planning process that serves as an organizing framework for the rest of the text.

Chapter 3 introduces students to the importance of evaluating opportunities in the external environments affecting marketing. This chapter also highlights the critical role of screening criteria for narrowing down from all possible opportunities to those that the firm will pursue. Then, Chapter 4 shows how analysis of the market relates to segmentation and differentiation decisions, as well as the criteria for narrowing down to a specific target market and marketing mix.

You have to understand customers in order to segment markets and satisfy target market needs. So the next two chapters take a closer look at *customers*. Chapter 5 studies the behavioral aspects of the final consumer market. Chapter 6 looks at how business and organizational customers—such as manufacturers, channel members, and government purchasers—are similar to and different from final consumers.

Chapter 7 presents a contemporary view of getting information—from marketing information systems and marketing research—for marketing planning. Chapter 7 includes discussion of how information technology—ranging from intranets to speedy collection of market research data—is transforming the marketing job. This sets the stage for discussions in later chapters about how research and marketing information improve each area of marketing strategy planning.

The next group of chapters—Chapters 8 through 18—is concerned with developing a marketing mix out of the Four Ps: Product, Place (involving channels of distribution, logistics, and distribution customer service), Promotion, and Price. These chapters are concerned with developing the "right" Product and making it available at the "right" Place with the "right" Promotion at the "right" Price to satisfy target customers and still meet the objectives of the business. These chapters are presented in an integrated, analytical way—as part of the overall framework for the marketing strategy planning process—so students' thinking about planning marketing strategies develops logically.

Chapters 8 and 9 focus on product planning for goods and services as well as managing product quality, new-product development, and the different strategy decisions that are required at different stages of the product life cycle. We emphasize the value of an organized new-product development process for developing truly new products that propel a firm to profitable growth. These chapters also detail how quality management approaches can improve implementation, including implementation of better service quality.

Chapters 10 through 12 focus on Place. Chapter 10 introduces decisions a manager must make about using direct distribution (for example, selling from the firm's own website) or working with other firms in a channel of distribution. We put special emphasis on the need for channel members to cooperate and coordinate to better meet the needs of customers. Chapter 11 focuses on the fast-changing arena of logistics and the strides that firms are making in using e-commerce to reduce the costs of storing, transporting, and handling products while improving the distribution service they provide customers. Chapter 12 provides a clear picture of retailers, wholesalers, and their strategy planning, including exchanges taking place via the Internet. This composite chapter helps students see why the big changes taking place in retailing are reshaping the channel systems for many consumer products.

Chapters 13 through 16 deal with Promotion. These chapters build on the concepts of integrated marketing communications, direct-response promotion, and customer-initiated digital communication, which are introduced in Chapter 13. Chapter 14 deals with the roles of personal selling, customer service, and sales technology in the promotion blend. Chapter 15 covers advertising and sales promotion, including the ways that managers are taking advantage of the Internet and other highly targeted media to communicate more effectively and efficiently. Chapter 16 is the newest chapter in the book and addresses publicity, broadly defined to include owned, earned, and social media.

Chapters 17 and 18 deal with Price. Chapter 17 focuses on pricing objectives and policies, including use of information technology to implement flexible pricing; pricing in the channel; and the use of discounts, allowances, and other variations from a list price. Chapter 18 covers cost-oriented and demand-oriented pricing approaches and how they fit in today's competitive environments. The careful coverage of marketing costs helps equip students to deal with the renewed cost-consciousness of the firms they will join.

The final chapter (19) considers how efficient the marketing process is. Here we evaluate the effectiveness of both micro- and macro-marketing—and we consider the competitive, technological, ethical, and social challenges facing marketing managers now and in the future. Chapter 19 also reinforces the integrative nature of marketing management and reviews the marketing strategy planning process that leads to creative marketing plans.

Four appendices can be used to supplement the main text material. Appendix A provides some traditional economic analysis of supply and demand that can be a useful tool in analyzing markets. Appendix B reviews some quantitative tools—or marketing arithmetic—which help marketing managers who want to use accounting data in analyzing marketing problems. Appendix B also reviews forecasting as a way to predict market potential and sales for a company's product. Students especially appreciate Appendix C—which is about career opportunities in marketing. Appendix D provides an example of a marketing plan for Hillside Veterinary Clinic. This example is referenced in Chapter 2 and with end-of-chapter exercises.

Following Appendix D are 46 written cases. The first eight of these cases are available to instructors in video format in the instructor resources in Connect. Most of the the next 38 short written cases have been updated with new information to make sure they reflect the realities of the current marketplace. Three of those cases are completely new to this edition. The focus of these cases is on problem solving. They encourage students to apply, and really get involved with, the concepts developed in the text. At the end of each chapter, we recommend particular cases that best relate to that chapter's content.

Two bonus chapters are available online and through custom printing. Bonus Chapter 1 "Implementing and Controlling Marketing Plans: Evolution and Revolution" was previously Chapter 18 in *Basic Marketing 19e*. This chapter provides a deeper dive on the concepts of implementation and control introduced in Chapter 2.

Bonus Chapter 2: "Managing Marketing's Link with Other Functional Areas" was previously Chapter 19 in *Basic Marketing 19e*. This chapter covers some of the important ways that marketing interacts with and relies on other functional areas: finance, production and operations, accounting, information systems and human resources.

Expanded Teaching and Learning Resources for the Fifteenth Edition

The authors of *Essentials of Marketing* and McGraw-Hill Higher Education have put together a variety of resources to supplement your teaching and learning experience.

Instructors will find the following resources posted in the Connect Library Instructor Resources for the Fifteenth Edition.

- *Connect Interactive Applications*—An online assignment and assessment solution that connects students with the tools and resources they'll need to achieve success. This is also where you will find our NEW Marketing Analytics: Data to Knowledge exercises and NEW iSeeIt! videos to engage student understanding of 17 key marketing concepts.
- *SmartBook*—Powered by LearnSmart, SmartBook is the adaptive reading experience that helps students learn faster, study more efficiently, and retain more knowledge.
- *Instructor's Manual and Digital Implementation Guide*—offers a single resource to make it easier for you to decide which resources to use when covering each chapter in the text.
- *Power Point Presentation Resources*—
  - *Chapter PowerPoint Slides.* For each chapter there is a set of PowerPoint presentations for a complete lecture that includes television commercials and short video clip examples, examples of print advertisements that demonstrate important concepts, and questions to use with "clickers" or simply to check if students are getting it.
  - *YouTube PowerPoint slides.* We have embedded YouTube videos into a collection with more than 80 slides, which bring virtual guest speakers, viral videos, case studies, and new ads to your classroom presentations.
  - *Multimedia Lecture Support Guide and Video Guide.* Now integrated into the Instructor's Manual and Digital Implementation Guide, you will find detailed lecture scripts and chapter outlines

for the presentation slides that make getting prepared for class fast and easy.
- *Author Blog*: Connect with the redesigned *Teach the 4 Ps* blog www.teachthe4ps.com for links to articles, blog posts, videos, video clips, and commercials—with tips on how to use them with *Essentials of Marketing*. The site is organized by topic—so you can easily find something for what you are teaching that day—and provides plenty of tips for bringing *active learning* to your classroom.
- *Practice Marketing Simulation*—An online and fully mobile interactive learning environment that simulates the full marketing mix as well as market segmentation and targeting. www.mhpractice.com.
- *Teaching Videos*—The video package includes 31 full-length videos and video cases that can be shown in class or assigned to students to view outside of class.
- *Test Bank*—Our test bank includes more than 5,000 objective test questions—every question developed or edited by the authors to ensure it works seamlessly with the text. McGraw-Hill's EZ-Test program facilitates the creation of tests.

Responsibilities of Leadership

In closing, we return to a point raised at the beginning of this preface. *Essentials of Marketing* has been a leading textbook in marketing since its first edition. We take the responsibilities of that leadership seriously. We know that you want and deserve the very best teaching and learning materials possible. It is our commitment to bring you those materials today with this edition and in future editions.

We recognize that fulfilling this commitment requires a process of continuous improvement. Because needs change, revisions, updates, and development of new elements must be ongoing. You are an important part of this evolution and of this leadership. We encourage your feedback. The most efficient way to get in touch with us is to send an e-mail message to Joe.Cannon@ColoState.edu. If you prefer the traditional approach, send a letter to Joe Cannon at Colorado State University, College of Business, Fort Collins, CO 80528-1278, United States of America. Thoughtful criticisms and suggestions from students and teachers alike have helped to make *Essentials of Marketing* what it is. We hope that you will help make it what it will be in the future.

William D. Perreault, Jr., Joseph P. Cannon, and E. Jerome McCarthy

Required=Results

McGraw-Hill Connect®
Learn Without Limits

Connect is a teaching and learning platform that is proven to deliver better results for students and instructors.

Connect empowers students by continually adapting to deliver precisely what they need, when they need it, and how they need it, so your class time is more engaging and effective.

Course outcomes improve with Connect.

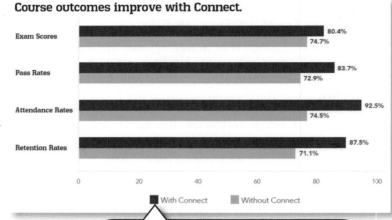

	With Connect	Without Connect
Exam Scores	80.4%	74.7%
Pass Rates	83.7%	72.9%
Attendance Rates	92.5%	74.5%
Retention Rates	87.5%	71.1%

88% of instructors who use **Connect** require it; instructor satisfaction **increases** by 38% when **Connect** is required.

> Using **Connect** improves passing rates by **10.8%** and retention by **16.4%**.

Analytics

Connect Insight®

Connect Insight is Connect's new one-of-a-kind visual analytics dashboard—now available for both instructors and students—that provides at-a-glance information regarding student performance, which is immediately actionable. By presenting assignment, assessment, and topical performance results together with a time metric that is easily visible for aggregate or individual results, Connect Insight gives the user the ability to take a just-in-time approach to teaching and learning, which was never before available. Connect Insight presents data that empowers students and helps instructors improve class performance in a way that is efficient and effective.

Connect helps students achieve better grades

	A	B	C	D	F
With Connect	36%	29.5%	22%	4.3%	8.2%
Without Connect	22.2%	22.3%	25.6%	9.8%	20%

Based on McGraw-Hill Education Connect Effectiveness Study 2013

> Students can view their results for any **Connect** course.

Mobile

Connect's new, intuitive mobile interface gives students and instructors flexible and convenient, anytime–anywhere access to all components of the Connect platform.

Adaptive

THE FIRST AND ONLY **ADAPTIVE READING EXPERIENCE** DESIGNED TO TRANSFORM THE WAY STUDENTS READ

More students earn **A's** and **B's** when they use McGraw-Hill Education **Adaptive** products.

SmartBook®

Proven to help students improve grades and study more efficiently, SmartBook contains the same content within the print book, but actively tailors that content to the needs of the individual. SmartBook's adaptive technology provides precise, personalized instruction on what the student should do next, guiding the student to master and remember key concepts, targeting gaps in knowledge and offering customized feedback, and driving the student toward comprehension and retention of the subject matter. Available on smartphones and tablets, SmartBook puts learning at the student's fingertips—anywhere, anytime.

Over **4 billion questions** have been answered, making McGraw-Hill Education products more intelligent, reliable, and precise.

STUDENTS WANT

Mc Graw Hill Education **SMARTBOOK®**

95% of students reported **SmartBook** to be a more effective way of reading material

100% of students want to use the Practice Quiz feature available within **SmartBook** to help them study

100% of students reported having reliable access to off-campus wifi

90% of students say they would purchase **SmartBook** over print alone

95% reported that **SmartBook** would impact their study skills in a positive way

Mc Graw Hill Education

*Findings based on a 2015 focus group survey at Pellissippi State Community College administered by McGraw-Hill Education

www.learnsmartadvantage.com

Acknowledgments

Essentials of Marketing has been influenced and improved by the input of more people than it is possible to list. We want to express our appreciation to those who have played the most significant roles, especially in this edition.

We are especially grateful to our many students who have criticized and made comments about materials in *Essentials of Marketing*. Indeed, in many ways, our students have been our best teachers.

Many improvements in recent editions were stimulated by feedback from a number of colleagues around the country. Their feedback took many forms. In particular, we would like to recognize the helpful contributions of:

Cliff Ashmead Abdool, *CUNY College of Staten Island*
Roshan (Bob) Ahuja, *Ramapo College of New Jersey*
Thomas Ainscough, *University of South Florida*
Ian Alam, *Ramapo College of New Jersey*
Mary Albrecht, *Maryville University*
David Andrus, *Kansas State University at Manhattan*
Chris Anicich, *Broome Community College*
Maria Aria, *Missouri State University*
April Atwood, *University of Washington*
Ainsworth Bailey, *University of Toledo*
Turina Bakker, *University of Wisconsin*
Jeff Bauer, *University of Cincinnati—Batavia*
Leta Beard, *Washington University*
Amy Beattie, *Nichols College of Champlain*
Cathleen Behan, *Northern VA Community College*
Patty Bellamy, *Black Hills State University*
Suzeanne Benet, *Grand Valley State University*
Shahid Bhuian, *Louisiana Tech University*
John S. Bishop, Jr., *Ohio State University*
David Blackmore, *University of Pittsburgh*
Ross Blankenship, *University of California Berkeley*
Maurice Bode, *Delgado Community College*
Jonathan Bohlman, *Purdue School of Management*
William J. Bont, *Grand Valley State University*
Laurie Brachman, *University of Wisconsin*
Kit Brenan, *Northland Community College*
John Brennan, *Florida State University*
Richard Brien, *De Anza College*
Elten Briggs, *University of Texas—Austin*
Denny Bristow, *St. Cloud State University*
Susan Brudvig, *Ball State University*
Kendrick W. Brunson, *Liberty University*
Derrell Bulls, *Texas Women's University*
Helen Burdenski, *Notre Dame College of Ohio*

Nancy Bush, *Wingate University*
Carmen Calabrese, *University of North Carolina—Pembroke*
Catherine Campbell, *University of Maryland University College*
James Carlson, *Manatee Community College*
Donald Caudill, *Bluefield State College*
Karen Cayo, *Kettering University*
Kenny Chan, *California State University—Chico*
E. Wayne Chandler, *Eastern Illinois University*
Chen Ho Chao, *Baruch College, City University of New York*
Valeri Chukhlomin, *Empire State College*
Margaret Clark, *Cincinnati State Technical and Community College*
Paris Cleanthous, *New York University—Stern School*
Thomas Cline, *St. Vincent College*
Gloria Cockerell, *Collin County Community College*
Linda Jane Coleman, *Salem State College*
Brian Connett, *California State University—Northridge*
Craig Conrad, *Western Illinois University*
Barbara Conte, *Florida Atlantic University*
Sherry Cook, *Southwest Missouri State*
Matt Critcher, *University of Arkansas Community College—Batesville*
Tammy Crutchfield, *Mercer University*
Brent Cunningham, *Jacksonville State University*
Madeline Damkar, *Cabrillo Community College/CSUEB*
Charles Davies, *Hillsdale College*
J. Charlene Davis, *Trinity University*
Scott Davis, *University of California at Davis*
Dwane Dean, *Manhattan College*
Larry Degaris, *California State University*
Nicholas Didow, *University of North Carolina—Chapel Hill*
Susan Higgins DeFago, *John Carroll University*
Oscar W. DeShields, Jr., *California State University—Northridge*
John E. Dillard, *University of Houston—Downtown*
Les Dlabay, *Lake Forest College*
Glenna Dod, *Wesleyan College*
Gary Donnelly, *Casper College*
Paul Dowling, *University of Utah*
Laura Downey, *Purdue University*
Phillip Downs, *Florida State University*
Michael Drafke, *College of DuPage*
John Drea, *Western Illinois University*
Colleen Dunn, *Bucks Community College*
Sean Dwyer, *Louisiana Technical University*
Judith Kay Eberhart, *Lindenwood University—Belleville*
Mary Edrington, *Drake University*
Steven Engel, *University of Colorado*
Dr. S. Altan Erdem, *University of Houston—Clear Lake*
Keith Fabes, *Berkeley College*

Peter Fader, *University of Pennsylvania*
Ken Fairweather, *LeTourneau University*
Phyllis Fein, *Westchester Community College*
Lori S. Feldman, *Purdue University*
Mark Fenton, *University of Wisconsin—Stout*
Jodie L. Ferguson, *Virginia Commonwealth University*
Richard Kent Fields, *Carthage College*
Lou Firenze, *Northwood University*
Michael Fitzmorris, *Park University*
Richard Fogg, *Kansas State University*
Kim Folkers, *Wartburg College*
Renee Foster, *Delta State University*
Frank Franzak, *Virginia Commonwealth University*
John Gaffney, *Hiram College*
John Gaskins, *Longwood University*
Carol Gaumer, *University of Maryland University College*
Karl Giulian, *Fairleigh Dickinson University—Madison*
Thomas Giese, *University of Richmond*
J. Lee Goen, *Oklahoma Baptist University*
Brent G. Goff, *University of Houston—Downtown*
David Good, *Central Missouri State University*
Pradeep Gopalakrishna, *Pace University*
Keith Gosselin, *California State University of Northbridge*
Rahul Govind, *University of Mississippi*
Norman Govoni, *Babson College*
Gary Grandison, *Alabama State University*
Wade Graves, *Grayson County College*
Mitch Griffin, *Bradley University*
Mike Griffith, *Cascade College*
Alice Griswold, *Clarke College*
Barbara Gross, *California State University—Northridge*
Susan Gupta, *University of Wisconsin at Milwaukee*
John Hadjmarcou, *University of Texas at El Paso*
Khalil Hairston, *Indiana Institute of Technology*
Adam Hall, *Western Kentucky University*
Bobby Hall, *Wayland Baptist University*
Joan Hall, *Macomb Community College*
David Hansen, *Schoolcraft College*
Dorothy Harpool, *Wichita State University*
LeaAnna Harrah, *Marion Technical College*
James Harvey, *George Mason University*
John S. Heise, *California State University—Northridge*
Lewis Hershey, *University of North Carolina—Pembroke*
James Hess, *Ivy Tech Community College*
Wolfgang Hinck, *Louisiana State University—Shreveport*
Pamela Homer, *California State University—Long Beach*
Ronald Hoverstad, *University of the Pacific*
John Howard, *Tulane University*
Doug Hughes, *Michigan State University—East Lansing*
Deborah Baker Hulse, *University of Texas at Tyler*
Janet Hunter, *Northland Pioneer College*
Phil Hupfer, *Elmhurst College*
Hector Iweka, *Lasell College*
Annette Jajko, *Triton College/College of DuPage*
Jean Jaymes, *West California State University—Bakersfield*
Carol Johanek, *Washington University*
Timothy Johnston, *University of Tennessee at Martin*
Keith Jones, *North Carolina A&T State University*
Sungwoo Jung, *Saint Louis University*
Fahri Karakaya, *University of Massachusetts*
Gary Karns, *Seattle Pacific University*

Pat Karush, *Thomas College*
Eileen Kearney, *Montgomery County Community College*
James Kellaris, *University of Cincinnati*
Robin Kelly, *Cuyahoga Community College*
Courtney Kernek, *Texas A&M University—Commerce*
Brian Kinard, *PennState University—University Park*
Rob Kleine, *Ohio Northern University*
Ken Knox, *Ohio State University—Athens*
Kathleen Krentler, *San Diego State University*
Claudia Kubowicz-Malhotra, *University of North Carolina—Chapel Hill*
Dmitri Kuksov, *Washington University*
Jean Laliberte, *Troy State University*
Tim Landry, *Kutztown University of Pennsylvania*
Geoffrey Lantos, *Oregon State University*
Linda Lamarca, *Tarleton State University*
Kevin Lambert, *Southeast Community College*
Richard LaRosa, *Indiana University of Pennsylvania*
Donald Larson, *The Ohio State University*
Dana-Nicoleta Lascu, *Richmond University*
Debra Laverie, *Texas Tech University*
Marilyn Lavin, *University of Wisconsin—Whitewater*
Freddy Lee, *California State University—Los Angeles*
Steven V. LeShay, *Wilmington University*
David Levy, *Bellevue University*
Dr. Jason Little, *Franklin Pierce University*
Doug Livermore, *Morningside College*
Lori Lohman, *Augsburg College*
Paul James Londrigan, *Mott Community College*
Guy Lochiatto, *California State University*
Sylvia Long-Tolbert, *University of Toledo*
Terry Lowe, *Heartland Community College*
Harold Lucius, *Rowan University*
Navneet Luthar, *Madison Area Technical College*
Richard Lutz, *University of Florida*
W. J. Mahony, *Southern Wesleyan University*
Rosalynn Martin, *MidSouth Community College*
Phyllis Mansfield, *Pennsylvania State University—Erie*
James McAloon, *Fitchburg State University*
Lee McCain, *Shaw University*
Christina McCale, *Regis University*
Michele McCarren, *Southern State Community College*
Kevin McEvoy, *University of Connecticut—Stamford*
Rajiv Mehta, *New Jersey Institute of Technology*
Sanjay Mehta, *Sam Houston State University*
Matt Meuter, *California State University—Chico*
Michael Mezja, *University of Las Vegas*
Margaret Klayton Mi, *Mary Washington College*
Herbert A. Miller, *Jr., University of Texas—Austin*
Linda Mitchell, *Lindon State College*
Ted Mitchell, *University of Nevada—Reno*
Robert Montgomery, *University of Evansville*
Todd Mooradian, *College of William and Mary*
Kelvyn A. Moore, *Clark Atlanta University*
Marlene Morris, *Georgetown University*
Brenda Moscool, *California State University—Bakersfield*
Ed Mosher, *Laramie Community College*
Reza Motameni, *California State University—Fresno*
Amit Mukherjee, *Providence College*
Steve Mumsford, *Gwynedd-Mercy College*
Clara Munson, *Albertus Magnus*

Thomas Myers, *University of Richmond*
Cynthia Newman, *Rider University*
Philip S. Nitse, *Idaho State University at Pocatello*
J. R. Ogden, *Kutztown University*
David Oh, *California State University—Los Angeles*
Okey Peter Onyia, *Lindenwood University*
Sam Okoroafo, *University of Toledo*
Jeannie O'Laughlin, *Dakota Wesleyan University*
Louis Osuki, *Chicago State University*
Daniel Padgett, *Auburn University*
Esther S. Page-Wood, *Western Michigan University*
Karen Palumbo, *University of St. Francis*
Terry Paridon, *Cameron University*
Dr. Amy Patrick, *Wilmington University*
Terry Paul, *Ohio State University*
Sheila Petcavage, *Cuyahoga Community College*
Stephen Peters, *Walla Walla Community College*
Man Phan, *Comsumnes River College*
Linda Plank, *Ferris State University*
Lucille Pointer, *University of Houston—Downtown*
Brenda Ponsford, *Clarion University*
Joel Poor, *University of Missouri*
Teresa Preston, *University of Arkansas at Little Rock*
Tracy Proulx, *Park University*
Brook Quigg, *Peirce College*
Anthony Racka, *Oakland Community College*
Kathleen Radionoff, *Cardinal Stritch University*
Daniel Rajaratnam, *Baylor University*
Catherine Rich-Duval, *Merrimack College*
Charles W. Richardson, Jr., *Clark Atlanta University*
Lee Richardson, *University of Baltimore*
Daniel Ricica, *Sinclair Community College*
Brent Richard, *Ramapo College of New Jersey*
Darlene Riedemann, *Eastern Illinois University*
Sandra Robertson, *Thomas Nelson Community College*
Kim Rocha, *Barton College*
Amy Rodie, *University of Nebraska—Omaha*
Carlos Rodriguez, *Governors State University*
Robert Roe, *University of Wyoming*
Ann R. Root, *Florida Atlantic University*
Mark Rosenbaum, *Northern Illinois University*
Donald Roy, *Middle Tennessee State University*
Joel Saegert, *University of Texas at San Antonio*
David Schalow, *University of Wisconsin—Stevens Point*
Nate Scharff, *Grossmont College*
Henry Schrader, *Ramapo College of New Jersey*
C. M. Sashi, *Florida Atlantic University*
Erika Schlomer-Fischer, *California Lutheran University*
Lewis Schlossinger, *Community College of Aurora*
Charles Schwepker, *Central Missouri State University*
Murphy Sewell, *University of Connecticut—Storrs*
Kenneth Shamley, *Sinclair College*
Doris Shaw, *Northern Kentucky University*
Donald Shifter, *Fontbonne College*
Jeremy Sierra, *New Mexico State University*
Lisa Simon, *California Polytech—San Luis Obispo*
Rob Simon, *University of Nebraska*
James Simpson, *University of Alabama in Huntsville*
Aditya Singh, *Pennsylvania State University—McKeesport*
Mandeep Singh, *Western Illinois University*
Jill Slomski, *Mercyhurst College*

Robert Smoot, *Lees College*
Don Soucy, *University of North Carolina—Pembroke*
Roland Sparks, *Johnson C. Smith University*
Joseph R. Stasio, *Merrimack College*
Gene Steidinger, *Loras College*
Jim Stephens, *Emporia State University*
Tom Stevenson, *University of North Carolina*
Geoffrey Stewart, *University of Louisiana at Lafayette*
Karen Stewart, *The Richard Stockton College of New Jersey*
Stephen Strange, *Henderson Community College*
Randy Stuart, *Kennesaw State University*
Rajneesh Suri, *Drexel University*
John Talbott, *Indiana University*
Uday Tate, *Marshall University*
A. J. Taylor, *Austin Peay State University*
Scott Taylor, *McHenry County College*
Janice Taylor, *Miami University*
Kimberly Taylor, *Florida International University*
Steven Taylor, *Illinois State University*
Jeff Thieme, *Syracuse University*
Scott Thompson, *University of Wisconsin—Oshkosh*
Dennis Tootelian, *California State University—Sacramento*
Gary Tschantz, *Walsh University*
Fran Ucci, *Triton College/College of DuPage*
Sue Umashankar, *University of Arizona*
David Urban, *Virginia Commonwealth University*
Kristin Uttech, *Madison Area Technical College*
Peter Vantine, *Georgia Tech*
Steve Vitucci, *Tarleton State University*
Sharon Wagner, *Missouri Western State College*
Suzanne Walchli, *University of the Pacific*
Jane Wayland, *Eastern Illinois University*
Danny "Peter" Weathers, *Louisiana State University*
Yinghong (Susan) Wei, *Oklahoma State University*
John Weiss, *Colorado State University*
M. G. M. Wetzeis, *Universiteit Maastrict, The Netherlands*
Fred Whitman, *Mary Washington College*
Judy Wilkinson, *Youngstown State University*
Phillip Wilson, *Midwestern State University*
Robert Witherspoon, *Triton College*
John Withey, *Indiana University—South Bend*
Brent Wren, *Manhattanville College*
Jim Wong, *Shenandoah University*
Joyce H. Wood, *N. Virginia Community College*
Newell Wright, *James Madison University*
Joseph Yasaian, *McIntosh College*
Gary Young, *Worcester State College*

We've always believed that the best way to build consistency and quality into the text and the other P.L.U.S. units is to do as much as possible ourselves. With the growth of multimedia technologies, it's darn hard to be an expert on them all. But we've had spectacular help in that regard.

The new chapter in this edition—Chapter 16—benefitted greatly from some "student" reviews along the way. Kelly Cannon, Ally Cannon, Ellery Miller, and Haley Wolfinger provided valuable feedback.

The lecture-support PowerPoints have been a tremendous effort over many editions. We appreciate the efforts of Luis Torres, Jay Carlson, Mandy Noelle Carlson, David Urban, Milt Pressley, and Lewis Hershey for their creative work on the lecture-support PowerPoint presentation slides. Ellery Miller was a huge help in putting together the YouTube PowerPoints in this edition.

Jon Firooz took our Computer-Aided Problems and updated them for use in Connect—they are now titled *Marketing Analytics: Data to Knowledge.*

We consider our "best in the business" video package a true team effort. Although the authors had input, the project has been led in recent years by Nick Childers at Shadows and Light Creative Services. For several editions, Judy Wilkinson has played a big role as producer of the video series for the book. In that capacity, she worked closely with us to come up with ideas, and she provided guidance to the talented group of marketing professors and managers who created or revised videos for this edition.

Of course, like other aspects of *Essentials of Marketing,* the video series has evolved and improved over time, and its current strength is partly due to the insights of Phil Niffenegger, who served as producer for our early video efforts. The video series also continues to benefit from the contributions of colleagues who developed videos in earlier editions. They are

Gary R. Brockway
James Burley
David Burns
Debra Childers
Martha O. Cooper
Carolyn Costley
Angie Fenton
W. Davis Folsom
Pam Girardo
Brenda Green
Douglas Hausknecht
Jean Jaymes
Scott Johnson
Bart Kittle
Claudia Kubowicz
Gene R. Lazniak
Freddy Lee
Bill Levy
Charles S. Madden
Don McBane
W. Glynn Mangold
Becky Manter
Robert Miller

J. R. Montgomery
Linda Mothersbaugh
Michael R. Mullen
Phillip Niffenegger
Okey Peter Onyia
Deborah Owens
Thomas G. Ponzurick
George Prough
Peter Rainsford
Jane Reid
Clinton Schertzer
Roger Schoenfeldt
Thomas Sherer
Jeanne M. Simmons
Walter Strange
Jeff Tanner
Ron Tatham
Rollie O. Tillman
Carla Vallone
Yinghong (Susan) Wei
Robert Welsh
Holt Wilson
Poh-Lin Yeou

Faculty and students at our current and past academic institutions—Michigan State University, University of North Carolina, Colorado State University, Emory, Notre Dame, University of Georgia, Northwestern University, University of Oregon, University of Minnesota, and Stanford University—have significantly shaped the book. Professor Andrew A. Brogowicz of Western Michigan University contributed many fine ideas to early editions of the text and supplements. Neil Morgan, Charlotte Mason, Rich Gooner, Gary Hunter, John Workman, Nicholas Didow, Barry Bayus, Jon Firooz, Ken Manning, and Ajay Menon have provided a constant flow of helpful suggestions.

We are also grateful to the colleagues with whom we collaborate to produce international adaptations of the text. In particular, Lindsey Meredith, Lynne Ricker, Stan Shapiro, Ken Wong, and Pascale G. Quester have all had a significant impact on *Essentials of Marketing.*

The designers, artists, editors, and production people at McGraw-Hill who worked with us on this edition warrant special recognition. All of them share our commitment to excellence and bring their own individual creativity to the project. First, we should salute Christine Vaughan, who has done a great (and patient) job as content production manager for the project. Without her adaptive problem solving, we could not have succeeded with a (very) rapid-response production schedule—which is exactly what it takes to be certain that teachers and students get the most current information possible.

Heather Darr worked as product developer on this edition; her insight and project management skills are much appreciated. Our executive brand manager, Kim Leistner, was new to this edition and brought great enthusiasm, energy, and ideas. We appreciated her valuable perspective on the *Essentials of Marketing* franchise.

The layout and design of the print and online versions of the text included a dedicated team of professionals. Keith McPherson is a long-time creative and valued contributor to *Essentials of Marketing.* He is a great talent and we sincerely appreciate his past efforts that continue to be reflected in the book's design. We sincerely appreciate the talents of Pam Verros who created the interior and Egzon Shaqiri who designed the cover for this edition of *Essentials of Marketing.* We also appreciate Mike Hruby, who again tracked down photos, ads, and permissions for the images we selected to illustrate important ideas.

We owe an ongoing debt of gratitude to Lin Davis. The book probably wouldn't exist without her—without her help, the book would've been just too overwhelming and we'd have quit! Lin was part of this team for more than 25 years. During that time, she has made contributions in every aspect of the text and package.

Kendra Miller joined the team with the 14th edition and has been a valuable addition. Kendra has brought new energy and insight along with a sharp eye for detail. Kendra's copyediting and photo/ad chasing have been very helpful. We like to bounce ideas off of Kendra—and she often shares her own insights—many of which have been added to the book.

Our families have been patient and consistent supporters through all phases in developing *Essentials of Marketing.* The support has been direct and substantive. Pam Perreault and Chris Cannon have provided valuable assistance and more encouragement than you could imagine. Our kids—Suzanne, Will, Kelly, Ally, and Mallory—provide valuable suggestions and ideas as well as encouragement and support while their dads are too often consumed with a never-ending set of deadlines.

We are indebted to all the firms that allowed us to reproduce their proprietary materials here. Similarly, we are grateful to associates from our business experiences who have shared their perspectives and feedback and enhanced our sensitivity to the key challenges of marketing management.

Our product must capsulize existing knowledge while bringing new perspectives and organization to enhance it. Our thinking has been shaped by the writings of literally thousands of marketing scholars and practitioners. In some cases, it is impossible to give unique credit for a particular idea or concept because so many people have played important roles in anticipating, suggesting, shaping, and developing it. We gratefully acknowledge these contributors—from the early thought-leaders to contemporary authors and researchers—who have shared their creative ideas. We respect their impact on the development of marketing and more specifically this book.

To all of these persons—and to the many publishers who graciously granted permission to use their materials—we are deeply grateful. Responsibility for any errors or omissions is certainly ours, but the book would not have been possible without the assistance of many others. Our sincere appreciation goes to all who contributed.

William D. Perreault, Jr.
Joseph P. Cannon
E. Jerome McCarthy

Brief Contents

Contents

1

CHAPTER ONE

Marketing's Value to Consumers, Firms, and Society 2

2

3

4

CHAPTER FOUR

Focusing Marketing Strategy with Segmentation and Positioning 86

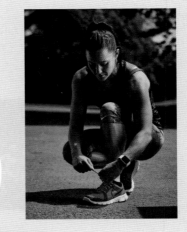

5

CHAPTER FIVE

Final Consumers and Their Buying Behavior 114

6

CHAPTER SIX
Business and Organizational Customers and Their Buying Behavior 142

7

CHAPTER SEVEN
Improving Decisions with Marketing Information 168

8

CHAPTER EIGHT

Elements of Product Planning for Goods and Services 196

9

CHAPTER NINE

Product Management and New-Product Development 226

10

CHAPTER TEN

Place and Development of Channel Systems 254

11

CHAPTER ELEVEN

Distribution Customer Service and Logistics 282

CHAPTER TWELVE

Retailers, Wholesalers, and Their Strategy Planning 304

CHAPTER THIRTEEN

Promotion—Introduction to Integrated Marketing Communications 334

14

15

18

19

A

BONUS CHAPTER 1

BONUS CHAPTER 2

Video Cases

Cases

Essentials of Marketing

A Marketing Strategy Planning Approach

CHAPTER ONE

1

Matthew Stockman/Getty Images.

Marketing's Value to Consumers, Firms, and Society

When it's time to roll out of bed in the morning, does the Spotify app on your Apple iPhone play your "Waking Up Happy" playlist, or is it your roommate blasting Luke Bryan? Do you throw on your Nike Flyknit shoes and get in a little run before breakfast? Not this morning. You slept in and now you barely have time to throw on your Levi's jeans, shirt from Zara, and Sperry Top-Sider shoes as you race off to class. You do need a quick bite at home before you go. Will it be a Chobani pineapple flavored Greek yogurt and an Einstein's bagel with Philadelphia Cream Cheese? Or maybe you grab a Chicken Apple Sausage breakfast sandwich at Caribou Coffee in the student union. If you hurry, your roommate can give you a ride to school in her new Ford Fiesta, although you could ride your Trek bicycle or take the bus that the city bought from Mercedes-Benz. Many choices.

When you think about it, you can't get very far into a day without bumping into marketing—and what the whole marketing system does for you. It affects every aspect of our lives—often in ways we don't even consider.

In other parts of the world, people wake up each day to different kinds of experiences. A family in rural Africa may have little choice about what food they will eat or where their clothing will come from. In some countries, economic decisions are still made by government officials. But in the world's most developed countries, consumers determine what's on store shelves. If no one buys a particular color, size, or style, then companies no longer produce it. So you may have trouble finding a Chicken Apple Sausage sandwich in Hangzhou, China, where the locals are more likely to join the line of people waiting for Ganqishi's breakfast of steamed buns.

One brand found around the world is Nike. How has Nike become the choice for so many professional and casual athletes around the world? Is it the more than $800 million Nike spends each year for endorsements from star athletes like Rory McIlroy and Cristiano Ronaldo? Maybe it's the innovations, like Nike's lightweight Flyknit running shoes and its Nike+ software apps. What part do the 24,000 retailers that carry Nike products play? Do Nike's connections with tens of millions of customers on Twitter, Instagram, and Facebook build customer relationships? Do these relationships increase sales?

Almost 50 years ago, Phil Knight and his college track coach, Bill Bowerman, founded Blue Ribbon Sports (later renamed Nike) to distribute Japanese running shoes. A few years later they were designing, producing, and selling athletic shoes. Today Nike is the 18th most valuable brand in the world, with annual sales of more than $28 billion. Part of its success comes from adapting its marketing strategy to changing market conditions—but Nike hasn't always adapted quickly. Back in the early 1980s, Nike was so focused on running shoes that it missed the aerobics shoe craze and fell behind rival Reebok. Nike profits plummeted and only aggressive cost-cutting saved the company.

After Nike signed Michael Jordan to endorse its basketball shoes in 1984, the Air Jordan line took the market by storm. Later, when Nike's advertising agency came up with the "Just Do It!" slogan and an ad campaign that covered television, magazines, and billboards around the world raced Nike further ahead. "Just Do It" helped carry Nike through the 1990s and its profits soared on rising sales aided by low-cost foreign production.

Then, in the late 1990s, the company came under attack when it was reported that some of its suppliers used child labor. At first Nike denied responsibility, claiming it couldn't control how its suppliers operated. But public protest showed that society expected more from a large, successful corporation, and Nike began to closely monitor its suppliers' labor practices. Since then, Nike's social responsibility efforts have turned around its reputation. For example, Nike leads a group of 10 partners in the GreenXchange, a web-based marketplace where member firms collaborate and share ideas to foster sustainability.

These days, Nike targets growth in emerging markets like China. Nike is courting Chinese consumers who are crazy about basketball (especially basketball superstar, LeBron James) by touting the NBA star in its ads. Nike works with Chinese athletes, too, including Olympic hurdler Liu Xiang and tennis player Li Na. Nike was one of the first brands to jump onto the Chinese mobile messaging service WeChat—directly connecting with hundreds of millions of Chinese consumers. To appeal to the more price-sensitive Chinese consumer, Nike's product line includes lower-priced shoes than those it sells in the United States. And because China doesn't have many large shopping malls, Nike has worked with retail partners to open 5,000 small stores—many focusing on a single sport. Nike is also ramping up online sales as Chinese customers grow increasingly comfortable with online buying.

Innovation continues to be an important part of Nike's culture. Some of Nike's recent innovations involve digital tools that create communities for its customers. For example, the Nike+ Training Club (N+TC) app runs on iPhone and Android devices and targets women at all fitness levels. The N+TC app has more than 100 workouts in 16 languages. Users can choose from dozens of different four-week programs designed to help them "Get Lean," "Get Strong," or "Get Focused." The programs feature Nike athletes like tennis star Serena Williams and gymnast Gabby Douglas who act as virtual trainers. The

app also lets users connect with friends and other users who motivate each other to work out. Similar Nike apps target runners, skate boarders, golfers, and more. And the apps are free! They help build long-term relationships (and future sales) with customers after they buy Nike workout gear. Innovations like these need to keep coming if Nike expects to continue to run ahead of a strong field of competitors that includes Adidas, Under Armour, and Chinese upstart Li Ning.[1]

LEARNING OBJECTIVES

In this chapter, you'll learn what marketing is all about and why it's important to you as a consumer. We'll also explore why it is so crucial to the success of individual firms and nonprofit organizations and the impact that it has on the quality of life in different societies.

When you finish this chapter, you should be able to

1 Know what marketing is and why you should learn about it.

2 Understand the difference between marketing and macro-marketing.

3 Know the marketing functions and why marketing specialists—including intermediaries and collaborators—develop to perform them.

4 Understand what a market-driven economy is and how it adjusts the macro-marketing system.

5 Know what the marketing concept is—and how it should guide a firm or nonprofit organization.

6 Understand what customer value is and why it is important to customer satisfaction.

7 Know how social responsibility and marketing ethics relate to the marketing concept.

8 Understand the important new terms (shown in red).

Marketing—What's It All About?

LO 1.1

Marketing is more than selling or advertising

How did all those bicycles get here?

Many people think that marketing means "selling" or "advertising." It's true that these are parts of marketing. But *marketing is much more than selling and advertising.*

To illustrate some of the other important things that are included in marketing, think about all the bicycles being pedaled with varying degrees of energy by bike riders around the world. Most of us don't make our own bicycles. Instead, they are made by firms such as Trek, Specialized, Mongoose, and Electra.

Most bikes do the same thing—get the rider from one place to another. But a bike rider can choose from a wide assortment of models. They are designed in different sizes and with or without gears. Off-road bikes have large knobby tires. Kids and older people may want more wheels—to make balancing easier. Some bikes need baskets or even trailers for cargo. You can buy a basic bike for less than $100. Or you can spend more than $5,000 for a custom frame.

Marketing helps make sure that customers get the bicycle that best meets their needs.
Left to right: Royalty-Free/CORBIS; ©Fotosearch/Publitek, Inc.; Pixtal/AGE Fotostock.

This variety of styles and features complicates the production and sale of bicycles. The following list shows some of the things a manager should do before and after deciding to produce and sell a bike.

1. Analyze the needs of people who might buy a bike and decide if they want more or different models.
2. Determine how many of these people will want to buy bicycles, where in the world they live, and when they will want to buy.
3. Identify competing companies that also produce bikes, what kind they sell, and at what prices.
4. Predict the designs of bikes—frame and handlebar styles, derailleurs, types of wheels, brakes, and other accessories—different customers will want, and decide which of these people the firm will try to satisfy.
5. Determine whether to sell bikes directly to consumers or through retailers—and if retailers, which ones should be used.
6. Decide how to tell potential customers about the firm's bikes.
7. Estimate the prices potential customers are willing to pay for their bikes and if the firm can make a profit selling at those prices.
8. Figure out how to provide customer service if a customer has a problem after buying a bike.

The above activities are not part of **production**—actually *making* goods or *performing* services. Rather, they are part of a larger process—called *marketing*—that provides needed direction for production and helps make sure that the right goods and services are produced and find their way to consumers.

You'll learn much more about marketing activities in Chapter 2. For now, it's enough to see that marketing plays an essential role in providing consumers with need-satisfying goods and services and, more generally, in creating customer satisfaction. Simply put, **customer satisfaction** is the extent to which a firm fulfills a customer's needs, desires, and expectations.

Marketing Is Important to You

Marketing is important to every consumer

Marketing affects almost every aspect of your daily life. The choices you have among the goods and services you buy, the stores where you shop, and the radio and TV programs you tune in to are all possible because of marketing. In the process of providing all these choices, marketing drives organizations to focus on what it takes to satisfy you, the customer. Most of the things you want or need are available conveniently *when* and *where* you want or need them.

Some courses are interesting when you take them but not directly relevant to your life once they're over. That's not so with marketing—you'll be a consumer dealing with marketing for the rest of your life regardless of what career you pursue. Moreover, as a consumer, you pay for the cost of marketing activities. In advanced economies, marketing costs about 50 cents of every consumer dollar. For some goods and services, the percentage is much higher. It makes sense to be an educated consumer and to understand what you get and don't get from all that spending.

Marketing will be important to your job

Another reason for studying marketing is that it offers many exciting and rewarding career opportunities. Throughout this book, you will find information about opportunities in different areas of marketing.

If you're aiming for a nonmarketing job, knowing about marketing will help you do your own job better. Throughout the book, we'll discuss ways that marketing relates to other functional areas. Further, marketing is important to the success of every organization. The same basic principles used to sell soap are also used to "sell" ideas, politicians, mass transportation, health care services, environmental sustainability, museums, and even colleges. Even your job résumé is part of a marketing campaign to sell yourself to some employer![2]

Use a marketing approach to get your next job

You will probably be seeking a job sometime soon, offering your services—as an accountant, a salesperson, a computer programmer, a financial analyst, or perhaps a store manager. Or maybe you will be looking for an opportunity with more responsibility or higher pay where you currently work. You will have more success getting the job you want when you take a marketing approach and try to figure out how to best satisfy the needs, interests, and desires of a prospective employer the same way a business looks at customers. Much of what you learn about how businesses use marketing can be applied in the job market. See Appendix C for more details on how to write your personal marketing plan.

Marketing affects innovation and standard of living

An even more basic reason for studying marketing is that marketing plays a big part in economic growth and development. One key reason is that marketing encourages research and **innovation**—the development and spread of new ideas, goods, and services. As firms offer new and better ways of satisfying consumer needs, customers have more choices among products and this fosters competition for consumers' money. This competition drives down prices. Moreover, when firms develop products that really satisfy customers, fuller employment and higher incomes can result. The combination of these forces means that marketing has a big impact on consumers' standard of living—and it is important to the future of all nations.[3]

How Should We Define Marketing?

There are micro and macro views of marketing

In our bicycle example, we saw that a producer of bicycles has to perform many customer-related activities besides just making bikes. The same is true for an insurance company or an art museum. This supports the idea of marketing as a set of activities done by an individual organization to satisfy its customers.

On the other hand, people can't survive on bicycles and art museums alone! In advanced economies, it takes goods and services from thousands of organizations to satisfy the many needs of society. Further, a society needs some sort of marketing system to organize the efforts of all the producers, wholesalers, and retailers required to satisfy the varied needs of all its citizens. So marketing is also an important social process.

We can view marketing in two ways: *from a micro view as a set of activities performed by organizations* and also *from a macro view as a social process.* Yet, in everyday use when people talk about marketing, they have the micro view in mind. So that is the way we will define marketing here. However, the broader macro view that looks at the whole production–distribution system is also important, so later we will provide a separate definition and discussion of macro-marketing.

Marketing defined

Marketing is the performance of activities that seek to accomplish an organization's objectives by anticipating customer or client needs and directing a flow of need-satisfying goods and services from producer to customer or client. Let's look at this definition.[4]

Applies to profit and nonprofit organizations

Marketing applies to both profit and nonprofit organizations. Profit is the objective for most business firms. But other types of organizations may seek more members or acceptance of an idea. Customers or clients may be individual consumers, business firms, nonprofit organizations, government agencies, or even foreign nations. Although most customers and clients pay for the goods and services they receive, others may receive them free of charge or at a reduced cost through private or government support.

More than just persuading customers

Marketing isn't just selling and advertising. Unfortunately, some executives still think of it that way. They feel that the job of marketing is to "get rid of" whatever the company happens to produce. In fact, the aim of marketing is to identify customers' needs and meet those needs so well that the product almost "sells itself." This is true whether the product is a physical good, a service, or even an idea. If the whole marketing job has been done well, customers don't need much persuading. They should be ready to buy. And after they buy, they'll be satisfied and ready to buy the same way the next time.

Begins with customer needs

Marketing should begin with potential customer needs—not with the production process. Marketing should try to anticipate needs. And then marketing, rather than production, should determine what goods and services are to be developed—including decisions about product features; design and packaging; prices or fees;

Marketing aims to identify customer needs and meet those needs so well that the product sells itself. Help Remedies found many customers looking for simple solutions to minor health problems.

transporting and storing policies; advertising and sales tactics; and, after the sale, installation, customer service, warranty, and perhaps even disposal and recycling policies.

Consider France's Sodebo, maker of fresh packaged meals (sandwiches and pasta) sold in grocery stores. Sodebo's consumer research found some customers had an unmet need: they wanted to satisfy mid-day hunger in a healthy way. The research showed that busy consumers would buy a high quality to-go salad, but found current choices skimpy and unsatisfying. Sodebo went to work developing salads that were convenient, delicious, and filling. On the way to market, Sodebo tested different recipes and packages to find what consumers and retailers liked best. By starting with customer needs, Sodebo's Salade & Compagnie line of 10 different boxed salads became a best seller.[5]

Does not do it alone

This does not mean that marketing should try to take over production, accounting, and financial activities. Rather, it means that marketing—by interpreting customers' needs—should provide direction for these activities and try to coordinate them.

Marketing involves exchanges

The idea that marketing involves a flow of need-satisfying offerings from a producer to a customer implies that there is an exchange of the need-satisfying offering for something else, such as the customer's money. Marketing focuses on facilitating exchanges. In fact, *marketing doesn't occur unless two or more parties are willing to exchange something for something else.* For example, in a **pure subsistence economy**—where each family unit produces everything it consumes—there is no need to exchange goods and services and no marketing is involved. (Although each producer–consumer unit is totally self-sufficient in such a situation, the standard of living is typically relatively low.)

Builds a relationship with the customer

Keep in mind that a marketing exchange is often part of an ongoing relationship, not just a single transaction. When marketing helps everyone in a firm really meet the needs of a customer before and after a purchase, the firm doesn't just get a single sale. Rather, it has a sale and an ongoing *relationship* with the customer. Then, in the future, when the customer has the same need again—or some other need that the firm can meet—other sales will follow. Often, the marketing *flow* of need-satisfying goods and services is not just for a single transaction but rather is part of building a long-lasting relationship that benefits both the firm and the customer.

The focus of this text— management-oriented micro-marketing

Because you are probably preparing for a career in management, the main focus of this text will be on managerial marketing, or the micro view of marketing. We will see marketing through the eyes of the marketing manager.

The marketing ideas we will be discussing throughout this text apply to a wide variety of situations. They are important for new ventures started by one person as well as big corporations, in domestic and international markets, and regardless of whether the focus is on marketing physical goods, services, or an idea or cause. They are equally critical whether the relevant customers or clients are individual consumers, businesses, or some other type of organization. For editorial convenience, we will sometimes use the term *firm* as a shorthand way of referring to any type of organization, whether it is a political party, a religious organization, a government agency, or the like. However, to reinforce the point that the ideas apply to all types of organizations, throughout the book we will illustrate marketing concepts in a wide variety of situations. For an example of effective micro-marketing, read "*What's Next?* Marketing helps India's rural poor."

Although marketing within individual firms (micro-marketing) is the primary focus of the text, marketing managers must remember that their organizations are just small parts of a larger macro-marketing system. Therefore, next we will briefly look at the macro view of marketing. Then, we will develop the managerial view more fully in later chapters.

What's Next? Marketing helps India's rural poor

In recent decades India has experienced rapid economic growth. Many of its citizens have more income and enjoy a higher quality of life. That helps to explain why Unilever's Indian subsidiary, Hindustan Unilever Limited (HUL), has worked hard to build a 40 percent share of the Indian market with its product lines that include soaps, toothpaste, and packaged foods.

Previously, HUL focused primarily on India's urban areas. Yet, almost three-fourths of India's one *billion* plus people still live in rural areas. About a third of these rural villagers still lack access to electricity—and less than half have basic sanitation. Many of them have an income of less than $2 a day. Conventional wisdom suggests that these poor rural villagers have too little money to be an attractive market. And it's expensive to distribute products to far-flung villages.

But now that is changing. HUL's marketing managers have decided that Indian villagers represent an opportunity for growth—and that villagers might benefit if they could purchase the soaps, toothpaste, and packaged food products that HUL is successfully selling in urban areas of India.

HUL has tailored a new marketing strategy to this target market. Many products have been repackaged in "sachets"—small bags that contain a one- or two-day supply. HUL prices the small sachets so that villagers can afford them—and that in turn gives customers a chance to try quality products that were previously unavailable.

HUL has created its "Shakti Ammas" (women entrepreneurs) program to communicate the benefits of its products and distribute them in remote rural areas. The program sets rural women up as home-based distributors and sales agents. These women stock HUL products at their homes and go door-to-door to sell them. They also organize meetings in local schools and at village fairs to educate their fellow villagers on health and hygiene issues.

This program continues to evolve. To provide wider distribution, male entrepreneurs (Shaktimaan) were recruited and given bicycles. The bikes allow each Shaktimaan to cover five or six nearby villages—far more than the Shakti Amma could previously cover on foot. A partnership with a leading Indian telecom provider gives Shakti entrepreneurs a new product line selling mobile phone services.

HUL will soon have more than 75,000 Shakti Ammas operating in 500,000 villages, reaching 600 million people across India. The Indian success spurred Unilever to adapt the model to developing countries around the globe. These women have a new source of income and are learning about business—while they bring the health benefits of improved hygiene to rural villages. And, of course, HUL hopes to clean up with a new source of growth. To see and hear more about Project Shakti, check out this video: http://youtu.be/E7Hvp_CCtYY.

How do we see parts of the definition of marketing playing out in this scenario? What customer needs does the Shakti Ammas program address? How does it build a relationship between HUL and the customer?[6]

Macro-Marketing

LO 1.2

Macro-marketing is a social process that directs an economy's flow of goods and services from producers to consumers in a way that effectively matches supply and demand and accomplishes the objectives of society.[7]

Emphasis is on whole system

With macro-marketing we are still concerned with the flow of need-satisfying goods and services from producer to consumer. However, the emphasis with macro-marketing is not on the activities of individual organizations. Instead, the emphasis is on *how the whole marketing system works*. This includes looking at how marketing affects society and vice versa.

Every society needs a macro-marketing system to help match supply and demand. Different producers in a society have different objectives, resources, and skills. Likewise, not all consumers share the same needs, preferences, and wealth. In other words, within every society there are both heterogeneous (highly varied) supply capabilities and heterogeneous demands for goods and services. The role of a macro-marketing system is to effectively match this heterogeneous supply and demand *and* at the same time accomplish society's objectives.

An effective macro-marketing system delivers the goods and services that consumers want and need. It gets products to them at the right time, in the right place, and at a price they're willing to pay. It keeps consumers satisfied after the sale and brings them back to purchase again when they are ready. That's not an easy job—especially if you think about the variety of goods and services a highly developed economy can produce and the many kinds of goods and services consumers want.

Separation between producers and consumers

Effective marketing in an advanced economy is difficult because producers and consumers are often separated in several ways. As Exhibit 1–1 shows, exchange between producers and consumers is hampered by *spatial separation; separation in time; separation of information; separation in values;* and *separation of ownership.* You may love your cell phone, but you probably don't know when or where it was produced or how it got to you. The people in the factory that produced it don't know about you or how you live. The producer knows it wants to make that phone at a low cost and isn't sure what features and benefits you are seeking.

In addition, most firms specialize in producing and selling large amounts of a narrow assortment of goods and services. This allows them to take advantage of mass production with its **economies of scale**—which means that as a company produces larger numbers of a particular product, the cost of each unit of the product goes down. Yet most consumers want to buy only a small quantity; they also want a wide assortment of different goods and services. These "discrepancies of quantity" and "discrepancies of assortment" further complicate exchange between producers and consumers (Exhibit 1–1). That is, each producer specializes in producing and selling large

Exhibit 1–1   Marketing Facilitates Production and Consumption

Production Sector
Specialization and division of labor result in heterogeneous supply capabilities

Discrepancies of Quantity Producers prefer to produce and sell in large quantities. Consumers prefer to buy and consume in small quantities.

Discrepancies of Assortment Producers specialize in producing a narrow assortment of goods and services. Consumers need a broad assortment.

Marketing needed to overcome discrepancies and separations

Spatial Separation Producers tend to locate where it is economical to produce, while consumers are located in many scattered places.

Separation in Time Consumers may not want to consume goods and services at the time producers would prefer to produce them, and time may be required to transport goods from producer to consumer.

Separation of Information Producers do not know who needs what, where, when, and at what price. Consumers do not know what is available from whom, where, when, and at what price.

Separation in Values Producers value goods and services in terms of costs and competitive prices. Consumers value them in terms of satisfying needs and their ability to pay.

Separation of Ownership Producers hold title to goods and services that they themselves do not want to consume. Consumers want goods and services that they do not own.

Consumption Sector
Heterogeneous demand for different goods and services and when and where they need to be to satisfy needs and wants

amounts of a narrow assortment of goods and services, but each consumer wants only small quantities of a wide assortment of goods and services.[8]

The purpose of a macro-marketing system is to overcome these separations and discrepancies. The "universal functions of marketing" help do this.

Marketing functions help narrow the gap

LO 1.3

The **universal functions of marketing** are buying, selling, transporting, storing, standardization and grading, financing, risk taking, and market information. They must be performed in all macro-marketing systems. *How* these functions are performed—and *by whom*—may differ among nations and economic systems. But they are needed in any macro-marketing system. Let's take a closer look at them now.

Any kind of exchange usually involves buying and selling. The **buying function** means looking for and evaluating goods and services. The **selling function** involves promoting the product. It includes the use of personal selling, advertising, customer service, and other direct and mass selling methods. This is probably the most visible function of marketing.

The **transporting function** means the movement of goods from one place to another. The **storing function** involves holding goods until customers need them.

Standardization and grading involve sorting products according to size and quality. This makes buying and selling easier because it reduces the need for inspection and sampling. **Financing** provides the necessary cash and credit to produce, transport, store, promote, sell, and buy products. **Risk taking** involves bearing the uncertainties that are part of the marketing process. A firm can never be sure that customers will want to buy its products. Products can also be damaged, stolen, or outdated. The **market information function** involves the collection, analysis, and distribution of all the information needed to plan, carry out, and control marketing activities, whether in the firm's own neighborhood or in a market overseas. Together these universal functions of marketing address the discrepancies and separations in Exhibit 1–1.

Producers, consumers, and marketing specialists perform functions

Producers and consumers sometimes handle some of the marketing functions themselves. However, exchanges are often easier or less expensive when a marketing specialist performs some of the marketing functions. For example, both producers and consumers may benefit when an **intermediary**—someone who specializes in trade

Acai berries are popular in the United States as a supplement and as an ingredient in juices and smoothies. A range of marketing functions are needed to overcome the spatial separation between the Central and South American farms, where the fruit is harvested from acai palms, and U.S. consumers. Consider the process: standardizing and grading the berries, transporting and storing the fruit and its juice, financing production of the acai end-products, as well as the buying and selling functions—all are necessary to bring a tasty fruit smoothie to a thirsty man in Hawaii.
SambaPhoto/Rogerio Assis/Getty Images; Brazil Photos/Getty Images; Brandon Tabiolo/Perspectives/ Getty Images.

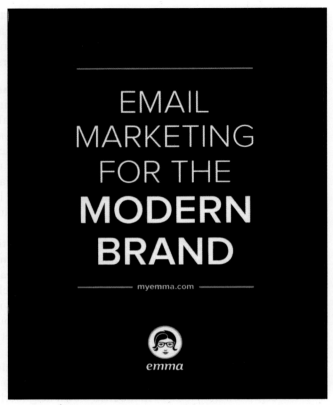

Intermediaries and collaborators develop and offer specialized services that facilitate exchange between producers and consumers. Companies that produce building supplies work with an intermediary such as Home Depot to better serve the electricians, plumbers, and carpenters that buy and use its products. EMMA helps organizations create, send, and track e-mail campaigns and online surveys. EMMA is a collaborator; it facilitates its clients selling and marketing information functions. ©2000–2015 Homer TLC, Inc. All Rights Reserved; Used with permission of myemma.com.

rather than production—plays a role in the exchange process. In Chapters 10, 11, and 12 we'll cover the variety of marketing functions performed by the two basic types of intermediaries: retailers and wholesalers. Imagine what it would be like to shop at many different factories and farms for the wide variety of brands of packaged foods that you like rather than at a well-stocked local grocery store. Although wholesalers and retailers must charge for services they provide, this charge is usually offset by the savings of time, effort, and expense that would be involved without them. So these intermediaries can help to make the whole macro-marketing system more efficient and effective.

A wide variety of other marketing specialists may also help smooth exchanges among producers, consumers, or intermediaries. These specialists are **collaborators**—firms that facilitate or provide one or more of the marketing functions other than buying. These collaborators include advertising agencies, marketing research firms, independent product-testing laboratories, Internet service providers, public warehouses, transporting firms, communications companies, and financial institutions (including banks).

New specialists develop to fill market needs

New types of marketing specialists develop or evolve when there are opportunities to make exchanges between producers and consumers more efficient or effective. The growth of the Internet provided one such opportunity and resulted in the rapid growth of e-commerce. **E-commerce** refers to exchanges between individuals or organizations—and activities that facilitate these exchanges—based on applications of information technology. Internet-based intermediaries—such as Amazon.com and eBay.com—help cut the costs of many marketing functions. Other marketing specialists have popped up online: Search engines such as Google facilitate information search, PayPal reduces consumer risks associated with paying for goods purchased online, and chat-based customer service firms help any company provide 24/7 customer support. Collectively, developments in e-commerce have significantly increased the efficiency and effectiveness of our macro-marketing system. At the same time, many individual firms take advantage of these innovations to improve profitability and customer satisfaction.[9]

Through innovation, specialization, or economies of scale, marketing intermediaries and collaborators are often able to perform the marketing functions better—and at a lower cost—than producers or consumers can. This allows producers and consumers to spend more time on production, consumption, or other activities—including leisure.

Functions can be shifted and shared

From a macro-marketing viewpoint, all of the marketing functions must be performed by someone—an individual producer or consumer, an intermediary, a marketing collaborator, or, in some cases, even a nation's government. No function can be completely eliminated. However, from a micro viewpoint, not every firm must perform all of the functions. Rather, responsibility for performing the marketing functions can be shifted and shared in a variety of ways. Further, not all goods and services require all the functions at every level of their production. "Pure services"—like a plane ride—don't need storing, for example. But storing is required in the production of the plane and while the plane is not in service.

Regardless of who performs the marketing functions, in general they must be performed effectively and efficiently or the performance of the whole macro-marketing system will suffer. With many different possible ways for marketing functions to be performed in a macro-marketing system, how can a society hope to arrive at a combination that best serves the needs of its citizens? To answer this question, we can look at the role of marketing in different types of economic systems.

The Role of Marketing in Economic Systems

LO 1.4

All societies must provide for the needs of their members. Therefore, every society needs some sort of **economic system**—the way an economy organizes to use scarce resources to produce goods and services and distribute them for consumption by various people and groups in the society.

How an economic system operates depends on a society's objectives and the nature of its political institutions.[10] But regardless of what form these take, all economic systems must develop some method—along with appropriate economic institutions—to decide what and how much is to be produced and distributed by whom, when, to whom, and why.

Government officials may make the decisions

In a **command economy**, government officials decide what and how much is to be produced and distributed by whom, when, to whom, and why. These decisions are usually part of an overall government plan, so command economies are also called "planned" economies. It sounds good for a government to have a plan, but as a practical matter, attempts by a government to dictate an economic plan often don't work out as intended.

Producers in a command economy generally have little choice about what goods and services to produce. Their main task is to meet the production quotas assigned in the plan. Prices are also set by government planners and tend to be very rigid—not changing according to supply and demand. Although consumers usually have some

Artists and craftsmen in developing economies often do not have a large local market for their products. Ten Thousand Villages operates retail stores and an e-commerce website to help artisans reach more customers and promote economic development in their communities. The stores open a market for Loeng Hanh's finely crafted ceramic pieces. Hanh's profits allow her to earn a living and save money for her four-year-old son's education.

freedom of choice—it's impossible to control every single detail—the assortment of goods and services may be limited.

Government planning in a command economy may work fairly well as long as an economy is very simple, with little variety in goods and services. However, modern first- and second-world economies are more complex, and government planning tends to break down. Although countries such as North Korea, Cuba, and Iran rely largely on command-oriented economic systems, there is a trend toward market-directed economic systems. They have proven more effective in meeting consumer needs.

A market-directed economy adjusts itself

In a **market-directed economy**, the individual decisions of the many producers and consumers make the macro-level decisions for the whole economy. In a pure market-directed economy, consumers make a society's production decisions when they make their choices in the marketplace. They decide what is to be produced and by whom—through their dollar "votes."

Price is a measure of value
Prices in the marketplace are a rough measure of how society values particular goods and services. If consumers are willing to pay the market prices, then apparently they feel they are getting at least their money's worth. Similarly, the cost of labor and materials is a rough measure of the value of the resources used in the production of goods and services to meet these needs. New consumer needs that can be served profitably—not just the needs of the majority—will probably be met by some profit-minded businesses.

Greatest freedom of choice
Consumers in a market-directed economy enjoy great freedom of choice. They are not forced to buy any goods or services, except those that must be provided for the good of society—things such as national defense, schools, police and fire protection, highway systems, and public-health services. These are provided by the community—and the citizens are taxed to pay for them.

Similarly, producers are free to do whatever they wish—provided that they stay within the rules of the game set by government *and* receive enough dollar "votes" from consumers. If they do their job well, they earn a profit and stay in business. But profit, survival, and growth are not guaranteed.

The role of government

The American economy and most other Western economies are mainly market-directed—but not completely. Society assigns supervision of the system to the government. For example, besides setting and enforcing the "rules of the game," government agencies control interest rates and the supply of money. They also set import and export rules that affect international competition, regulate radio and TV broadcasting, sometimes control wages and prices, and so on. Government also tries to be sure that property is protected, contracts are enforced, individuals are not exploited, no group unfairly monopolizes markets, and producers deliver the kinds and quality of goods and services they claim to be offering.[11]

Public interest groups and consumers spread the word

In many Western economies, public interest groups and consumers provide an additional check on a market-directed economy. For example, the Center for Science in the Public Interest (CSPI) is a consumer watchdog group that pressures food companies to make healthier products. CSPI regularly issues reports on unhealthy foods like the high fat content in movie theater popcorn and Chinese food. The consulting firm UL TerraChoice regularly exposes firms that make false or exaggerated environmental claims about their products.

Consumers can also report their satisfaction or dissatisfaction with companies by posting reviews on websites. Some customers make sure their dissatisfaction is heard. When musician Dave Carroll's guitar was damaged by United Airlines—and baggage handlers and the airline refused to compensate him—Carroll's band made a YouTube video. The funny video, "United Breaks Guitars," went viral, millions saw it, and lo and behold, United offered Carroll a new guitar. Prospective customers often search the web to learn about companies before buying. They can easily find positive and negative information on the Internet, giving firms an extra incentive to play by the socially accepted rules of the game.

Macro-marketing systems adjust over time

So far, we have described how a market-directed macro-marketing system adjusts to become more effective and efficient by responding to customer needs (see Exhibit 1–2). As you read this book, you'll learn more about how marketing affects society and vice

Exhibit 1–2 Model of a Market-Directed Macro-Marketing System versa. You'll also learn more about specific marketing activities and be better informed when drawing conclusions about how fair and effective the macro-marketing system is. For now, however, we'll return to our general emphasis on a managerial view of the role of marketing in individual organizations.

Marketing's Role Has Changed a Lot over the Years

It's clear that marketing decisions are very important to a firm's success. But marketing hasn't always been so complicated. In fact, understanding how marketing thinking has evolved makes the modern view clearer. So we will discuss five stages in marketing evolution: (1) the simple trade era, (2) the production era, (3) the sales era, (4) the marketing department era, and (5) the marketing company era. We'll talk about these eras as if they applied generally to all firms—but keep in mind that *some managers still have not made it to the final stages.* They are stuck in the past with old ways of thinking.

Simple trade era to production era

When societies first moved toward some specialization of production and away from a subsistence economy where each family raised and consumed everything it produced, traders played an important role. Early "producers for the market" made products that were needed by themselves and their neighbors. As bartering became more difficult, societies moved into the **simple trade era**—a time when families traded or sold their "surplus" output to local distributors. These specialists resold the goods to other consumers or other distributors. This was the early role of marketing—and it is still the focus of marketing in many of the less-developed areas of the world. In fact, even in the United States, the United Kingdom, and other more advanced economies, marketing didn't change much until the Industrial Revolution brought larger factories more than a 150 years ago.

From the production to the sales era

From the Industrial Revolution until the 1920s, many companies were in the production era—some still are today. The **production era** is a time when a company focuses on production of a few specific products—perhaps because few of these products are available in the market. "If we can make it, it will sell" is management thinking characteristic of the production era. Because of product shortages, many nations—including some of the post-communist republics of Eastern Europe—continue to operate with production era approaches.

By about 1930, most companies in the industrialized Western nations had more production capability than ever before. Now the problem wasn't just to produce—but to beat the competition and win customers. This led many firms to enter the sales era. The **sales era** is a time when a company emphasizes selling because of increased competition.

To the marketing department era

For most firms in advanced economies, the sales era continued until at least 1950. By then, sales were growing rapidly in most areas of the economy. The problem was deciding where to put the company's effort. Someone was needed to tie together the efforts of research, purchasing, production, shipping, and sales. As this situation became more common, the sales era was replaced by the marketing department era. The **marketing department era** is a time when all marketing activities are brought under the control of one department to improve short-run policy planning and to try to integrate the firm's activities.

To the marketing company era

Since 1960, most firms have developed at least some managers with a marketing management outlook. Many of these firms have even graduated from the marketing department era into the marketing company era. The **marketing company era** is a

In the past, many banks created products but left it to the marketing department to sell them. In today's more competitive environment, banks are doing research to discover customer needs. A bank that develops products that meet its users' needs will have more satisfied customers. When Bank of the Wichitas added an online branch, it decided to use an untraditional approach and called it Redneck Bank. Redneck Bank offers customers "flat out free checking" and convenience served with a healthy dollop of humor. The approach has been successful as the small bank from Oklahoma quickly added customers from all over the United States.
Courtesy of Bank of the Wichitas®.

time when, in addition to short-run marketing planning, marketing people develop long-range plans—sometimes five or more years ahead—and the whole company effort is guided by the marketing concept.

What Does the Marketing Concept Mean?

LO 1.5

The **marketing concept** means that an organization aims *all* of its efforts at satisfying its *customers*—at a *profit*. The marketing concept is a simple but very important idea.

The marketing concept is not a new idea—it's been around for a long time. But some managers show little interest in customers' needs. These managers still have a **production orientation**—making whatever products are easy to produce and *then* trying to sell them. They think of customers existing to buy the firm's output rather than of firms existing to serve customers and—more broadly—the needs of society.

Well-managed firms have replaced this production orientation with a marketing orientation. A **marketing orientation** means trying to carry out the marketing concept. Instead of just trying to get customers to buy what the firm has produced, a marketing-oriented firm tries to offer customers what they need.

Three basic ideas are included in the definition of the marketing concept: (1) customer satisfaction, (2) a total company effort, and (3) profit—not just sales—as an objective. See Exhibit 1–3. These ideas deserve more discussion.

Customer satisfaction guides the whole system

"Give the customers what they need" seems so obvious that it may be hard for you to see why the marketing concept requires special attention. However, people don't always do the logical thing—especially when it means changing what they've done in

Exhibit 1-3
Organizations with a
Marketing Orientation
Carry Out the Marketing
Concept

The whole company works together to satisfy customers

Survival and success require a profit

the past. When customers have choices, they choose companies that best meet their needs, desires, and expectations. They purchase again from these companies and they tell their friends about the great experience. This all starts with customer satisfaction.

Ideally, all managers should work together as a team. Every department may directly or indirectly impact customer satisfaction. But some managers tend to build "fences" around their own departments. There may be meetings to try to get them to work together—but they come and go from the meetings worried only about protecting their own turf.

We use the term *production orientation* as a shorthand way to refer to this kind of narrow thinking—and lack of a central focus—in a business firm. But keep in mind that this problem may be seen in sales-oriented sales representatives, advertising-oriented agency people, finance-oriented finance people, directors of nonprofit organizations, and so on. It is not a criticism of people who manage production. They aren't necessarily any more guilty of narrow thinking than anyone else.

The fences come down in an organization that has accepted the marketing concept. There may still be departments because specialization often makes sense. But the total system's effort is guided by satisfying customers' needs and wants—instead of what each department would like to do. The marketing concept provides a guiding focus that *all* departments adopt. It must be a philosophy of the whole organization, not just an idea that applies to the marketing department.

Firms must satisfy customers. But keep in mind that it may cost more to satisfy some needs than any customers are willing to pay. Or it may be much more costly to try to attract new customers than it is to build a strong relationship with—and encourage repeat purchases from—existing customers. So profit—the difference between a firm's revenue and its total costs—is the bottom-line measure of the firm's success and ability to survive. It is the balancing point that helps the firm determine what needs it will try to satisfy with its total (sometimes costly!) effort.

Some organizations have other measures of long-term success. Most nonprofit organizations need revenues to exceed costs to survive long term—but they may have other goals valued by employees and supporters. For example, a food bank may measure success by the number of meals it serves to the homeless. Many for-profit organizations consider more than profit; for example, many are concerned with the environment or their community.

Many organizations go beyond profit

Some organizations explicitly consider a **triple bottom line**—which measures an organization's economic, social, and environmental outcomes—as a measure of long-term success. Profit is the economic outcome. Social refers to how the company's business activities affect its employees and other people in the communities where it operates. The third bottom line takes into account environmental responsibility, usually seeking to at least not harm the natural environment. Together, these are sometimes referred to as measures of people, planet, and profit.[12]

Consider Namaste Solar, which actively seeks economic profits while also measuring the impact on its local community and the planet. For example, the company gives 20 percent of its after-tax earnings to support projects such as a community bicycle-recycling program or the local children's museum. Namaste Solar's core products help the planet, but it also offers grants of up to $30,000 to help schools and nonprofits install their own solar systems. The company also self-monitors and reduces its waste. It recycles or reuses 90 percent of its office supplies and employs a zero waste company kitchen. Many of Namaste Solar's customers and employees value its triple bottom line orientation.[13]

Adoption of the marketing concept is not universal

The marketing concept may seem obvious, but it is easy to maintain a production-oriented way of thinking. Producers of industrial commodities such as steel, coal, and chemicals have tended to remain production-oriented in part because buyers see little difference among competitors. Some industries with limited competition, including electric utilities and cable television providers, have also been slow to adopt the marketing concept. When an industry gets competitive, consumers have choices and flock to those that deliver customer satisfaction. This provides an incentive for more firms to practice the marketing concept.[14]

Take a look at Exhibit 1–4. It shows some differences in outlook between adopters of the marketing concept and typical production-oriented managers. As the exhibit suggests, the marketing concept forces the company to think through what it is doing—and why.

Exhibit 1–4 Some Differences in Outlook between Adopters of the Marketing Concept and Typical Production-Oriented Managers

Topic	Marketing Orientation	Production Orientation
Attitudes toward customers	Customer needs determine company plans	They should be glad we exist, trying to cut costs and bringing out better products
Product offering	Company makes what it can sell	Company sells what it can make
Role of marketing research	To determine customer needs and how well company is satisfying them	To determine customer reaction, if used at all
Interest in innovation	Focus is on locating new opportunities	Focus is on technology and cost cutting
Customer service	Satisfy customers after the sale and they'll come back again	An activity required to reduce consumer complaints
Focus of advertising	Need-satisfying benefits of goods and services	Product features and how products are made
Relationship with customer	Customer satisfaction before and after sale leads to a profitable long-run relationship	Relationship ends when a sale is made
Costs	Eliminate costs that do not give value to customer	Keep costs as low as possible

The Marketing Concept and Customer Value

LO 1.6

Take the customer's point of view

A manager who adopts the marketing concept sees customer satisfaction as the path to profits. To better understand what it takes to satisfy a customer, it is useful to take the customer's point of view.

A customer may look at a market offering from two perspectives. One deals with the potential benefits of that offering; the other concerns what the customer has to give up to get those benefits. Consider a student who has just finished an exam and is thinking about getting an iced coffee from Starbucks. Our coffee lover might see this as a great-tasting treat, a quick pick-me-up, a quiet place to relax and meet friends, and even as a way to get to know an attractive classmate. Clearly, different needs are associated with these different benefits. The cost of getting these benefits would include the price of the coffee and any tip to the server, but there might be other nondollar costs. For example, how difficult it will be to park is a convenience cost. Slow service would be an aggravation.

Customer value reflects benefits and costs

As this example suggests, both benefits and costs can take many different forms, perhaps ranging from economic to emotional. They also may vary depending on the situation. However, it is the customer's view of the various benefits and costs that is important. This leads us to the concept of **customer value**—the difference between the benefits a customer sees from a market offering and the costs of obtaining those benefits.

Some people think that higher customer value comes from a low price. But that may not be the case at all. A good or service that doesn't meet a customer's needs results in low customer value, even if the price is very low. A high price may be more than acceptable when it obtains the desired benefits. Think again about our Starbucks example. You can get a cup of coffee for a much lower price, but Starbucks offers more than just a cup of coffee. Customers find superior value when costs are lower and/or benefits are higher. This is indicated in the upper left-hand corner of Exhibit 1–5.

Customers may not think about it very much

It is useful for a manager to evaluate ways to improve the benefits, or reduce the costs, of what the firm offers customers. However, this doesn't mean that customers stop and compute some sort of customer value score before making each purchase. If they did, there wouldn't be much time in life for anything else. So a manager's objective and thorough analysis may not accurately reflect the customer's impressions. Yet it is the customer's view that matters—even when the customer has not thought about it.

Where does competition fit?

You can't afford to ignore competition. Consumers usually have choices about how they will meet their needs. So a firm that offers superior customer value is likely to win and keep customers.

Exhibit 1–5
Costs, Benefits, and Customer Value

Often the best way to improve customer value, and beat the competition, is to be first to satisfy a need that others have not even considered. The competition between Coca-Cola and Pepsi illustrates this. Coca-Cola and Pepsi were spending millions of dollars on promotion—fighting head-to-head for the same cola customers. They put so much emphasis on the cola competition that they missed other opportunities. That gave firms like Snapple the chance to enter the market and steal away customers. For these customers, the desired benefits—and the greatest customer value—came from the variety of a fruit-flavored drink, not from one more cola.

Build relationships with customer value

Firms that embrace the marketing concept seek ways to build a profitable long-term relationship with each customer. Even the most innovative firm faces competition sooner or later. Trying to get new customers by taking them away from a competitor is usually more costly than retaining current customers by really satisfying their needs. Satisfied customers buy again and again whereas dissatisfied customers often tell others not to buy. With a long-term relationship, the customer's buying job is easier, and it also increases the selling firm's profits.

Building relationships with customers requires that everyone in a firm work together to provide customer value before *and after* each purchase. If there is a problem with a customer's bill, the accounting people can't just leave it to the salesperson to straighten it out or, even worse, act like it's "the customer's problem." These hassles raise customers' costs of doing business. The long-term relationship with the customer—and the lifetime value of the customer's future purchases—is threatened unless everyone works together to make things right for the customer. Similarly, the firm's advertising might encourage a customer to buy once, but if the firm doesn't deliver on the benefits promised in its ads, the customer is likely to go elsewhere the next time the need arises. In other words, any time the customer value is reduced—because the benefits to the customer decrease or the costs increase—the relationship is weakened.[15]

Exhibit 1–6 summarizes these ideas. In a firm that has adopted the marketing concept, everyone focuses on customer satisfaction. They look for ways to offer superior customer value. That helps attract customers in the first place—and keeps them satisfied after they buy. So when they are ready to make repeat purchases, the firm is able to keep them as customers. Sales may increase further because satisfied customers are likely to buy other products offered by the firm. In this way, the firm builds profitable relationships with its customers. In other words, when a firm adopts the marketing concept, it wins and so do its customers.

Patagonia, a high-end brand of outdoor clothing, builds long-term relationships with its customers by helping them care for their clothing. Patagonia encourages customers to *not* buy new clothing but instead repair their Patagonia gear—and it helps them do that. Patagonia's Repair Department completes about 30,000 repairs per year and recently added a truck that brings repair services to the customer. This helps Patagonia deliver customer satisfaction and customer value and builds long-term relationships. Learn more at http://www.patagonia.com/us/worn-wear.
©Patagonia, Inc.

Exhibit 1-6 Satisfying Customers with Superior Customer Value to Build Profitable Relationships

Total company effort to satisfy customers → **Offer superior customer value** → **Attract customers** → **Satisfy customers** → **Retain customers** → **Increase sales to customers** → **Build profitable relationships with customers** →

Chipotle's value delivers satisfied customers—again and again

Chipotle Mexican Grill, a restaurant chain that specializes in tacos and burritos, illustrates these ideas. Since opening its first store in 1993, Chipotle has successfully built enduring relationships with customers looking for good food fast. Chipotle does relatively little advertising to acquire new customers. When Chipotle opens a new store, it usually gives away thousands of burritos to build buzz and generate publicity. New customers usually find value in Chipotle's fresh ingredients, great tasting menu, convenient locations, and fast service, even at $8 to $9 for a burrito and drink. Predictably, they tell their friends.

Chipotle's customers also get satisfaction knowing they are eating organically grown local produce and meat from animals raised on family farms without the use of antibiotics and added hormones. Chipotle lets customers know about its "food with integrity" values through its website, various promotions, advertising, and online videos. For example, Chipotle produces "Farmed and Dangerous," a comedy series that plays on Hulu and pokes fun at the "unsustainable world of industrial agriculture." In its stores, Chipotle's friendly staff and great food deliver customers high value, and they come back again and again. That's why Chipotle is one of the fastest-growing restaurant chains in the world.[16]

The Marketing Concept Applies in Nonprofit Organizations

Newcomers to marketing thinking

The marketing concept is as important for nonprofit organizations as it is for business firms. In fact, marketing applies to all sorts of public and private nonprofit organizations—ranging from government agencies, health care organizations, educational institutions, and religious groups to charities, political parties, and fine arts organizations.

Support may not come from satisfied "customers"

As with any business firm, a nonprofit organization needs resources and support to survive and achieve its objectives. Yet support often does not come directly from those who receive the benefits the organization produces. For example, the World Wildlife Fund protects animals. If supporters of the World Wildlife Fund are not satisfied with its efforts—don't think the benefits are worth what it costs to provide them—they will put their time and money elsewhere.

Just as most firms face competition for customers, most nonprofits face competition for the resources and support they need. The Air Force faces a big problem if it can't attract new recruits. A shelter for the homeless may fail if supporters decide to focus on some other cause, such as AIDS education.

What is the "bottom line"?

As with a business, a nonprofit must take in as much money as it spends or it won't survive. However, a nonprofit organization does not measure "profit" in the same way as a firm. And its key measures of long-term success are also different. The YMCA, colleges, symphony orchestras, and the United Way, for example, all seek to achieve different objectives and need different measures of success. When everyone in an organization agrees to *some* measure(s) of long-run success, it helps the organization focus its efforts.

May not be organized for marketing

Some nonprofits face other challenges in organizing to adopt the marketing concept. Often no one has overall responsibility for marketing activities. Even when some leaders do the marketing thinking, they may have trouble getting unpaid volunteers with many different interests to all agree with the marketing strategy. Volunteers tend to do what they feel like doing![17]

The Marketing Concept, Social Responsibility, and Marketing Ethics

LO 1.7

Society's needs must be considered

The marketing concept is so logical that it's hard to find fault with it. Yet when a firm focuses its efforts on satisfying some consumers—to achieve its objectives—there may be negative effects on society. For example, producers and consumers making free choices can cause conflicts and difficulties. This is called the **micro-macro dilemma**. What is "good" for some firms and consumers may not be good for society as a whole.

For instance, many people in New York City buy bottled water because they like the convenience of easy-to-carry disposable bottles with spill-proof caps. On the other hand, the city already provides citizens with good tasting, safe tap water at a fraction of the cost. Is this just a matter of free choice by consumers? It's certainly a popular choice! On the other hand, critics point out that it is an inefficient use of resources to waste oil making and transporting millions of plastic bottles that end up in landfills where they leach chemicals into the soil. That kind of thinking, about the good of society as a whole, explains why New York City has run ads that encourage consumers to "get your fill" of free city water. What do you think? Should future generations pay the environmental price for today's consumer conveniences?[18]

Questions like these are not easy to answer. The basic reason is that many different people may have a stake in the outcomes—and social consequences—of the choices made by individual managers *and* consumers in a market-directed system. This means that marketing managers should be concerned with **social responsibility**—a firm's obligation to improve its positive effects on society and reduce its negative effects. As you read this book and learn more about marketing, you will also learn more about social responsibility in marketing—and why it must be taken seriously. You'll also see that being socially responsible sometimes requires difficult trade-offs.

Social responsibility can be difficult to assess when the effects on society are mixed. Take hydraulic fracturing (fracking), a process that sends pressurized liquid deep into the ground to remove oil and natural gas. Some argue that fracking helps America become more energy independent, produces cleaner fuel compared to alternatives, and lowers gas prices, thus stimulating the economy. On the other hand, the chemicals and procedures used in fracking may harm the environment and cause earthquakes. The government and many oil and gas producers are working to minimize the negative effects, but as you can imagine there are no easy answers for these conflicts.[19]

New York City Department of Health/DCF Advertising.

Marketing is now widely accepted by many local, national, and international nonprofit organizations. The Copenhagen Zoo attracted attention with a series of eye-catching ads featuring some of the zoo's favorite attractions.
Advertising Agency Bates Y&R Copenhagen, Denmark; Creative Director: Ib Borup; Art Director: Peder Schack; Agecu Producers: Josephie Winther-Poupinel and Steen Nohr; Erich Karsholt.

The issue of social responsibility in marketing also raises other important questions—for which there are no easy answers.

Should all consumer needs be satisfied?

Some consumers want products that may not be safe or good for them in the long run. Some critics argue that businesses should not offer high-heeled shoes, alcoholic beverages, marijuana, gambling, or sugar-coated cereals because they aren't "good" for some consumers in the long run. Similarly, bicycles and roller blades are among the most dangerous products identified by the Consumer Product Safety Commission. Who should decide if these products will be offered to consumers?

Think about sugary soft drinks—consumers love them, but they add to a growing global obesity problem. Most consumers know the drinks are not good for them, and that they need to cut back, but some have trouble with this. New York City passed a law (later overturned in court) prohibiting the sale of sweetened drinks of more than 16 ounces. France passed a soda tax. Coca-Cola has, on its own, limited advertising to children, increased promotion of diet drinks, and promoted physical activity programs. Should governments or consumers make decisions about what products are offered to consumers?[20]

Do all marketers act responsibly?

Not all marketers act in a socially responsible manner. Sometimes firms or individuals advance their own short-term interests at the expense of customers. For example, during the housing boom in the mid-2000s, some mortgage brokers took advantage of trusting customers and sold them mortgages they could not afford while earning large commissions for themselves. As a result, many homebuyers were unable to pay for their homes, and this contributed to a global economic recession. When products are complicated, consumers may be vulnerable to unscrupulous sellers. In these circumstances we can debate whether it is better to "let the buyer beware" or enact stricter government regulation.

What if it cuts into profits?

There are times when being socially responsible can increase not only a firm's profits, but also its costs. Even though some consumers will pay premium prices to buy "fair trade" coffee, napkins made from recycled paper, hybrid cars that pollute less, or products made in overseas factories that pay a "fair wage," these items may cost more to produce. At the same time, other consumers attach little or no value to these social measures and refuse to pay a higher price for such products. Consequently, many firms selling to this second group are reluctant to be more socially responsible.

When a society feels that the social benefits are important, it may add regulations to create a level playing field for all firms and to assure that these benefits are provided. For example, there are laws that protect rivers from water pollution and that restrict the use

Ben & Jerry's runs its business with a very clear set of values. These values guide the ice cream maker's employees, including its marketing managers' ethics—the moral standards that guide marketing decisions and actions.
©Ben & Jerry's United States, Inc

of child labor. Still, it is difficult for governments to impose regulations that govern all circumstances where such trade-offs occur. So is the marketing concept really desirable?

Socially conscious marketing managers are trying to answer these questions. Their definition of customer satisfaction includes long-range effects—as well as immediate customer satisfaction. They try to balance consumer, company, and social interests.

The marketing concept guides marketing ethics

A manager cannot be truly consumer-oriented and at the same time intentionally unethical. However, at times, problems and criticism may arise because a manager did not fully consider the ethical implications of a decision. In either case, there is no excuse for sloppiness when it comes to **marketing ethics**—the moral standards that guide marketing decisions and actions. Each individual develops moral standards based on his or her own values. That helps explain why opinions about what is right or wrong often vary from one person to another, from one society to another, and among different groups within a society. It is sometimes difficult to say whose opinions are "correct." Even so, such opinions may have a very real influence on whether an individual's (or a firm's) marketing decisions and actions are accepted or rejected. So marketing ethics are not only a philosophical issue; they are also a pragmatic concern.

Problems may arise when some individual manager does not share the same marketing ethics as others in the organization. One person operating alone can damage a firm's reputation and even survival.

Exhibit 1-7 Summary of American Marketing Association Statement of Ethics

Preamble

The American Marketing Association commits itself to promoting the highest standard of professional ethical norms and values for its members (practitioners, academics, and students). Norms are established standards of conduct that are expected and maintained by society and/or professional organizations. Values represent the collective conception of what communities find desirable, important, and morally proper. Values also serve as the criteria for evaluating our own personal actions and the actions of others. As marketers, we recognize that we not only serve our organizations but also act as stewards of society in creating, facilitating, and executing the transactions that are part of the greater economy. In this role, marketers are expected to embrace the highest professional ethical norms and the ethical values implied by our responsibility toward multiple stakeholders (e.g., customers, employees, investors, peers, channel members, regulators, and the host community).

Ethical Norms

As Marketers, we must:

- Do no harm.

- Foster trust in the marketing system.

- Embrace ethical values.

Ethical Values

- Honesty—to be forthright in dealings with customers and stakeholders.

- Responsibility—to accept the consequences of our marketing decisions and strategies.

- Fairness—to balance justly the needs of the buyer with the interests of the seller.

- Respect—to acknowledge the basic human dignity of all stakeholders.

- Transparency—to create a spirit of openness in marketing operations.

- Citizenship—to fulfill the economic, legal, philanthropic, and societal responsibilities that serve stakeholders.

To be certain that standards for marketing ethics are as clear as possible, many organizations have developed their own written codes of ethics. These codes usually state—at least at a general level—the ethical standards that everyone in the firm should follow in dealing with customers and other people. Many professional societies also have such codes. For example, the American Marketing Association's code of ethics— see Exhibit 1–7—sets specific ethical standards for many aspects of marketing.[21]

Throughout the text, we will be discussing the types of ethical issues individual marketing managers face. But we won't be moralizing and trying to tell you how you should think on any given issue. Rather, by the end of the course we hope that *you* will have some firm personal opinions about what is and is not ethical in micro-marketing activities.[22]

Fortunately, the prevailing practice of most businesspeople is to be fair and honest. However, not all criticisms of marketing focus on ethical issues.

Ethical Dilemma

What would you do? A customer purchases a Canon digital camera that comes with a 90-day manufacturer's warranty on parts and labor. The salesperson suggests that the customer consider the store's three-year extended service to cover any problems with the camera. The customer replies, "I'm getting a Canon because it's a reputable brand—and at $98 the service agreement is one-third the cost of the camera." Four months later, the customer returns to the store and complains that the camera no longer takes pictures and that "the store needs to make it right." If you were the store manager, what would you say? Would your response be any different if you knew that the customer was going to post his complaint on a consumer website?

Exhibit 1-8 Sample Criticisms of Marketing

- Advertising is everywhere, and it's often annoying, misleading, or wasteful.

- The quality of products is poor and often they are not even safe.

- There are too many unnecessary products.

- Retailers add too much to the cost of distribution and just raise prices without providing anything in return.

- Marketing serves the rich and exploits the poor.

- Marketers overpromise service, and when a consumer has a problem, nobody cares.

- Marketing creates interest in products that pollute the environment.

- Private information about consumers is collected and used to sell them things they don't need.

- Marketing makes people too materialistic and motivates them toward "things" instead of social needs.

- Easy consumer credit makes people buy things they don't need and can't afford.

Marketing has its critics

We must admit that marketing—as it exists in the United States and other developed societies—has many critics. Marketing activity is especially open to criticism because it is the part of business most visible to the public.

A number of typical complaints about marketing are summarized in Exhibit 1–8. Think about these criticisms and whether you agree with them or not. What complaints do you have that are not covered by one of the categories in Exhibit 1–8?

Such complaints should not be taken lightly. They show that many people are unhappy with some parts of the marketing system. Certainly, the strong public support for consumer protection laws proves that not all consumers feel they are being treated like royalty.

As you consider the various criticisms of marketing, keep in mind that not all of them deal with the marketing practices of specific firms. Some of the complaints about marketing really focus on the basic idea of a market-directed macro-marketing system—and these criticisms often occur because people don't understand what marketing is or how it works.[23] As you go through this book, we'll discuss some of these criticisms. Then in our final chapter, we will return to a more complete appraisal of marketing in our consumer-oriented society.

CONCLUSION

The basic purpose of this chapter is to introduce you to marketing and highlight its value for consumers, firms, and society. In Chapter 2, we introduce a marketing strategy planning process that is the framework for ideas developed throughout the rest of the text—and that will guide your marketing thinking in the future. This chapter sets the stage for that by introducing basic principles that guide marketing thinking.

You've learned about two views of marketing, both of which are important. One takes a micro view and focuses on marketing activities by an individual business (or other type of organization). This is what most people (including most business managers) have in mind when they talk about mar-

keting. But it's important to understand that marketing also plays a more macro role. Macro-marketing is concerned with the way the whole marketing system works in a society or economy. It operates to make exchanges and relationships between producers and their customers more effective.

We discussed the functions of marketing and who performs them. This includes not only producers and their customers but also marketing specialists who serve as intermediaries between producers and consumers and other specialists (such as product-testing labs and advertising agencies) who are collaborators and facilitate marketing functions.

We explained how a market-directed economy works, through the macro-marketing system, to provide consumers with choices. We introduced macro-marketing in this chapter, and we'll consider macro-marketing issues throughout the text. But the major focus of this book is on marketing by individual organizations. Someone in an organization must plan and manage its activities to make certain that customer needs are satisfied.

That's why understanding the marketing concept is another objective. The marketing concept is the basic philosophy that provides direction to a marketing-oriented firm. It stresses that the company's efforts should focus on satisfying some target customers—at a profit. Production-oriented firms tend to forget this. The various departments within a production-oriented firm let their natural conflicts of interest get in the way of customer satisfaction.

We also introduced the customer value concept. It is marketing's responsibility to make certain that what the firm offers customers really provides them with value that is greater than they can obtain somewhere else. In today's competitive markets, a firm must offer superior customer value if it wants to attract customers, satisfy them, and build beneficial long-term relationships with them.

A final objective was for you to see how social responsibility and marketing ethics relate to the marketing concept. The chapter ends by considering criticisms of marketing—both of the way individual firms work and of the whole macro system. When you have finished reading this book, you will be better able to evaluate these criticisms.

By learning more about marketing-oriented decision making, you will be able to make more efficient and socially responsible decisions. This will help improve the performance of individual firms and organizations (your employers). Eventually it will help our macro-marketing system work better.

WHAT'S NOW?

This chapter introduced you to marketing, macro-marketing, social responsibility, and ethics. What is going on in the world today that reflects some of these concepts? To learn more about how these concepts are playing out in the world today, check out *What's Now?* at www.learnthe4ps.com/whatsnow/c1.

KEY TERMS

LO 1.8

production, 5	standardization and grading, 11	sales era, 16
customer satisfaction, 5	financing, 11	marketing department era, 16
innovation, 6	risk taking, 11	marketing company era, 16
marketing, 7	market information function, 11	marketing concept, 17
pure subsistence economy, 8	intermediary, 11	production orientation, 17
macro-marketing, 9	collaborators, 12	marketing orientation, 17
economies of scale, 10	e-commerce, 12	triple bottom line, 19
universal functions of marketing, 11	economic system, 13	customer value, 20
buying function, 11	command economy, 13	micro-macro dilemma, 23
selling function, 11	market-directed economy, 14	social responsibility, 23
transporting function, 11	simple trade era, 16	marketing ethics, 25
storing function, 11	production era, 16	

QUESTIONS AND PROBLEMS

1. The case that opens this chapter features Nike. Review this case and pull out as many examples as you can of different key terms and concepts. For example, Nike demonstrated social responsibility (key term) when it began to monitor its suppliers' labor practices.

2. Review the Nike case study that opens this chapter. In what ways does Nike appear to follow the marketing concept? Suggest three other activities Nike could do to follow the marketing concept.

3. List your activities for the first two hours after you woke up this morning. Briefly indicate how marketing affected your activities.

4. If a producer creates a revolutionary new product and consumers can learn about it and purchase it on a website, is any additional marketing effort really necessary? Explain your thinking.

5. Distinguish between the micro and macro views of marketing. Then explain how they are interrelated, if they are.

6. Refer to Exhibit 1–1 and give an example of a purchase you made recently that involved separation of information and separation in time between you and the producer. Briefly explain how these separations were overcome.

7. Describe a recent purchase you made. Indicate why that particular product was available at a store and, in particular, at the store where you bought it.

8. Define the functions of marketing in your own words. Using an example, explain how they can be shifted and shared.

9. Online computer shopping at websites makes it possible for individual consumers to get direct information from hundreds of companies they would not otherwise know about. Consumers can place an order for a purchase that is then shipped to them directly. Will growth of these services ultimately eliminate the need for retailers and wholesalers? Explain your thinking, giving specific attention to what marketing functions are involved in these "electronic purchases" and who performs them.

10. Explain why a small producer might want a marketing research firm to take over some of its information-gathering activities.

11. Distinguish between how economic decisions are made in a command economy and how they are made in a market-directed economy.

12. Would the functions that must be provided and the development of wholesaling and retailing systems be any different in a command economy from those in a market-directed economy?

13. Explain why a market-directed macro-marketing system encourages innovation. Give an example.

14. Define the marketing concept in your own words, and then explain why the notion of profit is usually included in this definition.

15. Define the marketing concept in your own words, and then suggest how acceptance of this concept might affect the organization and operation of your college.

16. Distinguish between production orientation and marketing orientation, illustrating with local examples.

17. Explain why a firm should view its internal activities as part of a total system. Illustrate your answer for (a) a large grocery products producer, (b) a plumbing wholesaler, (c) a department store chain, and (d) a cell phone service provider.

18. Give examples of some of the benefits and costs that might contribute to the customer value of each of the following products: (a) a wristwatch, (b) a weight-loss diet supplement, (c) a cruise on a luxury liner, and (d) a checking account from a bank.

19. What are examples of the benefits that you can provide to a prospective employer in your field? What are examples of the costs that employer would incur if it hired you? How do you think you can increase the value you offer a prospective employer?

20. Give an example of a recent purchase you made where the purchase wasn't just a single transaction but rather part of an ongoing relationship with the seller. Discuss what the seller has done (or could do better) to strengthen the relationship and increase the odds of you being a loyal customer in the future.

21. Discuss how the micro-macro dilemma relates to each of the following products: high-powered engines in cars, nuclear power, bank credit cards, and pesticides that improve farm production.

SUGGESTED CASES

1. McDonald's "Seniors" Restaurant
2. Nature's Way Foods, Inc.

18. West Tarrytown Volunteer Fire Department

Video Case 1. Chick-fil-A

MARKETING ANALYTICS: DATA TO KNOWLEDGE

CHAPTER 1: REVENUE, COST, AND PROFIT RELATIONSHIPS

This problem introduces you to the Marketing Analytics exercises, which are available in Connect (may require a separate purchase) for this text—and gets you started with the use of spreadsheet analysis for marketing decision making. Connect creates a spreadsheet to help you focus on the use of marketing analytics and not spreadsheet creation. In this case the problem is relatively simple. In fact, you could work it without the software. But by starting with a simple problem, you will learn how to use the program more quickly and see how it will help you with more complicated problems.

Sue Cline, the business manager at Magna University Student Bookstore, is developing plans for the next academic year. The bookstore is one of the university's nonprofit activities, but any "surplus" (profit) it earns is used to support the student activities center.

Two popular products at the bookstore are the student academic calendar and notebooks with the school name. Sue Cline

thinks that she can sell calendars to 90 percent of Magna's 3,000 students, so she has had 2,700 printed. The total cost, including artwork and printing, is $11,500. Last year the calendar sold for $5.00, but Sue is considering changing the price this year.

Sue thinks that the bookstore will be able to sell 6,000 notebooks if they are priced right. But she knows that many students will buy similar notebooks (without the school name) from stores in town if the bookstore price is too high.

Sue has entered the information about selling price, quantity, and costs for calendars and notebooks in the spreadsheet program so that it is easy to evaluate the effect of different decisions. The spreadsheet is also set up to calculate revenue and profit, based on

Revenue = (Selling price) × (Quantity sold) Profit = (Revenue) − (Total cost)

See Connect for the spreadsheet and questions needed to analyze this scenario.

Tristan Fewings/Getty Images.

Marketing Strategy Planning

There was a time when it didn't seem an exaggeration for Barnum & Bailey's ads to tout the circus as "the greatest show on earth." For one hundred years, circuses had brought excitement and family entertainment to towns all over the country. Parents hardly noticed the hard benches that they sat on as they watched their kids cheer for the acrobats, clowns, and animal acts. But by the 1980s, the popularity of traditional circuses was in decline; many simply went out of business.

You can imagine why this sad state of affairs would be a concern for Guy Laliberté—a stilt walker, accordion player, and fire-eater—and others in his band of performers. But instead of bemoaning the demise of the circus, they saw an opportunity for a new kind of entertainment—and their idea gave birth to "Cirque du Soleil."

Their new style of circus still traveled to audiences and set up the "big top" tent, but costly and controversial animal acts were eliminated. Instead, the entertainment focused on an innovative combination of acrobatics, music, and theater. This more sophisticated offering appealed to adults. Importantly, adults were willing to pay more for tickets when the show was targeted at them and not just kids—especially when the traditional circus benches were replaced with more comfortable seats.

Cirque du Soleil quickly struck a chord with audiences and soon the producers were developing new shows and expanding tours to reach new markets. Laliberté recognized and built on this breakthrough opportunity. At any one time, about a dozen different Cirque du Soleil shows travel across Europe, Asia, Australia, and North and South America. Each show performs in a host city from two weeks to three months. Nine other Cirque du Soleil shows have permanent homes and target tourists visiting Las Vegas, Nevada, and Orlando, Florida. Each of the shows has a unique theme. For example, OVO looks at the world of insects, Iris celebrates Hollywood movies, and Zumanity is an adult-themed cabaret-style show.

When considering new shows, each idea is evaluated on its creativity, uniqueness, and likelihood of becoming a real blockbuster. New shows can take more than five years and $100 million to develop. It is anticipated that these development costs will be recouped over each show's planned 10-year run. Some shows pay back even quicker. *Michael Jackson THE IMMORTAL World Tour* was a big hit—selling more than $140 million in tickets in its first full year on the road. That show's successes led to the development of *Michael Jackson ONE*, now based in Las Vegas.

As all of this suggests, Cirque du Soleil's marketing managers constantly evaluate new opportunities. A few years ago the company even considered a plan to diversify into hotels and spas based on the circus theme. This idea was screened out—at least for now—and instead the focus has been on developing new products for current customers. For example, in Las Vegas Cirque du Soleil created lounges with the Cirque du Soleil theme where customers could relax before or after one of their shows.

Cirque du Soleil reaches some new customers through television specials and DVDs. These small screen shows generate additional revenue while giving customers a taste of Cirque du Soleil—and whetting their appetite for a live show.

Once customers see a live Cirque du Soleil show, they want to see more. So Cirque advertises to encourage customers to see that first show. Ads in airline magazines target travelers heading to cities with permanent shows; traveling shows are heavily advertised in local media. Publicity and word-of-mouth are also important. Local newspapers and TV shows are interested in doing stories about touring productions before they come to town. Cirque du Soleil's website helps the press by providing photos, videos, and interviews for easy download. To encourage word-of-mouth, Cirque du Soleil invites influential people in the community to a gala opening night. The troupe also volunteers time to local art and charitable organizations, thereby building relationships with the community. After experiencing the magic, people often "spread the word" to friends and look forward to the next opportunity to see Cirque du Soleil in action.

Cirque du Soleil hopes to develop customers for life who love the shows and come back again and again. To keep that magic alive, they encourage customers to "Like" Cirque du Soleil's Facebook page, where regular updates feature video interviews with cast members, posts with Cirque du Soleil's latest news, and comments from other fans. For up-to-the-minute news, they can follow Cirque du Soleil on Twitter or download an app for their cell phones. Other fans prefer to watch that action on Cirque du Soleil's YouTube channel or follow photos on the brand's Instagram page or Pinterest boards. For anyone wishing to learn more, Cirque du Soleil's marketing managers also monitor and maintain Wikipedia pages and create home pages for each show.

Though Cirque du Soleil has been very successful, it must continue to focus on ways to improve its customers' experiences. Some recent shows were not adequately differentiated from one another—so Cirque du Soleil had trouble getting customers who had already seen Varekai to come to the new Totem show. Upstart imitators, such as the Canadian Cirque Éloize and Le Rêve in Las Vegas, offer similar entertainment fare. The well-known Cirque du Soleil brand name still gives the troupe a competitive advantage when it introduces new shows. It also allows Cirque to charge a premium price for tickets, which range from $40 to more than $200 for the exclusive *Tapis Rouge* (Red Carpet) tickets. Cirque du Soleil's carefully crafted marketing mix generates ticket sales that exceed half a billion dollars each year.[1]

LEARNING OBJECTIVES

Marketing managers at Cirque du Soleil make many decisions as they develop marketing strategies. Making good marketing strategy decisions is never easy, yet knowing what basic decision areas to consider helps you plan a more successful strategy. This chapter will get you started by giving you a framework for thinking about marketing strategy planning—which is what the rest of this book is all about.

When you finish this chapter, you should be able to

1 Understand what a marketing manager does.

2 Know what marketing strategy planning is—and why it is the focus of this book.

3 Understand target marketing.

4 Be familiar with the Four Ps in a marketing mix.

5 Know the difference between a marketing strategy, a marketing plan, and a marketing program.

6 Understand what customer lifetime value and customer equity are and why marketing strategy planners seek to increase them.

7 Be familiar with the text's framework for marketing strategy planning.

8 Know four broad types of marketing opportunities that help in identifying new strategies.

9 Understand why strategies for opportunities in international markets should be considered.

10 Understand the important new terms (shown in red).

The Management Job in Marketing

LO 2.1

In Chapter 1 you learned about the marketing concept—a philosophy to guide the whole firm toward satisfying customers at a profit. From the Cirque du Soleil case, it's clear that marketing decisions are very important to a firm's success. Let's look more closely at the marketing management process.

The **marketing management process** is the process of (1) *planning* marketing activities, (2) directing the *implementation* of the plans, and (3) *controlling* these plans. Planning, implementation, and control are basic jobs of all managers—but here we will emphasize what they mean to marketing managers.

Exhibit 2–1 shows the relationships among the three jobs in the marketing management process. The jobs are all connected to show that the marketing management process is continuous. In the planning job, managers set guidelines for the implementing job and specify expected results. They use these expected results in the control job to determine if everything has worked out as planned. The link from

Exhibit 2-1
The Marketing
Management Process

the control job to the planning job is especially important. This feedback often leads to changes in the plans or to new plans.

Managers should seek new opportunities

Managers are not satisfied just planning for the present market. Markets are dynamic. Consumers' needs, competitors, and the environment keep changing. Consider Hasbro, a company that seemed to have a "Monopoly" in family games. While it continued selling board games, firms such as Sony, Microsoft, and Nintendo zoomed in with video game competition. Then online multiplayer games such as World of Warcraft and Facebook-based Farmville grabbed consumers' attention, followed by mobile games such as Candy Crush and Trivia Crack. Bit by bit, Hasbro fell further behind customer trends. Of course, not every opportunity is good for every company. Really attractive opportunities are those that fit with what the whole company wants to do and is able to do well.

Strategic management planning concerns the whole firm

The job of planning strategies to guide a whole company is called **strategic (management) planning**—the managerial process of developing and maintaining a match between an organization's resources and its market opportunities. This is a top-management job. It includes planning not only for marketing but also for production, finance, human resources, and other areas.

Although marketing strategies are not whole-company plans, company plans should be market-oriented. And the marketing plan often sets the tone and direction for the whole company. So we will use *strategy planning* and *marketing strategy planning* to mean the same thing.[2]

What Is a Marketing Strategy?

Marketing strategy planning means finding attractive opportunities and developing profitable marketing strategies. But what is a "marketing strategy"? We have used these words rather casually so far. Now let's see what they really mean.

Exhibit 2-2
A Marketing Strategy

A **marketing strategy** specifies a target market and a related marketing mix. It is a big picture of what a firm will do in some market. Two interrelated parts are needed:

1. A **target market**—a fairly homogeneous (similar) group of customers to whom a company wishes to appeal.
2. A **marketing mix**—the controllable variables the company puts together to satisfy this target group.

The importance of target customers in this process can be seen in Exhibit 2–2, where the target market is at the center of the diagram. The target market is surrounded by the controllable variables that we call the "marketing mix." A typical marketing mix includes some product, offered at a price, with some promotion to tell potential customers about the product, and a way to reach the customer's place.

The marketing strategy for Herbal Essences hair care products aims at a specific group of target customers: young women in their late teens and early 20s. The products include various shampoos, conditioners, gels, and hairspray for different types of hair. The product names and brightly colored packaging grab customers' attention. Long Term Relationship (in bright red bottles) is formulated to add silkiness to long hair, and Body Envy (in orange bottles) adds body to flat hair. The curvy, matched, and nested shampoo and conditioner bottles subtly encourage customers to buy the products together. By seeking eye-level placement at stores such as Target and Walmart, Herbal Essences locates its products where most of its target customers shop for hair care essentials. The brand's print, television, and online advertising incorporate a mythical quality that supports the products' organic origins. Herbal Essences' homepage (www. herbalessences.com) includes hundreds of customer ratings and reviews, links to a Facebook Fan page (with more than 1 million fans), a Twitter feed, and a YouTube channel. The shampoo and conditioner retail for $6 to $8 a bottle, with occasional dollar-off coupons to encourage new customer trial. Fast-growing sales suggest this marketing mix hits the bulls-eye for this target market.[3]

© McGraw-Hill Education; Mark Dierker, photographer.

Selecting a Market-Oriented Strategy Is Target Marketing

Note that a marketing strategy specifies some *particular* target customers. This approach is called "target marketing" to distinguish it from "mass marketing." **Target marketing** says that a marketing mix is tailored to fit some specific target customers. In contrast, **mass marketing**—the typical production-oriented approach—vaguely aims at "everyone" with the same marketing mix. Mass marketing assumes that everyone is the same—and it considers everyone to be a potential customer. It may help to think of target marketing as the "rifle approach" and mass marketing as the "shotgun approach." See Exhibit 2–3.

Commonly used terms can be confusing here. The terms *mass marketing* and *mass marketers* do not mean the same thing. Far from it! *Mass marketing* means trying to sell to "everyone," as we explained earlier. *Mass marketers* such as Kraft Foods and Walmart are aiming at clearly defined target markets. The confusion with mass marketing occurs because their target markets usually are large and spread out.

Target marketing is not limited to small market segments—only to fairly homogeneous ones. A very large market—even what is sometimes called the "mass market"—may be

Exhibit 2-3
Production-Oriented and Marketing-Oriented Managers Have Different Views of the Market

Production-oriented manager sees everyone as basically similar and practices "mass marketing"

Marketing-oriented manager sees everyone as different and practices "target marketing"

fairly homogeneous, and a target marketer will deliberately aim at it. For example, a very large group of parents of young children are homogeneous on many dimensions, including their attitudes about changing baby diapers. In the United States alone, this group spends about $5 billion a year on disposable diapers—so it should be no surprise that it is a major target market for companies such as Kimberly-Clark (Huggies) and Procter & Gamble (Pampers). On the other hand, babies and their parents are not the only ones who need disposable diapers. Many elderly people, especially those who are in nursing homes and have mobility problems, use diapers. Needless to say, the

A marketing mix does not need to appeal to all customers. Target marketers recognize that every customer is different. They identify a target market to serve, and then create a marketing mix to match that market's needs. A $400 cooler is not for everyone, but YETI identified customers that value a high quality, durable cooler that keeps ice longer. People who fish a lot are one of the target markets that find YETI coolers to be a good value.

marketing mix that's right for babies isn't right for elder care. It's not just the sizes that are different, but also the forms. The elderly don't like the idea of needing "diapers"—so instead they wear disposable "pull ups."

The basic reason to focus on some specific target customers is so that you can develop a marketing mix that satisfies those customers' *specific* needs better than they are satisfied by some other firm. For example, E*TRADE uses a website (www.etrade.com) to target knowledgeable investors who want a convenient, low-cost way to buy and sell stocks online without a lot of advice (or pressure) from a salesperson.

Developing Marketing Mixes for Target Markets

There are many marketing mix decisions

There are many possible ways to satisfy the needs of target customers. A product might have many different features. It could be sold directly to customers via the Internet, offered only in stores, or both. Customer service levels before or after the sale can be adjusted. The package, brand name, and warranty can be changed. Various advertising media—newspapers, magazines, cable, the Internet—may be used. The company can develop social media sites on Facebook, Twitter, or Instagram. A company's own sales force or other sales specialists can be used. The price can be changed, discounts can be given, and so on. With so many possible variables, is there any way to help organize all these decisions and simplify the selection of marketing mixes? The answer is yes.

The "Four Ps" make up a marketing mix

It is useful to reduce all the variables in the marketing mix to four basic ones:

Product
Place
Promotion
Price

It helps to think of the four major parts of a marketing mix as the "*Four Ps.*"

Customer is not part of the marketing mix

The customer—the target market—is shown surrounded by the Four Ps in Exhibit 2–4. Some students assume that the customer is part of the marketing mix—but this is not so. The customer should be the *target* of all marketing efforts.

Exhibit 2–5 shows some of the strategy decision variables organized by the Four Ps. These will be discussed in later chapters. For now, let's just describe each P briefly.

Exhibit 2-4
A Marketing Strategy—Showing the Four Ps of a Marketing Mix

Product—the good or service for the target's needs

The Product area is concerned with developing the right "product" for the target market. This offering may involve a physical good, a service, or a blend of both. Whereas Coke Zero, Jeep Wrangler, and the Samsung Galaxy phone are physical goods, the product for Verizon Wireless is the communication service it provides—sending texts, completing phone calls, and connecting customers to the Internet. The Product of a political party is the policies it works to achieve. The important thing to remember is that your good or service should satisfy some customers' needs.

Along with other Product-area decisions such as branding, packaging, and warranties, we will talk about developing and managing new products, product quality, and whole product lines.

Exhibit 2-5 Strategy Decision Areas Organized by the Four Ps

Product	Place	Promotion	Price

• Physical good
• Service
• Features
• Benefits
• Quality level
• Accessories
• Installation
• Instructions
• Warranty
• Product lines
• Packaging
• Branding
	• Objectives
	• Channel type
	• Market exposure
	• Kinds of intermediaries
	• Kinds and locations of stores
	• How to handle transporting and storing
	• Service levels
	• Recruiting intermediaries
	• Managing channels
		• Objectives
		• Promotion blend
		• Salespeople
		  Kind
		  Number
		  Selection
		  Training
		  Motivation
		• Advertising
		  Targets
		  Kinds of ads
		  Media type
		  Copy thrust
		  Prepared by whom
		• Publicity
		• Sales promotion
			• Objectives
			• Flexibility
			• Level over product life cycle
			• Geographic terms
			• Discounts
			• Allowances

Place—reaching the target

Place is concerned with all the decisions involved in getting the right product to the target market's Place. A product isn't much good to a customer if it isn't available when and where it's wanted.

A product reaches customers through a channel of distribution. A **channel of distribution** is any series of firms (or individuals) that participate in the flow of products from producer to final user or consumer.

Sometimes a channel of distribution is short and runs directly from a producer to a final user or consumer. This is common in business markets and in the marketing of services. For example, GEICO sells its insurance directly to final consumers. However, as shown in Exhibit 2–6, channels are often more complex—as when Nestlé's packaged food products are handled by wholesalers and retailers before reaching consumers. When a marketing manager has several different target markets, several different channels of distribution may be needed.

We will also see how physical distribution service levels and decisions concerning logistics (transporting, storing, and handling products) relate to the other Place decisions and the rest of the marketing mix.

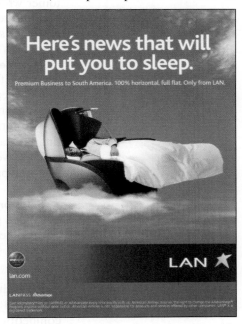

Here's news that will put you to sleep.

Premium Business to South America. 100% horizontal, full flat. Only from LAN.

LAN ✦

A firm's product may involve a physical good or a service or a combination of both. Chilean airline LAN provides a service, but the quality of its equipment, especially the special sleeper seats on its planes, helps the firm do a superior job in meeting the needs of international travelers.

Promotion—telling and selling the customer

The third P—Promotion—is concerned with telling the target market or others in the channel of distribution about the right product. Sometimes promotion is focused on acquiring new

Exhibit 2-6 Four Examples of Basic Channels of Distribution for Consumer Products

customers and sometimes it's focused on retaining current customers. Promotion includes personal selling, mass selling, and sales promotion. It is the marketing manager's job to blend these methods of communication.

Personal selling involves direct spoken communication between sellers and potential customers. Personal selling may happen face-to-face, over the telephone, or even via a videoconference over the Internet. Sometimes personal attention is required *after the sale.* **Customer service**—a personal communication between a seller and a customer who wants the seller to resolve a problem with a purchase—is often a key to building repeat business. Individual attention comes at a price; personal selling and customer service can be very expensive. Often this personal effort has to be blended with mass selling and sales promotion.

Mass selling is communicating with large numbers of customers at the same time. The main form of mass selling is **advertising**—any *paid* form of nonpersonal presentation of ideas, goods, or services by an identified sponsor. Advertising may appear in newspapers, on television, or over the Internet, among other places. **Publicity**—any *unpaid* form of nonpersonal presentation of ideas, goods, or services—includes getting favorable coverage in newspaper stories or on television. Publicity also involves creating web pages where a firm can tell interested customers more about its product. The web page could even be part of a social media tool such as Facebook, Twitter, or Pinterest.

Sales promotion refers to those promotion activities—other than advertising, publicity, and personal selling—that stimulate interest, trial, or purchase by final customers or others in the channel. This can involve the use of coupons, point-of-purchase materials, samples, signs, contests, events, catalogs, novelties, and circulars.

Price—making it right

In addition to developing the right Product, Place, and Promotion, marketing managers must also set the right Price. Price setting must consider the kind of competition in the target market and the cost of the whole marketing mix. A manager must also try to estimate customer reaction to possible prices. Besides this, the manager must know current practices as to markups, discounts, and other terms of sale. And if customers won't accept the Price, all of the planning effort is wasted.

Each of the Four Ps contributes to the whole

All Four Ps are needed in a marketing mix. In fact, they should all be tied together. But is any one more important than the others? Generally speaking, the answer is no—all contribute to one whole. When a marketing mix is being developed, all (final) decisions about the Ps should be made at the same time. That's why the Four Ps are arranged around the target market in a circle—to show that they all are equally important.

Let's sum up our discussion of marketing mix planning thus far. We develop a *Product* to satisfy the target customers. We find a way to reach our target customers' *Place*. We use *Promotion* to tell the target customers (and others in the channel) about the product that has been designed for them. And we set a *Price* after estimating expected customer reaction to the total offering and the costs of getting it to them.

Strategy jobs must be done together

It is important to stress—it cannot be overemphasized—that selecting a target market *and* developing a marketing mix are interrelated. Both parts of a marketing strategy must be decided together. It is *strategies* that must be evaluated against the company's objectives—not alternative target markets or alternative marketing mixes.

Ethical Dilemma

What would you do? You have been working for a major online retailer in the entertainment products category and have responsibility for DVD and Blu-ray movie sales. You've been approached by a company that offers a behavioral targeting software program. When a customer visits your website, this program can tell whether that customer has been "shopping around"—it knows if a customer has looked at DVD or Blu-ray movies at other online stores. Assuming this type of behavior means these customers are looking for a good deal, the new software allows you to charge a lower price only to these "shopping around" customers. The higher, regular prices will continue to be shown to other customers. The software seller claims his software will double your profits in the DVD and Blu-ray category. When you ask if it is fair that different customers pay different prices, the software salesperson says, "This is just how target marketing works today. One target market is price sensitive, so we give them a lower price. The other doesn't care about price, so we keep it higher." Would you purchase this service? How would customers paying the higher price feel if they found out other customers paid lower prices for the same movies? Explain your decision.

Understanding target markets leads to good strategies

The needs of a target market often virtually determine the nature of an appropriate marketing mix. So marketers must analyze their potential target markets with great care. This book will explore ways of identifying attractive market opportunities and developing appropriate strategies.

Let's look at the strategy planning process more closely in the classic case of Jeff Silverman and Toddler University (TU), Inc., a shoe company he started. During high school and college, Silverman worked as a salesperson at local shoe stores. He also gained valuable experience during a year working for Nike. From these jobs he learned a lot about customers' needs and interests. He also realized that some parents were not satisfied when it came to finding shoes for their preschool children.

Silverman saw there were many different types of customers for baby shoes, each group with a different set of needs. From his observations, there was one market that was underserved. These *Attentive Parents* wanted shoes that met a variety of needs. They wanted shoes to be fun and fashionable and functional. They didn't want just a good fit but also design and materials that were really right for baby play and learning to walk. These well-informed, upscale shoppers were likely to buy from a store that specialized in baby items. They were also willing to pay a premium price if they found the right product. Silverman saw an opportunity to serve the Attentive Parents target market with a marketing mix that combined, in

To smuggle durable, custom-fitted shoes into a kid's wardrobe, disguise them as sneakers.

Toddler University® presents a great leap forward for children's feet.

It's called the Higher Education™ Sneaker. And while its playful exterior may look like other sneakers, there the resemblance ends.

Because what you see here is footwear that gives kids who live in sneakers a significantly higher standard of living.

For instance, most companies that make lightweight shoes take the issue of fit all too lightly. Toddler U's come with custom-fitted footbeds that mold shoes to every contour of your child's feet. An exclusive process we call Tri-Dimensional Fit.™

Other sneaker soles are surprisingly inflexible when it comes to bending. But our Higher Education soles allow a child's feet to bend almost as easily as if they were barefoot, thanks to their pliant Flex Zones.®

And since destroying sneakers is among every kid's favorite sports, ours come with thicker leathers, molded rubber toe guards, and sturdy T.U. Custom Canvas.™ Making them the first sneakers specifically designed to finish last.

In other words, Higher Education is anything but a sneaker of the old school.

To see the complete line in a brilliant array of styles and colors, phone 1-800-237-6751 for the Toddler U dealer near you.

TODDLER UNIVERSITY®

Higher education for younger feet®

© 1990 Toddler U Inc.

Toddler University's marketing strategy was successful because it developed a distinctive marketing mix that was precisely relevant to the needs of its target market.
Courtesy Toddler University.

his words, "fit and function with fun and fashion." He developed a detailed marketing plan that attracted financial backers, and his company came to life.

Silverman contracted with a producer in Taiwan to make shoes to his specs with his Toddler University brand name. TU's specs were different—they improved the product for this target market. Unlike most rigid high-topped infant shoes, TU's shoes were softer with more comfortable rubber soles. The shoes were stitched rather than glued so they lasted longer and included an extra-wide opening so the shoes slipped easier onto squirming feet. A patented special insert allowed parents to adjust the shoes' width. The insert also helped win support from retailers. With 11 sizes of children's shoes—and five widths—retailers usually stocked 55 pairs of each style. TU's adjustable width reduced the stocking requirements, making the line more profitable than competing shoes. TU's Product and Place decisions worked together to provide customer value and also to give TU a competitive advantage.

For promotion, TU's print ads featured close-up photos of babies wearing the shoes and informative details about their special benefits. Creative packaging promoted the shoe and attracted customers in the store. For example, TU put one athletic-style shoe in a box that looked like a gray gym locker. TU also provided stores with "shoe rides"—electric-powered rocking replicas of its shoes. The rides attracted kids to the shoe department, and because they were coin-operated, they paid for themselves in a year.

TU priced most of its shoes at $35 to $40 a pair. This is a premium price, but the Attentive Parents typically have smaller families and are willing to spend more on each child.

In just four years, TU's sales jumped from $100,000 to more than $40 million. To keep growth going, Silverman expanded distribution to reach new markets in Europe. To take advantage of TU's relationship with its satisfied target customers, TU expanded its product line to offer shoes for older kids. Then Silverman made his biggest sale of all: He sold his company to Genesco, one of the biggest firms in the footwear business.[4]

The Marketing Plan Is a Guide to Implementation and Control

LO 2.5

Marketing plan fills out marketing strategy

As the Toddler University case illustrates, a marketing strategy sets a target market and a marketing mix. It is a big picture of what a firm will do in some market. A marketing plan goes farther. A **marketing plan** is a written statement of a marketing strategy *and* the time-related details for carrying out the strategy. It should spell out the following in detail: (1) what marketing mix will be offered, to whom (that is, the target market), and for how long; (2) what company resources (shown as costs) will be needed at what rate (month by month perhaps); and (3) what results are expected (sales and profits perhaps monthly or quarterly, customer satisfaction levels, and the like). The plan should also include some control procedures so that whoever is to carry out the plan will know if things are going wrong. This might be something as simple as comparing actual sales against expected sales with a warning flag to be raised whenever total sales fall below a certain level.

Appendix D provides a sample marketing plan for a veterinary clinic. At the end of each chapter, there is an exercise titled **Marketing Planning for Hillside Veterinary**

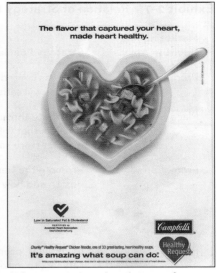

Campbell Soup Company has developed different soups (and related marketing mixes) that are targeted to the specific needs of different target markets. The marketing plan for each type of soup fits into Campbell's overall marketing program.
All images: © 2015 CSC Brands, L.P. All rights reserved.

Clinic that introduces you to aspects of a marketing plan as related to the topics in that chapter. This gives you a step-by-step way to learn how chapter concepts apply to marketing planning, and develop your plan-building skills as you progress through the text. In Chapter 19, we review all of the elements in a marketing plan. At that point, you will have learned about all of the major strategy decision areas (Exhibit 2–5) and how to blend them into an innovative strategy.

Implementation puts plans into operation

After a marketing plan is developed, a marketing manager knows *what* needs to be done. Then the manager is concerned with **implementation**—putting marketing plans into operation. Strategies work out as planned only when they are effectively implemented. Many **operational decisions**—short-run decisions to help implement strategies—may be needed.

Managers should make operational decisions within the guidelines set down during strategy planning. They develop product policies, place policies, and so on as part of strategy planning. Then operational decisions within these policies probably will be necessary—while carrying out the basic strategy. Note, however, that as long as these operational decisions stay within the policy guidelines, managers are making no change in the basic strategy. If the controls show that operational decisions are not producing the desired results, however, the managers may have to reevaluate the whole strategy—rather than just working harder at implementing it.

It's easier to see the difference between strategy decisions and operational decisions if we illustrate these ideas using our Toddler University example. Possible Four Ps or basic strategy policies are shown in the left-hand column in Exhibit 2–7, and examples of operational decisions are shown in the right-hand column.

It should be clear that some operational decisions are made regularly—even daily—and such decisions should not be confused with planning strategy. Certainly, a great deal of effort can be involved in these operational decisions. They might take a good part of the sales or advertising manager's time. But they are not the strategy decisions that will be our primary concern.

Analytical tools provide control

Our focus in this text is on developing marketing strategies. But eventually marketing managers must control the marketing plans that they develop and implement. The control job provides feedback so managers can change marketing strategies to

Exhibit 2-7 Relation of Strategy Policies to Operational Decisions for a Baby Shoe Company

Marketing Mix Decision Area	Strategy Policies	Likely Operational Decisions
Product	Carry as limited a line of colors, styles, and sizes as will satisfy the target market.	Add, change, or drop colors, styles, and/or sizes as customer tastes dictate.
Place	Distribute through selected "baby-products" retailers that will carry the full line and provide good in-store sales support and promotion.	In market areas where sales potential is not achieved, add new retail outlets and/or drop retailers whose performance is poor.
Promotion	Promote the benefits and value of the special design and how it meets customer needs.	When a retailer hires a new salesperson, send current training package with details on product line; increase use of local newspaper print ads during peak demand periods (e.g., before holidays).
Price	Maintain a "premium" price, but encourage retailers to make large-volume orders by offering discounts on quantity purchases.	Offer short-term introductory price "deals" to retailers when a new style is first introduced.

better meet customer needs. To maintain control, a marketing manager uses a number of analytical tools to learn more about customers and their buying habits. That might involve measuring customers' shopping behaviors and purchase decisions. In Chapter 19 we look more closely at how firms control marketing plans and programs. In addition, as we talk about each of the marketing decision areas in Chapters 8 through 18. we will discuss some of the analytical tools used to control each area. For example, we will discuss how companies evaluate the effectiveness of their advertising. At this time it is important for you to understand that marketing strategy is regularly evaluated and changed as feedback identifies what is working and what could work better.[5]

Several plans make a whole marketing program

Most companies implement more than one marketing strategy—and related marketing plan—at the same time. Procter & Gamble targets users of laundry detergent with at least three different strategies. Some consumers want Tide's superior cleaning capabilities; others prefer the color protection of Cheer or the pleasant scents of Gain. Each detergent has a different formulation and a different approach for letting its target market know about its benefits. Yet P&G must implement each of these marketing strategies at the same time—along with strategies for Bounty, Olay, Charmin, and many other brands.

A **marketing program** blends all of the firm's marketing plans into one "big" plan (see Exhibit 2–8). But the success of the marketing program depends on the

Exhibit 2-8 Elements of a Firm's Marketing Program

care that goes into planning the individual strategies and how well they work together to create value for customers and the firm.

Recognizing Customer Lifetime Value and Customer Equity

LO 2.6

In Chapter 1 we introduced the idea that building customer value attracts customers, and that satisfying those customers builds profitable long-term relationships. Let's take that a step further and understand how marketing strategies and marketing programs that build relationships with customers can create financial value for a marketer.

Relationships increase lifetime customer value

Loyal customers continue to buy brands that satisfy them, often seeking out other products from that same company. Many firms recognize this and measure the **customer lifetime value**, which is the total stream of purchases that a customer could contribute to the company over the length of the relationship. For example, a 22-year-old college graduate might purchase a new Honda Fit for $16,000. A few years later she could be in the market for a small sport utility vehicle, and if she was happy with how the Fit ran and the service she received, she might buy a Honda CR-V for $25,000. Maybe a couple of kids later, a Honda Odyssey minivan starts to look appealing, potentially followed over a few decades by additional Honda cars and trucks. A Honda lawn mower or two may be purchased along the way. If Honda continues to provide good value to this customer, her customer lifetime value could exceed $400,000.

This insight has changed how many firms approach marketing strategy planning. Financial analysis can demonstrate how important it is for a company to retain customers over time. A good marketing program develops multiple strategies to make it easy for satisfied customers to buy more from the company. For example, Honda has vehicles to satisfy customers across different stages of life.

Customer equity estimates profitability

We can carry the idea of customer lifetime value a step further by taking into account all of a firm's current and future customers and the costs associated with each. **Customer equity** is the expected earnings stream (profitability) of a firm's current and prospective customers over some period of time. Following the customer equity approach guides the marketing manager to make marketing decisions that enhance the firm's long-term profits—not just for the next quarter or year. By estimating the impacts that different marketing strategies and marketing programs have on customer equity, a firm can make marketing decisions with long-run financial implications in mind.

Too many marketing managers make decisions that stimulate short-term sales, while failing to consider the long-term implications. For example, the Tommy Hilfiger clothing brand used to be synonymous with fashion and thus commanded a premium price. The higher price also made it a more exclusive brand appealing to trendsetting customers. When marketing managers felt pressure to quickly grow sales volume, they discounted prices to acquire new customers. Loyal customers who bought Tommy Hilfiger because it signaled exclusivity and their sense of style saw "everyone" wearing the brand. As Hilfiger's prestige declined, department stores stopped placing the brand's clothing in prime locations and the Hilfiger clothes had to be put "on sale" to spur sales. Soon Tommy Hilfiger lost its reputation as a fashion leader—the brand was less profitable. The focus on short-term sales had long-run negative consequences for Tommy Hilfiger. Not every short-term

Ally Bank wants to grow its revenue and profitability from each customer—leading to greater customer equity. Ally Bank *acquires* many new customers who seek higher interest rates on their savings accounts—see the first advertisement. Those interest rates and Ally's 24 hour-a-day, 7 days a week telephone customer service help the bank *retain* customers. As an online bank, customers regularly visit the bank's website. Customer equity also grows when current customers buy other products from a company; Ally *enhances* customer equity when customers purchase additional financial services from Ally including CDs, IRAs, and auto loans.

Customer equity focuses on the revenues and costs of acquiring, retaining, and enhancing customers

Online Toolkit

Go the website for Wells Fargo bank (**www. wellsfargo.com**). Look through the "Personal" banking products and pages. What do you see at the site that is designed to attract new customers? What do you see to help retain its current customers? What offerings are designed to enhance customer value?

price cut has this type of effect, but marketing managers who focus on growing customer equity consider both short- and long-term profits.

Using the customer equity approach, marketing managers recognize three potential sources of new revenue—*acquiring* new customers, *retaining* current customers, and *enhancing* the customer value by increasing their purchases. Each of these efforts (acquiring, retaining, and enhancing) has its own costs and benefits as well. Many firms that have conducted this analysis find that it costs less to retain a customer than to acquire a new one—leading companies to increase investments to retain customers. The marketing manager should evaluate the effectiveness of a marketing mix in achieving each of these objectives, considering both revenues and costs over the long term. Typically a marketing plan includes different marketing strategies to address each of these goals. So, for example, a plan should recognize that as it acquires more customers, there will subsequently need to be greater investments in customer retention.

With growing concerns about the sustainability and global warming, many customers are seeking more environmentally friendly transportation. The electric car is one option. Tesla Motors' financial resources and research and development expertise around battery technology have helped it develop a line of electric vehicles that offer superior value to customers and will be difficult for competitors to copy. Part of the value includes giving its customers free access to "Superchargers" which recharge the Model S in minutes. Tesla's offering may be a *breakthrough opportunity.*
Tesla Motors, © 2015.

What Are Attractive Opportunities?

LO 2.7

Effective marketing strategy planning matches opportunities to the firm's resources (what it can do) and its objectives (what top management wants to do). Successful strategies get their start when a creative manager spots an attractive market opportunity. Yet an opportunity that is attractive for one firm may not be attractive for another. Attractive opportunities for a particular firm are those that the firm has some chance of doing something about—given its resources and objectives.

Breakthrough opportunities are best

Throughout this book, we will emphasize finding **breakthrough opportunities**—opportunities that help innovators develop hard-to-copy marketing strategies that will be very profitable for a long time. That's important because there are always imitators who want to "share" the innovator's profits—if they can. It's hard to continuously provide *superior* value to target customers if competitors can easily copy your marketing mix.

Competitive advantage is needed—at least

Even if a manager can't find a breakthrough opportunity, the firm should try to obtain a competitive advantage to increase its chances for profit or survival. **Competitive advantage** means that a firm has a marketing mix that the target market sees as better than a competitor's mix. A competitive advantage may result from efforts in different areas of the firm—cost cutting in production, innovative R&D, more effective purchasing of needed components, or financing for a new distribution facility. Similarly, a strong sales force, a well-known brand name, or good dealers may give it a competitive advantage in pursuing an opportunity. Whatever the source, an advantage succeeds only if it allows the firm to provide superior value and satisfy customers better than some competitor.[6]

Walgreens' source of competitive advantage emerges from being the largest drug retailing chain in the United States. The retailer operates 8,300 stores spread across all 50 states. Almost anywhere in the United States, consumers will find a Walgreens nearby. Many of Walgreens' target customers place a high value on convenience, making this source of competitive advantage particularly relevant. Because it would be costly to build as many stores, this strategy is hard for competitors to copy.

Avoid hit-or-miss marketing with a logical process

You can see why a manager *should* seek attractive opportunities. But that doesn't mean that everyone does—or that everyone can turn an opportunity into a successful strategy. It's all too easy for a well-intentioned manager to react in a piecemeal way to what appears to be an opportunity. Then by the time the problems are obvious, it's too late.

Exhibit 2-9 Overview
of Marketing Strategy
Planning Process

Note: Marketing manager narrows down from screening broad market opportunities to develop a focused marketing
strategy. S.W.O.T. denotes Strengths, Weaknesses, Opportunities, and Threats.

Developing a successful marketing strategy doesn't need to be a hit-or-miss proposition. And it won't be if you learn the marketing strategy planning process developed in this text. Exhibit 2–9 summarizes the marketing strategy planning process we'll be developing throughout the rest of the chapters.

Marketing Strategy Planning Process Highlights Opportunities

We've emphasized that a marketing strategy requires decisions about the specific customers the firm will target and the marketing mix the firm will develop to appeal to that target market. We can organize the many marketing mix decisions (review Exhibit 2–5) in terms of the Four Ps—Product, Place, Promotion, and Price. Thus, the "final" strategy decisions are represented by the target market surrounded by the Four Ps. However, the idea isn't just to come up with *some* strategy. After all, there are hundreds or even thousands of combinations of marketing mix decisions and target markets (i.e., strategies) that a firm might try. Rather, the challenge is to zero in on the *best* strategy.

**Process narrows
down from broad
opportunities to
specific strategy**

As Exhibit 2–9 suggests, it is useful to think of the marketing strategy planning process as a narrowing-down process. Later in this chapter and in Chapters 3 and 4 we will go into more detail about strategy decisions relevant to each of the terms in this figure. Then, throughout the rest of the book, we will present a variety of concepts and "how to" frameworks that will help you improve the way you make these strategy decisions. As a preview of what's coming, let's briefly overview the general logic of the process depicted in Exhibit 2–9.

The process starts with a broad look at a market—paying special attention to customer needs, the firm's objectives and resources, and competitors. This helps to identify new and unique opportunities that might be overlooked if the focus is narrowed too quickly.

Customers want to buy a product that is somehow different from what competitors offer. The Phillipines tourism office wants vacationers to know that visiting the Phillipine islands can offer similar scenery at a fraction of the price of a trip to Phuket, Thailand. Aleve wants customers to know that fewer pills can provide the same results as a multitude of its competitors' pills.

Screening criteria make it clear why you select a strategy

There are usually more opportunities—and strategy possibilities—than a firm can pursue. Each one has its own advantages and disadvantages. Trends in the external market environment may make a potential opportunity more or less attractive. These complications can make it difficult to zero in on the best target market and marketing mix. However, developing a set of specific qualitative and quantitative screening criteria can help a manager define what business and markets the firm wants to compete in. We will cover screening criteria in more detail in Chapter 3. For now, you should realize that the criteria you select in a specific situation grow out of an analysis of the company's objectives and resources.

S.W.O.T. analysis highlights advantages and disadvantages

A useful aid for organizing information from the broader market and developing relevant screening criteria is the **S.W.O.T. analysis**—which identifies and lists the firm's strengths, weaknesses, opportunities, and threats. The name S.W.O.T. is simply an abbreviation for the first letters in the words *s*trengths, *w*eaknesses, *o*pportunities, and *t*hreats. Strengths and weaknesses come from assessing the company's resources and capabilities. For example, a local farmer's market might have a great reputation in its community (strength) but have limited financial resources (weakness).

Opportunities and threats emerge from an examination of customers, competition, and the external market environment. The farmer's market might see an opportunity when a growing number of customers in its community show an interest in eating locally grown fruits and vegetables, whereas a threat could be a drought that limits local farmers' production. With a S.W.O.T. analysis, a marketing manager can begin to identify strategies that take advantage of the firm's strengths and opportunities while avoiding weaknesses and threats.

Segmentation helps pinpoint the target

In the early stages of a search for opportunities we're looking for customers with needs that are not being satisfied as well as they might be. Of course, potential customers are not all alike. They don't all have the same needs—nor do they always want to meet needs in the same way. Part of the reason is that there are different possible types of customers with many different characteristics. In spite of the many possible differences, there often are subgroups (segments) of consumers who are similar and could be satisfied with the same marketing mix. Thus, we try to identify and understand these different subgroups with market segmentation. We will explain approaches for segmenting markets later in Chapter 4. Then, in Chapters 5 and 6, we delve into the many interesting aspects of customer behavior. For now, however, you should know that understanding customers is at the heart of using market segmentation to narrow down to a specific target market. In other words, segmentation helps a manager decide to serve some segment(s)—subgroup(s) of customers—and not others.

Customers want something different

A marketing mix won't get a competitive advantage if it *just* meets needs in the same way as some other firm. Marketing managers want to identify customer needs that are not being addressed or might be met better than the competition. Combining analyses of customers, competitors, and the company help the marketing manager identify possible strategies that differentiate a marketing mix from the competition. **Differentiation** means that the marketing mix is distinct from what is available from a competitor. For some examples of differentiation, read "*What's Next?* Offering more by offering less." In Chapter 4 we will discuss differentiation and how it is used to help position a brand in a customer's mind.

Narrowing down to a superior marketing mix

Sometimes difference is based mainly on one important element of the marketing mix—say, an improved product or faster delivery. However, differentiation often requires that the firm fine-tune all of the elements of its marketing mix to the specific needs of a distinctive target market. Target customers are more likely to recognize differentiation when there is a consistent theme integrated across the Four Ps decision areas. The theme should emphasize the differences so target customers will think of the firm as being in a unique position to meet their needs.

For example, some people who use computers to play video games, consider fast, realistic on-screen graphics to be an important part of the gaming experience. Nvidia specializes in making graphics processors—the computer chips that control what we see on a computer screen. Nvidia's 900 series chips are small enough to be placed in notebook computers (instead of the desktops many elite game players are used to using)—yet offer high quality graphics and long battery life. Notebook computers with these chips are more expensive than other notebooks, but when a hard-core "gamer" buys a new notebook computer, he will look for a model with the Nvidia GeForce GTX graphics card inside. In Chapters 8 to 17 we'll cover many ways in which the Four Ps of the marketing mix can be developed to meet a target market's needs.

Copyright (©)2015 NVIDIA Corporation.

What's Next? Offering more by offering less

Just how much difference do customers think there is between Mobil and Exxon gasoline? Levi's and Lee jeans? Visa and MasterCard? Marriott and Holiday Inn hotels? American, Delta, and United Airlines? Although some customers see big differences and have their own favorite, many see little difference and end up buying the lowest-priced option. Marketing managers want to carefully craft a marketing mix that differs from what competitors offer and appeals to target customers.

Some brands differentiate by offering less than the competition in most areas—and then add a little something extra and unexpected for the category. Take a look at the airline JetBlue. When JetBlue entered the market in 2000, all the major airlines offered free meals on every flight, the choice of flying in first class, business class, or coach, and a wide range of different fares. JetBlue offered none of these benefits. But JetBlue wasn't a budget carrier either—every plane featured plush leather seats from the front to the back of the plane and satellite television in every seat. JetBlue also promised to never bump anyone from a flight. Over time, competitors followed JetBlue's lead, so its initial differentiation declined—yet many customers still see differences and remain loyal.

If you live in the western United States, you might find an In-N-Out Burger nearby. Unlike other fast-food joints, In-N-Out doesn't have kids' meals, salads, or desserts. In fact, the menu includes just six items! Yet there is more here than meets the eye. In-N-Out makes everything on the menu from scratch using fresh (not frozen) ingredients. Plus they have a "secret menu"; only insiders know what it means to ask for an order "Protein Style" or "Animal Style."

When IKEA brought its stores to the United States, selling ready-to-assemble furniture, appliances, and home accessories, there was nothing like it. American furniture shoppers were accustomed to high levels of customer service and wide selections of styles. IKEA arrived with only Danish-style furnishings, little sales help on the showroom floor, and no delivery service—and by the way, you had to put the furniture together yourself when you got it home. The furniture was cheap, just like the prices. IKEA told customers they should plan to replace it in a few years. Yet IKEA stores are not bare bones—each features a restaurant with smoked salmon and Swedish meatballs and free day care for the kids of shopping parents.

Some businesses differentiate by offering more than the competition—test drive a 740 horsepower Ferrari or stay at a luxurious Mandarin Oriental Hotel. But JetBlue, In-N-Out, and IKEA went the other direction. When competitors added more, these companies offered less—except for something special—and their most loyal customers like the difference.

What other brands can you think of that have differentiated by offering less?[7]

Exhibit 2–9 focuses on planning each strategy by carefully narrowing down to a specific marketing strategy. Of course this same approach works well when several strategies are to be planned. This may require different managers working together to develop a marketing program that increases customer equity.[8]

Types of Opportunities to Pursue

LO 2.8

Many opportunities seem obvious only after someone else identifies them. So early in the marketing strategy planning process it's useful for marketers to have a framework for thinking about the broad kinds of opportunities they may find. Exhibit 2–10 shows four broad possibilities: market penetration, market development, product development, and diversification. We will look at these separately to clarify the ideas. These opportunities differ depending on whether a firm targets customers in its current or new markets—and whether it uses present or new products. However, some firms pursue more than one type of opportunity at the same time.

Market penetration

Market penetration means trying to increase sales of a firm's present products in its present markets—probably through a more aggressive marketing mix. The firm

Exhibit 2–10
Four Basic Types
of Opportunities

may try to strengthen its relationship with customers to increase their rate of use or repeat purchases, or try to attract competitors' customers or current nonusers. Coleman got a 50 percent increase in sales of its outdoor equipment, such as camping lanterns and coolers, by reaching its target market with special promotional displays at outdoor events such as concerts, fishing tournaments, and NASCAR races. For example, about 250,000 auto racing fans camp on-site at NASCAR races each year—so a display at the campground is an effective way to reach customers when they have leisure time to browse through product displays and demos.[9]

New promotion appeals alone may not be effective. A firm may need to make it easier for customers to place repeat orders on the Internet. Or it may need to add more stores in present areas for greater convenience. Short-term price cuts or coupon offers may help.

Many firms try to increase market penetration by developing closer relationships with customers so that they will be loyal. Lands' End wants its customers to "Like" its Facebook page so the retailer can keep them informed of clothing they might want to buy.

Market development

Market development means trying to increase sales by selling present products in new markets. This may involve searching for new uses for a product. E-Z-Go, a producer of golf carts, has done this. Its carts are now a quiet way for workers to get around malls, airports, and big factories. The large units are popular as utility vehicles on farms, at outdoor sports events, and at resorts. E-Z-Go even fits carts with ice compartments and cash drawers so they can be used for mobile food services.[10]

Firms may also try advertising in different media to reach new target customers. Or they may add channels of distribution or new stores in new areas, including overseas. For example, Vievu originally produced body cameras for law enforcement officers; then Vievu found a new market for the same product among plumbers, electricians, and home-appliance repairmen. These service professionals use the body cameras, and the recordings they make, to help explain to customers what they did and why.[11]

Product development

Product development means offering new or improved products for present markets. By knowing the present market's needs, a firm may see new ways to satisfy customers. For example, Campbell Soup Company came out with a line of soups with 25 percent less sodium than its regular product. That may seem like a minor change, but the line had $650 million in sales because it was important to Campbell's health-conscious consumers. Many ski resorts have developed trails for hiking and mountain biking to bring their winter ski customers back in the summer.[12]

Diversification

Diversification means moving into totally different lines of business—perhaps entirely unfamiliar products, markets, or even levels in the production-marketing system. Products and customers that are very different from a firm's current base may look attractive to the optimists—but these opportunities are usually hard to evaluate. That's why diversification usually involves the biggest risk. McDonald's, for example, opened two hotels in Switzerland. The plan was to serve families on the weekend, but business travelers were the target during the week. Business travelers are not the group that

The Heinz ad is a clever visual reminder of the fresh taste of the tomatoes in Heinz Ketchup. The primary purpose of this type of promotion is to increase market penetration, which means increasing sales of a firm's present products in its present markets. Delta is well known for its faucets. Its new Touch O' Technology faucet is a product development that Delta hopes will capture yet more of the faucet market. The ability to stop and start the flow of water by simply touching the spout or handle has faucet shoppers talking and hopefully buying.

Courtesy McCann Erickson Advertising Ltd./London; © 2015 Delta Faucet Company.

McDonald's usually serves, and an upscale hotel is very different from a fast-food restaurant. This helps to explain why operation of the Golden Arch hotels was taken over by a hospitality management company after two years.

On the other hand, diversification can be successful—especially when the new strategy fits well with the firm's resources and marketing program. Consider computer chipmaker Intel's efforts to develop new types of inexpensive chips that can be placed in everything from your vacuum cleaner and alarm clock to your coffeepot and car door. The company is preparing for a future when these "things" talk to one another wirelessly, providing us with better insights. These new products open new markets, yet fit well with Intel's strengths.[13]

Which opportunities come first?

Usually firms find attractive opportunities fairly close to markets they already know. Most firms think first of greater market penetration. They want to increase profits and grow customer equity where they already have experience and strengths. On the other hand, many firms find that market development—including the move into new international markets—profitably takes advantage of current strengths.

International Opportunities Should Be Considered

LO 2.9

It's easy for a marketing manager to fall into the trap of ignoring international markets, especially when the firm's domestic market is prosperous. Yet there are good reasons to go to the trouble of looking elsewhere for opportunities.

The world is getting smaller

Many countries have reduced barriers, such as taxes on imports, which in the past made international trade more costly. These moves have increased international trade all over the world. In addition, advances in e-commerce, transportation, and communications are making it easier and cheaper to reach international customers. With a website and e-mail, even the smallest firm can provide international customers with a great deal of information—and easy ways to order—at very little expense.

Develop a competitive advantage at home and abroad

If customers in other countries are interested in the products a firm offers—or could offer—serving them may improve economies of scale. Lower costs (and prices) may

Levi Strauss & Co. created the dENiZEN™ brand because it saw a strong opportunity for great fitting, quality, and affordable jeans wear in markets like China where there is a significant emerging middle class consumer segment. The brand name combines "denim" with the Asian "zen"—which means "meditative state." The dENiZEN™ brand will eventually be available in Latin America and Africa also.
AP Photo/Eugene Hoshiko.

give a firm a competitive advantage both in its home markets *and* abroad. Black and Decker, for example, uses electric motors in many of its tools and appliances. By selling overseas as well as in the United States, it gets economies of scale and the cost per motor is very low.

Get an early start in a new market

A company facing tough competition, thin profit margins, and slow sales growth at home may get a fresh start in another country where demand for its product is just beginning to grow. A marketing manager may be able to transfer marketing know-how—or some other competitive advantage—the firm has already developed. Consider JLG, a Pennsylvania-based producer of equipment used to lift workers and tools at construction sites. Faced with tough competition, JLG's profits all but evaporated. By cutting costs, the company improved its domestic sales. But it got an even bigger boost from expanding overseas. In the first five years, its international sales were greater than what its total sales had been before. Then, when JLG added distribution in China, international sales grew to be half of its business. JLG sales in Europe benefit from new safety rules that require workers to be on an aerial platform if they're working up high. JLG continues to enjoy global growth.[14]

Find better trends in variables

Unfavorable trends in the market environment at home—or favorable trends in other countries—may make international marketing particularly attractive. For example, population growth in the United States has slowed and income is leveling off. In other places in the world, population and income are increasing rapidly. Many U.S. firms can no longer rely on the constant market growth that once drove increased domestic sales. Growth—and perhaps even survival—will come only by aiming at more distant customers. It doesn't make sense to casually assume that all of the best opportunities exist at home.[15]

Weigh the risks of going abroad

Marketing managers should consider international opportunities, but risks are often higher in foreign markets. Many firms fail because they don't know the foreign country's culture. Learning foreign regulations can be difficult and costly. Political or social unrest make it difficult to operate in some countries. Venezuela is a striking example. Current Venezuelan leaders have threatened to nationalize some international businesses that have located there. Careful planning can help reduce some of these risks, but ultimately managers must assess both the risks and opportunities that exist in each international market.

CONCLUSION

This chapter introduced you to the basic decision areas involved in marketing strategy planning and explained the logic for the marketing strategy planning process summarized in Exhibit 2-9. In the remainder of this book we'll rely on this exhibit as a way to highlight the organization of the topics we are discussing.

In this chapter, you learned that the marketing manager must constantly study the market environment—seeking attractive opportunities and planning new strategies. A marketing strategy specifies a target market and the marketing mix the firm will offer to provide that target market with superior customer value. A marketing mix has four major decision areas: the Four Ps—Product, Place, Promotion, and Price.

There are usually more potential opportunities than a firm can pursue, so possible target markets must be matched with marketing mixes the firm can offer. This is a narrowing-down process. The most attractive strategies—marketing plans and whole marketing programs—are chosen for implementation.

Marketing programs should recognize customer lifetime value and customer equity. These ideas can help marketing managers demonstrate the financial value for a firm that not only acquires customers, but satisfies them by offering superior customer value and sees repeat purchases over time.

Controls are needed to be sure that the plans are carried out successfully. If anything goes wrong along the way, continual feedback should cause the process to be started over again—with the marketing manager planning more attractive marketing strategies. Thus, the job of marketing management is one of continuous planning, implementation, and control. Strategies are not permanent; changes should be expected as market conditions change.

Firms need effective strategy planning to survive in our increasingly competitive markets. The challenge isn't just to come up with some strategy, but to zero in on the strategy that is best for the firm given its objectives and resources—and taking into consideration its strengths and weaknesses and the opportunities and threats that it faces. To improve your ability in this area, this chapter introduces a framework for marketing strategy planning. The rest of this text is organized to deepen your understanding of this framework and how to use it to develop profitable marketing mixes for clearly defined target markets. After several chapters on analyzing target markets, we will discuss each of the Four Ps in greater detail.

While market-oriented strategy planning is helpful to marketers, it is also needed by financial managers, accountants, production and personnel people, and all other specialists. A market-oriented plan lets everybody in the firm know what ballpark they are playing in and what they are trying to accomplish.

We will use the term *marketing manager* for editorial convenience, but really, when we talk about marketing strategy planning, we are talking about the planning that a market-oriented manager should do when developing a firm's strategic plans. This kind of thinking should be done—or at least understood—by everyone in the organization. And this includes even the entry-level salesperson, production supervisor, retail buyer, or human resources counselor.

WHAT'S NOW?

This chapter introduced you to marketing strategy planning. To learn more about how these concepts are playing out in the world today, check out *What's Now?* at www.learnthe4ps.com/whatsnow/c2.

KEY TERMS

marketing management process, 32

strategic (management) planning, 33

marketing strategy, 34

target market, 34

marketing mix, 34

target marketing, 34

mass marketing, 34

channel of distribution, 37

personal selling, 38

customer service, 38

mass selling, 38

advertising, 38

publicity, 38

sales promotion, 38

marketing plan, 40

implementation, 41

operational decisions, 41

marketing program, 42

customer lifetime value, 43

customer equity, 43

breakthrough opportunities, 45

competitive advantage, 45

S.W.O.T. analysis, 47

differentiation, 48

market penetration, 49

market development, 50

product development, 50

diversification, 50

QUESTIONS AND PROBLEMS

1. Review the Cirque du Soleil case study that opens the chapter. From this case, identify examples of different key terms and concepts covered in the chapter. For example, both the shows and DVDs are examples of product.

2. Review the Cirque du Soleil case study that opens the chapter. Offer an example of each of the four basic types of opportunities (see Exhibit 2-10 and related discussion) that Cirque du Soleil could pursue. These do not have to be examples that Cirque du Soleil is currently pursuing.

3. Distinguish clearly between a marketing strategy and a marketing mix. Use an example.

4. Distinguish clearly between mass marketing and target marketing. Use an example.

5. Why is the target market placed in the center of the Four Ps in the text diagram of a marketing strategy (Exhibit 2-4)? Explain using a specific example from your own experience.

6. If a company sells its products only from a website, which is accessible over the Internet to customers from all over the world, does it still need to worry about having a specific target market? Explain your thinking.

7. Explain, in your own words, what each of the Four Ps involves.

8. Evaluate the text's statement, "A marketing strategy sets the details of implementation."

9. Distinguish between strategy decisions and operational decisions, illustrating for a local retailer.

10. In your own words, explain what customer equity means and why it is important.

11. Consider two vastly different companies—one sells oral health care products (toothbrushes, toothpaste, mouthwash), the other is a fast food restaurant. For each of these companies, describe the firm's tactics (consider the Four Ps) in a) acquiring customers, b) retaining customers, and c) enhancing sales from customers.

12. Distinguish between a strategy, a marketing plan, and a marketing program, illustrating for a local retailer.

13. Outline a marketing strategy for each of the following new products: (a) a radically new design for a toothbrush, (b) a new fishing reel, (c) a new wonder drug, and (d) a new industrial stapling machine.

14. Provide a specific illustration of why marketing strategy planning is important for all businesspeople, not just for those in the marketing department.

15. Research has shown that only about three out of every four customers are, on average, satisfied by a firm's marketing programs. Give an example of a purchase you made where you were not satisfied and what the firm could have changed to satisfy you. If customer satisfaction is so important to firms, why don't they score better in this area?

16. Distinguish between an attractive opportunity and a breakthrough opportunity. Give an example.

17. Explain how new opportunities may be discovered by defining a firm's markets more precisely. Illustrate with a situation where you feel there is an opportunity—namely, an unsatisfied market segment—even if it is not very large.

18. In your own words, explain why the book suggests that you should think of marketing strategy planning as a narrowing-down process.

19. Explain the major differences among the four basic types of growth opportunities discussed in the text and cite examples for two of these types of opportunities.

20. Explain why a firm may want to pursue a market penetration opportunity before pursuing one involving product development or diversification.

21. In your own words, explain several reasons why a marketing manager should consider international markets when evaluating possible opportunities.

22. Give an example of a foreign-made product (other than an automobile) that you personally have purchased. Give some reasons why you purchased that product. Do you think that there was a good opportunity for a domestic firm to get your business? Explain why or why not.

MARKETING PLANNING FOR HILLSIDE VETERINARY CLINIC

Appendix D (the Appendices follow Chapter 19) includes a sample marketing plan for Hillside Veterinary Clinic. Skim through the different sections of the marketing plan. Look more closely at the "Marketing Strategy" section.

a. What is the target market for this marketing plan?

b. What is the strategy Hillside Veterinary Clinic intends to use?

c. What are your initial reactions to this strategy? Do you think it will be successful? Why or why not?

SUGGESTED CASES

3. Real NOCO United Soccer Academy
4. Computer Xperts
5. Polymer Dynamics
12. DrV.com—Custom Vitamins
29. Quality Iron Castings, Inc.

Video Case 1. Chick-fil-A
Video Case 2. Bass Pro Shops
Video Case 3. Potbelly Sandwich
Video Case 6. Big Brothers and Big Sisters of America

MARKETING ANALYTICS: DATA TO KNOWLEDGE

CHAPTER 2: TARGET MARKETING

Marko, Inc.'s managers are comparing the profitability of a target marketing strategy with a mass marketing "strategy." The spreadsheet gives information about both approaches.

The mass marketing strategy is aiming at a much bigger market. But a smaller percent of the consumers in the market will actually buy this product—because not everyone needs or can afford it. Moreover, because this marketing mix is not tailored to specific needs, Marko will get a smaller share of the business from those who do buy than it would with a more targeted marketing mix.

Just trying to reach the mass market will take more promotion and require more retail outlets in more locations—so promotion costs and distribution costs are higher than with the target marketing strategy. On the other hand, the cost of producing each unit is higher with the target marketing strategy—to build in a more satisfying set of features. But because the more targeted marketing mix is trying to satisfy the needs of a specific target market, those customers will be willing to pay a higher price.

In the spreadsheet, "quantity sold" (by the firm) is equal to the number of people in the market who will actually buy one each of the product—multiplied by the share of those purchases won by the firm's marketing mix. Thus, a change in the size of the market, the percent of people who purchase, or the share captured by the firm will affect quantity sold. And a change in quantity sold will affect total revenue, total cost, and profit.

See Connect for the spreadsheet and questions needed to analyze this scenario.

3

CHAPTER THREE

© Taylor Emrey Glascock.

Evaluating Opportunities in the Changing Market Environment

Back in 1995, when Amazon.com first went online, its founder Jeff Bezos saw a breakthrough opportunity in changing the retail shopping experience. Amazon's strategy took advantage of trends Bezos observed, especially a growing number of consumers shopping on the Internet. Laws back then didn't require the collection of sales tax on online sales, which offset charges for shipping and handling. Encouraged by a strong economy, early investors were patient as Amazon lost $3 billion from 1995 to 2003. They shared Bezos' belief that if Amazon consistently delivered value and satisfaction, customers would come back, buy more, and tell their friends. Bezos' and his investors' predictions were on target.

Amazon wasn't just "lucky" to be in the right place and time. Bezos pushed his firm to be innovative in every aspect of the customer experience online. He urged employees to keep the company's mission statement in mind: ". . . to be Earth's most customer-centric company, where customers can find and discover anything they might want to buy online, and endeavors to offer its customers the lowest possible prices." With this focus, Amazon pioneered community features such as customer reviews, which helped customers discover new products and make more informed decisions. Amazon developed "1-Click" checkout technology, making it faster and easier for customers to pay for items and arrange shipping. Amazon also expanded into new product markets, over time adding electronics, home and garden, health and beauty aids, industrial tools, cloud computing services, and more.

Amazon quickly pursued global growth, launching new sites in both the United Kingdom and Germany by 1998. These markets were attractive initial targets because, like the United States, each offered a large number of customers with access to the Internet and high incomes. It later opened sites serving customers in Brazil, Canada, Italy, France, Mexico, Spain, Japan, China, and India; now more than 45 percent of Amazon's sales come from abroad.

Amazon has become a leader in using customer data to deliver more personalized shopping experiences. For example, Amazon knows how its customers behave on the site—what pages they visit, what they buy and don't buy, and whether they read reviews or shop around before purchasing. Amazon combines this information with a customer's previous visits and knowledge gained from observing more than 200 million other customers to suggest products and serve up appropriate advertising.

Whether the economy is strong or weak, Amazon performs well—but for different reasons. In difficult economic times, customers look for value and Amazon's low prices deliver. In better economic times, customers buy more frequently and choose upscale products—which Amazon also sells.

Amazon makes online shopping convenient. For a $99 annual fee for Amazon Prime, customers receive free two-day shipping on select products and access to free videos, music, and more. Customers can place an Amazon Dash button in their home; when the button is pushed, an order is automatically sent to Amazon. For example, a customer might have a Dash button in their laundry room set to order Tide laundry detergent.

Amazon seeks a new competitive advantage by offering faster delivery options. It is setting up warehouses near major metro areas and is testing different approaches. The Amazon Now program offers customers same-day delivery in some markets. In Brooklyn, New York, bicycle couriers will deliver packages in less than an hour. Amazon hopes to someday use small drone aircraft to deliver small packages in 30 minutes or less. Legal restrictions—more than technology limitations—are holding this up for now.

Always testing new approaches is key to Amazon's success. Knowing the value of getting new customers when they are young, Amazon partnered with Purdue University to target students. It set up drop-off and pickup locations right on the Indiana college's campus. Students shopping at purdue.amazon.com find a custom online storefront where they can easily find text books for all their classes. Students receive next-day delivery of text books and other products; an e-mail or text message tells them when their order is ready for pickup.

Bezos believes in using technology to enhance customers' shopping experience. So Amazon produces shopping apps for tablet computers and smartphones. Amazon's Price Check can be used in a retail store. After scanning a bar code or speaking the product name into their phones, users can read Amazon reviews, see the Amazon price, and place an order if they like. Amazon aims to keep pace with its target customers' growing use of digital products to make their lives easier.

Although Amazon's heritage was built on print books, digital e-books are the future. Anticipating this trend, it developed the Kindle line of e-book readers and Kindle Fire tablets, with screens in sizes from 6 to 9 inches and holding up to 3,500 books. The top of the line Kindle Fire HD tablet comes with a 9-inch color screen that allows users to surf the web, watch videos, play games, run a wide range of apps—and, oh yeah, read books. That versatility makes Kindle Fire HD a hit with families.

Amazon closely monitors the strong competition in its markets. Amazon engages in price wars with Walmart over books, toys, and DVD's; fights Netflix and Hulu in video downloads; and battles Apple in tablet computers and online music. Amazon has never been afraid to tackle markets with strong competitors. To the contrary, it seeks large and growing markets where it can leverage its competitive strengths—company size, technology skills, efficient operations, and creative personnel. To grow in these competitive and fast-changing market environments, Amazon must continue to anticipate market trends and adjust its marketing strategies.[1]

LEARNING OBJECTIVES

The Amazon case shows that a marketing manager must understand customer needs and choose marketing strategy variables within the framework of a changing market environment. Opportunities need to fit with a firm's objectives and resources, and managers should screen for opportunities where there is a chance for competitive advantage and, if possible, favorable trends in the external environment.

When you finish this chapter, you should be able to

1 Know the variables that shape the environment of marketing strategy planning.

2 Understand why company objectives are important in guiding marketing strategy planning.

3 See how the resources of a firm affect the search for opportunities.

4 Know how to conduct a competitor analysis and how different types of competition affect strategy planning.

5 Understand how the economic and technological environments can affect strategy planning.

6 Know how elements of the political and legal environment affect marketing strategy planning.

7 Understand the cultural and social environment and how demographic trends affect strategy planning.

8 Understand how to screen and evaluate marketing strategy opportunities.

9 Understand the important new terms (shown in red).

The Market Environment

LO 3.1

The marketing strategy planning process (see Exhibit 2–9) requires narrowing down to the best opportunities and developing a strategy that gives the firm a competitive advantage and provides target customers with superior customer value. This narrowing-down process should consider the important elements of the market environment and how they are shifting.

A large number of forces shapes the market environment. The direct market environment includes customers, the company, and competitors. The external market environment is broader and includes four major areas:

1. Economic environment
2. Technological environment
3. Political and legal environment
4. Cultural and social environment

Exhibit 3–1 Marketing Strategy Planning, Competitors, Company, and External Market Environment

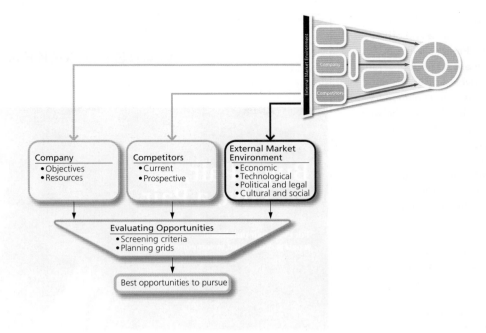

Managers can't alter the variables of the market environment. That's why it's useful to think of them as uncontrollable variables. On the other hand, a manager should analyze the environment when making decisions that can be controlled. For example, a manager can select a strategy that leads the firm into a market where competition is not yet strong or where trends in the external market are likely to support market growth.

In this chapter, we'll look at the key market environment variables shown in Exhibit 3–1 in more detail. We'll see how they shape opportunities—limiting some possibilities but making others more attractive.

Objectives Should Set Firm's Course

LO 3.2

A company must decide where it's going, or it may fall into the trap expressed so well by the quotation: "Having lost sight of our objective, we redoubled our efforts."[2] Company objectives should shape the direction and operation of the whole business.

It is difficult to set objectives that really guide the present and future development of a company. The marketing manager should be heard when the company is setting objectives. But setting whole company objectives—within resource limits—is ultimately the responsibility of top management. Top management must look at the whole business, relate its present objectives and resources to the external environment, and then decide what the firm wants to accomplish in the future.

A mission statement helps set the course

Each firm needs to develop its own objectives based on its own situation. This is important, but top executives often don't state their objectives clearly. If objectives aren't clear from the start, different managers may hold unspoken and conflicting objectives.

Many firms try to avoid this problem by developing a **mission statement**, which sets out the organization's basic purpose for being. A good mission statement focuses on a few key goals rather than embracing everything. It should guide managers in determining which opportunities to pursue.

Warby Parker sells fashion eyewear online and offline. Warby Parker's mission statement states its "...lofty objective: to offer designer eyewear at a revolutionary price, while leading the way for a socially conscious business. "This mission statement provides direction for more specific objectives that help it screen opportunities. For example, Warby Parker's fashionable glasses start at less than half the price of leading competitors," and for each pair Warby Parker sells, it donates a pair of glasses to someone in need.
© *Warby Parker.*

The mission statement for the American Red Cross provides this direction: "The American Red Cross prevents and alleviates human suffering in the face of emergencies by mobilizing the power of volunteers and the generosity of donors." This tells a Red Cross employee she should not pursue a grant that supports children's literacy—even if it's a good cause. On the other hand, the opportunity to develop a smartphone app that accepts donations for aid to Nepal following an earthquake fits right in this charity's mission. A mission statement may need to be revised as new market needs arise or as the market environment changes. This would be a fundamental change and not one that is made casually.[3]

The whole firm must work toward the same objectives

A mission statement is important, but it is not a substitute for more specific objectives that provide guidance in screening possible opportunities. For example, top management might set objectives such as "earn 25 percent annual return on investment" and "introduce at least three innovative and successful products in the next two years."

Of course, when there are a number of specific objectives stated by top management, it is critical that they be compatible. For example, the objective of introducing new products is reasonable. However, if the costs of developing and introducing the new products cannot be recouped within one year, the return on investment objective is impossible.

Company objectives should lead to marketing objectives

To avoid such problems, the marketing manager should at least be involved in setting company objectives. Company objectives guide managers as they search for and evaluate opportunities—and later plan marketing strategies. Particular *marketing* objectives should be set within the framework of larger company objectives. As shown in Exhibit 3–2, firms need a hierarchy of objectives—moving from company objectives

Exhibit 3-2 A Hierarchy
of Objectives

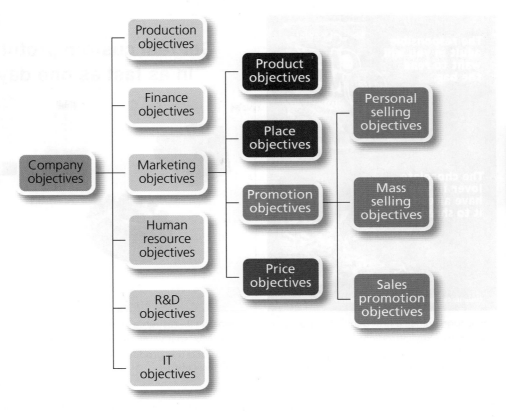

to marketing department objectives. For each marketing strategy, firms also need objectives for each of the Four Ps—as well as more detailed objectives. For example, in the Promotion area, we need objectives for personal selling, mass selling, *and* sales promotion.

Insurance company USAA provides an example. One of USAA's top objectives is to deliver high levels of customer satisfaction. Because customer service is a key driver of satisfaction, it is critical to have highly qualified and well-trained customer service representatives (CSRs) responding to customers' questions or problems. This leads to human resources objectives that guide the hiring and training of CSRs. Similarly, it's imperative for USAA's information technology group to develop software that increases the effectiveness of CSRs in their dealings with customers. So new software was designed to allow CSRs to view the same online screens as customers see on their PCs at home. With these capabilities, CSRs can solve customer problems more efficiently. USAA expects these efforts to deliver even higher levels of customer satisfaction and customer retention in the competitive insurance market.[4]

Both company objectives and marketing objectives should be realistic and achievable. Overly ambitious objectives are useless if the firm lacks the resources to achieve them.

Company Resources May Limit Search for Opportunities

LO 3.3

Every firm has some resources—hopefully some unique ones—that set it apart. Breakthrough opportunities—or at least some competitive advantage—come from making use of these strengths while avoiding direct competition with firms having similar strengths.

To find its strengths or recognize weaknesses, a firm must evaluate its functional areas (production, research and engineering, marketing, general management, and finance) as well as its present products and markets. The knowledge of people at the

The opportunities a firm decides to pursue may depend on its resources and capabilities. For example, General Mills was already producing a key ingredient for its new Chocolate Chex Mix, so it went ahead and launched Chex Mix Turtle. When 3-D printing technology became increasingly practical, Proto Labs added this production capability and faster services for its customers. *Left: © 2008 General Mills, Inc.; Right: Used with permission of Proto Labs, Inc.*

firm can also be a unique resource. By analyzing successes or failures in relation to the firm's resources, management can discover why the firm was successful—or why it failed—in the past. Let's take a closer look at three specific types of resources that guide marketing strategy planning—financial, production, and marketing.

Financial resources determine opportunities

Some opportunities require large amounts of capital just to get started. Money may be required for R&D, production facilities, marketing research, or advertising before a firm makes its first sale. And even a really good opportunity may not be profitable for years—so cash flow matters, too. If financial resources are limited, a firm may have to develop lower-cost and potentially riskier marketing plans. So lack of financial strength is often a barrier to entry into an otherwise attractive market.

What and how many can be produced? At what cost?

In many businesses, the cost of producing and selling each unit decreases as the quantity increases. This can place smaller firms at a production cost disadvantage when seeking to win business from larger competitors. On the other hand, new—or smaller—firms sometimes have the advantage of flexibility. They are not handicapped with large, special-purpose facilities that are obsolete or poorly located.

Many firms increase flexibility by not having any "in-house" manufacturing for their brands. Hanes is a good example. At one point, Hanes had U.S. factories for its underwear and T-shirts. But the factories were sold when most textile-related manufacturing moved to other countries with lower labor costs. Top managers for the brand said that they didn't have a competitive advantage in manufacturing anyway. Now, as Hanes' needs change, it has the flexibility to work with whatever suppliers around the world are best able to meet its specifications.

Marketing strategies often build on existing marketing resources

Marketing resources can create opportunities for a firm. In the product area, for example, a familiar brand can be a big strength. Starbucks is famous for its coffee beverages. When Starbucks introduced its coffee ice cream, many people quickly tried it because they knew what Starbucks flavor meant.[5]

Good relations with wholesalers and retailers can also be an important marketing resource—especially when introducing new products. Marketing managers at Clorox relied on this when they introduced the Green Works line of household cleaners. After years of working with the company on well-established products such as Clorox Bleach, retailers trusted Clorox to create an effective marketing strategy for Green Works. This trust opened doors that would've been closed to a new company. Other firms have a strong sales force or expertise in advertising, which should be recognized when developing a marketing strategy.

Firms can and often do develop new resources and capabilities when entering new markets. The lack of such resources should not rule out an opportunity, but an organization should recognize the costs required to develop the new capabilities.

Analyzing Competitors and the Competitive Environment

LO 3.4

Avoid head-on competition

The **competitive environment** affects the number and types of competitors the marketing manager faces and how they may behave. Although marketing managers usually can't control these factors, they can choose strategies that avoid head-on competition. And where competition is inevitable, they can plan for it.

Kinds of competitive situations

Economists describe four basic kinds of market (competitive) situations: monopoly, oligopoly, pure competition, and monopolistic competition. Understanding the differences among these market situations is helpful in analyzing the competitive environment, and our discussion assumes some familiarity with these concepts. (For a review, see Exhibit A–11 and the related discussion in Appendix A, following Chapter 19.)

Competitor-free environments are rare

Monopoly situations occur when one firm completely controls a broad product-market. These are relatively rare in market-directed economies. When monopolies are necessary, monopolists often face a great deal of government regulation. For example, in many parts of the world prices set by utility companies (electricity and water) must be approved by a government agency. Monopolists can be tempted to ignore customer needs, but a customer orientation can fend off increased government regulation and help the firm if competitors later enter the market.

Pure competition and oligopoly when there is little or no differentiation

Most product-markets head toward *pure competition*—or *oligopoly*—over the long run. In these situations, competitors offer very similar marketing mixes, and customers see the alternatives as close substitutes. In other words, competitors have failed to differentiate their offerings. In this situation, managers usually compete on low prices, and profit margins shrink. In oligopoly there are a few large firms competing, whereas in pure competition there are often many firms.

Avoiding these competitive situations is sensible and fits with our emphasis on finding a competitive advantage. Marketing managers can't just adopt the same "good" marketing strategy being used by other firms. That leads to head-on competition and a downward spiral in prices and profits. So target marketers try to offer a marketing mix better suited to target customers' needs than competitors' offerings.

Monopolistic competition is typical and a challenge

In *monopolistic competition,* different firms offer marketing mixes that at least some customers see as different. Each competitor tries to get control (a monopoly) in its "own" target market. But competition still exists because some customers see the various alternatives as substitutes. Most marketing managers in developed economies face monopolistic competition.

In monopolistic competition, marketing managers sometimes try to differentiate very similar products by relying on other elements of the marketing mix. For example, many consumers believe that most brands of gasoline are similar. This makes it difficult for a Texaco station to attract customers by claiming it offers better gasoline. So a Texaco station might compete on other parts of its offering, perhaps by serving Seattle's Best Coffee, giving discounted car washes, or maintaining longer hours of operation. Yet such approaches may not work for long if they are easily copied by competitors. So marketing managers should actively seek **sustainable competitive advantage,** a marketing mix that customers see as better than a competitor's mix and cannot be quickly or easily copied.

Analyze competitors to find competitive advantage

The best way for a marketing manager to avoid head-on competition is to find new or better ways to satisfy customers' needs and provide value. The search for a breakthrough opportunity—or some sort of competitive advantage—requires an understanding not only of customers but also of competitors. That's why marketing managers turn to **competitor analysis**—an organized approach for evaluating the strengths and weaknesses of current or potential competitors' marketing strategies.

The basic approach to competitor analysis is simple. You compare the strengths and weaknesses of your current (or planned) target market and marketing mix with what competitors are currently doing or are likely to do in response to your strategy.

The initial step in competitor analysis is to identify potential competitors. It's useful to start broadly and from the viewpoint of target customers. Companies may offer quite different products to meet the same needs, but they are competitors if customers see them as offering close substitutes. For example, disposable diapers, cloth diapers, and diaper rental services all compete in the same broad market concerned with baby care. Identifying a broad set of potential competitors helps marketing managers understand the different ways customers are currently meeting needs and sometimes points to new opportunities. Even parents who usually prefer the economy of cloth diapers may be interested in the convenience of disposables when they travel.

Marketing managers usually narrow the focus of their analysis to the set of **competitive rivals** that are their closest competitors. Rivals offering similar products are usually easy to identify. However, with a really new and different product concept, the closest competitor may be a firm that is currently serving similar needs with a different type of product. Although such firms may not appear to be close competitors, they are likely to fight back—perhaps with a directly competitive product—if another firm starts to take away customers.

Organize competitor analysis in a competitor matrix

A useful tool for organizing the competitor analysis is the **competitor matrix**, an organized table that compares the strengths and weaknesses of a company with those of its competitive rivals. A competitor matrix helps the marketing manager identify potential opportunities for differentiating the marketing mix.

Exhibit 3–3 provides an example of a competitor matrix that compares P&G's situation with those of two competitors in Japan. At this time, P&G was preparing to introduce a new version of its original Pampers, and the competitor analysis helped it develop a differentiated marketing mix. Because many Japanese grocery stores and drugstores are very small, frequent restocking by wholesalers is critical. Kao and Uni-Charm, the two leading Japanese competitors, both had better distribution networks than P&G. Kao also had a better computer system to handle reorders. With competitors having strengths in these areas, getting cooperation in the channel of distribution was going to be a challenge for P&G. To overcome this threat, P&G changed its packaging to take up less space and offered wholesalers and retailers better markups.[6]

Actively seek information about competitors

A marketing manager should actively seek information about current and potential competitors. Although most firms try to keep the specifics of their plans secret, much public information may be available. Sources of competitor information include trade publications, sales reps, suppliers, and other industry experts. In business markets, customers may be quick to explain what competing suppliers are offering.

Ethical issues may arise

The search for information about competitors can raise ethical issues. For example, people who change jobs and move to competing firms may have a great deal of information, but is

> ### Online Toolkit
>
> A marketing manager for Netflix may find it helpful to know more about how competitors advertise on search pages (such as Google and Yahoo!). The website KeywordSpy (**www.keywordspy.com**) offers that information and more. Go to the site and type "dvd rental" into its search bar and click "search." Click on the tab for PPC competitors. What competitors are identified? What information can you learn about Netflix and its competitors at this site? How could this information help Netflix's marketing manager?

Exhibit 3-3   Competitor Matrix Disposable Diaper Competition in Japan

	P&G's Current and Planned Strategy	Kao's Strengths (+) and Weaknesses (−)	Uni-Charm's Strengths (+) and Weaknesses (−)
Target Market(s)	Upscale, modern parents who can afford disposable diapers	Same as for P&G	Same as for P&G, but also budget-conscious segment that includes cloth diaper users (+)
Product	Improved fit and absorbency (+); brand name imagery weak in Japan (−)	Brand familiarity (+), but no longer the best performance (−)	Two brands—for different market segments—and more convenient package with handles (+)
Place	Distribution through independent wholesalers to both food stores and drugstores (+), but handled by fewer retailers (−)	Close relations with and control over wholesalers who carry only Kao products (+); computerized inventory reorder system (+)	Distribution through 80% of food stores in best locations (+); shelf space for two brands (+)
Promotion	Heaviest spending on daytime TV, heavy sales promotion, including free samples (+); small sales force (−)	Large, efficient sales force (+); lowest advertising spending (−) and out-of-date ad claims (−)	Advertising spending high (+); effective ads that appeal to Japanese mothers (+)
Price	High retail price (−), but lower unit price for larger quantities (+)	Highest retail price (−), but also best margins for wholesalers and retailers (+)	Lowest available retail price (+); price of premium brand comparable to P&G (−)
(Potential) Competitive Barriers	Patent protection (+), limits in access to retail shelf space (−)	Inferior product (−), excellent logistics support system (+)	Economies of scale and lower costs (+); loyal customers (+)
Likely Response(s)	Improve wholesaler and retailer margins; faster deliveries in channel; change package to require less shelf space	Press retailers to increase in-store promotion; change advertising and/or improve product	Increase short-term sales promotions; but if P&G takes customers, cut price on premium brand

it ethical for them to use it? Similarly, some firms have been criticized for going too far—like waiting at a landfill for competitors' trash to find copies of confidential company reports or "hacking" a competitor's computer network.

Beyond the moral issues, spying on competitors to obtain trade secrets is illegal. Damage awards can be huge. In one example, the courts ordered competing firms to pay Procter & Gamble about $125 million in damages for stealing secrets about its Duncan Hines soft cookies.[7]

Ethical Dilemma

What would you do? You are a salesperson for a company that manufactures industrial lighting used in factories. During a recent sales call, an engineer at your customer firm comments about a new energy-saving lightbulb that his company is testing for a competing supplier. Your company was not aware of the competitor's new product—which you think may make one of your product lines obsolete. Should you pass this competitive intelligence to your sales manager? Should you question the engineer or others at the customer firm to learn more? If you gather more information, should you share that with your company?

The Economic Environment

LO 3.5

The **economic environment** refers to macro-economic factors, including national income, economic growth, and inflation, that affect patterns of consumer and business spending. The rise and fall of the economy in general, within certain industries, or in specific parts of the world can have a big impact on what customers buy.

Economic conditions change rapidly

The economic environment can, and does, change quite rapidly. The effects can be far-reaching and require changes in marketing strategy.

Even a well-planned marketing strategy may fail if a country or region goes through a rapid business decline. You can see how quickly this can occur by considering what happened in the U.S. housing market just a few years ago. Earlier in the decade the economy was growing, household incomes were increasing, and interest rates were low. As a result, the housing market was hot. Manufacturers of building materials, home-builders, real estate firms, and mortgage companies all enjoyed strong profits as they scrambled to keep up with demand. By 2008 the economy was in a recession and the housing market abruptly collapsed. Firms that had done so well a year earlier were suffering huge losses—and many went bankrupt. Worse, millions of people lost their homes when they could not afford rising payments for variable-rate mortgages.

Interest rates and inflation affect buying

Changes in the economy are often accompanied by changes in the interest rate—the charge for borrowing money. Interest rates directly affect the total price borrowers must pay for products. So the interest rate affects when, and if, they will buy. This is an especially important factor in some business markets. But it also affects consumer purchases of homes, cars, and other items usually bought on credit.

Consider the situation of a home-buyer borrowing $150,000 on a 30-year mortgage at 4 percent interest. Monthly payments would be $716 (not including taxes). If the interest rate on that same 30-year loan was 7 percent, monthly payments would be $998—almost $300 more per month. You can see how high interest rates can cause many consumers to not buy a home, buy a smaller home, or buy the home but not new furniture or landscaping.

Interest rates usually increase during periods of inflation, and inflation is a fact of life in many economies. In some Latin American countries, inflation has exceeded 400 percent a year in recent years. In contrast, recent U.S. levels—3 to 20 percent—seem low. Still, inflation must be considered in strategy planning. When costs are rising rapidly and there are no more cost-cutting measures to take, a marketing manager may have to increase prices. For example, airlines and freight carriers can raise prices sharply in response to spiraling fuel costs.

Marketing managers must watch the economic environment carefully. In contrast to the cultural and social environment, economic conditions can move rapidly and require immediate strategy changes.[8]

The Technological Environment

Technology affects opportunities

Technology is the application of science to convert an economy's resources to output. Technology affects marketing in two basic ways: it creates opportunities for new products and it drives the development of new processes (ways of doing things). Throughout this book we offer many examples, so let's start by showing how anticipating technologies helps firms spot threats and opportunities.

Anticipate technologies and plan for the future

Although most technological developments don't come out of nowhere, it is not always clear how a technology just over the horizon might change a business. For example, producers of cameras and GPS systems might not have seen how quickly smartphones would cut into their business. Marketing managers should monitor technologies that might impact their industry—and engage in scenario planning to identify possible opportunities and threats.

What's Next? 3D printing set to save time, money, and lives

New approaches to manufacturing create fresh opportunities for marketing managers. 3D printing technology allows production of three-dimensional objects of any shape from a computer model. Computer-aided design (CAD) software is used to create a computer image of the object. A 3D printer uses that model to precisely build the object by adding layer upon layer of any material from plastic to titanium.

3D technology offers several benefits over traditional manufacturing. First, concepts go from idea to reality quickly. New product ideas can be prototyped, tested, and improved in hours, not weeks. Second, existing items can easily be scanned (in three dimensions) and quickly reproduced to create exact replicas or to improve an original. Third, 3D printing delivers cost savings in the form of lower shipping and packaging costs—especially on manufactured items produced in small numbers.

One promising application of 3D printing emerges from medicine, where the technology can be used to create body parts. Take the success story of Kaiba Gionfriddo. A birth defect caused his windpipe to collapse—threatening his life. So at age three months, doctors designed a custom splint they placed in Kaiba's throat to help him breathe. The 3D printed splint is made from a special plastic that degrades slowly (over three years) while Kaiba's body creates healthy tissue to replace it. Kaiba owes his life to a 3D printed part.

After a table saw accident mangled South African carpenter Richard Van As' fingers, he searched online for an affordable prosthesis. At thousands of dollars, all were beyond his means. While searching for help online, Van As ran across American special effects artist and puppeteer

Ivan Owen. The two developed an unlikely partnership that created technology to help Van As' dexterity. As publicity of their collaboration spread, they received a call from a woman whose five-year-old son was born without fingers on one hand. In less than a week, the two men created a crude mechanical hand, and later, 3D printed an improved version. The inventors posted the design and instructions for "Robohand" on a public website and now others can download the plans. Now, with a small 3D printer and less than $150 in parts, anyone can make a new hand.

Someday medical researchers expect to print human tissue, bones, and entire organs, but it doesn't stop there. Architectural engineers working with concrete hope to someday print whole buildings. An entrepreneur has already built a car using 3D printed plastic parts. And the military plans to use 3D printers on the battlefield to print parts to fix a tank or firearm.

Although new technologies create opportunities, there can also be threats. Plans for printing guns have already been posted on the Internet. When physical goods can be very easily copied, counterfeit goods may become more widespread. As with most new technologies, ethics, norms, and laws will emerge to provide guidance. But it appears that 3D printing will lead to breakthrough opportunities— "hands down" it's a winner.

There is considerable inventory in auto part stores and warehouses—and in hardware stores, too. What could large-scale adoption of 3D printing do to these businesses? If 3D printers were inexpensive enough that kids had them at home, how might this influence how kids play?[9]

Consider the possible impact of Google's driverless car project. Many expect that by the 2020s, most of us will be transported in robot-driven cars. There will be obvious effects in the automobile and insurance markets. Beyond that, did you know that in the United States, auto accidents account for 2 million emergency room visits each year? So driverless cars may reduce hospital demand for emergency services. Also, the nation's elderly might be able to live on their own longer if they can get around without having to drive, slowing demand for nursing homes. Bars and restaurants may see more business, and sell more alcohol, when patrons don't need to worry about driving home under the influence. Marketing managers who anticipate the impact of new technology can plan and adapt marketing strategies for the future.[10]

New production technologies create opportunities and threats. Read about one of these in *"What's Next?* 3D printing set to save time, money, and lives." Then think about how the growth of this technology might influence some industries.

Researchers at Coca-Cola developed a new technology for the plastic bottles used for many of its products. PlantBottle packaging looks and functions just like traditional PET plastic bottles—and it is recyclable. But because these bottles are partially made from plant material, they have a much smaller carbon footprint, making them better for the environment. Coke works with Ford, Heinz, Nike, and Procter & Gamble (not Pepsi) to accelerate future development of plant-based plastics. © 2006–2012 The Coca-Cola Company.

Technology changes marketing processes

Technology changes how customers and marketers do things. Facebook was founded in 2004 and just a dozen years later boasts more than 1.5 billion users. Now many organizations have Facebook pages or run highly targeted ads on the social network—fans of the Pittsburgh Steelers usually say that right on their Facebook page, identifying them as a target for ads for gear with their favorite football team's logo. The Internet has changed the nature of retailing as many consumers shop from their keyboard—or tablet device—and have purchases delivered to their homes. Hotels and airlines change prices depending on supply and demand on specific dates. Throughout this textbook you will read about how marketing is changing because of new applications of technology.

Technology comes with challenges

Technological change opens up many new opportunities, but it also poses challenges for marketers. For some marketing managers, change can be difficult, and they avoid technologies they do not understand. For others it is easy to fall in love with the latest technology—whether from the firm's R&D lab or a consultant selling social media tools—and blindly add it to the firm's marketing strategy. Both approaches can lead to a production-oriented way of thinking. That makes it more important than ever for marketing thinking to guide the process. Finding the best applications of technology still requires that marketing managers begin with customer needs.

Technology can pose ethical dilemmas

Breakthrough products can raise questions—do the benefits outweigh the costs? For example, many genetically modified foods can potentially increase crop yields and provide greater nutrition. Critics are concerned about human safety and other concerns. Aseptic drink boxes are convenient but difficult to recycle.

New technologies give marketers new ways to track consumers and perhaps deliver a more tailored experience—but does that invade consumers' privacy? Website visitors may not be aware that small computer files (called cookies) are often placed on their computers. Cookies allow the company to track what the customer does on the web.

Companies need to recognize and take advantage of changes in the technological environment. Deluxe Corporation was founded about 100 years ago. Soon thereafter it became a leader in the printing of paper checks and business forms used by consumers and businesses. Nowadays, as financial transactions are increasingly handled by electronic means, paper checks and business forms are going by the wayside. Deluxe has adapted its strategy, creating web-based services to help small businesses with logo design and website development.

This information can be used to give a web surfer a better online experience, perhaps serving up useful information, advertising, and discounts. On the other hand, users are often tracked without their knowledge and may prefer to retain their privacy.[11]

The Political Environment

LO 3.6

The attitudes and reactions of people, social critics, and governments all affect the political environment. Consumers in the same country usually share a common political environment, but the political environment can also affect opportunities at a local or international level.

Nationalism can be limiting in international markets

Strong sentiments of **nationalism**—an emphasis on a country's interests before everything else—affect how macro-marketing systems work. They can affect how marketing managers work as well. Nationalistic feelings can reduce sales—or even block all marketing activity—in some international markets. For many years, China has made it difficult for outside firms to do business there—in spite of the fact that the Chinese economy has experienced explosive growth as its factories have turned out larger and larger portions of the goods sold in the United States, Europe, and other parts of the world.

The "Buy American" policy in many government contracts and business purchases reflects this same attitude in the United States. There is broad consumer support for protecting U.S. producers—and jobs—from foreign competition. Automaker Chrysler draws on this sentiment in its "Imported from Detroit" campaign, which includes Detroit rap music artist Eminem and a two-minute Super Bowl commercial "Halftime in America" featuring Clint Eastwood. Both promote Chrysler's ties to Detroit, Michigan, Chrysler's American home.[12]

Trade agreements lower costs of trade

Important dimensions of the political environment are likely to be similar among nations that have banded together to have common regional economic boundaries. **Free trade** refers to agreements between countries to not restrict imports and exports.

オワリダ

THAT'S JAPANESE FOR "YOU'RE TOAST" IF YOUR WEBSITE CAN'T ACCOMMODATE OUR LANGUAGE AND CURRENCY.

adero›
The world wants your business™

WWW.ADERO.COM

Some countries have restrictions that raise the costs of importing, but free trade agreements drop those barriers. Since its inception in 1994, the North American Free Trade Agreement (NAFTA) has reshaped the rules of trade among the United States, Canada, and Mexico. Similar agreements exist among countries within Asia and Europe.[13]

The unification of European markets

Twenty years ago, each country in Europe had its own unique trade rules and regulations. These differences made it difficult and expensive to move products from one country to another. Now, the almost 30 countries of the European Union (EU) are reducing conflicting laws, taxes, and other obstacles to trade within Europe. This, in turn, is reducing costs and prices, and it is creating new jobs. Many of the member countries use the same currency (the euro), simplifying inter-European commerce and trade yet more.

Although Europe is becoming a large unified market, marketers will still encounter differences among European countries. What happened to Lands' End, the Wisconsin-based Internet and mail-order retailer, illustrates the issues. To better reach European consumers, Lands' End set up shop in England and Germany. As in the United States, its promotion and website touted the unconditional lifetime guarantee that is a key part of its strategy. However, German consumer protection rules prohibited promotion of the guarantee; the Germans argued that the promotion was a misleading gimmick (on the logic that the cost of the guarantee was "hidden" in higher prices that consumers would pay). German officials wanted this ban to apply even if the German consumer purchased the product from a Lands' End website in England. Quirky local rules like this could erode some of the benefits that should come from more European unification.[14]

The Legal Environment

Changes in the political environment often lead to changes in the legal environment and in the way existing laws are enforced. To illustrate the effects of the legal environment, we will discuss how it has evolved in the United States. However, laws often vary from one country to another.

Trying to encourage competition

American economic and legislative thinking is based on the idea that competition among many small firms helps the economy. Therefore, attempts by businesses to limit competition are considered contrary to the public interest.

Law	Product	Place	Promotion	Price
Sherman Act (1890) Monopoly or conspiracy in restraint of trade	Monopoly or conspiracy to control a product	Monopoly or conspiracy to control distribution channels		Monopoly or conspiracy to fix or control prices
Clayton Act (1914) Substantially lessens competition	Forcing sale of some products with others—tying contracts	Exclusive dealing contracts (limiting buyers' sources of supply)		Price discrimination by manufacturers
Federal Trade Commission Act (1914) Unfair methods of competition		Unfair policies	Deceptive ads or selling practices	Deceptive pricing
Robinson-Patman Act (1936) Tends to injure competition			Prohibits "fake" advertising allowances or discrimination in help offered	Prohibits price discrimination on goods of "like grade and quality" without cost justification, and limits quantity discounts
Wheeler-Lea Amendment (1938) Unfair or deceptive practices	Deceptive packaging or branding		Deceptive ads or selling claims	Deceptive pricing
Antimerger Act (1950) Lessens competition	Buying competitors	Buying producers or distributors		
Magnuson-Moss Act (1975) Unreasonable practices	Product warranties			

Starting in 1890, Congress passed a series of antimonopoly laws. Exhibit 3–4 shows the names and dates of these laws. Although the specific focus of each law is different, in general they are all intended to encourage competition.

Antimonopoly law and marketing mix planning

In later chapters, we will specifically apply antimonopoly law to the Four Ps. For now you should know what kind of proof the government must have to get a conviction under each of the major laws. You should also know which of the Four Ps are most affected by each law. Exhibit 3–4 provides such a summary—with a phrase following each law to show what the government must prove to get a conviction.

Prosecution is serious—you can go to jail

Businesses and *individual managers* are subject to both criminal and civil laws. Penalties for breaking civil laws are limited to blocking or forcing certain actions—along with fines. Where criminal law applies, jail sentences can be imposed. For example, several managers at Beech-Nut Nutrition Company were fined $100,000 each and sent to jail. In spite of ads claiming that Beech-Nut's apple juice was 100 percent natural, they tried to bolster profits by secretly using low-cost artificial ingredients.[15]

Consumer protection laws are not new

Although antimonopoly laws focus on protecting competition, the wording of the laws in Exhibit 3–4 has, over time, moved toward protecting consumers. Some consumer protections are also built into the English and U.S. common law systems. A seller has to tell the truth (if asked a direct question), meet contracts, and stand behind the firm's product (to some reasonable extent). Beyond this, it is expected that vigorous competition in the marketplace will protect consumers—*so long as they are careful.*

Yet focusing only on competition didn't protect consumers very well in some areas. So the government found it necessary to pass other laws. For example, various laws regulate packaging and labels, telemarketing, credit practices, and environmental claims. Usually, however, the laws focus on specific types of products.

Foods and drugs are controlled

Consumer protection laws in the United States go back to 1906 when Congress passed the Pure Food and Drug Act. Unsanitary meat-packing practices in the Chicago stockyards stirred consumer support for this act. Before the law, it was assumed that common law and the old warning "let the buyer beware" would take care of consumers.

Later acts corrected some loopholes in the law. The law now bans the shipment of unsanitary and poisonous products and requires extensive testing of drugs. The Food and Drug Administration (FDA) attempts to control manufacturers of these products. It can seize products that violate its rules—including regulations on branding and labeling.

Product safety is controlled

The Consumer Product Safety Act (of 1972), another important consumer protection law, set up the Consumer Product Safety Commission. This group has broad power to set safety standards and can impose penalties for failure to meet these standards. There is some question as to how much safety consumers really want—the commission found the bicycle the most hazardous product under its control!

But given that the commission has the power to *force* a product off the market—or require expensive recalls to correct problems—it is obvious that safety must be considered in product design. And safety must be treated seriously by marketing managers. There is no more tragic example of this than the recalls of Firestone tires used as original equipment on Ford's Explorer SUV. Hundreds of consumers were killed or seriously injured in accidents.[16]

State and local laws vary

Besides federal legislation—which affects interstate commerce—marketers must be aware of state and local laws. There are state and city laws regulating minimum prices and

In France, laws have been passed that put restrictions on car-sharing services like Uber.
© Uber USA, LLC.

the setting of prices, regulations for starting up a business (licenses, examinations, and even tax payments), and in some communities, regulations prohibiting certain activities—such as telephone selling or selling on Sundays or during evenings.

When electric carmaker Tesla Motors tried to bypass auto dealers and sell its vehicles directly to consumers, many states enacted laws prohibiting direct sales. And Airbnb, a service that allows people to temporarily rent rooms in their apartments and homes, was found to violate housing regulations in New York City. This tapestry of state and local laws may lead firms to specifically adapt marketing strategies to local requirements.[17]

The Cultural and Social Environment

LO 3.7

The **cultural and social environment** affects how and why people live and behave as they do—which affects customer buying behavior and eventually the economic, political, and legal environments. Many variables make up the cultural and social environment. Some examples are the languages people speak; the type of education they have; their religious beliefs; what type of food they eat; the style of clothing and housing they have; and how they view work, marriage, and family. Because the cultural and social environment has such broad effects, most people don't stop to think about it, how it may be changing, or how it may differ for other people.

Social cultural trends today

Some social cultural trends reflect broad changing attitudes. For example, many consumers are becoming more careful about the food they eat; organic foods have become more popular. You would think that might work well for Whole Foods Market, which has been selling organic groceries for more than 30 years. Unfortunately, as consumer demand grew, so did the interest of other retailers. Now Kroger sells its Simple Truth line of natural and organic foods—and Walmart stores carry some Wild Oats items. While that expansion might harm Whole Foods' bottom line, it helps organic farmers who are having trouble keeping up with demand.[18]

Where people are around the world

Other social cultural changes relate to demographic trends. So we now examine evolving trends related to population, age, income, literacy, and technology adoption across the globe and within the United States. This type of demographic data is also important to marketing strategy planning.

Exhibit 3–5 summarizes data for a number of representative countries from different regions around the world. Even with a current population of more than 316 million, the

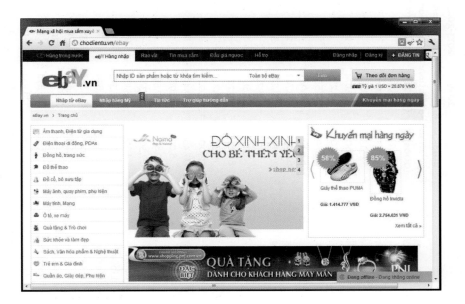

Marketing managers for eBay have found many opportunities for growth in fast-growing markets like Vietnam.
Copyright © 1995–2012 eBay Inc. All Rights Reserved.

Exhibit 3-5 Demographic Dimensions and Characteristics for Selected Countries

Country	2013 Population (000s)	2025 Projected Population (000s)	2013-2025 Projected Population Change (%)	Population Density per Sq. Mile*	Percent of Population in Urban Areas*	GNI Per Capita ($U.S.)*	GDP (billions of $U.S.)*	Estimated Literacy % of Population, 2011 (age 15+)	Mobile Phones/100 Inhabitants, 2008*	Percent Mobile Phone/100 Growth 2008-2013*	% of Population Using Internet*	% Internet User Growth 2008-2013
Algeria	39,210	45,841	17	16	70	5,330	210	73	101	33	17	70
Argentina	41,450	47,165	14	15	91	n/a	610	97	163	39	60	144
Australia	23,130	25,054	8	3	89	65,390	1,560	99	107	5	83	15
Bangladesh	156,600	197,674	26	1203	33	1,010	150	57	74	73	7	133
Brazil	200,400	218,259	9	24	85	11,690	2,246	90	135	71	52	50
Canada	35,160	37,559	7	4	81	52,200	1,827	99	81	23	86	12
China	1,357,000	1,394,639	3	145	53	6,560	9,240	94	89	85	46	100
Egypt	82,060	103,742	26	82	43	3,140	272	72	122	122	50	178
Ethiopia	94,100	131,261	39	94	19	470	48	43	27	1250	2	250
Finland	5,439	5,251	-4	18	84	48,820	267	99	172	34	92	10
France	6,031	68,680	4	121	79	43,460	2,806	99	98	5	82	15
Germany	80,620	79,226	-2	231	75	47,270	3,730	99	121	-5	84	8
Haiti	10,320	11,252	9	374	56	810	846	61	69	109	11	45
India	1,252,000	1,396,046	12	421	32	1,570	1,877	74	71	137	15	241
Iran	77,450	90,481	17	48	72	5,780	369	85	84	42	31	210
Israel	8,059	8,984	12	372	92	33,930	291	97	123	-2	71	20
Italy	59,830	62,591	5	203	69	35,860	2,149	98	159	5	59	31
Japan	127,300	123,386	-3	349	92	46,330	4,920	99	118	36	86	16
Kenya	4,350	53,196	20	78	25	1,160	55	87	72	71	39	333
Libya	6,202	7,375	19	4	78	12,930	62	89	165	31	17	295
Mexico	122,300	134,829	9	63	79	9,920	1,261	86	86	32	44	100
Nigeria	173,600	234,363	35	191	46	2,710	522	61	73	74	38	138
Norway	5,084	5,682	11	14	80	102,610	513	100	116	6	95	4
Pakistan	182,100	228,385	20	236	38	1,360	232	57	70	32	11	57
Romania	19,960	20,872	5	87	54	9,060	190	98	106	-5	50	54
Russia	143,500	128,180	-11	9	74	13,850	2,097	100	153	11	61	126
Saudi Arabia	28,830	31,877	11	13	83	26,260	749	96	184	34	61	69
Singapore	5,399	6,733	25	7,713	100	54,040	298	93	156	18	73	6
Somalia	10,500	13,274	26	17	39	150	1	38	49	600	2	100
Spain	46,650	51,415	10.2	94	79	39,920	1,393	98	107	-3	72	20
Switzerland	8,081	8,666	7	205	74	90,760	685	99	137	18	87	10
Turkey	74,930	90,498	21	249	72	10,970	822	95	93	-1	46	34
United Kingdom	64,100	67,244	5	265	82	41,680	2,678	99	125	3	90	15
United States	316,100	346,407	9	35	81	53,470	16,770	99	96	13	84	13
Vietnam	89,710	102,459	14.2	289	32	1,740	171	94	131	52	44	83

Sources: Data for projected population is from U.S. Census Bureau International Data Base. Urbanization data and literacy data from the CIA World Factbook. All other data from the World Bank.

*Data from 2013. Literacy data from 2009-2011, except for Algeria (2006), Argentina (2001), Australia (2001), Canada (2003), Egypt (2003), Finland (2000), France (2003), Germany (2003), Israel (2004), Italy (2001), Japan (2002), Mexico (2005), Pakistan (2013), Saudi Arabia (2012), Singapore (2000), Somalia (2001), Switzerland (2003), Turkey (2012), United Kingdom (2003), United States (2003), and Vietnam (2002).

United States makes up only 4.9 percent of the world's seven-billion-plus people. Marketing managers in any country may seek growth opportunities in other countries.

Although the size of a market is important, the population trend also matters. The world's population is growing fast, but that population growth varies dramatically from country to country. For example, between 2013 and 2025, the population is projected to grow more than 35 percent in both Ethiopia and Nigeria. During this same period, growth will be about 9 percent in the United States and 3 percent in China, while the population is predicted to decline in Japan, Russia, and many European countries. These trends have many marketing managers paying increased attention to fast-growing developing countries.[19]

A shift from rural to urban areas

Just 50 years ago, about two-thirds of the world's population lived in rural areas. Today about half live in urban areas, as more people move to cities for better job opportunities. The extent of urbanization varies widely across countries. While about 81 percent of U.S. residents live in urban areas, more than 90 percent do in Japan, Singapore, Israel, and Argentina (see Exhibit 3–5). By contrast, in Ethiopia and Kenya, 25 percent or less of the population lives in urban areas. The concentration of people in major cities often simplifies Place and Promotion decisions.

There's no market when there's no income

Profitable markets require income as well as people. The amount of money people can spend affects the products they are likely to buy. When considering international markets, income is often one of the most important demographic dimensions. There are a variety of different measures of national income. One widely used measure is **gross domestic product (GDP)**—the total market value of all goods and services provided in a country's economy in a year by both residents and nonresidents of that country. **Gross national income (GNI)** is a measure that is similar to GDP, but GNI does not include income earned by foreigners who own resources in that nation. By contrast, GDP does include foreign income.

When you compare countries with different patterns of international investment, the income measure you use can make a difference. For example, Ford has a factory in Thailand. The GDP measure for Thailand would include the profits from that factory because they were earned in that country. However, Ford is not a Thai firm, and most of its profit will ultimately flow out of Thailand. The Thai GNI would not include those profits. You should see that using GDP income measures can give the impression that people in less developed countries have more income than they really do. In addition, in a country with a large population, the income of the whole nation must be spread over more people. So *GNI per capita* (per person) is a useful figure because it gives some idea of the income level of people in the country.

Exhibit 3–5 gives an estimate of GNI per capita and GDP for each country listed. You can see that the more developed industrial nations—including the United States, Japan, and Germany—account for the biggest share of the world's GDP. In these countries, the GNI per capita is also quite high. This explains why so much trade takes place among these countries—and why many firms see them as the more important markets. In general, markets like these offer the best potential for products that are targeted at consumers with higher income levels. As a point of comparison, the GNI per capita in the United States is $53,740.[20]

Many managers, however, see great potential—and less competition—where GNI per capita is low. For example, Coca-Cola has made a push in Africa, where it hopes to establish a relationship with consumers now and turn that brand loyalty into profitable growth as consumer incomes rise.

Reading, writing, and marketing problems

The ability of a country's people to read and write has a direct influence on the development of its economy—and on marketing strategy planning. The degree of literacy affects the way information is delivered, which in marketing means promotion. The United Nations estimates that 16 percent of adults (age 15 or older) in the world cannot read and write. Two-thirds of them are women. You may be surprised by the

Online Toolkit

Michigan State University's Center for International Business Education and Research (CIBER) created globalEDGE—a website with information and tools for learning about global markets. Go to the globalEDGE homepage (**http://globaledge.msu.edu**) and search the dropdown menu by country for Italy. Select Italy and look through the "Statistics" and "Economy" pages. Check the same information for Brazil. How are these countries similar? How are they different? What marketing opportunities might be available in each country?

low literacy rates for some of the countries in Exhibit 3–5. Illiteracy creates challenges for product labels, instructions, and print advertising.[21]

Cell phone and Internet usage have increased rapidly around the world. These technologies may have their greatest impact in developing countries where, for example, they've completely skipped the adoption of landline phones and instead moved directly to a reliance on mobile phones.

Let's look at this phenomenon more closely. With the introduction of cell phones to the developing world came an ability to instantly communicate supply and demand to buyers and sellers. This has dramatically increased efficiency in some markets. For example, after fishermen in India began using cell phones, they called ashore to find out which ports had the most demand for their catch. This helped match supply and demand, lowering waste and stabilizing prices.[22]

Technology adoption races across continents

Adoption of these technologies varies across the globe (see Exhibit 3–5). Take cell phones, for example. Some people in Europe and Russia have separate phones for work and personal use, so the number of cell phones exceeds the population. Although penetration is lower in many of the poorest nations, those countries are experiencing very fast adoption rates. In Bangladesh, for instance, the 2013 ownership rate of 74 phones per 100 people represents a more than 73 percent increase from just five years earlier. Similar differences can be observed in Internet access. Marketing

Exhibit 3-6   2010 Population (in millions) and Projected Percentage Change by State 2010-2020*

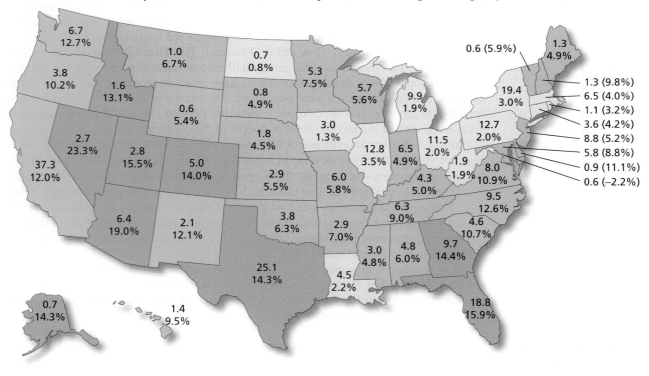

Percent change in population:
☐ Decreasing–4.2   ▨ 4.3–9.9   ▨ 10.0–12.9   ▨ 13.0 or higher

* Data from Weldon Cooper Center for Public Service, University of Virginia, Demographics & Workforce Group, 2013 update

managers need to recognize how target markets utilize this technology to determine its role in marketing strategy. For example, setting up a website in another language may be more useful in some countries than others.[23]

Population trends in the U.S. consumer market

While the U.S. population is not growing as quickly as in some other countries, Exhibit 3–6 shows that current population and population growth vary a lot in different regions of the country. The states shaded blue and green are growing at the fastest rate. The greatest growth is in the west and southeastern United States. These different rates of growth are important to marketers. Sudden growth in one area may create a demand for new shopping centers—whereas retailers in declining areas face tougher competition for a smaller number of customers.[24]

Boomers drive the graying of America

Another important dimension of U.S. society is its age distribution. In 1980, the median age of the U.S. population was 30—but by 2010 the median age rose to 37. The median age is growing because the percentage of the population in older age groups has increased. Exhibit 3–7 shows population trends by age groups. The graphic shows the number of people in the United States at various age groups in 2005, 2015, and 2025.

In Exhibit 3–7, these changes can be seen most dramatically when looking at the population of those older than age 60. The three age bands (60–69, 70–79, and 80+) each show a large increase by 2025. This will significantly increase the number of **senior citizens** (people older than 65). This increase is partly due to better health care and Americans living longer lives. It is also because **baby boomers**, those born

Exhibit 3–7   Population Distribution by Age Group in 2005, 2015, and 2025

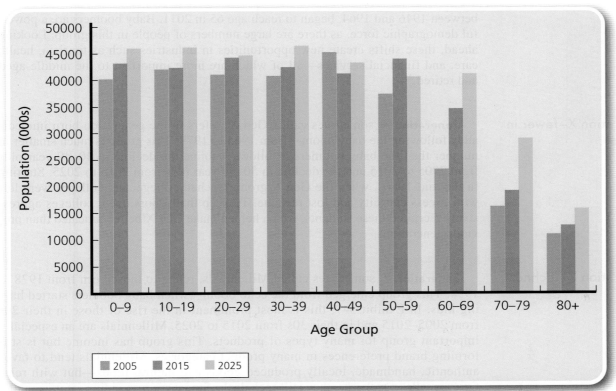

Source: U.S. Census Bureau.

Sales of minivans were in decline because new Gen X parents thought they were "uncool." Toyota responded with an online campaign featuring a couple rapping about life in the suburbs and driving their kids in their "Swagger Wagon." The campaign generated millions of online views and sales of Toyota's Sienna minivan jumped. Watch the videos at toyotaswaggerwagon.com.
© 2015 Toyota Motor Sales, U.S.A., Inc.

SWAGGER WAGON · Like · Share · More info · 0:09 / 2:36

between 1946 and 1964, began to reach age 65 in 2011. Baby boomers are a powerful demographic force, as there are large numbers of people in this group. Looking ahead, these shifts create new opportunities in industries such as tourism, health care, and financial services—all of which are more important to the middle-aged and retired.[25]

Generation X—fewer in number

Generation X, sometimes called Gen X, refers to the generation born immediately following the baby boom—from 1965 to 1977. This group is much smaller in number than the baby boomers it follows—notice the decline in 40–49 year olds from 2005 to 2015 and the decline in 50–59 year olds from 2015 to 2025. Starting in the mid-1980s, when the Gen X group reached college age, colleges were left with excess capacity and lost revenue. To keep their doors open, colleges aggressively recruited these students, which helped make Gen X better educated than previous generations.

Generation Y—techno savvy

Generation Y, sometimes called Millennials, refers to those born from 1978 to 1994. This group emerged from the echo boom—when baby boomers started having kids. In Exhibit 3–7, this is most prominent in the rise of those in their 20s from 2005–2015 and in their 30s from 2015 to 2025. Millennials are an especially important group for many types of products. This group has income but is still forming brand preferences in many product categories. Millennials tend to favor authentic, handmade, locally produced goods and natural foods—but with relatively smaller paychecks, they still seek deals. Stores are responding—for example,

Target has added more Greek yogurt, bagged coffee, craft beers, and gluten-free foods to appeal to Gen Y.[26]

Generation Z—more cautious

Generation Z refers to those born since 1995. This group is still young, so ideas about its emerging values are more speculative. These "digital natives" were born into a world that already used text messaging, cell phones, and the Internet. The Zs are also part of a more ethnically diverse United States than their parents knew, and they appear to be more accepting of different cultures, races, and religions. Growing up in the shadow of the 9/11 terrorist attacks and during the Great Recession, this group tends to have realistic (as opposed to optimistic) views of the world. The Zs may prefer brands that suggest long-term value, safety, and security. Marketing managers will closely monitor this group to identify other trends, patterns, and opportunities.[27]

Social and cultural changes come slowly

The trends and demographic data we've been reviewing show that changes in cultural values and social attitudes evolve slowly. They also reflect large groups of customers—not necessarily a firm's target market. Opportunities and threats can be identified early when marketing managers monitor and anticipate these changes.

Using Screening Criteria to Narrow Down to Strategies

Developing and applying screening criteria

After you analyze the firm's resources (for strengths and weaknesses), the environmental trends the firm faces, and the objectives of top management, you merge them all into a set of product-market screening criteria. These criteria should include both quantitative and qualitative components. The quantitative components summarize the firm's objectives: sales, profit, and return on investment (ROI) targets. (Note: ROI analysis is discussed briefly in Appendix B, which follows Chapter 19.) The qualitative components summarize what kinds of businesses the firm wants to be in, what businesses it wants to exclude, what weaknesses it should avoid, and what resources (strengths) and trends it should build on.[28]

Developing screening criteria is difficult but worth the effort. They summarize in one place what the firm wants to accomplish. When a manager can explain the specific criteria that are relevant to selecting (or screening out) an opportunity, others can understand the manager's logic. Thus, marketing decisions are not just made or accepted based on intuition and gut feel.

The criteria should be realistic—that is, they should be achievable. Opportunities that pass the screen should be viable strategies that the firm can implement with the resources it has. For example, Exhibit 3–8 illustrates some product-market screening criteria for a small retail and wholesale distributor.

Sustainability matters

Sometimes screening criteria can help bring focus to opportunities that fit well with trends in the external market environment. For example, General Electric (GE) operates many types of businesses, from jet aircraft engines and water treatment facilities to medical imaging and lightbulbs. Top management at GE believes that the really crucial needs of society relate to protecting the environment. They believe that efforts in this arena are so critical that they should be supported across all dimensions of the external environment. Thus, they want all GE managers to look for opportunities that fit what GE calls "ecomagination"—applying GE's creativity to solve problems related to ecology. GE is not alone in this kind of thinking. Many organizations now screen opportunities on **sustainability**—the idea that it's important to meet present needs without compromising the ability of future generations to meet their own needs. In many lines of business, that is a tall order. At GE that means lightbulbs that use less

Exhibit 3-8   An Example of Product-Market Screening Criteria for a Small Retail and Wholesale Distributor ($10 million annual sales)

1. **Quantitative criteria**

   a. Increase sales by $1,500,000 per year for the next five years.

   b. Earn ROI of at least 25 percent before taxes on new ventures.

   c. Break even within one year on new ventures.

   d. Opportunity must be large enough to justify interest (to help meet objectives) but small enough so company can handle with the resources available.

   e. Several opportunities should be pursued to reach the objectives—to spread the risks.

2. **Qualitative criteria**

   a. Nature of business preferred.

      (1) Should take advantage of our Internet order system and website promotion.

      (2) New goods and services for present customers to strengthen relationships and customer equity.

      (3) "Quality" products that do not cannibalize sales of current products.

      (4) Competition should be weak and opportunity should be hard to copy for several years.

      (5) There should be strongly felt (even unsatisfied) needs—to reduce promotion costs and permit "high" prices.

   b. Constraints.

      (1) Nature of businesses to exclude.

         (a) Manufacturing.

         (b) Any requiring large fixed capital investments.

         (c) Any requiring many support people who must be "good" all the time and would require much supervision.

      (2) Geographic.

         (a) United States, Mexico, and Canada only.

      (3) General.

         (a) Make use of current strengths.

         (b) Attractiveness of market should be reinforced by more than one of the following basic trends: technological, demographic, social, economic, political.

         (c) Address environmental problems.

energy, medical images with no toxic waste, jets that burn less fuel, and new ways to turn seawater into drinking water.[29]

Whole plans should be evaluated

You need to forecast the probable results of implementing a marketing strategy to apply the quantitative part of the screening criteria because only implemented plans generate sales, profits, and return on investment. For a rough screening, you need to estimate only the likely results of implementing each opportunity over a logical planning period. If a product's life is likely to be three years, for example, a good strategy may not produce profitable results for 6 to 12 months. But evaluated over the projected three-year life, the product may look like a winner. When evaluating the potential of possible opportunities (product-market strategies), it is important to evaluate similar things—that is, whole plans.

Total profit approach can help evaluate possible plans

Note that managers can evaluate different marketing plans at the same time. Exhibit 3–9 compares a much improved product and product concept (Product A) with a "me-too" product (Product B) for the same target market. In the short run, the me-too product will make a profit sooner and might look like the better choice—if managers consider only one year's results. The improved product, on the other hand, will take a good deal of pioneering—but over its five-year life it will be much more profitable.

Exhibit 3-9 Expected Sales and Cost Curves of Two Strategies over Five-Year Planning Periods

Planning Grids Help Evaluate a Portfolio of Opportunities

LO 3.8

When a firm has many scenarios to evaluate, comparisons are best made with graphical approaches—such as the nine-box strategic planning grid developed by General Electric and used by many other companies. Such grids can help evaluate a firm's whole portfolio of strategic plans or businesses.

General Electric looks for green positions

General Electric's (GE) strategic planning grid—see Exhibit 3–10—forces company managers to make three-part judgments (high, medium, and low) about the business strengths and industry attractiveness of all proposed or existing product-market plans. As you can see from Exhibit 3–10, this approach helps a manager organize information about the company's marketing environments (discussed earlier in this chapter) along with information about its strategy and translate it into relevant screening criteria.

The industry attractiveness dimension helps managers answer the question: Does this product-market plan look like a good idea? To answer that question, managers have to judge such factors (screening criteria) as the size of the market and its growth rate, the nature of competition, the plan's potential environmental or social impact, and how laws might affect it. Note that an opportunity may be attractive for *some* companies—but not well suited to the strengths (and weaknesses) of a particular firm. That is why the GE grid also considers the business strengths dimension.

The business strengths dimension focuses on the ability of the company to pursue a product-market plan effectively. To make judgments along this dimension, a manager evaluates whether the firm has people with the right talents and skills to implement the plan, whether the plan is consistent with the firm's image and profit objectives, and whether the firm could establish a profitable market share given its technical capability, costs, and size. Here again, these factors suggest screening criteria specific to this firm and market situation.

Exhibit 3-10 General Electric's Strategic Planning Grid

GE feels opportunities that fall into the green boxes in the upper left-hand corner of the grid are its best growth opportunities. Managers give these opportunities high marks on both industry attractiveness and business strengths. The red boxes in the lower right-hand corner of the grid, on the other hand, suggest a no-growth policy. Existing red businesses may continue to generate earnings, but they no longer deserve much investment. Yellow businesses are borderline cases—they can go either way. GE may continue to support an existing yellow business but will probably reject a proposal for a new one. It simply wouldn't look good enough on the relevant screening criteria.

GE's "stoplight" evaluation method is a subjective, multiple-factor approach. It avoids the traps and possible errors of trying to use oversimplified, single-number criteria—such as ROI or market share. Instead, top managers review detailed written summaries of many different screening criteria that help them make summary judgments. This approach helps everyone understand why the company supports some new opportunities and not others.[30]

General Electric considers factors that reflect its objectives. Another firm might modify the evaluation to emphasize other screening criteria—depending on its objectives and the type of product-market plans it is considering.

Evaluating Opportunities in International Markets

Evaluate the risks

The approaches we've discussed so far apply to international markets just as they do to domestic ones. But in international markets it is often harder to fully understand the market environment variables. This may make it more difficult to see the risks involved in particular opportunities. Some countries are politically unstable; their governments and constitutions come and go. An investment safe under one government might become a takeover target under another.

To reduce the risk of missing some basic variable that may help screen out a risky opportunity, marketing managers sometimes need a detailed analysis of the market environment they are considering entering. Such an analysis can reveal facts about an unfamiliar market that a manager in a distant country might otherwise overlook. Further, a local citizen who knows the market environment may be able to identify an

Lamb Weston and Click2Asia are successful in international markets because potatoes and cucumbers—in many different forms—are common in the diet of most cultures. Other products are much more sensitive to cultural differences.
Con Agra Foods Specialty Potato Products; Agency: Strahan Advertising; Courtesy Click2Asia.

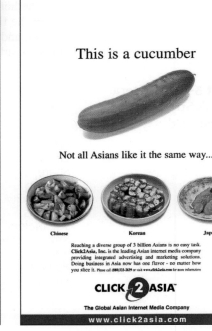

Exhibit 3-11 Continuum of Environmental Sensitivity

Insensitive		Sensitive
Industrial products	Basic commodity-type consumer products	Consumer products that are linked to cultural variables

"obvious" problem ignored even in a careful analysis. Thus, it is very useful for the analysis to include inputs from locals—perhaps cooperative distributors.[31]

Risks vary with environmental sensitivity

The farther you go from familiar territory, the greater the risk of making big mistakes. But not all products, or marketing mixes, involve the same risk. Think of the risks as running along a "continuum of environmental sensitivity." See Exhibit 3–11.

Some products are relatively insensitive to the economic and cultural environment into which they're placed. These products may be accepted as is—or they may require just a little adaptation to make them suitable for local use. Most industrial products are near the insensitive end of this continuum.

At the other end of the continuum, we find highly sensitive products that may be difficult or impossible to adapt to all international situations. Consumer products closely linked to other social or cultural variables are at this end. For example, some cultures view dieting as unhealthy; that explains why products such as Diet Pepsi, although popular in the United States, have sometimes done poorly in other countries. Many American quick-serve restaurants succeed in international markets only after adapting their menus to foreign tastes. McDonald's in India sells the Maharaja Mac, which is made from lamb or chicken, and in Japan it sells the Ebi Filet-O, which is a kind of shrimp burger.

This continuum helps explain why many of the early successes in international marketing were basic commodities such as gasoline, soap, transportation vehicles, mining equipment, and agricultural machinery. It also helps explain why some consumer products firms have been successful with basically the same promotion and products in different parts of the globe.

Yet some managers don't understand the reason for these successes. They think they can develop a global marketing mix for just about *any* product. They fail to see that firms producing and/or selling products near the sensitive end of the continuum should carefully analyze how their products will be seen and used in new environments—and plan their strategies accordingly.[32]

What if risks are still hard to judge?

If the risks of an international opportunity are hard to judge, it may be wise to look first for opportunities that involve exporting. This gives managers a chance to build experience, know-how, and confidence over time. Then the firm will be in a better position to judge the prospects and risks of taking further steps.

CONCLUSION

Businesses need innovative strategy planning to survive in our increasingly competitive markets. In this chapter, we discussed the variables that shape the broad environment of marketing strategy planning and how they may affect opportunities. First we looked at how the firm's own resources and objectives may help guide or limit the search for opportunities. Then we went on to look at the need to understand competition and how to do a competitive analysis. Next we shifted our focus to the external market environments. They are important because changes in these environments present new opportunities, as well as problems, that a marketing manager must deal with in marketing strategy planning.

The economic environment—including chances of recession or inflation—also affects the choice of strategies. And the marketer must try to anticipate, understand, and deal with these changes—as well as changes in the technology underlying the economic environment.

The marketing manager must also be aware of legal restrictions and be sensitive to changing political climates.

The acceptance of consumerism has already forced many changes.

The cultural and social environment affects how people behave and what marketing strategies will be successful.

Demographic data, including trends in population, income, and technology usage, provide an indicator of social trends. So we looked at these more closely.

Developing good marketing strategies within all these environments isn't easy. You can see that marketing planning is a challenging job that requires integration of information from many disciplines.

Eventually, managers need procedures for screening and evaluating opportunities. We explained an approach for developing qualitative and quantitative screening criteria—from an analysis of the strengths and weaknesses of the company's resources, the environmental trends it faces, and top management's objectives. We also discussed ways for evaluating and managing quite different opportunities—using the GE strategic planning grid.

Now we can go on in the rest of the book to discuss how to turn opportunities into profitable marketing plans and programs.

WHAT'S NOW?

This chapter discussed the dimensions of the broad external environment. What is going on in the world today that reflects some of the concepts you learned in this chapter? To learn more about how these concepts are playing out in the world today, check out *What's Now?* at www.learnthe4ps.com/whatsnow/c3.

KEY TERMS

LO 3.9

mission statement, 59

competitive environment, 63

sustainable competitive advantage, 63

competitor analysis, 64

competitive rivals, 64

competitor matrix, 64

economic environment, 66

technology, 66

nationalism, 69

free trade, 69

cultural and social environment, 73

gross domestic product (GDP), 75

gross national income (GNI), 75

senior citizens, 77

baby boomers, 77

Generation X, 78

Generation Y, 78

Generation Z, 79

sustainability, 79

QUESTIONS AND PROBLEMS

1. Review the Amazon case study that opens the chapter. From this case, identify examples of different key terms and concepts covered in the chapter. For example, Amazon's mission statement is noted and guides other decisions in the company.

2. Review the Amazon case study that opens this chapter. Create a table like the one below—and fill in the empty cells. If necessary look back at Chapter 2 to remind yourself of the definition of threat and opportunity. Then describe how each of the three trends could be seen as a threat or an opportunity for Amazon.

Trends	Threat	Opportunity
eBay becomes a larger competitive rival		
3D printing technology (see *What's Next?*)		
Faster Internet connections emerge across Africa		

3. Do you think it makes sense for a firm to base its mission statement on the type of product it produces? For example, would it be good for a division that produces electric motors to have as its mission: "We want to make the best (from our customers' point of view) electric motors available anywhere in the world"?

4. Explain how a firm's objectives may affect its search for opportunities.

5. Specifically, how would various company objectives affect the development of a marketing mix for a new type of Internet browser software? If this company were just being formed by a former programmer with limited financial resources, list the objectives the programmer might have. Then discuss how they would affect the development of the programmer's marketing strategy.

6. Explain how a firm's resources may limit its search for opportunities. Cite a specific example for a specific resource.

7. In your own words, explain how a marketing manager might use a competitor analysis to avoid situations that involve head-on competition.

8. The owner of a small hardware store—the only one in a medium-sized town in the mountains—has just learned that a large home improvement chain plans to open a new store nearby. How difficult will it be for the owner to plan for this new competitive threat? Explain your answer.

9. Discuss the probable impact on your hometown if a major breakthrough in air transportation allowed foreign producers to ship into any U.S. market for about the same transportation cost that domestic producers incur.

10. Will the elimination of trade barriers among countries in Europe eliminate the need to consider submarkets of European consumers? Why or why not?

11. What and who is the U.S. government attempting to protect in its effort to preserve and regulate competition?

12. For each of the *major* laws discussed in the text, indicate whether in the long run the law will promote or restrict competition (see Exhibit 3-4). As a consumer without any financial interest in business, what is your reaction to each of these laws?

13. Drawing on data in Exhibit 3-5, do you think that Romania would be an attractive market for a firm that produces home appliances? What about Finland? Discuss your reasons.

14. Discuss the value of gross domestic product and gross national income per capita as measures of market potential in international consumer markets. Refer to specific data in your answer.

15. Discuss how the worldwide trend toward urbanization is affecting opportunities for international marketing.

16. Discuss how slower population growth will affect businesses in your local community.

17. Discuss the impact of changes in the size and use of technology in the 18–29 age group on marketing strategy planning in the United States.

18. Name three specific examples of firms that developed a marketing mix to appeal to senior citizens.

19. Explain the product-market screening criteria that can be used to evaluate opportunities.

20. Explain General Electric's strategic planning grid approach to evaluating opportunities.

MARKETING PLANNING FOR HILLSIDE VETERINARY CLINIC

Appendix D (the Appendices follow Chapter 19) includes a sample marketing plan for Hillside Veterinary Clinic. The situation analysis section of the marketing plan includes sections labeled "Competitors" and "External Market Environment." Review those sections and answer the following questions.

a. In the Competitors section, what dimensions were used to analyze competitors? What other dimensions might have been examined?

b. How was competitor information gathered? How else could Hillside have gathered information about its competitors?

c. What aspects of the external market environment are included in the marketing plan? What do you think is the most important information in this section?

SUGGESTED CASES

2. Nature's Way Foods, Inc.
6. Steel Solutions
22. Bright Light Innovations: The Starlight Stove
33. Kennedy & Gaffney (K&G)

Video Case 4. Potbelly Sandwich
Video Case 5. Suburban Regional Shopping Malls

MARKETING ANALYTICS: DATA TO KNOWLEDGE

CHAPTER 3: COMPETITOR ANALYSIS

Mediquip, Inc., produces medical equipment and uses its own sales force to sell the equipment to hospitals. Recently, several hospitals have asked Mediquip to develop a laser-beam "scalpel" for eye surgery. Mediquip has the needed resources, and 200 hospitals will probably buy the equipment. But Mediquip managers have heard that Laser Technologies—another quality producer—is thinking of competing for the same business. Mediquip has other good opportunities it could pursue—so it wants to see if it would have a competitive advantage over Laser Tech.

Mediquip and Laser Tech are similar in most ways, but there are a few important differences. Laser Technologies already produces key parts that are needed for the new laser product—so its production costs would be lower. It would cost Mediquip more to design the product—and getting parts from outside suppliers would result in higher production costs.

On the other hand, Mediquip has marketing strengths. It already has a good reputation with hospitals—and its sales

force calls on only hospitals. Mediquip thinks that each of its current sales reps could spend some time selling the new product and that it could adjust sales territories so only four more sales reps would be needed for good coverage in the market. In contrast, Laser Tech's sales reps call on only industrial customers, so it would have to add 14 reps to cover the hospitals.

Hospitals have budget pressures—so the supplier with the lowest price is likely to get a larger share of the business. But Mediquip knows that both suppliers' prices will be set high enough to cover the added costs of designing, producing, and selling the new product—and leave something for profit.

Mediquip gathers information about its own likely costs and can estimate Laser Tech's costs from industry studies and Laser Tech's annual report. Mediquip has set up a spreadsheet to evaluate the proposed new product.

See Connect for the spreadsheet and questions needed to analyze this scenario.

CHAPTER FOUR

Focusing Marketing Strategy with Segmentation and Positioning

In the early 1930s in Billilund, Denmark, carpenter Ole Kirk Christiansen started a company that built wooden toys. He named his company LEGO, combining the first two letters from each word in the Danish phrase *leg godt,* which means "play well." Christiansen believed in quality—"only the best is good enough"—a value that stays with LEGO to this day.

During the 1950s, LEGO articulated its plastic bricks as part of a "system of play," based on learning through imagination, creativity, and problem solving. By 1958 LEGO had refined the design of the classic LEGO brick; those 1958 bricks still click and lock with any of the 40 billion bricks LEGO has made since. Buoyed by the tail end of the baby boom generation, LEGO grew rapidly in the 1960s and 1970s. That growth slowed during the 1980s when the "construction toy market" lost favor to electronic toys and software.

LEGO reacted by broadening its market. In the 1990s, LEGO opened three Legoland theme parks, developed video games and electronic toys, produced books and TV shows, and licensed watches and clothing. Although the new product lines increased sales, costs rose even more quickly. In 2004, LEGO lost more than $300 million. LEGO needed a strategy to turn things around—and fast!

To address the immediate financial weakness, LEGO sold off Legoland theme parks, outsourced production, and consolidated its product lines. In assessing its strengths, LEGO recognized 1) its brand name was widely trusted, and 2) its enduring system of play, building with bricks, provided a platform for innovation. To focus its new strategy, LEGO redefined its market around the iconic brick with a vision to equip children for the future through creative, playful learning. LEGO thought it could profitably grow in the "active play market."

LEGO next sought to get to know its customers better. So LEGO set loose teams of researchers who embedded with families to understand how seven- to nine-year-old boys in Germany and the United States lived and played. One finding shattered a myth that had guided LEGO's thinking much of the previous decade. LEGO had taken the wrong lessons from the growth of video games when it assumed kids needed immediate gratification. In response, LEGO had dumbed down many of its toys. But the new research found that kids wanted opportunities to demonstrate mastery—evidenced by the scoring, ranking, and sharing common in many computer games. LEGO also discovered that although kids lived very scheduled lives, they appreciated time to themselves. These findings guided new strategic thinking at LEGO.

For seven- to nine-year-old boys, LEGO focused on its kits—from LEGO City's fire station and police station to kits with *Harry Potter, Star Wars,* and *The Hobbit* movie themes. As boys get older, they appreciate LEGO products that bridge the virtual world of computers and the physical world. For example, teens go to LEGO Ideas, where they design their own kits and upload them to a website for others to see. Anyone can vote for their favorites and those with the most votes—such as The Big Bang Theory (based on the TV show)—are turned into limited edition kits. The new LEGO Fusion lets kids build their own towns, roads, shops, and restaurants in the real world—and then take a picture that moves their creations to a virtual world where they become part of a computer game.

Because of between-country differences in customer behavior, LEGO segments its customers by country. For example, whereas many German and American parents seek out toys that combine the values of learning and play, Japanese parents draw a sharper line between learning and play so don't tend to seek out educational toys. German parents are also much more likely to play LEGO with their kids as compared to American parents. So LEGO promotion varies among the countries.

The *Star Wars* kits and LEGO Mindstorm robots struck a chord with another market segment—adults. Thanks to the Internet, the dispersed adult fans of LEGO (they call themselves by the acronym AFOLs) found they weren't alone.

Forming online communities, like the LEGO User Group Network (www.LUGNET.biz), AFOLs meet and share their passion for bricks.

At first, LEGO didn't design a marketing mix for the AFOL segment. That changed when it found some AFOLs spending thousands of dollars a year on LEGO. When LEGO introduced the 3,104-piece, $299 Imperial Star Destroyer kit, it flew off store shelves. An AFOL in Chicago helped design the LEGO Architecture line which lets users build replicas of famous buildings such as the Eiffel Tower and Sydney Opera House. AFOLs account for 5 to 10 percent of all LEGO sales and influence even more.

Over the years, LEGO has made several failed attempts to crack the "girls active play market." LEGO research showed that after age 5, most girls lose interest in LEGO's products. With girls accounting for half the toy market, a big opportunity awaited if LEGO could do it right.

So LEGO again sent teams of researchers out to spend time with girls. The findings drove decisions for the LEGO Friends line. For example, whereas boys like to complete a kit before they start playing make-believe, girls like to play and pretend along the way. So the Friends kits now come with bagged parts, allowing the girls to start storytelling and rearranging sooner. Girls also had opinions about the LEGO figurines (LEGO calls them "mini-figs"). Whereas boys play with the mini-figs in the third person, girls project themselves onto each figure; further, girls found the traditional stubby mini-fig ugly—so Friends mini-figs look more like real people. Currently, the five main mini-fig characters in LEGO Friends come with names and backstories described in accompanying books. LEGO Friends works across cultures—showing strong sales in the United States, Germany, and the fast-growing Chinese market. Thanks to Friends, sales to girls went from 9 percent to 27 percent of LEGO's total sales.

Entering a new product-market, *The LEGO Movie* was a hit, taking in more than $450 million worldwide, while appealing to boys and girls. LEGO's profits now exceed $1 billion annually on sales of more than $4 billion. By "playing well" with adults, boys, and girls, LEGO has constructed the most valuable company in the toy business.[1]

LEARNING OBJECTIVES

As the LEGO case illustrates, a manager who develops an understanding of the needs and characteristics of specific groups of target customers within the broader market may see new, breakthrough opportunities. But it's not always obvious how to identify the real needs of a target market—or the marketing mix that those customers will see as different from, and better than, what is available from a competitor. This chapter covers concepts and approaches that will help you to succeed in the search for those opportunities.

When you finish this chapter, you should be able to

1 Define and describe generic markets and product-markets.

2 Know what market segmentation is and how to segment product-markets into submarkets.

3 Know three approaches to market-oriented strategy planning.

4 Know dimensions that may be useful for segmenting markets.

5 Recognize how some computer-aided methods are used in segmenting.

6 Know what positioning is and why it is useful.

7 Understand the important new terms (shown in red).

Search for Opportunities Can Begin by Understanding Markets

LO 4.1

Strategy planning is a narrowing-down process

In Chapter 2 we provided a framework for a logical marketing strategy planning process. It involves careful evaluation of the market opportunities available before narrowing down to focus on the most attractive target market and marketing mix. In Chapter 3, we focused on approaches for analyzing how competitors and the external market environment shape the evaluation of opportunities. In this chapter we discuss concepts that can guide the selection of specific target customers. See Exhibit 4–1 for an overview.

Exhibit 4-1 Focusing Marketing Strategy with Segmentation and Positioning

Segmentation and Targeting
- Defining generic markets and product-markets
- Understanding types of dimensions used to segment markets
- Knowing how to identify segments
- Deciding what segments to target
- Using segmentation approaches

Differentiation and Positioning
- Understanding customer's view
- Using positioning techniques
- Evaluating segment preferences
- Differentiating the marketing mix
- Knowing the relationship between positioning and targeting

In a broad sense, this chapter is about understanding and analyzing customers in a market. In Chapters 5 and 6 we will look more closely at specific influences on the behavior of both final consumers and organizational customers. However, this chapter sets the stage for that by explaining how marketing managers combine different types of information about customers to guide targeting decisions.

Because this chapter is about bringing focus to the search for market opportunities, a good place to start is by discussing what we really mean when we use the term *market*.

What is a company's market?

Identifying a company's market is an important but sticky issue. In general, a **market** is a group of potential customers with similar needs who are willing to exchange something of value with sellers offering various goods or services—that is, ways of satisfying those needs. However, within a general market, marketing-oriented managers develop marketing mixes for *specific* target markets. Getting the firm to focus on specific target markets is vital.

Don't just focus on the product

Some production-oriented managers don't understand this narrowing-down process. They get into trouble because they ignore the tough part of defining markets. To make the narrowing-down process easier, they just describe their markets in terms of *products* they sell. For example, producers and retailers of greeting cards might define their market as the "greeting card" market. But this production-oriented approach ignores customers—and customers make a market! This leads to missed opportunities.

Hallmark isn't missing these opportunities. Instead, Hallmark aims at the "personal-expression" market. The Hallmark.com online store, its Gold Crown stores, and other dealers offer all kinds of products that allow people to express their feelings by capturing and saving memories. As opportunities related to these needs change, Hallmark changes, too. For example, at a Hallmark store you can find both cards and picture frames. Hallmark also sells photo albums that allow customers to attach voice recordings to each picture. At Hallmark.com, subscribers will find tips about what to write in a graduation or birthday card, the etiquette to follow in writing a birth announcement, and a blog post on how to "Banish boredom with a Summer Fun List." The Hallmark eCards smartphone app lets users customize eCards with animated greetings—and send them by e-mail or post them on Facebook.[2]

From generic markets to product-markets

To understand the narrowing-down process, it's useful to think of two basic types of markets. A **generic market** is a market with *broadly* similar needs and sellers offering various, *often diverse,* ways of satisfying those needs. In contrast, a **product-market** is a market with *very* similar needs and sellers offering various *close substitute* ways of satisfying those needs.[3]

A generic market description looks at markets broadly and from a customer's viewpoint. Entertainment-seekers, for example, have several very different ways to satisfy their needs. An entertainment-seeker might buy a Blu-ray disc player and a high-definition TV (HDTV), sign up for a cruise on the Carnival Line, or reserve season tickets for the symphony. Any one of these *very different* products may satisfy this entertainment need. Sellers in this generic entertainment-seeker market have to focus on the need(s) the customers want satisfied—not on how one seller's product (HDTV system, vacation, or live music) is better than that of another producer.

It is sometimes hard to understand and define generic markets because *quite different product types may compete with one another.* For example, a person on a business trip to Italy might want a convenient way to record memories of the trip. Minolta's digital camera, a camera in a Samsung cell phone, Sony's video camcorder, and even postcards from local shops may all compete to serve our traveler's needs. If customers see all these products as substitutes—as competitors in the same generic market—then marketers must deal with this complication.

Camera makers try to stand out in a competitive product marketplace where each addresses customers' needs to capture and record memories. GoPro's Hero2 cameras attach to helmets, skis, and bikes to take photos while users are engaged in action sports; Fujifilm offers a waterproof model; and Lytro allows customers to focus different parts of the picture after the photo is taken.

Suppose, however, that our traveler decides to satisfy this need with a digital camera. Then—in this product-market—Canon, Sony, Olympus, Nikon, and many other brands may compete with one another for the customer's dollars. In this *product-*market concerned with digital cameras *and* needs to conveniently record memories, consumers compare similar products to satisfy their imaging needs.

Broaden market definitions to find opportunities

Broader market definitions—including both generic market definitions and product-market definitions—can help firms find opportunities. But deciding *how* broad to go isn't easy. Too narrow a definition limits a firm's opportunities—but too broad a

Nestlé targets customers in many different geographic markets around the world, but often the product-markets in one country are different than in another. For example, Nestlé created banana flavored milk ice on a stick to fit the local tastes and preferences of Chinese consumers. The same product would probably not have a following in other places.

All trademarks and Intellectual Property are owned by Société des Produits Nestlé S.A.,Vevey, Switzerland or used with permission

definition makes the company's efforts and resources seem insignificant. Consider, for example, the mighty Coca-Cola Company. It has great success and a huge market share in the U.S. soft drink market. On the other hand, its share of all beverage drinking worldwide is very small.

Here we try to match opportunities to a firm's resources and objectives. So the *relevant market for finding opportunities* should be bigger than the firm's present product-market—but not so big that the firm couldn't expand and be an important competitor. A small manufacturer of screwdrivers in Mexico, for example, shouldn't define its market as broadly as "the worldwide tool-users market" or as narrowly as "our present screwdriver customers." But it may have the capabilities to consider "the handyman's hand-tool market in North America." Carefully naming your product-market can help you see possible opportunities.

Naming Product-Markets and Generic Markets

Some managers think about markets just in terms of the product they already produce and sell. But this approach can lead to missed opportunities. For example, think about how digital pictures replaced photographic film and digital video recorders (DVRs) replaced VCRs. In the music world, streaming music has replaced MP3 players, which replaced portable CD players, which replaced portable cassette tape players, which replaced transistor radios.

As this suggests, when evaluating opportunities, product-related terms do not—by themselves—adequately describe a market. A complete product-market definition includes a four-part description.

What:	1. **Product type (type of good and type of service)**
To meet what:	2. **Customer (user) needs**
For whom:	3. **Customer types**
Where:	4. **Geographic area**

We refer to these four-part descriptions as product-market "names" because most managers label their markets when they think, write, or talk about them. Such a four-part definition can be clumsy, however, so we often use a nickname. And the nickname should refer to people—not products—because, as we emphasize, people make markets!

Product type describes the goods and/or services that customers want. Sometimes the product type is strictly a physical good or strictly a service. But marketing managers who ignore the possibility that *both* are important can miss opportunities.

Customer (user) needs refer to the needs the product type satisfies for the customer. At a very basic level, product types usually provide functional benefits such as nourishing, protecting, warming, cooling, transporting, cleaning, holding, and saving time. Although we need to identify such "basic" needs first, in advanced economies, we usually go on to emotional needs—such as needs for fun, excitement, pleasing appearance, or status. Correctly defining the need(s) relevant to a market is crucial and requires a good understanding of customers. We discuss these topics more fully in Chapters 5 and 6.

Customer type refers to the final consumer or user of a product type. Here we want to choose a name that describes all present (possible) types of customers. To define customer type, marketers should identify the final consumer or user of the product type, rather than the buyer—if they are different. For instance, producers should avoid treating intermediaries as a customer type—unless intermediaries actually use the product in their own business.

The *geographic area* is where a firm competes, or plans to compete, for customers. Naming the geographic area may seem trivial, but understanding the geographic boundaries of a market can suggest new opportunities. A firm aiming only at the domestic market, for example, may want to expand to other countries.

Product-market boundaries provide focus

This idea of making a decision about the boundaries of a market applies not just to geographic areas served but also to decisions about customer needs and product and customer types. Thus, naming the market is not simply an exercise in assigning labels. Rather, the manager's market definition sets the limits of the market(s) in which the firm will compete. For example, Canon targets a wide range of photographic needs and might approach a product-market named the "digital photographers market," defined as digital cameras (product type), that are easy to use and take high quality digital photographs (customer needs), for amateur photographers (customer types), in developing countries (geographic area). Canon's product line should appeal to this broad product-market. On the other hand, camera maker GoPro focuses on a more specific set of customer needs and has tighter boundaries on its market definition. GoPro might define the "adventure video market" as digital video cameras (product type), that are rugged, waterproof, and don't need to be operated by hand (customer needs), for adventure sports enthusiasts (customer types), who live anywhere in the world (geographic area). GoPro's video cameras attach to surfboards, handlebars, or helmets so that adventure sport enthusiasts can capture all the action. These product-market definitions give each company a focus that sharpens marketing strategy.

Exhibit 4-2
Relationship between Generic and Product-Market Definitions

No product type in generic market names

A generic market description *doesn't include any product-type terms.* It consists of only three parts of the product-market definition. This emphasizes that any product type that satisfies the customer's needs can compete in a generic market. Exhibit 4–2 shows the relationship between generic market and product-market definitions.

Later we'll study the many possible dimensions for segmenting markets. But for now you should see that defining markets only in terms of current products is not the best way to find new opportunities. Instead, the most effective way to find opportunities is to use market segmentation.

Market Segmentation Defines Possible Target Markets

LO 4.2

Market segmentation is a two-step process

Market segmentation is a two-step process of (1) *naming* broad product-markets and (2) *segmenting* these broad product-markets in order to select target markets and develop suitable marketing mixes.

This two-step process isn't well understood. First-time market segmentation efforts often fail because beginners start with the whole mass market and try to find one or two demographic characteristics to divide up (segment) this market. Customer behavior is usually too complex to be explained in terms of just one or two demographic characteristics. For example, a recent study of older adults without kids at home found that although half never visit social networking sites such as Facebook, almost one in five visited daily.[4]

Naming broad product-markets is disaggregating

The first step in effective market segmentation involves naming a broad product-market of interest to the firm. Marketers must break apart—disaggregate—all possible needs into some generic markets and broad product-markets in which the firm may be able to operate profitably (see Exhibit 4–3). No one firm can satisfy everyone's needs. So the naming—disaggregating—step involves brainstorming about very different solutions to various generic needs and selecting some broad areas—broad product-markets—where the firm has some resources and experience. This means that a car manufacturer would probably ignore all the possible opportunities in food and clothing

Exhibit 4-3 Narrowing Down to Target Markets

Exhibit 4-4 A Market Grid Diagram with Submarkets

Broad product-market (or generic market) name goes here
(The bicycle-riders product-market)

| Submarket 1 (Exercisers) | Submarket 3 (Transportation riders) | Submarket 4 (Socializers) |

Submarket 2 (Off-road adventurers)

Submarket 5 (Environmentalists)

markets and focus on the generic market, "transporting people in the world," and probably on the broad product-market, "cars, trucks, and utility vehicles for transporting people in the world."

Market grid is a visual aid to market segmentation

Assuming that any broad product-market (or generic market) may consist of submarkets, picture a market as a rectangle with boxes that represent the smaller, more homogeneous product-markets.

Exhibit 4–4, for example, represents the broad product-market of bicycle riders. The boxes show different submarkets. One submarket might focus on people who want basic transportation, another on people who want exercise, and so on. Alternatively, in the generic "transporting market" discussed earlier, we might see different product-markets of customers for bicycles, motorcycles, cars, airplanes, ships, buses, and "others."

Segmenting is an aggregating process

Marketing-oriented managers think of **segmenting** as an aggregating process—clustering people with similar needs into a "market segment." A **market segment** is a (relatively) homogeneous group of customers who will respond to a marketing mix in a similar way.

This part of the market segmentation process takes a different approach from the naming part. Here we look for similarities rather than basic differences in needs. Segmenters start with the idea that each person is one of a kind but that it may be possible to aggregate some similar people into a product-market.

Consumers associate the Clorox brand with strong cleaning power and bleach. Clorox uses the Green Works brand to target customers who want natural cleaning products that don't have harsh chemical fumes or residue.
Both ads: © 2012 The Clorox Company. Reprinted with permission.

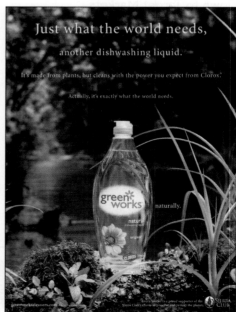

Exhibit 4-5
Every Individual Has His or Her Own Unique Position in a Market—Those with Similar Positions Can Be Aggregated into Potential Target Markets

A. Product-market showing three segments

B. Product-market showing six segments

Segmenters see each of these one-of-a-kind people as having a unique set of dimensions. Consider a product-market in which customers' needs differ on two important segmenting dimensions: need for status and need for dependability. In Exhibit 4–5A, each dot shows a person's position on the two dimensions. Although each person's position is unique, many of these people are similar in terms of how much status and dependability they want. So a segmenter may aggregate them into three (an arbitrary number) relatively homogeneous submarkets—A, B, and C. Group A might be called "status-oriented" and Group C "dependability-oriented." Members of Group B want both and might be called the "demanders."

How far should the aggregating go?

The segmenter wants to aggregate individual customers into some workable number of relatively homogeneous target markets and then treat each target market differently.

Look again at Exhibit 4–5A. Remember we talked about three segments. But this was an arbitrary number. As Exhibit 4–5B shows, there may really be six segments. What do you think—does this broad product-market consist of three segments or six?

Another difficulty with segmenting is that some potential customers just don't fit neatly into market segments. For example, not everyone in Exhibit 4–5B was put into one of the groups. Forcing them into one of the groups would have made these segments more heterogeneous and harder to please. Further, forming additional segments for them probably wouldn't be profitable. They are too few and not very similar in terms of the two dimensions. These people are simply too unique to be catered to and may have to be ignored—unless they are willing to pay a high price for special treatment.

The number of segments that should be formed depends more on judgment than on some scientific rule. But the following guidelines can help.

Criteria for segmenting a broad product-market

Ideally, "good" market segments meet the following criteria:

1. *Homogeneous (similar) within*—the customers in a market segment should be as similar as possible with respect to their likely responses to marketing mix variables *and* their segmenting dimensions.
2. *Heterogeneous (different) between*—the customers in different segments should be as different as possible with respect to their likely responses to marketing mix variables *and* their segmenting dimensions.
3. *Substantial*—the segment should be big enough to be profitable.
4. *Operational*—the segmenting dimensions should be useful for identifying customers and deciding on marketing mix variables.

Firms that compete in the oral health care market have developed a variety of products that appeal to the needs of different customer segments. Sensodyne targets consumers with sensitive teeth, Colgate Total Gum Defense aims at those concerned about the health of their gums, and Tom's Children's toothpaste emphasizes its use of natural ingredients.

It is especially important that segments be *operational*. This leads marketers to include demographic dimensions such as age, sex, income, location, and family size. In fact, it is difficult to make some Place and Promotion decisions without such information. For example, magazines, websites, and television shows have data on the demographic characteristics of their readers, visitors, and viewers. This makes it easier for a marketing manager to match these qualities with its target market.

Avoid segmenting dimensions that have no practical operational use. For example, you may find a personality trait such as moodiness among the traits of heavy buyers of a product, but how could you use this fact? Salespeople can't give a personality test to each buyer. Similarly, advertising couldn't make much use of this information. So although moodiness might be related in some way to previous purchases, it would not be a useful dimension for segmenting.

Target marketers aim at specific targets

LO 4.3

Once you accept the idea that broad product-markets may have submarkets, you can see that target marketers usually have a choice among many possible target markets.

There are three basic ways to develop market-oriented strategies in a broad product-market.

1. The **single target market approach**—segmenting the market and picking one of the homogeneous segments as the firm's target market.
2. The **multiple target market approach**—segmenting the market and choosing two or more segments, and then treating each as a separate target market needing a different marketing mix.
3. The **combined target market approach**—combining two or more submarkets into one larger target market as a basis for one strategy.

Note that all three approaches involve target marketing. They all aim at specific, clearly defined target markets (see Exhibit 4–6). For convenience, we call people who follow the first two approaches the "segmenters" and people who use the third approach the "combiners."

Exhibit 4-6
Segmenters and
Combiners Aim at
Specific Target
Markets

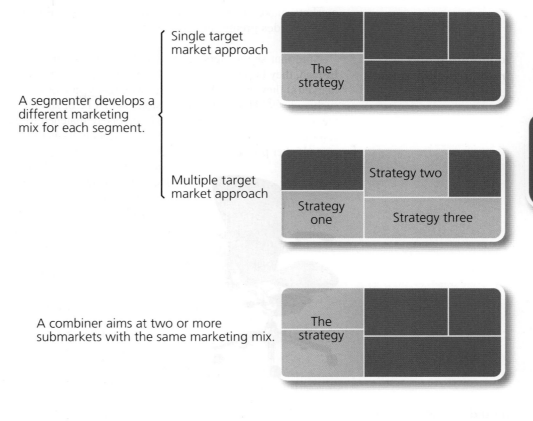

A segmenter develops a different marketing mix for each segment.

Single target market approach

Multiple target market approach

A combiner aims at two or more submarkets with the same marketing mix.

Combiners try to satisfy "pretty well"

Combiners try to increase the size of their target markets by combining two or more segments. Combiners look at various submarkets for similarities rather than differences. Then they try to extend or modify their basic offering to appeal to these "combined" customers with just one marketing mix. For example, a combiner who faces the broad bicycle-riders product-market shown in Exhibit 4–4 might try to develop a marketing mix that would do a pretty good job of appealing to both the *Exercisers* and the *Off-road adventurers*. The combined market would be bigger than either segment by itself. And although both submarkets might like fatter tires and multiple speeds, the *off-road adventurer* prefers a wider range of gears, a suspension system to handle bumps, and a more durable frame than the *exerciser* might want or need. On the other hand, comfort is more important to the *exerciser* who favors a more upright seating position. A single model of bicycle designed for both segments might not be the *best bike* for either segment.

Thus, a combiner makes compromises in developing the marketing mix. The combiner doesn't try to fine-tune each element of the marketing mix to appeal to each of the smaller submarkets. Rather, the marketing mix is selected to work fairly well with each segment.

A combined target market approach may help achieve some economies of scale. It may also require less investment than developing different marketing mixes for different segments—making it especially attractive for firms with limited resources.

Segmenters try to satisfy "very well"

Segmenters aim at one or more homogeneous segments and try to develop a different marketing mix for each segment. Segmenters usually fine-tune their marketing mixes for each target market—perhaps making basic changes in the product itself—because they want to satisfy each segment very well.

Instead of assuming that the whole market consists of a fairly similar set of customers (like the mass marketer does) or merging various submarkets together (like the combiner), segmenters believe that aiming at one, or some, of these smaller markets makes it possible to provide superior value and satisfy them better. This then provides greater profit potential for the firm.

Segmenting may produce bigger sales

Note that segmenters are not settling for a smaller sales potential or lower profits. Instead, they hope to increase sales by getting a much larger share of the business in the market(s) they target. A segmenter who really satisfies the target market can often build such a close relationship with customers that he or she faces no real competition. A segmenter who offers a marketing mix precisely matched to the needs of the target market can often charge a higher price, thus producing higher profits. Customers are willing to pay a higher price because the whole marketing mix provides better customer value.

Consider the success of the Aeron desk chair developed by Herman Miller (HM), an 80-year-old company that makes office furniture. Most firms that sell office furniture offered similar lines of executive desk chairs that were padded for comfort and conveyed the look of success. Marketing managers at HM realized that some customers felt that these traditional chairs were boring. Further, in an e-commerce world, even top executives sit at computers and want a chair that provides both good support and good looks. So to satisfy this upscale segment, HM designed a new type of chair from scratch. There's no fabric or padding, but everything about it adjusts to your body. It's so comfortable that HM positions it as "the chair you can wear." With a price tag of $750 or more, the Aeron chair became a status symbol for high-tech managers and has been as profitable as it is popular.[5]

© William D. Perreault, Jr., Ph.D.

Should you segment or combine?

Which approach should a firm use? This depends on the firm's resources, the nature of competition, and—most important—the similarity of customer needs, attitudes, and buying behavior.

It's usually safer to be a segmenter—that is, to try to satisfy some customers *very* well instead of many just *fairly* well. That's why many firms use the single or multiple target market approach instead of the combined target market approach. For example, Procter & Gamble produces both Tide and Cheer laundry detergents, which have different marketing mixes. Even within the Tide brand, there are different formulas. Tide Free & Gentle is free from dye and perfumes and targets families with newborn babies or individuals with allergies. Tide plus Febreze Sport is designed for washing sports apparel, which might have grass or blood stains. The Product, Promotion, and Place differ between these and other Tide specialty detergents. Though extremely effective, this approach may not be possible for a smaller firm with more limited resources. A smaller firm may have to use the single target market approach—focusing all its efforts at the one submarket niche where it sees the best opportunity.[6]

Kaepa, Inc., is a good example. Sales of its all-purpose sneakers plummeted as larger firms such as Nike and Reebok stole customers with a multiple target market approach. They developed innovative products and aimed their promotion at specific needs—such as jogging, aerobics, cross-training, and walking. Kaepa turned things around by catering to the needs of cheerleaders. Cheerleading squads can order Kaepa shoes with custom team logos and colors. The soles of the shoes feature finger grooves that make it easier for cheerleaders to build human pyramids. Kaepa also carefully targets its market research and promotion. Kaepa salespeople attend the cheerleading camps that each summer draw 40,000 enthusiasts. Kaepa even arranges for the cheering teams it sponsors to do demos at retail stores. This generates publicity and pulls in buyers, so retailers put more emphasis on the Kaepa line.[7]

Profit is the balancing point

In practice, cost considerations often encourage more aggregating and favor combining submarkets as costs often drop due to economies of scale. On the other hand, many customers prefer to have their needs satisfied more exactly—and will be more satisfied by a segmenter that develops a marketing mix that more closely matches their needs. When the rest of the marketing mix better matches their needs, customers are often willing to pay a higher price. Profit is the balancing point. It determines how unique a marketing mix the firm can afford to offer to a particular market segment.

What Dimensions Are Used to Segment Markets?

LO 4.4

Segmenting dimensions guide marketing mix planning

Market segmentation forces a marketing manager to decide which product-market dimensions might be useful for planning marketing strategies. The dimensions should help guide marketing mix planning. Exhibit 4–7 shows the basic kinds of dimensions we'll be talking about in Chapters 5 and 6—and their probable effect on the Four Ps. Ideally, we want to describe any potential product-market in terms of all three types of customer-related dimensions—plus a product-type description—because these dimensions help us develop better marketing mixes.

Many segmenting dimensions may be considered

Customers can be described by many specific dimensions. Exhibit 4–8 shows some dimensions useful for segmenting consumer markets. A few are behavioral dimensions; others are geographic and demographic. We discuss these final consumer segmenting dimensions in Chapters 3 and 5. Exhibit 4–9 shows some additional dimensions for segmenting markets when the customers are businesses, government agencies, or other types of organizations. These dimensions for segmenting organizational customers are covered in Chapter 6. Regardless of whether customers are final consumers or organizations, segmenting a broad product-market *usually* requires using several different dimensions at the same time.[8]

What are the qualifying and determining dimensions?

To select the important segmenting dimensions, think about two different types of dimensions. **Qualifying dimensions** are those relevant to including a customer type in a product-market. **Determining dimensions** are those that actually affect the customer's purchase of a *specific* product or brand in a product-market.

A prospective car buyer, for example, has to have enough money—or credit—to buy a car and insure it. Our buyer also needs a driver's license. This still doesn't guarantee a purchase. He or she must have a real need—such as a job that requires "wheels" or kids who have to be carpooled. This need may motivate the purchase of *some* car. But these qualifying dimensions don't determine what specific brand or model car the person might buy. That depends on more specific interests—such as the kind of safety,

Exhibit 4-7 Relation of Potential Target Market Dimensions to Marketing Strategy Decision Areas

Potential Target Market Dimensions	Effects on Strategy Decision Areas
1. Behavioral needs, attitudes, and how present and potential goods and services fit into customers' consumption patterns.	Affects *Product* (features, packaging, product line assortment, branding) and *Promotion* (what potential customers need and want to know about the firm's offering, and what appeals should be used).
2. Urgency to get need satisfied and desire and willingness to seek information, compare, and shop.	Affects *Place* (how directly products are distributed from producer to customer, how extensively they are made available, and the level of service needed) and *Price* (how much potential customers are willing to pay).
3. Geographic location and other demographic characteristics of potential customers.	Affects size of *Target Markets* (economic potential), *Place* (where products should be made available), and *Promotion* (where and to whom to target with advertising, publicity, sales promotion and personal selling).

Exhibit 4-8   Possible Segmenting Dimensions and Typical Breakdowns for Consumer Markets

Behavioral

Needs	Economic, functional, physiological, psychological, social, and more detailed needs.
Benefits sought	Situation specific, but to satisfy specific or general needs.
Thoughts	Favorable or unfavorable attitudes, interests, opinions, beliefs.
Rate of use	Heavy, medium, light, nonusers.
Purchase relationship	Positive and ongoing, intermittent, no relationship, bad relationship.
Brand familiarity	Insistence, preference, recognition, nonrecognition, rejection.
Kind of shopping	Convenience, comparison shopping, specialty, none (unsought product).
Type of problem solving	Routinized response, limited, extensive.
Information required	Low, medium, high.

Geographic

Region of world, country	North America (United States, Canada), Europe (France, Italy, Germany), and so on.
Region in country	(Examples in United States): Pacific, Mountain, West North Central, West South Central, East North Central, East South Central, South Atlantic, Middle Atlantic, New England.
Size of city	No city; population under 5,000; 5,000–19,999; 20,000–49,999; 50,000–99,999; 100,000–249,999; 250,000–499,999; 500,000–999,999; 1,000,000–3,999,999; 4,000,000 or over.

Demographic

Income	Less than $10,000; $10,000–24,999; $25,000–49,999; $50,000–74,999; $75,000–99,999; $100,000–149,999; $150,000–249,999; $250,000 or more.
Gender	Male, female.
Age	Infant; younger than 6; 6–11; 12–17; 18–24; 25–34; 35–49; 50–64; 65 or older.
Family size	1, 2, 3–4, 5 or more.
Family life cycle	Young, single; young, married, no children; young, married, youngest child younger than 6; young, married, youngest child older than 6; older, married, with children; older, married, no children younger than 18; older, single; other variations for single parents, divorced, etc.
Occupation	Professional and technical; managers, officials, and proprietors; clerical sales; craftspeople; foremen; operatives; farmers; retired; students; housewives; unemployed.
Education	Grade school or less; some high school; high school graduate; some college; college graduate; some graduate school; graduate degree.
Ethnicity	Asian, Black, Hispanic, Native American, White, multiracial.
Social class	Lower-lower, upper-lower, lower-middle, upper-middle, lower-upper, upper-upper.

Note: Terms used in this table are explained in detail later in the text.

performance, or appearance the customer wants. Determining dimensions related to these needs affect the specific car the customer purchases. If safety is a determining dimension for a customer, a Volvo wagon that offers side impact protection, air bags, and all-wheel drive might be the customer's first choice.

Consider Ford's efforts to sell cars in Vietnam. When Ford arrived in the country a few years ago, many consumers didn't even know how to drive a car—an important *qualifying* dimension when you are selling cars. To increase the size of its market, Ford created a free driving school for Vietnamese wanting to learn how to drive. Ford hoped that training drivers using Ford cars would build brand preference that would become a *determining* dimension for future Vietnamese drivers.[9]

Determining dimensions may be very specific

How specific the determining dimensions are depends on whether you are concerned with a general product type or a specific brand (see Exhibit 4–10). The more

Exhibit 4-9
Possible Segmenting Dimensions for Business/Organizational Markets

Kind of relationship	Weak loyalty → strong loyalty to vendor Single source → multiple vendors "Arm's length" dealings → close partnership
Type of customer	Manufacturer, service producer, government agency, military, nonprofit, wholesaler or retailer (when end user), and so on
Demographics	Geographic location (region of world, country, region within country, urban → rural); Size (number of employees, sales volume); Primary business or industry (North American Industry Classification System); Number of facilities
How customer will use product	Installations, components, accessories, raw materials, supplies, professional services
Type of buying situation	Decentralized → centralized Buyer → multiple buying influence Straight rebuy → modified rebuy → new-task buying
Purchasing methods	Vendor analysis, purchasing specifications, Internet bids, negotiated contracts, long-term contracts, e-commerce websites

Note: Terms used in this table are explained in detail later in the text.

specific you want to be, the more particular the determining dimensions may be. In a particular case, the determining dimensions may seem minor. But they are important because they *are* the determining dimensions.

Marketers at General Mills know this. Lots of people try to check e-mail or drive a car while eating breakfast or lunch. General Mills has figured out that for many of these target customers the real determining dimension in picking a snack is whether it can be eaten "one-handed."

Qualifying dimensions are important too

The qualifying dimensions help identify the "core benefits" that must be offered to everyone in a product-market. For example, people won't choose General Mills' one-handed snacks unless they qualify as being tasty. Qualifying and determining dimensions work together in marketing strategy planning.

Exhibit 4-10   Finding the Relevant Segmenting Dimensions

Segmenting dimensions become more specific when the target segment seeks to purchase a particular brand of the product

All potential dimensions	Qualifying dimensions	Determining dimensions (product type)	Determining dimensions (brand specific)
Dimensions generally relevant to purchasing behavior	Dimensions relevant to including a customer type in the product-market	Dimensions that affect the customer's purchase of a specific type of product	Dimensions that affect the customer's choice of a specific brand

People who are out in the sun should protect their skin. This safety need is a qualifying dimension of consumers in the market for sunscreen products. However, parents may especially seek Banana Boat Baby and Kids Sunblock Lotion and Baby Sprays because they are easy on kids' eyes and don't cause tearing. For these parents this is a determining need. There are a variety of ways that Coffee-Mate is different from cream, but this ad focuses on the idea that it does not need to be refrigerated. For some consumers, that determines what they will buy.

© 1999-2015 Edgewell. *Creative Director/Copywriter: Emily Smeraldo; Art Director: Wayne Kan & Jonathan Lee; School: School of Visual Arts, New York; Instructors: Richard Pels & Paul Jarvis.*

Different dimensions needed for different submarkets

Personas give segments life

International marketing requires even more segmenting

Note that each different submarket within a broad product-market may be motivated by a different set of dimensions. In the snack food market, for example, health food enthusiasts are interested in nutrition, dieters worry about calories, and economical shoppers with lots of kids may want volume to "fill them up."

Sometimes a marketing manager must decide whether a firm should serve customers it really doesn't want to serve. For example, banks sometimes offer marketing mixes that are attractive to wealthy customers but drive off low-income consumers.

After creating segments, some firms create *buyer personas*—fictional depictions of customers illustrative of each target segment. These depictions often turn into elaborate background "stories" that describe a typical segment member's demographic characteristics and behavior patterns—related (and unrelated) to buying, motivations, and goals. A buyer persona emerges from customer research, usually personal interviews with several members of the target market segment.

For example, a bicycle maker might develop buyer personas for different target segments. If it targets commuters, the following might reflect the beginnings of a buyer persona:

Sam is a single 29-year-old male who lives in Seattle, Washington. He rides 10 miles each way to his job where he earns $85,000 a year as a computer programmer. On weekends he likes to hang with his girlfriend and race mountain bikes. Sam is price sensitive with his commuter bike (he spends more lavishly on his mountain bikes). The commuter bike must be safe and reliable; it should have fenders and a chain guard to deal with the regular rains in Seattle.

This description of Sam might continue with details on Sam's favorite websites, social media behavior, reading selections, long- and short-term goals, and his history of riding. Personas often include a photo. Because people relate best to people (rather than abstract "segments"), personas help everyone across the organization (research and development, customer service, advertising, website development, and more) to better empathize with target customers and develop a marketing orientation.[10]

Success in international marketing requires even more attention to segmenting. There are more than 192 nations with their own unique cultures! And they differ greatly in language, customs (including business ethics), beliefs, religions, race, and income distribution patterns. (We discuss some of these differences in Chapters 3, 5, and 6) These additional differences can complicate the segmenting process. Even worse, critical data are often less available—and less dependable—as firms move into international markets. This is one reason why some firms insist that local operations and decisions be handled by natives. They, at least, have a feel for their markets.

Segmenting international markets may require more dimensions. But one practical method adds just one step to the approach discussed earlier. First, marketers segment by country or region—looking at demographic, cultural, and other characteristics, including stage of economic development. This may help them find regional or national submarkets that are fairly similar. Then—depending on whether the firm is aiming at final consumers or business markets—they apply the same basic approaches presented before.

Smart segmenters win in international markets

Many firms make only modest changes to marketing mixes when they enter developing countries. So sellers can really stand out when they show a respect for and focus on local customers. A few years ago Korea's LG Electronics started tailoring products to the Indian market. As one example, LG's Charcoal Lighting Heater Microwave includes an autocook menu with settings for more than 130 Indian dishes. The move paid off when LG was chosen as the most trusted consumer durable brand in India.

Ethical issues in selecting segmenting dimensions

Marketing managers sometimes face ethical decisions when selecting segmenting dimensions. Problems may arise if a firm targets customers who are somehow at a disadvantage in dealing with the firm or who are unlikely to see the negative effects of their own choices. For example, some people criticize athletic shoe companies for targeting poor, inner-city kids who see expensive athletic shoes as an important status symbol. Many firms, including producers of infant formula, have been criticized for targeting consumers in less-developed nations. Some nutritionists criticize firms that market soft drinks, candy, and snack foods to children.

Ethical Dilemma

What would you do? You just started your dream job as marketing manager for Appy Day Games (ADG). You are its sixth and latest employee, and the first dedicated to marketing. ADG's games are fun, easy to learn, and sell for a dollar each on the Android and Apple app stores. Unfortunately, with many competitors offering games for free, ADG sales are modest and it is not yet profitable. Shortly after starting, the company founder (Rachel) tells you about a new opportunity. She has received an enticing offer from DataMatic. DataMatic wants to put a software code into each of ADG's games. The code would collect data from every ADG customer's smartphone. The data, including all the e-mail addresses and phone numbers stored in the phones, would be sent back to DataMatic, which would package and sell it to its customers who are looking for leads. DataMatic's offer would instantly make ADG profitable. DataMatic says its software already resides on half the games on the "App Store Top 50" anyway. Rachel likes the idea and figures that if it's legal and everyone else does it, why shouldn't ADG? What do you think of DataMatic's proposal? Would you advise Rachel to accept the offer? Why or why not?[11]

More Sophisticated Techniques May Help in Segmenting and Targeting

LO 4.5

Marketing researchers and managers often turn to computer-aided methods for help with the segmenting job. A detailed review of the possibilities is beyond the scope of this book. But a brief discussion will give you a flavor of how computer-aided methods work. In addition, the Marketing Analytics: Data to Knowledge problem for this chapter (Chapter 4, Segmenting Customers) on the text website gives you a hands-on feel for how managers use them.

Clustering usually requires a computer

Clustering techniques try to find similar patterns within sets of data. Clustering groups customers who are similar on their segmenting dimensions into homogeneous segments. Clustering approaches use computers to do what previously was done with much intuition and judgment.

The data to be clustered might include such dimensions as demographic characteristics, the importance of different needs, attitudes toward the product, and past buying behavior. The computer searches all the data for homogeneous groups of people. When it finds them, marketers study the dimensions of the people in the groups to see why the computer clustered them together. The results sometimes suggest new, or at least better, marketing strategies.[12]

A cluster analysis of the toothpaste market, for example, might show that some people buy toothpaste because it tastes good (the sensory segment), whereas others are concerned with the effect of clean teeth and fresh breath on their social image (the sociables). Still others worry about decay or gum disease (the worriers), and some are just interested in the best value for their money (the value seekers). Each of these market segments calls for a different marketing mix—although some of the Four Ps may be similar.

Customer database can focus the effort

A variation of the clustering approach relies on **customer relationship management (CRM)**, where the seller fine-tunes

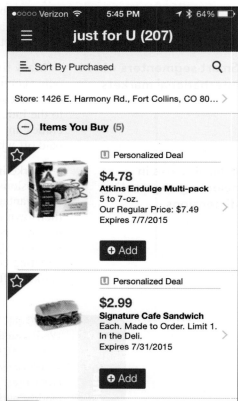

Safeway gathers customer data from its shoppers' use of customer loyalty cards. These data are used to tailor marketing mixes to each customer. So a customer who has purchased a Signature Cafe Sandwich may receive special offers for this item in the future and maybe for chips, too. These offers can be seen on the customer's smartphone and the Safeway Just for U™ app.

the marketing effort with information from a detailed customer database. The database stores information that is useful for segmentation. Analytic software aids in identifying customer segments, so that each can be delivered to a different marketing mix.

Consider the efforts of InterContinental Hotels Group (IHG), which built a database with information from members of its Priority Club rewards program. The database includes details on each traveler, such as income level, where they live, frequent travel destinations, whether each prefers family-style or business-travel accommodations, and more. IHG communicates regularly by e-mail to these important customers. In the past IHG divided the database into as many as 15 segments, with each group receiving a different e-mail message. Now IHG has more data and more finely tuned customer segments—sometimes IHG sends more than 1,500 *different* e-mails in a single campaign. So for example, one segment typically stays on weekends, redeems reward points for gift cards, and usually registers through the hotel's marketing partners. The e-mail message those customers receive offers special pricing and lets them know of upcoming weekend events in locations they favor. IHG's more personalized and more directed messages have resulted in 35 percent more customers accepting offers than when it had only 15 segments. For another example of how a firm used its CRM database to target customers, see "*What's Next?* Target reads its customers' minds."[13]

Targeting a segment of one

The ultimate in personalization occurs when firms consider each customer his or her own segment. Business-to-business markets, with very large customers, have typically treated customers individually as "segments of one." CRM helps consumer marketers do the same. The first time a guest reserves a room at the Mandarin Oriental hotel, she's asked about her personal preferences, which are saved in a database for future visits. On her next visit, the guest finds the room thermostat set to her preferred temperature, the phone's color touch screen shows the weather back home, and the three down feather pillows she enjoys are already on the bed.

Smartphones help target customers by current location

Many marketing managers would like to know when target customers are near their stores. With that information, they might be able to make those customers an offer to get them to visit the store and make a purchase. That kind of information is becoming a reality.

Today more than two-thirds of Americans and Europeans have smartphones. These phones send out signals, so an advertiser knows where the phone (and presumably its owner) is at any given moment. This helps retailers send messages to potential customers when they get within set distances of their stores. For example, customers who download the Macy's app to their phones are reminded of products they "liked" in the app when they enter a Macy's store. Audi's mobile ads direct customers to their nearest Audi dealer. Marketing managers and advertising agencies are just figuring out how to use location data—but we can expect this to grow, allowing marketers to more easily identify and reach customers.[14]

Differentiation and Positioning
Take the Customer Point of View

LO 4.6

Differentiate the marketing mix—to serve customers better

As we've emphasized throughout, the reason for focusing on a specific target market—by using marketing segmentation approaches or tools such as cluster analysis or CRM—is so that you can fine-tune the whole marketing mix to provide some group of potential customers with superior value. By *differentiating* the marketing mix to do a better job meeting customers' needs, the firm builds competitive advantage. When this happens, target customers view the firm's marketing mix as uniquely suited to their preferences and needs.

Although the marketing manager may want customers to see the firm's offering as unique, that is not always possible. Me-too imitators may come along and copy the firm's strategy. Further, even if a firm's marketing mix is different, consumers may not know or care. They're busy and, simply put, the firm's product may not be that important in their lives. This is where another important concept, *positioning,* comes in.

Positioning is based on customers' views

Positioning refers to how customers think about proposed or present brands in a market. Without a realistic view of how customers think about offerings in the market, it's hard for the marketing manager to differentiate. At the same time, the manager should know how he or she *wants* target customers to think about the firm's marketing mix. Positioning issues are especially important when competitors in a market appear to be very similar. For example, many people think that there isn't much difference between one provider of home owner's insurance and another. But State Farm Insurance uses advertising to emphasize the value of the service and personal attention from its agents, who live right in the customer's neighborhood. Low-price insurers who sell from websites or toll-free numbers can't make that claim.

Figuring out what customers really think about competing products isn't easy, but there are approaches that help. Most of them require some formal marketing research. The results are usually plotted on graphs to help show how consumers view the competing products. Usually, the products' positions are related to two or three product features that are important to the target customers.

Managers make the graphs for positioning decisions by asking consumers to make judgments about different brands—including their "ideal" brand—and then use computer programs to summarize the ratings and plot the results. The details of positioning

Sanuk wants to create a fun image for its footwear. The brand takes its name from the Thai word for fun, its products are known for a funky sense of style, and its promotion is creative and humorous. These contribute to the brand's positioning and Sanuk's target customers perceiving the brand as fun and irreverent. © 2015 Deckers Brands.

What's Next? Target reads its customers' minds

A few years ago a man walked into a Target store outside Minneapolis demanding to see a manager. The man was upset that Target was sending his teenage daughter coupons for baby clothes and cribs. "Are you trying to encourage her to get pregnant?" he asked the manager. The store manager promised to look into it, but a few days later the father called back and sheepishly admitted that there was more going on in his house than he knew about. His daughter was due in August. How did Target know? Why would Target care?

Consumers' shopping habits are hard to break. Once customers start shopping at a particular store for groceries, DVDs, or greeting cards, they get into a routine and don't even consider shopping at other stores. It turns out that a few major life events—new job, new home, marriage, and yes, new baby—significantly weaken those habits, at least for a short time. At those vulnerable moments, a competing store has an opportunity to steal a customer away—perhaps encouraging a switch with some well-timed promotions—and maybe help them develop a new shopping habit.

So how does a retail store such as Target segment its market and target pregnant shoppers? Target's marketing managers wondered if their customer relationship management (CRM) database might hold an answer. The database includes information on the shopping behavior of customers who sign up for the store's loyalty card or use a credit card. Along with additional data Target purchases from third parties, the database offers a detailed profile of millions of Target customers.

A small number of these customers told Target they were pregnant by signing up for the store's baby registry, where they also recorded the date the baby was due to be born. Target's statisticians used data from the customers they knew were pregnant and "mined" their CRM data to try to determine how their shopping behavior changed during pregnancy.

The statisticians discovered 25 products that were purchased more frequently during pregnancy. For example, although many people buy lotions, about six months before their due date purchases of unscented lotions bump up. Around that same time pregnant women stock up on supplements such as calcium, magnesium, and zinc. A few months later there is an uptick in purchases of scent-free soap, extra-large bags of cotton balls, hand sanitizers, and washcloths.

The statisticians use this information to develop a prediction score for each customer in Target's CRM database—predicting whether each is pregnant and when she will deliver. Customers with high scores receive customized direct mailings with coupons for a new crib or disposable diapers. Target wants these customers to start buying groceries and other products at Target, too. So it makes sure the mailings also include other products these customers haven't yet bought at Target. Many of these customers soon make Target their primary shopping location. So the next time you open a promotion for something you are thinking about buying, the store may be reading your mind—via its CRM database.

When this story became public, some customers questioned whether Target had crossed an ethical line. They found Target's behavior creepy. What do you think? Are Target's practices ethical? Should a retailer use data to predict customer behavior? Why or why not?[15]

techniques—sometimes called *perceptual mapping*—are beyond the scope of this text. But Exhibit 4–11 shows the possibilities.[16]

Exhibit 4–11 shows the "product space" for different brands of bar soap using two dimensions—the extent to which consumers think the soaps moisturize and deodorize their skin. For example, consumers see Dove as quite high on moisturizing but low on deodorizing. Dove and Tone are close together—implying that consumers think of them as similar on these characteristics. Dial is viewed as different from Dove and Tone and at a distance from them on the graph. Remember that positioning maps are based on *customers' perceptions*—the actual characteristics of the products (as determined by a chemical test) might be different!

Each segment may have its own preferences

The circles in Exhibit 4–11 show different sets (submarkets) of consumers clustered near their ideal soap preferences. Groups of respondents with a similar ideal

Exhibit 4-11 "Product Space" Representing Consumers' Perceptions for Different Brands of Bar Soap

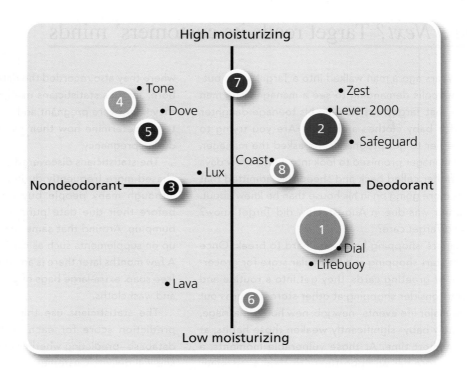

product are circled to show apparent customer concentrations. In this graph, the size of the circles suggests the size of the segments for the different ideals.

Ideal clusters 1 and 2 are the largest and are close to two popular brands—Dial and Lever 2000. It appears that customers in cluster 2 want more moisturizing than they see in Dial. However, exactly what this brand should do about this isn't clear. Perhaps Dial should leave its physical product alone—but emphasize moisturizing more in its promotion to make a stronger appeal to those who want moisturizers. A marketing manager talking about this approach might simply refer to it as "positioning the brand as a good moisturizer." Of course, whether the effort is successful depends on whether the whole marketing mix delivers on the promise of the positioning communication.

Note that ideal cluster 7 is not near any of the present brands. This may suggest an opportunity for introducing a new product—a strong moisturizer with some deodorizers. A firm that chooses to follow this approach would be making a segmenting effort.

Combining versus segmenting

Positioning analysis may lead a firm to combining—rather than segmenting—if managers think they can make several general appeals to different parts of a "combined" market. For example, by varying its promotion, Coast might try to appeal to segments 8, 1, and 2 with one product. These segments are all quite similar (close together) in what they want in an ideal brand. On the other hand, there may be clearly defined submarkets—and some parts of the market may be "owned" by one product or brand. In this case, segmenting efforts may be practical—moving the firm's own product into another segment of the general market area where competition is weaker.

Positioning as part of broader analysis

A positioning analysis helps managers understand how customers see their market. It is a visual aid to understanding a product-market. The first time such an analysis is done, managers may be shocked to see how much customers' perceptions of a market differ from their own. For this reason alone, positioning analysis may be crucial. But a positioning analysis usually focuses on specific product features and brands that are close competitors in the product-market. Thus, it is a product-oriented approach. Important *customer*-related dimensions—including needs and attitudes—may be overlooked.

Premature emphasis on product features is dangerous in other ways as well. As our bar soap example shows, starting with a product-oriented definition of a market and how bar soaps compete against other bar soaps can make a firm miss more basic shifts in markets. For example, bars have lost popularity to liquid soaps. Other products, such as bath oils or body washes for use in the shower, are now part of the relevant competition also. Managers wouldn't see these shifts if they looked only at alternative bar soap brands—the focus is just too narrow.

It's also important to realize that the way consumers look at a product isn't just a matter of chance. Let's return to our bar soap example. Although many consumers do think about soap in terms of moisturizing and deodorizing, other needs shouldn't be overlooked. For example, some consumers are especially concerned about wiping out germs. Marketers for Dial soap recognized this need and developed ads that positioned Dial as "the choice" for these target customers. This helped Dial win new customers, including those who switched from Lifebuoy—which was otherwise similar to Dial (see Exhibit 4–11). In fact, what happened to Lifebuoy highlights what happens if managers don't update their marketing strategy as customer needs and competition change. Lifebuoy was the first deodorant soap on the market; it was a leading brand for more than 100 years. But it gradually lost sales to competitors with stronger marketing mixes (clearer differentiation, better positioning, and superior customer value) until sales declined and Lever stopped selling it.

Sometimes repositioning is needed

Sometimes research shows the marketing manager that target customers are not viewing the brand in the desired way—it needs to be *repositioned*. Changing customers' perceptions of a brand is not easy—and requires changes to the marketing mix. In the mid-2000s Korean carmaker Hyundai found that its positioning was not helping it sell more vehicles. It conducted research that showed pictures of the Hyundai Veracruz, with the Hyundai name hidden, to a group of potential car buyers—71 percent said they would buy one. Another group of buyers was shown the same pictures *with* the Hyundai name—only 52 percent were interested this time. Hyundai learned that it had a reputation as a "cheap low quality" car, even though data showed its vehicles among the best made in the world. To reposition the brand, Hyundai gave buyers a 10-year, 100,000-mile warranty on every car and ran ads that emphasized its high safety and quality ratings. Soon Hyundai wasn't seen as cheap; instead, it was "more value for your money." With the new positioning, Hyundai's market share jumped 70 percent in three years.[17]

Positioning statement provides direction for marketing strategy

Sometimes marketing managers use a positioning statement to provide focus for a marketing mix. A **positioning statement** concisely identifies the firm's desired target market, product type, primary benefit or point of differentiation, and the main reasons a buyer should believe the firm's claims. The one or two benefits highlighted in the statement should be those most important to the target market—and unique to the brand. It's important that everyone involved in planning the marketing strategy agree with the positioning statement because it helps narrow options and guide the selection of a marketing mix.

Some firms use a template like the following to aid in preparation of a positioning statement:

For (*our target market*), (*our brand*) of all (*product type*) delivers (*key benefit or point of differentiation*) because (*our brand*) is (*reasons to believe*).

© 2015 PEPSICO, INC.

A few years ago, marketing managers for Mountain Dew used this template to develop the following positioning statement:

> For 16- to 24-year-old males, who embrace excitement, adventure, and fun, Mountain Dew of all carbonated soft drinks, delivers great taste that exhilarates like no other because Mountain Dew is energizing, thirst-quenching, and has a one-of-a-kind citrus flavor.

The positioning statement provided Mountain Dew's advertising agency with a direction to follow that led to a series of television and print advertisements that reinforced this positioning. The statement guided decisions about packaging, point-of-purchase promotion, sponsorships, the look and feel of a website, and choices for new flavors. The marketing strategy based on this positioning helped Mountain Dew gain market share with this target market.[18]

As we emphasize throughout the text, you must understand potential needs and attitudes when planning marketing strategies. If customers treat different products as substitutes, then a firm has to position itself against those products too. Customers won't always be conscious of all of the detailed ways that a firm's marketing mix might be different, but careful positioning can help highlight a unifying theme or benefits that relate to the determining dimensions of the target market. Thus, it's useful to think of positioning as part of the broader strategy planning process—because the purpose is to ensure that the whole marketing mix is positioned for competitive advantage.

CONCLUSION

Chapters 2 and 3 introduced a framework for strategy planning that starts with analysis of the broad market and then narrows down to a specific target market and marketing mix. The basic purpose of this chapter is to show how marketing managers use market segmentation and positioning to guide that narrowing-down process.

Now that you've read this chapter you should understand how to carefully define generic markets and product-markets and how that can help in identifying and evaluating opportunities. We stressed the shortcomings of a too-narrow,

product-oriented view of markets and explained why it's better to take a broader view that also includes consideration of customer needs, the product type, the customer type, and the geographic area.

We also discussed approaches for market segmentation—the process of naming and then segmenting broad product-markets to find potentially attractive target markets. Some people try to segment markets by starting with the mass market and then dividing it into smaller submarkets based on a few demographic characteristics. But this can lead to poor results. Instead, market segmentation should first focus on a broad product-market and then group similar customers into homogeneous submarkets. The more similar the potential customers are, the larger the submarkets can be. Four criteria for evaluating possible product-market segments were presented.

Once a broad product-market is segmented, marketing managers can use one of three approaches to market-oriented strategy planning: (1) the single target market approach, (2) the multiple target market approach, or (3) the combined target market approach. In general, we encourage marketers to be segmenters rather than combiners.

We also cover computer-aided approaches such as clustering techniques, CRM, and positioning. We emphasize the role of positioning in providing a focus or theme to the various elements of a differentiated marketing mix that fits the preferences of target customers.

In summary, good marketers should be experts on markets and the dimensions that segment them. By thoughtfully segmenting markets, they may spot opportunities—even breakthrough opportunities—and help their firms succeed against aggressive competitors offering similar products.

In Chapters 5 and 6 you'll learn more about the buying behavior of final consumers and organizational customers. As you enrich your understanding of customers and how they behave, you will develop command of a broader set of dimensions that are important for segmentation and positioning.

WHAT'S NOW?

This chapter digs into segmentation, targeting, differentiation, and positioning. For some current real-world examples and learnings, check out *What's Now?* at www.learnthe4ps.com/whatsnow/c4.

KEY TERMS

LO 4.7

market, 93

generic market, 93

product-market, 94

market segmentation, 97

segmenting, 98

market segment, 98

single target market approach, 100

multiple target market approach, 100

combined target market approach, 100

combiners, 100

segmenters, 101

qualifying dimensions, 103

determining dimensions, 103

clustering techniques, 108

customer relationship management (CRM), 108

positioning, 110

QUESTIONS AND PROBLEMS

1. Review the LEGO case study that opens the chapter. From this case, identify examples of different key terms and concepts covered in the chapter. For example, LEGO operated in the construction toy product-market.

2. Review the LEGO case study that opens this chapter. Applying concepts from the chapter, how else could LEGO segment the market? Use at least two segmenting dimensions not discussed in the current case and describe each market segment. Describe three marketing tactics that could be used in developing a strategy for each target market.

3. Distinguish between a generic market and a product-market. Illustrate your answer.

4. Explain what market segmentation is.

5. List the types of potential segmenting dimensions, and explain which you would try to apply first, second, and third in a particular situation. If the nature of the situation would affect your answer, explain how.

6. Explain why segmentation efforts based on attempts to divide the mass market using a few demographic dimensions may be very disappointing.

7. Illustrate the concept that segmenting is an aggregating process by referring to the admissions policies of your own college and a nearby college or university.

8. Review the types of segmenting dimensions listed in Exhibits 4–8 and 4–9, and select the ones you think should be combined to fully explain the market segment you personally would be in if you were planning to buy a new watch today. List several dimensions and try to develop a shorthand name, like "fashion-oriented," to describe your own personal market segment. Then try to estimate what proportion of the total watch market would be in your market segment. Next, explain if there are any offerings that come close to meeting the needs of your market. If not, what sort of a marketing mix is needed? Would it be economically attractive for anyone to try to satisfy your market segment? Why or why not?

9. Identify the determining dimension or dimensions that explain why you bought the specific brand you did in your most recent purchase of a (a) soft drink, (b) shampoo, (c) shirt or blouse, and (d) larger, more expensive item, such as a bicycle, camera, or boat. Try to express the

determining dimension(s) in terms of your own personal characteristics rather than the product's characteristics. Estimate what share of the market would probably be motivated by the same determining dimension(s).

10. Consider the market for off-campus apartments in your city. Identify some submarkets that have different needs

and determining dimensions. Then evaluate how well the needs in these market segments are being met in your geographic area. Is there an obvious breakthrough opportunity waiting for someone?

11. Explain how positioning analysis can help a marketing manager identify target market opportunities.

MARKETING PLANNING FOR HILLSIDE VETERINARY CLINIC

Appendix D (the Appendices follow Chapter 19) includes a sample marketing plan for Hillside Veterinary Clinic. Look through the "Customers" section.

a. How does the marketing plan segment the market?

b. Can you think of other segmentation dimensions that could be used?

c. What do you think of the approach Hillside used to determine target markets? Is it using a single target market, multiple target market, or combined target market approach?

d. How does Hillside plan to differentiate and position its offering?

SUGGESTED CASES

3. Real NOCO Soccer Academy
7. Waimate Mountain Lodge
10. Sampson's Ice Center
30. Walker-Winkle Mills, Ltd.

Video Case 2. Bass Pro Shops
Video Case 4. Potbelly Sandwich
Video Case 7. Invacare
Video Case 8. Segway

MARKETING ANALYTICS: DATA TO KNOWLEDGE

CHAPTER 4: SEGMENTING CUSTOMERS

The marketing manager for Audiotronics Software Company is seeking new market opportunities. He is focusing on the voice recognition market and has narrowed down to three segments: the Fearful Typists, the Power Users, and the Professional Specialists. The Fearful Typists don't know much about computers—they just want a fast way to create e-mail messages, letters, and simple reports without errors. They don't need a lot of special features. They want simple instructions and a program that's easy to learn. The Power Users know a lot about computers, use them often, and want a voice recognition

program with many special features. All computer programs seem easy to them—so they aren't worried about learning to use the various features. The Professional Specialists have jobs that require a lot of writing. They don't know much about computers but are willing to learn. They want special features needed for their work—but only if they aren't too hard to learn and use.

The marketing manager prepared a table summarizing the importance of each of three key needs in the three segments (see table that follows).

Market Segment	Importance of Need (1 = not important; 10 = very important)		
	Features	Easy to Use	Easy to Learn
Fearful Typists	3	8	9
Power Users	9	2	2
Professional Specialists	7	5	6

Audiotronics' sales staff conducted interviews with seven potential customers who were asked to rate how important each of these three needs were in their work. The manager

prepared a spreadsheet to help him cluster (aggregate) each person into one of the segments—along with other similar people. Each person's ratings are entered in the spreadsheet, and the clustering procedure computes a similarity score that indicates how similar (a low score) or dissimilar (a high score) the person is to the typical person in each of the segments. The manager can then "aggregate" potential customers into the segment that is most similar (that is, the one with the *lowest* similarity score).

Potential Customer	Importance of Need (1 = not important; 10 = very important)			
	Features	Easy to Use	Easy to Learn	Type of Computer
A.	8	1	2	Dell laptop
B.	6	6	5	HP desktop
C.	4	9	8	Apple
D.	2	6	7	Apple
E.	5	6	5	HP desktop
F.	8	3	1	Dell laptop
G.	4	6	8	Apple

See Connect for the spreadsheet and questions needed to analyze this scenario.

Future Publishing/Getty Images.

Final Consumers and Their Buying Behavior

When Sony introduced its Walkman in the late 1970s, it quickly became a popular way for on-the-go music lovers to play tapes of their favorite music—anywhere they went. Competing players quickly emerged, but Sony kept its lead by improving its Walkman and then offering models for CDs and digital audiotapes when those media came on the market.

In the late 1990s, the new MP3 format offered quality music from a small digital file that played on a computer or portable player. Diamond Multimedia's Rio was the first MP3 player. The Rio was innovative, but users had to download music from virus-ridden websites such as Napster—or use special software to "rip" CDs to MP3 format. Many music buffs liked the idea of having songs at their fingertips, but getting the digital files was just too complicated. Further, music companies filed lawsuits charging some with illegally downloading MP3 music files. All of this slowed the initial adoption of MP3 players.

Attitudes quickly changed when Apple offered an innovative marketing mix that addressed these customer needs. The online iTunes store offered legal downloads of songs at a reasonable price and without the risk of viruses. Apple's free iTunes software made it easy to organize digital music on a computer and transfer it to Apple's iPod. The iPod was designed to be stylish and easy to use. Apple's ads generated awareness and interest among customers of the new concept with the promise of "a thousand songs in your pocket." Even skeptics who ignored the ads couldn't help but notice the distinctive white iPod cords dangling from the ears of a friend who was "in" on this cool new product. That prompted a lot of product conversations and on-the-spot iPod demos. Testimonials on blogs, online consumer reviews, and posts on MySpace (there was no Facebook yet) also helped spread the word.

Although most iPod owners were satisfied with their purchases, competitors such as Microsoft, Sony, and Creative Labs raised expectations in the market by promoting benefits such as longer battery life, capacity for more songs, and lower prices. For some consumers, all of this choice required a more careful purchase decision. For example, some would search for information and reviews on the Internet or talk with salespeople in stores to figure out which model was best.

Cell phones that played music were already on the market when Apple introduced the iPhone, but most consumers couldn't see the benefits. The iPhone changed that. The iPhone's colorful touchscreen display, ability to search the web, and music player wowed consumers. Soon iPhone owners customized their phones with software applications ("apps") from the iTunes store that let them play games such as "Angry Birds" and "Words with Friends," watch YouTube videos, or check their Facebook page or Twitter feed—right on their iPhones.

Many customers buy Apple's products sight unseen; the first iPad tablet computer had almost a half million preorders from customers who had never even held one in their hands. These loyal Apple customers trusted the iPad to live up to expectations based on their previous experiences with other Apple products. The iPad changed the way people looked at their personal computers—with many buying the tablet instead of a laptop or desktop computer. Later the iPad mini attracted customers seeking a less expensive version.

Apple mania became a global phenomenon. Apple sees a big opportunity in Asia, especially in China, with its rapidly growing middle class. In China, Apple found consumer behavior different than in the West. Most Chinese buy iPhones based on word-of-mouth; they especially like to buy what their friends or people they admire own. So Apple's marketing strategy in China has focused on getting key opinion leaders and celebrities to use the iPhone. In developing countries, most consumers' income goes to food and housing, so few have enough remaining to purchase expensive electronics like an iPhone. Apple hopes that many will purchase used versions of earlier iPhones and become used to the technology.

Many wondered what needs the Apple Watch would fill when it was first introduced. The Watch offers the convenience of paying at the cash register with a wave of the Watch (and Apple Pay) and hundreds of apps enhance the Watch's functionality. Would filling these needs get people to pay $350 or more (much more) for a smart watch?

Apple produced three models of the Watch to match different customer needs—each model came in a smaller 38 mm and larger 42 mm size. Apple Watch Sport (at $349 or $399) was designed for fitness buffs and thriftier shoppers. Sport models come with sweat proof bands in five colors—including neon green or pink. Fitness-minded buyers would appreciate the Watch's ability to monitor and motivate routine activity (amount of time spent standing for example) and more intense exercise.

The mid-priced ($550 to $1100) Apple Watch model—stainless steel case trimmed with either a leather or stainless steel band—better complements a business suit or night on the town. Businesspeople appreciate that the Watch reminds them of an upcoming next appointment or lets them check an e-mail or text message without pulling out their iPhones.

Customers with a lot of discretionary income and a high need for status could buy the Apple Watch Edition. Although the functionality on this model is no different than the other models, it comes with a choice of rose or yellow gold cases, fancier band choices, and sells for $10,000 to $17,000.

The Watch moves Apple into the emerging "wearable electronics" product-market where Apple already found competitors such as Google and Samsung. Those companies, along with Amazon, Microsoft, Facebook, and Spotify, are just some of the competitors that want a piece of Apple's large pie. All this competition means new features and more choices for consumers, but it also complicates the consumer decision process for new phone, tablet computer, and watch buyers. That is, except for those most loyal customers who trust Apple will continue to identify new and better ways to meet customer needs.[1]

LEARNING OBJECTIVES

Many variables influence consumer buying behavior. As the Apple case highlights, successful marketing strategy planning requires a clear understanding of how target consumers buy—and what factors affect their decisions. The learning objectives for this chapter will help you develop that understanding.

When you finish this chapter, you should be able to

1 Describe how economic needs influence the buyer decision process.

2 Understand how psychological variables affect an individual's buying behavior.

3 Understand how social influences affect an individual's buying behavior.

4 Describe how culture and ethnicity influence consumer buying behavior.

5 Explain how characteristics of the purchase situation influence consumer behavior.

6 Explain the process by which consumers make buying decisions.

7 Understand important new terms (shown in red).

Consumer Behavior: Why Do They Buy What They Buy?

The Apple case shows the in-depth customer knowledge needed for effective marketing strategy planning. Without that understanding, it would be difficult to zero in on the right target market, or to develop and adapt a marketing mix that will be the best value for customers.

Understanding consumer behavior can be a challenge. Specific behaviors vary a great deal for different people, products, and purchase situations. In today's global markets the variations are countless. That makes it impractical to catalog all the possibilities. But there are general behavioral principles—frameworks—that marketing managers can apply to better understand their specific target markets. In this chapter our approach focuses on developing your skill in working with these frameworks by exploring thinking from economics, psychology, sociology, and other behavioral disciplines. We'll take a look at the topics overviewed in Exhibit 5–1, which includes a simplified model of consumer behavior.

We will begin with a discussion of influences on the consumer decision process: economic needs, psychological variables, social influences, culture/ethnicity, and the purchase situation. Exhibit 5–2 provides an expanded look at these influences. Following our discussion of these different categories of influences, we will look more closely at the consumer decision process.

Exhibit 5-1 Consumer Behavior for Marketing Strategy Planning

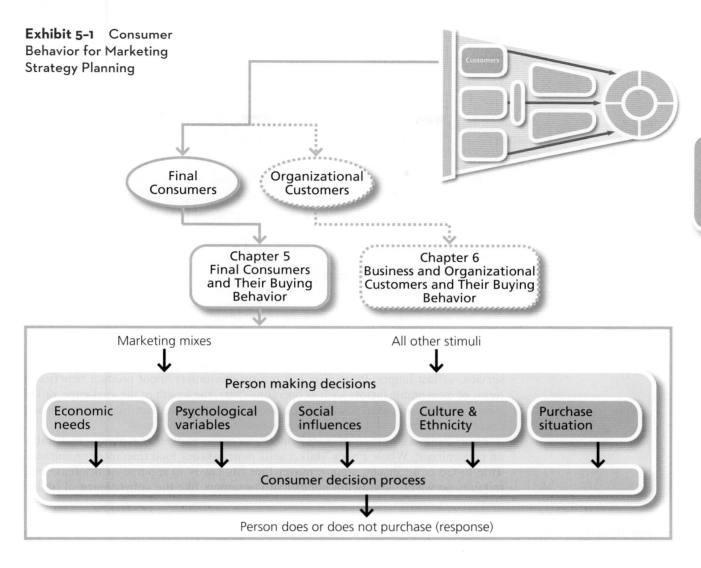

Economic Needs Affect Most Buying Decisions

Economic buyers seek the best uses of time and money

Most economists assume that consumers are **economic buyers**—people who know all the facts and logically compare choices to get the greatest satisfaction from spending their time and money. The economic-buyer theory says that consumers decide what to buy based on **economic needs**, which are concerned with making the best use of a consumer's time and money—as the consumer judges it. Some consumers look for the lowest price. Others will pay extra for convenience. And others may weigh price and quality for the best value. Some economic needs include:

1. Economy of purchase or use
2. Efficiency in operation or use
3. Dependability in use
4. Improvement of earnings
5. Convenience

Clearly, marketing managers must be alert to new ways to appeal to economic needs. Most consumers appreciate firms that offer them improved economic value for the money they spend. But improved value does not just mean offering lower and

Exhibit 5-2   A Model of Influences on Consumer Behavior

Marketing mixes   All other stimuli

Person making decisions

| **Economic needs** | **Psychological variables** | **Social influences** | **Culture & Ethnicity** | **Purchase situation** |
| • Economy of purchase
• Convenience
• Efficiency
• Dependability | • Motivation
• Perception
• Learning
• Attitude
• Trust
• Lifestyle | • Family
• Social class
• Reference groups | • Culture
• Ethnicity
• International | • Purchase reason
• Time
• Surroundings |

Consumer decision process

Person does or does not purchase (response)

lower prices. For example, products can be designed to work better, require less service, or last longer. Promotion can inform consumers about product benefits in terms of measurable factors such as operating costs, the length of the guarantee, or the time a product will save. Carefully planned Place decisions can make it easier and faster for customers who face a poverty of time to make a purchase.

Many firms adjust their marketing mixes for target markets that place a high value on convenience. Whole Foods Market sells more takeout food than most restaurants. Tide-to-Go is an instant stain remover that fits easily in a purse or briefcase and requires no water. A growing number of consumers like the convenience of online shopping at Zappos.

Income affects needs

The ability to satisfy economic needs largely depends on how much money a consumer has available—which in turn depends a great deal on household income.

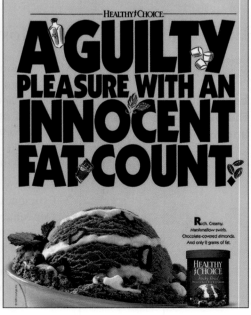

Economic needs affect many buying decisions, but for some purchases the behavioral influences on a consumer are more important.
Left: All text and images are copywritten with permission from GEICO; Right: © ConAgra Foods, Inc. All Rights Reserved.

In the United States, income distribution varies widely. In 2013, 24 percent of households reported an income of less than $25,000, and the median income—where half the households earned more and half earned less—was $51,939. After taking account of inflation, the median income declined about 5 percent in the previous decade. During this same period, America's middle-income consumers have been hit hard by the rising costs of necessities.[2]

In most households, people don't have enough income to buy everything they want. For many products, these people can't be customers even if they want to be. For example, most families spend a good portion of their income on such necessities as food, rent or house payments, home furnishings, transportation, and insurance. A family's purchase of "luxuries" comes from **discretionary income**—what is left of income after paying taxes and paying for necessities.

Discretionary income is an elusive concept because the definition of necessities varies from family to family and over time. It depends on what they think is necessary for their lifestyle. High-speed Internet service purchased out of discretionary income by a lower-income family may be considered a necessity by a higher-income family.[3]

Consumer confidence affects spending

Economic conditions affect consumer confidence and spending. In a strong economy, consumers feel confident and secure in their jobs, so they are more likely to borrow money to buy a larger house, a new car, or vacation in an exotic locale. On the other hand, when consumers worry about job prospects or their retirement savings decline, they are more cautious spenders.

Economic value and income are important factors in many purchase decisions. But most marketing managers think that buyer behavior is not as simple as the economic-buyer model suggests. So let's look more closely at the psychological variables that influence buying behavior (see Exhibit 5–2).

Psychological Influences within an Individual

LO 5.2

Needs motivate consumers

Everybody is motivated by needs and wants. **Needs** are the basic forces that motivate a person to do something. Some needs involve a person's physical well-being, others the individual's self-view and relationship with others. Needs are more basic than wants. **Wants** are "needs" that are learned during a person's life. For example, everyone needs water or some kind of liquid, but some people also have learned to want Clearly Canadian's raspberry-flavored sparkling water on the rocks.

When a need is not satisfied, it may lead to a drive. The need for liquid, for example, leads to a thirst drive. A **drive** is a strong stimulus that encourages action to reduce a need. Drives are internal—they are the reasons behind certain behavior patterns. In marketing, a product purchase results from a drive to satisfy some need.

Some critics imply that marketers can somehow manipulate consumers to buy products against their will. But trying to get consumers to act against their will is a waste of time. Instead, a good

Whether a product is a want or a need depends on what a consumer has learned during his or her life.

© 2010 Nissan. Nissan, Nissan model names and the Nissan logo are registered trademarks of Nissan.

Exhibit 5-3   Possible Needs Motivating a Person to Some Action

Types of Needs	Specific Examples			
Physiological needs	Food Sex	Rest Liquid	Activity Self-preservation	Sleep Warmth/coolness
Psychological needs	Nurturing Playing-relaxing Self-identification	Curiosity Order Power	Independence Personal fulfillment Pride	Love Playing/competition Self-expression
Desire for ...	A better world Acceptance Affiliation Esteem Knowledge	Respect Status Achievement Appreciation Sympathy	Beauty Happiness Self-satisfaction Variety Affection	Companionship Distinctiveness Recognition Sociability Fun
Freedom from ...	Fear Pain	Depression Stress	Loss Sadness	Anxiety Illness

marketing manager studies what consumer drives, needs, and wants already exist and how they can be satisfied better.

Consumers seek benefits to meet needs

We're all a bundle of needs and wants. Exhibit 5–3 lists some important needs that might motivate a person to some action. This list, of course, is not complete. But thinking about such needs can help you see what *benefits* consumers might seek from a marketing mix.

When a marketing manager defines a product-market, the needs may be quite specific. For example, the food need might be as specific as wanting a Domino's thick-crust pepperoni pizza—delivered to your door hot and ready to eat.

Several needs at the same time

Consumer psychologists often argue that a person may have several reasons for buying—sometimes at the same time. Maslow is well known for his five-level hierarchy of needs. We will discuss a similar four-level hierarchy that is easier to apply to consumer behavior. Exhibit 5–4 illustrates the four levels along with an example showing how a company has tried to appeal to each need. Generally, lower-level needs must be addressed before consumers seek to satisfy the higher-level needs. The lowest-level needs are physiological, then come safety, social, and personal needs (PSSP).[4]

Physiological needs are concerned with biological needs—food, liquid, rest, and sex. **Safety needs** are concerned with protection and physical well-being (perhaps involving health, financial security, medicine, and exercise). Marketers that offer *solutions* to consumer problems build brand loyalty. Charmin addressed such a need for holiday shoppers in New York City. Because it can be difficult to find a public restroom—and coffee shops don't like it when noncustomers use their facilities—Charmin's "holiday gift to the City" was luxury public restrooms located in Times Square. Many users will remember Charmin's gift the next time they buy toilet tissue.

Social needs are concerned with love, friendship, status, and esteem—things that involve a person's interaction with others. Marketers that help people *connect* with others inspire positive feelings about their own brands. Coca-Cola addressed this need with a series of viral videos around the theme of delivering happiness. One featured a bright red Coca-Cola truck that stopped on streets in Brazil. A sign on the back of the truck told consumers to "Push" a large button. When they did, the truck dispensed happiness in the form of Cokes and fun items such as t-shirts, soccer balls, and even a surfboard. The truck created on-the-street social connections. The fun video created more social connection when viewers forwarded a link to friends and family.

Personal needs, on the other hand, are concerned with an individual's need for personal satisfaction—unrelated to what others think or do. Examples include

Exhibit 5-4 The PSSP Hierarchy of Needs

Newman's Own
(donates 100% of after-tax profits to progressive causes)

Harley Owners Group
(connecting motorcycle riders to one another)

Tylenol Feel Better
(website identifies top headache triggers)

Aquafina
("pure water, perfect taste")

Need for: a better world, accomplishment, fun, freedom, and relaxation

Need for: love, friendship, status, esteem, and connecting with others

Need for: solutions, protection, and physical well-being (perhaps involving health, security, and exercise)

Need for: food, liquid, rest, and sex

Personal needs

Social needs

Safety needs

Physiological needs

PSSP name

Example needs

accomplishment, fun, freedom, and relaxation—as well as a desire to make the world a better place. Many people want to make food choices that enable them to achieve a healthier balance in their lives. So ConAgra Foods (maker of healthy foods such as SmartPop! Popcorn and Egg Beaters) developed an online tool to help. Members complete a survey at "Start Making Choices" and then receive feedback and advice on nutrition, activity, and well-being based on a calculated "Balanced Life Index." Weekly contact between the company and its customers keeps the relationship alive.

Often marketing managers are able to address multiple needs. Consider the California Milk Processing Board (creators of "Got Milk?") and its online game "Get the Glass." The game appealed to kids—the group that needs milk the most—and, besides being fun, it educated players on why milk is important (personal needs). It could be played with family—or forwarded to friends (social needs). Of course drinking milk addresses thirst (physiological needs) and promotes strong bones (safety needs). In the online game's first two months, more than 6 million people visited the site, with 650,000 reaching the Glass at Fort Fridge. The game was credited with helping boost sales of milk by more than 10 million gallons compared to the same period a year earlier.[5]

Perception determines what consumers see and feel

Consumers select varying ways to meet their needs sometimes because of differences in **perception**—how we gather and interpret information from the world around us.

We are constantly bombarded by marketing stimuli —ads, products, signs, stores— yet we notice only a small number of these. This is because we apply the following selective processes:

1. **Selective exposure**—our eyes and minds seek out and notice only information that interests us. This often relates to current needs. So when we are hungry, we notice signs for restaurants; when we are looking for a new sports car, we notice ads for sports cars.

The Consumer Safety Institute in the Netherlands wants to remind parents that children see those cleaning supplies under the sink differently. As consumers approached this outdoor ad, the image changed from the one on the left to the one on the right (and back). *Both ads: Courtesy eiligheidNL; Agency: Lemz/Netherlands.*

The ad shows two different images when viewed from different angles (lenticular effect).

2. **Selective perception**—we screen out or modify ideas, messages, and information that conflict with previously learned attitudes and beliefs. So if we believe that Apple products are cool, we ignore ads by Samsung that suggest Apple is uncool.

3. **Selective retention**—we remember only what we want to remember. Even when we notice stimuli in the market, we may not place it in memory if we don't believe it or don't feel that information will be useful to us. If we read an article about Taco Bell removing artificial ingredients from its food, but we don't eat at Taco Bell, then we won't commit this new information to memory.

Recognizing that consumers use these selective processes, marketing managers try to engage with customers when they are likely to be open to their messages. So Mazda advertises its sports car on websites such as Edmunds.com where consumers research cars. A marketing manager for Ben & Jerry's Ice Cream sends a $1.00 off coupon to a customer's smartphone just as they pull into their local grocery store.

Learning determines what response is likely

Learning is a change in a person's thought processes caused by prior experience. Learning is often based on direct experience: A little girl tastes her first cone of Ben & Jerry's Cherry Garcia flavor ice cream, and learning occurs! Learning may also be based on indirect experience or associations. If you watch an ad that shows other people enjoying Ben & Jerry's Chocolate Fudge Brownie low-fat frozen yogurt, you might conclude that you'd like it too.

Consumer learning may result from things that marketers do, or it may result from stimuli that have nothing to do with marketing. Either way, almost all consumer behavior is learned.[6]

Experts describe a number of steps in the learning process. We've already discussed the idea of a drive as a strong stimulus that encourages action. Depending on the **cues**—products, signs, ads, and other stimuli in the environment—an individual chooses some specific response. A **response** is an effort to satisfy a drive. The specific response chosen depends on the cues and the person's past experience.

Exhibit 5-5 The Learning Process

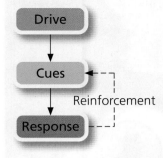

Sales take off after Febreze learns a lesson

Reinforcement of the learning process occurs when the response is followed by satisfaction—that is, reduction in the drive. Reinforcement strengthens the relationship between the cue and the response. And it may lead to a similar response the next time the drive occurs. Repeated reinforcement leads to development of a habit—making the individual's decision process routine. Exhibit 5–5 shows the relationships of the important variables in the learning process.

Marketing managers for Febreze used the learning process to develop a best-selling product, but first they had to get the drive, cue, response, and reinforcement just right. Febreze contains a chemical very effective at eliminating odors—spray it on clothing, furniture, or carpet and smells magically disappear. Febreze's marketing managers figured that most consumers desired a home free of offensive odors (drive), so the first television ads for Febreze focused on smells around the house. For example, one showed a dog on a couch and a woman saying, "Sophie will always smell like Sophie, but now my couch doesn't have to" (cue). In the ad, the woman sprays Febreze on the couch (response) and the dog smell disappears (reinforcement).

In spite of an aggressive advertising campaign, Febreze sold poorly when it was initially launched. To learn why, marketing researchers interviewed customers in their homes. They discovered two problems. First, many people living in the smelliest homes simply didn't realize their homes smelled at all. They had become desensitized to the smells of their pets, cigarette smoke, or other odors, so for them, the desired cue didn't exist. Second, what Febreze provided—lack of a smell—didn't provide positive reinforcement for the customer.

So Febreze's marketing managers went back to the drawing board. They interviewed more customers and reviewed video tape of people cleaning their homes. They identified another market, people who wanted a clean house (drive). When they saw a messy home (cue), they cleaned the house (response) and finished by rewarding themselves with something relaxing or happy—maybe just a smile (reinforcement). Here marketing managers realized that a scented version of Febreze might provide positive reinforcement—something that could signal the cleaning job was done. So Febreze added scents and new advertising that showed homemakers spraying a room with Febreze after cleaning (reinforcement). Sales took off; now Febreze sells more than $1 billion a year. And Febreze's marketing managers learned a valuable lesson.[7]

Many needs are culturally learned

Many needs are culturally (or socially) learned. The need for food, for instance, may lead to many specific food wants. Many Japanese enjoy sushi (raw fish), and their children learn to like it. Fewer Americans, however, have learned to enjoy it.

Ethics question: do consumers learn needs from marketing?

Some critics argue that marketing efforts encourage people to spend money on learned wants totally unrelated to any basic need. Consumer needs are internal, but advertising can make consumers aware of their needs—and suggest a way to satisfy these needs. For example, a customer may have thirst as a basic need; advertising helps him become aware of Simply Lemonade brand as a tasty way to satisfy his need. The next time he is thirsty, he may want Simply Lemonade. So advertising does not create needs—but it can make consumers more aware of an existing need and create a want for a specific product.[8]

Attitudes relate to buying

An **attitude** is a person's point of view toward something. The "something" may be a product, an advertisement, a salesperson, a firm, or an idea. Attitudes are an important topic because they affect the selective processes, learning, and the buying decisions.

Because attitudes are usually thought of as involving liking or disliking, they have some action implications. Beliefs are not so action-oriented. A **belief** is a person's opinion about something. Beliefs may help shape a consumer's attitudes but don't necessarily involve any liking or disliking. It is possible to have a belief—say, that Listerine PocketPak strips have a medicinal taste—without really caring what they

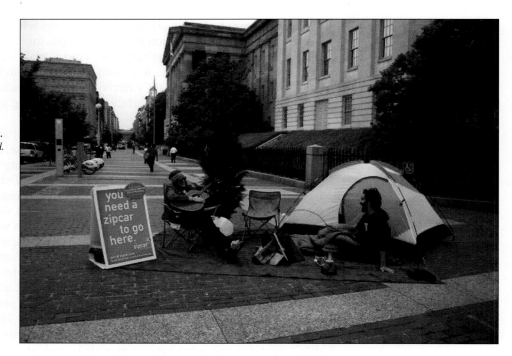

Zipcar appeals to urban consumers who do not have their own car. For three weeks in Washington, DC, Zipcar set up installations (like the one shown here) to change consumer attitudes about renting a car to get out of town.

taste like. On the other hand, beliefs about a product may have a positive or negative effect in shaping consumers' attitudes. For example, promotion for Splenda, a no-calorie sweetener in a yellow packet, informs consumers that it's "made from sugar so it tastes like sugar." A dieter who believes that Splenda will taste better because it is made from sugar might try it instead of just routinely rebuying another brand, like Equal. On the other hand, a person with diabetes might believe that he should avoid Splenda—like he avoids other products made from sugar—even though Splenda is actually suitable for people with diabetes.[9]

In an attempt to relate attitude more closely to purchase behavior, some marketers stretch the attitude concept to include consumer "preferences" or "intention to buy." Managers who must forecast how much of their brand customers will buy are particularly interested in the intention to buy. Forecasts would be easier if attitudes were good predictors of intentions to buy. Unfortunately, the relationships usually are not that simple. A person may have a positive attitude toward hot tubs, but have no intention to buy one.

"Green" attitudes and beliefs change marketing mixes

A growing number of consumers believe that making "greener" purchases has a positive effect on the environment. Marketing managers have responded by developing marketing mixes to address these ecological interests. Subway sandwich shops have added recycling bins. GM and Nissan introduced all-electric cars. Malt-O-Meal breakfast cereals, a low-cost brand that has always been packaged in bags, touted the environmental benefits of this packaging. Its "Bag the Box" campaign garnered publicity on a small budget. Many consumers have positive attitudes toward brands that try to make a difference in this area.[10]

Online Toolkit

Climate Counts is a nonprofit organization that provides information to help consumers make choices that have a positive impact on the planet. Go to the Climate Counts website (**www.climatecounts.org**), click on the "Climate Scores" link, choose a market sector, and compare the different companies. Do you think this information will affect how *consumers* behave? Do you think the information will affect how *companies* behave? What will be the effect on consumer and company behavior if some consumers use Twitter or e-mail to share ratings with others?

Consumer attitudes can affect their purchasing (and donating) behavior. The World Wildlife Fund knows consumers have more favorable attitudes toward panda bears as compared to bluefin tuna—but both species are endangered and need support.
© World Wildlife Fund.

"WOULD YOU CARE MORE IF I WAS A PANDA?"

Most marketers work with existing attitudes

Because consumer attitudes tend to be enduring, it's usually more economical for marketers to work with them than try to change them. Changing negative attitudes is probably the most difficult job marketers face.[11]

Follow changing attitudes

Changing attitudes about sustainability have been accompanied by changing beliefs about sharing and ownership. Toward that end, many consumers in the United States and Europe—where consumers have long-striven for car *ownership*—are looking more at sharing cars. The product-market for transporting people is changing. Read more in "*What's Next?* Will sharing replace owning?"

Ethical issues may arise

Part of the marketing job is to inform and persuade consumers about a firm's offering. An ethical issue sometimes arises, however, if consumers have *inaccurate* beliefs. For example, promotion of a "children's cold formula" may play off parents' fears that adult medicines are too strong—even though the basic ingredients in the children's formula are the same and only the dosage is different.

Marketers must also be careful about promotion that might encourage false beliefs, even if the advertising is not explicitly misleading. For example, ads for Ultra Slim-Fast low-fat beverage don't claim that anyone who buys the product will lose weight and look like the slim models who appear in the ads—but some critics argue that the advertising gives that impression.

Meeting expectations is important

Attitudes and beliefs sometimes combine to form an **expectation**—an outcome or event that a person anticipates or looks forward to. Consumer expectations often focus on the benefits or value that the consumer expects from a firm's marketing mix. This is an important issue for marketers because a consumer is likely to be dissatisfied if his or her expectations are not met. Promotion that overpromises can create this problem. Finding the right balance, however, can be difficult. A few years ago Van Heusen came up with a new way to treat its wash-and-wear shirts so that they look better when they come out of the wash. Van Heusen promoted these shirts as "wrinkle-free." The new shirt is an improvement, but consumers who expect it to look as if it had been ironed are disappointed.[12]

Building consumer trust builds sales

Trust is the confidence a person has in the promises or actions of another person, brand, or company. Trust drives expectations, because when people trust, they *expect* the other party to fulfill promises or perform capably.

Customers may come to trust through experience with a company or person. For example, if your dog always happily chows down Purina dog food—and remains healthy and active—you might come to trust the Purina brand. A customer might trust a travel agent who previously planned enjoyable vacations for her family. Trust can also relate to recommenders—for example, many consumers trust *Consumer Reports* magazine and put a lot of stock in its product reviews and ratings.

Highly trusted people, brands, and companies have many advantages in the marketplace. Consumers prefer to buy from and are more loyal to brands they trust. Trusted brands are less susceptible to price-based competition. For example, few people would switch from a trusted hair stylist just to save a few dollars.

Trust can be very important in some purchase situations. For example, many customers interested in foods with natural ingredients trust Whole Foods. This trust allows customers who value these qualities to buy anything at the store without having to read every label. Similarly, when buying a family car, many shoppers want a very safe and reliable car. Although many car companies make this claim, customers must decide which brand they believe will really deliver. For many years Toyota had a strong reputation in this area, but reports of unintended acceleration caused many customers to lose trust in the carmaker. Trust can be fragile and companies must work to maintain the customer trust that has been built—sometimes over many decades.[13]

Psychographics focus on activities, interests, and opinions

Psychographics or **lifestyle analysis** is the analysis of a person's day-to-day pattern of living as expressed in that person's *A*ctivities, *I*nterests, and *O*pinions—sometimes referred to as *AIOs*. Exhibit 5–6 shows a number of variables for each of the AIO dimensions—along with some demographics used to add detail to the lifestyle profile of a target market.

Understanding the lifestyle of target customers has been especially helpful in providing ideas for advertising themes. Let's see how it adds to a typical demographic description. It may not help Dodge marketing managers much to know that an average member of the target market for a Dodge Dart is 34.8 years old, married, lives in a three-bedroom home, and has 2.3 children. Lifestyles help marketers paint a more human portrait of the target market. For example, lifestyle analysis might show that the 34.8-year-old is also a community-oriented consumer with traditional values who especially enjoys spectator sports and spends much time in other family activities. An ad might show the Veracruz being used by a happy family at a ball game so the target market could really identify with the ad. And the ad might be placed on an ESPN show whose viewers match the target lifestyle profile.[14]

What's Next? Will sharing replace owning?

Except for some big city dwellers, consumers in much of the United States and Europe have long viewed car ownership as a necessary evil. That is beginning to change. Evolving needs, attitudes, and lifestyles are creating opportunities for new transportation services. Whether captivated by changing values or simple economics, many consumers are giving up or sharing their cars.

There is an economic case for turning in the keys. Monthly payments, insurance, parking, gas, depreciation, and maintenance, add up to an average of $8,000 per year for car owners. Let's look at a few new ways customers are getting around in cars without owning one.

Car-sharing services like Zipcar are growing fast. Signing up for Zipcar is simple; customers hop online, fill out an application, and pay a $70 annual membership fee. Applicants with a good driving record receive a Zipcard in the mail a few days later. Renting a car is even easier. A member (called a Zipster) logs on to Zipcar's website, searches for cars in their area, and makes a reservation. Cars are typically parked on a street, in gas stations, or in parking lots, making them easy to locate. At the reserved time, a Zipster unlocks the car with a wave of a smartphone (equipped of course with the Zipcar app) and drives off, returning the car to the same general area when done.

Another approach lets individual car owners share their vehicles (and earn a few bucks) through a *peer-to-peer* network. A car (or truck) owner can list a vehicle at RelayRides.com by posting photos and a brief description. They also set daily and weekly rental rates. Prescreened renters search the site, click on a car, and wait to hear if it's available from the owner. RelayRides takes a cut and provides insurance coverage. The company facilitates hundreds of thousands of transactions a year. Car owners can earn $4,000 or more a year.

Some non-car owners are *ridesharing*. Although carpooling has been around a long time, ridesharing uses the Internet to connect riders with drivers going on the same route at the same time. Frédéric Mazzella, founder of BlaBlaCar (more on the name in a moment), came up with the idea on a holiday trip to see his family. Mazzella noticed most of the cars on the road contained only the driver. He thought there had to be a way to fill some of those empty seats.

BlaBlaCar members create a brief profile with a photo and an indication of their how much they like to talk—a single "Bla" means not very chatty, "BlaBla" people are talkative, and "BlaBlaBlas" can't shut up. Drivers post where they are going, when, and how much a customer needs to "chip in" on expenses (usually a fraction of the cost of a corresponding rail or bus ticket). Passengers search for rides, and drivers have a choice about who they carry. After the ride, drivers and passengers rate each other to help future riders make better choices.

Consumers' attitudes on sharing have been changing. Music has already moved from owning physical goods—records, tapes, and CD's—to renting music from a streaming service like Spotify. Other people share a bedroom or entire home on services such as Airbnb and VRBO.

In what other product-markets are consumers sharing, borrowing, and renting instead of owning? What product-markets do you think might see a shift from ownership to sharing? Why?[15]

Exhibit 5-6 Lifestyle Dimensions (and Some Related Demographic Dimensions)

Dimension		Examples	
Activities	Work Hobbies Social events	Vacation Entertainment Club membership	Surfing web Shopping Sports
Interests	Family Home Job	Community Recreation Fashion	Food Media Achievements
Opinions	Themselves Social issues Politics	Business Economics Education	Products Future Culture
Demographics	Income Age Family life cycle	Geographic area Ethnicity Dwelling	Occupation Family size Education

Social Influences Affect Consumer Behavior

LO 5.3

We've been discussing some of the ways needs, attitudes, and other psychological variables influence the buying process. Now we'll look at how a consumer's family, social class, and reference groups influence the consumer decision process.

Family life cycle influences needs

Relationships with other family members influence many aspects of consumer behavior. Family members may share many attitudes and values, consider one another's opinions, and divide various buying tasks. Marital status, age, and the age of any children in the family have an especially important effect on how people spend their income. Put together, these dimensions tell us about the life-cycle stage of a family. Exhibit 5–7 shows a summary of stages in the family life cycle. Let's take a closer look at how a few of these stages influence buying behavior.

Young people and families accept new ideas

Singles and young couples seem to be more willing to try new products and brands—and they are careful, price-conscious shoppers. Although many young people are waiting longer to marry, most tie the knot eventually. These younger families—especially those with no children—are still accumulating durable goods, such as automobiles and home furnishings. Only as children arrive and grow does family spending shift to soft goods and services, such as education, medical, and personal care. To meet expenses, people in this age group often make more purchases on credit, and they save less of their income.[16]

Divorce—increasingly a fact of American life—disrupts the traditional family life-cycle pattern. The mother usually has custody of the children, and the father may pay child support. The mother and children typically have much less income than two-parent families. Such families spend a larger portion of their income on housing, child care, and other necessities, leaving little for discretionary purchases. If a single parent remarries, the family life cycle may start over again.[17]

Exhibit 5-7 Stages in Modern Family Life Cycles

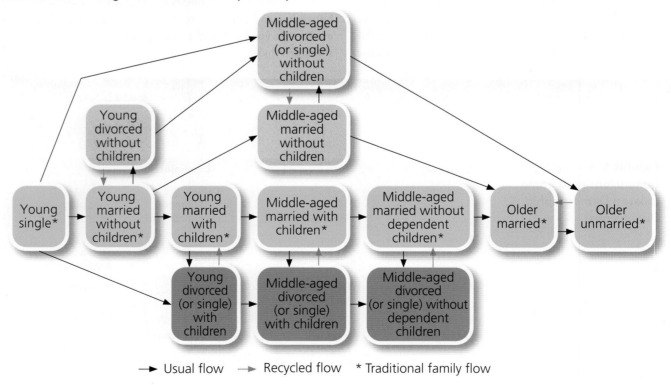

→ Usual flow   → Recycled flow   * Traditional family flow

Schwan's home delivery of food products and complete meals appeals to dual-career families and professionals who place a high value on their time. *Courtesy Hunt Adkins; Art Director: Mark Fairbanks; Copywriter: Rob Franks.*

Reallocation for teenagers

Once children become teenagers, further shifts in spending occur. Teenagers eat more, want to wear expensive clothes, like music, and develop recreation and education needs that are hard on the family budget. American teens currently spend almost $200 billion a year. They are a target for many firms; Bausch & Lomb's contact-lens sales hit record levels when the firm refocused its marketing efforts on teens.[18]

Selling to the empty nesters

Another important category is the **empty nesters**—people whose children are grown and who are now able to spend their money in other ways. This tends to be a high-income period, especially for white-collar workers. Empty nesters are an attractive market for many items. Often they spend more on travel and other things they couldn't afford earlier in life. Much depends on their income, of course.[19]

Who is the real decision maker in family purchases?

In years past, most marketers in the United States targeted the wife as the family purchasing agent. Now, with sex-role stereotypes changed and with night and weekend shopping more popular, men and older children take more responsibility for shopping and decision making. Family roles vary from one culture to another.

Buying responsibility and influence vary greatly depending on the product and the family. Although often only one family member goes to the store for a specific purchase, other family members may influence the decision or really decide what to buy. Still others may use the product.[20]

Social class affects attitudes, values, and buying

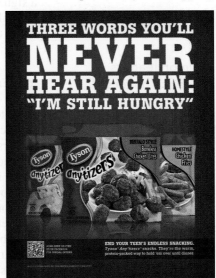

It is estimated that teenagers make or directly influence more than $200 billion in spending in the United States. Tyson recognizes this fact and appeals to parents who have heard their teens cry, "I'm still hungry."
®/© 2013, Tyson Foods, Inc.

Up to now, we've been concerned with individuals and their family relationships. Now let's consider how society looks at an individual and perhaps the family—in terms of social class. A **social class** is a group of people who have approximately equal social position as viewed by others in the society.

Almost every society has some social class structure. In most countries, social class is closely related to a person's occupation, but it may also be influenced by education, community participation, where a person lives, income, possessions, social skills, and other factors—including what family a person is born into.

In most countries—including the United States—there is *some* general relationship between income level and social class. But people with the same income level may be in different social classes. So income by itself is usually not a good measure of social class. And people in different social classes may spend, save, and borrow money in very different ways.

The U.S. class system is far less rigid than those in most countries. Children start out in the same social class as their parents—but they can move to a different social class depending on their education and job. By contrast, India's social structure is much more rigid, and individuals can't easily move up in the class system.

Marketers want to know what buyers in various social classes are like. In the United States, simple approaches for measuring social class groupings are based on a person's *occupation, education,* and *type and location of housing*. By using marketing research surveys or available census data, marketers can get a feel for the social class of a target market.

What do these classes mean?

Although many people think of America as a middle-class society, studies suggest that in many marketing situations distinctive social class groups do exist. Various classes shop at different stores. They prefer different treatment from salespeople. They buy different brands of products—even though prices are about the same. And they have different attitudes toward spending and saving—even when they have the same income level.

Reference groups help people form attitudes

A **reference group** refers to the people to whom an individual looks when forming attitudes about a particular topic. People normally have several reference groups for different topics. Some they meet face-to-face; others they just wish to imitate—for example, performers or athletes. In either case, they may take values from these reference groups and make buying decisions based on what the group might accept.

Reference influence is stronger for products that others "see" and which relate to status in the group. For example, whereas one group might view owning a fur coat as a sign of "having arrived," a group of animal lovers may see the same purchase as bad judgment.[21]

Opinion leaders influence buyers

An **opinion leader** is a person who influences others. Opinion leaders aren't necessarily wealthier or better educated. And opinion leaders on one subject aren't necessarily opinion leaders on another. For example, you may have a friend who is ahead of the curve in knowing about videogames, but you might not want that friend's opinion about new clothing styles and cosmetics. Opinion leaders can influence both what product categories a consumer considers and what brands he or she purchases.

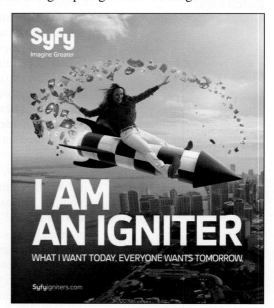

Marketing managers often target opinion leaders because they influence others. The Syfy television network wants advertisers to know that many of its viewers are opinion leaders.

Social media boosts social influence

Social media such as Facebook, Twitter, and Snapchat, make it easier for consumers to influence one another. On social media it is easy to follow people from a various reference groups whether that means Justin Bieber's Twitter feed or an old high school friend's Facebook posts. These give consumers access to new reference groups that may influence their buying decision process.

Social media can also amplify the voices of opinion leaders. A traveler can have a lot of influence by posting a long, detailed review of a sight that "can't be missed" in Thailand. A friend can rave (or rage) about the new *Star Wars* movie—and influence who goes (and who stays home). Marketing managers are trying to figure out how to manage this type of influence—and we will discuss it more in Chapter 16.[22]

Culture, Ethnicity, and Consumer Behavior

LO 5.4

Cultural variation across ethnic groups or countries can result in differences in how consumers make purchase choices. As we discussed in Chapter 3, these differences create opportunities for resourceful firms. In this section we discuss how culture, ethnicity, and international boundaries influence consumer behavior.

Culture surrounds the other influences

Culture is the whole set of beliefs, attitudes, and ways of doing things of a reasonably homogeneous set of people. In this chapter, as well as Chapter 3, we look at the broad impact of culture.

We can think of the American culture, the French culture, or the Chinese culture. People within these cultural groupings tend to be more similar in outlook and behavior. But often it is useful to think of subcultures within such groupings. For example, within the American culture, there are various religious, ethnic, and regional subcultures.

Failure to consider cultural differences, even subtle ones, can result in problems. To promote their product and get people to try it, marketers for Pepto-Bismol often provide free samples at festivals and street fairs. Their idea is that people tend to overindulge at such events. However, when they distributed sample packets at a festival in San Francisco's Chinatown, they insulted many of the people they wanted to influence. Booths with Chinese delicacies lined the streets, and many of the participants interpreted the sample packets (which featured the word "Nauseous" in large letters) as suggesting that Chinese delicacies were nauseating. The possibility of this misinterpretation may seem obvious in hindsight, but if it had been that obvious in advance, the whole promotion would have been handled differently.[23]

Do ethnic groups buy differently?

America may be called the melting pot, but ethnic groups deserve special attention when analyzing markets. One basic reason is that people from different ethnic groups may be influenced by very different cultural variables. They may have quite varied needs and their own ways of thinking. Moreover, Americans value diversity and the United States is becoming a multicultural market. As a result, rather than disappearing in a melting pot, some important cultural and ethnic dimensions are being preserved and highlighted. This creates both opportunities and challenges for marketers.

Stereotypes are common—and misleading

A marketer needs to study ethnic dimensions very carefully because they can be subtle and fast-changing. This is also an area where stereotyped thinking is the most common—and misleading. Many firms make the mistake of treating all consumers in a particular ethnic group as homogeneous. For example, some marketing managers treat all 41.8 million African American consumers as "the black market," ignoring the great variability among African American households on other segmenting dimensions.

Ethnic markets are becoming more important

More marketers pay attention to ethnic groups now because the number of ethnic consumers is growing at a much faster rate than the overall society. Much of this growth results from immigration. In addition, however, the median age of Asian Americans, African Americans, and Hispanics is much lower than that of whites—and the birthrate is higher. In combination, these factors have a dramatic effect.

The buying power of ethnic submarkets is also increasing rapidly. Estimates indicate that Hispanics and African Americans each spend more than $1 trillion a year and Asian Americans more than $500 billion a year. It's also important to marketers that much of this buying power is concentrated in certain cities and states, which makes targeted promotion and distribution more efficient. For example, more than 30 percent of San Francisco residents are Asians.

Hispanic market is growing

Let's take a closer look at Hispanic Americans. Hispanics are the largest and fastest growing ethnic group in the United States. In 2013, the Hispanic population was about 54.1 million and made up 17 percent of the total U.S. population—up from 35.3 million and 12.5 percent in 2000. We can expect more growth because in 2010, 23.1 percent of all children younger than age 18 were Hispanic. Their relative youth and the growth potential suggest the Hispanic market offers great marketing opportunities.[24]

Many companies are responding to this trend. For example, Wells Fargo branches in the Southwest have added Latin-style decor, bicultural tellers, and Spanish-language promotion. Efforts such as these have significantly increased Wells Fargo's business. P&G found Hispanic consumers like using fragrances in their homes and developed Febreze Destinations Collections, a line of air fresheners targeting this market. The growth is reflected in media that target Hispanics, too. ESPN Deportes (Spanish for "ESPN Sports")—a 24-hour cable television channel and companion website—focuses on the particular interests of the Hispanic sports fan.

Asian American market is growing fast, too

Although there are fewer Asian Americans (about 16.8 million in 2013, representing 5.3 percent of the population), the number has more than tripled since 1980. Asian Americans have the highest median family income (about $66,000) of the major ethnic groups. Because of this growth and income, companies as varied as Kraft, Walmart, and Allstate are targeting these consumers—especially in California, New York, and Texas, where half the Asian American population is concentrated.[25]

Many firms are developing strategies to appeal to the fast-growing Hispanic market. Goya wants to let grocers know that demand for coconut milk spikes during the holidays because it is a vital part of many Hispanic celebrations. Nestle's Coffee Mate brand is bringing flavors popular in Mexico and South America to the United States.
Left: Copyright © 2015 Goya Foods, Inc. All Rights Reserved.; Right: All trademarks and Intellectual Property are owned by Société des Produits Nestlé S.A.,Vevey, Switzerland or used with permission.

| Culture varies in international markets | Planning strategies that consider cultural differences in international markets can be even harder—and such cultures usually vary more. Each foreign market may need to be treated as a separate market with its own submarkets. Ignoring cultural differences—or assuming that they are not important—almost guarantees failure in international markets. |

Consider the situation faced by marketers as they introduced Swiffer, the fast-selling wet mop, in Italy. Research showed that Italian women wash their floors four times more often than Americans. Based on that, you might predict a big success for Swiffer in Italy. Yet many new cleaning products flop there. Fortunately, the research suggested a reason. Many Italians have negative attitudes about ad claims that a product makes cleaning *easier*. Although this benefit has wide appeal in the United States, many Italian women doubt that something that works easily will meet their standards for cleanliness. So for the Italian market Swiffer was modified and beeswax was added to polish floors after they have been mopped. Now Swiffer is a top seller in Italy.[26]

Sometimes an understanding of local culture points out new ways to blend the Four Ps. For example, Nestlé knew that free samples would kickstart the adoption process of its new line of food flavorings in Brazil. In the United States, it's common to distribute free samples at stores, but that would seem strange to Brazilians. Local Nestlé managers in Brazil posed a more culturally acceptable approach to distribute the samples. In Brazil, people cook on gas stoves and deliverymen regularly bring canisters of gas to their homes. So Nestlé paid these local gas deliverymen to offer their customers samples of the flavorings and explain how to use them. Consumers showed more interest in the samples when the conversation took place with someone they trusted right by the stove where the flavorings would be used.[27]

Individuals Are Affected by the Purchase Situation

LO 5.5

The **purchase situation** takes into account the purpose, time available, and location where a purchase is made.

| Consumers consider the purpose for the purchase | Consumers can buy the same type of product yet they have completely different *purposes* for the purchase. This influences buying behavior. For example, how a consumer buys a bunch of flowers depends on whether they are for a mother who lives far away, the host of a dinner party, or a girlfriend following a little disagreement. The reason for the purchase influences how the buyer evaluates options and, ultimately, the choice made. |

| Time affects what happens | Time influences a purchase situation. When consumers make a purchase—and the time they have available for shopping—will influence their behavior. Socializing with friends at a Starbucks induces different behavior than grabbing a quick cup of 7-Eleven coffee on the way to work. The urgency of the need is another time-related factor. Shopping for tires is much more urgent when one has a flat as compared to when one notices that the tread is just starting to wear thin. When the need is urgent, customers will be less inclined to evaluate a range of options—and place more emphasis on speed and convenience. |

| Surroundings affect buying too | Where a purchase is made and the surrounding location can affect buying behavior. The excitement at an on-site auction may stimulate impulse buying. Checking out an auction online might lead to a different response. Consider how the warehouse-like setting in a Sam's Club store signals low-cost operations and price reductions.[28] |

Consumer behavior varies with situational factors. Consumers shop differently when buying gifts—and BoConcept tries to make gift-buying easier by presenting a range of ideas. The time a consumer has available to shop also affects his or her behavior. Woot uses this to its advantage. The online retailer offers one deeply discounted product each day—customers must buy that day or forget about it.

Left: BoConcept © 1999–2015.; Right: © WOOT, INC. or its affiliates. All rights reserved.

Needs, benefits sought, attitudes, motivation, and even how a consumer selects certain products all vary depending on the purchase situation. So different purchase situations may require different marketing mixes—even when the same target market is involved.

The Consumer Decision Process

LO 5.6

The model in Exhibit 5–2 organizes the many different influences on consumer behavior. It helps explain *why* consumers make the decisions they make. Now, we'll expand that model with a closer look at the steps in the consumer decision process and a focus on *how* consumers make decisions.[29] See Exhibit 5–8.

Recognizing a need creates a problem for the consumer

The consumer decision process begins when a consumer becomes aware of an unmet need. The consumer's problem-solving process then focuses on how best to meet that need. Problem recognition often happens quickly. A student on the way to class, for example, may realize that she's thirsty and wants something to drink. Or problem recognition may take shape over time. For example, a recent grad with a new apartment might want a comfortable place to sit while watching TV in the evening. These situations present problems that may be solved with a purchase. But what purchase should it be?

Do the web and social media drive needs?

The web and social media potentially expose consumers to many goods, services, experiences, and people. Does this activity affect consumer awareness of wants and needs? For example, have you ever noticed a Facebook friend with a new car, new shirt, or on a fun vacation, and found yourself thinking about making a similar purchase? Other sites, like the photo-sharing site Pinterest, encourage people to look at photos—often products—that friends have "pinned" (see Online Toolkit featuring Pinterest).

Exhibit 5-8   An Expanded Model of Consumer Behavior

While advertising often tries to raise awareness of needs, consumers who see friends or family addressing certain needs may find themselves with new wants and needs.

Three levels of problem solving are useful

How a consumer solves the problem depends on the situation. Exhibit 5–9 highlights the basic problem-solving steps a consumer may go through to satisfy a need. A consumer may search for information, identify alternatives, decide what factors (criteria) are important, and then evaluate one or more alternative products that meet the need. These activities may require a lot of time and effort on the part of a consumer, very little time, or be skipped altogether.

How much effort is put into a buying decision depends in part on the economic needs, psychological variables, social influences, and purchase situation factors discussed earlier in this chapter. It's also tied to the amount of risk a buyer sees in making a wrong choice. For instance, when a buyer has little involvement in the purchase

Online Toolkit

Pinterest is a photo-sharing site that allows users to create and share "pinboards" around a particular topic of interest. When users find an image online, they can add it to one of their pinboards. Go to the Pinterest website (**www.pinterest.com**). This exercise will require you to set up an account if you do not have one. Account registration is fast and can be deleted after completing the exercise. Click and open "Categories" (as of this writing, a symbol in the upper left corner of the site). Choose "Cars & Motorcycles" or "Weddings" and look through several dozen images that have been pinned in the category. How could this activity make interested followers of the category aware of needs they might not have had previously? How could a marketing manager who sells hub caps or wedding dresses take advantage of this phenomenon?

Exhibit 5-9 Consumer
Problem Solving

or the expense is small, a poor buying decision will result in little financial or social risk. Under these circumstances the buyer usually puts little effort into the buying decision. On the other hand, when a buyer is highly involved and cares deeply about the choice, or when the price is high, there may be more risk in making a bad decision. So the buyer often extends more effort in order to be more confident. Exhibit 5–10 suggests three levels of problem solving that relate to the amount of effort the buyer puts into the decision.

Consumers use **extensive problem solving** when they put much effort into deciding how to satisfy a need—as is likely for a completely new purchase or to satisfy an important need. At this level of problem solving, consumers conduct more information search, identify more alternatives, have more criteria for evaluation, and spend more time evaluating options (see Exhibit 5–9). For example, an avid computer "gamer" may put a great deal of effort into buying a new gaming computer. Our gamer might solicit friends' opinions about the graphics speed and audio quality for different models before going online to compare options and prices and read technical reviews. Then, the gamer might visit a local store for a hands-on demo of a favorite game on a few computers. To narrow down to a final choice, the gamer could evaluate customer-service support and warranties. This is certainly not an impulse purchase! The decision to buy—and what to buy—comes only after an extensive effort.

Limited problem solving is used by consumers when *some* effort is required in deciding the best way to satisfy a need. This is typical when the consumer has some previous experience with a product but isn't quite sure which choice to make at the moment. A seasoned computer gamer, for instance, may already know that he likes sports games and what store has the newest releases. At the store he might get the salesperson's advice and check out the video quality on a few games before deciding which to buy. This is a deliberate purchase, but only a limited amount of effort is expended before making the decision.

A consumer uses **routinized response behavior** when he or she regularly selects a particular way of satisfying a need when it occurs. Routinized response is typical when a consumer has considerable experience in how to meet a specific need and requires no new information. For example, our gamer might automatically buy the latest version of "Madden NFL" as soon as EA Sports makes it available. Routinized response also may occur when a buyer trusts a company, brand, or a friend's recommendation. Because trust lowers the risk of making the wrong choice, less effort is required from the buyer.

Routinized response behavior is also typical for **low-involvement purchases**—purchases that have little importance or relevance for the customer. Let's face it, for most of us, buying a box of salt is probably not one of the burning issues in your life.[30]

Buying isn't always rational

The idea of a decision process does *not* imply that consumers always apply *rational* processes in their buying decisions. To the contrary, consumers don't always seek accurate information or make smart choices that provide the best economic value. This is often because of the influences on consumer behavior that we discussed earlier in the chapter. For example, most sport utility vehicles never leave the paved road, but buyers like the image of driving an SUV and *knowing* they can get off the paved

Exhibit 5-10 Problem-Solving Continuum

Low involvement Frequently purchased Inexpensive Little risk Little information needed	Routinized response behavior	Limited problem solving	Extensive problem solving	High involvement Infrequently purchased Expensive High risk Much information desired

road if they want to. When a tourist spends 1,000 euros on a Loewe leather purse, it may simply be that she loves the style, can afford it, and "has to have it." Needs are operating in such a purchase, but they are higher-level needs and not some sort of functional "requirement."

To buy or not to buy

A customer who is ready to buy may have to decide which brand to purchase and where to make the purchase (that is, which store or location). There may be related decisions about colors, features, or other options as well. Buying can be complicated—and sometimes the complexity of all the choices causes customers to delay the purchase.

When a consumer decides to delay a purchase, oftentimes the sale is lost. He or she may never return. For that reason, some marketers make it easy for customers to come back later and purchase. For example, Walmart recently instituted a Christmas layaway program. When using layaway, a customer makes incremental payments on a purchase—and does not take it home until it is paid in full. Similarly, online retailers often allow customers to place items on a "Wish List" or "Save to Favorites" so they are easy to find when they return to the site.

When a customer gets close to making a purchase, marketing managers want to help "tip the scales." At this point, offers of special financing or free delivery might be helpful in overcoming a delayed purchase.

Consumers can have second thoughts after a purchase

After making a purchase, buyers often have second thoughts and wonder if they made the right choice. The resulting tension is called **dissonance**—a feeling of uncertainty about whether the correct decision was made. (In layman's terms, this is known as "buyer's remorse.") This may lead a customer to seek additional information to confirm the wisdom of the purchase.[31]

Post-purchase regret is a bigger problem

Sometimes uncertainty isn't the issue. Rather the consumer is certain about being unhappy with a purchase. When a post-purchase experience fails to live up to expectations, a customer will be disappointed. For example, going out for an expensive dinner—and then getting slow service and cold food—results in considerable dissatisfaction and regret over the choice. The diner is much less likely to visit that restaurant again. A consumer may regret making a purchase for a variety of reasons that the consumer didn't anticipate when making the purchase. But, whatever the reason, regret is not likely to lead to the same decision in the future.

Some consumers spread the word after they buy

Many consumers talk about their purchases and share opinions about their good and bad experiences. Recommendations from friends can have a big influence on whether we try a new restaurant, buy a hybrid car, or choose a veterinarian. Consumers are even more likely to share stories about being dissatisfied than satisfied. This is important for a marketer to remember. At times, his or her career might call for countering negative publicity—damage control—to save a product's image.[32]

New concepts require an adoption process

When consumers face a really new concept, their previous experience may not be relevant. These situations involve the **adoption process**—the steps individuals go through on the way to accepting or rejecting a new idea. Although the adoption process is similar to the decision-making process, learning plays a clearer role and promotion's contribution to a marketing mix is more visible.

In the adoption process, an individual moves through some fairly definite steps:

1. *Awareness*—the potential customer comes to know about the product but lacks details. The consumer may not even know how it works or what it will do.
2. *Interest*—if the consumer becomes interested, he or she will gather general information and facts about the product.
3. *Evaluation*—a consumer begins to give the product a mental trial, applying it to his or her personal situation.

4. *Trial*—the consumer may buy the product to experiment with it in use. A product that is either too expensive to try or isn't available for trial may never be adopted.

5. *Decision*—the consumer decides on either adoption or rejection. A satisfactory evaluation and trial may lead to adoption of the product and regular use. According to psychological learning theory, reinforcement leads to adoption.

6. *Confirmation*—the adopter continues to rethink the decision and searches for support for the decision—that is, further reinforcement.[33]

Dropbox had to work with the adoption process when it introduced cloud (online) data storage—an idea that was not familiar to many computer users. Dropbox lets users create a file folder on their devices—say their laptop, tablet, or smartphone—and share it with the others. For example, if a consumer places a photo, song, or document in the Dropbox folder on their laptop, it would automatically be replicated on their phone and tablet computer. The file is also backed up on the Internet. Furthermore, folders can also be shared with friends or work colleagues.

© grzegorz knec/Alamy.

Dropbox first targeted techies, who are comfortable with technology. The techies quickly downloaded Dropbox because it filled a need—these users tend to have many digital devices. Dropbox came with 2 GB of online storage. To encourage early customers to spread *awareness* and *generate* interest in Dropbox, they were given additional storage space for each person they referred to Dropbox. Many techies found good value in Dropbox and were happy to spread the word. A video on its website demonstrated how Dropbox works, making it easy for customers to *evaluate* its usefulness to them. The software was easy to install and it was free, making *trial* easy, too. As others used Dropbox, many began to share files with friends, family, and co-workers. This acted as *confirmation* and *reinforced* their decision. Some customers use the service so much they pay for additional storage space.

CONCLUSION

In this chapter, we analyzed the individual consumer as a problem solver who is influenced by economic needs, psychological variables, social influences, cultural factors, and the purchase situation. We showed how these variables influence the consumer decision process, what the steps in that process are, and why it is important to consider these steps when planning a marketing strategy. For example, we discussed three levels of problem solving that you can use to evaluate how consumers approach different types of purchase decisions—from the simple, routinized response behavior to the complex, extensive problem-solving behavior. We also discussed how the consumer's experience after the purchase impacts what that consumer will do in the future.

From a broader perspective, this chapter makes it clear that each consumer and purchase decision is somewhat unique. It isn't possible to catalog all of the individual possibilities. Rather, the overall focus of this chapter is to provide general frameworks you can use to analyze consumers regardless of the particular product or decision. This also helps you identify the dimensions of consumer behavior most important for segmenting the market and developing a targeted marketing mix.

By now it should be clear that expensive marketing errors can be made when you assume that other consumers will behave in the same manner as you or your family and friends. That's why we rely on the social and behavioral sciences for insight about consumer behavior and why marketing research is so important to marketing managers when they are developing a marketing strategy for a particular target market. When managers understand how and why consumers behave the way they do, they are better able to develop effective marketing mixes that really meet the needs of their target market.

WHAT'S NOW?

This chapter examines how consumers make buying decisions—and the factors influencing their decision process. For some current real-world examples and learnings, check out *What's Now?* at www.learnthe4ps.com/whatsnow/c5

KEY TERMS

LO 5.7

economic buyers, 117
economic needs, 117
discretionary income, 119
needs, 119
wants, 119
drive, 119
physiological needs, 120
safety needs, 120
social needs, 120
personal needs, 120
perception, 121
selective exposure, 121

selective perception, 122
selective retention, 122
learning, 122
cues, 122
response, 122
reinforcement, 123
attitude, 123
belief, 123
expectation, 124
trust, 126
psychographics, 126
lifestyle analysis, 126

empty nesters, 129
social class, 129
reference group, 130
opinion leader, 130
culture, 131
purchase situation, 133
extensive problem solving, 136
limited problem solving, 136
routinized response behavior, 136
low-involvement purchases, 136
dissonance, 137
adoption process, 137

QUESTIONS AND PROBLEMS

1. Review the Apple case study that opens the chapter. From this case, identify examples of different key terms and concepts covered in the chapter. For example, on-the-spot demos of the iPod are conducted by an opinion leader.

2. Review the Apple case study that opens this chapter. Applying concepts from the chapter, what else could Apple do to enhance the launch and subsequent sales of the Apple Watch? Offer some specific strategy suggestions and justify each by referring to concepts from this chapter.

3. In your own words, explain economic needs and how they relate to the economic-buyer model of consumer behavior. Give an example of a purchase you recently made that is consistent with the economic-buyer model. Give another that is not explained by the economic-buyer model. Explain your thinking.

4. Explain what is meant by a hierarchy of needs and provide examples of one or more products that enable you to satisfy each of the four levels of need.

5. Cut out or photocopy two recent advertisements: one full-page color ad from a magazine and one large display ad from a newspaper. In each case, indicate to which needs the ads appeal.

6. Explain how an understanding of consumers' learning processes might affect marketing strategy planning. Give an example.

7. Briefly describe your own *beliefs* about the potential value of low-energy compact fluorescent lightbulbs, your *attitude* toward them, and your *intention* about buying one the next time you need to replace a bulb.

8. Give an example of a recent purchase experience in which you were dissatisfied because a firm's marketing mix did not meet your expectations. Indicate how the purchase fell short of your expectations—and also explain whether your expectations were formed based on the firm's promotion or on something else. Will it affect how much you trust that firm or brand in the future?

9. Explain psychographics and lifestyle analysis. Explain how they might be useful for planning marketing strategies to reach college students, as opposed to average consumers.

10. A supermarket chain is planning to open a number of new stores to appeal to Hispanics in southern California. Give

some examples that indicate how the Four Ps might be adjusted to appeal to the Hispanic subculture.

11. How should social class influences affect the planning of a new restaurant in a large city? How might the Four Ps be adjusted?

12. Illustrate how the reference group concept may apply in practice by explaining how you personally are influenced by some reference group for some product. What are the implications of such behavior for marketing managers?

13. Give two examples of recent purchases where the specific purchase situation influenced your purchase decision. Briefly explain how your decision was affected.

14. Give an example of a recent purchase in which you used extensive problem solving. What sources of information did you use in making the decision?

15. On the basis of the data and analysis presented in Chapter 5, what kind of buying behavior would you expect to find for the following products: (a) a haircut, (b) a shampoo, (c) a digital camera, (d) a tennis racket, (e) a dress belt, (f) a cell phone, (g) life insurance, (h) an ice cream cone, and (i) a new checking account? Set up a chart for your answer with products along the left-hand margin as the row headings and the following factors as headings for the columns: (a) how consumers would shop for these products, (b) how far they would travel to buy the product, (c) whether they would buy by brand, (d) whether they would compare with other products, and (e) any other factors they should consider. Insert short answers—words or phrases are satisfactory—in the various boxes. Be prepared to discuss how the answers you put in the chart would affect each product's marketing mix.

16. Review the model in Exhibit 5-2 and then reread the Apple case at the beginning of this chapter. List and briefly describe specific points in the case that illustrate the model.

17. Interview a friend or family member about two recent purchase decisions. One decision should be an important purchase, perhaps the choice of an automobile, a place to live, or a college. The second purchase should be more routine, such as a meal from a fast-food restaurant or a regularly purchased grocery item. For each purchase, ask your friend questions that will help you understand how the decision was made. Use the model in Exhibit 5-8 to guide your questions. Describe the similarities and differences between the two purchase decisions.

MARKETING PLANNING FOR HILLSIDE VETERINARY CLINIC

Appendix D (the Appendices follow Chapter 19) includes a sample marketing plan for Hillside Veterinary Clinic. Look through the "Customers" section and consider the following questions.

a. Based on the marketing plan, what do we know about the consumer behavior of the target market?

b. What additional information do you think would be helpful before developing a marketing strategy for Hillside?

SUGGESTED CASES

1. McDonald's "Seniors" Restaurant
9. Restful Night Motel
12. DrV.com—Custom Vitamins

3. Real NOCO Soccer Academy
10. Sampson's Ice Center
30. Walker-Winkle Mills, Ltd.

8. Salvaggio's Trattoria
11. Run Free

MARKETING ANALYTICS: DATA TO KNOWLEDGE

CHAPTER 5: SELECTIVE PROCESSES

Submag, Inc., uses direct-mail promotion to sell magazine subscriptions. Magazine publishers pay Submag $3.12 for each new subscription. Submag's costs include the expenses of printing, addressing, and mailing each direct-mail advertisement plus the cost of using a mailing list. There are many suppliers of mailing lists, and the cost and quality of different lists vary.

Submag's marketing manager, Shandra Debose, is trying to choose between two possible mailing lists. One list has been generated from phone directories. It is less expensive than the other list, but the supplier acknowledges that about 10 percent of the names are out-of-date (addresses where people have moved away). A competing supplier offers a list of active members of professional associations. This list costs 4 cents per name more than the phone list, but only 8 percent of the addresses are out-of-date.

In addition to concerns about out-of-date names, not every consumer who receives a mailing buys a subscription. For example, *selective exposure* is a problem. Some target customers never see the offer—they just toss out junk mail without even opening the envelope. Industry studies show that this wastes about 10 percent of each mailing—although the precise percentage varies from one mailing list to another.

Selective perception influences some consumers who do open the mailing. Some are simply not interested. Others don't want to deal with a subscription service. Although the price is good, these consumers worry that they'll never get the magazines. Submag's previous experience is that selective perception causes more than half of those who read the offer to reject it.

Of those who perceive the message as intended, many are interested. But *selective retention* can be a problem. Some people set the information aside and then forget to send in the subscription order.

Submag can mail about 25,000 pieces per week. Shandra Debose has set up a spreadsheet to help her study effects of the various relationships discussed earlier and to choose between the two mailing lists.

See Connect for the spreadsheet and questions needed to analyze this scenario.

6
CHAPTER SIX

© Paulo Whitaker/Reuters Pictures.

Business and Organizational Customers and Their Buying Behavior

MetoKote Corporation specializes in protective coating applications, such as powder-coat and liquid paint, that other manufacturers need for the parts and equipment they make. For example, when you see John Deere agricultural, construction, or lawn- and grounds-care equipment, many of the components have likely been coated (painted) in a MetoKote facility. In fact, Deere and MetoKote have a close buyer-seller relationship. Although Deere uses a variety of methods to identify suppliers and get competitive bids for many items it needs, it's different with MetoKote. Deere isn't going to switch to some other supplier just because other options provide cheaper coatings. MetoKote not only provides protective coatings for many Deere products, it has built facilities right next to some Deere plants. When it's time for a component to be coated, a conveyer belt moves the part out of the Deere plant and into the MetoKote facility. A short time later it's back—and it's green or yellow.

Many people were involved in the decision to purchase coating services in this way. The responsibility for choosing a painting vendor didn't just rest with Deere's purchasing department but involved input from people in finance, quality control, and production employees. They worked together—often with MetoKote personnel—to figure out exactly what was needed to provide the high-quality protective finish Deere's customers expect on each piece of Deere equipment. A decision like this was not easy, so Deere's buying team took its time gathering information and reviewing different suppliers.

Once they decided to work with MetoKote, it was a long-term decision. Deere trusts MetoKote will consistently offer quality paint jobs, but also appreciates that the supplier's experts keep up with all of the environmental regulations and new technologies for coatings.

Deere does all this because it knows how demanding the customers in its agricultural, commercial, and construction equipment markets can be. Deere's organizational customers differ from the consumers that buy its riding lawnmowers. There are fewer business customers, but many of them spend more than a $100,000 a year on Deere equipment. And they do a lot of analysis to make sure those investments pay off in the long run. Like Deere, they want good value—and Deere is known for delivering that. Business buyers are experts, too, highly trained in what they buy. And while there are many farmers across the globe, there are many more consumers.

John Deere sees some of its biggest opportunities in developing markets such as India and South America. Brazil, for example, now produces more than half of the world's orange juice—almost all for export. Farms in Brazil can be very large; a single farm might stretch over 200,000 acres and purchase millions of dollars in farm equipment each year. So when John Deere managers asked, farmers in Brazil responded that they wanted powerful tractors capable of hauling wider planters and other implements. When the new 8R tractor was introduced, it sold well in spite of the fact that it cost more than other tractors on the market. Brazilian farmers found it helped them get more done with fewer tractors and less labor. Those savings, plus the greater reliability and durability of Deere equipment, create value.

Until recently, John Deere sales in South America grew more than 30 percent per year. But sales to farmers also depend on the weather and the economy. When a drought and recession hit Brazil, farmers were forced to tighten their belts and cut back on spending. The delayed purchases of new farm equipment slowed Deere's sales in South America.

Although some customers buy directly from John Deere, most purchase from a John Deere dealer. These dealers buy what their customers want. And the dealers know Deere's reputation for quality service is just as important as the company's reputation for quality products. So Deere has streamlined distribution with the goal of giving customers and dealers better service. It's dropping dealers who don't measure up to its goals for customer satisfaction—and encouraging the dealers that remain to consolidate so that they will have economies of scale in purchasing, be able to afford more specialists in important areas like e-commerce, and be able to share inventory among multiple locations. Dealers appreciate that Deere set up the MachineFinder website and Facebook page, which help customers find used Deere equipment being sold by its dealers. Deere even finances used purchases through John Deere Credit.

Deere designs marketing strategies that solve particular customer problems. For example, golf course managers buy Deere equipment to maintain their fairways, greens, and sand traps because they value the reliability and durability of the brand's products. However, they also need a variety of operating supplies—ranging from grass seed and irrigation equipment to ball washers and chemicals. Golf course managers have many responsibilities besides purchasing, so Deere introduced its One Source service, which provides golf course managers with a "one-stop shop" for the things they need—all backed by the trusted Deere name. One Source saves time and strengthens Deere's relationships with both its dealers and their golf course

customers. Of course, it creates new challenges for Deere's purchasing department. It must identify, evaluate, monitor, and recommend the suppliers for the products that golf courses need. Deere's dealers and golf course customers rely on Deere's purchasing specialists to make the right decisions, but that's part of the value that Deere provides.

Innovative approaches to delivering customer value make Deere the supplier of choice for all kinds of business customers.[1]

LEARNING OBJECTIVES

As the John Deere case illustrates, the buying behavior of organizational customers can be very different from the buying behavior of final consumers. Marketing strategy planning requires a solid understanding of who these organizational customers are and how they buy.

When you finish this chapter, you should be able to

1 Name and give examples of the different types of business and organizational buyers.

2 Describe how organizational and business markets differ from consumer markets.

3 Describe each step in the model of organizational/business buying.

4 Explain the different types of buying processes.

5 Understand the different types of buyer–seller relationships and their benefits and limitations.

6 Know about the number and distribution of manufacturers and why they are an important customer group.

7 Know how buying by service firms, retailers, wholesalers, and governments is similar to—and different from—buying by manufacturers.

8 Understand important new terms (shown in red).

Business and Organizational Customers—A Big Opportunity

LO 6.1

Most people think about an individual final consumer when they hear the term *customer*. But many marketing managers aim at customers who are not final consumers. In fact, more purchases are made by businesses and other organizations than by final consumers.

Business and organizational customers are any buyers who buy for resale or to produce other goods and services. There are many different types of organizational customers, including the following:

- *Producers of goods and services*—including manufacturers, farmers, real estate developers, hotels, banks, and even doctors and lawyers
- *Intermediaries*—wholesalers and retailers
- *Government units*—federal agencies in the United States and other countries as well as state and local governments
- *Nonprofit organizations*—national organizations such as the American Red Cross and Girl Scouts as well as local organizations such as museums and churches

Exhibit 6-1 Understanding Business and Organizational Customers for Marketing Strategy Planning

As this suggests, not all organizational customers are business firms. Even so, they are sometimes loosely referred to as *business buyers, intermediate buyers,* or *industrial buyers*—and marketing managers often refer to organizational customers collectively as the "business-to-business" market, or simply, the *B2B market.*

In this chapter, we'll focus on organizational customers and their buying behavior (see Exhibit 6–1). In Chapter 5 we focused on buying by final consumers, so here we'll start by covering important ways that organizational buying differs from buying by final consumers. Next, we will look at a model of business and organizational buying. Finally, we'll focus on some key differences among the specific types of organizational customers.

So keep in mind that, for many firms, marketing strategy planning is about meeting the needs of organizational customers, not final consumers. A firm can target both final consumers and organizations, but different marketing mixes may be needed. As you learn about the buying behavior of organizations, think about how a firm's marketing mix may need to be different and how it may be adjusted.

Organizational Customers Are Different

LO 6.2

In some ways, organizational buying is similar to the model of consumer behavior introduced in Chapter 5. Businesses and organizations make purchases to solve problems, they seek information, and the decision-making process varies depending on the

Exhibit 6-2
Differences between
Organizational
Customers and Final
Consumers

nature of the purchase. Yet organizational customers and their buying behaviors differ from final consumers and their buying behaviors. These differences have important implications for the marketing strategy planning process (see Exhibit 6–2).

Customers are fewer in number but each spends more dollars

As compared to the consumer market, the organizational market includes far fewer buyers—yet the dollars spent by each are, on average, much greater. Consider that Procter & Gamble sales to Walmart are more than $11 billion. Although that case reflects an extreme, most B2B sellers have many customers that provide each of them with thousands—if not hundreds of thousands—of dollars in revenue. This allows business marketers the opportunity to invest more marketing resources into satisfying each customer.

Economic needs are primary

Organizations intently focus on economic factors when they make purchase decisions. Buyers try to account for the total cost of selecting a supplier and its particular marketing mix, not just the initial price of the product. For example, a hospital that needs a new type of digital X-ray equipment might look at both the original cost and ongoing costs, how it would affect doctor productivity, and, of course, the quality of the images it produces. The hospital might also consider the seller's reliability and its ability to provide speedy maintenance and repair.

The matter of reliability deserves further emphasis. Companies count on reliable suppliers—suppliers that deliver consistent quality on time. An organization may not be able to function if purchases don't arrive when they're expected. For example, imagine what would happen on a Buick assembly line if Nexteer Automotive was a few days late delivering its adaptive steering wheels. Buick might have to shut down the assembly line. This would affect other suppliers—raising their costs—and Buick's dealers might not be happy if they lost car sales.

The cost of poor quality can also be significant. Airbags made by Takata were found to be defective—but that was after 30 million cars (in the United States alone) were already on the road with the faulty safety device. The total cost of replacing all those airbags was more than half a billion dollars, not counting the harm to the reputations of the automakers involved.[2]

Behavioral needs still matter

Although economic needs are primary, B2B sellers know that organizational buyers are also influenced by noneconomic factors. Many of the behavioral dimensions

A seller's marketing mix may need to consider both the needs of the company and the individual. Buyers want to avoid taking risks that reflect badly on their decisions. Honda reminds customers that its reputation for reliability is something they can count on—that lowers the risk a buyer might feel buying an unknown brand. A.O. Smith knows that organizational buyers want to save their company money, but they also want to feel good about their choices.

mentioned in Chapter 5, such as security, status, and a sense of accomplishment, are relevant here, too. Purchasing managers and others involved in buying decisions are human, and they want friendly relationships with suppliers.

The purchasing people in some firms are eager to imitate progressive competitors or even to be the first to try new products. Such "innovators" deserve special attention when new products are being introduced. Most members of the buying center want to do their jobs well, and good suppliers try to help them accomplish that. A recent survey found that buyers are more motivated to receive and open e-mails from marketers who offer fresh insight and ideas.[3]

For many purchases, buyers know that choosing a supplier who delivers poor quality or late deliveries can be very costly—but it also means the buyer may be blamed. Buyers want to avoid this risk—and a marketer who develops a marketing mix that lowers the buyer's risk puts himself or herself in a stronger position.

A seller's marketing mix should satisfy *both* the needs of the customer company and the needs of individuals who influence the purchase. Therefore, sellers need to find an overlapping area where both can be satisfied. See Exhibit 6–3 for a summary of this idea.

Exhibit 6–3
Overlapping Needs of Individual Influencers and the Customer Organization

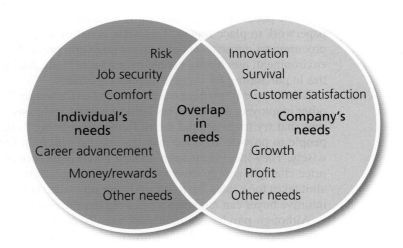

While consumers have ethical issues to consider when making purchases, organizational buyers must be careful to avoid a conflict between their own self-interest and company outcomes. This can be difficult; sometimes the ethical line can be blurry. Consequently, some firms set strict ethical guidelines. Marketers must be careful here. A salesperson offering a company pen to a prospect may view the giveaway as part of the promotion effort—but the customer firm may have a policy against employees accepting any gift from a supplier.

Although most organizational buyers act in an ethical manner, there have been highly publicized abuses. For example, Omnicare Inc., which provides pharmaceutical drugs to customers that include nursing homes, was charged with soliciting and receiving kickback payments from its nursing home customers and drug maker suppliers, including Johnson & Johnson (J&J). J&J and Omnicare apparently sold the drug Risperdal to nursing homes as a treatment for dementia and anxiety, conditions for which it was not approved. The two companies also agreed to downplay risks of diabetes and weight gain when talking to patients and doctors. The case may cost the two firms more than $1 billion in fines and other charges—plus untold damage to their reputations.

Marketers need to take concerns about conflict of interest very seriously. Part of the promotion job is to persuade different individuals who may influence an organization's purchase. Yet the whole marketing effort may be tainted if it even *appears* that a marketer has encouraged a person who influences a decision to put personal gain ahead of company interest. The pressure marketing managers feel to make sales goals must be tempered by ethical choices.[4]

Ethical Dilemma

What would you do? Assume that you are a salesperson in a small company. For months you've been trying to get a big order from a large firm. A purchasing manager at the firm casually mentions that she is trying to help two friends find tickets for a big hockey game. Your boss has season tickets for entertaining customers, but you know that the purchasing manager's company strictly prohibits any gift to employees. When you ask your boss what to do, the reply is, "Well, the tickets would be used by the friends and not the customer firm's employee, so you can offer them if you think you should." *What should you do?* What are the pros and cons of your decision?

Many organizations rely on specialists to ensure that purchases are handled sensibly. These specialists have different titles in different firms (such as procurement officer, supply manager, purchasing agent, or buyer), but basically they are all **purchasing managers**—buying specialists for their employers. In large organizations, they usually specialize by product area and are real experts.

Some people think purchasing is handled by clerks who sit in cubicles and do the paperwork to place orders. That view is out of date. Today, most firms look to their procurement departments to help cut costs and provide competitive advantage. In this environment, purchasing people have a lot of clout. And there are good job opportunities in purchasing for capable business graduates.

Salespeople often have to see a purchasing manager first—before they contact any other employee. These buyers hold important positions and take a dim view of sales reps that try to go around them. Rather than being "sold," these buyers want salespeople to provide accurate information that will help them solve problems and buy wisely. They like information on new goods and services, as well as tips on potential price changes, supply shortages, and other changes in market conditions. Sometimes all it takes for a sales rep to keep a buyer up to date is to send an occasional e-mail. An intuitive buyer can tell when a sales rep has the customer firm's best interests at heart.

Although purchasing managers usually coordinate relationships with suppliers, other people may also play important roles in influencing the purchase decision.[5]

Multiple buying influence in a buying center

Multiple buying influence means that several people—perhaps even top management—play a part in making a purchase decision. Possible buying influences include the following:

1. *Users*—perhaps production line workers or their supervisors.
2. *Influencers*—perhaps engineering or R&D people who help write specifications or supply information for evaluating alternatives.
3. *Buyers*—the purchasing managers who have the responsibility for working with suppliers and arranging the terms of the sale.
4. *Deciders*—the people in the organization who have the power to select or approve the supplier—often a purchasing manager but perhaps top management for larger purchases.
5. *Gatekeepers*—people who control the flow of information within the organization. Gatekeepers might include purchasing managers, receptionists, secretaries, research assistants, bookkeepers, and many more.

BASF plastics can be used in automobile parts—replacing heavier metal parts. The lower weight can increase fuel efficiency. BASF personnel work with purchasing managers and engineers at automakers to determine where plastic parts offer the greatest benefit to the end user (car buyer). *Copyright © BASF Corporation 2015.*

The following example portrays how different buying influences work in the purchase of a corporate jet. A company that already owns a corporate jet may decide it is time to lease a new one. The current lease is expiring and a newer jet would have better fuel efficiency and be more reliable. Middle and upper management (users) would be likely to provide comments on features they would like to see in the new model. Thus, they play the roles of influencers. The expert knowledge of the chief pilot and the airplane mechanic would make them significant influencers on the purchase. The chief pilot might also serve as gatekeeper by deciding which information and how much of his expertise he shares with others. A finance executive would also be likely to weigh in (another influencer) with thoughts on costs and financing the purchase. An assistant to the purchasing manager (gatekeeper) does online searches for information and decides what information to put into a report. After recommendations have been made, a large multimillion-dollar purchase like a corporate jet might go before the board of directors (deciders) for final approval. After all these buying influences are considered and a particular jet is selected, one of the purchasing agents for

A company's purchase of a corporate jet is likely to involve many different people in the buying process.
© 2015, Cessna Aircraft Company. All Rights Reserved. Cessna Aircraft Company [Cessna] is a wholly owned subsidiary of Textron Inc.

the firm (the buyer) works with the chosen supplier to arrange the terms of the sale, including delivery dates, payment, installation, and after-sale service.

It is helpful to think of a **buying center** as all the people who participate in (or influence) a purchase. Because different people may make up a buying center from one decision to the next, the salesperson must study each case carefully. Just learning whom to talk with may be hard, but thinking about the various roles in the buying center can help.

The salesperson may have to talk to every member of the buying center—stressing different topics for each. This not only complicates the promotion job but also lengthens it. Approval of a routine order may take anywhere from a day to several months. On very important purchases—a new building, major equipment, or a new information system—the selling period may take a year or more.[6]

Buying procedures are standardized

Buying organizations often establish formal procedures governing how purchases are made. For example, if a contract exists with an office supply vendor, everyone in the organization may be required to make their purchases through a special website. A person who needs to purchase something may have to complete a **requisition**—a request to buy something. For larger purchases, there may be rules requiring that multiple suppliers are contacted so that prices can be compared.

If a large organization has facilities at dispersed locations, much of the purchasing work may be done at a central location. With centralized buying, a sales rep may be able to sell to facilities all over a country—or even across several countries—without leaving the base city. Walmart handles many of the purchase decisions for stores in its retail chain from its headquarters in Arkansas. Many purchasing decisions for agencies of the U.S. government are handled in Washington, D.C.

The general procedures for organizational buying are outlined in the next section.

A Model of Business and Organizational Buying

LO 6.3

Business and organizational buying generally follows the three-step approach shown in Exhibit 6–4. Depending on the nature of the purchase, how each step plays out can vary—and the third step is not always routinely reviewed. The next few sections of this chapter will examine more closely these three steps. Let's begin by looking at how organizations define the problem by narrowing down from problem recognition to specifying a particular solution.[7]

Exhibit 6-4 A Model of Organizational Buying

Step 1: Defining the Problem
- Problem recognition
- Describing the need
- Specifying the product

Step 2: Decision-Making Process
- Establish buying process
- Gather information
- Solicit proposals/bids
- Select the supplier

Step 3: Managing the Buyer–Seller Relationship
- Structure the relationship
- Monitor supplier performance

Step 1: Define the Problem

Organizations make purchases to satisfy needs. Generally speaking, most organizations make purchases for the same basic reason: They buy goods and services that will help them meet the demand for the goods and services that they in turn supply to their markets. In other words, their basic need is to satisfy their own customers and clients. A producer buys because it wants to earn a profit by making and selling goods or services. A wholesaler or retailer buys products it can profitably resell to its customers. A town government wants to meet legal and social obligations to its citizens.

From recognizing problems to describing needs

At their earliest stages, problems may not be well understood. A manufacturer might be seeking a way to speed up production. A dentist might wonder if there is a better way to bill her customers. A clothing retailer may be looking for spring fashions to appeal to its target market. A school district may be seeking a way to provide more students with access to computers. Each of these realizations can trigger the organization to seek more details about the problem at hand.

Ultimately, the problem should be narrowed down to a more specific need. What product or service can solve the client's problem? Selling organizations often try to get in at this stage. Some sellers even help the buyer realize they have a problem—for example, a seller of medical office management software might send direct mail to dentists describing the benefits other dental offices have received after using its software.

Specifications describe the product

In other situations, an organization may simply decide what it wants and move quickly through this stage. Often larger organizations, with formal procedures, spend more time detailing the purchase requirements. In this case, organizational buyers may buy on the basis of a set of **purchasing specifications**—a written description of what the firm wants to buy. When quality is highly standardized, as is often the case with manufactured items, the specification may simply consist of a brand name or part number.

Often, however, when the purchase requirements are more complicated, the specifications may set out detailed information about the performance standards the product must meet. Purchase specifications for services tend to be detailed because services are less standardized and usually are not performed until after they're purchased.

Eastman Chemical Co. developed Eastman Tritan, an innovative copolyester (plasticlike) material. Tritan is durable, heat resistant, and offers design flexibility and ease of processing. It is ideal for the molded parts needed by kitchen appliance manufacturers. Promotion from Eastman Chemical, possibly through ads like this one or a salesperson calling on a buyer, will help the buying firm recognize a need and see that Tritan is the solution.
© 2015 Eastman Chemical Company or its subsidiaries. All rights reserved.

Customers may expect quality certification

Organizational customers considering a new supplier or one from overseas may be concerned about product quality. However, this is becoming less of an obstacle because of ISO 9000. **ISO 9000** is a way for a supplier to document its quality procedures according to internationally recognized standards.

ISO 9000 assures a customer that the supplier has effective quality checks in place, without the customer having to conduct its own costly and time-consuming audit. Some customers won't buy from any supplier who doesn't have it. To get ISO 9000 certified, a company must prove to outside auditors that it documents how the company operates and who is responsible for quality every step of the way.[8]

Step 2: The Decision-Making Process

LO 6.4

After the buying organization defines the problem, describes the need, and specifies the product, the next step involves the decision-making process—how a firm decides what to buy, whether to buy, and if they buy. In this step buyers gather information, solicit proposals from suppliers, and finally choose a supplier. The decision-making process can vary depending on the nature of the purchase—so we start by looking at different buying processes (see Exhibit 6–5).[9]

Three kinds of buying processes are useful

New-task buying occurs when a customer organization has a new need and wants a great deal of information. New-task buying can involve setting product specifications, evaluating sources of supply, and establishing an order routine that can be followed in the future if results are satisfactory. Multiple buying influence is most often found in new-task buying.

A **straight rebuy** is a routine repurchase that may have been made many times before. Buyers probably don't bother looking for new information or new sources of supply. Most of a company's small or recurring purchases are of this type—but they take only a small part of an organized buyer's time. Important purchases may be made this way too—but only after the firm has decided what procedure will be "routine."

The **modified rebuy** is the in-between process where some review of the buying situation is done—though not as much as in new-task buying. Sometimes a competitor will get lazy enjoying a straight rebuy situation. An alert marketer can turn these situations into opportunities by providing more information or a better marketing mix.

Straight rebuys often use e-commerce order systems

E-commerce computer systems *automatically* handle a large portion of straight rebuys. Buyers program decision rules that tell the computer how to order and leave the details of following through to the computer. For example, when an order comes in that requires certain materials or parts, the computer information system automatically orders them from the appropriate suppliers, sets the delivery date, and schedules production.

Exhibit 6–5
Organizational Buying Processes

Characteristics	Type of Process		
	New-Task Buying	Modified Rebuy	Straight Rebuy
Time Required	Much	Medium	Little
Multiple Influence	Much	Some	Little
Review of Suppliers	Much	Some	None
Information Needed	Much	Some	Little

Exhibit 6–6
Major Sources of
Information Used by
Organizational Buyers

	Marketing sources	Nonmarketing sources
Personal sources	• Salespeople • Others from supplier firms • Trade shows	• Buying center members • Outside business associates • Consultants and outside experts
Impersonal sources	• Online events and virtual trade shows • Sales literature and catalogs • E-mails and newsletters • Website content including blogs, video, case studies, and white papers • Social media (a company LinkedIn page)	• Online searches • Rating services • Trade associations • News publications • Product directories • Online communities • Social media (comments on LinkedIn)

If conditions change, buyers modify the computer instructions. When nothing unusual happens, however, the computer system continues to routinely rebuy as needs develop—electronically sending purchase orders to the regular supplier.

New-task buying requires the most information

While buyers want to stay current on all facets of purchasing, new-task buying situations motivate them to seek specific information. Often a new-task buy starts with a *user* who becomes aware of a need and begins researching solutions. Even though a wide variety of information sources are available (see Exhibit 6–6), business buyers will use the sources they trust. To build trust, a marketer must make sure its information is reliable and useful to the buyer. Sellers should present information objectively; if it appears too self-serving and biased toward the suppliers' offering, it may not be trusted or used by the buyer.

How much information a customer collects depends on the importance of the purchase and the level of uncertainty about what choice might be best. The time and expense of searching for information may not be justified for a minor purchase. But a major purchase often involves real detective work by the buyer.

New-task buying situations provide a good opportunity for a new supplier to make inroads with a customer. With a buyer actively searching for information, the seller's promotion has a much greater chance of being noticed and having an impact. Advertising, trade show exhibits, e-mails, and salespeople can all help build the buyer's attention, but an informative website may be essential for getting attention in the first place.[10]

Search engines—a first step to gathering information

Most purchasing managers start with an Internet search when they need to identify new suppliers, better ways to meet needs, or information to improve decisions. Buyers often rely on highly specialized search engines—like one that finds all types of steel that meet certain technical specifications and then compares prices. But buyers also use general-purpose search engines such as Google. A search across the whole web can often locate off-the-shelf products that eliminate the need to buy expensive, custom-made items. For example, a firm in Saudi Arabia ordered $1,000 worth of tiny rubber grommets from Allstates Rubber & Tool, a small firm in the suburbs of Chicago. If the buyer's search hadn't located Allstates's website, the only alternative would have been to pay much more for custom-made grommets—and Allstates wouldn't have picked up a new customer.[11]

Marketing managers know that it is critical to have a website that buyers can find. That's why suppliers often pay for a sponsored link (an ad) that appears when certain

Online Toolkit

Go to the Buyer Zone website (**www.buyerzone.com**). Type "office chairs" into the search box. On this page, look at the Buyer's Guide—there are several links. Look at the Buyer's Guides for other products as well. What other features are available on this site? What can be learned about buying different products from BuyerZone.com? For a marketing manager targeting small businesses, how could this site be useful?

keywords are included in a search. A supplier might also change its website so that it is more likely to appear high on a list of searches.

Buyers want sites with useful content

Having useful content on a website not only moves it higher on the buyer's search results, but also gives buyers a reason to fully explore the seller's website. Instead of trying to sell the customer, a supplier needs to educate buyers about their needs and present the advantages and disadvantages of the seller's products. Buyers like to read targeted **white papers** (an authoritative report or guide that addresses important issues in an industry and offers solutions). White papers may advocate a seller's solution, but if they appear objective, they can help establish a firm as a thought leader in a particular area. Buyers also like to read case studies to learn about how other companies have addressed similar needs. Video content and blogs can also make a seller's website more useful.

Buyers share experiences in online communities

Buyers especially value recommendations from others who have already dealt with a similar need. Sometimes they turn to their LinkedIn network to solicit advice from colleagues. Others turn to online communities. For example, at Spiceworks Community (www.spiceworks.com), IT professionals ask and answer technical questions, research best practices, and learn what others think about a product or service they are considering. Buyers trust this source of information, and similar online communities have developed around other industries. As buyers rely more on social networks, communications from marketers may have less influence on buyers' attitudes and choices.[12]

Solicit proposals from suppliers

When buyers in B2B markets identify potential suppliers, they contact one or more suppliers for proposals. A supplier may simply send a brochure or product catalog, or it may have a salesperson contact the buyer over the phone. In more complex buying situations, there may be formal presentations from different suppliers that also submit detailed proposals.

Buyers ask for competitive bids to compare offerings

Sometimes buyers will ask suppliers to submit a **competitive bid**—the terms of sale offered by the supplier in response to the purchase specifications posted by a buyer. If different suppliers' quality, dependability, and delivery schedules all meet the specs, the buyer will select the low-price bid. But a creative marketer needs to look carefully at the buyer's specs—and the need—to see if changing other elements of the marketing mix could provide a competitive advantage.

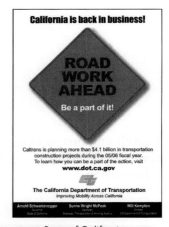

© 2015 State of California,

Rather than search for suppliers, buyers sometimes post their requirements and invite qualified suppliers to submit a bid. Some firms set up or participate in a procurement website that directs suppliers to companies (or divisions of a company) that need to make purchases. These sites make it easy for suppliers to find out about the purchase needs of the organizations that sponsor the sites. This helps increase the number of suppliers competing for the business and that can drive down prices or provide more beneficial terms of sale. For example, when the California Department of Transportation was planning $4 billion in new construction projects, it established a procurement site so that potential suppliers knew each project's requirements for submitting a competitive bid.

Evaluating and selecting suppliers

Considering all of the factors relevant to a purchase decision can be very complex. A supplier or product that is best in one way may not be best in others. To try to deal with these situations, many firms use **vendor analysis**—a formal rating of

What's Next? Saving money *and* the planet

Attention to sustainability often identifies savings that previously were not obvious. Sometimes all that is involved is a simple change from what's routine. For example, when Falconbridge Limited's aluminum smelter changed to more efficient (but more expensive) lightbulbs, it saved almost $100,000 per year in energy bills. When the Fairmont Hotel in Vancouver searched for alternative chemicals to use in its pool, it found new ones that were healthier for guests and cut costs by $2,000. Hotels everywhere cleaned up when they stopped rewashing all of their linens every day. All it took was a card in the bath that says, "If you'd like us to replace a towel with a clean one, put it on the floor." The cards cost pennies, whereas the hot water, detergent, labor, and wear on linens cost millions.

Retailers and wholesalers must be guided by what customers want; putting green products on their shelves will just rack up losses unless there's customer demand. But firms such as Walmart and Home Depot advertise their sustainable choices because many consumers do want them. Walmart took note when—in one year—its customers bought 100 million eco-friendly fluorescent lightbulbs. Home Depot has identified more than 4,000 Eco Option products that meet government specifications for water conservation, energy efficiency, clean air, and sustainable forestry. Both retailers are building more energy-efficient stores and prodding their suppliers to think green by using less packaging.

When governments are doing the buying, they need to demonstrate an economic return for a sustainable purchase. Some consumers might spend a premium for an electric car, but buses need to have a reasonable payback. Electric bus maker Proterra is building the case for its $850,000 electric bus. The 80 passenger bus is whisper quiet but sells for more than twice the price of a comparable diesel-powered bus. Depending on the price of gas and electricity, the buses can pay back in anywhere from 2 to 6 years—and cities such as Reno, Nevada, and Greenville, South Carolina, can justify the up-front expense.

Some progressive firms don't need to see financial benefits; they simply make sustainability an essential buying criterion. New Belgium Brewing Company put sustainable values in its mission statement; that means its purchasing people select more energy efficient (but higher-priced) brew kettles, use wind-powered electricity, and build facilities that are more costly but use the latest green ideas. Many nonprofit organizations take this altruistic approach. It's hard to imagine an environmental organization such as the Sierra Club not having sustainability as a value when it's time to make purchases.

So what's next for sustainability? Should businesses and nonprofit organizations only buy more sustainable products that also save the green (dollars, that is)? What are other benefits of making more sustainable purchasing?[14]

suppliers on all relevant areas of performance. The purpose isn't just to get a low price from the supplier on a given part or service. Rather, the goal is to lower the *total costs* associated with purchases. Analysis might show that the best vendor is the one that helps the customer reduce costs of excess inventory, retooling of equipment, or defective parts.[13]

Procedures like vendor analysis can be applied to many different situations. In "*What's Next?* Saving money *and* the planet" we look at how some firms are making buying decisions that are sustainable for the bottom line and the environment.

Which buying procedure becomes routine is critical

From our earlier discussion, you can see that buyers make important decisions about how to deal with one or more suppliers. At one extreme, a buyer might want to rely on competition among all available vendors to get the best price on each and every order it places. At the other extreme, it might just routinely buy from one vendor with whom it already has a good relationship. In practice, there are many important and common variations between these extremes. To better understand the variations, let's take a closer look at the benefits and limitations of different types of buyer–seller relationships.

Step 3: Managing Buyer–Seller Relationships in Business Markets

LO 6.5

After selecting a supplier, the buyer and seller must figure out how to structure and manage the relationship. Many organizational purchases are ongoing—a buyer will make regular purchases. Other purchases, might involve a single transaction—buying a replacement part for example. Buyers and suppliers should work together to figure out the best way to structure the relationship. In this section we look at the many different considerations for managing buyer–seller relationships.

Close relationships may produce mutual benefits

There are often significant benefits of a close working relationship between a supplier and a customer firm. And such relationships are becoming common. Many firms are reducing the number of suppliers with whom they work—expecting more in return from the suppliers that remain. The best relationships involve real partnerships where there's mutual trust and a long-term outlook. Closely tied firms often share tasks at lower total cost than would be possible working at arm's length.

The partnership between AlliedSignal and Betz Laboratories, for example, shows the benefits of a good relationship. A while back, Betz was just one of several suppliers that sold Allied chemicals to keep the water in its plants from gunking up pipes and rusting machinery. But Betz didn't stop at selling commodity powders. Teams of Betz experts and Allied engineers studied each plant to find places where water was being wasted. In less than a year, a team in one plant found $2.5 million in potential cost savings. For example, by adding a few valves to recycle the water in a cooling tower, Betz was able to save 300 gallons of water a minute, resulting in savings of more than $100,000 a year and reduced environmental impact. Because of ideas like this, Allied's overall use of water treatment chemicals decreased. However, Betz sales to Allied doubled because it became Allied's only supplier of water chemicals.[15]

Relationships can involve many from both sides

As the Allied–Betz Laboratories collaboration shows, some buyer–seller relationships can involve multiple buying influence—more than just a purchasing agent and a salesperson. To develop effective solutions, those closest to the problems should be directly involved. This may mean bringing people together from accounting, finance, production, information systems, and/or other functional areas of both the buyer and seller firms.

Relationships may not make sense

Although close relationships can produce benefits, they are not always best. For buyers, long-term commitments can also reduce flexibility. When competition drives down prices and spurs innovation, customers may be better off letting suppliers compete for their business. It may not be worth the customer's investment to build a relationship for purchases that are not particularly

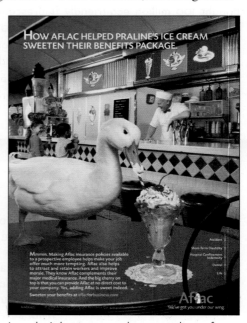

In today's business markets, suppliers of both goods and services are working to build closer relationships with their business customers—to meet needs better and create a competitive advantage. Aflac provides cost-effective insurance products that help companies attract and retain employees. Aflac builds close relationships with customers to assure they see these benefits. *Source: Used with permission of American Family Life Assurance Company of Columbus.*

Exhibit 6-7

Key Dimensions of Relationships in Business Markets

important or made that frequently. Besides that, close relationships take time and attention to build and manage.

Sellers don't usually want closer relationships with all of their customers either. Some customers may place orders that are too small or require so much special attention that the relationship would never be profitable for the seller. Also, in situations where a customer doesn't want a relationship, trying to build one may cost more than it's worth. Buyers and sellers should choose closer relationships where the benefits outweigh the costs.[16]

Relationships have many dimensions

Relationships are not "all or nothing" arrangements. Many firms may have a close relationship in some ways and not in others. Thus, it's useful to think about five key dimensions that help characterize most buyer–seller relationships: cooperation, information sharing, operational linkages, legal bonds, and relationship-specific adaptations. Purchasing managers for the buying firm and salespeople for the supplier usually coordinate the different dimensions of a relationship. However, as shown in Exhibit 6–7, close relationships often involve direct contacts between a number of people from other areas in both firms.[17]

Cooperation treats problems as joint responsibilities

In cooperative relationships, the buyer and seller work together to achieve both mutual and individual objectives. The two firms treat problems that arise as a joint responsibility. National Semiconductor (NS) and Siltec, a supplier of silicon wafers, found clever ways to cooperate and cut costs. Workers at the NS plant used to throw away the expensive plastic cassettes that Siltec uses to ship the silicon wafers. Now Siltec and NS cooperate to recycle the cassettes. This helps the environment and also saves more than $300,000 a year. Siltec passes along most of that to NS as lower prices.[18]

Shared information is useful but may be risky

Some relationships involve open sharing of information. This might include the exchange of proprietary cost data or demand forecasts or working jointly on new product designs. Information might be shared in discussions between personnel, or through information systems connected via the Internet, a key facet of B2B e-commerce. The electronic approach has a big advantage in that it is fast and easy to update the information. It also saves time. A customer can check detailed product specs or the status of a job on the production line without having to wait for someone to respond.

Information sharing can lead to better decisions and better planning. However, firms don't want to share information if there's a risk that a partner might misuse it. For example, one of General Motors' suppliers shared some of its planned technology to the automaker. It later found out that General Motors' purchasing chief showed blueprints of that secret technology to competing suppliers. Violations of trust in a relationship are an ethical matter and should be taken seriously.

Suppliers can be wary of sharing bad news with an important customer. For example, a supplier may wait to tell a customer of financial problems—and that can cause trouble. When Edscha, a German supplier of sunroofs to BMW, unexpectedly filed for insolvency, BMW had a crisis in the making. BMW was about to launch its new Z4 convertible—and Edscha supplied all the tops. Getting a new supplier up-to-speed would have taken six months, so BMW scrambled to support Edscha and launch the Z4 on schedule. A more trusting and open relationship might have provided more lead time to work out problems.[19]

Operational linkages share functions between firms

Operational linkages are direct ties between the internal operations of the buyer and seller firms. These linkages usually involve ongoing coordination of activities between the firms. Shared activities are especially important when neither firm, working on its own, can perform a function as well as the two firms can working together.

Business customers often require operational linkages to reduce total inventory costs, maintain adequate inventory levels, and keep production lines moving. On the other hand, keeping too much inventory is expensive. Providing a customer with inventory when it's needed may require that a supplier be able to provide **just-in-time delivery**—reliably getting products there *just* before the customer needs them. We'll discuss just-in-time systems in more detail in Chapter 11. For now, it's enough to know that closer relationships between buyers and sellers involve operational linkages that lower costs and increase efficiency.

Contracts spell out obligations

Many purchases in business markets are simple transactions. The seller's responsibility is to transfer title to goods or perform services, and the buyer's responsibility is to pay the agreed price. However, more complex relationships may be spelled out in detailed legal contracts. An agreement may apply only for a short period, but long-term contracts are also common.

For example, a customer might ask a supplier to guarantee a 6 percent price reduction for a particular part for each of the next three years and pledge to virtually eliminate defects. In return, the customer might offer to double its orders and help the supplier boost productivity.

Spain's EmpordAigua offers consulting services to help firms manage water quality and usage. EmpordAigua believes that no two drops of water are alike—nor are any two customers' water needs. So EmpordAigua develops close buyer–seller relationships based on cooperation, information sharing, and relationship-specific adaptations to develop custom water solutions for each of its client's needs. *Courtesy EmpordAigUA® Water Design & Technology.*

Sometimes the buyer and seller know roughly what is needed but can't fix all the details in advance. For example, specifications or total requirements may change over time. Then the relationship may involve **negotiated contract buying**, which means agreeing to contracts that allow for changes in the purchase arrangements. In such cases, the general project and basic price is described but with provision for changes and price adjustments up or down.

Some managers figure that even a detailed contract isn't a good substitute for regular good-faith reviews to make sure that neither party gets hurt by changing business conditions. Harley-Davidson used this approach when it moved toward closer relationships with a smaller number of suppliers. Purchasing executives tossed out detailed contracts and replaced them with a short statement of principles to guide relationships between Harley and its suppliers.

Specific adaptations invest in the relationship

Relationship-specific adaptations involve changes in a firm's product or procedures that are unique to the needs or capabilities of a relationship partner. Industrial suppliers often custom design a new product for just one customer; this may require investments in R&D or new manufacturing technologies. MetoKote, in its relationship with John Deere in the case at the beginning of this chapter, made a specific adaptation by building its coating plant right next door to Deere's factory.

Buying firms may also adapt to a particular supplier. When Apple designed MacBook computers with an Intel computer chip, it made it difficult later to change to a different chipmaker. However, buyers are often hesitant to make big investments that increase dependence on a specific supplier. Typically, they do it only when there isn't a good alternative—perhaps because only one or a few suppliers are available to meet a need—or if the benefits of the investment are clear before it's made.

Specific adaptations are usually made when the buying organization chooses to **outsource**—contract with an outside firm to produce goods or services rather than to produce them internally. Many firms have turned to outsourcing to cut costs—and that's why much outsourcing is handled by suppliers in countries where labor costs are lower. For example, many American companies are outsourcing production to firms in China and customer service to India.[20]

Powerful customer may control the relationship

Although a marketing manager may want to work in a cooperative partnership, that may be impossible with large customers who have the power to dictate how the relationship will work. Often a powerful customer negotiates lower prices from suppliers. For example, when Hewlett-Packard started selling personal computers through Walmart stores, it knew a rock-bottom price would be required. So it used its large sales volume to demand lower prices from its suppliers and the contract manufacturers that assembled the PCs. This helped H-P offer lower priced computers while maintaining higher profit margins than its competition.[21]

Buyers usually use several sources to spread their risk

Even if a marketing manager develops the best marketing mix possible and cultivates a close relationship with the customer, the customer may not give *all* of its business to one supplier. Buyers often look for several dependable sources of supply to protect themselves from unpredictable events such as strikes, fires, or floods in one of their suppliers' plants. For example, Western Digital, the world's largest provider of hard-disk drives, produces most of its drives in Thailand. When flooding in Thailand closed down many of Western Digital's manufacturing plants, it significantly tightened the world's supply of personal computers.[22]

Even when buyers don't want a single source of supply, a good marketing mix is still likely to win a larger share of the total business—which can prove to be very important. From a buyer's point of view, it may not seem like a big deal to give a particular supplier a 40 percent share of the orders rather than a 20 percent share. But for the seller that doubles their sales with that one customer—a 100 percent increase.

Buyers monitor supplier performance

Organizations routinely monitor supplier performance. Suppliers that fail to meet a buyer's performance expectations may be dropped. The process can be good for both buyer and supplier. Suppliers that perform well may find their share of a buyer's purchases go up. Suppliers that listen to feedback from customers can learn how to improve and increase the value of the relationship. Good buying organizations provide regular feedback to their suppliers without being asked—and smart suppliers listen closely and respond to them. Honda, for example, provides a monthly report card that details the supplier's performance in five areas: quality, delivery, quantity delivered, performance history, and any special incidents. The report fosters an ongoing dialogue between Honda suppliers about ways that both Honda and the supplier can work together to improve supplier performance.[23]

Variations in buying by customer type

We've been discussing aspects of relationships and buying approaches that generally apply with different types of customer organizations—in both the United States and internationally. However, it's also useful to have more detail about specific types of customers. Knowing the size, number, geographic location, and buying procedures of manufacturers, service firms, retailers, wholesalers, and governments help marketing managers to segment markets, identify targets, and create more effective marketing mixes.

Manufacturers Are Important Customers

LO 6.6

There are not many big ones

One of the most striking facts about manufacturers is how few there are compared to final consumers. This is true in every country. In the United States, for example, there are about 330,000 factories. The majority of these are quite small—more than half have less than 10 workers. In small plants, the owners often do the buying. And they buy less formally than buyers in the relatively few large manufacturing plants—which employ most of the workers and produce a large share of the value added by manufacturing. For example, only about 3 percent of all plants have 250 or more employees, yet they employ almost half of the production workers and produce about 60 percent of the value added by manufacturers.

Customers cluster in geographic areas

In addition to concentration by company size, industrial markets are concentrated in certain geographic areas. Internationally, industrial customers are concentrated in countries that are at the more advanced stages of economic development. From all the talk in the news about the United States shifting from an industrial economy to a service and information economy, you might conclude that the United States is an exception—that the industrial market in this country is shrinking. It is true that the number of people employed in manufacturing has been shrinking, but U.S. manufacturing output is higher than at any other time in the nation's history. The rate of growth, however, is fastest in countries where labor is cheap.[24]

Within a country, there is often further concentration of manufacturing in specific areas. In the United States, many factories are concentrated in big metropolitan areas—especially in New York, Pennsylvania, Ohio, Illinois, Texas, and California. There is also concentration by industry. In Germany, for example, the steel industry is concentrated in the Ruhr Valley. Similarly, U.S. manufacturers of high-tech electronics are concentrated in California's famous Silicon Valley near San Francisco.

Business data often classify industries

The products an industrial customer needs to buy depend on the business it is in. Because of this, sales of a product are often concentrated among customers in similar businesses. For example, apparel manufacturers are the main customers for zippers. Marketing managers must focus their marketing mixes on prospective customers who exhibit characteristics similar to their current customers.

Detailed information is often available to help a marketing manager learn more about customers in different lines of business. The U.S. government collects and publishes data by the **North American Industry Classification System (NAICS) codes**—groups of firms in similar lines of business. (NAICS is pronounced like "nakes.") The number of establishments, sales volumes, and number of employees—broken down by geographic areas—are given for each NAICS code. A number of

A firm like Alcoa Aluminum is likely to find that the majority of customers that use aluminum are concentrated within a few industries that it can identify by their North American Industry Classification System code number.
Left: Fotosearch/Getty Images; Top Right: Alejandro da Silva Farias/ Getty Images; Bottom Right: Thomas Trustschel/Getty Images

other countries collect similar data, and some of them try to coordinate their efforts with an international variation of the NAICS system. However, in many countries data on business customers are incomplete or inaccurate.

So let's take a closer look at how the NAICS codes work. The NAICS code breakdowns start with broad industry categories such as construction (23), manufacturing (31), retail trade (44), and so on (see Exhibit 6–8). Within each two-digit industry breakdown, much more detailed data may be available for three-digit industries (that is, subindustries of the two-digit industries). For example, within the two-digit manufacturing industry (code 31) there are manufacturers of food (311), leather (316), and others, including apparel manufacturers (315). Then each three-digit group of firms is further subdivided into more detailed four-, five-, and six-digit classifications. For instance, within the three-digit (315) apparel manufacturers there are four-digit subgroups for knitting mills (3151), cut and sew

Exhibit 6-8 Illustrative NAICS Code Breakdown for Apparel Manufacturers apparel (3152), and producers of apparel accessories (3159). Exhibit 6–8 illustrates that breakdowns become more detailed as you move to codes with more digits. However, detailed data (say, broken down at the four-digit level) aren't available for all industries in every geographic area. The government does not provide detail when only one or two plants are located in an area.

Many firms find their *current* customers' NAICS codes and then look at NAICS-coded lists for similar companies that may need the same goods and services. Other companies look at which NAICS categories are growing or declining to discover new opportunities.[25]

Producers of Services—Smaller and More Spread Out

LO 6.7

The service side of the U.S. economy is large and has been growing fast. Service operations are also growing in some other countries. There are many good opportunities to provide these service companies with the products they need to support their operations. But there are also challenges.

The United States has almost 6 million service firms—more than 17 times as many as it has manufacturers. Some of these are big companies with international operations. Examples include AT&T, Hilton Hotels, Prudential Insurance, PricewaterhouseCoopers, Wells Fargo, and Accenture. These firms have purchasing departments that are like those in large manufacturing organizations. But as you might guess given the large number of service firms, most of them are small—Evans Dental Group, North Coast Maid Service, and Affordable Computer Repair. They're also more spread out around the country than manufacturing concerns. Factories often locate where transportation facilities are good, raw materials are available, and it is less costly to produce goods in quantity. Service operations, in contrast, often have to be close to their customers.

Buying may not be as formal

Purchases by small service firms are often handled by whoever is in charge or their administrative assistant. This may be a doctor, lawyer, owner of a local insurance agency, hotel manager, or office manager. Suppliers who usually deal with purchasing specialists in large organizations may have trouble adjusting to this market. Personal selling is still an important part of promotion, but reaching these customers in the first place often requires more advertising. And small service firms may need much more help in buying than a large corporation.

Small service customers like Internet buying

Small service companies that don't attract much personal attention from salespeople often rely on e-commerce for many of their purchases. Purchases by small customers can add up—so for many suppliers these customers are an important target market. Increasingly suppliers cater to the needs of these customers with specially designed websites. A well-designed website can be efficient for both customers and suppliers. Customers can get information, place orders, or follow up with a call or e-mail for personal attention from a salesperson or customer service rep when it's needed.

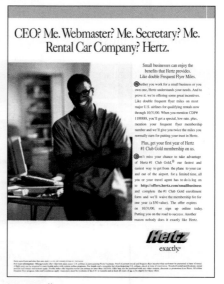

In a smaller service organization, purchases may be made by the person who is in charge rather than a person with full-time responsibility for purchasing.
© 2014 The Hertz Corporation.

Retailers and Wholesalers Buy for Their Customers

Most retail and wholesale buyers see themselves as purchasing agents for their target customers—remembering the old saying that "Goods well bought are half sold." For example, the buying specialist at Walgreens Drugstores who handles products targeted at ethnic consumers is a real expert. He knows what ethnic customers want and won't be persuaded by a sales rep for a manufacturer who can't provide it. He might also work closely with Televisa, a manufacturer of haircare and skincare products, to produce a line of products targeting the growing Hispanic market.

Committee buying is impersonal

Space in retail stores is limited, and buyers for retail chains simply are not interested in carrying every product that some salesperson wants them to sell. In an average week, 150 to 250 new items are offered to the buying offices of a large chain such as Safeway. If the chain accepted all of them, it would add 10,000 new items during a single year! Obviously, these firms need a way to deal with this overload. Most retailers carefully evaluate products. A product has to prove itself before gaining widespread adoption.

Decisions to add or drop lines or change buying policies may be handled by a *buying committee*. The seller still calls on and gives a pitch to a buyer—but the buyer does not have final responsibility. Instead, the buyer prepares forms summarizing proposals for new products and passes them on to the committee for evaluation. The seller may not get to present her story to the buying committee in person. This rational, almost cold-blooded, approach certainly reduces the impact of a persuasive salesperson. On the other hand, it may favor a firm that has hard data on how its whole marketing mix will help the retailer to attract and keep customers.

The entrepreneurs who started PenAgain (a uniquely shaped writing tool), for example, had to have more than a distinct product to get shelf space at Walmart. Their presentation to Walmart had to include hard data showing their marketing mix already worked well in other retail stores and evidence of their ability to supply the large quantities a retailer the size of Walmart would need. After that, Walmart would want first-hand data, offering to sell PenAgain in a limited number of stores before selling it in all their stores.[26]

Buyers watch computer output closely

Most larger firms use sophisticated computerized inventory replenishment systems. Scanners at retail checkout counters keep track of what goes out the door—and computers use these data to update the records. Even small retailers and wholesalers use automated control systems that create daily reports showing sales of every product. Buyers with this kind of information know, in detail, the profitability of the different competing products. If a product isn't moving, the retailer isn't likely to be impressed by a salesperson's request for more in-store attention or added shelf space.

Retailers see themselves as buying agents for their target customers—but they also have to determine what they can profitably sell. Retailers are attracted to well-known brands such as Dove because they know their consumers are more likely to buy brands they know. Chiquita wants to remind convenience stores that selling bananas can bring profits.
Left: DOVE® is a registered trademark of Mars, Incorporated. This trademark and advertisement are used with permission. Mars, Incorporated is not associated with McGraw-Hill Higher Education; Right: © 2014 Chiquita Brands L.L.C. All Rights Reserved.

Reorders are straight rebuys

Retailers and wholesalers usually carry a large number of products. A drug wholesaler, for example, may carry up to 125,000 products. Because they deal with so many products, most intermediaries buy their products on a routine, automatic reorder basis—straight rebuys—once they make the initial decision to stock specific items. Automatic computer ordering is a natural outgrowth of computerized checkout systems. Sellers to these markets must understand the size of the buyer's job and have something useful to say and do when they call.

The Government Market

Size and diversity

Some marketers ignore the government market because they think that government red tape is more trouble than it's worth. They probably don't realize how big the government market really is. Government is the largest customer group in many countries—including the United States. About 30 percent of the U.S. gross domestic product is spent by various government units. Different government units buy almost every kind of product. They run not only schools, police departments, and military organizations, but also supermarkets, public utilities, research laboratories, offices, hospitals, and even liquor stores. These huge government expenditures cannot be ignored by an aggressive marketing manager.

Competitive bids may be required

Government buyers in the United States are expected to spend money wisely—in the public interest—so their purchases are usually subject to much public review. To avoid charges of favoritism, most government customers buy by specification using a mandatory bidding procedure. Often the government buyer must accept the lowest bid that meets the specifications. You can see how important it is for the buyer to write precise and complete specifications. Otherwise, sellers may submit a bid that fits the specs but doesn't really match what is needed. By law, a government unit might have to accept the lowest bid—even for an unwanted product.

The approved supplier list

Specification and bidding difficulties aren't problems in all government orders. Items that are bought frequently—or for which there are widely accepted standards—are purchased routinely. The government unit simply places an order at a previously approved price. To share in this business, a supplier must be on the list of approved suppliers and agree on a price that will stay the same for a specific period—perhaps a year.[27]

Learning what government wants

In the United States, there are more than 89,527 local government units (school districts, cities, counties, and states) as well as many federal agencies that make purchases. Some firms sell directly to government agencies; others work with prime contractors that resell to the government. Both are good opportunities for many businesses. Often small and medium-size businesses find it easier to sell to prime contractors rather than win a contract with a large government agency. Potential suppliers should focus on the government units or prime contractors they want to cater to and learn the bidding methods of those units. Then, they should monitor websites where government contracts are advertised. Target marketing can make a big contribution

The City of San Jose worked with a number of suppliers when it built the Lake Cunningham Regional Skate Park. One of the city's vendors, California Skateparks of Upland, California, used 800 cubic yards of a special spray concrete mixture to create the park's bowls, halfpipes, and walls. To light the park evenly, without shadows, the city turned to Musco Lighting from Oskaloosa, Iowa, which lit the park with 10 50-foot poles, each bearing three 1500-watt fixtures. To give the park's 50,000 annual visitors a shady place to rest, Robert A. Bothman, Inc., from San Jose, California, created five planters that were filled with wildflowers, native grasses, and palms.
© Dave Lauridsen.

here—making sure the marketing mixes are well matched with the different bid procedures.

Because government agencies want to promote competition for their business, marketers are provided with a lot of information—in print form and online. The U.S. government has a central source and USA.gov is a great place to start. There are also resources at FedBizOpps. gov (www.fbo.gov), including videos, publications, and a search tool to find opportunities to fit a firm's strategy. The General Services Administration handles vendor contracts for off-the-shelf goods and services; information for vendors is available at www.gsa.gov. Every federal government agency has a separate office devoted to small businesses with direct links to prime contractors. Various state and local governments also offer guidance, as do government units in other countries.

Courtesy USA.gov.

Dealing with foreign governments

Foreign governments offer a good opportunity for some organizations. But sellers should recognize that selling to government units in foreign countries can be a real challenge, one that should be approached with caution. In many cases, a firm must get permission from the government in its own country to sell to a foreign government. Moreover, most government contracts favor domestic suppliers if they are available. Even if such favoritism is not explicit, public sentiment may make it very difficult for a foreign competitor to get a contract. Or the government bureaucracy may simply bury a foreign supplier in so much red tape that there's no way to win.

Is it unethical to "buy help"?

In some countries, government officials expect small payments (grease money) just to speed up processing of routine paperwork, inspections, or decisions from the local bureaucracy. Outright influence peddling—where government officials or their friends request bribe money to sway a purchase decision—is common in some markets. In the past, marketers from some countries have looked at such bribes as a cost of doing business. However, the **Foreign Corrupt Practices Act**, passed by the U.S. Congress in 1977, prohibits U.S. firms from paying bribes to foreign officials. A person who pays bribes, or authorizes an agent to pay them, can face stiff penalties. However, the law was amended in 1988 to allow small grease money payments if they are customary in a local culture. Since 1998, the law applies to foreign firms or foreign individuals who accept payments while in the United States. In recent years, prosecutions under this statute have increased thanks to more rigorous enforcement and greater cooperation with foreign governments. For example, in 2012 more than 80 firms were under investigation for violating the Foreign Corrupt Practices Act. This included Wal-Mart Stores, Inc., which was alleged to have bribed officials in Mexico to quickly obtain permits to open stores. The Sarbanes-Oxley Act of 2002 makes individual executives responsible for their company's financial disclosures; and a bribe mischaracterized as a legitimate expense may violate the law. Managers need to be careful and up-front about such payments.[28]

CONCLUSION

In this chapter, we examined organizational buying and how it differs from final consumer buying. We saw that organizational buyers rely heavily on economic factors and cost-benefit analysis to make purchase decisions. Organizational buyers generally prefer to avoid risk. This chapter showed how multiple influences are important in buying decisions—and how marketing managers must recognize and attend to the needs of all members of the buying center.

Chapter 6 introduced a three-step model of business and organizational buying. The first step—defining the problem—described how buyers recognize problems and then find solutions by determining buying needs. The second step—the decision-making process—examined three organizational buying processes: new-task buying, modified rebuy, and the straight rebuy. Each process involves different levels of information gathering, and this section reviewed how buyers gather information for buying. The third step—managing the buyer–seller relationship—looked at different aspects of these relationships in practice. Buying behavior and marketing opportunities may change when there's a close relationship between a supplier and a customer. There are different ways that a supplier can build close relationships with its customers. We identified key dimensions of relationships and their benefits and limitations.

We saw that organizational buyers buy for resale or to produce other goods and services—this group includes manufacturers, farmers, distributors, retailers, government agencies, and nonprofit organizations. The chapter concluded by providing insights about buying practices particular to manufacturers, service firms, intermediaries, and governments.

Understanding how organizations buy can help marketing managers identify logical dimensions for segmenting markets and developing marketing mixes. The unique nature of each product will likely require further adjustments in the mix. Different product classes are discussed in Chapter 8. Variations by product may provide additional segmenting dimensions to help a marketing manager fine-tune a marketing strategy.

WHAT'S NOW?

This chapter examined organizational buying. For some current real-world examples and learnings, check out *What's Now?* at www.learnthe4ps.com/whatsnow/c6

KEY TERMS

LO 6.8

business and organizational customers, 144

purchasing managers, 148

multiple buying influence, 149

buying center, 150

requisition, 150

purchasing specifications, 151

ISO 9000, 152

new-task buying, 152

straight rebuy, 152

modified rebuy, 152

white paper, 153

competitive bid, 153

vendor analysis, 153

just-in-time delivery, 158

negotiated contract buying, 159

outsource, 159

North American Industry Classification System (NAICS) codes, 160

Foreign Corrupt Practices Act, 165

QUESTIONS AND PROBLEMS

1. Review the John Deere case study that opens the chapter. From this case, identify examples of different key terms and concepts covered in the chapter. For example, when MetoKote built a paint plant right next door to John Deere's manufacturing plant, this was an example of a relationship-specific adaptation.

2. Review the John Deere case study that opens this chapter. Applying concepts from the chapter, what else could be done to build a more effective buyer–supplier relationship with MetoKote? How should John Deere manage a relationship with a supplier of cleaning supplies for its manufacturing plant? Offer some specific recommendations based on what you learned in this chapter.

3. In your own words, explain how the buying behavior of business customers in different countries may have been a factor in speeding the spread of international marketing.

4. Compare and contrast the buying behavior of final consumers and organizational buyers. In what ways are they most similar and in what ways are they most different?

5. Briefly discuss why a marketing manager should think about who is likely to be involved in the buying center for a particular purchase. Is the buying center idea useful in consumer buying? Explain your answer.

6. If a nonprofit hospital were planning to buy expensive MRI scanning equipment (to detect tumors), who might be involved in the buying center? Explain your answer and describe the types of influence that different people might have.

7. Describe the situations that would lead to the use of the three different buying processes for a particular product—lightweight bumpers for a pickup truck.

8. Why would an organizational buyer want to get competitive bids? What are some of the situations when competitive bidding can't be used?

9. How likely is it that each of the following would use competitive bids? (a) a small town that needs a road resurfaced, (b) a scouting organization that needs a printer to print its scouting handbook, (c) a hardware retailer that wants to add a new lawnmower line, (d) a grocery store

chain that wants to install new checkout scanners, and (e) a sorority that wants to buy a computer to keep track of member dues. Explain your answers.

10. Discuss the advantages and disadvantages of just-in-time supply relationships from an organizational buyer's point of view. Are the advantages and disadvantages merely reversed from the seller's point of view?

11. Explain why a customer might be willing to work more co-operatively with a small number of suppliers rather than pitting suppliers in a competition against one another. Give an example that illustrates your points.

12. Would a tool manufacturer need a different marketing strategy for a big retail chain such as Home Depot than for a single hardware store run by its owner? Discuss your answer.

13. How do you think a furniture manufacturer's buying habits and practices would be affected by the specific type of product to be purchased? Consider fabric for upholstered furniture, a lathe for the production line, cardboard for shipping cartons, and lubricants for production machinery.

14. Discuss the importance of target marketing when analyzing organizational markets. How easy is it to isolate homogeneous market segments in these markets?

15. Explain how NAICS codes might be helpful in evaluating and understanding business markets. Give an example.

16. Considering the nature of retail buying, outline the basic ingredients of promotion to retail buyers. Does it make any difference what kinds of products are involved? Are any other factors relevant?

17. The government market is obviously an extremely large one, yet it is often slighted or even ignored by many firms. Red tape is certainly one reason, but there are others. Discuss the situation and be sure to include the possibility of segmenting in your analysis.

18. Some critics argue that the Foreign Corrupt Practices Act puts U.S. businesses at a disadvantage when competing in foreign markets with suppliers from other countries that do not have similar laws. Do you think that this is a reasonable criticism? Explain your answer.

MARKETING PLANNING FOR HILLSIDE VETERINARY CLINIC

Appendix D (the Appendices follow Chapter 19) includes a sample marketing plan for Hillside Veterinary Clinic. Hillside decided to focus on final consumers and their pets rather than include organizational customers who might need veterinary care for animals. Such customers might range from dog breeders and farmers to animal protection shelters and law enforcement agencies who work with dogs. Would it be easy or hard for Hillside to expand its focus to serve customers who are not final consumers? Explain your thinking.

SUGGESTED CASES

5. Polymer Dynamics
6. Steel Solutions

MARKETING ANALYTICS: DATA TO KNOWLEDGE

CHAPTER 6 VENDOR ANALYSIS

CompuTech, Inc., makes circuit boards for personal computers. It is evaluating two possible suppliers of electronic memory chips.

The chips do the same job. Although manufacturing quality has been improving, some chips are always defective. Both suppliers will replace defective chips. But the only practical way to test for a defective chip is to assemble a circuit board and "burn it in"—run it and see if it works. When one chip on a board is defective at that point, it costs $2.00 for the extra labor time to replace it. Supplier 1 guarantees a chip failure rate of not more than 1 per 100 (that is, a defect rate of 1 percent). The second supplier's 2 percent defective rate is higher, but its price is lower.

Supplier 1 has been able to improve its quality because it uses a heavier plastic case to hold the chip. The only disadvantage of the heavier case is that it requires CompuTech to use a connector that is somewhat more expensive.

Transportation costs are added to the price quoted by either supplier, but Supplier 2 is further away so transportation costs are higher. And because of the distance, delays in supplies reaching CompuTech are sometimes a problem. To ensure that a sufficient supply is on hand to keep production going, CompuTech must maintain a backup inventory—and this increases inventory costs. CompuTech figures inventory costs—the expenses of finance and storage—as a percentage of the total order cost.

To make its vendor analysis easier, CompuTech's purchasing agent has entered data about the two suppliers on a spreadsheet. He based his estimates on the quantity he thinks he will need over a full year.

See Connect for the spreadsheet and questions needed to analyze this scenario.

CHAPTER SEVEN

Boston Globe/Getty Images.

Improving Decisions with Marketing Information

In 1946 Bill Rosenberg launched Industrial Luncheon Services, delivering meals, snacks, and coffee to factory workers in the Boston area. From his daily sales totals, Rosenberg knew his working class customers loved his coffee and doughnuts. Rosenberg thought a sit-down restaurant with these two menu items could be a success, and a few years later Dunkin' Donuts was born. Back then Dunkin' charged just 5 cents for one of its 52 varieties of doughnuts. Although Dunkin's 10 cent cup of coffee sounds like a bargain today, it was double the going rate. Nevertheless, customers saw its higher quality coffee—always served fast and hot—as a good value.

By 2005 Dunkin' had grown to 6,000 franchised locations in the United States and abroad. Coffee represented almost two-thirds of its sales; doughnuts and sandwiches each accounted for about 17 percent. Dunkin's flavored coffees, lattes, Chai, iced coffee, and other beverages put it in direct competition with Starbucks. With 90 percent of its stores in the northeastern United States, it saw a big opportunity for growth. Yet Dunkin's marketing managers wondered if they should change its marketing strategy to better fit evolving customer behavior, changing competition, and new target markets.

Dunkin' managers knew they had many options: for example, adding new sandwiches, offering catering and delivery services, and providing cozier seating. Copernicus Marketing conducted research and designed Dunkin's "store of the future." Product design software evaluated more than two billion combinations by varying portion sizes, exterior store design, interior music selection, and more. With data from a nationally representative sample of more than 1,000 customers and prospects, sales and costs were forecast for each combination and the most profitable options identified. This research guided the construction of experimental prototype stores—which emphasized Dunkin's quality coffee and its speed of service at the counter and drive-through window. When the new stores exceeded sales and profit targets, its managers knew they had a future direction.

Dunkin' Donuts knew it needed to better understand its loyal coffee drinkers—and those of its chief rival, Starbucks. So, the company paid dozens of its most dedicated customers to buy coffee at Starbucks—while simultaneously paying a similar number of Starbucks loyalists to come to Dunkin' Donuts.

After debriefing interviews, the two groups were found to be so different that Dunkin' researchers dubbed them "tribes."

What each tribe detested about its rival's store was exactly what made it love its usual outlet. For example, Starbucks' regulars found Dunkin' outlets boring, austere, and unoriginal. They didn't like that workers dumped standard amounts of milk and sugar in their drinks—they didn't feel special at Dunkin' Donuts. Although Dunkin' tribe members wanted newer looking stores, the Starbucks experience turned them off. All those laptop users made it hard to find a seat—and they wondered why coffee shops needed couches. They complained about Starbucks' higher prices and the slower speed of service. They didn't like Starbucks' "tall," "grande," and "venti" lingo; just give us "small," "medium," and "large" please! This exercise convinced Dunkin' that there were customers out there who wanted an alternative to Starbucks—and it could fine-tune a marketing strategy to provide it.

A psychographic survey offered further insight on the attitudes, values, and interests of Dunkin' tribe members. They're busy, love routine, prefer simple with no frills, and see themselves as down-to-earth folks without pretensions. One-third of Americans fit this profile, but these people are more common in the Midwest and South than in the Northeast. So Dunkin' quickly targeted new stores in cities in Ohio, Tennessee, and Florida. This research also guided the "America Runs on Dunkin'" advertising campaign featuring office and construction workers getting through their days with the chain's help.

Dunkin' Donuts' Executive Chef Jeff Miller (see picture) and his staff whip up innovative additions to the menu. But before these foods go to market they get input from customers. Dunkin' chefs developed a new line of hearty snacks for drive-through customers looking for an on-the-go snack. Focus groups liked the smoothies and hot flatbreads, but the tiny stuffed pinwheels did not satisfy their hunger. They liked it better when Dunkin' came back with larger size "bites" filled with pork and other ingredients.

Dunkin' encourages customer feedback and listens closely for ideas to fine-tune its marketing strategy. A group of its best customers serve on the Dunkin' Advisory Panel where they regularly complete online surveys and participate in online focus groups. The company also closely monitors its website and social media efforts—reading what Facebook fans and Twitter followers write and using analytical software to collect and analyze buzz on the Internet. Dunkin' knows why and how people come to its website.

Data even drives the precise location of each Dunkin' Donuts shop; a software program analyzes data on demographics, competition, and traffic patterns at the neighborhood level. This program predicted sales would increase at one store by adding a drive-through lane and moving the store just 100 yards—from one end of a strip mall to the other. After the move, sales jumped more than 50 percent.

Dunkin' Donuts wondered if the costs and discounts of a loyalty program would be offset by higher sales and profits. So they conducted an experiment. A group of customers' purchases were monitored before and after they received a prototype Dunkin' Donuts loyalty card.

After getting the card, customers visited Dunkin' 30 percent more often and spent 40 percent more. Decision made. Now more than 3 million customers have a DD Perks Rewards

card. The new cards bring in more data—data that Dunkin' uses to target sales promotions. With 60 percent of sales coming before 11 a.m., there are opportunities to grow sales later in the day. Therefore, DD Perks members who regularly visit Dunkin' in the morning are offered big discounts to come back for an afternoon snack—which often becomes a new habit.

Dunkin' is still growing—it has more than 11,000 stores in 36 countries. To keep growing, Dunkin' Donuts will keep collecting, analyzing, and acting on data for its marketing strategy planning, implementation, and control.[1]

LEARNING OBJECTIVES

The Dunkin' Donuts case shows that successful marketing strategies require information about potential target markets and their likely responses to marketing mixes—as well as information about competitors and other market environment variables. Managers also need information for implementation and control. Without good information, managers are left to guess—and in today's fast-changing markets, that invites failure. In this chapter, we discuss how marketing managers get the information that they need.

When you finish this chapter, you should be able to

1 Discuss marketing information systems.

2 Understand the scientific approach to marketing research.

3 Cite methods for collecting secondary and primary data.

4 Understand the role of observing, questioning, and using experimental methods in marketing research.

5 Understand the challenges to interpreting marketing research data.

6 Recognize how market research information aids marketing planning in international markets.

7 Understand important new terms (shown in red).

Effective Marketing Requires Good Information

LO 7.1

Information is a bridge to the market

To make good marketing decisions, managers need accurate information about what is happening in the market. They usually can't get all of the information they'd like, but part of their job is to find cost-effective ways to get the information that is imperative.

In this chapter, we'll focus on the two sources that marketing managers utilize for information to help them make better decisions. One source is **marketing research**—procedures that develop and analyze new information about a market. Marketing research involves a wide range of techniques, including Internet searches, customer surveys, experiments, direct observation of customers, and many more. Marketing managers often find that one-at-a-time marketing research projects can be too costly or take too long to get the desired information. So, in many companies, marketing managers also routinely get help from a **marketing information system (MIS)**—which is an organized way of continually gathering, accessing, and analyzing information that marketing managers need to make ongoing decisions.

Marketing managers may need marketing research, an MIS, or a combination of both to get the information they need to make decisions during any step in the marketing strategy planning process—or to improve implementation and control (see Exhibit 7–1).

Exhibit 7-1 Marketing Information Inputs to Marketing Strategy Planning Decisions

Marketing information systems
- Multimedia data
- Data warehouses
- Decision support systems
- Marketing models

Marketing research
- Role of research specialists
- Scientific method
- Steps in marketing research
  1. Define problem
  2. Analyze situation
  3. Gather problem-specific data
  4. Interpret the data
  5. Solve the problem

In this chapter, we'll discuss ways to make marketing research and an MIS more useful, and the key issues that marketing managers face in using them.

Big companies turn to marketing research specialists

Most large companies have a separate marketing research department to plan and manage research projects. People in these departments usually rely on outside specialists to carry out the work on particular projects. Further, they may call in specialized marketing consultants and marketing research organizations to take charge of a whole project.

Smaller companies usually don't have separate marketing research departments. They depend on their salespeople or managers to conduct what research they do. Non-profit organizations rarely did market research in the past, but more have begun to see its value and often use outside specialists.

IT and marketing cooperate to create the MIS

When it comes to setting up an MIS, a company usually turns to information technology (IT) experts. Sometimes this expertise resides in an organization's IT department. Even small firms may have a person who handles most of the technical work on its computer systems. Many small and large firms look to outside consultants and service providers for help with increasingly complex information systems.

Whether these activities are conducted inside the company or outsourced, it is very important that marketing managers be closely involved in the design of marketing research or an MIS. Specialists in research and IT can make sure that the technical aspects are handled correctly, but marketing managers need to make sure they can access information to guide marketing strategy planning or implementation and control.

Changes Are Under Way in Marketing Information Systems

Marketing managers for some companies make decisions based heavily on their own judgment—with very little hard data. The manager may not even know that he or she is about to make the same mistake that the previous person in that job already made!

When it's time to make a decision, they may wish they had more information. But by then it's too late, so they do without.

An MIS makes information available and accessible

Many firms realize that it doesn't pay to wait until you have important questions you can't answer. They anticipate the information they will need. They work to develop a continual flow of information that is available and quickly accessible from an MIS when it's needed.

We won't cover all of the technical details of planning for an MIS. But you should understand what an MIS is so you know some of the possibilities. We'll be discussing the elements of a complete MIS as shown in Exhibit 7–2. As part of that review, we'll highlight how new sources of data and technology are changing MIS use.

The big data explosion

Many of today's businesses are awash in data. Estimates suggest that organizations today process more than 1,000 times as much data as they did in the year 2000. The explosion of data comes as organizations collect and store more information from internal sources (for example, e-mails, spreadsheets, documents, financial reports, and clickstreams—which track customers as they move through a

Marketing managers have greater access to data and increasingly powerful software which makes it easier and less expensive for companies to gather, analyze, and access marketing information.

Exhibit 7–2 Elements of a Complete Marketing Information System company's website), external sources (for example, government sources such as the U.S. Census, social media websites such as Facebook and LinkedIn, and digital sensors placed on industrial equipment, automobiles, and shipping crates), and market research studies (for example, results from surveys and experiments). The amount of data that organizations collect doubles every two years—so the stored data available to marketing managers continues to grow. This explosion is often referred to as **big data**—data sets too large and complex to work with typical database management tools.[2]

"Data" from new sources

Part of that massive growth in data comes as marketing managers figure out how to collect and analyze new sources of data. For example, some companies have figured out how to determine emotions from facial expressions. Honda uses cameras and software to measure customer emotions while using a new product. Coca-Cola takes data from webcams that monitor consumer's facial expressions while watching its ads. Other companies have machines that analyze photos on sites such as Instagram. From a photo, software can identify a social media user's emotion, the activity they are engaged in, logos on their clothing, and products they might be carrying. The technology will allow companies to mine photos on Instagram and Facebook to learn more about products and customers. Smartphones track the owner of the phone's movement through the day as well as online search activity. Companies like Verizon Wireless sell that information to interested marketing companies. All of this data is collected and stored with the idea of learning more about customers and better serving up ads or products that capture their interest.[3]

Store data in a warehouse

An MIS organizes all of this incoming data and information into a **data warehouse**—a place where databases are stored so that they are available when needed. You can think of a data warehouse as an electronic library, where all of the information is indexed. With big data, firms have had to build larger data warehouses and find new ways to store, index, and access a wide variety of data.[4]

From data to information, knowledge, and wisdom

All that *data* in its raw form is not useful to a marketing manager. So an MIS includes software programs that convert the data to information that is useful to managers. Sales data becomes *information* when it provides answers to questions of "who," "what," "where," "how much," and "when." So for example, sales data might be presented in a table that shows the sales of different products over time and in different geographic locations—answering questions such as *Who is buying our product? Where do they live? How much do they buy? What products are they buying?*

Information becomes *knowledge* when it helps a marketing manager answer "how" and "why" questions. Marketing managers can combine their experience in a market with information to generate knowledge. Or, the marketing manager might use the information to design a new marketing research project to generate knowledge. *How did they decide to buy our product instead of the competition? Why did that Facebook post generate so many comments? Why did they wait so long to buy?*

For example, a marketing manager at Frito-Lay might have *information* indicating that customers in the northeast United States are not satisfied with a recently launched snack food. This might cause the marketing manager to engage in a marketing research project to find out the reasons (why) for the dissatisfaction—*knowledge*. As the marketing manager gains experience and understanding of why things happened in the past, she can put that together to build *wisdom* and better predict what will happen in the future. This helps the marketing manager to better evaluate possible marketing strategy decisions.[5]

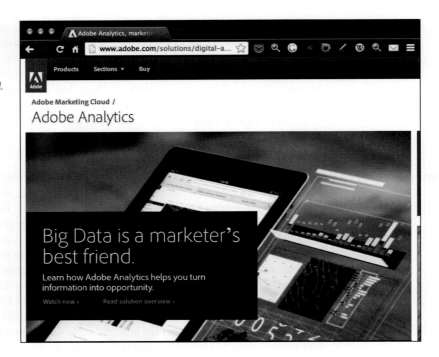

Many firms look to outside experts, like Adobe, to help them analyze and draw insights from big data.

Get more accurate information faster and easier

Accessing all the information in an MIS is not easy—especially with the wide variety of different types of data and information. Fortunately, advances in information technology have ushered in improvements in marketing information systems. With good search software, much of the information is instantly available, often just a mouse click away. Many firms, even small ones, have their own **intranet**—a system for linking computers *within* a company. An intranet works like the Internet. However, to maintain security, access to websites or data on an intranet is usually limited to employees. Even so, information can be searched and available on demand. Further, it's a simple matter to "publish" new information to a website as soon as it becomes available.

Decision support systems can convert information to knowledge

With so much information available, marketing managers look to software programs for aid in interpreting what they find in the MIS. It can be helpful to have a **decision support system (DSS)**—a computer program that makes it easy for a marketing manager to obtain and use information. These types of programs help marketing managers convert information into knowledge that allows them to make informed marketing strategy decisions. Let's look at a couple of types of decision support systems.

Marketing dashboards monitor the market

One way to interface with a data warehouse and DSS is through a **marketing dashboard**, which displays up-to-the-minute marketing data in an easy-to-read format—much like a car's dashboard shows the speedometer and fuel gauge. Marketing dashboards are usually customized to a manager's areas of responsibility. For example, a dashboard for a customer service manager at Verizon Wireless might show the percentage of customer calls dropped by cell towers, the location of repair trucks in the field, and the number of callers "on hold" waiting for customer service help. With early warning about potential problems, the manager can quickly make corrections. For example, a manager might call in extra customer service help if too many customers are "on hold."[6]

Information for planning, implementation, and control

Some decision support systems go even further—helping a marketing manager improve all aspects of their planning—blending individual Ps, combining the Four Ps into mixes, and developing and selecting plans. Further, they can monitor

What's Next? Big data predicts pop music hits

Forecasting the success of a new product can be a dicey proposition, but it's particularly challenging to anticipate the fickle tastes of teenage music junkies. Traditionally, the music industry relied on the intuition of record label executives. These music veterans traveled the country listening to acts in bars and clubs trying to find the next Beyoncé, Kanye West, or Taylor Swift. Record labels are motivated to find that next superstar—the top 1 percent of musicians earn about three quarters of all the recorded music revenue. Now big data is coming to the rescue—helping the music industry to better project that next hit song or star artist.

One company bringing data to this quest is Shazam. Shazam is a smartphone app that identifies music; the app listens to a brief sample of a song, compares it to a large database, and then tells the user the song title, artist, and album. Users think of Shazam as a handy way to find out the name of an unfamiliar tune, but music executives see it as a leading indicator of the next pop hit. With more than 20 million searches each day, Shazam gets a pretty good picture of what people don't yet recognize, but know they like.

Shazam helps a record label decide if it really has a hit on its hands. For example, Republic Records thought it might have a future star in SoMo—and that his first hit could be "Ride." So they tested the song in the small (population 63,000) town of Victoria, Texas, where just one radio station played "Ride." Soon it was the most tagged song on Shazam in Victoria, and they knew they had a hit. With added promotion, "Ride" later reached #20 on U.S. R&B charts. By adding critic reviews to search data, Shazam helps record labels decide where its promotional investment might get the best return.

Another music-related data collection venture, Next Big Sound (NBS), evolved from a student project in a Northwestern University entrepreneurship class. NBS scours the web for all kinds of music data—the number of plays a song has on Pandora or its digital downloads and the number of new Facebook likes or Twitter mentions of an artist. NBS puts this on a digital dashboard for its clients. Years before they became household names, NBS predicted stardom for Iggy Azalea, A$AP Rocky, and Macklemore & Lewis. NBS's Find product mines that data to identify obscure bands with breakout potential. NBS's patented "likelihood of success" algorithm predicts sales with 20% accuracy for 85% of artists—giving labels a much better idea about where to spend their promotion budgets. For example, NBS analysis showed that getting on Conan O'Brien's show offers a bigger boost than other late night shows.

Big data is being used in all parts of the music industry—from personalized radio to songwriting. Streaming music services such as Pandora and Spotify use proprietary algorithms to determine what songs a listener hears next. Hit Song Science analyzes a song for patterns in rhythm, chord progression, length, lyrics, and more—yielding a "hit score" from 1 to 10. Some songwriters revise songs to get higher scores.

Therein lies a concern of some in the music industry. Listeners already favor the familiar—"Today's Top Hits" and "Today's Hits" are the top stations on Spotify and Pandora. If songwriters and streaming services are copying what worked in the past, will a lot of good songs never get airplay? Are we likely to hear minor variations on what we already know and like? Will new and creative music break through? Will it get the chance? What does that mean for the future of creativity around music?[7]

the implementation of current plans, comparing results against plans and making necessary changes more quickly. Drawing on data on the demographics in a geographic area, customers' online behavior, or how a marketing strategy worked in the past, a DSS can make estimates using a marketing model. A **marketing model** is a statement of relationships among marketing variables. It enables a manager to look at the sales (and costs) expected with different types of promotion and select the marketing mix that is best for a particular target market.[8]

For example, auto parts retailer AutoZone uses data and marketing models to better meet customer needs. Although AutoZone offers more than a million items, each store can hold only about 40,000. So it helps to know what customers might be looking for when they come in. So AutoZone supplements sales histories at each outlet with outside databases. For example, it knows what types of cars are being driven in the local areas around each outlet. When all this data is plugged into a marketing model, AutoZone can decide just what products to carry at each store.[9]

Marketing managers want the ability to monitor the market and success of marketing strategies anywhere and anytime with marketing dashboards.

Although data drives many marketing strategy decisions, one might not expect "art" to be as predictable. But the ease and availability of big data is now influencing musicians, authors, and television producers and the products they produce. Check out how in "*What's Next?* Big data predicts pop music hits."

Many firms resist adding an MIS

Of course not every organization has a useful MIS. For some firms, the challenge and cost of setting up an MIS have made it a lower priority. In other organizations, marketing managers just aren't comfortable with data and don't press for an MIS.

These firms may be missing an opportunity. Falling data storage costs and low-cost, easy-to-use analytical tools are changing things quickly. It is now fairly easy and inexpensive to find out, for example, which web pages are most popular on a firm's website, how long visitors stay at each page, how they came to the page, and much more. The free program, Google Analytics, makes this analysis inexpensive and easy.

The Scientific Method and Marketing Research

LO 7.2

Marketing research—combined with the strategy planning framework we discussed in Chapter 2—can also help marketing managers make better decisions.

Marketing research is guided by the **scientific method**, a decision-making approach that focuses on being objective and orderly in *testing* ideas before accepting them. With the scientific method, managers don't just *assume* that their intuition is correct. Instead, they use their intuition and observations to develop **hypotheses**—educated guesses about the relationships between things or about what will happen in the future. Then they test their hypotheses before making final decisions.

A manager who relies only on intuition might introduce a new product without testing consumer response. But a manager who uses the scientific method might say, "I think (hypothesize) that consumers currently using the most popular brand will prefer our new product. Let's run some consumer tests. If at least 60 percent of the consumers prefer our product, we can introduce it in a regional test market. If it doesn't pass the consumer test there, we can make some changes and try again." With this approach, decisions are based on evidence, not just hunches.

The scientific method forces an orderly research process. Some managers don't carefully specify what information they need. They blindly move ahead—hoping that research will provide "the answer." Other managers may have a clearly defined problem or question but lose their way after that. These hit-or-miss approaches waste both time and money.

Five-Step Approach to Marketing Research

The **marketing research process** is a five-step application of the scientific method that includes:

1. Defining the problem
2. Analyzing the situation
3. Getting problem-specific data
4. Interpreting the data
5. Solving the problem

Exhibit 7–3 shows the five steps in the process. Note that the process may lead to a solution before all of the steps are completed. Or as the feedback arrows show, researchers may return to an earlier step if needed. For example, the interpreting step may point to a new question—or reveal the need for additional information—before a final decision can be made.

Exhibit 7–3 Five-Step Scientific Approach to Marketing Research Process

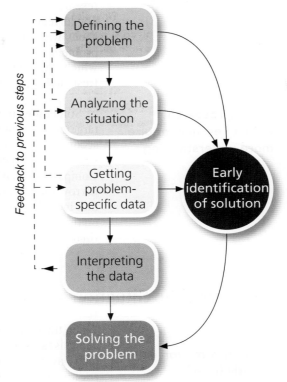

Effective research usually requires cooperation

Good marketing research requires cooperation between researchers and marketing managers. Researchers must be sure their research focuses on real problems.

Marketing managers must be able to explain what their problems are and what kinds of information they need. They should be able to communicate with specialists in the specialists' language. Marketing managers may only be "consumers" of research, but they should be informed consumers—able to explain exactly what they want from the research. They should also know about some of the basic decisions made during the research process so they know the limitations of the findings.

For this reason, our discussion of marketing research won't emphasize mechanics but rather how to plan and evaluate the work of marketing researchers.[10]

Defining the Problem—Step 1

Defining the problem is often the most difficult step in the marketing research process. But it's important for the objectives of the research to be clearly defined. The best research job on the wrong problem is wasted effort.

Pinpointing and identifying the problem is half the battle

Our strategy planning framework is useful for guiding the problem definition step. It can help the researcher identify the real problem area and what information is needed. Do we really know enough about our target markets to work out all of the Four Ps? Before deciding how to position our product, do we understand our competitor's strengths and weaknesses? Do we know enough to decide what celebrity to use in an ad or how to handle the price war in New York City or Tokyo? If not, we may want to do research rather than rely on intuition.

Don't confuse problems with symptoms

The problem definition step sounds simple—and that's the danger. It's easy to confuse problems with symptoms.

Marketers for Kiwi shoe polish encountered this situation. Marketing managers blamed sluggish sales on a lack of innovation in shoe polish. So Kiwi managers conducted a number of consumer studies on the problem of how to improve its polish. Yet none of the new product ideas clicked with consumers. Things changed when a new CEO realized that the slow sales and lack of interest in new polish products was just a symptom of the fact that today's footwear is made less from leather and more from synthetic materials. Today's shoes need less polish. So the CEO changed the focus of research to another problem—figure out what feet- and footwear-related needs were not currently being met. That research showed that having comfortable, fresh-smelling shoes was a top priority for women. Further research focusing on how to solve that problem led to the development of several new products, including Kiwi Fresh'ins, which are lightly scented disposable and ultrathin shoe inserts that keep feet feeling fresh and comfortable all day.[11]

Setting research objectives may require more understanding

Sometimes the research objectives are very clear. A manager wants to know if the targeted households have tried a new product and what percent of them bought it a second time. But research objectives aren't always so simple. The manager might also want to know *why* some didn't buy or whether they had even heard of the product. Companies rarely have enough time and money to study everything. A manager must narrow the research objectives. One good way is to develop a list of research questions that includes all the possible problem areas. Then the manager can consider the items on the list more completely—in the situation analysis step—before narrowing down to final research objectives.

Analyzing the Situation—Step 2

LO 7.3

What information do we already have?

When the marketing manager thinks the real problem has begun to surface, a situation analysis is useful. A **situation analysis** is an informal study of what information is already available in the problem area. It can help define the problem and specify what additional information, if any, is needed.

The situation analysis may begin with quick research—perhaps an Internet search; a closer look at information in an MIS; and phone calls or informal talks with people familiar with the industry, problem, or situation.

Let's consider a situation facing the marketing manager for the Hershey's candy company. She reviews last month's sales and finds that sales in the Chicago region are down by 5 percent, which concerns her. She could begin a situation analysis by digging deeper into the MIS and discover that sales of Hershey chocolate bars at one large grocery store chain are down by 25 percent. Otherwise sales in this region are up. Her next step might be an e-mail or phone call to the salesperson who calls on this grocery store chain. A phone call might reveal that last month the store had a big promotion going with a competitor's candy bars. Through this type of situation analysis, you can see that the marketing manager turned data into information and knowledge—she now knows why sales are down. This type of analysis might lead to an early solution—perhaps talking with the salesperson about how to set up a future promotion to try to gain back lost sales.

Situation analysis helps educate a researcher

The situation analysis is especially important if the marketing manager is dealing with unfamiliar areas or if the researcher is a specialist who doesn't know much about the management decisions to be made. They *both* must be sure they understand the problem area—including the nature of the target market, the marketing mix, competition, and other external factors. Otherwise, the researcher may rush ahead and make costly mistakes or simply discover facts that management already knows. The following case illustrates this danger.

A marketing manager at the home office of a large retail chain hired a research firm to do in-store interviews to learn what customers liked most, and least, about some of

Exhibit 7-4   Examples of Sources, Techniques, and Tools for Gathering Secondary and Primary Data

All data types

Secondary data

Inside company   Review company files, intranet, reports. Search marketing information systems. Analyze sales and cost data.

Outside company   Search the Internet, library, and government databases. Talk to researchers at universities and private research organizations.

Primary data

Observation   Use video to observe customers shopping. Track consumer clicks on a website. Purchase loyalty card data from retailers.

Questioning   Conduct focus group or in-depth interviews with customers to learn their needs. Use online, phone, or surveys of customers to measure customer satisfaction.

its stores in other cities. Interviewers diligently filled out their questionnaires. When the results came in, it was apparent that neither the marketing manager nor the researcher had done their homework. No one had even talked with the local store managers! Several of the stores were in the middle of some messy remodeling—so all the customers' responses concerned the noise and dust from the construction. The research was a waste of money.

Secondary data may provide the answers—or some background

The situation analysis should also find relevant **secondary data**—information that has been collected or published already. Later, in Step 3, we will cover **primary data**—information specifically collected to solve a current problem. Too often researchers rush to gather primary data when much relevant secondary information is already available—at little or no cost (see Exhibit 7–4)!

Much secondary data are available

Ideally, much secondary data are already available from the firm's MIS. Data that have not been organized in an MIS may be available from the company's files and reports. Secondary data also are available from libraries, trade associations, government agencies, and private research organizations; increasingly, these organizations put their information online. So one of the first places a researcher should look for secondary data is on the Internet.

Search the web better

Marketing managers can find a treasure trove of useful information on the Internet. It's all readily accessible from a computer, tablet, or smartphone. But available is not the same as reliable. Anyone can post anything on the Internet. So, as with any other research source, you should carefully evaluate the accuracy of Internet sources.

The key to the Internet is finding what's needed. If you have a pretty clear idea about what you are seeking, search engines such as Google are a good place to start. A major problem is that searches often identify too many irrelevant sources. There are techniques to getting better search results. If you have not had formal training on Internet search, you might look for an online tutorial to sharpen your search skills. At Google Search Education Online (www.powersearchingwithgoogle.com) you can learn how search works, search tips and tricks, and more. Check it out!

But don't stick to one search engine. Each search engine uses a different algorithm. Although many people default to Google, other search engines, including Bing, Yahoo,

DuckDuckGo, and Dogpile can yield different results. Also, when searching for international information, use a search engine's international platform for better results. Google has sites tailored to different countries—google.co.uk (for the United Kingdom) or Google.co.jp (for Japan), for examples.

Monitor chatter on the web

Sometimes it can be useful to review or monitor what others are saying about your company or its products. There are useful tools that allow a marketing manager to quickly access what is being said online. For example, a marketing manager can simply enter a brand name at search.twitter.com or socialmention.com to find tweets, blog posts, comments, and other online mentions of that brand. By scanning these online posts, a marketing manager can get a sense of how customers feel about the brand. Social Mention takes this a step further and aggregates all kinds of content from users—bookmarks, blog posts, Twitter, Facebook, and many more. Social Mention's software automatically analyzes all of these sources and performs a *sentiment analysis* that categorizes each mention as positive, negative, or neutral.

These monitoring tools are alluring; they generate a lot of information very quickly and many are free. Yet this information is selective—choosing Internet users who choose to be vocal—and may not accurately reflect the sentiment of the target market. When Skittles launched a new website, its marketing managers were alarmed by early criticism of the site in social media outlets including blogs, Facebook, and Twitter. When Skittles managers tapped a broader set of customers, they found little need for concern.

> ### Online Toolkit
>
> Marketing managers like to know what is being said online about their brand—and their competitors'. SocialMention is a service that searches social media and aggregates the content it finds. Go to **www.socialmention.com** and compare three activity trackers. Conduct three separate searches using "Fitbit," "Garmin Vivosmart," and "Acer Liquid Leap"—for each, search in "All." Which activity tracker has the most positive sentiment? Negative sentiment? What is the ratio of positive to negative sentiment for each? Click on "negative" for each to learn the reasons for negative comments. Look at the measures of strength, sentiment, passion, and reach (hover over each to learn what it means) for each brand. How could this information be used by a marketing manager for Fitbit?

However, online monitoring may provide a "head's up" about consumer attitudes or problems. If Kryptonite had monitored the web, it might have responded more quickly to YouTube videos showing how easy it was to pick its bicycle locks. When the videos went viral, the company's reputation was badly damaged.[12]

Government data are inexpensive

Federal and state governments publish data on many subjects. Government data are often useful in estimating the size of markets. In Chapters 3 and 5 we gave a number of examples of the different types of data that are available. Almost all government data are immediately usable in inexpensive print and digital publications, on websites, and in downloads ready for further analysis.

Sometimes it's more practical to use summary publications with links or references that lead to more detailed reports. For the U.S. market, the United States Census Bureau Topics page (http://www.census.gov/topics.html) and its Data and Statistics page (www.usa.gov/Topics/Reference-Shelf/Data.shtml) are good starting places. Another useful summary reference is the *Statistical Abstract of the United States,* which provides a summary of statistics on the social, political, and economic organization of the United States—though it must be purchased or accessed through a library. Similarly, the *United Nations Statistical Yearbook* is one of the best summaries of worldwide data; it can be downloaded in PDF format (http://unstats.un.org/unsd/syb/).

Secondary data are very limited on some international markets. However, most countries with advanced economies have government agencies that help researchers get the data they need. For example, *Statistics Canada* (www.statcan.gc.ca/) compiles a great deal of information on the Canadian market. *Eurostat* (http://ec.europa.eu/eurostat), the statistical office for the European Union countries, offers many publications packed with data on Europe, and data.australia.gov.au is an online source for the Australian government's public information datasets. In the United States, data.gov is an initiative to make a wide variety of government data more readily accessible. Some city and state governments have similar agencies for local data.

Situation analysis yields a lot—for very little	The virtue of a good situation analysis is that it can be very informative and takes little time. It's also inexpensive compared with more formal research efforts—like a large-scale survey. A phone, access to the Internet, and time might be all a marketing manager needs to gather a lot of insight. Situation analysis can help focus further research or even eliminate the need for it entirely. The situation analyst is really trying to determine the exact nature of the situation and the problem. This can lead the researcher back to Step 1, defining the problem, to an early identification of the solution, or to identifying problem-specific data needs.
Determine what else is needed	At the end of the situation analysis, you can see which research questions—from the list developed during the problem definition step—remain unanswered. Then you have to decide exactly what information you need to answer those questions and how to get it. This may require discussion between technical experts and the marketing manager. Often companies use a written **research proposal**—a plan that specifies what information will be obtained and how—to be sure no misunderstandings occur later. The research plan may include information about costs, what data will be collected, how it will be collected, who will analyze it and how, and how long the process will take.

Getting Problem-Specific Data—Step 3

LO 7.4 **Gathering primary data**	There are different methods for collecting primary data. Which approach to use depends on the nature of the problem and how much time and money are available. In most primary data collection, the researcher tries to learn what customers think about some topic or how they behave under some conditions. There are two basic methods for obtaining information about customers: *questioning* and *observing*. Questioning can be qualitative or quantitative; observing can take many forms.
Qualitative questioning— open-ended with a hidden purpose	**Qualitative research** seeks in-depth, open-ended responses, not yes or no answers. The researcher tries to get people to share their thoughts on a topic—without giving them many directions or guidelines about what to say. One qualitative research method uses *non-directive interviews,* where an interviewer asks questions that encourage the interviewee to provide details. For example, a researcher might ask, "Please tell me about your last grocery shopping trip." Whereas some respondents talk about their preparation for the trip (preparing a list), another might talk about characteristics of the store, and another about prices and selection. Follow-up questions might just ask the respondent to elaborate. The real advantage of this approach is *depth*. Each person can be asked follow-up questions so the researcher really understands what *that* respondent is thinking. The depth of the qualitative approach gets at the details—even if the researcher needs a lot of judgment to summarize it all.
Focus groups stimulate discussion	One widely used form of qualitative questioning in marketing research is the **focus group interview**, which involves simultaneously interviewing 6 to 10 people in an informal group setting. A focus group also uses open-ended questions, but here an interviewer seeks group interaction—to stimulate thinking and get immediate reactions. Focus groups can be conducted in-person or online. MOD-PAC, a large printing company, faced a problem: business from its traditional large customers was drying up. MOD-PAC managers wanted to know if there were niche markets willing to buy printing services over the Internet. So they conducted online focus groups, each with prospects from a different target market. The focus groups helped MOD-PAC managers see that each group had different needs and used different terms to discuss its problems. Each focus group also indicated that there was interest in buying printing services online. In response, MOD-PAC developed its "Print Lizard" website; the home page uses tabs to route customers from different segments to the part of the site that caters to their specific needs.[13]

Online communities and panels as well as webcam interviews may be used to conduct qualitative or quantitative research.

Online focus groups help offset some of the limitations of traditional face-to-face focus groups. Participants who meet online usually feel freer to express their honest thoughts—and an aggressive individual is less likely to dominate the group. Regardless of how a focus group is conducted, conclusions reached from a session usually vary depending on who watches it. A typical problem—and serious limitation—with qualitative research is that it's hard to measure the results objectively. The results seem to depend largely on the viewpoint of the researcher. In addition, people willing to participate in a focus group—especially those who talk the most—may not be representative of the broader target market.

Focus groups can be conducted quickly and at relatively low cost—on average about $4,000 each. This is part of their appeal. But focus groups are probably being overused. It's easy to fall into the trap of treating an idea arising from a focus group as a "fact" that applies to a broad target market. To avoid this trap, some researchers use qualitative research to prepare for quantitative research. Qualitative research can provide good ideas—hypotheses. But we often need other approaches—based on more representative samples and objective measures—to test the hypotheses.

Structured questioning gives more objective results

When researchers use identical questions and response alternatives, they can summarize the information quantitatively. Samples can be larger and more representative, and various statistics can be used to draw conclusions. For these reasons, most survey research is **quantitative research**—which seeks structured responses that can be summarized in numbers, such as percentages, averages, or other statistics. For example, a marketing researcher might calculate what percentage of respondents have tried a new product and then figure an average score for how satisfied they were.

Fixed responses speed answering and analysis

Survey questionnaires usually provide fixed responses to questions to simplify analysis of the replies. This multiple-choice approach also makes it easier and faster for respondents to reply. Simple fill-in-a-number questions are also widely used in quantitative research. Fixed responses are also more convenient for computer analysis, which is how most surveys are analyzed.

Surveys come in many forms

Decisions about what specific questions to ask and how to ask them usually depend on how respondents will be contacted—by mail, e-mail, on the phone, or in person. What question and response approach is used may also affect the survey. There are many possibilities. For example, whether the survey is self-administered or handled by an interviewer, the questionnaire may be on paper or online. The online survey can be programmed to skip certain questions, depending on answers given. Online surveys also allow the researcher to show pictures or play audio/video clips (for example, to get reactions to a television ad).

Mail and online surveys are common and convenient

A questionnaire distributed by mail or online is useful when extensive questioning is necessary. Respondents can complete the questions at their convenience. They may be more willing to provide personal information—because a questionnaire can be completed anonymously. But the questions must be simple and easy to follow because no interviewer is there to help. If the respondent is likely to be a computer user, a questionnaire on a website can include a help feature with additional directions for people who need them.

A big problem with questionnaires is that many people don't complete them. The widespread use of surveys means that many are now ignored. The **response rate**—the percentage of people contacted who complete the questionnaire—is often low and respondents may not be representative. Mail and online surveys are economical if a large number of people respond. But they may be quite expensive if the response rate is low. Worse, the results may be misleading if the respondents are not representative. For example, people who complete online questionnaires tend to be younger and better educated than the population as a whole.[14]

Online surveys are often used to measure customer satisfaction—often soon after transacting business with an organization. Many retailers have a code on a receipt to encourage a shopper to fill out an online survey. Response rates are low as most shoppers don't remember to complete the survey.

Some airlines are getting the survey part right, seeing 10 to 20 percent response rates to e-mailed surveys. Most airlines send at least some fliers in an e-mail with a link to a survey shortly after a flight. And airlines are learning from and acting on

Online Toolkit

Survey Monkey is one of several websites that host and help you create an online survey. Go to Survey Monkey's website (**www.surveymonkey.com**) and click on the "How It Works" link. Scroll down and click around to learn more about how the product works. What are some advantages of using Survey Monkey versus hiring an outside firm to develop a survey? What are some disadvantages? What types of research problems might be addressed with this type of survey?

Southwest uses surveys and other types of research to "listen" to customer inputs. It also has a blog at www.blogsouthwest.com where it encourages customers and employees to share their opinions. For example, when Southwest changed how its frequent flyer loyalty program worked, the blog allowed customers to ask questions and comment on the change. *Both images: © 2015 Southwest Airlines Co. All Rights Reserved.*

these surveys. For example, they know that on-time performance is the biggest driver to customer satisfaction. They also discovered that a service failure (lost bags or delayed flight) can be an opportunity; if the airline handles the problem quickly and keeps travelers informed, customer satisfaction doesn't suffer. Insights like these have improved the experiences airlines deliver.[15]

Surveys have limitations. Sometimes it takes a while to compile data—though online surveys are faster. It can be difficult to get respondents to expand on particular points in mail or online surveys. In markets where illiteracy is a problem, it may not be possible to get any response. In spite of these limitations, the convenience and economy of self-administered surveys makes them popular.

Telephone surveys—fast but maybe not trustworthy

Telephone interviews can be effective for getting quick answers to simple questions or when there is a need to probe and really learn what the respondent is thinking. With computer-aided telephone interviewing, answers are immediately recorded on a computer, resulting in fast data analysis.

Unfortunately, many respondents simply don't answer the phone when they don't recognize the number—or refuse to participate in a phone survey. A recent study found that only 9 percent of households initially contacted actually completed a survey—down from 36 percent in the late 1990s. Because of these concerns, telephone survey use is in decline.

Personal interview surveys—can be in-depth

A personal interview survey is usually much more expensive per interview than online, mail, or telephone surveys. But it's easier to get and keep the respondent's attention when the interviewer is right there. The interviewer can also help explain complicated directions and perhaps get better responses. For these reasons, personal interviews are commonly used for research on business customers. To reduce the cost of locating consumer respondents, interviews are sometimes done at a store or shopping mall. This is called a mall intercept interview because the interviewer stops a shopper and asks for responses to the survey.

Researchers have to be careful that having an interviewer involved doesn't affect the respondent's answers. Sometimes people won't give an answer they consider embarrassing. Or they may try to impress or please the interviewer. Further, in some cultures people don't want to give any information. For example, many people in Africa, Latin America, and Eastern Europe are reluctant to be interviewed. This is also a problem in many low-income, inner-city areas in the United States; even Census Bureau interviewers have trouble getting cooperation.[16]

Market research online communities combine qualitative and quantitative research methods

The Internet enables firms to explore and use a variety of research techniques. One technique combines qualitative and quantitative approaches in private online communities. A **market research online community (MROC)** is an online group of participants who are joined together by a common interest and who participate in ongoing research. Online communities are recruited to fit a desired psychographic, lifestyle, or demographic profile and may be comprised of 50 to several hundred members. Members spend months, possibly years, online together brainstorming ideas and conversing with other customers and the firm's marketing managers. Communities often include online focus groups and question-and-answer sessions, as well as quantitative approaches such as polls and surveys.

Hallmark Cards is one of the pioneers in this area. In the "Hallmark Idea Exchange," an online group of 200 mothers of young children are asked about everything from Hallmark's merchandising strategy to its pricing. Participants meet for at least a half hour each week and discuss their wants, needs, and preferences. Hallmark marketing managers stimulate discussion of relevant topics by posting questions. Sometimes they take polls to get a wider range of opinions on what it thinks are some of the best ideas. Hallmark Idea Exchange generates at least 10 to 15 concrete ideas each month.

Marketing managers need to be cautious when gathering data online. "Tricia," that 41-year-old mother from Wisconsin, may actually be "Jake," a 24-year-old bartender in Oregon who is just looking to score a few free gift cards or some extra cash by joining an online community. Nevertheless, with careful monitoring online communities can provide valuable insights.[17]

Questioning has limitations

Questioning—whether qualitative or quantitative—has its limitations. Respondents sometimes give answers that they think the questioner wants to hear, or they may not accurately recall past events. When that is the case, observing may be more accurate or economical.

Observing—what you see is what you get

Observing—as a method of collecting data—focuses on a well-defined problem. Here we are not talking about the casual observations that may stimulate ideas in the early steps of a research project. With the observation method, researchers try to see or record what the subject does naturally. They don't want the observing to *influence* the subject's behavior.

For example, marketing managers for Heinz Ketchup knew they had an opportunity if they could make it easier to eat French fries while driving. To learn more, marketing managers sat behind a one-way mirror and watched consumers sitting in minivans put ketchup on fries, burgers, and chicken nuggets during a simulated driving experience. They saw some people tear the corners off packets with their teeth and others squirt ketchup in their mouth before adding fries. Insights from this research fueled development of Heinz "Dip and Squeeze" ketchup packets, which can be squeezed

© Fortunato M. Ramin.

from one end like the traditional foil pouch or opened by peeling back the lid, for those who prefer dipping. Consumers like the new packaging and fast-food restaurants are selling more French fries out of the drive-through window.[18]

Ethnographic research looks at customers in their own environment

Ethnographic research has roots in anthropology, which studies different cultures by observing participants in their natural habitat. In marketing research, ethnography involves studying customers in their homes or at work.

Video cameras can be useful for ethnography because subjects often don't know their behavior is being recorded. Some researchers use this technique to study the routes

Ethnographic research into the grooming habits of people in rural China helped P&G better understand these customers needs. For example, the relative scarcity of water means women might have only a few cups of water to rinse hair that extends to the middle of their backs. P&G developed a leave-in hair conditioner that required no rinsing. It also created face soaps and hair dyes requiring little or no water.
Benjamin Lowy/Getty Images.

consumers follow through a store or how they select products. A dog food manufacturer put video cameras on the pet food aisle in supermarkets to learn more about how people choose dog food and treats. The videos showed that kids often picked the treats, but that the kids' parents chose the food. The videos also revealed that kids couldn't reach treats when they were on higher shelves. Sales increased when the treats were moved to lower shelves.[19]

Bloomberg/Getty Images.

Walk a mile in the customer's shoes

Sometimes the best way to observe a customer is for a marketing manager to become a customer. By calling his firm's own customer service number and pretending to be a customer, a marketing manager can discover how long it takes someone to answer the phone—or the ability of a customer service rep to politely and efficiently solve a problem.

Marketing managers at Walgreens drugstores wanted to better understand the challenges facing senior citizens—an important and growing target market. So they donned glasses that blurred vision and wore large rubber gloves that simulated arthritic hands. After experiencing firsthand the difficulties facing seniors, Walgreens managers began to use larger print in the weekly circular and installed call buttons near heavy items such as bottled water and laundry detergent.[20]

Observing is common in advertising research

Observation methods are common in advertising research. For example, Nielsen Media Research (www.nielsenmedia.com) uses a device called the "people meter" that adapts the observation method to television audience research. Individuals wear the device which detects hidden audio tones in a TV or radio broadcast. Of course the device cannot track whether someone is actually listening to or watching an ad.[21]

Observing website visitors

Website analysis software allows marketing managers to observe customer behavior at a firm's website. For example, there are tools that help marketing managers understand how a customer came to a website—was it the keyword used in a Google search, a response to an e-mail promotion, or a link from an online review site? Reports show the series of clicks made by visitors and how long they stayed on each page. This information can help marketing managers make changes to the site so that it attracts the right customers and offers useful information so they stay and make purchases.

Online retailer Shipwreck Beads wanted to promote a summer sale of fire-polished beads, so it e-mailed 76,000 customers and placed banner ads on the websites for *BeadStyle* and *Bead and Button* magazines. Website analysis tools showed which promotions and which keywords generated the most leads. Because the answers were available very quickly, the firm revised the advertising copy to include more instances of the phrase "fire-polished beads." This simple change improved placement on search pages and, within a month, hits to its website increased fourfold.

Checkout scanners see a lot

Computerized scanners at retail checkout counters help researchers collect very specific, and useful, information. Often this type of data feeds directly into a firm's MIS. Managers of a large chain of stores can see exactly what products have sold each day and how much money each department in each store has earned. But the scanner also has wider applications for marketing research.

Information Resources, Inc. (www.infores.com) and ACNielsen (www.acnielsen.com) use **consumer panels**—a group of consumers who provide information on a continuing basis. Whenever a panel member shops for groceries, he or she gives an ID card to the clerk, who scans the number. Then the scanner records every purchase—including brands, sizes, prices, and any coupons used. In a variation of this approach, consumers use a handheld scanner to record purchases once they get home. Sometimes members of a panel answer questions and the answers are merged with the scanner data.

Data captured by electronic scanners are equally important to e-commerce in business-to-business markets. Increasingly, firms mark their shipping cartons and packages with computer-readable bar codes that make it fast and easy to track inventory, shipments, orders, and the like. As information about product sales or shipments becomes available, it is instantly included in the MIS and accessible over the Internet.

Experimental method controls conditions

A marketing manager can get a different kind of information—with either questioning or observing—using the experimental method. With the **experimental method**, researchers compare the responses of two (or more) groups that are similar except on the characteristic being tested. The experimental method is sometimes called A/B testing, because it compares options labeled A and B. Researchers want to learn if the specific characteristic—which varies among groups—*causes* differences in some response among the groups. For example, a researcher might be interested in comparing responses of consumers who had seen an ad for a new product with consumers who had not seen the ad. The "response" might be an observed behavior—like the purchase of a product—or the answer to a specific question—like "How interested are you in this new product?" See Exhibit 7–5.

Marketing managers for Mars—the company that makes Snickers candy bars—used the experimental method to help solve a problem. They wanted to know if making their candy bar bigger would increase sales enough to offset the higher cost. To decide, they conducted a marketing experiment in which the company carefully varied the size of candy bars sold in *different* markets. Otherwise, the marketing mix stayed the same. Then researchers tracked sales in each market area to see the effect of the different sizes. They saw a big difference immediately; the added sales more than offset the cost of a bigger candy bar.

Online experiments can quickly generate knowledge

Online companies can conduct experiments and often get answers in just a few days. An online retailer might try two different versions of a web page and then see which one generates more sales. For example, online retailer Zappos thought that adding short product demonstration videos to each product page would increase sales (a hypothesis). Zappos knew that there would be some cost to creating so many videos, so it needed to know whether the videos would increase sales. Customers that linked on the tested products were randomly shown a product page with a video or an identical page without a video. Zappos found that purchases increased about 10 percent

Exhibit 7-5 Illustration of Experimental Method in Comparing Effectiveness of Two Ads

DHL Express Australia wanted to find out if the gender of the courier shown on its website would result in different rates of conversion for the DHL website. So the company conducted an A/B test. It showed some visitors to its website Version A (on the left) with a female courier, and others Version B with a male courier. Do you think the gender of the courier made any difference in the rate of lead conversions? If so, which image do you think performed better? *See the actual results by scrolling to the footnote at the bottom of this page.
2015 © DHL International GmbH. All rights reserved.

when pages included the video description. That experiment justified the production of more than 50,000 videos—and higher sales.

Test marketing of new products is another type of marketing experiment. In a typical approach, a company tries variations on its planned marketing mix in a few geographic market areas. The results of the tests help to identify problems or refine the marketing mix—before the decision is made to go to broader distribution. However, alert competitors may disrupt such tests—perhaps by increasing promotion or offering retailers extra discounts.[22]

Syndicated research shares data collection costs

Some private research firms specialize in collecting data and then sell them to managers in many different client firms. Often the marketing manager subscribes to the research service and gets regular updates. About 40 percent of marketing research spending is for syndicated research, and this helps explain why it can be an economical approach when marketing managers from many different firms need the same type of data. For example, many different auto producers use J. D. Power's (www.jdpa.com) surveys of customer satisfaction—often as the basis for advertising claims. Subscription data services are available for many different industries—ranging from food services to prescription drugs to microelectronic devices.[23]

A combination of research methods may be needed

Using one research method to solve an initial problem may identify new questions that are best answered with different research methods. Consider WD-40, a popular all-purpose lubricant sold in a blue-and-yellow spray can. To find potential new uses of WD-40, researchers visited mechanics and watched them as they worked. These observers realized that even small cans of WD-40 were difficult for mechanics to handle in tight spaces. In addition, the spray created drips and messes because it was difficult to control the amount being applied.

To address these problems, the new-product team developed a prototype for the No Mess Pen, a small marker that delivers a precise amount of the lubricant. Then, researchers

* Based on previous research in Norway (where a female image generated 25% more lead lead conversions), marketing managers hypothesized the female image would be more successful in Australia as well. This hypothesis was confirmed and the female image generated 15% more lead conversions. So DHL changed the image on its site. Source: Best of A/B Testing—DHL Ethnicity & Gender Testing," Business 2 Community, (see http://goo.gl/OJucHK, accessed August 27, 2015).

held focus groups to get reactions from mechanics. They weren't encouraging. Mechanics didn't think that the small unit would handle their large application needs. Yet many thought their spouses might like the pen for small household lubrication jobs. To follow up on this idea, WD-40 conducted online surveys. More than two-thirds of the women respondents said they would buy the product. To fine-tune targeting and promotion, WD-40 then conducted more than 40 in-home studies to learn how families actually used the No Mess Pen. This research confirmed that women were the primary target market, but that men used the pens as well. Moreover, the pen didn't replace the can of WD-40 already found in most households; rather, pens were stored in desk drawers, cars, and toolboxes so they'd be handy. WD-40 used different research methods to address different problems, but in combination they contributed to making the No Mess Pen a great success.[24]

Understand the costs and benefits of research

Whether collecting secondary data for a situation analysis or primary data from a focus group or survey, marketing research takes time and money. A good marketing manager knows that the value of additional information lies in the ability to design more effective marketing strategies. Similarly, different research methods provide different insights—and come at different costs. Marketing managers do not need to spend $100,000 to determine whether to spend $50,000 on advertising.

There are also benefits to getting information quickly—particularly in some markets. For example, competition and customer behavior can change quickly in high-technology markets. If a study takes six months to complete, the marketing manager may be developing a marketing strategy for a market that no longer exists—or, at best, looks quite different.

Small companies with limited budgets must be especially creative in identifying low-cost ways to get the information they need. Marketing managers can learn a lot by simply making sure they listen to what their firm's customers have to say. Even when doing informal research, marketers should have objectives for their questions. They can also learn a lot by studying competitors' websites and promotional materials or by shopping in their stores. When conducting formal research, they should be careful not to be too frugal. Skipping the pretesting of a questionnaire or using employees instead of real customers in a focus group may give managers a false sense of confidence—and worse, the wrong solution to a problem.[25]

When marketing managers at an ice cream manufacturer wanted consumers to pick the favorite of 48 proposed flavor names, they backed up mall intercept interviews with a quantitative online survey. Both methods produced the same favorite flavor—but online was faster and more cost efficient.
Courtesy Greenfield Online.

Interpreting the Data—Step 4

LO 7.5

What does it really mean?

After someone collects the data, they have to be analyzed to decide what they all mean. In quantitative research, this step usually involves statistics. **Statistical packages**—easy-to-use computer programs that analyze data—have made this step easier. As we noted earlier, some firms provide *decision support systems* so managers can use a statistical package to interpret data themselves. More often, however, technical specialists are involved at the interpretation step.

Exhibit 7-6　Cross-Tabulation Breakdown of Responses on a Survey of Smartphone Usage*

Have you used your smartphone for___?	What is your age?		
	18-29	30-49	50+
Text messaging	100%	98%	92%
Internet use	97%	90%	80%
Voice/video calls	93%	91%	94%
Email	91%	87%	87%
Social networking service access	91%	77%	55%
Video	75%	46%	31%
Music	64%	39%	21%

Respondents were contacted 14 times over the course of a week—twice per day. Each respondent was asked if during the previous hour, they had used their smartphone for any of the features listed. Respondents are recorded if they answered yes to each feature at least once.

*"U.S. Smartphone Use in 2015" *Pew Research Center*, April 2015

Cross-tabulation is one of the most frequently used approaches for analyzing and interpreting marketing research data. It shows the relationship of answers to two different questions. Exhibit 7–6 is an example. The cross-tab analysis shows that people of all ages use smartphones for text messaging and voice or video calls. On the other hand, young people are much more likely to use a smartphone to access social networking sites, watch videos, or listen to music.

There are many other approaches for statistical analysis—the best one depends on the situation. The details of statistical analysis are beyond the scope of this book. But a good manager should know enough to understand what a research project can and can't do.[26]

Is your sample really representative?

It's usually impossible for marketing managers to collect all the information they want about everyone in a **population**—the total group they are interested in. Marketing researchers typically study only a **sample**, a part of the relevant population. How well a sample *represents* the total population affects the results. Results from a sample that is not representative may not give a true picture.

The manager of a retail store might want a phone survey to learn what consumers think about the store's hours. If interviewers make all of the calls during the day, consumers who work outside the home during the day won't be represented. Those interviewed might say the limited store hours are "satisfactory." Yet it would be a mistake to assume that *all* consumers are satisfied.

Research results are not exact

An estimate from a sample, even a representative one, usually varies somewhat from the true value for a total population. Managers sometimes forget this. They assume that survey results are exact. Instead, when interpreting sample estimates, managers should think of them as *suggesting* the approximate value.

If random selection is used to develop the sample, researchers can use statistical methods to help determine the likely accuracy of the sample value. This is done in terms of **confidence intervals**—the range on either side of an estimate that is likely to contain the true value for the whole population. Some managers are surprised to learn how wide that range can be.

Consider a wholesaler who has 2,000 retail customers and wants to learn how many of these retailers carry a product from a competing supplier. If the wholesaler randomly samples 100 retailers and 20 say yes, then the sample estimate is 20 percent. But with that information the wholesaler can only be 95 percent confident that the percentage of all retailers is in the confidence interval between 12 and 28 percent. The larger the

Surveys may not be valid when the sample does not accurately represent the target population. Survey Sampling and i.think_inc. help marketing researchers develop samples that are highly representative of the target market.
© 2015 Survey Sampling International.
© i.think.com 2015.

sample size, the greater the accuracy of estimates from a random sample. With a larger sample, a few unusual responses are less likely to make a big difference.[27]

Validity problems can destroy research

Even if the sampling is carefully planned, it is also important to evaluate the quality of the research data itself.

Managers and researchers should be sure that research data really measure what they are supposed to measure. Many of the variables marketing managers are interested in are difficult to measure accurately. Questionnaires may let us assign numbers to consumer responses, but that still doesn't mean that the result is precise. An interviewer might ask, "How much did you spend on soft drinks last week?" A respondent may be perfectly willing to cooperate—and be part of the representative sample—but just not be able to remember. Or the respondent may contribute to inaccurate data by just "guessing."

Validity concerns the extent to which data measure what they are intended to measure. Validity problems are important in marketing research because many people will try to answer even when they don't know what they're talking about. Further, a poorly worded question can mean different things to different people and invalidate the results. Often, pretests of a research project are required to evaluate the quality of the questions and measures and to ensure that potential problems have been identified.

Ethics involved in interpreting and presenting results

Marketing managers want information they can trust when they make marketing decisions. But research often involves many hidden details. A person who wants to misuse research to pursue a personal agenda can often do so.

Ethical Dilemma

What would you do? You're the new marketing manager for a small firm that offers computer repair services. The company's owner approves your proposal for a telephone survey to learn more about the needs of firms that are not current customers. You identify local firms for the sample and hire a researcher to call them. The interviewer tells respondents that their answers will be anonymous and used only for research purposes. About halfway through the data collection, the interviewer tells you that respondents are confused by one of the questions and that their answers to that question are probably useless. The question concerns the issue that is most important to your new boss. Do you admit the problem to others in your company? If the sales manager asks for the completed questionnaires, including all the names and responses, what would you say?

Perhaps the most common ethical issues concern decisions to withhold certain information about the research. For example, a manager might selectively share only those results that support his or her viewpoint. Others involved in a decision might never know that they are getting only partial truths.[28]

Solving the Problem—Step 5

The last step is solving the problem

In the problem solution step, managers use the research results to make marketing decisions.

Some researchers, and some managers, are fascinated by the interesting tidbits of information that come from the research process. They are excited if the research reveals something they didn't know before. But if research doesn't have action implications, it has little value and suggests poor planning by the researcher and the manager.

When the research process is finished, the marketing manager should be able to apply the findings in marketing strategy planning—the choice of a target market or the mix of the Four Ps. If the research doesn't provide information to help guide these decisions, the company has wasted research time and money.

We emphasize this step because it is the reason for and logical conclusion to the whole research process. This final step must be anticipated at each of the earlier steps.

International Marketing Research

LO 7.6

Research contributes to international success

Marketing research on overseas markets is often a major contributor toward international marketing success. Conversely, export failures are often due to a lack of home office expertise concerning customer interests, needs, and other segmenting dimensions as well as environmental factors such as competitors' prices and products. Effective marketing research can help to overcome these problems.

There are a large number of international marketing research firms that offer specialized services to marketing managers. *Courtesy P. Robert & Partners. © 2015 Fieldwork Inc.*

Accurate data may be hard to find

In many countries, it is difficult—especially for a foreigner—to gather accurate information. Let's look at the challenge in China. Because the economy is growing so rapidly, secondary data that are out of date may be much more inaccurate than would be the case in a country with slow growth. Some important secondary data (such as the *China Statistical Yearbook*) are now available in an English language version, but that is often not the case. There are other problems, such as no explanation of the methods used to collect the data. That's important because the Chinese market is both large and complicated. Imagine how you would try to complete a competitor analysis when there are more than 1,000 Chinese firms that brew beer! Collecting primary data is difficult, too. Western researchers feel that Chinese managers and consumers are not very receptive to direct questioning. Those who agree to cooperate may be hesitant to say anything negative about their own companies or anything favorable about competitors. So it takes experienced interviewers to carefully interpret responses.[29]

Avoid mistakes with local researchers

Whether a firm is small and entering overseas markets for the first time or large and already well established internationally, there are often advantages to working with local marketing research firms. They know the local situation and are less likely to make mistakes based on misunderstanding the customs, language, or circumstances of the customers they study.

Many large research firms have a network of local offices around the world to help with such efforts. Similarly, multinational or local advertising agencies and intermediaries can often provide leads on identifying the best research suppliers.

Some coordination and standardization makes sense

When a firm is doing similar research projects in different markets around the world, it makes sense for the marketing manager to coordinate the efforts. If the manager doesn't establish some basic guidelines at the outset, the different research projects may all vary so much that the results can't be compared from one market area to another. Such comparisons give a home office manager a better chance of understanding how the markets are similar and how they differ.[30]

CONCLUSION

Marketing managers face difficult decisions in selecting target markets and managing marketing mixes, but they rarely have all the information they would like to have before making those decisions. Even less information may be available in international markets. This doesn't mean that managers have to rely solely on intuition; they can usually obtain some good information that will improve the quality of their decisions. Both large and small firms can take advantage of Internet and intranet capabilities to develop marketing information systems (MIS) that help to ensure routinely needed data are available and quickly accessible.

Some questions can only be answered with marketing research. Marketing research should be guided by the scientific method. This approach to solving marketing problems involves five steps: (1) defining the problem, (2) analyzing the situation, (3) obtaining data, (4) interpreting

data, and (5) developing and implementing a solution. This objective and organized approach helps to keep problem solving on task. It reduces the risk of doing costly and unnecessary research that doesn't achieve the desired end—solving the marketing problem.

Our strategy planning framework can be very helpful in evaluating marketing research. By finding and focusing on real problems, researchers and marketing managers may be able to move more quickly to a useful solution during the situation analysis stage—without the costs and risks of gathering primary data. With imagination, they may even be able to find answers in their MIS or in readily available secondary data. However, primary data from questioning, observing, or conducting experiments may be needed. Qualitative data often provide initial insights or hypotheses—which might be tested with more representative samples and quantitative approaches.

WHAT'S NOW?

This chapter examined how marketing managers make better strategy decisions with marketing information. To see some examples of new techniques, approaches and examples of marketing research, check out *What's Now?* at www.learnthe4ps.com/whatsnow/c7

KEY TERMS

marketing research, 170

marketing information system (MIS), 170

big data, 172

data warehouse, 173

intranet, 174

decision support system (DSS), 174

marketing dashboard, 174

marketing model, 175

scientific method, 176

hypotheses, 176

marketing research process, 177

situation analysis, 178

secondary data, 179

primary data, 179

research proposal, 181

qualitative research, 181

focus group interview, 181

quantitative research, 182

response rate, 183

market research online community (MROC), 184

consumer panels, 186

experimental method, 187

statistical packages, 189

population, 190

sample, 190

confidence intervals, 190

validity, 191

QUESTIONS AND PROBLEMS

1. Review the Dunkin' Donuts case study that opens the chapter. From this case, identify examples of different key terms and concepts covered in the chapter. For example, the first paragraph describes "daily sales totals," which are examples of secondary data.

2. Review the Dunkin' case study that opens this chapter. Imagine you are in charge of Dunkin' Donuts expansion into Russia. Identify five different types of research you would conduct before opening your first store in Moscow.

3. Discuss the concept of a marketing information system and why it is important for marketing managers to be involved in planning the system.

4. In your own words, explain why a decision support system (DSS) can add to the value of a marketing information system. Give an example of how a decision support system might help.

5. Discuss how output from a marketing information system (MIS) might differ from the output of a typical marketing research department.

6. Discuss some of the likely problems facing the marketing manager in a small firm who plans to search the Internet for information on competitors' marketing plans.

7. Explain the key characteristics of the scientific method and show why these are important to managers concerned with research.

8. How is the situation analysis different from the data collection step? Can both these steps be done at the same time to obtain answers sooner? Is this wise?

9. Distinguish between primary data and secondary data and illustrate your answer.

10. With so much secondary information now available free or at low cost over the Internet, why would a firm ever want to spend the money to do primary research?

11. If a firm were interested in estimating the distribution of income in the state of California, how could it proceed? Be specific.

12. If a firm were interested in estimating sand and clay production in Georgia, how could it proceed? Be specific.

13. Go to the library (or get on the Internet) and find (in some government publication or website) three marketing-oriented "facts" on international markets that you did not know existed or were available. Record on one page and show sources.

14. Explain why a company might want to do focus group interviews rather than individual interviews with the same people.

15. Distinguish between qualitative and quantitative approaches to research—and give some of the key advantages and limitations of each approach.

16. Define response rate and discuss why a marketing manager might be concerned about the response rate achieved in a particular survey. Give an example.

17. Prepare a table that summarizes some of the key advantages and limitations of mail, e-mail, telephone, and personal interview approaches for administering questionnaires.

18. Would a firm want to subscribe to a shared cost data service if the same data were going to be available to competitors? Discuss your reasoning.

19. Explain how you might use different types of research (focus groups, observation, survey, and experiment) to forecast market reaction to a new kind of disposable baby diaper, which is to receive no promotion other than what the retailer will give it. Further, assume that the new diaper's name will not be associated with other known products. The product will be offered at competitive prices.

20. Marketing research involves expense—sometimes considerable expense. Why does the text recommend the use of marketing research even though a highly experienced marketing executive is available?

21. A marketing manager is considering opportunities to export her firm's current consumer products to several different countries. She is interested in getting secondary data that will help her narrow down choices to countries that offer the best potential. The manager then plans to do more detailed primary research with consumers in those markets. What suggestions would you give her about how to proceed?

22. Discuss the concept that some information may be too expensive to obtain in relation to its value. Illustrate.

MARKETING PLANNING FOR HILLSIDE VETERINARY CLINIC

Appendix D (the Appendices follow Chapter 19) includes a sample marketing plan for Hillside Veterinary Clinic. Look through the "Customers" and "Competitors" sections in the Situation Analysis and consider the following questions.

a. What different types of marketing research were conducted to fill out these sections of the marketing plan?

b. What are the strengths of the research conducted? What are the weaknesses?

c. Keeping in mind probable cost and time to complete, what additional research would you recommend?

SUGGESTED CASES

3. Real NOCO Soccer Academy   8. Salvaggio's Trattoria   9. Restful Night Motel

MARKETING ANALYTICS: DATA TO KNOWLEDGE

CHAPTER 7 MARKETING RESEARCH

Texmac, Inc., has an idea for a new type of weaving machine that could replace the machines now used by many textile manufacturers. Texmac has done a telephone survey to estimate how many of the old-style machines are now in use. Respondents using the present machines were also asked if they would buy the improved machine at a price of $10,000.

Texmac researchers identified a population of about 5,000 textile factories as potential customers. A sample of these were surveyed, and Texmac received 500 responses. Researchers think the total potential market is about 10 times larger than the sample of respondents. Two hundred twenty of the respondents indicated that their firms used old machines like the one the new machine was intended to replace. Forty percent of those firms said that they would be interested in buying the new Texmac machine.

Texmac thinks the sample respondents are representative of the total population, but the marketing manager realizes that estimates based on a sample may not be exact when applied to the whole population. He wants to see how sampling error would affect profit estimates. Data for this problem appear in the spreadsheet. Quantity estimates for the whole market are computed from the sample estimates. These quantity estimates are used in computing likely sales, costs, and profit contribution.

See Connect for the spreadsheet and questions needed to analyze this scenario.

CHAPTER EIGHT

National Basketball Association/Getty Images.

Elements of Product Planning for Goods and Services

Kevin Plank was a business major and football player at the University of Maryland when he spotted an opportunity. He and his teammates wore cotton T-shirts under their football pads, but the T-shirts quickly became sweat-soaked, heavy, and uncomfortable during practices and games. When Plank began looking for a product that would perform better than a T-shirt, he learned about new types of fabrics and performance clothing for bicyclists and hikers.

In New York City's garment district, Plank learned about a polyester-Lycra-blend fabric that didn't trap moisture. He worked with a tailor to develop several prototype shirts and then asked friends who were players in the National Football League to try them. The players really liked the skintight compression shirts. They fit comfortably under football gear and wicked away sweat—keeping the players cooler, drier, and lighter. When Plank's friends clamored for more shirts, he knew he was on to something. However, he couldn't afford a big ad campaign to tout the benefits of his product, and he didn't have relationships with retailers who could help build demand with final consumers. So Plank moved to commercialize his shirts with a focus on a target market he knew: college football teams.

Plank went back to New York and ordered 500 shirts, the first products with the Under Armour brand name and the start of what became the Heat-Gear warm weather product line. Then he loaded his shirts in his SUV and traveled to colleges across the Southeast. He tried to persuade coaches, players, and equipment managers about the benefits of his unique shirts. Many were not initially convinced of the value—especially because the price was three to five times the price of a T-shirt. But the shirt's advantages were clear after a player would try one for a football practice. Praise for the product spread quickly.

Success with college and professional athletes helped the company build credibility. Soon Under Armour was expanding its product line—adding shoes, bottoms, backpacks, and accessories and moving into new sports including baseball, golf, soccer, and volleyball. It even went right at one of Nike's strengths —the basketball shoe market. Under Armour's signing of NBA star Stephen Curry to an endorsement deal turned into a coup when Curry won the league's Most Valuable Player award and his team won the NBA championship.

Under Armour's success attracted Nike and Adidas—and later dealer brands such as Kohl's Tek Gear and J.C. Penney's Simply for Sports—to the performance clothing market. The dealer brands' lower prices appealed to customers who saw all the brands as the same. So Under Armour put more emphasis on innovation and creative promotion to build customer preference for the Under Armour brand. For example, Under Armour ran TV and print ads featuring professional athletes such as Dallas Cowboy (and former Plank teammate) Eric Ogbogu. When the muscular Ogbogu barked the firm's tag line, "Protect This House," it instantly became a part of popular sports culture and a rallying cry of players and fans in football stadiums across the country.

Although Under Armour's roots are in male team sports, a big opportunity for future growth lies in the women's market. Just a few years ago, Under Armour's women's line made up less than 20 percent of revenues. Its "shrink it and pink it" approach—simply making smaller sizes and pastel colors of its men's line—didn't sell very well. Research showed that although women were aware of the Under Armour brand, it didn't have the same appeal as Lululemon and Nike. The opportunity is great; the female athletic clothing market of clothes-buying athletes is actually larger (55 percent) than the male side.

So Plank stepped up investment in the women's market. He hired a new product manager and built a marketing team of 10 (up from one) and design team of 20 who focused solely on women's apparel, accessories, and footwear. New products emerged that were fashion forward and offered a better fit for the female body. To appeal to women more likely to work out at the gym or do yoga, its "What's Beautiful" advertising campaign encouraged women with the "No matter what, sweat every day" tagline. Social media (Tumblr, Pinterest, and Facebook) promoted an online community where women created profiles, set goals, and provided encouragement. The plan worked and Under Armour's share of the market of "female athletes" grew quickly.

Under Armour sees a bigger opportunity in another segment of the women's market; "athletic females" are comfortable wearing athletic gear outside the gym. Under Armour's more fashionable gear fits their workout and running-about lifestyles. A new campaign, "I Will What I Want" campaign featured American Ballet Theater's Misty Copeland and supermodel Giselle Bündchen. The campaign highlights the physical and mental fortitude driving their success. Copeland's ad, with more than 8 million YouTube views, features Copeland's muscular physique with a voice-over rejection from a top ballet school, "you have the wrong body for ballet." The new product lines and targeted campaigns resonate with their target market; women's lines now account for 30 percent of Under Armour's sales.

Under Armour's future may depend on its ability to connect digital technology with fitness. In an effort to lose weight or stay fit, many casual athletes are using software apps to track and analyze workouts and eating habits. Under Armour developed apps for these customers, but its brand awareness and market share in the fitness app market was limited. So it spent more than $700 million to acquire three fitness apps—MyFitnessPal, Endomondo, and MapMyFitness—and their 120 million users. The

data from the apps and the increased brand awareness should fuel more growth.

In less than 20 years, Under Armour went from a start-up in Plank's grandmother's basement to a firm with more than $3.5 billion in annual sales. Of course, growth in the performance clothing market is slowing, and competition from Nike, Adidas, and a growing number of dealer brands creates price competition, but Kevin Plank is used to taking on big competitors. Once during his college football days, the 5-foot 11-inch, 229-pound Plank was assigned to block his 6-foot 4-inch, 269-pound buddy Ogbogu, and the bigger man ended up on his back with a concussion. Watch out Nike![1]

LEARNING OBJECTIVES

Developing a marketing mix that provides superior customer value for target customers is ultimately the focus of the marketing strategy planning process. To develop a successful marketing mix requires that each of the Four Ps is carefully planned and works well with all the others. Many important strategy decisions are required. This chapter focuses on key ideas related to strategy planning for Product.

When you finish this chapter, you should be able to

1 Understand what "Product" really means.

2 Cite the key differences between goods and services.

3 Understand what branding is and how to use it in strategy planning.

4 Understand the importance of packaging in strategy planning.

5 Understand the role of warranties in strategy planning.

6 Know the differences among various consumer and business product classes.

7 Understand how product classes can help a marketing manager plan marketing strategies.

8 Understand important new terms (shown in red).

The Product Area Involves Many Strategy Decisions

The Under Armour case highlights some of the important topics and strategy decision areas that we'll discuss in this chapter and in Chapter 9. As shown in Exhibit 8–1, there are many strategy decisions in the Product area. They're the focus of this chapter. Then, in Chapter 9, we'll take a "how to" look at developing new products and also explain how strategy usually changes as products move through their life in the market.

We'll start here by looking at Product through the eyes of the customer. This focuses attention on the total benefits provided by the Product—regardless of whether it is a physical good, a service, or both. Then we'll review strategy decisions for three important Product areas: branding, packaging, and warranties. We'll conclude by considering product classes, which are based on how customers think about and shop for products. They help show how strategy decisions for Product relate to decisions for Place, Promotion, and Price.

Exhibit 8-1 Product Decisions for Marketing Strategy Planning

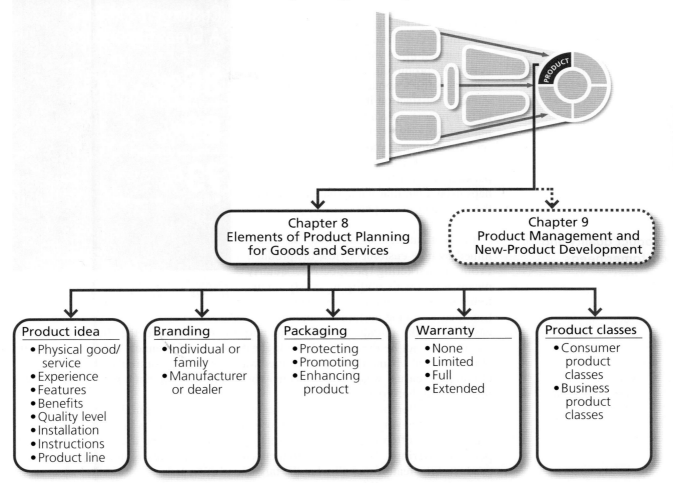

Chapter 8 Elements of Product Planning for Goods and Services	Chapter 9 Product Management and New-Product Development

Product idea	Branding	Packaging	Warranty	Product classes

• Physical good/
  service
• Experience
• Features
• Benefits
• Quality level
• Installation
• Instructions
• Product line
	• Individual or
	  family
	• Manufacturer
	  or dealer
		• Protecting
		• Promoting
		• Enhancing
		  product
			• None
			• Limited
			• Full
			• Extended
				• Consumer
				  product
				  classes
				• Business
				  product
				  classes

What Is a Product?

LO 8.1

Customers buy satisfaction

When Jif sells its peanut butter, is it just selling roasted peanuts, sugar, salt, and oil?

When Air Jamaica sells a ticket for a flight to the Caribbean, is it just selling wear and tear on an airplane and pilot fatigue?

The answer to these questions is *no*. Instead, what these companies are really selling is the satisfaction, use, or benefit the customer wants.

Consumers care that their Jif peanut butter tastes great, easily spreads on bread for a fast sandwich, and offers a source of protein in their diet. If they worry about too much fat or sugar in their diet, they can buy Jif Reduced Fat or Simply Jif. Of course retailers who sell peanut butter are satisfied, because Jif tells customers about the brand in advertising and packages the peanut butter in bright eye-catching colors that help the brand sell.

Similarly, Air Jamaica's customers want a safe, comfortable on-time flight—but they also want easy online reservations, low prices, smooth check-in at the airport, and luggage that arrives undamaged and on time. In other words, purchases deliver the highest level of satisfaction when the customer's entire *experience* with the product meets or exceeds the customer's needs.

Product means the need-satisfying offering of a firm. The idea of "Product" as potential customer satisfaction or benefits is very important. Many business managers get wrapped up in the technical details involved in producing a product. But most customers think about a product in terms of the total satisfaction it provides. That satisfaction may require a "total" product offering that is really a combination of excellent service, a physical good along with the right features, useful instructions, a convenient package, a trustworthy warranty, and perhaps even a familiar name that has satisfied the consumer in the past.

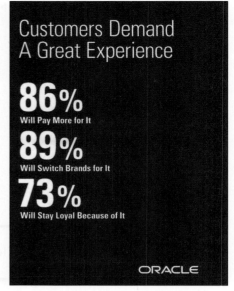

Product quality and customer needs

Product quality should also be determined by how customers view the product. From a marketing perspective, **quality** means a product's ability to satisfy a customer's needs or requirements. This definition focuses on the customer—and how the customer thinks a product will fit some purpose. For example, the "best" satellite TV service may not be the one with the highest number of channels but the one that includes a local channel that a consumer wants to watch. Similarly, the best-quality clothing for casual wear on campus may be a pair of jeans, not a pair of dress slacks made of a higher-grade fabric.

Among different types of jeans, the one with the most durable fabric might be thought of as having the highest grade or *relative quality* for its product type. Marketing managers often focus on relative quality when comparing their products to competitors' offerings. However, a product with better features is not a higher-quality product if the features aren't what the target market wants.

In Chapter 9, we'll look at ways to manage product quality. For now, however, it is important to see that quality and satisfaction depend on the total product offering. If

OPERA TO PUNK ROCK MP3s

BIGPOND MUSIC

For Big Pond Music, a product line includes the different songs that fall within a particular music genre—for example punk rock MP3s. An individual product would be a particular song. The product assortment includes all the different music genres and songs.
Copyright 2015 Belgiovane Williams Mackay/Sydney. All rights reserved.

potato chips get stale on the shelf because of poor packaging, the consumer will be dissatisfied. A broken button on a shirt will disappoint the customer—even if the laundry did a nice job cleaning and pressing the collar.[2]

Ethical Dilemma

What would you do? Your construction firm was the low price bidder on a plan to build three new runways at an airport. After winning the contract, you assured the airport commissioner that your work would far exceed the minimum quality specs in the contract. However, a test of the batch of concrete for the second runway shows that it's not as strong as the concrete you've been using. It does exceed the specs in the contract, but barely. Throwing the concrete away would eat up most of the profit expected from the job and also delay the airport in using the runway. There are various options. You could proceed with the project and be quiet about it, later admitting what happened. Alternatively, you could call the commissioner, reveal everything, and then ask for approval to proceed (chancing denial—an outcome that would seriously hurt your company). With or without approval, you could offer a special warranty. Explain what you would do. What, if anything, would you say to your employees about your decision?[3]

Sorting out product lines, product assortments, and individual products

An **individual product** is a particular product within a product line. A **product line** is a set of individual products that are closely related. It usually is differentiated by brand, level of service offered, price, or some other characteristic. For example, each size and scent of a brand of soap is an individual product. Intermediaries usually think of each separate product as a stock-keeping unit (SKU) and assign it a unique SKU number. A **product assortment** is the set of all product lines and individual products that a firm sells. The seller may see the products in a line as related because they're produced or operate in a similar way, sold to the same target market, sold through the same types of outlets, or priced at about the same level. Sara Lee, for example, has many product lines in its product assortment—including beverages, luncheon meats, desserts, insecticides, body care, air care, and shoe care. But Enterprise has one product line—different types of vehicles to rent.

Product lines require strategy decisions

Marketing managers have several decisions to make about product lines. One strategy decision involves *product line length*—the number of individual products in a product line. Sometimes extending the length of the product line offers marketing managers new opportunities. Firms can add more colors, flavors, styles, and sizes to appeal to a wider range of customers. For example, Subway offers breakfast sandwiches, which appeal to a new market segment. Coca-Cola in recent years has added Vanilla Coke, Cherry Coke, and Coke Zero to appeal to a wider range of customers.

Marketing managers should make product line length decisions with knowledge about the needs and wants of both end customers and intermediaries—as well as the company's own costs. Extending product line length can raise production and distribution costs and might confuse customers. UPS's My Choice service offers residential customers greater flexibility about when and where they receive package deliveries from UPS. For example, for a five dollar fee, a consumer can reroute a package (perhaps to a work address) or select a two-hour delivery window. UPS must weigh the costs of adding this new service against the benefits of additional revenue and higher customer satisfaction.

Each individual product and target market may require a separate strategy. For example, Clorox's strategy for selling Clorox Scented Bleach will differ from its strategy for selling Clorox Regular Bleach. In this book and the first marketing course, we'll focus mainly on developing one marketing strategy at a time. But remember that a marketing manager may have to plan *several* strategies to develop an effective marketing program for a product line or whole company.[4]

Differences between Goods and Services

LO 8.2

Goods and/or services are the product

A product may be a tangible, physical *good.* Or a product may be a **service**—an intangible offering involving a deed, performance, or effort. A service is not physical or tangible. Many products are a *blend of both*—part good and part service. Exhibit 8–2 shows that a product can range from a 100 percent emphasis on a physical good—for a commodity like steel pipe—to a 100 percent emphasis on service—for a product like satellite radio from SiriusXM. Many products include a combination of goods and services. When you eat out, you are buying food (a physical good) that is prepared and served by a restaurant's staff (a service).

Regardless of the blend of goods and services involved, the marketing manager must consider most of the same elements in planning products and marketing mixes. Given this, we usually won't make a distinction between goods and services but will call all of them Products. However, understanding key differences in goods and services can help fine-tune marketing strategy planning. So let's look at some of these differences next.

How tangible is the product?

Because a good is a physical thing, it can be seen and touched. You can try on a pair of Timberland shoes, smell Starbucks beans as they roast, and page through the latest issue of *People* magazine. A good is a *tangible* item. It's usually easy to know exactly what you will get before you decide to buy it. And once you've bought it, you own it.

In contrast, services are not physical—they are *intangible*. When you provide a customer with a service, the customer can't keep it. Rather, a service is experienced, used, or consumed. You go to a DreamWorks Pictures movie, but afterward all you have is a memory. You can buy a pass to ski at Vail and enjoy the experience, but you don't own the ski lift. Sometimes it's a challenge that customers can't see, feel, or smell a service before they buy it. For example, a person who wants advice from an accountant doesn't know in advance how good the advice will be.

To reduce this uncertainty, service customers often seek referrals from friends or advice from online reviews. They may also look for cues to help them judge the quality of a service before they buy. That's why some service providers emphasize physical evidence of quality. A lawyer is likely to have diplomas on the wall, shelves loaded with books, and furnishings that suggest success.

Where the product is produced

Goods are typically mass-produced in a factory far away from the customer. A service is usually produced in person—where the customer is located—*after* the customer has committed to making the purchase. It is often difficult to achieve economies of scale with personal services. One reason is that service suppliers often need duplicate equipment and staff at places where the service is actually provided. Merrill Lynch sells investment advice along with financial products worldwide. That advice could, perhaps, be produced more economically in a single building in New York City

Exhibit 8-2 Examples of Possible Blends of Physical Goods and Services in a Product

Canned soup, steel pipe, paper towels

Restaurant meal, cell phone, automobile tune-up

Satellite radio, hair styling, postal service

100% physical good emphasis

100% service emphasis

Blend of physical good and service

A consumer can't hold a service and look at it before purchasing, so service firms often use messages and images in their promotion that helps make the benefits of the service experience more valid. Allstate's "Mayhem" ads are a vivid reminder of the value of a good insurance policy.
Video frames: © 2015 Allstate Insurance Company; Agency: Leo Burnett North America.

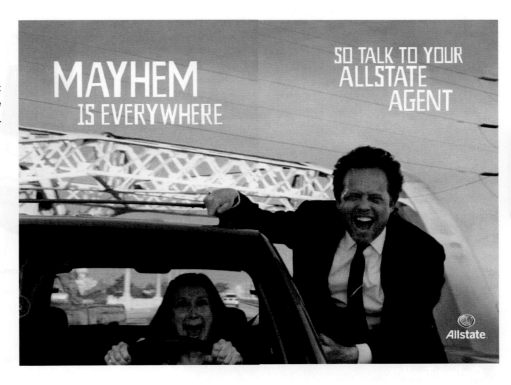

and made available only on its website. But Merrill Lynch has offices all over the world because many customers want a personal touch from their stockbroker.

Quality consistency

A worker in a factory that makes Whirlpool appliances can be in a bad mood and customers will never know. Even if there are production problems, quality controls are likely to catch defective goods before they leave the factory. Service quality often isn't that consistent; one reason is that it's hard to separate the service experience from the person who provides it. A rude teller in a bank can drive customers away. Service providers also vary in their ability, and problems with the service they deliver are usually obvious to customers. In addition, when many people must all work well together—as in a hospital or on a cruise ship—it's even more of a challenge to deliver consistent service quality.

Services cannot be stored

Services are perishable. They can't be produced and then stored to sell at some future time when more customers want to buy. This makes it difficult to balance supply and demand, especially if demand varies a lot. At Thanksgiving, Southwest Airlines has to turn away customers because most of its flights are fully booked; other airlines may get that business. Perhaps Southwest could buy more planes and hire more pilots, but most of the time that would result in costly excess capacity—planes flying with empty seats. The revenue that could have come from any empty seats is lost forever.

Because of problems like this, airlines, doctors, hotels, and other service firms sometimes charge fees to clients who don't show up when they say they will. Service organizations also use a variety of approaches to shift customer demand to less busy times. Movie tickets are cheaper for afternoon shows, restaurants offer early-bird specials, and hotels that cater to business travelers promote weekend getaways. Firms also try to reduce the dissatisfaction that customers may feel if they must wait for service. Golf courses provide practice greens, and some doctors' offices provide comfortable seating and magazines.[5]

Adding services to goods to differentiate

When competitors focus only on physical goods, a firm may differentiate its offering by adding a service valued by the target market. Many companies make high-quality

IKEA furniture usually needs to be assembled after a buyer gets it home. Many customers like the "goods" (IKEA furniture) but also appreciate that IKEA offers furniture assembly "services."
© Inter IKEA Systems B.V. 1999–2012; Agency: Grabarz & Partner/ Hamburg.

HDTVs, but Panasonic's research revealed that some consumers worried about how to set up an HDTV when they got it home. So Panasonic added Plasma Concierge service to support its HDTV customers with well-trained advisors and priority in-home service.

Software apps can offer services that add value to goods. Paint producer Benjamin Moore's "ben Color Capture" allows iPhone users to take a picture of any color and automatically match it to a Benjamin Moore paint color. Some firms are linking goods and services on the Internet to create value for customers. Read more in "*What's Next? The Internet of Things connects products.*"

This idea also works when the emphasis is on services, where goods in the offering provide differentiation. An overnight stay at a Westin Hotel has a service emphasis, but Westin's ads highlight the Heavenly Bed—which includes a high-quality mattress, extra pillows, and luxury linens.

Branding Is a Strategy Decision

LO 8.3

There are so many brands—and we're so used to seeing them—that we take them for granted. But branding is an important decision area, so we will treat it in some detail.

What is branding?

Branding means the use of a name, term, symbol, or design—or a combination of these—to identify a product. It includes the use of brand names, trademarks, and practically all other means of product identification.

Brand name has a narrower meaning. A **brand name** is a word, letter, or a group of words or letters. Examples include Verizon Wireless, WD-40, 3M Post-its, and GoPro Hero.

Trademark is a legal term. A **trademark** includes only those words, symbols, or marks that are legally registered for use by a single company. So for example, Power-Point, Bubble Wrap, and Q-Tips are all trademarks, which refer to products from Microsoft, Sealed Air Corporation, and Unilever, respectively. A **service mark** is the same as a trademark except that it refers to a service offering.[6]

What's Next? The Internet of things connects products

Think about some of the physical objects you see and use every day: a car tire, T-shirt, stop sign, thermostat, coffeemaker, smartphone, garage door, traffic light, or a sprinkler system. Inside each of these objects, a sensor, actuator, or data communications technology can be embedded to connect the object with the Internet or some other data network. Once connected, the objects can be tracked, coordinated, and controlled. The Internet allows these goods to be supplemented with additional services. This collection of interconnected objects is being called the "Internet of Things." Let's take a look at some of the features and benefits the Internet of Things could soon deliver.

Imagine your alarm clock rings and tells your coffeemaker to start brewing your morning cup so it is ready by the time you get to the kitchen. In fact the clock learns (by simply observing when it rings and when you grab the coffee) that you take 20 minutes to shower and brush your teeth before you get to the coffee—so it delays the brewing to be fresh and hot at that time. The sprinkler system in your yard knows how long and when to run—its sensors know about recent rainfall *and* the weather forecast for the next few days. As you leave home to go shopping, your house closes the garage door and turns off the lights.

As you enter the grocery store parking lot, cameras recognize your license plate and tie this data to your store loyalty card, and your phone receives coupons based on your past purchases. In the store your smartphone loads a shopping list prepared by your refrigerator

and pantry—where sensors know what you like to keep on hand and can tell what's there and what you need. Arriving at the cash register, you find that your cartload has already been rung up and charged to your bank account—just bag it all up and be on your way. That evening, as you approach your favorite local watering hole for a drink, your phone warns you that your "ex" is inside. Uh oh, the next move is yours.

Businesses and governments already leverage IoT technology for sustainability and efficiency. Videocameras at businesses know when everyone has gone home; at that point, the building automatically turns out the lights and adjusts the heating or cooling to save energy. Delivery routes are programmed to minimize delay—and adjust on the fly as traffic patterns change throughout the day. Visual sensors on railroad cars inspect tracks in real time, providing feedback on sections of track most in need of repair. Sensors in roads adjust the timing of traffic lights to optimize traffic flow.

With sensor prices plummeting, analysts predict that by the early 2020s, more than 50 billion "things" will contain this technology. Enhancing goods with services has the potential to offer individuals, businesses, and governments more convenience and greater efficiency. The challenge for marketing managers will be to recognize real customer needs—and figure out how the IoT can deliver them.

How could a connection to the Internet of Things add value for owners of an automobile? a refrigerator? a lawn mower?[7]

The word *FedEx* can be used to explain these differences. The FedEx overnight delivery service is branded under the brand name FedEx (whether it's spoken or printed in any manner). When "FedEx" is printed in a certain typeface, however, it becomes a trademark. A trademark need not be attached to the product. It need not even be a word—it can be a symbol. Exhibit 8–3 shows some common trademarks.

These differences may seem technical. But they are very important to business firms that spend a lot of money to protect and promote their brands. Sometimes a firm's brand name is the only element in its marketing mix that a competitor can't copy.

Brands meet needs   Well-recognized brands make shopping easier. Think of trying to buy groceries, for example, if you had to evaluate each of the 25,000 items every time you went to a supermarket. Many customers are willing to buy new things—but having gambled and won, they like to buy a sure thing the next time. Brand names connect a product

Exhibit 8-3   Recognized Trademarks and Symbols Help in Promotion

with the benefits a customer can expect. The connection may be learned from past consumer experience, from the firm's promotion, or in other ways. Customers *trust* the brand name if they consistently have a positive experience with the brand or they hear good things from the firm's promotion or other customers. If their marketing mixes work, customers trust that every time they eat *Certified Angus Beef* it will be "tender, high-quality meat" and that their oil changes at *Jiffy Lube* will always be "fast and convenient." If a brand consistently delivers on a promise that target customers consider important, those customers will pay a premium price for the certainty that comes with that brand name.

Brand promotion has other advantages for branders as well as customers. A good brand reduces the marketer's selling time and effort. Good brands can also improve the company's image—speeding acceptance of new products marketed under the same name. For example, many consumers quickly tried Listerine PocketPaks breath fresheners when they appeared because they already knew they trusted Listerine mouthwash.[8]

Thinking its image might be getting a bit stale, Tropicana updated the packaging for its orange juice. So it ditched the longtime Tropicana brand symbol of a colorful orange pierced by a straw for the package on the right showing a muted glass of orange juice. Sales fell as some loyal Tropicana customers failed to recognize their regular brand on store shelves. Soon the original package design was back in stores. Customers appreciate a familiar brand name.
© Joseph P. Cannon Ph.D.

What conditions favor branding?

Although branding helps customers make buying decisions, branding is not always easy to do. Building a well-respected brand name can be costly. It doesn't always make sense as part of a marketing strategy. In some industries, well-known brands are just not that common. Think about it. Can you recall a brand name for file folders, bed frames, electric extension cords, or nails? The following are conditions that can make a market more favorable to successful branding:

1. The product is easy to label and identify by brand or trademark.
2. The product quality is easy to maintain and the best value for the price.
3. Dependable and widespread availability is possible. When customers start using a brand, they want to be able to continue using it.
4. Demand is strong enough that the market price can be high enough to make the branding effort profitable.
5. There are economies of scale. If the branding is really successful, costs should drop and profits should increase.
6. Favorable shelf locations or display space in stores will help. This is something retailers can control when they brand their own products.

In general, these conditions are less common in developing economies, and that may explain why efforts to build brands in emerging markets often fail. For example, one study found Chinese consumers willing to pay a premium of only 2 percent for branded products they regularly purchase—as compared to premiums of 20 percent or more in developed countries.[9]

Achieving Brand Familiarity Is Not Easy

Today, familiar brands exist for most product categories, ranging from crayons (Crayola) to real estate services (RE/MAX). Nevertheless, brand acceptance must be earned with a good product and regular promotion. **Brand familiarity** means how well customers recognize and accept a company's brand. The degree of brand familiarity affects the planning for the rest of the marketing mix—especially where the product should be offered and what promotion is needed.

Five levels of brand familiarity

Five levels of brand familiarity are useful for strategy planning: (1) rejection, (2) nonrecognition, (3) recognition, (4) preference, and (5) insistence.

Some brands have been tried and found wanting. **Brand rejection** means that potential customers won't buy a brand unless its image is changed—or if the customers have no other choice. Rejection may suggest a change in the product or perhaps only a shift to target customers who have a better image of the brand. Overcoming a negative image is difficult and can be very expensive. Sometimes customers have no other choice. Many music and sports fans would like to reject Ticketmaster, which sells tickets to sports and music events. But customers often have little choice when it comes time to buy tickets to see their favorite band or team perform live. Recently, comedian Louis C.K. sold tickets directly to his fans to avoid associating with Ticketmaster. This attitude has helped jump-start competitors for Ticketmaster, though the company is working hard to reverse that negative customer attitude.[10]

Brand rejection is a big concern for service-oriented businesses because it's hard to control the quality of service. A business traveler who gets a dirty room in a Hilton Hotel in Caracas, Venezuela, might not return to a Hilton anywhere. Yet it's difficult for Hilton to ensure that every maid does a good job every time.

Some products are seen as basically the same. **Brand nonrecognition** means final consumers don't recognize a brand at all—even though intermediaries may use the brand name for identification and inventory control. Examples include school supplies, inexpensive dinnerware, many of the items that you'd find in a hardware store, and thousands of dot-coms on the Internet.

Brand recognition means that customers remember the brand. This may not seem like much, but it can be a big advantage if there are many "nothing" brands on the market. Even if consumers can't recall the brand without help, they may be reminded when they see it in a store among other less familiar brands.

Most branders would like to win **brand preference**—which means that target customers usually choose the brand over other brands, perhaps because of habit or favorable past experience. **Brand insistence** means customers insist on a firm's branded product and are willing to search for it. That loyalty is one benefit, but customers that insist on a brand are most likely to let others know of their "love" and exhibit positive word-of-mouth.[11]

A brand is likely to have target customers at each level of brand familiarity. Ideally, customers move to higher levels of brand familiarity (brand preference and brand insistence) over time. Marketing strategies often aim to encourage this movement. Consider the café-bakery chain Panera Bread. It's possible that some target customers may reject the brand because of a bad previous experience. However, if Panera provides consistently excellent service and tries to recognize and compensate for (hopefully) rare instances of poor service, those who reject the brand should be a very small group. Other customers in the target market may not recognize the brand and need promotion that is directly aimed at them, possibly in the form of advertising. With successful promotion, these customers will likely move to the brand recognition level. Because higher levels of brand familiarity will probably require first-hand experience, coupons or additional promotion efforts may be needed to encourage an actual visit to a café. If Panera delivers an enjoyable time (good food and service at a fair price), then more customers are likely to develop brand preference. Customers who are truly delighted may move to brand insistence and recommend Panera to their friends and family.[12]

The right brand name can help

A good brand name can help build brand familiarity. It can help tell something important about the company or its product. For more than 50 years, Kraft Foods used the name A.1. Steak Sauce. As steak declined in popularity, Kraft dropped "Steak" from the name to give the product broader appeal. A name change to an iconic 50-year-old brand is not taken lightly.

Naming a brand can be art and science. Exhibit 8–4 lists some characteristics of a good brand name. Lululemon, Outback, Jelly Belly, Bonobos, and DieHard are examples of successful brand names that fit some of these criteria. Can you think of others?

Companies that compete in international markets face a special problem in selecting brand names. A name that conveys a positive image in one language may be meaningless in another. Or, worse, it may have unintended meanings. British food company Sharwood discovered this after spending millions of dollars launching a curry sauce called *Bundh*. Unfortunately many Punjabi speakers, who were one of the target

Many of In-N-Out Burger's customers insist on the brand. This loyal and fanatical fan base anxiously awaits the opening of an In-N-Out Burger in their town. When In-N-Out opened in Frisco, Texas, customers waited in lines for more than an hour to get their favorite burger and fries. Manufacturers with strong brands have a leg up in the battle of the brands. Consumers' trust of the Morton brand name helped the brand gain retail distribution and consumer trial when it introduced ice melters.
Michael Ainsworth/The Dallas Morning News. Copyright © 1995-2015 Morton Salt, Inc. All rights reserved. Morton Salt Inc. is part of the K+S Group.

Exhibit 8-4
Characteristics of a Good
Brand Name

• Short and simple	• Suggestive of product benefits
• Easy to spell and read	• Adaptable to packaging/labeling needs
• Easy to recognize and remember	• No undesirable imagery
• Easy to pronounce	• Always timely (does not go out of date)
• Can be pronounced in only one way	• Adaptable to any advertising medium
• Can be pronounced in all languages (for international markets)	• Legally available for use (not in use by another firm)

markets, thought the word sounded more like the Punjabi word for "backside." IKEA uses Swedish and Norwegian words as brand names, bringing a unique character to the brand. But when IKEA opened a store in Thailand, it discovered the *Redalen* bed and *Jättebra* plant pot sounded a lot like crude Thai terms related to sex.[13]

A respected name builds brand equity

Because it's costly to build brand recognition, some firms prefer to acquire established brands rather than try to build their own. The value of a brand to its current owner or to a firm that wants to buy it is sometimes called **brand equity**—the value of a brand's overall strength in the market. For example, brand equity is likely to be higher if many satisfied customers insist on buying the brand and if retailers are eager to stock it. That almost guarantees ongoing profits.

The financial value of the Coca-Cola brand illustrates brand equity. What is Coca-Cola but water, sugar, and flavoring? There is a unique flavor, but much of the value comes from associations people have with the brand name. In a research study, subjects' brains were scanned while they drank Coke and Pepsi in a taste test. When they drank the two soft drinks unlabeled (not knowing the brand) the subjects' preferences were evenly split. When the drinks were labeled, three-fourths chose Coke—and the brain scans suggested those favoring Coke used an area of the brain associated with memories. This suggested that Coke created pleasure because of people's experience with the brand. That type of association creates a competitive advantage that cannot be easily overcome. Many consumers have this positive association. Findings like these help explain the power of the Coca-Cola brand in building consumer preference and long-term profits. In 2015, the Coca-Cola brand was among the 10 most valuable in the world, estimated to be worth more than $84 billion.[14]

Protecting Brand Names and Trademarks

U.S. common law and civil law protect the rights of trademark and brand name owners. The **Lanham Act** (of 1946) spells out what kinds of marks (including brand names) can be protected and the exact method of protecting them. The law applies to goods shipped in interstate or foreign commerce.

The Lanham Act does not force registration. But registering under the Lanham Act is often a first step toward protecting a trademark to be used in international markets. That's because some nations require that a trademark be registered in its home country before they will register or protect it.

You must protect your own

A brand can be a real asset to a company. Each firm should try to see that its brand doesn't become a common descriptive term for its kind of product. When this happens, the brand name or trademark becomes public property—and the owner loses all rights to it. This happened with the names cellophane, aspirin, shredded wheat, and kerosene.

Burger chain In-N-Out's menu and the colors in its restaurant are part of its trademark. Before In-N-Out had restaurants in Utah, a restaurant called Chadder's opened using In-N-Out's same menu and color scheme. If In-N-Out were to let this stand, these features might become public property. In-N-Out sued Chadder's, a judge ruled against Chadder's and it soon went out of business.[15]

Trademarks need to be protected around the globe

When introducing a new brand name, marketing managers must be sure to have rights to the trademark in all of its markets. Apple got into a dispute over the iPad trademark after the product was launched. Apple purchased rights to the name from a Taiwanese firm which held rights to the iPad name in several Asian countries—including, Apple believed, China. But when the iPad was launched, a Chinese firm claimed it still owned the rights to the iPad name. After battles in Chinese courts, Apple eventually settled by paying Proview Technology $60 million for the Chinese rights to the iPad name.

Counterfeiting is accepted in some cultures

Even when products are properly registered, counterfeiters may make unauthorized copies. Counterfeit products cause a brand to lose sales and jeopardize its reputation. Many well-known brands—ranging from Levi's jeans to Rolex watches to Zantax medicine—face this problem. International trade in counterfeit and pirated goods may exceed $500 billion annually. Counterfeiting continues to grow and is especially common in developing countries where regulation is weak or cultural values differ. In Azerbaijan and Bulgaria, BP discovered counterfeit BP service stations—with low-quality fuel. And in a knockoff Apple Store in China, many employees think they are working in the real thing.[16]

What Kind of Brand to Use?

Keep it in the family

Branders of more than one product must decide whether they are going to use a **family brand**—the same brand name for several products—or individual brands for each product. Examples of family brands are Keebler snack food products and Sears Kenmore appliances.

The use of the same brand for many products makes sense if all are similar in type and quality. The main benefit is that the goodwill attached to one or two products may help the others. Money spent to promote the brand name benefits more than one product, which cuts promotion costs for each product.

A special kind of family brand is a **licensed brand**—a well-known brand that sellers pay a fee to use. For example, the familiar Sunkist brand name has been licensed to many companies for use on more than 400 products in 30 countries. Betty Crocker sells Sunkist Lemon Bar mix, Jelly Belly makes Sunkist Fruit Gems candy, and Dr Pepper produces Sunkist orange soda. Sunkist earns extra revenue and its partners get instant brand recognition. That said, Sunkist must carefully choose partners that sell quality products and promote the brand in ways that won't harm its carefully curated image.[17]

Individual brands for outside and inside competition

A company uses **individual brands**—separate brand names for each product—when it's important for the products to each have a separate identity, as when products vary in quality or type.

If the products are really different, such as Elmer's glue and Borden's ice cream, individual brands can avoid confusion. Some firms use individual brands with similar products to make segmentation and positioning efforts easier. For example, when General Mills introduced a line of organic cereals, it used the Cascadian Farm name and the Big G logo was not on the box. The rationale was that consumers who try to avoid additives might not trust a big corporate brand.[18]

Generic "brands"

Products that some consumers see as commodities may be difficult or expensive to brand. Some manufacturers and intermediaries have responded to this problem with **generic products**—products that have no brand at all other than identification of their contents and the manufacturer or intermediary. Generic products are usually offered in plain packages at lower prices. They are quite common in less-developed nations.[19]

Who Should Do the Branding?

Manufacturer brands versus dealer brands

Manufacturer brands are brands created by producers. These are sometimes called national brands because the brand is promoted all across the country or in large regions. Note, however, that many manufacturer brands are now distributed globally. Such brands include Nabisco, Colgate, Northwestern Mutual Life, Marriott, Master-Card, and McDonald's.

Dealer brands, also called **private brands** (or private label), are brands created by intermediaries. Examples of dealer brands include Craftsman and Kenmore (Sears), Primo Taglio and Priority Pet (Safeway), Up & Up (Target), and Sam's Choice and Equate (Walmart).

Who's winning the battle of the brands?

Manufacturer and dealer brands often sell in the same retail stores. The **battle of the brands**, the competition between dealer brands and manufacturer brands, is just a question of which brands will be more popular and who will be in control. At one time, manufacturer brands were much more popular than dealer brands. In some categories, such as soft drinks, they still are. But in categories such as milk and cheese, dealer brands are very strong contenders. In the United States, almost 30 percent of grocery store purchases are now dealer brands, with percentages much higher in many European countries and very low in most of Asia and South America. Over the past 30 years, dealer brands have been slowly gaining an upper hand. During the recent economic downturn, more consumers were motivated to try dealer brands—and many were pleasantly surprised by the quality and the variety they found.

Brand names tend to do better in some categories. For example, in the United States, private label accounts for less than 2 percent of hair care sales. Hair care brands tend to be innovative and have a high level of advertising, which results in higher perceived product differentiation and more loyal customers. On the other hand, in developed countries about 40 percent of all milk sales are from dealer brands. Milk buyers tend to purchase frequently and see little differentiation among brands.[20]

Retailers are motivated to develop dealer brands

There is plenty of motivation for intermediaries to develop dealer brands. The intermediary usually earns a better margin on the sale of a dealer brand. Strong dealer brands also give an intermediary leverage in negotiations with the manufacturer brand.

In the grocery trade, retailers are putting more attention behind new dealer brand products. Kroger and Safeway recently hired marketing managers with experience at major national brands. Recently, almost a third of all new product introductions were for dealer brands, up from less than 10 percent just a few years ago. Traditionally, dealer brands were knockoffs of manufacturer brands—often of lower quality with lower prices. Now some dealer brands sell premium products. Kroger's popular "Private Selection" line of frozen pizzas is priced the same as the national brand DiGiorno. Kroger conducts its own market research, which recently led to changes in the packaging of its Pet Pride pet food brand. It

General Mills and Cascadian Farm are both manufacturer brands, while Food Lion (a grocery store chain) is a dealer brand.
© William D. Perreault, Jr., Ph.D.

learned that dog owners like to see packages with dogs and owners playing together, while cat owners just want to see a happy cat. New packages reflect those changes.

Intermediaries have some advantages in this battle. With the number of large retail chains growing, they are better able to arrange reliable sources of supply at low cost. They can also give dealer brands special shelf position and promotion. Because manufacturer brands typically need to build strong brand preference or brand insistence through heavy promotion and quality ingredients—both of which raise costs and lead to higher prices—national brands' prices are about 30 percent higher on average. Still, national brands are not going to disappear. Intermediaries know that many customers are still attracted to Mountain Dew, Colgate, Tide, and Cheerios.[21]

Packaging Promotes, Protects, and Enhances

LO 8.4

Packaging involves promoting, protecting, and enhancing the product. Packaging can be important to both sellers and customers (see Exhibit 8–5). It can make a product more convenient to use or store. It can prevent spoiling or damage. Good packaging makes products easier to identify and promotes the brand at the point of purchase and even in use.

Packaging can lower distribution costs

Better protective packaging is very important to manufacturers and wholesalers. They sometimes have to pay the cost of goods damaged in shipment. Retailers need protective packaging too. It can reduce storing costs by cutting breakage, spoilage, and theft. Good packages also save space and weight so they are easier to transport, handle, and display—and better for the environment.[22]

Exhibit 8–5 Some Ways Packaging Benefits Consumers and Marketers

Opportunity to Add Value	Some Decision Factors	Examples
Promoting	Link product to promotion	The bunny on the Energizer battery package is a reminder that it "keeps going and going."
	Branding at point of purchase or consumption	Coke's logo greets almost everyone each time the refrigerator is opened.
	Product information	Nabisco's nutrition label helps consumers decide which cookie to buy, and a UPC code reduces checkout time and errors.
Protecting	For shipping and storing	Cardboard inserts and a box protect the Roku streaming player.
	From tampering	Tylenol's safety seal prevents tampering.
	From shoplifting	Cardboard hang-tag on Gillette razor blades is too large to hide in hand.
	From spoiling	Kraft's shredded cheese has a resealable zipper package to keep it fresh.
Enhancing product	The environment	Tide detergent bottle can be recycled.
	Convenience in use	The package for Better Oats brand oatmeal includes a built-in measuring cup pouch so consumers don't need a measuring cup.
	Added product functions	Plastic tub is useful for refrigerator leftovers after the Cool Whip is gone.

When customers are likely to make a brand decision at the store shelf, packaging can call attention to a new product. Frontera promotes its line of corn chips by using bright bag colors, bold graphics, and chip viewing windows. The convenience of squeezeable packaging for baby food enhances the product for busy parents.
With permission of Frontera Foods, Inc. © McGraw-Hill Education; Mark Dierker, photographer.

Greener packaging creates value for buyers and sellers

U.S. shoppers generate much more trash per person than anywhere else on earth. Much of what is tossed out is packaging. It overloads landfills, litters streets, and pollutes the environment. For years plastic seemed to be the perfect packaging material because it is clean, light, and durable; unfortunately, this means it's everywhere and lasts forever. Even colorful package graphics are troublesome. The ink to print them often has toxins that later creep into the soil and water. Firms should try to give consumers what they want, but in applying that logic to packaging, many people have been short-sighted. Businesses and consumers alike have acted as if there was nothing an *individual* could do to reduce environmental problems. Now that attitude is changing.

Growing numbers of consumers are interested in making greener choices. Firms are making packaging choices that are better for the environment. For example, Timberland makes its shoe boxes with 100 percent recycled materials, soy-based inks, and water-based glues. Whole Foods Market uses salad bar containers made from sugarcane waste that they safely turn into compost within about 90 days. It makes sense for firms to publicize such efforts to attract like-minded consumers. Publicity also calls attention to the idea that even small changes can add up to big improvements.

Most sustainable packaging initiatives lower costs for producers too. For big brands, small changes can have huge impacts—on the environment and bottom line. Unilever has been a leader in this area. When it changed shipping cases for its Wishbone salad dressing, Unilever saved 21 metric tons of cardboard. A redesigned bottle and cap for Suave shampoo and conditioner is 15 percent lighter—reducing annual resin needed by 670 tons a year in the United States alone. Appliance manufacturers have eliminated cardboard in packaging, replacing it with foam blocks on corners. The foam is lighter and reduces shipping costs and damages that occur during loading, unloading, and transportation.[23]

The **Federal Fair Packaging and Labeling Act** (of 1966) requires that consumer goods be clearly labeled in easy-to-understand terms to give consumers more information. The law also calls on industry to try to reduce the confusing number of package sizes and make labels more useful. Since then, there have been further guidelines. The most far-reaching are based on the Nutrition Labeling and Education Act of 1990. It requires food manufacturers to use a uniform format that allows consumers to compare the nutritional value of different products. Recently there have been more changes, including requirements to clearly show the fat content of food and ingredients that trigger common food allergies.

The Courts tend to rule against misleading labels. For example, the Supreme Court ruled that Coca-Cola (which makes many different lines of juices) could be sued by POM Wonderful for calling one of its juices "Pomegranate-Blueberry" even though it had less than 1 percent pomegranate juice.[24]

© William D. Perreault, Jr., Ph.D.

Although various laws provide guidance on many packaging issues, many areas still require marketing managers to make ethical choices. For example, some firms have been criticized for designing packages that conceal a downsized product, giving consumers less for their money. Similarly, some retailers design packages and labels for their private-label products that look just like, and are easily confused with, manufacturer brands. Are efforts such as these unethical, or are they simply an attempt to make packaging a more effective part of a marketing mix? Different people will answer differently.

Many critics think that labeling information is too often incomplete or misleading. For example, what does it really mean if a label says a food product is "organic" or "low fat"? How far should a marketing manager go in putting potentially negative information on a package? Should Häagen-Dazs affix a label that says "this product will clog your arteries"? That sounds extreme, but what type of information *is* appropriate?

Many consumers like the convenience that accompanies the myriad product and packaging choices available. Is it unethical for a marketing manager to give consumers with different preferences a choice? Some critics argue that it is. Others praise firms that give consumers choices.[25]

Warranty Policies Are a Part of Strategy Planning

A **warranty** explains what the seller promises about its product. A marketing manager should decide whether to offer a specific warranty, and if so what the warranty will cover and how it will be communicated to target customers. This is an area where the legal environment—as well as customer needs and competitive offerings—must be considered.

U.S. common law says that producers must stand behind their products—even if they don't offer a specific warranty. A written warranty provided by the seller may promise more than the common law provides. However, it may actually *reduce* the responsibility a producer would have under common law.

The federal **Magnuson-Moss Act** (of 1975) says that producers must provide a clearly written warranty if they choose to offer any warranty. The warranty does not have to be strong. However, Federal Trade Commission (FTC) guidelines try to ensure that warranties are clear and definite and not deceptive or unfair. A warranty must also be available for inspection before the purchase.

A company has to make it clear whether it's offering a full or limited warranty—and the law defines what *full* means. Most firms offer a limited warranty if they offer one at all. In recent years, many firms have reduced the period of warranty coverage. Apple's popular iPod music player, for example, has a standard one-year warranty on hardware, but only a 90-day warranty on phone support. Apple *sells* a supplemental warranty to extend hardware and phone coverage for two years from date of purchase.

Service guarantees

Service guarantees are becoming more common as a way to attract, and keep, customers. Some Pizza Hut locations guarantee a luncheon pizza in five minutes or it's free. L.L. Bean and Lands' End have satisfaction guarantees, which allow customers to return products at any time for any reason. Hampton Inn, Garden Inn, and Embassy Suites (all Hilton brand hotels) also promise satisfaction or a guest does not pay. Guarantees such as these increase a customer's confidence that the brand can deliver on its promise and reduce the risk a customer might feel.[26]

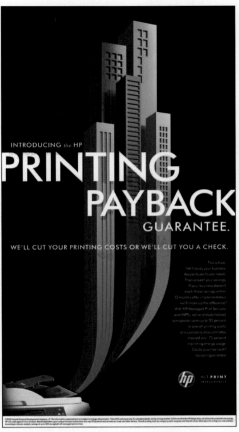

In a competitive market, a product's warranty or guarantee can be the critical difference in a firm's marketing mix.
© 2015 Hewlett-Packard Development Company, L.P.

Product Classes Help Plan Marketing Strategies

LO 8.6

So far in this chapter, we've focused on key strategy decisions for Product (see Exhibit 8–1). Managers usually try to blend those decisions in a unique way to differentiate the firm's offering and create superior customer value. However, you don't have to treat *every* product as unique when planning strategies—some classes of products benefit from similar marketing mixes. So now we'll introduce these product classes and show why they are a useful starting point for developing marketing mixes for new products and for evaluating present mixes.

Product classes start with type of customer

All products fit into one of two broad groups—based on the type of customer that will use them. **Consumer products** are products meant for the final consumer. **Business products** are products meant for use in producing other products.

The same product—like Bertolli Olive Oil—*might* be both a consumer product and a business product. Consumers buy it to use in their own kitchens, but food processing companies and restaurants buy it in large quantities as an ingredient in the products they sell. Selling the same product to both final consumers and business customers requires (at least) two different strategies.

There are product classes within each group. Consumer product classes are based on how consumers think about and shop for products. Business product classes are based on how buyers think about products and how they'll be used.

Consumer Product Classes

LO 8.7

Consumer product classes divide into four groups: (1) convenience, (2) shopping, (3) specialty, and (4) unsought. *Each class is based on the way people think about and shop for products.* See Exhibit 8–6 for a summary of how these product classes relate to marketing mixes.[27]

Convenience products— purchased quickly with little effort

Convenience products are products a consumer needs but isn't willing to spend much time or effort shopping for. These products are bought often, require little service or selling, don't cost much, and may even be bought by habit. A convenience product may be a staple, impulse product, or emergency product.

Staples are products that are bought often, routinely, and without much thought—such as breakfast cereal, canned soup, and most other packaged foods used almost every day in almost every household.

Impulse products are products that are bought quickly—as *unplanned* purchases—because of a strongly felt need. True impulse products are items that the customer hadn't planned to buy, decides to buy on sight, may have bought the same way many times before, and wants right now. If the buyer doesn't see an impulse product at the right time, the sale may be lost.[28]

Exhibit 8-6   Consumer Product Classes and Marketing Mix Planning

Consumer Product Class	Marketing Mix Considerations	Consumer Behavior
Convenience products		
Staples	Maximum exposure with widespread, low-cost distribution; mass selling by producer; usually low price; branding is important.	Routinized (habitual); low effort; frequent purchases; low involvement.
Impulse	Widespread distribution with display at point of purchase.	Unplanned purchases bought quickly.
Emergency	Need widespread distribution near probable point of need; price sensitivity low.	Purchase made with time pressure when a need is great.
Shopping products		
Homogeneous	Need enough exposure to facilitate price comparison; price sensitivity high.	Customers see little difference among alternatives and seek lowest price.
Heterogeneous	Need distribution near similar products; promotion (including personal selling) to highlight product advantages; less price sensitivity.	Extensive problem solving; consumer may need help in making a decision (salesperson, website, etc.).
Specialty products	Price sensitivity is likely to be low; limited distribution may be acceptable, but should be treated as a convenience or shopping product (in whichever category product would typically be included) to reach persons not yet sold on its specialty product status.	Willing to expend effort to get specific product, even if not necessary; strong preferences make it an important purchase; Internet becoming important information source.
Unsought products		
New unsought	Must be available in places where similar (or related) products are sought; needs attention-getting promotion.	Need for product not strongly felt; unaware of benefits or not yet gone through adoption process.
Regularly unsought	Requires very aggressive promotion, usually personal selling.	Aware of product but not interested; attitude toward product may even be negative.

Emergency products are products that are purchased immediately when the need is great. The customer doesn't have time to shop around when a traffic accident occurs, a thunderstorm begins, or an impromptu party starts. The price of the ambulance service, raincoat, or ice cubes won't be important.

Shopping products are compared

Shopping products are products that a customer feels are worth the time and effort to compare with competing products. Shopping products can be divided into two types, homogeneous or heterogeneous, depending on what customers are comparing. The exact same products can be homogeneous or heterogeneous. It just depends on how a particular target market thinks about and shops for the product.

Homogeneous shopping products are items the customer sees as basically the same and wants at the lowest price. So, for example, a target market that believes "all gasoline is the same" seeks out and buys gas at the station with the lowest prices. Another target market could believe that all 32-inch LED televisions are basically the same—so they shop the Internet for the lowest price. A low cost producer might try to promote that its products are "just as good as" higher priced alternatives. Vizio has used this strategy with considerable success in the television market.

Heterogeneous shopping products are items the customer sees as different and wants to inspect for quality and suitability—furniture, clothing, and membership in a spa are good examples. In this situation, target consumers seek information from a knowledgeable salesperson or a reputable website. Case in point: *Some* customers who *do* see 32-inch televisions as different will visit a local store to see various models and talk to a salesperson, then go to websites like CNET.com to read professional and user reviews.

For heterogeneous shopping products, quality, features, and style matter more than price. In fact, once the customer finds the right product, price may not matter as long as it's reasonable. For instance, you may have asked a friend to recommend a good dentist without even asking what the dentist charges.

Branding may be less important for heterogeneous shopping products. The more carefully consumers compare price and quality, the less they rely on brand names or labels. Some retailers carry competing brands so consumers won't go to a competitor to compare items.

For some target customers, Easter candy is an impulse purchase. It is important to display it where easily seen by the target market. Fresh Brothers hopes that many of its customers view its pizza as a specialty product and customers make a special effort to find one of its restaurants. Fresh Brothers Facebook page reminds its biggest fans about their pizza and communicates specials.

Left: © Ira Berger/Alamy; Right: Courtesy Fresh Brothers

Specialty products—no substitutes please!

Specialty products are consumer products that the customer really wants and makes a special effort to find. Shopping for a specialty product doesn't mean comparing—the buyer wants that special product and is willing to search for it. It's the customer's *willingness to search*—not the extent of searching—that makes it a specialty product.

Any branded product that consumers insist on by name is a specialty product. Marketing managers want customers to see their products as specialty products and ask for them over and over again. Building that kind of relationship isn't easy. It means satisfying the customer every time. However, that's easier and a lot less costly than trying to win back dissatisfied customers or attract new customers who are not seeking the product at all.

Unsought products need promotion

Unsought products are products that potential customers don't yet want or know they can buy. So they don't search for them at all. In fact, consumers probably won't buy these products if they see them—unless promotion can show their value.

There are two types of unsought products. **New unsought products** are products offering really new ideas that potential customers don't know about yet. Informative promotion can help convince customers to accept the product, ending its unsought status. Dannon's yogurt and Litton's microwave ovens are popular items now, but initially they were new unsought products.

Brand managers for pain reliever Panadol Ultra faced two challenges in rural Guatemala: 1) a high level of illiteracy and 2) an unsought product because many in the target market didn't know about using pills for pain relief. Panadol created a sponge in the shape of the pill that local women could use as a cushion when carrying heavy items on their heads—a common practice. Soon women became a walking ad for the brand and sales increased by 45 percent among the target market.
Courtesy Panadol Ultra; Agency: Saatchi & Saatchi/Guatemala.

Regularly unsought products are products—such as gravestones, life insurance, and nursing homes—that stay unsought but not unbought forever. There may be a need, but potential customers aren't motivated to satisfy it. For this kind of product, personal selling is *very* important.

Many nonprofit organizations try to "sell" their unsought products. For example, the American Red Cross regularly holds blood drives to remind prospective donors of how important it is to give blood.

One product may be seen in several ways

The same product might be seen in different ways by different target markets at the same time. For example, a product viewed as a staple by most consumers in the United States, Canada, or some similar affluent country might be seen as a heterogeneous shopping product by consumers in another country. The price might be much higher when considered as a proportion of the consumer's budget, and the available choices might be very different. Similarly, for some people salsa is seen as a staple; for others—who, for example, think it is worth tracking down W. B. Williams Georgia Style Peach Salsa on the Internet—it is a specialty product.

Business Products Are Different

Business product classes are different from consumer product classes because they relate to how and why business firms make purchases. Thus, knowing the specific classes of business products helps in strategy planning. First, however, it's useful to

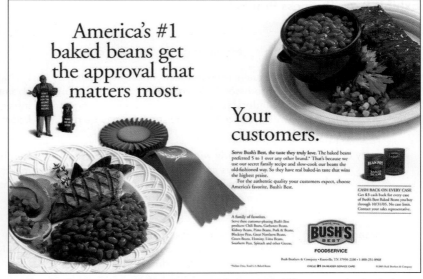

Many items in Bush's Best line of food products sell as both consumer and business products, and different marketing mixes are required to reach the different target markets.

Both images: Copyright © Bush Brothers & Company. All Rights Reserved.

note some important ways that the market for business products is different from the market for consumer products.

One demand derived from another

The big difference between the consumer products market and the business products market is **derived demand**—the demand for business products derives from the demand for final consumer products. For example, car manufacturers buy about one-fifth of all steel products. But if demand for cars drops, they'll buy less steel. Then even the steel supplier with the best marketing mix is likely to lose sales.[29]

Price increases might not reduce quantity purchased

Total *industry* demand for business products is fairly inelastic. Business firms must buy what they need to produce their own products. Even if the cost of basic silicon doubles, for example, Intel needs it to make computer chips. However, sharp business buyers try to buy as economically as possible. So the demand facing *individual sellers* may be extremely elastic—if similar products are available at a lower price.

Tax treatment affects buying too

How a firm's accountants—and the tax laws—treat a purchase is also important to business customers. An **expense item** is a product whose total cost is treated as a business expense in the year it's purchased. A **capital item** is a long-lasting product that can be used and depreciated for many years. Often it's very expensive. Customers pay for the capital item when they buy it, but for tax purposes the cost is spread over a number of years. This may reduce the cash available for other purchases.

Business Product Classes—How They Are Defined

Business product classes are based on how buyers think about products and how the products will be used. The classes of business products are (1) installations, (2) accessories, (3) raw materials, (4) components, (5) supplies, and (6) professional services. Exhibit 8–7 relates these product classes to marketing mix planning.

Installations—a boom-or-bust business

Installations—such as buildings, land rights, and major equipment—are important capital items. One-of-a-kind installations—such as office buildings and custom-made machines—generally require special negotiations for each sale. Negotiations often

Exhibit 8-7 Business Product Classes and Marketing Mix Planning

Business Product Classes	Marketing Mix Considerations	Buying Behavior
Installations	Usually requires skillful personal selling by producer, including technical contacts, or understanding of applications; leasing and specialized support services may be required.	Multiple buying influence (including top management) and new-task buying are common; infrequent purchase, long decision period, and boom-or-bust demand are typical.
Accessory equipment	Need fairly widespread distribution and numerous contacts by experienced and sometimes technically trained personnel; price competition is often intense, but quality is important.	Purchasing and operating personnel typically make decisions; shorter decision period than for installations; Internet sourcing.
Raw materials	Grading is important, and transportation and storing can be crucial because of seasonal production and/or perishable products; markets tend to be very competitive.	Long-term contract may be required to ensure supply; online auctions.
Component parts and materials	Product quality and delivery reliability are usually extremely important; negotiation and technical selling typical on less-standardized items; replacement after-market may require different strategies.	Multiple buying influence is common; online competitive bids used to encourage competitive pricing.
Maintenance, repair, and operating (MRO) supplies	Typically require widespread distribution or fast delivery (repair items); arrangements with appropriate intermediaries may be crucial.	Often handled as straight rebuys, except important operating supplies may be treated much more seriously and involve multiple buying influence.
Professional services	Services customized to buyer's need; personal selling very important; inelastic demand often supports high prices.	Customer may compare outside service with what internal people could provide; needs may be very specialized.

involve top management and can stretch over months or even years. Standardized major equipment is treated more routinely.

Installations are a boom-or-bust business. During growth periods, firms may buy installations to increase capacity. But during a downswing, sales fall off sharply.[30]

Specialized services are needed as part of the product

Suppliers sometimes include special services with an installation at no extra cost. A firm that sells (or leases) equipment to dentists, for example, may install it and help the dentist learn to use it.

Accessories—important but short-lived capital items

Accessories are short-lived capital items—tools and equipment used in production or office activities—such as Canon's small copy machines, Rockwell's portable drills, and Steelcase's filing cabinets. Accessories are more standardized than installations and they're usually needed by more customers.

Because these products cost less and last a shorter time than installations, multiple buying influence is less important. Operating people and purchasing agents, rather than top managers, may make the purchase decision. As with installations, some customers may wish to lease or rent—to expense the cost.

Raw materials become part of a physical good

Raw materials are unprocessed expense items—such as logs, iron ore, and wheat—that are moved to the next production process with little handling. Unlike installations and accessories, *raw materials become part of a physical good and are expense items*.

There are two types of raw materials: (1) farm products and (2) natural products. **Farm products** are grown by farmers—examples are oranges, sugar cane, and cattle. **Natural products** are products that occur in nature—such as timber, iron ore, oil, and coal.

The need for grading is one of the important differences between raw materials and other business products. Nature produces what it will—and someone must sort and grade raw materials to satisfy various market segments.

Most buyers of raw materials want ample supplies in the right grades for specific uses—fresh vegetables for Green Giant's production lines or logs for Weyerhaeuser's paper mills. To ensure steady quantities, raw materials customers often sign long-term contracts, sometimes at guaranteed prices.

Component parts and materials must meet specifications

Components are processed expense items that become part of a finished product. Component *parts* are finished (or nearly finished) items that are ready for assembly into the final product. Intel's microprocessors included in personal computers and TRW's air bags in cars are examples. Component *materials* are items such as wire, plastic, or textiles. They have already been processed but must be processed further before becoming part of the final product. Quality is important with components because they become part of the firm's own product.

Some components are custom-made. Then teamwork between the buyer and seller may be needed to arrive at the right specifications. So a buyer may develop a close partnership with a dependable supplier. In contrast, standardized component materials are more likely to be purchased online using a competitive bidding system.

Because component parts go into finished products, a replacement market often develops. Car tires are components originally sold in the *OEM (original equipment market)* that become consumer products in the *aftermarket*.[31]

Supplies for maintenance, repair, and operations

Supplies are expense items that do not become part of a finished product. Supplies can be divided into three types: (1) maintenance, (2) repair, and (3) operating supplies—giving them their common name: MRO supplies.

Maintenance and small operating supplies are like convenience products. The item will be ordered because it is needed—but buyers won't spend much time on it. For such "nuisance" purchases branding is important, and so are breadth of assortment and the seller's dependability. Intermediaries usually handle the many supply items. They are often purchased via online catalog sites.[32]

Business product classes are based on what buyers think about products and how the product will be used. Grainger is a wholesaler that offers a wide range of maintenance, repair, and operating supplies (often called MRO supplies). Accenture is a consulting firm that offers its professional services to a wide range of companies.

Important operating supplies, such as coal and fuel oil, receive special treatment. Usually there are several sources for such commodity products—and large volumes may be purchased at global exchanges on the Internet.

Professional services—pay to get it done

Professional services are specialized services that support a firm's operations. They are usually expense items. Management consulting services can improve the company's efficiency. Information technology services can maintain a company's networks and websites. Advertising agencies can help promote the firm's products. And food services can improve morale.

Managers compare the cost of buying professional services outside the firm (*outsourcing*) to the cost of having company people do them. Work that was previously done by an employee is now often purchased from an independent specialist. Clearly, the number of service specialists is growing in our complex economy.

CONCLUSION

In this chapter, we looked at Product broadly—which is the right vantage point for marketing strategy planning. We saw that a product may be a good or a service, or some combination of both. And we saw that a firm's Product is what it offers to *satisfy the needs of its target market*—which may include the customer's experience both before and after the purchase. We also described some key marketing differences between goods and services.

We reviewed the Product area strategy decisions required for branding and packaging—and saw how the right decisions can add value for customers and give a product a competitive edge. Customers view a brand as a guarantee of quality, which leads to repeat purchases, lower promotion costs, higher sales figures, and greater customer equity. Packaging offers promotional opportunities and informs customers. Variations in packaging can also help a product

appeal to different segments of the market. And packaging can help protect the product anywhere in the channel of distribution. We also saw how warranties can play an important role in strategy planning—by reducing buying risk. Customers see warranties as a signal of quality.

The brand familiarity a product earns is a measure of the marketing manager's ability to carve out a separate market. Therefore, ultimately, brand familiarity affects Place, Price, and Promotion decisions. Strategy planning for the marketing mix will vary across product classes. We introduced both consumer product classes (based on *how consumers think about and shop for products*) and business product classes (based on *how buyers think about products and how they'll be used*). In addition, we showed how the product classes affect planning marketing mixes.

WHAT'S NOW?

This chapter introduced product planning for goods and services. For some current real-world examples and learnings, check out *What's Now?* at www.learnthe4ps.com/whatsnow/c8

KEY TERMS

LO 8.8

product, 200	brand name, 204	brand preference, 208
quality, 200	trademark, 204	brand insistence, 208
individual product, 201	service mark, 204	brand equity, 209
product line, 201	brand familiarity, 207	Lanham Act, 209
product assortment, 201	brand rejection, 207	family brand, 210
service, 202	brand nonrecognition, 207	licensed brand, 210
branding, 201	brand recognition, 207	individual brands, 210

QUESTIONS AND PROBLEMS

1. Review the Under Armour case study that opens this chapter. From this case, identify examples of different key terms and concepts covered in the chapter. For example, Kohl's Tek Gear is an example of a dealer brand.

2. Review the Under Armour case study that opens this chapter. Using three different consumer product classes as an example, describe how a customer would think about and buy Under Armour products. Then examine the marketing mix considerations in Exhibit 8–6 for each of the product classes you chose. What would Under Armour need to do to support the marketing strategy for each?

3. Define, in your own words, what a Product is.

4. Discuss several ways in which physical goods are different from pure services. Give an example of a good and then an example of a service that illustrates each of the differences.

5. What products are being offered by a shop that specializes in bicycles? By a travel agent? By a supermarket? By a new car dealer?

6. Consumer services tend to be intangible, and goods tend to be tangible. Use an example to explain how the lack of a physical good in a pure service might affect efforts to promote the service.

7. Explain some of the different aspects of the customer experience that could be managed to improve customer satisfaction if you were the marketing manager for: (a) an airport branch of a rental car agency, (b) a fast-food restaurant, (c) an online firm selling software directly to consumers from a website, and (d) a hardware store selling lawn mowers.

8. Is there any difference between a brand name and a trademark? If so, why is this difference important?

9. Is a well-known brand valuable only to the owner of the brand?

10. Suggest an example of a product and a competitive situation where it would not be profitable for a firm to spend large sums of money to establish a brand.

11. List five brand names and indicate what product is associated with the brand name. Evaluate the strengths and weaknesses of the brand name.

12. Explain family brands. Should Best Buy carry its own dealer brands to compete with some of the popular manufacturer brands it carries? Explain your reasons.

13. In the past, Sears emphasized its own dealer brands. Now it is carrying more well-known manufacturer brands. What are the benefits to Sears of carrying more manufacturer brands?

14. What does the degree of brand familiarity imply about previous and future promotion efforts? How does the degree of brand familiarity affect the Place and Price variables?

15. You operate a small hardware store with an emphasis on manufacturer brands and have barely been breaking even. Evaluate the proposal of a large wholesaler that offers a full line of dealer-branded hardware items at substantially lower prices. Specify any assumptions necessary to obtain a definite answer.

16. Give an example where packaging costs probably (a) lower total distribution costs and (b) raise total distribution costs.

17. How would the marketing mix for a staple convenience product differ from the mix for a homogeneous shopping product? How would the mix for a specialty product differ from the mix for a heterogeneous shopping product? Use examples.

18. Give an example of a product that is a *new* unsought product for most people. Briefly explain why it is an unsought product.

19. In what types of stores would you expect to find (a) convenience products, (b) shopping products, (c) specialty products, and (d) unsought products?

20. What kinds of consumer products are the following: (a) watches, (b) automobiles, and (c) toothpastes? Explain your reasoning.

21. Cite two examples of business products that require a substantial amount of service in order to be useful.

22. Explain why a new law office might want to lease furniture rather than buy it.

23. Would you expect to find any wholesalers selling the various types of business products? Are retail stores required (or something like retail stores)?

24. What kinds of business products are the following: (a) lubricating oil, (b) electric motors, and (c) a firm that provides landscaping and grass mowing for an apartment complex? Explain your reasoning.

25. How do raw materials differ from other business products? Do the differences have any impact on their marketing mixes? If so, what specifically?

26. For the kinds of business products described in this chapter, complete the following table (be brief, use one or a few well-chosen words).

    1. *Kind of distribution facility(ies) needed and functions they will provide.*

    2. *Caliber of salespeople required.*

    3. *Kind of advertising required.*

Products	1	2	3
Installations			
Buildings and land rights			
Major equipment			
Standard			
Custom-made			
Accessories			
Raw materials			
Farm products			
Natural products			
Components			
Supplies			
Maintenance and small operating supplies			
Important operating supplies			
Professional services			

MARKETING PLANNING FOR HILLSIDE VETERINARY CLINIC

Appendix D (the Appendices follow Chapter 19) includes a sample marketing plan for Hillside Veterinary Clinic. Look through the "Marketing Strategy" section.

a. What goods does Hillside Veterinary Clinic sell?

b. What services does Hillside Veterinary Clinic sell?

c. What consumer product classes are offered by Hillside Veterinary Clinic?

d. The discussion of product classes in this chapter indicates what marketing mix is typical for different classes of products. Does the marketing strategy recommended in Hillside's marketing plan fit with those considerations? Why or why not?

SUGGESTED CASES

1. McDonald's "Senior" Restaurant
3. Real NOCO Soccer Academy
13. AAA Office World
31. Bowman Home Health Services

Video Case 3. Toyota Prius
Video Case 7. Invacare

MARKETING ANALYTICS: DATA TO KNOWLEDGE

CHAPTER 8 BRANDING DECISION

Wholesteen Dairy, Inc., produces and sells Wholesteen brand condensed milk to grocery retailers. The overall market for condensed milk is fairly mature, and there's sharp competition among dairies for retailers' business. Wholesteen's regular price to retailers is $8.88 a case (24 cans). FoodWorld—a fast-growing supermarket chain and Wholesteen's largest customer—buys 20,000 cases of Wholesteen's condensed milk

a year. That's 20 percent of Wholesteen's total sales volume of 100,000 cases per year.

FoodWorld is proposing that Wholesteen produce private-label condensed milk to be sold with the FoodWorld brand name. FoodWorld proposes to buy the same total quantity as it does now, but it wants half (10,000 cases) with the Wholesteen brand and half with the FoodWorld brand. FoodWorld wants Wholesteen to reduce costs by using a lower-quality can for the FoodWorld brand. That change will cost Wholesteen $.01 less per can than it costs for the cans that Wholesteen uses for its own brand. FoodWorld will also provide preprinted labels with its brand name—which will save Wholesteen an additional $.02 a can.

Wholesteen spends $70,000 a year on promotion to increase familiarity with the Wholesteen brand. In addition, Wholesteen gives retailers an allowance of $.25 per case for their local advertising, which features the Wholesteen brand. FoodWorld has agreed to give up the advertising allowance for its own brand, but it is only willing to pay $7.40 a case for the milk that will be sold with the FoodWorld brand name. It will continue under the old terms for the rest of its purchases.

Sue Glick, Wholesteen's marketing manager, is considering the FoodWorld proposal. She has entered cost and revenue data on a spreadsheet—so she can see more clearly how the proposal might affect revenue and profits.

See Connect for the spreadsheet and questions needed to analyze this scenario.

9

CHAPTER NINE

Product Management and New-Product Development

The founders of iRobot didn't know that their company would become the world leader in home robots. However, from the start they didn't intend to just imitate other firms' products. Instead they wanted to create totally new product concepts that would change society. That is where they're headed, with products that help consumers around the house—such as Roomba, Scooba, and Looj—and products for business, government, and the military—such as Ava 500 and PackBot. Ava 500 will allow a new level of collaboration for office environments. The military used PackBot to clear roadside bombs in Iraq and search caves in Afghanistan. Let's take a closer look at how iRobot got to where it is today.

When iRobot started, the company focused on just military and business products. One project with S. C. Johnson involved industrial cleaning robots. iRobot later entered the consumer market, developing concepts for robotic toys for Hasbro. Here it learned the importance of cost control; for two years, many toy ideas iRobot pitched to Hasbro were rejected. They were technically elegant but too expensive. These experiences helped iRobot focus on an idea for a low-priced robotic vacuum cleaner—later named the Roomba.

Roomba's new-product developers knew the importance of taking the customer's perspective. So early prototypes of the Roomba went home with iRobot employees, where their spouses, friends, and neighbors could test them. The developers gained valuable feedback and quickly learned that not everyone was technically savvy. So when design engineers talked about how best to train customers to use the Roomba, the team realized that was backward. Instead of training customers, they designed Roomba's software to figure out what to do when a customer pushed the start button. The Roomba is so simple to use that the owner's manual is only a few pages long, and most people don't need it.

The original idea was for Roomba to just have sweeper brushes. However, in focus groups consumers said that the Roomba also needed a vacuum. Responding to this consumer input added extra expense late in the project, but iRobot was ready because of the cost-control lessons learned from working with Hasbro. With Roomba, developers had controlled every penny from the outset and were able to add the vacuum and value consumers wanted.

Before iRobot introduced the Roomba, the vacuum cleaner market was mature, with few breakthrough product ideas. Then came Roomba. It's a slick looking, 15-inch disk, less than 4 inches tall. It's a robot but requires no programming. You simply place it on the floor, press a button to turn it on, and Roomba scurries around the room doing its job. It can scoot under the sofa, avoid the furniture, and return to the battery charger when the job is done.

Marketing managers wanted to sell Roomba to a large market segment—people who hate to vacuum. But they were concerned the Roomba's appeal might be limited to a small market of gadget-loving techies. To offset consumer concerns about the complexity of the technology, introductory promotion described the Roomba as an intelligent vacuum cleaner. For the first three years, the word robot didn't even appear on the package (except in the iRobot company name).

For its launch, iRobot worked with specialty retailers such as Sharper Image and Brookstone. These retailers were willing to show videos of Roomba in action and train their salespeople to explain and demonstrate Roomba in their stores. The extra promotion push was important because initially customers didn't know the brand name and were not looking for this sort of product. However, iRobot quickly generated publicity for the Roomba—with everything from appearances on the "Today" show and videos on YouTube, to reviews in magazines, newspapers, and at CNET.com. All of this media attention—and some traditional advertising—propelled sales and quickly made Roomba a familiar brand. Soon iRobot expanded distribution to Bed Bath and Beyond, Target, and Amazon.com.

By controlling costs, iRobot initially priced Roomba at $200. A higher price might have been acceptable to some customers, but that low price helped fend off potential competitors, at least for a while. Soon other competitors, including Electrolux, P3, iTouchless, and Infinuvo jumped into the market. But Roomba's established brand kept it ahead of the pack.

iRobot's sales grew quickly, and it is now a well-known brand with more than 13 million home robots, with Roomba leading the charge, sold. iRobot's product managers are always listening to the market to identify customer needs. Then they work with iRobot's engineers to develop new features. For example, some models include Dirt Detect Series 2. This new feature uses sensors that recognize the dirtiest areas, which then receive more concentrated cleaning. Differentiation helps iRobot generate higher margins and better return on investment on all its Roomba models—which range in price from $350 to $700.

An aging population and rising health care costs offer a new opportunity for iRobot in the medical field. iRobot partnered with InTouch Health in developing RP-VITA (short for Remote Presence Virtual + Independent Telemedicine Assistant). RP-VITA is designed to deliver acute care and remote consultation by bringing doctors to patients. With more than 150 different types of medical specialties, few hospitals have ready access to all of them. So RP-VITA brings specialists, who are usually located in large urban hospitals, to patients in need of their expertise. For example, a vascular surgeon in Houston can check on a stroke victim at the St. Charles Medical Center in Redmond, Oregon. With a touch of his iPad, the doctor tells RP-VITA (in Redmond) which patient he wants to see. The robot navigates busy hallways and enters the patient's room. Two-way video lets the surgeon talk with the patient, read her chart, and even check her eyes for dilated pupils. Then he recommends the next stage of treatment and monitors the outcomes. Robots like RP-VITA offer one way to tame rising health care costs.

iRobot's creative product development and marketing strategy have resulted in remarkable growth. Sales have grown from $54 million in 2003 to more than $600 million just 12 years later. To keep that going, iRobot must continue to fill its pipeline with new products that meet tomorrow's customers' needs.[1]

LEARNING OBJECTIVES

Developing new products and managing them for profitable growth are keys to success for most firms. Yet many new products fail. Even products that succeed face new challenges as competition becomes more intense. So the marketing strategy that supported the product's initial success usually needs to change as the market evolves. This chapter will help you understand this evolution and how it relates to effective new-product development and creative strategy changes for existing products—both of which are crucial to attracting and retaining target customers.

When you finish this chapter, you should be able to

1 Understand how product life cycles affect strategy planning.

2 Describe what is involved in designing new products and what "new products" really are.

3 Understand the new-product development process.

4 Appreciate the team effort that goes into new-product development.

5 Understand the need for product or brand managers.

6 Understand how total quality management can improve goods and services.

7 Understand important new terms (shown in red).

Innovation and Market Changes Create Opportunities

Successful new products, like those in the iRobot case, are critical in driving profitable growth for both new and established companies. iRobot pioneered a fast-growing new product-market—and "computer-controlled cleaning tools" are meeting customer needs in new ways. Similarly, in Chapter 5, we looked at how the iPod, iPhone, and other innovations in digital media have changed personal entertainment. In fact, all around us there is a constant life-and-death struggle where old products are replaced by new products. Before Crest Whitening Strips, the only path to whiter teeth was expensive processes in a dentist's office. And who knows whether new Meow Mix Tender Centers will revolutionize cat food or Nabisco Belvita Breakfast Biscuits will change the way Americans eat breakfast. These recent new product launches have attracted initial interest from consumers.[2]

These innovations show that products, customer behavior, and competition change over time. These changes create opportunities for marketing managers and pose challenges as well. Developing new products and managing existing products to meet changing conditions are important to the success of every firm. In Chapter 8 we looked at important strategy planning decisions that need to be made for new products and sometimes changed for existing products. In this chapter, we'll look at how successful new products are developed in the first place—and what marketing managers need to know and do to manage their growth. We'll start by explaining the cycle of growth and decline that new product innovations go through. When you understand the stages in this cycle, you can see *why* it is so critical for a firm to have an effective new-product development process—and why the challenges of managing a product change as it matures (see Exhibit 9–1).

Managing Products over Their Life Cycles

LO 9.1

Revolutionary products create new product-markets. But competitors are always developing and copying new ideas and products—making existing products out of date more quickly than ever. Products, like consumers, go through life cycles.

Product life cycle has four major stages

The **product life cycle** describes the stages a really new product idea goes through from beginning to end. The product life cycle is divided into four major stages: (1) market introduction, (2) market growth, (3) market maturity, and (4) sales decline. The product life cycle is concerned with new types (or categories) of products in the market, not just what happens to an individual brand.

Exhibit 9-2
Typical Life Cycle of a
New-Product Concept

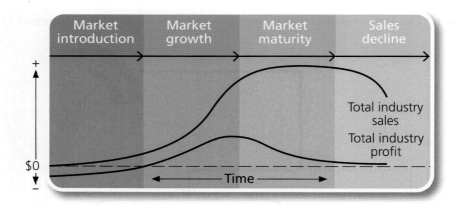

A particular firm's marketing mix usually must change during the product life cycle. There are several reasons why customers' attitudes and needs may change over the product life cycle. The product may be aimed at entirely different target markets at different stages. And the nature of competition moves toward pure competition or oligopoly.

Further, total sales of the product—by all competitors in the industry—vary in each of its four stages. They move from very low in the market introduction stage to high at market maturity and then back to low in the sales decline stage. More important, the profit picture changes too. These general relationships can be seen in Exhibit 9–2. Note that sales and profits do not move together over time. *Industry profits decline while industry sales are still rising.*[3]

Market introduction—investing in the future

In the **market introduction** stage, sales are low as a new idea is first introduced to a market. Customers aren't looking for the product. Even if the product offers superior value, customers don't even know about it. Informative promotion is needed to tell potential customers about the advantages and uses of the new-product concept.

Even though a firm promotes its new product, it takes time for customers to learn that the product is available. Most companies experience losses during the introduction stage because they spend so much money for Product, Place, and Promotion development. Of course, they invest the money in the hope of future profits.

Market growth—profits go up and down

In the **market growth** stage, industry sales grow fast—but industry profits rise and then start falling. The innovator begins to make big profits as more and more customers buy. But competitors see the opportunity and enter the market. After East African Breweries created a sensation in Nigeria with its non-alcoholic malt beverage Alvaro, Coca-Cola followed eight months later with its own malt drink Novida.[4] Some just copy the most successful product or try to improve it to compete better. Others try to refine their offerings to do a better job of appealing to some target markets. The new entries result in much product variety. So monopolistic competition—with down-sloping demand curves—is typical of the market growth stage.

This is the time of biggest profits *for the industry.* It is also a time of rapid sales and earnings growth for companies with effective strategies. *But it is toward the end of this stage when industry profits begin to decline* as competition and consumer price sensitivity increase (see Exhibit 9–2).

Market maturity—sales level off, profits decline

The **market maturity** stage occurs when industry sales level off and competition gets tougher. Many aggressive competitors have entered the race for profits—except in oligopoly situations. Industry profits go down throughout the market maturity stage because promotion costs rise and some competitors cut prices to attract business. Less efficient firms can't compete with this pressure—and they drop out of the market. There is a long-run downward pressure on prices.

In market maturity, persuasive advertising shows how brands are different.
Left: ®™ Trademarks © Mars, Incorporated 2015; Right: © Jardiland

New firms may still enter the market at this stage—increasing competition even more. Note that late entries skip the early life-cycle stages, including the profitable market growth stage. And they must try to take a share of the saturated market from established firms, which is difficult and expensive. The market leaders have a lot at stake, so they fight hard to defend their share. Customers who are happy with their current relationship won't switch to a new brand. So late entrants usually have a tough battle.

Persuasive promotion becomes even more important during the market maturity stage. Products may differ only slightly. Most competitors have discovered effective appeals or just copied the leaders. As the various products become almost the same in the minds of potential consumers, price sensitivity is a real factor.[5]

In the United States, the markets for most cars, most household appliances, and many consumer packaged goods such as breakfast cereal, carbonated soft drinks, and laundry detergent are in market maturity. This stage may continue for many years—until a basically new product idea comes along—even though individual brands or models come and go.

Sales decline—a time of replacement

During the **sales decline** stage, new products replace the old. Price competition from dying products becomes more vigorous—but firms with strong brands may make profits until the end because they have successfully differentiated their products.

As the new products go through their introduction stage, the old ones may keep some sales by appealing to their most loyal customers or those who are slow to try new ideas. These conservative buyers might switch later—smoothing the sales decline.

Product life cycles don't relate to individual products

Product life cycles describe *industry* sales and profits for a *product idea* within a particular product-market. The sales and profits of an individual brand may not, and often do not, follow the life-cycle pattern. They may vary up and down throughout the life cycle—sometimes moving in the opposite direction of industry sales and profits.

A firm may introduce or drop a specific product during *any* stage of the product life cycle. A "me-too" brand introduced during the market growth stage, for example, may never get sales at all and suffer a quick death. For example, Walmart tried to rent DVDs by mail after Netflix was already established as the market leader. When customers did not see Walmart's marketing mix as better, it failed to attract enough customers and closed operations.

Each market should be carefully defined	A product idea can also be in a different life-cycle stage in different markets. For example, in the United States, milk is in the market maturity stage. U.S. consumers drink 18 times more milk than Asian consumers do—where milk is in the market introduction stage. Some firms in the dairy business are trying to grow the Asian market. To appeal to the Asian palate, they are selling milk with added flavors such as ginger and honey.[6]

Strategy planners who naïvely expect sales of an individual product to follow the general product life-cycle pattern are likely to be surprised. In fact, it might be more sensible to think in terms of "product-market life cycles" rather than product life cycles— but we will use the term *product life cycle* because it is commonly accepted and widely used. |

Product Life Cycles Vary in Length

How long a whole product life cycle takes—and the length of each stage—varies wildly across products. The cycle may vary from a few years—in the case of pocket-size video cameras (which were quickly replaced by smartphones)—to more than 100 years for gas-powered cars.

The product life-cycle concept does not tell a manager precisely *how long* the cycle will last. But a manager can often make a good guess based on the life cycles for similar products. Sometimes marketing research can help too.

Product life cycles are getting shorter	Although the life cycles for different products vary, in general, product life cycles are getting shorter. This is partly due to rapidly changing technology. One new invention may make possible many new products that replace old ones. Tiny electronic microchips led to thousands of new products—from Texas Instruments calculators in the early days to microchip-controlled heart valves now.

Think about how many years it took for some of the world's major innovations to reach 25 percent of the U.S. population: it took electricity 46 years; the telephone, 35 years; the personal computer, 16 years; and the Internet, 7 years. How soon will it be before 25 percent of the American population has drones or driverless cars? |
| **Why some products grow more quickly** | A new-product idea will move quickly through the early stages of the product life cycle when the innovation has certain characteristics. For example, the greater the *comparative advantage* of a new product over those already on the market, the more rapidly its sales will grow. Sales growth is also faster when the product is *easy to use* and if its advantages are *easy to communicate*. If the product *can be tried* on a limited basis—without a lot of risk to the customer—it can usually be introduced more quickly. Finally, if the product is *compatible* with the values and experiences of target customers, they are likely to buy it more quickly.[7]

The fast adoption of DVD players is a good example. The idea of renting or buying movies to view at home was already *compatible* with consumer lifestyles, but many consumers hesitated before buying a DVD player. They also saw DVD rental as *compatible* when they went to a video rental store and saw video tapes and a growing number of DVDs to rent. A demo of a DVD movie at a store or a friend's house made for compelling *communication* of the *comparative advantage* of better picture and audio quality. Another advantage was highlighted in ads showing DVD extras such as deleted scenes and interviews with directors. Some consumers didn't see the value when DVD players were priced at several hundred dollars—but when prices dropped, these customers quickly bought DVD players. Now media streaming players, including Apple TV, Roku, Chromecast and others, offer many of these same characteristics and are moving into the market growth stage and are likely to replace DVD players.[8] |

New products that do a better job of meeting the needs of specific target customers are more likely to move quickly and successfully through the introductory stage of the product life cycle. Square register allows individuals and retailers to accept credit cards on their smartphone or tablet computer. Such convenience, coupled with low cost, helped the product swiftly move into the market growth stage of the product life cycle.

© 2009–2015 Square, Inc.

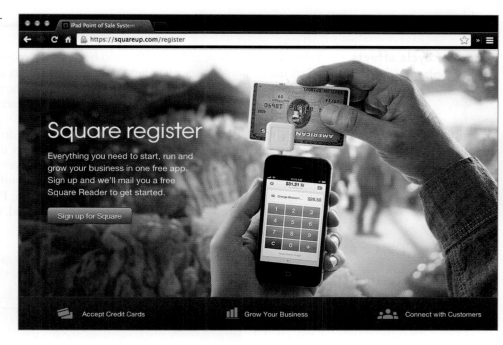

Pioneer or follower—which strategy works best?

The product life cycle means that firms must be developing new products all the time. Further, they must try to use marketing mixes that will make the most of the market growth stage—when profits are highest. The question becomes, is it better to be the *pioneer*—the first to market with a new-product idea—or a *follower?*

On average, pioneers tend to be less profitable over the long run—in part because many do not survive. That said, there are some real success stories among pioneers. For example, FedEx invented overnight delivery and remains the market leader. More often, though, there is an advantage to being the *second-mover*—one that quickly follows the pioneer. Second-movers that have a strong customer focus and respond quickly with a superior marketing mix can build market share during the market growth stage.

There are many examples of successful second-movers. Although many consider Apple to be an innovator, the iPod, iPhone, and iPad were not the first of their kind to market. Yet Apple responded quickly with a better marketing mix in each of these product categories. Likewise, Amazon wasn't the first online bookstore. Bookstacks launched the online Books.com (a site later sold to Barnes & Noble) three years before Amazon. RC Cola had the first diet cola on the market—but Coke and Pepsi quickly copied the idea and took over the market. An observant second-mover can learn from the pioneer's mistakes and quickly come to market with a marketing mix that provides superior value.[9]

The short happy life of fashions and fads

The sales of some products are influenced by **fashion**—the currently accepted or popular style. Fashion-related products tend to have short life cycles. What is currently popular can shift rapidly. A certain color or style of clothing—baggy jeans, miniskirts, wayfarer glasses, or four-inch-wide ties—may be in fashion one season and outdated the next. Marketing managers who work with fashions often have to make really fast product changes.

A **fad** is an idea that is fashionable only to certain groups who are enthusiastic about it. But these groups are so fickle that a fad is even more short lived than a regular fashion. Many toys—whether digital pets like Tomagatchi or shaped rubber bands like Silly Bandz—are fads, but do well during a short-lived cycle.[10]

Planning for Different Stages of the Product Life Cycle

Length of cycle affects strategy planning

Where a product is in its life cycle—and how fast it's moving to the next stage—should affect marketing strategy planning. Marketing managers must make realistic plans for the later stages. Exhibit 9–3 shows the relationship of the product life cycle to the marketing mix variables. The technical terms in this figure are discussed later in the book.

Introducing new products

Exhibit 9–3 shows that a marketing manager has to do a lot of strategy planning to introduce a really new product. Money must be spent developing the new product. Even if the product is unique, this doesn't mean that everyone will immediately come running to the producer's door. The firm will have to build channels of distribution—perhaps offering special incentives to win cooperation. Promotion is needed to build demand *for the whole idea* not just to sell a specific brand. Because all this is expensive,

Exhibit 9-3
Typical Changes in the Marketing Mix over the Product Life Cycle

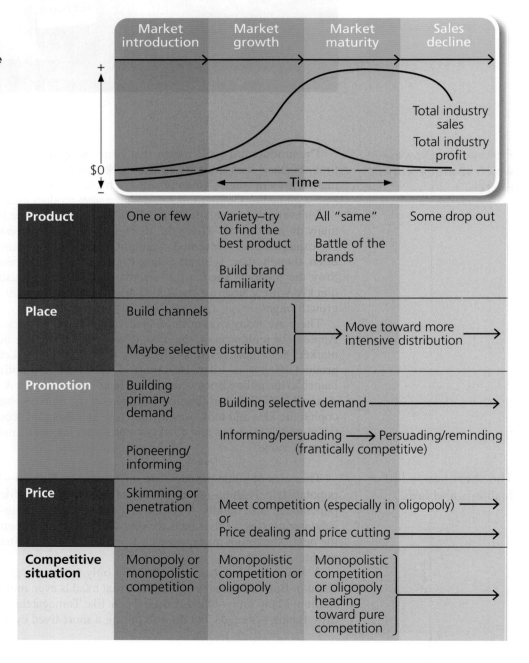

	Market introduction	Market growth	Market maturity	Sales decline
Product	One or few	Variety—try to find the best product Build brand familiarity	All "same" Battle of the brands	Some drop out
Place	Build channels Maybe selective distribution	Move toward more intensive distribution →		
Promotion	Building primary demand Pioneering/informing	Building selective demand ————————→ Informing/persuading → Persuading/reminding (frantically competitive)		
Price	Skimming or penetration	Meet competition (especially in oligopoly) ———→ or Price dealing and price cutting ————————→		
Competitive situation	Monopoly or monopolistic competition	Monopolistic competition or oligopoly	Monopolistic competition or oligopoly heading toward pure competition →	

it may lead the marketing manager to try to "skim" the market—charging a relatively high price to help pay for the introductory costs.

The correct strategy, however, depends on how quickly the new idea will be accepted by customers—and how quickly competitors will follow with their own versions of the product. When the early stages of the cycle will be fast, a low initial (penetration) price may make sense to help develop loyal customers early and keep competitors out.

Be prepared to pivot to a new marketing mix

It can be difficult to predict customer response to a really new product. So marketing managers need to carefully monitor initial customer reactions and be prepared to *pivot*—or move to a new marketing mix. After all the effort of planning a new product, this can be difficult for some marketing managers. Yet this is what the developers of "Game Neverending," a massive multiplayer online game, did following the game's launch. The game did not catch on as the developers had hoped, but they noticed that a photo-sharing element of the game was a popular feature. Soon the game was gone, but a photo-sharing service called Flickr was born. Flickr became a great success—more than 50 million photos are uploaded each month—because of the developers' willingness to pivot to a different marketing mix.

Pioneers may need help

Sometimes, before an innovation can take off, a number of different companies need to come together. For example, electric cars require charging stations—or drivers can't wander too far from home. Similarly, Hulu and HBO GO needed widespread availability of low-cost high speed Internet service for customers to utilize their streaming video services.

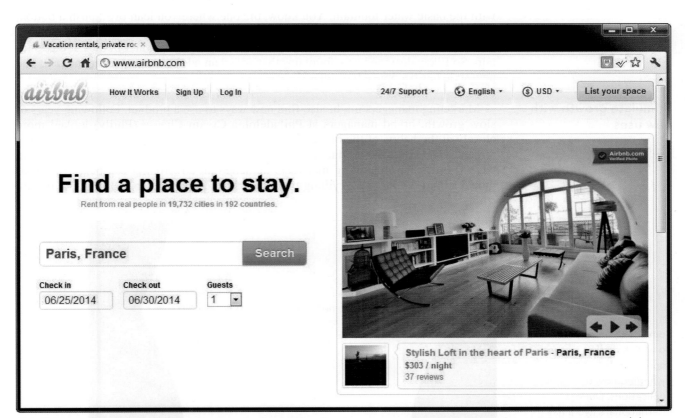

Airbnb is a community marketplace to discover, list, and book unique accommodations in more than 25,000 cities around the world. Airbnb hosts list their extra space, be it a private island, a tree house, an igloo, or a castle, and guests discover and book these spaces for short- or long-term stays. Because this was a new idea to many of Airbnb's target customers, Airbnb had to build primary demand in the market introduction stage; it used promotion to tell its target market how the service works. E-mail campaigns, listings on Craigslist, publicity, and positive word-of-mouth have helped it rapidly grow in room nights booked.
© Airbnb, Inc.

Managing maturing products

It's important for a firm to have some competitive advantage as it moves into market maturity. Even a small advantage can make a big difference—and some firms do very well by carefully managing their maturing products. They are able to capitalize on a slightly better product or perhaps lower production or marketing costs. Or they are simply more successful at promotion—allowing them to differentiate their more or less homogeneous product from competitors. For example, graham crackers were competing in a mature market and sales were flat. Nabisco used the same ingredients to create bite-sized Teddy Grahams and then promoted them heavily. These changes captured new sales and profits for Nabisco.[11]

Product life cycles keep moving. But that doesn't mean a firm should just sit by as its sales decline. There are other choices. A firm can improve its product or develop an innovative new product for the same market. Or it can develop a new strategy targeted at a new market where the life cycle is not so far along. That approach is working for InSinkErator. It has an 80 percent share of all garbage disposals, but in the mature U.S. market, disposals are already in more than half of all homes. In contrast, garbage disposals are in only about 10 percent of homes in many areas of Europe. Although many households there can afford a disposal, until recently most cities prohibited them on environmental grounds. When research showed that garbage disposals actually provide environmental benefits, InSinkErator adapted its strategy and sales in Europe have grown quickly.[12]

Add value in mature product-markets

In the highly competitive market maturity stage of the product life cycle, many firms slash prices to maintain market share. Creative marketers will find other ways to create value and maintain their margins. That is what Elkay Manufacturing Co. did with the basic water fountain. You know, the one where you lean over, push a button, and slurp a drink. After making those water fountains for decades, Elkay noticed changes in consumer behavior. More consumers were filling water bottles at the fountain. So Elkay designed new fountains that added an additional top-filling nozzle. The new style has become a big seller.[13]

Stimulate growth with new uses

Marketing managers might also find new ways to use a product. Following years of slow growth, brand managers at Philadelphia Cream Cheese (Philly) looked more closely at the habits of the brand's most frequent buyers. They discovered these customers were using the product as an ingredient—not just as something to smear on bagels. European marketing managers launched an advertising campaign that promoted adding Philly to everything from spaghetti to Spanish tapas. Hoping to inspire

Some companies continue to do well in market maturity by improving their products or by finding new uses and applications. DuPont International's Lycra has expanded from personal apparel to furniture upholstery.
Courtesy DuPont Textiles & Interiors' LYCRA®; Agency: Saatchi & Saatchi/ Zurich.

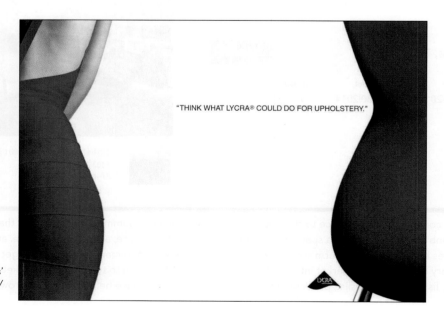

"THINK WHAT LYCRA® COULD DO FOR UPHOLSTERY."

The market for traditional shoe polish has been in decline as leather shoes become less common and people have less time to polish their own shoes. Even in the sales decline stage, market leader Kiwi develops new products like Kiwi Express Shine.

creative home cooks, they persuaded Tesco, the U.K.'s leading grocer, to place Philly next to main-dish staples like salmon. Now the number of Philly customers in the U.K. using it as an ingredient is almost 40 percent—double the level before the campaign. And sales have grown more than 20 percent in a mature market.[14]

Phase out dying products

Not all strategies are exciting growth strategies. If prospects are poor in a product-market, a phase-out strategy may be needed. The need for phasing out becomes more obvious as the sales decline stage arrives. But even in market maturity, it may be clear that a particular product is not going to be profitable enough to reach the company's objectives. In any case, it is wise to remember that marketing plans are implemented as ongoing strategies. Salespeople make calls, inventory moves in the channel, advertising is scheduled for several months into the future, and so on. So the firm usually experiences losses if managers end a plan too abruptly. Because of this, it's sometimes better to phase out the product gradually.

Phasing out a product may involve some difficult implementation problems. But phase-out is also a *strategy*—and it must be market-oriented to cut losses. In fact, it is possible to milk a dying product for some time if competitors move out more quickly and there is ongoing (though declining) demand. Some customers are willing to pay attractive prices to get their old favorite.

New-Product Planning

LO 9.2

In most markets, progress marches on. Firms must develop new products or modify their current products to meet changing customer needs and competitors' actions. Not having an active new-product development process means that, consciously or subconsciously, the firm decides to milk its current products and eventually go out of business. New-product planning is not optional; it is essential for survival in today's dynamic markets.[15]

What is a new product?

In discussing the introductory stage of product life cycles, we focused on the types of really new product innovations that tend to disrupt old ways of doing things. However, each year firms introduce many products that are basically refinements of existing products. So a **new product** is one that is new *in any way* for the company concerned. But customers don't see all new products in the same way.

New products, or innovations, can be loosely grouped into three categories based on the extent to which customers have to change their behavior to adopt the new product.

Customers readily adopt continuous innovations

Continuous innovations don't require customers to learn new behaviors. Such products usually entail minor variations on existing products. A new toothpaste flavor, a low-calorie iced tea, or a new style of earring would fit in this category. Customers can readily understand and use these new products. Promotion for this type of innovation emphasizes awareness—often with new packaging or advertising that touts an added feature.

Dynamically continuous innovation

Dynamically continuous innovations require minor changes in customer behavior. For example, 3M developed a Bluetooth-enabled stethoscope, which works like a traditional stethoscope, except that it wirelessly records and stores the sounds of the heart, lung, and other body parts in digital computer files. The innovation requires new behaviors by removing the need to key in information. Doctors can attach the sound files to computer records, as well as send them to other doctors or specialists for help diagnosing and treating patients. Promotion for dynamically continuous innovations needs to clearly communicate the benefits of the innovation.

Customers must learn new behaviors for discontinuous innovations

A *discontinuous innovation* requires that customers adopting the innovation significantly change their behavior. This type of innovation often results in a completely new product-market and new-product life cycle. Appliance maker Godrej needed to think differently about refrigeration in rural India. In this part of the world, where most families make less than $5 a day and electricity is unreliable or unavailable, there is little demand for the major appliances Godrej produces. Customers generally don't purchase food that requires staying cool for more than a couple of hours. These consumers have basic needs—they would like to keep milk, vegetables, and fruit cool for a day or two. Then they could shop less frequently and prepare a broader range of meals. For this market, Godrej engineers created ChotuKool ("little cool" in Hindi), a portable cooler which runs on DC current or an external battery. The design minimizes heat loss and power usage. The innovation is life-altering for people in this part of the world and changes how they shop and cook. Promotion for a discontinuous innovation like ChotuKool usually requires personal selling and product demonstrations to educate customers about new behaviors.[16]

FTC says product is "new" for only six months

A firm can call its product new for only a limited time. Six months is the limit according to the **Federal Trade Commission (FTC)**—the federal government agency that polices antimonopoly laws. To be called new, says the FTC, a product must be entirely new or changed in a "functionally significant or substantial respect."[17]

New products can be classified by the extent to which customers need to change behavior in order to adopt the innovation. For continuous innovations, like the Jelly Belly Chocolate Dips, customers don't need to learn new behaviors. The Nest Thermostat programs itself, so customers need to learn not to change the thermostat on their own; adopting requires a modest change in consumer behavior . Adoption of a discontinuous innovation, like the self-driving car will significantly change customers' behavior. *Left: © 2011–2014 Jelly Belly Candy Company. All Rights Reserved. Middle: © 2015 Nest Labs; Right: Rex Features via AP Images.*

Patent and copyright laws protect inventors

When developing a new product, a firm can file with a government for a **patent**, which grants the inventor the ability to "exclude others from making, using, offering for sales, or selling the invention." Patent law provides an incentive for inventors to share their new technology with the world in exchange for a short-term monopoly on its use. Many firms with a competitive advantage for innovative products file patents and vigorously protect them to keep competitors from stealing their technology. Apple and Samsung have filed various suits against each other regarding technology and innovation in smartphones and tablet computers.[18]

In the United States and many other countries, *copyright* law protects the producer of a creative work (literary, musical, dramatics, or artistic), giving them exclusive rights to reproduce the work. There are some limitations to copyright. These laws are designed to protect inventors and provide an incentive for innovation.[19]

Ethical issues in new-product planning

New-product decisions—and decisions to abandon old products—often involve ethical considerations. For example, some firms (including firms that develop drugs) have been criticized for holding back important new-product innovations until patents run out, or sales slow down, on their existing products.

At the same time, others have been criticized for *planned obsolescence*—releasing new products that the company plans to soon replace with improved new versions. Similarly, wholesalers and retailers complain that producers too often keep their new-product introduction plans a secret and leave intermediaries with dated inventory that they can sell only at a loss.

Companies also face ethical dilemmas when they decide to stop supplying a product or the service and replacement parts to keep it useful. An old model of a Cuisinart food processor, for example, might be in perfect shape except for a crack in the plastic mixing bowl. It's sensible for the company to improve the design if the crack is a frequent problem, but if consumers can't get a replacement part for the model they already own, they're left holding the bag.

Different marketing managers might have very different reactions to such criticisms. However, product management decisions often have a significant effect on customers and intermediaries. A too-casual decision may lead to a negative backlash that affects the firm's strategy or reputation.[20]

An Organized New-Product Development Process Is Critical

LO 9.3

Identifying and developing new-product ideas—and effective strategies to go with them—is often the key to a firm's success and survival. But the costs of new-product development and the risks of failure are high. Experts estimate that consumer packaged-goods companies spend more than $20 million to introduce a new brand—and 80 to 95 percent of those new brands flop. That's a big expense—and a waste. In the service sector, the front-end cost of a failed effort may not be as high, but it can have a devastating long-term effect if dissatisfied consumers turn elsewhere for help.[21]

Why most new products fail

A new product may fail for many reasons. Most often, companies fail to offer a unique benefit or underestimate the competition. Sometimes the idea is good but the company has design problems—or the product costs much more to produce than was expected. Some companies rush to get a product on the market without developing a complete marketing plan.[22]

But moving too slowly can be a problem too. The longer new-product development takes, the more likely it is that customer needs will be different when the product is actually introduced. When consumer interest in trucks and SUVs was high, General Motors started planning new models. A few years later gas prices soared and the new General Motors vehicles did not sell.

Exhibit 9-4 New-Product Development Process

Idea generation	Screening	Idea evaluation	Development	Commercialization

Ideas from:
Customers and
  users
Marketing
  research
Competitors
Other markets
Company people
Intermediaries, etc.
	Strengths and
	  weaknesses
	Fit with
	  objectives
	Market trends
	Rough ROI
	  estimate
		Concept testing
		Reactions from
		  customers
		Rough estimates
		  of costs, sales,
		  and profits
			R&D
			Develop model
			  or service
			  prototype
			Test marketing
			  mix
			Revise plans as
			  needed
			ROI estimate
				Finalize product
				  and marketing
				  plan
				Start production
				  and marketing
				  "Roll out" in
				  select markets
				Final ROI
				  estimate

A formal new-product development process

To move quickly and also avoid expensive new-product failures, companies should follow an organized new-product development process. The following pages describe such a process, which moves logically through five steps: (1) idea generation, (2) screening, (3) idea evaluation, (4) development (of product and marketing mix), and (5) commercialization. See Exhibit 9–4.

The general process is similar for both consumer and business markets—and for both goods and services. There are some significant differences, but we will emphasize the similarities in the following discussion.

Process tries to kill new ideas—economically

An important element in the new-product development process is continued evaluation of a new idea's likely profitability and return on investment. The hypothesis tested is that the new idea will *not* be profitable. This puts the burden on the new idea—to prove itself or be rejected. As shown in Exhibit 9–5, as the process moves along, the number of ideas retained declines over time. Such a process may seem harsh, but experience shows that most new ideas have some flaw. Marketers try to discover those flaws early and either find a remedy or reject the idea completely.

Applying this process requires much analysis of the idea *before* the company spends money to develop and market a product. Over time, those ideas that survive receive increasingly large investment (see Exhibit 9–5). The costs in the latter stages of the new-product development can be high, so the process assures that the best ideas receive the most investment. This is a major departure from the usual production-oriented approach—in which a company develops a product first and then asks sales to "get rid of it."

Step 1: Idea generation

Finding new-product ideas can't be left to chance. Instead, firms need a formal procedure to generate a continuous flow of ideas. For some companies, a constant investment in research and development results in a flow of new technology with new-product applications. But new ideas can come from a company's own sales or production staff, wholesalers or retailers, competitors, consumer surveys, or

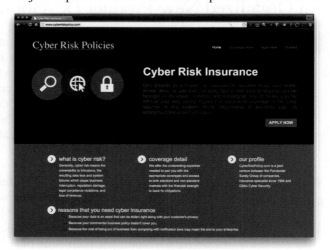

A computer system breach by a hacker or a computer virus can be very costly for a business. As this practice became more common, customers asked insurance companies for help in reducing that risk. Insurers developed new products to meet those needs.
Used with permission of Poindexter Surety Group.

Exhibit 9-5 New-Product Development Process: Number of Ideas and Investment in Each Idea

other sources such as trade associations, advertising agencies, or government agencies. By analyzing new and different views of the company's markets and studying present consumer behavior, a marketing manager can spot opportunities that have not yet occurred to competitors or even to potential customers. Let's look at some examples of how this works.

Ideas from customers

Customers can be a great source of new ideas—and if they suggest the idea, they are more likely to buy it. Companies such as Rubbermaid and eBags comb through customer reviews for new-product ideas. T-shirt maker Threadless takes this approach to another level. Threadless community members submit T-shirt designs as part of a contest. Winning designs are chosen based on ratings and comments from other members—a process called *crowdsourcing*. Threadless then produces the winners and sells them on its website—and because community members tell them which shirts to make, almost every product sells out.

As customers leave "data exhaust" from their online and offline behavior, companies that analyze it are finding new-product ideas. For example, online retailer CafePress sells themed gifts and user-customized products. Its products tie to popular culture and current events, so CafePress examines what customers enter into its search bar. Recently "Class of 2015" and "Zombies" were popular searches on the site—so CafePress quickly added products to address these customer needs. As an offline example of "data exhaust," Coca-Cola gathers data from its Freestyle drink machines. The fountain machines let consumers choose from 125 different flavors and drinks. The data on what they buy are sent back to Coke. When Coke sees a trend or regional variation, it can bottle a new drink for wider distribution.[23]

Online Toolkit

Starbucks asks customers for new-product ideas at its **www.mystarbucksidea.com** website. Go to this site and click on "View Ideas." Next, click on "Popular Ideas." Choose two popular ideas and read the ideas and comments. How do you think Starbucks benefits from this site? What could be done to improve this site?

Ideas from other companies and markets

No one firm can always be first with the best new ideas. So companies should pay attention to what competitors are doing. Some firms use what's called *reverse engineering*. For example, new-product specialists at Ford Motor Company buy other firms' cars as soon as they're available. Then they take the cars apart to look for new ideas or improvements. British Airways talks to travel agents to learn about new services offered by competitors.

Sometimes ideas from one product-market can be adapted for another—where it will be a *new* product. To get such ideas, some firms "shop" in international markets. For instance, food companies in Europe are experimenting with an innovation from Japan—a clear, odorless, natural film for wrapping food. Consumers don't have to unwrap it; when they put the product in boiling water or a microwave, the wrapper vanishes. For more sources of ideas, see "*What's Next?* New product ideas from nature."[24]

Step 2: Screening

Screening involves evaluating the new ideas with the type of S.W.O.T. analysis described in Chapter 2 and the product-market screening criteria described in Chapter 3. Recall that these criteria include the combined output of a resources (strengths and weaknesses) analysis, a long-run trends analysis, and a thorough understanding of the company's objectives. See Exhibit 2–9 and Exhibit 3–8. A "good" new idea should eventually lead to a product (and marketing mix) that will give the firm a competitive advantage—hopefully, a lasting one.

The life-cycle stage at which a firm's new product enters the market has a direct bearing on its prospects for growth. So screening should consider how the strategy for a new product will hold up over the whole product life cycle.

Safety must be considered

Real acceptance of the marketing concept prompts managers to screen new products on the basis of how safe they are. Safety is not a casual matter. The U.S. **Consumer Product Safety Act** (of 1972) set up the Consumer Product Safety Commission to encourage safety in product design and better quality control. The commission has a great deal of power. It can set safety standards for products. It can order costly repairs or the return of unsafe products. And it can back up its orders with fines and jail sentences. The Food and Drug Administration has similar powers for foods and drugs.

Product safety complicates strategy planning because not all customers—even those who want better safety features—are willing to pay more for safer products. Some features cost a lot to add and increase prices considerably. These safety concerns must be considered at the screening step because a firm can later be held liable for unsafe products.

Products can turn to liabilities

Product liability means the legal obligation of sellers to pay damages to individuals who are injured by defective or unsafe products. Product liability is a serious matter. Liability settlements may exceed not only a company's insurance coverage but its total assets!

Relative to most other countries, U.S. courts enforce a strict product liability standard. Sellers may be held responsible for injuries related to their products no matter how the items are used or how well they're designed. In one widely publicized judgment, McDonald's paid a huge settlement to a woman who suffered third-degree burns when her coffee spilled. The court concluded that there was not enough warning about how hot the coffee was.

Product liability is a serious ethical and legal matter. Many countries are attempting to change their laws so that they will be fair to both firms and consumers. But until product liability questions are resolved, marketing managers must be even more sensitive when screening new-product ideas.[25]

What's next? New product ideas from nature

Over the last 3 billion or so years, nature has found ways to solve a wide range of problems. Biomimicry studies nature's best ideas and adapts them to create new products. So maybe if we just ask nature, it will give us new-product ideas.

How does nature create a flexible fastener? Perhaps the best-known example of biomimicry is Velcro, which was invented in 1941 by a Swiss engineer who was curious why burrs stubbornly stuck to his dog's fur following a hike in the woods. Placing the burrs under a microscope, he saw the miniature hooks that grabbed tiny loops found on clothes, socks, and animal fur. This inspired the two-part Velcro fastener; one side with tiny hooks and the other with matching loops.

How does nature create strong bonds? A professor at Oregon State University wondered how mussels keep such a tight grip on underwater rocks with waves persistently pounding down on them. Subsequent research found the mussels secrete proteins known as byssal threads. The threads create an adhesive with superior strength and flexibility. This finding inspired development

of a soy-based adhesive Columbia Forest products used to create its PureBond plywood. The adhesive replaces formaldehyde, a toxic chemical used in most plywood.

How does nature manage temperature variation? On the African savannas, temperatures can range from 35 to 110 degrees Fahrenheit in a single day. Termites there build and live in mounds that can reach more than 15 feet in height and maintain virtually constant temperatures inside. Looking closer at the termite mounds, scientists discovered the insects' secrets; they constantly open and close vents to draw in cool air at the base and ventilate hot air through chimneys. Drawing on these insights, architects designed Eastgate Center, a high-rise building in Zimbabwe that consumes less than 10 percent of the energy used in similarly sized buildings.

Nature's problem-solving experience draws on millions of years of adaptation. For more ideas, you can ask your own questions—and see answers—at www.asknature.org. Firms need to look everywhere for new-product ideas and nature has much to share.[26]

ROI is a crucial screening criterion

Getting by the initial screening criteria doesn't guarantee success for the new idea. But it does show that at least the new idea is in the right ballpark *for this firm.* If many ideas pass the screening criteria, a firm must set priorities to determine which ones go on to the next step in the process. This can be done by comparing the ROI (return on investment) for each idea—assuming the firm is ROI-oriented. The most attractive alternatives are pursued first.

Step 3: Idea evaluation

When an idea moves past the screening step, it is evaluated more carefully. This stage involves getting more reactions from customers, even though at this stage an actual product has yet to be developed. Although this can make getting customer input more difficult, firms need extensive feedback before adding the expense of producing the product.

At this stage, marketing managers should describe and relate the assumptions they are making about each new idea. The product idea represents a hypothesis, or educated guess, about how to meet customer needs. For example, a law firm may assume its corporate clients care enough about convenience to pay a premium price for a new web-based document sharing service. By making assumptions—like the value customers place on convenience—explicit, marketing managers can conduct research to find out as quickly as possible if assumptions are true.

Initial evaluation may come from informal focus groups. Their reactions can be helpful—especially if they show that potential users are not excited about the new idea. A more formal method uses **concept testing**—getting reactions from customers about how well a new-product idea fits their needs. Concept testing uses market research—ranging from focus groups to surveys of potential customers. Some firms

Ideas that survive to the development stage receive more attention. An automaker might develop a scale model of a car or a full-fledged, operational prototype. Honda's Micro Commuter and BMW's i8 Spyder may be on the market if they survive continued scrutiny from customers and show signs of a positive ROI.
Bloomberg/Getty Images. AP Photo/Alexander F. Yuan.

run concept tests online, which can lower costs and speed feedback. It can be fast and easy to show some photos or a video of a concept, along with possible prices, to a sample of target customers. Follow-up survey questions gauge consumer reactions.

Writers for Disney Channel's TV show *Sofia the First* have found concept testing helps. The writers share scripts and plotlines with kids at a nearby preschool to learn what kids like and understand. For example, an episode intended to be called "Sofia's First Slumber Party" didn't resonate; kids were unfamiliar with the phrase "slumber party." So the episode was changed to "The Big Sleepover."[27]

Marketing research can also help identify the size of potential markets and that helps companies to estimate likely costs, revenue, and profitability. Together, all this information helps marketing managers decide whether there is an opportunity, whether it fits with the firm's resources, *and* whether there is a basis for developing a competitive advantage. With such information, the firm can develop a more reliable estimate of ROI in various market segments and decide whether to continue the new-product development process.[28]

Step 4: Development

Product ideas that survive the screening and idea evaluation steps get further investment of time and money. Usually, this involves more research and development (R&D) to design and develop the physical part of the product. Or, in the case of a new service offering, the firm works out the details of what training, equipment, staff, and so on will be needed to deliver on the idea. Input from a firm's earlier efforts helps guide this technical work.

Customers react to prototypes

Passing that test often leads next to the creation of a **prototype**—an early sample or model built to test a concept. A service firm may try to train a small group of service providers and test the service on real customers. 3-D printing technology allows a computer-designed drawing to quickly be converted into a three-dimensional replica, often at a relatively low cost. For example, automakers can "print" a life-size car fender, door, or even an auto body. This allows for checking fit, finish, and styling.

Customers may even be involved in a *co-creation process*—where customers react to prototypes and suggest improvements. This process uses *rapid prototyping,* where customer input is received and quickly designed into a revision of the product— and then fed back to customers for further input. The repetitive process in rapid prototyping encourages innovations to "fail early and fail often" so the best ideas get to market more quickly. Google uses this approach to test new features it wants to add to its family of online services (Google, Gmail, Google+ and others)—often incorporating feedback in less than 24 hours and then seeking additional feedback from a test group.[29]

With actual goods and services, potential customers can more realistically react to how well a product meets their needs. Focus groups, panels, and surveys provide feedback on features and the whole product idea. Sometimes that reaction kills the idea. For example, Coca-Cola Foods believed it had a great idea with Minute Maid Squeeze-Fresh—frozen orange juice concentrate in a squeeze bottle. In tests, however, Squeeze-Fresh bombed. Consumers loved the idea but hated the product. In real life, it was messy to use, and no one knew how much concentrate to squeeze in the glass.[30]

Market testing uses real market conditions

Firms often use full-scale *market testing* to get customer reactions under real market conditions or to test variations in the marketing mix. For example, a firm may test alternative brand names, prices, or advertising copy in different test cities. Note that the firm tests the whole marketing mix, not just the product. For example, a hotel chain might test a new service offering at one location to see how it goes over. Running market tests is costly, but *not* testing is risky. Frito-Lay was so sure it understood consumers' snack preferences that it introduced a three-item cracker line without market testing. Even with network TV ad support, MaxSnax suffered overwhelming consumer indifference. By the time Frito-Lay pulled the product from store shelves, it had lost $52 million.[31]

Step 5: Commercialization

A product idea that survives this far can finally be placed on the market. Putting a product on the market is expensive, and success usually requires cooperation of the whole company. Manufacturing or service facilities have to be set up. Goods have to be produced to fill the channels of distribution, or people must be hired and trained to provide services. Further, introductory promotion is costly—especially if the company is entering a very competitive market.

Because of the size of the job, some firms introduce their products city by city or region by region—in a gradual "rollout"—until they have complete market coverage. Rollouts also permit more market testing, but the main purpose is to do a good job implementing the marketing plan. Marketing managers also need to pay close attention to control—to ensure that the implementation effort is working and that the strategy is on target.

Steps should not be skipped

Because speed can be important, it's always tempting to skip needed steps when some part of the process seems to indicate that the company has a "really good idea." But the process moves in steps—gathering different kinds of information along the way. By skipping steps, a firm may miss an important aspect that could make a whole strategy less profitable or actually cause it to fail.

Ethical Dilemma

What would you do? You are the marketing manager for a company that creates video games. A big competitor has just released an action game that appeals to kids who own your best-selling game. Your competitor's release is a better game because it takes advantage of features available in a hot new video game system. Your firm's updated release won't be available for at least four months. One of your game developers suggests that you preannounce your game will be ready in two months—which is about as long as gamers are likely to wait. Should you announce that your new version is coming or just wait until you know more? If a reporter for a popular gaming magazine calls and asks for a statement about when your firm's release will be on the market, should you say two months, four months, or "we don't know yet"? If your product is preannounced but then not ready by that date, what should your firm communicate to customers? Explain your thinking.

New-Product Development: A Total Company Effort

LO 9.4

We've been discussing the steps in a logical, new-product development process. However, as shown in Exhibit 9–6, many factors can impact the success of the effort.[32]

Top-level support is vital

Companies that are particularly successful at developing new goods and services seem to have one key trait in common: enthusiastic top-management support for new-product development. New products tend to upset old routines that managers of established products often try in subtle but effective ways to maintain. So someone with top-level support, and authority to get things done, needs to be responsible for new-product development.

A culture of innovation

Top management also drives the organization's culture. A culture of innovation consists of people open to exchanging ideas, willing to listen to others, and pushing good ideas forward. Some companies formally encourage employees to pursue innovation—by giving them time. For example, Google allows all employees the freedom to spend 20 percent of their time working on new ideas, even if the ideas are unrelated to their job description. A culture that supports innovation generates more ideas.[33]

Put someone in charge

Rather than leaving new-product development to anyone in engineering, R&D, or sales who happens to be interested in taking the initiative, successful companies *put* someone in charge. It may be a person, department, or team. But it's not a casual thing. It's a major responsibility of the job.

> ### Online Toolkit
>
> A company called Quirky draws on an online community to move products through the new-product development process. Go to the Quirky website (**www.quirky.com**). Scroll down and watch the short video overview and peruse the site. What advantages and disadvantages does Quirky have compared to a corporation or individual inventor? What would you do to improve the site?

Balance market needs and company resources

From idea generation to commercialization, a company's R&D specialists, operations, and marketing personnel must work together to evaluate the feasibility of new ideas. Everyone should be guided by a clear understanding of customer needs. It doesn't make

Exhibit 9–6 New-Product Development Success Factors

sense for R&D people to develop a technology or product that doesn't have potential for the firm and its markets.

Marketing managers must recognize that new-product projects need to meet return-on-investment goals. Team members from R&D and production should provide insights about the company's capabilities and costs to produce. It isn't sensible for a marketing manager to develop elaborate marketing plans for goods or services that the firm simply can't produce—or produce profitably.

Clearly, a balancing act is involved here. But the critical point is one we've been emphasizing throughout the whole book: *Marketing-oriented firms seek to satisfy customer needs at a profit with an integrated, whole company effort.*

New-product success

Savvy marketing managers generate products the market values. They must put together comprehensive marketing plans, communicating the features and benefits of a new product, identifying the right price and the best distribution channels, pinpointing competition, and establishing a budget. The same marketing manager who shepherded the product through new-product development may manage it in regular operations. Or there may be a handoff to a product manager. In either case, after a new product launches, activities that assure long-term success must follow.

Need for Product Managers

LO 9.5

Product variety leads to product managers

When a firm has only one or a few related products, everyone is interested in them. But when a firm has products in several different product categories, management may decide to put someone in charge of each category, or each brand, to be sure that attention to these products is not lost in the rush of everyday business. **Product managers** or **brand managers** manage specific products—often taking over the jobs formerly handled by an advertising manager. That gives a clue to what is often their major responsibility—Promotion—because the products have already been developed by the new-product people. However, some brand managers start at the new-product development stage and carry on from there.

Product managers are especially common in large companies that produce many kinds of products. Several product managers may serve under a marketing manager. Sometimes these product managers are responsible for the profitable operation of a particular product's whole marketing effort. Then they have to coordinate their efforts with others, including the sales manager, advertising agencies, production and research people, and even channel members. This is likely to lead to difficulties if product managers have no control over the marketing strategy for other related brands or authority over other functional areas whose efforts they are expected to direct and coordinate.

To avoid these problems, in some companies the product manager serves mainly as a "product champion"—concerned with planning and getting the promotion effort implemented. A higher-level marketing manager with more authority coordinates the efforts and integrates the marketing strategies for different products into an overall plan.

P&G has some of the world's best known brands, including Crest toothpaste, Gillette razors, Head & Shoulders shampoo, Downy, Gain, Tide, and Ariel laundry detergents, and many more. Each product or brand has a manager who primarily manages Promotion for that brand.
© McGraw-Hill Education; Mark Dierker, photographer.

The activities of product managers vary a lot depending on their experience and aggressiveness and the company's organizational philosophy. Today, companies are emphasizing marketing experience—because this important job takes more than academic training and enthusiasm. But it is clear that someone must be responsible for developing and implementing product-related plans, especially when a company has many products.[34]

Adapting products for international markets

Product managers may work with managers in other countries to decide whether and how to adapt products for different markets. Some adaptations may be required and fairly simple—for example, many countries have different electrical voltages, necessitating different plugs for electrical products. Other adaptations demand more creativity. Nestlé adapted its Kit Kat chocolate candy bars for the Japanese palate with 19 unique flavors including soy sauce, miso, sweet potato, and blueberry. In Germany, Kit Kat lemon yogurt bars are popular; in the U.K., it's peanut butter. Nestlé adapts many of its other products to international preferences also. Whereas in the United States, fruit-flavored ice "popsicles" are a summertime treat all kids crave, in China, Nestlé created flavored milk ice on a stick to fit local preferences—the most popular flavor, banana.[35]

Managing Product Quality

LO 9.6

Total quality management meets customer requirements

In Chapter 8 we explained that product quality means the ability of a product to satisfy a customer's needs or requirements. Now we'll expand that idea and discuss some ways a manager can improve the quality of a firm's goods and services. We'll develop these ideas from the perspective of **total quality management (TQM)**, the philosophy that everyone in the organization is concerned about quality, throughout all of the firm's activities, to better serve customer needs.

The cost of poor quality is lost customers

Most of the early attention in quality management focused on reducing defects in goods produced in factories. At one time most firms assumed defects were an inevitable part of mass production. They saw the cost of replacing defective parts or goods as just a cost of doing business—an insignificant one compared to the advantages of mass production. However, many firms were forced to rethink this assumption when Japanese producers of cars, electronics, and cameras showed that defects weren't inevitable. Much to the surprise of some production-oriented managers, the Japanese experience showed that it is less expensive to do something right the first time than it is to pay to do it poorly and then pay again to fix problems. And their success in taking customers away from established competitors made it clear that the cost of defects wasn't just the cost of replacement!

From the customer's point of view, getting a defective product and having to complain about it is a big headache. The customer can't use the defective product and suffers the inconvenience of waiting for someone to fix the problem—*if* someone gets around to it. It certainly doesn't deliver superior value. Rather, it erodes goodwill and leaves customers dissatisfied, less trusting of the brand, and possibly spreading their dismay to others via word-of-mouth or the Internet. The big cost of poor quality is the cost of lost customers.

Firms that adopted TQM methods to reduce manufacturing defects soon used the same approaches to overcome many other problems. Their success brought attention to what is possible with TQM—whether the problem concerns poor customer service, flimsy packaging, or salespeople who can't answer customers' questions.

Getting a handle on doing things right the first time

The idea of identifying customer needs and doing things right the first time seems obvious, but it's easier said than done. Problems always come up, and it's not always clear what isn't being done as well as it could be. People tend to ignore problems that don't pose an immediate crisis. But firms that adopt TQM always look for ways to

A firm that understands the needs of its target customers can focus on those aspects of quality that are most important for developing superior customer value. Toronto's Hospital for Sick Children (also called SickKids) treats thousands of kids with cancer each year. To help these kids manage the pain they experience during treatments, these young patients keep track of their pain twice daily in a "pain journal." That isn't always easy for kids who are tired and discouraged after receiving chemotherapy treatments, so SickKids worked with an outside firm to develop a video game. Each patient receives an iPhone with the Pain Squad Mobile App that makes a fun game out of keeping a pain journal. Compliance is now 90%. Success! These young cancer patients are better managing their pain and receiving higher quality treatment from SickKids.

improve implementation with **continuous improvement**—a commitment to constantly make things better one step at a time. Once you accept the idea that there *may* be a better way to do something and you look for it, you may just find it!

Data drives quality improvement

In Chapter 7 we discussed big data and how firms now have access to more information about how customers behave and use their products. Firms are beginning to figure out how to evaluate this information to drive product improvements. For example, industrial equipment makers have added smart meters and digital sensors to products so they can be constantly monitored and provide an early warning of failure. Parts can be replaced before they fail—and possibly be improved in future models.

Another example happens in publishing, where e-books have created opportunities for authors and publishers to learn more about just how their products are consumed. For example, data show what lines users have highlighted, how long it takes them to read a book, what parts are read most quickly, how much they read in one sitting, and for those who fail to finish the book—when do they quit? Barnes and Noble shares this information with publishers and authors to help them create books that might better hold people's attention.

Building quality into services

Services create particular quality management challenges. Most products involve some service component whether it is primarily a service, primarily a physical good, or a blend of both. Even a manufacturer of ball bearings isn't just providing wholesalers or producers with round pieces of steel. Customers need information about deliveries, they need orders filled properly, and they may have questions to ask the firm's accountant or engineers. Because almost every firm must manage the service it provides customers, let's focus on some of the special concerns of managing service quality.

Deliver quality at each touchpoint

Marketing managers must deliver quality throughout the entire customer experience. If they do not, even one problem can affect how the customer perceives the firm's quality. Think about how an otherwise great restaurant experience could be ruined by a rude waiter. The purchase and consumption process for many products involves multiple *touchpoints*, or points where there is contact between the customer and the company. There are usually more touchpoints for services than for goods.

Photo by David McNew/Getty Images.

Consider everything that needs to go right for a customer getting an oil change at a Jiffy Lube. The experience might begin at the Jiffy Lube website, where a customer seeks information about the services offered, prices, hours of operation, and the phone number and address of a local Jiffy Lube. Is this information easy to find? A phone call to a local Jiffy Lube outlet should be promptly answered by a friendly, knowledgeable person. Upon arrival, is the driveway well-marked? Is there a long queue for service? The attendant may have entered the license plate number and could already have the customer's details on his computer screen—or not. Is the check-in process quick? Is the attendant courteous? The waiting area should be clean and perhaps offer Wi-Fi. What happens if another customer has noisy young children—does that affect the quality of the oil change experience? The payment process should be fast—and offer the customer information about his or her car. The car should be clean when it is picked up. Finally, the car should not experience any service problems immediately following the oil change. Whew! That is a lot of things to get right, every time, if Jiffy Lube is to deliver high quality to its customers. Other types of products can have greater or fewer touchpoints, but a marketing manager should recognize that all of them contribute to the customer's perception of quality.

Train people and empower them to serve

A service provider usually deals directly with the customer, making it difficult to provide consistent service quality. People are just not as consistent in their actions as machines or computers are. In addition, service quality often depends on a service provider interpreting each customer's needs. For example, a hair stylist has to ask good questions and successfully interpret the customer's responses before it's possible to provide the right cut. As a result, a person doing a specific service job may perform one specific task correctly but fail the customer in a host of other ways. Two keys to improving service quality are: (1) training and (2) empowerment.

All employees in contact with customers need training—many firms see 40 hours a year of training as a minimum. Good training usually includes role-playing on handling different types of customer requests and problems. A rental car attendant who is rude or inattentive when a customer is trying to turn in a car may leave the customer dissatisfied—even if the rental car was perfect.

Companies can't afford an army of managers to inspect how each employee implements a strategy—and such a system usually doesn't work anyway. Quality cannot be "inspected in." It must come from the people who do the service jobs. So firms that commit to service quality empower employees to figure out how to best satisfy customers' needs. **Empowerment** means giving employees the authority to correct a problem without first checking with management. At a hotel, for instance, an empowered room-service employee knows it's OK to run across the street to buy the specific brand of bottled water a guest requests.[36]

Specify jobs and measure performance

Managers who develop successful quality programs clearly specify and write out exactly what tasks need to be done, how, and by whom. This may seem unnecessary. After all, most people know, in general, what they're supposed to do. However, if the tasks are clearly specified, it's easier to see what criteria should be used to measure performance. Once criteria are established, there needs to be some basis on which to evaluate the job being done.

Getting a return on quality is important

While the cost of poor quality is lost customers, the type of quality efforts we've been discussing can also increase costs. It's easy to fall into the trap of running up unnecessary costs trying to improve some facet of quality that really isn't that important to customer satisfaction or customer retention. When that happens, customers may still be satisfied, but the firm can't make a profit because of the higher costs. In other words, there isn't a financial return on the money spent to improve quality. A manager should focus on quality efforts that really provide the customer with superior value—quality that costs no more to provide than customers will ultimately be willing to pay.[37]

CONCLUSION

This chapter introduced the product life-cycle concept and showed how life cycles affect marketing strategy planning. The product life-cycle concept shows why new products are so important to growth in markets and also helps to explain why different strategies—including strategies for new, improved products—need to be developed over time. Innovators—or fast copiers—who successfully bring new products to market are usually the ones who achieve the greatest growth in customer equity.

In today's highly competitive marketplace it is no longer profitable to simply sell "me-too" products. Markets, competition, and product life cycles are changing at a fast pace. New products help a company appeal to new target markets by appealing to unmet needs. New products can also encourage current customers to purchase more. In addition, they can help retain customers by adapting to changing customer needs.

Just because a product is new to a company doesn't mean that it is a really new innovation and starts a new-product life cycle. However, from a marketing manager's perspective, a product is new to the firm if it is new in any way or to any target market. Firms don't just develop and introduce new products; they do so within the context of the whole marketing strategy.

Many new products fail. But we presented an organized new-product development process that helps to prevent that fate. The process makes it clear that new-product success isn't just the responsibility of people from R&D or marketing but rather requires a total company effort.

We also described product and brand management. To help a product or brand grow, managers in these positions usually recommend ways to adjust all of the elements of the marketing mix, but the emphasis is often on Promotion.

Poor product quality results in dissatisfied customers. So alert marketers look for ways to design better quality into new products and to improve the quality of ones they already have. Approaches developed in the total quality management (TQM) movement can be a big help in this regard. Ultimately, the challenge is for the manager to focus on aspects of quality that really matter to the target customer. Otherwise, the cost of the quality offered may be higher than what target customers are willing to pay.

In combination, this chapter and Chapter 8 introduce strategy decision areas for Product and important frameworks that help you see how Product fits within an overall strategy. These chapters also start you down the path to a deeper understanding of the Four Ps. In Chapter 10, we expand on that base by focusing on the role of Place in the marketing mix.

WHAT'S NOW?

This chapter examines the product life cycle and new-product development. For current real-world examples and learnings, check out *What's Now?* at www.learnthe4ps.com/whatsnow/c9

KEY TERMS

LO 9.7

product life cycle, 229
market introduction, 230
market growth, 230
market maturity, 230
sales decline, 231
fashion, 233
fad, 233

new product, 237
Federal Trade Commission (FTC), 238
patent, 239
Consumer Product Safety Act, 242
product liability, 242
concept testing, 243

prototype, 244
product managers, 247
brand managers, 247
total quality management (TQM), 248
continuous improvement, 249
empowerment, 250

QUESTIONS AND PROBLEMS

1. Review the iRobot case study that opens the chapter. From this case, identify examples of different key terms and concepts covered in the chapter. For example, the AVA 500 robot appears to be a discontinuous innovation.

2. Review the iRobot case study that opens this chapter. Assume that iRobot is trying to develop a home health care robot. This robot would help the elderly around the house with basic tasks such as reminders to take medicines and basic cleaning. Describe how this might look at each step in the new-product development process. Provide as much detail—even if you are speculating—as possible.

3. Explain how industry sales and industry profits behave over the product life cycle.

4. Cite two examples of products that you think are currently in each of the product life-cycle stages. Consider services as well as physical goods.

5. Explain how you might reach different conclusions about the correct product life-cycle stage(s) in the worldwide automobile market.

6. Explain why individual brands may not follow the product life-cycle pattern. Give an example of a new brand that is not entering the life cycle at the market introduction stage.

7. Discuss the life cycle of a product in terms of its probable impact on a manufacturer's marketing mix. Illustrate using personal computers.

8. What characteristics of a new product will help it to move through the early stages of the product life cycle more quickly? Briefly discuss each characteristic—illustrating with a product of your choice. Indicate how each characteristic might be viewed in some other country.

9. What is a new product? Illustrate your answer.

10. Explain the importance of an organized new-product development process and illustrate how it might be used for (a) a new hair care product, (b) a new children's toy, and (c) a new subscribers-only cable television channel.

11. Discuss how you might use the new-product development process if you were thinking about offering some kind of summer service to residents in a beach resort town.

12. Explain the role of product or brand managers. When would it make sense for one of a company's current brand managers to be in charge of the new-product development process? Explain your thinking.

13. If a firm offers one of its brands in a number of different countries, would it make sense for one brand manager to be in charge, or would each country require its own brand manager? Explain your thinking.

14. Discuss the social value of new-product development activities that seem to encourage people to discard products that are not all worn out. Is this an economic waste? How worn out is all worn out? Must a shirt have holes in it? How big?

15. What are the major advantages of total quality management as an approach for improving the quality of goods and services? What limitations can you think of?

MARKETING PLANNING FOR HILLSIDE VETERINARY CLINIC

Appendix D (the Appendices follow Chapter 19) includes a sample marketing plan for Hillside Veterinary Clinic. Look through the "Marketing Strategy" section.

a. Hillside offers many different products. Identify several of these products and indicate where you think each one is in its product life cycle.

b. Exhibit 9-3 summarizes some marketing mix characteristics based on where a product fits in the product life cycle. Is Hillside's marketing plan consistent with what this exhibit suggests? Why or why not?

SUGGESTED CASES

6. Steel Solutions

20. Minnehaha Marine & Camp

22. Brightlight Innovations: The Starlight Stove

Video Case 3. Toyota Prius

Video Case 8. Segway

MARKETING ANALYTICS: DATA TO KNOWLEDGE

CHAPTER 9 GROWTH STAGE COMPETITION

AgriChem, Inc., has introduced an innovative new product—a combination fertilizer, weed killer, and insecticide that makes it much easier for soybean farmers to produce a profitable crop. The product introduction was quite successful, with 1 million units sold in the year of introduction. And AgriChem's profits are increasing. Total market demand is expected to grow at a rate of 200,000 units a year for the next five years. Even so,

AgriChem's marketing managers are concerned about what will happen to sales and profits during this period.

Based on past experience with similar situations, they expect one new competitor to enter the market during each of the next five years. They think this competitive pressure will drive prices down about 6 percent a year. Further, although the total market is growing, they know that new competitors will chip away at AgriChem's market share—even with the 10 percent a year increase planned for the promotion budget. In spite of the competitive pressure, the marketing managers are sure that familiarity with AgriChem's brand will help it hold a large share of the total market and give AgriChem greater economies of scale than competitors. In fact, they expect that the ratio of profit to dollar sales for AgriChem should be about 10 percent higher than for competitors.

AgriChem's marketing managers have decided the best way to get a handle on the situation is to organize the data in a spreadsheet. They have set up the spreadsheet so they can change the "years in the future" value and see what is likely to happen to AgriChem and the rest of the industry. The starting spreadsheet shows the current situation with data from the first full year of production.

See Connect for the spreadsheet and questions needed to analyze this scenario.

Imaginechina via AP Images.

Place and Development of Channel Systems

In the 1970s the early "microcomputers" were very hard to set up and difficult to use, so few people wanted them. That also explains why there were no computer stores. Altair, one of the first brands, initially sold mainly at "electronics fairs." Most of these gatherings were in California; often buyers and sellers just met in an open market on Saturday mornings. Then Heath introduced its more powerful H89 computer through mail-order catalogs as a build-it-yourself kit. Heath added value with good telephone technical support.

Soon after that, Xerox used its competitive advantage in distribution to introduce its 820 model. Business customers liked buying computers from the same wholesalers that regularly handled their Xerox copiers. By 1980, Radio Shack's large retail store network helped the easy-to-use TRS-80 become the best-selling computer. Customers appreciated the accessibility of Radio Shack's in-store staff and tech support specialists.

As you read this, it probably occurs to you that most of the firms mentioned no longer sell computers. These early firms couldn't adjust quickly enough when IBM introduced its first PC. The pull of IBM's familiar brand gave more customers the confidence to buy. Sales of PCs surged as IBM established a chain of its own retail stores and worked closely with select dealers who promised to pay special attention to the IBM brand. Big-business customers bought in quantity directly from IBM's aggressive sales force. After IBM's design became an industry standard, firms such as Compaq, HP, and Toshiba quickly jumped in with PC models of their own—often selling through independent computer dealers.

Soon after, Michael Dell, then just a freshman in college, started buying and reselling computers from his dorm room. Dell figured a target market of price-conscious customers would respond to a different marketing mix. He used direct-response advertising in computer magazines; customers called a toll-free number to order a computer with the exact features they wanted. Then Dell used UPS to ship directly to the customer. Prices were low, too, because the direct channel eliminated retailer markup and the build-to-order approach reduced inventory costs. Dell also built reliable machines and delivered superior customer service. It would have been tough to centralize all of this if he had been working with thousands of retailers.

Although Dell's direct model worked well with tech-savvy consumers and small businesses, it struggled to make inroads with big government and corporate buyers. Eventually Dell adapted its strategy, using a sales force and building relationships, making some progress with these buyers.

At the same time, HP and other firms tried to imitate Dell's successful direct-order approach. However, this move created conflict with the retailers already selling most of HP's PCs; the retailers were not happy with competition from their own supplier! When these retailers responded by pushing other brands, HP limited the models sold online and added programs to support their dealers; for example, providing quick turnaround for retailers placing orders for custom-built computers.

Looking for ways to grow, Dell saw prospects in international markets. After success in Europe, it went after Asia. China was a huge market with a small but growing middle class and many small and medium-size businesses. But Dell ran into a well-entrenched Chinese competitor: state-supported PC maker Legend (later renamed Lenovo) already owned the small but growing market. Dell struggled to gain distribution outside of big Chinese cities where Lenovo had a strong distribution network.

This is where our story of the PC market shifts; Lenovo built a strong foundation in China to eventually become a global PC powerhouse. Back in the 1990s, it was just a distributor that adapted foreign PCs with local software and helped customers with Internet connectivity. Later, Lenovo moved up the value chain by manufacturing its own computers. Lenovo's presence in thousands of retail shops across the country was reassuring to first-time computer buyers who wanted to feel and touch a computer before purchasing.

Many customers became more comfortable with PC buying and sought the lower-cost option of buying direct from the manufacturer. So Lenovo added a direct selling channel for these customers. A more agile supply chain and a just-in-time delivery system also kept Lenovo's costs low. This strategy was important in the price-sensitive Chinese consumer market. At the time, it took several months' salary for a middle class Chinese consumer to buy a PC. Yet many Chinese consumers found a way because education is so highly valued in Chinese culture.

Back in 2005, Lenovo was little known outside of China. Then it made a bold move: Lenovo bought IBM's then struggling PC business. IBM's move out of the highly competitive PC market was just what Lenovo needed to jump-start a worldwide distribution network. IBM's ThinkPad was popular with business customers around the world, so the acquisition gave

Lenovo access to IBM's network of value-added resellers—firms that purchase PCs, tailor software and accessories, and finalize pricing to fit business customer needs. Lenovo's agile supply chain lowered the ThinkPad's production costs without sacrificing its reputation for power and durability. Lenovo continued innovating with products like Yoga—a laptop computer with a fold-back touchscreen that operates as a tablet.

Lenovo cannot forget its roots—which are still very profitable. Although rural Chinese may not be buying the latest technology, $400 desktop computers are the mainstay for suburban and urban Chinese. Competitors have yet to keep pace with Lenovo's vision to have a store selling its products within 30 miles of every person in China.

Dell continues to battle, but the former global market share leader is now in third place behind #1 Lenovo and #2 HP. Lenovo's strategy of different products and distribution models in different parts of the world continues to help it grow. But it is not stopping there. As the PC market matures and moves into decline, Lenovo pursues new growth opportunities. Lenovo recently purchased the Motorola mobile phone business from Google. Lenovo plans to leverage its strong distribution in India and China—where smartphones are just starting to take off—to dominate a new product category. With only 6 percent market share, and established competitors such as Apple and Samsung, the road ahead will be tough. But Lenovo's managers are confident that its supply chain and distribution network will once again deliver the goods.[1]

LEARNING OBJECTIVES

This case shows that offering customers a good product at a reasonable price is not the whole story. Marketing managers must make decisions about how they will make goods and services available to a target customer's Place when the customer wants them. This chapter's learning objectives will help you understand the role of Place in marketing strategy.

When you finish this chapter, you should be able to

1 Understand what product classes suggest about Place objectives.

2 Understand why some firms use direct channel systems whereas others work with intermediaries and indirect systems.

3 Understand how and why marketing specialists develop strategies to make channel systems more effective.

4 Understand how to develop cooperative relationships and avoid conflict in channel systems.

5 Know how channel members in vertical marketing systems shift and share functions to meet customer needs.

6 Understand the differences between intensive, selective, and exclusive distribution.

7 Know how multichannel distribution and reverse channels operate.

8 Know the main approaches firms use to reach customers in international markets.

9 Understand important new terms (shown in red).

Marketing Strategy Planning Decisions for Place

Managers must think about **Place**—making goods and services available in the right quantities and locations, when customers want them. And when different target markets have different needs, a number of Place variations may be required. Our opening case makes it clear that new Place arrangements can dramatically change the competition in a product-market. This is especially important in business today because information technology, including websites and e-commerce, makes it easier for firms to work together more efficiently and also to reach customers directly.

In this chapter and the two that follow, we'll deal with the many important marketing strategy decisions that a marketing manager must make concerning Place. Exhibit 10–1

Exhibit 10-1   Marketing Strategy Planning Decisions for Place

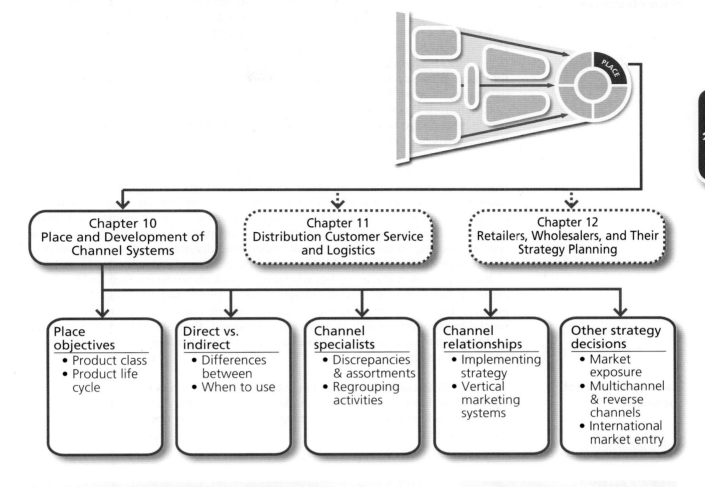

gives an overview. We'll start here with a discussion of Place objectives and how they relate to product classes and the product life cycle—ideas introduced in the Product chapters (8 and 9). We'll then discuss the type of channel that most aptly meets customers' needs. We'll show why specialists are often involved and how they come together to form a **channel of distribution**—any series of firms or individuals who participate in the flow of products from producer to final user or consumer. We'll also consider how to manage relations among channel members to reduce conflict and improve cooperation. This chapter concludes by considering the desired level of market exposure (and how many channel outlets are needed) as well as approaches for reaching customers in international markets.

In Chapter 11, we'll expand the Place discussion to decisions that a marketing manager makes about physical distribution, including customer service level, transporting, and storing. Then, in Chapter 12, we'll take a closer look at the many different types of retailing and wholesaling firms. We'll consider their role in channels as well as the strategy decisions they make to satisfy their own customers.

Place Decisions Are Guided by "Ideal" Place Objectives

LO 10.1

All marketing managers want to be sure that their goods and services are available in the right quantities and locations—when customers want them. But customers may have different needs in these areas as they make different purchases.

Product classes suggest Place objectives

In Chapter 8 we introduced the product classes, which summarize consumers' urgency to have needs satisfied and their willingness to seek information, shop, and compare. Now you should be able to use the product classes to handle Place decisions.

Exhibit 8–6 shows the relationship between consumer product classes and ideal Place objectives. Similarly, Exhibit 8–7 shows the business product classes and how they relate to customer needs. Study these exhibits carefully. They set the framework for making Place decisions. In particular, the product classes help us decide how much market exposure we'll need in each geographic area.

Recall from Chapter 8 that customers won't spend much time shopping for convenience products; so widespread distribution is needed to make products available when the need strikes. If customers want to compare shopping products, some distribution channels can make that process easier. For example, online sellers often carry a broad assortment of products to make this easier, and some physical stores offer similar advantages. *Heterogeneous* shopping goods should have outlets that provide information—knowledgeable salespeople who can provide insights about different brands and models and online stores with videos or information. *Homogeneous* shopping goods favor low-cost retailers as customers focus mostly on low prices. Customers will search for specialty goods, so the higher cost of widespread distribution may not be needed. Unsought products should be sold at locations where other, related products are available.

Business product classes reflect what buyers think about the products and how they are used. Accessory equipment and maintenance, repair, and operating (MRO) supplies are used frequently, requiring widespread distribution. Raw materials often have special transportation needs that must be considered. Reliable delivery is critical for component parts and materials. Professional services are usually delivered in person, so location matters.

Place system is not automatic

Several different product classes may be involved if different market segments view a product in different ways. Thus, marketing managers may need to develop several strategies, each with its own Place arrangements. There may not be one Place arrangement that is best.

For most target customers, the Iams brand of premium dog food is a staple or heterogeneous shopping product. So Iams distributes through supermarkets, pet superstores, and mass merchandisers, displaying it near competing products. On the other hand, iVet's super-premium dog food is likely to be perceived as a specialty product. Consequently it is sold only through veterinarians who give the product an extra push with their recommendation.
Left: © The Procter & Gamble Company. Used by permission; Right: Copyright © 2015 iVet Professional Formulas.

For example, many consumers view Tide laundry detergent as a staple for doing laundry at home. To meet their needs, it is widely distributed in grocery and discount stores. Customers who run out of detergent while doing wash at a laundromat see Tide as an emergency product and want small boxes available in a vending machine. And some hotels look at Tide as an operating supply that the housekeeping department needs to provide guests with clean sheets and towels. For these hotels, Tide comes in large drums that are sold and delivered by wholesalers of housekeeping supplies.

Place decisions have long-run effects

The marketing manager must also consider Place objectives in relation to the product life cycle; see again Exhibit 9–3. Place decisions often have long-run effects. They're usually harder to change than Product, Promotion, and Price decisions. Many firms that thought they could quickly establish effective websites for direct online sales, for example, found that it took several years and millions of dollars to work out the kinks. It can take even longer and cost more to develop effective working relationships with others in the channel. Legal contracts with channel partners may limit changes. And it's hard to move retail stores and wholesale facilities once they are set up. Yet as products mature, they typically need broader distribution to reach different target customers. Marketing managers need to keep the future in mind when they develop Place objectives.

Channel System May Be Direct or Indirect

LO 10.2

One of the most basic Place decisions producers must make is whether to handle the whole distribution job themselves— perhaps by relying on direct-to-customer e-commerce selling or opening their own stores—or use wholesalers, retailers, and other specialists.

Many firms prefer to distribute directly to the final customer or consumer because they want to control the whole marketing job. They may think that they can serve target customers at a lower cost or do the work more effectively than intermediaries. Although this can be true, marketing managers should carefully assess the value intermediaries add for end customers.

Direct distribution maintains control

One reason a producer chooses direct distribution is because it wants to maintain control of the marketing mix. Wholesalers and retailers usually carry competing products and will make decisions that are in their own interests—and this may not always be aligned with the interests of an individual producer. For example, Goodyear wants its target customers to know that its Assurance Triple-Tred All-Season tires get 21 percent better wet traction than a leading competitor. But if Roadmasters Auto and Tire Centers makes a bigger profit on that "leading competitor," the salesperson at Roadmasters may not deliver that "better

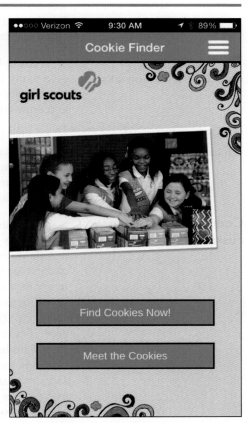

Girl Scouts sell their cookies direct to customers. But you need to know when and where a girl scout will be selling the cookies. So Girl Scouts of America created the Cookie Locator app for the iPhone. Customers just enter their zip code and they are directed to the nearest source of the tasty treats.
© 2015 Girl Scouts of the United States of America. A501(c) (3)Organization. All Rights Reserved.

Ela Family Farms in Hotchkiss, Colorado sells its organic tree fruits—along with jams, sauces, and nectars—direct to consumers. Consumers can find their tasty product line at their farmer's market stand or by ordering online with direct home delivery. Business products are often sold direct. GE Aviation has only a few very large customers that buy its commercial jet engines direct from the producer.

Left: © Ela Family Farms; Right: © 2015 General Electric

wet traction" message. If Goodyear had a promotion to sell this tire at a lower price, Roadmasters may choose to not pass it along to its customers. At its own online store, Goodyear can be sure that customers receive the message and price Goodyear prefers.

The Internet makes direct distribution easier

Website-based e-commerce systems and delivery services such as UPS and FedEx give many firms direct access to customers whom it would have been impossible to reach in the past. Even small, specialized firms may be able to establish a web page and draw customers from all over the world.

Direct contact with customers

Another benefit to direct distribution is that it puts a firm in direct contact with its customers; it is more aware of changes in customer attitudes. It is in a better position to adjust its marketing mix quickly because there is no need to convince other channel members to help. If a product needs an aggressive selling effort or special technical service, the marketing manager can ensure that salespeople receive the necessary training and motivation.

Common with business customers and services

Many business products are sold direct-to-customer. Alcan sells aluminum to General Motors direct. Woodward produces products such as pumps and fuel nozzles that it sells directly to aircraft makers such as Boeing, Airbus, and Gulfstream. This is understandable because in business markets there are fewer transactions, orders are larger, and customers may be concentrated in one geographic area. Further, once relationships are established, e-commerce systems can efficiently handle orders.

Service firms often use direct channels. If the service must be produced in the presence of customers, there may be little need for intermediaries. An accounting firm like PricewaterhouseCoopers, for example, must deal directly with its customers.

Firms that produce physical goods turn to channel specialists to help provide the services customers expect. GE may hope that its authorized appliance dealers don't get many repair calls, but the service is available when customers need it. Here the intermediary produces the service.[2]

When suitable intermediaries are not available

A firm may have to go direct if suitable intermediaries are not available or will not cooperate. Sometimes intermediaries that have the best contacts with the target market may be hesitant to add unproven vendors or new products. For example, when Glacéau began selling its now popular Vitaminwater, wholesale distributors had no interest in carrying it. So the owner of the company delivered the bottled water directly to small retailers in New York City. Once he proved his product would sell, distributor interest grew. On the other hand, to enter the California market, Glacéau gave distribution rights to just one distributor. As a result, it was in this distributor's interest to work closely with Glacéau to

Keurig and Nespresso are two companies that sell single-serve coffee and the equipment for brewing it. Keurig sells most of its products through retailers, with some direct sales via its website. Nespresso uses a direct model, selling only through its website. Both companies have been successful with these business models.
Left: © Keurig, Incorporated 2013. All rights reserved., Right: © 2013 Nestlé Nespresso SA.

build the market. Eventually Coca-Cola purchased Glacéau; at that point, Coke added many of its own distributors. Glacéau became a success by slowly building support from retailers and wholesalers, but many new products fail because the producer can't find willing channel partners and doesn't have the resources to handle direct distribution.[3]

In the United States, the Census Bureau publishes detailed data concerning wholesalers and retailers, including breakdowns by kind of business, product line, and geographic territory. Similar information is available for many other countries. It can be very valuable in strategy planning—especially to learn whether potential channel members are serving a target market. You can also learn what sales volume current intermediaries are achieving.

Some consumer products are sold "direct"

Many companies that produce consumer products have websites where a consumer can place a direct order. But for most consumer products this is still a small part of total sales. Most consumer products are sold through intermediaries.

Of course, some consumer products are sold direct to consumers where they live or work. Mary Kay and Avon cosmetics, Electrolux vacuum cleaners, Amway Global household products, and Tupperware are examples. These firms and many others are finding that this is a good way to crack open international markets ranging from India and China to Brazil, Africa, and the U.K. Most of these firms rely on direct selling, which involves personal sales contact between a representative of the company and an individual consumer.

However, most of these "salespeople" are *not* company employees. Rather, they usually work independently and the companies that they sell for refer to them as *dealers, distributors, agents,* or some similar term. So in a strict technical sense, this is not really direct producer-to-consumer distribution.[4]

Don't be confused by the term *direct marketing*

Even though most consumer products are sold through intermediaries, an increasing number of firms rely on **direct marketing**—direct communication between a seller and an individual customer using a promotion method other than face-to-face personal selling. Sometimes direct marketing promotion is coupled with direct distribution from a producer to consumers.

It was difficult for Solar Sisters to find distribution channel partners when it tried to sell its solar lamps, solar phone chargers, and solar panels in Uganda, Tanazania, and Nigeria. So it used a different strategy. Now women entrepreneurs in these countries buy the lights and sell them to others in their villages. Since the women salespeople are not employed by Solar Sister, this is technically not direct distribution.

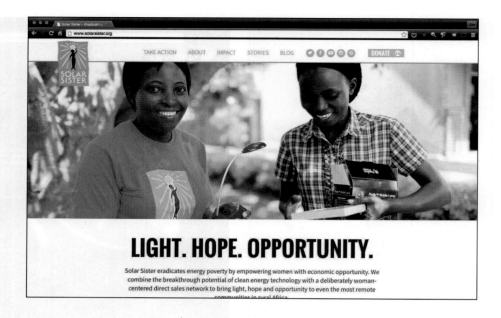

LIGHT. HOPE. OPPORTUNITY.

Solar Sister eradicates energy poverty by empowering women with economic opportunity. We combine the breakthrough potential of clean energy technology with a deliberately woman-centered direct sales network to bring light, hope and opportunity to even the most remote communities in rural Africa.

However, many firms that use direct marketing promotion distribute their products through intermediaries. For example, Logitech, which produces personal computer peripherals, uses e-mails to communicate directly with customers who purchase Logitech products through retailers. So the term direct marketing is primarily concerned with the Promotion area, not Place decisions. We'll talk about direct marketing promotion in more detail in Chapter 13.[5]

When indirect channels are best

Even if a producer wants to handle the whole distribution job, sometimes it's simply not possible. Customers often have established buying patterns. For example, Square D, a producer of electrical supplies, might want to sell directly to electrical contractors. It can certainly set up a website for online orders or even open sales offices in key markets. But if contractors like to make all of their purchases in one convenient stop—at a local electrical wholesaler—the only practical way to reach them is through a wholesaler. Similarly, most consumers prefer the convenience of picking up milk, bread, meat, fruit, and vegetables in a single shopping trip. So most producers of these food items don't try to sell directly to consumers.

In general, consumers of household goods prefer to shop for certain products at specific places. Some consumers, for instance, see Sears as *the* place to shop for large home appliances, so they'll buy only the brands that Sears carries. This is one reason most firms that produce consumer products rely so heavily on indirect channels (see Exhibit 2–6).[6]

Intermediaries may supply needed information

Specialists often help provide information to bring buyers and sellers together. For example, most consumers don't know much about the wide variety of home and auto insurance policies available. A local independent insurance agent may help them decide which policy, and which insurance company, best fits their needs.

Intermediaries who are close to their customers are often able to anticipate customer needs and forecast demand more accurately. This information can help reduce inventory costs in the whole channel—and it may help the producer smooth out production.

Most producers seek help from specialists when they first enter international markets. Specialists can provide crucial information about customer needs and insights into differences in the market environment.

Intermediaries provide working capital and credit

Direct distribution usually requires a significant investment in facilities, people, and information technology. A company that has limited financial resources or that wants to retain flexibility may want to avoid that investment by working with established intermediaries.

Intermediaries may further reduce a producer's need for working capital by buying the producer's output and carrying it in inventory until it's sold. If customers want a good "right now," there must be inventory available to make the sale. And if customers are spread over a large area, it will probably be necessary to have widespread distribution.

Some wholesalers play a critical role by providing credit to customers at the end of the channel. A wholesaler who knows local customers can help reduce credit risks. As sales via the Internet grow, sellers are looking for faster and better ways to check the credit ratings of distant customers. It's an unhappy day when the marketing manager learns that a customer who was shipped goods based on an online order can't pay the invoice.

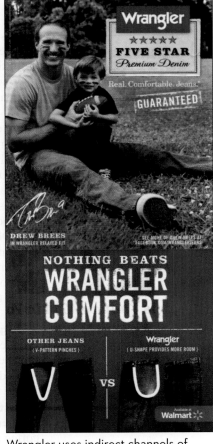

Wrangler uses indirect channels of distribution. In this ad, Wrangler lets customers know they can find Wrangler jeans at Walmart.
© 2015 VF Corporation. All Rights Reserved.

Cost and effectiveness should determine direct/indirect decision

The most important reason for using an indirect channel of distribution is that an intermediary can often help producers serve customer needs better and at lower cost. Marketing managers should carefully evaluate each target market's needs and determine its customers' willingness to pay. A firm should also understand its capabilities and those of willing intermediaries. This will help the marketing manager determine whether to use intermediaries and, if so, which intermediaries would work best.

Some firms use direct and indirect channels

When a company serves multiple target markets, it may choose to sell direct and through intermediaries. For example, a company like Autolite uses direct channels to sell its spark plugs to automakers like Ford. Yet it also sells to consumers through intermediaries like Pep Boys. Traditionally, most firms targeting consumers relied on indirect channels, but that is changing. For example, although Bose electronics, Under Armour athletic gear, and Samsonite luggage sell through retail outlets, each also sells directly through its own outlet stores and online at the company's website.

Online Toolkit

Under Armour sells directly to consumers and indirectly through intermediaries such as Dick's Sporting Goods. Go to Dick's Sporting Good's website (**www.dickssportinggoods.com**) and search for Under Armour. Find an Under Armour shirt and save that page. Then go to the Under Armour site (**www.underarmour.com**) and search for the same item. Could you find it? If not, try to find a very similar item. Compare and contrast the promotion, pricing, and delivery charges between the two products and distribution channels. Why does Under Armour compete with one of its retailers? How do you think Dick's Sporting Goods feels about Under Armour selling direct to consumers?

Deciding whether to sell directly, indirectly, or both requires an understanding of discrepancies and separations (introduced briefly in Chapter 1). Now we'll go into more detail.

Channel Specialists May Reduce Discrepancies and Separations

LO 10.3

The assortment and quantity of products customers want may be different from the assortment and quantity of products companies produce. Producers are often located far from their customers and may not know how best to reach them. Customers in turn may not know about their choices. Specialists develop strategies to adjust these discrepancies and separations.[7]

Discrepancies of quantity and assortment

Discrepancy of quantity means the difference between the quantity of products it is economical for a producer to make and the quantity final users or consumers normally want. For example, most manufacturers of golf balls produce large quantities—perhaps 200,000 to 500,000 in a given time period. The average golfer, however, wants only a few balls at a time. Adjusting for this discrepancy usually requires intermediaries—wholesalers and retailers.

Producers typically specialize by product—and therefore another discrepancy develops. **Discrepancy of assortment** means the difference between the lines a typical producer makes and the assortment final consumers or users want. Most golfers, for example, need more than golf balls. They want golf shoes, gloves, clubs, a bag, and, of course, a golf course to play on. And they usually don't want to shop for each item separately. So, again, there is a need for wholesalers and retailers to adjust these discrepancies.

Channel specialists adjust discrepancies with regrouping activities

Regrouping activities adjust the quantities or assortments of products handled at each level in a channel of distribution. There are four regrouping activities: accumulating, bulk-breaking, sorting, and assorting. When one or more of these activities is needed, a marketing specialist may develop them to fill this need.

Adjusting quantity discrepancies by accumulating and bulk-breaking

Accumulating involves collecting products from many small producers. Much of the coffee that comes from Colombia is grown on small farms in the mountains. Accumulating the small crops into larger quantities is a way of getting the lowest transporting rate and making it more convenient for distant food processing companies to buy and handle it. Accumulating is especially important in less-developed countries and in other situations, like agricultural markets, where there are many small producers.

Because FedEx offers specialized services that facilitate exchange between producers and consumers, it helps to reduce discrepancies and separations.
Photo by Reed/Bloomberg via Getty Images.

What's Next? Bits and bytes need distribution, too

Virtual products need distribution, too. Music, television programs, movies, books, video games, and software all exist in an intangible, digital form—though some are also sold as physical goods. Many service products are purchased, selected, and sometimes delivered in part through digital channels—hotels, airline tickets, and banking, for example. Distribution costs can be very low for digital products because most can travel over the World Wide Web at little or no cost. Yet even without a physical form, distribution remains an important marketing strategy decision for firms with digital products.

Take video entertainment, for example. It was just a couple of decades ago that most viewers selected from television programming that happened to be on the few major networks at a particular time. But in today's marketplace, an explosion of networks, channels, and programming make it almost impossible to keep up with all the choices. Even the variety of programming shown on a single network such as ESPN or HBO is a lot for most viewers to evaluate. As a result, online intermediaries such as Hulu are coming on the scene. As with other intermediaries, Hulu collects programming from television networks and movie studios and streams it over the Internet to smartphones, computers, and TV sets.

As a channel specialist, Hulu reduces discrepancies and separations between consumers (viewers of video content) and producers (primarily creators of television programming and movies). Hulu matches the assortment and quantity of programming viewers want with the assortment and quantity of programming available. TV viewers face *discrepancies of quantity*—there are millions of hours of television programming produced, but most viewers need only a couple hours or less at a time. Viewers also face *discrepancies of assortment*; for instance, a viewer may enjoy watching nature programs, but that type of program is shown on Discovery Channel, National Geographic Channel, the Public Broadcasting Service, and MSNBC.

So Hulu performs *regrouping* activities to better satisfy viewer needs. For example, by bringing together programming from multiple networks, Hulu *accumulates* content; this makes it easier for consumers to visit one site where they can search and find the desired programming. Hulu does *bulk-breaking*; it receives programming from networks in bulk—all the episodes of *Family Guy*, for example—and then offers them for viewing one episode at a time. By providing its viewers with features that tag and rate programs, Hulu also performs a *sorting* activity. The tagging system combines with other categories developed by Hulu to create an *assorting* activity that helps consumers view collections of programs that match their interests.

As you can see from this short case on video entertainment, producers of digital products face many of the same challenges facing producers of physical goods. Now see if you can conduct the same type of analysis conducted here on the airline travel and ebook markets. Go to the websites Expedia.com (for airline tickets) and Amazon.com and its Kindle product (for ebooks) to learn how these sellers operate. How does each of these companies operate to reduce discrepancies of quantity and assortment? Conduct an analysis similar for each similar to what we have done in the previous two paragraphs for Hulu.[8]

Accumulating is also important with professional services because they often involve the combined work of a number of individuals, each of whom is a specialized producer. A hospital makes it easier for patients by accumulating the services of a number of health care specialists, many of whom may not actually work for the hospital.

Many wholesalers and retailers who operate from Internet websites focus on accumulating. Specialized sites for everything from Chinese art to Dutch flower bulbs bring together the output of many producers.

Bulk-breaking involves dividing larger quantities into smaller quantities as products get closer to the final market. The bulk-breaking may involve several levels in the channel. Wholesalers may sell smaller quantities to other wholesalers or directly to retailers. Retailers continue breaking bulk as they sell individual items to their customers.

Adjusting assortment discrepancies by sorting and assorting

Different types of specialists adjust assortment discrepancies. They perform two types of regrouping activities: sorting and assorting.

Sorting means separating products into grades and qualities desired by different target markets. For example, an investment firm might offer its customers shares in a mutual fund made up only of stocks for companies that pay regular dividends. Similarly, a wholesaler that specializes in serving convenience stores may focus on smaller packages of frequently used products.

Assorting means putting together a variety of products to give a target market what it wants. This usually is done by those closest to the final consumer or user—retailers or wholesalers who try to supply a wide assortment of products for the convenience of their customers. Thus, a wholesaler selling Yazoo tractors and mowers to golf courses might also carry Pennington grass seed and Scott fertilizer.

Although digital products are not distributed in the same manner as physical goods, these products also experience discrepancies of quantity and assortment. Read about how this works in *"What's Next?* Bits and bytes need distribution, too."

Adding or subtracting channels can add value and differentiate

Specialists develop strategies to adjust separations and discrepancies if they need to be adjusted. Sometimes spotting such a need creates an opportunity. For example, many office workers in big cities don't have time to run out to a restaurant for lunch every day. The growth of food trucks in urban areas emerged as a new channel for some restaurants.

On the other hand, there is no point in having intermediaries just because that's the way it's always been done. Eliminating intermediaries might create other opportunities. Some manufacturers of business products now reach more customers in distant markets with a website than was previously possible for them to reach with independent manufacturers' reps who sold on commission (but otherwise left distribution to the firm). The website cost advantage can translate to lower prices and a marketing mix that is a better value for some target segments.[9]

Channel Relationships Must Be Managed

Marketing manager must choose type of channel relationship

Intermediary specialists can help make a channel more efficient. But there may be problems getting the different firms in a channel to work together well. How well they work together depends on the type of relationship they have. This should be carefully considered because marketing managers usually have choices about what type of channel system to join or develop.

The whole channel should have a product-market commitment

Ideally, all of the members of a channel system should have a shared *product-market commitment*—with all members focusing on the same target market at the end of the channel and sharing the various marketing functions in appropriate ways. When members of a channel do this, they are better able to compete effectively for the customer's business. Unfortunately, many marketing managers overlook this idea because it's not the way their firms have traditionally handled channel relationships.

Traditional channel systems involve weak relationships

In **traditional channel systems**, the various channel members make little or no effort to cooperate with one another. They buy and sell from one another—and that's the extent of their relationship. Each channel member does only what it considers to be in its own best interest. It doesn't worry about other members of the channel. This is shortsighted, but it's easy to see how it can happen. The objectives of the various channel members may be different. For example, Cooper Industries wants a wholesaler of electrical building supplies to sell Cooper products. But a wholesaler who works with different producers may not care whose products get sold. The wholesaler just wants happy customers and a good profit margin.[10]

Conflict gets in the way

Specialization can make a channel more efficient—but not if the specialists are so independent that the channel doesn't work smoothly. Because members of traditional

STIHL sells its high-quality chain saws through 8,000 independent STIHL dealers nationwide. These dealers provide product demonstrations, good advice, and expert on-site service. STIHL limits horizontal conflict by not selling through home-improvement warehouses or online stores that put more emphasis on price competition and less on service.
The STIHL name and the STIHL logo are protected names and trademarks of ANDREAS STIHL AG & Co. KG.

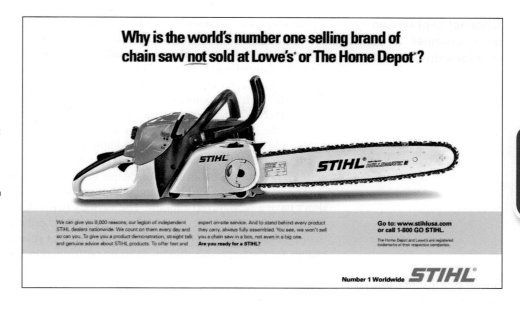

channel systems often have different objectives—and different ideas about how things should be done—conflict is common.

There are two basic types of conflict in channels of distribution. *Vertical conflicts* occur between firms at different levels in the channel of distribution. A vertical conflict may occur if a producer and a retailer disagree about how much promotion effort the retailer should give the producer's product. For example, when GameStop started selling used video games, game publishers were concerned the move would steal sales from new games. Not only would revenue from new games decrease, but the game publishers would not earn any revenue on used game sales.[11]

Horizontal conflicts occur between firms at the same level in a distribution channel. For example, a bicycle store that keeps a complete line of bikes on display, has a knowledgeable sales staff, and lets customers take test rides isn't happy to find out that an online store with little inventory and no salespeople offers customers lower prices on the same models. The online retailer gets a free ride on the competing store's investments in inventory and sales staff.

Managing channel conflict

Some level of conflict may be inevitable—or even useful if that is what it takes for customers at the end of the channel to receive better value. However, most marketing managers try to avoid conflicts that harm relationships with channel partners. To appease channel partners, manufacturers often try to serve different market segments through each channel. For example, convenience stores like 7-11 and membership stores like Costco both sell Coke—but one offers it cold in individual servings at many convenient location, whereas the other offers it warm and 24 cans at a time at a warehouse store. Each offers a different marketing mix to a different target market.

Other firms manage conflict by offering different products through each channel. Gibson stopped selling guitars on its website after complaints from its traditional retailers and distributors. On the other hand, Gibson's website continued to sell a wide variety of accessories that most retailers did not want to stock. Gibson's competitor, Fender, also decided to sell direct to consumer's and created conflict with its dealers. Many Fender dealers think customers will test out a new guitar in their stores and buy on the Fender website. Fender promises not to undercut its dealers prices. Some dealers may nudge customers toward Gibson in the long run.[12]

In general, treating channel partners fairly—even when one partner is more powerful—tends to build trust and reduce conflict. Trusting relationships lead to greater cooperation in the channel. As a consequence, channel members are better able to satisfy the needs of target customers at the end of the channel.[13]

Channel captain can guide channel relationships

Although each channel system should act as a unit, some firms are in a better position to take the lead in the relationship and in coordinating the whole channel effort. This situation calls for a **channel captain**—a manager who helps direct the activities of a whole channel and tries to avoid or solve channel conflicts.

For example, when Harley-Davidson wanted to expand sales of fashion accessories, it was difficult for motorcycle dealers to devote enough space to all of the different styles. Harley considered selling the items directly from its own website, but that would take sales away from dealers who were working hard to help Harley sell both cycles and fashions. So Harley's president asked a group of dealers and Harley managers to work together to come up with a plan they all liked. The result was a website that sells Harley products through the dealer that is closest to the customer.[14]

The concept of a single channel captain is logical. But most traditional channels don't have a recognized captain. The various firms don't act as a coordinated system. Yet firms are interrelated, even if poorly, by their policies. So it makes sense to try to avoid channel conflicts by planning for channel relations. The channel captain arranges for the necessary functions to be performed in the most effective way.[15]

Some producers lead their channels

Sometimes producers take the lead in channel relations. Typically this occurs when the producer is large, dominates a category, or wields a powerful brand name. In this case, intermediaries usually take a back seat and support the producer. They often negotiate a situation that is profitable for both parties, but the producer usually has a stronger hand.

Acting as channel captains in their respective channels, both Peterson and Electrolux are able to get cooperation from many independent wholesalers and retailers as well as big chains like Lowe's because they develop marketing strategies that help the whole channel compete more effectively. This also helps everyone in the channel do a better job of meeting the needs of target customers at the end of the channel.

Left: Copyright © 2007, Peterson Manufacturing Company. All rights reserved., Right: Courtesy ELECTROLUX North America.

Exhibit 10-2 How Channel Functions May Be Shifted and Shared in Different Channel Systems

A. How strategy decisions are handled in a producer-led channel

B. How strategy decisions are handled in a retailer-led channel

Exhibit 10–2A shows this type of producer-led channel system. Here the producer has selected the target market and developed the Product, set the Price structure, invested in consumer and channel Promotion, and developed the Place setup. Intermediaries are then expected to finish the Promotion job in their respective places. Of course, in a retailer-dominated channel system, the marketing jobs would be handled in a different way.

Boar's Head, maker of premium meat products sold at deli counters across the United States, offers an example of a producer-led channel system. Boar's Head gained this position by outspending its rivals on advertising and earning brand preference and brand insistence from consumers. Boar's Head negotiates with retailers so that its signage dominates the deli department and it is often the only premium brand in the store. The brand commands a premium price. Prudent marketing decisions help Boar's Head maintain good margins.

Powerful retailers can lead channels

Sometimes wholesalers or retailers take the lead. They are closer to the final user or consumer and are in an ideal position to assume the channel captain role. Intermediaries find that the ability to gather, analyze, and interpret data generates insights about customer needs. They can then seek out producers who can meet these needs with products at reasonable prices. Powerful retail chains such as Walmart, Toys "R" Us, and Tesco now dominate the channel systems for many products in the United States, Asia, and Europe. In these situations the retailer often suggests new products suppliers should make. They also have a strong influence on prices. Exhibit 10–2B shows how marketing strategy might be handled in this sort of retailer-led channel system.[16]

Vertical Marketing Systems Focus on Final Customers

LO 10.5

Many marketing managers accept the view that a coordinated channel system can help everyone in the channel. These managers are moving their firms away from traditional channel systems and instead developing or joining vertical marketing systems.

Exhibit 10-3 Characteristics of Traditional and Vertical Marketing Systems

Characteristics	Traditional	Type of Channel Vertical Marketing Systems		
		Administered	Contractual	Corporate
Amount of cooperation	Little or none	Some to good	Fairly good to good	Complete
Control maintained by	None	Economic power and leadership	Contracts	Ownership by one company
Examples	Typical channel of "independents"	General Electric, Miller Beer, Scotts Miracle-Gro	McDonald's, Holiday Inn, Ace Hardware, Super Valu, Coca-Cola, Chevrolet	Florsheim Shoes, Sherwin-Williams

Vertical marketing systems are channel systems in which the whole channel focuses on the same target market at the end of the channel. Such systems make sense, and are growing, because if the final customer doesn't buy the product, the whole channel suffers. There are three types of vertical marketing systems—corporate, administered, and contractual. Exhibit 10–3 summarizes some characteristics of these systems and compares them with traditional systems.

Corporate channel systems shorten channels

Some corporations develop their own vertical marketing systems by internal expansion or by buying other firms, or both. With **corporate channel systems**—corporate ownership all along the channel—we might say the firm is going "direct." But actually the firm may be handling manufacturing, wholesaling, *and* retailing—so it's more accurate to think of the firm as a vertical marketing system.

Corporate channel systems may develop by **vertical integration**—acquiring firms at different levels of channel activity. For example, in England, most of the quaint local pubs are now actually owned and operated by the large breweries.

Vertical integration has potential advantages—stable sources of supplies, better control of distribution and quality, greater buying power, and lower executive overhead. Provided that the discrepancies of quantity and assortment are not too great at each level in a channel, vertical integration can be profitable. However, many managers have found that it's hard to be really good at running manufacturing, wholesaling, and retailing businesses that are very different from one another. Instead, they try to be more efficient at what they do best and focus on ways to get cooperation in the channel for the other activities.[17]

Administered and contractual systems may work well

Firms can often gain the advantages of vertical integration without building a costly corporate channel. A manager can develop administered or contractual channel systems instead. In **administered channel systems**, the channel members informally agree to cooperate with one another. They can agree to routinize ordering, share inventory and sales information over computer networks, standardize accounting, and coordinate promotion efforts. In **contractual channel systems**, the channel members agree by contract to cooperate with one another. With both of these systems, the members retain some of the flexibility of a traditional channel system.

Vertical marketing systems dominate the marketplace

Vertical systems in the consumer products area have a healthy majority of retail sales and should continue to increase their share in the future. Vertical marketing systems are becoming the major competitive units in the U.S. distribution system—and they are growing rapidly in other parts of the world as well.[18]

Exhibit 10-4 Comparing Levels of Market Exposure

| | Level of Market Exposure | | |
	Intensive	Selective	Exclusive
Number of outlets	Many	Some—a few in each geographic area	Few—one per geographic area
Used when . . .	Convenience products, business supplies, and higher sales volume offset higher distribution costs	Widespread coverage is needed, but also special attention from intermediaries	Fewer customers so support needed from intermediaries or when franchisees demand protected markets
Examples	Coca-Cola, Wrigley's chewing gum, Butterfinger candy bars	Oakley sunglasses, Vera Bradley handbags, Goodyear tires	Audi cars, Sub-Zero appliances, Piaget watches, Five Guys restaurants

The Best Channel System Should Achieve Ideal Market Exposure

LO 10.6

You may think that all marketing managers want their products to have maximum exposure to potential customers. This isn't true. Some product classes require much less market exposure than others. **Ideal market exposure** makes a product available widely enough to satisfy target customers' needs but not exceed them. Too much exposure only increases the total cost of marketing.

Ideal exposure may be intensive, selective, or exclusive

Intensive distribution is selling a product through all responsible and suitable wholesalers or retailers who will stock or sell the product. **Selective distribution** is selling through only those intermediaries who will give the product special attention. **Exclusive distribution** is selling through only one intermediary in a particular geographic area. For an overview, see Exhibit 10–4. As we move from intensive to exclusive distribution, we give up exposure in return for some other advantage—including, but not limited to, lower cost.

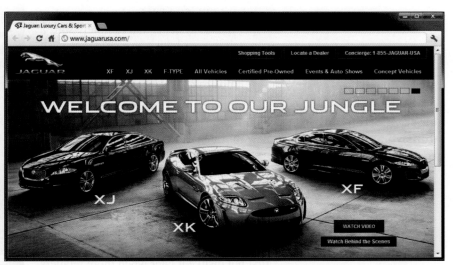

Starburst is a convenience product and is sold using intensive distribution. On the other hand, most members of Jaguar's target market view the car as a heterogeneous shopping or specialty product—so the car-maker uses exclusive distribution.

Intensive distribution—sell it where they buy it

Intensive distribution is commonly needed for convenience products and business supplies—such as laser printer cartridges, ring binders, and copier paper—used by all offices. Customers want such products nearby. For example, Rayovac batteries were not selling well even though their performance was very similar to other batteries. Part of that was due to heavier advertising for Duracell and Energizer. But consumers usually don't go shopping for batteries. They're purchased on impulse 83 percent of the time. To get a larger share of purchases, Rayovac had to be in more stores. It offered retailers a marketing mix with less advertising and a lower price. In three years, the brand moved from being available in 36,000 stores to 82,000 stores—and that increase gave sales a big charge.[19]

Selective distribution—sell it where it sells best

Selective distribution covers the broad area of market exposure between intensive and exclusive distribution. It may be suitable for all categories of products. Only the better intermediaries are used here. Companies commonly use selective distribution to gain some of the advantages of exclusive distribution—while still achieving fairly widespread market coverage.

Reduce costs and get better partners

A selective policy might be used to avoid selling to wholesalers or retailers that (1) place orders that are too small to justify making calls, (2) make too many returns or request too much service, (3) have a poor credit rating, or (4) are not in a position to do a satisfactory job.

Selective distribution is becoming more popular than intensive distribution as firms see that they don't need 100 percent coverage of a market to support national advertising. Interested customers without a local store can often buy online. Often the majority of sales come from relatively few customers—and the others buy too little compared to the cost of working with them. This is called the 80/20 rule—80 percent of a company's sales often come from only 20 percent of its customers.

Get special effort from channel members

Selective distribution can produce greater profits not only for the producer but for all channel members. Wholesalers and retailers are more willing to promote products aggressively if they know they're going to obtain the majority of sales through their own efforts. They may carry wider lines, do more promotion, and provide more service—all of which lead to more sales. Viper makes systems that remotely start a car—sit in your house on a cold day, push a button, and your car starts. Its selective distribution (just a few outlets per city) gets it stronger support from its dealers.

Selective often moves to intensive as market grows

In the early part of the life cycle of a new unsought good, a producer may have to use selective distribution. Well-known wholesalers and retailers may have the power to get such a product introduced, but sometimes on their own terms. That often means limiting the number of competing wholesalers and retailers. The producer may be happy with such an arrangement at first but dislike it later when more retailers want to carry the product.

Exclusive distribution sometimes makes sense

Exclusive distribution is just an extreme case of selective distribution—the firm selects only one wholesaler or

WE'RE NEW TO THE AREA. SO BE A GOOD NEIGHBOR AND INTRODUCE YOURSELF.

As demand for premium coffee increased, Dunkin' Donuts took advantage of its brand reputation and the quality of its product to obtain distribution in supermarkets.

retailer in each geographic area. Besides the various advantages of selective distribution, producers may want to use exclusive distribution to help control prices and the service offered in a channel. Franchisors such as McDonald's and 1-800-GOT-JUNK? offer franchisees exclusive territories.

Is limiting market exposure legal? It depends

Exclusive distribution is an area considered under U.S. antimonopoly laws. Courts currently focus on whether an exclusive distribution arrangement hurts competition.

Horizontal arrangements—among *competing* retailers, wholesalers, or producers—to limit sales by customer or territory have consistently been ruled illegal by the U.S. Supreme Court. Courts consider such arrangements obvious collusion that reduces competition and harms customers.

The legality of vertical arrangements—between producers and intermediaries—is not as clear-cut. A 1977 Supreme Court decision (involving Sylvania and the distribution of TV sets) reversed an earlier ruling that it was always illegal to set up vertical relationships limiting territories or customers. Now courts can weigh the possible good effects against the possible restrictions on competition. They look at competition between whole channels rather than just focusing on competition at one level of distribution. The Sylvania decision does not mean that all vertical arrangements are legal. Rather, it says that a firm has to be able to legally justify any exclusive arrangements.

Thus, firms should be cautious about entering into *any* exclusive distribution arrangement. The courts can force a change in relationships that were expensive to develop. And even worse, the courts can award triple damages if they rule that competition has been hurt.

The same cautions apply to selective distribution. Here, however, less formal arrangements are typical—and the possible impact on competition is more remote. It is now more acceptable to carefully select channel members when building a channel system. Refusing to sell to some intermediaries, however, should be part of a logical plan with long-term benefits to consumers.[20]

Multichannel Distribution and Reverse Channels

LO 10.7

Trying to achieve the desired degree of market exposure can lead to complex channels of distribution. Firms may need different channels to reach different segments of a broad product-market or to be sure they reach each segment at different stages of the purchase process. Sometimes this results in competition and conflict among different channels. Sometimes additional channels must be developed to return or recycle products. Let's look closer at multichannel distribution and then reverse channels.

Many firms use more than one channel of distribution

Consider the different channels used by a company that publishes computer books. See Exhibit 10–5. This publisher sells through a general book wholesaler that in turn sells to Internet book retailers and independent book retailers. The publisher might also sell through a computer supplies wholesaler that serves electronics superstores like Best Buy. It may also sell some of its best sellers through a large chain or even to consumers who order directly from its website. An Internet retailer might offer books in print and as e-book downloads. All these channels can cause problems because different wholesalers and retailers want different markups. It also increases competition, including price competition. And the competition among different intermediaries may lead to conflicts between the intermediaries and the publisher. Managers must consider the impact of conflict if they choose to increase market exposure by using more channels of distribution.

Multichannel distribution is becoming more common

Multichannel distribution occurs when a producer uses several competing channels to reach the same target market—perhaps using several intermediaries in addition to selling directly. Multichannel distribution is becoming more common. A single target

Exhibit 10-5 An Example of Different Channels of Distribution Used by a Publisher of Computer Books

Note: Channel members may target different market segments; however, in some cases they may compete for the same customers. And the channels shown here may also compete with channels for similar books by another publisher.

market can buy a new Apple iPad at Apple's website, an Apple store, an online retailer, or a physical store such as Target or a college bookstore. Dr. Pepper also uses multichannel distribution; you can buy a Dr. Pepper at a convenience store, grocery store, vending machine, or fast food restaurant.

Sometimes producers use multichannel distribution because their present channels do a poor job or fail to reach some potential customers. For example, Reebok International had been relying on local sporting goods stores to sell its shoes to high school and college athletic teams. But Reebok wasn't getting much of the business. Sales jumped when it set up its own sales department team to sell directly to the schools. The schools could still buy from a local sporting goods store, but now they had a second option.[21]

Multichannel distribution reflects customer behavior

The main reason for the growth of multichannel distribution is that it reflects how customers want to shop. Customers may find that different channels are more effective at different stages in the purchase process. When customers search for information, evaluate products, and make purchases in different channels, they are multichannel shopping. For example, a customer may go on Amazon's website to read customer reviews of a new James Patterson novel—but then want the convenience of picking the book up while shopping at Walmart.

Ethical decisions may be required

If competition changes or customers' Place requirements shift, the current channel system may not be effective. The changes required to serve customer needs may hurt one or more members of the channel. Ethical dilemmas in the channel area arise in situations like this—because not everyone in the channel can win.

For example, wholesalers and the independent retailers that they serve in a channel of distribution may trust a producer channel captain to develop marketing strategies that will work for the whole channel. However, the producer may decide that consumers, and its own business, are best served by a change (say, dropping current wholesalers and selling directly to big retail chains). A move of this sort, if implemented immediately, may not give current wholesaler-partners a chance to make adjustments of their own. The more dependent they are on the producer, the more severe the impact

The *Guardian* is a British daily newspaper. *The Guardian* has adapted to changing consumer behavior with a multichannel distribution approach to deliver the news—using print, a website, and apps for tablet computers and cell phones. The multichannel approach format provides for new services (for example, reader comments on articles posted online). To highlight the multichannel approach and these new features, *The Guardian* created a short video that shows how *The Guardian* might cover the classic fairy tale, "The Three Little Pigs." The entertaining video has an unexpected conclusion that you can see at http://youtu.be/vDGrfhJH1P4. © *Guardian News & Media Ltd 2012.*

is likely to be. It's not easy to determine the best or most ethical solution in these situations. However, marketing managers must think carefully about the consequences of Place strategy changes for other channel members. In channels, as in any business dealing, relationships of trust must be treated with care.[22]

Ethical Dilemma

What would you do? Assume you are the sales manager for a small producer of hip-hop fashions. As you arrive at a trade show to promote your firm's new line, your assistant pulls you aside to warn you that some of the owners of shops that usually carry your line are looking for you—and several are hopping mad. They've heard rumors that a big retail chain will be carrying your new line in all of its stores. In the past, your firm has distributed its fashions only through these small, "independent" retail shops, and they see the big chains as threats. Although you have had some negotiations with a buyer for the big retail chain, no deal has been reached yet. What will you say to the owners of the small shops, many of whom helped your firm get started and have always supported your marketing plans? If you are certain that most of these small retailers will *not* place any orders if they think the big chain will be carrying the same line, will you respond differently? Explain your thinking.

Reverse channels are important too

Most firms focus on getting products to their customers. But some marketing managers must also plan for **reverse channels**—channels used to retrieve products that customers no longer want. The need for reverse channels may arise in a variety of different situations. Toy companies, automobile firms, drug companies, and others sometimes have to recall products because of safety problems. A firm that makes an error in completing an order may have to take returns. If a ViewSonic computer monitor breaks while it's still under warranty, someone needs to get it to the repair center. Soft-drink companies may need to recycle empty bottles. And, of course, consumers sometimes buy something in error and want to return it. This is common with online purchases where consumers can't see, touch, or try the product before purchasing it.[23]

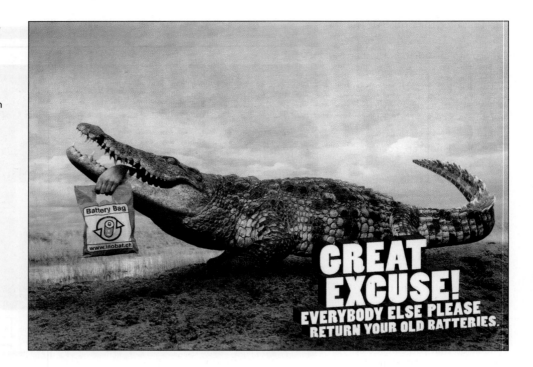

Disposing of batteries in the trash can be harmful to the environment. So the Swiss government created INOBAT, an organization that promotes recycling with creative promotion and an easy return bag.
Courtesy INOBAT.

New laws require reverse channels in some industries

Many firms have moved reluctantly to improve reverse channels—often doing so only when required by new laws designed to help the environment. For example, some "take back" laws require manufacturers to recycle or reuse hazardous materials or products at the end of their useful life—at no additional cost to the customer. In Europe, automakers must take back and recycle or reuse 85 percent of any vehicle made after 2004, and the European Community's Waste Electrical and Electronic Equipment (WEEE) Directive has firms taking back products such as computers and televisions. Similar laws are cropping up in the United States.

Reverse channels— sustainable and profitable

While reverse channels help the environment, many firms find them profitable, too. In rural China, for example, it's cheaper for Coke to reuse glass bottles than to rely on plastic packages or cans. Recycling has been even more important to Xerox. Customers responded well to Xerox's offer to dispose of old copy machines with the purchase of new models. But in the first year of the program, Xerox saved $50 million by refurbishing and then reselling parts from the recycled models.

Reverse channels are also a way to give customers environmentally friendly choices. For example, new Ecoworx carpet tiles from Shaw Floors are manufactured using recycled carpets. Shaw also promises that when the time comes it will pick up and recycle the tiles at no cost to the customer. To make it easy for the customer to follow up, Shaw's telephone number is on the back of each tile. Firms such as Sony, Office Depot, and Best Buy are viewed as good (and green) corporate citizens as well because they help consumers recycle electronics.[24]

Plan for reverse channels

When marketing managers don't plan for reverse channels, the firm's customers may be left to solve "their" problem. That usually doesn't make

Online Toolkit

Some websites are willing to buy your used electronics components. Go to Gazelle (**www.gazelle.com**) and enter information about your cell phone or other electronic product. What were you offered? Would you be interested in using this type of service? What concerns do you think phone makers Samsung or Apple might have?

sense. So a complete plan for Place may need to consider an efficient way to return products—with policies that different channel members agree on. It may also require specialists who were not involved in getting the product to the consumer. But if that's what it takes to satisfy customers, it should be part of marketing strategy planning.[25]

Entering International Markets

LO 10.8

All of the strategy decisions for Place (see again Exhibit 10–1) apply whether a firm is just focused on its domestic market or is also trying to reach target customers in international markets. However, marketing managers typically face differences in international markets that require additional choices. In the external market environment, culture and laws are almost always different from those with which the marketing manager is familiar. Developing countries may have less stable economies, and political environments involve more risk. Financial reporting requirements may or may not be as rigorous—so evaluating a customer's creditworthiness can be a challenge. Still, many small and medium-sized businesses see international sales as a growth opportunity worth the risk.

There are five basic ways to enter international markets (see Exhibit 10–6). As a rule, the approaches with greater risk and required investment offer the benefit of greater control over the marketing mix used.

Exporting often comes first

Some companies get into international marketing just by **exporting**—selling some of what the firm produces to foreign markets. Some firms start exporting just to take advantage of excess capacity—or even to get rid of surplus inventory. Some firms decide to change little if anything about the product, the label, or even the instructions. This explains why some early efforts at exporting are not very satisfactory. Other firms work closely with intermediaries who develop appropriate marketing mix changes and handle problems such as customs, import and export taxes, shipping, exchange rates, and recruiting or working with wholesalers and retailers in the foreign country.

American firm Sono-Tek Corporation produces ultrasonic spray coating technology used in many electronic manufacturing processes. The company gets 60 percent of its revenue from exporting, mostly into Europe and many parts of Asia. Even exporting has higher costs though, as Sono-Tek estimates that it spends 80 percent of its sales and marketing budget overseas.[26]

Licensing is often an easy way

Licensing means selling the right to use some process, trademark, patent, or other right for a fee or royalty. The licensee in the foreign market takes most of the risk because it must make some initial investment to get started. The licensee also does most of the marketing strategy planning for the markets it is licensed to serve. If good partners are available, this can be an effective way to enter a market. Gerber entered the Japanese baby food market this way, but exports to other countries.

Exhibit 10-6 Basic Approaches for Entering International Markets

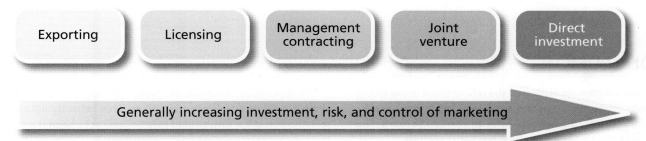

Management contracting sells know-how

Management contracting means that the seller provides only management and marketing skills—others own the production and distribution facilities. Some mines and oil refineries are operated this way—and Hilton operates hotels all over the world for local owners using this method. This is another relatively low-risk approach to international marketing. The low level of commitment to fixed facilities makes the approach attractive in developing nations or ones where the government is less stable.

Some firms tailor their websites to sell directly to export customers in foreign countries. Nike used this approach in Argentina.
© 2015 Nike, Inc. All Rights Reserved.

Joint venturing increases involvement

In a **joint venture** a domestic firm enters into a partnership with a foreign firm. As with any partnership, there can be honest disagreements over objectives—for example, how much profit is desired and how fast it should be paid out—as well as operating policies. Where a close working relationship can be developed—perhaps based on one firm's technical and marketing know-how and the foreign partner's knowledge of the market and political connections—this approach can be very attractive to both parties. Typically the two partners must make significant investments and agree on the marketing strategy. Once a joint venture is formed, it can be difficult to end if things aren't working out. American investment bank J.P. Morgan used this approach to enter China, where stiff regulations prohibited a foreign firm from owning a controlling share of a Chinese investment bank or money management firm.

Direct investment involves ownership

When a foreign market looks really promising, a firm may want to take a bigger step with a direct investment. **Direct investment** means that a parent firm has a division (or owns a separate subsidiary firm) in a foreign market. This gives the parent firm complete control of marketing strategy planning. Direct investment is a big commitment and usually entails greater risks. If a local market has economic or political problems, the firm cannot easily leave. On the other hand, by providing local jobs, a company builds a strong presence in a new market. This helps the firm develop a good reputation with the government and customers in the host country. And the firm does not have to share profits with a partner.

Direct investment also helps a firm learn more about a new market. For example, U.S.-based quick-lube chain Grease Monkey entered the Chinese market by opening company-owned locations. It quickly discovered Chinese customers wanted a much broader range of services than was customary in the United States. Grease Monkey added the services—and greater profits followed.[27]

CONCLUSION

In this chapter, we discussed the role of Place in marketing strategy. Place decisions are especially important because they may be difficult and expensive to change. So marketing managers must make Place decisions very carefully.

We discussed how product classes and the product life cycle are related to Place objectives. This helps us determine how much a firm should rely on indirect channel systems with intermediaries or direct systems.

Marketing specialists and channel systems develop to adjust discrepancies of quantity and assortment. Their regrouping activities are basic in any economic system. Adjusting discrepancies provide opportunities for creative marketers.

Channels of distribution tend to work best when there is cooperation among the members of a channel—and conflict is avoided. So we discussed the importance of planning channel systems and the role of a channel captain.

We stressed that channel systems compete with one another and that vertical marketing systems seem to be winning.

Channel planning also requires firms to decide on the degree of market exposure they want. The ideal level of exposure may be intensive, selective, or exclusive. We discussed the legal issues marketing managers must consider in developing channel systems. Finally, we examined different approaches for entering international markets.

WHAT'S NOW?

This chapter introduces you to a range of decisions marketing managers make around Place. For some current real-world examples and learnings, check out *What's Now?* at www.learnthe4ps.com/whatsnow/c10

KEY TERMS

LO 10.9

place, 256
channel of distribution, 257
direct marketing, 261
discrepancy of quantity, 264
discrepancy of assortment, 264
regrouping activities, 264
accumulating, 264
bulk-breaking, 265
sorting, 266
assorting, 266

traditional channel systems, 266
channel captain, 268
vertical marketing systems, 270
corporate channel systems, 270
vertical integration, 270
administered channel systems, 270
contractual channel systems, 270
ideal market exposure, 271
intensive distribution, 271
selective distribution, 271

exclusive distribution, 271
multichannel distribution, 273
reverse channels, 275
exporting, 277
licensing, 277
management contracting, 278
joint venture, 278
direct investment, 278

QUESTIONS AND PROBLEMS

1. Review the PC industry case study that opens the chapter. From this case, identify examples of different key terms and concepts covered in the chapter. For example, channel conflict is shown when HP added direct distribution in response to Dell.

2. Review the PC industry case study that opens this chapter. Applying Place concepts from the chapter, what should Lenovo do to gain a stronger position in the smartphone market?

3. Give two examples of service firms that work with other channel specialists to sell their products to final consumers. What marketing functions can the specialist provide in each case?

4. Discuss some reasons why a firm that produces installations might use direct distribution in its domestic market but use intermediaries to reach overseas customers.

5. Explain discrepancies of quantity and assortment using the clothing business as an example. How does the application of these concepts change when selling steel to the automobile industry? What impact does this have on the number and kinds of marketing specialists required?

6. Explain the four regrouping activities with an example from the building supply industry (nails, paint, flooring, plumbing fixtures, etc.). Do you think that many specialists develop in this industry, or do producers handle the job themselves? What kinds of marketing channels would you expect to find in this industry, and what functions would various channel members provide?

7. Insurance agents are intermediaries who help other members of the channel by providing information and handling the selling function. Does it make sense for an insurance agent to specialize and work exclusively with one insurance provider? Why or why not?

8. Discuss the Place objectives and distribution arrangements that are appropriate for the following products (indicate any special assumptions you have to make to obtain an answer):

   a. A postal scale for products weighing up to 2 pounds.
   b. Children's toys: (1) radio-controlled model airplanes costing $80 or more and (2) small rubber balls.
   c. Heavy-duty, rechargeable, battery-powered nut tighteners for factory production lines.
   d. Fiberglass fabric used in making roofing shingles.

9. Give an example of a producer that uses two or more different channels of distribution. Briefly discuss what problems this might cause.

10. Explain how a channel captain can help traditional independent firms compete with a corporate (integrated) channel system.

11. Find an example of vertical integration within your city. Are there any particular advantages to this vertical integration? If so, what are they? If there are no advantages, how do you explain the integration?

12. What would happen if retailer-organized channels (either formally integrated or administered) dominated consumer products marketing?

13. How does the nature of the product relate to the degree of market exposure desired?

14. Why would intermediaries want to be exclusive distributors for a product? Why would producers want exclusive distribution? Would intermediaries be equally anxious to get exclusive distribution for any type of product? Why or why not? Explain with reference to the following products: candy bars, batteries, golf clubs, golf balls, steak knives, televisions, and industrial woodworking machinery.

15. Explain the present legal status of exclusive distribution. Describe a situation where exclusive distribution is almost sure to be legal. Describe the nature and size of competitors and the industry, as well as the nature of the exclusive arrangement. Would this exclusive arrangement be of any value to the producer or intermediary?

16. Discuss the promotion a new grocery products producer would need in order to develop appropriate channels and move products through those channels. Would the nature of this job change for a new producer of dresses? How about for a new, small producer of installations?

17. Describe the advantages and disadvantages of the approaches to international market entry discussed in this chapter.

MARKETING PLANNING FOR HILLSIDE VETERINARY CLINIC

Appendix D (the Appendices follow Chapter 19) includes a sample marketing plan for Hillside Veterinary Clinic. Look through the "Marketing Strategy" section.

a. Why does Hillside sell its product directly instead of indirectly?

b. Hillside has a small selection of pet supplies that it sells to people who bring in their pets. What products does it resell at retail? What channel functions does it provide, and what channel functions are performed by its suppliers?

SUGGESTED CASES

13. AAA Office World
15. The Olentangy Group
16. Tall Timber Lumber Supply

32. Lever Ltd.
34. Chess Aluminum Worldwide

MARKETING ANALYTICS: DATA TO KNOWLEDGE

CHAPTER 10 INTENSIVE VERSUS SELECTIVE DISTRIBUTION

Hydropump, Inc., produces and sells high-quality pumps to business customers. Its marketing research shows a growing market for a similar type of pump aimed at final consumers—for use with Jacuzzi-style tubs in home remodeling jobs. Hydropump will have to develop new channels of distribution to reach this target market because most consumers rely on a retailer for advice about the combination of tub, pump, heater, and related plumbing fixtures they need. Hydropump's marketing manager, Robert Black, is trying to decide between intensive and selective distribution. With intensive distribution, he would try to sell through all the plumbing supply, bathroom fixture, and hot-tub retailers who will carry the pump. He estimates

that about 5,600 suitable retailers would be willing to carry a new pump. With selective distribution, he would focus on about 280 of the best hot-tub dealers (2 or 3 in the 100 largest metropolitan areas).

Intensive distribution would require Hydropump to do more mass selling—primarily advertising in home renovation magazines—to help stimulate consumer familiarity with the brand and convince retailers that Hydropump equipment will sell. The price to the retailer might have to be lower too (to permit a bigger markup) so they will be motivated to sell Hydropump rather than some other brand offering a smaller markup.

With intensive distribution, each Hydropump sales rep could probably handle about 300 retailers effectively. With selective distribution, each sales rep could handle only about

70 retailers because more merchandising help would be necessary. Managing the smaller sales force and fewer retailers with the selective approach, would require less manager overhead cost.

Going to all suitable and available retailers would make the pump available through about 20 times as many retailers and have the potential of reaching more customers. However, many customers shop at more than one retailer before making a final choice—so selective distribution would reach almost as many potential customers. Further, if Hydropump is using selective distribution, it would get more in-store sales attention for its pump and a larger share of pump purchases at each retailer.

Black has decided to use a spreadsheet to analyze the benefits and costs of intensive versus selective distribution. **See Connect for the spreadsheet and questions needed to analyze this scenario.**

11

Distribution Customer Service and Logistics

If you want a Coca-Cola, there's usually one close by—no matter where you might be in the world. And that's no accident. An executive for the best-known brand name in the world stated the goal simply: "Make Coca-Cola available within an arm's reach of desire." To achieve that objective, Coke works with many different channels of distribution. But that's just the start. Think about what it takes for a bottle, can, or cup of Coke to be there whenever you're thirsty. In warehouses and distribution centers, on trucks, in restaurants and sports arenas, and thousands of other retail outlets, Coke handles, stores, and transports more than 400 billion servings of the soft drink a year. Getting all that product to consumers could be a logistical nightmare, but Coke does it effectively and at a low cost.

Fast information about what the market needs helps keep Coke's distribution on target. Coke uses an Internet-based data system that links about one million retailers and other sellers to Coke and its bottlers. The system lets Coke bottlers and retailers exchange orders, invoices, and pricing information online. Orders are processed instantly—so sales to consumers at the end of the channel aren't lost because of stock-outs. Similarly, computer systems show Coke managers exactly what's selling in each market; they can even estimate the effects of seasonal changes and promotions as they plan inventories and deliveries. Coke products move efficiently through the channel. In Cincinnati, for example, Coke built the beverage industry's first fully automated distribution center. And when Coke's truck drivers get to the retail store, they knowingly stock the shelves with the correct mix of products.

Coke's strategies in international markets rely on many of the same ideas. But the stage of market development varies in different countries, so Coke's emphasis varies as well. To increase sales in France, for example, Coke installed thousands of soft-drink coolers in French supermarkets. In Great Britain, Coke emphasizes multipacks because it wants to have more inventory at the point of consumption—in consumers' homes. In Japan, by contrast, Coke relies heavily on an army of truck drivers to constantly restock one million Coke vending machines, more per capita than anywhere else in the world. Japanese customers can even use their cell phones to buy a Coke from one of these vending machines. Coke's bottlers are buying more trucks and increasing the frequency of delivery to keep up with fast growth in Thailand.

In less developed areas, the focus may be on different challenges—especially if the limitations of the Place system can make Coke products hard to find or costly. In Africa, where per capita consumption of Coke products is one-tenth of that in the United States, Coca-Cola wants its products to be cold and available everywhere—even in the lowest income areas. So for example, in Kabira, a Kenyan slum, a local distributor uses three shipping containers as a portable warehouse. Dirt and gravel roads make it easier to deliver by hand, so delivery personnel stack a couple dozen crates onto two-wheeled carts and fan out to 345 small shops delivering Coke, Fanta, and Stoney Ginger Beer. Deliveries might occur once or twice a day because the small shops hold so little inventory. Coke provides shops with plenty of "red"—Coke signage, tablecloths, and refrigerated coolers. Returnable glass bottles help keep costs down and at prices of less than 25 cents (U.S.), Coke becomes a treat on hot days.

Fortune magazine recently put the spotlight on Coca-Cola's commitment to sustainability, and decisions in the logistics area have had big environmental effects. For example, Coca-Cola helped develop vending machines that are HFC-free and 40 to 50 percent more energy efficient than conventional beverage equipment. Similarly, in the U.S. and Canada, Coca-Cola's gas-electric hybrid delivery trucks cut emissions and fuel consumption by a third. In spite of positive steps like these, Coca-Cola still faces some challenges concerning sustainability and logistics. For example, critics argue that in a society where there is already a safe supply of tap water it doesn't make sense to bottle water (Coke's brand is Dasani), transport it in trucks that consume fuel and contribute to pollution, and then add worry about how best to dispose of the empty bottles and bottle tops.

In parts of the world where access to clean water remains a challenge, shipping in bottled water can be costly. Inventor and entrepreneur Dean Kamen designed a water purification unit called Slingshot that could eventually cost less than $2000/unit to produce. Kamen is now working with Coca-Cola to distribute Slingshot to some of the more than one billion people in remote parts of Africa, Asia, and Latin America who lack access to clean water. Coca-Cola places Slingshot in a little red store called Ekocenter, where locals can shop for convenience items (like a Coke) and get their water purified at no charge.

With a 70 percent market share, Coca-Cola dominates the fountain channel for soft drinks. Building on that strength, Coca-Cola developed an innovative self-serve fountain dispenser that delivers custom-flavored soft drinks to customers and big data to Coca-Cola managers. The Coca-Cola Freestyle allows customers to pour up to 125 different flavors of soda—how about Grape Sprite or Peach Diet Coke? Freestyle also gives Coca-Cola lots of useful data. For example, Freestyle wirelessly communicates when any of the 30 flavor cartridges start to run low. It also uploads data to Coke's headquarters showing which flavors and combinations are most popular and how that varies by time of day and part of the country. This data helps fast-food outlets and Coke's marketing managers identify when and where to launch new products and guides promotion efforts.

Coca-Cola's worldwide distribution network delivers a sustainable competitive advantage. Of course Pepsi, Dr. Pepper, Red Bull Energy Drink, and Hansen's Natural Sodas are competing for distributors' attention and retail shelf space. Coke is pushing new products as well. The battle to quench customers' thirsts depends on each brand's marketing programs—but clearly Place has an important role to play.[1]

LEARNING OBJECTIVES

Choosing the right distribution channels is crucial in getting products to the target market's Place. But, as the Coca-Cola case shows, that alone doesn't ensure that products are placed "within an arm's reach of desire"—when, where, in the quantities that customers want them, and at a price they're willing to pay. In this chapter, we discuss how marketing managers ensure that they also have physical distribution systems that meet their customers' needs—at both an acceptable service level and an affordable cost.

When you finish this chapter, you should be able to

1 Understand why logistics (physical distribution) is such an important part of Place and marketing strategy planning.

2 Understand why the physical distribution customer service level is a key marketing strategy variable.

3 Understand the physical distribution concept and why the coordination of storing, transporting, and related activities is so important.

4 See how firms can cooperate and share logistics activities that will provide added value to their customers.

5 Know about the advantages and disadvantages of various transportation methods.

6 Know how inventory and storage decisions affect marketing strategy.

7 Understand the distribution center concept.

8 Understand important new terms (shown in red).

Physical Distribution Gets It to Customers

LO 11.1

Whenever Product includes a physical good, Place requires logistics decisions. **Logistics** is the transporting, storing, and handling of goods in ways that match target customers' needs with a firm's marketing mix—both within individual firms and along a channel of distribution. **Physical distribution (PD)** is another common name for logistics.

There are many different combinations of logistics decisions. Each combination can result in a different level of distribution service and different costs. So companies must determine the best way to provide the level of distribution service that customers want and are willing to pay for. We start this chapter by considering these critical logistics decisions (see Exhibit 11–1). Next, we describe the choice among different modes of transportation: Each has its own costs and benefits. We conclude with decisions about inventory and the use of distribution centers.

Logistics costs are very important to both companies and consumers. These costs vary from firm to firm and, from a macro-marketing perspective, from country to

Exhibit 11-1 The Role of Logistics and Physical Distribution Customer Service in Marketing Strategy

PLACE

Chapter 10
Place and Development of Channel Systems

Chapter 11
Distribution Customer Service and Logistics

Chapter 12
Retailers, Wholesalers, and Their Strategy Planning

Logistics customer service
- What is logistics customer service?
- Level to offer
- Cost considerations
- Using JIT and EDI to coordinate logistics

Transporting
- Transportation modes
- Benefits and limitations

Storing
- Storage and strategy planning
- Inventory costs
- Storage facilities
- Distribution centers

country. For some products, a company may spend half or more of its total marketing dollars on physical distribution activities. As lawmakers debate the high cost of health care, logistics costs represent more than one-third the expense attached to hospital supplies. Although this is down from about 50 percent a few decades ago, there's still room for improvement.

Differences in logistics costs across countries can be substantial. Developed economies in the United States and Europe spend about 9 to 15 percent of GDP on logistics-related costs—whereas in the developing economies of Latin America and Africa, costs are 30 percent or more. Marketing managers must carefully consider these costs when entering new markets.[2]

Physical Distribution Customer Service

LO 11.2

From the beginning, we've emphasized that marketing strategy planning is based on meeting customers' needs. Planning for logistics and Place is no exception. So let's start by looking at logistics through a customer's eyes.

Customers want products, not excuses

Customers don't care how a product was moved or stored or what some channel member had to do to provide it. Rather, customers think in terms of the physical distribution **customer service level**—how rapidly and dependably a firm can deliver what they, the customers, want.

The best shipping method for any given product is usually a balancing act between service and cost. Trains provide a slower, less expensive shipping approach as compared to air freight.
Left: © scanrail/iStock/Getty Images; Right: © FedEx 1995-2015; Agency: DM9 DDB/São Paulo, Brazil.

What does this really mean? It means that Toyota wants to have enough windshields delivered to make cars *that* day—not late so production stops *or* early so there are a lot of extras to move around or store. It means that business executives who rent cars from Hertz want them to be ready when they get off their planes. It means that when you order a blue shirt at the Lands' End website you receive blue, not pink. It means you want your Tostitos to be whole when you buy a bag at the snack bar—not crushed into crumbs from rough handling in a warehouse.

Physical distribution is invisible to most consumers

PD is, and should be, a part of marketing that is "invisible" to most consumers. It gets their attention only when something goes wrong. At that point, it may be too late to do anything that will keep them happy.

In countries where physical distribution systems are inefficient, consumers face shortages of the products they need. By contrast, most consumers in the United States and Canada don't think much about physical distribution. This probably means that these market-directed macro-marketing systems work pretty well—that a lot of individual marketing managers have made good decisions in this area. But it doesn't mean that the decisions are always clear-cut or simple. In fact, many trade-offs may be required.

Trade-offs of costs, service, and sales

Most customers would prefer very good service at a very low price. But that combination is hard to provide because it usually costs more to provide higher levels of service. So most physical distribution decisions involve trade-offs among costs, the customer service level, and sales.

If you want a new HP computer and the Best Buy store where you would like to buy it doesn't have it on hand, you're likely to buy it elsewhere; or if that model HP is hard to get, you might just switch to some other brand. Assuming your Best Buy store can locate the computer you desire at another Best Buy or in stock at HP's factory, perhaps it could keep your business by guaranteeing two-day delivery to your home. This will cost the store manager some airfreight charges. In this case, the manager trades the savings of storing inventory for the extra cost of speedy delivery. Missing one sale may not seem that important, but it all adds up; consider, a few years ago a computer company lost more than $500 million in sales because its computers weren't available when and where customers were ready to buy them.

Exhibit 11–2 illustrates trade-off relationships like that highlighted in the HP example just mentioned. The exhibit shows costs on the vertical axis and customer

Exhibit 11–2
Trade-Offs among
Physical Distribution
Costs, Customer Service
Level, and Sales

*Note: Sales may be lost because of poor customer service or because of the high price charged to pay for too high a customer service level.

service level (measured as the percent of customers receiving delivery within one day) on the horizontal axis. Note the following:

- As service level increases (moving left to right), transportation costs (in blue) initially fall as the firm makes larger shipments—and then rise a bit as shipments become more frequent.
- Inventory costs (black line) rise as the retailer carries more computers to meet any level of demand.
- Cost of lost sales (green line) initially falls because customers are not likely to buy a different product when the model they want is in stock. However, as customer service climbs to higher levels (mostly rising inventory carrying costs), the seller must raise prices to cover the higher service levels. This leads to some customers choosing alternatives—and raises the cost of lost sales.
- When all of the costs above are added together, the total costs (red line) fall as service level increases—but then rise. The optimum level of customer service occurs where the total costs are minimized (X on the graph).

Exhibit 11–2 provides a starting point to discuss the trade-offs marketing managers must make. For instance, faster but more expensive transportation may reduce the need for a costly inventory of computers. However, if the target customers have even higher expectations, they will buy elsewhere and sales will be lost. Alternatively, the seller may hope that a higher service level will attract more customers. But if the service level is higher than customers want or are willing to pay for, sales will be lost to competitors.

Trade-offs more complicated with more products

Trade-offs that must be made in physical distribution can be even more complicated. The approach demonstrated in Exhibit 11–2 focuses on the sale of a single item. But a customer dissatisfied by not finding the item she wanted may soon shop elsewhere—reducing the lifetime customer value. For example, a few years ago cost-cutting efforts at Walmart resulted in reduced inventory—and some empty shelves. Some of those disappointed Walmart customers decide to shop elsewhere, and losses were far greater than the failure to sell particular items on a particular day or two. Similar problems occurred when Target entered Canada a few years ago. Target could not deliver quickly enough and empty shelves made a bad first impression. Target never recovered and closed all 133 stores it operated there.

Information technology can improve service levels and cut costs at the same time. Better information flows make it easier to coordinate activities, improve efficiency, and add value for the customer.[3]

Physical Distribution Concept Focuses on the Whole Distribution System

LO 11.3

The physical distribution concept

The **physical distribution (PD) concept** says that all transporting, storing, and product-handling activities of a business and a whole channel system should be coordinated as one system that seeks to minimize the cost of distribution for a given customer service level. Both lower costs and better service help to increase customer value. This seems like common sense, but until recently most companies treated physical distribution functions as separate and unrelated activities.

Traditionally, responsibility for different logistics activities was spread among various departments in a firm—production, shipping, sales, warehousing, purchasing, and others. No one person was responsible for coordinating storing and shipping decisions or customer service levels. It was even rarer for different firms in the channel to collaborate. Each just did its own thing. Unfortunately, in too many firms these old-fashioned ways persist—with a focus on individual functional activities rather than the whole physical distribution system.[4]

Decide what service level to offer

With broader adoption of the physical distribution concept, this is changing. Firms work together to decide what aspects of service are most important to customers at the end of the channel. Then they focus on finding the least expensive way to achieve the target level of service.

Exhibit 11–3 shows a variety of factors that may influence the customer service level (at each level in the channel). The most important aspects of customer service depend on target market needs. Xerox might focus on how long it takes to deliver copy machine repair parts once it receives an order. When a copier breaks down, customers want the repair "yesterday." The service level might be stated as "we will deliver 90 percent of all emergency repair parts within 24 hours." This might require that commonly needed parts be available on the service truck, that order processing be very fast, and that parts not available locally be sent by airfreight. Obviously, supplying this service level will affect the total cost of the PD system. But it may also beat competitors.

Fast PD service can be critical for retailers that appeal to consumers who are eager to get a new product that is in hot demand—the latest movie release, bestselling book, or popular toy or video game.

Customers increasingly expect more convenience and speed as part of their PD service—and at a low cost. After examining their own strengths and weaknesses, as well as the needs of their target customers, two of the largest retailers in the United States have taken divergent strategic paths. As an almost completely online player, Amazon continues to focus on offering its customers faster delivery. Amazon Prime customers (numbering in the tens of millions) already get free two-day delivery with a low-cost option to upgrade to next-day delivery. Now with investments in warehouses around the country, Amazon offers same-day delivery to many customers.

Exhibit 11–3
Examples of Factors that Affect PD Service Levels

- Advance information on product availability
- Time to enter and process orders
- Backorder procedures
- Where inventory is stored
- Accuracy in filling orders
- Damage in shipping, storing, and handling
- Online status information
- Advance information on delays
- Time needed to deliver an order
- Reliability in meeting delivery date
- Complying with customer's instructions
- Defect-free deliveries
- How needed adjustments are handled
- Procedures for handling returns

Amazon's Prime Pantry program allows customers to pay a $5.99 flat fee to receive low-priced grocery, household, and pet care items.

In contrast, Walmart has chosen to more tightly integrate its stores and online offerings; instead of faster home delivery it uses the web to make for a faster in-store experience. Walmart's site to store program allows customers to shop online and get free shipping to a Walmart store or select FedEx Office locations, where customers pick up their order. The store is also testing Walmart To-Go, where customers order groceries (and other merchandise) online and pick them up at a local store (for free) or have them delivered for $5 to $7.[5]

Find the lowest total cost for the right service level

In selecting a PD system, the **total cost approach** involves evaluating each possible PD system and identifying *all* of the costs of each alternative. This approach uses the tools of cost accounting and economics. Costs that otherwise might be ignored—like inventory carrying costs—are considered. The possible costs of lost sales due to a lower customer service level may also be considered.

"The dog ate your order."

When it comes to on-time delivery of your shipment, any excuse is a bad excuse. You want it fast, accurate and complete regardless of the size. And Sauder delivers. Thanks to our computerized invoice and inventory system, private truck fleet and four million square feet of manufacturing and warehouse space. When it comes to keeping customers happy, we've done our homework. That experience has made us the world's largest manufacturer of ready-to-assemble furniture. Find out what it can do for you.

SAUDER woodworking

502 MIDDLE ST. • ARCHBOLD, OH 43502 • (419) 446-2711

Sauder tries to help customer firms do a better job of tracking the status of orders and making certain that products are where they are needed at the right time.

For example, Vegpro Kenya compared different PD systems for shipping ready-to-eat fresh produce from fields in Kenya to grocery stores in major European cities. The analysis showed that the costs of airfreight transportation were significantly higher than using trucks and ships. But the firm also found that costs of spoilage and inventory could be much lower when airfreight is used. The faster airfreight-based PD system brought customers fresher produce at about the same total cost. So Vegpro cleans, chops, and packages vegetables in its 27,000 square-foot air-conditioned facility at the Nairobi airport—using low-cost African labor. And the next day, fresh beans, baby carrots, and other vegetables are on store shelves in Madrid, London, and Paris.[6]

Coordinating Logistics Activities among Firms

LO 11.4

Functions can be shifted and shared in the channel

As a marketing manager develops the Place part of a strategy, it is important to decide how physical distribution functions can and should be divided within the channel. Who will store, handle, and transport the goods—and who will pay for these services? Who will coordinate all of the PD activities?

There is no right sharing arrangement. Physical distribution can be varied endlessly in a marketing mix and in a channel system. And competitors may share these functions in different ways—with different costs and results.

How PD is shared affects the rest of a strategy

How the PD functions are shared affects the other three Ps—especially Price. The sharing arrangement can also make (or break) a strategy. Consider Channel Master, a firm that wanted to take advantage of the growing market for the dishlike antennas used to receive TV signals from satellites. The product looked like it could be a big success, but the small company didn't have the money to invest in a large inventory. So

Channel Master decided to work only with wholesalers who were willing to buy (and pay for) several units—to be used for demonstrations and to ensure that buyers got immediate delivery.

In the first few months Channel Master earned $2 million in revenues—just by providing inventory for the channel. And the wholesalers paid the interest cost of carrying inventory—more than $300,000 the first year. Here the wholesalers helped share the risk of the new venture, but it was a good decision for them, too. They won many sales from a competing channel whose customers had to wait several months for delivery. And by getting off to a strong start, Channel Master became a market leader.

JIT requires a coordinated effort

If firms in the channel do not plan and coordinate how they will share PD activities, PD is likely to be a source of conflict rather than a basis for competitive advantage. Let's consider this point by taking a closer look at *just-in-time (JIT) delivery* systems, which we introduced in Chapter 6 and defined as reliably getting products there just before the customer needs them.

A key advantage of JIT for business customers is that it reduces their PD costs—especially storing and handling costs. However, if the customer doesn't have any backup inventory, there's no security blanket if a supplier's delivery truck gets stuck in traffic, there's an error in what's shipped, or there are any quality problems. Thus, a JIT system requires that a supplier have extremely high quality control in every PD activity.

A JIT system usually requires that a supplier respond to very short order lead times and the customer's production schedule. Thus, e-commerce order systems and information sharing over computer networks are often required. JIT suppliers often locate their facilities close to important customers. Trucks may make smaller and more frequent deliveries—perhaps even several times a day.

A JIT system shifts greater responsibility for PD activities backward in the channel. If the supplier can be more efficient than the customer could be in controlling PD costs—and still provide the customer with the service level required—this approach can work well for everyone in the channel. However, JIT is not always the best approach. It may be better for a supplier to produce and ship in larger, more economical quantities—if the savings offset the distribution system's total inventory and handling costs.[7]

Supply chain may involve even more firms

In our discussion, we have taken the point of view of a marketing manager. This focuses on how logistics should be coordinated to meet the needs of customers at the end of the channel of distribution. Now, however, we should broaden the picture somewhat because the relationships within the distribution channel are sometimes part of a broader network of relationships in the **supply chain**—the complete set of firms and facilities and logistics activities that are involved in procuring materials, transforming them into intermediate or finished products, and distributing them to customers.

For example, Manitowoc is one of the world's largest manufacturers of cranes. Its huge mobile cranes are used at construction sites all around the world. Robert Ward, who is in charge of purchasing for Manitowoc, must ensure an unbroken flow of parts and materials so that Manitowoc can keep its promises to customers regarding crane delivery dates. This is difficult because each crane has component parts from many suppliers around the globe. Further, any supplier may be held up by problems with its own suppliers. In

Manitowoc Mobile Crane

Boom: steel iron source fabricated in Belgium & U.S.

Counterweights: Poland & France

Cable: U.S.

Hook: Netherlands & Belgium

Chasis: steel from Sweden & Germany, fabricated in Poland

Tires: France, Japan & China

Steel rims: Germany & China

Cabs: Germany

What's Next? Disaster relief logistics are life and death

Hurricanes, tsunamis, and earthquakes create immediate needs for emergency relief supplies. And the logistics involved in delivering them include many of the same activities found in the physical delivery of other goods. However, in a disaster situation, life and death often hinge upon the speed with which food, water, and medical supplies can be delivered. Yet, when bridges, roads, and airports are destroyed, local transportation can be complicated, if not impossible. And, even worse, there is no advance warning when or where aid will be needed. Imagine what it would be like for one business to be instantly ready to distribute millions of products to a target market that usually doesn't exist, moves around the world, and then without notice pops up somewhere with insatiable needs.

People in advanced societies have high expectations that help will be immediate when disaster strikes. Yet, it's nearly impossible for relief agencies to meet those expectations. Still, improved performance is on the way from both disaster relief agencies and private businesses, which have learned from recent efforts. For example, instead of stockpiling drugs, tents, and blankets, agencies are learning to rely on outsourcing. Agencies arrange open orders with suppliers who must be prepared to instantly ship supplies whenever and wherever they are needed.

Organizations with logistics expertise also lend a helping hand. Immediately following disasters in all parts of the world, transportation giants like FedEx, DHL, and China Southern Airlines have responded quickly with planes and trucks that facilitate delivery of needed supplies. Walmart and its Japanese Seiyu stores have responded more quickly than governmental organizations to disasters like Hurricane Katrina and Japan's Fukushima earthquake. The Fritz Institute analyzes past relief efforts and consults with agencies to help them better prepare for future responses.

When chaos hits, coordination of relief efforts is possible only if there is good information. Agencies need to know what supplies are available, where they're located, what needs are greatest, and where and how quickly deliveries can be made. Having one central communication hub—to collect and share this type of information—and IT systems specifically dedicated to the task are key. A new system called Suma allows relief workers to manage incoming donations, put them in the right storage places, and establish shipping priorities. It also helps to receive communications from victims, and solar phone chargers and lanterns are often dropped from planes along with tents and water.

Other physical distribution solutions are decidedly low-tech, but equally important. For example, boxes need to be color coded so it's obvious which ones contain critical medical supplies and perishable food. And donated goods must be packed in cartons light enough to be carried on foot where roads have been so damaged that they're impassable in a vehicle.

Explain how other concepts from this chapter might be used to manage disasters?[8]

---

one case, Manitowoc's German factory was having trouble getting key chassis parts from two suppliers in Poland. Ward traced the problem back to a Scandinavian steel mill that was behind on shipments to the Polish firms. Manitowoc buys a lot of steel and has a lot of leverage with steel distributors, so Ward scoured Europe for distributors who had extra inventory of steel plate. The steel he found was more expensive than buying the steel directly from the mill, but the mill couldn't keep supplies flowing and the distributors could. By helping to coordinate the whole supply chain, Manitowoc was able to keep its promises and deliver cranes to its customers on schedule.[9]

Work to meet the needs of the customer at the end of the supply chain

Ideally, all of the firms in the supply chain should work together to meet the needs of the customer at the very end of the chain. That way, at each link along the chain, the shifting and sharing of logistics functions and costs are handled to result in the most value for the final customer. This makes a supply chain more efficient and effective—giving it a competitive advantage against other supply chains competing to serve the same target market.[10]

There are few supply chain challenges greater than getting relief to victims of a disaster. The demand for a fast response is critical. Read more in *"What's Next?* Disaster relief logistics are life and death."

291

Better information helps coordinate PD

Coordinating all of the elements of PD has always been a challenge—even in a single firm. Trying to coordinate orders, inventory, and transportation throughout the whole supply chain is even tougher. But information shared over the Internet and at websites has been important in finding solutions to these challenges. Physical distribution decisions will continue to improve as more firms are able to have their computers "talk" to each other directly and as websites help managers get access to up-to-date information whenever they need it.

Electronic data interchange sets a standard

Until recently, differences in computer systems from one firm to another hampered the flow of information. Many firms attacked this problem by adopting **electronic data interchange (EDI)**—an approach that puts information in a standardized format easily shared between different computer systems. In many firms, purchase orders, shipping reports, and other paper documents were replaced with computerized EDI. With EDI, a customer transmits his or her order information directly to the supplier's computer. The supplier's computer immediately processes the order and schedules production, order assembly, and transportation. Inventory information is automatically updated, and status reports are available instantly. The supplier might then use EDI to send the updated information to the transportation provider's computer. In fact, most international transportation firms rely on EDI links with their customers.[11]

Improved information flow and better coordination of PD activities is a key reason for the success of Pepperidge Farm's line of premium cookies. Most of the company's delivery truck drivers use handheld computers to record the inventory at each stop along their routes. They use a wireless Internet connection to instantly transmit the information into a computer at the bakeries, and cookies in short supply are produced. The right assortment of fresh cookies is quickly shipped to local markets, and delivery trucks are loaded with what retailers need that day. Pepperidge Farm moves cookies from its bakeries to store shelves in about three days; most cookie producers take about

Companies such as Marsh and IBM provide consulting services and software to help firms manage complex supply chains. *Left: © 2015 MARSH LLC. ALL RIGHTS RESERVED; Right: © Copyright IBM Corporation 1994, 2015.*

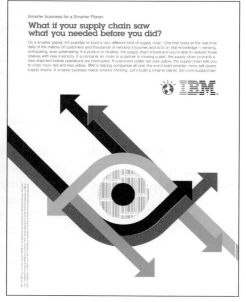

10 days. That means fresher cookies for consumers and helps to support Pepperidge Farm's high-quality positioning and premium price.[12]

Ethical issues may arise

Some ethical issues that arise in the PD area concern communications about product availability. For example, some critics say that Internet sellers too often take orders for products that are not available or which they cannot deliver as quickly as customers expect. Yet a marketing manager can't always know precisely how long it will take before a product will be available. It doesn't make sense for the marketer to lose a customer if it appears that he or she can satisfy the customer's needs. But the customer may be inconvenienced or face added cost if the marketer's best guess isn't accurate. Similarly, some critics say that stores too often run out of products that they promote to attract consumers to the store. Yet it may not be possible for the marketer to predict demand or to know when placing an ad that deliveries won't arrive. Different people have different views about how a firm should handle such situations. Some retailers just offer rain checks.

Ethical Dilemma

What would you do? Many major firms, ranging from Nike and Starbucks to Walmart and IKEA, have been criticized for selling products from overseas suppliers whose workers toil in bad conditions for long hours and at low pay. Defenders of the companies point out that overseas sourcing provides jobs that are better than what workers would have without it. Critics think that companies that sell products in wealthy countries have a social responsibility to see that suppliers in less-developed nations pay a fair wage and provide healthy working conditions. What do you think? Should U.S. firms be required to monitor the employment practices of suppliers in their supply chains? Should all suppliers be held to Western legal or moral standards? What solutions or compromises might be offered?[13]

The Transporting Function Adds Value to a Marketing Strategy

LO 11.5

Transporting aids economic development and exchange

Transporting is the marketing function of moving goods. Transportation makes products available when and where they need to be—at a cost. But the cost is less than the value added to products by moving them, or there is little reason to ship in the first place.

Transporting can help achieve economies of scale in production. If production costs can be reduced by producing larger quantities in one location, these savings may more than offset the added cost of transporting the finished products to customers. Without

The cost of transportation adds little to the total cost of products like pharmaceutical drugs, which are already expensive relative to their size and weight. On the other hand, transporting costs can be a large part of the total cost for heavy products that are low in value, like sheet aluminum.
Left: © Allan Hunter Shoemake Photography, Inc; Right: © Steve Smith

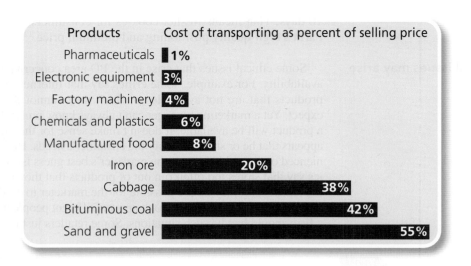

Products	Cost of transporting as percent of selling price
Pharmaceuticals	1%
Electronic equipment	3%
Factory machinery	4%
Chemicals and plastics	6%
Manufactured food	8%
Iron ore	20%
Cabbage	38%
Bituminous coal	42%
Sand and gravel	55%

low-cost transportation, both within countries and internationally, there would be no mass distribution as we know it today.

Transporting can be costly

Transporting costs limit the target markets a marketing manager can serve. Shipping costs increase delivered cost—and that's what really interests customers. Transport costs add little to the cost of products that are already valuable relative to their size and weight. A case of medicine, for example, might be shipped to a drugstore at low cost. But transporting costs can be a large part of the total cost for heavy products of low value—such as many minerals and raw materials. You can imagine that shipping a massive roll of aluminum to a producer of soft-drink cans is an expensive proposition. Exhibit 11–4 shows transporting costs as a percent of total sales dollars for several products.[14]

Governments may influence transportation

Government often plays an important role in the development of a country's transportation system, including its roads, harbors, railroads, and airports. And different countries regulate transportation differently, although regulation has in general been decreasing.

As regulations decreased in the United States, competition in the transportation industry increased. As a result, a marketing manager generally has many carriers in one or more modes competing for the firm's transporting business. Or a firm can do its own transporting. So knowing about the different modes is important.[15]

Which Transporting Alternative Is Best?

Transporting function must fit the whole strategy

The transporting function should fit into the whole marketing strategy. But picking the best transporting alternative depends on the product, other physical distribution decisions, and what service level the company wants to offer. The best alternative should provide the level of service (for example, speed and dependability) required at as low a cost as possible. Exhibit 11–5 shows that different modes of transportation have different strengths and weaknesses. Low transporting cost is *not* the only criterion for selecting the best mode.[16]

Railroads—large loads moved at low cost

Railroads are still the workhorse of the U.S. transportation system. They carry more freight over more miles than any other mode. However, they account for less than 10 percent of transport revenues. They carry heavy and bulky goods—such as coal, steel, and chemicals—over long distances at relatively low cost. Because railroad freight usually moves more slowly than truck shipments, it is not as well suited

Exhibit 11-5   Benefits and Limitations of Different Transport Modes

			Transporting Features			
Mode	Cost	Delivery Speed	Number of Locations Served	Ability to Handle a Variety of Goods	Frequency of Scheduled Shipments	Dependability in Meeting Schedules
Truck	High	Fast	Very extensive	High	High	High
Rail	Medium	Average	Extensive	High	Low	Medium
Water	Very low	Very slow	Limited	Very high	Very low	Medium
Air	Very high	Very fast	Extensive	Limited	High	High
Pipeline	Low	Slow	Very limited	Very limited	Medium	High

for perishable items or those in urgent demand. Railroads are most efficient at handling full carloads of goods. Less-than-carload (LCL) shipments take a lot of handling, which means they usually move more slowly and at a higher price per pound than carload shipments.[17]

Trucks are more expensive, but flexible and essential

The flexibility and speed of trucks make them better at moving small quantities of goods for shorter distances. They can travel on almost any road. They go where the rails can't. They are also reliable in meeting delivery schedules, which is an essential requirement for logistics systems that provide rapid replenishment of inventory after a sale. In combination these factors explain why at least 75 percent of U.S. consumer products travel at least part of the way from producer to consumer by truck. And in countries with good highway systems, trucks can give extremely fast service. Trucks compete for high-value items. Trucks are essential for firms that deliver to people's homes—the so-called "last mile" for e-commerce. They will become even more critical as online sales and same-day delivery become important parts of some retailers' marketing strategies.[18]

Low labor costs in developing countries can make transportation costs relatively low—especially for short distances. In Egypt one-third of McDonald's sales involve delivery.
Photo by Peter Macdiarmid/Getty Images.

Ship it overseas, but slowly

Water transportation is the slowest shipping mode, but it is usually the lowest-cost way of shipping heavy freight. Water transportation is very important for international shipments and often the only practical approach. This explains why port cities such as Boston, New York City, Rotterdam, Osaka, and Singapore are important centers for international trade.

Inland waterways are important too

Inland waterways (such as the Mississippi River and Great Lakes in the United States and the Rhine and Danube in Europe) are also important, especially for bulky, nonperishable products such as iron ore, grain, and gravel. However, when winter ice closes freshwater harbors, alternate transportation must be used.

Pipelines move oil and gas

Pipelines are used primarily to move oil and natural gas. So pipelines are important both in the oil-producing and oil-consuming countries. Only a few major cities in the United States, Canada, Mexico, and Latin America are more than 200 miles from a major pipeline system. However, the majority of the pipelines in the United States are located in the Southwest, connecting oil fields and refineries.

Airfreight is expensive, but fast and growing

The most expensive cargo transporting mode is airplane—but it is fast! Airfreight rates are on average three times higher than trucking rates—but the greater speed may offset the added cost.

High-value, low-weight goods—such as high-fashion clothing and parts for the electronics industry—are often shipped by air. Perishable products that previously could not be shipped are now being flown across continents and oceans. Flowers and bulbs from Holland, for example, now are jet-flown to points all over the world. And airfreight has become very important for small emergency deliveries, like repair parts.

But airplanes may cut the total cost of distribution

Using planes may reduce the cost of packing, unpacking, and preparing goods for sale and may help a firm reduce inventory costs by eliminating outlying warehouses. Valuable benefits of airfreight's speed are less spoilage, theft, and damage. Although the *transporting* cost of air shipments may be higher, the *total* cost of distribution may be lower. As more firms realize this, airfreight firms—such as DHL Worldwide Express, FedEx, and Emery Air Freight—have enjoyed rapid growth.[19]

Will drones deliver soon?

Small unmanned aircraft, called drones, have been used in the military and by hobbyists. They are now being used for delivery services. In Germany, DHL uses drones to deliver medicine to a small island off the German coast. Swiss Post has been testing drone delivery of mail. And Amazon is testing drones for delivery in Canada (the Federal Aviation Administration in the United States has slowed testing here).[20]

Put it in a container—and move between modes easily

Products often move by several different modes and carriers during their journey. This is especially common for international shipments. Japanese firms, like Sony, ship stereos to the United States, Canada, and Europe by boat. When they arrive at the dock, they are loaded on trains and sent across the country. Then the units are delivered to a wholesaler by truck or rail.

To better coordinate the flow of products between modes, transportation companies like CSX offer customers a complete choice of different transportation modes. Then CSX, not the customer, figures out the best and lowest-cost way to shift and share transporting functions among the modes.[21]

© Olivier Lantzendörffer/iStockphoto.

Loading and unloading goods several times used to be a real problem. Parts of a shipment would become separated, damaged, or even stolen. And handling the goods, perhaps many times, raised costs and slowed delivery. Many of these problems are reduced with **containerization**—grouping individual items into an economical shipping quantity and sealing them in protective containers for transit to the final destination. This protects the products and simplifies handling during shipping. Some containers are as large as truck bodies.

Transportation costs higher in developing countries

Transportation choices are usually not so good in developing countries. Roads are often poor, rail systems may be limited, and ports may be undeveloped. Local firms that specialize in logistics services may not exist at all. Even so, firms that are willing to invest the effort can reap benefits and help their customers overcome the effects of these problems.

Metro AG, a firm based in Germany that has opened wholesale facilities in Bangalore and several other major cities in India, illustrates this point. Metro focuses on selling food products and other supplies to the thousands of restaurants, hotels, and other small businesses in the markets it serves. When Metro started in India, 40 percent of the fruits and vegetables it purchased from farmers were spoiled, damaged, or lost by the time they got to Metro. These problems piled up because the produce traveled from the fields over rough roads and was handled by as many as seven intermediaries along the way. To overcome these problems, Metro gave farmers crates to protect freshly picked crops from damage and to keep them away from dirt and bacteria that would shorten their shelf life. Further, crates were loaded and unloaded only once because Metro bought its own refrigerated trucks to pick up produce and bring it directly to its outlets. Metro used the same ideas to speed fresh seafood from fishermen's boats. Many of Metro's restaurant customers previously bought what they needed from a variety of small suppliers, many of whom would run out of stock. Now the restaurant owners save time and money with one-stop shopping at Metro. Metro is growing fast in India because it has quality products that are in stock when they're needed, and it's bringing down food costs for its customers.[22]

Transportation choices have environmental costs too

Marketing managers must be sensitive to the environmental effects of transportation decisions. Trucks, trains, airplanes, and ships contribute to air pollution and global warming; estimates suggest that on average more than half of a firm's total carbon emissions come from transportation. There are other problems as well. For example, a damaged pipeline or oil tanker can spew thousands of gallons of oil before it can be repaired.

Many firms are taking steps to reduce such problems. FedEx and UPS are revamping their fleets to use more electric and alternative fuel vehicles. Rail is usually the

When Metro set up its cash-and-carry wholesale operations in India, it could not rely on the same logistics systems it used in Germany. Rather, Metro had to create its own fleet of refrigerated trucks to pick up produce directly from farmers. However, this reduced stock-outs and helped Metro offer customers better-quality produce at lower prices.
© METRO Cash & Carry India Pvt. Ltd. 2015.

cleanest way to move land freight a long distance, but General Electric's recently introduced Evolution locomotives have 5 percent better fuel economy and 40 percent lower emissions compared to previous models. GE is already working on a hybrid locomotive that will improve fuel economy another 10 percent. Truck manufacturers are also working to improve fuel efficiency and environmental impact. Peterbilt and International are among firms working to build diesel-hybrid 18-wheelers. The U.S. government supports these initiatives through the Environmental Protection Agency's SmartWay program (www.epa.gov/smartway/). It helps freight carriers, shippers, and logistics companies improve fuel efficiency and reduce environmental impact. Both trucking and railroad firms have procedures to ensure that transporting toxic cargo is safer. Today the public *expects* companies to manufacture, transport, sell, and dispose of products in an environmentally sound manner.[23]

Transportation analytics aid the environment and lower costs

Transportation companies routinely place sensors on trucks and train cars to monitor their movement. These sensors generate a lot of data. Managers use this to identify opportunities to more effectively manage the economic and environmental costs of transportation. For example, UPS uses global positioning data to learn and recommend routes for its drivers—routes that maximize service and minimize fuel consumption. Trucking company U.S. Xpress monitors the location and driving behavior of each of its 10,000 trucks; it knows how many times a driver brakes hard, whether he sends a text message to a customer to let him know he's running late, and how long he takes for each rest stop. U.S. Xpress uses these data to show drivers how to improve service and save fuel. For instance, when a U.S. Xpress driver gets a 10-hour break, air conditioning lowers the cab temperature to 70 degrees for the first two hours, before kicking up to 78 degrees. This move alone saved the company $24 million in one year and also lowered U.S. Xpress's environmental impact.[24]

The Storing Function and Marketing Strategy

LO 11.6

Store it and smooth out sales and increase profits and consumer satisfaction

Storing varies in the channel system

Storing is the marketing function of holding goods so they're available when they're needed. **Inventory** is the amount of goods being stored.

Storing is necessary when production of goods doesn't match consumption. This is common with mass production. Nippon Steel, for example, might produce thousands of steel bars of one size before changing the machines to produce another size. It's often cheaper to produce large quantities of one size, and store the unsold quantity, than to have shorter production runs. Thus, storing goods allows the producer to achieve economies of scale in production.

Storing allows producers and intermediaries to keep stocks at convenient locations, ready to meet customers' needs. In fact, storing is one of the major activities of some intermediaries.

Most channel members provide the storing function for some length of time. Even final consumers store some things for their future needs. Which channel members store the product, and for how long, affects the behavior of all channel members. For example, the

Menasha, a supplier of innovative packaging, wants its client firms to realize that its package designs can help to reduce both logistics costs and environmental impacts.
© 2015 Menasha Corporation

Exhibit 11-6 Many Expenses Contribute to Total Inventory Cost

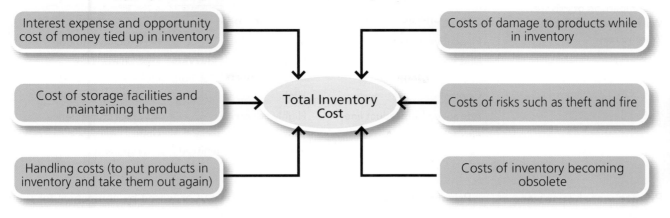

producer of Snapper lawn mowers tries to get wholesalers to inventory a wide selection of its machines. That way, retailers can carry smaller inventories because they can be sure of dependable local supplies from wholesalers. And the retailers might decide to sell Snapper—rather than Toro or some other brand that they would have to store at their own expense.

If consumers "store" the product, more of it may be used or consumed. That's why Breyer's likes customers to buy its half-gallon packages. The "inventory" is right there in the freezer—and ready to be eaten—whenever the impulse hits.

Goods are stored at a cost

Storing can increase the value of goods, but *storing always involves costs* too. Different kinds of cost are involved (see Exhibit 11–6). Car dealers, for example, must store cars on their lots—waiting for the right customer. The interest expense of money tied up in the inventory is a major cost. In addition, if a new car on the lot is dented or scratched, there is a repair cost. If a car isn't sold before the new models come out, its value drops. There is also a risk of fire or theft—so the retailer must carry insurance. And, of course, dealers incur the cost of leasing or owning the display lot where they store the cars.

In today's competitive markets, most firms watch their inventories closely. They try to cut unnecessary inventory because it can make the difference between a profitable strategy and a loser. On the other hand, a marketing manager must be very careful in making the distinction between unnecessary inventory and inventory needed to provide the distribution service level customers expect. Shipments of Boeing's 787 Dreamliner aircraft were significantly delayed by a shortage of bolts that hold the jet airplanes together. The lack of availability of this relatively small part cost Boeing millions of dollars.[25]

Rapid response cuts inventory costs

Many firms are finding that they can cut inventory costs and still provide the desired customer service level—if they can reduce the time it takes to replace items that are sold. This is one important reason that JIT has been widely adopted. The firms involved use EDI, the Internet, and similar computerized approaches to share information and speed up the order cycle and delivery process.

Specialized Storing Facilities May Be Required

New cars can be stored outside on the dealer's lot. Fuel oil can be stored in a specially designed tank. Coal and other raw materials can be stored in open pits. But most products must be stored inside protective buildings. Often, firms can choose among different types of specialized storing facilities. The right choice may reduce costs and serve customers better.

Exhibit 11-7

A Comparison of Private Warehouses and Public Warehouses

Characteristics	Type of Warehouse	
	Private	**Public**
Fixed investment	Very high	No fixed investment
Unit cost	High if volume is low Very low if volume is very high	Low: charges are made only for space needed
Control	High	Low managerial control
Adequacy for product line	Highly adequate	May lack convenience
Flexibility	Low: fixed costs have already been committed	High: easy to end arrangement

Private warehouses are common

Private warehouses are storing facilities owned or leased by companies for their own use. Most manufacturers, wholesalers, and retailers have some storing facilities either in their main buildings or in a separate location. A sales manager often is responsible for managing a manufacturer's finished-goods warehouse, especially if regional sales branches aren't near the factory.

Firms use private warehouses when a large volume of goods must be stored regularly. Yet private warehouses can be expensive. If the need changes, the extra space may be hard, or impossible, to rent to others.

Public warehouses fill special needs

Public warehouses are independent storing facilities. They can provide all the services that a company's own warehouse can provide. A company might choose a public warehouse if it doesn't have a regular need for space. For example, Tonka Toys uses public warehouses because its business is seasonal. Tonka pays for the space only when it is used. Public warehouses are also useful for manufacturers that must maintain stocks in many locations, including foreign countries. See Exhibit 11–7 for a comparison of private and public warehouses.[26]

Warehousing facilities cut handling costs too

The cost of physical handling is a major storing cost. Goods must be handled once when put into storage and again when removed to be sold. To reduce these costs, modern one-story buildings away from downtown traffic have replaced most old multistory warehouses. They eliminate the need for elevators and permit the use of power-operated lift trucks, battery-operated motor scooters, roller-skating order pickers, electric hoists for heavy items, and hydraulic ramps to speed loading and unloading.

Bar codes, Universal Product Code (UPC) numbers, and electronic radio frequency identification (RFID) tags make it easy for computers to monitor inventory, order needed stock, and track storing and shipping costs. For example, clothing retailer Zara puts RFID tags on every piece of merchandise. The tags allow Zara to know where every piece of merchandise is at any given time—greatly simplifying the process of taking inventory. Each time Zara sells a garment, the tag immediately notifies the stockroom to bring up another from the stockroom. Chips in the tags make it easier to find similar garments—in the store or at a nearby store.

The Distribution Center—A Different Kind of Warehouse

LO 11.7

Is storing really needed?

Discrepancies of assortment or quantity between one channel level and another are often adjusted at the place where goods are stored. It reduces handling costs to regroup and store at the same place—*if both functions are required.* But sometimes regrouping is required when storing isn't.

Don't store it, distribute it

A **distribution center** is a special kind of warehouse designed to speed the flow of goods and avoid unnecessary storing costs. Today, the distribution center concept is widely used by firms at all channel levels. Many products buzz through a distribution center without ever tarrying on a shelf; workers and equipment immediately sort the products as they come in and then move them to an outgoing loading dock and the vehicle that will take them to their next stop. Technology is key to making distribution centers efficient.

Consider how food distributor Sysco addresses the challenge of shipping more than 21.5 million tons of fruit, vegetables, meats, and other food-related products each year. Sysco's customers include one in every three restaurants, school cafeterias, and other food service outlets in the United States and Canada. Because Sysco delivers so many products in so many different forms—from boxes of frozen French fries, crates of Granny Smith apples, and 80-pound tubs of flour to pots, pans, and utensils—its handling needs vary widely.

To move all these goods efficiently and quickly, Sysco relies on technology. It uses supply chain management software and an EDI system to automatically direct supplies from vendors such as Kraft and Kellogg to one of two Sysco "redistribution centers." There, orders are quickly consolidated and moved to one of Sysco's 177 distribution centers. The 400,000+ square-foot distribution centers are organized by weight and temperature; heavier items—such as cans weighing 40 to 50 pounds—are housed on one side, and lighter items—such as boxes of potato chips—on the other. To fill orders, custom software supplies fork-lift drivers with printouts telling them which items to pick first and how to stack them on a pallet based on the weight of the items, their location in the distribution center, and their ultimate destination. After calculating delivery routes that optimize time and fuel use, the software also provides instructions for loading the trucks.

Sysco delivers more than food to its customers. On the "Customer Solutions" section of Sysco's website, restaurateurs are connected with business resources (such as payroll and marketing tools) and managers of school lunch programs or nursing home meals can learn about Sysco's profitability consultation, menu analysis, and safety training. To-

Robotic order fulfillment systems are common in many large warehouses.
iStock/Getty Images

gether Sysco's combination of efficient operations, service and support, and quality products provide excellent value for its target market.[27]

Direct store delivery skips the distribution center

Some firms prefer to skip the distribution center altogether and ship products directly from where they are manufactured to retail stores. This may move products more quickly, but usually at a higher cost. Frito-Lay uses this approach. It handles more than 10,000 direct delivery routes to more than 200,000 small-store customers. The route drivers build close relationships with the many small retailers. That helps Frito-Lay better understand end consumers and adapt product mixes to particular stores. These extra services result in more shelf space and higher prices at the small stores.[28]

Managers must be innovative to provide customers with superior value

More competitive markets, improved technology, coordination among firms, and efficient new distribution centers are bringing big improvements to the PD area. Yet the biggest challenges may be more basic. As we've emphasized here, physical distribution activities transcend departmental, corporate, and even national boundaries. So taking advantage of ways to improve often requires cooperation all along the channel system. Too often, such cooperation doesn't exist—and changing ingrained ways of doing things is hard. But marketing managers who push for innovations in these areas are likely to win customers away from firms and whole channel systems that are stuck doing things the old way.[29]

CONCLUSION

This chapter explained the major logistics activities and how they contribute to the value of products by getting them to the place that customers want or need them. If the distribution customer service level meets their needs and can be provided at a reasonable cost, customers may not even think about the logistics activities that occur behind the scenes. But if products are not available when and where they need to be, a strategy will fail. So decisions in these areas are an important part of Place and marketing strategy planning.

We emphasized the relation between customer service level, transporting, and storing. The physical distribution concept focuses on coordinating all the storing, transporting, and product-handling activities into a smoothly working system—to deliver the desired service level and customer value at the lowest total cost.

Marketing managers often want to improve service and may select a higher-cost alternative to improve their marketing mix. The total cost approach might reveal that it is possible both to reduce costs and to improve customer service—perhaps by working closely with other members of the supply chain.

We discussed various modes of transporting and their advantages and disadvantages. We also discussed ways to reduce inventory costs. For example, distribution centers are an important way to cut storing and handling costs, and computerized information links—within firms and among firms in the channel—are increasingly important in blending all of the logistics activities into a smooth-running system.

Effective marketing managers make important strategy decisions about physical distribution. Creative strategy decisions may result in lower PD costs while maintaining or improving the customer service level. And production-oriented competitors may not even understand what is happening.

WHAT'S NOW?

This chapter examined logistics decisions—the transporting, storing, and handling of goods in ways that match target customers' needs. For some current real-world examples and learnings, check out *What's Now?* at www.learnthe4ps.com/whatsnow/c11

KEY TERMS

LO 11.8

logistics, 284

physical distribution (PD), 284

customer service level, 285

physical distribution (PD) concept, 288

total cost approach, 289

supply chain, 290

electronic data interchange (EDI), 292

transporting, 293

containerization, 297

storing, 298

inventory, 298

private warehouses, 300

public warehouses, 300

distribution center, 300

QUESTIONS AND PROBLEMS

1. Review the Coca-Cola case study that opens the chapter. From this case, identify examples of different key terms and concepts covered in the chapter. For example, a distribution center is discussed in the second paragraph.

2. Review the Coca-Cola case study that opens this chapter. Assume that Coca-Cola is adding packaged fresh fruit snacks (they have a two-week shelf life) to its product line. Would the current physical distribution system for its drinks work for snacks? Why or why not? What changes might be needed?

3. Explain how adjusting the customer service level could improve a marketing mix. Illustrate with your own example.

4. Briefly explain which aspects of customer service you think would be most important for a producer that sells fabric to a firm that manufactures furniture.

5. Briefly describe a purchase you made where the customer service level had an effect on the product you selected or where you purchased it.

6. Discuss the types of trade-offs involved in PD costs, service levels, and sales.

7. Give an example of why it is important for different firms in the supply chain to coordinate logistics activities.

8. Discuss some of the ways computers are being used to improve PD decisions.

9. Explain why a just-in-time delivery system would require a supplier to pay attention to quality control. Give an example to illustrate your points.

10. Discuss the problems a supplier might encounter in using a just-in-time delivery system with a customer in a foreign country.

11. Review the list of factors that affect PD service levels in Exhibit 11–3. Indicate which factors are most likely to be improved by EDI links between a supplier and its customers.

12. Explain the total cost approach and why it may cause conflicts in some firms. Give examples of how conflicts might occur between different departments.

13. Discuss the relative advantages and disadvantages of railroads, trucks, and airlines as transporting methods.

14. Discuss why economies of scale in transportation might encourage a producer to include a regional merchant wholesaler in the channel of distribution for its consumer product.

15. Discuss some of the ways that air transportation can change other aspects of a Place system.

16. Explain which transportation mode would probably be most suitable for shipping the following goods to a large Los Angeles department store:

   a. 300 pounds of Maine lobster
   b. 15 pounds of screwdrivers from Ohio
   c. Three dining room tables from High Point, North Carolina
   d. 500 high-fashion dresses from the fashion district in Paris
   e. A 10,000-pound shipment of exercise equipment from Germany
   f. 600,000 pounds of various appliances from Evansville, Indiana

17. Indicate the nearest location where you would expect to find large storage facilities. What kinds of products would be stored there? Why are they stored there instead of some other place?

18. When would a producer or intermediary find it desirable to use a public warehouse rather than a private warehouse? Illustrate, using a specific product or situation.

19. Discuss the distribution center concept. Is this likely to eliminate the storing function of conventional wholesalers? Is it applicable to all products? If not, cite several examples.

20. Clearly differentiate between a warehouse and a distribution center. Explain how a specific product would be handled differently by each.

21. If a retailer operates only from a website and ships all orders by UPS, is it freed from the logistics issues that face traditional retailers? Explain your thinking.

MARKETING PLANNING FOR HILLSIDE VETERINARY CLINIC

Appendix D (the Appendices follow Chapter 19) includes a sample marketing plan for Hillside Veterinary Clinic. Look through the "Marketing Strategy" section. To provide veterinary care to pets, Hillside needs to have a variety of medical supplies on hand. To handle that, it relies on deliveries from suppliers and its own inventory decisions. It also sells some retail pet products to customers, and that requires a separate set of decisions about how it will handle inventory.

a. What logistics issues related to medical supplies should Hillside consider? Can you think of ways in which delivery from its suppliers or its own inventory decisions will be important in its ability to help its patients?

b. With respect to the retail pet products that Hillside sells, what level of customer service should customers expect?

c. What issues are involved in the storage of pet supplies?

SUGGESTED CASES

16. Tall Timber Lumber Supply
26. Abundant Harvest

MARKETING ANALYTICS: DATA TO KNOWLEDGE

CHAPTER 11 TOTAL DISTRIBUTION COST

Proto Company has been producing various items made of plastic. It recently added a line of plain plastic cards that other firms (such as banks and retail stores) will imprint to produce credit cards. Proto offers its customers the plastic cards in different colors, but they all sell for $40 per box of 1,000. Tom Phillips, Proto's product manager for this line, is considering two possible physical distribution systems. He estimates that if Proto uses airfreight, transportation costs will be $7.50 a box,

and its cost of carrying inventory will be 5 percent of total annual sales dollars. Alternatively, Proto could ship by rail for $2 a box. But rail transport will require renting space at four regional warehouses—at $26,000 a year each. Inventory carrying cost with this system will be 10 percent of total annual sales dollars. Phillips prepared a spreadsheet to compare the cost of the two alternative physical distribution systems.

See Connect for the spreadsheet and questions needed to analyze this scenario.

Retailers, Wholesalers, and Their Strategy Planning

From 1843 to 1855 Rowland Hussey Macy opened—and closed—four general stores that specialized in "dry goods," mainly textiles and ready-to-wear clothing. Learning from those early failures, Macy finally hit on a formula that worked with the R.H. Macy Dry Goods store he opened in New York City in 1858. Macy was soon adding departments with new product lines and moving into nearby buildings. Resembling a collection of specialty shops, Macy's became one of the world's first department stores. Innovative from the start, Macy's was the first store to offer visits with Santa Claus. It also led the way in illuminating window displays to lure customers into its stores. In 1902, the original store moved uptown to Herald Square, where it remains today as the flagship in the 800+ store Macy's chain.

Department stores proved to be popular with American shoppers; the concept was in the growth stage of its life cycle for more than a century before sales topped out in the 1970s. Department stores' large product assortment and attentive customer service appealed to many customers. Typically located in city centers or regional malls, department stores pulled customers from a wide geographic area. In the early 1900s, Sears and Marshall Field's branched out with mail-order catalogs and brought the department store to rural America. In the 1970s, department stores began to lose market share; first to mass-merchandisers and later to supercenters such as Target and Walmart, which offered convenient neighborhood locations and lower prices. To compete, department stores pushed sale prices, but profits declined and customer service suffered. Many thought the arrival of Internet retailing in the late 1990s signaled the death knell for department stores. But some department stores successfully adapted their marketing mixes, making them relevant again. Macy's has been particularly successful.

Macy's revival stems from changes across its marketing strategy. Macy's started by clearly defining its target markets. Macy's saw an opportunity with teens and the slightly older millennials (ages 19–30), who spend $60 billion a year and 50 percent more per person than the average population. Within that segment, Macy's defined four distinct target markets: teen girls, teen boys, millennial women, and millennial men. Each segment has unique needs and shopping behaviors.

High school age teens want stylish clothes and spend a lot of time online. So Macy's connects with them through Tumblr, Pinterest, Facebook, and text messages. Macy's social media feauture a mix of content that appeals to teens: videos with the latest fashion trends, online shopping, and m.mix, where teens can discover new bands, download music, and get tips on decorating a college dorm room. Macy's has also developed exclusive lines for this market, including Marilyn Monroe clothing (for girls), G-Star Raw clothing (for boys), Keds collection shoes, and a Glee-themed line based on the popular television program. In the store, this group prefers to "self-serve," so Macy's trained its sales staff to be available but not pushy with teens.

The millennial market might be found in college, starting a career, or maybe having a family. These customers prefer to hear from Macy's via e-mail, catalog, or direct mail. Macy's created its Impulse Shop with products for this group. Shoppers will find Inglot Cosmetics, DV by Dolce Vita Shoes, and Else from Joe's Jeans here. This target market favors fast-fashion retailers such as Zara and H&M that produce a collection of clothes and get it into a store in just a couple of weeks. Macy's needed to do the same and spurred its supply chain to respond quickly to fashion trends. These customers appreciate suggestions and advice from Macy's salespeople. So in the Impulse Shop at Macys.com, a black handbag might be suggested to complement the black shoes a shopper puts into her shopping cart. And in the store, Macy's salespeople are friendlier and offer more suggestions to millennials than to teens.

The My Macy's program mines customer data to adapt marketing communications to *individual* customers. Macy's customer relationship management database includes a great deal of insight about each customer: previous purchases, responses to e-mails, online shopping behavior, and other information collected over time. Macy's uses these data to customize promotions in e-mails and direct mail. For example, Macy's sent out 30,000 different versions of a direct mailing; the pieces varied from 32 to 76 pages long and featured merchandise designed to appeal to each customer. As a result, footwear fanatics saw more shoes and moms saw more kids' clothes.

Macy's recognizes that teens and millennials are multichannel shoppers, and Macy's wants to be in all those channels. Macy's developed its "omnichannel" strategy to create a seamless shopping experience across its mobile, online, and brick-and-mortar stores. So when the shoes a customer loves at the store are not in stock in his size, they are delivered to the customer's home two days later direct from Macys.com. When a customer finds Macys.com doesn't have a navy blue Lacoste polo shirt he wants to buy in stock, the order can be shipped today from a local store that has one on its shelf.

In retail, not everything goes out the front door. Sometimes even Macy's One-Day Sale prices don't move the merchandise. When that happens, or when returns cannot be restocked, other channels of distribution are needed. Macy's Wholesale sells pallet loads of returned clothing and unsold merchandise to clearance centers or other countries.

Macy's is leading a department store revival with its blend of online, mobile, and 800+ stores, an ability to transform big data into personalized shopping experiences, and a focus on the needs of its teen and millennial target markets. Still, Macy's faces fierce competition from department stores such as Nordstrom and Kohl's, specialty shops such as Buckle and American Eagle, and online stores such as eBay and Zappos. To keep growing, Macy's must continue adapting its marketing mix to meet its customers' evolving needs.[1]

LEARNING OBJECTIVES

Retail and wholesale organizations exist as members of marketing channel systems. But they also do their own strategy planning as they compete for target customers. As the Macy's case shows, these firms make decisions about Product, Place, Promotion, and Price. This chapter overviews the strategy planning decisions of different types of retailers and wholesalers. The chapter shows how retailing and wholesaling are evolving—to give you a sense of how things may change in the future.

When you finish this chapter, you should be able to

1 Understand the nature and basic structure of retailing.

2 Understand how retailers plan their marketing strategies.

3 Know about the many kinds of retailers that work with producers and wholesalers as members of channel systems.

4 Understand what is different about retailing on the Internet.

5 Understand how and why retailers evolve, including the roles of technology, scrambled merchandising, and the "wheel of retailing."

6 Understand some of the differences in retailing in different nations.

7 Know what progressive wholesalers are doing to modernize their operations and marketing strategies.

8 Know the various kinds of merchant and agent wholesalers and the strategies they use.

9 Understand important new terms (shown in red).

Retailers and Wholesalers Plan Their Own Strategies

As we saw in Chapter 10, retailers and wholesalers perform a vital role in channel systems. Now we'll look at the decisions that retailers and wholesalers make in developing their own strategies. But first, study Exhibit 12–1 for a visual of how everything fits together.

Producers can choose a variety of different paths to deliver products to target customers (see Exhibit 12–2). In Chapter 10 we discussed how some producers deliver goods or services directly to customers. We also saw how in some industries,

Exhibit 12-1 Marketing Strategy Planning for Retailers and Wholesalers

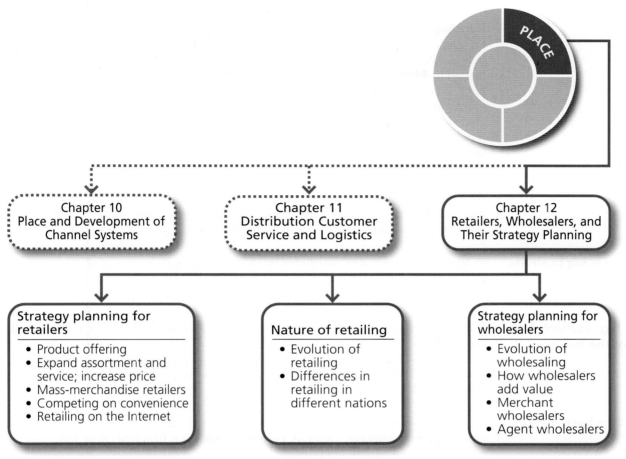

Chapter 10
Place and Development of
Channel Systems

Chapter 11
Distribution Customer
Service and Logistics

Chapter 12
Retailers, Wholesalers, and
Their Strategy Planning

Strategy planning for retailers
- Product offering
- Expand assortment and service; increase price
- Mass-merchandise retailers
- Competing on convenience
- Retailing on the Internet

Nature of retailing
- Evolution of retailing
- Differences in retailing in different nations

Strategy planning for wholesalers
- Evolution of wholesaling
- How wholesalers add value
- Merchant wholesalers
- Agent wholesalers

retailers and/or wholesalers add value so it makes sense to use indirect channels. And of course, many producers use more than one of these paths to get products to customers.

When marketing managers decide to use intermediaries in their marketing strategy, they can choose among many different types of retailers and wholesalers. Retailers and wholesalers have different target markets and different marketing mixes, and a producer should select intermediaries that best facilitate its strategy.

To better understand these options, we begin the chapter with a discussion of strategy planning for retailers (back to Exhibit 12–1). Retailers must create a marketing mix that provides value for a target market. We also discuss how retailing has evolved and where it stands today, including some important international differences. Chapter 12 concludes by considering strategy planning and the services offered by different types of wholesalers.

Exhibit 12-2 Wholesalers and Retailers in a Typical Channel of Distribution

The Nature of Retailing

Retailing covers all of the activities involved in the sale of products to final consumers. Retailers range from large chains of specialized stores, such as Toys "R" Us, to individual merchants like the woman who sells baskets from an open stall in the central market in Ibadan, Nigeria. Some retailers operate from stores and others operate without a store—by selling online, on TV, with a printed catalog, from vending machines, or even in consumers' homes. Most retailers sell physical goods produced by someone else. But in the case of service retailing—such as dry cleaning, fast food, tourist attractions, online bank accounts, or hair salons—the retailer is often the producer. Because they serve individual consumers, even the largest retailers face the challenge of handling many small transactions.

The nature of retailing and its rate of change are generally related to the stage and speed of a country's economic development. In the United States, retailing is more varied and dynamic than in most other countries. By studying the U.S. system, you will better understand where retailing is headed in other parts of the world.

Retailing is big business.

Retailing is crucial to consumers in every macro-marketing system. For example, consumers spend about $4.7 *trillion* (that's $4,700,000,000,000!) a year buying goods and services from U.S. retailers.

A few big retailers do most of the business

There are more than a million retailers in the United States, but most of these retailers are small; more than half report annual sales of less than $1 million. The larger retail stores—those selling more than $5 million annually—do most of the business. Less than 15 percent of the retail stores are this big, yet they account for almost 75 percent of all retail sales.[2]

Big chains have market clout

One reason for the dominance of large retailers is that many achieve economies of scale from a corporate chain. A **corporate chain** is a firm that owns and manages more than one store—and often it's many. Chains—including Nordstrom's, Walmart, Kroger, 7-11, and Chipotle—have grown rapidly and now account for about half of all retail sales. Chains can buy in larger quantities and earn lower prices, they get operational efficiencies from running many stores, and they can apply advertising and other promotion costs over many stores. You can expect chains to continue to grow and take business from independent stores.[3]

Some businesspeople like to open retail franchises with brand names consumers already know—brands with track records of success, like Dunkin' Donuts and Baskin Robbins.

Retail through cooperatives and franchisors

Because size offers such an advantage, many retailers not connected to a chain join cooperatives or franchises. Retailers' cooperatives pool purchasing and marketing expenses to increase efficiency and effectiveness. Piggly Wiggly grocery, Ace Hardware, NAPA Auto Parts stores, and Carpet One are examples of cooperatives.

In a **franchise operation**, the franchisor develops a good marketing strategy, and the retail franchise holders carry out the strategy in their own units. Each franchise holder benefits from its relationship with the larger company and its experience, buying power, promotion, and image. In return, the franchise holder signs a contract, agreeing to pay fees and commissions and strictly follow franchise rules designed to continue the successful strategy. Franchise holders' sales account for about a third of all retail sales. Hampton Hotels, Anytime Fitness, Subway, and Supercuts are examples of franchises.[4]

Small retailers specialize

While big chains and franchises dominate the sales volume, 85% of all retailers are small. But it is not easy for small retailers; the failure rate of small retailers is high. A recent study found less than half were operating four years after starting in business. Without the same economies of scale, small retailers that survive usually develop a specialty and become highly knowledgeable about a market niche. For example, online retailer Wicker Central specializes in outdoor wicker furniture. With four toy stores in Charleston, South Carolina, Wonder Works survives because it offers visitors a unique experience on each visit. These stores compete with larger competitors based on intimate knowledge of their markets and high levels of customer service.[5]

Planning a Retailer's Strategy

LO 12.2

Retailers interact directly with final consumers—so strategy planning is critical to their survival. If a retailer loses a customer to a competitor, the retailer is the one who suffers. Producers and wholesalers still make *their* sale regardless of which retailer sells the product. So let's look closer at strategy planning for retailers.

Consumers have reasons for buying from particular retailers

Different consumers prefer different kinds of retailers. But many retailers either don't know or don't care why. All too often, beginning retailers just rent a store and assume customers will show up. As a result, in the United States about three-fourths of new retailing ventures fail during the first year. Even an established retailer will quickly lose if its customers find a better way to meet their needs. To avoid this fate, a retailer should carefully identify possible target markets and try to understand why these people buy where they do. In this way, the retailer can fine-tune its marketing mix to the needs of specific target markets.[6]

Retailers make decisions about the whole marketing mix

Like other organizations, retailers make marketing mix decisions about target market, Product, Place, Promotion, and Price (see Exhibit 12–3). For retailers, some of the Product decisions include choices about what products to carry, how wide an assortment to offer, and which services to support. Place decisions include where stores will be located (online and/or brick-and-mortar), the number of stores, as well as store layout and design. Promotion involves

Retailers make decisions about the whole marketing mix. Drugstore CVS created its myCVS smartphone app that helps its customers manage and quickly refill their prescriptions, find out about deals, place orders for merchandise to be picked up later, and much more.
© 2013 CVS Caremark; Phone image: © Jacek Lasa/Alamy.

Exhibit 12-3   Examples of Marketing Strategy Decisions for Retailers

Product
- Product selection (width and depth of assortment, brands, quality)
- After-sale service
- Special services (special orders, entertainment, gift wrap)

Place
- Physical stores and/or sales over the Internet
- Number and location of stores
- Shopping atmosphere (comfort, safety)
- Store size, layout, and design
- Store hours

Price
- Credit cards—whether to offer a store card
- Discount policies
- Frequency and level of sales prices
- Charge (or not) for delivery or other services

Promotion
- Advertising
- Publicity (Facebook, Twitter, Pinterest)
- Salespeople (number and training)
- Helpful information (demonstrations, displays, online videos, online reviews)

letting customers know about the business and the goods and services offered through its in-store and out-of-store signage, advertising, salespeople, publicity (including social media), and other approaches. Price decisions are varied as well, and include, for example, whether to accept credit cards or charge for delivery, and how frequently to offer products at discounted sales prices.

Strategy requires carefully setting policies

In developing a strategy, a retailer should consciously make decisions that set policies on *all* of these marketing mix issues. Each of them can impact a customer's view of the costs and benefits of choosing that retailer. The combination of these marketing mix decisions differentiates one retailer's offering from another. These decisions affect its positioning in the market—how customers think about the retailer compared to others. A retailer must consider its target customers' economic, social, and emotional needs. If the combination doesn't provide superior value to some target market, the retailer will fail.

Consider the marketing strategies for two very different, yet successful, shoe retailers. Usually located in malls and shopping centers, Payless ShoeSource's primary target market is families looking for moderately priced shoes. Although its shoes can be ordered online, most sales occur in one of its 4,500 brick-and-mortar stores. The stores have a self-service design that encourages customers to select and try on shoes without the help of a salesperson. Even though each store carries an average of 500 styles and 6,700 pairs of shoes—including dress, casual, boots, and athletic—for men, women, and children, Payless' product line is relatively narrow for a shoe retailer and includes mostly lesser-known brands. Payless' advertising in local newspapers emphasizes value and usually promotes its low prices. Further, Payless' Facebook page, with more than 750,000 "likes," keeps its most ardent fans informed of the next deal.[7]

Zappos.com offers a different marketing mix that appeals to a different target market. Zappos operates several online storefronts in addition to Zappos—including Zappos Couture with high fashion shoes and Zappos Running. Although Zappos recently added clothing, handbags, housewares, and beauty supplies to its product assortment, its core product line remains shoes. Zappos' wide product line includes more than 150,000 styles and 1,400 brands—including many styles in well-known brands such as Nike, Timberland, and Bandolino. Because shoppers are understandably reluctant to buy shoes without first trying them on, Zappos devotes a whole page to each shoe. There it provides eight or more photos from different angles, customer reviews, videos, and detailed descriptions. Zappos also offers free shipping and free returns—for up to 365 days after purchase! The retailer wins praise for its customer service, available 24/7 on the phone or the web. That service helps build positive word-of-mouth for Zappos, and more than 75 percent of its customers are repeat buyers. It has a relatively small budget for its advertising on television, print, online, and the bottom of the plastic bins in airport security lines. A free monthly digital magazine for tablet computers, *Zappos Now,* keeps customers informed about fashion trends and offers tips about Zappos products. CEO and author Tony Hsieh's Twitter feed has more than 2.8 million followers. Zappos and Payless ShoeSource developed very different marketing mixes, but each keeps target customers coming back.[8]

Different types of retailers emphasize different strategies

Retailers have an almost unlimited number of ways in which to alter their offerings—their marketing mixes—to appeal to a target market. Because of all the variations, it's oversimplified to classify retailers and their strategies on the basis of a single characteristic—such as merchandise, services, sales volume, or even whether they operate in cyberspace. But a good place to start is by considering basic types of retailers and some differences in their strategies.

Conventional Retailers—Try to Avoid Price Competition

LO 12.3

Single-line, limited-line retailers specialize by product

About 150 years ago, **general stores**—which carried anything they could sell in reasonable volume—were the main retailers in the United States. But with the growing number of consumer products after the Civil War, general stores couldn't offer enough variety in all their traditional lines. So some stores began specializing in dry goods, apparel, furniture, or groceries.

Exhibit 12-4 Types of Retailers and the Nature of Their Offerings (*with examples*)

Now most *conventional* retailers are **single-line** or **limited-line stores**—stores that specialize in certain lines of related products rather than a wide assortment. Many specialize not only in a single line, such as clothing, but also in a *limited line* within the broader line. Within the clothing line, a retailer might carry *only* shoes, formal wear, or even neckties but offer depth in that limited line.

Single-line, limited-line stores are being squeezed

The main advantage of limited-line retailers is that they can satisfy some target markets better. Perhaps some are just more conveniently located. But most adjust to suit specific customers. They build a relationship with their customers and earn a position as *the* place to shop for a certain type of product. But these retailers face the costly problem of having to stock some slow-moving items in order to satisfy their target markets. Many of these stores are small—with high expenses relative to sales. So they try to keep their prices up by avoiding competition on identical products.

Conventional retailers like this have been around for a long time and are still found in every community. They are a durable lot and clearly satisfy some people's needs. In fact, in most countries conventional retailers still handle the vast majority of all retailing sales. However, this situation is changing fast. Nowhere is the change clearer than in the United States. Conventional retailers are being squeezed by retailers who modify their mixes in the various ways suggested in Exhibit 12–4. Let's look closer at some of these other types of retailers.

Expand Assortment and Service—To Compete at a High Price

Specialty shops usually sell shopping products

A **specialty shop**—a type of conventional limited-line store—is usually small and has a distinct "personality." Specialty shops sell special types of shopping products, such as high-quality sporting goods, exclusive clothing, baked goods, or even antiques. They aim at a carefully defined target market by offering a unique product assortment, knowledgeable salesclerks, and better service.

Catering to certain types of customers whom the management and salespeople know well simplifies buying, speeds turnover, and cuts costs due to obsolescence and style changes. Specialty shops probably will continue to be a part of the retailing scene as long as customers have varied tastes and the money to satisfy them.[9]

Department stores combine many limited-line stores and specialty shops

Department stores are larger stores that are organized into many separate departments and offer many product lines. Each department is like a separate limited-line store and handles a wide variety of shopping products, such as men's wear or housewares. They are usually strong in customer services, including credit, merchandise return, delivery, and sales help.

Department stores are still a major force in big cities. Although they have staged a bit of a comeback recently in the United States, the number of department stores, the average sales per store, and their share of retail business has declined significantly since the 1970s. Well-run limited-line stores compete with good service and often carry the same brands. In the United States and many other countries, mass-merchandising retailers have posed an even bigger threat.[10]

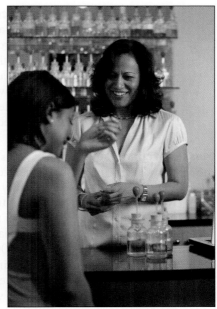

Specialty shops and department stores often rely on well-trained salespeople who deliver expertise and customer service.
John Henley/Getty Images

Evolution of Mass-Merchandising Retailers

Mass-merchandising is different from conventional retailing

The conventional retailers just discussed think that demand in their area is fixed—and they have a "buy low and sell high" philosophy. Many modern retailers reject these ideas. Instead, they accept the **mass-merchandising concept**—which says that retailers should offer low prices to get faster turnover and greater sales volumes—by appealing to larger markets. The mass-merchandising concept applies to many types of retailers, including both those that operate stores and those that sell online. But to understand mass-merchandising better, let's look at its evolution from the development of supermarkets and discounters to modern mass-merchandisers such as Walmart in the United States, Tesco in the U.K., and Amazon.com on the Internet.

Supermarkets started the move to mass-merchandising

The basic idea for **supermarkets**, large stores specializing in groceries with self-service and wide assortments, developed in the United States during the 1930s Depression. In earlier days, customers entered a store and a clerk, from behind a counter, fetched requested items. Then some innovators introduced self-service as a way to cut costs while also providing a broad assortment in large bare-bones stores.[11]

Today's supermarkets carry 20,000 to 40,000 items and per-store sales are about $20 million a year, with about 75 percent of that in food. The average size of a supermarket is 40,000 square feet. In the United States, there are about 35,000 supermarkets, and competition in most areas is intense. More recently, supermarket operators have opened superstores of 50,000 to 100,000 square feet with extensive selection.[12]

Supermarkets are planned for maximum efficiency. Scanners at checkout make it possible to carefully analyze the sales of each item and allocate more shelf space to faster-moving and higher-profit items. Survival depends on efficiency and high sales volume. Net profits in supermarkets usually run a thin 1 to 2 percent of sales or less!

Discount houses upset conventional retailers

After World War II, some retailers started to focus on discount prices. These **discount houses** offered "hard goods" (cameras, TVs, and appliances) at substantial price cuts to customers who would go to the discounter's low-rent store, pay cash, and take care of any service or repair problems themselves. These retailers sold at 20 to 30 percent off the list price being charged by conventional retailers.

In the early 1950s, with war shortages finally over, manufacturer brands became more available. The discount houses were able to get any brands they wanted and to offer wider assortments. At this stage, many discounters turned respectable—moving to better locations and offering more services and guarantees. It was from these origins that today's mass-merchandisers developed.

Mass-merchandisers are more than discounters

Mass-merchandisers are large self-service stores with many departments that emphasize "soft goods" (housewares, clothing, and fabrics) and staples (like health and beauty aids) but still follow the discount house's emphasis on lower margins to get faster turnover. Mass-merchandisers, such as Walmart and Target, have checkout counters in the front of the store and little sales help on the floor. Today, the average mass-merchandiser has nearly 60,000 square feet of floor space, but many new stores are 100,000 square feet or more. Mass-merchandisers grew rapidly—and they've become the primary place to shop for many frequently purchased consumer products. To move into new markets—big cities or small towns—some of these retailers are opening stores with smaller footprints.

Supercenters meet all routine needs

Some supermarkets and mass-merchandisers have moved toward becoming **supercenters (hypermarkets)**—very large stores that try to carry not only food and drug items but all goods and services that the consumer purchases *routinely*. These superstores look a lot like a combination of the supermarkets, drugstores, and mass-merchandisers from which they have evolved, but the concept is different. A supercenter is trying to meet *all* the customer's routine needs at a low price. Supercenter operators include Meijer, Fred Meyer, Target, and Walmart. In fact, Walmart's supercenters have turned it into the largest food retailer in the United States.

Supercenters average more than 150,000 square feet and carry about 50,000 items. Their assortment in one place is convenient, but many time-pressured consumers think that the crowds, lines, and "wandering around" time in the store are not. Some supercenters have responded by reducing product line depth. For example, Walmart recently decided that it didn't need to carry 24 tape measures and now carries just four.[13]

New mass-merchandising formats keep coming

The warehouse club is another retailing format that quickly gained popularity. Sam's Club and Costco are two of the largest. Consumers usually pay an annual membership fee to shop in these large, no-frills facilities. Among the 3,500 items per store, they carry food, appliances, yard tools, tires, and other items that many consumers see as homogeneous shopping items and want at the lowest possible price. The growth of these clubs has also been fueled by sales to small-business customers. That's why some people refer to these outlets as wholesale clubs. However, when half or more of a firm's sales are to final consumers, it is classified as a retailer, not a wholesaler.[14]

Warehouse club store Costco offers its target customers a limited assortment, warehouse ambiance, and low prices.
AP Photo/Rick Bowmer.

Single-line mass-merchandisers rise and fall

Since 1980, many retailers focusing on single product lines have adopted the mass-merchandisers' approach with great success. Toys "R" Us pioneered this trend. Similarly, IKEA (furniture), Home Depot (home improvements), Best Buy (electronics), and Staples (office supplies) attract large numbers of customers with their large assortment and low prices in specific product categories. These stores are called *category killers* because it's so hard for less specialized retailers to compete. Now online retailers offering greater assortment and even lower prices threaten the category killers.[15]

Some Retailers Focus on Added Convenience

Convenience (food) stores must have the right assortment

Convenience (food) stores are a convenience-oriented variation of the conventional limited-line food stores. Instead of expanding their assortment, however, convenience stores limit their stock to pickup or fill-in items such as bread, milk, beer, and eat-on-the-go snacks. Many also sell gas. Stores such as 7-Eleven and Stop-N-Go aim to fill consumers' needs between trips to a supermarket, and many of them are competing with fast-food outlets. They offer convenience, not assortment, and often charge prices 10 to 20 percent higher than nearby supermarkets. However, as many other retailers have expanded their hours, intense competition is driving down convenience store prices and profits.[16]

Vending machines are convenient

Automatic vending is selling and delivering products through vending machines. Vending machine sales account for only about 1.5 percent of total U.S. retail sales. Yet for some target markets this retailing method can't be ignored.

Although vending machines can be costly to operate, consumers like their convenience. Many vending machines are becoming more convenient by accepting credit cards and mobile payment. Traditionally, soft drinks, candy bars, and snack foods have been sold by vending machines. Now some higher-margin products are beginning to use this channel. For example, Standard Hotels uses poolside vending machines to sell bathing suits.[17]

Stores come to the home—in person, on television, and in catalogs

In-home shopping in the United States started in the pioneer days with **door-to-door selling**—a salesperson going directly to the consumer's home. Variations on this approach are still important for firms such as Amway Global and Mary Kay. It meets some consumers' need for convenient personal attention. Although gaining popularity in some international markets such as China and parts of Africa, it now accounts for less than 1 percent of retail sales in the United States.

Some target markets value the convenience of automatic vending and door-to-door selling.
Left: Used with permission of Utique, Inc.; Right: Bloomberg/Getty Images.

Customers can also shop at home by watching cable television channels dedicated to shopping and then calling in their orders by phone. QVC and Home Shopping Network operate in the United States, Japan, and some European countries. Similarly, catalogs allow customers to page through merchandise and place orders on the phone or online. Deliveries will usually occur a few days later, handled by shippers UPS or FedEx. Both of these home shopping methods use a multichannel approach by adding a website.[18]

Internet retailing has quickly become the most popular way to shop at home (and sometimes at work). Let's take a closer look at online retailing.

Retailing and the Internet

Internet retailing is growing fast

Internet retailing is still in the growth stage. In 2015, online sales in the United States topped $350 billion and grew to more than 7 percent of all retail sales. Online sales are predicted to top 10 percent of all U.S. sales by 2018. Online sales are growing about 15 percent per year whereas total retail sales grow less than 2 percent. In some categories, the share of online sales is even greater; more than half of all computer hardware and software, and more than a quarter of all books, are sold online. The impact of the Internet on retail sales is even greater—as many shoppers go to the Internet (often visiting online retail sites) for information before buying in a physical store.

Internet retailers and physical (sometimes called brick-and-mortar) stores are waging an intense battle for consumer shopping attention. See Exhibit 12–5 for a comparison of these two shopping methods.[19] Innovative Internet retailers are finding ways to offset some of the advantages of physical stores—and physical stores are figuring out how to use the Internet to their advantage. This battle between online and offline retailers has fueled a period of innovation unlike anything retailing has ever seen—and it is likely to continue. Let's take a closer look at how retailers are adapting their strategies for the online customer.[20]

Online retail offers low prices and wide assortment

With no storefront and limited sales help, online retailers usually have lower operating costs than brick-and-mortar stores. Customers may not have to pay sales taxes either—though that is changing. These advantages lead many online stores to use low prices to attract customers. But because the Internet makes it easy to compare products and prices from different online sellers, price-sensitive shoppers usually choose the store with the lowest price. That puts constant price pressure on Internet sellers to figure out how to differentiate their offerings.

Online stores offer a very wide assortment of products—often from different sellers. It is easy to click from site to site or simply conduct a search for a specific brand/

Exhibit 12–5 Comparing the Advantages of Shopping Online with Shopping at a Physical Store

Advantages of Shopping Online	Advantages of Shopping at a Physical Store
• Rich variety of product information from many sources	• Ability to hold, try on, or test products before purchase
• Reviews and tips from customers who've already used the product	• Personal help and interaction
• Wide assortment	• Edited assortment—easier to decide
• Fast and convenient purchase/checkout	• Convenient product returns
• Simplified price and product feature comparison	• Help with setup and ongoing service needs
• Anytime and anywhere access	• Instant access to products and instant gratification
	• Shopping with friends or family is a social activity

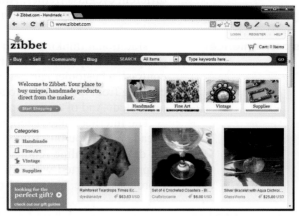

Online retailers have different marketing strategies. Wayfair specializes in furniture and other products for the home. Its family of brands includes AllModern.com, which specializes in modern design, and Birch Lane, which offers classic furnishings and timeless home décor. Zibbet is an online global marketplace that connects buyers and sellers of handmade goods, fine art, vintage items, and crafting supplies.

Left: © 2002–2015 by Wayfair LLC, 4 Copley Place, Floor 7, Boston, MA. 02116.; Right: © 2012 Zibbet Pty Ltd.

model and find multiple sites offering the same thing. Sites such as Amazon.com and eBay bring different sellers together to offer customers even more choices. To counter that online advantage, many brick-and-mortar stores are adding in-store computer terminals so customers can buy online what they might not find in the store.

Lowering the risk of shopping online

Although customers can find low prices online, sometimes prices aren't what they seem. Many online retailers add charges for handling and delivery. Returns and exchanges can create more expense and hassle. Customer concerns about fraud and security create hidden costs. Some customers worry about how an online retailer handles personal information such as e-mail addresses and credit card numbers.

The most successful online retailers have found ways to overcome these customer concerns. Many offer free shipping. Some offer free exchanges or returns and pack bar-coded return labels with the original shipment to make returns easy. Other stores provide excellent customer service and build a good reputation, because word-of-mouth matters online. Organizations such as TRUSTe place a seal of approval on sites that meet certain privacy standards, and sites such as ResellerRatings and Google Shopping collect customer reviews of retailers. Together these efforts help lower the costs, worries, and hassles of online shopping.

Obtaining purchase information

For many purchases, consumers seek information to help them make the purchase decision. It used to be inconvenient to shop online because there just wasn't a lot of product information available. That has changed. In many physical retail stores cost-cutting measures have resulted in fewer or less-well-trained salespeople, making it difficult to get helpful buying information. Online it can be easy to learn about a product; with the click of a mouse, an online shopper can access product descriptions and specifications, photos and videos, and reviews posted by other consumers. Some sites make virtual salesclerks available to chat—online or on the phone—at any time.

However, for some purchases the ultimate information comes from physically inspecting a product before purchase. That is one reason that clothing sells best in physical stores—about 30 percent of clothing bought online is returned. To try to overcome this limitation, many online stores show photos and videos that demonstrate its products. At eyeglass retailer EyeBuyDirect.com, customers can upload a photo of themselves and then see what they look like when they virtually "try on" different eyeglass frames. Another online eyeglass retailer, Warby Parker, allows customers to select up to five frames to try on at home before placing an order.[21]

What is convenience?

Traditional thinking about retail stores considered shopping convenience from the perspective of product assortment, store location, and store hours. On the Internet, by contrast, a customer can get to a very wide assortment on a single retailer's site or by clicking from one website to another. Product assortment on the Internet can be almost unlimited. And of course online stores are open 24 hours a day 7 days a week.

The Internet makes shopping inconvenient in other ways however. You have to plan ahead. When you buy something, you've actually just ordered it and you have to wait for delivery. Online retailers are trying to overcome these disadvantages with faster shipping. It started with low-cost two-day shipping, then one-day shipping became more reasonable. Now some online retailers offer same-day delivery.

Online retailers use big data to personalize shopping

Online retailers have lots of information on their customers' shopping behavior. For example, an online retailer can see just how customers move through its website, what information about each product is being consumed (do they watch videos or read reviews?), what competitive products are considered, and what (if anything) is ultimately purchased. Cookies (small data files placed on a customer's computer) can even tell a retailer what a shopper does at a competitor's site and pull information from a customer's Facebook page. All those data offer a retailer a great deal of insight into each of its customers.

The ability to collect and analyze big data in real time (while customers are shopping) gives online retailers the opportunity to provide a more personalized shopping experience. So for example, a customer known to have shopped at a competitor's site might be seen as a "price-oriented shopper" and could receive a targeted discount. Knowing that a customer previously purchased a sweater from the store, an online retailer might show more sweaters of a similar style on the front page when the customer returns. When a customer shops for a DVD at Amazon.com, the site makes recommendations for other videos based on that customer's previous purchases and past purchases of movie buyers with similar interests. That intimate knowledge should make such recommendations more on-target and relevant. All of these activities provide customers with a shopping experience tailored to their needs and interests.

Shoppers go mobile with tablets and smartphones

As consumers get more comfortable with multichannel shopping, many access the Internet "on the go" with their mobile device. Physical retailers see an opportunity to leverage this trend with websites and apps that work with tablet computers and smartphones. For example, ShopRite Supermarkets developed an app for iPhone and Android that allows users to buy groceries, check out the weekly sales, manage their shopping lists, clip coupons, and discover new recipes. The

© Joseph P. Cannon Ph.D.

app also allows customers to shop from home; they can even scan items currently in their pantries, and then send their order to ShopRite for pickup or delivery. Shopping on mobile devices is a new consumer behavior, and leading retailers are watching closely for opportunities to develop services that enhance target customers' shopping experience.

Customers expect to use the larger screen on tablet computers differently from the way they use their smartphones. Retailers such as Amazon, IKEA, Fab, and Nordstrom have created tablet computer apps that turn traditional catalogs into more interactive experiences. Consumers appear to put their feet up, relax, and shop on their tablets. Many use the apps to discover new products or to gather information for future purchases. This creates a different shopping experience than sitting at a desk with a computer.

Retailers that figure out ways to provide target customers with improved shopping experiences on their tablets will grow sales.

Multichannel shoppers shop many stores but buy at only one

Some customers are **multichannel shoppers** who use different channels as they move through the purchase process. This can occur within the same retailer, like when a customer goes to Home Depot to buy an electronic light switch, and while standing at the shelf, pulls out their smartphone, opens the Home Depot site, and reads reviews of the product. Another a multichannel shopper seeking a new tennis racquet might read customer reviews of the Wilson Blade tennis racquet at The-Tennis-Store.com, go to a pro shop at a local tennis club to hit some balls with the Blade, and then ultimately purchase the tennis racquet at a steep discount from another online retailer.

Multichannel shopping can cause problems for retailers. When consumers go to a brick-and-mortar store to inspect a product (a showroom) and then purchase from an online retailer with a lower price, this practice is called *showrooming*. Smartphone apps make the practice easy, allowing customers to scan products in a retail store and then see prices from across the web. As online stores offer more information to consumers, the trend has started flowing in the other direction. Many shoppers are now *webrooming*—gathering information at an online store and then purchasing at the brick-and-mortar store. Unfortunately, the only retailer making money on this shopping trip is the one the customer buys from, not the others from whom the customer gleaned information along the purchase journey.[22]

> ### Online Toolkit
>
> The Amazon App for iPhone (and Android) allows a shopper in a physical store to scan a product's bar code and then check prices for the product at Amazon.com. Go to Amazon's website and read about this app (**http://tinyurl.com/4qdw9bt**). How will this type of application affect retailers and their marketing mix decisions? Which types of stores will see Amazon App as a threat? How is this an opportunity for Amazon.com?

The seamless multichannel shopping experience

Many brick-and-mortar retailers view these trends—shopping on mobile devices and webrooming—as an opportunity. Some brick-and-mortar retailers are using their physical stores as a source of competitive advantage. These retailers use a strategy called omnichannel. **Omnichannel** is a multichannel selling approach where a single retailer provides a seamless customer shopping experience from desktop computer, mobile device, telephone, or brick-and-mortar store. We talked about multichannel distribution in Chapter 10, and omnichannel is an example of multichannel with a high level of coordination across the channels.

So for example, when an online shopper at Crate & Barrel's website moves from desktop to mobile device—anything placed in the cart while on a smartphone will still be there when they open the site on their desktop computer. Websites for Best Buy and Home Depot allow customers to view the actual inventory of particular items at a local store—customers know what is in stock before they arrive. Both stores let customers buy online and pick up in the store. Omnichannel strategies are winning over multi-channel shoppers.[23]

Why Retailers Evolve and Change

LO 12.5

The Internet and online shopping and the competitive threat it poses to traditional retailing has been a big motivator of change in retailing. In this section, we discuss some broader retailing trends and consider how technology influences the in-store shopping experience.

The wheel of retailing keeps rolling

The **wheel of retailing theory** says that new types of retailers enter the market as low-status, low-margin, low-price operators and then, if successful, evolve into more conventional retailers offering more services with higher operating costs and higher prices. Then they're threatened by new low-status, low-margin, low-price retailers—and the wheel turns again. Department stores, supermarkets, and mass-merchandisers went through this cycle. Some Internet sellers are on this path.

The wheel of retailing theory doesn't explain all major retailing developments. Vending machines enter as high-cost, high-margin operations. Convenience food stores are high-priced. Suburban shopping centers don't emphasize low price.

Scrambled merchandising—mixing product lines for higher profits

Conventional retailers tend to specialize by product line. But many modern retailers are moving toward **scrambled merchandising**—carrying any product lines they think they can sell profitably. Supermarkets and drugstores sell anything they can move in volume—panty hose, phone cards, one-hour photo processing, motor oil, potted plants, and computer software. Mass-merchandisers don't just sell everyday items but also cell phones, computer printers, and jewelry.[24]

Product life-cycle concept applies to retailer types too

A retailer with a new idea may have big profits—for a while. But if it's a really good idea, the retailer can count on speedy imitation and a squeeze on profits. Other retailers will copy the new format or scramble their product mix to sell products that offer them higher margins or faster turnover. That puts pressure on the original firm to change or lose its market.

Some conventional retailers are in decline as these life and death cycles continue. Recent innovators, like the Internet merchants, are still in the market growth stage (see Exhibit 12–6). Some retailing formats that are mature in the United States are only now beginning to grow in other countries.

Technology drives retail evolution

Retailers are also using technology to enhance the in-store shopping experience—and this is motivating further evolution and change in retailing. You can read more about that in "*What's Next?* Technology derives strategy changes in brick-and-mortar retail."

Ethical issues for retailers

Let's look more closely at the ethical challenges that emerge from these new technologies and other retail practices. As you read in our discussion of online retailing and in the *What's Next?* box, retailers gather and use information to offer customers a

Exhibit 12–6 Retailer Life Cycles—Timing and Years to Market Maturity

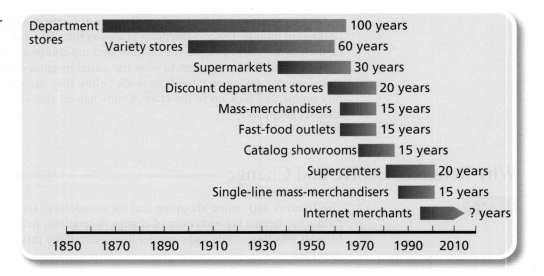

Department stores	100 years
Variety stores	60 years
Supermarkets	30 years
Discount department stores	20 years
Mass-merchandisers	15 years
Fast-food outlets	15 years
Catalog showrooms	15 years
Supercenters	20 years
Single-line mass-merchandisers	15 years
Internet merchants	? years

1850   1870   1890   1910   1930   1950   1970   1990   2010

What's Next? Technology drives strategy changes in brick-and-mortar retail

Technology has often fueled evolution in retail. We have already seen how the Internet and the collection and analysis of customers' online activity are changing retailing. Brick-and-mortar retail stores are also leveraging technology to improve the in-store shopping experience. To get an idea of where in-store retailing might be heading next, let's take a look at some leaders in this area.

Kroger is a forerunner in the use of technology to enhance the customer shopping experience. A few years ago, the average wait in a checkout line at its supermarkets was four minutes. Then Kroger installed special infrared cameras at each store entrance and above cash registers. A computer algorithm interprets the camera data and software automatically signals a manager when more than two customers are waiting in line. The store manager can then open additional checkout lanes—and the home office monitors service levels at every Kroger store. Average wait time fell to less than 30 seconds.

Walmart is testing a different way to keep customers out of lines. Its "Scan & Go" program lets customers scan bar codes of items while they shop—putting them right into bags already in their shopping cart. At the self-checkout lane, they simply wave their iPhone at the screen, wirelessly pay, and walk out the door. Starbucks' smartphone app lets customers skip the line altogether. With Order Ahead, a customer places an order and indicates the time they want to pick it up. Payment occurs automatically through the app.

In-store tracking provides retailers with information useful for store layout, merchandising, and sales promotion. Some stores utilize video cameras, others use sensors or track cell phones to monitor customer movement around stores. Jeweler Alex & Ani learned where customers lingered longer and which items were picked up most often—leading to changes in product placement. Other retailers are testing targeted promotions based on tracking data. For example, a customer who has visited a store three times without making a purchase might be targeted with a 10 percent off coupon.

Other retailers are enhancing the in-store experience with technology. Designer Rebecca Minkoff's new stores in New York and San Francisco provide a glimpse into the future. Customers can browse merchandise on an oversized touchscreen, tapping to request specific items and sizes to try on. A text message lets a customer know when the items are waiting in a fitting room. Inside the fitting room, customers tap a touchscreen mirror to request further assistance or additional merchandise. Sales clerks tote iPads that allow them to respond to customer requests or to check out anywhere in the store.

Technologies that save customers money or time, or create a more pleasant in-store shopping experience, are changing the future of shopping. Consider a McDonald's restaurant and a college bookstore—how could some of the ideas discussed above be used to improve customer experiences at each of these locales? What other technologies could they employ?[25]

---

more personalized shopping experience, which appears consistent with the marketing concept. But is it ethical to monitor customers' shopping behavior without their knowledge? Do retailers need customers' permission? Does it depend on how this information is used?

Most retailers face intense competitive pressure. The desperation that comes with such pressure has pushed some retailers toward questionable marketing practices.

Critics argue, for example, that retailers too often advertise special sale items to bring price-sensitive shoppers into the store or to a website but then don't stock enough to meet demand. Other retailers are criticized for pushing consumers to trade up to more expensive items. What is ethical and unethical in situations like these, however, is subject to debate. Retailers can't always anticipate demand perfectly, and deliveries may not arrive on time. Similarly, trading up may be a sensible part of a strategy—if it's done honestly.

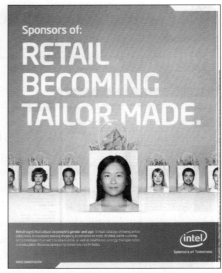

Many retailers use technology to enhance the shopping experience. In South Korea, Homeplus wanted to expand its market share without the high cost of opening new stores. So Homeplus placed "virtual stores" in subway stations in Korean cities. The stores have no actual stock, only images with QR codes. On their way home from work, customers scan the QR codes of items they wish to purchase. Shortly after they arrive home, their order is delivered. Intel is working on developing signage that recognizes the age and gender of customers standing in front of its signs. The signs can then display messages tailored to each customer.
Left: Rex Features via AP Images.; Right: © Intel Corporation.

The marketing concept should guide firms away from unethical treatment of customers. However, a retailer on the edge of going out of business may lose perspective on the need to satisfy customers in both the short and the long term.[26]

Differences in Retailing in Different Nations

LO 12.6

New ideas spread across countries

Mass-merchandising requires mass markets

New retailing approaches that succeed in one part of the world are often quickly adapted to other countries. Self-service approaches that started with supermarkets in the United States are now found in retail operations worldwide. The supercenter concept, on the other hand, initially developed in Europe.

The low prices, selections, and efficient operations offered by mass-merchandisers might be attractive to consumers everywhere, but consumers in less-developed nations often don't have the income to support mass distribution. The small shops that survive in these economies sell in very small quantities, often to a small number of consumers.

Coca-Cola's desire to put its products "within an arm's reach of desire" anywhere in the world requires selling through a variety of different retail channels.
Left: © Joel Rafkin/PhotoEdit.; Middle: Photo by Marco Di Lauro/Getty Images.; Right: AP Photo/Peter Morgan.

Retailers moving to international markets must adapt marketing strategies

Slow growth at home has prompted some large retail chains to move into international markets. They think that the competitive advantages that worked well in one market can provide a similar advantage in another country. But legal and cultural differences in international markets can make success difficult. Despite success in Latin America and Canada, Walmart has struggled in Germany and Japan. Similarly, French mass-merchandiser Carrefour expanded in Europe and South America, but its U.S. stores failed and it experienced legal problems in Indonesia.

Other retailers, such as California-based My Dollarstore, have successfully adapted for quick international growth. My Dollarstore franchises the "dollar store" concept worldwide and adapts its marketing strategy to local markets. In India, the price of each product is 99 rupees or about two dollars. Dollar stores in the United States target lower-income consumers, but in India the "Made in America" label attracts many higher-income consumers. Initially the merchandise in the Indian stores was the same as in U.S. stores. However, My Dollarstore quickly discovered what sold (Hershey's syrup is a hit) and what didn't (papaya and carrot juice). It also offered money-back guarantees, an unusual practice in India. Adaptations like these helped entice consumers into My Dollarstore's Indian franchises.[28]

Online retailing varies across nations

Online shopping behavior, and therefore online retailing, varies considerably across countries. For example, in the United Kingdom about half of all consumers regularly purchase online, whereas in emerging markets online sales are almost nonexistent. The most obvious prerequisite for online retailing is access to the Internet—in particular, broadband (fast) connections. Chapter 3 discussed technology and the uneven adoption of the Internet and mobile phones across the globe. A reliable national postal system (lacking in many countries) is also needed for delivering online purchases.

Even when infrastructure is in place, cultural factors influence preferences for online shopping. For example, a European study of 20,000 clothing shoppers identified seven segments based on their shopping needs. One segment, nicknamed "time-pressed optimizers," was particularly interested in online shopping. With very busy lives, this group had less time for in-store shopping so they sought the best possible product by doing research online. Yet only 3 percent of Italian shoppers and 6 percent of French shoppers fell into this segment—as compared to 16 percent of Brits and 18 percent of Germans. Another segment, "price-oriented bargain hunters," enjoyed going to many stores and rummaging to find bargain merchandise. This group was most common in Italy (31 percent of shoppers), and helps to explain why only about 10 percent of Italians regularly purchased online.[29]

What Is a Wholesaler?

LO 12.7

It's hard to define what a wholesaler is because there are so many different wholesalers doing different jobs. Some of their activities may even seem like manufacturing. As a result, some wholesalers describe themselves as "manufacturer and dealer." Some like to identify themselves with such general terms as *merchant, agent, dealer,* or *distributor.* And others just take the name commonly used in their trade—without really thinking about what it means.

To avoid a long technical discussion on the nature of wholesaling, we'll use the U.S. Census Bureau definition:

Wholesaling is concerned with the *activities* of those persons or establishments that sell to retailers and other merchants, or to industrial, institutional, and commercial users, but that do not sell in large amounts to final consumers. So **wholesalers** are firms whose main function is providing wholesaling activities. Wholesalers sell to all of the different types of organizational customers described in Chapter 6.

Wholesaling activities are just variations of the basic marketing functions—gathering and providing information, buying and selling, grading, storing, transporting, financing, and risk taking—we discussed in Chapter 1. You can understand wholesalers' strategies better if you look at them as members of channels. They add value by doing jobs for their customers and for their suppliers.

> ### Online Toolkit
>
> China-based Alibaba is the world's largest B2B trading platform for small businesses. Go to the Alibaba website (**www.alibaba.com**). Search for an "iPhone case." Check out three different cases. What are the prices for each? What are the minimum order quantities? Notice the Response Rate information to the right of many cases—click on the rate. How much of an impact do you think this has on the decision to buy? Then look around at other product categories. What kinds of business product classes (see Exhibit 8-7) do you think Alibaba would best support?

Wholesaling Is Changing with the Times

A hundred years ago wholesalers dominated distribution channels in the United States and most other countries. The many small producers and small retailers needed their services. This situation still exists in less-developed economies.

Wholesaling is in decline

However, in developed nations, as producers became larger many bypassed the wholesalers. Cost-conscious buyers at some large retail chains, including Walmart and Lowe's, even refuse to deal with some wholesalers who represent small producers. Efficient delivery services from UPS and FedEx make it easier for many producers to ship directly to their customers, even those in foreign markets. The Internet also puts pressure on wholesalers whose primary role is providing information to bring buyers and sellers together. These factors

With permission of Fear No Fruit Productions.

have combined to decrease the number of wholesalers in the United States; there are about 400,000 wholesalers today—following a steady decline over the last 20 years.

Opportunities remain for progressive wholesalers

Those that have survived are adapting their marketing strategies and finding new ways to add value in the channel. Progressive wholesalers are becoming more concerned with their customers and with channel systems. Many are using technology to offer better service. Some of the biggest B2B e-commerce sites on the Internet are wholesaler operations, and many wholesalers are enjoying significant growth. Others develop voluntary chains that bind them more closely to their customers.

Frieda's, Inc., is a good example; it is a wholesaler that each year supplies supermarkets and food-service distributors with $30 million worth of exotic fruits and vegetables. It was started by Frieda Caplan in 1962; today her daughters Karen and Jackie run the company. It is a sign of the marketing savvy of these women that artichokes, Chinese donut peaches, alfalfa sprouts, and spaghetti squash no longer seem very exotic. All of these crops were once viewed as unusual. Few farmers grew them, supermarkets didn't handle them, and consumers didn't know about them. Caplan helped to change all of that. She realized that some supermarkets wanted to attract less price-sensitive consumers who preferred more interesting choices in the hard-to-manage produce department. So she looked for products that would help her retailer-customers meet this need. For example, the funny looking kiwi fruit with its fuzzy brown skin was popular in New Zealand but virtually unknown to U.S. consumers. Caplan worked with small farmer-producers to ensure that she could provide her retailer-customers with a steady supply. She packaged kiwi with interesting recipes and promoted it to consumers. Because of her efforts, demand has grown and most supermarkets now carry kiwi. That has attracted competition from larger wholesalers. But that doesn't bother the Caplans. When one of their specialty items becomes a commodity with low profit margins, another novel item replaces it. In a typical year, Frieda's introduces about 40 new products—such as Asian pears, kiwano melons, sun-dried yellow tomatoes, and hot Asian chiles.

Frieda's also has an advantage because of the special services it provides. It was the first wholesaler to routinely use airfreight for orders and send produce managers a weekly "hot sheet" about the best sellers. The Caplans also use seminars and press releases to inform produce buyers about how to improve sales. For example, one attention-getting story about Frieda's "El Mercado de Frieda" line helped retailers do a better job serving Hispanic customers. Similarly, Frieda's website attracts final consumers with helpful tips and recipes. And now that more consumers are eating out, Frieda's has established a separate division to serve the special needs of food-service distributors.[30]

Wholesalers need to add value

Progressive wholesalers need to be efficient, but that doesn't mean they all have low costs. Some wholesalers' higher operating expenses result from the strategies they select, including the special services they offer to some customers. Let's look more closely at different types of wholesalers and the different ways they add value to channels of distribution.

Wholesalers Add Value in Different Ways

LO 12.8

Exhibit 12–7 compares the number, sales volume, and costs of some major types of wholesalers. The differences in operating costs suggest that each of these types performs, or does not perform, certain wholesaling functions. But which ones and why? And why do manufacturers use merchant wholesalers—costing 13.1 percent of sales—when agent wholesalers cost only 3.7 percent?

To answer these questions, we must understand what these wholesalers do and don't do. Exhibit 12–8 gives a big-picture view of the major types of wholesalers we'll be

Exhibit 12-7 U.S. Wholesale Trade by Type of Wholesale Operation

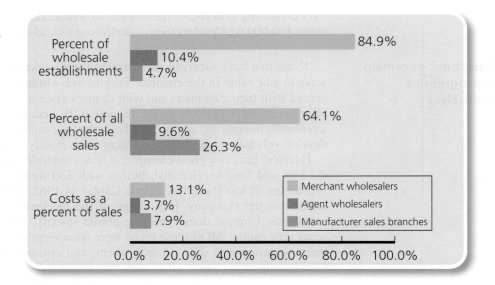

Percent of wholesale establishments: 84.9%, 10.4%, 4.7%

Percent of all wholesale sales: 64.1%, 9.6%, 26.3%

Costs as a percent of sales: 13.1%, 3.7%, 7.9%

Merchant wholesalers
Agent wholesalers
Manufacturer sales branches

0.0% 20.0% 40.0% 60.0% 80.0% 100.0%

discussing. There are lots more specialized types, but our discussion will give you a sense of the diversity. Note that a major difference between merchant and agent wholesalers is whether they *own* the products they sell. Before discussing these wholesalers, we'll briefly consider producers who handle their own wholesaling activities.

Manufacturers' sales branches are considered wholesalers

Manufacturers who just take over some wholesaling activities are not considered wholesalers. However, when they have **manufacturers' sales branches**—warehouses that producers set up at separate locations away from their factories—they're classified as wholesalers by the U.S. Census Bureau and by government agencies in many other countries.

In the United States, these manufacturer-owned branch operations account for about 4.7 percent of wholesale facilities—but they handle 26.3 percent of total wholesale sales. One reason sales per branch are so high is that the branches are usually placed in

Exhibit 12-8 Types of Wholesalers

Does wholesaler own the products?

Yes (merchant wholesalers)

No (agent wholesalers)

How many functions does the wholesaler provide?

Agent wholesalers
Auction companies
Brokers
Manufacturers' agents
Selling agents

All the functions

Some functions

Service merchant wholesaler
General merchandise wholesalers (or mill supply houses)
Single-line or general-line wholesalers
Specialty wholesalers

Limited-function merchant wholesaler
Cash-and-carry wholesalers
Drop-shippers
Truck wholesalers
Rack jobbers
Catalog wholesalers

the best market areas. This also helps explain why their operating costs, as a percent of sales, are often lower. It's also easier for a manufacturer to coordinate information and logistics functions with its own branch operations than with independent wholesalers.[31]

Merchant Wholesalers Are the Most Numerous

Merchant wholesalers own (take title to) the products they sell. They often specialize by certain types of products or customers. For example, Fastenal is a wholesaler that specializes in distributing threaded fasteners used by a variety of manufacturers. It owns (takes title to) the fasteners for some period before selling to its customers. If you think all merchant wholesalers are fading away, Fastenal is proof that they can serve a needed role. In the last decade Fastenal's profits have grown at about the same pace as Microsoft's.[32]

Exhibit 12–7 shows that almost 85 percent of the wholesaling establishments in the United States are merchant wholesalers—and they handle more than 64 percent of wholesale sales. Merchant wholesalers are even more common in other countries. Japan is an extreme example. Products are often bought and sold by a series of merchant wholesalers on their way to the business user or retailer.[33]

Service wholesalers provide all the functions

Service wholesalers are merchant wholesalers that provide all the wholesaling functions. Within this basic group are three types: (1) general merchandise, (2) single-line, and (3) specialty.

General merchandise wholesalers are service wholesalers that carry a wide variety of nonperishable items such as hardware, electrical supplies, furniture, drugs, cosmetics, and automobile equipment. With their broad line of convenience and shopping products, they serve hardware stores, drugstores, and small department stores. *Mill supply houses* operate in a similar way, but they carry a broad variety of accessories and supplies to serve the needs of manufacturers.

Single-line (or general-line) wholesalers are service wholesalers that carry a narrower line of merchandise than general merchandise wholesalers. For example, they might carry only food, apparel, or certain types of industrial tools or supplies. In consumer products, they serve the single- and limited-line stores. In business products, they cover a wider geographic area and offer more specialized service.

Specialty wholesalers are service wholesalers that carry a very narrow range of products and offer more information and service than other service wholesalers. For example, a firm that produces specialized lights for vehicles might rely on specialty wholesalers to help reach automakers in different countries. A consumer products specialty wholesaler might carry only health foods instead of a full line of groceries. Some limited-line and specialty wholesalers are growing by helping independent retailer-customers compete with mass-merchandisers. But in general, many consumer-products wholesalers have been hit hard by the growth of retail chains that set up their own distribution centers and deal directly with producers.

A specialty wholesaler of business products might limit itself to fields requiring special technical knowledge or service. Richardson Electronics is an interesting example. One of its specialties is in distributing replacement parts, such as electron tubes, for old equipment that many manufacturers still use on the factory floor. Richardson describes itself as "on the trailing edge of technology," but many of its customers operate in countries where new technologies are not yet common. Richardson gives them easy access to information from its website (www.rell.com) and makes its products available quickly by stocking them in locations around the world.[34]

Limited-function wholesalers provide some functions

Limited-function wholesalers provide only *some* wholesaling functions. In the following paragraphs, we briefly discuss the main features of these wholesalers. Although less numerous in some countries, these wholesalers are very important for some products.

Cash-and-carry wholesalers want cash

Cash-and-carry wholesalers operate like service wholesalers—except that the customer must pay cash. In the United States, big warehouse clubs have taken much of this business. But cash-and-carry operators are common in less-developed nations where very small retailers handle the bulk of retail transactions. Full-service wholesalers often refuse to grant credit to small businesses that may have trouble paying their bills.

Drop-shippers do not handle the products

Drop-shippers own (take title to) the products they sell—but they do *not* actually handle, stock, or deliver them. These wholesalers are mainly involved in selling. They get orders and pass them on to producers. Then the producer ships the order directly to the customer. Drop-shippers commonly sell bulky products (like lumber) for which additional handling would be expensive and possibly damaging. Drop-shippers in the United States are already feeling the squeeze from buyers and sellers connecting directly via the Internet. But the progressive ones are fighting back by setting up their own websites and getting fees for referrals.

Truck wholesalers deliver—at a cost

Truck wholesalers specialize in delivering products that they stock in their own trucks. Their big advantage is that they promptly deliver perishable products that regular wholesalers prefer not to carry. A 7-Eleven store that runs out of potato chips on a busy Friday night doesn't want to be out of stock all weekend! They help retailers keep a tight rein on inventory, and they seem to meet a need.

Rack jobbers sell hard-to-handle assortments

Rack jobbers specialize in hard-to-handle assortments of products that a retailer doesn't want to manage—and rack jobbers usually display the products on their own wire racks. For example, a grocery store or mass-merchandiser might rely on a rack jobber to decide which paperback books or magazines it sells. The wholesaler knows which titles sell in the local area and applies that knowledge in many stores.

Catalog wholesalers reach outlying areas

Catalog wholesalers sell through catalogs that may be distributed widely to smaller industrial customers or to retailers that might not be called on by other wholesalers. Customers place orders at a website or by mail, e-mail, fax, or telephone. These wholesalers sell lines such as hardware, jewelry, sporting goods, and computers. For example, Inmac uses a catalog that is printed in six languages and a website (www.inmac.com) to sell a complete line of computer accessories. Many of its customers don't have a local wholesaler, but they can place orders from anywhere in the world. Most catalog wholesalers quickly adapted to the Internet. It fits what they were already doing and makes it easier. But they're facing more competition too; the Internet allows customers to compare prices from more sources of supply.[35]

Agents Are Strong on Selling

They don't own the products

Agent wholesalers are wholesalers who do *not* own the products they sell. Their main purpose is to help in buying and selling. Agent wholesalers normally specialize by customer type and by product or product line. But they usually provide even fewer functions than the limited-function wholesalers. They operate at relatively low cost—sometimes 2 to 6 percent of their selling price—or less in the case of website–based agents who simply bring buyers and sellers together.

They are important in international trade

Agents are common in international trade. Many markets have only a few well-financed merchant wholesalers. The best many producers can do is get local representation through agents and then arrange financing through banks that specialize in international trade.

Agent wholesalers are usually experts on local business customs and regulations in their own countries. Sometimes a marketing manager can't work through a foreign government's red tape without the help of a local agent.

Manufacturers' agents provide selling expertise

A **manufacturers' agent** sells similar products for several noncompeting producers—for a commission on what is actually sold. Such agents work almost as members of each company's sales force, but they're really independent wholesalers. More than half of all agent wholesalers are manufacturers' agents. Their big plus is that they already call on some customers and can add another product line at relatively low cost—and at no cost to the producer until something sells! If an area's sales potential is low, a company may use a manufacturers' agent because the agent can do the job at low cost. Small producers often use agents everywhere because their sales volume is too small to justify their own sales force.

Agents can be especially useful for introducing new products. For this service, they may earn 10 to 15 percent commission. (In contrast, their commission on large-volume established products may be quite low—perhaps only 2 percent.) A 10 to 15 percent commission rate may seem small for a new product with low sales. Once a product sells well, however, a producer may think the rate is high and begin using its own sales reps.

Electronic Manufacturers' Agents is a company of manufacturers' agents that represents 20 different suppliers of electronics parts. EMA reps make sales calls on customers in the southeastern United States.
Photo courtesy of Joseph Sandusky/EMA.

Export and import agents are experts in international trade

Export or **import agents** are basically manufacturers' agents who specialize in international trade. These agent wholesalers operate in every country and help international firms adjust to unfamiliar market conditions in foreign countries.

Manufacturers' reps will continue to play an important role in businesses that need an agent to perform order-getting tasks. But manufacturers' reps everywhere

330

are feeling pressure when it comes to routine business contacts. More producers are turning to telephone selling, websites, e-mail, teleconferencing, and faxes to contact customers directly.[36]

Brokers offer market information and knowledge

Brokers bring buyers and sellers together. Brokers usually have a *temporary* relationship with the buyer and seller while a particular deal is negotiated. They are especially useful when buyers and sellers don't come into the market very often. The broker's product is information about what buyers need and what supplies are available. If the transaction is completed, they earn a commission from whichever party hired them. **Export** and **import brokers** operate like other brokers, but they specialize in bringing together buyers and sellers from different countries. Smart brokers quickly saw new opportunities to expand their reach by using the Internet. As the Internet causes consolidation, it will also provide more value. A smaller number of cyberbrokers will cut costs and dominate the business with larger databases of buyers and sellers.

Selling agents—almost marketing managers

Selling agents take over the whole marketing job of producers—not just the selling function. A selling agent may handle the entire output of one or more producers, even competing producers, with almost complete control of pricing, selling, and advertising. In effect, the agent becomes each producer's marketing manager.

Financial trouble is one of the main reasons a producer calls in a selling

IronPlanet uses auctions to connect buyers and sellers of used heavy equipment such as cranes, tractors, and trucks.
Copyright © 1999–2015 IronPlanet, Inc. All Rights Reserved.

agent. The selling agent may provide working capital and may also take over the affairs of the business. But selling agents also work internationally. A **combination export manager** is a blend of manufacturers' agent and selling agent—handling the entire export function for several producers of similar but noncompeting lines.

Auction companies speed up the sale

Auction companies provide a place where buyers and sellers can come together and bid to complete a transaction. Traditionally they were important in certain lines—such as livestock, fur, tobacco, and used cars—where demand and supply conditions change rapidly.

CONCLUSION

In this chapter, we explored evolving approaches to retailing and wholesaling. We also examined how marketers are finding an efficient and effective balance of technology and the personal touch that works for their target markets.

Modern retailing is scrambled—and we'll see more changes in the future. In such a dynamic environment, a producer's marketing manager must choose carefully among the available kinds of retailers. And retailers must plan their marketing mixes with target customers' needs in mind—while becoming part of an effective channel system.

There are many different types of retailers, each offering different marketing mixes to appeal to different target customers. Lower margins and faster turnover are the modern philosophy for mass-merchandisers, but this is no guarantee of success as retailers' life cycles move on. Online retailing is growing quickly, and many physical retailers include the Internet in their marketing mixes.

Retailing tends to evolve in predictable patterns—and we discussed the wheel of retailing theory to help understand this. But the growth of chains and scrambled merchandising continues, as retailing evolves to meet changing consumer demands.

Wholesalers can provide functions for those both above and below them in a channel of distribution. These services are closely related to the basic marketing functions. There are many types of wholesalers. Some provide all the wholesaling functions—whereas others specialize in only a few. Eliminating wholesalers does not eliminate the need for the functions they now provide, but technology is helping firms to perform these functions in more efficient ways.

Despite predictions that the Internet would eliminate the "middleman," wholesalers continue to exist. The more progressive ones are adapting to a changing environment. But some less-progressive wholesalers will fail. On the other hand, new types of intermediaries are evolving. Some are creating new ways of helping producers and their customers achieve their objectives by finding new ways to add value.

One thing is certain, the evolving Internet and yet-to-emerge technologies won't allow marketers to rest on their laurels. Successes will be short-lived as retail and wholesale competitors keep looking for new ways to satisfy customer needs. The most agile retailers and wholesalers are the most likely to survive.

WHAT'S NOW?

This chapter examined the nature of retailing and wholesaling. Whereas wholesaling changes rather slowly, there are many changes going on in retailing. For some current real-world examples and learnings, check out *What's Now?* at www.learnthe4ps.com/whatsnow/c12

KEY TERMS

retailing, 308

corporate chain, 308

franchise operation, 308

general stores, 311

single-line stores, 312

limited-line stores, 312

specialty shop, 312

department stores, 313

mass-merchandising concept, 313

supermarkets, 313

discount houses, 313

mass-merchandisers, 314

supercenters (hypermarkets), 314

convenience (food) stores, 315

automatic vending, 315

door-to-door selling, 315

multichannel shoppers, 319

omnichannel, 319

wheel of retailing theory, 320

scrambled merchandising, 320

wholesaling, 324

wholesalers, 324

manufacturers' sales branches, 326

merchant wholesalers, 327

service wholesalers, 327

general merchandise wholesalers, 327

single-line (or general-line) wholesalers, 327

specialty wholesalers, 327

limited-function wholesalers, 327

cash-and-carry wholesalers, 328

drop-shippers, 328

truck wholesalers, 328

rack jobbers, 328

catalog wholesalers, 328

agent wholesalers, 329

manufacturers' agent, 329

export agents, 329

import agents, 329

brokers, 330

export brokers, 330

import brokers, 330

selling agents, 330

combination export manager, 330

auction companies, 330

QUESTIONS AND PROBLEMS

1. Review the Macy's case study that opens the chapter. From this case, identify examples of different key terms and concepts covered in the chapter. For example, Macy's is an example of a department store.

2. Review the Macy's case study that opens this chapter. Go to the Macys.com website and consider the discussion in this chapter of online retailing and omnichannel. What else could Macy's do to improve its online and offline shopping experience for customers.

3. Compare and contrast the marketing mix and target market for a bike shop in your community with the online bicycle retailer Performance Bicycle (www.performancebike.com).

Use your best judgment to identify each retailer's primary target market and some of its Product, Place, Promotion, and Price decisions.

4. What sort of a "product" are specialty shops offering? What are the prospects for organizing a chain of specialty shops?

5. Distinguish among discount houses, price-cutting by conventional retailers, and mass-merchandising. Forecast the future of low-price selling in food, clothing, and appliances. How will the Internet affect that future?

6. Discuss a few changes in the market environment that you think help to explain why telephone, mail-order, and Internet retailing have been growing so rapidly.

7. What are some advantages and disadvantages to using the Internet for shopping?

8. Apply the wheel of retailing theory to your local community. What changes seem likely? Will established retailers see the need for change, or will entirely new firms have to develop?

9. What advantages does a retail chain have over a retailer who operates with a single store? Does a small retailer have any advantages in competing against a chain? Explain your answer.

10. Many producers are now seeking new opportunities in international markets. Are the opportunities for international expansion equally good for retailers? Explain your answer.

11. Discuss how computer systems affect wholesalers' and retailers' operations.

12. Consider the evolution of wholesaling in relation to the evolution of retailing. List several changes that are similar and several that are fundamentally different.

13. Do wholesalers and retailers need to worry about new-product planning just as a producer needs to have an organized new-product development process? Explain your answer.

14. How do you think a retailer of Maytag washing machines would react if Maytag set up a website, sold direct to consumers, and shipped direct from its distribution center? Explain your thinking.

15. What risks do merchant wholesalers assume by taking title to goods? Is the size of this risk about constant for all merchant wholesalers?

16. Why would a manufacturer set up its own sales branches if established wholesalers were already available?

17. What is an agent wholesaler's marketing mix?

18. Why do you think that many merchant wholesalers handle competing products from different producers, whereas manufacturers' agents usually handle only noncompeting products from different producers?

19. What alternatives does a producer have if it is trying to expand distribution in a foreign market and finds that the best existing merchant wholesalers won't handle imported products?

20. Discuss the future growth and nature of wholesaling if chains, scrambled merchandising, and the Internet continue to become more important. How will wholesalers have to adjust their mixes? Will wholesalers be eliminated? If not, what wholesaling functions will be most important? Are there any particular lines of trade where wholesalers may have increasing difficulty?

MARKETING PLANNING FOR HILLSIDE VETERINARY CLINIC

Appendix D (the Appendices follow Chapter 19) includes a sample marketing plan for Hillside Veterinary Clinic. Look through the "Marketing Strategy" section.

a. What kind of retail operation is the vet clinic? Does it fit any of the types described in this chapter?

b. How could Hillside make use of a website?

c. The marketing plan notes future plans to offer kennel (boarding) services and pet supplies. How will this change Hillside's current strategy? Does the marketing plan provide a good sense of what needs to be done? Do you have other recommendations for Hillside?

SUGGESTED CASES

11. Run Free

12. DrV.com—Custom Vitamins

14. Schrock and Oh

15. The Olentangy Group

16. Tall Timber Lumber Supply

Video Case 2. Bass Pro Shops

Video Case 5. Suburban Regional Shopping Malls

MARKETING ANALYTICS: DATA TO KNOWLEDGE

CHAPTER 12: SELECTING CHANNEL INTERMEDIARIES

Art Glass Productions, a producer of decorative glass gift items, wants to expand into a new territory. Managers at Art Glass know that unit sales in the new territory will be affected by consumer response to the products. But sales will also be affected by which combination of wholesalers and retailers Art Glass selects. There is a choice between two wholesalers. One wholesaler, Giftware Distributing, is a merchant wholesaler that specializes in gift items; it sells to gift shops, department stores, and some mass-merchandisers.

The other wholesaler, Margaret Degan & Associates, is a manufacturers' agent who calls on many of the gift shops in the territory.

Art Glass makes a variety of glass items, but the cost of making an item is usually about the same—$5.20 a unit. The items would sell to Giftware Distributing at $12.00 each—and in turn the merchant wholesaler's price to retailers would be $14.00—leaving Giftware with a $2.00 markup to cover costs and profit. Giftware Distributing is the only reputable merchant wholesaler in the territory, and it has agreed to carry the line only if Art

Glass is willing to advertise in a trade magazine aimed at retail buyers for gift items. These ads will cost $8,000 a year.

As a manufacturers' agent, Margaret Degan would cover all of her own expenses and would earn 8 percent of the $14.00 price per unit charged the gift shops. Individual orders would be shipped directly to the retail gift shops by Art Glass, using United Parcel Service (UPS). Art Glass would pay the UPS charges at an average cost of $2.00 per item. In contrast, Giftware Distributing would anticipate demand and place larger orders in advance. This would reduce the shipping costs, which Art Glass would pay, to about $.60 a unit.

Art Glass' marketing manager thinks that Degan would be able to sell only about 75 percent as many items as Giftware Distributing—since she doesn't have time to call on all of the smaller shops and doesn't call on any department stores. On the other hand, the merchant wholesaler's demand for $8,000 worth of supporting advertising requires a significant outlay.

The marketing manager at Art Glass decided to use a spreadsheet to determine how large sales would have to be to make it more profitable to work with Giftware and to see how the different channel arrangements would contribute to profits at different sales levels.

See Connect for the spreadsheet and questions needed to analyze this scenario.

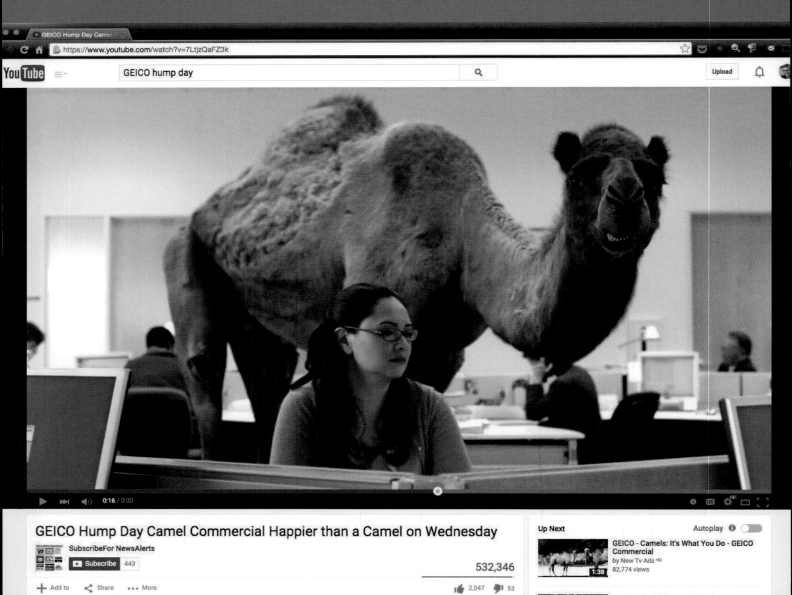

GEICO Hump Day Camel

C https://www.youtube.com/watch?v=7LtjzQaFZ3k

You Tube ☰ ·   GEICO hump day   🔍   Upload   🔔

0:16 / 0:30

GEICO Hump Day Camel Commercial Happier than a Camel on Wednesday

SubscribeFor NewsAlerts

▶ Subscribe 443   532,346

➕ Add to   ⬐ Share   ••• More   👍 2,047   👎 53

Up Next   Autoplay ⓘ ⬤

GEICO - Camels: It's What You Do - GEICO
Commercial
by New Tv Ads HD
1:38   82,774 views

Camel - The Opening Farewell

Promotion—Introduction to Integrated Marketing Communications

Back in the 1930s, in the depths of the Great Depression, Leo and Lillian Goodwin started the Government Employees Insurance Company—GEICO. GEICO kept operating costs low by selling auto insurance only to two low-risk target markets: federal employees and military personnel. GEICO passed the savings on in the form of lower premiums—and sales steadily grew for decades.

After becoming a wholly-owned subsidiary of Berkshire Hathaway in 1996, GEICO's management sought to accelerate earnings growth by targeting new markets. However, getting growth in the mature auto insurance market meant that GEICO would need to take customers away from better known competitors such as Allstate and State Farm. As if that wasn't difficult enough, many prospects didn't even know about GEICO. Ted Ward, GEICO's vice president of marketing, discussed this situation with the firm's ad agency, The Martin Agency of Richmond, Virginia. Together they decided that an aggressive advertising campaign could achieve the objectives of increasing awareness of GEICO and bringing in new customers.

The GEICO campaign that emerged used an animated, talking lizard to help get attention and communicate the firm's message. In the first commercial, the charming reptile with the British accent stated, "I am a gecko, not to be confused with GEICO, which could save you hundreds on car insurance. So stop calling me!" The humorous ads quickly generated awareness and interest among target customers, many of whom had never heard of GEICO. The original plan was for the Gecko campaign to run for a short time, but research said customers loved the Gecko, and he continues to be an important part of GEICO's image and promotions.

GEICO wants customers to know it offers good value—great car insurance at low prices. But to prove this, customers have to reach out for a price quote. It's quick and easy to get a quote at GEICO's website, so to spur the target audience to action, GEICO ads remind them that "15 minutes could save you 15 percent or more on car insurance." GEICO likes to have a variety of ads—and has had talking pigs and camels (remember "hump day"?) star in its funny television ads. GEICO also posts many of its ads on YouTube—where ads play immediately before videos. YouTube lets customers skip those videos after watching for five seconds—so GEICO makes sure its ads got the point across in those first five seconds—before customers skip over it.

Although GEICO aims for its target market with advertising, it knows that many customers interested in insurance start the information gathering process on their own. GEICO knows when people type "auto insurance" into Google, they are probably looking to buy insurance. GEICO uses various techniques to make sure GEICO.com appears near the top of the organic search results. Just in case customers don't see that, it also pays for a sponsored link (advertisement) assuring that GEICO will join other ads at the side of the search results. Clicking on a link in the search results lands them on a page that asks for their ZIP code, the first step toward getting a price quote from GEICO. Or they can look at the GEICO.com website to learn more about the company and its portfolio of insurance products.

All this promotion helped make GEICO a familiar name, but many insurance buyers still want to talk to a real person before deciding what to do. These customers can visit with a GEICO salesperson at one of its local offices or call GEICO's toll-free number and talk on the phone with an inside sales rep. GEICO selects capable salespeople who are licensed insurance agents, and then trains them to develop an understanding of each customer's needs and concerns so that the agents can then explain GEICO's benefits to the customer in a persuasive way.

Of course, GEICO seeks to build an ongoing relationship with customers after they sign up for a policy. Regular contacts and updates are handled with promotional e-mails. Customers can call a GEICO salesperson to learn more about other GEICO products, such as less familiar umbrella insurance policies. Later, if a customer who purchases a policy has a problem, GEICO's highly rated customer service team works quickly to resolve it.

Current GEICO customers also visit its website. The website is a type of "owned media"—GEICO owns and manages it—unlike television or radio advertising that GEICO pays to access. GEICO.com uses the website to engage with its customers and continue communication after the sale. At GEICO.com, customers can manage and update their policy or make an insurance claim. They can also learn more about GEICO's other insurance products, various discounts, local gas prices, and more. The site also links to GEICO's social media pages.

GEICO uses social media to build relationships with its current customers and connect with potential new customers. GEICO maintains a blog, a YouTube channel, Flickr photostream, Instagram, and Pinterest pinboards. Its most popular social media tool is its Facebook page, which more than 400,000 people have "liked"—though some customers prefer the Gecko's personal Facebook page. The Facebook page lets customers see the latest television ads and photos of the Gecko. Customers can also "like" or "share" an ad or other post with their own Facebook friends. A potential customer is more likely to consider GEICO when they have seen a friend "like" the brand.

GEICO's promotion brings together advertising, personal selling, and online

media; in combination, they help GEICO acquire and retain customers. That recipe—along with a great product—has moved GEICO from less than a 3 percent share of the auto insurance market in 1996 to more than a 10 percent share and the industry's #2 position today.[1]

LEARNING OBJECTIVES

As the GEICO example shows, there are many decisions that a marketing manager must make concerning Promotion, and it is an important part of marketing strategy planning. Marketing managers usually blend a variety of different promotion methods to achieve promotion objectives because each method has its own strengths and limitations. In this chapter we introduce the major promotion options and how to integrate them into an effective whole.

When you finish this chapter, you should be able to

1 Know the advantages and disadvantages of the promotion methods a marketing manager can use in strategy planning.

2 Understand the integrated marketing communications concept and why firms use a blend of different promotion methods.

3 Understand the importance of promotion objectives.

4 Know how the traditional communication process affects promotion planning.

5 Understand how customer-initiated interactive communication is different.

6 Know how typical promotion plans are blended to get an extra push from wholesalers and retailers, as well as help from customers in pulling products through the channel.

7 Understand how promotion blends typically vary over the adoption curve and product life cycle.

8 Understand how to determine how much to spend on promotion efforts.

9 Understand important new terms (shown in red).

Promotion Communicates to Target Markets

LO 13.1

Promotion is communicating information between the seller and potential buyer or others in the channel to influence attitudes and behavior. The promotion part of the marketing mix involves telling target customers that the right Product is available at the right Place at the right Price. Just as Promotion must be fine-tuned for a specific target market, it must fit with the other variables of the marketing mix and reinforce the strategy's differentiation and positioning.

This is the first of four chapters that discuss issues pertinent to Promotion. We begin with an overview of the major promotion methods. Marketing managers can choose from several basic types of promotion: personal selling, mass selling, sales promotion, and publicity (see Exhibit 13–1). Because these methods have different strengths and limitations, a marketing manager typically uses them in combination to achieve specific objectives. We also discuss the specialists who are involved in managing

Exhibit 13-1 Promotion and Marketing Strategy Planning

| Chapter 13 Promotion—Introduction to Integrated Marketing Communications | Chapter 14 Personal Selling and Customer Service | Chapter 15 Advertising and Sales Promotion | Chapter 16 Publicity: Promotion Using Owned Media, Earned Media, and Social Media |

Promotion methods	**Managing promotion**	**Effective communication**	**Blending promotion**

• Personal selling and customer service
• Mass selling
  • Advertising
  • Publicity
• Sales promotion
	• Promotion managers
	• Integrated marketing communications
	• Objectives drive decisions
		• Traditional communication process
		• Customer-initiated communication process
			• Push and pull
			• Adoption processes
			• Product life cycle
			• Budget setting

different types of promotion and why it is important for them to work together as a team. This chapter also provides models that will help you understand how communication works—including when companies broadcast information to target markets and when target customers seek information on their own. Finally, we look at some concepts that help marketing managers develop the best promotion blend.

In Chapter 14, we take a closer look at the important promotion strategy decisions marketing and sales managers make in personal selling and customer service. Chapter 15 provides a closer look at advertising and sales promotion—two forms of mass selling. Chapter 16 examines publicity, which may occur through a range of nontraditional media.

In this chapter we'll go into some detail about the different promotion methods—a key challenge for marketing managers is how best to blend them. So it's helpful to begin with a brief overview of the promotion methods available.

Several Promotion Methods Are Available

Personal selling—flexibility is its strength

Personal selling involves direct spoken communication between sellers and potential customers. Customer service is a form of personal communication between a customer and seller to resolve a problem with a purchase. Salespeople get immediate feedback, which helps them to adapt. Although some personal selling is included in most marketing mixes, it can be very expensive. So it's often desirable to combine personal selling with mass selling and sales promotion.

Everyone loves free snacks, so it's not surprising that many customers engaged with McDonald's outdoor ad. Customers use their cell phone to snap a picture of a particular snack (on this day a sundae), then they bring the photo to the nearby McDonald's for their reward. Sales promotion activities like this stimulate consumer interest and trial.

Mass selling involves advertising and publicity

Mass selling is communicating with large numbers of potential customers at the same time. It's less flexible than personal selling, but when the target market is large and scattered, mass selling can be less expensive.

Advertising is a primary form of mass selling. **Advertising** is any *paid* form of non-personal presentation of ideas, goods, or services by an identified sponsor. It includes the use of traditional media such as magazines, newspapers, radio and TV, signs, and direct mail as well as new media such as the Internet. Marketing managers pay for advertising to be placed on specific media, but another form of mass selling doesn't involve paying media costs.

Publicity avoids media costs

Publicity is any *unpaid* form of nonpersonal presentation of ideas, goods, or services. Of course, publicity people are paid. But they try to attract attention to the firm and its offerings *without having to pay media costs.* Publicity includes a wide range of different types of media: a company's website and the material it posts on the website, viral videos, word-of-mouth communication, a company's Facebook page, and its "tweets" on Twitter. It can also include coverage it receives in the press—for example when a movie is reviewed in the newspaper.

Sales promotion tries to spark immediate interest

Sales promotion refers to promotion activities—other than advertising, publicity, and personal selling—that stimulate interest, trial, or purchase by final customers or others in the channel. Sales promotion may be aimed at consumers, at intermediaries, or at a firm's own employees. Examples include contests and coupons aimed at consumers, trade shows or calendars for wholesalers or retailers, or sales contests and meetings aimed at a company's own sales force. Relative to other promotion methods, sales promotion can usually be implemented quickly and get results sooner. In fact, most sales promotion efforts are designed to produce immediate results.

Less is spent on advertising than personal selling or sales promotion

Many people incorrectly believe that promotion money gets spent primarily on advertising—because advertising is all around them. But all the special sales promotions—coupons, sweepstakes, trade shows, and the like—add up to even more money. Similarly, much personal selling goes on in the channels and in other business markets. In total, firms spend less money on advertising than on personal selling or sales promotion.

Someone Must Plan, Integrate, and Manage the Promotion Blend

LO 13.2

Each promotion method has its own strengths and weaknesses. In combination, they complement one another. Each method also involves its own distinct activities and requires different types of expertise. As a result, it's usually the responsibility of specialists—such as sales managers, advertising managers, sales promotion managers, public relations, and social media managers—to develop and implement the detailed plans for the various parts of the overall promotion blend.

Sales managers manage salespeople

Sales managers are concerned with managing personal selling. Often the sales manager is responsible for building good distribution channels and implementing Place policies. In smaller companies, the sales manager may also act as the marketing manager and be responsible for advertising and sales promotion.

Advertising managers work with ads and agencies

Advertising managers manage their company's mass-selling effort—in television, newspapers, magazines, and other media. Their job is choosing the right media and developing the ads. Advertising may be handled in-house, by departments existing within the firms, or it may be contracted to outside advertising agencies.

Sales promotion managers need many talents

Sales promotion managers manage their company's sales promotion effort. In some companies, a sales promotion manager has independent status and reports directly to the marketing manager. If a firm's sales promotion spending is substantial, it probably *should* have a specific sales promotion manager. Sometimes, however, the sales or advertising departments handle sales promotion efforts—or sales promotion is left as a responsibility of individual brand managers. Regardless of who the manager is, sales promotion activities vary so much that many firms use both inside and outside specialists.

Publicity may be managed by many

An advertising manager may handle publicity, but in larger firms there may be someone who manages **public relations**—communication with noncustomers, including the press, labor, public interest groups, stockholders, and the government. A *social media manager* may be in charge of a company's social media (Facebook page, Twitter feed, LinkedIn page, etc.) and possibly its website. Any of these jobs may be outsourced—though a firm that manages public relations probably differs from one that manages social media or a firm's website.

Marketing manager talks to all, blends all

Although many specialists may be involved in planning for and implementing specific promotion methods, determining the blend of promotion methods is a strategy decision—and it is the responsibility of the *marketing manager*. With all of the promotion options, determining the best blend is a challenging responsibility.

The marketing manager must weigh the pros and cons of the various promotion methods and then devise an effective promotion blend—fitting in the various departments and personalities and coordinating their efforts. Then the advertising, sales, and sales promotion managers should develop the details consistent with what the marketing manager wants to accomplish.

> ## Online Toolkit
>
> Adweek sponsors a blog titled *AdFreak* (**www. adfreak.com**), which makes daily posts with the "best and worst of advertising, branding, and design." Go to this page and check out three recent posts. How could regularly reading this blog help an advertising or social media manager?

In China, Pepsi depends on a blend of integrated marketing communications, including in-store sampling, outdoor advertising, and web-based publicity. The web page shown here promotes the "Pepsi Soccer Carnival" on Tencent, China's most popular social media site. Soccer fans can play online games, gamble, and use instant messaging to win prizes such as virtual "cans" of Pepsi and phone calls from soccer stars such as Jose Torres and Didier Drogba.
Top: © 2015 PEPSICO, INC; Bottom Left: Photo by China Photos/Getty Images; Bottom Right: Photo by Adrian Bradshaw/Getty Images.

Send a consistent and complete message with integrated marketing communications

Effective blending of all of the firm's promotion efforts should produce **integrated marketing communications**—the intentional coordination of every communication from a firm to a target customer to convey a consistent and complete message.

The GEICO case at the start of this chapter is a good example of integrated marketing communications. Different promotion methods handle different parts of the job. Yet the methods are coordinated so that the sum is greater than the parts. The separate messages are complementary, but also consistent.

It seems obvious that a firm's different communications to a target market should be consistent. However, when a number of different people are working on different promotion elements, they are likely to see the same big picture only if a marketing manager ensures that it happens. Getting consistency is harder when different firms handle different aspects of the promotion effort. For example, different firms in the channel may have conflicting objectives.

To get effective coordination, everyone involved with the promotion effort must clearly understand the plan for the overall marketing strategy. They all need to understand how each promotion method will contribute to achieve specific promotion objectives.[2]

Which Methods to Use Depends on Promotion Objectives

`LO 13.3`

Overall objective is to affect behavior

A marketing manager usually has to set priorities for the promotion objectives. The ultimate objective is to encourage customers to choose a *specific* product. However, which promotion objectives are of highest priority will depend on the market situation and target market. For example, as we saw in Chapters 5 and 6, customers often move along a step-by-step buying path—and the path may differ for different types of purchases. Sometimes customers are familiar with the product and sometimes it is completely new to them. Objectives should be guided by what we know about target customers. In this section, we discuss different types of promotion objectives and tie them to frameworks describing the purchase process.

Informing, persuading, and reminding are basic promotion objectives

Promotion objectives must be clearly defined—because the right promotion blend depends on what the firm wants to accomplish. It's helpful to think of three basic promotion objectives: *informing, persuading,* and *reminding* target customers about the company and its marketing mix. All try to affect buyer behavior by providing customers with information.

It's also useful to set more specific promotion objectives that state *exactly whom* you want to inform, persuade, or remind, and *why*. This is unique to each company's strategy—and specific objectives vary by promotion method. We'll talk about more specific promotion objectives in Chapters 14, 15, and 16. Here we'll focus on the three basic promotion objectives and then link them to the adoption process and a new model.

Informing is educating

Potential customers must know something about a product if they are to buy it. A firm with a really new product may not have to do anything but inform consumers of the product's features and benefits. An *informing* objective can show that it meets consumer needs better than other products can. Imagine a customer moving to a new town with an interest in joining a health club where he can work out. A health club might place brochures in local apartment complexes or run ads in the newspaper to let target customers know about the features at its facility. A small business might want to have a service regularly clean its offices. The owner might begin by searching on the Internet. There she might find a local cleaning company's website with information about various services.

Persuading usually becomes necessary

When competitors offer similar products, the firm must not only inform customers that its product is available but also persuade them to buy it. A *persuading* objective means the firm will try to develop a favorable set of attitudes so customers will buy, and keep buying, its product. A persuading objective often tries to demonstrate how one brand is better than others. To convince consumers to buy Brawny paper towels, ads show Brawny as the towel that's best for tough cleanup jobs. A salesperson for Andersen Windows tries to convince homebuilders about the quality and affordability of Andersen Windows as compared to those of a competitor, so the builder chooses Andersen for future housing projects.

The Boston Celtics Instagram page *reminds* fans of their favorite team.

Reminding may be enough

If target customers already have positive attitudes about a firm's marketing mix—or a good relationship with a firm—a *reminding* objective might be suitable. Customers who have been attracted and sold once are still targets for competitors' appeals. Reminding them of their past satisfaction may keep them from shifting to a competitor. An accountant working for a small local firm might phone her customers once every few months to "check in" and see if they have any questions. This serves as a reminder that the accountant is there and available.

Promotion objectives relate to adoption processes

In Chapter 5, we looked at consumer buying as a step-by-step problem-solving process through which buyers go on the way to adopting (or rejecting) an idea or product. The three basic promotion objectives relate to these steps. See the first two columns in Exhibit 13–2. *Informing* and *persuading* may be needed to affect the potential customer's knowledge and attitudes about a product and then bring about its adoption. Later, promotion can simply *remind* the customer about that favorable experience and confirm the adoption decision.

The AIDA model is a practical approach

The basic promotion objectives and adoption process fit very neatly with another action-oriented model—called AIDA—that we will use in this chapter and in Chapters 14 and 15 to guide some of our discussion. The **AIDA model** consists of four promotion jobs: (1) to get *Attention,* (2) to hold *Interest,* (3) to arouse *Desire,* and (4) to obtain *Action.*

The last two columns in Exhibit 13–2 show the relationship of the promotion objectives and adoption process to the AIDA jobs. Getting attention is necessary to make consumers aware of the company's offering. Holding interest gives the communication a chance to build the consumer's interest in the product. Arousing desire affects the evaluation process, perhaps building preference. And obtaining

Exhibit 13–2
Relation of Promotion Objectives, Adoption Process, and AIDA Model

Promotion Objectives	Adoption Process	AIDA Model
Informing	{ Awareness Interest	Attention Interest
Persuading	Evaluation Trial }	Desire
Reminding	Decision Confirmation }	Action

What's Next? Once upon a time...

Does telling a story work? A study found that Super Bowl ads following a classic story pattern—exposition, rising action, climax, falling action, denouement (resolution)—were more popular than those that did not. Budweiser's "Lost Dog" Super Bowl ad followed this story arc. Watch the ad at: https://youtu.be/xAsjRRMMg_Q. The ad begins on a ranch, showing the connection between a puppy and one of the Budweiser Clydesdale horses (exposition). When the puppy gets lost in the city, the rancher worries and posts "lost dog" posters (rising action). The puppy journeys toward home but with the ranch in the distance, we see a wolf stalking the pup (more rising action). Back at the ranch, the Clydesdales hear the pup, so they escape the barn, coming to our puppy's rescue (climax). The Clydesdales and puppy run home together (falling action) and the muddy puppy gets a bath (denouement). That one-minute story won the *USA Today Super Bowl Admeter*—a survey of viewers—and generated attention and interest for Budweiser.

Other stories get customers' interest because they explain how a company solves problems. Louisville Slugger makes baseball bats—but its brand purpose is "to make players great." Louisville Slugger's origin story goes back to 1884. That's when seventeen-year-old Bud Hillerich, a fan of the Louisville Eclipse baseball club, brought the team's star player, Pete Browning, to Bud's father's woodworking shop.

Browning, stuck in a hitting slump, had broken his bat, and Bud offered to make him a new one. The next day Browning had three hits, and a legend—and a new business—was born.

Lifebuoy soap uses story to focus people on an important problem. Each year diarrhea and pneumonia claim the lives of two million kids before they reach age five. Research shows that regular hand-washing with soap significantly cuts the risk of diarrhea and infection. Lifebuoy soap wanted to try to get this message to people in third-world countries, so it created its "Help a Child Reach 5" campaign. As a demonstration, Lifebuoy adopted the Indian village Thesgora and showed how hand-washing lowered diarrhea from 36 percent to 5 percent. Lifebuoy created a three-minute video story (see https://youtu.be/UF7oU_YSbBQ) showing a father walking on his hands through town to a religious shrine to offer thanks. We then see that this is his son's fifth birthday—and that his previous children had never reached this milestone. This is also the Lifebuoy story—the essence of the brand—that hand-washing saves lives.

Stories that resonate with target markets catch attention and interest—and help them remember a brand's message. Describe a story your college or university could tell that might resonate with prospective students. How could that story be turned into a short television ad or YouTube video?[3]

Home improvement retailer Lowe's uses different promotions to achieve different objectives. "Lowe's Fix in Six" uses the social media tool Vine to post 6-second how-to videos that *educate* customers. This one shows customers how to use a rubber band on a stripped screw. For more tips, search the hash tag "#lowesfixinsix." When the promotion objective is *reminding*, Lowe's billboards remind customers of projects they need to complete.

action includes gaining trial, which may lead to a purchase decision. Continuing promotion is needed to confirm the decision and encourage an ongoing relationship and additional purchases.

British marketers for Pampers disposable diapers generated attention and interest with TV ads that showed the world from a baby's perspective. To encourage desire and action, they used creative in-store and point-of-purchase advertising. For example, on the doors of restrooms with baby-changing facilities, fake door knobs were placed unreachably high, with the message: "Babies have to stretch for things. That's why they like the extra stretchiness of Pampers Active fit." And on store shelves, in a play on babies' disobedient nature, pull-out Pampers information cards were marked "Do Not Pull."[4]

Good stories are another way to grab customer attention and hold their interest. In *"What's Next?* Once upon a time…" we can see how promotion that tells a story can have a happy ending.

Promotion Requires Effective Communication

LO 13.4

Communication starts with a trusted source and a receiver

Promotion is wasted when it doesn't communicate effectively. There are many reasons why a promotion message can be misunderstood or not heard at all. To understand this, it's useful to think about a whole **communication process**—which means a source trying to reach a receiver with a message. Exhibit 13–3 shows the elements of the communication process. Here we see that a **source**—the sender of a message—is trying to deliver a message to a **receiver**—a potential customer.

Customers evaluate the source of the message in terms of trustworthiness and credibility. For example, American Dental Association (ADA) studies show that Listerine mouthwash helps reduce plaque buildup on teeth. Listerine mentions the ADA endorsement in its promotion to help make the promotion message credible. If a salesperson (source) is not trusted, then the message being delivered will not be used by the receiver.

A major advantage of personal selling is that the source—the seller—can get immediate feedback from the receiver. It's easier to judge how the message is being received and to change it if necessary. Mass sellers usually must depend on marketing research or total sales figures for feedback—and that can take too long. Many marketers include toll-free telephone numbers and website addresses as ways of building direct-response feedback from consumers into their mass-selling efforts.

Noise distracts the message

The **noise**—shown in Exhibit 13–3—is any distraction that reduces the effectiveness of the communication process. Conversations and snack-getting during TV ads

Exhibit 13-3 The Traditional Communication Process

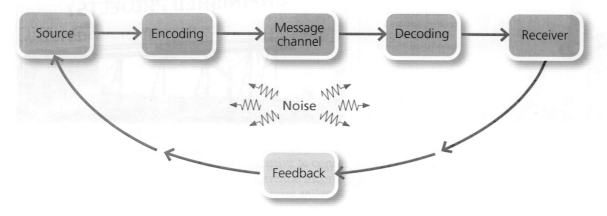

344

are noise. An industrial buyer reading a text message during a salesperson's presentation is noise. Advertisers who plan messages must recognize that many possible distractions—noise—can interfere with communications.

Encoding and decoding depend on a common frame of reference

The basic difficulty in the communication process occurs during encoding and decoding. **Encoding** is the source deciding what it wants to say and translating it into words or symbols that will have the same meaning to the receiver. **Decoding** is the receiver translating the message. This process can be very tricky. The meanings of various words and symbols may differ depending on the attitudes and experiences of the two groups. People need a common frame of reference to communicate effectively (see Exhibit 13–4).

Exhibit 13-4 This Same Message May Be Interpreted Differently

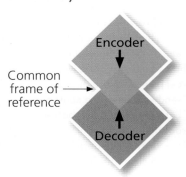

Maidenform encountered this problem with a promotion aimed at working women. The company ran a series of ads depicting female stockbrokers and doctors wearing Maidenform lingerie. The men in the ads were fully dressed. Maidenform was trying to encode the message that women worked in positions of authority, but some women decoded the message as portraying them as sex objects. In this case, the promotion people who encoded the message didn't understand the attitudes of the target market and how they would decode the message.[5]

The same message may be interpreted differently

Different audiences may interpret a message differently. Such differences are common in international marketing when cultural differences or translation are problems. In Taiwan, the translation of the Pepsi slogan "Come alive with the Pepsi Generation" came out as "Pepsi will bring your ancestors back from the dead." The Swedish brand Samarin thought it would avoid these problems with ads showing three simple drawings—and no words. The first picture shows a man holding his stomach in obvious pain, in the second he is drinking Samarin, and in the last he is smiling and happy. Worked great—except in the Middle East where people read from right to left. Uh oh! Many firms run into problems like this.[6]

Message channel is important too

The communication process is complicated even more because the message is coming from a source through some **message channel**—the carrier of the message. A source can use many message channels to deliver a message. The salesperson does it in person with voice and action. Advertising must do it with media such as magazines, TV, e-mail, or Internet websites. A particular message channel may enhance or detract from a message. A TV ad, for example, can *show* that Dawn dishwashing detergent "takes the grease away"; the same claim might not be convincing if it arrived in a consumer's e-mail.

Feedback takes many forms

The last element in the traditional communication process is *feedback*—communication from the receiver back to the source. Feedback may take many different forms: a customer may simply have a different attitude, seek more information, visit a store, or purchase the product. Objectives should state the desired feedback and marketing managers should measure whether the communication is having the anticipated response.

Integrated direct response seeks immediate feedback

Sometimes marketing managers want to get immediate feedback from *specific* customers. This prompts firms to turn to direct marketing—direct communication between a seller and an individual customer using a promotion method other than face-to-face personal selling. Most direct marketing communications are designed to prompt immediate feedback—a direct response—by customers. That's why this type of communication is often called *direct-response promotion.*

USG used a clever direct mailer to promote its Securock roofing material. On the outside is what looks like a brown-paper sandwich bag. The headline on the bag reads: "We've figured out how to make roofing work a real picnic." In the bag is a "sandwich" with the sentence: "Let the hands-down better roof board hand your crew a free lunch." The details on how to claim the free lunch are included. To get their meal, the roofers have to listen to a sales pitch, but this mailer has made it appetizing.
© 2015 USG Corporation.

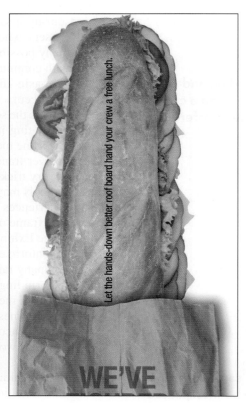

Direct mail and e-mail are two tools commonly used for direct-response promotion. A carefully selected mailing list—perhaps from the firm's customer relationship management (CRM) database—allows advertisers to reach customers with specific interests. For the best response, marketing managers carefully segment their customers and use mail or e-mail to deliver targeted messages.

E-mail can be low cost and targeted

Most customers use e-mail these days, and communicating via e-mail offers benefits to buyers and sellers. Sellers like the relatively low cost compared to direct mail. E-mails give customers a chance to click through to photos and videos. Media tools such as these help them decide whether to make a donation or place an order.

Of course getting to the message in the e-mail necessitates a customer opening the e-mail. Personalized and creative messages can get customers attention in a crowded e-mail inbox. To get opened, an e-mail subject line should grab target customers attention. For example, when a customer buys eyeglasses at Warby Parker, the retailer asks when the prescription expires. Two weeks before it expires, you get an e-mail with the subject line: "Uh-oh your prescription is expiring." This catches the reader's attention—the subject line is true—and increases the odds of the e-mail being opened.[7]

When Customers Initiate the Communication Process

LO 13.5

The traditional process in Exhibit 13–3 assumes that it's the seller ("source") who initiates communication. Let's look closer at another communication model, shown in Exhibit 13–5, where a customer ("receiver") initiates the communication process. For example, consumers google "pizza delivery" or ask retail salespeople for help, and organizational buyers phone salespeople to ask questions or request bids. The growth of the Internet makes it much easier for customers to initiate the information gathering

Exhibit 13-5
A Model of Customer-
Initiated Interactive
Communication

process, and more customers are doing just that. Although this process has many of the same components as the traditional process we considered earlier, the differences and implications for Promotion are significant.

Customer initiates communication with a search process

In the process in Exhibit 13–5, a customer (*receiver*) initiates communication with a decision to *search* for information in a particular message channel. The most common and far-reaching *message channel* used for information searching is the Internet—usually queried through a search engine such as Google or Bing and accessed by a personal computer, tablet, or cell phone. Sometimes a buyer immediately links to a particular seller's web page to seek out information. The message channel is still the carrier of the message, as was the case before, but searchable message channels usually feature an archive of existing messages on a number of topics. There may be many available topics—even millions.

Customer decides how much information to get

The receiver then reviews and screens the various options and decides which messages to pursue. A search engine returns a list of results that includes paid advertisements and free listings. A search can also occur at the website of a producer, retailer, or wholesaler. For example, a business customer may visit a distributor of janitorial supplies and search for industrial cleaning solutions—and then click on pricing information or perhaps the safety of the ingredients. Similarly, a consumer might visit Netflix and search for horror movies and then look for the director, actors, or the comments of people who have already seen the movie. The customer chooses the information of interest to her—not the marketing manager.

Marketers must grab attention to be selected

Because a customer now has so many options, it's important for a marketer to be among the first to grab that customer's attention. That means that an online retailer that sells golf gear wants to be near the top of the search results when someone searches for "Big Bertha golf," Callaway's popular line of golf clubs. In this case, the retailer can pay a search engine company to put a sponsored (advertising) link near the top of the list.

When the receiver looks more closely at the information on screen, he decides whether to stay or leave the site. Usually more information is just a click away—and that click can be to dig deeper into the marketer's site or to click away to another website. Marketing managers need to make sure that the page holds the receiver's interest or begins to arouse desire. Noise can still be a problem as well—and lead the searcher in a different direction. For example, a confusing website may make it difficult to figure out a retailer's return policy and discourage a customer from buying.

Understanding customers online search behavior helps brands develop websites that attract target customers. Polish women love to search for and share recipes—the best-selling magazine in Poland is all about recipe sharing. International food brand Knorr wanted to appear more local and trustworthy to Polish consumers, so it decided to become the country's best source of recipes and cooking ideas. Knorr found that the Polish word for recipe, "przepisy," was available as a URL. Knorr then built a branded website, a Facebook page, and mobile apps around recipe sharing. Whenever someone searches Google.pl for "przepisy" (recipe), Knorr's site comes up on top—helping to drive more traffic to the branded site. As online recipe sharing grows, so do visitors to the site. The average visitor spends almost 8 minutes on the site, the Facebook page has more than a half million "Likes," and the mobile app has been downloaded more than 300,000 times. Most important, the Knorr brand has closed the gap on its local competition with respect to trustworthiness and brand image.

Left: © M. Hruby; Right: © 2015 Unilever United States.

As this short scenario depicts, consumers can collect information from a wide range of sources before making purchase decisions. Although many of those are outside the control of a marketing manager, that doesn't mean those sources should be ignored. Marketing managers can still make sure that they have plenty of product pictures—and that they are easy to post on Pinterest and Instagram. They can also monitor what is being said about the brand online. Whereas online compliments let the firm know what it is doing well, complaints can highlight unmet customer needs—and give managers a chance to turn things around.

Promotion timing and relevance have an impact

Communication that customers receive during the customer-initiated communication process is usually timely—it often occurs when a customer is actively gathering purchase information. Consequently, customers more readily pay attention and are more likely to be interested in promotional information.

When customers surf the Internet, they often signal they are ready to make a purchase. For example, reading articles about different kinds of bicycles, visiting a couple of websites, and "Liking" the local bike shop on Facebook might all be indications of an impending bicycle purchase.

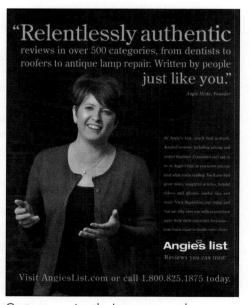

Customers using the Internet to gather information before making a purchase look for trusted, unbiased sources. Angie's List is a website that offers its subscribers access to consumer reviews of service providers such as plumbers, housekeepers, and family physicians.
© Copyright 1999–2014, Angie's List. All Rights Reserved.

There are companies that monitor and track consumers as they surf the web. Customers often leave telltale signs that they might be interested in buying certain products. Marketing managers can identify target customers interested in buying their products and deliver timely and relevant online (and offline) advertising to these customers.

Be ready for customers who initiate communication

When customers have the power to decide where to click next, marketing managers need to create a different kind of promotion. The first challenge is for marketing managers to figure out how to appear high on target customers' searches. Second, the marketing managers must have truly useful information—or customers will quickly click to something that will help them make a better purchase decision. And finally, promotion needs to keep them there to learn more about the seller's offering.

We will discuss specific tools that can be used when we cover publicity in Chapter 16. Until then, an example will demonstrate what we mean by capturing and retaining the inbound customer. The travel agency Discover Africa creates content that attracts customers to its website and keeps them coming back. Discover Africa started by identifying nine different target markets that it thought it could serve (for example, "Mr. Business," "The Campers," and "The Student/Backpacker"). Then Discover Africa created articles, videos, and travel guides for its website—each designed to appeal to one or more target groups. With a little outbound promotion of the discoverafrica.net website and its content, others started noticing and linking to the site. This helped discoverafrica.net appear near the top of online searches related to travel in Africa. Discover Africa was soon viewed as an authority on African travel, and sales began to climb.[8]

Online Toolkit

Reputation.com offers services to help companies and individuals monitor and manage their online reputations. Go to the company's website (**www.reputation.com**) and view the services it offers for businesses. What types of companies might find this service useful? Why? Is there any ethical issue with managing your online reputation? Why or why not?

Ethical issues in marketing communications

Promotion is one of the most frequently criticized areas of marketing. Many criticisms focus on whether communications are honest and fair. Marketers must sometimes make ethical judgments in considering these charges and in planning their promotion.

For example, we often look to the source of a communication to decide whether we believe it is credible. When a TV news program broadcasts a video publicity release, consumers don't know it was prepared to achieve marketing objectives. They think the news staff is the source. That may make the message more credible, but is it fair? Many say yes—as long as the publicity information is truthful. Similar concerns are raised about the use of celebrities in advertisements. A person who plays the role of an honest and trustworthy person on a popular TV series may be a credible message source in an ad, but is using such a person misleading to consumers? Some critics believe it is. Others argue that consumers recognize advertising when they see it and know celebrities are paid for their endorsements.

The most common criticisms of promotion relate to exaggerated claims. If an advertisement or a salesperson claims that a product is the "best available," is that just a personal opinion or should every statement be backed up by proof? What type of proof should be required? Some promotions do misrepresent the benefits of a product. Customers look to online reviews for objective opinions. What about posting fake favorable reviews for your company or its products—or negative reviews about a competitor? Real reviews offer a way for consumers to see beyond potential exaggerated claims. But if consumers feel that at least some reviews are phony, they may distrust all reviews. Some people believe that the Internet will eventually expose dishonest players in the market.

There are also issues related to consumer privacy. Most consumers are unaware that their web-surfing habits are being tracked. Many websites place "cookies" (electronic files) on a customer's computer so that when the customer revisits their site, the system "remembers" the customer. Although this sort of tracking offers them the potential benefit of more personalized communications, some consumers might want to remain anonymous.

Most marketing managers realize that the ultimate proof comes when the customer makes the purchase. Customers won't spread positive word-of-mouth or come back if the marketing mix doesn't deliver what the promotion promises. As a result, most marketing managers work to make promotion claims specific and believable.[9]

How Typical Promotion Plans Are Blended and Integrated

LO 13.6

There is no one right blend

Get a push in the channel with promotion to intermediaries

There is no one *right* promotion blend for all situations. Each one must be developed as part of a marketing mix and should be designed to achieve the firm's promotion objectives in each marketing strategy. So let's take a closer look at typical promotion blends in different situations.

When a channel of distribution involves intermediaries, their cooperation can be crucial to the success of the overall marketing strategy. **Pushing** (a product through a channel) means using normal promotion effort—personal selling, advertising, and sales promotion—to help sell the whole marketing mix to possible channel members. This approach emphasizes the importance of securing the wholehearted cooperation of channel members to promote the product in the channel and to the final user.

Producers usually take on much of the responsibility for the pushing effort in the channel. However, wholesalers often handle at least some of the promotion to retailers. Similarly, retailers often handle promotion in their local markets. The overall effort is most likely to be effective when all of the individual messages are carefully integrated.

Promotion to intermediaries emphasizes personal selling and sales promotion

Salespeople handle most of the important communication with wholesalers and retailers. These clients don't want empty promises. They want to know what they can expect in return for their cooperation and help. A salesperson can answer questions about what promotion will be directed toward the final consumer, each channel member's part in marketing the product, and important details on pricing, markups, promotion assistance, and allowances. A salesperson can also help the firm determine when it should adjust its marketing mix from one intermediary to another.

When suppliers offer similar products and compete for attention and shelf space, intermediaries usually pay attention to the one with the best profit potential. So sales promotions targeted at intermediaries usually focus on short-term arrangements that will improve the intermediary's profits. For example, a soft-drink bottler might offer a convenience store a free case of drinks with every two cases it buys. The free case improves the store's profit margin on the whole purchase.

Green Mountain Coffee uses both push and pull to support its coffees. Green Mountain's website and membership program promote a "Deal of the Week" directly to consumers. The ad on the right targets purchasing agents at grocery stores, letting them know that Green Mountain's family of brands will bring volume and profits to their stores.

Keurig Green Mountain, Inc. 33 Coffee Lane, Waterbury, VT. 05676 USA © 1999-2015 All rights reserved.

Firms run ads in trade magazines to recruit new intermediaries or to inform channel members about a new offering. Trade ads usually encourage intermediaries to contact the supplier for more information, and then a salesperson takes over.

Push within a firm—with promotion to employees

Some firms emphasize promotion to their own employees—especially salespeople or others in contact with customers. This type of *internal marketing* effort is basically a variation on the pushing approach. One objective of an annual sales meeting is to inform reps about important elements of the marketing strategy—so they'll work together as a team to implement it. Some firms use promotion to motivate employees to provide better customer service or achieve higher sales. This is typical in services where the quality of the employees' efforts is a big part of the product. For example, at one time, advertising for McDonald's used the theme "We love to see you smile." The ads communicate to customers but also remind employees that the service they provide is crucial to customer satisfaction.

Pulling policy—customer demand pulls the product through the channel

Most producers focus a significant amount of promotion on customers at the end of the channel. This helps to stimulate demand and pull the product through the channel of distribution. **Pulling** means getting customers to ask intermediaries for the product.

Pulling and pushing are usually used in combination (see Exhibit 13–6). However, if intermediaries won't work with a producer—perhaps because they're already carrying a competing brand—a producer may try to use a pulling approach by itself. This involves highly aggressive promotion to final consumers or users—perhaps using coupons or samples—temporarily bypassing intermediaries. If the promotion works, the intermediaries are forced to carry the product to satisfy customer requests. However, this approach is risky. Customers may lose interest before reluctant intermediaries make the product available. At a minimum, intermediaries should be told about the planned pulling effort—so they can be ready if the promotion succeeds.

Who handles promotion to final customers at the end of the channel varies in different channel systems, depending on the mix of pushing and pulling. Further, the promotion blend typically varies depending on whether customers are final consumers or business users.[10]

Exhibit 13-6 Promotion May Encourage Pushing in the Channel, Pulling by Customers, or Both

Promotion to final consumers

The large number of consumers almost forces producers of consumer products and retailers to emphasize advertising, publicity, and sales promotion. Sales promotion—such as coupons, contests, or free samples—builds consumer interest and short-term sales of a product. An informative website that includes customer reviews and video demonstrations helps customers build favorable impressions of a company and its products. Effective mass selling may build enough brand familiarity so that little personal selling is needed, as in self-service and discount operations.[11]

Personal selling can be effective too. Aggressive personal selling to final consumers usually is found in channel systems for expensive products, such as those for financial services, furniture, fine jewelry, consumer electronics, designer clothing, and automobiles.

Promotion to business customers

Producers and wholesalers that target business customers often emphasize personal selling. This is practical because there are fewer of these customers and their purchases are typically larger. Sales reps can be more flexible in adjusting their companies' appeals to suit each customer—and personal contact is usually required to close a sale. A salesperson is also able to call back later to follow up, resolve any problems, and nurture the relationship with the customer.

Although personal selling dominates in business markets, mass selling is necessary too. A typical sales call on a business customer costs about $500. That's because salespeople spend less than half their time actually selling. The rest is consumed by such tasks as traveling, paperwork, sales meetings, and strictly service calls. So it's seldom practical for salespeople to carry the whole promotion load.

Business buyers often engage in Internet search to identify solutions for current needs. So it's important for a seller's website to appear near the top of the search results. Otherwise, it has no opportunity to draw buyers' attention and build interest for the firm's products. Ads in trade magazines or at a B2B e-commerce website, for instance, can inform potential customers that a product is available. Most trade ads give a toll-free telephone number and an e-mail or website address to stimulate direct inquiries.

HP offers hardware, software, and consulting services to help firms with their information technology needs. As cloud computing grew in importance, HP wanted its customers to know HP could help them design a custom cloud computing solution. Ads and a direct mail brochure (complete with umbrella) drove customers to HP's website where they could find technical papers and sign up for HP Discovery Workshops and Cloud Roadmap services. The website also included an interactive feature that allowed users to literally create a cloud in any shape they wanted. HP's salespeople followed up on the leads in this integrated marketing comunications campaign.
© 2011 Hewlett-Packard Development Company, L.P.

Domestic and international trade shows also help identify prospects. Even so, most sellers who target business customers spend only a small percentage of their promotion budget on mass selling and sales promotion.

Each market segment may need a unique blend

Knowing what type of promotion is typically emphasized with different targets is useful in planning the promotion blend. But each unique market segment may need a separate marketing mix and a different promotion blend. You should be careful not to slip into a shotgun approach (using a single promotion across market segments) when what you really need is a rifle approach (a specific mix for a particular target market). This can result from too much combining, as discussed in Chapter 4.

Marketing managers blend push and pull activities because of the specific needs of those target markets. Another way to segment a market depends on where customers are in the adoption process, and we discuss these needs next.

Adoption Processes Can Guide Promotion Planning

LO 13.7

The AIDA and adoption processes look at individuals. This emphasis on individuals helps us understand how promotion affects the way that people behave. But it's also useful to look at markets as a whole. Different segments of customers within a market may behave differently—with some taking the lead in trying new products and, in turn, influencing others.

Promotion must vary for different adopter groups

Research on how markets accept new ideas has led to the adoption curve model. The **adoption curve** shows when different groups accept ideas. It emphasizes the relations among groups and shows that individuals in some groups act as leaders in

Exhibit 13-7 The Adoption Curve

| Innovators (3–5%) | Early adopters (10–15%) | Early majority (34%) | Late majority (34%) | Laggards or nonadopters (5–16%) |

Percent adoption

90

50

20

5
0

Time

accepting a new idea. Promotion efforts usually need to change over time to adjust to differences among the adopter groups.

Exhibit 13–7 shows the adoption curve for a typical successful product. Some of the important characteristics of each of these customer groups are discussed next. Which one are you? Does your group change for different products?

Innovators don't mind taking some risks

The **innovators** are the first to adopt. They are eager to try a new idea and willing to take risks. Innovators tend to be young and well educated. They are likely to be mobile and have many contacts outside their local social group and community. Business firms in the innovator group are often specialized and willing to take the risk of doing something new.

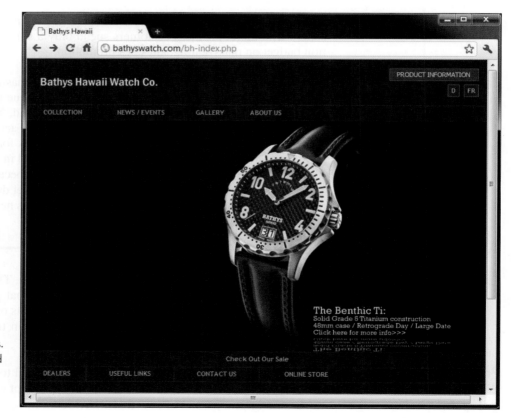

The website for Bathys Hawaii Watch Co. was getting about 60 hits a day until Gizmodo. com, a blog on new consumer technology that appeals to technology opinion leaders, wrote about the Bathys watch designed especially for surfers. After that, website hits jumped to 1,800 per day, and sales increased by 300 percent.
© 2008 Bathys Hawaii.

Innovators tend to rely on impersonal and scientific information sources, or other innovators, rather than salespeople. They often search for information on the Internet, read articles in technical publications, or look for informative ads in special-interest magazines.

Early adopters are often opinion leaders

Early adopters are well respected by their peers and often are opinion leaders. They tend to be younger, more mobile, and more creative than later adopters. But unlike innovators, they have fewer contacts outside their own social group or community. Business firms in this category also tend to be specialized.

Of all the groups, this one tends to have the greatest contact with salespeople. Mass media are important information sources too. Marketers should be very concerned with attracting and selling to the early adopter group. Their acceptance is crucial. The next group, the early majority, look to the early adopters for guidance. The early adopters can help the promotion effort by spreading *word-of-mouth* information and advice among other consumers.

Early majority group is deliberate

The **early majority** avoids risk and waits to consider a new idea after many early adopters have tried it—and liked it. Average-sized business firms that are less specialized often fit in this category. If successful companies in their industry adopt the new idea, they will too.

The early majority have a great deal of contact with mass media, salespeople, and early adopter opinion leaders. Members usually aren't opinion leaders themselves.

Late majority is cautious

The **late majority** is cautious about new ideas. Often they are older and more set in their ways, so they are less likely to follow early adopters. In fact, strong social pressure from their own peer group may be needed before they adopt a new product. Business firms in this group tend to be conservative, smaller-sized firms with little specialization.

The late majority makes little use of marketing sources of information—mass media and salespeople. They tend to be oriented more toward other late adopters rather than outside sources they don't trust.

Laggards or nonadopters hang on to tradition

Laggards or **nonadopters** prefer to do things the way they've been done in the past and are very suspicious of new ideas. They tend to be older and less well educated. The smallest businesses with the least specialization often fit this category. They cling to the status quo and think it's the safe way.

The main source of information for laggards is other laggards. This certainly is bad news for marketers. In fact, it may not pay to bother with this group.[12]

Promotion Blends Vary over the Product Life Cycle

Stage of product in its life cycle

The adoption curve helps explain why a new product goes through the product life-cycle stages described in Chapter 9. Promotion blends usually have to change to achieve different promotion objectives at different life-cycle stages.

Market introduction stage—"this new idea is good"

During market introduction, the basic promotion objective is informing. If the product is a really new idea, the promotion must build **primary demand**—demand for the general product idea—not just for the company's own brand. Rooftop solar panels and "smart" appliances (that connect to the Internet) are good examples of product concepts where primary demand is just beginning to grow. There may be few potential innovators during the introduction stage, and personal selling can help find them. Firms also need salespeople to find good channel members and persuade them to carry the new product. Sales promotion may be targeted at salespeople or channel members to get them interested in selling the new product. And sales promotion may also encourage customers to try it.

Market growth stage—"our brand is best"

In the market growth stage, more competitors enter the market, and promotion emphasis shifts from building primary demand to stimulating **selective demand**—demand for a company's own brand. The main job is to persuade customers to buy, and keep buying, the company's product.

Now that there are more potential customers, mass selling becomes more economical. But salespeople and personal selling must still work in the channels, expanding the number of outlets and cementing relationships with channel members.

The evolution of promotion for Banquet Homestyle Bakes illustrates these first two stages. When ConAgra Foods introduced Homestyle Bakes, it was the first shelf-stable meal kit with the meat already in the package. ConAgra, also the producer of Armour processed meats, had the expertise to create a tasty product that a consumer could prepare in a few minutes and then just stick in the oven. When Homestyle Bakes came out, there was no direct competition. The sales force used market research data to convince retailers to give the product shelf space, and ads used humor to highlight that the package was unusually heavy because it already included meat. However, over time new competition entered the market with similar offerings. So promotion shifted to emphasize why Homestyle Bakes was better, with a variety of new flavors and 10 percent more meat. Similarly, to keep customers interested in the Homestyle brand, the sales force shifted its efforts to get retailers to participate in Homestyle Bakes' "Super Meals/Super Moms" contests, which offered harried moms prizes such as a visit to a spa.[13]

Market maturity stage—"our brand is better, really"

In the market maturity stage, mass selling and sales promotion may dominate the promotion blends of consumer products firms. Business products may require more aggressive personal selling—perhaps supplemented by more advertising. The total dollars allocated to promotion may rise as competition increases.

If a firm already has high sales—relative to competitors—it may have a real advantage in promotion at this stage. For example, sales of Tylenol tablets are about four times the sales of Motrin competing tablets. If both Tylenol and Motrin spend the same percentage of sales (say 35 percent) on promotion, Tylenol will spend four times as much as its smaller competitor and will probably communicate to more people.

Strong brands may use promotion to remind customers about the product. For example, Oreo cookies is a strong brand. Devoted customers follow Oreo Cookie on Twitter and enjoy regular tweets and clever Vine videos. This Tweet includes a link to an Oreo-themed game and mouth-watering Oreo fun at PlayWithOreo.com.
© Mondelēz International. All Rights Reserved.

Firms that have differentiated their marketing mixes may favor mass selling because they have something to talk about. For instance, a firm with a strong brand may use reminder-type advertising or target frequent-buyer promotions at current customers to strengthen the relationship and keep customers loyal. This may be more effective than costly efforts to win customers away from competitors.

However, as a market drifts toward pure competition, some companies resort to price-cutting. This may temporarily increase the number of units sold, but it is also likely to reduce total revenue and the money available for promotion. The temporary sales gains disappear and prices are dragged down even lower when competitors retaliate with their own short-term sales promotions, like price-off coupons. As cash flowing into the business declines, spending may have to be cut back.[14]

In the market maturity stage, brands need to tell customers why their brand is better. Car batteries are a mature market, so Interstate lets target customers know its car batteries last a long time.
© 2015 Interstate Batteries.

Sales decline stage— "let's tell those who still want our product"

During the sales decline stage, the total amount spent on promotion usually decreases as firms try to cut costs to remain profitable. Because some people may still want the product, firms need more targeted promotion to reach these customers.

On the other hand, some firms may increase promotion to try to slow the cycle, at least temporarily. Crayola had almost all of the market for children's crayons, but sales were slowly declining as new kinds of markers came along. Crayola increased ad spending to urge parents to buy their kids a "fresh box."

Setting the Promotion Budget

LO 13.8

Size of budget affects promotion efficiency and blend

There are some economies of scale in promotion. An ad on national TV might cost less *per person* reached than an ad on local TV. Similarly, citywide radio, TV, and newspapers may be cheaper than neighborhood newspapers or direct personal contact. But the *total cost* for some mass media may force small firms, or those with small promotion budgets, to use promotion alternatives that are more expensive per contact. For example, a small retailer might want to use local television but finds that there is only enough money for a web page, an ad in the Yellow Pages, and an occasional newspaper ad.

Find the task, budget for it

The most common method of budgeting for promotion expenditures is to compute a percentage of either past sales or sales expected in the future. The virtue of this method is its simplicity. However, just because this mechanical approach is common doesn't mean that it's smart. It leads to expanding marketing expenditures when business is good and cutting back when business is poor. When business is poor, this approach may just make the problem worse—if weak promotion is the reason for declining sales.

In light of our continuing focus on planning marketing strategies to reach objectives, the most sensible approach to budgeting promotion expenditures is the **task method**—basing the budget on the job to be done. It helps a marketing manager to set priorities so that the money spent on promotion produces specific and desired

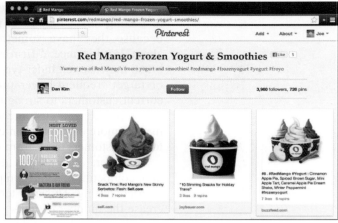

Red Mango is a frozen yogurt and smoothie brand. The brand uses social media as part of its promotion blend. With more than 700,000 "likes" on Facebook, Red Mango can communicate directly with fans through their Facebook newsfeeds. Red Mango also maintains a Pinterest account. While marketing managers like that there is little cost to put promotional messages and photos on these sites, they must remember to budget for the costs of maintaining these pages. Ongoing maintenance can be costly. The cost per person reached can be relatively low for a brand like Red Mango, with its large following. But for every brand with hundreds of thousands of followers, there are hundreds with less than a thousand followers.
Both images: © 2013 Red Mango, Inc

results. In fact, this approach makes sense for *any* marketing expenditure, but here we'll focus on promotion.

A practical approach is to determine which promotion methods are most economical and effective for the tasks that need to be completed to achieve communication objectives. The costs of these tasks are then totaled to determine how much should be budgeted for promotion (just as money is allocated for other marketing activities required by the strategy). In other words, the firm can assemble its total promotion budget directly from detailed plans rather than by simply relying on historical patterns or ratios.

Of course this makes the process sound simpler than it really is. Some promotion activities and objectives can be readily measured. Setting a target of adding 10,000 new "Likes" to Taco Bell's Facebook page and then offering discount coupons to each new "Like" is pretty straightforward. Taco Bell can measure the cost of the promotion (coupons plus any advertising) and the number of new "Likes" on the Facebook page. On the other hand, what if the objective is to change the level of brand familiarity of Bonobos pants for fashion-conscious men by running ads in select men's magazines? The results here can be more difficult to measure, but not impossible. Even when evaluation is difficult, marketing managers should still try to evaluate costs and returns to develop a realistic budget.[15]

CONCLUSION

Promotion is an important part of any marketing mix. Most consumers and intermediate customers can choose from among many products. To be successful, a producer must not only offer a good product at a reasonable price but also inform potential customers about the product and where they can buy it. Further, producers must tell wholesalers and retailers in the channel about their product and marketing mix. These intermediaries, in turn, must use promotion to reach their customers. And the promotion blend must fit with the rest of the marketing mix and the target market.

In this chapter, we introduced different promotion methods and we discussed the advantages and disadvantages of each method. We also discussed the integrated marketing communications concept and explained why most firms use a blend of different promotion methods. While the overall promotion objective is to affect buying behavior, the basic promotion objectives are informing, persuading, and reminding. These objectives help guide the marketing manager's decisions about the promotion blend.

Models from the behavioral sciences help us understand the communication process and how it can break down. These models recognize different ways to communicate. We discussed direct-response promotion for developing more targeted promotion blends. And we described an approach where customers initiate and interact with the marketer's communications. It provides new and different challenges for marketing managers.

This chapter also recognized other factors that influence decisions about promotion blends. Marketing managers must make decisions about how to split promotion that is directed at final consumers or business customers—and at channel members. Promotion blends are also influenced by the adoption curve and the product life-cycle stages. Finally, we described how promotion budgets are set and influence promotion decisions.

In this chapter, we considered some basic concepts that apply to all areas of promotion. In Chapters 14, 15, and 16 we'll discuss personal selling, customer service, advertising, publicity, and sales promotion in more detail.

WHAT'S NOW?

This chapter introduced different types of promotion. Promotion is one of the most interesting and fastest changing aspects of marketing. For some current real-world examples and learnings, check out *What's Now?* at www.learnthe4ps.com/whatsnow/c13

KEY TERMS

LO 13.9

promotion, 336

personal selling, 337

mass selling, 338

advertising, 338

publicity, 338

sales promotion, 338

sales managers, 339

advertising managers, 339

sales promotion managers, 339

public relations, 339

integrated marketing communications, 340

AIDA model, 342

communication process, 344

source, 344

receiver, 344

noise, 344

encoding, 345

decoding, 345

message channel, 345

pushing, 350

pulling, 351

adoption curve, 353

innovators, 354

early adopters, 355

early majority, 355

late majority, 355

laggards, 355

nonadopters, 355

primary demand, 355

selective demand, 356

task method, 357

QUESTIONS AND PROBLEMS

1. Review the GEICO case study that opens the chapter. From this case, identify examples of different key terms and concepts covered in the chapter. For example, advertising is represented by the Gecko ads.

2. Review the GEICO case study that opens this chapter. Then go to GEICO's Facebook page and Twitter feed. Suggest three different posts for each site—one each aiming to inform, persuade, and remind.

3. Briefly explain the nature of the three basic promotion methods available to a marketing manager. What are the main strengths and limitations of each?

4. In your own words, discuss the integrated marketing communications concept. Explain what its emphasis on "consistent" and "complete" messages implies with respect to promotion blends.

5. Relate the three basic promotion objectives to the four jobs (AIDA) of promotion using a specific example.

6. Discuss the communication process in relation to a producer's promotion of an accessory product—say, a new electronic security system businesses use to limit access to areas where they store confidential records.

7. If a company wants its promotion to appeal to a new group of target customers in a foreign country, how can it protect against its communications being misinterpreted?

8. Promotion has been the target of considerable criticism. What specific types of promotion are probably the object of this criticism? Give a particular example that illustrates your thinking.

9. With direct-response promotion, customers provide feedback to marketing communications. How can a marketing

manager use this feedback to improve the effectiveness of the overall promotion blend?

10. How can a promotion manager aim a message at a certain target market with electronic media (like the Internet) when the customer initiates the communication? Give an example.

11. What promotion blend would be most appropriate for producers of the following established products? Assume average- to large-sized firms in each case and support your answer.

    a. Chocolate candy bars.
    b. Car batteries.
    c. Panty hose.
    d. Castings for truck engines.
    e. A special computer used by manufacturers for control of production equipment.
    f. Inexpensive plastic rainhats.
    g. A digital tape recorder that has achieved specialty-product status.

12. A small company has developed an innovative new spray-on glass cleaner that prevents the buildup of electrostatic dust on computer screens and TVs. Give examples of some low-cost ways the firm might effectively promote its product. Be certain to consider both push and pull approaches.

13. Would promotion be successful in expanding the general demand for: (a) almonds, (b) air travel, (c) golf clubs, (d) walking shoes, (e) high-octane unleaded gasoline, (f) single-serving, frozen gourmet dinners, and (g) bricks? Explain why or why not in each case.

14. Explain how an understanding of the adoption process would help you develop a promotion blend for digital tape recorders, a new consumer electronics product that produces high-quality recordings. Explain why you might change the promotion blend during the course of the adoption process.

15. Explain how opinion leaders affect a firm's promotion planning.

16. Discuss how the adoption curve should be used to plan the promotion blend(s) for a new automobile accessory—an electronic radar system that alerts a driver if he or she is about to change lanes into the path of a car that is passing through a blind spot in the driver's mirrors.

17. If a marketing manager uses the task method to budget for marketing promotions, are competitors' promotion spending levels ignored? Explain your thinking and give an example that supports your point of view.

18. Discuss the potential conflict among the various promotion managers. How could this be reduced?

MARKETING PLANNING AT HILLSIDE VETERINARY CLINIC

Appendix D (the Appendices follow Chapter 19) includes a sample marketing plan for Hillside Veterinary Clinic. Look through the "Marketing Strategy" section.

a. What are Hillside's promotion objectives? How do they differ for the various goods and services the company offers?

b. Do the promotion activities recommended in the plan fit with the promotion objectives? Create a table to compare them. Label the columns: good/service, promotion objective, and promotion activities.

c. Based on the situation analysis, target market, and intended positioning, recommend other (low-cost) promotion activities for Hillside.

SUGGESTED CASES

18. West Tarrytown Volunteer Fire Department
19. UltimateWedding.com

MARKETING ANALYTICS: DATA TO KNOWLEDGE

CHAPTER 13 SELECTING A COMMUNICATIONS CHANNEL

Helen Troy, owner of three Sound Haus stereo equipment stores, is deciding what message channel (advertising medium) to use to promote her newest store. Her current promotion blend includes direct-mail ads that are effective for reaching her current customers. She also has knowledgeable salespeople who work well with consumers once they're in the store. However, a key objective in opening a new store is to attract new customers. Her best prospects are professionals in the

25–44 age range with incomes over $38,000 a year. But only some of the people in this group are audiophiles who want the top-of-the-line brands she carries. Troy has decided to use local advertising to reach new customers.

Troy narrowed her choice to two advertising media: Pandora, a music streaming service that offers localized advertising services, and a biweekly magazine that focuses on entertainment in her city. Many of the magazine's readers are out-of-town visitors interested in concerts, plays, and restaurants. They usually buy stereo equipment at home. But the magazine's audience research shows that many local professionals do subscribe to the magazine. Troy doesn't think that the objective can be achieved with a single ad. However, she believes that ads in six issues will generate good local awareness with her target market. In addition, the magazine's color format will let her present the prestige image she wants to convey in an ad. She thinks that will help convert aware prospects to buyers. Specialists at a local advertising agency will prepare a high-impact ad for $2,000, and then Troy will pay for the magazine space.

Pandora can target an audience similar to Troy's own target market. She knows repeated ads will be needed to be sure that most of her target audience is exposed to her ads. Troy thinks it will take daily ads for several months to create adequate awareness among her target market. Pandora will provide an announcer and prepare a recording of Troy's ad for a one-time fee of $200. All she has to do is tell them what the message content for the ad should say.

Both Pandora and the magazine gave Troy reports summarizing recent audience research. She decides that comparing the two media in a spreadsheet will help her make a better decision.

See Connect for the spreadsheet and questions needed to analyze this scenario.

CHAPTER FOURTEEN

© William D. Perreault, Jr., Ph.D.

Personal Selling and Customer Service

As a student in the College of Business at the University of Illinois, Pooja Gupta wanted a job that would offer interesting challenges, give opportunities for professional growth, and value her enthusiasm. She found what she wanted with Ferguson. Ferguson was actively recruiting on college campuses to find the brightest and best candidates for its sales jobs—so, in a way, the job found her.

Gupta knew that motivated young people often find the best opportunities in fast-growing companies. She didn't expect, however, that her fast-growing company would be a wholesaler of plumbing supplies, pipes, valves, and fittings. To the contrary, she'd heard that many wholesalers were declining. But that didn't apply to Ferguson. For decades it has doubled in size about every five years—and now it's the largest U.S. distributor of plumbing products. And in a business that serves such a wide variety of customer types—large industrial firms, city waterworks, commercial builders and subcontractors, kitchen and bath dealers, and final consumers—you don't get that kind of growth without an effective sales force.

It's Ferguson's sales force that gets the initial orders with new customers, builds the relationships that instill customer loyalty, and provides the customer service support that Ferguson emphasizes. Its sales reps understand their customers' business problems and how Ferguson's products, e-commerce, and state-of-the-art logistics systems can help solve them. This expertise and focus on customer needs make Ferguson salespeople trusted partners. Because they're real experts on the company's products and how to cut customer costs, they proved invaluable during the recent economic downturn when demand for Ferguson's core plumbing products plunged along with new home construction.

An effective sales force like the one at Ferguson doesn't just happen. Someone needs to figure out the promotion jobs that require personal selling and then get the right people on the job. That is why Ferguson's marketing managers work closely with sales managers.

Ferguson carries more than a million products, provides service centers at 1,300 locations, and has divisions that specialize by different customer segments. It would be futile for sales reps to try to be experts in everything. Instead, sales managers carefully match each salesperson to particular territories, customers, and product lines. Gupta, for example, helps contractors in the Virginia market figure out how to satisfy the needs of final consumers for whom they are building or remodeling homes. She knows the current fashions for kitchen and bath renovations, how to reduce "behind-the-wall" plumbing installation costs for a big new apartment building, and the advantages and limitations of hundreds of brands from companies such as Kohler, Elkay, Moen, and Jacuzzi.

Other Ferguson salespeople work with cities and huge waterworks contractors on infrastructure projects such as updating water purification facilities. And salespeople for Ferguson's Integrated Systems Division (ISD) are really selling a big business idea rather than "pipe." They show top executives at customer firms why they should invest millions of dollars in a full-service supply relationship where Ferguson does all of the purchasing and warehousing for entire manufacturing facilities. In stark contrast, the main sales job in one of Ferguson's new self-service Xpress outlets is to ring up sales when hurried plumbers need repair parts.

To recruit talented people for these varied jobs, Ferguson's sales managers use a wide variety of methods. For example, the careers section of Ferguson's website collects job applicant profiles on an ongoing basis. When a position opens up, qualified candidates are notified. And Ferguson actively recruits on college campuses, typically hiring about 700 graduates every year. After a pre-interview on campus, select candidates go to a regional office and meet a number of managers from that area.

After the best people are selected, Ferguson provides the sales training to make them even better. Of course, the training is different for different people. For example, most new college recruits work for a short time in a Ferguson warehouse, which helps them understand the company's logistics system, its products, and its industry as well as the company's "can-do" culture. Other training methods range from self-study online modules to role playing to working in the field with experienced managers who help them build professional problem-solving skills as well as technical knowledge.

Even experienced sales reps need ongoing training on new strategies or policies. When Ferguson's management saw an opportunity to enhance customer loyalty, a training program was developed and implemented with Ferguson's 19,000 associates. They participated in face-to-face and online courses covering topics such as "the difference between customer satisfaction and loyalty" and "how to earn loyal customers." The return on investment for the training program was estimated at more than 400 percent.

To be sure that each salesperson is highly motivated, Ferguson's sales managers make certain that sales compensation arrangements and benefits reward salespeople for producing needed results. For example, the evaluation considers how well individuals work within a team—because in the customer service culture at Ferguson, great

teamwork is critical. Those investments paid off when the economy and home building recently picked up. Ferguson's experienced reps were ready to help contractors, builders, and home buyers choose the right supplies and fuel Ferguson's growth.[1]

LEARNING OBJECTIVES

Promotion is communicating with potential customers and others in the channel. As the Ferguson case suggests, personal selling is often the best way to do it. While face to face with prospects, salespeople can adjust what actions they take in response to the prospect's interests, needs, questions, and feedback. If, and when, the prospect is ready to buy, the salesperson is there to ask for the order. And afterward, the salesperson works to be certain that the customer is satisfied and will buy again in the future. In this chapter, you'll learn about the key strategy decisions related to personal selling that marketing managers and the sales managers who work with them make.

When you finish this chapter, you should be able to

1 Understand the importance and nature of personal selling.

2 Know the three basic sales tasks—order-getting, order-taking, and supporting—and what various kinds of salespeople can be expected to do.

3 Understand why customer service presents different challenges than other personal selling tasks.

4 Know the different ways sales managers can organize salespeople so that personal selling jobs are handled effectively.

5 Know how sales technology affects the way sales tasks are performed.

6 Know what the sales manager must do, including selecting, training, and organizing salespeople to carry out the personal selling job.

7 Understand how the right compensation plan can help motivate and control salespeople.

8 Understand when and where to use the three types of sales presentations.

9 Understand important new terms (shown in red).

The Importance and Role of Personal Selling

LO 14.1

Personal selling requires strategy decisions

In this chapter, we'll discuss the importance and nature of personal selling and customer service so you'll understand the strategy decisions in this area (see Exhibit 14–1).

We'll also discuss a number of frameworks and how-to approaches that guide these strategy decisions. Because these approaches apply equally to domestic and international markets, we won't emphasize that distinction in this chapter. This does not mean, however, that personal selling techniques don't vary from one country to another. To the contrary, in dealing with *any* customer, the salesperson must adjust for cultural influences and other factors that might affect communication. For example, a Japanese customer and an Arab customer might respond differently to subtle aspects of a salesperson's behavior. The Arab customer might expect to be physically very close to a salesperson, perhaps only two feet away, while they talk. The Japanese customer might consider that distance rude. Similarly, what topics of discussion are considered sensitive, how messages are interpreted, and which

Exhibit 14-1   Strategy Planning and Personal Selling

negotiating styles are used vary from one country to another. A salesperson must know how to communicate effectively with each customer—wherever and whoever that customer is.[2]

Personal selling is important

Personal selling is absolutely essential in the promotion blends of some firms. Consider how you would feel if you regularly had to meet payrolls and somehow, almost miraculously, your salespeople kept coming in with orders just in time to keep the business profitable.

Personal selling is often a company's largest single operating expense. This is another reason why it is important to understand sales management decisions. Bad ones are costly in both lost sales and in actual out-of-pocket expenses.

Every economy needs and uses many salespeople. In the United States, *one person out of every ten in the total labor force is involved in sales work*. By comparison, that's about 20 times more people than are employed in advertising. Any occupation that employs so many people and is so important to the economy deserves study. Looking at what salespeople do is a good way to start.

Helping to buy is good selling

Good salespeople don't just try to *sell* the customer. Rather, they try to *help the customer buy*—by understanding the customer's needs and presenting the advantages and disadvantages of their products. Such helpfulness results in satisfied customers

Good salespeople help customers find solutions to problems. Often that requires a trusting relationship that comes from carefully listening to a customers and learning how best to address their needs.

and long-term relationships. And strong relationships often form the basis for a competitive advantage, especially in business markets.

Not only the salespeople sell

Selling may be done by almost anyone in the organization. When you ask the butcher at your local supermarket for advice, his assistance will help you buy the right cut. The butcher is selling. When your auto mechanic helps you buy the appropriate motor oil for your oil change, the mechanic is selling. When a web page designer helps a marketing manager build a site that meets customer needs, the designer is selling. We may not call each of these people a salesperson, but they are all helping customers buy. Although this chapter focuses on more traditional salesperson roles, smart companies make sure that everyone in the organization who talks to customers knows at least something about selling.[3]

Salespeople represent the whole company— and customers too

The salesperson is often a representative of the whole company—responsible for explaining its total effort to customers rather than just pushing products. The salesperson may provide information about products, explain company policies, and even negotiate prices or diagnose technical problems.

The sales rep is often the only link between the firm and its customers, especially if customers are far away. When a number of people from the firm work with the customer organization—which is common when suppliers and customers form close relationships—it is usually the sales rep who coordinates the relationship for his or her firm (see Exhibit 6–6).

As evidence of these changing responsibilities, some companies give their salespeople such titles as account representative, field manager, sales consultant, market specialist, or sales engineer.

Sales force aids in marketing information function as well

The salesperson also represents the customers' interests inside the firm. The sales force can aid in the marketing information function too. The sales rep may be the first to hear about a new competitor or a competitor's new strategy. And sales reps who are well attuned to customers' needs can be a key source of ideas for new products or new uses for existing products.

It was a salesperson for Material Sciences Corporation (MSC) who spotted an opportunity for the firm in the automotive market. The sales rep worked closely with the Ford team developing the new F-150 truck. When he asked for more information about how Ford was trying to reduce road noise, he, in effect, opened the door for a potential application of MSC's Quiet Steel product. Quiet Steel had not previously been used in the automotive market. It was a perfect fit. These insights helped MSC gain a foothold with other automakers. A couple of questions from a salesperson helped consumers get quieter cars and trucks.[4]

Salespeople can be strategy planners too

Some salespeople are expected to be marketing managers in their own territories. And some become marketing managers by default because top management hasn't provided detailed strategy guidelines. Either way, the salesperson may have choices about (1) which customers to target, (2) which particular products to emphasize, (3) which intermediaries to rely on for help, (4) what message to communicate and how to use promotion money, and (5) how to adjust prices. A salesperson who can put together profitable strategies and implement them well can rise very rapidly. The opportunity is there for those prepared and willing to work.[5]

What Kinds of Personal Selling Are Needed?

LO 14.2

If a firm has too few salespeople, or the wrong kind, some important personal selling tasks may not be completed. And having too many salespeople wastes money. In addition, the balance that is right may change over time with other changes in strategy or the market environment. That's why many firms have to restructure their sales forces.

One of the difficulties of determining the right number and kind of salespeople is that every sales job is different. Whereas an engineer or accountant can look forward to fairly specific duties, the salesperson's job changes constantly. However, there are three basic types of sales tasks (see Exhibit 14–2). This gives us a starting point for understanding what sales tasks need to be done and how many people are needed to do them.

Exhibit 14–2 Basic Sales Tasks

Personal selling is divided into three tasks

The three **basic sales tasks** are order-getting, order-taking, and supporting. For convenience, we'll describe salespeople by these terms—referring to their primary task—*although one person may do two or all three tasks in some situations*.

Order Getters Develop New Business Relationships

Order getters are concerned with establishing relationships with new customers and developing new business. **Order-getting** means seeking possible buyers with a well-organized sales presentation designed to sell a good, service, or idea.

Order getters must know what they're talking about, not just be personal contacts. Order-getting salespeople normally are well paid—many earn more than $100,000 a year!

Producers' order getters—find new opportunities

Producers of all kinds of products, especially business products, have a great need for order getters. They use order getters to locate new prospects, open new accounts, see new opportunities, and help establish and build channel relationships.

Top-level customers are more interested in ways to save or make more money than in technical details. Good order getters cater to this interest. They help the customer identify ways to solve problems; then they sell concepts and ideas, not just physical products. The goods and services they supply are merely the means of achieving the customer's end.

To be effective at this sort of "solutions selling," an order getter often needs to understand a customer's whole business as well as technical details about the product and its applications. For example, a salesperson for automated manufacturing equipment must understand a prospect's production process as well as the technical details of converting to computer-controlled equipment.

Order getters for professional services—and other products where service is a crucial element of the marketing mix—face a special challenge. The customer usually can't inspect a service before deciding to buy. The order getter's communication and relationship with the customer may be the only basis for evaluating the quality of the supplier.

Wholesalers' order getters—almost hand it to the customer

Salespeople for agent wholesalers are often order getters—particularly the more aggressive manufacturers' agents and brokers. They face the same tasks as producers' order getters. But, unfortunately for them, once the order-getting is done and the customers become established and loyal, producers may try to eliminate the agents and save money with their own order takers.

Retail order getters influence consumer behavior

Convincing consumers about the value of products they haven't seriously considered takes a high level of personal selling ability. Order getters for unsought consumer products must help customers see how a new product can satisfy needs now being filled by something else. Without order getters, many common products—ranging from mutual funds to air conditioners—might have died in the market introduction stage. The order getter helps bring products out of the introduction stage into the market growth stage.

Order getters are also helpful for selling *heterogeneous* shopping products. Consumers shop for many of these items on the basis of suitability and value. They welcome useful information.

Order Takers Nurture Relationships to Keep the Business Coming

Order takers sell to the regular or established customers, complete most sales transactions, and maintain relationships with their customers. After a customer becomes interested in a firm's products through an order getter, supporting salesperson, or through advertising or sales promotion, an order taker usually answers any final questions and completes the sale. **Order-taking** is the routine completion of sales made regularly to target customers. It usually requires ongoing follow-up to make certain that the customer is totally satisfied.

Producers' order takers—train, explain, and collaborate

Order takers work on improving the whole relationship with their accounts, not just on completing a single sale. Even in e-commerce, where customers place routine orders with computerized order systems, order takers do a variety of important jobs that are essential to the business relationship. Someone has to explain details, make adjustments, handle complaints, explain new prices or terms, place sales promotion materials, and keep customers informed of new developments. An order taker who fails to meet a customer's expectations on any of these activities might jeopardize the relationship and future sales.

Firms sometimes use order-taking jobs to train potential order getters and managers. Such jobs give them an opportunity to meet customers and better understand their needs. And, frequently, they run into some order-getting opportunities.

Order takers who are alert to order-getting possibilities can make the big difference in generating new sales. Some firms lose sales just because no one ever asks for the order. Banks try to avoid this problem. For example, when a customer walks into a First Bank branch to make a deposit, the teller's computer screen shows information about the customer's accounts. If the balance in a checking account is high and the customer does not use any of the bank's other investment services, the teller is trained to ask if the customer would be interested in learning about the bank's certificates of deposit. Some firms use more sophisticated customer relationship management (CRM) database systems that figure out which specific financial service would be best for the teller to recommend.[6]

Wholesalers' order takers—not getting orders but keeping them

Whereas producers' order takers usually handle relatively few items, wholesalers' order takers often sell thousands of items. Sales reps who handle that many items may single out a few of the newer or more profitable items for special attention, but it's not possible to give aggressive sales effort to many. So the main job of wholesalers' order takers is to maintain close contact with customers, place orders, and check to be sure the company fills orders promptly. Order takers also handle any adjustments or complaints and generally act as liaisons between the company and its customers.

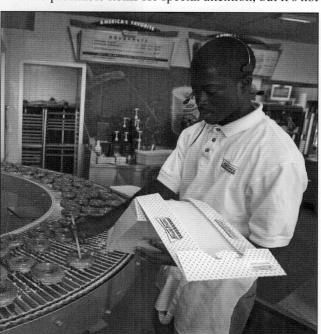

In retail, salesclerks are usually order takers

Order-taking may be almost mechanical at the retail level—for example, at the supermarket checkout counter. Some retail clerks perform poorly because they receive little training. Turnover can be high, too, as many receive little more than the mini-

Friendly and capable retail order takers can play an important role in building good relations with customers.
AP Photo/Chuck Burton.

mum wage. Even so, retail order takers play a vital role in a retailer's marketing mix. Customers expect prompt and friendly service. They will find a new place to shop, or to do their banking or have their car serviced, rather than deal with a salesclerk who is inept or rude or acts annoyed by having to complete a sale.

Supporting Sales Force Informs and Promotes in the Channel

Supporting salespeople help the order-oriented salespeople, but they don't try to get orders themselves. Their activities are aimed at enhancing the relationship with the customer and getting sales in the long run. For the short run, however, they are ambassadors of goodwill who may provide specialized services and information. There are three types of supporting salespeople: missionary salespeople, technical specialists, and customer service reps.

Missionary salespeople can increase sales

Missionary salespeople are supporting salespeople who work for producers—calling on intermediaries and their customers. They try to develop goodwill and stimulate

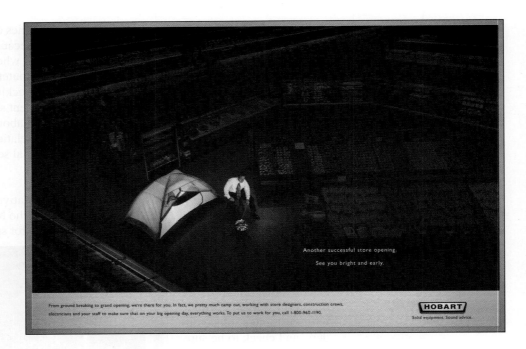

Another successful store opening.

See you bright and early.

From ground breaking to grand opening, we're there for you. In fact, we pretty much camp out, working with store designers, construction crews, electricians and your staff to make sure that on your big opening day, everything works. To put us to work for you, call 1-800-960-1190.

HOBART
Solid equipment. Sound advice.

demand, help intermediaries train their salespeople, and often take orders for delivery by intermediaries. Missionary salespeople are sometimes called *merchandisers* or *detailers*.

Producers who rely on merchant wholesalers or e-commerce to obtain widespread distribution often use missionary salespeople. The sales rep can give a promotion boost to a product that otherwise wouldn't get much attention because it's just one of many. A missionary salesperson for Vicks' cold remedy products, for example, might visit pharmacists during the cold season and encourage them to use a special end-of-aisle display for Vicks' cough syrup—and then help set it up. The wholesaler that supplies the drugstore would benefit from any increased sales but might not take the time to urge use of the special display.

An imaginative missionary salesperson can double or triple sales for a company. Naturally, this doesn't go unnoticed. Missionary sales jobs are often a route to order-oriented jobs.

Technical specialists are experts who know product applications

Technical specialists are supporting salespeople who provide technical assistance to order-oriented salespeople. Technical specialists are often science or engineering graduates with the know-how to understand the customer's applications and explain the advantages of the company's product. They are usually more skilled in showing the technical details of their product than in trying to persuade customers to buy it. Before the specialist's visit, an order getter probably has stimulated interest. The technical specialist provides the details.

Customer service reps solve problems after a purchase

Customer service reps work with customers to resolve problems that arise with a purchase, usually after the purchase has been made. Unlike other supporting sales activities, which are needed only in certain selling situations, *every* marketing-oriented company needs good people to handle customer service. Customer service is important to both business customers and final consumers. There are times when a customer's problem simply can't be resolved without a personal touch.

In general, all types of personal selling help to win customers, but effective customer service is especially critical in keeping them. It is often the key to building repeat business. It's useful to think of customer service reps as *the salespeople who promote a customer's next purchase by being sure that the customer is satisfied with a previous purchase.* In this chapter, you'll see that the strategy decisions for customer service reps are the same as for others involved in personal selling. In spite of this, some firms don't view customer service as a personal selling activity—or as part of the firm's integrated marketing communications. They manage it as a production operation where output consists of responses to questions from "problem customers." That approach is one reason that customer service is often a problem area for firms. So it's useful to take a closer look at why customer service activities are so important and why firms should manage them as part of the personal selling effort.

Customer Service Promotes the Next Purchase

LO 14.3

Customer service is not the product

People sometimes use the term *customer service* as a catch-all expression for anything that helps customers. Our focus here is on the service that is required *to solve a problem that a customer encounters with a purchase.* This highlights an important distinction in how customers look at their purchase experience. In that regard, it is useful to think about the difference between customer service and the service (or support) that is part of the product that a customer buys.

In Chapter 8, we discussed the idea that a firm's product is its need-satisfying offering, and that it may be a physical good, a service, or a combination of the two (see Exhibit 8–2). Wells Fargo offers consumers credit card services for a fee. Wolf Camera makes prints from customers' digital images. Dell sells computer hardware and software that is supported with telephone or website technical support for some period of time after the purchase. In all of these situations, customers see service as an important aspect of what they are purchasing.

However, from a customer's perspective, that kind of service is different from the customer service that is required to fix a problem when something doesn't work as the customer hopes or expects. For example, our customer doesn't expect the Wells Fargo ATM to eat her credit card when she's on a trip, doesn't want Wolf to charge more than the advertised price for her pictures, and isn't planning on Dell sending the wrong computer. These problems are breakdowns in the firms' marketing mixes. What the customer expected from the seller is not what the customer got.

When a customer service rep works to solve a customer's problem, it often involves taking steps to remedy what went wrong. But repairing a negative experience is fundamentally different from providing a positive experience in the first place. No matter how effective the customer service solution, the problem is an inconvenience or involves other types of costs to the customer. Thus, the customer value from the firm's marketing mix is lower than what the customer bargained for. Often it's also less than the value the firm *intended* to provide.

In Spain, cell phone operator Vodafone has set up customer service hotlines with representatives who can speak 11 languages from Arabic to Romanian. That's because Spain has one of Europe's fastest growing immigrant populations, with more than 600,000 foreigners arriving annually. Vodafone's customer service efforts help the company acquire *and* retain these new customers.

© 2015 Vodafone Group. Vodafone Group Plc.

Why customer service is part of promotion

We mentioned before that customers weigh negative experiences more heavily than positive experiences when they decide whether to buy the same product (or from the same company) again. They are also more likely to tell other people about bad experiences with a company than about good ones. The practical matter is that customer service interactions arise because the customer is unhappy. So, if the firm doesn't have an effective way to provide customer service, it is, consciously or unconsciously, making a decision to kiss that customer good-bye. In today's highly competitive markets, that can be a big mistake, especially in situations where it's costly to acquire new customers or when the lifetime value of a customer is significant. Poor customer service reduces the firm's customer equity.

This is why firms should view customer service reps as a key part of personal selling. They are not just fixing the customer's problem, but rather fixing the company's problem, which is the risk of losing customers.

Big data and social media can create proactive customer service

We have portrayed customer service as a reactive form of communication—companies waiting for customers to call or write in with a complaint. Many customers don't bother contacting a company—they just stop doing business with the offending firm or voice their complaints online. Then there are companies that try to solve customers' problems even when the customers don't ask for help. They are monitoring the web and using big data analytics to provide *proactive* customer service. These companies reach out to unhappy customers before their frustration boils over.

Consider Comcast, which developed a well-earned reputation for poor customer service over the last couple of decades. Now the company has begun to turn that reputation around—though turning a reputation around takes time. While Comcast continues to use inbound telemarketing to answer and respond to customer questions, another group inside the company trolls the Internet and accesses big data from Facebook, Twitter, blogs, and discussion forums to find anyone complaining about Comcast. Then Comcast reaches out to those customers to address their complaints. This proactive approach is beginning to turn Comcast's reputation around.[7]

Customer service reps are customer advocates

A breakdown in any element of the marketing mix can result in a requirement for customer service. Ideally, a firm should deliver what it promises, but marketing is a human process and mistakes do happen. Consider, for example, a customer who decides to use Verizon cell phone service because its ad—or the salesperson at the Radio Shack who sold the phone—said that the first month of service would be free. If Verizon bills the customer for the first month, is it a pricing problem, a promotion problem, or a lack of coordination in the channel? From the customer's perspective, it really doesn't matter. What does matter is that expectations have been dashed. The customer doesn't need explanations or excuses but instead needs an advocate to make things right.

Sometimes the marketing mix is fine, but the customer makes a purchase that is a mistake. Or customers may simply change their minds. Either way, customers usually expect sellers to help fix purchasing errors. Firms need policies about how customer service reps should deal with customer errors. But most firms simply can't afford to alienate customers, even ones who have made an error, if they expect them to come back in the future. Sometimes the toughest sales job is figuring out how to keep a customer who is unhappy.

Regardless of whether the firm or customer causes the problem, customer service reps need to be effective communicators, have good judgment, and realize that they are advocates not only for their firm but also for its customers. As that implies, the rest of the company needs to be organized to provide the support reps need to fix problems.

The Right Structure Helps Assign Responsibility

LO 14.4

We have described three sales tasks—order-getting, order-taking, and supporting. A sales manager must organize the sales force so that all the necessary tasks are done well. In many situations, a particular salesperson might be given two, or all three, of these tasks. For example, 10 percent of a particular job may be order-getting, 80 percent order-taking, and the additional 10 percent customer service. On the other hand, organizations are often structured to have different salespeople specialize in different sales tasks and by the target markets they serve.[8]

Sales tasks may be handled by a team

If different people handle different sales tasks, firms often rely on **team selling**—when different people work together on a specific account. Sometimes members of a sales team are not from the sales department at all. If improving the relationship with the customer calls for input from the quality control manager, then that person becomes a part of the team, at least temporarily. Producers of big-ticket items often use team selling. IBM uses team selling to sell information technology solutions for a whole business. Different specialists handle different parts of the job—but the whole team coordinates its efforts to achieve the desired result.

Different target markets need different sales tasks

Sales managers often divide sales force responsibilities based on the type of customer involved. For example, Bigelow—a company that makes quality carpet for homes and office buildings—divided its sales force into groups of specialists. Some Bigelow salespeople call only on architects to help them choose the best type of carpet for new office buildings. These reps know all the technical details, such as how well a certain carpet fiber will wear or its effectiveness in reducing noise from office equipment. Often no sale is involved because the architect only suggests specifications and doesn't actually buy the carpet. Other Bigelow salespeople call on retail carpet stores. These reps encourage the store manager to keep a variety of Bigelow carpets in stock. They also introduce new products, help train the store's salespeople, and try to solve any problems that occur. Bigelow also has a group of customer service reps who are available via a toll-free number. They help final consumers who have purchased carpet but have a problem that the carpet store can't resolve.

Big accounts get special treatment

Very large customers often require special sales efforts—and relationships with them are treated differently. Moen, a maker of plumbing fixtures, has a regular sales force to call on building material wholesalers and an elite **major accounts sales force** that sells directly to large accounts—such as Lowe's, Home Depot, or other major retail chains that carry plumbing fixtures.

You can see why this sort of special attention is justified when you consider Procter & Gamble's relationship with Walmart. Walmart accounts for one-fourth or more of

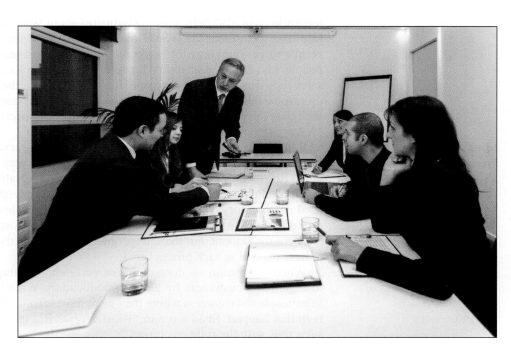

Some sellers use sales teams to sell to its very large accounts. These teams work together to address the customer's needs.
© Minerva Studio/iStock

the total national sales in many of the product categories in which P&G competes. For instance, Walmart sells about one-third of the toothpaste in the United States. If P&G wants to grow its share of the toothpaste market, it has to make certain that it stimulates an effective sales effort with Walmart.

Some salespeople specialize in telephone selling

Some firms have a group of salespeople who specialize in **telemarketing**—using the telephone to call on customers or prospects. The National Do Not Call Registry in the United States and similar laws in other countries have largely eliminated telemarketing to consumers. Registered users cannot be called except by nonprofits and a few other select groups. However, the reception to telephone selling in business markets is often quite different.

In business markets, an "inside" sales force can often build profitable relationships with small or hard-to-reach customers the firm might otherwise have to ignore. Telephone selling is also used to extend personal selling efforts to new target markets or increase the frequency of contact with current customers. The big advantage of telephone selling by an inside sales group in these situations is that it saves time and money for the seller, and it gives customers a fast and easy way to solve a purchasing problem. For example, many firms use toll-free incoming telephone lines to make it convenient for customers to call the inside sales force for assistance or to place an order. Telephone contact may supplement a good website; the website provides standard information and an inside salesperson answers specific questions on the phone.

Companies that produce goods and services for final consumers also rely heavily on toll-free telephone lines to give final consumers easy access to customer service reps. In most cases, there is no other practical way for the producer to be sure that retailers are taking care of customers or their problems. A customer service call center provides a way for the producer to get direct feedback from customers—and perhaps find solutions to potential problems.[9]

Sales tasks are done in sales territories

Often companies organize selling tasks on the basis of a **sales territory**—a geographic area that is the responsibility of one salesperson or several working together. A territory might be a region of a country, a state, or part of a city, depending on the market potential. An airplane manufacturer like Boeing might consider a whole country as *part* of a sales territory for one salesperson.

Carefully set territories can reduce travel time and the cost of sales calls. Assigning territories can also help reduce confusion about who has responsibility for a set of sales tasks. Consider the Hyatt Hotel chain. At one time, each hotel had its own salespeople to get bookings for big conferences and business meetings. That meant that people who had responsibility for selecting meeting locations might be called on by sales reps from 20 or 30 different Hyatt hotels. Now, the Hyatt central office divides up responsibility for working with specific accounts; one rep calls on an account and then tries to sell space in the Hyatt facility that best meets the customer's needs.

Specializing by product lines brings more expertise to customers

Sometimes simple geographic division doesn't serve customers' best interests. When companies sell different products that require very different knowledge or selling skills, it can make sense to have salespeople specialized by product line. For example, DuPont makes special films for hospital X-ray departments as well as chemicals used in laboratory blood tests. Dupont uses different salespeople (each an expert in its product line) that call on different people in the same hospitals. It might be a little less efficient for Dupont, but the salespeople are more effective and customers are happier to have experts in each product area.

When most selling is done online or via telephone, there are no major cost savings to organizing customers by geographic location. What if it were possible to assign salespeople to customers where they were most effective? Data is being used today to help that happen. Read more in *"What's Next?* Big data matchmaking puts the right sales reps with the right customers."

What's Next? Big data matchmaking puts the right sales reps with the right customers

Assurant Solutions sells credit insurance. Credit insurance pays the insured person's mortgage, car, or credit card payments if he loses his job or experiences major medical problems. Customers often buy credit insurance as an add-on when making very large purchases, such as a house or car. When customers make payments, they see an additional monthly fee for the credit insurance. Sometimes that monthly fee gets some customers second-guessing their need for the insurance; they decide they might be better off taking their chances. When that happens, they call Assurant's customer service team to cancel the policy. This team's job is to prevent customers from dropping the coverage.

As for other companies in the financial services industry, customer retention is key to profitability. The customer service team is the last chance for Assurant to retain customers who call in to drop the insurance. Assurant's customer service group used to be operationally optimized—staffing to assure 80 percent of customers waited less than 20 seconds to speak to a customer service representative (CSR). Inbound phone calls were routed to CSRs with expertise in the product the customer owned, and computer screens displayed scripts that CSRs followed and offers they could make to try to keep a customer from following through on canceling his or her policy. With all those efforts, Assurant's CSRs retained just 16 percent of those calling to cancel—above average for the industry, but not good enough. With five of every six customers not convinced to keep their policy, or at least buy a different product, Assurant figured there was an opportunity for improvement. So it turned to analytics.

Insurance companies are data-driven by nature—they forecast the likelihood of accidents, deaths, and product failures—so it made sense for Assurant to take an analytical approach to managing customer service. Assurant's customer service managers have access to lots of data: on customers, products, CSRs, and of course the outcome from each transaction. Assurant also has plenty of statisticians and actuaries who know how to predict outcomes by mining data for insights. With some deep analysis of past transactions, they identified patterns that helped predict success (retaining a customer) and failure when customers call in to cancel a policy.

Assurant discovered that different CSRs were more successful dealing with certain kinds of customers and problems. So the analysts built math models to predict which CSRs would be most effective with each type of customer. Inbound calls are analyzed in real-time, so each call is instantly routed to the CSR with the best chance of keeping the customer's business. If the best CSR for a specific customer is busy on another call, then it rolls to the next-best CSR, and so on down the line. By matching customers with CSRs, Assurant's retention rate *doubled*. The new system also ensures that customers with the biggest premiums are assigned to the best customer service reps, so the dollars retained *tripled* as compared to before.

Although the analytics don't tell *why* some reps outperform others, data matching customers and CSRs seems to work. Assurant's customer service managers attribute the success to rapport. The analytics know enough about each customer and CSR to create matches where the possibility of connecting is greatest. Creating the right match makes it easier to build a foundation of trust, and persuasion and retention are likely to follow.

Discuss how analytics like those described here could be used at a company like Ferguson Enterprises (the chapter opening case). How could it be done? Would it be practical?[10]

Size of sales force depends on workload

Once the important sales tasks are specified and the responsibilities divided, the sales manager must decide how many salespeople are needed. The first step is estimating how much work can be done by one person in some time period. Then the sales manager can make an educated guess about how many people are required in total, as the following example shows.

For many years, the Parker Jewelry Company was very successful selling its silver jewelry to department and jewelry stores in the southwestern region of the United States. But top managers wanted to expand into the big urban markets in the northeastern states. They realized that most of the work for the first few years would require order getters. They felt that a salesperson would need to call on each account at least once a month to get a share of this competitive business. They estimated that a salesperson could make only five calls a day on prospective buyers and still allow time for travel, waiting, and follow-up on orders that came in. This meant that a sales rep who made calls 20 days per month could handle about 100 stores (5/day × 20 days).

AlignMix software helps sales managers design sales territories to reduce travel time and costs while maximizing sales potential.
© Cozmix Inc. 2005–2015. All Rights Reserved.

The managers purchased a database that included all of the telephone Yellow Pages listings for the country. Then they simply divided the total number of stores by 100 to estimate the number of salespeople needed. This also helped them set up territories—by defining areas that included about 100 stores for each salesperson. Obviously, managers might want to fine-tune this estimate for differences in territories—such as travel time. But the basic approach can be adapted to many different situations.[11]

Some managers forget that over time the right number of salespeople may change as sales tasks change. Then when a problem becomes obvious, they try to change everything in a hurry—a big mistake. Consideration should be ongoing as to what type and how many salespeople are needed. If the sales force needs to be reduced, it doesn't make sense to let a lot of people go all at once, especially when that could be avoided with some planning.

Sometimes technology can substitute for or complement personal selling

Some sales tasks that have traditionally been handled by a person can now be handled effectively and at lower cost by an e-commerce system or other technology. The situation that the firm faces may influence which approach makes the most sense and how many salespeople are really needed (see Exhibit 14–3).

In many selling situations, there is a great deal of problem solving and coordination needed. These more complicated sales require a salesperson to create and build relationships. When information is not standardized—in other words, the information swapped back and forth is changing all the time—we need to focus on personal selling alone (see lower right box in Exhibit 14–3). A salesperson selling trucking

Exhibit 14–3
Examples of Possible Personal Selling Emphasis

Standardized information exchanged on a recurring basis (orders, invoices, delivery status, product information, prices)

High — Emphasis on standardized e-commerce (with customer service) | Emphasis on both personal selling & customized e-commerce

Low — Emphasis on digital self-service | Emphasis on personal selling

Low | High
Relationship building required (problem solving, coordination, support, cooperation)

services may find that each transaction and price is unique—so technology doesn't substitute for personal selling.

If relationships are needed, but there is a great deal of standard information—for example, routine ordering, pricing, and delivery status—then the salesperson should be supplemented by a customized e-commerce system that allows the buyer to check information as needed (upper right box in Exhibit 14–3). Walmart's relationship with a large supplier like Procter & Gamble may have this type of relationship. There is plenty of planning and coordination that requires a salesperson (or sales team), but with thousands of products and hundreds of stores, regular orders and invoicing are pretty standardized. Computers are best to manage that flow of information.

There are a growing number of situations where little or no salesperson relationship building is needed. If there is a lot of standardized information flowing, but no relationship building needed (upper left box in Exhibit 14–3), then setting up a standard e-commerce system where computers exchange information about stock levels and orders may be sufficient. Customer service can be contacted for exceptions. Many supplier–wholesaler relationships find this type of exchange to be efficient and effective.

Other situations have less frequent transactions, and no need for relationship building (lower left box in Exhibit 14–3). This is a situation where digital self-service makes sense. This is the role of ATMs for banks. If the customer needs money at an airport in the middle of the night, the ATM provides better support than the customer could get with a real person at the bank. Many firms provide self-service at their websites. For example, at HPShopping.com customers configure computers to their own specs. When looking at options such as "How much memory to buy," customers simply click on the "Help me decide" button for more information.

When customer service is digital and self-service, customers get fast service

Because customers want problems resolved quickly, many firms rely on the Internet to deliver rapid and low-cost customer service. Websites can list FAQs (Frequently Asked Questions—with answers), provide copies of instructions, and show video demonstrations. Some firms even set up online communities where customers help one another with problems. The searchable communities make it easy to find someone else who has experienced the same problem—and see how it was fixed.

Consider Logitech, a maker of computer keyboards and mice, webcams, remote controls for television and home theater systems, and many other consumer electronics products. Most of Logitech's products work in conjunction with a non-Logitech product a consumer already owns. As a result, many customers have problems getting their new Logitech product to work perfectly right out of the box. Logitech's product support website lists a toll-free number and includes a FAQ section for each product. Logitech also set up a community support forum—where customers interact with one another (and Logitech experts). Many customers visit the forum to ask questions or to search for others with similar problems; some visit just because they enjoy answering questions. Because Logitech monitors the forum to answer questions and discover any issues with its products, it can quickly add a new FAQ or rewrite the instructions included in a product's package. Because each question and subsequent response live indefinitely in the searchable forums, the next customer seeing "blurry laggy video" with his new Logitech webcam can search and find the solution KachiWachi (a screen name) offered on July 10, 2008. Some customers prefer these quick and proven answers, and Logitech likes the low cost.[12]

Online Toolkit

Go to the Logitech community support forum at **http://forums.logitech.com**. Scroll down the list to "Harmony Remotes" and then choose "Harmony Remotes." Click on a few of the topics with a high number of "replies." Are customers getting their questions answered? How quickly do they get answers? How do you think this affects customer satisfaction for Logitech?

We've focused on technology that substitutes for personal contact by a salesperson. But marketing managers also need to make decisions about providing sales technology support to help salespeople communicate more effectively.

Information Technology Provides Tools to Do the Job

Changes in how sales tasks are handled

New sales technology tools are changing how sales tasks and responsibilities are planned and handled. It is usually the sales manager's job—perhaps with help from specialists in technology—to decide what types of tools are needed and how they will be used.

To get a sense of what is involved, consider a day in the life of a sales rep for a large consumer packaged goods firm. Over a hasty breakfast, she plans the day's sales calls on her laptop's organizer, checks a LinkedIn contact to learn more about a customer she will meet for the first time that afternoon, watches a 15-minute video presentation for a new product, and sorts through a dozen e-mail messages. One e-mail is from a buyer for a supermarket chain. Sales in the chain's paper towel category are off 10 percent, and he wants to know if the rep can help. The rep downloads sales trend data for the chain and its competitors from her firm's intranet. A spreadsheet analysis of the data reveals that the sales decline is due to new competition from warehouse clubs.

After a videoconference with a brand manager and a company sales promotion specialist to seek advice, she prepares a PowerPoint presentation, complete with a proposed shelf-space plan that recommends the buyer promote larger-size packages of both her company's and competitors' brands. Before leaving home, the rep e-mails an advance copy of the report to the buyer and her manager. In her car, she calls the buyer to schedule an appointment.[13]

New software and hardware provide a competitive advantage

The sales rep in this example relies on support from an array of software and hardware, some of which wasn't even available a decade ago. Software for customer relationship management, spreadsheet sales analysis, digital presentations, time management, sales forecasting, customer contact, and shelf-space management is at the salesperson's fingertips—most of it available right online. Commonplace hardware includes everything from smartphones and tablet computers to personal videoconferencing systems. In many situations, these technologies give sales reps new ways to meet customers' needs while achieving the objectives of their jobs.

Technology tools can help at different stages of the buying process. Car configurators allow consumers to go to a website and "build" their dream car in the colors and with the options they want. Dreaming about a new car moves customers forward in the purchase process and brings ready and prepared customers to car dealers to meet a salesperson and take a test drive. Hobart sells large commercial kitchen equipment typically purchased by restaurants. This makes it difficult to demonstrate the products on a sales call. So Hobart created the Hobart Spotlight App for iPad. The app allows Hobart salespeople to *virtually* demonstrate the entire product line with videos and information.
Left: © 2015 Toyota Motor Sales, U.S.A., Inc.; Right: Hobart © 2015 All Rights Reserved.

These tools change how well the job is done. Yet this is not simply a matter that is best left to individual sales reps. Use of these tools may be necessary just to compete effectively. For example, if a customer expects a sales rep to access data on past sales and provide an updated sales forecast, a sales organization that doesn't have this capability will be at a real disadvantage in keeping that customer's business.

On the other hand, these tools have costs. There is an obvious expense of buying the technology. But there is also the training cost of keeping everyone up to date. Often that is not an easy matter. Some salespeople who have done the sales job well for a long time "the old-fashioned way" resent being told that they have to change what they are doing, even if it's what customers expect. So if a firm expects salespeople to be able to use these technologies, that requirement needs to be included in selecting and training people for the job.[14]

Sound Selection and Training to Build a Sales Force

LO 14.6

Selecting good salespeople takes judgment

It is important to hire *well-qualified* salespeople who will do a good job. But selection in many companies is done without serious thought about exactly what kind of person the firm needs. Managers may hire friends and relations, or whoever is available, because they feel that the only qualification for a sales job is a friendly personality. This approach leads to poor sales, lost customers, and costly sales force turnover.

Progressive companies are more careful. They constantly update a list of possible job candidates. They invite applications at the company's website. They schedule candidates for multiple interviews with various executives and do thorough background checks. Unfortunately, such techniques don't guarantee success. But a systematic approach based on several different inputs results in a better sales force.

One problem in selecting salespeople is that two different sales jobs with identical titles may involve very different selling or supporting tasks and require different skills. A carefully prepared job description helps avoid this problem.

Job descriptions should be in writing and specific

A **job description** is a written statement of what a salesperson is expected to do. It might list 10 to 20 specific tasks—as well as routine prospecting and sales report writing. Each company must write its own job specifications. And it should provide clear guidelines about what selling tasks the job involves. This is critical to determine the kind of salespeople who should be selected—and later it provides a basis for seeing how they should be trained, how well they are performing, and how they should be paid.

Good salespeople are trained, not born

The idea that good salespeople are born that way may have some truth—but it isn't the whole story. A salesperson needs to be taught about the company and its products, giving effective sales presentations, using appropriate sales technology, and building relationships with customers. But this isn't always done. Many salespeople do a poor job because they haven't had good training. Firms often hire new salespeople and immediately send them out on the road, or the retail selling floor, with no grounding in the basic selling steps and no information about the product or the customer. They just get a price list and a pat on the back. This isn't enough!

All salespeople need some training

It's up to sales and marketing management to be sure that salespeople know what they're supposed to do and how to do it. Hewlett-Packard Co. recently faced this problem. For years the company was organized into divisions based on different product lines—printers, network servers, and the like. However, sales reps who specialized in the products of one division often couldn't compete well against firms that could offer customers total solutions to computing problems. When a new top executive came in and reorganized the company, all sales reps needed training in their new responsibilities, how they would be organized, and what they should say to their customers about the benefits of the reorganization.

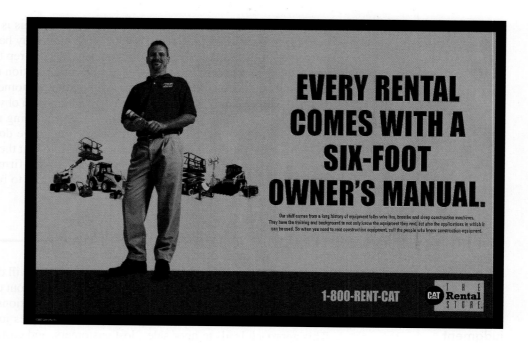

Customers who rent heavy construction equipment want to deal with a knowledgeable salesperson. So CAT selects salespeople who have experience with the applications for which the equipment will be used and gives them training on CAT products and new developments in the market. *Caterpillar © 2015. All Rights Reserved.*

Sales training should be modified based on the experience and skills of the group involved. But the company's sales training program should cover at least the following areas: (1) company policies and practices, (2) product information, (3) building relationships with customer firms, and (4) professional selling skills.

Selling skills can be learned

Many companies spend the bulk of their training time on product information and company policy. They neglect training in selling techniques because they think selling is something anyone can do. But training in selling skills can pay off. Estée Lauder, for example, has selling skills for the "beauty advisors" who sell its cosmetics down to a fine art—and its training manual and seminars cover every detail. Its advisors who take the training seriously immediately double their sales.[15] Training can also help salespeople learn how to be more effective in cold calls on new prospects, in listening carefully to identify a customer's real objections, in closing the sale, and in working with customers in difficult customer service situations.

Training often starts in the classroom with lectures, case studies, and videotaped trial presentations and demonstrations. But a complete training program adds on-the-job observation of effective salespeople and coaching from sales supervisors. Many companies also use web-based training, weekly sales meetings or work sessions, annual conventions, and regular e-mail messages and newsletters, as well as ongoing training sessions, to keep salespeople up to date.[16]

Online Toolkit

Sales managers need to think about what training their salespeople need, but sales reps also need to take the initiative and stay up to date on what is happening in the sales profession. *Selling Power* magazine maintains a website at **www.sellingpower.com**. Go to the website and identify several ideas that could be used by a salesperson to enhance his or her skills.

Compensating and Motivating Salespeople

LO 14.7

To recruit, motivate, and keep good salespeople, a firm has to develop an effective compensation plan. Ideally, sales reps should be paid in such a way that what they want to do—for personal interest and gain—is in the company's interest too. Most companies focus on financial motivation—but public recognition, sales contests, and simple personal recognition for a job well done can be highly effective in encouraging greater sales effort.[17] Our main emphasis here, however, will be on financial motivation.[18]

Two basic decisions must be made in developing a compensation plan: (1) the level of compensation and (2) the method of payment.

Compensation varies with job and needed skills

To build a competitive sales force, a company must pay at least the going market wage for different kinds of salespeople. To be sure it can afford a specific type of salesperson, the company should estimate—when the job description is written—how valuable such a salesperson will be. A good order getter may be worth $100,000 or more to one company but only $15,000 to $25,000 to another—just because the second firm doesn't have enough to sell! In such a case, the second company should rethink its job specifications, or completely change its promotion plans, because the going rate for order getters is much higher than $15,000 a year.

If a job requires extensive travel, aggressive order-getting, or customer service contacts with troublesome customers, the pay may have to be higher. But the salesperson's compensation level should compare, at least roughly, with the pay scale of the rest of the firm. Normally, salespeople earn more than the office or production force but less than top management.

Payment methods vary

Given some competitive level of compensation, there are three basic methods of payment: (1) straight salary, (2) straight commission (incentive), or (3) a combination plan. A straight salary offers the most security for the salesperson. Commission pay, in contrast, offers the most incentive and is tied to results actually achieved. A commission is often based on a percentage of dollar sales, but it may be a financial incentive based on other outcomes—such as the number of new accounts, customer satisfaction ratings, or customer service problems resolved in some time period. Most salespeople want some security, and most companies want salespeople to have some incentive to do better work, so the most popular method is a combination plan that includes some salary and some commission. Bonuses, profit sharing, pensions, stock plans, insurance, and other fringe benefits may be included, too.

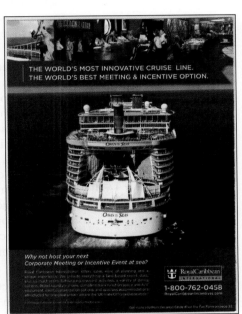

Salespeople that meet certain sales targets may win travel.
© 2015 Royal Caribbean International.

Salary gives control— if there is close supervision

A salesperson on straight salary earns the same amount regardless of how he or she spends time. So the salaried salesperson is expected to do what the sales manager asks—whether it is order-taking, supporting sales activities, solving customer service problems, or completing sales call reports. However, the sales manager maintains control *only* by close supervision. As a result, straight salary or a large salary element in the compensation plan increases the amount of sales supervision needed.

Commissions can both motivate and direct

If personal supervision would be difficult, a firm may get better control with a compensation plan that includes some commission, or even a straight commission plan, with built-in direction. One trucking company, for example, has a sales incentive plan that pays higher commissions on business needed to balance freight shipments—depending on how heavily traffic has been moving in one direction or another. Another company that wants to motivate its salespeople to devote more time to developing new accounts could pay higher commissions on shipments to new customers. However, a salesperson on a straight commission tends to be his or her own boss. The sales manager is less likely to get help on sales activities that won't increase the salesperson's earnings.

Incentives should link efforts to results

The incentive portion of a sales rep's compensation should be large only if there is a direct relationship between the salesperson's efforts and results. Otherwise, a salesperson in a growing territory might have rapidly increasing earnings, while the sales rep in a poor area will have little to show for the same amount of work. Such a situation isn't fair, and it can lead to high turnover and much dissatisfaction. A sales manager can take such differences into consideration when setting a salesperson's **sales quota**—the specific sales or profit objective a salesperson is expected to achieve. Often a salesperson receives a bonus for meeting the sales quota.

Commissions reduce need for working capital

Small companies that have limited working capital or uncertain markets often prefer straight commission, or combination plans with a large commission element. When sales drop off, costs do too. Such flexibility is similar to using manufacturers' agents who get paid only if they deliver sales. This advantage often dominates in selecting a sales compensation method. Exhibit 14–4 shows the general relation between personal selling expense and sales volume for each of the basic compensation alternatives.

Compensation plans should be clear

Salespeople are likely to be dissatisfied if they can't see the relationship between the results they produce and their pay. A compensation plan that includes different commissions for different products or types of customers can become quite complicated. Simplicity is best achieved with straight salary. But in practice, it's usually better to sacrifice some simplicity to gain some incentive, flexibility, and control. The best combination of these factors depends on the job description and the company's objectives.

To make it easier for a sales rep to see the relationship between effort and compensation, some firms provide the rep with that information online. For example, sales reps at Oracle, a company that sells database systems, can check a website and see how they are doing. As new sales results come in, the report at the website is updated. Sales managers can also make changes quickly—for example, by putting a higher commission on a product or more weight on customer satisfaction scores.[19]

Sales managers must plan, implement, and control

Managers must regularly evaluate each salesperson's performance and be certain that all the needed tasks are being done well. The compensation plan may have to be changed if the pay and work are out of line. And by evaluating performance, firms can also identify areas that need more attention—by the salesperson or management.[20]

Exhibit 14-4 Relation between Total Selling Expense and Sales Volume

Personal Selling Techniques—Prospecting and Presenting

LO 14.8

We've stressed the importance of training in selling techniques. Now let's discuss these ideas in more detail so you understand the basic steps each salesperson should follow—including prospecting and selecting target customers, planning sales presentations, making sales presentations, and following up after the sale. Exhibit 14–5 shows the steps we'll consider. You can see that the salesperson is just carrying out a planned communication process, as we discussed in Chapter 13.[21]

Prospecting—narrowing down to the right target

Narrowing the personal selling effort down to the right target requires constant, detailed analysis of markets and much prospecting. Basically, **prospecting** involves following all the leads in the target market to identify potential customers.

Finding live prospects who will help make the buying decision isn't as easy as it sounds. In business markets, for example, the salesperson may need to do some hard detective work to find the real purchase decision makers.

Some companies provide prospect lists or a customer relationship management (CRM) database to make this part of the selling job easier. The CRM database may be integrated with other marketing communication tools to help salespeople spend more time working on the best prospects. ThoughtLava, a website design firm, uses its CRM database to initially contact prospects by e-mail. It uses software that tracks which prospects open the e-mail, which click through to the firm's website, and even

Exhibit 14-5 Key Steps in the Personal Selling Process

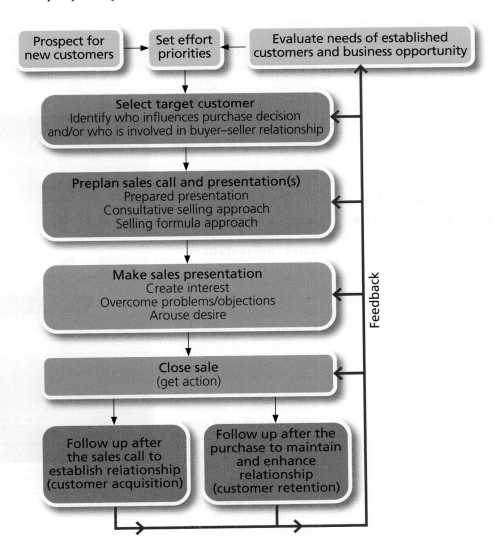

which pages they visit. Given this information, ThoughtLava's salespeople know in advance which of the firm's services interest each prospect, and that helps them decide which prospects to focus on.[22]

All customers are not equal

Although prospecting focuses on identifying new customers, established customers require attention too. It's often time-consuming and expensive to establish a relationship with a customer, so once established it makes sense to keep the relationship healthy. That requires the rep to routinely review active accounts, rethink customers' needs, and reevaluate each customer's long-term business potential. Some small accounts may have the potential to become big accounts, and some accounts that previously required a lot of costly attention may no longer warrant it. So a sales rep may need to set priorities both for new prospects and existing customers.

How long to spend with whom?

Once a set of prospects and customers who need attention has been identified, the salesperson must decide how much time to spend with each one. A sales rep must qualify customers—to see if they deserve more effort. The salesperson usually makes these decisions by weighing the potential sales volume as well as the likelihood of a sale. This requires judgment. But well-organized salespeople usually develop some system because they have too many demands on their time.[23]

Many firms provide their reps with CRM systems to help with this process also. Most of them use some grading scheme. A sales rep might estimate how much each prospect is likely to purchase and the probability of getting and keeping the business, given the competition. The computer then combines this information and grades each prospect. Attractive accounts may be labeled A—and the salesperson may plan to call on them weekly until the sale is made, the relationship is in good shape, or the customer is moved into a lower category. B customers might offer somewhat lower potential and be called on monthly. C accounts might be called on only once a year—unless they happen to contact the salesperson. And D accounts might be transferred to a telemarketing group.[24]

Three kinds of sales presentations may be useful

Once the salesperson selects a target customer, it's necessary to make a **sales presentation**—a salesperson's effort to make a sale or address a customer's problem. But someone has to plan what kind of sales presentation to make. This is a strategy decision. The kind of presentation should be set before the sales rep goes calling. And in situations where the customer comes to the salesperson—in a retail store, for instance— planners have to make sure that prospects are brought together with salespeople.

A marketing manager can choose two basically

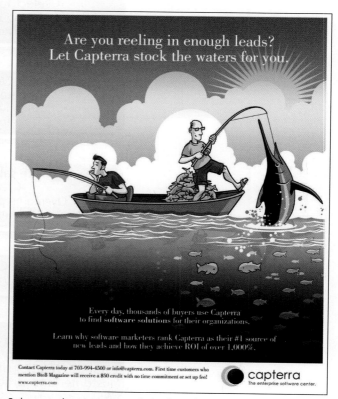

Are you reeling in enough leads? Let Capterra stock the waters for you.

Every day, thousands of buyers use Capterra to find software solutions for their organizations.

Learn why software marketers rank Capterra as their #1 source of new leads and how they achieve ROI of over 1,000%.

Contact Capterra today at 703-994-4500 or info@capterra.com. First time customers who mention BtoB Magazine will receive a $50 credit with no time commitment or set up fee! www.capterra.com

capterra
The enterprise software center.

Salespeople are constantly looking for ways to be more efficient in identifying sales leads and prospects.
Capterra, Inc.; Agency: RMR & Associates.

different approaches to making sales presentations: the prepared approach or the consultative selling approach. Another approach, the selling formula approach, is a combination of the two. Each of these has its place.

The prepared sales presentation

The **prepared sales presentation** approach uses a memorized presentation that is not adapted to each individual customer. This approach says that a customer faced with a particular stimulus will give the desired response—in this case, a yes answer to the salesperson's prepared statement, which includes a **close**, the salesperson's request for an order.

If one trial close doesn't work, the sales rep tries another prepared presentation and attempts another closing. This can go on for some time—until the salesperson runs out of material or the customer either buys or decides to leave. Exhibit 14–6 shows the relative participation of the salesperson and customer in the prepared approach. Note that the salesperson does most of the talking.

Exhibit 14-6 Prepared Approach to Sales Presentation

Firms may rely on this canned approach when only a short presentation is practical. It's also sensible when salespeople aren't very skilled. The company can control what they say and in what order. The approach is often used by telemarketers who may have only a few minutes to get a customer's attention and generate interest. For example, Novartis uses missionary salespeople to tell doctors about new drugs when they're introduced. Doctors are busy, so they give the rep only a minute or two. That's just enough time to give a short, prepared pitch and leave some samples. To get the most out of the presentation, Novartis refines it based on feedback from doctors whom it pays to participate in focus groups.[25]

But a canned approach has a weakness. It treats all potential customers alike. It may work for some and not for others. A prepared approach may be suitable for simple order-taking—but it is no longer considered good selling for complicated situations.

Consultative selling builds on the marketing concept

The **consultative selling approach** involves developing a good understanding of the individual customer's needs before trying to close the sale. This name is used because the salesperson is almost acting as a consultant to help identify and solve the customer's problem. With this approach, the sales rep makes some general benefit statements to get the customer's attention and interest. Then the salesperson asks questions and *listens carefully* to understand the customer's needs. Once they agree on needs, the seller tries to show the customer how the product fills those needs and to close the sale. This is a problem-solving approach—in which the customer and salesperson

Exhibit 14-7 Consultative Selling Approach to Sales Presentation

work together to satisfy the customer's needs. That's why it's sometimes called the need-satisfaction approach. Exhibit 14–7 shows the participation of the customer and the salesperson during such a sales presentation.

The consultative selling approach takes skill and time. The salesperson must be able to analyze what motivates a particular customer and show how the company's offering would help the customer satisfy those needs. The sales rep may even conclude that the customer's problem is really better solved with someone else's product. That might result in one lost sale, but it also is likely to build real trust and more sales opportunities over the life of the relationship with the customer.

Although consultative selling is commonly used in B2B markets, retailers can build relationships with customers by using this approach. Salespeople at Nordstrom's department stores are well known for their attention to customers. They often know their regular customers and will ask a range of questions to make sure they get exactly what they need. A customer looking for a pair of dress pants may be asked a half-dozen questions by a salesperson—"What will you be using them for?" "Do you expect to travel with them?" "Do you prefer something lightweight for summer, or do you want to wear them year-round?" And more. These questions help the salesperson recommend pants that fit the customer's precise needs. This retail salesperson is the customer's consultant on pants. Customers are rewarded with the "perfect fit," and the salesperson and Nordstrom earn the customer's loyalty.[26]

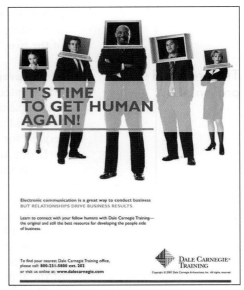

Many firms turn to outside training specialists, like Dale Carnegie Training, for programs that can help salespeople learn how to connect with customers.
LaForce + Stevens Agency/New York.

Selling formula approach—some of both

The **selling formula approach** starts with a prepared presentation outline—much like the prepared approach—and leads the customer through some logical steps to a final close. The prepared steps are logical because we assume that we know something about the target customer's needs and attitudes.

Exhibit 14–8 shows the selling formula approach. The salesperson does most of the talking at the beginning of the presentation—to communicate key points early. This part of the presentation may even have been prepared as part of the marketing strategy. As the sales presentation moves along, however, the salesperson brings the customer into the discussion to help clarify just what needs this customer has. The salesperson's job is to discover the needs of a particular customer to know how to proceed. Once it is clear what kind of customer this is, the salesperson comes back to show how the product satisfies this specific customer's needs and to close the sale.

Exhibit 14-8 Selling Formula Approach to Sales Presentation

AIDA helps plan sales presentations

AIDA—Attention, Interest, Desire, Action: Most sales presentations follow this AIDA sequence. The time a sales rep spends on each of the steps varies depending on the situation and the selling approach being used. But it is still necessary to begin a presentation by getting the prospect's *attention* and, hopefully, to move the customer to *action*.[27]

Ethical issues may arise

As in every other area of marketing communications, ethical issues arise in the personal selling area. The most basic issue, plain and simple, is whether a salesperson's presentation is honest and truthful. But addressing that issue is a no-brainer. No company is served well by a salesperson who lies or manipulates customers to get their business.

What would you do? Assume that you are a sales rep and sell costly electronic systems for use in automated factories. You made a sales presentation to a customer, but he didn't place an order—and then wouldn't take your calls when you tried to inform him that your company was coming out with a more reliable model at the same price. Months later, he faxes a purchase order for immediate delivery on the model you originally discussed. You have the old model in stock, and it will be difficult to sell once the new model arrives in two weeks. In fact, your company has doubled the usual commission rate to clear out the old model. Do you try to contact the customer again to tell him about the new model, or do you do what he has requested and immediately fill the order with the old model? Either way, if you make the sale, the commission will pay for your upcoming vacation to the Caribbean. Explain what you would do and why.

On the other hand, most sales reps sooner or later face a sales situation in which they must make more difficult ethical decisions about how to balance company interests, customer interests, and personal interests. Conflicts are less likely to arise if the firm's marketing mix really meets the needs of its target market. Similarly, they are less likely to occur when the firm sees the value of developing a long-term relationship with the customer. Then the salesperson is arranging a happy marriage. By contrast, ethical conflicts are more likely when the sales rep's personal outcomes (such as commission income) or the selling firm's profits hinge on making sales to customers whose needs are only partially met by the firm's offering. A number of financial services firms, for example, have garnered bad publicity—and even legal problems—from situations like this.

Ideally, companies can avoid the whole problem by supporting their salespeople with a marketing mix that really offers target customers unique benefits. Moreover, top executives, marketing managers, and sales managers set the tone for the ethical climate in which a salesperson operates. If they set impossible goals or project a "do-what-you-need-to-do" attitude, a desperate salesperson may yield to the pressure of the moment. When a firm clearly advocates ethical selling behavior and makes it clear that manipulative selling techniques are not acceptable, the salesperson is not left trying to swim against the flow.[28]

CONCLUSION

In this chapter, we discussed the importance and nature of personal selling. Selling is much more than just getting rid of the product. In fact, a salesperson who is not given strategy guidelines may have to become the strategy planner for the market he or she serves. Ideally, however, the sales manager and marketing manager work together to set some strategy guidelines: the kind and number of salespeople needed, what sales technology support will be provided, the kind of sales presentation desired, and selection, training, and motivation approaches.

We discussed the three basic sales tasks: (1) order-getting, (2) order-taking, and (3) supporting. Most sales jobs combine at least two of these three tasks. We also considered the role of customer service and why it is so important to a firm and its customers. Once a firm specifies the important tasks, it can decide on the structure of its sales

organization and the number of salespeople it needs. The nature of the job and the level and method of compensation also depend on the blend of these tasks. Firms should develop a job description for each sales job. This, in turn, provides guidelines for selecting, training, and compensating salespeople.

Once the marketing manager agrees to the basic plan and sets the budget, the sales manager must implement the plan, including directing and controlling the sales force. This includes assigning sales territories and controlling performance. A sales manager is deeply involved with the basic management tasks of planning and control—as well as ongoing implementation of the personal selling effort.

We also reviewed some basic selling techniques and identified three kinds of sales presentations. Each has its place—but the consultative selling approach seems best for higher-level sales jobs. In these kinds of jobs, personal selling is achieving a new, professional status because of the competence and level of personal responsibility required of the salesperson. The day of the old-time glad-hander is passing in favor of the specialist who is creative, industrious, persuasive, knowledgeable, highly trained, and therefore able to help the buyer. This type of salesperson always has been, and probably always will be, in short supply. And the demand for high-level salespeople is growing.

WHAT'S NOW?

This chapter examined how consumers make buying decisions—and the factors influencing their decision process. For some current real-world examples and learnings, check out *What's Now?* at www.learnthe4ps.com/whatsnow/c14

KEY TERMS

LO 14.9

basic sales tasks, 367
order getters, 367
order-getting, 367
order takers, 368
order-taking, 368
supporting salespeople, 369
missionary salespeople, 369

technical specialists, 370
customer service reps, 370
team selling, 373
major accounts sales force, 373
telemarketing, 374
sales territory, 374
job description, 379

sales quota, 382
prospecting, 383
sales presentation, 384
prepared sales presentation, 385
close, 385
consultative selling approach, 385
selling formula approach, 386

QUESTIONS AND PROBLEMS

1. Review the Ferguson case study that opens the chapter. From this case, identify examples of different key terms and concepts covered in the chapter. For example, it mentions that salespeople specialize by customer segments—part of getting the right structure.

2. Review the Ferguson case study that opens the chapter. The case does not mention how the sales force is compensated—salary, commission, or some combination. Assume they are compensated by straight (100 percent) salary and the company changes to a straight (100 percent) commission compensation. How might this affect how the salespeople behave? What behaviors might become more common? What behaviors might become less common?

3. What strategy decisions are needed in the personal selling area? Why should the marketing manager make these strategy decisions?

4. What kind of salesperson (or what blend of the basic sales tasks) is required to sell the following products? If there are several selling jobs in the channel for each product, indicate the kinds of salespeople required. Specify any assumptions necessary to give definite answers.
   a. Laundry detergent
   b. Costume jewelry
   c. Office furniture
   d. Men's underwear
   e. Mattresses
   f. Corn
   g. Life insurance

5. Distinguish among the jobs of producers', wholesalers', and retailers' order-getting salespeople. If one order getter is needed, must all the salespeople in a channel be order getters? Illustrate.

6. Discuss the role of the manufacturers' agent in a marketing manager's promotion plans. What kind of salesperson is a manufacturers' agent? What type of compensation plan is used for a manufacturers' agent?

7. Discuss the future of the specialty shop if producers place greater emphasis on mass selling because of the inadequacy of retail order-taking.

8. Compare and contrast missionary salespeople and technical specialists.

9. Think about a situation when you or a friend or family member encountered a problem with a purchase and tried to get help from a firm's customer service representative. Briefly describe the problem, how the firm handled it, and what you think about the firm's response. How could it have been improved?

10. Would it make sense for your school to have a person or group whose main job is to handle "customer service" problems? Explain your thinking.

11. A firm that produces mixes for cakes, cookies, and other baked items has an incoming toll-free line for customer service calls. The manager of the customer service reps has decided to base about a third of their pay on the number of calls they handle per month and on the average amount of time on the phone with each customer.

What do you think are the benefits and limitations of this incentive pay system? What would you recommend to improve it?

12. Explain how a compensation plan could be developed to provide incentives for experienced salespeople and yet make some provision for trainees who have not yet learned the job.

13. Cite an actual local example of each of the three kinds of sales presentations discussed in the chapter. Explain for each situation whether a different type of presentation would have been better.

14. Are the benefits and limitations of a canned presentation any different if it is supported with a PowerPoint presentation or DVD than if it is just a person talking? Why or why not?

15. Describe a consultative selling sales presentation that you experienced recently. How could it have been improved by fuller use of the AIDA framework?

16. How would our economy operate if personal salespeople were outlawed? Could the economy work? If so, how? If not, what is the minimum personal selling effort necessary? Could this minimum personal selling effort be controlled by law?

MARKETING PLANNING FOR HILLSIDE VETERINARY CLINIC

Appendix D (the Appendices follow Chapter 19) includes a sample marketing plan for Hillside Veterinary Clinic. Look through the "Marketing Strategy" section.

a. What personal selling tasks are performed at Hillside Veterinary Clinic and who does them?

b. If Hillside wanted to put more emphasis on "order-getting" to promote growth, what ideas do you have for how to do it?

c. Based on the situation analysis, target market, and intended positioning, recommend some ways that Hillside could actively work to improve its reputation for customer service.

SUGGESTED CASES

12. DrV.com—Custom Vitamins
21. Geonovo Chemical, Inc. (GCI)

23. Schmidt Furniture
28. AAT Tools (AAT)

MARKETING ANALYTICS: DATA TO KNOWLEDGE

CHAPTER 14 SALES COMPENSATION

Franco Welles, sales manager for Nanek, Inc., is trying to decide whether to pay a sales rep for a new territory with straight commission or a combination plan. He wants to evaluate possible plans—to compare the compensation costs and profitability of each. Welles knows that sales reps in similar jobs at other firms make about $36,000 a year.

The sales rep will sell two products. Welles is planning a higher commission for Product B—because he wants it to get extra effort. From experience with similar products, he has some rough estimates of expected sales volume under the different plans and various ideas about commission rates. The details are found in the spreadsheet. The program computes compensation and how much the sales rep will contribute to profit. "Profit contribution" is equal to the total revenue generated by the sales rep minus sales compensation costs and the costs of producing the units.

See Connect for the spreadsheet and questions needed to analyze this scenario.

15

CHAPTER FIFTEEN

SUBWAY

Advertising and Sales Promotion

In the summer of 1965, 17-year-old Fred DeLuca was trying to figure out how to pay for college. A family friend suggested that Fred open a sandwich shop—and then the friend invested $1,000 to help get it started. Within a month, they opened their first shop. From that humble start grew the Subway franchise chain, with more than 44,000 outlets in 110 countries.

Targeted advertising, timely publicity, and sales promotion have been important to Subway's growth. For more than a decade, memorable Subway ads have featured Jared Fogle, a college student who was overweight but lost 245 pounds by eating only Subway's low-fat sandwiches such as the "Veggie Delite." Jared says it was a fluke that he ended up in Subway's ads. Subway learned about Jared after a friend wrote a story about his "Subway sandwich diet" in the college newspaper. Subway's strategy at that time focused on its line of seven different sandwiches with less than 6 grams of fat. The objective was to set Subway fare apart from other fast food, position it to appeal to health-conscious eaters, and spark new sales growth. Jared already knew he liked Subway sandwiches, but the "7 under 6" promotion inspired him to incorporate them into his diet.

As soon as Jared's ads began to run, word of his inspiring story spread, and consumer awareness of Subway and its healthy fare increased. It's always hard to isolate the exact impact of ads on sales, but sales grew more than 18 percent that year. The ads also attracted the attention of potential franchisees. Many of them chose to learn more about Subway at local seminars or by watching a video at Subway's website. Interested franchisees also meet with representatives of Subway at franchising trade shows.

Franchisees can develop their own promotions. A south Florida franchisee wanted to boost weekend sales at his two stores, so he offered footlong subs for $5 on Saturdays and Sundays. Business boomed, with lines streaming out the door. A down economy had made customers particularly price-sensitive, so the bargain had wide appeal. And the promotion was profitable because the increased volume of sandwiches made up for the lower margin on each footlong. Word got out and soon other franchisees were selling $5 footlongs. Then the franchisees' advertising group voted to take it nationwide for four weeks, later extending it indefinitely. Soon it was hard to find someone who didn't recognize the five-finger signs and catchy (yet annoying) jingle from the campaign developed by the MMB ad agency. Awareness of the campaign reached 90 percent among 18–64-year-olds.

Subway tries to balance its menu and promotion to appeal to three segments: customers interested in low fat, those most concerned about taste, and those seeking a good value. The "eat fresh" theme and copy thrust of some of Subway's ads appeal to the first two target markets, while in-store signage promotes its "value meals." For those most concerned about taste, Subway counters higher end fare from Panera Bread and Quiznos Subs with its "Subway Selects" line of sandwiches. Subway reinforces its healthy positioning with "Famous Fan" spokespeople such as NBA All-Star Russell Westbrook, Major League Baseball star Mike Trout, and Australian snowboarder Torah Bright, among others.

Subway knows that some media target very specific customer groups. Young people are a major target market for Subway. So it posts banner and video ads on CollegeHumor.com. With so many people now on smartphones, Subway has also created 30-second mobile video ads to let customers know about its avocado-inspired summer sandwiches. The ads get people's attention and interest; then, to turn desire into action, consumers tap on their phone's screen to open a map to the nearest Subway.

Besides spending more time on their mobile devices, many of Subway's target customers spend time on Facebook. Many of these Facebook users are already fans of Subway, as evidenced by the 25 million likes on its page. These customers get regular updates from Subway in their Facebook news feed. Other target customers see Subway's sponsored messages (a fancy name for ads) on Facebook. Ads like these let customers know about new sandwiches or special promotions. For example, one recent Facebook ad asked viewers for "likes" and promised that when the ad reached 40,000 likes, Subway would release a "Free Subs for a Year" promotion. The result was more than 60,000 likes, 800+ comments, and 1,500 shares—bringing a lot more Facebook fans and a lot of attention and awareness for Subway and its promotion—and one lucky winner.

Another Subway target market is families interested in healthy fast food. This group gets a different promotion blend. For example, Subway's Fresh Fit menu for kids and the Fresh Fit for Kids website offer family-friendly advice and reinforces Subway's healthy positioning. Subway sponsors Little League Baseball and Softball, advertises in *Little League* magazine, and targets little leaguers and their parents via direct mail and with point-of-sale materials. Of course the right cartoon characters appeal to Subway's target market of children. So Subway develops kids meals that tie into movies such as *Frozen* and *Inside Out*. The characters from these Disney films can be found in some of Subway's outdoor, cinema, and television advertising as well as on cups and in-store signage.

It has taken more than great promotion to achieve this success—although the more than $500 million Subway spends helps. Convenient locations, a tasty and healthy product, and good value combine to deliver a great customer experience for Subway's target markets, while earning it plenty of positive word-of-mouth along the way. Subway's great Product, Place, and Price don't matter if no one knows about it. So Subway's effective Promotion spreads the message and Subway continues to deliver profitable growth to its owners and franchisees.[1]

LEARNING OBJECTIVES

The Subway case shows that promotion—in particular, advertising and sales promotion—are often critical elements in the success or failure of a strategy. But many firms do a poor job with all three—so just copying how other firms handle these important strategy decisions is not "good enough." There is no sense in imitating bad practices. This chapter helps you understand important decisions that make effective use of advertising, publicity, and sales promotion.

When you finish this chapter, you should be able to

1   Recognize the importance of advertising in the economy.

2   Understand why a marketing manager sets specific objectives to guide the advertising effort.

3   Understand when the various kinds of advertising are needed.

4   Understand how to choose the "best" medium.

5   Understand the main ways that digital advertising differs from advertising in other media.

6   Understand how to plan the "best" message—that is, the copy thrust.

7   Understand what advertising agencies do.

8   Describe the challenges and methods used to measure advertising effectiveness.

9   Understand how to advertise legally.

10 Understand the importance and nature of sales promotion.

11 Know the advantages and limitations of different types of sales promotion.

12 Understand important new terms (shown in red).

Advertising, Sales Promotion, and Marketing Strategy Planning

Advertising and sales promotion can play a central role in the Promotion blend because they reach many customers at the same time. On a per-contact basis, these promotion methods provide a relatively low-cost way to inform, persuade, and activate customers. Advertising and sales promotion can position a firm's marketing mix as the one that meets customer needs. They can help motivate channel members or a firm's own employees, as well as final customers.

Unfortunately the results that marketers *actually achieve* with advertising and sales promotion are very uneven. It has been said that half of the money spent on these activities is wasted—but most managers don't know which half. Mass selling can be exciting and involving, or it can be downright obnoxious. Sometimes it's based on careful research, yet much of it is based on someone's pet idea. A creative idea may produce great results or be a colossal waste of money. Ads can stir emotions or go unnoticed.[2]

This chapter explains approaches to help you understand how successful advertising, publicity, and sales promotion work (see Exhibit 15–1). After a brief overview of the

Exhibit 15–1   Marketing Strategy Planning, Advertising, and Sales Promotion

| Chapter 13 Promotion—Introduction to Integrated Marketing Communications | Chapter 14 Personal Selling and Customer Service | Chapter 15 Advertising and Sales Promotion | Chapter 16 Publicity: Promotion Using Owned Media, Earned Media, and Social Media |

Advertising spending
- Total spending
- Largest advertisers
- Jobs in advertising

Advertising strategy decisions
- Advertising objectives
- Target audience
- Types of advertising
- Media types
- Copy thrust
- Who does the work

Advertising and the law
- Deceptive and unfair advertising
- Standards evolving

Sales promotion decisions
- Objectives
- Challenges
- Match with target market

cost of advertising, we look at the different decisions marketing managers—and the advertising agencies they may work with—have to make: (1) what they want to achieve through advertising, (2) who the target audience is, (3) what kind of advertising to use, (4) which media to use to reach target customers, (5) what to say (the copy thrust), and (6) who will do the work—the firm's own marketing or advertising people or outside agencies. We also discuss legal issues in advertising. There are challenges in managing sales promotion, but it offers advantages over advertising for some objectives. So, this chapter also presents decisions that must be made with respect to different types of sales promotion for different targets.

International dimensions are important

The basic strategy planning decisions for advertising, publicity, and sales promotion are the same regardless of where in the world the target market is located. However, the look and feel can vary a lot in different countries. The choices available

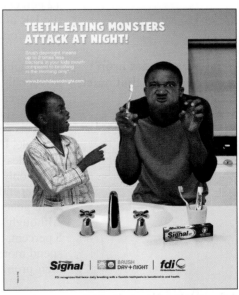

In some parts of Africa, there has not been a long tradition of brushing teeth, so Signal's advertising educates consumers on the importance of regular tooth-brushing.
© 2015 Unilever.

to a marketing manager within each of the decision areas may also vary dramatically from one country to another.

Commercial television may not be available. If it is, government rules may limit the type of advertising permitted or when ads can be shown. For example, privacy laws are stricter in Europe as compared to the United States, making it more difficult to track consumers' online behavior and deliver highly targeted advertising. Radio broadcasts in a market area may not be in the target market's language. The target audience may not be able to read. Access to interactive media such as the Internet may be nonexistent. Cultural influences may limit ad messages. Ad agencies that already know a nation's unique advertising environment may not be available.

Sales promotion can also differ in some international markets. For example, a typical Japanese grocery retailer with only 250 square feet of space doesn't have room for *any* special end-of-aisle displays. Consumer promotions may be affected, too. In some developing nations, samples can't be distributed through the mail because they're routinely stolen before they get to target customers. And some countries ban consumer sweepstakes because they see them as a form of gambling.

In this chapter we'll consider a number of these international issues, but we'll focus on the array of choices available in the United States and other advanced economies.

Advertising Is Big Business

LO 15.1

Total spending is big—and growing internationally

As an economy grows, advertising becomes more important—because more consumers have income and advertising can get results. But good advertising results cost money. And spending on advertising is significant. In 1946, U.S. advertising spending on media (the largest and most easily tracked expense) alone was slightly more than $3 billion. By 2015, it was almost $200 billion—and projected to continue growing about 5 percent per year.[3]

Over the last decade, the rate of advertising spending has increased even more rapidly in other countries. Total ad media spending worldwide was estimated to be at more than $570 billion in 2015. Advertising in the United States accounts for about 32 percent of worldwide ad spending. Advertising in China (the world's second largest advertising market) is growing fast—accounting for about $71 billion in 2015 (about 12 percent of the total worldwide). The next biggest spenders are Japan, Germany, and the UK at $37 billion, $28 billion, and $27 billion respectively. North America, Asia, and Europe are where most advertising money is spent.

Most advertisers aren't really spending that much

Although total spending on advertising seems high, U.S. corporations spend an average of only about 2.5 percent of their sales dollars on advertising. Worldwide, the percentage is even smaller. Exhibit 15–2 shows, however, that advertising spending as a percent of sales dollars varies significantly across product categories. Producers of consumer products generally spend a larger percent than firms that produce business products. For example, U.S. companies that make perfume and cosmetics spend about 20.3 percent of their sales dollars on advertising. However, companies that sell plastics to manufacturers spend only about 1.7 percent on advertising. Some business products companies—those that depend on e-commerce or personal selling—may spend less than 1/10 of 1 percent.

In general, the percent is smaller for retailers and wholesalers than for producers. Although some large chains such as Kohl's, Macy's, and JCPenney spend more than 5 percent, other retailers and wholesalers spend 2 percent or less. Individual firms may spend more or less than others in the industry, depending on the role of advertising in their promotion blend.[4]

Advertising doesn't employ that many people

Although total advertising expenditures are large, the advertising industry itself employs relatively few people. The major expense is for media time and space. Many students hope for a glamorous job in advertising, but there are fewer jobs in advertising than you might think. In the United States, only about 500,000 people work directly in the advertising industry. Advertising agencies employ less than half of all these people.[5]

Exhibit 15-2 Advertising Spending as Percent of Sales for Illustrative Product Categories

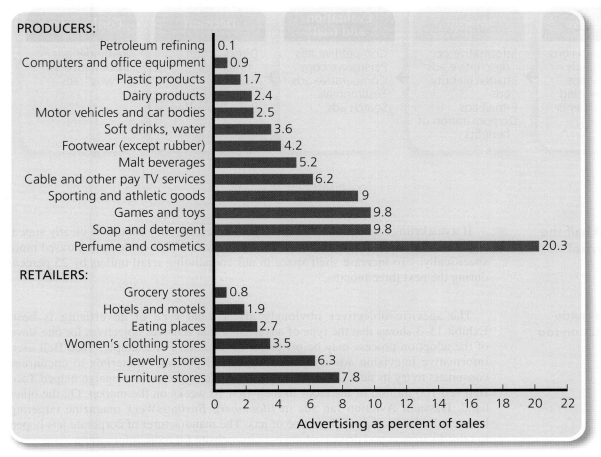

PRODUCERS:

Category	Advertising as percent of sales
Petroleum refining	0.1
Computers and office equipment	0.9
Plastic products	1.7
Dairy products	2.4
Motor vehicles and car bodies	2.5
Soft drinks, water	3.6
Footwear (except rubber)	4.2
Malt beverages	5.2
Cable and other pay TV services	6.2
Sporting and athletic goods	9
Games and toys	9.8
Soap and detergent	9.8
Perfume and cosmetics	20.3

RETAILERS:

Category	Advertising as percent of sales
Grocery stores	0.8
Hotels and motels	1.9
Eating places	2.7
Women's clothing stores	3.5
Jewelry stores	6.3
Furniture stores	7.8

Advertising as percent of sales

Advertising Objectives Are a Strategy Decision

LO 15.2

Advertising objectives must be specific

Every ad and every advertising campaign should have clearly defined objectives. These should grow out of the firm's overall marketing strategy and the promotion jobs assigned to advertising. It isn't enough for the marketing manager to say, "Promote the product." The marketing manager must decide exactly what advertising should do.

Advertising objectives should be more specific than personal selling objectives. One of the advantages of personal selling is that a salesperson can shift the presentation for a specific customer. Each ad, however, must be effective not just for one customer but for thousands, or millions, of them.

The marketing manager sets the overall direction

Advertising objectives usually start with the marketing manager, who works with the advertising manager to develop the objectives and an appropriate budget to accomplish them. The following list contains some potential advertising objectives:

1. For our target market, position the new product as the most technologically advanced in the industry.
2. Increase awareness of our brand to 50 percent in our primary target market.
3. In our new geographic market, obtain trial of our product from 20 percent of our customers by the end of the year.
4. Increase sales of our product by 10 percent.
5. Get 100,000 new customers to visit the website and click through to view information about our new product.

Exhibit 15-3 Examples of Different Types of Advertising over Adoption Process Stages

Awareness	Interest	Evaluation and trial	Decision	Confirmation
Teaser campaigns Pioneering ads Jingles/slogans Viral advertising Announcements	Informative or descriptive ads Image/celebrity ads E-mail ads Demonstration of benefits	Competitive ads Persuasive copy Comparative ads Testimonials Search ads	Direct-action retail ads Point-of-purchase ads Price deal offers	Reminder ads Informative "why" ads

If you want half the market, say so!

If a marketing manager really wants specific results, they should be clearly stated. A general objective is "To help expand market share." This could be rephrased more specifically: "To increase shelf space in our cooperating retail outlets by 25 percent during the next three months."

Objectives guide implementation too

The specific objectives obviously affect what type of advertising is best. Exhibit 15–3 shows that the type of advertising that achieves objectives for one stage of the adoption process may be off target for another. For example, Taco Bell used informative television ads and in-store point-of-purchase materials to encourage consumers to try its new Doritos Locos Tacos. The aggressive campaign helped Taco Bell sell 100 million of the tacos in their first 10 weeks on the market. On the other hand, Dassault Aviation ran ads in *Bloomberg BusinessWeek* magazine targeting business leaders with its Falcon line of jets. The manufacturer of corporate jets hoped to raise awareness and drive customers to its website for more information.

Coordinating advertising across the channel to achieve objectives

Sometimes advertising objectives can be accomplished more effectively or more economically by someone else in the channel. Firms should work closely with other channel members to coordinate advertising efforts to get the best results. For example, a producer of office supplies like Avery Dennison may find that the most economical use of its advertising dollars is the weekly flyer of a retail chain like Office Depot. So Avery Dennison offers **advertising allowances**—price reductions to firms further along in the channel—to encourage them to advertise or otherwise promote the firm's products locally.

Cooperative advertising involves producers sharing in the cost of ads with wholesalers or retailers. This helps the intermediaries compete in their local markets. It also helps the producer get more promotion for its advertising dollars because media usually give local advertisers lower rates than national or international firms. In addition, a retailer or wholesaler who is paying a share of the cost is more likely to follow through.[6]

Objectives Determine the Kinds of Advertising Needed

The chosen advertising objectives largely determine which of two basic types of advertising to use—product or institutional (see Exhibit 15–4). **Product advertising** tries to sell a product. We will discuss three categories of product advertising—pioneering, competitive, and reminder—which focus on getting consumers to know, like, and remember something. Then we will discuss **institutional advertising**, which promotes an organization's image, reputation, or ideas rather than a specific product.

Exhibit 15-4 Types of Advertising

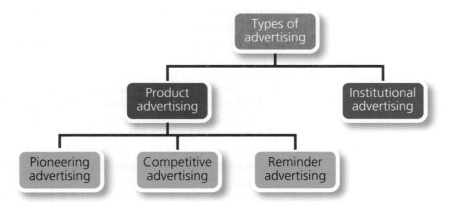

Pioneering advertising builds primary demand

Pioneering advertising tries to develop primary demand for a product category rather than demand for a specific brand. Pioneering advertising is usually done in the early stages of the product life cycle; it informs potential customers about the new product and helps turn them into adopters. When digital cameras first came out, consumers didn't know their benefits or why they might want one—and at the same time they worried about how they could get printed pictures. So advertising for the early products in the market had to explain these basics and build primary demand.

Competitive advertising emphasizes selective demand

Competitive advertising tries to develop selective demand for a specific brand. A firm is forced into competitive advertising as the product life cycle moves along—to hold its own against competitors. For example, as digital cameras moved to the growth stage of the product life cycle, advertising emphasized features and benefits to persuade customers that they needed more megapixels, lower prices, or face recognition.

Competitive advertising may be either direct or indirect. **Direct competitive advertising** aims for immediate buying action. **Indirect competitive advertising** points out product advantages to affect future buying decisions.

Most of Delta Airlines' advertising is of the competitive variety. Much of it tries for immediate sales—so the ads are the direct type with prices, timetables, and phone numbers to call for reservations. Some of its ads are the indirect type. They focus on the quality of service and suggest you check Delta's website the next time you travel.

Mini Cooper's Dutch advertising agency had multiple objectives when it left large empty boxes with torn ribbons and wrapping paper around Amsterdam shortly after Christmas. The boxes created awareness for the Mini Cooper and reinforced its positioning as small, different, and "fun"—like a toy.
Courtesy Ubachswisbrun/ JWT Amsterdam.

Comparative advertising means making specific brand comparisons—using actual product names. Verizon touted its superior coverage with ads showing maps that highlighted its service as compared to AT&T. An Audi television ad shows a guy driving down the highway in his BMW. At full speed, he jumps out of his car and climbs onto a passing truck that is carrying a delivery of new Audi Q5s.

Many countries forbid comparative advertising. But, in the United States, the Federal Trade Commission decided to encourage comparative ads because it thought they would increase competition and provide consumers with more useful information. Superiority claims are supposed to be supported by research evidence—but the guidelines aren't clear. When P&G's Dryel did not fare well in independent test comparisons with stain removal by professional dry cleaners, P&G changed its ad claims. However, some firms just keep running tests until they get the results they want. Others talk about minor differences that don't reflect real customer value. Comparative ads can also backfire by calling attention to competing products that consumers had not previously considered.

Reminder advertising reinforces a favorable relationship

Reminder advertising tries to keep the product's name before the public. It may be useful when the product has achieved brand preference or insistence, perhaps in the market maturity or sales decline stages. It is used primarily to reinforce previous promotion. Here the advertiser may use soft-sell ads that just mention or show the name—as a reminder. Hallmark, for example, often relies on reminder ads because most consumers already know the brand name and, after years of promotion, associate it with high-quality cards and gifts.

Institutional advertising—remember our name

Institutional advertising usually focuses on the name and prestige of an organization or industry. It may seek to inform, persuade, or remind. Its basic objective is to develop goodwill or improve an organization's relations with various groups—not only customers but also current and prospective channel members, suppliers, shareholders, employees, and the general public. The British government, for instance, uses institutional advertising to promote England as a place to do business. Many Japanese firms, like Hitachi, emphasize institutional advertising, in part because they often use the company name as a brand name.

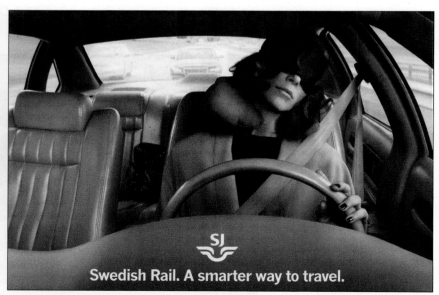

Purex Complete with Zout uses a direct type of competitive advertising; the ad offers a free sample to encourage immediate action. The indirect competitive ad for Swedish Rail points out advantages of taking the train as compared to driving.
Left: © 2015 Henkel Corporation. ALL RIGHTS RESERVED; Right: Courtesy King/Stockholm.

Companies sometimes rely on institutional advertising to present the company in a favorable light, perhaps to overcome image problems. Other organizations use institutional advertising to advocate a specific cause or idea. Insurance companies and organizations such as Mothers Against Drunk Driving, for example, use these advocacy ads to encourage people not to drink and drive.[7]

Choosing the "Best" Medium—How to Deliver the Message

LO 15.4

Advertising media are the various means by which the message is communicated to the target market. The first column of Exhibit 15–5 lists some of the most common kinds of media.[8] Marketing managers seek the best medium, which varies with the situation. Effectiveness depends on how well the medium fits with the rest of a marketing strategy—that is, it depends on (1) your promotion objectives, (2) what target markets you want to reach, (3) the funds available for advertising, and (4) the nature of the media, including whom they *reach,* with what *frequency,* with what *impact,* and at what *cost.*

Exhibit 15–5 shows estimated ad spending for 2015 and 2018, as well as relative shares and growth. It also indicates some pros and cons of major kinds of media. As the exhibit shows, television continues to draw the largest share of advertising spending, though it is projected to see a slight decline in coming years. Digital media sources are the next largest media outlay, though desktop and laptop are in decline and the largest growth occurs in advertising on mobile devices. The combined digital spending is projected to be greater than television in the next few years. Radio advertising and print advertising in newspapers and magazines each receive less than 10 percent of the total media spend—and all are in decline.[9]

Although digital advertising media are clearly the growth opportunity for advertising, more traditional media sources will still receive the majority of media spending in the near future. And that will be even truer in most countries around the world where access to the Internet lags the United States and major western markets (see Exhibit 3–5). So our discussion of advertising media will begin with a closer look at this important part of the advertising media budget. A discussion of digital and mobile as advertising media follows.

Medium should fit promotion objectives

The medium should support the promotion objectives. If the objective requires demonstrating product benefits, TV or Internet with video may be the best alternative. If the objective is to inform, telling a detailed story and using precise pictures, then Internet advertising might be right. Newspapers work well for businesses operating in local markets. Alternatively, with a broad target market or when there is a need to show color, magazines may be better. For example, when Jockey wanted to show customers the variety of styles and colors in its men's underwear, it was concerned about showing men just wearing underwear on television. So Jockey switched its advertising to magazines, where it felt more comfortable showing those images.[10]

Match your market with the media

To guarantee good media selection, the advertiser first must *clearly* specify its target market. Then the advertiser can choose media that reach those target customers. Most media firms use marketing research to develop profiles of their audiences. Generally, this research focuses on demographic characteristics rather than the segmenting dimensions specific to the planning needs of *each* different advertiser.

Advertisers pay for the whole audience

Advertisers pay for the whole audience to whom the media delivers, including those who aren't potential customers. For example, Delta Faucet, a faucet manufacturer that wanted its ads to reach plumbers, placed ads on ESPN's Saturday college football telecasts. Research showed that many plumbers watched the ESPN games. Yet plumbers are only a very small portion of the total college football audience—and the size of the total audience determined the cost of the advertising time.[11]

Exhibit 15-5 Estimated U.S. Ad Spending and Projected Growth, and Advantages and Disadvantages of Major Advertising Media

Kind of Media	2015 Ad Spending ($ billions)	Share of 2015 ad spending (%)	2018 Ad Spending ($ billions)	Share of 2018 ad spending (%)	Change 2015-2018 (%)	Advantage	Disadvantages
TV (broadcast & cable)	70.6	37.3	67.6	35.7	-4.3	Demonstrations, image building, good attention, wide reach, cable can be targeted	"Clutter"—ads compete for attention, expensive, limited time (usually 30 seconds or less), often skipped by viewers
Digital - Desktop/laptop	32.0	16.9	20.6	10.9	-35.5	Ads link to more detailed website, some "pay for results," easier to track results, can be highly targeted	Hard to compare costs with other media
Digital - Mobile	26.5	14.0	50.0	26.4	88.6	Same as above – plus location based	Same as above
Newspapers	16.3	8.6	13.4	7.1	-17.4	Flexible, timely, local market, covers a lot in a geographic area	"Clutter"—ads compete for attention, poor photo reproduction, declining readership of newspapers, usually focused on sales
Radio	15.5	8.2	13.4	7.1	-13.4	Wide reach, segmented audience, inexpensive, use of sound and voices can help create certain image of business	Weak attention, many different rates, short exposure, declining audience, listeners cannot review the ad, ads interrupt entertainment
Magazines	15.0	7.9	13.1	6.9	-12.7	High reader involvement, very targeted, good detail, some "pass along", image quality high – better for photos	Inflexible, long lead times, cost can be high, limited flexibility on location of ad within magazine
Outdoor and cinema	7.4	3.9	6.8	3.6	-7.7	Captive audience, can be geographic and local	Outdoor—"glance" medium Cinema—primarily a younger audience
Directories	5.9	3.1	4.4	2.3	-25.8	Reaches local customers ready to buy, relatively inexpensive	Many competitors listed in same place, hard to differentiate, declining use, pages look cluttered
Total	189.4		220.6		16.5		

Data for advertising spending differs depending on the source, but the overall ratios and trends are similar. For another source, see IAB internet advertising revenue report, 2014 full year results, April 2015, an industry survey conducted by PwC and sponsored by the Interactive Advertising Bureau. These data come from : "Total US Ad Spending to See Largest Increase Since 2004," *eMarketer*, July 2, 2014

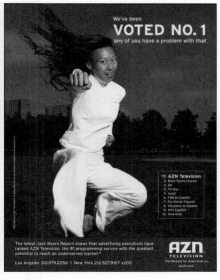

Cable television can offer targeted messages to specific demographic, social, and cultural groups.

Select media to zero in on specific target markets

Today, advertisers direct more attention to reaching smaller, more defined target markets. Even traditional media are becoming more targeted. TV is a good example. Cable TV channels—such as CNN, Nickelodeon, ESPN, MTV, and the Golf Channel—are taking advertisers away from the networks because they target specific audiences. The Golf Channel, for example, averages around 130,000 viewers at a time, but these upscale consumers are *the* target market for makers of golf clubs, balls, and accessories. So advertising on the networks for golf products isn't nearly as efficient as advertising on a single cable channel. Moreover, being specialized doesn't necessarily mean that the target market is small. MTV appeals most strongly to young viewers, but its programming is seen in about 400 million homes worldwide.

Using big data, TV tailors ads to individual households

As discussed in Chapter 7, research firms are collecting big data from consumers' credit and loyalty cards, online activities, and other sources to build profiles of individual households. This information allows advertisers to have a more in-depth understanding of each household and to target individual households with desired characteristics. Now this information is being combined with technology that allows cable television operators to deliver particular ads to different households—even when the different households are watching the same show. This capability allows cable TV to deliver ads exactly where it wants them to be seen.

The U.S. Army has used this technology to aim recruitment ads at specific target markets. For example, its "family influencers" target market received a TV ad showing a daughter discussing her enlistment decision with her parents. At the same time, households fitting the "youth ethnic 1" segment saw an ad showing African American men testing and repairing military equipment. Other groups saw ads customized to their demographic background and role in the enlistment decision. This may be the future of television advertising.[12]

Magazines sort readers by special interests

Many magazines serve only special interest groups, such as cooks, new parents, and personal computer users. Others target people working in particular fields such as furniture retailing and electrical wholesaling. The most profitable magazines seem to be the ones aimed at clearly defined target markets. With the right campaign, magazines deliver results.

For example, LEGO had a promotion objective of getting parents to use its Duplo line of building blocks as a way for them to play *with* their kids—instead of sending

Advertising managers often look to grab attention with alternative media. The yellow stripes were already part of the Swiss crosswalk and the red package was added for Zurifest, a well-attended event in Switzerland.
© 2010-2015 McDonald's. All Rights Reserved. Agency: TBWA/Zurich.

kids off to play on their own. So they turned to *Parents* magazine. LEGO managers created a pull-out calendar that featured 31 activities for parents to do with their kids. LEGO asked parents to post pictures of themselves doing the Duplo activities with their kids to the Duplo Facebook page. Following the ad, LEGO research saw a jump in parents' purchase intention and belief that Duplo made their kids smarter.[13]

Internet cuts into newspapers and directories

Newspapers and directories such as the *Yellow Pages* used to be "must buys" for local businesses. Now consumers just turn to Google, Craigslist, or an app like Urban Spoon for local information. Advertising in newspapers and directories is in decline, with no revival in sight. Hungry families used to grab the *Yellow Pages* and flip to "Pizza"—now they just type "Pizza" or "Papa John's" into a search engine.

Specialized media are small, but gaining

The advertising media listed in Exhibit 15–5 attract the vast majority of advertising media budgets. But advertising specialists always look for cost-effective new media that will help advertisers reach their target markets. For example, one company successfully sells space for signs on bike racks that it places in front of 7-Eleven stores. A new generation of ATMs shows video ads while customers wait to get their money.

Some B2B advertisers are using specialized media to target difficult-to-reach target markets. Companies with products for doctors and medical offices can be a particular challenge to reach. Practice Fusion developed ad-supported software that organizes medical records. In exchange for the free software, doctors get a daily dose of advertising. The doctors are so difficult to reach that advertisers pay 20 times as much to run ads on Practice Fusion's software as they would to run the same ad on Yahoo! or Facebook. The Internet offers advertisers many creative opportunities, so let's examine this medium in more detail.[14]

Digital and Mobile Advertising

LO 15.5

Customer viewing moves to new screens

As Exhibit 15–5 demonstrates, the Internet—accessible through computers and, more frequently, mobile phones—is where advertisers expect to spend an increasing share of their media budget. This change in media spending follows trends observed in how Americans spend time with different media. For example, research shows the average American's daily time with *print* newspapers and magazines dropped from about 50 minutes in 2010 to 26 minutes in 2014. During that same time period, Americans' time with digital media went from just over 3 hours per day to almost 6 hours per day. That increase in digital media consumption has been driven largely by mobile devices—which went from less than 30 minutes to almost three hours per day. As time spent online grows—especially accessing the Internet from mobile devices—it only makes sense that advertisers will follow.[15]

The Internet allows consumers to socialize with friends, review news and other information, enjoy entertainment like videos, and shop. This change in consumer behavior creates new challenges and opportunities for marketing managers targeting specific customers or segments through digital media (computers and mobile devices). Chapter 16 discusses how marketing managers use *unpaid* media—often on the Internet—to communicate with customers. In this section, we look at how *paid media*—via online and mobile *advertising*—are used in marketing strategy planning. We begin by highlighting some of digital advertising's unique qualities and then describe some of the main types of digital and online advertising.

Most advertisers pay only if ads deliver

Advertisers often pay for online ads differently than with other media. Most media charge customers based on the number of people who see an ad—the number of viewers of a television show or readers of a magazine, for example. Most websites, on the other hand, use a **pay-per-click** advertising model, where advertisers pay media costs only when a customer clicks on the ad and links to the advertiser's website. Pay-per-click advertising is a big shift from traditional media where firms pay for ads based on an estimate of how many people will see the ad. Many firms like this ability to directly track the cost of advertising and resulting sales—this allows a marketing manager to set a budget and track return on investment.

Consider Omaha Steaks, which sells frozen meat by mail order and uses Google search ads. Its ads appear when any of about 1,600 keywords, including *Omaha steaks* or *filet mignon,* are entered at Google. Omaha Steaks pays about 30–35 cents for each click-through. "Omaha Steaks" gets about 200–300 clicks per day.[16]

The Internet offers some unique benefits for advertisers. The advertisement on the left appeared on the website for NBCNews.com after one of the authors made a purchase at the online clothing retailer Territory Ahead. The shirt featured in the ad was one the author considered but did not purchase. This is an example of retargeting. VW wants customers to understand that drivers can start the new Tiguan with their keys in their pocket, by simply pressing a button. To demonstrate this feature online, customers first click their cursor on the ad. Next, the customer is asked to touch their webcam—at which time the viewer hears the car start and sees it drive out of the ad.
Left: © territory ahead. All rights reserved; Right: © 2015 Volkswagen of America, Inc.

Exhibit 15-6   Types of Digital Advertising, Examples, Advantages and Disadvantages

Type of Digital Ad	Advantages	Disadvantages
Banner ads (including pop-up ads)	Relatively low cost, banner ads work best for building a brand and image, good tracking tools can measure effectiveness, targeted ads can bring in customers	Some types (especially pop-up) can be seen as intrusive, browser ad blockers may limit reach, banner ads so prevalent that people tend to ignore them
Directories and classifieds (e.g., Craigslist)	Low cost, highly targeted, best for customers ready to buy	Does not work for brand building, does not fit for large companies
Search advertising (e.g., Google Adwords)	Easy to set budget and control costs, targets users in information gathering stage of the buying process, easy to measure return on investment, highly targeted; high credibility	Bidding process for keywords can become costly, information overload for customers, limited space for copy thrust, limited/no image capability
Social network advertising (on Facebook, Twitter and other social media sites)	High knowledge of individuals, potentially wide reach, can stimulate viral, can be narrowly targeted, relatively low cost, "endorsements" from friends likes can be powerful, easy to set a budget	Users of social media actively avoid advertising, advertiser generally has less data than from other sources
Mobile advertising (often includes search and social networks advertising on smartphones)	A large and growing audience, works best for high involvement/utilitarian products, potential for location-based targeting, works well for immediate purchase	Technical limitations (small screen, bandwidth, data transfer), not user friendly, not very interactive, measurement tools still emerging

Online ads know where customers have been on the web

Advertising online also allows customers to be tracked. Some websites place a small file called a cookie on the computer of people who visit their sites. The customer can be tracked—allowing the advertiser to target specific customers who have demonstrated an interest in their company. **Retargeting** (or *behavioral retargeting*) displays ads to a web user based on sites they have previously visited. When that customer fails to make a purchase, she may receive ads at other (unrelated) websites reminding her of previous website visits. So for example, when a customer checks out desk chairs at online retailer Overstock.com—but decides not to purchase—the customer may soon see ads for those same desk chairs on other websites. Perhaps you have experienced advertising "stalking" you online.

The cookies left on a person's computer also make it possible to infer a customer's interests. A California theme park used this approach to increase vacation package sales at its website. Special ads were delivered to web surfers whose computers had cookies indicating they lived in specific western states and had visited a travel site in the previous two weeks. Although this proved to be a cost-effective way to target ads and boost online sales, some web surfers find the invasion of privacy a bit creepy.[17]

Different types of digital advertising

There are many different types of digital advertising. Exhibit 15–6 lists some examples of the main types of digital advertising. Each offers some advantages and disadvantages.[18]

Most online advertisers seek a direct response—they entice a customer to click on a link, gather information, and engage. Advertising on the Internet has evolved quickly, with marketing managers receiving rapid feedback and then having the ability to quickly implement changes based on that feedback. Further, advances in technology continually open doors for new types of advertising. To get the attention of web surfers, Internet advertisers have created different types of ads. Most of these ads also utilize pay-per-click and engage in retargeting as described above.

Banner and pop-up ads build brands

Banner ads are a type of online advertising that places an ad on a web page—often across the top or to the side of the page's primary content. *Pop-up ads* are similar to banner ads, but usually cover an entire browser window—"popping up" in front of (or sometimes behind) a user's browser page. The ads are often used to create awareness or build a brand. The *click-through-rate*—number of people who click on the ad divided by the number of people the ad is presented to—is very low (about 1 in 1,000). That rate can be bumped up a bit when video or other active media are presented. These ads are often annoying to users—and many people install pop-up blocker software that prevents the ads from opening up.[19]

Directory and classified ads

When customers know what they want, they may turn to a directory or classified ad. People looking for a used car might look on Craigslist or a directory service such as Cars.com. These sites can be low cost and work well for local businesses, but don't generally work well for generating awareness or brand building.

Search engine ads know what you want

Google and Facebook are battling for the future of advertising. Google's (and other search engines such as Bing and Yahoo!) advantage is that customers often turn to the site to help with a purchase decision. Search may occur when a customer has a problem—but no solution—or it may occur when a customer knows exactly what he wants to buy. Statistics show that more than 80 percent of consumers use search engines for at least some of their shopping. So when customers are shopping, the sponsored search ads that appear along with the organic search results are usually relevant and helpful. Retailers like REI capitalize on this knowledge by paying a search engine firm for a sponsored search ad. For example, REI will pay for one of its ads to appear above or next to the results of a search on "hiking boots."

Some firms use keywords associated with competitors—and "hijack" potential customers. For example, when a customer typed "iphone 6s" into Google, he laughed when an ad appeared for an iPhone competitor, which stated, "Awkward You Obviously – Mean S6 – Samsung.com" (Samsung's Galaxy S6 phone). Is this competitive? Does it cross an ethical line?

Social media sites know who you are

Facebook's advantage follows from the detailed knowledge it has of each of its users. When Facebook users fill out a profile, they give Facebook demographic information. And with each new status update, photo, friend, "Like," and clicked link, a user gives Facebook more and more insights about themselves, their preferences, and their values. Facebook knows most of its users' ages, ethnicities, jobs, relationship statuses, restaurant preferences, favorite music groups, birthdays, and much more. Facebook analyzes this information to offer advertisers very specific profiles that help advertisers target ads. The challenge for Facebook is that users don't go to the social network with buying in mind—they go to see what their friends are doing. Users tend to ignore various types of advertising that Facebook has tried, and the click-through rate on Facebook ads has been very low.

Specialized media offer opportunities for highly targeted messages. Ford Motorcraft services Ford cars needing repair or maintenance. The need for such services rises in bad weather. So Ford Motocraft worked with the Weather Channel UK to place ads on the backdrops for the Weather Channel app. The ads would appear only during specific weather conditions—including snow, rain, and fog.
© 2015 Ford Motor Company. ©2001-2015, The Weather Channel LLC weather.com®.

Are smartphones an advertising game-changer?

Smartphones are becoming increasingly ubiquitous in developed countries. In the United States, more than three out of four 18–34-year-olds have smartphones. And we have already noted how much more time people are spending on mobile devices as compared to the time they spend on their computers. This creates a new opportunity for advertisers. The biggest players in mobile advertising are Google and Facebook, which offer search and social networking services through mobile devices—and deliver advertising at the same time. Because mobile devices track customers' whereabouts (through GPS), the segmenting dimension of physical location at a specific time can be added to target marketing. Many businesses—bars, restaurants, and retail stores—find it useful to target customers based on this dimension. For example, a Panera restaurant could benefit from advertising to customers who are walking within a few blocks of the restaurant around lunch time. At the very least, because customers are conducting searches and accessing social media from mobile devices, advertisers should consider having mobile friendly versions of their ads.[20]

Big data helps advertisers serve timely ads

Let's look at an example of how one company leveraged big data and a mobile platform to deliver relevant advertising to customers. After examining billions of flu-related web searches over a five-year period, Google found it could predict where flu outbreaks were occurring two weeks before published reports from the Centers for Disease Control and Prevention. Google Flu Trends allows anyone to access this information. Marketing managers for Vicks Behind Ear Thermometer saw an opportunity to leverage Google's big data on flu trends. Vicks wanted to target mothers—and Pandora (streaming music service) had data that allowed them to identify listeners with kids. Vicks further segmented moms by delivering ads only in areas of the country experiencing flu outbreaks with the message: "Flu levels in your area are high. Be prepared with Vicks revolutionary Behind Ear Thermometer." Tapping the ad would direct the mom to the nearest store that sold the thermometer: "Buy at Walgreens 0.5 miles away." Big data and mobile advertising allowed Vicks to narrowly segment the market and deliver timely, relevant messages moms were grateful to receive.[21]

Ethics and digital advertising

There are a number of ethical issues surrounding online advertising—particularly with regard to deception and privacy. The U.S. government has been critical of Google, Yahoo, and Bing—claiming these search engines do little to distinguish the natural or organic search results offered by a search engine from the paid advertising. Because customers tend to favor organic results, this can be misleading and potentially deceptive. Back in 2002, the FTC asked search engines to use shading, borders, text differences, or labels to clearly differentiate the search results from paid advertising. Over the last dozen or so years, the search engines have made such differences less apparent.[22]

Advertisers don't mind paying when interested customers click on their ads. However *click fraud* occurs when a person or software program automatically clicks on an ad without having any interest in the ad's subject. The intent is to defraud the advertiser and make money for an unscrupulous website. Consider Martin Fleischmann, for example. As owner of the insurance quote site MostChoice.com, he found that many of the click-throughs on his ads came from "customers" in Botswana, Mongolia, and Syria—where MostChoice did not do business. After investigating, Fleischmann discovered he was paying for clicks on sites with names like insurance1472.com—where uninterested people were being paid by the owners of these sites to simply click on the ads placed there by Google. The owners of these sites host the ads and get paid because their ads generate click-throughs. Some unscrupulous characters even employ "robots" (online software) to automatically click on the ads on their sites. Recently Google estimated that about half of all online ads are seen only by robots. This is a serious issue that will have to be fixed if online advertising is to get credibility with advertisers.[23]

Cookies and mobile advertising both raise questions about privacy. Cookies track a person's whereabouts on the Internet. Mobile advertising is based on an advertiser knowing where a customer is physically located at any given time. Some question if it

What's Next? Does advertising that's everywhere get us anywhere?

There's no holiday from advertising. You get to the beach, look down, and see huge versions of the Skippy peanut butter logo embossed in the sand. You roll your eyes in dismay and catch a view of a plane pulling a 100-foot-long banner ad with Catherine Zeta-Jones urging you to "Sign up for T-Mobile's free Friday minutes." You walk down the street and try to ignore the billboards and bus stop shelter ads. But it's hard not to notice trucks whose trailers are billboards and yes, those are ads on the trucks' mud flaps, too. Is that a picture of Colonel Sanders on a fire hydrant making your mouth water for KFC's "fiery" chicken wings? A bus drives by wrapped in an ad for McDonald's and you see a taxicab with hubcaps advertising Taco Bell.

You are getting hungry, but you packed a lunch and seek refuge in a nearby park. Not quite an escape from ads—the bench you sit on is an ad for a check-cashing service and for good measure the banana you pull out of your lunch bag has a sticker advertising Florida oranges. A couple of girls walk by wearing T-shirts emblazoned with "Abercrombie and Fitch" and "Old Navy." Then you hear a deep voice but it's just a cell phone; the ring tone of the guy sitting next to you is promoting Stephen King's new movie with the author's voice. You think, "What next?" when a text message offers you discounted admission at a club a block away from where you are sitting—do they know where you are?

You need to get away from this commercial overload, so you head back to your condo to kick back, watch a movie, play computer games, and maybe read e-mail. But this is no escape! An ad and discount for the local Hard Rock Café are printed on the key to your rented condo. The "ad-free" pay-per-view movie has product placements from Red Bull, Blackberry, and Mercedes Benz. You pull out your laptop to play "The Sims" video game and see a virtual gift from a friend—a "Dunkin' Donuts Big and Toasted" breakfast sandwich. So you close the game and check your e-mail. You sort through your e-mails—half of which are uninvited spam messages. Scanning your Facebook you see a "sponsored message" from Subway and a friend sharing a T-Mobile commercial featuring Kim Kardashian #KimsDataStash. Did you really need to see that? Maybe you can read a book and escape. At least you paid the extra $20 for the ad-free version of the Amazon Kindle e-reader. Is there no place to hide?

There are many cases where promotion benefits consumers and companies. After all, it is revenues from advertising that cover the cost of lots of great stuff consumers get for free. Yet sometimes you can't help but wish that you—and your wallet—were not the target of so many companies! What do you think of *all* this advertising? How is it good and bad for individuals? Society? Advertisers?[24]

---

is appropriate for advertisers to track people—especially because most have not knowingly given the advertiser permission to track their whereabouts. Research has suggested that these are serious concerns for many consumers—marketing managers need to tread carefully or they may invite regulation.[25]

Privacy is also an issue with social networking ads. At least here customers are knowingly giving their personal data to Facebook—though many Facebook users may not be aware of how Facebook uses their data.

Marketing managers can choose from many different advertising media—online and off—to deliver their messages. It raises questions about whether this much advertising hits its target and how many targets it hits. Ponder the value of advertising as you read, *"What's Next?* Does advertising that's everywhere get us anywhere?"

Planning the "Best" Message—What to Communicate

LO 15.6

Specifying the copy thrust

Once you decide *how* the messages will reach the target audience, you have to decide on the **copy thrust**—what the words and illustrations should communicate. Carrying out the copy thrust is the job of advertising specialists. But the advertising manager and the marketing manager need to understand the process to be sure that the job is done well.[26]

The copy thrust—both the text and the image—in this ad for Lurpak butter grabs attention and holds interest.
© LURPAK 2014-2015; Agency: Saatchi & Saatchi/London.

Let AIDA help guide message planning

Basically, the overall marketing strategy should determine *what* the message should say. Then management judgment, perhaps aided by marketing research, can help decide how to encode this content so it will be decoded as intended.

As a guide to message planning, we can use the AIDA concept: getting Attention, holding Interest, arousing Desire, and obtaining Action.

Getting attention

Getting attention is an ad's first job. Many readers leaf through magazines without paying attention to any of the ads, and viewers get snacks during TV commercials. When watching a program on TiVo, they may zip past the commercial with a flick of a button. On the Internet, they may use a pop-up blocker or click on the next website before the ad message finishes loading onto the screen.

Many attention-getting devices are available. A large headline, computer animations, shocking statements, attractive models, animals, online games, special effects—anything different or eye-catching—may do the trick. However, the attention-getting device can't detract from, and hopefully should lead to, the next step: holding interest.

Holding interest

Holding interest is more difficult. A humorous ad, an unusual video effect, or a clever photo may get your attention—but once you've seen it, then what? If there is no relation between what got your attention and the marketing mix or the ad does not address your needs, you'll move on. To hold interest, the tone and language of the ad must fit with the experiences and attitudes of the target customers and their reference groups. As a result, many advertisers develop ads that relate to specific emotions. They hope that the good feeling about the ad will stick, even if its details are forgotten.

Arousing desire

Arousing desire to buy a particular product is one of an ad's most difficult jobs. The ad must convince customers that the product can meet their needs. Testimonials may persuade a consumer that other people with similar needs like the product. Product comparisons may highlight the advantages of a particular brand.

To arouse desire, an ad should usually focus on a *unique selling proposition* that aims at an important unsatisfied need. This can help differentiate the firm's marketing mix and position its brand as offering superior value to the target market. Too many advertisers ignore the idea of a unique selling proposition. Rather than using an integrated blend of communications to tell the whole story, they cram too much into each ad—and then none of it has any impact.

Obtaining action

Getting action is the final requirement—and not an easy one. From communication research, we now know that prospective customers must be led beyond considering how the product *might* fit into their lives to actually trying it.

Direct-response ads can sometimes help promote action by encouraging interested consumers to do *something* even if they are not ready to make a purchase. For example,

Fidelity Investments has run TV ads featuring colorful graphs, a sign with "Wow!" and the company's phone number and website address. And just in case viewers don't "get it," Blondie's song "Call Me" plays in the background. Fidelity wants to encourage interested consumers to make the first step in building a relationship.[27]

Is native advertising ethical?

Sometimes the "best messages" are disguised—and not obviously advertising. Consumers tend to have their "guard" up when they know something is advertising—and advertisers try to bring that guard down. One approach makes it difficult to distinguish between advertising and media content. *Native advertising* is advertising designed to not look like ads; it mimics the look and feel of the platform on which the ad appears. For example, an advertiser might write an article to promote a product and post it on a newspaper's website—and the font, layout, and writing style of the "ad" make it appear to be another article at the site. Native advertising may also be placed on the radio, in a magazine, or on a podcast. Native advertisements are typically accompanied with phrases such as "sponsored by" or "posted by" that indicate the name of the advertiser.

For example, carmaker Mini USA published "25 Places That Look Not Normal," in collaboration with online news site BuzzFeed. The post said, "Prepare to have your mind blown. We tip our hats to those who see things differently" (link to http://goo.gl/wME-BgA). Below the title, you see Mini USA listed unobtrusively in text. Then, following 25 pretty awesome looking places, you see Mini's slogan "We tip our hats to those who see things differently. MINI. NOT NORMAL," followed by a video advertisement for Mini.

Advertisers have found that native advertising works—catchy headlines get people's attention and people engage with the content. Consumers find these ads more credible than traditional advertising—perhaps because they don't think they are ads. With many print publications and their websites struggling for profits, native advertising is viewed as a promising revenue source—and its use has increased in recent years. Critics charge that native advertising deceives readers and is therefore unethical. The Federal Trade Commission, which regulates advertising, has had hearings to determine whether and how to regulate the practice, but has not issued guidance to this point.[28]

Ethical Dilemma

What would you do? You are the director of marketing for an online dating company. Your company is an upstart in the industry—still trying hard to get attention in a world where Match.com, OKCupid, Tinder, and others are well known. *NewsSpace*, an online site known for its cleverness in attracting readers with its entertaining and provocative headlines, has approached your marketing team with an offer to advertise an article it will post on the site. Your company slogan is "Mating Habits for Humans." *NewsSpace* wants to post an article "9 Awesome Animal Mating Habits"—which would provide a photo of how different animals show care and concern for others of their kind. *NewsSpace* proposes that #9 on the list would be something for humans and feature your company's website. A video ad for your company would be in the #10 slot. The company has ideas for ranking 1 through 8, but you can influence those in any way you like. The ad would appear to be just another article at the site—using the same format and function as other articles—but in small type it would be noted "Sponsored by. . . . " A couple people on your team think this is a great idea. A few others wonder if the practice might be deceptive or possibly even illegal. The representative from *NewsSpace* says that it is legal and they get few complaints. Would you run this type of ad? If yes, explain why and what you would tell those who oppose the ad. If no, explain why and what you would tell those who are in favor.[29]

Advertising Agencies Often Do the Work

LO 15.7

An advertising manager manages a company's advertising effort. Many advertising managers, especially those working for large retailers, have their own advertising departments that plan specific advertising campaigns and carry out the details. Others turn over much of the advertising work to specialists—the advertising agencies.

Ad agencies are specialists

Advertising agencies are specialists in planning and handling mass selling details for advertisers. Agencies play a useful role. They are independent of the advertiser and have an outside viewpoint. They bring experience to an individual client's problems because they work for many other clients. They can often do the job more economically than a company's own department. And if an agency isn't doing a good job, the client can select another. However, ending a relationship with an agency is a serious decision. Too many marketing managers just use their advertising agency as a scapegoat. Whenever anything goes wrong, they blame the agency.

Some full-service agencies handle any activity related to advertising, publicity, or sales promotion. They may even handle overall marketing strategy planning as well as marketing research, product and package development, and sales promotion. Other agencies are more specialized. For example, in recent years there has been rapid growth of digital agencies that specialize in developing Internet ads and online publicity and sales promotion.

The biggest agencies handle much of the advertising

The vast majority of advertising agencies are small, with 10 or fewer employees. But the largest agencies account for most of the billings. Over the past two decades many of the big agencies merged, creating mega-agencies with worldwide networks. In fact, the "Big Three" advertising agency networks account for more than half of all advertising/media agency revenue. These three giant agency groups are each composed of large ad agencies with local or global presence.

The mega-agency can offer varied services, wherever in the world a marketing manager needs them. This may be especially important for managers in large corporations—such as Toyota, Unilever, NEC, and PepsiCo—that advertise worldwide. That said, some firms use different agencies for different tasks in different parts of the world.[30]

The really big agencies are less interested in smaller accounts. Smaller agencies will continue to appeal to customers who want more personal attention and a close relationship that is more attuned to their marketing needs.

Ethical conflicts may arise

Ad agencies usually work closely with their clients, and they often have access to confidential information. This can create ethical conflicts if an agency is working with two or more competing clients. Most agencies are sensitive to the potential problems and keep people and information from competing accounts separated. Even so, that doesn't always happen. For example, PepsiCo got a restraining order to stop an ad agency from assigning four people who had worked on advertising for its Aquafina bottled water to the account for Coca-Cola's competing brand, Dasani. Coca-Cola, in turn, yanked the account away from the agency. Because of situations like this, many advertisers refuse to work with any agency that handles any competing accounts, even if they are handled in different offices.[31]

Measuring Advertising Effectiveness Is Not Easy

LO 15.8

Success depends on the total marketing mix

It would be convenient if we could measure the results of advertising by looking at sales. Some breakthrough ads do have a very direct effect on a company's sales—and the advertising literature is filled with success stories that "prove" advertising increases sales. Similarly, market research firms such as Information Resources can sometimes compare sales levels before and after the period of an ad campaign. Yet we usually can't measure advertising success just by looking at sales. Advertising managers should measure effectiveness against the advertising objectives. The total marketing mix—not just advertising—is responsible for the sales result. Sales results are also affected by what competitors do and by other changes in the external market environment.

Research and testing can improve the odds

Ideally, advertisers should pretest advertising before it runs rather than relying solely on their own guesses about how good an ad will be. The judgment of creative people or advertising experts may not help much. They often judge only on the basis of originality or cleverness of the copy and illustrations.

Many progressive advertisers now demand laboratory or market tests to evaluate an ad's effectiveness. A/B testing involves an experiment to compare two conditions. For example, in test markets, some consumers will see ads on their cable TV system, whereas others do not. Sales are then compared between the two groups. Scanner sales data from retailers in those test markets can provide an estimate of how an ad is likely to affect sales. This approach will become even more powerful in the future as more cable systems allow viewers to provide immediate feedback to an ad as it appears on TV or on the Internet. A/B testing is more common with online and digital advertising. A website can easily serve half the customers that visit a site one ad and the other half another ad—and then see which ad results in more click-throughs and more purchases. This works best when the advertising objective is a direct response.

Some companies use big data and artificial intelligence to learn how individual customers shop, what brands they prefer, and when they are in the market to buy particular products. When customers see advertising relevant to their current needs, the messages are more effective.
© 2013 RocketFuel Inc.

Hindsight may lead to foresight

After ads run, researchers may try to measure how much consumers recall about specific products or ads. The response to radio or television commercials or magazine readership can be estimated using various survey methods to check the size and composition of audiences. Similarly, most Internet advertisers keep track of how many "hits" on the firm's website come from ads placed at other websites.[32]

Avoid Unfair Advertising

LO 15.9

Government agencies may say what is fair

In most countries, the government takes an active role in deciding what kinds of advertising are allowable, fair, and appropriate. For example, France and Japan limit the use of cartoon characters in advertising to children, and Canada bans *any* advertising targeted directly at children. In Switzerland, an advertiser cannot use an actor to represent a consumer. New Zealand limits political ads on TV. In the United States, print ads must be identified so they aren't confused with editorial matter; in other countries ads and editorial copy can be intermixed. Most countries limit the number and length of commercials on broadcast media.

What is seen as positioning in one country may be viewed as unfair or deceptive in another. For example, when Pepsi was advertising its cola as "the choice of the new generation" in most countries, Japan's Fair Trade Committee didn't allow it—because in Japan Pepsi was not "the choice." China's relatively unrestricted advertising climate has recently become more restrictive. P&G was fined almost $1 million for promising its Crest whitening toothpaste would bring whiter teeth in "just one day."[33]

Differences in rules mean that a marketing manager may face very specific limits in different countries, and local experts may be required to ensure that a firm doesn't waste money developing ads that will never be shown or which consumers will think are deceptive.

In the United States, the Federal Trade Commission (FTC) has the power to control unfair or deceptive business practices, including deceptive advertising. The FTC has been policing deceptive advertising for many years. And it may be getting results now that advertising agencies, as well as advertisers, must share equal responsibility for false, misleading, or unfair ads.

This is a serious matter. If the FTC decides that a particular practice is unfair or deceptive, it has the power to require affirmative disclosures—such as the health warnings on cigarettes—or **corrective advertising**—ads to correct deceptive advertising. The FTC forced Bayer to run corrective advertising after Bayer made unproven claims about its drug Yaz's efficacy for treating acne and premenstrual syndrome. Other advertisers learn from these cases. The possibility of large financial penalties or the need to pay for corrective ads causes most advertisers to stay well within the law.[34]

However, sometimes ad claims seem to get out of hand anyway. The FTC has started to crack down on claims related to weight loss and health. For example, KFC quickly stopped running several of its TV ads after the FTC objected to the ads and opened an investigation. KFC's ads positioned fried chicken as a healthy choice in fast food, but there was also lots of small print at the bottom of the screen to qualify the claims. Skechers and Reebok claimed that their shoes would help customers lose weight and strengthen muscles. The FTC took issue with the unfounded claims and the two firms had to return millions of dollars to consumers.[35]

What constitutes unfair and deceptive advertising is a difficult question. The law provides some guidelines, but the marketing manager must make personal judgments as well. The social and political environment is changing worldwide. Practices considered acceptable some years ago are now questioned or considered deceptive. Saying or even implying that your product is *best* may be viewed as deceptive. And a 1988 revision of the Lanham Act protects firms whose brand names are unfairly tarnished in comparative ads.

It's really not hard to figure out how to avoid criticisms of being unfair and deceptive. Making a vague claim that cannot be proved or disproved (sometimes called "puffery") is acceptable—the FTC won't bring charges for ads that claim "the best hamburger in the world." But marketing managers need to put a stop to the typical production-oriented approach of trying to use advertising to differentiate me-too products that are not different and don't offer customers better value.[36]

Sales Promotion—Do Something Different to Stimulate Change

Sales promotion refers to those Promotion activities—other than advertising, publicity, and personal selling—that stimulate interest, trial, or purchase by final customers or others in the channel. Exhibit 15–7 shows examples of typical sales promotions targeted at final customers, channel members, or a firm's own employees.

Sales promotion is generally used to complement the other promotion methods. Although advertising campaigns and sales force strategy decisions tend to have longer-term effects, a particular sales promotion activity usually lasts for only a limited time period. Sales promotion can often be implemented quickly and get sales results sooner than advertising. Further, sales promotion objectives usually focus on prompting some short-term action. For an intermediary, such an action might be a decision to stock a product, provide a special display space, or give the product extra sales emphasis. For a consumer, the desired action might be to try a new product, switch from another brand, or buy more of a product. The desired action by an employee might be a special effort to satisfy customers.

Exhibit 15-7 Example of Sales Promotion Activities

Aimed at final consumers or users	Aimed at wholesalers or retailers	Aimed at company's own sales force
Contests	Price deals	Contests
Coupons	Promotion allowances	Bonuses
Aisle displays	Sales contests	Meetings
Samples	Calendars	Portfolios
Trade shows	Gifts	Displays
Point-of-purchase materials	Trade shows	Sales aids
Banners and streamers	Meetings	Training materials
Frequent buyer programs	Catalogs	
Sponsored events	Merchandising aids	
	Videos	

Sales promotion objectives and situation should influence decision

There are many different types of sales promotion, but what type is appropriate depends on the situation and objectives. For example, Exhibit 15–8 shows some possible ways that a short-term promotion might affect sales. The sales pattern in the graph on the left might occur if Hellmann's issues coupons to help clear its excess mayonnaise inventory. Some consumers might buy earlier to take advantage of the coupon, but unless they use extra mayonnaise, their next purchase will be delayed. In the center graph, kids might convince parents to eat more Big Macs while McDonald's has a Monopoly game promotion, but when it ends, things go back to normal. The graph on the right shows a Burger King marketer's dream come true: free samples of a new style of french fries quickly pull in new customers who like what they try and keep coming back after the promotion ends. This is the best-case scenario—a sales promotion encourages trial, and customers change their habits. From these examples, you can see that the situation and the objective of the sales promotion should determine what type is best.

Sales promotion spending has grown in mature markets

Sales promotion involves so many different types of activities that it is difficult to estimate accurately how much is spent in total. There is general consensus, however, that the total spending on sales promotion exceeds spending on advertising.[37]

One reason for increased use of sales promotion by many consumer products firms is that they are generally competing in mature markets. There's only so much soap that consumers want to buy, regardless of how many brands there are vying for their

Exhibit 15-8 Some Possible Effects of a Sales Promotion on Sales

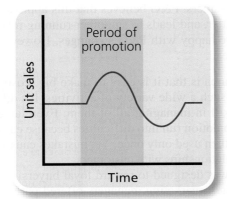

Sales temporarily increase, then decrease, then return to regular level

Sales temporarily increase and then return to regular level

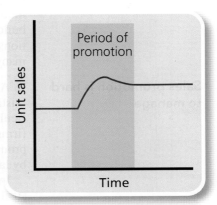

Sales increase and then remain at higher level

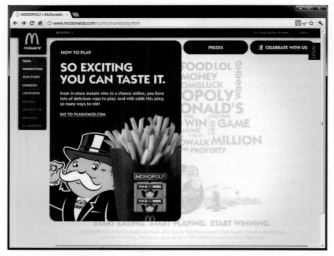

The McDonalds' Monopoly game promotion brings customers into restaurants to eat and to play the game.
© 2010–2015 McDonald's. All Rights Reserved.

dollars. There's also only so much shelf space that retailers will allocate to a particular product category.

The competitive situation is intensified by the growth of large, powerful retail chains. They have put more emphasis on their own dealer brands and also demanded more sales promotion support for the manufacturer brands they do carry.

Perhaps in part because of this competition, many consumers have become more price sensitive. Many sales promotions, like coupons, have the effect of lowering the prices consumers pay. So sales promotion has been used as a tool to overcome consumer price resistance, creating a downward cycle of pricing and promotion.

The growth of sales promotion has also been fostered by the availability of more ad agencies and specialists who plan and implement sales promotion programs. Of course, the most basic reason for the growth of spending on sales promotion is that it can be very effective if it is done properly. But there are challenges in the sales promotion area.

Challenges in Managing Sales Promotion

Does sales promotion erode brand loyalty?

Some experts think that marketing managers—especially those who deal with consumer packaged goods—put too much emphasis on sales promotion. They argue that the effect of most sales promotion is temporary and that money spent on advertising and personal selling helps the firm more over the long term. When the market is not growing, sales promotion may just encourage "deal-prone" customers (and intermediaries) to switch back and forth among brands. Here, all the expense of the sales promotion simply contributes to lower profits. It also increases the prices that consumers pay because it increases selling costs.

However, once a marketing manager is in this situation there may be little choice other than to continue. In mature markets, frequent sales promotions may be needed just to offset the effects of competitors' promotions. One escape from this competitive rat race is for the marketing manager to seek new opportunities—with a strategy that doesn't rely solely on short-term sales promotions for competitive advantage.

There are alternatives

Procter & Gamble is a company that changed its strategy, and promotion blend, to decrease its reliance on sales promotion targeted at intermediaries. It is offering intermediaries lower prices on many of its products and supporting those products with more advertising and promotion to final consumers. P&G believes that this approach builds its brand equity, serves consumers better, and leads to smoother-running relationships in its channels. Not all retailers are happy with P&G's changes. However, many other producers are following P&G's lead.

Sales promotion is hard to manage

Another problem in the sales promotion area is that it is easy to make big, costly mistakes. Because sales promotion includes such a wide variety of activities, it's difficult for the typical company to develop skill in managing all of them. Even large firms and agencies that specialize in sales promotion run into difficulties because each promotion is typically custom-designed and then used only once. Yet mistakes caused by lack of experience can be costly or hurt relationships with customers.

In a promotion for Pampers diapers that was designed to reward loyal buyers and steal customers away from competing Huggies, marketing managers offered parents Fisher-Price toys if they collected points printed on Pampers' packages. At first the promotion seemed to be a big success because so many parents were collecting points. But that turned into a problem when Fisher-Price couldn't produce enough toys to redeem all the points. Pampers had to add 50 toll-free phone lines to handle all the complaints, and a lot of angry parents stopped buying Pampers for good. Problems like this are common.[38]

Not a sideline for amateurs

Sales promotion mistakes are likely to be worse when a company has no sales promotion manager. If the personal selling or advertising managers are responsible for sales promotion, they often give it less attention. They allocate money to sales promotion if there is any "left over" or if a crisis develops. This approach misuses a valuable element of the promotion blend.

Making sales promotion work is a learned skill, not a sideline for amateurs. That's why specialists in sales promotion have developed, both inside larger firms and as outside consultants. Some of these people are real experts. But it's the marketing manager's responsibility to set sales promotion objectives and policies that will fit in with the rest of each marketing strategy.[39]

Most M&M's® are sold as consumer products, but M&M's® printed with special messages or brand logos are a sweet way to remind business customers about a firm.
© 2015 Mars, Incorporated and its Affiliates. All Rights Reserved.

Different Types of Sales Promotion for Different Targets

LO 15.11

Tie consumer sales promotions to objectives

Much of the sales promotion aimed at final consumers or users tries to increase demand, perhaps temporarily, or to speed up the time of purchase. Such promotion might involve developing materials to be displayed in retailers' stores, including banners, sample packages, calendars, and various point-of-purchase materials. It might include sweepstakes contests as well as coupons designed to get customers to buy a product by a certain date.

All of these sales promotion efforts are aimed at specific objectives. When customers already have a favorite brand, free samples can be used to get them to try something new. For example, Amazon.com's "Free Chapter" feature allows a customer to view part of a book before buying. When Starbucks launched its new coffee-flavored ice creams, it offered coupons for a free pint to fans on its Facebook page. In this type of situation, sales of the product might start to pick up as soon as customers try the product and find that they like it. And sales will continue at the higher level after the promotion is over if satisfied customers make repeat purchases. Thus, the cost of the sales promotion in this situation might be viewed as a long-term investment.

Once a product is established, consumer sales promotion usually focuses on short-term sales increases. For example, after a price-off coupon for a soft drink is distributed, sales might temporarily pick up as customers take advantage of buying at a lower price. When the objective of the promotion is focused primarily on producing a short-term increase in sales, it's sensible for the marketing manager to evaluate the cost of the promotion relative to the extra sales expected. If the increase in sales won't at least cover the cost of the promotion, it probably doesn't make sense to do it. Otherwise, the firm is "buying sales" at the cost of reduced profit.

John Deere created buzz about its new 764 high-speed dozer (described as a cross between a tractor and a bulldozer) by launching it at the biggest trade show event of the year—the ConExpo show at the Las Vegas Convention Center. Promotion included e-mail, Internet, live CNBC broadcast, press conferences, electronic press kits, magazine articles, and various sales promotion items. All of this was intended to "whet the appetite of the marketplace so when the 764 hit the ground, people would line up to buy it." And it worked. Customers raised their hands and said, "I want one."

Copyright © 2015 Deere & Company. All Rights Reserved.

B2B promotions move products or generate leads

Sales promotion directed at industrial customers might use the same kinds of ideas. In addition, the sales promotion people might set up and staff trade show exhibits that generate attention and interest for a firm and its products. Trade shows usually occur in one city over a period of three to seven days. Customers attend to learn from industry experts. For example, the Consumer Electronics Show in Las Vegas each January lasts four days and attracts more than 2,500 electronics exhibitors and 140,000 attendees. After the show, these customers become leads for the company's salespeople who try to convert customer interest to actual sales. Trade shows are big events that require significant planning.

Many customers would like to attend trade shows, but the cost in time or money make it difficult. So now many trade shows occur online. These virtual trade show "attendees" sit at their desks and choose which speakers to watch and which exhibits to visit. Virtual trade shows may be kept up year-round, making it convenient for customers to gather information when they are most interested in making a purchase.

Some sellers give promotion items—pen sets, watches, or clothing (perhaps with the firm's brand name on them)—to remind business customers of their products. This is common, but it can be a problem. Some companies do not allow buyers to accept any gifts.[40]

Trade promotion aims at intermediaries

Trade promotion refers to sales promotion aimed at intermediaries. There is a range of tools that may be used depending on the promotion objective (see Exhibit 15–7). Sometimes a producer uses trade promotion to get the intermediary's sales force to pay more attention to the producer's products. Sales contests can help achieve that goal. Intermediary salespeople earn prizes for exceeding sales targets. Another approach is to train intermediary salespeople on the product, perhaps at a producer-sponsored sales meeting in a desirable location (so that attendance has its own rewards, in addition to professional growth).

About half of sales promotion spending targeting intermediaries has the effect of reducing the price in some manner or another. Discounting products can give a wholesaler or retailer an incentive to sell the product more quickly—with either extra effort or a lower price. We will discuss the various types of price-related promotions in Chapter 16.

Sales promotion for own employees

Sales promotion aimed at the company's own sales force might try to encourage providing better service, getting new customers, selling a new product, or selling the company's whole line. Depending on the objectives, the tools might be contests, bonuses on sales or number of new accounts, and holding sales meetings at fancy resorts to raise everyone's spirits.

Ongoing sales promotion work might also be aimed at the sales force—to help sales management. Sales promotion might be responsible for preparing sales portfolios, digital videos, PowerPoint presentations, displays, and other sales aids, as well as sales training materials.

Service-oriented firms such as hotels and restaurants use sales promotions targeted at their employees. Some, for example, give a monthly cash prize for the employee who provides the "best service." And the employee's picture is displayed to give recognition.[41]

CONCLUSION

It may seem simple to develop an advertising campaign. Just pick the medium and develop a message. But it's not that easy.

This chapter discussed why marketing managers should set specific objectives to guide the entire advertising effort. Knowing what they want to achieve, marketing managers can determine what kind of advertising—product or institutional—to use. We also discussed three basic types of product advertising: pioneering, competitive (direct and indirect), and reminder.

Marketing managers must also choose from various media—so we discussed their advantages and disadvantages. Because the Internet and mobile devices offer new

advertising opportunities and challenges, we discussed how it is similar to and different from other media. And, of course, marketing managers must determine the message—or copy thrust—that will appear in ads.

Many technical details are involved in mass selling. Advertising agencies often handle these jobs. But specific objectives must be set for agencies, or their advertising may have little direction and be almost impossible to evaluate. This chapter also discussed how to make sure that advertising is done legally.

Sales promotion spending is big and growing. This approach is especially important in prompting action—by customers, intermediaries, or salespeople. There are many different types of sales promotion, and it is a problem area in many firms because it is difficult for a firm to develop expertise with all of the possibilities.

Advertising and sales promotion are often important parts of a promotion blend, but as many customers tune out advertising, other forms of media are gaining a greater share of the promotion budget. In Chapter 16 we will explore different forms of publicity, owned media, earned media, and social media.

WHAT'S NOW?

This chapter examined advertising and sales promotion. For some current real-world examples and learnings, check out *What's Now?* at www.learnthe4ps.com/whatsnow/c15

KEY TERMS

LO 15.12

advertising allowances, 396
cooperative advertising, 396
product advertising, 396
institutional advertising, 396
pioneering advertising, 397
competitive advertising, 397

direct competitive advertising, 397
indirect competitive advertising, 397
comparative advertising, 398
reminder advertising, 398
advertising media, 399
pay-per-click, 403

retargeting, 404
copy thrust, 407
advertising agencies, 410
corrective advertising, 412

QUESTIONS AND PROBLEMS

1. Review the Subway case study that opens the chapter. From this case, identify examples of different key terms and concepts covered in the chapter. For example, it is mentioned that the "Jared" ads increased consumer awareness.

2. Review the Subway case study that opens the chapter. Consider the digital and mobile advertising section of the chapter. Develop a plan with three specific ideas about how Subway could develop digital and mobile programs consistent with its target markets and positioning. Explain why your ideas would work.

3. Identify the strategy decisions a marketing manager must make in the advertising arena.

4. Discuss the relation of advertising objectives to marketing strategy planning and the kinds of advertising actually needed. Illustrate with examples.

5. List several media that might be effective for reaching consumers in a developing nation with low per capita income and a high level of illiteracy. Briefly discuss the limitations and advantages of each medium you suggest.

6. Give three examples where advertising to intermediaries might be necessary. What is(are) the objective(s) of such advertising?

7. What does it mean to say that "money is invested in advertising"? Is all advertising an investment? Illustrate with examples.

8. Find advertisements to final consumers that illustrate the following types of advertising: (a) institutional, (b) pioneering, (c) competitive, and (d) reminder. What objective(s) does each of these ads have? List the needs each ad addresses.

9. Describe the type of media that might be most suitable for promoting: (a) tomato soup, (b) greeting cards, (c) a business component material, and (d) playground equipment. Specify any assumptions necessary to obtain a definite answer.

10. Briefly discuss some of the pros and cons an advertising manager for a producer of sports equipment might want to think about in deciding whether to advertise on the Internet.

11. Discuss the use of testimonials in advertising. Which of the four AIDA steps might testimonials accomplish? Are testimonials suitable for all types of products? If not, for which types are they most suitable?

12. Find a magazine ad that you think does a particularly good job of communicating to the target audience. Would the ad communicate well to an audience in another country? Explain your thinking.

13. Discuss the future of smaller advertising agencies now that many of the largest are merging to form mega-agencies.

14. Does advertising cost too much? How can this be measured?

15. Is it unfair to criticize a competitor's product in an ad? Explain your thinking.

16. Name two companies that you think would have success building a Facebook page. Why do you think they should choose to build a page? What type of content should each company place on its page?

17. How would your local newspaper be affected if local supermarkets switched their weekly advertising and instead used a service that delivered weekly freestanding ads directly to each home?

18. Explain why P&G and other consumer packaged goods firms are trying to cut back on some types of sales promotion like coupons for consumers and short-term trade promotions such as "buy a case and get a case free."

19. Discuss some ways that a firm can link its sales promotion activities to its advertising and personal selling efforts—so that all of its promotion efforts result in an integrated effort.

20. Indicate the type of sales promotion that a producer might use in each of the following situations and briefly explain your reasons:

   a. A firm has developed an improved razor blade and obtained distribution, but customers are not motivated to buy it.

   b. A competitor is about to do a test market for a new brand and wants to track sales in test market areas to fine-tune its marketing mix.

   c. A big grocery chain won't stock a firm's new popcorn-based snack product because it doesn't think there will be much consumer demand.

21. Why wouldn't a producer of toothpaste just lower the price of its product rather than offer consumers a price-off coupon?

22. If sales promotion spending continues to grow—often at the expense of media advertising—how do you think this might affect the rates charged by mass media for advertising time or space? How do you think it might affect advertising agencies?

MARKETING PLANNING FOR HILLSIDE VETERINARY CLINIC

Appendix D (the Appendices follow Chapter 19) includes a sample marketing plan for Hillside Veterinary Clinic. Look through the "Marketing Strategy" section.

a. What are Hillside's advertising objectives?

b. What types of advertising and media are being proposed? Why are these types used and not others?

c. What type of copy thrust is recommended? Why?

d. What sales promotion activities are being planned? What are the goals of sales promotion?

SUGGESTED CASES

MARKETING ANALYTICS: DATA TO KNOWLEDGE

CHAPTER 15 SALES PROMOTION

As a community service, disc jockeys from radio station WMKT formed a basketball team to help raise money for local nonprofit organizations. The host organization finds or fields a competing team and charges $5 admission to the game. Money from ticket sales goes to the nonprofit organization.

Ticket sales were disappointing at recent games, averaging only about 300 people per game. When WMKT's marketing manager, Bruce Miller, heard about the problem, he suggested using sales promotion to improve ticket sales. The PTA for the local high school—the sponsor for the next game—is interested in the idea but is concerned that its budget doesn't include any promotion money. Miller tries to help them by reviewing his idea in more detail.

Specifically, he proposes that the PTA give a free T-shirt (printed with the school name and date of the game) to the first 500 ticket buyers. He thinks the T-shirt giveaway will create a lot of interest. In fact, he says he is almost certain the promotion would help the PTA sell 600 tickets, double the usual number. He speculates that the PTA might even have a sellout of all 900 seats in the school gym. Further, he notes that the T-shirts will more than pay for themselves if the PTA sells 600 tickets.

A local firm that specializes in sales promotion items agrees to supply the shirts and do the printing for $2.40 a shirt if the PTA places an order for at least 400 shirts. The PTA thinks the idea is interesting but wants to look at it more closely to see what will happen if the promotion doesn't increase ticket sales. To help the PTA evaluate the alternatives, Miller sets up a spreadsheet with the relevant information.

See Connect for the spreadsheet and questions needed to analyze this scenario.

Photo by Boston Globe/Getty Images.

Publicity: Promotion Using Earned Media, Owned Media, and Social Media

Brian Halligan and Dharmesh Shah met in 2004 while MBA students at MIT. While helping entrepreneurs with their marketing, Halligan noticed that many traditional marketing tactics—sending out massive numbers of e-mails, advertising, cold calling customers, and attending trade shows—were becoming less effective. Customers had become pretty good at avoiding many advertising and sales efforts. About the same time, Shah was attracting many readers to his OnStartups blog without any advertising or traditional promotion.

These experiences led the friends to long talks about traditional approaches to promotion. They started calling advertising and cold-call selling "outbound" promotion—because the approach was about sending communication *out* to customers. But buyers no longer passively waited for seller communications; the Internet made it easy to actively search for solutions to their problems. If customers were searching, companies that created useful content would be found; they called this content "inbound" promotion.

If inbound reflected customer behavior and was so much more effective, why weren't more businesses using it? Halligan and Shah found that a major impediment involved just getting started; for most marketing managers the process was daunting—build a website, write a blog, record a podcast, design a business page on Facebook. It seemed much easier to keep doing things the old way. So in 2006, Halligan and Shah created software that simplified inbound promotion. They called their software HubSpot. The inbound process works best when customers are looking for information and education before making a purchase. Many B2B buyers buy this way—and a surprising number of consumer purchases as well.

HubSpot (the company) approaches its marketing following the same four phases it recommends to its customers: 1) acquiring—getting awareness and interest, 2) converting—moving customers to desire and action (i.e., purchasing a subscription to the software), 3) onboarding—helping customers with installation and training on the software, and 4) ongoing—analyzing results and increasing product usage. Promotion methods change as customers move through the process.

For HubSpot, customer acquisition begins with making customers aware of the inbound philosophy and the problems it solves, thus fostering interest in the software. The founders got some attention with their book, *Inbound Marketing: Get Found Using Google, Social Media, and Blogs*. Other customers learned about HubSpot from its "Marketing Grader," a free online tool which measures the effectiveness of a user's website. This tool evaluates a site and offers pointers for improving grades—tips HubSpot software helps implement.

HubSpot employees publish new content weekly, including blog articles, case studies, white papers, a podcast, online seminars (webinars), and e-books. It's all offered free of charge. Some web pages ask for customer contact information (for example, name, e-mail address, and job title), which HubSpot compiles in a database to learn more about each customer's particular needs and interests. Some of HubSpot's customers keep up with the company on social media; when followers "like" a Hubspot Facebook post, "favorite" a Tweet, or comment on the Inbound Marketers group on LinkedIn (which HubSpot runs), they pass along an endorsement of HubSpot and its message to *their* friends and colleagues.

Many potential customers find HubSpot when they perform an online search—all that content helps HubSpot appear high in search results. Others might read a blog post by a business expert who links to HubSpot's "State of Inbound Marketing" research report or one of its blog posts. HubSpot tracks every customer interaction, from the web to e-mail to the phone. It knows what keywords customers search to find its site, what content they download, and which blog posts they read and forward to someone else at their company. These analytical insights help HubSpot identify the kind of content that customers find most useful—so it can produce more.

Finding this valuable trove of marketing insight, many customers sign up for HubSpot's e-mail list. HubSpot creates customized e-mails, sending each customer only the information relevant to their job, industry, or interests. It monitors individual customers, to see which have the highest levels of engagement. For example, it can record which customers open e-mails and follow those who frequently return to the HubSpot website. These customers are usually the most promising leads, so a a salesperson contacts these prospects directly. Using a consultative selling approach, the salesperson learns the customers' needs, often ending with an online demonstration of the HubSpot software. The sales process may continue for weeks (or months) as HubSpot's salesperson educates a customer about inbound promotion, the web, and their unique software. The salesperson recommends the best combination of HubSpot services—usually resulting in a new subscriber (customers pay $250 to $1,500 per month for the software).

The next two phases—onboarding and ongoing—are central to customer retention. If customers don't see value in HubSpot's software, they cancel their subscription. So HubSpot works closely with customers during installation and training. It also monitors ongoing customer usage, and offers more tips and training to customers who are not taking full advantage of the software. Customers also find value in HubSpot's Success Community, where fellow customers and HubSpot technical support people offer more tips and answer questions.

A typical HubSpot customer is Marcus Sheridan, owner of River Pools and Spas, which constructs inground pools in the Washington DC area. Sheridan turned to HubSpot when he noticed his company's radio, direct mail, and *Yellow Pages* ads were not bringing in customers like they used to. Sheridan, who had no previous experience running a website, used HubSpot software to add photos, advice, and informational blog posts. This content was found by customers searching online for information about an inground pool. His website became a powerful sales engine. HubSpot's software also tells him that blog posts like "How much does a fiberglass pool cost?" are especially effective bringing in customers who are considering building a new pool. Soon River's blog had more than 7,000 visitors a month and he cut his advertising budget to almost nothing. The low-pressure, high information content of the site fostered customer trust in River Pools and Spas—and soon sales soared.

River Pools and Spas is just one of many satisfied HubSpot customers. HubSpot recently ranked #1 in customer satisfaction among marketing automation software vendors. HubSpot's customers appreciate the information and insights HubSpot shares; it helps them them grow their businesses. All that sharing helps HubSpot grow, too; HubSpot's sales have grown more than 50% per year.[1]

LEARNING OBJECTIVES

As the HubSpot case points out, many organizations are finding new approaches to telling customers about their products. This chapter provides you with a broad overview of new promotion tools that utilize earned media, owned media, and social media.

When you finish this chapter, you should be able to

1 Explain how publicity fits into the promotion blend.

2 Understand the differences between paid, earned, and owned media.

3 Explain how customers obtain information from search, pass-along, and experience.

4 Describe different types of owned media.

5 Describe how to use public relations to earn attention from the press.

6 Describe how to earn word-of-mouth from customers.

7 Explain what social media is and how it differs from traditional media.

8 Compare and contrast the major social media platforms.

9 Describe how firms use software to measure, manage, and automate online promotion.

10 Understand important new terms (shown in red).

Publicity, the Promotion Blend, and Marketing Strategy Planning

LO 16.1

This is the fourth chapter covering Promotion (see Exhibit 16–1). Chapter 13 introduced the different ways a seller tells target customers about a product—through personal and mass selling. Chapter 13 also described communication models to help

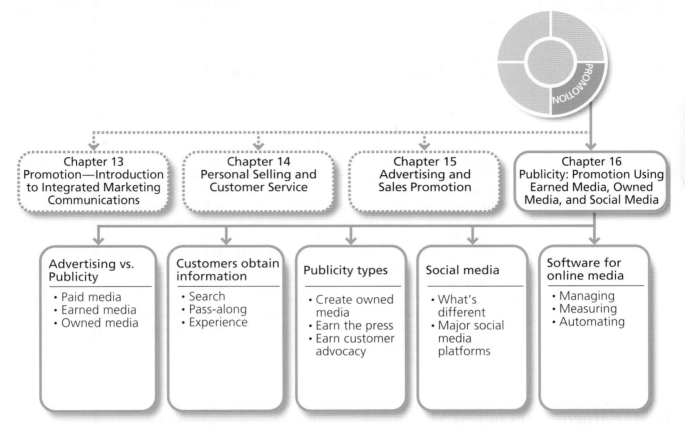

us understand and design promotion more effectively. Chapter 14 explained personal selling—direct spoken communication between buyers and sellers—and customer service. Chapter 15 covered two types of mass selling—advertising and sales promotion—where communication occurs with a large number of potential customers at the same time. This chapter digs into publicity. *Publicity* refers to any *unpaid* form of nonpersonal presentation of ideas, goods, or services.

Publicity requires strategy decisions

This chapter takes a close look at different types of publicity. The chapter begins by comparing advertising (paid promotion) to different types of publicity (unpaid promotion). Then the concepts of paid media, earned media, and owned media are introduced—explaining how each has advantages and disadvantages in the promotion blend. After briefly describing how information flows through search, pass-along, and branded experiences, we provide more details on different types of owned and earned media. Finally, we explain the different types of social media. This chapter examines the following questions:

- How does a seller attract potential customers' attention to its *own* media?
- How does a seller *earn* favorable coverage in news media or recommendations from other customers?
- How can a seller encourage target customers to come to its brand pages? "Like" its Facebook page? Follow its Twitter feed? Sign up for its e-mail newsletters?
- What is unique about *social media* and how do marketing managers utilize it in their promotion blends?
- How can software be used to manage and monitor this media portfolio?

Integrating publicity into the promotion blend

Publicity works best when it is integrated into the entire marketing mix. A marketing manager must understand how the right promotion moves a customer through the buying process. As a customer moves through the process, different types of information are needed.

Consider the different types of promotion involved in Kat's purchase of a backpack. Kat likes to hike and was thinking about buying a new backpack. She sees a magazine ad for an Osprey backpack and recalls a friend's recommendation of the brand—capturing Kat's attention and interest. So she visits the Osprey website, sees and reads about different backpacks, compares features, and watches a short video. While there, Kat finds links to stores that sell the packs. Then she reads reviews at eBags.com and learns of some new features she should consider when buying a new backpack. Not quite ready to buy, Kat puts the purchase on hold. A week later, while scrolling through Facebook, a sponsored post from Osprey Packs rekindles Kat's interest and desire for a new backpack. By the time she arrives at her local REI store, Kat has narrowed her choices to three Osprey models. A helpful salesperson shows her the bags, answers some questions, and tells her about a sale with discounted prices; she buys the Osprey Aura 65 AG EX. After all this, Kat feels like part of the Osprey family—she likes to show fellow hikers all the features of her new backpack whenever asked. Kat also likes to stay informed and follows Osprey Packs on Instagram—often "liking" the posted images.

Various elements of Osprey's promotion blend combine to help move Kat through the purchase process for an Osprey backpack. At different stages, advertising, sales promotion, publicity, and personal selling contributed to the decision to purchase. This chapter discusses assorted media and shows how they can be integrated to achieve communication objectives.

Paid, Earned, and Owned Media

To better understand publicity, it helps to compare it with advertising. Advertising was covered in Chapter 15. Advertising and publicity are both types of mass selling—in this chapter, we will differentiate them. We have already mentioned that advertising uses *paid media;* advertisers pay for placement on television, radio, online, and so on. Within publicity, we have two types of unpaid media—owned media and earned media. This section defines, describes, and compares paid, owned, and earned media (see Exhibit 16–2).

Advertising uses *paid media*

Media refers to the means used for mass communication. For example, advertising utilizes **paid media** or messages generated by a brand (or company or nonprofit organization) and communicated through a message channel the brand pays to access. The source of the message is the organization doing the advertising.

Publicity relies on *unpaid media—owned* or *earned*

Owned media refers to promotional messages generated by a brand (or company or nonprofit organization) communicated through a message channel the brand directly controls. Owned media includes the brochures and catalogs a company mails to target customers. A brand's product website, blog, and social media pages—YouTube channel, Facebook page, or Instagram—are also examples of owned media. As with paid media, the selling company is the source of the message.

Earned media refers to promotional messages *not* directly generated by the company or brand, but rather by third parties such as journalists or customers. The company or brand is assumed to *earn* the attention of journalists or customers because there is an interesting story to tell or because others would value this information. Earned media can be positive or negative. Poor customer service might earn a restaurant a bad review on Yelp.

Exhibit 16-2 Paid, Owned, and Earned Media

Journalists' messages can appear as editorial content in a newspaper, magazine, or on a website that provides news. Many newspapers and magazines (online and offline) publish restaurant, theater, book, and movie reviews—or review new products. Trade magazines write articles about new goods and services of interest to its readers.

A company or brand can also *earn* word-of-mouth communication from customers. **User-generated content** refers to any type of communication created by customers for other customers. User-generated content can take many forms. Customers can recommend their hairdresser to a friend or demonstrate their new Samsung Galaxy phone to a co-worker. A customer can also send a tweet praising a new book—or post a review at Amazon describing what he likes (and doesn't like) about his new nonstick frying pan. All of these types of user-generated content are examples of earned media.[2]

Promotion and customer trust

Chapters 5 and 6 describe how customers can gather and use information before making a buying decision. In Chapter 13, we noted that a customer's trust of a source influences whether they believe and act on information. As shown in Exhibit 16–2, these three general categories of media include different sources which are associated with different levels of trust. Research shows that customers generally view earned and owned media as more credible and trustworthy than paid media is.

A recent study of 29,000 Internet consumers from 58 countries found the four most highly trusted sources for buying information are forms of publicity, not advertising (see Exhibit 16–3). Consumers trust information from *earned* media sources most: 84 percent of respondents trust recommendations from people they know, 68 percent trust online consumer opinions (reviews), and 67 percent trust editorial content such as newspaper articles. Branded websites (a form of *owned* media) are trusted by 69 percent of respondents. These levels of trust were significantly higher than various types of advertising (paid) media. Among various advertising (paid) media, trust ranged from 37 percent for text ads on mobile phones to 62 percent for television advertising.[3]

Exhibit 16-3   Customer Trust in Various Sources of Information

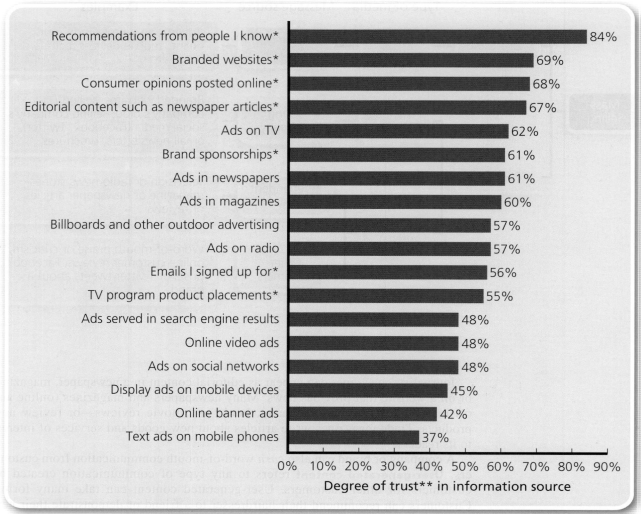

Recommendations from people I know*	84%
Branded websites*	69%
Consumer opinions posted online*	68%
Editorial content such as newspaper articles*	67%
Ads on TV	62%
Brand sponsorships*	61%
Ads in newspapers	61%
Ads in magazines	60%
Billboards and other outdoor advertising	57%
Ads on radio	57%
Emails I signed up for*	56%
TV program product placements*	55%
Ads served in search engine results	48%
Online video ads	48%
Ads on social networks	48%
Display ads on mobile devices	45%
Online banner ads	42%
Text ads on mobile phones	37%

0% 10% 20% 30% 40% 50% 60% 70% 80% 90%

Degree of trust** in information source

*Sources of earned or owned media, others are forms of paid media.
**Percentages reflect those responding that they "completely trust" or "somewhat trust" the information source.

Benefits and challenges for each media type

The general differences among these three types of media extend beyond trust. Let's look at the benefits and challenges facing each (see Exhibit 16–4).

Paid media—high message control yet becoming less effective

Chapter 15 addressed many of the benefits of advertising. Marketing managers (or their advertising agencies) develop the copy thrust and therefore control the words and images in the messages customers receive. Most advertising is designed to target a large number of customers at once, whereas specialized media target fewer customers more precisely.

On the other hand, customers are getting better at avoiding advertising messages. Most customers see advertising as an interruption of something they would rather be doing—watching their favorite TV program, not a television commercial; listening to a popular song on the radio, not an advertising jingle; getting to a favorite website without waiting for an ad to be served up. New technology helps many customers to sidestep advertising messages. Digital video recorders (DVRs) let consumers skip right past television commercials. Online music streaming services such as Spotify allow subscribers to listen ad-free, and pop-up blockers or simply clicking to another page lets Internet

Exhibit 16-4 Benefits and Challenges of Advertising Media, Owned Publicity Media, and Earned Publicity Media

Media type	Benefits	Challenges
Paid media (advertising)	• High message control • More precise targeting • Potentially large audience	• Not trusted • Customers easily avoid • More costly, declining effectiveness
Owned media	• High message control • Relatively low cost • Niche audiences • Versatile in message content and format	• Need to drive or attract customers to sites and create value to assure their return • Requires resources to manage and maintain
Earned media	• Most trusted information source • Customers most likely to act on this information	• Very little message control • Can be negative toward brand • Difficult to measure • Difficult to create • Difficult to target

surfers bypass ads. Combine these behaviors with customers' lack of trust in advertising and it's easy to understand why advertising effectiveness has been declining.

Owned media—high message control and lower cost

Owned media allows a marketing manager to craft the precise message customers receive. Marketing managers can choose what information is displayed in a brochure or on the company website, YouTube channel, Instagram, Pinterest page, or Twitter feed. A website may include an information page that provides details about a product's features with information to show how a customer can find retailers that carry the

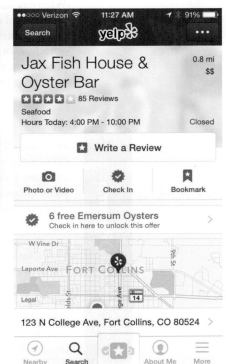

Jax Fish House, a restaurant in Fort Collins, Colorado, maintains an Instagram page. Jax uses this form of owned media to post pictures of its delicious food and wine. Jax controls what gets posted on Instagram. On the other hand, Jax does not directly control what is said in the 85 reviews it has on Yelp. Fortunately, delivering a great dining experience helps the restaurant to earn high praise.

product. Owned media also allows a manager a great deal of versatility with the messaging. For example, a web page might contain a short video overview of a product with a link to a detailed text-heavy web page for those customers desiring technical specifications. While owned media has low media costs—and usually lower costs overall—marketing managers need to remember that there is a cost to create and maintain owned media channels.

The challenges for marketing managers include maintaining owned media and making sure customers find their information when it is needed in the buying process. A website or social media feed needs regular updating and monitoring to ensure the site contains content customers find helpful. Additionally, the site must be easy to navigate and search. Later in this chapter we discuss approaches for developing owned media that attracts customers by creating value for them.[4]

Customers act on earned media, but it has risks

Marketing managers are usually thrilled when positive articles are written about their products or customers post positive reviews on social media sites. These are the most powerful messages a target customer can receive—customers trust and act on this information. Think about your own experience. How likely are you to visit a new restaurant when you see an advertisement in the newspaper? How does that compare to having a friend tell you, "We had a great dinner last night at that new Italian restaurant on Main Street"?

On the other hand, earned media creates challenges for a brand. These influential message sources are out of a marketing manager's control. When a restaurant critic writes a negative review in the newspaper or an unhappy customer posts a less-than-flattering review on Yelp, customers are much less likely to visit that business. This chapter also includes discussion about how marketing managers can foster positive earned media while managing negative media.[5]

Customers Obtain Information from Search, Pass-Along, and Experience

LO 16.3

Whereas advertising media is generally broadcast to customers, customers discover owned and earned media through different processes. So before we look at different types of media, it is helpful to understand three other processes by which customers obtain information—search, pass-along, and experience. By understanding how each process works, marketing managers can select the best tools and practices to achieve particular promotion objectives.

Ethical Dilemma

What would you do? Imagine you work in marketing for online retailer Ozzy World (OW). OW imports Australian products for sale in the United States, selling mostly via the Internet. Your company is looking to improve its listing on search engines, so it sought advice from a company that specializes in SEO. These SEO experts guarantee that their enhancements will double a client's number of new customers within two months (or their money back). As it turns out, OW uses "black hat" SEO techniques designed to trick search engines. So-called black hat techniques include practices such as "invisible text," where long lists of keywords are put on a company's web page in the same color font as the background—so only search engines can "see" these words. You have heard that some search engines will ban sites that use black hat techniques, but these SEO experts say they know how to get around that. After the meeting, your boss pulls you into his office and asks your opinion. What would you say? Is this approach ethical? What would make you more or less likely to support this approach to improving OW's placement in search rankings?[6]

What's Next? Take STEPPS to go viral

Customers spreading a positive message far and wide . . . that's a marketing manager's dream. Consider the boost in sales Blendtec enjoyed when it released the "Will It Blend" series of videos (http://www.willitblend.com) featuring Blendtec's CEO using one of the company's industrial strength blenders to grind up cell phones, golf balls, and even a solar lamp. The videos have generated more than 27 million views and a lot of awareness and interest in its blenders.

For every highly contagious message, hundreds don't get much pass-along. According to Jonah Berger, there are characteristics of an idea or message that make it contagious. He suggests six STEPPS—Social currency, Triggers, Emotion, Public, Practical value, and Stories—to increase pass-along.

Social currency occurs when the sharer looks good by sharing. When a new bar called Please Don't Tell opened in New York City, it had a secret. There was no front door to get into the bar; the only entry was through a phone booth in the corner of a neighboring hot dog restaurant. Those who knew the secret gained social currency when they shared this tip with friends. Many did and now the bar is a hit—without advertising, a street sign, or front door.

Triggers make a topic easy to remember and encourage others to talk about it. When Philadelphia's fine steakhouse, Barclay Prime, added a $100 cheesesteak sandwich to the menu, people started talking. Cheesesteak sandwiches typically sell for five bucks. The home of the original cheesesteak, Philadelphia has hundreds of cheesesteak shops whose mere existence trigger conversations about Barclay Prime's budget-buster.

Humor is one *emotion* people like to share. Alas, this contagious story didn't help United Airlines. After the airline's baggage handlers damaged musician Dave Carroll's guitar and its customer service failed to show any concern, the musician created a music video (see https://youtu.be/5YGc4zOqozo) about the experience and posted it on YouTube. Carroll's frustration and sense of humor connected with people. The video generated 14 million views over the next eight months, and United's image took a hit.

When a product's features are noticeably *public*, they spread more quickly. When Apple introduced the iPod, most headphones were black with black cords. Apple's white headphones stood out. Designer Christian Louboutin's shoes have red soles—they draw attention when wearers walk down a street.

People also like to pass along interesting *stories*, especially stories with *practical value*. Stories capture the imagination and make an idea easy to remember and therefore share. Stories with practical value make the sharer look smart and helpful. Subway sandwiches' story of Jared Fogle losing 245 pounds by eating only low-fat Subway sandwiches is a simple story with value to many.

Going viral is not easy, but when a marketing manager takes the right STEPPS, he or she increases the chances that their message becomes contagious. Describe how a nonprofit organization focused on raising money for AIDS prevention in Africa could use each of the STEPPS to increase likelihood of its message and mission going viral.[7]

Marketers want to be found when customers search

Because customers often search for information during the shopping process, marketing managers need to make sure that when target customers search, online material useful to them is "found." Most customers use a search engine such as Google, Bing, or Yahoo—and most favor the organic search results rather than the paid ads at the side of the search (see Chapter 15 for more on search advertising). When conducting an online search, most users don't look past the 10 results on a typical first page of search; studies find that half of those who click on an organic search choose the first or second result and about three quarters pick one of the top five. So when customers are looking, it pays to get near the top of that first page of results.

To appear high on organic search results, marketing managers often use **search engine optimization (SEO)**, which is the process of designing a website so that it ranks high in a search engine's unpaid results. SEO considers how target customers search, what key words they use in a search, and how the search engine prioritizes its results. Although the technical elements of SEO are beyond the scope of this textbook, you should know marketing managers can employ many techniques to influence standing in search results.[8]

Customers search offline, too	Customers search for answers offline as well. This may lead them to a salesperson who can answer their questions. It might also lead them to a neighbor or friend who might help them "find a new dentist" or "recommend a preschool." In these latter two situations, the information often leads to other customers sharing information with one another directly—a form of pass-along.
Pass-along from trusted sources	**Pass-along** occurs when one customer makes a recommendation for (or against) a specific brand to another customer. Customers pass along videos, articles, coupons, or websites to other customers. They also recommend brands when the seller has earned an endorsement—or advise against a brand that deserves it. Sellers can earn more recommendations by making it easy for customers to share recommendations or content.
The ultimate in pass-along—going viral	When customers quickly spread a message far and wide, it's called "viral" promotion. When Evian created its "Roller Skating Babies" video to promote its bottled water and posted it on YouTube, friends passed along the link in e-mails, with "You have to watch this!" in the subject line. The video—essentially an ad for Evian—has been viewed more than 100 million times on YouTube! Getting a video to go viral is not easy. But there is growing research about how pass-along works. You can read more in "*What's Next?* Take STEPPS to go viral."
Customers experience branded services	Customers gain experience with a brand in many ways. Most often customers gain experience with a brand by using its Product—its goods and/or services. Some firms use Promotion to enhance customer experiences. **Branded services** are valued services a brand provides that are not directly connected to a core product offering. Branded services are usually free or low cost and offer target customers benefits that leave a positive impression. This helps customers perceive a company or brand as caring about the customers' welfare. Customers *experience* these benefits and develop a positive attitude that fosters trust. Customers had a positive experience with Samsung when the electronics maker put charging stations (with Samsung signage) in more than 100 major airports. It positioned itself as a "lifesaver" and built favorable attitudes with lucrative business travelers—who tend to buy a lot of consumer electronics. Now, Samsung is targeting another gadget-loving group—students—by putting its charging stations on college campuses.[9]

Create Owned Media Content Your Customers Can Use

	When solving a problem, customers have choices about where to go to find information. When faced with a new problem or need, many customers turn first to the Internet. When a business or organization creates owned media content that helps customers solve their problems, their messages get into buyers' minds. In this section, we will examine different types of owned media. Exhibit 16–5 provides an overview of the types of owned media discussed in this section. Social media (such as Facebook and Twitter) often operate as owned media and are covered later in this chapter. Exhibit 16–5 also describes how customers typically discover each type of media and representative promotion objectives. Understanding how customers discover owned media helps a firm develop other promotional efforts which direct target customers to owned media.
Educate customers and start a conversation	A website, salesperson, or book that helps a customer solve a problem also earns that customer's trust. Customers who find content useful will pass along the site to others. Those types of connections also help a firm with its search engine optimization—creating a virtual circle. Content can fill a customer's need without requiring that the customer make a purchase. When customers see a company providing useful information but not asking for something in return, customers trust the content provider. This eventually leads to more sales.

Exhibit 16-5 Types of Owned Media—How Customers Find It and Typical Promotional Objectives

Type of owned media	How customers typically discover each type of owned media	Typical promotion objectives
Educational web pages	• Customers search so firms should optimize pages to be found when customers seek to solve problems	• Build awareness • Educate and inform customers • Foster customer trust
White papers and case studies	• Customers typically search for answers to problems and seek out white papers and case studies • Advertising can also drive traffic to this type of content in B2B	• Generate awareness • Educate and inform customers • Build reputation as thought leader • Foster customer trust
Landing pages	• Ads designed to drive customers to relevant landing pages • Optimize pages to be found when customers try to solve problems	• Build awareness • Start a relationship • Generate leads
Blogs	• Some posts motivate pass-along • Blog posts boost a whole site's visibility on search engines • Regularly delivering value to keep customers coming back	• Maintain interest • Build reputation as thought leader
Infographics	• Frequently infographics are passed along	• Grab attention • Inform customers
Branded apps	• Positive, unique experiences lead to pass-along • Provides positive experience	• Support brand positioning
Brand communities	• New members often discover through search • When customers value they will share site with others who have similar interests	• Provide value for customers • Remind customers
E-mail newsletter	• E-mail newsletters with useful content to promote pass-along • If experience is not useful, customers will not read or unsubscribe	• Maintain relationship • Remind customers • Cross-sell to customers

Online jewelry retailer Blue Nile uses its website to educate target customers. Young men seeking a diamond engagement ring appreciate Blue Nile's efforts to educate them about diamonds. That appreciation often leads to a sale.
© 1999–2015 Blue Nile Inc.

Home Depot created and posted "How to Build a Fence" on YouTube, and more than 860,000 customers watched it. A video with this many views appears high in a search for "building a fence," gets passed along by satisfied viewers, and provides customers with a positive Home Depot experience. It also moves a consumer on to the next step in the buying process—which might include a visit to a Home Depot store and a conversation with a sales clerk who can help the consumer design a fence and gather the materials needed to build it.

Business customers seek solutions

Organizational buyers often jump right on the Internet when they discover a new need. Often they seek out "thought leaders" in the industry to learn more about their options. For a company to establish itself as such a leader, it might publish white papers. A **white paper** is an authoritative report or guide that addresses important issues in an industry and offers solutions. Some companies will self-publish an extended version of a white paper as an *e-book*. E-books and white papers are most successful when, in addition to describing a problem, they help the customer solve it without promoting a particular company's products. An objective tone helps the provider build trust and credibility with potential customers. Business customers also like to read **case studies**—success stories about how a company helped another customer.[10]

Online Toolkit

Go to HubSpot.com (**www.hubspot.com**). Click on "Case Studies," then choose "Industry," and then "Travel and Leisure." Read two of the case studies that appear. How could these case studies help a firm in the travel business? How do the case studies encourage a customer to get more information from HubSpot?

Some firms ask customers to leave contact information before downloading a white paper, case study, or even an e-book. For example, a seller may ask for a customer's name, e-mail address, and job title. This feeds into a lead management system the seller can use for follow-up with an e-mail or phone call from a salesperson.

Landing pages to engage customers

A **landing page** is a customized web page that logically follows from clicking on an organic search result, online advertisement, or other link. Landing pages may be linked from social media, an e-mail campaign, or search engine optimization around specific key terms. The goal of a landing page is to move customers along in the purchase process. Because customers can easily click away from a web page, a landing page that directly addresses a customer's needs minimizes click-away. Often a landing page will make an offer to the customer— perhaps the opportunity to download a white paper— and ask for their contact information in return.[11]

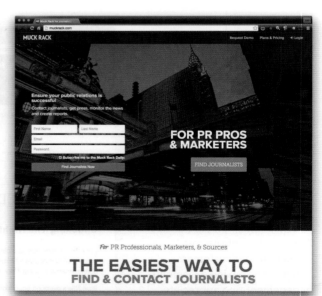

Some customers "land" on the home page

Some organizations and brands are so well known that customers simply jump to a home page. When a company serves multiple target markets, the home page should quickly help each target market get to the information it needs. Consider the New York Public Library, which serves, among others,

Muck Rack is a website designed to help journalists and public relations professionals. Muck Rack's "landing page" offers target customers a free daily e-mail with useful news in exchange for their contact information.
Copyright 2015 Sawhorse Media, LLC.

academic researchers from around the world who seek access to the library's online resources, Spanish-speaking residents of the Bronx who are interested in local classes (in Spanish) on how to use a computer, tourists in New York City who want to visit the architecturally stunning main library building on Fifth Avenue, and individuals and foundations that donate to the library. The library's home page has links to "Research," "Locations," "Classes and Events," and "Support the Library" that take each target market to the information it needs with one click.

Product web pages drive desire and action

By the time a customer comes to a web page developed for a specific product, the customer is probably already aware and interested. The product page should be designed to give customers the kind of information needed to promote desire and action—possibly detailed product information, pictures or videos, or links to where a purchase can be made. In other situations, a product page may be needed for a recent buyer of the product to get more information.

Blogs informally communicate with customers

A **blog** is a regularly updated website, usually managed by one person or a small group and written in an informal, conversational style. Many companies use blogs as a way to regularly communicate with customers. A blog allows a company or individual to get their ideas out to interested target customers. Some firms use a blog to position a firm or individual as a thought leader on a particular topic or to just demonstrate

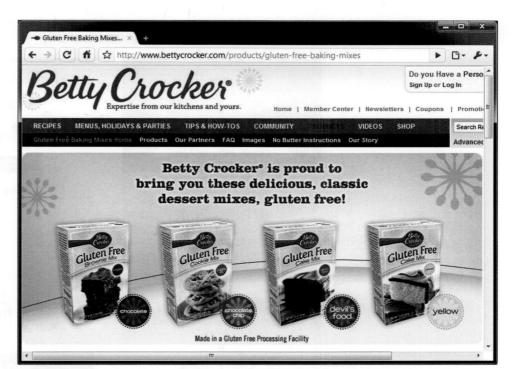

About 2 percent of all people suffer from an intolerance to gluten, whether due to celiac disease or wheat allergies. This small target market didn't attract much interest from big companies like General Mills and its Betty Crocker brand. However, when rumors of gluten-free Betty Crocker baked goods spread rapidly across the Internet, its brand managers realized that almost no advertising would be needed to attract the gluten-free group and make the line a success. Upon further research, brand managers learned that the first thing recently diagnosed celiac patients do is conduct online research to figure out what they can eat. So General Mills marketing managers went ahead with product development and built a website with information about its gluten-free line. When a firm has a product that closely meets the needs of a closely knit target market, promotion through publicity can be especially cost effective.

their helpfulness and concern. Customers like to do business with experts and caring people and companies.

Larry McGlynn, president and CEO of McGlynn, Clinton & Hall Insurance Agencies uses his "Massachusetts Family Insurance" blog to connect with current and potential customers. Larry is a funny guy who cares about his customers. Some of his blog posts, like the one with the YouTube video from a demolition derby titled, "When does an insurance agent enjoy a car crash?" highlight his humor. Other posts offer serious information—like when he explained law on distracted driving in "no txt'g while drv'g!" The posts get McGlynn new business indirectly—he uses the posts as a way to stay in touch with clients by e-mailing them a link to each new post. Many pass the e-mail to friends and family—some of whom become customers.[12]

Infographics get attention and pass-along

In a world of text messages and short attention spans, many firms turn to images to capture customers' attention and interest. One type of image is an **infographic**—a visual image such as a chart or diagram used to represent information or data. The visual images, often combined with minimal text, grab attention, simplify complex information, and highlight trends or patterns. A well-designed infographic quickly conveys useful information and gets passed along more readily than a text-heavy website.[13]

Branded apps solve customer problems

Some brands are finding ways to deliver branded services directly to where customers can use them most easily—through apps on their mobile devices. **Branded apps** are sponsored software applications that benefit customers by providing entertainment, solving a problem, and/or saving time. A branded app can be a positive reminder for the brand, especially when its function ties closely to the core product.

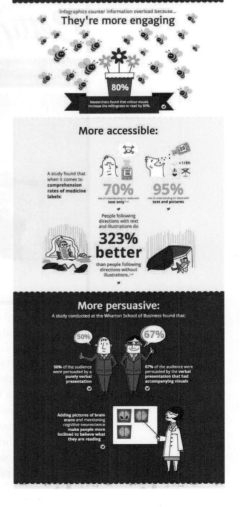

This infographic explains how and why infographics work.
Neoman Studios Limited/ Manchester, United Kingdom M1 1EZ.

Charmin toilet paper takes a decidedly humorous approach to helping on-the-go customers with their personal needs. The SitORSquat app for smartphones uses GPS to show customers nearby public restrooms that, based on customer reviews, are clean (you can sit) or dirty (you better squat).

Online communities connect customers

A **brand community** is a group of customers joined around a particular brand or common set of shared interests. A brand community should be designed to serve the interests of its members—and the brand often enjoys increased customer loyalty, larger purchases, or simply being viewed as a trusted partner. One long-running brand community is the Harley Owner's Group (HOG). HOGs operate locally to organize motorcycle owners around the lifestyle and attitude represented by Harley-Davidson. The group's social interactions and activities enhance the value customers get from owning a Harley and ultimately increases

American Express helps its target market of small business owners to thrive with its Open Forum website. The site is filled with helpful content on everything from leadership and compensation to advertising. An open community allows contributions from guest bloggers who offer advice, tips, and tricks these customers appreciate. While visiting the site, small business owners can easily link to all of American Express's business services. The site helps American Express build a closer relationship with its small business target market.

customer loyalty. Companies as diverse as LEGO (toys), Oracle (database software), and H&R Block (tax preparation services) have also developed successful brand communities.[14]

Build customer relationships with e-mail

When people think of companies sending out e-mail, many think of *spam*—unwanted, irrelevant messages sent out to a large number of recipients. These days effective spam filters limit unwanted e-mails, and marketers have found that customers like to receive only pertinent and timely messages from companies they want to do business with. However, effective e-mail newsletters help companies build ongoing customer relationships that lead to increased purchases. E-mail newsletters are an important part of many retailers' promotion blends.

Newsletters can tell customers about new products, existing products, or special sale prices. Some companies develop different e-mail newsletters tailored to specific customer interests—and desired frequency of communication. For example, online retailer Lands' End allows customers to share their interests (Men's, Women's, Kids', School Uniforms, or Home) and determine mailing frequency (daily, weekly, monthly, or stop e-mailing me). Ethical companies ask customers for permission before sending e-mails and make it easy to unsubscribe from newsletters.[15]

Earned Media from Public Relations and the Press

LO 16.5

We mentioned that media coverage can be earned from customers—or from the press. Let's look first at how it works with the press and then from the vantage point of customer advocacy.

Get coverage in the press

Some companies *earn* editorial coverage—with their goods and services or good works featured in articles, stories, and reviews in magazines, newspapers, or on television. If a firm has a really new message, a published article may get more attention than advertising can. Trade magazines carry articles featuring the newsworthy products of interest to people in a particular job or industry.

This kind of coverage doesn't usually happen by luck or accident. A good public relations effort often lays the groundwork for companies that get positive attention in the press. Sometimes a firm's public relations people write the basic copy of an article and then try to convince magazine or newspaper editors to print it.

Get found when the press searches for a story

Southwest Airlines uses press releases to generate publicity in the popular press. When it wants to promote its special fares and new routes, its PR staff uses a targeted approach to get attention from news reporters. Because many reporters research story ideas on specialized search engines, such as PRWeb and Google News, the PR staff at Southwest writes press releases so they appear at the top of the reporters' search lists. Southwest's PR staff practices SEO and researches the keywords reporters use most frequently on these search engines, later using those words in press releases. For example, Southwest's press releases use the phrase "cheap airfare" because it is in four times as many search requests as "cheap airline tickets." Southwest also puts a hot link to its special low-fare web page at the very start of each press release. The link allows Southwest PR staff to track which press releases work best—then it uses that information to fine-tune other messages. These extra efforts have paid off. In one case Southwest generated $1.5 million in online ticket sales with just four press releases.[16]

Bloggers are the new press

Independent bloggers often "publish" their own stories on topics of interest. Readers often view these citizen "journalists" as objective sources of information. Many bloggers become experts on a particular topic and have readers interested in what they have to say. Identifying influential bloggers who have the attention of target customers can be helpful.

Kimberly-Clark, maker of disposable diapers and other baby products, has moms for a target market. It

The Mom Blog Society is a collection of writers who target parents (mostly moms) with helpful parenting advice that can include product recommendations. *Copyright © 2014 Mom Blog Society.*

recognized a growing cadre of "mommy bloggers," stay-at-home moms who write blogs about childrearing. With a loyal readership, these bloggers can influence many people. So Kimberly-Clark sent samples of its new Huggies Pure & Natural premium diapers to 500 of them.[17]

Ethics and the law require disclosing blogger connections

When a blogger (or someone posting on social media) offers an endorsement or testimonial for a product, it must be disclosed. When two bloggers tripped across country and wrote nice stories about Walmart, it gave the impression they were completely objective. It was later discovered that the bloggers were supported by the organization, Working Families for Walmart—and paid indirectly by Walmart. Walmart suffered through some negative publicity.[18]

Online pressrooms help journalists

A public relations (PR) person or staff can make it easier for the press. A PR group can develop press kits, including promotional materials specifically designed for the media. Many businesses and nonprofits have a "Press" section on their website that posts press releases, photos, and sometimes videos geared to the press. For its traveling performances, Cirque du Soleil relies on local newspaper and television to produce stories that stoke interest and demand for tickets. Cirque du Soleil's online pressroom provides the press with hundreds of photos and videos of its performances.

Earned Media from Customer Advocacy

LO 16.6

Customers trust and act on recommendations from friends, family, and colleagues. Even recommendations from strangers often have a stronger influence on buying decisions than advertising does. Research has also found that customers acquired from word-of-mouth are more loyal and have greater lifetime value than customers acquired from other means.[19]

That said, although information from other customers is influential, it is much more difficult to control than the messages a marketing manager crafts for an advertisement, sales promotion, or owned media. When customers control the message, the words might be exactly what the marketing manager wants, or they could be incorrect, inappropriate, or harmful to the company. Let's take a closer look at how customer-to-customer communication works and some strategies for fostering the more positive forms of this promotion.

Opinion leaders help spread the word—good and bad

Opinion leaders like to share their views—they also get attention from other customers who respect their views. Marketers value personal recommendations from opinion leaders. For example, some movie fans like to be the first to see new flicks. If they like a movie, they quickly tell their friends and word-of-mouth publicity does the real selling job. When online grocer FreshDirect opened in New York City, positive word-of-mouth was key to its fast growth.

However, consumers are even more likely to talk about negative experiences than positive ones. So, if early groups reject the product, it may never get off the ground. In one study, 64 percent of consumers said they would not shop at a store after being told about someone else's negative experience there.[20]

Paying for opinion leaders

To help motivate consumers to spread the word, a company called BzzAgent helps marketing managers start conversations. BzzAgent works with about 800,000 "agents" in the United States, Canada, and the United Kingdom. Agents who sign up to help with a particular campaign receive product samples and information. If they like

> **Online Toolkit**
>
> BzzAgent has a code of conduct for its agents, but even so it has received some negative publicity that questions the ethics of its agents. Go to the BzzAgent site (**www.BzzAgent.com**) and scroll to the bottom of the page. Here you will find a link for "Code of Conduct." Click on that link and read through the code. If a BzzAgent follows the guidelines in the code, do you think the practice is ethical? In your opinion, what actions would make a BzzAgent's behavior unethical?

the product, they are urged to pass the word. Although such behavior could be deceptive, BzzAgent encourages its agents to be ethical and disclose their status as "BzzAgents." Kraft Foods, General Mills, and Dockers are among the companies that have run campaigns through BzzAgent.[21]

Most customers are reluctant to recommend

Most customers are reluctant to recommend products—even when they do have a great experience. There are a number of reasons why customers hold back. Some worry a recommendation may result in a dissatisfying experience for a friend. This fear of negative consequences often outweighs the benefits of a friend having a good experience. People also worry about the personal costs of recommendations. If a business they recommend gets busier, service quality may decline or prices might go up. Some products can be difficult to explain to others—and people don't want to be put on the spot when trying to explain them. People also hold back if they feel the recommendation doesn't make them look good. Or they worry that others might question their ethics, perhaps believing they receive some type of kickback for making the recommendation.[22]

Encouraging word-of-mouth

For customers to share their great experiences, they must see doing so as safe, fun, and worthwhile. First, a company must offer a great product. Consistently high performance gives a customer confidence that it happens all the time—and increases confidence that anyone they recommend it to will have a similar experience. Second, companies must give customers a specific story to share—anything from delighting (far exceeding customer expectations) to creating an unusual experience. Sometimes unusual is simple—imagine if the cable TV repairperson called to say he would be twenty minutes *early* and asked if that was inconvenient. You might be surprised enough to tell some friends. Third, companies shouldn't be afraid to ask for recommendations. It doesn't hurt to come out and ask satisfied customers to leave reviews or tell their friends. A link to a review site following a purchase makes this easier. Fourth, some organizations offer easily shareable content on their social media sites—making it easy for customers to click and share information. Social media sharing "buttons" can be placed next to online content to facilitate pass-along.

Referral programs give customers incentives to recommend

Another way to motivate positive word-of-mouth is through a referral program. A **referral program** offers a current customer an incentive for recommending a new customer to a business. Usually referral programs require the new customer to make a purchase. To give both the person giving and the person receiving the referral an incentive, both are usually offered some sort of discount. So for example, after a customer gives a positive review at AirBnB (a website where customers can rent out lodging), they are asked if they would like to refer a friend. The friend is sent a $25 discount—and after the friend books a place to stay through AirBnB, a similar credit is given to the person who made the referral.[23]

These types of programs are often used by online companies because of the simplicity and low cost of giving and receiving referrals over the Internet. It is also easy for a company to experiment with different levels of compensation and find the offers that work best.

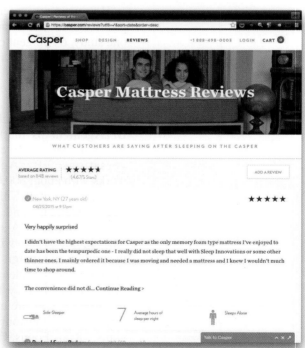

Ratings and reviews let customers do the selling

Reviews allow customers to sell to one another. Reviews can have a strong influence on purchase behavior because readers view reviews as objective reports that share first-hand

Casper Mattress sells mattresses online. Reviews are an important part of its promotion mix. Customers usually like to lie down on a mattress before purchasing. Positive reviews and some explanations about the purchase can reduce the risk of buying without trying.
© 2015 Casper Sleep, Inc.

knowledge. As a result, many companies include rating and review capabilities on their owned media. Most major retailers find reviews increase sales.

Manage negative reviews when they come along

Whereas online compliments let the firm know what it is doing well, complaints can highlight unmet customer needs—and give managers a chance to turn things around. Marketing managers should not ignore negative reviews—they should respond and fix the problems.

That is what the owner of a California spa did. She was horrified to learn her spa had only a two-and-a-half-star rating (out of five) on the popular review site Yelp. com. She set out to fix things. First, she e-mailed the unhappy reviewers in an effort to make things right. Then she encouraged her satisfied customers to post reviews. She also fixed areas of concern. Soon the spa had an acceptable four-star rating on Yelp, and rather than scaring off prospects, the review site was spurring them to action.[24]

The ethics and danger of falsifying earned media

Companies need to be careful they are not too zealous in seeking positive word-of-mouth. Not only is it unethical, firms are often easily exposed when they engage in unethical practices. For example, a Honda manager went on the Facebook page for the Honda Crosstour and raved about the new car's design—when most other comments were negative. Some readers recognized the manager's name from articles in the automobile press and cried foul. Honda ended up embarrassed when the deception was reported on *Autoblog* and other sites. Sometimes TripAdvisor suspects some of the reviews on its site are fake—like when a hotel's employees post reviews that build up their facility and tear down a competitor. To prevent fake reviews from harming the credibility of its own site, TripAdvisor flags suspicious reviews with a red disclaimer.[25]

Social media simplifies and amplifies pass-along

People are more likely to pass-along when it is easy to do. So social media sites such as Facebook and Twitter make it as easy as clicking on a "like," "share," or "retweet" button. Social media also amplifies customer word-of-mouth—as one person can have hundreds or even thousands of followers. So let's take a closer look at social media and its role in the promotion blend.

Social Media Differs from Traditional Media

LO 16.7

In Chapter 15 we learned about traditional media—including television, magazines, radio, and so on. Advertisers would place their messages on these media to communicate to other customers. The growth of the Internet led to a rise in different types of social media. **Social media** refers to websites or software applications that allow users to create and share ideas, information, photos and videos, and interact in a social network. Examples of social media include Facebook, Twitter, Instagram, Pinterest, and LinkedIn. About 7 in 10 Americans are on at least one social media platform. Among those who are 18 to 29 years old, the number is 9 in 10. Let's look closely at how social media differ from traditional media before we focus on how social media can work in the promotion blend.[26]

Social media—paid, owned, and earned

Paid, owned, and earned media may appear on social media. Chapter 15 describes advertising (paid media) on social media sites. On Facebook for example, a seller can choose to run a "sponsored message" (paid media) on the site. That same seller might also create a Facebook page (owned media) so that a brand's fans can "like" the page and keep up with messages it sends out. When a customer clicks "like" on a brand page or writes something on that brand's wall, the customer's friends see it (earned media). Most of the major social networking sites provide similar paid, earned, and owned media opportunities.

Social media—no media placement cost but not free

Most social media has no *direct* media cost, but that doesn't mean social media is free. A company needs to hire staff or an agency to manage its presence on social media. Once a company starts a Facebook page or Twitter stream, it should regularly maintain the page—or customers may wonder if the company has gone out of business.

Social media—many-to-many communication

Advertising is a one-to-many model of communication—a brand sends a message to many customers at once. Social media operates in a different way; social media offers a many-to-many model of communication. When a brand posts on Facebook, some customers engage and respond—and others simply follow the back-and-forth interaction. Many brands respond to Tweets and Facebook posts in order to engage with customers. Those conversations appear in public—so other customers can read and (if they like) enter into the conversation.

Advertising plans, social media reacts

Advertising through paid media typically involves a relatively long planning cycle. Evaluating concepts, approving ideas, and producing a print, radio, television, or online advertisement can take months. Although marketing managers should have a social media plan, this form of communication offers the ability to react to current or emerging events/comments immediately. Many social media managers monitor news and events that may have a relationship to, or potential interest in, the brand's target market.

It is those in-the-moment reactions that can get some social media posts more attention. A few years ago, the Super Bowl had a blackout in the middle of the football game. Oreo's fast-thinking social media manager tweeted "Power Out? No Problem" and posted a photo of an Oreo cookie with the caption: "You can still dunk in the dark." The clever joke was retweeted more than 15,000 times and generated plenty of conversations around Oreo.

Major Social Media Platforms

LO 16.8

There are many different social media platforms—and there seem to be new ones appearing weekly. In recent years, five social media sites have attracted considerable attention in the United States and around the world: Facebook, Twitter, Instagram, Pinterest, and

This series of images shows how Facebook can be used to deliver paid, owned, and earned media. The first image shows an advertisement for Sonos that will appear in target customers' newsfeeds (paid media). A second image shows Sonos' Facebook page (owned media). Comments by current customers on one of Sonos' posts results in endorsements from other customers (earned media).
© 2004-2015 Sonos, Inc.

Exhibit 16-6   Big Five Social Media Platforms—User Demographics

	Facebook	Twitter	Instagram	Pinterest	LinkedIn
2014 % of U.S. population using	58	19	21	22	23
Growth rate 2012–14 (%)	6	44	100	87	40
Frequency of use					
Check in: daily/ weekly/less often	70/17/12	36/24/40	49/24/26	17/29/52	13/25/61
Average minutes on site per day	40	17	21	21	10
Usage % among online adults					
Male/female usage (%)	66/77[a]	24/21	22/29	13/42	28/27
Age 18–29 (%)	87[b]	37	53	34	23
Age 30–49 (%)	73	25	25	28	31
Age 50–64 (%)	63	12	11	27	30
Age 65+ (%)	56	10	6	17	21
Owned media: how companies, nonprofits, or brands create owned media on platform	Company and/or brand pages	Create one or more Twitter profiles, create hashtags	Build an Instagram page, add images and hashtags	Create a Pinterest page and pinboards	Build a company page, post company news
Earned media: how customers demonstrate support	Customers "Like," "Share," and comment	Customers can "Follow," "Tweet," "Retweet," and comment	"Follows," "Likes," and comments	Customers save ("Pin") favorites to their own pinboards, follow others	News gets "Likes" or comments from other LinkedIn users

[a] Read as among all online adults, 66% of males online use Facebook and 77% of females online use Facebook.

[b] Read as 87% of those age 18–29 are on Facebook.

Sources: *Social Media Update 2014*, Pew Research Center, January 9, 2015; CMO's *Guide to the Social Landscape*, 2015, "Younger Users Spend More Daily Time on Social Networks," *eMarketer*, November 18, 2014.

LinkedIn. Each has more than 250 million users visiting their sites at least once a month. Facebook has more than 1.4 billion users. Each of these sites offers something different to users and to the promotion blend. This section digs a little deeper into the social networking leaders summarized in Exhibit 16–6.[27]

Facebook—the king of social media

Facebook is an online social networking website that allows registered users to create profiles, upload photos and video, and send messages to friends, family, and colleagues.[28] Facebook dominates social media; in 2014 the site reached more than 1.4 billion users globally and 58% of the U.S. adult population. Facebook is visited more frequently than any of the other social media sites; 70% of Facebook users check in daily—most from mobile devices—and spend an average of 40 minutes per day on the site. Facebook is especially effective among older adults—more than half of online adults over age 50 are on Facebook.

Users typically scroll through their "newsfeed" with posts (videos, photos, status updates) from "Friends," "Liked" businesses or organizations, and sponsored posts (paid advertising). Because the average user has hundreds of friends, Facebook has an algorithm that decides what content is placed in the user's newsfeed. The algorithm favors posts from friends and brands that the user actively engages with by clicking or commenting on posts.

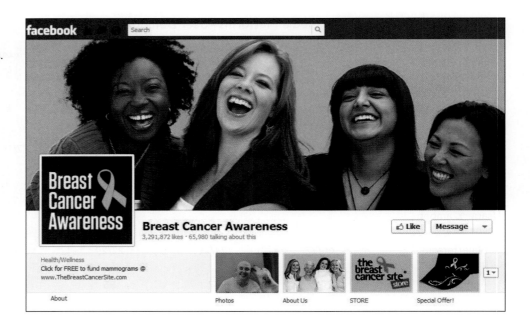

On Facebook anyone can set up pages to promote a business or nonprofit. Business pages might feature photos, videos, links to a company's homepage, reviews, and other information. After a business or nonprofit sets up and publishes a Facebook page, users can choose to click the "Like" button and become a "fan" of that page. Fans receive updates from the brand in their newsfeed. Some large brands, including McDonald's, MTV, Disney, and Red Bull, boast more than 40 million fans.

Facebook's size makes presence a must for many companies

Facebook's sheer size—and its use by many different customer segments—makes it necessary for many organizations to have at least some presence. Because customers have to choose to "like" a brand page, the target for messages should be current customers. Sales contests and discounts are sometimes used to engage fans. Most brands try to post engaging content to encourage fans to click through or share the content with their friends, which (by coming from a friend) offers additional credibility. Nike maintains a corporate Facebook page, but also keeps specialty pages dedicated to specific sports including Nike Golf, Nike Basketball, Nike Running, and more.

Twitter microblogging service

Twitter is a social networking microblogging service that allows registered users to send out short (140 characters or less) messages called "tweets."[29] Measured by size and engagement, Twitter is much smaller than Facebook. In 2014, Twitter had fewer than 288 million users globally and reached about 19 percent of the U.S. adult population. Twitter is growing faster than Facebook. The demographics of the average user skew young, with 37 percent of online adults aged 18 to 29 using Twitter, but only 12 percent from age 50 to 64, and 10 percent of online adults 65 and older. Just over one-third (36 percent) of Twitter users check in daily, with the average user spending about 17 minutes—those aged 18 to 29 average 30 minutes per day.

Twitter operates like a public message board, with most tweets available for anyone (even people not signed up for Twitter) able to see them. Most Twitter users follow friends, celebrities, news sites, and brands. Among active users, tweets tend to be more frequent and less personal as compared to Facebook.

Tweets are short and sweet

Because of the 140 character limit, tweets are concise—for example, this tweet from Starbucks: "Buy any fall drink (hot or iced), get one free. 2-6 pm, 9/17-9/21, participating US stores." However, at times, brand tweets include a link to more details on a landing page. The payroll management company ADP tweets links to content (produced by ADP or not) relevant to the payroll industry; many of its sales reps retweet (a way of forwarding a tweet) to their follower-customers. By frequently passing along non-ADP content, ADP and its sales force earned a reputation for being trusted experts in their field. A simple "hashtag" (#) allows fans to pass along support for well-known brands and helps marketing managers assess engagement and interact with potential leads. Nike fans can post using a Nike hashtag (#Nike) or the Nike tagline (#justdoit).

Instagram—when a picture is worth a thousand words

Images and video have long been a prominent part of the copy thrust in print and television advertising. Social media users often skim through content; image and video sharing is what tends to capture people's attention. Photographs and videos can tell short stories and connect people to a brand or seller—it can inspire them, solve everyday problems, or simply entertain.

Instagram is a free online photo and video sharing service geared to mobile phones. Photos and videos can be taken with the Instagram smartphone app (or other camera app) and shared on other social networking sites including Facebook, Twitter, and Tumblr. In 2014, Instagram was the fastest growing major social media platform—doubling its number of users from 2012. In 2014, Instagram had about 300 million users around the world. Instagram's penetration is greatest among younger age groups. Although accurate data is not available for those younger than 18, 53 percent of online adults aged 18 to 29 use Instagram—and about half use Instagram on a daily basis. Brands including *National Geographic* magazine, Nike, and *The Ellen DeGeneres Show* each have more than 10 million followers.[30]

Instagram can work well for many small businesses, where an owner or part-time marketing manager may find it less time consuming to take pictures as compared to writing stories or posts. Businesses in the restaurant, clothing, fashion, travel, and entertainment fields often post images on Instagram to maintain or stoke customer interest in their goods and services.

Pinterest lets users share wish lists

Pinterest is a website that allows registered users to share ideas and images they find online with fellow users. The ideas and images are organized into pinboards (a kind of online bulletin board). In 2015, it was estimated that Pinterest had about 70 million users globally, with 48 million in the United States. About three-quarters of Pinterest users are female. Although the site is most frequently used by younger people, it maintains appeal to some in older age groups.[31]

Users create boards around a wide range of topics that work well with images, including art, fashion, travel, and home décor. For many users, it is kind of a "wish

Home improvement retailer Lowe's Pinterest page includes many photos of different around-the-house projects that customers could choose to complete – hopefully shopping at Lowe's to pick up some materials to make the job easier.

list"—so marketing managers want to make sure they post images on their own websites that can easily pin to Pinterest. Retailers can put "Pin It" buttons next to images so that customers can create a wish list that other followers see as well—promoting pass-along and earned media. Retailers such as LL Bean, Nordstrom, and Lowe's, each with more than 3 million followers, are among the biggest brands on Pinterest.

Businesses get social on LinkedIn

LinkedIn is a social networking website for businesspeople who create personal or company profiles. In 2014, LinkedIn claimed almost 350 million registered users worldwide, with more than 115 million in the United States. Demographics show that penetration among online adults is highest in ages 30 to 64 (around 30 percent) but that growth is fastest among students and recent college graduates. Individuals may have hundreds or thousands of connections; companies such as Microsoft, General Electric, and HP have more than a million followers. Media companies that target businesspeople, including the *Wall Street Journal* and *Forbes* magazine, use LinkedIn to distribute articles.[32]

Businesspeople used to think of LinkedIn as a place to network for jobs. Now many companies and salespeople use LinkedIn to communicate with customers. Companies posting news, white papers, and reports develop a reputation as trusted industry experts. Salespeople identify and qualify leads and share knowledge with customers.

Other social networks

We have highlighted some of the most popular social networks, but depending on the target market and promotion objectives, other social networks should be considered. Google+ is very large, but includes a less engaged user base. Tumblr is a microblogging site that makes it easy for users to share all types of media from browser, phone, desktop, or e-mail.

For firms targeting millennials and Gen Z, the fast-growing photo/video sharing app Snapchat has been a hit. Video and photo sharing services are among the fastest growing social networks and include YouTube, Vimeo, Snapchat, Flickr, Vine, and Periscope. Specialized social networks target very specific audiences. For example, Allrecipes.com can get a nutritionist, caterer, or personal chef in front of relevant target markets. Home remodelers and architects can show their wares on Houzz—a site with more than six million photos of different home remodeling projects.

Different networks around the world

While all of the social networks discussed here have a significant global presence, marketing managers doing business internationally should be aware of various localized social media. Some of these can be quite large. For example, China's QZone's more than 600 million active users write blogs, maintain diaries, share photos, watch videos, and listen to music on the site. Sina Weibo, another Chinese site that is kind of a combination of Twitter and Facebook, has more than 300 million users. Although available in several languages, the Facebook-like site VK (formerly VKontakte) is especially popular among Russian speakers and has more than 280 million registered users. Each provides a promotion opportunity if target customers use the site.

Many ways to offer value to social media fans and followers

Ultimately, social media needs fans and followers—or no one sees the content. Target customers follow companies and brands that deliver some sort of value and followers will show support for valued posts by "liking," sharing," "retweeting," or commenting. There are many different ways to deliver value; a brand can offer discounted prices, make followers laugh, or provide fast customer service. The TEDx Youth Conference in Sydney, Australia, gave free coffee to anyone who posted a photo from the event or a comment on Instagram, Twitter, or Facebook—that got a lot of "likes." Some of the different kinds of value social media can deliver—with examples—are shown in Exhibit 16–7.

Exhibit 16-7 Different Types of Social Media Content and Examples

Type of content	Examples
Humor	• Vine: Oreo's funny "snack hacks" video series. • Twitter and Facebook: Taco Bell makes humorous posts. • YouTube: Samuel Adams introduces a new beer using helium as an ingredient—April Fools!
Deals and discounts	• Facebook: Online beauty retailer Sephora sometimes offers "Facebook fans only" deals. • Twitter: In the UK, Domino's pizza reduced the price of pizza based on how many people tweeted in time for lunch.
Contests	• Instagram: Habitat for Humanity runs a photo contest to highlight onsite volunteers. • Facebook, Twitter, Pinterest, Instagram, and YouTube: Lay's "Do Us a Flavor" contest asked customers to submit and vote on new chip flavors. • Instagram: Starbucks' "White Cup Challenge" asked customers to design Starbucks cups.
Insider knowledge	• Snapchat: Acura NSX game allowed the first 100 followers a glimpse of its new super car prototype racing on a test track. • Instagram: Fashion designer Oscar de la Renta offers followers a sneak peek of its upcoming fashion lines. • LinkedIn: Microsoft's LinkedIn home page includes peeks behind the scenes at the company, blogs, and Q&A. • Instagram: General Electric gives followers a peek into the science driving GE's cutting-edge technology.
Educational	• Snapchat: World Wildlife Fund highlighted endangered species with its #LastSelfie campaign. • Vine: General Electric had users create "Six Second Science" videos.
Useful ideas, information, and practices	• LinkedIn: The Four Seasons hotel's company page provides helpful videos and articles about destinations where it has accommodations. • Facebook: Marketing consulting firm Marketo posts articles and white papers on Facebook. • Pinterest: Whole Foods has more than 60 different boards with topics ranging from baking to gardening.
Product launches and updates	• Twitter: Retailer H&M shows many of its latest fashions on Twitter. • Snapchat: Madonna launched a new song on Snapchat to target its younger user base.
Customer service	• Twitter: Delta Airlines offers customer service on Twitter. • Twitter: Xbox video game's customer support team has more than 600,000 followers and responds quickly to customer questions.
Image and lifestyle	• Pinterest: Retailer Nordstrom posts products and lifestyle inspiration images daily. • Facebook: Motorcycle accessory maker Biltwell encouraged fans to post motorcycle helmet art. • Instagram: GoPro posts a customer "Photo of the Day" that highlights the lifestyle of GoPro users.

Social media objectives—build relationships, not just fans

Some companies make the mistake of focusing on short-term objectives like generating millions of Facebook fans or thousands of followers on Instagram. Although these objectives are easy to measure, they don't necessarily have any impact on the company's bottom line.

Promotional efforts utilizing social media are best focused on increasing target customers' purchase likelihood. And because customers generally follow brands they already know and like, social media works best when the target market is already a customer. In most situations, social media as earned and owned media is *not* aimed at making target customers aware of the brand or encouraging trial. Instead, promotion objectives for social media usually focus on (a) enhancing brand familiarity by growing the number of customers that prefer or insist on a brand or (b) growing customer equity by encouraging customers to increase their purchases.

Software Can Manage, Measure, and Automate Online Media

LO 16.9

Implementing paid, owned, earned, and social media requires that managers follow many of the principles discussed elsewhere in this textbook. Segmentation remains important—with the lower costs of owned media and social media allowing firms to efficiently target smaller segments. Promotion objectives must be kept in mind. For most organizations, owned, earned, and social media are parts of a larger promotion blend—the marketing manager must carefully pull these pieces together to be efficient and effective. The AIDA model (see Exhibit 13–2) and promotion objectives should guide the copy thrust as well as the amount and type of information provided. For firms that have earned, owned, and social media online, new software helps manage, measure, and automate these media.

Software can manage social media

Because different types of earned, owned, and social media occur online, software can be used to monitor and manage the process. One popular tool is Hootsuite, a dashboard that offers marketing managers the ability to submit messages to Facebook, Twitter, LinkedIn, and other social media on a scheduled basis. The posts can be scheduled weeks or months in advance. Hootsuite and other software can also collect and analyze data from various social media.[33]

Measure results from online media

For many firms, earned, owned, and social media happen online—which makes monitoring and measuring the results faster and easier. So, for example, when Dollar Shave Club posts on Facebook, it can very quickly see how many users "Like" the post and what comments are made. When the company posts a video on Twitter, it can count how many followers retweet (forward) the message and how many watch the video. When Dollar Shave Club runs an ad on television, it can count how many customers come to its website, how many sign up for its service, and how long those customers continue to buy.

Software tools allow marketing managers to track many different online marketing measures. So for example, managers can track the number of visitors to a site, how many stay (and how many bounce to another site in only a few seconds), how long those customers stay, and how they found the site (a link from another page? A Google search and keywords used in the search?). Marketing managers can also track what customers purchase, how much they spend, and discover how the biggest spenders found the site. These are just a few of the many different online measures. Tracking this data allows marketing managers to see what works—and what doesn't—and then adjust their marketing strategy in a very short time. Many firms use the free Google Analytics, a software designed for this analysis.

Software carries customers through the purchase process

Software can also be programmed to help firms respond to particular customer actions. **Marketing automation software** tracks individual customers' behavior and triggers actions in response to specific customer actions. For organizations with customers who spend a lot of time online, this software provides a low-cost way to learn more about customers and deliver the right messages at the right time. For example, a customer who visits a site three times might automatically be delivered a "pop-up" question "Can I answer any questions for you?" that links to a waiting salesperson.

Another example deals with a troubling issue for online retailers. Studies estimate that about two-thirds of all online shopping carts are abandoned before checkout. This means a customer has come to an online store, placed something in the cart, and then left without completing the purchase. Some online retailers use marketing automation to send customers that abandon a cart an e-mail that reminds them of the purchase. The e-mail may even include an offer for free shipping or a discount.[34]

Marketing automation software can be more sophisticated for B2B sellers. Earlier in this chapter, we noted that many companies post white papers and case studies designed to demonstrate solutions to business problems. So imagine a marketing manager seeking to find a better way to "manage social media." A Google search on the topic might lead to a landing page for Hootsuite (the software mentioned previously)

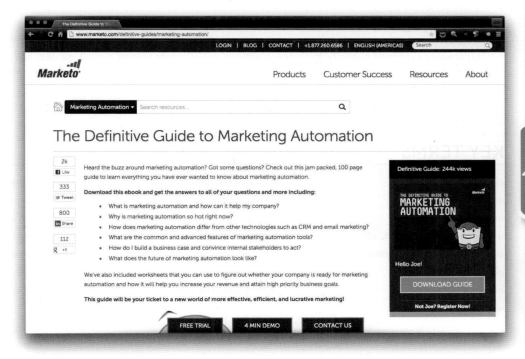

that offers a seven-page white paper titled "8 Tips for Social Business." The paper educates the customer on social media without overly promoting the Hootsuite solution. This paper isn't exactly free—before downloading, an interested customer must surrender some information valuable to Hootsuite: name, e-mail address, company, job title, and phone number. This information is used to start a file on the customer. The white paper also includes a link to other online readings—some of which are not created by Hootsuite—but all of this activity can be tracked. The customer's behavior is used to determine whether a salesperson should phone the prospect—and if the salesperson calls, she can review the file to know what material the customer has found most useful. The HubSpot software described in the chapter-opening case is an example of this type of tool.[35]

CONCLUSION

This is the fourth chapter on Promotion. The different options for promotion have grown in recent years. For decades, most promotion efforts revolved around salespeople, advertising, and sales promotion. Although marketing managers understood the importance of word-of-mouth, it was difficult to directly influence, and most customers had trouble finding it when they needed it.

The Internet was the technology that triggered a great deal of change in promotion. The Web changed customer behavior—with many customers looking online for information to help them make better purchase choices. People's "screen time" moved from television to the computer and now the phone, where they often access the Internet and social media. Marketing managers have responded to these new customer behaviors with new forms of promotion.

This chapter provided an introduction to the wide range of tools available to marketing managers in the forms of earned media, owned media, and social media. The chapter showed how these alternative media compare to paid media (advertising)—with most earned and owned media more trusted by customers than traditional advertising. The chapter highlights how the Internet makes it easier for customers to learn about products from companies and other customers.

With social media grabbing so much customer attention, the chapter examines five of the largest platforms—Facebook, Twitter, Instagram, Pinterest, and LinkedIn. Although these social networks are most popular with teens and Millennials, they have had an impact on many target markets. The chapter concludes with a discussion of software used to manage, monitor, and even automate some of these processes—further lowering their costs and increasing their effectiveness.

WHAT'S NOW?

This chapter examined publicity. With new practices and concepts around owned, earned, and social media emerging regularly, make sure you are caught up some of the latest in this area. Check out *What's Now?* at www.learnthe4ps.com/whatsnow/c16

KEY TERMS

LO 16.10

paid media, 424

owned media, 424

earned media, 424

user-generated content, 425

search engine optimization (SEO), 428

pass-along, 430

branded services, 430

white paper, 432

case studies, 432

landing page, 432

blog, 433

infographic, 434

branded apps, 434

brand community, 435

referral program, 438

social media, 439

Facebook, 441

Twitter, 442

Instagram, 443

Pinterest, 443

LinkedIn, 444

marketing automation software, 446

QUESTIONS AND PROBLEMS

1. Review the HubSpot case study that opens the chapter. From this case, identify examples of different key terms and concepts covered in the chapter. For example, the case mentions customers "liking" a HubSpot Facebook post—this is an example of pass-along and earned media.

2. Review the HubSpot case study that opens the chapter. Suggest how the company might utilize some other form of earned, owned, or social media in its promotion blend.

3. Describe the general (earned, owned, and paid) and specific (see examples in this chapter) type of media that might be most suitable for promoting: (a) a neighborhood sandwich shop, (b) toothpaste, (c) a hairdresser, and (d) accounting software for small businesses. Specify any assumptions necessary to obtain a definite answer.

4. Which of the following products are good candidates for user-generated content: (a) men's underwear, (b) women's fashion jeans, (c) brand of salsa, (d) lumber used in home construction.

5. For each of the following products, indicate how search, pass-along, and experience would (or would not) operate for customers seeking information: (a) a brand of shampoo, (b) a pair of jeans, (c) a real estate agent, (d) a company that sells chemicals to a manufacturer, (e) a local shoe store. [Sample Answer for (a): for shampoo, a customer might search online for a shampoo to treat dandruff or oily hair, pass-along might occur if someone asks a friend for a recommendation of a shampoo—but it is unlikely that someone offers an unsolicited recommendation for a shampoo, and branded experience might occur if the shampoo was offered at a hotel or in the showers at a health club.]

6. Briefly discuss some of the pros and cons of earned and owned media for a producer of golf clubs and for a dance studio.

7. Find a web page that you think does a particularly good job of communicating to the target audience. Would it communicate well to an audience in another country (assume it is translated to the foreign language)? Explain your thinking.

8. Find a Facebook page for a brand or company. Evaluate that page. What do you think are the promotion objectives? Does the Facebook page foster engagement (are many followers posting messages directed at the brand)?

9. Name two companies that you think would have success building a Pinterest page. Why do you think they should choose to build a page? What type of content should each company place on its pinboards?

10. What kinds of publicity would work best at a company that markets tractors, combines, and other farm equipment to farmers? Why would the publicity you suggest be effective?

11. Search online and find examples of: (a) case study, (b) infographic, (c) blog, and (d) branded community. Describe the promotion objective you believe each is trying to achieve.

12. Go to the Facebook page for Olive Garden (Italian restaurant chain)—choose the main company page, not an individual location. Scan through the page and open different tabs. Critique the pages. What do you think works well? What could be improved?

MARKETING PLANNING FOR HILLSIDE VETERINARY CLINIC

Appendix D (the Appendices follow Chapter 19) includes a sample marketing plan for Hillside Veterinary Clinic. Look through the "Marketing Strategy" section of the plan.

a. Identify key elements of earned and owned media that Hillside plans to use.

b. Suggest two additional ways that Hillside Veterinary Clinic could promote earned media and two ways it could add owned media.

c. How could Hillside use two additional aspects of social media?

SUGGESTED CASES

3. Real NOCO Soccer Academy
18. West Tarrytown Volunteer Fire Department

19. UltimateWedding.com
36. Silverglade Homes

MARKETING ANALYTICS: DATA TO KNOWLEDGE

CHAPTER 16 SALES ANALYTICS

Janet runs an online business selling homemade crafts. Looking at the online analytics for her store, she recognized a problem with shopping cart abandonment. Customers would come to her online store, place items in a cart, and then never complete the purchase. Janet began sending reminder emails to customers with abandoned carts and many came back to the store and completed their purchases. But there was still room for significant improvement. Her analysis shows an abandon rate of 65%. That is, 65% of the people who add items to their online cart didn't actually complete the transaction and place an order. Janet wonders if it would help to offer some sort of discount to these customers to provide an extra incentive to complete the transaction. To evaluate the idea she decides to create a spreadsheet to analyze her options.

See Connect for the spreadsheet and questions needed to analyze this scenario.

CHAPTER SEVENTEEN

Pricing Objectives and Policies

Twenty-somethings Adam Lowry and Eric Ryan shared a San Francisco apartment and an interest in starting a business. Back in 2000, after studying chemistry, Lowry was a climate scientist with a passion for sustainability. Ryan had studied marketing and he worked in the advertising business; his interest was design. While hanging out drinking beer and on road trips to the mountains, the two talked about products they thought were cool and uncool—and what markets might be ripe for disruption.

They spotted opportunity in the $17 billion household cleaning product-market. They saw a mature market with little differentiation among brands. Dealer brands were viewed as lower quality at lower prices. National brands gave retailers price deals and advertising allowances in exchange for shelf space. Consumer promotion debated minor differences in cleaning efficacy, with coupons and sale prices used to woo shoppers whose brand loyalty was more habit than commitment.

The external market environment suggested a path building on the entrepreneurs' strengths. Scientific studies showed that many household cleaning chemicals were not healthy over the long haul. The green movement was picking up steam. Mass merchandiser Target was successfully selling everyday items with a designer flair. Lowry and Ryan thought a line of stylish, sustainable products made with safe ingredients that "cleaned like heck and smelled like heaven" could find a niche in this market.

Soon Method Products was born. Lowry and Ryan tested batches of cleaning products they mixed in their bathtub and beer pitchers labeled "Do Not Drink." They filled clear spray bottles with samples of their first four products—cleaners for kitchen, shower, bath, and glass. Then they ambushed independent grocery store managers in early morning hours and pitched their products. That's how the owner of Mollie Stone's discovered Method. He was their first customer. Method placed an order with its contract manufacturer and produced its first large batches.

Later that summer, as sales began to take off, Ryan revisited packaging design. Without money to advertise, he thought something unique would garner attention and interest at point-of-purchase. Method approached well-known industrial designer Karim Rashid with a pitch to "reinvent soap." Intrigued, Rashid came on board. Rashid's designs got Method noticed. A lot of Method customers discover the brand in a store—they love the cool package and figure at least the soap looks good sitting on the counter. But customers find they also like how well the cleaners work and keep buying.

Method's green promise also resonated with customers. Method's "people against dirty" campaign told the brand's story: most cleaners leave behind toxic chemical residues, leaving homes "dirty" after being cleaned. And when these chemicals go down the drain, they contaminate the natural environment. "People against dirty" got the message across to Method's target market. Design and green proved to be powerful differentiators and allowed Method to charge a price about 20 percent higher than leading brands.

Their first really big sale was to Target. Method's stylish packaging was a perfect fit with Target's market and its design focus. After successful test markets in San Francisco and Chicago, Target took Method nationwide. But Method doesn't appeal to every retailer. For example, Walmart customers thought Method was too expensive, and the line was dropped.

In spite of its premium price and impressive retail contracts, Method struggled for profitability. By 2006, the brand held only 0.5 percent in market share and less than $100 million in sales. The problem: Method's production and operating costs were higher than giant, mega-brand competitors such as Procter & Gamble; in fact, brands like Dawn sold in stores for less than Method's cost to produce. Suppliers didn't give Method the same quantity discounts and it didn't have similar manufacturing economies of scale.

Growth had other costs. For example, retailers and wholesalers expected up-front cash payments or a few free cases of product before taking a chance on Method. New products are risky; retailers don't know how much they'll sell.

Fortunately for Method, its financial backers were initially concerned with market share and sales volume rather than profitability. They continued to invest in building support for the brand and developing innovative new products.

Method's innovations in the laundry category show how a little company can influence a big (make that huge) market. When Method introduced a laundry soap three times as concentrated as market leader Tide, most consumers thought Method was much more expensive than the larger bottles on the shelf. Method had to teach customers that it took less Method to get the same clean. After learning how to properly "dose" Method, customers appreciated the convenience of the smaller bottle. Retailers immediately recognized the value of lower handling costs and a smaller shelf footprint (so they could stock more products) and pressured Method's competitors to offer similar concentrates.

A few years later, Method launched an improved laundry detergent. Its "smartclean technology" was eight times the concentration of regular detergent. Moms could hold a 20-ounce bottle (fifty-loads) in one hand and their baby in the other. Those same moms like the dye-free, hypoallergenic free + clear version, whereas other customers prefer the Fresh Air or Peony Blossom fragrances. Of course the detergent has an environmentally friendly, biodegradable formulation. A simple squirt system makes it easy to measure the right dose of detergent, although those savings are lost on the majority of consumers who pour too much detergent into each load of laundry.

For price-sensitive shoppers, Method's $15.49 list price ($12.99 at Target) might not look like a great deal next to Target's own Up & Up brand for $8.38 (75 loads of laundry) or Tide's 100-ounce, 64-load jug at $11.99. Even after a coupon, a package bun-

dled with fabric softener, or a refill with the Method pouch, customers pay more per load of laundry for Method.

So how is Method growing? Because Method's whole marketing mix offers superior value to its narrow target market. Customers might try Method because of its stylish packaging and green roots or maybe its clever advertising, sales promotion, and publicity efforts attracted their attention. But Method's customers buy again (and again) because its products clean well and they can find the brand where they shop, online or off. With Method's focus, that little corner of the market where they're cleaning up will surely keep growing.[1]

LEARNING OBJECTIVES

The Method case demonstrates the importance of Price and how it interacts with the other marketing mix variables to create value and influence customer behavior. This chapter will help you better understand pricing objectives and policies that influence how firms make pricing decisions.

When you finish this chapter, you should be able to

1 Explain the dimensions of price and value.

2 Understand how pricing objectives should guide strategy planning for pricing decisions.

3 Understand choices marketing managers must make about price flexibility.

4 Know what a marketing manager should consider when setting the price level for a product in the early stages of the product life cycle.

5 Understand the many possible variations of a price structure, including discounts, allowances, and who pays transportation costs.

6 Understand the value pricing concept and its role in obtaining a competitive advantage by offering target customers superior value.

7 Understand the legality of price level and price flexibility policies.

8 Understand important new terms (shown in red).

Price Has Many Strategy Dimensions

LO 17.1

Price is one of the four major strategy decision variables that a marketing manager controls. Pricing decisions affect both the number of sales a firm makes and how much money it earns. Price is what a customer must give up to get the benefits offered by the rest of a firm's marketing mix, so it plays a direct role in shaping customer value.

Guided by the company's objectives, marketing managers develop specific pricing objectives (see Exhibit 17–1). These objectives drive decisions about key pricing policies: (1) how flexible prices will be, (2) the level of prices over the product life cycle, (3) to whom and when discounts and allowances will be given, and (4) how transportation costs will be handled. After we've looked at these specific areas, we will discuss how they combine to impact customer value as well as laws that are relevant. In Chapter 18, we will discuss how prices are set.

It's not easy to define price in real-life situations because price reflects many dimensions. People who don't realize this can make big mistakes.

Exhibit 17–1   Strategy Planning and Pricing Objectives and Policies

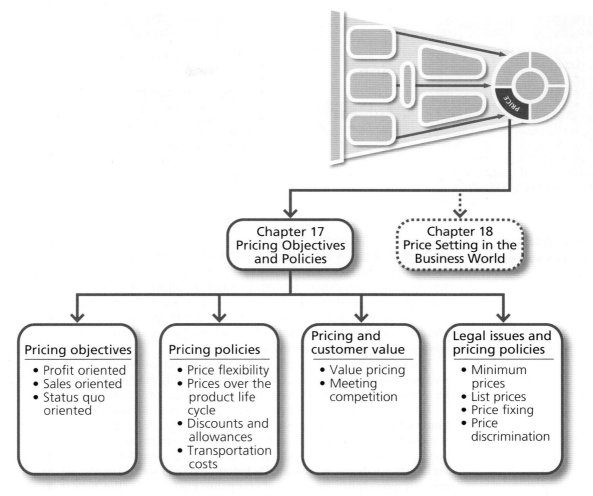

Chapter 17
Pricing Objectives
and Policies

Chapter 18
Price Setting in the
Business World

Pricing objectives
- Profit oriented
- Sales oriented
- Status quo oriented

Pricing policies
- Price flexibility
- Prices over the product life cycle
- Discounts and allowances
- Transportation costs

Pricing and customer value
- Value pricing
- Meeting competition

Legal issues and pricing policies
- Minimum prices
- List prices
- Price fixing
- Price discrimination

Suppose you've been saving to buy a new car and you see in an ad that, after a $1,000 rebate, the base price for the new-year model is $16,494—5 percent lower than the previous year. At first this might seem like a real bargain. However, your view of this deal might change if you found out you also had to pay a $400 transportation charge and an extra $480 for an extended service warranty. The price might look even less attractive if you discovered that the navigation system, side air bags, and moonroof that were standard the previous year are now options that cost $1,900. The cost of the higher interest rate on the car loan and the sales tax on all of this might come as an unpleasant surprise too. Further, how would you feel if you bought the car anyway and then learned that a friend who just bought the exact same model got a much lower price from the dealer by using a broker he found on the Internet?[2]

IKEA's clever—and carefully located—promotional signs remind customers that its price is a good value compared to what they pay for other everyday goods and services.
© Inter IKEA Systems B.V. 1999–2015.

Exhibit 17–2 Price Exchanged for Something of Value (as seen by consumers or users)

Price	Something of Value
List Price Less: Discounts • Quantity • Seasonal • Cash • Temporary sales Less: Allowances • Trade-ins • Damaged goods Less: Rebate and coupon value Plus: Transportation and taxes	Product • Physical good • Service • Assurance of quality • Repair facilities • Packaging • Warranty • Psychic benefit Place of delivery or when available

Exchange

The price equation: Price equals something of value

This example emphasizes that when a seller quotes a price, it is related to *some* assortment of goods and services. So **Price** is the amount of money that is charged for "something" of value. Of course, price may be called different things in different settings. Colleges charge tuition. Landlords collect rent. Motels post a room rate. Country clubs get dues. Banks ask for interest when they loan money. Airlines have fares. Doctors set fees. Employees want a wage. People may call it different things, but *almost every business transaction in our modern economy involves an exchange of money—the Price—for something.*

The something can be a physical product in various stages of completion, with or without supporting services, with or without quality guarantees, and so on. Or it could be a pure service—dry cleaning, a lawyer's advice, or insurance on your car.

The nature and extent of this something determine the amount of money exchanged. Some customers pay list price. Others obtain large discounts or allowances because something is *not* provided. Exhibit 17–2 summarizes some possible variations for consumers or users, and Exhibit 17–3 does the same for channel members. These variations are discussed more fully below, and then we'll consider the customer value concept more fully—in terms of competitive advantage. But here it should be clear

Exhibit 17–3 Price Exchanged for Something of Value (as seen by channel members)

Price	Something of Value
List price Less: Discounts • Quantity • Seasonal • Cash • Trade or functional • Temporary "deals" Less: Allowances • Damaged goods • Advertising • Push money • Stocking fees Plus: Transportation, taxes, tariffs, and costs of handling or disposal	Product • Branded—well known • Guaranteed • Warranted • Service—repair facilities • Convenient packaging for handling Place • Availability—when and where Promotion • Promotion aimed at end-user customers Price • Price-level guarantee • Sufficient margin and inventory turns to allow for profit

Exchange

Exhibit 17-4 Possible Pricing Objectives

that Price has many dimensions. How each of these dimensions is handled affects customer value. If a customer sees greater value in spending money in some other way, no exchange will occur.

Objectives Should Guide Strategy Planning for Price

LO 17.2

Pricing objectives should flow from, and fit within, company-level and marketing objectives. Pricing objectives should be *explicitly stated* because they have a direct effect on pricing policies as well as the methods used to set prices. Exhibit 17–4 shows the various types of pricing objectives we'll discuss.

Profit-Oriented Objectives

Target returns provide specific guidelines

Over the long term, and often over the short term, marketing managers should set objectives oriented toward making a profit. A **target return objective** sets a specific level of profit as an objective. Often this amount is stated as a percentage of sales or of capital investment. A large manufacturer such as Motorola might aim for a 15 percent return on investment. The target for Safeway and other supermarket chains might be a 1 percent return on sales.

A target return objective has administrative advantages in a large company. Performance can be compared against the target. Some companies eliminate divisions, or drop products, that aren't yielding the target rate of return. For example, General Electric sold its small appliance division to Black & Decker because it felt it could earn higher returns in other product-markets.

Some just want satisfactory profits

Some managers aim for only satisfactory returns. They just want returns that ensure the firm's survival and convince stockholders they're doing a good job. Similarly, some small family-run businesses aim for a profit that will provide a comfortable lifestyle.[3]

Many private and public nonprofit organizations set a price level that will just recover costs. In other words, their target return figure is zero. For example, a government agency may charge motorists a toll for using a bridge but then drop the toll when the cost of the bridge is paid.

Similarly, firms that provide critical public services—including many utilities, insurance companies, and defense contractors—sometimes pursue only satisfactory long-run targets. They are well aware that the public expects them to set prices that are in the public interest. They may also have to face public or government agencies that review and approve prices.[4]

Profit maximization can be socially responsible

A **profit maximization objective** seeks to get as much profit as possible. It might be stated as a desire to earn a rapid return on investment—or, more bluntly, to charge all the traffic will bear.

Pricing to achieve profit maximization doesn't always lead to high prices. Low prices may expand the size of the market and result in greater sales and profits. For example, when prices of cell phones were very high, only businesses and wealthy people bought them. When producers lowered prices, nearly everyone bought one.

Some products have no direct competitors. If customers value those products, then firms will have more flexibility in choosing prices to maximize profits. After arriving at a theater, a moviegoer has no snack options beyond the theater's snack bar.
™/® are trademarks of Just Born, Inc., Bethlehem, PA. 18017. All rights reserved. © 2015.

If a firm is earning a very large profit, other firms will try to copy or improve on what the company offers. Frequently, this leads to lower prices.

Sales-Oriented Objectives

Sales growth doesn't necessarily mean big profits

A **sales-oriented objective** seeks some level of unit sales, dollar sales, or share of market—*without referring to profit.*

Some managers are more concerned about sales growth than profits. They think sales growth always leads to more profits. This sometimes makes sense over the short term. For example, many Procter & Gamble brands in product categories such as shampoo, soap, and diapers lost market share during the recent recession. When the economy began to recover, P&G kept prices low and sacrificed profits in order to grow with the recovering economy. It might also work well when products are in the introductory or early growth stages of the product life cycle. However, over the long term this kind of thinking causes problems when a firm's costs are growing faster than sales. Although some firms have periods of declining profits in spite of growth in sales, business managers should usually pay more attention to profits, not just sales.

Some nonprofit organizations set prices to increase market share—precisely because they are *not* trying to earn a profit. For example, many cities set low fares to fill up their buses, reduce traffic, and help the environment. Buses cost the same to run empty or full, and there's more benefit when they're full even if the total revenue is no greater.

Market share objectives are popular

Many firms seek to gain a specified share (percent) of a market. If a company has a large market share, it may have better economies of scale than its competitors. In addition, it's usually easier to measure a firm's market share than to determine if profits are being maximized.

Michelin wants its customers to know that its more efficient tires make them a good value. Lumension Security reminds customers of the high cost of lax computer security.
Left: Copyright ©2015 Michelin North America Inc. All rights reserved. Right: © 2000-2015 Lumension Security, Inc. all rights reserved.; Agency: Lois Paul & Partners/ Woburn, MA.

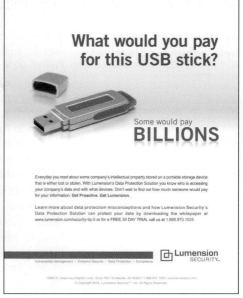

A company with a longer-run view may aim for increased market share when the market is growing. The hope is that future volume will justify sacrificing some profit in the short run. HP, Dell, and Acer have waged pricing battles in an effort to gain market share in the personal computer market. High market share offers economies of scale and negotiating power with suppliers. Companies as diverse as 3M and Coca-Cola look at opportunities in Eastern Europe and Southeast Asia this way.

Of course, market share objectives have the same limitations as straight sales growth objectives. A larger market share, if gained at too low a price, may lead to profitless "success."

Status Quo Pricing Objectives

Don't-rock-the-boat objectives

Managers satisfied with their current market share and profits sometimes adopt **status quo objectives**—don't-rock-the-*pricing*-boat objectives. Managers may say that they want to stabilize prices, or meet competition, or even avoid competition. This don't-rock-the-boat thinking is most common when the total market is not growing.

Sometimes firms in an industry make price changes very carefully—and only if others follow their lead. This tends to prevent price wars, which can drag down all firms' profits. For example, the airline industry typically raises prices collectively. One airline might add a fuel surcharge—if the others do not follow, that airline backs off and all maintain the status quo.

Or stress nonprice competition instead

A status quo pricing objective may be part of an aggressive overall marketing strategy focusing on **nonprice competition**—aggressive action on one or more of the Ps other than Price. Some companies that sell through the Internet originally thought that they'd compete with low prices and still earn high profits from volume. However, when they didn't get the sales volume they hoped for, they realized that there were also some nonprice ways to compete. For example, Zappos.com offers free shipping and guarantees that it will meet local shoe store prices. But it wins customers with its enormous selection of shoes, a website that makes it easy for customers to find what they want, and excellent customer service before and after the sale.

Most Firms Set Specific Pricing Policies—To Reach Objectives

Administered prices help achieve objectives

Price policies usually lead to **administered prices**—consciously set prices. In other words, instead of letting daily market forces (or auctions) decide their prices, most firms set their own prices. They may hold prices steady for long periods of time or change them more frequently if that's what's required to meet objectives.

If a firm doesn't sell directly to final customers, it usually wants to administer both the price it receives from intermediaries and the price final customers pay. After all, the price final customers pay will ultimately affect the quantity it sells.

Yet it is often difficult to administer prices throughout the channel. Other channel members may also wish to administer prices to achieve their own objectives. This is what happened to Alcoa, one of the largest aluminum producers. To reduce its excess inventory, Alcoa offered its wholesalers a 30 percent discount off its normal price. Alcoa expected the wholesalers to pass most of the discount along to their customers to stimulate sales throughout the channel. Instead, wholesalers bought *their* aluminum at the lower price but passed on only a small discount to customers. As a result, the quantity Alcoa sold didn't increase much, and it still had excess inventory, while the wholesalers made much more profit on the aluminum they did sell.[5]

Some firms don't even try to administer prices. They just meet competition—or worse, mark up their costs with little thought to demand. They act as if they have no choice in selecting a price policy.

Remember that Price has many dimensions. Managers usually *do* have many choices. They *should* administer their prices. And they should do it carefully because, ultimately, customers must be willing to pay these prices before a whole marketing mix succeeds. In the rest of this chapter, we'll talk about policies a marketing manager must set to do an effective job of administering Price.[6]

Price Flexibility Policies

LO 17.3

One-price policy—the same price for everyone

One of the first decisions a marketing manager has to make is whether to use a one-price or a flexible-price policy. A **one-price policy** means offering the same price to all customers who purchase products under essentially the same conditions and in the same quantities. The majority of U.S. firms use a one-price policy—mainly for administrative convenience and to maintain goodwill among customers. But that is changing thanks to technology and the ability to identify different customer segments to which a firm wishes to charge higher or lower prices.

A one-price policy makes pricing easier. But a marketing manager must be careful to avoid a rigid one-price policy. This can amount to broadcasting a price that competitors can undercut, especially if the price is somewhat high. One reason for the growth of mass-merchandisers is that conventional retailers rigidly applied traditional margins and stuck to them. This left an opportunity for mass-merchandisers to undercut conventional retailers on price, allowing them to gain market share.

Flexible-price policy—different prices for different customers

A **flexible-price policy** means offering the same product and quantities to different customers at different prices. When computers are used to implement flexible pricing, the decisions focus more on what type of customer will get a price break. As firms learn how to analyze big data, more organizations are moving from a one-price policy to a flexible-price policy.

Pricing databases make flexible pricing easier

Various forms of flexible pricing are more common now that most prices are maintained in a central computer database. Frequent changes are easier. You see this when supermarket chains give loyalty club cardholders reduced prices on weekly specials. The checkout scanner reads the code on the package, and then the computer looks up the club price or the regular price depending on whether a club card has been scanned.

Some marketing managers set up relationships with Internet companies whose ads invite customers to "set your own price." For example, at www.priceline.com, visitors specify the desired schedule for a hotel. Hotels that use the site offer rooms that don't appear to have high demand at deeply discounted prices. So for example, if a hotel is only expected to be half full next weekend, the hotel offers big discounts through Priceline. Even at a discount, the hotel rooms can be profitable. It may appear that these marketing managers have given up on administering prices. Just the opposite is true. They are carefully administering a flexible price. They adapt the price based on supply and demand—offering few discounts if the hotel is close to capacity and more discounts when demand is low.

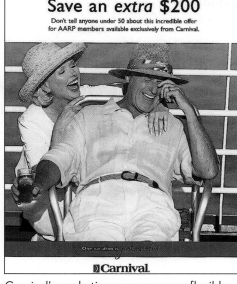

Carnival's marketing managers use flexible pricing, including discounts for members of the AARP who are older than age 50.

Big data helps managers make the most of flexible pricing

Many firms use big data to more accurately identify target customers and offer them particular prices depending on the firm's marketing strategy. Many sources of big data can be read in real-time, so pricing "experiments" can be run. For example, an online retailer can cut prices for a day or even a few hours to see whether it stimulates demand and raises profits. Another example of big data at work in real time is Office Depot.com's adjustment of prices depending on a customer's browsing history and the physical location of the computer from which he is browsing.

Even brick-and-mortar retailers will use knowledge of individual customers to offer targeted price discounts to certain customers. For example, a grocery store can identify a customer as she shops the store—using her cell phone signal. The store can then offer discounts to new or infrequent shoppers to encourage greater loyalty. On the other hand, the retailer may prefer to offer discounts to reward its best customers—and further cement loyalty. Retailers can then follow those customers' future purchases to determine whether targeting one or both groups with discounts yields more profits.

Dynamic pricing means prices change with demand

Dynamic pricing offers products at a price that changes according to the level of demand, the type of customer, or the state of the weather. Big data can be used to more accurately predict future demand and adapt prices to maximize revenue and profit. So for example, airlines typically adjust prices over time. If United Airlines sees that early morning Tuesday flights from St. Louis to Miami are not selling well, the airline can lower the price to stimulate demand—perhaps encouraging some flyers to fly out on Tuesday morning instead of Monday night when there are fewer available seats. It is better to sell some seats at a discount than to have the flight leave with half the seats empty.

Sports teams are increasing ticket revenue by analyzing big data and implementing dynamic pricing. For example, the San Francisco Giants baseball team adjusts ticket prices to maximize attendance and revenue for each game. Ticket prices for each seat at each game can be adjusted after crunching numbers that examine past ticket sales, the day of the week, time of the game, the opposing team's record, the pitching matchup, the going price at ticket resale sites like StubHub, and even the weather forecast. The Giants were expecting an additional $5 million in revenue the first year using the system. Other teams are following the Giants' lead.[7]

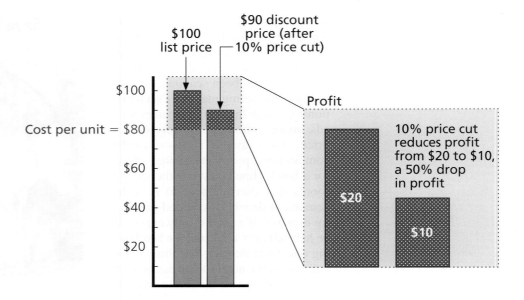

Exhibit 17-5 Impact of Price Cut on Profit

$100 list price

$90 discount price (after 10% price cut)

Cost per unit = $80

Profit

10% price cut reduces profit from $20 to $10, a 50% drop in profit

$20

$10

Salespeople can adjust prices to the situation

Flexible pricing is most common in the channels, in direct sales of business products, and at retail for expensive shopping products. Retail shopkeepers in less-developed economies typically use flexible pricing—shopkeepers start with high prices but bargain to try to make a sale at a price the customer will accept while still providing maximum profit to the seller. These situations usually involve personal selling, not mass selling. The advantage of flexible pricing is that the salesperson can adjust price—considering prices charged by competitors, the relationship with the customer, and the customer's bargaining ability. Flexible-price policies often specify a *range* in which the actual price charged must fall.[8]

Too much price-cutting erodes profits

Some sales reps let price-cutting become a habit. This can lead to a lower price level and lower profit. A small price cut may not seem like much; but keep in mind that all of the revenue that is lost would go to profit. If salespeople for a producer that usually earns profits equal to 20 percent of its sales cut prices by an average of about 10 percent, profits would drop by half (see Exhibit 17–5)!

Disadvantages of flexible pricing

Flexible pricing does have disadvantages. A customer who finds that others paid lower prices for the same marketing mix will be unhappy. This can cause real conflict in channels. For example, the Winn-Dixie supermarket chain stopped carrying products of some suppliers who refused to give Winn-Dixie the same prices available to chains in other regions of the country. Similarly, companies that post different prices for different segments on a website that all can see often get complaints.

If buyers learn that negotiating is in their interest, the time needed for bargaining will increase. This can increase selling costs and reduce profits. It can also frustrate customers. For example, most auto dealers use flexible pricing and bargain for what they can get. Inexperienced consumers, reluctant to bargain, often pay hundreds of dollars more than the dealer is willing to accept. By contrast, CarMax has earned high customer-satisfaction ratings by offering haggle-weary consumers a one-price policy.[9]

Price-Level Policies—Over the Product Life Cycle

LO 17.4

Marketing managers who administer prices must consciously set a price-level policy. As they enter the market, they have to set introductory prices that may have long-run effects. They must consider where the product life cycle is and how fast it's moving.

And they must decide if their prices should be above, below, or somewhere in between relative to the market.

Let's look for a moment at a new product in the market introduction stage of its product life cycle. There are few (or no) direct substitute marketing mixes. So the price-level decision should focus first on the nature of market demand. A high price may lead to higher profit from each sale but also to fewer units sold. A lower price might appeal to more potential customers. With this in mind, should the firm set a high or low price?

Skimming pricing— feeling out demand at a high price

A **skimming price policy** tries to sell the top (skim the cream) of a market—the top of the demand curve—at a high price before aiming at more price-sensitive customers. Skimming may maximize profits in the market introduction stage for an innovation, especially if there are few substitutes or if some customers are not price sensitive. Skimming is also useful when you don't know very much about the shape of the demand curve. It's sometimes safer to start with a high price that can be reduced if customers balk.

Skimming has critics

Some critics argue that firms should not try to maximize profits by using a skimming policy on new products that have important social consequences—a patent-protected, life-saving drug or a technique that increases crop yields, for example. Many of those who need the product may not have the money to buy it. This is a serious concern. However, it's also a serious problem if firms don't have any incentive to take risks and develop new products.[10]

Price moves down the demand curve

A skimming policy usually involves a slow reduction in price over time (see Exhibit 17–6). Note that as price is reduced, new target markets are probably being sought. So as the price level steps down the demand curve, new Place, Product, and Promotion policies may be needed too.

Let's take a closer look at how this trend played out in cellular phone service. When McCaw Cellular Communications—the firm that pioneered cellular phone service and was later bought out by AT&T—first came on the market, it set a high price. Each wireless minute cost about $1, and customers had to pay about $675 for a large, clunky phone. McCaw used dealers to sell the premium-priced packages because they could

Exhibit 17-6   Alternative Introductory Pricing Policies explain the value of the system and get orders. They mainly targeted firms that gave phones to their on-the-go executives and salespeople. Many of these customers were not price sensitive because no good substitute was available. However, that changed as other cellular providers came into the market.

To improve the value of its offering, McCaw bought large quantities of phones from Motorola at low cost and then packaged them with a service contract at a high discount. As the market grew, economies of scale kicked in and McCaw cut prices even more. McCaw also did more advertising and started to sell cellular services through a variety of retail outlets, including mass-merchandisers. These Promotion and Place changes cut selling costs and helped reach the growing number of families who wanted cell service. Free weekend and evening minutes for consumers when demand from business customers was low sweetened the deal. In addition, prices on phones had come down so much that retailers gave away a phone with a one-year service contract—and offered family plans where additional family members were added to a contract for about $10 each. By then, AT&T was relying more heavily on television advertising that encouraged customers to sign up at an AT&T store or at the AT&T website—which helped cut channel markups from the selling price.

Promotion and discounting became even more aggressive as cell phone services merged, but AT&T was able to build its share because it was the exclusive service provider for Apple's hot iPhone. However, Sprint didn't just roll over and let AT&T win the competition for the growing number of smartphone users. Rather, it slashed the total costs of using smartphones with its "Simply Everything" plan. For $99 a month it offered customers unlimited talking, web browsing, text, picture and video messaging, music downloads, and even 150 radio stations. As this example suggests, as the skimming price in the market changes, it is often accompanied by a series of changes in marketing strategy, not just a stepping down of prices.[11]

Penetration pricing—get volume at a low price

A **penetration pricing policy** tries to sell the whole market at one low price. This approach might be wise when the elite market—those willing to pay a high price—is small. This is the case when the whole demand curve is fairly elastic. See Exhibit 17–6. A penetration policy is even more attractive if selling larger quantities results in lower costs because of economies of scale. Penetration pricing may be wise if the firm expects strong competition very soon after introduction.

Sony relied on penetration pricing when it battled with Toshiba to introduce a next-generation optical disc player. Sony's Blu-ray format and Toshiba's HD-DVD format were incompatible formats. Sony had to win market acceptance quickly. If Toshiba's HD-DVD format became the standard, Sony's investment to develop and promote Blu-ray would go down the drain.

To motivate buyers, Sony cut the price on its Blu-ray players to the bone. Getting adoptions quickly was critical because studios would distribute movies in the format most popular with consumers. Sony saw an opportunity to kick-start its efforts by including a Blu-ray disc drive in its PS3 third-generation game console. When it came out in late 2006, the PS3 was more expensive than competing consoles because it had more power and a Blu-ray drive. However, Sony priced it below its current production cost. This move was part of Sony's penetration pricing plan for Blu-ray. All the PS3 consoles that Sony sold that Christmas contributed to economies of scale and lower prices on the regular Blu-ray players. In addition, all of the excited people who clamored to buy PS3s for their favorite games also used them for their Blu-ray movies. This added to Sony's Blu-ray market share with consumers and gave it an advantage with studios. By spring of 2008, Sony had a clear lead and Toshiba threw in the towel on its HD-DVD format.[12]

Of course, even a low penetration price doesn't keep competitors out of a market permanently. Product life cycles do march on. However, a firm that gets a head start in a new market can often maintain its advantage.

Marketers often use introductory price dealing—in the form of temporary price cuts, introductory coupons, or trade-in allowances—to speed new products into a market.
Left: © 2005 Spectrum Brands, Inc. All Rights Reserved.
Right: ©2015 Google.

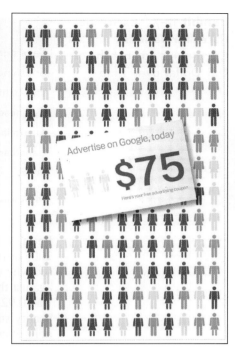

Introductory price dealing—temporary price cuts

Low prices do attract customers. Therefore, marketers often use **introductory price dealing**—temporary price cuts—to speed new products into a market and get customers to try them. However, don't confuse these *temporary* price cuts with low penetration prices. The plan here is to raise prices as soon as the introductory offer is over. By then, hopefully, target customers will have decided it is worth buying again at the regular price. Introductory price dealing should be part of a larger marketing strategy. For example, some developers of software applications (or "apps") for smartphones, such as those sold on Apple's iTunes, know that getting onto the store's list of "Top Apps" gets attention, which drives sales. So some app makers price the app low at launch to encourage sales, which moves it up the rankings. Then they raise prices to optimize profits.

Established competitors often choose not to meet introductory price dealing—as long as the introductory period is not too long or too successful. However, some competitors match introductory price deals with their own short-term sale prices to discourage customers from shopping around.

When trade occurs across national boundaries, exchange rates affect prices

We've been talking about the price level of a firm's product. But a nation's money also has a price level—what it is worth in some other currency. For example, on April 16, 2011, one U.S. dollar was worth 0.61 British pounds. In other words, the exchange rate for the British pound against the U.S. dollar was 0.61. Exhibit 17–7 lists exchange rates for money from several countries over a number of years. From this exhibit you can see that exchange rates change over time—and sometimes the changes are significant. For example, on April 16, 2005, a U.S. dollar was worth 42.89 Thai baht; just three years later the U.S. dollar was worth 27 percent less—only 31.44 Thai baht.

As the following example shows, exchange rate changes can have a significant effect on international trade and how a firm's price is viewed by customers in an overseas market. Jacquelyn Tran started BeautyEncounter.com, an online retail cosmetics website, in 1999. Before long, her domestic business was doing well and she was also attracting some sales from the United Kingdom, France, Germany, Japan, Canada, and

Exhibit 17-7 Exchange Rates for Various Currencies against the U.S. Dollar over Time

Base currency	Number of Units of Base Currency per U.S. Dollar*			
	2005	2008	2011	2014
British pound	0.64	0.50	0.61	2.25
Thai baht	42.89	31.44	30.13	32.25
Japanese yen	120.04	101.40	83.30	102.29
Australian dollar	1.64	1.06	0.95	1.07
Canadian dollar	1.46	1.00	0.96	1.10
Euro	0.92	0.63	0.69	0.72

* Units shown are for April 16th in each year.

Latin America. Her sales to international customers grew at an even faster rate after 2005 as the U.S. dollar weakened against other currencies (see Exhibit 17–7). You can see why this would happen by looking at the change in the exchange rate of the euro against the dollar. In April of 2005, the exchange rate for the euro against the dollar was 0.92, so a customer living in Europe paid 92 euros to purchase $100 worth of beauty supplies. Three years later, the exchange rate had dropped to 0.63, so at that point it cost the customer only 63 euros to purchase the same $100 worth of supplies. So, from the perspective of a European customer, the change in the exchange rate over that time period had the same effect as a price cut. Yet many of those customers didn't just buy the same beauty supplies and pocket the extra 29 euros. Instead, they continued to spend the same amount in their home currency (92 euros), which in 2008 was equal to $146. In effect, these customers increased the size of their orders from Beauty Encounter by 46 percent (from $100 to $146). The shift in exchange rates also made the firm's cosmetics cheaper relative to competing cosmetics retailers in Europe, and that attracted new overseas customers.

Beauty Encounter's export business benefited from exchange rates from 2005 to 2008. But by 2011 the exchange rate for the euro had climbed to 0.69. If a European customer continued to spend the same amount in 2011 as she did in 2008 (92 euros), then she would be purchasing just $133 worth of goods, not $146 as in 2008. The change in rates had a negative impact on Beauty Encounter's sales because it amounted to a price hike.[13]

Online Toolkit

There is a website (**www.x-rates.com**) that converts one country's currency to another. Go to the website, click on "Currency Calculator," and determine how much $100 U.S. is worth in Thai bahts, British pounds, and euros. How do those numbers compare with April 2014 (see Exhibit 17-7)?

Discount Policies—Reductions from List Prices

LO 17.5

Prices start with a list price

Most price structures are built around a base price schedule or list price. **Basic list prices** are the prices final customers or users are normally asked to pay for products. In this book, unless noted otherwise, list price refers to basic list price.

In Chapter 18, we discuss how firms set these list prices. For now, however, we'll consider variations from list price and why they are made.

Discounts are reductions from list price

Discounts are reductions from list price given by a seller to buyers who either give up some marketing function or provide the function themselves. Discounts can be useful in marketing strategy planning. In the following discussion, think about what function the buyers are giving up, or providing, when they get each of these discounts.

Quantity discounts encourage volume buying

Quantity discounts are discounts offered to encourage customers to buy in larger amounts. This lets a seller get more of a buyer's business, or shifts some of the storing function to the buyer, or reduces shipping and selling costs—or all of these. There are two kinds of quantity discounts: cumulative and noncumulative.

Cumulative quantity discounts apply to purchases over a given period—such as a year—and the discount usually increases as the amount purchased increases. Cumulative discounts encourage *repeat* buying by reducing the customer's cost for additional purchases. This is a way to develop loyalty and ongoing relationships with customers. For example, a Lowe's lumberyard might give a cumulative quantity discount to a building contractor who is not able to buy all of the needed materials at once. Lowe's wants to reward the contractor's patronage and discourage shopping around.

A cumulative quantity discount is often attractive to business customers who don't want to run up their inventory costs. They are rewarded for buying large quantities, even though individual orders may be smaller.

Noncumulative quantity discounts apply only to individual orders. Such discounts encourage larger orders but do not tie a buyer to the seller after that one purchase. Lowe's lumberyard may resell insulation products made by several competing producers. Owens-Corning might try to encourage Lowe's to stock larger quantities of its pink insulation by offering a noncumulative quantity discount.

Customers who buy six applications of Frontline Plus flea protection get two more for free—essentially a quantity discount of 25 percent.

®FRONTLINE, MERIAL, CERTIFECT, ORAVET, HEARTGARD and the Dog & Hand logo are registered trademarks, and ™SATISFACTION PLUS GUARANTEE is a trademark, of Merial. All other marks are the property of their respective owners. ©2013 Merial Limited, Duluth, GA. All rights reserved.

Seasonal discounts—buy sooner

Seasonal discounts are discounts offered to encourage buyers to buy earlier than present demand requires. If used by a manufacturer, this discount tends to shift the storing function further along in the channel. It also tends to even out sales over the year. For example, Kyota offers wholesalers a lower price on its garden tillers if they buy in the fall, when sales are slow.

Service firms that face irregular demand or excess capacity often use seasonal discounts. For example, some tourist attractions, such as ski resorts, offer lower weekday rates when attendance would otherwise be down.

Payment terms and cash discounts set payment dates

Most sales to businesses are made on credit. The seller sends a bill (invoice) by mail or electronically, and the buyer's accounting department processes it for payment. Some firms depend on their suppliers for temporary working capital (credit). Therefore, it is very important for both sides to clearly state the terms of payment—including the availability of cash discounts—and to understand the commonly used payment terms.

Net means that payment for the face value of the invoice is due immediately. These terms are sometimes changed to net 10 or net 30, which means payment is due within 10 or 30 days of the date on the invoice.

Cash discounts are reductions in price to encourage buyers to pay their bills quickly. The terms for a cash discount usually modify the net terms.

2/10, net 30 means the buyer can take a 2 percent discount off the face value of the invoice if the invoice is paid within 10 days. Otherwise, the full face value is due within 30 days. And it usually is stated or understood that an interest charge will be added after the 30-day free-credit period.

Smart buyers carefully evaluate cash discounts. A discount of 2/10, net 30 may not look like much at first. But the buyer earns a 2 percent discount for paying the invoice just 20 days sooner than it should be paid anyway. By not taking the discount, the company in effect is borrowing at an annual rate of 36 percent. That is, assuming a 360-day year and dividing by 20 days, there are 18 periods during which the company could earn 2 percent—and 18 times 2 equals 36 percent a year.

Some firms help buyers who cannot afford to pay for their products all at once by offering some form of installment plan. Installment involves making small payments over time—usually with interest payments built in. This approach has been used to open rural markets in the developing countries of Africa and Latin America to portable solar energy. Many of these rural villages are located off the electric grid and rely on kerosene lamps for light. Kerosene isn't a healthy or economic alternative to electricity—but until recently, many of these customers had little choice. When low-cost solar power first became available, these customers couldn't afford the $50 to $100 cost to install a small rooftop system. Then many solar suppliers developed installment plans. Customers might pay $10 for installation and then $1.50 a week (half the price of kerosene) for perhaps a year or two.[14]

Another example is cars. Many are leased—where consumers pay a monthly fee over a specified time period (usually three years). A monthly payment of $199 a month sounds more affordable to most consumers than buying the car for $21,495. Of course at the end of three years, the person leasing a car has to purchase it or return it, while the purchaser still owns their car.

Credit sales are also important to retailers. Credit cards are the most common method for customers to pay over time. Retailers usually accept credit cards from services such as Visa or MasterCard and pay a percent of the revenue from each credit sale for the service. Some retailers also have aggressive promotions to sign up customers for their own credit cards because customers who carry a store's credit card may spend more money at the store. Generous credit terms, such as "no interest or payments for one full year" do stimulate sales. However, credit that is too easy exposes retailers to the risk of losses when the economy turns down.

There are also ethical concerns about credit card companies and retailers that make it too easy for consumers to buy things they really can't afford. The problem becomes worse when an unpaid balance on a credit card carries a very high interest rate. This can significantly increase the price a consumer pays. Even worse, it leaves many low-income consumers trapped in debt.

College students have traditionally been a target market for credit cards—in part because credit card issuers covet customers who don't have any previous card loyalties. Of course many students also arrive at college with no job, no income, few assets, and

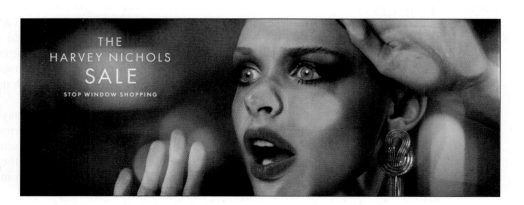

Sale prices encourage consumers to purchase products immediately. To get the sale price, customers give up the convenience of buying when they want to buy and instead buy when the seller wants to sell.
Harvey Nichols 2015; Agency: Adam & Eve DDB/London; Photographer: Marc Philbert.

a sparse credit report. Wooed with free food or gifts, many sign up for cards and return home with significant debt. So the U.S. Congress passed the Credit CARD Act of 2009, which offers protections for college-age students. Anyone younger than 21 must now have a cosigner or prove they can repay any debt.[15]

Trade discounts are often set by tradition

A **trade (functional) discount** is a list price reduction given to channel members for the job they are going to do. A manufacturer, for example, might allow a retailer a 30 percent trade discount from the suggested retail list price to cover the cost of carrying inventory and providing knowledgeable salespeople to demonstrate the manufacturer's products. Similarly, the manufacturer might allow wholesalers a *chain* discount of 30 percent and 10 percent off the suggested retail price. In this case, the wholesalers would be expected to pass the 30 percent discount on to retailers.

Special sales reduce list prices—temporarily

A **sale price** is a temporary discount from the list price. Sale price discounts encourage immediate buying. In other words, to get the sale price, customers give up the convenience of buying when they want to buy and instead buy when the seller wants to sell.

Special sales provide a marketing manager with a quick way to respond to changing market conditions without changing the basic marketing strategy. For example, a retailer might use a sale to help clear extra inventory or to meet a competing store's price.

In recent years, sale prices and deals have become much more common. Some retailers have sales so often that consumers just wait to purchase when there's a sale. Others check out a website such as www.fatwallet.com to figure out where the product they want is already on sale. At first it may seem that consumers benefit from all this. But prices that change constantly erode brand loyalty.

To avoid these problems, some firms that sell consumer convenience products offer **everyday low pricing**—setting a low list price rather than relying on frequent sales, discounts, or allowances. Some supermarkets use this approach.

> **Online Toolkit**
>
> camelcamelcamel (**camelcamelcamel.com**) is a website that automatically tracks prices at Amazon.com. The site allows users to track prices, showing a product's price history for a year or more into the past. Users can also ask to be sent an e-mail alert when the price drops to a certain level. Go to Amazon.com and find a popular toy (pick one that has been out at least a year). Copy the URL (web address) for that toy and paste it into the bar at the top of the camelcamelcamel site. How much has the price varied in the last year? What was the highest price? Lowest price? Current price?

Sale prices should be used carefully, consistent with well-thought-out pricing objectives and policies. A marketing manager who constantly uses temporary sales to adjust the price level probably has not done a good job setting the normal price or creating a marketing mix that offers sustainable competitive advantage.[16]

Allowance Policies—Off List Prices

Allowances, like discounts, are given to final consumers, business customers, or channel members for doing something or accepting less of something.

Advertising allowances— something for something

Advertising allowances are price reductions given to firms in the channel to encourage them to advertise or otherwise promote the supplier's products locally. For example, Sony might give an allowance (3 percent of sales) to its retailers. They, in turn, are expected to spend the allowance on local advertising.

Stocking allowances— get attention and shelf space

Stocking allowances—sometimes called *slotting allowances*—are given to an intermediary to get shelf space for a product. For example, a producer might offer a retailer cash or free merchandise to stock a new item. Stocking allowances are commonly used to get supermarket chains to handle new products. Supermarkets are more willing to give space to a new product if the supplier will offset their handling costs and risks.

With a big stocking allowance, the intermediary makes extra profit—even if a new product fails and the producer loses money.[17]

PMs—push for cash

Push money (or prize money) allowances—sometimes called *PMs* or *spiffs*—are given to retailers by manufacturers or wholesalers to pass on to the retailers' salesclerks for aggressively selling certain items. PM allowances are used for new items, slower-moving items, or higher-margin items. They are often used for pushing furniture, clothing, consumer electronics, and cosmetics. A salesclerk, for example, might earn an additional $5 for each new model Panasonic DVD player sold.

Bring in the old, ring up the new—with trade-ins

A **trade-in allowance** is a price reduction given for used products when similar new products are bought. Trade-ins give the marketing manager an easy way to lower the effective price without reducing list price. Sometimes producers want to get older products off the market or move them to a new market. Apple offered trade-in incentives for its iPhones and shipped the older models to developing countries that could not afford the higher price of a new phone.

Some Customers Get Something Extra

Coupons—more for less

Many producers and retailers offer discounts (or free items) through coupons distributed in packages, mailings, print ads, at the store, or online. By presenting a coupon to a retailer, the consumer is given a discount off list price. The fastest-growing distribution approach is online—where consumers can search for coupons and print them out, send them to their cell phone, or directly add them to their store loyalty card. This is especially common in the consumer packaged goods business—but the use of price-off coupons is also growing in other lines of business.

Retailers are willing to redeem producers' coupons because it increases their sales and they usually are paid for the trouble of handling the coupons. For example, a retailer that redeems a 50 cents off coupon might be repaid 75 cents.[18]

"Deal-of-the-Day" sites give big discounts

Most coupons offer discounts of $0.50 to $1.00—which isn't enough to move some customers to action. So "Deal-of-the-Day" websites such as Groupon and Living Social offer customers real bargains—often half off or more. The bargain offers come from local businesses—usually retailers, restaurants, or service providers—and arrive in daily e-mails customers sign up to receive. Customers must purchase the deal that day—perhaps buying a certificate for $180 worth of auto detailing services for $90. Businesses offering these big discounts hope to attract new customers who will make future purchases at regular prices or purchase more than the amount on the certificate. But marketers should be careful with such promotions; many deal-seekers are only loyal to the next deal—and not the business offering it.

Rebates—cash back

Some firms offer **rebates**—refunds paid to consumers after a purchase. Sometimes the rebate is very large. Some automakers offer rebates of $500 to $6,000 to promote sales of slow-moving models. Rebates are also used on lower-priced items, ranging from Duracell batteries to Logitech webcams and Paul Masson wines. Rebates give a producer a way to be certain that final consumers actually get the price reduction. If the rebate amount were just taken off the price charged to intermediaries, they might not pass the savings along to consumers.

But rebates have their critics. While rebates prompt many consumers to make a purchase, many rebates—even high-value rebates—are never redeemed. A few years ago TiVo offered a $100 holiday season rebate, but half of the consumers eligible failed to even request their rebate. For many customers the paperwork and hassle deter them; others simply forget after they leave the store. The growing consumer backlash against rebates and the threat of government regulation have prompted many firms to drop rebates from their marketing strategies.[19]

Coupons are often used to encourage customers to try a new brand or to attract customers who might not purchase without a discount.
© Ben & Jerry's.

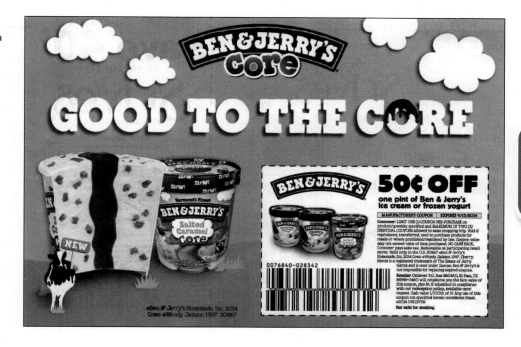

Coupons, deals, and rebates can segment the market

Coupons, deals, and rebates can help marketing managers attract new customers or move customers who are interested in a product to take action and buy. However, many marketing managers want to sell not only to customers looking for a bargain but also to customers willing to pay full price. But it's hard for a firm to appeal to both groups with the same price. For instance, if a firm persists in offering only higher prices, then sales are lost to the price-sensitive customer who wants only the lowest price. On the other hand, if a firm lowers its prices to appeal to the bargain hunters, then profits will be low from all customers—even those willing to pay a higher price.

To appeal to both groups and maximize profits, many firms now offer a variety of coupons, deals, and rebates. These discounts are an effective way to segment the market. For example, bargain hunters are willing to spend the time and energy necessary to find discounts—before purchasing the firm's products—and probably would not purchase without them. This makes the discounts a useful part of the price equation for these shoppers. But other customers will still pay full price because they value the whole marketing mix. They don't need the added incentive of a deal and won't look for the discounts. As a result, a marketing manager can increase total profits by segmenting the market and targeting each group separately.

List Price May Depend on Geographic Pricing Policies

Retail list prices sometimes include free delivery. Or free delivery may be offered to some customers as an aid to closing the sale. But deciding who pays the freight charge is more important on sales to business customers than to final consumers because more money is involved. Purchase orders usually specify place, time, method of delivery, freight costs, insurance, handling, and other charges. There are many possible variations for an imaginative marketing manager, and some specialized terms have developed.

F.O.B. pricing is easy

A commonly used transportation term is **F.O.B.**—which means "free on board" some vehicle at some place. Typically a location is associated with F.O.B. and often the terms *F.O.B. shipping point* or *F.O.B. destination* are used. Whatever place is listed refers to the point where title passes from the seller to the buyer. So F.O.B. shipping point means that the buyer has responsibility as soon as the product is loaded onto a vehicle at the seller's point of shipment (perhaps its warehouse). The buyer then pays the cost of shipping, insurance, and other costs from the point of shipping. When something is shipped F.O.B. destination, title does not pass to the buyer until the product is delivered. The seller has responsibility for shipping costs and any damage that might occur in shipping.

F.O.B. shipping point pricing simplifies the seller's pricing—but it may narrow the market. Because the delivered cost varies depending on the buyer's location, a customer located farther from the seller must pay more and might buy from closer suppliers.

Zone pricing smooths delivered prices

Zone pricing means making an average freight charge to all buyers within specific geographic areas. The seller pays the actual freight charges and bills each customer for an average charge. For example, a company in Canada might divide the United States into seven zones, then bill all customers in the same zone the same amount for freight even though actual shipping costs might vary.

Zone pricing reduces the wide variation in delivered prices that results from an F.O.B. shipping point pricing policy. It also simplifies transportation charges.

Uniform delivered pricing—one price to all

Uniform delivered pricing means making an average freight charge to all buyers. It is a kind of zone pricing—an entire country may be considered as one zone—that includes the average cost of delivery in the price. Uniform delivered pricing is most often used when (1) transportation costs are relatively low and (2) the seller wishes to sell in all geographic areas at one price, perhaps a nationally advertised price.

In today's competitive markets, a marketing manager must look for ways to enhance customer value from the firm's marketing mix. L.L. Bean uses free shipping; the U.S. Post Office offers the simplicity and convenience of shipping to any state for one low rate.
Left: L.L. Bean® is a registered trademark of L.L. Bean Inc. Copyright 2015.
Right: Copyright © 2015 USPS. All Rights Reserved.

Freight-absorption pricing—competing on equal ground in another territory

When all firms in an industry use F.O.B. shipping point pricing, a firm usually competes well near its shipping point but not farther away. As sales reps look for business farther away, delivered prices rise and the firm finds itself priced out of the market.

This problem can be reduced with **freight-absorption pricing**—which means absorbing freight cost so that a firm's delivered price meets that of the nearest competitor. This amounts to cutting list price to appeal to new market segments. Some firms look at international markets this way; they just figure that any profit from export sales is a bonus.

Pricing Policies Combine to Impact Customer Value

Look at Price from the customer's viewpoint

We've discussed pricing policies separately so far, but from the customer's view they all combine to impact customer value. So when we talk about Price we are really talking about the whole set of price policies that define the real price level. On the other hand, superior value isn't just based on having a lower price than some competitor but rather on the whole marketing mix.

Value pricing leads to superior customer value

Smart marketers look for the combination of Price decisions that results in value pricing. **Value pricing** means setting a fair price level for a marketing mix that really gives the target market superior customer value.

Value pricing doesn't necessarily mean cheap if cheap means bare-bones or low-grade. It doesn't mean high prestige either if the prestige is not accompanied by the right quality goods and services. Rather, the focus is on the customer's requirements and how the whole marketing mix meets those needs.

Honda is a firm that has been effective with value pricing. It has different marketing mixes for different target markets. From the $15,000 Fit to the $36,000 S2000 Roadster and $40,000 four-wheel drive Pilot, Honda offers high quality at reasonable prices. Among fast-food restaurants, Wendy's was one of the first to create a Dollar Menu. This has helped to give it a reputation for value pricing.

Companies that use value pricing deliver on their promises. They try to give the consumer pleasant surprises—like an unexpected service—because it increases value and builds customer loyalty. They return the price if the customer isn't completely satisfied. They avoid unrealistic price levels—prices that are high only because consumers already know the brand name. They build relationships so customers will come back time and again.

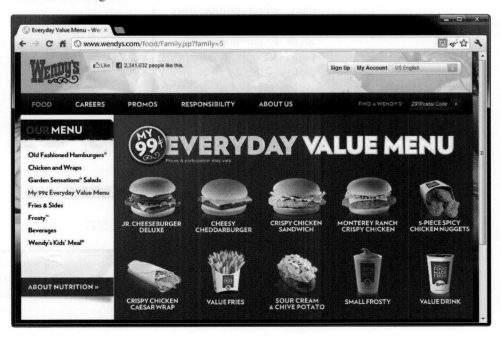

Wendy's $0.99 Everyday Value Menu communicates value to its customers.
© 2014 Oldemark LLC. Wendy's International, LLC.

There are Price choices in most markets

Some marketing managers miss the advantages of value pricing. They've heard economists say that in perfect competition it's foolish to offer products above or below the market price. But most firms *don't* operate in perfect competition where what firms offer is exactly the same.

Most operate in monopolistic competition, where products and whole marketing mixes are *not* exactly the same. This means that there are pricing options. At one extreme, some firms are clearly above the market—they may even brag about it. Tiffany's is well known as one of the most expensive jewelry stores in the world. Other firms emphasize below-the-market prices in their marketing mixes. Prices offered by discounters and mass-merchandisers, such as Walmart and Tesco, illustrate this approach. They may even promote their pricing policy with catchy slogans such as "guaranteed lowest prices."

Value pricers define the target market and the competition

In making price decisions and using value pricing, it is important to clearly define the *relevant target market* and *competitors* when making price comparisons.

Consider Walmart prices again from this view. Walmart may have lower prices on electronics products such as flat-panel televisions, but it offers less expertise from the store's sales staff, less selection, and no help installing or setting up a new television. Walmart may appeal to budget-oriented shoppers who compare prices *and* value among different mass-merchandisers. But a specialty electronics store appeals to different customers and may not even be a direct competitor!

A producer of flat-panel televisions with this point of view may offer the specialty electronics store models that are not available to Walmart—to ensure that customers don't view price as the only difference between the two stores. Further, the specialty store needs to clearly communicate to its target market *how* it offers superior value. Walmart is certainly going to communicate that it offers low prices. If that's all customers hear, they will see no differences between retailers except for price. The specialty retailer must emphasize its expertise, selection, or the superior performance of its product line—so that target customers who value these differences know where to find them.

Meeting competitors' prices may be necessary

In a mature market there is downward pressure on both prices and profit margins. Moreover, differentiating the value a firm offers may not be easy when competitors can quickly copy new ideas. Extending our flat-panel example, if our speciality store is in a city with a number of similar stores with the same products, there may not be a way to convince consumers that one beats all of the others. In such circumstances there may be no real pricing choice other than to "meet the competition." With profit margins already thin, they would quickly disappear or turn into losses at a lower price. And a higher price would simply prompt competitors to promote their price advantage.[20]

Consumers often use websites such as PriceGrabber.com that search for the best prices on particular items. When it's easy for customers to compare prices, marketers must clearly communicate to the customer how the rest of the marketing mix is better and why it justifies a higher price. *Copyright © 2015 PriceGrabber.com, Inc. All Rights Reserved.*

What's Next? Putting a price (and value) on life

What is the value of one more day of life? One more month? One more year? These are the difficult decisions that doctors, patients, and public policy makers are having to make. Life-extending medical treatments can be very expensive—and while the costs are borne partly by patients, most of the cost falls on insurance companies and the government. When most patients have a costly procedure or treatment, private insurance or a government program such as Medicare or Medicaid pays most of the bill—and that means other insured people and taxpayers foot the bill. This leaves lawmakers and voters needing to make decisions about the value of one more day, one more month, or one more year of life.

A few years ago, doctors at Memorial Sloan-Kettering Cancer Center made a big decision: they decided to boycott the colorectal cancer drug Zaltrap. The required three-month treatment with Zaltrap cost more than $30,000—more than twice as much as an equally effective competitive treatment. Both drugs have similar side effects. Both drugs offer patients an average of 42 days more of life. Making a decision to remove a potentially life-extending medicine from doctors' options because of cost was unheard of.

Perhaps this choice shouldn't have been a big deal. In most product-markets, an equally effective product costing twice as much has no value—so it would not even be brought to market. But this is the world of medicine. When faced with life-threatening conditions, patients and doctors don't often consider cost when making deciding on a course of action.

The question of "value" gets more complicated when no equivalent treatments exist. Consider Novartis' "miracle pill," Gleevec, which treats a rare cancer—chronic myeloid leukemia. With an 80 percent survival rate 10 years from diagnosis, Gleevec has no equally effective competitors. But an annual supply sells for $76,000 at wholesale and a total cost to patients (and their insurer) typically exceeds $100,000. Every year!

Gilead Science's Sovaldi was another breakthrough—boasting a 95 percent rate of *curing* hepatitis C. The cure costs $84,000. A daily does for 12 weeks breaks down to $1,000 a pill. A less expensive competing treatment has severe side effects and doesn't cure as many patients. Gilead claims that its cure *saves* the health care system in the long run. Cured of hepatitis C, these patients will never experience (and the health care system won't incur the cost of) the longer-term tolls of this disease, which include liver scarring, cirrhosis, cancer, and organ failure.

Drug companies come back to the hundreds of millions of dollars invested in research, development, and bringing a new product to market. Many new product efforts fail along the way. High prices cover those costs and assure future breakthroughs can be funded. Critics wonder if these companies are perhaps taking advantage of their situation. They wonder if the price justifies the value—to the individual and to society (which ends up paying much of the cost). Will society one day have to decide between millions of childhood vaccinations and hundreds of cancer treatments?

The value of one more day, one more month, or one more year may be priceless. But in the end, someone has to pay for breakthrough drugs. What do you think? Are the prices of these drugs fair? Do they deliver proportionate value? How should a company determine prices for breakthrough drugs? Should society—because it pays in part through insurance and taxes—have a say about whether such drugs are covered by insurance plans?[21]

Even though competition can be intense, too many marketers give up too easily. They often can find a way to differentiate, even if it's something that competitors dismiss as less important. For example, Kellogg was facing soggy sales and tough competition in the dry cereal category. Dealer brands made price competition even tougher. However, when Kellogg added freeze-dried fruit to create Special K Red Berries, it attracted many customers away from competing brands. The berries did increase costs, but Kellogg's profits still improved. In Europe, where price sensitivity was greatest, Kellogg kept the price the same but reduced the size of the Red Berries box. In the United States, the size of the box is standard but the price was increased enough to provide profit margins. Even though General Mills later copied the idea, Kellogg had a head start and quickly came out with other fruit-added cereals. And both producers benefited by having a way to differentiate from the low-price store brands in their category.[22]

There may be little choice about Price in oligopoly situations. Pricing at the market—that is, meeting competition—may be the only sensible policy. To raise prices might lead to a large loss in sales, unless competitors adopt the higher price too. And cutting prices would probably lead to similar reductions by competitors—downward along an inelastic industry demand curve. This can lead only to a decrease in total revenue for the industry and probably for each firm. The major airlines faced these problems recently.

Price and customer perceptions of quality

Prices also influence how customers view quality. Without other information, most customers associate higher prices with a higher quality product. Marketing managers should be aware that charging lower prices than competitors might have a detrimental effect on how customers view relative product quality.

Online glasses retailer Warby Parker considered this issue when starting up. The first business plan called for selling eyeglasses that typically cost $500 for less than $50. Warby Parker figured it could be profitable at that price. However, upon reflection, Warby Parker's founders worried that the dramatic price gap might adversely affect customer perceptions of its product quality and optical-related services. Sure enough, research showed Warby Parker that prices below about $100 raised customer suspicions about the quality. So it priced its glasses at $95. It used some of the extra margin to offer better service. For example, it created a "Home Try-On Program" that allows customers to request up to five frames, try them on for five days, and then return the frames, all at no cost to the customer. Even with online rivals such as Zenni Optical and GlassesUSA.com charging half of Warby Parker's prices, Warby Parker continues to capture customers' trust, and consequently, prosper.[23]

Value pricing fits with market-oriented strategy planning

There are times when the marketing manager's hands are tied and there is little that can be done to differentiate the marketing mix. However, most marketing managers do have choices—many choices. They can vary strategy decisions with respect to all of the marketing mix variables, not just Price, to offer target customers superior value. And when a marketer's hands are really tied, it's time to look for new opportunities that offer more promise.

Value can have societal and ethical dimensions

Value is a subjective appraisal. It may differ for each person. This can be more complicated when society has to pay part of the "price." This can be the case for many projects where the government is involved. For example, is it a good investment to build a new interstate highway or build a new school. All taxpayers contribute, but only some benefit.

The issue is the same for healthcare—especially because Medicare and Medicaid are government programs that pay for the health care of many elderly U.S. citizens. With an aging population and rising health care costs, value is becoming a growing concern in the health care debate. The breakthrough innovations in healthcare have costs and benefits that create challenges for a society deciding how they should be valued. Read more about this complicated value issue in *"What's Next?* Putting a price (and value) on life."

Legality of Pricing Policies

This chapter discusses the many pricing decisions that must be made. However, some pricing decisions are limited by government legislation. The first step to understanding pricing legislation is to know the thinking of legislators and the courts. Our focus will be on U.S. legislation but most countries have similar laws. Still, marketing managers may find that some countries have more restrictive laws. Intel was fined $1.45 billion by European regulators for price discounting practices that were used to keep competitors out of the market.[24]

Minimum prices are sometimes controlled

Unfair trade practice acts put a lower limit on prices, especially at the wholesale and retail levels. They have been passed in more than half the states in the United States.

Selling below cost in these states is illegal. Wholesalers and retailers are usually required to take a certain minimum percentage markup over their merchandise-plus-transportation costs. The practical effect of these laws is to protect certain limited-line food retailers—such as dairy stores—from the kind of "ruinous" competition supermarkets might offer if they sold milk as a leader, offering it below cost for a long time.

The United States and most other countries control the minimum price of imported products with antidumping laws. **Dumping** is pricing a product sold in a foreign market below the cost of producing it or at a price lower than in its domestic market. These laws are usually designed to protect the country's domestic producers and jobs. U.S. steelmakers have accused China of dumping and encouraged the U.S. government to take action.

Regulators can set prices

In some industries, often where there is little competition, a state government may control prices. For example, many utilities—such as electric and gas—have little or no competition to keep prices in check, so states will usually have a board that governs the prices they charge. To assure all citizens have access to affordable auto insurance, most states control auto insurance rates as well. Still, to maintain competition, there are several important regulations in the pricing area.

You can't lie about prices

Phony list prices are prices customers are shown to suggest that the price has been discounted from list. Some customers seem more interested in the supposed discount than in the actual price. Most businesses, trade associations, and government agencies consider the use of phony list prices unethical. In the United States, the FTC tries to stop such pricing—using the **Wheeler Lea Amendment**, which bans "unfair or deceptive acts in commerce."[25]

A few years ago, some electronics retailers were criticized on these grounds. They'd advertise a $300 discount on a computer when the customer signed up for an Internet service provider, but it might not be clear to the consumer that a three-year commitment—costing more than $700—was required.

Price fixing is illegal—you can go to jail

Difficulties with pricing—and violations of pricing legislation—usually occur when competing marketing mixes are quite similar. When the success of an entire marketing strategy depends on price, there is pressure (and temptation) to make agreements with competitors (conspire). And **price fixing**—competitors getting together to raise, lower, or stabilize prices—is common and relatively easy. *But it is also completely illegal in the United States.* It is considered "conspiracy" under the Sherman Act and the Federal Trade Commission Act. To discourage price fixing, both companies and individual managers are held responsible. In a recent case, an executive at Archer Daniels Midland (ADM) Company was sentenced to three years in jail and the company was fined $100 million.[26]

Different countries have different rules concerning price fixing, and this has created problems in international trade. Japan, for example, allows price fixing, especially if it strengthens the position of Japanese producers in world markets.

Producers may set minimum retail prices

Manufacturers usually suggest a retail list price and then leave it up to retailers to decide what to charge in their local markets. In fact, until recently the courts prohibited manufacturers from imposing a minimum price at which their goods could be sold. This was viewed as a form of price fixing and a violation of the Sherman Antitrust Act. However, the ruling in a recent Supreme Court case changes that. The case involved Leegin Creative Leather Products and Kay's Kloset, a retailer that had been discounting Leegin's handbags. To prevent the discounting, Leegin stopped selling to Kay's Kloset. Kay's Kloset brought suit and said that retailers should be free to set their own prices—which, in turn, would keep prices lower for consumers. However, Leegin argued that its strategy focused on building the reputation of its brand with excellent service and advertising. Its retailers couldn't provide that level of service and promotion if they didn't charge a price that offered a sufficient profit margin. Leegin also argued that if one retailer ignored the strategy and cut its price on Leegin products, other retailers would follow suit—and soon the retailers wouldn't be able to provide the backing Leegin bags needed to compete. The court ruling, which supported Leegin, marks an important change because it gives manufacturers more power to control retail pricing.[27]

U.S. antimonopoly laws ban price discrimination unless…

Price level and price flexibility policies can lead to price discrimination. The **Robinson-Patman Act** (of 1936) makes illegal any **price discrimination**—selling the same products to different buyers at different prices—*if it injures competition*. The law does permit some price differences—but they must be based on (1) cost differences or (2) the need to meet competition. Both buyers and sellers are considered guilty if they know they're entering into discriminatory agreements.

What does "like grade and quality" mean?

Firms in businesses as varied as transportation services, book publishing, and auto parts have been charged with violations of the Robinson-Patman Act in recent, nationally publicized cases. Competitors who have been injured by a violation of the law have incentive to go to court because they can receive a settlement that is three times larger than the damage suffered.

The Robinson-Patman Act allows a marketing manager to charge different prices for similar products if they are *not* of "like grade and quality." But the FTC says that if the physical characteristics of a product are similar, then they are of like grade and quality. A landmark U.S. Supreme Court ruling against the Borden Company upheld the FTC's view that a well-known label *alone* does not make a product different from one with an unknown label. The company agreed that the canned milk it sold at different prices under different labels was basically the same.

But the FTC's victory in the Borden case was not complete. The U.S. Court of Appeals found no evidence of injury to competition and further noted that there could be no injury unless Borden's price differential exceeded the "recognized consumer appeal of the Borden label." How to measure "consumer appeal" was not spelled out, so producers who want to sell several brands—or dealer brands at lower prices than their main brand—probably should offer physical differences, and differences that are really useful.[28]

Can cost analysis justify price differences?

The Robinson-Patman Act allows price differences if there are cost differences—say, for larger quantity shipments or because intermediaries take over some of the physical distribution functions. But justifying cost differences is a difficult job. And the justification must be developed *before* different prices are set. The seller can't wait until a competitor, disgruntled customer, or the FTC brings a charge. At that point, it's too late.[29]

Can you legally meet price cuts?

Under the Robinson-Patman Act, meeting a competitor's price is permitted as a defense in price discrimination cases. A major objective of antimonopoly laws is to protect competition, not competitors. And "meeting competition in good faith" still seems to be legal.

Special promotion allowances might not be allowed

Some firms violate the Robinson-Patman Act by providing push money, advertising allowances, and other promotion aids to some customers and not others. The act prohibits such special allowances, *unless they are made available to all customers on "proportionately equal" terms*.[30]

How to avoid discriminating

Because price discrimination laws are complicated and penalties for violations heavy, many business managers follow the safest course by offering few or no quantity discounts and the same cost-based prices to *all* customers. This is *too* conservative a reaction. But when firms consider price differences, they may need a lawyer involved in the discussion!

© William D. Perreault, Jr., Ph.D.

CONCLUSION

The price variable offers an alert marketing manager many possibilities for varying marketing mixes. This chapter began by discussing how a firm's pricing objectives may be oriented toward profit, sales, or maintaining the status quo. Clear pricing objectives help in making decisions about the firm's important pricing policies.

This chapter discussed the pros and cons of flexible pricing and some of the approaches that firms use to implement it. It also considered the initial price level decision—skim the cream or penetration—that the marketing manager must make with new products at the introductory stage of their life cycle. We also discussed a variety of ways that marketing managers adjust the basic list price under different circumstances—by using different types of discounts, allowances, and transportation costs. These policies need to be clearly defined by the marketing manager.

The chapter described how the different components of price are traded off against the other marketing mix variables to create something of value for the customer. We also discussed value pricing and how to create a competitive advantage by offering customers superior value—which isn't the same as just offering lower and lower prices.

Pricing comes under greater scrutiny from the law than some other marketing mix variables. So it is important to understand key legal constraints that influence pricing decisions.

This chapter provided a foundation for understanding the objectives and policies that guide pricing decisions. This information provides input into the price-setting process, which we describe in greater detail in the following chapter when we look at both cost- and demand-oriented approaches to pricing.

WHAT'S NOW?

This chapter examined pricing objectives, policies, and practices. For some current real-world examples and applications, check out *What's Now?* at www.learnthe4ps.com/whatsnow/c17

KEY TERMS

LO 17.8

price, 454

target return objective, 455

profit maximization objective, 456

sales-oriented objective, 456

status quo objectives, 457

nonprice competition, 457

administered prices, 458

one-price policy, 458

flexible-price policy, 458

skimming price policy, 461

penetration pricing policy, 462

introductory price dealing, 463

basic list prices, 464

discounts, 464

quantity discounts, 464

cumulative quantity discounts, 465

noncumulative quantity discounts, 465

seasonal discounts, 465

net, 465

cash discounts, 465

2/10, net 30, 465

trade (functional) discount, 467

sale price, 467

everyday low pricing, 467

allowances, 467

advertising allowances, 467

stocking allowances, 467

push money (or prize money) allowances, 468

trade-in allowance, 468

rebates, 468

F.O.B, 470

zone pricing, 470

uniform delivered pricing, 470

freight-absorption pricing, 471

value pricing, 471

unfair trade practice acts, 474

dumping, 475

phony list prices, 475

Wheeler Lea Amendment, 475

price fixing, 475

Robinson-Patman Act, 476

price discrimination, 476

QUESTIONS AND PROBLEMS

1. Review the Method case study that opens the chapter. From this case, identify examples of different key terms and concepts covered in the chapter. For example, early on the company had a sales-oriented pricing objective thanks to financial backers concerned with market share and sales volume.

2. Review the Method case study that opens this chapter. Considering what you have learned in the class thus far (other elements of the marketing mix), and, more specifically, pricing lessons in this chapter, offer strategy suggestions for: 1) prices and other marketing mix decisions over the product life cycle in the laundry category, and 2) how

value pricing would work for Method's laundry products—how does it deliver and communicate value?

3. Identify the strategy decisions a marketing manager must make in the Price area. Illustrate your answer for a local retailer.

4. How should the acceptance of a profit-oriented, a sales-oriented, or a status quo–oriented pricing objective affect the development of a company's marketing strategy? Illustrate for each.

5. Distinguish between one-price and flexible-price policies. Which is most appropriate for a hardware store? Why?

6. What pricing objective(s) is a skimming pricing policy most likely implementing? Is the same true for a penetration pricing policy? Which policy is probably most appropriate for each of the following products: (a) a new type of home lawn-sprinkling system, (b) a skin patch drug to help smokers quit, (c) a DVD of a best-selling movie, and (d) a new children's toy?

7. How would differences in exchange rates between different countries affect a firm's decisions concerning the use of flexible-price policies in different foreign markets?

8. Are seasonal discounts appropriate in agricultural businesses (which are certainly seasonal)?

9. What are the effective annual interest rates for the following cash discount terms: (a) 1/10, net 20; (b) 1/5, net 10; and (c) net 25?

10. Why would a manufacturer offer a rebate instead of lowering the suggested list price?

11. How can a marketing manager change a firm's F.O.B. terms to make an otherwise competitive marketing mix more attractive?

12. What type of geographic pricing policy is most appropriate for the following products (specify any assumptions necessary to obtain a definite answer): (a) a chemical by-product, (b) nationally advertised candy bars, (c) rebuilt auto parts, and (d) tricycles?

13. How would a ban on freight absorption (that is, requiring F.O.B. factory pricing) affect a producer with substantial economies of scale in production?

14. Give an example of a marketing mix that has a high price level but that you see as a good value. Briefly explain what makes it a good value.

15. Think about a business from which you regularly make purchases even though there are competing firms with similar prices. Explain what the firm offers that improves value and keeps you coming back.

16. Cite two examples of continuously selling above the market price. Describe the situations.

17. Explain the types of competitive situations that might lead to a meeting-competition pricing policy.

18. Would consumers be better off if all nations dropped their antidumping laws? Explain your thinking.

19. How would our marketing system change if manufacturers were required to set fixed prices on *all* products sold at retail and *all* retailers were required to use these prices? Would a manufacturer's marketing mix be easier to develop? What kind of an operation would retailing be in this situation? Would consumers receive more or less service?

20. Is price discrimination involved if a large oil company sells gasoline to taxicab associations for 2.5 cents less than the price charged to retail service stations? The gas sold to the cab associations will be resold to taxi drivers. What happens if the cab associations resell gasoline not only to taxicab operators but also to the general public?

MARKETING PLANNING FOR HILLSIDE VETERINARY CLINIC

Appendix D (the Appendices follow Chapter 19) includes a sample marketing plan for Hillside Veterinary Clinic. Look through the "Marketing Strategy" section.

a. A veterinary clinic located in another town gives its customers a 10 percent discount on their next vet bill if they refer a new pet owner to the clinic. Do you think that this would be a good idea for Hillside? Does it fit with Hillside's strategy?

b. The same clinic offered customers a sort of cumulative discount—an end-of-year refund if their total spending at the clinic exceeded a certain level. That clinic sees it as a way of being nice to people whose pets have had a lot of problems. Do you think that this is a good idea for Hillside? Why or why not?

SUGGESTED CASES

MARKETING ANALYTICS: DATA TO KNOWLEDGE

CHAPTER 17 CASH DISCOUNTS

Joe Tulkin owns Tulkin Wholesale Co. He sells paper, tape, file folders, and other office supplies to about 120 retailers in nearby cities. His average retailer-customer spends about $900 a month. When Tulkin started business in 1991, competing wholesalers were giving retailers invoice terms of 3/10, net 30. Tulkin never gave the issue much thought—he just used the same invoice terms when he billed customers. At that time, about half of his customers took the discount. Recently, he noticed a change in the way his customers were paying their bills. Checking his records, he found that 90 percent of the retailers were taking the cash discount. With so many retailers taking the cash discount, it seems to have become a price reduction.

In addition, Tulkin learned that other wholesalers were changing their invoice terms.

Tulkin decides he should rethink his invoice terms. He knows he could change the percent rate on the cash discount, the number of days the discount is offered, or the number of days before the face amount is due. Changing any of these, or any combination, will change the interest rate at which a buyer is, in effect, borrowing money if he does not take the discount. Tulkin decides that it will be easier to evaluate the effect of different invoice terms if he sets up a spreadsheet to let him change the terms and quickly see the effective interest rate for each change.

See Connect for the spreadsheet and questions needed to analyze this scenario.

Photo by Tasos Katopodis/Getty Images for Samsung.

Price Setting in the Business World

Back in the 1990s, American consumers saw Samsung as a second-tier producer of commodity electronics. In the United States it was known for cheap microwave ovens and color televisions—little more. The company operated on thin margins—and even lost money during the Asian economic crisis in the late 1990s. Samsung figured it could earn higher margins if it could develop more product lines and differentiate each more clearly. Samsung decided to re-position itself as a high-quality producer known for innovation and design.

Samsung set up design studios around the world, developed a more globally oriented corporate culture, and focused on getting new technology to market more quickly. This change in strategy worked. Samsung is now the largest consumer electronics company in the world—with the leading market share in many product categories and a reputation for quality and design. The TV market is a microcosm of many changes in Samsung and consumer electronics. So let's look at how the TV market has evolved and how it has influenced Samsung's strategy planning, especially pricing.

Samsung was a major player in the LCD panel market in the 1990s—producing the LCD panels that go into computer monitors and the first flat-panel televisions. In fact, Samsung sold LCD panels to many of its competitors in the TV market. Because it was costly to produce the larger LCD panels needed for televisions, prices were high. By 2001, the average price for flat-panel TVs was about $10,000. At this price, demand was limited. Flat screens were mostly sold by commercial audio-video suppliers to business customers.

As prices came down over the next few years, consumer demand grew and Samsung started to distribute its flat-panel TVs through electronics chains such as Best Buy and Circuit City. That helped to bring down selling costs, and more important, economies of scale in production kicked in to further lower costs and prices.

Anticipating rapid growth in the television market, suppliers of LCD panels invested billions of dollars in new factories to make panels for the ever-expanding range of TV screens. LCD suppliers (including Samsung) wanted to protect those investments, so they secretly met to set prices (and were later found guilty of price fixing). Even those efforts didn't keep prices of LCD panels from dropping as suppliers desperately tried to capture sales through pricing incentives, though they probably fell more slowly than expected in a perfectly competitive market.

By 2005, the price of a 30-inch high-definition Samsung LCD television had dropped below $3,000. Still, with a similar size tube-style television available for less than $800, the size of the consumer market for LCD televisions remained limited. On the other hand, the new technology had strong support from retailers, who enjoyed the 30 percent margins they earned on LCD TVs. Samsung kept pushing technology boundaries and gained a name for itself with its ultra-thin LCD TVs. Its reputation for quality was also starting to turn around. And because Samsung was vertically integrated and produced the LCD panels for its own TVs, its costs were lower than most of its competitors'. Samsung used this advantage to offer low prices and build market share.

Over the next couple of years, Samsung experienced new competition from almost 100 upstart TV makers. Vizio proved to be one of the most successful. Vizio handled design and marketing itself but left production to contract manufacturers in China. As a result, its overhead costs were less than 1 percent of sales; Samsung's overhead costs were 10 to 20 percent of sales. To gain market share, Vizio settled for slim profit margins of just 2 percent, much lower than Samsung's desired returns. Vizio didn't try to offer a TV that had the most advanced video standards or technology. Rather, it just tried to have an inexpensive TV in each of the most popular sizes. This strategy gave Vizio a significant price advantage on the retail floor and helped it gain distribution in discount stores such as Walmart and Costco. Vizio did not advertise. The promotion job was left to retailers who found they could easily draw in customers with Vizio's low prices.

Retailers pressured TV makers, like Samsung, to cut prices too. This caused a price war, after which the price of LCD flat screens continued to tumble and dropped 40 percent in less than a year. Over time, most of the low-priced competitors left the market, and prices stabilized. Samsung and Sony then tried to reduce competition for their retailers by imposing a minimum price strategy. While many of the retailers were pleased to have the higher margins, Samsung eventually allowed retailers to compete on price—fearing it would lose share to Panasonic and Vizio. And soon retailers complained of "selling $2,000 TVs and making $10."

The ongoing focus on price in this market threatened to turn TVs into a commodity—where brand and features didn't matter, only price. To maintain economies of scale, Samsung offers a full line of TVs. For example, it has 55" TVs with suggested retail prices ranging from $1,599 to $4,999—though street prices (what most retailers actually charge) go from $699 to $2,499.

Samsung wants to move consumers to the higher priced models in its line, where its margins—and those of its retailers—are higher. So Samsung listens to customers and tries to anticipate their needs. For example, its "smart TVs" have built-in Internet connections and apps to allow for easy viewing of services such as Hulu, Vudu, and Netflix. When consumers asked for thinner flat-panel TVs, Samsung responded with the thinnest models on the market. Samsung's curved screen UHD (ultra high definition) TVs command a premium price because aficionados of viewing from multiple angles will sacrifice for this viewability. Yet not all innovations appeal to enough consumers to be deemed successful. Although Samsung was one of the first TV makers to jump into 3D TVs, consumers haven't fully bought into this innovation.

Communicating the benefits of new features has been a challenge for Samsung and others in this market. Samsung may innovate, but competitors soon follow. Samsung continues to be attacked from the low end by firms like Vizio, while also getting strong competition from Panasonic, Sony, and Sharp at the high end. Yet Samsung keeps effectively adapting its whole marketing strategy and keeps communicating and delivering value to its target customers—outcome being, perseverance pays.[1]

LEARNING OBJECTIVES

Ultimately, the price that a firm charges must cover the costs of the whole marketing mix, or the firm will not make a profit. So it's important for marketing managers to understand costs and how they relate to pricing. On the other hand, it doesn't make sense to set prices based just on costs, because customers won't buy a product if they don't think that it represents a good value for their money. So setting prices is not an easy task, and marketing managers must carefully balance costs, customer price sensitivity, and other factors. This chapter will help you better understand these issues and how to evaluate them in setting prices.

When you finish this chapter, you should be able to

1 Understand how most wholesalers and retailers set their prices by using markups.

2 Understand why turnover is so important in pricing.

3 Understand the advantages and disadvantages of average-cost pricing.

4 Know how to use break-even analysis to evaluate possible prices.

5 Understand the advantages of marginal analysis and how to use it for price setting.

6 Understand other demand-oriented factors that influence price setting.

7 Explain full-line pricing and factors influencing such decisions.

8 Understand how bid pricing and negotiated prices work.

9 Understand important new terms (shown in red).

Price Setting Is a Key Strategy Decision

In Chapter 17 we discussed the idea that pricing objectives and policies should guide pricing decisions. We described different dimensions of the pricing decision and how they combine to create value for customers. This chapter builds on those concepts—all of which influence price setting—and gives you additional frameworks that will help you understand how marketing managers set prices. See Exhibit 18–1.

There are many ways to set prices. But, for simplicity, they can be reduced to two basic approaches—*cost-oriented* and *demand-oriented* price setting. We will discuss cost-oriented approaches first because they are most common. Also, understanding the problems of relying on a cost-oriented approach shows why a marketing manager must consider customer demand and price sensitivity to make good Price decisions. We conclude the chapter with a discussion of some special price-setting issues—pricing full lines of products, bid pricing, and negotiated pricing.

Some Firms Just Use Markups

Markups guide pricing by intermediaries

Some firms, including most retailers and wholesalers, set prices by using a **markup**—a dollar amount added to the cost of products to get the selling price. For example, suppose that a CVS drugstore buys a bottle of Pert Plus shampoo and conditioner for $2.40. To make a profit, the drugstore obviously must sell Pert Plus for more than $2.40. If it adds $1.20 to cover operating expenses and provide a profit, we say that the store is marking up the item $1.20.

Markups, however, usually are stated as percentages rather than dollar amounts. And this is where confusion sometimes arises. Is a markup of $1.20 on a cost of $2.40 a markup of 50 percent? Or should the markup be figured as a percentage of the selling price—$3.60—and therefore be 33⅓ percent? A clear definition is necessary.

Markup percent is based on selling price—a convenient rule

Unless otherwise stated, **markup (percent)** means the percentage of selling price that is added to the cost to get the selling price. So the $1.20 markup on the $3.60 selling price is a markup of 33⅓ percent. Markups are related to selling price for convenience.

There's nothing wrong with the idea of markup on cost. However, to avoid confusion, it's important to state clearly which markup percent you're using.

A manager may want to change a markup on selling price to one based on cost, or vice versa. The calculations used to do this are simple. (See the section on markup conversion in Appendix B on marketing arithmetic. The appendices follow Chapter 19.)[2]

Many retailers have a standard markup on products, like Powerade and Burt's Bees personal care products.
Left: Photo by Andrew Burton/Getty Images; Right: Tony Cenicola/The New York Times/Redux

Many use a standard markup percent

Many intermediaries select a standard markup percent and then apply it to all their products. This makes pricing easier. When you think of the large number of items the average retailer and wholesaler carry—and the small sales volume of any one item—this approach may make sense. Spending the time to find the best price to charge on every item in stock (day to day or week to week) might not pay.

Moreover, different companies in the same line of business often use the same markup percent. There is a reason for this: Their operating expenses are usually similar. So they see a standard markup as acceptable as long as it's large enough to cover the firm's operating expenses and provide a reasonable profit.

Markups are related to gross margins

How does a manager decide on a standard markup in the first place? A standard markup is often set close to the firm's *gross margin*. Managers regularly see gross margins on their operating (profit and loss) statements. The gross margin is the amount left—after subtracting the cost of sales (cost of goods sold) from net sales—to cover the expenses of selling products and operating the business. (See Appendix B on marketing arithmetic if you are unfamiliar with these ideas.) Our CVS manager knows that there won't be any profit if the gross margin is not large enough. For this reason, CVS might accept a markup percent on Pert Plus that is close to the store's usual gross margin percent.

Smart producers pay attention to the gross margins and standard markups of intermediaries in their channel. They usually allow discounts similar to the standard markups these intermediaries expect.

Markup chain may be used in channel pricing

Different firms in a channel often use different markups. A **markup chain**—the sequence of markups firms use at different levels in a channel—determines the price structure in the whole channel. The markup is figured on the *selling price* at each level of the channel.

For example, Black & Decker's selling price for a cordless electric drill becomes the cost the Ace Hardware wholesaler pays. The wholesaler's selling price becomes the hardware retailer's cost. And this cost plus a retail markup becomes the retail selling price. Each markup should cover the costs of running the business and leave a profit.

Exhibit 18–2 illustrates the markup chain for a cordless electric drill at each level of the channel system. The production (factory) cost of the drill is $43.20. In this case, the producer takes a 10 percent markup and sells the product for $48. The markup is 10 percent of $48 or $4.80. The producer's selling price now becomes the wholesaler's cost—$48. If the wholesaler is used to taking a 20 percent markup on selling price, the markup is $12—and the wholesaler's selling price becomes $60. The $60 now becomes the cost for the hardware retailer. And a retailer who is used to a 40 percent markup adds $40, and the retail selling price becomes $100.

Exhibit 18-2 Example of a Markup Chain and Channel Pricing

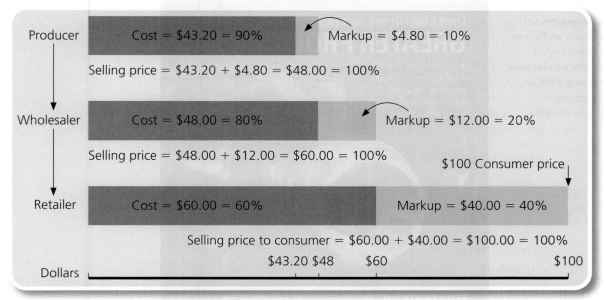

High markups don't always mean big profits

Some people, including many conventional retailers, think high markups mean big profits. Often this isn't true. A high markup may result in a price that's too high—a price at which few customers will buy. You can't earn much if you don't sell much, no matter how high your markup on a single item. So high markups may lead to low profits.

Lower markups can speed turnover and the stockturn rate

LO 18.2

Some retailers and wholesalers, however, try to speed turnover to increase profit—even if this means reducing their markups. They realize that a business runs up costs over time. If they can sell a much greater amount in the same time period, they may be able to take a lower markup and still earn higher profits at the end of the period.

An important idea here is the **stockturn rate**—the number of times the average inventory is sold in a year. Various methods of figuring stockturn rates can be used (see the section "Computing the Stockturn Rate" in Appendix B). A low stockturn rate may be bad for profits.

At the very least, a low stockturn rate increases inventory carrying cost and ties up working capital. If a firm with a stockturn of 1 (once per year) sells products that cost it $100,000, it has that much tied up in inventory all the time. But a stockturn of 5 requires only $20,000 worth of inventory ($100,000 cost ÷ 5 turnovers a year). If annual inventory carrying cost is about 20 percent of the inventory value, that reduces costs by $16,000 a year. That's a big difference on $100,000 in sales!

Whether a stockturn rate is high or low depends on the industry and the product involved. An electrical parts wholesaler may expect an annual rate of 2—whereas a supermarket might expect 8 stockturns on average but 20 stockturns for soaps and 70 stockturns for fresh fruits and vegetables.

Mass-merchandisers run in fast company

Although some intermediaries use the same standard markup percent on all their products, this policy ignores the importance of fast turnover. Mass-merchandisers know this. They put low markups on fast-selling items and higher markups on items that sell less frequently. For example, Walmart may put a small markup on fast-selling health and beauty aids (such as toothpaste or shampoo) but higher markups on appliances and clothing.

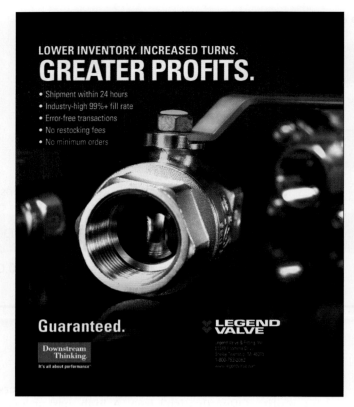

Where does the markup chain start?

Some markups eventually become standard in a trade. Most channel members tend to follow a similar process—adding a certain percentage to the previous price. But who sets price in the first place? The firm that brands a product is usually the one that sets its basic list price. It may be a large retailer, a large wholesaler, or most often, the producer.

Some producers just start with a cost per unit figure and add a markup—perhaps a standard markup—to obtain their selling price. Or they may use some rule-of-thumb formula such as:

$$\text{Selling price} = \text{Average production cost per unit} \times 3$$

A producer who uses this approach might develop rules and markups related to its own costs and objectives. Yet even the first step—selecting the appropriate cost per unit to build on—isn't easy. Let's discuss several approaches to see how cost-oriented price setting really works.

Average-Cost Pricing Is Common and Can Be Dangerous

LO 18.3

Although later in this chapter we will discuss better methods for setting prices, average-cost pricing is so commonly employed that it is important for you to understand this method and its weaknesses. And when demand is constant and predictable, average-cost pricing may be appropriate.

Average-cost pricing means adding a reasonable markup to the average cost of a product. A manager usually finds the average cost per unit by studying past records. Dividing the total cost for the last year by all the units produced and sold in that period gives an estimate of the average cost per unit for the next year. If the cost was $32,000 for all labor and materials and $30,000 for fixed overhead expenses—such as selling expenses, rent, and manager salaries—then the total cost is $62,000. See Exhibit 18–3A. If

Exhibit 18-3 Results of Average-Cost Pricing

A. Calculation of Planned Profit If 40,000 Items Are Sold		B. Calculation of Actual Profit If Only 20,000 Items Are Sold	
Calculation of Costs:		**Calculation of Costs:**	
Fixed overhead expenses	$30,000	Fixed overhead expenses	$30,000
Labor and materials ($0.80 a unit)	32,000	Labor and materials ($0.80 a unit)	16,000
Total costs	$62,000	Total costs	$46,000
"Planned" profit	18,000		
Total costs and planned profit	$80,000		
Calculation of Profit (or Loss):		**Calculation of Profit (or Loss):**	
Actual unit sales × Price ($2.00*)	$80,000	Actual unit sales price × ($2.00*)	$40,000
Minus: total costs	62,000	Minus: total costs	46,000
Profit (loss)	$18,000	Profit (loss)	($6,000)
Result:		**Result:**	
Planned profit of $18,000 is earned if 40,000 items are sold at $2.00 each.		Planned profit of $18,000 is not earned. Instead, $6,000 loss results if 20,000 items are sold at $2.00 each.	

*Calculation of "reasonable" price: $\dfrac{\text{Expected total costs and planned profit}}{\text{Planned number of items to be sold}} = \dfrac{\$80,000}{40,000} = \$2.00$

the company produced 40,000 items in that time period, the average cost is $62,000 divided by 40,000 units, or $1.55 per unit. To get the price, the producer decides how much profit per unit to add to the average cost per unit. If the company considers 45 cents a reasonable profit for each unit, it sets the new price at $2.00. Exhibit 18–3A shows that this approach produces the desired profit if the company sells 40,000 units.

It does not make allowances for cost variations as output changes

It's always a useful input to pricing decisions to understand how costs operate at different levels of output. Further, average-cost pricing is simple. But it can also be dangerous. It's easy to lose money with average-cost pricing. To see why, let's follow this example further.

First, remember that the average price of $2.00 per unit was based on output of 40,000 units. But if the firm is able to produce and sell only 20,000 units in the next year, it may be in trouble (see Exhibit 18–3B). Twenty thousand units sold at $2.00 each ($1.55 cost plus $0.45 for expected profit) yield a total revenue of only $40,000. The overhead is still fixed at $30,000, and the variable material and labor cost drops by half to $16,000—for a total cost of $46,000. This means a loss of $6,000, or 30 cents a unit. The method that was supposed to allow a profit of 45 cents a unit actually causes a loss of 30 cents a unit!

The basic problem with the average-cost approach is that it doesn't consider cost variations at different levels of output. In a typical situation, costs are high with low output, and then economies of

GoToMyPC: It's this easy.

GoToMyPC lets you instantly work on your office computer from any Internet connection, with complete access to your email, programs and files. The automatic setup takes just minutes, and there's no hardware needed. Just click and take your office with you wherever you go.

FREE 30-Day Trial
gotomypc.com | promo code: inc

GoToMyPC

by CITRIX

When developing a new product, software companies and online services like GoToMyPC have high fixed overhead expenses relative to the variable cost for each additional user. This cost structure can make average-cost pricing especially dangerous.

scale set in—the average cost per unit drops as the quantity produced increases. This is why mass production and mass distribution often make sense. It's also why it's important to develop a better understanding of the different types of costs a marketing manager should consider when setting a price.

Marketing Managers Must Consider Various Kinds of Costs

LO 18.4

Average-cost pricing may lead to losses because there are a variety of costs—and each changes in a *different* way as output changes. Any pricing method that uses cost must consider these changes. To understand why, we need to define six types of cost.

There are three kinds of total cost

1. **Total fixed cost** is the sum of those costs that are fixed in total—no matter how much is produced. Among these fixed costs are rent, depreciation, managers' salaries, property taxes, and insurance. Such costs stay the same even if production stops temporarily.
2. **Total variable cost**, on the other hand, is the sum of those changing expenses that are closely related to output—expenses for parts, wages, packaging materials, outgoing freight, and sales commissions.

At zero output, total variable cost is zero. As output increases, so do variable costs. If Levi's doubles its output of jeans in a year, its total cost for denim cloth also (roughly) doubles.

3. **Total cost** is the sum of total fixed and total variable costs. Changes in total cost depend on variations in total variable cost, because total fixed cost stays the same.

There are three kinds of average cost

The pricing manager usually is more interested in cost per unit than total cost, because prices are usually quoted per unit.

1. **Average cost (per unit)** is obtained by dividing total cost by the related quantity (that is, the total quantity that causes the total cost).
2. **Average fixed cost (per unit)** is obtained by dividing total fixed cost by the related quantity.
3. **Average variable cost (per unit)** is obtained by dividing total variable cost by the related quantity.

An example shows cost relations

A good way to get a feel for these different types of costs is to extend our average-cost pricing example (Exhibit 18–3A). Exhibit 18–4 shows the six types of cost and how they vary at different levels of output. The line for 40,000 units is highlighted because that was the expected level of sales in our average-cost pricing example. For simplicity, we assume that average variable cost is the same for each unit. Notice, however, that total variable cost increases when quantity increases.

Exhibit 18–5 shows the three average cost curves from Exhibit 18–4. Notice that average fixed cost goes down steadily as the quantity increases. Although the average variable cost remains the same, average cost decreases continually too. This is because average fixed cost is decreasing. With these relations in mind, let's reconsider the problem with average-cost pricing.

Ignoring demand is the major weakness of average-cost pricing

Average-cost pricing works well if the firm actually sells the quantity it used to set the average-cost price. Losses may result, however, if actual sales are much lower than expected. On the other hand, if sales are much higher than expected, then profits may be very good. But this will only happen by luck—because the firm's demand is much larger than expected.

To use average-cost pricing, a marketing manager must make *some* estimate of the quantity to be sold in the coming period. Without a quantity estimate, it isn't possible to compute average cost. But unless this quantity is related to price—that is,

Exhibit 18-4   Cost Structure of a Firm

Quantity (Q)	Total Fixed Costs (TFC)	Average Fixed Costs (AFC)	Average Variable Costs (AVC)	Total Variable Costs (TVC)	Total Cost (TC)	Average Cost (AC)
0	$30,000	—	—	—	$ 30,000	—
10,000	30,000	$3.00	$0.80	$ 8,000	38,000	$3.80
20,000	30,000	1.50	0.80	16,000	46,000	2.30
30,000	30,000	1.00	0.80	24,000	54,000	1.80
40,000	30,000	0.75	0.80	32,000	62,000	1.55
50,000	30,000	0.60	0.80	40,000	70,000	1.40
60,000	30,000	0.50	0.80	48,000	78,000	1.30
70,000	30,000	0.43	0.80	56,000	86,000	1.23
80,000	30,000	0.38	0.80	64,000	94,000	1.18
90,000	30,000	0.33	0.80	72,000	102,000	1.13
100,000	30,000	0.30	0.80	80,000	110,000	1.10

$$0.30\ (AFC) = \frac{30{,}000\ (TFC)}{100{,}000\ (Q)}$$

$$\begin{bmatrix} 100{,}000 & (Q) \\ \times 0.80 & (AVC) \\ \hline 80{,}000 & (TVC) \end{bmatrix}$$

$$\begin{bmatrix} 30{,}000 & (TFC) \\ +80{,}000 & (TVC) \\ \hline 110{,}000 & (TC) \end{bmatrix}$$

$$1.10\ (AC) = \frac{110{,}000\ (TC)}{100{,}000\ (Q)}$$

unless the firm's demand curve is considered—the marketing manager may set a price that doesn't even cover a firm's total cost! You saw this happen in Exhibit 18–3B, when the firm's price of $2.00 resulted in demand for only 20,000 units and a loss of $6,000.

The demand curve is still important even if a manager has not taken time to think about it. For example, Exhibit 18–6 shows the demand curve for the firm we're discussing. This demand curve shows *why* the firm lost money when it tried to use average-cost pricing. At the $2.00 price, quantity demanded is only 20,000. With this demand curve and the costs in Exhibit 18–4, the firm will incur a loss whether management sets the price at a high $3 or a low $1.20. At $3, the firm will sell only 10,000 units for a total revenue of $30,000. But total cost will be $38,000—for a loss of $8,000. At the

Exhibit 18-5   Typical Shape of Cost (per unit) Curves When Average Variable Cost per Unit Is Constant

Exhibit 18–6 Evaluation of Various Prices along a Firm's Demand Curve

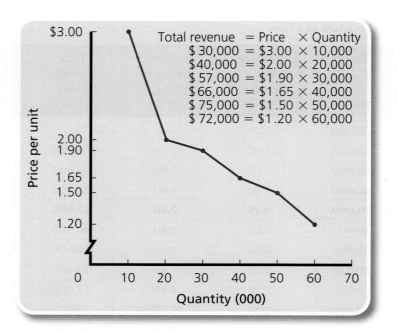

Total revenue	= Price	× Quantity
$ 30,000	= $3.00	× 10,000
$ 40,000	= $2.00	× 20,000
$ 57,000	= $1.90	× 30,000
$ 66,000	= $1.65	× 40,000
$ 75,000	= $1.50	× 50,000
$ 72,000	= $1.20	× 60,000

$1.20 price, it will sell 60,000 units—at a loss of $6,000. However, the curve suggests that at a price of $1.65 consumers will demand about 40,000 units, producing a profit of about $4,000.

In short, average-cost pricing is simple in theory but often fails in practice. In stable situations, prices set by this method may yield profits but not necessarily *maximum* profits. And note that such cost-based prices may be higher than a price that would be more profitable for the firm, as shown in Exhibit 18–6. When demand conditions are changing, average-cost pricing is even more risky.

Exhibit 18–7 summarizes the relationships just discussed. Cost-oriented pricing requires an estimate of the total number of units to be sold. That estimate determines the *average* fixed cost per unit and thus the average total cost. Then the firm adds the desired profit per unit to the average total cost to get the cost-oriented selling price. How customers react to that price determines the actual quantity the firm will be able to sell. But that quantity may not be the quantity used to compute the average cost![3]

Exhibit 18–7 Summary of Relationships among Quantity, Cost, and Price Using Cost-Oriented Pricing

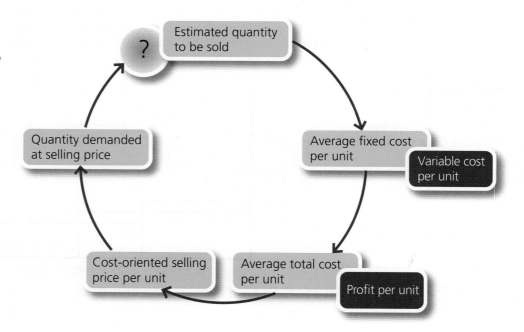

Don't ignore competitors' costs

Another danger of average-cost pricing is that it ignores competitors' costs and prices. Just as the price of a firm's own product influences demand, the price of available substitutes may impact demand. By finding ways to cut costs, a firm may be able to offer prices lower than competitors and still make an attractive profit.

Break-Even Analysis Can Evaluate Possible Prices

Some price setters use break-even analysis in their pricing. **Break-even analysis** evaluates whether the firm will be able to break even—that is, cover all its costs—with a particular price. This is important because a firm must cover all costs in the long run or there is not much point being in business. This method focuses on the **break-even point (BEP)**—the quantity where the firm's total cost will just equal its total revenue.

Break-even charts help find the BEP

To help understand how break-even analysis works, look at Exhibit 18–8, an example of the typical break-even chart. *The chart is based on a particular selling price*—in this case $1.20 a unit. The chart has lines that show total costs (total variable plus total fixed costs) and total revenues at different levels of production. The break-even point on the chart is at 75,000 units, where the total cost and total revenue lines intersect. At that production level, total cost and total revenue are the same—$90,000.

The difference between the total revenue and total cost at a given quantity is the profit—or loss! The chart shows that below the break-even point, total cost is higher than total revenue and the firm incurs a loss. The firm would make a profit above the break-even point. However, the firm would only reach the break-even point, or get beyond it into the profit area *if* it could sell at least 75,000 units at the $1.20 price.

Break-even analysis can be helpful if used properly, so let's look at this approach more closely.

How to compute a break-even point

A break-even chart is an easy-to-understand visual aid, but it's also useful to be able to compute the break-even point.

The BEP, in units, can be found by dividing total fixed costs (TFC) by the **fixed-cost (FC) contribution per unit**—the assumed selling price per unit minus the variable cost per unit. This can be stated as a simple formula:

$$\text{BEP (in units)} = \frac{\text{Total fixed cost}}{\text{Fixed cost contribution per unit}}$$

Exhibit 18–8
Break-Even Chart for a Particular Situation

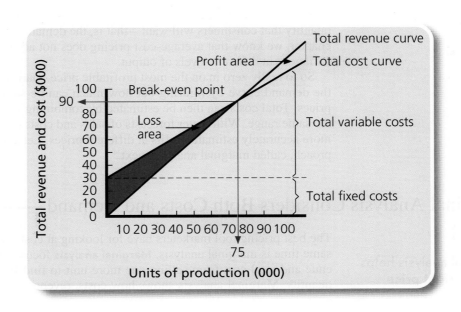

This formula makes sense when we think about it. To break even, we must cover total fixed costs. Therefore, we must figure the contribution each unit will make to covering the total fixed costs (after paying for the variable costs to produce the item). When we divide this per-unit contribution into the total fixed costs that must be covered, we have the BEP (in units).

To illustrate the formula, let's use the cost and price information in Exhibit 18–8. The price per unit is $1.20. The average variable cost per unit is 80 cents. So the FC contribution per unit is 40 cents ($1.20 − $0.80). The total fixed cost is $30,000 (see Exhibit 18–8). Substituting in the formula:

$$\text{BEP} = \frac{\$30,000}{\$0.40} = 75,000 \text{ units}$$

From this you can see that if this firm sells 75,000 units, it will exactly cover all its fixed and variable costs. If it sells even one more unit, it will begin to show a profit—in this case, 40 cents per unit. Note that once the fixed costs are covered, the part of revenue formerly going to cover fixed costs is now *all profit*.

BEP can be stated in dollars too

The BEP can also be figured in dollars. The easiest way is to compute the BEP in units and then multiply by the assumed per-unit price. If you multiply the selling price ($1.20) by the BEP in units (75,000) you get $90,000—the BEP in dollars.

Each possible price has its own break-even point

Often it's useful to compute the break-even point for each of several possible prices and then compare the BEP for each price to likely demand at that price. The marketing manager can quickly reject some price possibilities when the expected quantity demanded at a given price is way below the break-even point for that price.

Break-even analysis is helpful—but not a pricing solution

Break-even analysis is helpful for evaluating alternatives. It is also popular because it's easy to use. Yet break-even analysis is too often misunderstood. Beyond the BEP, profits seem to be growing continually. And the graph—with its straight-line total revenue curve—makes it seem that any quantity can be sold at the assumed price. But this usually isn't true. It is the same as assuming a perfectly horizontal demand curve at that price. In fact, most managers face down-sloping demand situations. And their total revenue curves do *not* keep going straight up.

Break-even analysis is a useful tool for analyzing costs and evaluating what might happen to profits in different market environments. But it is a cost-oriented approach. Like other cost-oriented approaches, it does not consider the effect of price on the quantity that consumers will want—that is, the demand curve. And from earlier in the chapter, we know that average-cost pricing does not accurately take into account cost variations at different levels of output.

So to really zero in on the most profitable price, marketers are better off estimating the demand curve by figuring out how much can be sold across a range of feasible prices. Total costs can then be estimated by combining variable and fixed costs across the same range. With better forecasts of sales and costs data, a marketing manager can more accurately estimate profits at different prices. Let's look more closely at this approach, called marginal analysis, next.[4]

Marginal Analysis Considers Both Costs and Demand

LO 18.5

Marginal analysis helps find the right price

The best pricing tool marketers have for looking at costs and revenue (demand) at the same time is marginal analysis. **Marginal analysis** focuses on the changes in total revenue and total cost from selling one more unit to find the most profitable price and quantity. Marginal analysis shows how costs, revenue, and profit change at different

Exhibit 18-9
Revenue, Cost, and Profit at Different Prices for a Firm

(1) Price (P)	(2) Quantity (Q)	(3) Total Revenue (TR = P × Q)	(4) Total Variable Cost (TVC)	(5) Fixed Cost (FC)	(6) Total Cost (TC = TVC + FC)	(7) Profit (Prf = TR − TC)
$200	0	$0	$0	$200	$200	−$200
175	1	175	60	200	260	285
160	2	320	120	200	320	0
145	3	435	180	200	380	55
135	4	540	240	200	440	100
125	5	625	300	200	500	125
115	**6**	**690**	**360**	**200**	**560**	**130**
105	7	735	420	200	620	115
95	8	760	480	200	680	80
85	9	765	540	200	740	25
75	10	750	600	200	800	−50
65	11	715	660	200	860	−145
55	12	660	720	200	920	−260

prices. The price that maximizes profit is the one that results in the greatest difference between total revenue and total cost.[5]

Demand estimates involve "if-then" thinking

Because the price determines what quantity will be sold, a manager needs an estimate of the demand curve to compute total revenue. A practical approach here is for managers to think about a price that appears to be too high and one that is too low. Then, for a number of prices between these two extremes, the manager estimates what quantity it might be possible to sell. You can think of this as a summary of the answers to a series of what-if questions—*What* quantity will be sold *if* a particular price is selected?

Profit is the difference between total revenue and total cost

The first two columns in Exhibit 18–9 give price and quantity combinations (demand) for an example firm. In this case, a manager estimates that sales will be zero at a price of $200; at a price of $175, one unit is predicted to sell; at a price of $160, two units, and so forth. Total revenue in column 3 of Exhibit 18–9 is equal to a price multiplied by its related quantity. Costs at the different quantities are also shown. The total variable costs are $60 per unit and fixed costs are $200 no matter how many units are sold. Column 6 shows the total cost by adding total variable cost and the fixed cost at each price and predicted quantity. The profit (column 7) at each quantity and price is the difference between total revenue and total cost. In this example, the best price is $115 (and a quantity of six units are expected to be sold) because that combination results in the highest profit ($130).

Profit maximization with total revenue and total cost curves

Exhibit 18–10 graphs the total revenue, total cost, and total profit relationships for the numbers we've been working with in Exhibit 18–9. The highest point on the total profit curve is at a quantity of six units. This is also the quantity where we find the greatest vertical distance between the total revenue curve and the total cost curve. Exhibit 18–9 shows that it is the $115 price that results in selling six units, so $115 is the price that leads to the highest profit. A price lower than $115 results in a higher sales volume, but

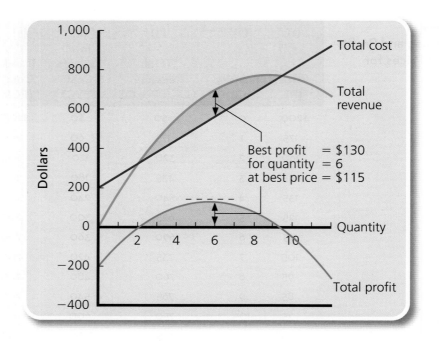

Best profit = $130
for quantity = 6
at best price = $115

you can see that the total profit curve declines beyond a quantity of six units. So a profit-maximizing marketing manager would not be interested in setting a lower price.

A profit range is reassuring

Marginal analysis focuses on the price that earns the highest profit. But a slight miss doesn't mean failure, because demand estimates don't have to be exact. There is usually a range of profitable prices. You can see this in Exhibit 18–9 and in the section of Exhibit 18–10 shown in yellow. Although the price that would result in the highest profit is $115, the firm's strategy would be profitable all the way from a price of $85 to $145. So the effort of trying to estimate demand will probably lead to being someplace in the profitable range. In contrast, the mechanical use of average-cost pricing could lead to a price that is much too high—or much too low.

A rough demand estimate is better than none

Some managers don't take advantage of marginal analysis because they think they can't determine the exact shape of the demand curve. But that view misses the point of marginal analysis. Marginal analysis encourages managers to think carefully about what they *do know* about costs and demand. Only rarely is either type of information exact. So, in practice, the focus of marginal analysis is not on finding the precise price that will maximize profit. Rather, the focus is on getting an estimate of how profit might vary across a *range of relevant prices*. Further, a number of practical demand-oriented approaches can help a marketing manager do a better job of understanding the likely shape of the demand curve for a target market. We'll discuss these approaches next.

Additional Demand-Oriented Approaches for Setting Prices

LO 18.6

Evaluating the customer's price sensitivity

A manager who knows what influences target customers' price sensitivity can do a better job estimating the demand curve that the firm faces. Marketing researchers have identified a number of factors that influence price sensitivity across many different market situations.

The first is the most basic. When customers have *substitute ways* of meeting a need, they are likely to be more price sensitive. A cook who wants a cappuccino maker to be able to serve something distinctive to guests at a dinner party may be willing to pay a high price. However, if different machines are available and our cook sees them as pretty similar, price sensitivity will be greater. It's important not to ignore dissimilar alternatives if the customer sees them as substitutes. If a machine for espresso were much less expensive than one for cappuccino, our cook might decide that an espresso machine would meet her needs just as well.

The impact of substitutes on price sensitivity is greatest when it is easy for customers to *compare prices*. For example, unit prices make it easier for our cook to compare the prices of espresso and cappuccino grinds on the grocery store shelf. Many people believe that the ease of comparing prices on the Internet increases price sensitivity and brings down prices. New smartphone technology makes comparisons possible while shopping in brick-and-mortar retail stores. Several smartphone software apps allow consumers to scan a product's bar code and then check prices for the product at other online stores. If nothing else, it may make sellers more aware of competing prices.

People tend to be less price sensitive when someone else *pays the bill* or *shares the cost*. Perhaps this is just human nature. Insurance companies think that consumers would reject high medical fees if they were paying all of their own bills. And executives might plan longer in advance to get better discounts on airline flights if their companies weren't footing the bills.

Customers tend to be more price sensitive the greater the *total expenditure*. Sometimes a big expenditure can be broken into smaller pieces. Mercedes knows this. When its ads focused on the cost of a monthly lease rather than the total price of the car, more consumers got interested in biting the bullet.

Customers are less price sensitive the greater the *significance of the end benefit* of the purchase. Computer makers will pay more to get Intel processors if they believe that having an "Intel inside" sells more machines. Positioning efforts often focus on emotional benefits of a purchase to increase the significance of a benefit. Ads for L'Oréal hair color, for example, show closeups of beautiful hair while popular celebrities tell women

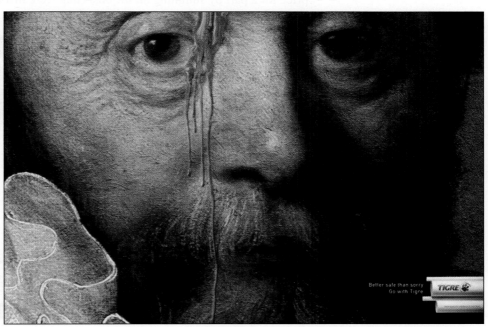

Business customers can be price sensitive unless given a reason to pay a higher price. Tigre sells pipes, fittings, and accessories for construction products—including an extensive line to prevent leaks. With this ad, "Better safe than sorry. Go with Tigre," Tigre wants to remind customers of the potential costs of a leaky pipe.
© 2015 Tigre S/A.

to buy it "because you're worth it." A consumer who cares about the price of a bottle of hair color might still have no question that she's worth the difference in price.

Customers are sometimes less price sensitive if there are *switching costs*—costs that a customer faces when buying a product that is different from what has been purchased or used in the past. For example, if a hair salon raises its prices, many customers will not switch to a new salon. The hassles of looking for a new stylist—and the risk of ending up with a bad hair day—usually make it easier to simply pay the higher price. The same thing can happen in a business context, where switching costs can be quite high. If Adobe raises the price of its Photoshop software, most managers are reluctant to add the costs of finding an alternative and training employees on a new product. Firms entering new markets like this need to find creative ways to lower switching costs. Incentives such as free trials or introductory price discounts may be used.

These factors apply in many different purchase situations, so it makes sense for a marketing manager to consider each of them in refining estimates of how customers might respond at different prices.[6]

Competitor analysis and price sensitivity

Customer demand depends on available alternatives. So a marketing manager can often improve pricing decisions and profitability by considering customer price sensitivity as part of a competitor analysis. The new CEO of Parker Hannifin (PH), a large industrial parts maker, realized this. Before he arrived, PH managers usually set the price for a part by summing all the costs that were involved in making it and then adding a 35 percent markup. Managers liked this approach; it was easy and also left some

Value in use pricing considers what a customer will save by buying a product. Both ClimateMaster and Hytorc tout the savings realized by switching to their products.
Left: © ClimateMaster, Inc. 2011. Right: Copyright © 2015 – HYTORC DIV UNEX Corporation; Agency: Stein Rogan & Partners, Chief Creative Officer: Tom Stein, Associate Creative Director/ Copywriter: Michael Ruby, Senior Art Director: Annabella Martamendi.

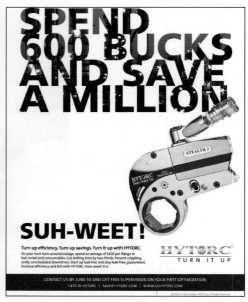

room for haggling. Yet the new CEO saw that they could improve what they were doing. First, he asked them to classify every product—and there were thousands—into categories. At one extreme, there was a new category for PH parts that were basically commodities and just like what competitors offered. At the other extreme, there was a category for PH parts that were important to customers and that were only available from PH. This category included a high-pressure valve that was used on airplane doors; no other supplier had a valve that worked as well for this critical application. Prices on parts in this last category were raised by 5 percent or more—as long as the price still represented a good value. On commodity parts, prices were reduced by 5 percent to beat competitors. And, of course, there were a number of other levels of price adjustment for categories between the extremes. Fine-tuning PH prices to consider competition was simple, but it increased profits by 25 percent.[7]

Value in use pricing— how much will the customer save?

Organizational buyers think about how a purchase will affect their total costs. Many marketers who aim at business markets keep this in mind when estimating demand and setting prices. They use **value in use pricing**—which means setting prices that will capture some of what customers will save by substituting the firm's product for the one currently being used.

For example, a producer of computer-controlled machines used to assemble cars knows that the machine doesn't just replace a standard machine. It also reduces labor costs, quality control costs, and—after the car is sold—costs of warranty repairs. The marketer can estimate what each auto producer will save by using the machine—and then set a price that makes it less expensive for the auto producer to buy the computerized machine than to stick with the old methods. The number of customers who have different levels of potential savings also provides some idea about the shape of the demand curve.

Creating a superior product that could save customers money doesn't guarantee that customers will be willing to pay a higher price. To capture the value created, the seller must convince buyers of the savings—and buyers are likely to be skeptical. A salesperson needs to be able to show proof of the claims.[8]

Auctions show what a customer will pay

Auctions have always been a way to determine exactly what some group of potential customers would pay, or not pay, for a product. However, the use of online auctions has dramatically broadened the use of this approach for both consumer and business products. Millions of auctions are on eBay each day. And some firms are setting up their own auctions, especially for products in short supply. The U.S. government is using online auctions as well. For example, the Federal Communications Commission (FCC) auctions rights to use airwaves for cell phones and other wireless devices. Count on more growth in online auctions.[9]

Some sellers use sequential price reductions

Some sellers are taking the auction approach and adapting it by using sequential price reductions over time. The basic idea is that the seller starts with a relatively high price and sells as much of the product as possible at that price, but plans from the start on a series of step-by-step price reductions until the product is sold out. This approach is most commonly used with products that have a short life or are in short supply, but which would just run up inventory costs if they are not sold. Retailers like TJ Maxx use this approach with women's fashions, and grocery stores use it with perishable food such as fruits and vegetables. Cruise lines sell space this way; they don't want the ship to sail with empty cabins. Some people may think of this as a "clearance" sale. But the difference here is that the plan from the outset is to work down the demand curve in steps—appealing to segments who are least price sensitive first—until all of a product is sold. However, sellers hope that if they offer the right products they'll never get to price reductions (which earn lower margins). Rather, they prefer to be bringing in the next round of products to start the process over again.

Customers may have reference prices

Some people don't devote much thought to what they pay for the products they buy, including some frequently purchased goods and services. But consumers often have a **reference price**—the price they expect to pay—for many of the products they purchase. And different customers may have different reference prices for the same basic type of purchase. For example, a person who really enjoys reading might have a higher reference price for a popular paperback book than another person who is only an occasional reader.[10]

If a firm's price is lower than a customer's reference price, customers may view the product as a better value and demand may increase. Sometimes a firm will try to position the benefits of its product in such a way that consumers compare it with a product that has a higher reference price. Public Broadcasting System TV stations do this when they ask viewers to make donations that match what they pay for "just one month of cable service." Insurance companies frame the price of premiums for homeowners' coverage in terms of the price to repair flood damage—and advertising makes the damage very vivid.

Leader pricing—make it low to attract customers

Leader pricing means setting some very low prices—real bargains—to get customers into retail stores. The idea is not only to sell large quantities of the leader items but also to get customers into the store to buy other products. Certain products are picked for their promotion value and priced low but above cost. In food stores, the leader prices are the "specials" that are advertised regularly to give an image of low prices. Leader pricing is normally used with products for which consumers do have a specific reference price.

Leader pricing can backfire if customers buy only the low-priced leaders. To avoid hurting profits, managers often select leader items that aren't directly competitive with major lines—as when bargain-priced blank CDs are a leader for an electronics store.[11]

Grocery stores often use leader pricing on milk. The stores hope to attract customers who will purchase more than just milk when they visit.

Used by Permission of Deutsch Inc. as Agent for National Fluid Milk Processor Promotion Board.

When is "free" a price?

Maybe the ultimate price from a consumer standpoint is "free"—with the expectation that at least some customers will pay later. In *"What's Next? Making money by giving your product away"* you can read more about this strategy.

Bait pricing—offer a steal, but sell under protest

Bait pricing is setting some very low prices to attract customers but trying to sell more expensive models or brands once the customer is in the store. For example, a furniture store may advertise a color TV for $199. But once bargain hunters come to the store, salespeople point out the disadvantages of the low-priced TV and try to convince them to trade up to a better, more expensive, set. Bait pricing is something like leader pricing. But here the seller *doesn't* plan to sell many at the low price.

If bait pricing is successful, the demand for higher-quality products expands. This approach may be a sensible part of a strategy to trade up customers. And customers may be well served if—once in the store—they find a higher-priced product offers features better suited to their needs. But bait pricing is also criticized as unethical.

Is bait pricing ethical?

Extremely aggressive and sometimes dishonest bait-pricing advertising has given this method a bad reputation. Some stores make it very difficult to buy the bait item. The Federal Trade Commission considers this type of bait pricing a deceptive act and

What's Next? Making money by giving your product away

One way to generate customer demand is to give your product away. This not-so-new approach to pricing is gaining popularity. There are a few reasons for the resurgence of this tactic. First, many digital products have near-zero variable costs. It costs almost nothing for Facebook to add another user or for one more customer to download Google's Picasa photo organizing and editing software. Direct distribution over the web adds no additional cost. Offering something for free generates buzz, and the promotional benefit often outweighs the cost of the giveaway—at least for a while. Finally, in some product categories, consumers expect things to be free. For example, most readers of online newspapers and magazines refuse to pay when publishers try to charge for subscriptions.

So how do firms give something away and still make money? One approach counts on advertisers to provide the revenue. "Free" attracts customer eyeballs, and advertisers pay for access to eyeballs. For example, Japanese photocopy shop Tadacopy offers college students free photocopies—with advertising on the back of each page. Because websites for CNN, Facebook, Google, and ESPN are free, each draws a larger audience than pay-to-view-websites. These larger audiences attract advertisers who pay fees to place ads. And Facebook and Google users give companies something more than space/exposure—they provide information about the "eyeballs" searching for products. These data are valuable to marketing managers trying to understand their target market.

Some companies offer a basic product for free, while charging for more for customers interested in premium—a strategy called "freemium" (combining the words "free" and "premium"). For example, Dropbox offers customers 2 gigabytes of free storage—and customers can pay for more. The revenue from paying customers allows Dropbox to cover the freeloaders. Many software applications—especially those on the Android Market and iPhone App Store—are given away for free, but include "in-app purchases." The "free" app serves as a risk-free customer trial.

The Brazilian music group Banda Calypso uses a variation of this approach. It gives street vendors masters of its CDs and CD liner art at no charge. The street vendors then burn CDs and sell them on the street. Sales of high-quality, low-priced CDs bring in new fans, and Banda Calypso benefits when some of these fans pay for tickets to the band's live performances.

A "free" strategy must be managed carefully. Once customers get something for free, they can be reluctant to pay for it later. The *New York Times* and other online news sites have struggled to get customers to pay a subscription fee. Before a firm offers something for nothing, it's important to think through what the firm gets in exchange—and how that achieves the firm's pricing objectives. "Free" usually works best when customers need to experience the value of the firm's offering to recognize the benefits.

Think about the examples shown here and other "free" products you know about. What is it about these products that allows them to make money while giving their products away? For what types of products would this business model not be likely to work?[12]

---

has banned its use in interstate commerce. Even well-known chains like Sears have been criticized for bait pricing.

Psychological pricing—some prices just seem right

Psychological pricing means setting prices that have special appeal to target customers. Some people think there are whole ranges of prices that potential customers see as the same. So price cuts in these ranges do not increase the quantity sold. But just below this range, customers may buy more. Then, at even lower prices, the quantity demanded stays the same again—and so on. Exhibit 18–11 shows the kind of demand curve that leads to psychological pricing. Vertical drops mark the price ranges that customers see as the same. Pricing research shows that there *are* such demand curves.[13]

Exhibit 18–11 Demand Curve When Psychological Pricing Is Appropriate

Odd-even pricing is setting prices that end in certain numbers. For example, products selling below $50 often end in the number 5 or the number 9—such as 49 cents or $24.95. Prices for higher-priced products are often $1 or $2 below the next even dollar figure—such as $99 rather than $100.

Some marketers use odd-even pricing because they think consumers react better to these prices—perhaps seeing them as "substantially" lower than the next highest even price. Marketers using these prices seem to assume that they have a rather jagged demand curve—that slightly higher prices will substantially reduce the quantity demanded.[14]

Price lining—a few prices cover the field

Price lining is setting a few price levels for a product line and then marking all items at these prices. This approach assumes that customers have a certain reference price in mind that they expect to pay for a product. For example, many neckties are priced between $20 and $50. In price lining, there are only a few prices within this range. Ties will not be priced at $20, $21, $22, $23, and so on. They might be priced at four levels—$20, $30, $40, and $50.

Price lining has advantages other than just matching prices to what consumers expect to pay. The main advantage is simplicity—for both salespeople and customers. It is less confusing than having many prices. Some customers may consider items in only one price class. Their big decision, then, is which item(s) to choose at that price.

For retailers, price lining has several advantages. Sales may increase because (1) they can offer a bigger variety in each price class and (2) it's easier to get customers to make decisions within one price class. Stock planning is simpler because demand is larger at the relatively few prices. Price lining can also reduce costs because inventory needs are lower.

Demand-backward pricing and prestige pricing

Demand-backward pricing is setting an acceptable final consumer price and working backward to what a producer can charge. It is commonly used by producers of consumer products, especially shopping products such as women's clothing and appliances. It is also used with gift items for which customers will spend a specific amount—because they are seeking a $10 or a $15 gift. Many of Mexico's low-income consumers carry only 5 or 10 peso coins. So Ace laundry detergent developed a new version of its product that adjusted features and manufacturing costs to meet a 10 peso price point.[15]

A restaurant may use demand-backward pricing to set a meal price that final consumers find attractive—while adjusting what food is included so that it's still profitable. Ferrari uses prestige pricing to signify the high quality and exclusivity of its sports cars.
Left: © 2015 TEXAS ROADHOUSE, INC. Right: Ferrari S.p.A. Copyright 2015 – All rights reserved.

Exhibit 18-12 Demand Curve Showing a Prestige Pricing Situation

The producer starts with the retail (reference) price for a particular item and then works backward—subtracting the typical margins that channel members expect. This gives the approximate price the producer can charge. Then the average or planned marketing expenses can be subtracted from this price to find how much can be spent producing the item. Candy companies do this. They alter the size of the candy bar to keep the bar at the expected price.

Prestige pricing is setting a rather high price to suggest high quality or high status. Some target customers want the best, so they will buy at a high price. But if the price seems cheap, they worry about quality and don't buy. Prestige pricing is most common for luxury products such as furs, jewelry, and perfume.

It is also common in service industries, where the customer can't see the product in advance and relies on price to judge its quality. Target customers who respond to prestige pricing give the marketing manager an unusual demand curve. Instead of a normal down-sloping curve, the curve goes down for a while and then bends back to the left again (see Exhibit 18–12).[16]

Pricing a Full Line

LO 18.7

Our emphasis has been, and will continue to be, on the problem of pricing an individual product mainly because this makes our discussion clearer. But most marketing managers are responsible for more than one product. In fact their "product" may be the whole company line! So we'll discuss this matter briefly.

Full-line pricing—market- or firm-oriented

Full-line pricing is setting prices for a whole line of products. How to do this depends on which of two basic situations a firm is facing.

In one case, all products in the company's line are aimed at the same general target market, which makes it important for all prices and value to be logically related. This is a common approach with shopping products. A producer of refrigerators might offer several models with different features at different prices to give its target customers some choice. The difference among the prices and benefits should appear reasonable when the target customers are evaluating them. Customer perceptions can be important here. A low-priced item, even one that is a good value at that price, may drag down the image of the higher end of the line. Alternatively, one item that consumers do not see as a good value may spill over to how they judge other products in the line. A marketing manager sometimes adds a higher-priced item to an existing product line to influence customer reference prices. The highest-priced product might not get many sales, but it makes the second-highest-product in the line appear less expensive by comparison.

> **Online Toolkit**
>
> Abt is an online retailer of appliances and electronics. Go to Abt's online site (**www.abt.com**). Enter "KitchenAid refrigerator" into the search bar. Then narrow the search by choosing "Side-by-Side Refrigerators." How many refrigerators come up? Scroll down and check the box marked "Compare" underneath two of the models and then click COMPARE. What is the price of each model? What additional features are available on more expensive models? Which model do you think sells the best? Why?

In other cases, the different products in the line are aimed at entirely different target markets so there doesn't have to be any relation between the various prices. A chemical producer of a wide variety of products with several target markets, for example, probably should price each product separately.

| Costs are complicated in full-line pricing | The marketing manager must try to recover all costs on the whole line—perhaps by pricing quite low on more competitive items and much higher on ones with unique benefits. However, estimating costs for each product is a challenge because there is no single right way to assign a company's fixed costs to each of the products. Regardless of how costs are allocated, any cost-oriented pricing method that doesn't consider demand can lead to very unrealistic prices. To avoid mistakes, the marketing manager should judge demand for the whole line as well as demand for each individual product in each target market. |

Costs are complicated in full-line pricing

The marketing manager must try to recover all costs on the whole line—perhaps by pricing quite low on more competitive items and much higher on ones with unique benefits. However, estimating costs for each product is a challenge because there is no single right way to assign a company's fixed costs to each of the products. Regardless of how costs are allocated, any cost-oriented pricing method that doesn't consider demand can lead to very unrealistic prices. To avoid mistakes, the marketing manager should judge demand for the whole line as well as demand for each individual product in each target market.

Complementary product pricing

Complementary product pricing is setting prices on several products as a group. This may lead to one product being priced very low so that the profits from another product will increase, thus increasing the product group's total profits. When Gillette introduced the M3Power battery-powered wet-shaving system, the shaver, two blade cartridges, and a Duracell battery had a relatively low suggested retail price of $14.99. However, the blade refill cartridges, which must be replaced frequently, come in a package of four at a hefty price of $10.99.

Complementary product pricing differs from full-line pricing because different production facilities may be involved—so there's no cost allocation problem. Instead, the problem is really understanding the target market and the demand curves for each of the complementary products. Then various combinations of prices can be tried to see what set will be best for reaching the company's pricing objectives.[17]

Product-bundle pricing— one price for several products

A firm that offers its target market several different products may use **product-bundle pricing**—setting one price for a set of products. Firms that use product-bundle pricing usually set the overall price so that it's cheaper for the customer to buy the products at the same time than separately. A bank may offer a product-bundle price for a safe-deposit box, traveler's checks, and a savings account. Bundling encourages customers to spend more and buy products that they might not otherwise buy; because the added cost of the extras is not as high as it would normally be, the value is better.

Most firms that use product-bundle pricing also set individual prices for the unbundled products. This may increase demand by attracting customers who want one item in a product assortment but don't want the extras. Many firms treat services this way. A software company may have a product-bundle price for its software and access to a toll-free telephone assistance service. However, customers who don't need help can pay a lower price and get just the software. Spirit Airlines successfully differentiates its offering from other airlines by *un*bundling the services most airlines offer. Spirit sells deeply discounted airfares and then charges customers for boarding passes, carry-on bags, water, and peanuts—all extras fliers usually receive for "free" on other airlines.[18]

Pizza Hut offers a bundle that includes pizza, wings, and Pepsi for a special price.
©2015 Pizza Hut, Inc. All rights reserved. The Pizza Hut name, logos, and related material are trademarks of Pizza Hut, Inc.

Bid Pricing and Negotiated Pricing Depend Heavily on Costs

LO 18.8

A new price for every job

We introduced the issue of competitive bidding in Chapter 6. But now let's take a closer look at bid pricing. **Bid pricing** means offering a specific price for each possible job rather than setting a price that applies for all customers. When submitting a bid price for a standardized product, the marketing manager may have to decide the firm's lowest acceptable price and how close to that price should be the bid. But in many situations bid pricing is more complicated. For example, building contractors and companies selling services (such as cleaning or data processing) often bid on large projects with many variables.

A big problem in bid pricing on a complicated job is estimating all the costs that will apply. This may sound easy, but a complicated bid may involve thousands of cost components. Further, management must include an overhead charge and a charge for profit.

Because many firms use an e-mail distribution list or website to solicit bids, the process is fast and easy for the buyer. But a seller has to be geared up to set a price and respond quickly. However, this system does allow the seller to set a price based on the precise situation and what costs and revenue are involved.

Bids are usually based on purchase specifications provided by the customer. The specs may be sent by e-mail or posted on a website. Sometimes the seller can win the business, even with a higher bid price, by suggesting changes in the specs that save the customer money.

At times, it isn't possible to figure out specs or costs in advance. This may lead to a negotiated contract where the customer agrees to pay the supplier's total cost plus an agreed-on profit figure (say, 10 percent of costs or a dollar amount)—after the job is finished.

Ethical issues in cost-plus bid pricing

Some unethical sellers give bid prices based on cost-plus contracts a bad reputation by faking their records to make costs seem higher than they really are. In other cases, there may be honest debate about what costs should be allowed. We've already considered, for instance, the difficulties in allocating fixed costs.

Demand must be considered too

Competition must be considered when adding in overhead and profit for a bid price. Usually, the customer will get several bids and accept the lowest one. So unthinking addition of typical overhead and profit rates should be avoided. Some bidders use the same overhead and profit rates on all jobs, regardless of competition, and then are surprised when they don't get some jobs.[19]

Many firms use software from companies such as Bid2Win to help manage the complex process of estimating costs and setting a bid price. *Copyright © B2W Software Inc. 1993-2015. All Rights Reserved.*

Negotiated prices—what will a specific customer pay?

Sometimes the customer asks for bids and then singles out the company that submits the *most attractive* bid, not necessarily the lowest, for further bargaining. What a customer will buy—if the customer buys at all—depends on the **negotiated price**, a price that is set based on bargaining between the buyer and seller. As with simple bid pricing, negotiated pricing is most common in situations where the marketing mix is adjusted for each customer—so bargaining may involve the whole marketing mix, not just the price level. Through the bargaining process, the seller tries to determine what aspects of the marketing mix are most important—and worth the most—to the customer.

Sellers must know their costs to negotiate prices effectively. However, negotiated pricing is a demand-oriented approach. Here the seller analyzes very carefully a particular customer's position on a demand curve, or on different possible demand curves based on different offerings, rather than the overall demand curve for a group of customers.

CONCLUSION

In this chapter, we discussed various approaches to price setting. Generally, retailers and wholesalers use markups. Some just use the same markups for all their items because it is simpler, but this is usually not the best approach. It's more effective to consider customer demand, competition, and how markups relate to turnover and profit.

It's important for marketing managers to understand costs; if customers are not willing to pay a price that is at least high enough to cover all of the costs of the marketing mix, the firm won't be profitable. So we describe the different types of cost that a marketing manager needs to understand and how average-cost pricing is used to set prices. But we note that this approach can fail because it ignores demand. We look at break-even analysis, which is a variation of the cost-oriented approach. It is useful for analyzing possible prices. However, managers must estimate demand to evaluate the chance of reaching these possible break-even points.

The major difficulty with demand-oriented pricing involves estimating the demand curve. But experienced managers, perhaps aided by marketing research, can estimate the nature of demand for their products. Even if estimates are not exact, they can help to get prices in the right ballpark—and there's usually a profitable range around the most profitable price. So marketers should consider demand when setting prices. We see this with value in use pricing, psychological pricing, odd-even pricing, full-line pricing, and even bid pricing. Understanding the factors that influence customer price sensitivity can make these approaches more effective.

Although we do not recommend that cost-oriented approaches be used by themselves, they do help the marketing manager understand the firm's profitability. Pricing decisions should consider the cost of offering the whole marketing mix. But smart marketers do not accept cost as a given—target marketers always look for ways to be more efficient—to reduce costs while improving the value that they offer customers.

WHAT'S NOW?

This chapter examined how managers set prices. For some current real-world examples and learnings, check out *What's Now?* at www.learnthe4ps.com/whatsnow/c18

KEY TERMS

LO 18.9

markup, 483	average variable cost (per unit), 488	odd-even pricing, 500
markup (percent), 483	break-even analysis, 491	price lining, 500
markup chain, 484	break-even point (BEP), 491	demand-backward pricing, 500
stockturn rate, 485	fixed-cost (FC) contribution per unit, 491	prestige pricing, 501
average-cost pricing, 486	marginal analysis, 492	full-line pricing, 501
total fixed cost, 488	value in use pricing, 497	complementary product pricing, 502
total variable cost, 488	reference price, 497	product-bundle pricing, 502
total cost, 488	leader pricing, 498	bid pricing, 503
average cost (per unit), 488	bait pricing, 498	negotiated price, 504
average fixed cost (per unit), 488	psychological pricing, 499	

QUESTIONS AND PROBLEMS

1. Review the Samsung case study that opens the chapter. From this case, identify examples of different key terms and concepts covered in the chapter. For example, "selling $2,000 and making $10" refers to markup.

2. Review the Samsung case study that opens this chapter. Explain how Samsung could make changes to its marketing strategy to address: a) price sensitivity, b) value in use pricing, and c) reference prices. How does it use product-line pricing? Go to the section of Samsung's website where its TVs are shown to better understand its television product line.

3. Why do many department stores seek a markup of about 30 percent when some discount houses operate on a 20 percent markup?

4. A producer distributed its riding lawn mowers through wholesalers and retailers. The retail selling price was $800, and the manufacturing cost to the company was $312. The retail markup was 35 percent and the wholesale markup 20 percent. What was the cost to the wholesaler? To the retailer? What percentage markup did the producer take?

5. Relate the concept of stock turnover to the growth of mass-merchandising. Use a simple example in your answer.

6. If total fixed costs are $200,000 and total variable costs are $100,000 at the output of 20,000 units, what are the probable total fixed costs and total variable costs at an output of 10,000 units? What are the average fixed costs, average variable costs, and average costs at these two output levels? Explain what additional information you would want to determine what price should be charged.

7. Construct an example showing that mechanical use of a very large or a very small markup might still lead to unprofitable operation whereas some intermediate price would be profitable. Draw a graph and show the break-even point(s).

8. The Davis Company's fixed costs for the year are estimated at $200,000. Its product sells for $250. The variable cost per unit is $200. Sales for the coming year are expected to reach $1,250,000. What is the break-even point? Expected profit? If sales are forecast at only $875,000, should the Davis Company shut down operations? Why?

9. Discuss the idea of drawing separate demand curves for different market segments. It seems logical because each target market should have its own marketing mix. But won't this lead to many demand curves and possible prices? And what will this mean with respect to discounts and varying prices in the marketplace? Will it be legal? Will it be practical?

10. Distinguish between leader pricing and bait pricing. What do they have in common? How can their use affect a marketing mix?

11. Cite a local example of psychological pricing and evaluate whether it makes sense.

12. Cite a local example of odd-even pricing and evaluate whether it makes sense.

13. How does a prestige pricing policy fit into a marketing mix? Would exclusive distribution be necessary?

14. Is a full-line pricing policy available only to producers? Cite local examples of full-line pricing. Why is full-line pricing important?

MARKETING PLANNING FOR HILLSIDE VETERINARY CLINIC

Appendix D (the Appendices follow Chapter 19) includes a sample marketing plan for Hillside Veterinary Clinic. Look through the "Marketing Strategy" section.

a. A veterinary clinic must have some system for dealing with emergencies that occur on weekends and at night when the clinic is closed. Individual vets usually rotate so that someone is always on call to handle emergencies. The price for emergency care is usually 50 percent higher than the price for care during normal hours. Do you think that Hillside should charge higher prices for emergency care? Does it fit with Hillside's strategy?

b. Some customers have expensive pedigree dogs and cats and are less price sensitive than others about fees for veterinary care. Do you think that it would be possible for Hillside to charge higher prices in caring for expensive pets? Why or why not?

SUGGESTED CASES

17. Simply Pure H2O4U, Inc.
24. WireX

27. Advanced Molding, Inc.
35. Skipper's Pizza Pies

MARKETING ANALYTICS: DATA TO KNOWLEDGE

CHAPTER 18 BREAK-EVEN/PROFIT ANALYSIS

This problem lets you see the dynamics of break-even analysis. The starting values (costs, revenues, etc.) for this problem are from the break-even analysis example in this chapter (see Exhibit 18–8).

The first column computes a break-even point. You can change costs and prices to figure new break-even points (in units and dol-

lars). The second column goes further. There you can specify target profit level, and the unit and dollar sales needed to achieve your target profit level will be computed. You can also estimate possible sales quantities, and the program will compute costs, sales, and profits. Use a spreadsheet to address these issues.

See Connect for the spreadsheet and questions needed to analyze this scenario.

CHAPTER NINETEEN

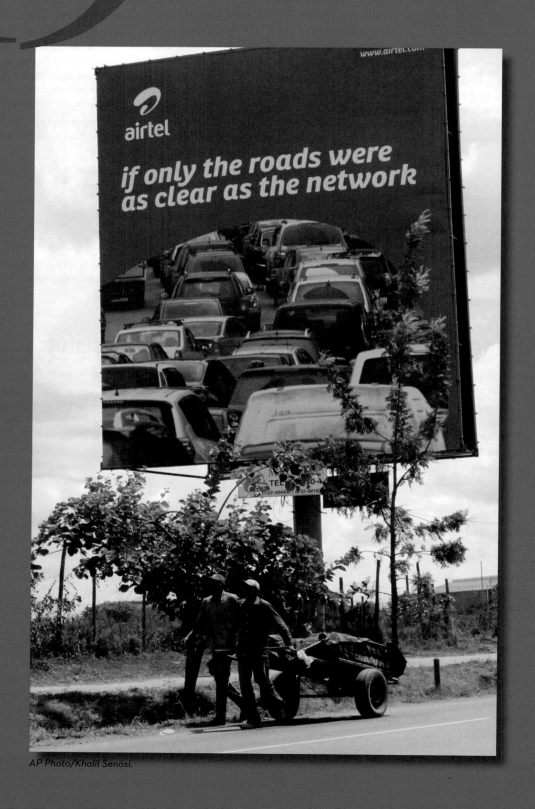

AP Photo/Khalil Senosi.

Ethical Marketing in a Consumer-Oriented World: Appraisal and Challenges

While consumers want marketplace choice, on a global scale we're not there yet. Someone in a village in Uganda may be able to get a glimpse of the quality of life that consumers in advanced Western economies enjoy, but for that person it doesn't seem real. What is real is the struggle of everyday life—living without electricity or running water—and, in fact, worrying about malnutrition, disease, and hunger. Cell phone carriers see growth opportunities in some of the world's poorest countries, yet average monthly billings are often less than $5. The vast majority of consumer-citizens in these societies can still only wonder if they'll ever have choices among a wide variety of goods and services—and the income to buy them—that most consumers take for granted in the United States, Canada, England, most countries in Western Europe, Australia, and a few other advanced economies.

Even in the face of a serious global economic downturn, the challenges faced by consumers and marketing managers in advanced economies seem minor by contrast. In England, for example, some consumers who live in villages that are off the beaten path may worry, instead, that they are not included in the 96 percent of the British population served by Tesco delivery vans. Tesco, the largest supermarket chain in England, created its online shopping service for groceries (and hundreds of other products) just a few years ago, but now its fleet of vans make hundreds of thousands of deliveries a week.

If online shopping for groceries has had a slower start in the United States, it just may be because many Americans are more interested in instant gratification. We expect the corner convenience store to have a nice selection of frozen gourmet dinners that we can prepare in minutes in a microwave oven. Or perhaps that's too much hassle. After all, Domino's will deliver a hot pizza in less than 30 minutes. And McDonald's has our Egg McMuffin ready when we pull up at the drive-thru at 7:00 in the morning. In a relative sense, few of the world's consumers can expect so much and get so much of what they expect.

But is it a good thing that firms give us what we want? Think about how automakers offered SUVs to appeal to consumers. SUVs do satisfy many of the needs of suburban lifestyles. But most are gas guzzlers and pollute our air. Some critics even charge that the United States has jumped into wars in the Middle East because of such over-reliance on oil. On the other hand, as both gas prices and consumer environmental sensitivity have increased, producers have responded with hybrid technologies and electric vehicles. Clean hydrogen vehicles may even be in our future. Of course, such adjustments take time.

Much national attention is now directed toward problems of obesity, especially among children. In the United States, more than a third of children and adolescents weigh too much. Actually, the surge of obesity among children is a global trend. Nutritionists say that in the United States and elsewhere, the key culprits are too much fat, starch, and sugar in diets. World Health Organization experts say that today's levels of childhood obesity will later lead to an explosion of illnesses (such as heart disease, diabetes, and hypertension) that will drain economies, create enormous suffering, and cause premature deaths. Many nutritionists and public health officials point the finger of blame at food processors and fast food. When a group of obese teenagers sued McDonald's, claiming that it made them fat, the widely publicized case was fodder for jokes on late-night TV shows. But fast-food companies are not laughing. The judge threw out the case but left open the door for future suits. Some legal experts say that this is just the beginning of legal actions—and they draw the parallel with suits against tobacco companies 30 years ago. Many fast-food companies are scrambling to add salads, fruit, and other low-fat fare to their menus. Do you think consumers should have the right to choose high-fat foods if that is what they want?

When you think about the contrast between problems of starvation and too much fast food, it's not hard to decide which consumers are better off. But is that just a straw man comparison? Is the situation in less-developed nations one extreme, with the system in the United States and similar societies just as extreme—only in a different way?

Would we be better off if we didn't put quite so much emphasis on marketing? Do we need so many brands of products? Does all the money we spend on advertising really help consumers? Should we expect access to fast food any hour of the day—or to order groceries over the Internet and have a van deliver them to our front door? Conversely, do all of these choices just increase the prices consumers pay without really adding anything of value? More generally, does marketing serve society well?

These questions are what this chapter is about. Now that you have a better understanding of what marketing is all about, and how the marketing manager contributes to the macro-marketing process, you should be able to decide whether marketing costs too much.[1]

LEARNING OBJECTIVES

Throughout the text, we've discussed ways that marketing can help customers while also meeting a firm's objectives. We've also considered many related ethical and societal questions. In this chapter, we evaluate the overall costs and benefits of marketing to society. This leads into an explanation of how to prepare a marketing plan—because the marketing plan integrates all of the decisions in the marketing strategy planning process and thus guides the firm toward more effective marketing.

When you finish this chapter, you should be able to

1 Understand why marketing must be evaluated differently at the micro and macro levels.

2 Understand why this text argues that micro-marketing costs too much.

3 Understand why this text argues that macro-marketing does not cost too much.

4 Understand all of the elements of the marketing strategy planning process and strategy decisions for the Four Ps.

5 Know how to prepare a marketing plan and how it relates to the marketing strategy planning process.

6 Know some of the challenges marketers face as they work to develop ethical marketing strategies that serve consumers' needs.

How Should Marketing Be Evaluated?

LO 19.1

We must evaluate at two levels

We've stressed the need for marketing to satisfy customers at a cost that customers consider a good value. So in this final chapter we'll focus on both customer satisfaction and the costs of marketing as we evaluate marketing's impact on society (see Exhibit 19–1). As we discussed in Chapter 1, it's useful to distinguish between two levels of marketing. Managerial (micro) marketing concerns the marketing activities of an individual firm, whereas macro-marketing concerns how the whole marketing system works. Some complaints against marketing are aimed at only one of these levels at a time. In other cases, the criticisms seem to be directed to one level but actually are aimed at the other. Some critics of specific ads, for example, probably would not be satisfied with any advertising. When evaluating marketing, we must treat each of these levels separately.

Nation's objectives affect evaluation

Different nations have different social and economic objectives. Dictatorships, for example, may be mainly concerned with satisfying the needs of society as seen by the political elite. In a socialist state, the objective might be to satisfy society's needs as defined by government planners. In some societies, the objectives are defined by religious leaders. In others, it's whoever controls the military.

Exhibit 19-1 Ethical Marketing in a Consumer-Oriented World

Marketing's Impact on Society: Micro and Macro Views

Evaluating marketing
- Micro versus macro criteria
- Measuring consumer satisfaction
- Micro-marketing often costs too much
- Macro-marketing does not cost too much

Putting together innovative marketing plans
- Strategy planning process
- Understanding customers
- Blending marketing mix
- Content of the marketing plan

Challenges facing marketers
- Opportunities for improvement
- Marketing managers and social responsibility
- How far should the marketing concept go?

Consumer satisfaction is the objective in the United States

In the United States, *the basic objective of our market-directed economic system has been to satisfy consumer needs as they, the consumers, see them.* This objective implies that political freedom and economic freedom go hand in hand and that citizens in a free society have the right to live as they choose. The majority of American consumers would be unwilling to give up the freedom of choice they now enjoy. The same can be said for Canada, Great Britain, and most other countries in the European Union. To maintain focus, we will concentrate on marketing as it exists in American society.

Therefore, let's try to evaluate the operation of marketing in the American economy—where the present objective is to satisfy consumer needs *as consumers see them.* This is the essence of our system.

Can Consumer Satisfaction Be Measured?

Because consumer satisfaction is our objective, marketing's effectiveness must be measured by *how well* it satisfies consumers. There have been various efforts to measure overall consumer satisfaction—not only in the United States but also in other countries. For example, a team of researchers at the University of Michigan has created the American Customer Satisfaction Index based on regular interviews with tens of thousands of customers of about 230 companies in 43 industries. Similar studies are available for member countries of the European Union.

Satisfaction depends on individual aspirations

This sort of index makes it possible to track changes in consumer satisfaction measures over time and even allows comparison among countries. That's potentially useful. Yet there are limits to interpreting any measure of consumer satisfaction when we try to evaluate macro-marketing effectiveness in any absolute sense. One basic issue is that satisfaction depends on and is *relative to* your level of aspiration or expectation. Less prosperous consumers begin to expect more out of an economy as they see the higher living standards of others. Also, aspiration levels tend to rise with repeated successes and fall with failures. Products considered satisfactory one day may not be satisfactory the next day, or vice versa. Thirty years ago, most people were satisfied with a 21-inch color TV that pulled in three or four channels. But once you become accustomed to a large-screen HD model and enjoy all the options possible with a digital satellite receiver, on-demand programs, and a DVR, that old TV is never the same again.

In addition, consumer satisfaction is a highly personal concept. Thus, looking at the "average" satisfaction of a whole society does not provide a complete picture for evaluating macro-marketing effectiveness. At a minimum, some consumers are more satisfied than others. So, although efforts to measure satisfaction are useful, any evaluation of macro-marketing effectiveness has to be in part subjective.

Probably the supreme test is whether the macro-marketing system satisfies enough individual consumer-citizens so that they vote—in the ballot box—to keep it running. So far, we've done so in the United States.[2]

There are many measures of micro-marketing effectiveness

Measuring the marketing effectiveness of an individual firm is also difficult, but it can be done. Expectations may change just as other aspects of the market environment change—so firms have to do a good job of coping with the change. Individual business firms can and should try to measure how well their marketing mixes satisfy their customers (or why they fail). In fact, most large firms now have some type of ongoing effort to determine whether they're satisfying their target markets. For example, the J.D. Power and Associates marketing research firm is well known for its studies of consumer satisfaction with different makes of automobiles and computers. And the American Customer Satisfaction Index is also used to rate individual companies.

Planetfeedback.com makes it easy for consumers to give feedback to companies.

Many large and small firms measure customer satisfaction with attitude research studies. Other widely used methods include comment cards, e-mail response features on websites, unsolicited consumer responses (usually complaints), opinions of intermediaries and salespeople, market test results, and profits. Of course, customers may be very satisfied with some aspects of what a firm is doing but dissatisfied about other dimensions of performance.[3]

In our market-directed system, it's up to each customer to decide how effectively individual firms satisfy his or her needs. Usually, customers will buy more of the products that satisfy them—and they'll do it repeatedly. That's why firms that develop really satisfying marketing mixes are able to develop profitable long-term relationships with the customers that they serve. Because efficient marketing plans can increase profits, profits can be used as a rough measure of a firm's efficiency in satisfying customers. Nonprofit organizations have a different bottom line, but they too will fail if they don't satisfy supporters and get the resources they need to continue to operate.

Evaluating marketing effectiveness is difficult, but not impossible

It's easy to see why opinions differ concerning the effectiveness of micro- and macro-marketing. If the objective of the economy is clearly defined, however—and the argument is stripped of emotion—the big questions about marketing effectiveness probably *can* be answered.

In this chapter, we argue that micro-marketing (how individual firms and channels operate) frequently *does* cost too much but that macro-marketing (how the whole marketing system operates) *does not* cost too much, *given the present objective of the American economy—consumer satisfaction.* Don't accept this position as *the* answer but rather as a point of view. In the end, you'll have to make your own judgment.[4]

Micro-Marketing Often Does Cost Too Much

LO 19.2

Throughout the text, we've explored what marketing managers could or should do to help their firms do a better job of satisfying customers—while achieving company objectives. Many firms implement highly successful marketing programs, but others are still too production-oriented and inefficient. For customers of these latter firms, micro-marketing often does cost too much.

Research shows that many consumers are not satisfied; but you know that already. All of us have had experiences when we weren't satisfied—when some firm didn't deliver on its promises. And the problem is much bigger than some marketers want to believe. Research suggests that the majority of consumer complaints are never reported. Worse, many complaints that are reported never get fully resolved.

Coke spent many millions of dollars to develop and promote Blak, a fusion of cola and coffee that was sold in the energy drink category. After more than a year of investments to build the brand, Coke finally abandoned the effort. Even companies with outstanding marketing talents sometimes make expensive marketing mistakes.
© William D. Perreault, Jr., Ph.d.

The failure rate is high

Further evidence that too many firms are too production-oriented—and not nearly as efficient as they could be—is the fact that so many new products fail. New and old businesses—even ones that in the past were leaders in their markets—fail regularly too.

Generally speaking, marketing inefficiencies are due to one or both of these reasons:

1. Lack of interest in or understanding of the sometimes fickle customer.
2. Improper blending of the Four Ps—lack of understanding of or adjustment to the market environment, especially what competitors do.

Either of these problems can easily be a fatal flaw—the sort of thing that leads to business failures. A firm can't create value if it doesn't have a clue what customers think or say. Even if a firm listens to the "voice of the customer," there's no incentive for the customer to buy if the benefits of the marketing mix don't exceed the costs. And if the firm succeeds in coming up with a marketing mix with benefits greater than costs, it still won't be a superior value unless it's better than what competitors offer.

The high cost of missed opportunities

Another sign of failure is the inability of firms to identify new target markets and new opportunities. A new marketing mix that isn't offered doesn't fail—but the lost opportunity can be significant for both a firm and society. Too many managers seize on whatever strategy seems easiest rather than seeking really new ways to satisfy customers. Too many companies stifle really innovative thinking. Layers of bureaucracy and a "that's not the way we do things" mentality can snuff it out.

On the other hand, not every new idea is a good idea for every company. Many firms have lost millions of dollars with failed efforts to jump on the "what's new" bandwagon—without stopping to figure out how it is going to really satisfy the customer and result in profit for the firm. That is as much a ticket for failure as being too slow or bureaucratic.

Ethical Dilemma

What would you do? Your firm has a new strategy that will make its established product obsolete. However, it will take a year before you are ready to implement the new strategy. If you announce your plan in advance, profits will disappear because many customers and intermediaries will delay purchases until the new product is released. If you don't announce the new plan, customers and intermediaries will continue to buy the established product as their needs dictate, but some will be stuck owning the inferior product and won't do business with you again in the future. How would you handle this situation? Explain the reasoning for your decisions.

Micro-marketing does cost too much, but things are changing

For reasons like these, marketing does cost too much in many firms. Despite much publicity, the marketing concept is not applied in many places.

But not all firms and marketers deserve criticism. More of them *are* becoming customer-oriented. And many are paying more attention to market-oriented planning to carry out the marketing concept more effectively. Throughout the text, we've highlighted firms and strategies that are making a difference. The successes of innovative firms—such as Nike, Cirque du Soleil, Amazon.com, LEGO, Apple, iRobot, Method, and GEICO—do not go unnoticed. Yes, they make some mistakes. That's human—and marketing is a human enterprise. But they have also shown the results that market-oriented strategy planning can produce.

Another encouraging sign is that more companies are recognizing that they need a diverse set of backgrounds and talents to meet the increasingly varied needs of their increasingly global customers. They're shedding "not-invented-here" biases and embracing new technologies, comparing what they do with the best practices of firms in totally different industries, and teaming up with outside specialists who can bring a fresh perspective.

Chipotle's target market appreciates its commitment to offering "food with integrity." That requires a total company effort—from organizational buyers who make sure the ingredients are sustainably raised to the servers in the stores that offer a friendly smile and fast service. This leads to high customer satisfaction and profits for Chipotle.

© 2015 Chiopotle Mexican Grill.

Managers who adopt the marketing concept as a way of business life do a better job. They look for target market opportunities and carefully blend the elements of the marketing mix to meet their customers' needs. As more of these managers rise in business, we can look forward to much lower micro-marketing costs and strategies that do a better job of satisfying customer needs.

Macro-Marketing Does Not Cost Too Much

LO 19.3

Some critics of marketing take aim at the macro-marketing system. They typically argue that the macro-marketing system causes a poor use of resources and leads to an unfair distribution of income. Most of these complaints imply that some marketing activities by individual firms should not be permitted—and because they are, our macro-marketing system does a less-than-satisfactory job. Let's look at some of these positions to help you form your own opinion.

Micro-efforts help the economy grow

Some critics feel that marketing helps create a monopoly or at least monopolistic competition. Further, they think this leads to higher prices, restricted output, and reduction in national income and employment.

It's true that firms in a market-directed economy try to carve out separate monopolistic markets for themselves with new products. But consumers do have a choice. They don't *have* to buy the new product unless they think it's a better value. The old products are still available. In fact, to meet the new competition, prices of the old products usually drop. And that makes them even more affordable.

Over several years, the innovator's profits may rise—but rising profits also encourage further innovation by competitors. This leads to new investments, which contribute to economic growth and higher levels of national income and employment. Around the world, many countries failed to achieve their potential for economic growth under command systems because this type of profit incentive didn't exist.

Increased profits also attract competition. Profits and prices then begin to drop as new competitors enter the market and begin producing somewhat similar products. (Recall the rise and fall of industry profit during the product life cycle.)

Is advertising a waste of resources?

Advertising is the most criticized of all micro-marketing activities. Indeed, many ads *are* annoying, insulting, misleading, and downright ineffective. This is one reason why micro-marketing often does cost too much. However, advertising can also make both the micro- and macro-marketing processes work better.

Advertising is an economical way to inform large numbers of potential customers about a firm's products. Provided that a product satisfies customer needs, advertising can increase demand for the product—resulting in economies of scale in manufacturing, distribution, and sales. Because these economies may more than offset advertising costs, advertising can actually *lower* prices to the consumer.[5]

Consumers are not puppets

The idea that firms can manipulate consumers to buy anything the company chooses to produce simply isn't true. A consumer who buys a soft drink that tastes terrible won't buy another can of that brand, regardless of how much it's advertised. In fact, many new products fail the test of the market. Not even large corporations are assured of success every time they launch a new product. Consider, for example, the dismal fate of Pets.com and eToys.com, Ford's Edsel, Sony's beta format VCRs, Xerox's personal computers, and half of the TV programs put on the air in recent years. And if powerful corporations know some way to get people to buy products against their will, would companies such as Lucent, General Motors, and Eastern Airlines ever have gone through long periods losing hundreds of millions of dollars?

Needs and wants change

Consumer needs and wants change constantly. Few of us would care to live the way our grandparents lived when they were our age. Marketing's job is not just to satisfy consumer wants as they exist at any particular point in time. Rather, marketing must keep looking for new *and* better ways to create value and serve consumers.[6]

Does marketing make people materialistic?

There is no doubt that marketing caters to materialistic values. However, people disagree as to whether marketing creates these values or simply appeals to values already there.

Even in the most primitive societies, people want to accumulate possessions. The tendency for ancient pharaohs to surround themselves with wealth and treasures can hardly be attributed to the persuasive powers of advertising agencies!

Products do improve the quality of life

Clearly, the quality of life can't be measured just in terms of quantities of material goods. But when we view products as the means to an end rather than the end itself, they *do* make it possible to satisfy higher-level needs. The Internet, for example, empowers people with information in ways that few of us could have even imagined a decade ago.

Marketing reflects our own values

Critics say that advertising elevates the wrong values—for example, by relying on sex appeal to get attention—and generally sending the signal that what really matters most is self-gratification. For example, GoDaddy.com sells Internet domain names and related services. Its stated objective for a Super Bowl ad was to create the most talked about ad ever, and it figured that a risqué ad was the way to go. The ad that it ultimately aired (after trying another dozen or so ideas that were rejected as inappropriate for TV) was a spoof on Janet Jackson's "wardrobe malfunction" during the Super Bowl halftime show the previous year. The sexy woman dancing around in the commercial doesn't have anything to do with GoDaddy.com, but she did get a lot of attention and GoDaddy's awareness levels went up significantly. A survey showed that it was one of the four most liked commercials during the Super Bowl and the year, but also one of the four most disliked. There are thousands of other ads that rely on something related to sex to get attention. But is it advertising that creates interest in sex or something else? Experts who study values seem to agree that, in the short run, marketing reflects social values while in the long run it enhances and reinforces them. Further, many companies work hard to figure out their customers' beliefs and values. Then they refuse to use ads that would be offensive to their target customers.[7]

Micro-marketing does not cost too much when firms understand and address customer needs and wants with an effective marketing mix. Some customers prefer not to use dangerous chemicals on their skin to keep bugs and mosquitoes away, so Shieldtox Naturgard uses natural ingredients to offer continuous control of flying insects. Saridon's clever advertising reminds customers that its tablets are a good way to manage a headache.

Left: © Copyright Reckitt Benckiser Group plc. All rights reserved; Agency: Euro RSCG Bangkok. Right: BBDO Guerrero/Proximity Philippines; Chief Executive Officer: David Guerrero; Executive Creative Director: Brandie Tan; Creative Director: Gary Amante' Creative Director: Rey Tiempo; Account Director: Cindy Evangelista; Senior Account Manager: Iking Uy; Print Producer: Al Salvador; Photographers: Paolo Gripo & Abet Bagay; Retouchers: Oliver Brillantes & Vilma Magsino; Client: Bayer Philippines/Consumer Care; Brand Managers: Edward Go & Christian Galvez.

Not all needs are met

Some critics argue that our macro-marketing system is flawed because it does not provide solutions to important problems, such as questions about how to help the homeless, the uneducated, dependent children, minorities who have suffered discrimination, the elderly poor, and the sick. Many of these people do live in dire circumstances. But is that the result of a market-directed system?

There is no doubt that many firms focus their effort on people who can pay for what they have to offer. But, as the forces of competition drive down prices, more people are able to afford more of what they need. And the matching of supply and demand stimulates economic growth, creates jobs, and spreads income among more people. In other words, a market-directed economy makes efficient use of resources. However, it can't guarantee that government aid programs are effective. It doesn't ensure that all voters and politicians agree on which problems should be solved first—or how taxes should be set and allocated. It can't eliminate the possibility of a child being ignored.

These are important societal issues. Consumer-citizens in a democratic society assign some responsibilities to business and some to government. Ultimately, consumer-citizens vote in the ballot box for how they want governments to deal with these concerns—just as they vote with their dollars for which firms to support. As more managers in the public sector understand and apply marketing concepts, we should be able to do a better job meeting the needs of all people.

Marketing Strategy Planning Process Requires Logic and Creativity

LO 19.4

We've said that our macro-marketing system *does not* cost too much, given that customer satisfaction is the present objective of our economy. But we admit that the performance of many business firms leaves a lot to be desired. This presents a challenge to serious-minded students and marketers—and raises the question: What needs to be done?

Exhibit 19-2 Overview of Marketing Strategy Planning Process

We hope that this book has convinced you that a large part of the answer to that question is that the *effectiveness and value of marketing efforts in individual firms is improved significantly when managers take the marketing concept seriously—and when they apply the marketing strategy planning process we've presented.* So let's briefly review these ideas and show how they can be integrated into a marketing plan.

Marketing strategy planning process brings focus to efforts

Developing a good marketing strategy and turning the strategy into a marketing plan requires creative blending of the ideas we've discussed throughout this text. Exhibit 19–2 provides a broad overview of the major areas we've been talking about. You first saw this exhibit in Chapter 2—before you learned what's really involved in each idea. Now we must integrate ideas about these different areas to narrow down to a specific target market and marketing mix that represents a real opportunity. This narrowing-down process requires a thorough understanding of the market. That understanding is enhanced by careful analysis of customers' needs, current or prospective competitors, and the firm's own objectives and resources. Similarly, trends in the external market environment may make a potential opportunity more or less attractive.

There are usually more different strategy possibilities than a firm can pursue. Each possible strategy usually has a number of different potential advantages and disadvantages. This can make it difficult to zero in on the best target market and marketing mix. However, as we discussed in Chapter 3, developing a set of specific qualitative and quantitative screening criteria—to define what business and market(s) the firm wants to compete in—can help eliminate potential strategies that are not well suited to the firm.

Careful analysis helps the manager focus on a strategy that takes advantage of the firm's strengths and opportunities while avoiding its weaknesses and threats to its success. These strengths and weaknesses can be compared with the pros and cons of strategies that are considered. For example, if a firm is considering a strategy that focuses on a target market that is already satisfied by a competitor's offering, finding a competitive advantage might require an innovative new product, improved distribution, more effective promotion, or a better price. Just offering a

Bolthouse Farms saw an opportunity to sell more baby carrots. Because teenagers were their target market, they knew that a "healthy snack" positioning was probably not the best approach. So they developed a creative marketing strategy to appeal to this target market: "Eat 'em like junk food." Creative packaging, fun promotion, and distribution in school lunchroom vending machines were just part of the strategy that helped grow a previously stagnant market for baby carrots.

Courtesy HL Group/New York.

marketing mix similar to the competition's usually doesn't provide any real basis for the firm to position or differentiate its marketing mix as offering superior customer value.

Marketing manager must blend the Four Ps

Exhibit 19–3 reviews the major marketing strategy decision areas organized by the Four Ps. Each of these requires careful decision making. Yet marketing planning involves much more than just independent decisions and assembling the parts into a marketing mix. The Four Ps must be creatively *blended*—so the firm develops the best

Exhibit 19-3
Strategy Decision Areas Organized by the Four Ps

Product	Place	Promotion	Price

• Physical good
• Service
• Features
• Benefits
• Quality level
• Accessories
• Installation
• Instructions
• Warranty
• Product lines
• Packaging
• Branding
	• Objectives
	• Channel type
	• Market exposure
	• Kinds of intermediaries
	• Kinds and locations of stores
	• How to handle transporting and storing
	• Service levels
	• Recruiting intermediaries
	• Managing channels
		• Objectives
		• Promotion blend
		• Salespeople
		  Kind
		  Number
		  Selection
		  Training
		  Motivation
		• Advertising
		  Targets
		  Kinds of ads
		  Media type
		  Copy thrust
		  Prepared by whom
		• Publicity
		• Sales promotion
			• Objectives
			• Flexibility
			• Level over product life cycle
			• Geographic terms
			• Discounts
			• Allowances

mix for its target market. In other words, each decision must work well with all of the others to make a logical whole.

In our discussion, we've given the job of integrating the Four Ps strategy decisions to the marketing manager. Now you should see the need for this integrating role. It is easy for specialists to focus on their own areas and expect the rest of the company to work for or around them. This is especially true in larger firms where the size of the whole marketing job is too big for one person. Yet the ideas of the product manager, the advertising manager, the sales manager, the logistics manager, and whoever makes pricing decisions may have to be adjusted to improve the whole mix. It's critical that each marketing mix decision work well with all of the others. A breakdown in any one decision area may doom the whole strategy to failure.

The Marketing Plan Brings All the Details Together

LO 19.5

Marketing plan provides a blueprint for implementation

Once the manager has selected the target market, decided on the (integrated) marketing mix to meet that target market's needs, and developed estimates of the costs and revenues for that strategy, it's time to put it all together in the marketing plan. As we explained in Chapter 2, a marketing plan includes the time-related details—including costs and revenues—for a marketing strategy. Thus, the plan basically serves as a blueprint for what the firm will do.

Exhibit 19–4 provides a summary outline of the different sections of a complete marketing plan. You can see that this outline is basically an abridged overview of the topics we've covered throughout the text. Thus, you can flesh out your thinking for any portion of a marketing plan by reviewing the section of the book where that topic is discussed in more detail. Further, the Hillside Veterinary Clinic case in Appendix D provides a real example of the types of thinking and detail that are included.

Marketing plan spells out the timing of the strategy

Some time schedule is implicit in any strategy. A marketing plan simply spells out this time period and the time-related details. Usually, we think in terms of some reasonable length of time—such as six months, a year, or a few years. But it might be only a month or two in some cases, especially when rapid changes in fashion or technology are important. Or a strategy might be implemented over several years, perhaps the length of the early stages of the product's life.

Although the outline in Exhibit 19–4 does not explicitly show a place for the time frame for the plan or the specific costs for each decision area, these should be included in the plan—along with expected estimates of sales and profit—so that the plan can be compared with *actual performance* in the future. In other words, the plan not only makes it clear to everyone what is to be accomplished and how—it also provides a basis for the control process after the plan is implemented.[8]

A complete plan spells out the reasons for decisions

The plan outline shown in Exhibit 19–4 is quite complete. It doesn't just provide information about marketing mix decisions—it also includes information about customers (including segmenting dimensions), competitors' strategies, other aspects of the market environment, and the company's objectives and resources. This material provides important background information relevant to the "why" of the marketing mix and target market decisions.

Too often, managers do not include this information; their plans just lay out the details of the target market and the marketing mix strategy decisions. This shortcut approach is more common when the plan is really just an update of a strategy that has been in place for some time. However, that approach can be risky.

Managers too often make the mistake of casually updating plans in minor ways—perhaps just changing some costs or sales forecasts—but otherwise sticking with

<u>**Situation Analysis**</u>
Company Analysis
    Company objectives and overall marketing objectives
    Company resources (marketing, production, financial, human, etc.)
    Other marketing plans (marketing program)
    Previous marketing strategy
    Major screening criteria relevant to product-market opportunity selected
        Quantitative (ROI, profitability, risk level, etc.)
        Qualitative (nature of business preferred, social responsibility, environment, etc.)
    Major constraints
    Marketing collaborators (current and potential)
Customer Analysis (organizational customers and/or final consumers)
    Product-market
    Possible segmenting dimensions (customer needs, other characteristics)
        Qualifying dimensions and determining dimensions
    Identify target market(s) (one or more specific segments)
        Operational characteristics (demographics, geographic locations, etc.)
    Potential size (number of people, dollar purchase potential, etc.) and likely growth
    Key economic, psychological, and social influences on buying
    Type of buying situation
    Nature of relationship with customers
Competitor Analysis
    Nature of current/likely competition
    Current and prospective competitors (or rivals)
        Current strategies and likely responses to plan
    Competitive barriers to overcome and sources of potential competitive advantage
Analysis of the Market Context—External Market Environment
    Economic environment
    Technological environment
    Political and legal environment
    Cultural and social environment
Key Factors from Situation Analysis
    S.W.O.T.: Strengths, weaknesses, opportunities, and threats from situation analysis
<u>**Marketing Plan Objectives**</u>
    Specific objectives to be achieved with the marketing strategy
<u>**Differentiation and Positioning**</u>
    How will marketing mix be differentiated from the competition?
    How will the market offering be positioned?
    Positioning statement
<u>**Marketing Strategy**</u>
Overview of the Marketing Strategy
    General direction for the marketing strategy
    Description of how the Four Ps fit together
Target Market(s)
    Summary of characteristics of the target market(s) to be approached
Product
    Product class (type of consumer or business product)
    Current product life-cycle stage
    New-product development requirements (people, dollars, time, etc.)
    Product liability, safety, and social responsibility considerations
    Specification of core physical good or service
        Features, quality, etc.
    Supporting service(s) needed
    Warranty (what is covered, timing, who will support, etc.)
    Branding (manufacturer versus dealer, family versus individual, etc.)

continued

Packaging
  Promotion and labeling needs
  Protection needs
Cultural sensitivity of product
Fit with product line
Place
  Objectives
    Degree of market exposure required
    Distribution customer service level required
  Type of channel (direct, indirect)
    Other channel members or collaborators required
    Type/number of wholesalers (agent, merchant, etc.)
    Type/number of retailers
    How discrepancies and separations will be handled
    How marketing functions will be shared
  Coordination needed in company, channel, and supply chain
    Information requirements (EDI, the Internet, e-mail, etc.)
  Transportation requirements
  Inventory product-handling requirements
  Facilities required (warehousing, distribution centers, etc.)
  Reverse channels (for returns, recalls, etc.)
Promotion
  Objectives
  Major message theme(s) (for integrated marketing communications/positioning)
  Promotion blend
    Advertising (type, media, copy thrust, etc.)
    Personal selling (type and number of salespeople, compensation, effort allocation, etc.)
    Publicity
    Sales promotion (for customers, channel members, employees)
    Interactive media
  Mix of push and pull required
  Who will do the work?
Price
  Nature of demand (price sensitivity, price of substitutes)
  Demand and cost analyses (marginal analysis)
  Markup chain in channel
  Price flexibility
  Price level(s) (under what conditions) and impact on customer value
  Adjustments to list price (geographic terms, discounts, allowances, etc.)
Marketing Information Requirements
  Marketing research needs (with respect to customers, Four Ps, external environment, etc.)
  Secondary and primary data needs
  Marketing information system needs, models to be used, and so on
Implementation and Control
Special Implementation Problems to Overcome
  People required
  Manufacturing, financial, and other resources needed
Control
  Marketing information systems and data needed
  Criterion measures/comparison with objectives (customer satisfaction, sales, cost, performance analysis, etc.)
Budget, Sales Forecasts, and Estimates of Profit
  Costs (all elements in plan, over time)
  Sales (by market, over time, etc.)
  Estimated operating statement (pro forma)
Timing
  Specific sequence of activities and events, and so on
  Likely changes over the product life cycle
Risk Factors and Contingency Plans

what was done in the past. A big problem with this approach is that it's easy to lose sight of why those strategy decisions were made in the first place. When the market situation changes, the original reasons may no longer apply. Yet if the logic for those strategy decisions is not retained, it's easy to miss changes taking place that should result in a plan being reconsidered. For example, a plan that was established in the growth stage of the product life cycle may have been very successful for a number of years. But a marketing manager can't be complacent and assume that success will continue forever. When market maturity hits, the firm may be in for big trouble—unless the basic strategy and plan are modified. If a plan spells out the details of the market analysis and logic for the marketing mix and target market selected, then it is a simple matter to routinely check and update it. Remember: The idea is for all of the analysis and strategy decisions to fit together as an integrated whole. Thus, as some of the elements of the plan or market environment change, the whole plan may need a fresh approach.

Challenges Facing Marketers

LO 19.6

Marketers face the challenge of preparing creative and innovative marketing plans, but that in itself will not improve the value of marketing to society. We need to face up to other basic challenges that require new ways of thinking.

Change is the only thing that's constant

We need better marketing performance at the firm level. Progressive firms pay attention to changes in the market—including trends in the market environment—and how marketing strategies need to be improved to consider these changes. Exhibit 19–5 lists some of the important trends and changes we've discussed throughout this text.

Most of the changes and trends summarized in Exhibit 19–5 are having a positive effect on how marketers serve society. And this ongoing improvement is self-directing. As consumers shift their support to firms that do meet their needs, laggard businesses are forced to either improve or get out of the way.

If it ain't broke, improve it

Marketing managers must constantly evaluate their strategies to be sure they're not being left in the dust by competitors who see new and better ways of doing things. It's crazy for a marketing manager to constantly change a strategy that's working well. But too many managers fail to see or plan for needed changes. They're afraid to do anything different and adhere to the idea that "if it ain't broke, don't fix it." But a firm can't always wait until a problem becomes completely obvious to do something about it. When customers move on and profits disappear, it may be too late to fix the problem. Marketing managers who take the lead in finding innovative new markets and approaches get a competitive advantage.

We need to welcome international competition

Marketers can't afford to bury their heads in the sand and hope that international competition will go away. Rather, they must realize that it is part of today's market environment. It creates even more pressure on marketing managers to figure out what it takes to gain a competitive advantage—both at home and in foreign markets. But with the challenge comes opportunities. The forces of competition in and among market-directed economies will help speed the diffusion of marketing advances to consumers everywhere. As macro-marketing systems improve worldwide, more consumers will have income to buy products—from wherever in the world those products come.

We need to use technology wisely

We live in a time of dramatic new technologies. Many marketers hate the idea that what they've learned from years of on-the-job experience may no longer apply when a technology like the Internet comes along. Or they feel that it's the job of the technical specialist to figure out how a new technology can help the firm serve its customers.

Exhibit 19-5 Some Important Changes and Trends Affecting Marketing Strategy Planning

Communication Technologies
The Internet and intranets
Satellite communications and Wi-Fi
Video conferencing and Internet telephony
Growing use of smartphones
Consumer online "search" shopping
More interactive communications with customers

Role of Computerization
E-commerce, websites
Wireless networks
Scanners, bar codes, and RFID for tracking
Multimedia integration
"Cloud" computing
Mobile web access

Marketing Research
Search engines and web analytics
Online research—surveys, focus groups, online communities
Growth of marketing information systems
Decision support systems
Single source data (and scanner panels)
Data warehouses and data mining
Customer relationship management (CRM) systems
Big data

Demographic Patterns
Technology usage around the globe
Explosion in senior and ethnic submarkets
Aging of the baby boomers
Population growth slowdown in United States
Geographic shifts in population
Slower real income growth in United States

Business and Organizational Customers
Closer relationships and single sourcing
Just-in-time inventory systems/EDI
Web portals and Internet sourcing
Interactive bidding and proposal requests
Internet as source of information
ISO 9000
E-commerce and supply chain management

Product
More attention to "really new" products
Growth of dealer brands and private label
Faster new-product development
R&D teams with market-driven focus
Role of customer experience
More attention to quality
More attention to service technologies
More attention to sustainable design
Category management
3D printing
Patent trolls tie up patents
Internet of Things

Channels and Logistics
Internet selling (wholesale and retail)
More vertical marketing systems
Clicks and bricks (multichannel)
More multichannel shopping
Larger, more powerful retail chains
More attention to distribution service

Real-time inventory replenishment
Radio frequency identification (RFID)
Automated warehousing and handling
Cross-docking at distribution centers
Logistics outsourcing

Sales Promotion
Database-directed promotion
Point-of-purchase promotion
Trade promotion becoming more sensible
Event sponsorships
Customer loyalty programs
Customer acquisition cost analysis

Personal Selling
Post-sale customer service
Sales technology
Major accounts specialization
More telemarketing and team selling

Mass Selling
Interactive media (Internet ads, etc.)
Increasing role of publicity
More emphasis on "found" media
Role of customer reviews and ratings
Integrated marketing communications
Growth of more targeted media
Growth of interactive agencies
Consolidation of global agencies
Consolidation of media companies
Changing agency compensation
Shrinking media budgets
Social media
Inbound communications

Pricing
Electronic bid pricing and auctions
Value pricing
Overuse of sales and deals
Bigger differences in discounts
More attention to exchange rate effects
Lower markups on higher stockturn items
Use of "free" as a price
Comparison price shopping easier

International Marketing
More international market development
Global competitors—at home and abroad
Global communication over the Internet
New trade rules (NAFTA, WTO, EU, etc.)
More attention to exporting by small firms
International expansion by retailers
Impact of "pop" culture on traditional cultures
Tensions between "have" and "have-not" cultures
Growing income and population in emerging markets

General
Economic decline
S.W.O.T. analysis
Privacy issues
More attention to positioning and differentiation
Shift away from diversification
More attention to profitability, not just sales
Greater attention to superior value
Addressing environmental concerns

But marketers can't just pawn that responsibility off on "somebody else." If that means learning about new technologies, then that is just part of the marketing job.

At a broader level, firms face the challenge of determining what technologies are acceptable and which are not. For example, gene research has opened the door to life-saving medicines, genetically altered crops that resist drought or disease, and even cloning of human beings. Yet in all of these arenas there is intense conflict among different groups about what is appropriate. How should these decisions be made? There is no simple answer to this question, but it's clear that old production-oriented views are *not* the answer. Perhaps we will move toward developing answers if some of the marketing ideas that have been applied to understanding individual needs can be extended to better understand the needs of society as a whole.

Internet for consumers—sunny or partly cloudy

The Internet promised to create a more transparent business environment for customers. By shining "sunlight" on bad practices, the costs rise for firms producing a defective product or engaging in unethical behavior. In some ways this has proven to be the case. Early adopter customers review purchases on websites. Reports of a boring book, misleading product descriptions, poorly designed products, or bad customer service help prospective customers make more informed choices. On the other hand, there are growing reports of companies gaming the review system with fake reviews—leading consumers to question this source of information.

Along the same lines, companies must work hard to bury negative information about their brands. Sometimes this is justified, as the web allows anyone with a gripe (valid or not) to post complaints. But now marketing managers have become much more clever about controlling their brand image online. It wasn't too long ago that when typing Nike into Google, the first page of the search returned several links questioning the company's ethics and practices. Now the same search turns up only positive messages. In part this is because Nike has responded to critics and actively engages in more sustainable and socially responsible practices. It is also because Nike is more aware of how to manage search results to effectively bury its critics.

A constant challenge for food producers is assuring product safety. Instrumentation, like that sold by Japanese firm Leco, is often used to monitor food quality and safety. One safety lapse can harm a brand's reputation. The headline of the ad reads, "I am inside your taste of goodness."
Client: LECO Japan; Ad Tetsuro Tandai; Designer: Masashi Fujiyoshi; Copywriter: Hiroyuki Iwase; Computer Graphics: Takashi Taniai.

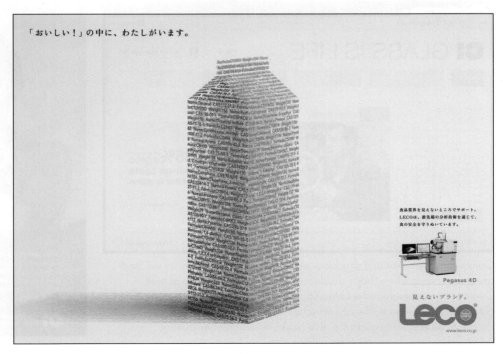

In general, the Internet has helped to shine a light that helps consumers make more informed choices. The risk is that increasingly web-savvy brands find ways to clean up their image without cleaning up their practices.[9]

We must consider *long-run* consumer welfare

Throughout this book we have emphasized the importance of the marketing concept—satisfying customers through a total company effort at a profit. Unfortunately, some firms take too short-run a view. They satisfy customers in the near term and take their profits, without worrying about longer-term problems. For example, some banks, mortgage brokers, and credit card companies made credit too easy to get. Some customers enjoyed this for a while, but many purchased homes or built up credit card debt that they couldn't afford. Although this helped companies earn high profits in the short term, many customers later defaulted on loans. Eventually, such activities harmed customers—and wreaked havoc on our global economy. Marketing managers must have a long-run view of customer satisfaction and recognize their social responsibility.

May need more social responsibility

Good business managers put themselves in the consumer's position. A useful rule to follow might be: Do unto others as you would have others do unto you. Sometimes called the "Golden Rule," this approach is found in many religions and philosophies. In practice, this means developing satisfying marketing mixes for specific target markets. It may mean building in more quality or more safety. The consumer's long-run satisfaction should be considered too. How will the product hold up in use? What about service guarantees? While trying to serve the needs of some target market, does the marketing strategy disregard the rights and needs of other consumers or create problems that will be left for future generations?[10]

We need the truth

Promotion provides powerful ways to communicate with customers. Yet too many firms lapse into telling only half the truth. This is most obvious when there is a shift in consumer interest. For example, a firm's ad may accurately proclaim that its food product has no "trans fat"—but do consumers think that means it's healthy, low calorie, or even low in fat? Today we're also seeing a lot of incomplete or misleading

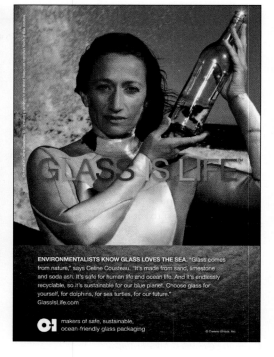

Companies that produce products with environmental benefits will find greater success when those products deliver other benefits as well. Owens Illinois developed a campaign that points out all the benefits of glass. Besides being endlessly recyclable, things taste better in glass. Products packaged in glass are also healthier and higher quality.
© 2015 O-I.

"greenwashing" claims about firms' environmental practices and eco-friendly products. It's good for a firm to create a biodegradable package and promote it, but the cleaning product in the package shouldn't contain chemicals that will be harmful once they're in the sewer system.

Growing consumer cynicism about promotion is also a problem. As it gets worse, firms as well as consumers suffer. Regulations say that marketing communications shouldn't be false or misleading, but managers need to take seriously the responsibility to be truthful to their customers. Marketing communications should be helpful—not just legal. Managers who don't get this message are likely to learn a hard lesson from activists who spread criticisms of their firms across the web and other media. The potential harm to a brand's reputation from this sort of negative publicity has many firms cautious about overstating their claims, including ones related to sustainability efforts.[11]

The environment is everyone's need

Marketers need to work harder and smarter at finding ways to satisfy consumer needs without sacrificing the environment. All consumers need the environment, whether they realize it yet or not. We are only beginning to understand the consequences of the environmental damage that's already been done. Acid rain, depletion of the ozone layer, global warming, and toxic waste in water supplies—to mention but a few current environmental problems—have catastrophic effects.

In the past, most firms didn't pass the cost of environmental damage on to consumers in the prices that they paid. Pollution was a hidden and unmeasured cost for most companies. That is changing rapidly. Firms are already paying billions of dollars to correct problems, including problems created years ago. The government isn't accepting the excuse that "nobody knew it was a big problem."[12]

Consumer privacy needs to be protected

Marketers must also be sensitive to consumers' rights and privacy. Today, sophisticated marketing research methods, the Internet, and other technologies make it easier to abuse these rights. For example, credit card records—which reveal much about consumers' purchases and private lives—are routinely sold to anybody who pays for the computer file. Many people place loads of personal information on social networking

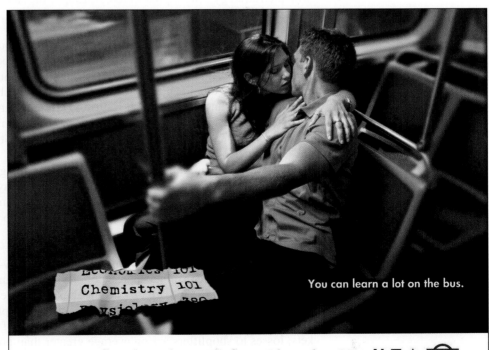

The Utah Transit Authority (UTA) thought that more university students would ride the bus long term if they were motivated by personal benefit rather than environmental or social conscience. For most people, the pros and cons of riding the bus, like other product choices, are more a personal matter. So UTA decided it should offer an answer to the question, "What's in it for me?" The answer in this particular UTA ad is "social opportunities." Although public transit is not exactly a sexy product, the ad employs a "sex sells" approach. What do you think? Is this a good idea? Why? Photo by: Bob Wolter & Associates.

You can learn a lot on the bus.

University of Utah students ride free with student I.D. **UTA** websites, such as Facebook, assuming they have some privacy. This is often not the case. For example, a rogue marketer with an e-mail list can go to Facebook and quickly find a name, gender, friends, age, interests, job, location, and education level for each e-mail address.

Most consumers don't realize how much data about their personal lives—some of it incorrect but treated as fact—are collected and available. A simple computer billing error may land consumers on a bad-credit list without their knowledge. Worse, poor security can result in identity theft. Marketing managers should use technology responsibly to improve the quality of life, not disrupt it. If you don't think privacy is a serious matter, enter your social security number in an Internet search engine and see what pops up. You may be surprised.[13]

May need to change laws and how they are enforced

One of the advantages of a market-directed economic system is that it operates automatically. But in our version of this system, consumer-citizens provide certain constraints (laws), which can be modified at any time. Managers who ignore consumer attitudes must realize that their actions may cause new restraints.

Before piling on too many new rules, however, some of the ones we have may need to be revised—and others may need to be enforced more carefully. Antitrust laws, for example, are often applied to protect competitors from one another—but they were originally intended to encourage competition.

Specifically, U.S. antitrust laws were developed so that all firms in a market would compete on a level playing field. But in many markets, that level playing field no longer exists. In our global economy, individual U.S. firms now compete with foreign firms whose governments urge them to cooperate with one another. Such foreign firms don't see one another as competitors; rather they see U.S. firms, as a group, as the competitors.

Laws should affect top managers

Strict enforcement of present laws could have far-reaching results if more price fixers, fraudulent or deceptive advertisers, and others who violate existing laws—thus affecting the performance of the macro-marketing system—were sent to jail or given heavy fines. A quick change in attitudes might occur if unethical top managers—those who plan strategy—were prosecuted, instead of the salespeople or advertisers expected to deliver on weak or undifferentiated strategies.

Laws merely define minimal ethical standards

Whether a marketer is operating in his or her own country or in a foreign nation, the legal environment sets the *minimal* standards of ethical behavior as defined by a society. In addition, the American Marketing Association's Statement of Ethics (Exhibit 1–7) provides basic guidelines that a marketing manager should observe. But marketing managers constantly face ethical issues where there are no clearly defined answers. Every marketing manager should make a personal commitment to carefully evaluate the ethical consequences of marketing strategy decisions. Stretch your thinking by reading "*What's Next?* Marketers use big data—cool or creepy."

On the other hand, innovative new marketing strategies *do* sometimes cause problems for those who have a vested interest in the old ways. Some people try to portray anything that disrupts their own personal interest as unethical. But that is not an appropriate ethical standard. The basic ethical charge to marketers is to find new *and* better ways to serve society's needs.

Need socially responsible consumers

We've stressed that marketers should act responsibly—but consumers have responsibilities too. Some consumers abuse policies about returning goods, change price tags in self-service stores, and are downright abusive to salespeople. Others think nothing of ripping off businesses because "they're rich." Shoplifting is a major problem for most traditional retailers, averaging almost 2 percent of sales nationally. In supermarkets, losses to shoplifters are on average greater than profits. Online retailers, in turn, must fight the use of stolen or fraudulent credit cards. Honest consumers pay for the cost of this theft in higher prices.

What's Next? Marketers use big data—cool or creepy

Throughout this book we have discussed big data (see Chapter 7 for a deeper discussion). Marketing managers use big data to build "social profiles" of individual consumers. These profiles are developed by analyzing customers' clicks, conversations, Facebook "Likes," Twitter "tweets," cell phone activity, and credit card and loyalty card purchases. The social profiles allow marketing managers to deliver highly targeted, personalized (and presumably more relevant and appealing) marketing mixes. In exchange, customers give up some privacy.

Is this new practice cool? Or is it creepy? To better understand how the big data revolution affects customers, let's take a closer look at how this might play out in real life by looking at two fictional college students, Nick and Shelby.

Nick often eats fast food and regularly receives e-mail coupons for fast-food purchases. Saving money sounds cool. Nick's profile shows that he usually spends significantly more than the coupon amount, and computer analysis of Nick's photos and comments on Facebook suggest he is overweight. Soon Nick starts seeing ads for diets; he also receives a special introductory offer from a local health club. Cool or creepy? Nick's Facebook newsfeed and Twitter feed include "articles" from news sites on healthy eating with an emphasis on Kellogg's Special K diet products and weight-loss tips from South Beach Diet products. Cool or creepy? Some days, as Nick walks home from school, his Snapchat shows a picture of a bowl of ice cream (and $0.50 off)—just a block before he passes Baskin Robbins Ice Cream store. Timely. Cool or creepy?

Shelby's friends know she works out regularly and maintains a healthy diet. Last week she was online reading articles about mountain bikes—now when she surfs the web, she sees ads for mountain bikes. Cool or creepy? As Shelby walks into her grocery store, her phone lights up with an offer for a dollar off on Ben & Jerry's Greek Frozen Yogurt—she loves that stuff, but rarely eats it unless she's feeling down. Did the grocery store know she and her boyfriend just broke up? Yes, it did. It "saw" her Facebook status update. Cool or creepy? Shelby often receives direct-mail offers for low-interest credit cards; Nick doesn't get those. Does the financial institution figure that healthier behavior is a sign of self-discipline and, therefore, financial responsibility? Will insurance companies draw the same conclusions and adjust rates accordingly? Cool or creepy?

These examples are not the future—they happen today. Marketing managers use big data to customize advertising, promotion, pricing, and online content. Tracked by your cell phone's GPS, messages target your location. If a $0.50 coupon motivates Nick to buy ice cream, but it takes $1.00 off to move Shelby, each gets a different coupon. The "articles" served to your news feed might be written by someone paid by a brand prominently featured in the article.

Cool or creepy? Probably depends on your values. As we move into a brave new world where customers surrender privacy (usually without their knowledge), you should have questions. Do you want to trade your privacy for personalized marketing mixes? What do you have to gain or lose? Who owns your data? Should governments regulate this—or should it be up to you? There are no easy answers. Is this cool? Creepy? A little of both? A lot of both?[14]

Americans tend to perform their dual role of consumer-citizens with a split personality. We often behave differently at the cash register than we do on our soap box. For example, we say that we want to protect the environment, but when it comes to making our own purchase decisions, we're likely to pick the product that is more convenient or lower priced rather than the one that is the sustainable choice. We protest sex and violence in the media, but some of the

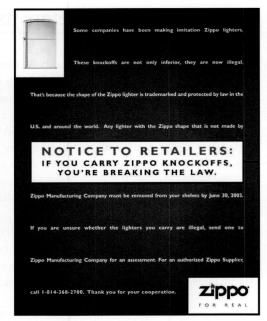

Consumers should act in a socially aware/responsible manner. They must be cautious with their personal data and credit cards. Most identity thieves gather information from purses and wallets. Consumer demand for lower prices and willingness to purchase counterfeit products harms honest retailers and firms that produce legitimate products.
Left: Courtesy Your Credit Card Companies. Right: © 2015 Zippo Manufacturing Company.

most profitable websites on the Internet are purveyors of pornography. Parents complain about advertising aimed at children but use TV as a Saturday morning babysitter.

Unethical or illegal behavior is widespread. In a major survey of workers, managers, and executives from a wide range of industries, 48 percent admitted to taking unethical or illegal actions in the past year. Offenses included things such as cheating on expense accounts, paying or accepting kickbacks, trading sex for sales, lying to customers, leaking company secrets, and looking the other way when environmental laws are violated. Think about it—we're talking about half of the workforce.[15]

As consumer-citizens, each of us shares the responsibility for preserving an effective macro-marketing system. And we should take this responsibility seriously. That even includes the responsibility to be smarter customers. Let's face it, a majority of consumers ignore most of the available information that could help them spend money (and guide the marketing process) more wisely. Consumerism has encouraged nutritional labeling, unit pricing, truth-in-lending, plain-language contracts and warranties, and so on. Many companies provide extensive information at their websites or in brochures. Government agencies publish many consumer buying guides on everything from tires to appliances, as do organizations such as Consumers Union. Most of this information is available from home over the Internet. It makes sense to use it.

How Far Should the Marketing Concept Go?

Should marketing managers limit consumers' freedom of choice?

Achieving a better macro-marketing system is certainly a desirable objective. But what part should a marketer play in deciding what products to offer?

This is extremely important because some marketing managers, especially those in large corporations, can have an impact far larger than they do in their roles as consumer-citizens. For example, should they refuse to produce hazardous products, such as skis or motorcycles, even though such products are in strong demand? Should they install safety devices that increase costs and raise prices that customers don't want to pay?

These are difficult questions to answer. Some things marketing managers do clearly benefit both the firm and consumers because they lower costs or improve consumers' options. But other decisions may actually reduce consumer choice and conflict with a desire to improve the effectiveness of our macro-marketing system.

Consumer-citizens should vote on the changes

It seems fair to suggest, therefore, that marketing managers should be expected to improve and expand the range of goods and services they make available—always trying to add value and better satisfy consumers' needs and preferences. This is the job we've assigned to business.

If pursuing this objective makes excessive demands on scarce resources or has an unacceptable ecological effect, then consumer-citizens have the responsibility to vote for laws restricting individual firms that are trying to satisfy consumers' needs. This is the role that we, as consumers, have assigned to the government—to ensure that the macro-marketing system works effectively.

It is important to recognize that some *seemingly minor* modifications in our present system *might* result in very big, unintended problems. Allowing some government agency to prohibit the sale of products for seemingly good reasons could lead to major changes we never expected and could seriously reduce consumers' present rights to freedom of choice, including "bad" choices.

CONCLUSION

Macro-marketing does *not* cost too much. Consumers have assigned business the role of satisfying their needs. Customers find it satisfactory and even desirable to permit businesses to cater to them and even to stimulate wants. As long as consumers are satisfied, macro-marketing will not cost too much—and business firms will be permitted to continue as profit-making entities.

But business exists at the consumer's discretion. It's mainly by satisfying the consumer that a particular firm—and *our* economic system—can justify its existence and hope to keep operating.

In carrying out this role—granted by consumers—business firms are not always as effective as they could be. Many business managers don't understand the marketing concept or the role that marketing plays in our way of life. They seem to feel that business has a basic right to operate as it chooses. And they proceed in their typical production-oriented ways. Further, many managers have had little or no training in business management and are not as competent as they should be. Others fail to adjust to the changes taking place around them. And a few dishonest or unethical managers can do a great deal of damage before consumer-citizens take steps to stop them. As a result, marketing by individual firms often *does* cost too much. But the situation is improving. More business training is now available, and more competent people are being attracted to marketing

and business generally. Clearly, you have a role to play in improving marketing activities in the future.

The marketing strategy planning process presented in this book provides a framework that will guide you to more effective marketing decisions—and marketing that really does deliver superior value to customers. It also benefits the firm, through profits and growth. It's truly a "win–win" situation. And in our competitive, market-driven economy, managers and firms that lead the way in creating these successes will not go unnoticed. As effective marketing management spreads to more companies, the whole macro-marketing system will be more efficient and effective.

To keep our system working effectively, individual firms should implement the marketing concept in a more efficient, ethical, and socially responsible way. At the same time, we—as consumers—should consume goods and services in an intelligent and socially responsible way. Further, we have the responsibility to vote and ensure that we get the kind of macro-marketing system we want. What kind do you want? What should you do to ensure that fellow consumer-citizens will vote for your system? Is your system likely to satisfy you as well as another macro-marketing system? You don't have to answer these questions right now—but your answers will affect the future you'll live in and how satisfied you'll be.

WHAT'S NOW?

This chapter covered the roles of marketing in society. There are constantly new issues that marketing faces in society. For some current real-world examples and applications, check out *What's Now?* at www.learnthe4ps.com/whatsnow/c19

QUESTIONS AND PROBLEMS

1. Review the case study that opens this chapter. From this case, identify examples of different key terms and concepts covered in the chapter. For example, highlight examples of micro- versus macro-marketing criteria.

2. Review the case study that opens this chapter and look at the section "Challenges Facing Marketers." If you could advise the U.S. government, would you increase regulation around those challenges? Why or why not? Offer specific examples.

3. Explain why marketing must be evaluated at two levels. What criteria should be used to evaluate each level of marketing? Defend your answer. Explain why your criteria are better than alternative criteria.

4. Discuss the merits of various economic system objectives. Is the objective of the American economic system sensible? Could it achieve more consumer satisfaction if sociologists or public officials determined how to satisfy the needs of lower-income or less-educated consumers? If so, what education or income level should be required before an individual is granted free choice?

5. Should the objective of our economy be maximum efficiency? If your answer is yes, efficiency in what? If not, what should the objective be?

6. Discuss the conflict of interests among production, finance, accounting, and marketing executives. How does this conflict affect the operation of an individual firm? The economic system? Why does this conflict exist?

7. Why does adoption of the marketing concept encourage a firm to operate more efficiently? Be specific about the impact of the marketing concept on the various departments of a firm.

8. In the short run, competition sometimes leads to inefficiency in the operation of our economic system. Many people argue for monopoly in order to eliminate this inefficiency. Discuss this solution.

9. How would officially granted monopolies affect the operation of our economic system? Consider the effect on allocation of resources, the level of income and employment, and the distribution of income. Is the effect any different if a firm obtains a monopoly by winning out in a competitive market?

10. Comment on the following statement: "Ultimately, the high cost of marketing is due only to consumers."

11. Distinguish clearly between a marketing strategy and a marketing plan. If a firm has a really good strategy, does it need to worry about developing a written plan?

12. How far should the marketing concept go? How should we decide this issue?

13. Should marketing managers, or business managers in general, refrain from producing profitable products that some target customers want, but that may not be in their long-run best interest? Should firms be expected to produce "good" but less profitable products? What if such products break even? What if they are unprofitable but the company makes other profitable products—so on balance it still makes some profit? What criteria are you using for each of your answers?

14. Should a marketing manager or a business refuse to produce an "energy-gobbling" appliance that some consumers are demanding? Should a firm install an expensive safety device that will increase costs but that customers don't want? Are the same principles involved in both these questions? Explain.

15. Discuss how one or more of the trends or changes shown in Exhibit 19–5 are affecting marketing strategy planning for a specific firm that serves the market where you live.

16. Discuss how slower economic growth or no economic growth would affect your college community—in particular, its marketing institutions.

MARKETING PLANNING FOR HILLSIDE VETERINARY CLINIC

Appendix D (the Appendices follow this chapter) includes a sample marketing plan for Hillside Veterinary Clinic. Review the entire marketing plan.

a. How do the pieces fit together?

b. Does the marketing strategy logically follow from the target market dimensions?

c. Does the marketing strategy logically follow from the differentiation and positioning?

d. Does the plan appear reasonable given the stated objectives?

SUGGESTED CASES

17. Simply Pure H2O4U, Inc.
22. Bright Light Innovations: The Starlight Stove
27. Advanced Molding, Inc.
28. AAT Tools
30. Walker-Winkle Mills

31. Bowman Home Health Services
32. Lever Ltd.
34. Chess Aluminum Worldwide
Video Case 4. Potbelly Sandwich
Video Case 6. Big Brothers and Big Sisters of America

A Economics Fundamentals

Products and Markets as Seen by Customers and Potential Customers

Economists see individual customers choosing among alternatives

A basic idea from economics is that most customers have a limited income and simply cannot buy everything they want. They must balance their needs and the prices of various products. Economists usually assume that customers have a fairly definite set of preferences and that they evaluate alternatives in terms of whether the alternatives will make them feel better or in some way improve their situation.

But what exactly is the nature of a customer's desire for a particular product?

Usually economists answer this question in terms of the extra utility the customer can obtain by buying more of a particular product—or how much utility would be lost if the customer had less of the product. It is easier to understand the idea of utility if we look at what happens when the price of one of the customer's usual purchases changes.

The law of diminishing demand

LO A.1

Suppose that consumers buy potatoes in 10-pound bags at the same time they buy other foods such as bread and rice. If the consumers are mainly interested in buying a certain amount of food and the price of the potatoes drops, it seems reasonable to expect that they will switch some of their food money to potatoes and away from some other foods. But if the price of potatoes rises, you expect our consumers to buy fewer potatoes and more of other foods.

The general relationship between price and quantity demanded illustrated by this food example is called the **law of diminishing demand**—which says that if the price of a product is raised, a smaller quantity will be demanded, and if the price of a product is lowered, a greater quantity will be demanded. Experience supports this relationship between price and total demand in a market, especially for broad product categories or commodities such as potatoes.

The relationship between price and quantity demanded in a market is what economists call a *demand schedule.* An example is shown in Exhibit A–1. For each row in the table, column 2 shows the quantity consumers will want (demand) if they have to pay the price given in column 1. The third column shows that the total revenue (sales) in the potato market is equal to the quantity demanded at a given price times that price. Note that as prices drop, the total *unit* quantity increases, yet the total *revenue* decreases. Fill in the blank lines in the third column and observe the behavior of total revenue, an important number for the marketing manager. We will explain what you should have noticed, and why, a little later.

The demand curve— usually down-sloping

If your interest is seeing only at which price the company will earn the greatest total revenue, the demand schedule may be adequate. But a demand curve shows more. A **demand curve** is a graph of the relationship between price and quantity demanded in a market, assuming that all other things stay the same. Exhibit A–2 shows the demand curve for potatoes—really just a plotting of the demand schedule in Exhibit A–1. It shows how many potatoes potential customers will demand at various possible prices. This is a "down-sloping demand curve."

Most demand curves are down-sloping. This just means that if prices are decreased, the quantity customers demand will increase.

Exhibit A–1
Demand Schedule for
Potatoes (10-pound bags)

Point	(1) Price of Potatoes per Bag (P)	(2) Quantity Demanded (bags per month) (Q)	(3) Total Revenue per Month ($P \times Q =$ TR)
A	$1.60	8,000,000	$12,800,000
B	1.30	9,000,000	_____
C	1.00	11,000,000	11,000,000
D	0.70	14,000,000	_____
E	0.40	19,000,000	_____

Exhibit A–2
Demand Curve for
Potatoes (10-pound bags)

Demand curves always show the price on the vertical axis and the quantity demanded on the horizontal axis. In Exhibit A–2, we have shown the price in dollars. For consistency, we will use dollars in other examples. However, keep in mind that these same ideas hold regardless of what money unit (dollars, yen, euros, pounds, etc.) is used to represent price. Even at this early point, you should keep in mind that markets are not necessarily limited by national boundaries—or by one type of money.

Note that the demand curve shows only how customers will react to various possible prices. In a market, we see only one price at a time, not all of these prices. The curve, however, shows what quantities will be demanded, depending on what price is set.

Microwave oven demand
curve looks different

To get a more complete picture of demand-curve analysis, let's consider another product that has a different demand schedule and curve. A demand schedule for standard 1-cubic-foot microwave ovens is shown in Exhibit A–3. Column 3 shows the total revenue that will be obtained at various possible prices and quantities. Again, as the price goes down, the quantity demanded goes up. But here, unlike the potato example, total revenue increases as prices go down—at least until the price drops to $100.

Every market has a
demand curve, for some
time period

These general demand relationships are typical for all products. But each product has its own demand schedule and curve in each potential market, no matter how small the market. In other words, a particular demand curve has meaning only for a particular market. We can think of demand curves for individuals, groups of individuals who form a target market, regions, and even countries. And the time period covered really should be specified, although this is often neglected because we usually think of monthly or yearly periods.

Exhibit A–3
Demand Schedule
for 1-Cubic-Foot
Microwave Ovens

Point	(1) Price per Microwave Oven (P)	(2) Quantity Demanded per Year (Q)	(3) Total Revenue (TR) per Year (P × Q = TR)
A	$300	20,000	$ 6,000,000
B	250	70,000	17,500,000
C	200	130,000	26,000,000
D	150	210,000	31,500,000
E	100	310,000	31,000,000

Exhibit A-4
Demand Curve for
1-Cubic-Foot Microwave
Ovens

The difference between
elastic and inelastic

The demand curve for microwave ovens (see Exhibit A–4) is down-sloping—but note that it is flatter than the curve for potatoes. It is important to understand what this flatness means.

We will consider the flatness in terms of total revenue because this is what interests business managers.*

When you filled in the total revenue column for potatoes, you should have noticed that total revenue drops continually if the price is reduced. This looks undesirable for sellers and illustrates inelastic demand. **Inelastic demand** means that although the quantity demanded increases if the price is decreased, the quantity demanded will not "stretch" enough—that is, it is not elastic enough—to avoid a decrease in total revenue.

In contrast, **elastic demand** means that if prices are dropped, the quantity demanded will stretch (increase) enough to increase total revenue. The upper part of the microwave oven demand curve is an example of elastic demand.

But note that if the microwave oven price is dropped from $150 to $100, total revenue will decrease. We can say, therefore, that between $150 and $100, demand is inelastic—that is, total revenue will decrease if price is lowered from $150 to $100.

Thus, elasticity can be defined in terms of changes in total revenue. *If total revenue will increase if price is lowered, then demand is elastic. If total revenue will decrease if price is lowered, then demand is inelastic.* (Note: A special case known as "unitary elasticity of demand" occurs if total revenue stays the same when prices change.)

Total revenue may
increase if price is raised

A point often missed in discussions of demand is what happens when prices are raised instead of lowered. With elastic demand, total revenue will *decrease* if the price is *raised.* With inelastic demand, however, total revenue will *increase* if the price is *raised.*

The possibility of raising price and increasing dollar sales (total revenue) at the same time is attractive to managers. This occurs only if the demand curve is inelastic. Here total revenue will increase if price is raised, but total costs probably will not increase—and may actually go down—with smaller quantities. Keep in mind that profit is equal to total revenue minus total costs. So when demand is inelastic, profit will increase as price is increased!

The ways total revenue changes as prices are raised are shown in Exhibit A–5. Here total revenue is the rectangular area formed by a price and its related quantity. The larger the rectangular area, the greater the total revenue.

---

* Strictly speaking, two curves should not be compared for flatness if the graph scales are different, but for our purposes now we will do so to illustrate the idea of "elasticity of demand." Actually, it would be more accurate to compare two curves for one product on the same graph. Then both the shape of the demand curve and its position on the graph would be important.

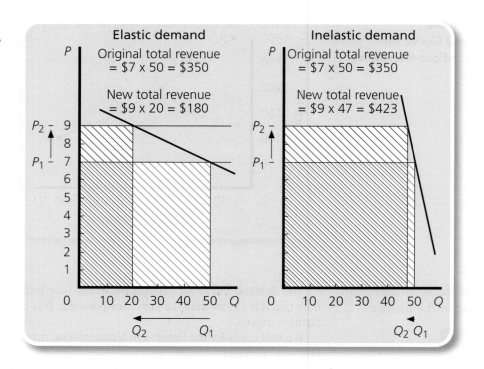

P_1 is the original price here, and the total potential revenue with this original price is shown by the area with blue shading. The area with red shading shows the total revenue with the new price, P_2. There is some overlap in the total revenue areas, so the important areas are those with only one color. Note that in the left-hand figure—where demand is elastic—the revenue added (the red-only area) when the price is increased is less than the revenue lost (the blue-only area). Now let's contrast this to the right-hand figure, when demand is inelastic. Only a small blue revenue area is given up for a much larger (red) one when price is raised.

An entire curve is not elastic or inelastic

It is important to see that it is *wrong to refer to a whole demand curve as elastic or inelastic*. Rather, elasticity for a particular demand curve refers to the change in total revenue between two points on the curve, not along the whole curve. You saw the change from elastic to inelastic in the microwave oven example. Generally, however, nearby points are either elastic or inelastic—so it is common to refer to a whole curve by the degree of elasticity in the price range that normally is of interest—the *relevant range*.

Demand elasticities affected by availability of substitutes and urgency of need

LO A.3

At first, it may be difficult to see why one product has an elastic demand and another an inelastic demand. Many factors affect elasticity, such as the availability of substitutes, the importance of the item in the customer's budget, and the urgency of the customer's need and its relation to other needs. By looking more closely at one of these factors—the availability of substitutes—you will better understand why demand elasticities vary.

Substitutes are products that offer the buyer a choice. For example, many consumers see grapefruit as a substitute for oranges and hot dogs as a substitute for hamburgers. The greater the number of "good" substitutes available, the greater will be the elasticity of demand. From the consumer's perspective, products are "good" substitutes if they are very similar (homogeneous). If consumers see products as extremely different, or heterogeneous, then a particular need cannot easily be satisfied by substitutes. And the demand for the most satisfactory product may be quite inelastic.

As an example, if the price of hamburger is lowered (and other prices stay the same), the quantity demanded will increase a lot, as will total revenue. The reason is

Exhibit A–6
Demand Curve for Hamburger (a product with many substitutes)

that not only will regular hamburger users buy more hamburger, but some consumers who formerly bought hot dogs or steaks probably will buy hamburger too. But if the price of hamburger is raised, the quantity demanded will decrease, perhaps sharply. Still, consumers will buy some hamburger, depending on how much the price has risen, their individual tastes, and what their guests expect (see Exhibit A–6).

In contrast to a product with many "substitutes"—such as hamburger—consider a product with few or no substitutes. Its demand curve will tend to be inelastic. Motor oil is a good example. Motor oil is needed to keep cars running. Yet no one person or family uses great quantities of motor oil. So it is not likely that the quantity of motor oil purchased will change much as long as price changes are *within a reasonable range*. Of course, if the price is raised to a staggering figure, many people will buy less oil (change their oil less frequently). If the price is dropped to an extremely low level, manufacturers may buy more—say, as a lower-cost substitute for other chemicals typically used in making plastic (Exhibit A–7). But these extremes are outside the relevant range.

Demand curves are introduced here because the degree of elasticity of demand shows how potential customers feel about a product—and especially whether they see substitutes for the product. But to get a better understanding of markets, we must extend this economic analysis.

Markets as Seen by Suppliers

Customers may want some product—but if suppliers are not willing to supply it, then there is no market. So we'll study the economist's analysis of supply. And then we'll bring supply and demand together for a more complete understanding of markets.

Exhibit A–7
Demand Curve for Motor Oil (a product with few substitutes)

Exhibit A–8
Supply Schedule for Potatoes (10-pound bags)

Point	Possible Market Price per 10-lb. Bag	Number of Bags Sellers Will Supply per Month at Each Possible Market Price
A	$1.60	17,000,000
B	1.30	14,000,000
C	1.00	11,000,000
D	0.70	8,000,000
E	0.40	3,000,000

Note: These data and the resulting supply curve in Exhibit A–9 are for a single month to emphasize that farmers might have some control over when they deliver their potatoes. There would be different data, and consequently a different curve, for each month.

Economists often use the kind of analysis we are discussing here to explain pricing in the marketplace. But that is not our intention. Here we are interested in how and why markets work and the interaction of customers and potential suppliers. Later in this appendix we will review how competition affects prices, but how individual firms set prices, or should set prices, is discussed fully in Chapters 17 and 18.

Supply curves reflect supplier thinking

Generally speaking, suppliers' costs affect the quantity of products they are willing to offer in a market during any period. In other words, their costs affect their supply schedules and supply curves. Whereas a demand curve shows the quantity of products customers will be willing to buy at various prices, a **supply curve** shows the quantity of products that will be supplied at various possible prices. Eventually, only one quantity will be offered and purchased. So a supply curve is really a hypothetical (what-if) description of what will be offered at various prices. It is, however, a very important curve. Together with a demand curve, it summarizes the attitudes and probable behavior of buyers and sellers about a particular product in a particular market—that is, in a product-market.

Some supply curves are vertical

We usually assume that supply curves tend to slope upward—that is, suppliers will be willing to offer greater quantities at higher prices. If a product's market price is very high, it seems only reasonable that producers will be anxious to produce more of the product and even put workers on overtime or perhaps hire more workers to increase the quantity they can offer. Going further, it seems likely that producers of other products will switch their resources (farms, factories, labor, or retail facilities) to the product that is in great demand.

On the other hand, if consumers are only willing to pay a very low price for a particular product, it's reasonable to expect that producers will switch to other products, thus reducing supply. A supply schedule (Exhibit A–8) and a supply curve (Exhibit A–9) for

Exhibit A–9
Supply Curve for Potatoes (10-pound bags)

potatoes illustrate these ideas. This supply curve shows how many potatoes would be produced and offered for sale at each possible market price in a given month.

In the very short run (say, over a few hours, a day, or a week), a supplier may not be able to change the supply at all. In this situation, we would see a vertical supply curve. This situation is often relevant in the market for fresh produce. Fresh strawberries, for example, continue to ripen, and a supplier wants to sell them quickly—preferably at a higher price—but in any case, they must be sold.

If the product is a service, it may not be easy to expand the supply in the short run. Additional barbers or medical doctors are not quickly trained and licensed, and they have only so much time to give each day. Further, the prospect of much higher prices in the near future cannot easily expand the supply of many services. For example, a hit play or an "in" restaurant or nightclub is limited in the amount of product it can offer at a particular time.

Elasticity of supply

The term *elasticity* also is used to describe supply curves. An extremely steep or almost vertical supply curve, often found in the short run, is called **inelastic supply** because the quantity supplied does not stretch much (if at all) if the price is raised. A flatter curve is called **elastic supply** because the quantity supplied does stretch more if the price is raised. A slightly up-sloping supply curve is typical in longer-run market situations. Given more time, suppliers have a chance to adjust their offerings, and competitors may enter or leave the market.

Demand and Supply Interact to Determine the Size of the Market and Price Level

We have treated market demand and supply forces separately. Now we must bring them together to show their interaction. The *intersection* of these two forces determines the size of the market and the market price—at which point (price and quantity) the market is said to be in *equilibrium.*

The intersection of demand and supply is shown for the potato data discussed earlier. In Exhibit A–10, the demand curve for potatoes is now graphed against the supply curve in Exhibit A–9.

In this potato market, demand is inelastic—the total revenue of all the potato producers would be greater at higher prices. But the market price is at the **equilibrium point**—where the quantity and the price sellers are willing to offer are equal to the quantity and price that buyers are willing to accept. The $1.00 equilibrium price for potatoes yields a smaller *total revenue* to potato producers than a higher price would. This lower equilibrium price comes about because the many producers are willing to supply enough potatoes at the lower price. *Demand is not the only determiner of price level. Cost also must be considered—via the supply curve.*

Exhibit A–10
Equilibrium of Supply and Demand for Potatoes (10-pound bags)

Some consumers get a surplus

Presumably, a sale takes place only if both buyer and seller feel they will be better off after the sale. But sometimes the price a consumer pays in a sales transaction is less than what he or she would be willing to pay.

The reason for this is that demand curves are typically down-sloping, and some of the demand curve is above the equilibrium price. This is simply another way of showing that some customers would have been willing to pay more than the equilibrium price—if they had to. In effect, some of them are getting a bargain by being able to buy at the equilibrium price. Economists have traditionally called these bargains the **consumer surplus**—that is, the difference to consumers between the value of a purchase and the price they pay.

Some business critics assume that consumers do badly in any business transaction. In fact, sales take place only if consumers feel they are at least getting their money's worth. As we can see here, some are willing to pay much more than the market price.

Demand and Supply Help Us Understand the Nature of Competition

LO A.5

The elasticity of demand and supply curves and their interaction help predict the nature of competition a marketing manager is likely to face. For example, an extremely inelastic demand curve means that the manager will have much choice in strategy planning, especially price setting. Apparently customers like the product and see few substitutes. They are willing to pay higher prices before cutting back much on their purchases.

The elasticity of a firm's demand curve is not the only factor that affects the nature of competition. Other factors are the number and size of competitors and the uniqueness of each firm's marketing mix. Understanding these market situations is important because the freedom of a marketing manager, especially control over price, is greatly reduced in some situations.

A marketing manager operates in one of four kinds of market situations. We'll discuss three kinds: pure competition, oligopoly, and monopolistic competition. The fourth kind, monopoly, isn't found very often and is like monopolistic competition. The important dimensions of these situations are shown in Exhibit A–11.

Exhibit A–11
Some Important Dimensions Regarding Market Situations

Important Dimensions	Types of Situations			
	Pure Competition	Oligopoly	Monopolistic Competition	Monopoly
Uniqueness of each firm's product	None	None	Some	Unique
Number of competitors	Many	Few	Few to many	None
Size of competitors (compared to size of market)	Small	Large	Large to small	None
Elasticity of demand facing firm	Completely elastic	Kinked demand curve (elastic and inelastic)	Either	Either
Elasticity of industry demand	Either	Inelastic	Either	Either
Control of price by firm	None	Some (with care)	Some	Complete

When competition is pure	**Many competitors offer about the same thing**

Many competitors offer about the same thing

Pure competition is a market situation that develops when a market has

1. Homogeneous (similar) products.
2. Many buyers and sellers who have full knowledge of the market.
3. Ease of entry for buyers and sellers; that is, new firms have little difficulty starting in business—and new customers can easily come into the market.

More or less pure competition is found in many agricultural markets. In the potato market, for example, there are thousands of small producers—and they are in pure competition. Let's look more closely at these producers.

Although the potato market as a whole has a down-sloping demand curve, each of the many small producers in the industry is in pure competition, and each of them faces a flat demand curve at the equilibrium price. This is shown in Exhibit A–12.

As shown at the right of Exhibit A–12, an individual producer can sell as many bags of potatoes as he chooses at $1—the market equilibrium price. The equilibrium price is determined by the quantity that all producers choose to sell given the demand curve they face.

But a small producer has little effect on overall supply (or on the equilibrium price). If this individual farmer raises 1/10,000th of the quantity offered in the market, for example, you can see that there will be little effect if the farmer goes out of business—or doubles production.

The reason an individual producer's demand curve is flat is that the farmer probably couldn't sell any potatoes above the market price. And there is no point in selling below the market price! So, in effect, the individual producer has no control over price.

Markets tend to become more competitive

Not many markets are *purely* competitive. But many are close enough so we can talk about "almost" pure competition situations—those in which the marketing manager has to accept the going price.

Such highly competitive situations aren't limited to agriculture. Wherever *many* competitors sell *homogeneous* products—such as textiles, lumber, coal, printing, and laundry services—the demand curve seen by *each producer* tends to be flat.

Markets tend to become more competitive, moving toward pure competition (except in oligopolies—see below). On the way to pure competition, prices and profits are pushed down until some competitors are forced out of business. Eventually, in

Exhibit A–12 Interaction of Demand and Supply in the Potato Industry and the Resulting Demand Curve Facing Individual Potato Producers long-run equilibrium, the price level is only high enough to keep the survivors in business. No one makes any profit—they just cover costs. It's tough to be a marketing manager in this situation!

When competition is oligopolistic

A few competitors offer similar things

Not all markets move toward pure competition. Some become oligopolies. **Oligopoly** situations are special market situations that develop when a market has

1. Essentially homogeneous products—such as basic industrial chemicals or gasoline.
2. Relatively few sellers—or a few large firms and many smaller ones who follow the lead of the larger ones.
3. Fairly inelastic industry demand curves.

The demand curve facing each firm is unusual in an oligopoly situation. Although the industry demand curve is inelastic throughout the relevant range, the demand curve facing each competitor looks "kinked" (see Exhibit A–13). The current market price is at the kink.

There is a market price because the competing firms watch one another carefully—and they know it's wise to be at the kink. Each firm must expect that raising its own price above the market price will cause a big loss in sales. Few, if any, competitors will follow the price increase. So the firm's demand curve is relatively flat above the market price. If the firm lowers its price, it must expect competitors to follow. Given inelastic industry demand, the firm's own demand curve is inelastic at lower prices, assuming it keeps its share of this market at lower prices. Because lowering prices along such a curve will drop total revenue, the firm should leave its price at the kink—the market price.

Sometimes there are price fluctuations in oligopolistic markets. This can be caused by firms that don't understand the market situation and cut their prices to try to get business. In other cases, big increases in demand or supply change the basic nature of the situation and lead to price cutting. Price cuts can be drastic, such as Du Pont's price cut of 25 percent for Dacron. This happened when Du Pont decided that industry production capacity already exceeded demand, and more plants were due to start production.

It's important to keep in mind that oligopoly situations don't just apply to whole industries and national markets. Competitors who are focusing on the same local target market often face oligopoly situations. A suburban community might have several gas stations, all of which provide essentially the same product. In this case,

Exhibit A-13
Oligopoly–Kinked Demand Curve– Situation

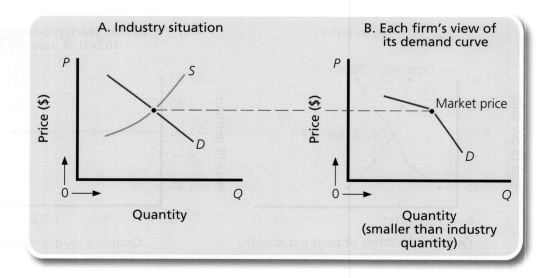

A. Industry situation

B. Each firm's view of its demand curve

the "industry" consists of the gas stations competing with one another in the local product-market.

As in pure competition, oligopolists face a long-run trend toward an equilibrium level, with profits driven toward zero. This may not happen immediately—and a marketing manager may try to delay price competition by relying more on other elements in the marketing mix.

When competition is monopolistic

A price must be set

You can see why marketing managers want to avoid pure competition or oligopoly situations. They prefer a market in which they have more control. **Monopolistic competition** is a market situation that develops when a market has

1. Different (heterogeneous) products—in the eyes of some customers.
2. Sellers who feel they do have some competition in this market.

The word *monopolistic* means that each firm is trying to get control in its own little market. But the word *competition* means that there are still substitutes. The vigorous competition of a purely competitive market is reduced. Each firm has its own down-sloping demand curve. But the shape of the curve depends on the similarity of competitors' products and marketing mixes. Each monopolistic competitor has freedom—but not complete freedom—in its own market.

Judging elasticity will help set the price

Because a firm in monopolistic competition has its own down-sloping demand curve, it must make a decision about price level as part of its marketing strategy planning. Here, estimating the elasticity of the firm's own demand curve is helpful. If it is highly inelastic, the firm may decide to raise prices to increase total revenue. But if demand is highly elastic, this may mean there are many competitors with acceptable substitutes. Then the price may have to be set near that of the competition. And the marketing manager probably should try to develop a better marketing mix.

CONCLUSION

The economist's traditional demand and supply analysis provides a useful tool for analyzing the nature of demand and competition. It is especially important that you master the concepts of a demand curve and demand elasticity. How demand and supply interact helps determine the size of a market and its price level. The interaction of supply and demand also helps explain the nature of competition in different market situations. We discussed three competitive situations: pure competition, oligopoly, and monopolistic competition. The fourth kind, monopoly, isn't found very often and is like monopolistic competition.

The nature of supply and demand—and competition—is very important in marketing strategy planning. We discuss these topics more fully in Chapters 3 and 4 and then build on them throughout the text. This appendix provides a good foundation on these topics.

KEY TERMS

LO A.6

law of diminishing demand, 533

demand curve, 533

inelastic demand, 535

elastic demand, 535

substitutes, 536

supply curve, 538

inelastic supply, 539

elastic supply, 539

equilibrium point, 539

consumer surplus, 540

pure competition, 541

oligopoly, 542

monopolistic competition, 543

QUESTIONS AND PROBLEMS

1. Explain in your own words how economists look at markets and arrive at the "law of diminishing demand."

2. Explain what a demand curve is and why it is usually down-sloping. Then give an example of a product for which the demand curve might not be down-sloping over some possible price ranges. Explain the reason for your choice.

3. What is the length of life of the typical demand curve? Illustrate your answer.

4. If the general market demand for men's shoes is fairly elastic, how does the demand for men's dress shoes compare to it? How does the demand curve for women's shoes compare to the demand curve for men's shoes?

5. If the demand for perfume is inelastic above and below the present price, should the price be raised? Why or why not?

6. If the demand for shrimp is highly elastic below the present price, should the price be lowered?

7. Discuss what factors lead to inelastic demand and supply curves. Are they likely to be found together in the same situation?

8. Why would a marketing manager prefer to sell a product that has no close substitutes? Are high profits almost guaranteed?

9. If a manufacturer's well-known product is sold at the same price by many retailers in the same community, is this an example of pure competition? When a community has many small grocery stores, are they in pure competition? What characteristics are needed to have a purely competitive market?

10. List three products that are sold in purely competitive markets and three that are sold in monopolistically competitive markets. Do any of these products have anything in common? Can any generalizations be made about competitive situations and marketing mix planning?

11. Cite a local example of an oligopoly, and explain why it is an oligopoly.

Marketing Arithmetic

LEARNING OBJECTIVES

Marketing students must become familiar with the essentials of the language of business. Businesspeople commonly use accounting terms when talking about costs, prices, and profit. And using accounting data is a practical tool in analyzing marketing problems. The objectives of this appendix and the sections that follow will help you understand these concepts and how they are used by marketing managers.

When you finish this appendix, you should be able to

1 Understand the components of an operating statement (profit and loss statement).

2 Know how to compute the stockturn rate.

3 Understand how operating ratios can be used to analyze a business.

4 Understand how to calculate markups and markdowns.

5 Understand how to calculate a return on investment (ROI) and return on assets (ROA).

6 Understand the basic forecasting approaches and why they are used.

7 Understand important new terms (shown in red).

The Operating Statement

LO B.1

An **operating statement** is a simple summary of the financial results of a company's operations over a specified period of time. Some beginning students may feel that the operating statement is complex, but as we'll soon see, this really isn't true. *The main purpose of the operating statement is determining the net profit figure and presenting data to support that figure.* This is why the operating statement is often referred to as the *profit and loss statement.*

Exhibit B-1
An Operating Statement (Profit and Loss Statement)

Perry Company Operating Statement For the Year Ended December 31, 201X			
Gross sales			$540,000
Less: Returns and allowances			40,000
Net sales			$500,000
Cost of sales:			
Beginning inventory at cost		$80,000	
Purchases at billed cost	$310,000		
Less: Purchase discounts	40,000		
Purchases at net cost	270,000		
Plus: freight-in	20,000		
Net cost of delivered purchases		290,000	
Cost of goods available for sale		370,000	
Less: Ending inventory at cost		70,000	
Cost of sales			300,000
Gross margin (gross profit)			200,000
Expenses:			
Selling expenses:			
Sales salaries	60,000		
Advertising expense	20,000		
Website updates	10,000		
Delivery expense	10,000		
Total selling expense		100,000	
Administrative expense:			
Office salaries	30,000		
Office supplies	10,000		
Miscellaneous administrative expense	5,000		
Total administrative expense		45,000	
General expense:			
Rent expense	10,000		
Miscellaneous general expenses	5,000		
Total general expense		15,000	
Total expenses			160,000
Net profit from operation			$ 40,000

Exhibit B-1 shows an operating statement for a wholesale or retail business. The statement is complete and detailed so you will see the framework throughout the discussion, but the amount of detail on an operating statement is *not* standardized. Many companies use financial statements with much less detail than this one. They emphasize clarity and readability rather than detail. To really understand an operating statement, however, you must know about its components.

Only three basic components

The basic components of an operating statement are *sales*—which come from the sale of goods and services; *costs*—which come from the producing and selling process; and the balance (called *profit* or *loss*)—which is just the difference between sales and costs. So there are only three basic components in the statement: sales, costs, and profit (or loss). Other items on an operating statement are there only to provide supporting details.

Time period covered may vary

There is no one time period an operating statement covers. Rather, statements are prepared to satisfy the needs of a particular business. This may be at the end of each day or at the end of each week. Usually, however, an operating statement summarizes results for one month, three months, six months, or a full year. Because the time period does vary, this information is included in the heading of the statement as follows:

**Perry Company
Operating Statement
For the (Period) Ended (Date)**

Also see Exhibit B–1.

Management's uses of operating statements

Before going on to a more detailed discussion of the components of our operating statement, let's think about some of the uses for such a statement. Exhibit B–1 shows that a lot of information is presented in a clear and concise manner. With this information, a manager can easily find the relation of net sales to the cost of sales, the gross margin, expenses, and net profit. Opening and closing inventory figures are available—as is the amount spent during the period for the purchase of goods for resale. Total expenses are listed to make it easier to compare them with previous statements and to help control these expenses.

All this information is important to a company's managers. Assume that a particular company prepares monthly operating statements. A series of these statements is a valuable tool for directing and controlling the business. By comparing results from one month to the next, managers can uncover unfavorable trends in the sales, costs, or profit areas of the business and take any needed action.

A skeleton statement gets down to essential details

Let's refer to Exhibit B–1 and begin to analyze this seemingly detailed statement to get first-hand knowledge of the components of the operating statement.

As a first step, suppose we take all the items that have dollar amounts extended to the third, or right-hand, column. Using these items only, the operating statement looks like this:

Gross sales	$540,000
Less: Returns and allowances	40,000
Net sales	500,000
Less: Cost of sales	300,000
Gross margin	200,000
Less: Total expenses	160,000
Net profit (loss)	$ 40,000

Is this a complete operating statement? The answer is *yes*. This skeleton statement differs from Exhibit B–1 only in supporting detail. All the basic components are included. In fact, the only items we must list to have a complete operating statement are

Net sales	$500,000
Less: Costs	460,000
Net profit (loss)	$ 40,000

These three items are the essentials of an operating statement. All other subdivisions or details are just useful additions.

Meaning of sales

Now let's define the meaning of the terms in the skeleton statement.

The first item is sales. What do we mean by sales? The term **gross sales** is the total amount charged to all customers during some time period. However, there is always some customer dissatisfaction or just plain errors in ordering and shipping goods. This results in returns and allowances, which reduce gross sales.

A **return** occurs when a customer sends back purchased products. The company either refunds the purchase price or allows the customer dollar credit on other purchases.

An **allowance** usually occurs when a customer is not satisfied with a purchase for some reason. The company gives a price reduction on the original invoice (bill), but the customer keeps the goods and services.

These refunds and price reductions must be considered when the firm computes its net sales figure for the period. Really, we're only interested in the revenue the company manages to keep. This is **net sales**—the actual sales dollars the company receives. Therefore, all reductions, refunds, cancellations, and so forth made because of returns and allowances are deducted from the original total (gross sales) to get net sales. This is shown below.

Gross sales	$540,000
Less: Returns and allowances	40,000
Net sales	$500,000

Meaning of cost of sales

The next item in the operating statement—**cost of sales**—is the total value (at cost) of the sales during the period. We'll discuss this computation later. Meanwhile, note that after we obtain the cost of sales figure, we subtract it from the net sales figure to get the gross margin.

Meaning of gross margin and expenses

Gross margin (gross profit) is the money left to cover the expenses of selling the products and operating the business. Firms hope that a profit will be left after subtracting these expenses.

Selling expense is commonly the major expense below the gross margin. Note that in Exhibit B–1, **expenses** are all the remaining costs subtracted from the gross margin to get the net profit. The expenses in this case are the selling, administrative, and general expenses. (Note that the cost of purchases and cost of sales are not included in this total expense figure—they were subtracted from net sales earlier to get the gross margin. Note, also, that some accountants refer to cost of sales as cost of goods sold.)

Net profit—at the bottom of the statement—is what the company earned from its operations during a particular period. It is the amount left after the cost of sales and the expenses are subtracted from net sales. *Net sales and net profit are not the same.* Many firms have large sales and no profits—they may even have losses! That's why understanding costs, and controlling them, is important.

Detailed Analysis of Sections of the Operating Statement

Cost of sales for a wholesale or retail company

The cost of sales section includes details that are used to find the cost of sales ($300,000 in our example).

In Exhibit B–1, you can see that beginning and ending inventory, purchases, purchase discounts, and freight-in are all necessary to calculate cost of sales. If we pull the cost of sales section from the operating statement, it looks like this:

Cost of sales:			
Beginning inventory at cost.		$80,000	
Purchases at billed cost	$310,000		
Less: Purchase discounts.	40,000		
Purchases at net cost.	270,000		
Plus: freight-in.	20,000		
Net cost of delivered purchases		290,000	
Cost of goods available for sale		370,000	
Less: Ending inventory at cost		70,000	
Cost of sales.			$300,000

Cost of sales is the cost value of what is *sold,* not the cost of goods on hand at any given time.

Inventory figures merely show the cost of goods on hand at the beginning and end of the period the statement covers. These figures may be obtained by physically counting goods on hand on these dates or estimated from perpetual inventory records that show the inventory balance at any given time. The methods used to determine the inventory should be as accurate as possible because these figures affect the cost of sales during the period and net profit.

The net cost of delivered purchases must include freight charges and purchase discounts received because these items affect the money actually spent to buy goods and bring them to the place of business. A **purchase discount** is a reduction of the original invoice amount for some business reason. For example, a cash discount may be given for prompt payment of the amount due. We subtract the total of such discounts from the original invoice cost of purchases to get the *net* cost of purchases. To this figure we add the freight charges for bringing the goods to the place of business. This gives the net cost of *delivered* purchases. When we add the net cost of delivered purchases to the beginning inventory at cost, we have the total cost of goods available for sale during the period. If we now subtract the ending inventory at cost from the cost of the goods available for sale, we get the cost of sales.

One important point should be noted about cost of sales. The way the value of inventory is calculated varies from one company to another—and it can cause big differences in the cost of sales and the operating statement. (See any basic accounting textbook for how the various inventory valuation methods work.)

Exhibit B–1 shows the way the manager of a wholesale or retail business arrives at her cost of sales. Such a business *purchases* finished products and resells them. In a manufacturing company, the purchases section of this operating statement is replaced by a section called cost of production. This section includes purchases of raw materials and parts, direct and indirect labor costs, and factory overhead charges (such as heat, light, and power) that are necessary to produce finished products. The cost of production is added to the beginning finished products inventory to arrive at the cost of products available for sale. Often, a separate cost of production statement is prepared, and only the total cost of production is shown in the operating statement. See Exhibit B–2 for an illustration of the cost of sales section of an operating statement for a manufacturing company.

Expenses

Expenses go below the gross margin. They usually include the costs of selling and the costs of administering the business. They do not include the cost of sales, either purchased or produced.

There is no right method for classifying the expense accounts or arranging them on the operating statement. They can just as easily be arranged alphabetically or according to amount, with the largest placed at the top and so on down the line. In a business of any size, though, it is clearer to group the expenses in some way and use subtotals by groups for analysis and control purposes. This was done in Exhibit B–1.

Summary on operating statements

The statement presented in Exhibit B–1 contains all the major categories in an operating statement—together with a normal amount of supporting detail. Further detail can be added to the statement under any of the major categories without changing the nature of the statement. The amount of detail normally is determined by how the statement will be used. A stockholder may be given an abbreviated operating statement—whereas the one prepared for internal company use may have a lot of detail.

Computing the Stockturn Rate

LO B.2

A detailed operating statement can provide the data needed to compute the **stockturn rate**—a measure of the number of times the average inventory is sold during a year. Note that the stockturn rate is related to the *turnover during a year,* not the length of time covered by a particular operating statement.

Exhibit B-2 Cost of Sales Section of an Operating Statement for a Manufacturing Firm

Cost of sales:		
Finished products inventory (beginning)........	$ 20,000	
Cost of production (Schedule 1)...............	100,000	
Total cost of finished products available for sale.	120,000	
Less: Finished products inventory (ending) ...	30,000	
Cost of sales............................		$ 90,000

Schedule 1, Schedule of cost of production		
Beginning work in process inventory.............		15,000
Raw materials:		
Beginning raw materials inventory.............	10,000	
Net cost of delivered purchases...............	80,000	
Total cost of materials available for use	90,000	
Less: Ending raw materials inventory.........	15,000	
Cost of materials placed in production	75,000	
Direct labor.....................................	20,000	
Manufacturing expenses:		
Indirect labor............................... $4,000		
Maintenance and repairs 3,000		
Factory supplies 1,000		
Heat, light, and power....................... 2,000		
Total manufacturing expenses	10,000	
Total manufacturing costs.......................		105,000
Total work in process during period..............		120,000
Less: Ending work in process inventory		20,000
Cost of production		$100,000

The stockturn rate is a very important measure because it shows how rapidly the firm's inventory is moving. Some businesses typically have slower turnover than others. But a drop in turnover in a particular business can be very alarming. It may mean that the firm's assortment of products is no longer as attractive as it was. Also, it may mean that the firm will need more working capital to handle the same volume of sales. Most businesses pay a lot of attention to the stockturn rate, trying to get faster turnover (and lower inventory costs).

Three methods, all basically similar, can be used to compute the stockturn rate. Which method is used depends on the data available. These three methods, which usually give approximately the same results, are shown below.*

$$(1) \quad \frac{\text{Cost of sales}}{\text{Average inventory at cost}}$$

$$(2) \quad \frac{\text{Net sales}}{\text{Average inventory at selling price}}$$

$$(3) \quad \frac{\text{Sales in units}}{\text{Average inventory in units}}$$

Computing the stockturn rate will be illustrated only for Formula 1, because all are similar. The only difference is that the cost figures used in Formula 1 are changed to a selling price or numerical count basis in Formulas 2 and 3. (*Note:* Regardless of

---

* Differences occur because of varied markups and nonhomogeneous product assortments. In an assortment of tires, for example, those with low markups might have sold much better than those with high markups. But with Formula 3, all tires would be treated equally.

the method used, you must have both the numerator and denominator of the formula in the same terms.)

If the inventory level varies a lot during the year, you may need detailed information about the inventory level at different times to compute the average inventory. If it stays at about the same level during the year, however, it's easy to get an estimate. For example, using Formula 1, the average inventory at cost is computed by adding the beginning and ending inventories at cost and dividing by 2. This average inventory figure is then divided into the cost of sales (in cost terms) to get the stockturn rate.

For example, suppose that the cost of sales for one year was $1,000,000. Beginning inventory was $250,000 and ending inventory $150,000. Adding the two inventory figures and dividing by 2, we get an average inventory of $200,000. We next divide the cost of sales by the average inventory ($1,000,000 ÷ $200,000) and get a stockturn rate of 5. The stockturn rate is covered further in Chapter 18.

Operating Ratios Help Analyze the Business

LO B.3

Many businesspeople use the operating statement to calculate **operating ratios**—the ratio of items on the operating statement to net sales—and to compare these ratios from one time period to another. They can also compare their own operating ratios with those of competitors. Such competitive data are often available through trade associations. Each firm may report its results to a trade association, which then distributes summary results to its members. These ratios help managers control their operations. If some expense ratios are rising, for example, those particular costs are singled out for special attention.

Operating ratios are computed by dividing net sales into the various operating statement items that appear below the net sales level in the operating statement. The net sales figure is used as the denominator in the operating ratio because it shows the sales the firm actually won.

We can see the relation of operating ratios to the operating statement if we think of there being another column to the right of the dollar figures in an operating statement. This column contains percentage figures, using net sales as 100 percent. This approach can be seen below.

Gross sales	$540,000	
Less: Returns and allowances	40,000	
Net sales	500,000	100%
Less: Cost of sales	300,000	60
Gross margin	200,000	40
Less: Total expenses	160,000	32
Net profit	$ 40,000	8%

The 40 percent ratio of gross margin to net sales in the preceding example shows that 40 percent of the net sales dollar is available to cover selling and administrative expenses and provide a profit. Note that the ratio of expenses to sales added to the ratio of profit to sales equals the 40 percent gross margin ratio. The net profit ratio of 8 percent shows that 8 percent of the net sales dollar is left for profit.

The value of percentage ratios should be obvious. The percentages are easily figured and much easier to compare than large dollar figures.

Note that because these operating statement categories are interrelated, only a few pieces of information are needed to figure the others. In this case, for example, knowing the gross margin percent and net profit percent makes it possible to figure the expenses and cost of sales percentages. Further, knowing just one dollar amount and the percentages lets you figure all the other dollar amounts.

Markups

A **markup** is the dollar amount added to the cost of sales to get the selling price. The markup usually is similar to the firm's gross margin because the markup amount added onto the unit cost of a product by a retailer or wholesaler is expected to cover the selling and administrative expenses and to provide a profit.

The markup approach to pricing is discussed in Chapter 18, so it will not be discussed at length here. But a simple example illustrates the idea. If a retailer buys an article that costs $1 when delivered to his store, he must sell it for more than this cost if he hopes to make a profit. So he might add 50 cents onto the cost of the article to cover his selling and other costs and, hopefully, to provide a profit. The 50 cents is the markup.

The 50 cents is also the gross margin or gross profit from that item *if* it is sold. But note that it is *not* the net profit. Selling expenses may amount to 35 cents, 45 cents, or even 55 cents. In other words, there is no guarantee the markup will cover costs. Further, there is no guarantee customers will buy at the marked-up price. This may require markdowns, which are discussed later in this appendix.

Markup conversions

Often it is convenient to use markups as percentages rather than focusing on the actual dollar amounts. But markups can be figured as a percent of cost or selling price. To have some agreement, *markup (percent)* will mean percentage of selling price unless stated otherwise. So the 50-cent markup built into the $1.50 *selling price* is a markup of 33⅓ percent. On the other hand, the 50-cent markup is a 50 percent markup on *cost*.

Some retailers and wholesalers use markup conversion tables or spreadsheets to easily convert from cost to selling price, depending on the markup on selling price they want. To see the interrelation, look at the two formulas below. They can be used to convert either type of markup to the other.

$$(4) \quad \frac{\text{Percent markup}}{\text{on selling price}} = \frac{\text{Percent markup on cost}}{100\% + \text{Percent markup on cost}}$$

$$(5) \quad \frac{\text{Percent markup}}{\text{on cost}} = \frac{\text{Percent markup on selling price}}{100\% - \text{Percent markup on selling price}}$$

In the previous example, we had a cost of $1, a markup of 50 cents, and a selling price of $1.50. We saw that the markup on selling price was 33⅓ percent—and on cost, it was 50 percent. Let's substitute these percentage figures—in Formulas 4 and 5—to see how to convert from one basis to the other. Assume first of all that we know only the markup on selling price and want to convert to markup on cost. Using Formula 5, we get

$$\text{Percent markup on cost} = \frac{33\tfrac{1}{3}\%}{100\% - 33\tfrac{1}{3}\%} = \frac{33\tfrac{1}{3}\%}{66\tfrac{1}{3}\%} = 50\%$$

On the other hand, if we know only the percent markup on cost, we can convert to markup on selling price as follows:

$$\text{Percent markup on selling price} = \frac{50\%}{100\% + 50\%} = \frac{50\%}{150\%} = 33\tfrac{1}{3}\%$$

These results can be proved and summarized as follows:

Markup $0.50 = 50% of cost, or 33⅓% of selling price

+ Cost $1.00 = 100% of cost, or 66⅔% of selling price

Selling price $1.50 = 150% of cost, or 100% of selling price

Note that when the selling price ($1.50) is the base for a markup calculation, the markup percent (33⅓ percent = $0.50/$1.50) must be less than 100 percent. As you can see, that's because the markup percent and the cost percent (66⅔ percent = $1.00/$1.50) sum to exactly 100 percent. So if you see a reference to a markup percent that is greater than 100 percent, it could not be based on the selling price and instead must be based on cost.

Markdown Ratios Help Control Retail Operations

The ratios we discussed previously were concerned with figures on the operating statement. Another important ratio, the **markdown ratio**, is a tool many retailers use to measure the efficiency of various departments and their whole business. But note that it is *not directly related to the operating statement*. It requires special calculations.

A **markdown** is a retail price reduction required because customers won't buy some item at the originally marked-up price. This refusal to buy may be due to a variety of reasons—soiling, style changes, fading, damage caused by handling, or an original price that was too high. To get rid of these products, the retailer offers them at a lower price.

Markdowns are generally considered to be due to business errors, perhaps because of poor buying, original markups that are too high, and other reasons. (Note, however, that some retailers use markdowns as a way of doing business rather than a way to correct errors. For example, a store that buys overstocked fashions from other retailers may start by marking each item with a high price and then reduce the price each week until it sells.) Regardless of the reason, however, markdowns are reductions in the original price—and they are important to managers who want to measure the effectiveness of their operations.

Markdowns are similar to allowances, because price reductions are made. Thus, in computing a markdown ratio, markdowns and allowances are usually added together and then divided by net sales. The markdown ratio is computed as follows:

$$\text{Markdown \%} = \frac{\$ \text{ Markdowns} + \$ \text{ Allowances}}{\$ \text{ Net sales}} \times 100$$

The 100 is multiplied by the fraction to get rid of decimal points.

Returns are *not* included when figuring the markdown ratio. Returns are treated as consumer errors, not business errors, and therefore are not included in this measure of business efficiency.

Retailers who use markdown ratios usually keep a record of the amount of markdowns and allowances in each department and then divide the total by the net sales in each department. Over a period of time, these ratios give management one measure of the efficiency of buyers and salespeople in various departments.

It should be stressed again that the markdown ratio is not calculated directly from data on the operating statement because the markdowns take place before the products are sold. In fact, some products may be marked down and still not sold. Even if the marked-down items are not sold, the markdowns—that is, the reevaluations of their value—are included in the calculations in the time period when they are taken.

The markdown ratio is calculated for a whole department (or profit center), *not* individual items. What we are seeking is a measure of the effectiveness of a whole department, not how well the department did on individual items.

Return on Investment (ROI) Reflects Asset Use

LO B.5

Another off-the-operating-statement ratio is **return on investment (ROI)**—the ratio of net profit (after taxes) to the investment used to make the net profit, multiplied by 100 to get rid of decimals. Investment is not shown on the operating statement. But it is shown on the **balance sheet** (statement of financial condition), which is another accounting statement that shows a company's assets, liabilities, and net worth. It may take some digging or special analysis, however, to find the right investment number.

Investment means the dollar resources the firm has invested in a project or business. For example, a new product may require $4 million in new money—for inventory, accounts receivable, promotion, and so on—and its attractiveness may be judged by its likely ROI. If the net profit (after taxes) for this new product is expected to be $1 million in the first year, then the ROI is 25 percent—that is, ($1 million ÷ $4 million) × 100.

There are two ways to figure ROI. The *direct* way is

$$\text{ROI (in \%)} = \frac{\text{Net profit (after taxes)}}{\text{Investment}} \times 100$$

The *indirect* way is

$$\text{ROI (in \%)} = \frac{\text{Net profit (after taxes)}}{\text{sales}} = \frac{\text{Sales}}{\text{Investment}} \times 100$$

This way is concerned with net profit margin and turnover—that is,

$$\text{ROI (in \%)} = \text{Net profit margin} \times \text{Turnover} \times 100$$

This indirect way makes it clearer how to *increase* ROI. There are three ways:

1. Increase profit margin (with lower costs or a higher price)
2. Increase sales
3. Decrease investment

Effective marketing strategy planning and implementation can increase profit margins, sales, or both. And careful asset management can decrease investment.

ROI is a revealing measure of how well managers are doing. Most companies have alternative uses for their funds. If the returns in a business aren't at least as high as outside uses, then the money probably should be shifted to the more profitable uses.

Some firms borrow more than others to make investments. In other words, they invest less of their own money to acquire assets—what we called *investments*. If ROI calculations use only the firm's own investment, this gives higher ROI figures to those who borrow a lot—which is called *leveraging*. To adjust for different borrowing proportions—to make comparisons among projects, departments, divisions, and companies easier—another ratio has come into use. **Return on assets (ROA)** is the ratio of net profit (after taxes) to the assets used to make the net profit—times 100. Both ROI and ROA measures are trying to get at the same thing—how effectively the company is using resources. These measures became increasingly popular as profit rates dropped and it became more obvious that increasing sales volume doesn't necessarily lead to higher profits—or ROI or ROA. Inflation and higher costs for borrowed funds also force more concern for ROI and ROA. Marketers must include these measures in their thinking, or top managers are likely to ignore their plans and requests for financial resources.

Forecasting Target Market Potential and Sales

LO B.6

Effective strategy planning and developing a marketing plan require estimates of future sales, costs, and profits. Without such information, it's hard to know if a strategy is potentially profitable.

The marketing manager's estimates of sales, costs, and profits are usually based on a forecast (estimate) of target **market potential**—what a whole market segment might buy—and a **sales forecast**—an estimate of how much an industry or firm hopes to sell to a market segment. Usually we must first try to judge market potential before we can estimate what share a particular firm may be able to win with its particular marketing mix.

Three levels of forecasts are useful

We're interested in forecasting the potential in specific market segments. To do this, it helps to make three levels of forecasts.

Some economic conditions affect the entire global economy. Others may influence only one country or a particular industry. And some may affect only one company or one product's sales potential. For this reason, a common top-down approach to forecasting is to

1. Develop a *national income forecast* (for each country in which the firm operates) and use this to
2. Develop an *industry sales forecast,* which then is used to
3. Develop forecasts for a *specific company,* its *specific products,* and the *segments* it targets.

Generally, a marketing manager doesn't have to make forecasts for a national economy or the broad industry. This kind of forecasting—basically trend projecting—is a specialty in itself. Such forecasts are available in business and government publications, and large companies often have their own technical specialists. Managers can use just one source's forecast or combine several. Unfortunately, however, the more targeted the marketing manager's earlier segmenting efforts have been, the less likely that industry forecasts will match the firm's product-markets. So managers have to move directly to estimating potential for their own companies and for their specific products.

Two approaches to forecasting

Many methods are used to forecast market potential and sales, but they can all be grouped into two basic approaches: (1) extending past behavior and (2) predicting future behavior. The large number of methods may seem confusing at first, but this variety has an advantage. Forecasts are so important that managers often develop forecasts in two or three different ways and then compare the differences before preparing a final forecast.

Extending past behavior can miss important turning points

When we forecast for existing products, we usually have some past data to go on. The basic approach, called **trend extension,** extends past experience into the future. With existing products, for example, the past trend of actual sales may be extended into the future (see Exhibit B–3).

Ideally, when extending past sales behavior, we should decide why sales vary. This is the difficult and time-consuming part of sales forecasting. Usually we can gather a lot of data about the product or market or about changes in the market environment. But unless we know the *reason* for past sales variations, it's hard to predict in what direction, and by how much, sales will move. Graphing the data and statistical techniques—including correlation and regression analysis—can be useful here. (These techniques, which are beyond our scope, are discussed in beginning statistics courses.)

Once we know why sales vary, we can usually develop a specific forecast. Sales may be moving directly up as population grows in a specific market segment, for example. So we can just estimate how population is expected to grow and project the impact on sales.

The weakness of the trend extension method is that it assumes past conditions will continue unchanged into the future. In fact, the future isn't always like the past. An agent wholesaler's business may have been on a steady path, but the development of the Internet may have added a totally new factor. The past trend for the agent's sales has changed because now the agent can quickly reach a broader market.

Exhibit B-3 Straight-Line Trend Projection—Extends Past Sales into the Future

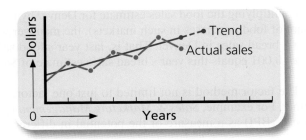

As another example, for years the trend in sales of disposable diapers moved closely with the number of new births. However, as the number of women in the workforce increased and as more women returned to jobs after babies were born, use of disposable diapers increased, and the trend changed. As in these examples, trend extension estimates will be wrong whenever big changes occur. For this reason—although they may extend past behavior for one estimate—most managers look for another way to help them forecast sharp market changes.

Predicting future behavior takes judgment

When we try to predict what will happen in the future instead of just extending the past, we have to use other methods and add more judgment. Some of these methods (to be discussed later) include juries of executive opinion, salespeople's estimates, surveys, panels, and market tests.

Forecasting Company and Product Sales by Extending Past Behavior

Past sales can be extended

At the very least, a marketing manager ought to know what the firm's present markets look like and what it has sold to them in the past. A detailed sales analysis for products and geographic areas helps to project future results.

Just extending past sales into the future may not seem like much of a forecasting method. But it's better than just assuming that next year's total sales will be the same as this year's.

Factor method includes more than time

A simple extension of past sales gives one forecast. But it's usually desirable to tie future sales to something more than the passage of time.

The factor method tries to do this. The **factor method** tries to forecast sales by finding a relation between the company's sales and some other factor (or factors). The basic formula is: Something (past sales, industry sales, etc.) *times* some factor *equals* sales forecast. A **factor** is a variable that shows the relation of some other variable to the item being forecast. For instance, in the preceding example, both the birthrate and the number of working mothers are factors related to sales of disposable diapers.

A bread producer example

The following example, about a bread producer, shows how firms can make forecasts for many geographic market segments using the factor method and available data. This general approach can be useful for any firm—producer, wholesaler, or retailer.

Analysis of past sales relationships showed that the bread manufacturer regularly sold one-tenth of 1 percent (0.001) of the total retail food sales in its various target markets. This is a single factor. By using this single factor, a manager could estimate the producer's sales in a new market for the coming period by multiplying a forecast of expected retail food sales by 0.001.

Sales & Marketing Management magazine makes retail food sales estimates each year. Exhibit B–4 shows the kind of geographically detailed data available.

Let's carry this bread example further—using the data in Exhibit B–4 for the Denver, Colorado, metro area. Denver's food sales were $4,700,116,000 for the previous year. By simply accepting last year's food sales as an estimate of next year's sales and multiplying the food sales estimate for Denver by the 0.001 factor (the firm's usual share of food purchases in such markets), the manager would have an estimate of next year's bread sales in Denver. That is, last year's food sales estimate ($4,700,116,000) times 0.001 equals this year's bread sales estimate of $4,700,116.

Factor method can use several factors

The factor method is not limited to just one factor; several factors can be used together. For example, *Sales & Marketing Management* regularly gives a "buying power index" (BPI) as a measure of the potential in different geographic areas (see Exhibit

Exhibit B-4 Illustrative Page from Sales & Marketing Management's Survey of Buying Power: Metro and County Totals

COLORADO

METRO AREA County City	Total Population (000s)	% Population by Age Group				House-holds (000s)	Total Retail Sales	Food & Beverage Stores	Food Service & Drinking Establish-ments	General Merchan-dise	Furniture & Home Furnish. & Electron. & Appliances	Motor Vehicle & Parts Dealers	Total EBI ($000)	Median Hsld. EBI	Effective Buying Income % of Hslds: by EBI Group			Buying Power Index
		18-24	25-34	35-49	50+										A $20,000-$34,999	B $35,000-$49,999	C $50,000 & Over	
BOULDER-LONGMONT	**303.7**	**13.6**	**15.5**	**25.6**	**22.4**	**119.6**	**5,081,227**	**1,001,555**	**556,377**	**448,453**	**247,484**	**1,220,087**	**7,716,546**	**51,714**	**17.8**	**17.1**	**51.6**	**0.1360**
BOULDER	303.7	13.6	15.5	25.6	22.4	119.6	5,081,227	1,001,555	556,377	448,453	247,484	1,220,087	7,716,546	51,714	17.8	17.1	51.6	0.1360
.Boulder	97.1	26.4	18.8	20.0	20.1	40.7	2,147,663	439,133	267,970	121,357	117,520	447,464	2,480,204	43,427	21.5	15.8	43.1	0.0479
.Longmont	74.6	8.7	14.6	25.3	23.6	28.0	1,126,804	250,483	122,965	125,103	40,068	272,449	1,531,271	47,526	19.4	20.1	46.8	0.0290
COLORADO SPRINGS	**537.3**	**10.7**	**14.4**	**24.7**	**22.6**	**200.1**	**7,883,675**	**819,826**	**647,101**	**984,753**	**465,488**	**2,031,112**	**10,259,019**	**42,082**	**24.7**	**21.0**	**38.7**	**0.1994**
EL PASO	537.3	10.7	14.4	24.7	22.6	200.1	7,883,675	819,826	647,101	984,753	465,488	2,031,112	10,259,019	42,082	24.7	21.0	38.7	0.1994
.Colorado Springs	373.1	10.5	14.8	24.5	23.7	146.5	6,786,693	628,690	549,107	858,048	443,063	1,848,219	7,353,670	41,212	24.9	20.9	37.5	0.1515
DENVER	**2,199.5**	**9.2**	**16.2**	**25.0**	**23.8**	**858.0**	**33,750,880**	**4,700,116**	**3,232,590**	**3,615,646**	**2,518,616**	**9,368,057**	**52,585,220**	**49,109**	**18.8**	**19.0**	**48.9**	**0.9282**
ADAMS	382.9	10.5	16.7	23.3	21.1	134.3	4,558,882	670,017	371,810	416,956	385,657	1,466,781	6,459,840	42,802	22.5	22.4	38.7	0.1253
Thornton	87.3	9.7	17.5	24.9	18.0	30.6	707,386	152,812	68,679	122,478	40,099	150,769	1,594,293	48,053	19.4	22.4	46.8	0.0270
Westminster	105.4	9.9	17.1	26.0	20.3	40.1	1,052,771	153,993	114,177	292,678	100,304	88,416	2,368,971	51,512	17.0	21.6	51.9	0.0384
ARAPAHOE	505.4	8.8	15.1	25.7	23.9	197.5	9,846,119	1,160,676	872,314	963,885	595,477	4,049,257	13,314,002	52,887	18.2	18.6	53.1	0.2422
Aurora	286.8	10.4	17.2	24.0	21.0	109.0	3,889,713	531,245	378,269	566,166	225,882	1,236,463	5,874,943	47,398	20.7	21.5	46.0	0.1076
DENVER	568.5	11.1	19.9	22.1	25.1	243.7	9,287,630	1,235,129	1,270,413	730,810	755,362	1,701,220	13,899,851	42,540	21.6	18.4	41.0	0.2474
.Denver	568.5	11.1	19.9	22.1	25.1	243.7	9,275,551	1,224,988	1,269,426	730,810	755,362	1,700,815	13,899,851	42,540	21.6	18.4	41.0	0.2474
DOUGLAS	200.7	4.9	15.9	29.6	18.0	69.6	2,725,601	517,182	250,871	294,714	289,389	355,394	5,147,699	59,715	10.9	18.2	64.7	0.0851
JEFFERSON	542.0	8.3	13.2	26.8	26.5	212.9	7,332,648	1,117,112	467,182	1,209,281	492,731	1,795,405	13,763,828	54,470	16.4	18.6	55.1	0.2282
Arvada	104.0	8.0	11.9	25.9	28.1	40.0	1,007,245	224,707	79,597	133,524	60,181	74,965	2,332,241	51,557	18.1	19.3	51.8	0.0376
Lakewood	148.0	9.9	15.2	24.1	28.8	62.3	2,065,827	297,529	149,068	292,832	124,879	561,796	3,451,207	46,782	20.8	21.1	45.2	0.0599
DENVER-BOULDER-GREELEY																		
CONSOLIDATED AREA	**2,695.8**	**10.0**	**15.9**	**24.9**	**23.6**	**1,044.7**	**40,882,936**	**5,939,206**	**3,929,714**	**4,267,775**	**2,809,610**	**11,246,398**	**63,170,157**	**48,397**	**19.2**	**19.0**	**47.9**	**1.1216**

B–4). This index considers (1) the population in a market, (2) the retail sales in that market, and (3) income in that market. The BPI for the Denver, Colorado, metro area, for example, is 0.9282—that is, Denver accounts for 0.9282 percent of the total U.S. buying power. This means that consumers who live in Denver have higher than average buying power. We know this because Denver accounts for about 0.77 percent of the U.S. population.

Using several factors rather than only one uses more information. And in the case of the BPI, it gives a single measure of a market's potential. Rather than falling back on using population only, or income only, or trying to develop a special index, the BPI can be used in the same way that we used the 0.001 factor in the bread example.

Predicting Future Behavior Calls for More Judgment and Some Opinions

These past-extending methods use quantitative data—projecting past experience into the future and assuming that the future will be like the past. But this is risky in competitive markets. Usually, it's desirable to add some judgment to other forecasts before making the final forecast yourself.

Jury of executive opinion adds judgment

One of the oldest and simplest methods of forecasting—the **jury of executive opinion**—combines the opinions of experienced executives, perhaps from marketing, production, finance, purchasing, and top management. Each executive estimates market potential and sales for the *coming years.* Then they try to work out a consensus.

The main advantage of the jury approach is that it can be done quickly and easily. On the other hand, the results may not be very good. There may be too much extending of the past. Some of the executives may have little contact with outside market influences. But their estimates could point to major shifts in customer demand or competition.

Estimates from salespeople can help too

Using salespeople's estimates to forecast is like the jury approach. But salespeople are more likely than home office managers to be familiar with customer reactions and what competitors are doing. Their estimates are especially useful in some business markets where the few customers may be well known to the salespeople. But this approach can be useful in any type of market.

However, managers who use estimates from salespeople should be aware of the limitations. For example, new salespeople may not know much about their markets. Even experienced salespeople may not be aware of possible changes in the economic climate or the firm's other environments. And if salespeople think the manager is going to use the estimates to set sales quotas, the estimates may be low!

Surveys, panels, and market tests

Special surveys of final buyers, retailers, or wholesalers can show what's happening in different market segments. Some firms use panels of stores—or final consumers—to keep track of buying behavior and to decide when just extending past behavior isn't enough.

Surveys are sometimes combined with market tests when the company wants to estimate customers' reactions to possible changes in its marketing mix. A market test might show that a product increased its share of the market by 10 percent when its price was dropped 1 cent below competition. But this extra business might be quickly lost if the price were increased 1 cent above competition. Such market experiments help the marketing manager make good estimates of future sales when one or more of the Four Ps is changed.

Accuracy depends on the marketing mix

Forecasting can help a marketing manager estimate the size of possible market opportunities. But the accuracy of any sales forecast depends on whether the firm selects and implements a marketing mix that turns these opportunities into sales and profits.

KEY TERMS

operating statement, 545

gross sales, 547

return, 547

allowance, 548

net sales, 548

cost of sales, 548

gross margin (gross profit), 548

expenses, 548

net profit, 548

purchase discount, 549

stockturn rate, 549

operating ratios, 551

markup, 551

markdown ratio, 553

markdown, 553

return on investment (ROI), 553

balance sheet, 554

return on assets (ROA), 554

market potential, 554

sales forecast, 554

trend extension, 555

factor method, 556

factor, 556

jury of executive opinion, 558

QUESTIONS AND PROBLEMS

1. Distinguish between the following pairs of items that appear on operating statements: (a) gross sales and net sales, and (b) purchases at billed cost and purchases at net cost.

2. How does gross margin differ from gross profit? From net profit?

3. Explain the similarity between markups and gross margin. What connection do markdowns have with the operating statement?

4. Compute the net profit for a company with the following data:

Beginning inventory (cost)	$ 150,000
Purchases at billed cost.	330,000
Sales returns and allowances.	250,000
Rent	60,000
Salaries.	400,000
Heat and light.	180,000
Ending inventory (cost)	250,000
Freight cost (inbound)	80,000
Gross sales	1,300,000

5. Construct an operating statement from the following data:

Returns and allowances.	$ 150,000
Expenses.	20%
Closing inventory at cost	600,000
Markdowns	2%
Inward transportation	30,000
Purchases	1,000,000
Net profit (5%)	300,000

6. Compute net sales and percent of markdowns for the following data:

Markdowns	$ 40,000
Gross sales	400,000
Returns.	32,000
Allowances	48,000

7. (a) What percentage markups on cost are equivalent to the following percentage markups on selling price: 20, $37\frac{1}{2}$, 50, and $66\frac{2}{3}$? (b) What percentage markups on selling price are equivalent to the following percentage markups on cost: $33\frac{1}{3}$, 20, 40, and 50?

8. What net sales volume is required to obtain a stockturn rate of 20 times a year on an average inventory at cost of $100,000 with a gross margin of 25 percent?

9. Explain how the general manager of a department store might use the markdown ratios computed for her various departments. Is this a fair measure? Of what?

10. Compare and contrast return on investment (ROI) and return on assets (ROA) measures. Which would be best for a retailer with no bank borrowing or other outside sources of funds (that is, the retailer has put up all the money that the business needs)?

11. Explain the difference between a forecast of market potential and a sales forecast.

12. Suggest a plausible explanation for sales fluctuations for (a) computers, (b) ice cream, (c) washing machines, (d) tennis rackets, (e) oats, (f) disposable diapers, and (g) latex for rubber-based paint.

13. Explain the factor method of forecasting. Illustrate your answer.

14. Based on data in Exhibit B-4, discuss the relative market potential of the city of Boulder, Colorado, and the city of Lakewood, Colorado, for (a) prepared cereals, (b) automobiles, and (c) furniture.

Career Planning in Marketing

There's a Place in Marketing for You

LO C.1

We're happy to tell you that many opportunities are available in marketing. There's a place in marketing for everyone, from a service provider in a fast-food restaurant to a vice president of marketing in a large company such as Microsoft or Procter & Gamble. The opportunities range widely, so it will help to be more specific. In the following pages, we'll discuss (1) the typical pay for different marketing jobs, (2) setting your own objectives and evaluating your interests and abilities, and (3) the kinds of jobs available in marketing. We'll also provide some ideas about using the Internet to get more information and perhaps apply for a job or post your own information; this material is in the What's Next box with the title "Getting wired for a career in marketing."

There Are Many Marketing Jobs, and They Can Pay Well

LO C.2

There are many interesting and challenging jobs for those with marketing training. You may not know it, but more than half of graduating college students take their initial job in a sales, marketing, or customer service position regardless of their stated major. So you'll have a head start because you've been studying marketing, and companies are always looking for people who already have skills in place. In terms of upward mobility, more CEOs have come from the sales and marketing side than all other fields combined. The sky is the limit for those who enter the sales and marketing profession prepared for the future!

Further, marketing jobs open to college-level students do pay well. According to the most recent salary surveys from the National Association of Colleges and Employers, at the time this book went to press, marketing graduates were being offered starting salaries around $40,000, with a range from $25,000 to more than $60,000. Students with a master's in marketing averaged about $60,000; those with an MBA averaged about $75,000. Starting salaries can vary considerably, depending on your background, experience, and location.

Starting salaries in marketing compare favorably with many other fields. They are lower than those in such fields as computer science and electrical engineering where college graduates are currently in demand. But there is even better opportunity for personal growth, variety, and income in many marketing positions. The *American Almanac of Jobs and Salaries* ranks the median income of marketers number 10 in a list of 125 professions. Marketing also supplies about 50 percent of the people who achieve senior management ranks.

How far and fast your career and income rise above the starting level, however, depends on many factors, including your willingness to work, how well you get along with people, and your individual abilities. But most of all, it depends on *getting results*—individually and through other people. And this is where many marketing jobs offer the newcomer great opportunities. It is possible to show initiative, ability, creativity, and judgment in marketing jobs. And some young people move up very rapidly in marketing. Some even end up at the top in large companies or as owners of their own businesses.

Marketing is often the route to the top

Marketing is where the action is! In the final analysis, a firm's success or failure depends on the effectiveness of its marketing program. This doesn't mean the other functional areas aren't important. It merely reflects the fact that a firm won't have much need for accountants, finance people, production managers, and so on if it can't successfully meet customers' needs and sell its products.

Because marketing is so vital to a firm's survival, many companies look for people with training and experience in marketing when filling key executive positions. In general, chief executive officers for the nation's largest corporations are more likely to have backgrounds in marketing and distribution than in other fields such as production, finance, and engineering.

Develop Your Own Personal Marketing Strategy

Now that you know there are many opportunities in marketing, your problem is matching the opportunities to your own personal objectives and strengths. Basically the problem is a marketing problem: developing a marketing strategy to sell a product—yourself—to potential employers. Just as in planning strategies for products, developing your own strategy takes careful thought. Exhibit C–1 shows how you can organize your own strategy planning. This exhibit shows that you should evaluate yourself first—a personal analysis—and then analyze the environment for opportunities. This will help you sharpen your own long- and short-run objectives, which will lead to

Exhibit C-1
Organizing Your Own
Personal Marketing
Strategy Planning

developing a strategy. Finally, you should start implementing your own personal marketing strategy. These ideas are explained more fully next.

Conduct Your Own Personal Analysis

You are the product you are going to include in your own marketing plan. So first you have to decide what your long-run objectives are—what you want to do, how hard you want to work, and how quickly you want to reach your objectives. Be honest with yourself—or you will eventually face frustration. Evaluate your own personal strengths and weaknesses—and decide what factors may become the key to your success. Finally, as part of your personal analysis, set some preliminary timetables to guide your strategy planning and implementation efforts. Let's spell this out in detail.

Set broad long-run objectives

Your strategy planning may require some trial-and-error decision making. But at the very beginning, you should make some tentative decisions about your own objectives—what you want out of a job and out of life. At the very least, you should decide whether you are just looking for a job or whether you want to build a career. Beyond this, do you want the position to be personally satisfying—or is the financial return enough? And just how much financial return do you need? Some people work only to support themselves (and their families) and their leisure-time activities. These people try to find job opportunities that provide adequate financial returns but aren't too demanding of their time or effort.

Other people look first for satisfaction in their job—and they seek opportunities for career advancement. Financial rewards may be important too, but these are used mainly as measures of success. In the extreme, the career-oriented individual may be willing to sacrifice a lot, including leisure and social activities, to achieve success in a career.

Once you've tentatively decided these matters, then you can get more serious about whether you should seek a job or a career in marketing. If you decide to pursue a career, you should set your broad long-run objectives to achieve it. For example, one

What's Next? Getting wired for a career

The Internet is a virtual treasure trove of resources for every stage of career planning and job hunting. It can help you learn: how to do a self-assessment, the outlook for different industries and jobs, what firms have jobs open, how to improve a résumé and post it online, and just about anything else you can imagine. Here we'll highlight just a few ideas and websites that can help you get started. However, if you start with some of these suggestions, each website you visit will provide links to other relevant sites that will give you new ideas.

If you are not sure about a career direction, a few sites can help you learn about potential jobs and careers. O*Net (http://www.onetonline.org/) allows you to explore different careers and find detailed descriptions of many types of jobs. The Vault (http://www.vault.com/) can be used to research industries and companies. WetFeet (http://www.wetfeet.com/) also provides access to articles, guides, and useful insights. Career One Stop (www.careeronestop.org), sponsored by the United States Department of Labor, provides a wide range of career and job search information. You can learn about average salary amounts and benefits, get advice about writing résumés and cover letters, and much more. You might also go to *The Wall Street Journal's* Career Journal site (www.careerjournal.com) where you can find job listings, job-hunting advice, career articles from *The Wall Street Journal,* and more. You can create and post a résumé there as well. Professional associations are another great resource.

LinkedIn.com (https://www.linkedin.com/) is the social networking site for business professionals. It has become sort of a must for job seekers. Set up your own LinkedIn page and begin networking; start by connecting with your instructors, fellow students, and business professionals you know and meet during the job search process. When you ask people to connect, personalize the invitation by reminding them of how you know each other or why you want to link specifically with them.

To learn more about jobs in marketing, you could start with the site www.marketingjobs.com, which has listings of marketing jobs, links to a number of companies with openings, a résumé center with ideas for preparing a résumé and posting it on the Internet, and lists of helpful periodicals. Other sites relevant to marketing professionals include the American Marketing Association (www.marketingpower.com), the Sales and Marketing Executives International (www.smei.org), and the Council of Supply Chain Management Professionals (www.cscmp.org). Similar professional sites exist for other careers.

Your college's career center may have additional resources you can check out—sometimes the career center subscribes to sites, so you can access pay sites at no charge. Of course a search engine can provide more specific insights—perhaps to employers in a particular area of the country or a very specific field.

---

long-run objective might be to pursue a career in marketing management (or marketing research). This might require more academic training than you planned, as well as a different kind of training. If your objective is to get a job that pays well, on the other hand, then this calls for a different kind of training and different kinds of job experiences before completing your academic work.

Evaluate personal strengths and weaknesses

What kind of a job is right for you?

Because of the great variety of marketing jobs, it's hard to generalize regarding the aptitudes you should have to pursue a career in marketing. Different jobs attract people with various interests and abilities. We'll give you some guidelines about what kinds of interests and abilities marketers should have. However, if you're completely lost about your own interests and abilities, see your campus career counselor and take some vocational aptitude and interest tests. These tests will help you to compare yourself with people who are now working in various career positions. They will *not* tell you what you should do, but they can help, especially in eliminating possibilities you are less interested in or less able to do well in.

Are you people-oriented or thing-oriented?

One useful approach is to decide whether you are basically "people-oriented" or "thing-oriented." This is a very important decision. A people-oriented person might be very unhappy in an inventory management job, for example, whereas a thing-oriented person might be miserable in a personal selling or retail management job that involves a lot of customer contact.

Marketing has both people-oriented and thing-oriented jobs. People-oriented jobs are primarily in the promotion area—where company representatives must make contact with potential customers. This may be direct personal selling or customer service activities—for example, in technical service or installation and repair. Thing-oriented jobs focus more on creative activities and analyzing data—as in advertising and marketing research—or on organizing and scheduling work—as in operating warehouses, transportation agencies, or the back-end of retailers.

People-oriented jobs tend to pay more, in part because such jobs are more likely to affect sales, the lifeblood of any business. Thing-oriented jobs, on the other hand, are often seen as cost generators rather than sales generators. Taking a big view of the whole company's operations, the thing-oriented jobs are certainly necessary—but without sales, no one is needed to do them.

Thing-oriented jobs are usually done at a company's facilities. Further, especially in lower-level jobs, the amount of work to be done and even the nature of the work may be spelled out quite clearly. The time it takes to design questionnaires and tabulate results, for example, can be estimated with reasonable accuracy. Similarly, running a warehouse, analyzing inventory reports, scheduling outgoing shipments, and so on are more like production operations. It's fairly easy to measure an employee's effectiveness and productivity in a thing-oriented job. At the least, time spent can be used to measure an employee's contribution.

A sales rep, on the other hand, might spend all weekend thinking and planning how to make a half-hour sales presentation on Monday. For what should the sales rep be compensated—the half-hour presentation, all of the planning and thinking that went into it, or the results? Typically, sales reps are rewarded for results—and this helps account for the sometimes extremely high salaries paid to effective order getters. At the same time, some people-oriented jobs can be routinized and are lower paid. For example, salespeople in some retail stores are paid at or near the minimum wage.

Managers needed for both kinds of jobs

Here we have oversimplified deliberately to emphasize the differences among types of jobs. Actually, of course, there are many variations between the two extremes. Some sales reps must do a great deal of analytical work before they make a presentation. Similarly, some marketing researchers must be extremely people-sensitive to get potential customers to reveal their true feelings. But the division is still useful because it focuses on the primary emphasis in different kinds of jobs.

Managers are needed for the people in both kinds of jobs. Managing others requires a blend of both people and analytical skills—but people skills may be the more important of the two. Therefore, people-oriented individuals are often promoted into managerial positions more quickly.

What will differentiate your product?

After deciding whether you're generally people-oriented or thing-oriented, you're ready for the next step—trying to identify your specific strengths (to be built on) and weaknesses (to be avoided or remedied). It is important to be as specific as possible so you can develop a better marketing plan. For example, if you decide you are more people-oriented, are you more skilled in verbal or written communication? Or if you are more thing-oriented, what specific analytical or technical skills do you have? Are you good at working with numbers, using a computer, solving complex problems, or coming to the root of a problem? Other possible strengths include past experience (career-related or otherwise), academic performance, an outgoing personality, enthusiasm, drive, and motivation.

It is important to see that your plan should build on your strengths. An employer will be hiring you to do something—so promote yourself as someone who is able to do something *well*. In other words, find your competitive advantage in your unique strengths—and then communicate these unique things about *you* and what you can do. Give an employer a reason to pick you over other candidates by showing that you'll add superior value to the company.

While trying to identify strengths, you also must realize that you may have some important weaknesses, depending on your objectives. If you are seeking a career that requires technical skills, for example, then you need to get those skills. Or if you are seeking a career that requires independence and self-confidence, then you should try to develop those characteristics in yourself—or change your objectives.

Set some timetables

At this point in your strategy planning process, set some timetables to organize your thinking and the rest of your planning. You need to make some decisions at this point to be sure you see where you're going. You might simply focus on getting your first job, or you might decide to work on two marketing plans: (1) a short-run plan to get your first job and (2) a longer-run plan—perhaps a five-year plan—to show how you're going to accomplish your long-run objectives. People who are basically job-oriented may get away with only a short-run plan, just drifting from one opportunity to another as their own objectives and opportunities change. But those interested in careers need a longer-run plan. Otherwise, they may find themselves pursuing attractive first-job opportunities that satisfy short-run objectives but quickly leave them frustrated when they realize that they can't achieve their long-run objectives without additional training or other experiences that require starting over again on a new career path.

Opportunities in Marketing

Strategy planning is a matching process. For your own strategy planning, this means matching yourself to career opportunities. So let's look at opportunities available in the market environment. (The same approach applies, of course, in the whole business area.) Exhibit C–2 shows some of the possibilities and salary ranges. The exhibit is assembled from salary data at www.salary.com. The salary ranges reflect the 25th percentile to the 75th percentile in the summer of 2013. For more information, look at Salary.com, where you can find job descriptions and data adjusted to different parts of the country. You can also find information about other career paths common to marketing majors—including logistics and purchasing/procurement management.

Keep in mind that the salary ranges in Exhibit C–2 are rough estimates. Salaries for a particular job often vary depending on a variety of factors, including company size, industry, and geographic area. People in some firms also get big bonuses that are not counted in their salaries. There are many other sources of salary information. For example, *Advertising Age* publishes an annual survey of salary levels for different marketing and advertising jobs, with breakdowns by company size and other factors. Many trade associations, across a variety of different industries, also publish surveys, and the U.S. government's Bureau of Labor Statistics (www.bls.gov) includes salary data. If you use the search engine at www.google.com and do a search on *salary survey,* you will find hundreds of such surveys for a number of different industries.

Identifying current opportunities in marketing

Because of the wide range of opportunities in marketing, it's helpful to narrow your possibilities. After deciding on your own objectives, strengths, and weaknesses, think about where in the marketing system you might like to work. Would you like to work for manufacturers, or wholesalers, or retailers? Or does it really matter? Do you want to be involved with consumer products or business products? By analyzing your feelings about these possibilities, you can begin to zero in on the kind of job and the functional area that might interest you most.

One simple way to get a better idea of the kinds of jobs available in marketing is to review the chapters of this text—this time with an eye for job opportunities rather than new concepts. The following paragraphs contain brief descriptions of job areas that

Exhibit C-2   Some Career Paths and Compensation Ranges*

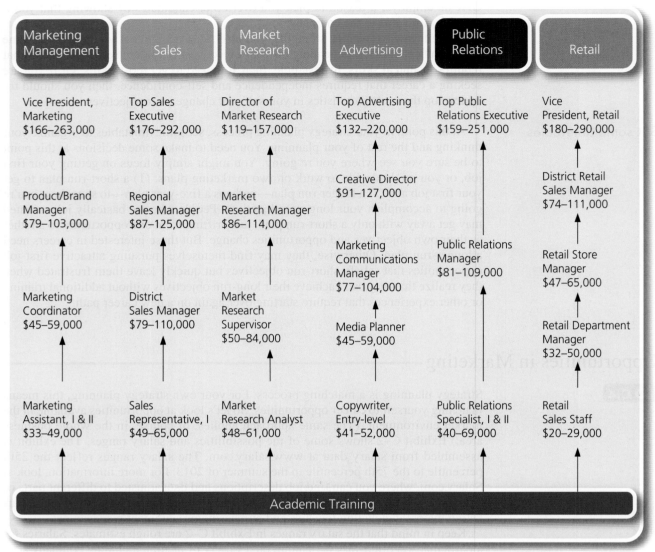

Marketing Management	Sales	Market Research	Advertising	Public Relations	Retail
Vice President, Marketing $166–263,000	Top Sales Executive $176–292,000	Director of Market Research $119–157,000	Top Advertising Executive $132–220,000	Top Public Relations Executive $159–251,000	Vice President, Retail $180–290,000
					District Retail Sales Manager $74–111,000
Product/Brand Manager $79–103,000	Regional Sales Manager $87–125,000	Market Research Manager $86–114,000	Creative Director $91–127,000		
			Marketing Communications Manager $77–104,000	Public Relations Manager $81–109,000	Retail Store Manager $47–65,000
Marketing Coordinator $45–59,000	District Sales Manager $79–110,000	Market Research Supervisor $50–84,000			
			Media Planner $45–59,000		Retail Department Manager $32–50,000
Marketing Assistant, I & II $33–49,000	Sales Representative, I $49–65,000	Market Research Analyst $48–61,000	Copywriter, Entry-level $41–52,000	Public Relations Specialist, I & II $40–69,000	Retail Sales Staff $20–29,000

Academic Training

* Salaries are based on data from Salary.com and represent the range for a salary plus bonus from the 25th to the 75th percentile as of July 2013, rounded to the nearest $1,000. Salary for retail vice president was estimated.

marketing graduates are often interested in with references to specific chapters in the text. Some, as noted, offer good starting opportunities, whereas others do not. While reading these paragraphs, keep your own objectives, interests, and strengths in mind.

Marketing manager (Chapter 2)
This is usually not an entry-level job, although aggressive students may move quickly into this role in smaller companies.

Customer or market analyst (Chapters 3 through 5)
Opportunities as consumer analysts and market analysts are commonly found in large companies, marketing research organizations, advertising agencies, and some consulting firms. Investment banking firms also hire entry-level analysts; they want to know what the market for a new business is like before investing. Beginning market analysts start in thing-oriented jobs until their judgment and people-oriented skills are tested.

opportunities in customer service. Many firms need qualified customer service representatives who work with customers to fulfill their needs and help ensure customer satisfaction. Customer service reps may interact with customers on the phone, by online chat, or via e-mail. But other service representatives help customers at their businesses with installations or equipment repair. Although some of the entry-level positions that require only high school education are being outsourced to other countries, positions requiring strong communication skills and a good education provide an opportunity for marketing majors. There are also management positions that develop customer service strategies, control costs, and focus on hiring, training, and retaining customer service reps and enhancing customer satisfaction.

Advertising opportunities (Chapters 13 , 15, and 16)

Job opportunities in this area are varied and highly competitive. And because the ability to communicate and a knowledge of the behavioral sciences are important, marketing and advertising graduates often find themselves competing with majors from fields such as English, communication, psychology, and sociology. There are thing-oriented jobs such as copywriting, media buying, art, computer graphics, and so on. Competition for these jobs is very strong—and they go to people with a track record. So the entry-level positions are as assistant to a copywriter, media buyer, or art director. There are also people-oriented positions involving work with clients, which are probably of more interest to marketing graduates. This is a glamorous but small and extremely competitive industry where young people can rise very rapidly—but they can also be as easily displaced by new bright young people. Entry-level salaries in advertising are typically low. There are sometimes good opportunities to get started in advertising with a retail chain that prepares its advertising internally. Another way to get more experience with advertising is to take a job with one of the media, perhaps in sales or as a customer consultant. Selling advertising space on a website or cable TV station or newspaper may not seem as glamorous as developing TV ads, but media salespeople help their customers solve promotion problems and get experience dealing with both the business and creative side of advertising.

Publicity and public relations opportunities (Chapters 13 and 16)

Although the number of entry-level positions in publicity and public relations is expected to continue to grow rapidly, competition for jobs will be stiff. College graduates with degrees in journalism, public relations, communications, and marketing may qualify for these openings. Many are attracted to these high-profile jobs. In addition to the popular press, more firms are placing useful content on the Internet to inform and influence customers. To a large degree, the tools used in these fields rely on emerging technologies. This bodes well for recent college graduates who may be more comfortable using newer technologies than "old hands" in publicity and public relations. International experience and proficiency in a second language can sometimes help job candidates stand out.

Sales promotion opportunities (Chapters 13 and 15)

The number of entry-level positions in the sales promotion area is growing because the number of specialists in this area is growing. For example, specialists might help a company plan a special event for employees, figure out procedures to distribute free samples, or perhaps set up a database to send customers a newsletter. Because clients' needs are often different, creativity and judgment are required. It is usually difficult for an inexperienced person to show evidence of these skills right out of school, so entry-level people often work with a project manager until they learn the ropes. In companies that handle their own sales promotion work, a beginner usually starts by getting some experience in sales or advertising.

Earned, owned, and social media management (Chapters 13, 15, and 16)

The opportunities for managing owned, earned, and social media are growing rapidly. As we saw in Chapters 13, 15, and 16, marketing managers are investing an increasing share of their promotion budgets into these forms of media. Although the media cost is relatively low, there is a need for people to create, update, and manage the content on owned media, including the company's web pages and/or social media platforms. Young people have some advantage here, as they are often consumers of social media and are not intimidated (as some of the "old guard" might be). A social media manager must be comfortable creating content—so they should be a good writer and creative as well as understand the company's customers and products. They may be required to write blog posts or write about products on web pages. There are opportunities to analyze the data generated by websites. Sometimes these jobs require someone to facilitate a company's online community or to respond to customer comments and reviews.

Pricing opportunities (Chapters 17 and 18)

Pricing decisions are usually handled by experienced executives. However, in some large companies and consulting firms there are opportunities as pricing analysts for marketing graduates who have quantitative skills. These people work as assistants to higher-level executives and collect and analyze information about competitors' prices and costs as well as the firm's own costs. Thus, being able to work with accounting numbers and computer spreadsheets is often important in these jobs. However, sometimes the route to these jobs is through experience in marketing research or product management.

Credit management opportunities

Specialists in credit have a continuing need for employees who are interested in evaluating customers' credit ratings and ensuring that money gets collected. Both people skills and thing skills can be useful here. Entry-level positions normally involve a training program and then working under the supervision of others until your judgment and abilities are tested.

International marketing opportunities

Many marketing students are intrigued with the adventure and foreign travel promised by careers in international marketing. Some firms hire recent college graduates for positions in international marketing, but more often these positions go to MBA graduates. However, that is changing as more and more firms pursue international markets. It's an advantage in seeking an international marketing job to know a second language and to know about the culture of countries where you would like to work. Your college may have courses or international exchange programs that would help in these areas. Graduates aiming for a career in international marketing usually must spend time mastering the firm's domestic marketing operations before being sent abroad. So a good way to start is to focus on firms that are already involved in international marketing, or that are planning to move in that direction soon. On the other hand, there are many websites with listings of international jobs. For example, you might want to visit www.overseasjobs.com.

Customer relations/consumer affairs opportunities (Chapters 13 and 19)

Most firms are becoming more concerned about their relations with customers and the general public. Employees in this kind of work, however, usually have held various positions with the firm before doing customer relations.

Study trends that may affect your opportunities

A strategy planner should always be evaluating the future because it's easier to go along with trends than to buck them. This means you should watch for political, technical, or economic changes that might open or close career opportunities.

If you can spot a trend early, you may be able to prepare yourself to take advantage of it as part of your long-run strategy planning. Other trends might mean you should avoid certain career options. For example, technological changes in computers and communications, including the Internet, are leading to major changes in retailing and advertising as well as in personal selling. Cable television, telephone selling, and direct-mail selling may reduce the need for routine order takers, while increasing the need for higher-level order

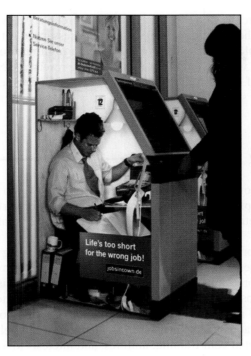

getters. More targeted and imaginative sales presentations for delivery by mail, e-mail, phone, or Internet websites may be needed. The retailers that prosper will have a better understanding of their target markets. And they may need to be supported by wholesalers and manufacturers that can plan targeted promotions that make economic sense. This will require a better understanding of the production and physical distribution side of business, as well as the financial side. And this means better training in accounting, finance, inventory control, and so on. So plan your personal strategy with such trends in mind.

This humorous ad on the side of a vending machine says, "Life's too short for the wrong job!" Planning for the right job—like planning a marketing strategy—pays off.
© Matthias Spactgens/Scholz & Friends/Berlin

One good way to get more detailed analysis is to go to the U.S. Bureau of Labor Statistics website at http://stats.bls.gov and do a search for *occupational outlook*. The Bureau provides detailed comments about the outlook for employment and growth in different types of jobs, industries, and regions.

Evaluate business practices

Finally, you need to know how businesses really operate and the kind of training required for various jobs. We've already seen that there are many opportunities in marketing—but not all jobs are open to everyone, and not all jobs are entry-level jobs. Positions such as marketing manager, brand manager, and sales manager are higher rungs on the marketing career ladder. They become available only when you have a few years of experience and have shown leadership and judgment. Some positions require more education than others. So take a hard look at your long-run objectives—and then see what degree you may need for the kinds of opportunities you might like.

Develop Objectives

LO C.5

Once you've done a personal analysis and environment analysis—identifying your personal interests, your strengths and weaknesses, and the opportunities in the environment—define your short-run and long-run objectives more specifically.

Develop long-run objectives

Your long-run objectives should clearly state what you want to do and what you will do for potential employers. You might be as specific as indicating the exact career area you want to pursue over the next 5 to 10 years. For example, your long-run objective might be to apply a set of marketing research and marketing management tools to the food manufacturing industry, with the objective of becoming director of marketing research in a small food manufacturing company.

Your long-run objectives should be realistic and attainable. They should be objectives you have thought about and for which you think you have the necessary skills (or the capabilities to develop those skills) as well as the motivation to reach.

Develop short-run objectives

To achieve your long-run objective(s), you should develop one or more short-run objectives. These should spell out what is needed to reach your long-run objective(s). For example, you might need to develop a variety of marketing research skills *and* marketing management skills—because both are needed to reach the longer-run objective. Or you might need an entry-level position in marketing research for a large food manufacturer to gain experience and background. An even shorter-run objective might be to take the academic courses that are necessary to get that desired entry-level job. In this example, you would probably need a minimum of an undergraduate degree in marketing, with an emphasis on marketing research. (Note that, given the longer-run objective of managerial responsibility, a business degree would probably be better than a degree in statistics or psychology.)

Developing Your Marketing Plan

Now that you've developed your objectives, move on to developing your own personal marketing plan. This means zeroing in on likely opportunities and developing a specific marketing strategy for these opportunities. Let's talk about that now.

Identify likely opportunities

An important step in strategy planning is identifying potentially attractive opportunities. Depending on where you are in your academic training, this can vary all the way from preliminary exploration to making detailed lists of companies that offer the kinds of jobs that interest you. If you're just getting started, talk to your school's career counselors and placement officers about the kinds of jobs being offered to your school's graduates. Your marketing instructors can help you be realistic about ways you can match your training, abilities, and interests to job opportunities. Also, it helps to read business publications such as *Bloomberg BusinessWeek, Fortune, The Wall Street Journal,* and *Advertising Age.* If you are interested in opportunities in a particular industry, check at your library or on the Internet to see if there are trade publications or websites that can bring you up to speed on the marketing issues in that area. Your library or college may also have an online service to make it easier to search for articles about specific companies or industries. And many companies have their own websites that can be a very useful source of information.

Don't overlook the business sections of your local newspapers to keep in touch with marketing developments in your area. And take advantage of any opportunity to talk with marketers directly. Ask them what they're doing and what satisfactions they find in their jobs. Also, if your college has a marketing club, join it and participate actively in the club's programs. It will help you meet marketers and students with serious interest in the field. Some may have had interesting job experiences and can provide you with leads on part-time jobs or exciting career opportunities.

If you're far along in your present academic training, list companies that you know something about or are willing to investigate, trying to match your skills and interests with possible opportunities. Narrow your list to a few companies you might like to work for.

If you have trouble narrowing down to specific companies, make a list of your personal interest areas—sports, travel, reading, music, or whatever. Think about the companies that compete in markets related to these interests. Often your own knowledge about these areas and interest in them can give you a competitive advantage in getting a job. This helps you focus on companies that serve needs you think are important or interesting. A related approach is to do a search on the Internet for websites related to your areas of interest. Websites often display ads or links to firms that are involved in that specific interest area. Further, many companies post job openings on their own websites or at websites that specialize in promoting job searches by many companies.

Then do some research on these companies. Find out how they are organized, their product lines, and their overall strategies. Try to get clear job descriptions for the kinds of positions you're seeking. Match these job descriptions against your understanding of these jobs and your objectives. Jobs with similar titles may offer very different opportunities. By researching job positions and companies in depth, you should begin to have a feel for where you would be comfortable as an employee. This will help you narrow your target market of possible employers to perhaps five firms. For example, you may decide that your target market for an entry-level position consists of large corporations with (1) in-depth training programs, (2) a wide product line, and (3) a wide variety of marketing jobs that will enable you to get a range of experiences and responsibilities within the same company.

Planning your product

Just like any strategy planner, you must decide what product features are necessary to appeal to your target market. Identify which credentials are mandatory and which are optional. For example, is your present academic program enough, or will you need more training? Also, identify what technical skills are needed, such as computer programming or accounting. Further, are there any business experiences or extracurricular activities that might help make your product more attractive to employers? This might involve active participation in college organizations or work experience, either on the job or in internships.

Planning your promotion

Once you identify target companies and develop a product you hope will be attractive to them, you have to tell these potential customers about your product. You can write directly to prospective employers, sending a carefully developed résumé that reflects your strategy planning. Or you can visit them in person (with your résumé). Many colleges run well-organized interviewing services. Seek their advice early in your strategy planning effort.

Implementing Your Marketing Plan

When you complete your personal marketing plan, you have to implement it, starting with working to accomplish your short-run objectives. If, as part of your plan, you decide that you need specific outside experience, then arrange to get it. This may mean taking a low-paying job or even volunteering to work in political organizations or volunteer organizations where you can get that kind of experience. If you decide that you need skills you can learn in academic courses, plan to take these courses. Similarly, if you don't have a good understanding of your opportunities, then learn as much as you can about possible jobs by talking to professors, taking advanced courses, and talking to businesspeople. Of course, trends and opportunities can change—so continue to read business publications, talk with professionals in your areas of interest, and be sure that the planning you've done still makes sense.

Strategy planning must adapt to the environment. If the environment changes or your personal objectives change, you have to develop a new plan. This is an ongoing process—and you may never be completely satisfied with your strategy planning. But even trying will make you look much more impressive when you begin your job interviews. Remember, although all employers would like to hire a Superman or a Wonder Woman, they are also impressed with candidates who know what they want to do and are looking for a place where they can fit in and make a contribution. So planning a personal strategy and implementing it almost guarantee you'll do a better job of career planning, and this will help ensure that you reach your own objectives, whatever they are.

Whether or not you decide to pursue a marketing career, the authors wish you the best of luck in your search for a challenging and rewarding career, wherever your interests and abilities may take you.

Hillside Veterinary Clinic Marketing Plan[1]

TABLE OF CONTENTS

1. Executive Summary

Hillside Veterinary Clinic (HVC) is a small animal veterinary clinic operating in Wellington, Colorado, owned and operated by Dr. Kelly Hardy. The clinic has one full-time veterinarian and four full-time vet techs who provide service in a small but fast-growing community in northern Colorado. The clinic has been in operation for six years and has tentative plans (two to three years from now) to move into a new building—where it will add the sale of pet supplies and kennel services to its veterinary services. To fund its new building, HVC must grow sales. The clinic prides itself on offering compassionate and personal care to pets and pet owners.

Current customers appear to be very satisfied with Hillside Veterinary Clinic and customer retention is high. There are many competitors in nearby Fort Collins—some of whom serve Wellington residents. The rapid growth of the town of Wellington creates many opportunities for acquiring customers who are new to the area.

This plan focuses only on the veterinary services offered to customers and Hillside's growth objectives over the next two years. The specific objectives of this marketing plan are:

- Within two years, the number of customers (currently 1,200) will increase by 15 percent or by 180 customers (to 1,380).
  - Most of this new growth will come from new homeowners in the area. However, additional growth will occur by converting local customers to HVC through promotional efforts.
- The retention rate of current customers will remain at 95 percent (not counting those who leave the area).
  - This is an estimate of the current customer retention rate.
- Within two years, 30 percent of customers will have annual dental examinations and teeth cleanings done on their dogs (up from 5 to 10 percent today).
- Within two years, 30 percent of customers will have well-pet health test screening on their dogs or cats at least every two years (up from 7 percent today).

This results in two related marketing strategies—the first of which targets acquiring new customers. HVC will use a variety of marketing tactics to generate awareness, especially among those moving to Wellington. The second set of tactics targets current customers and focuses on retaining these customers, thus growing its business. In particular, HVC hopes to enhance sales of its prevention services by bundling related services with attractive pricing and promotion tools (including signs and brochures). HVC will also make sure that it retains its current positioning as a vet clinic that is compassionate with pets and their owners.

2. Situation Analysis

This marketing plan begins with an analysis of the market facing Hillside Veterinary Clinic (HVC). It includes an assessment of the company, customers, competitors, and external market environment. This information is then summarized with a S.W.O.T. (Strengths, Weaknesses, Opportunities, and Threats) analysis.

2.1 Company Analysis

Hillside Veterinary Clinic is located in the town of Wellington, Colorado. Wellington, with a population of around 6,800, is located about 10 miles north of Fort Collins (a city of 152,000) in Larimer County. Wellington is also located 65 miles north of Denver, Colorado, and 25 miles south of the Wyoming border. The nearest city north of Wellington is Cheyenne, Wyoming, about 35 miles north.

Hillside Veterinary Clinic has been in operation for six years—opened by Dr. Kelly Hardy after she earned her Doctorate in Veterinary Medicine in 2000. The clinic focuses on small animals—most of its patients being dogs and cats with some other small pets such as rabbits, ferrets, hamsters, and guinea pigs. The clinic does not handle larger animals such as horses, cows, or pigs. HVC now has six full-time employees—including one veterinarian (Dr. Kelly Hardy), four veterinary technicians, and one office manager. More details about the clinic are noted in the following sections.

2.1.1 Company Objectives and Marketing Objectives

In evaluating any new opportunities, Dr. Hardy tries to keep focused on the values and goals she has for her business. Her company has developed a mission statement, a set of general goals, and a more specific set of marketing objectives.

Dr. Hardy aims to keep her business focused with the following mission statement:

It is the mission of the Hillside Veterinary Clinic—doctors and staff—to provide progressive, high-quality veterinary medical and surgical services to our clients and their pets. Our team is committed to improving the quality of life of pets and their owners by strengthening the human–animal bond.

Dr. Hardy describes the general goals of her organization as follows:

- To place its greatest emphasis on compassionate care for pets and their owners, no matter how large HVC becomes. (This will always be HVC's highest priority because it is consistent with Dr. Hardy's personal values.)
- To build a larger, more accommodating facility and to offer more pet-related services to the community—including kennel services and the sale of pet supplies.
- To purchase the latest state-of-the-art anesthesia machines and monitoring equipment so HVC can continue to provide the most humane care for its clients.
- To hire more staff so that individual pet care can be maintained and enhanced.
- To invest in more in-clinic diagnostic equipment.
- To provide greater information to customers about preventive health care such as vaccinations, parasite prevention, regular physical exams and lab screening, dental prophylaxis, as well as weight control/nutrition programs for pets.

When asked about the objectives for her organization, Dr. Hardy indicated the following:

- In two years, by July 2017, HVC will add on to the facility. This add-on will include additional kennel space and a remodel of the basement apartment, allowing a staff member to live on site and provide after-hours care.
- In five years, by July 2020, HVC will increase its current sales volume by 50 percent.
  - We need the sales growth to justify the facility addition.
  - Most of this new growth will come from new services planned to coincide with additional services. These services are not the focus of this marketing plan, but are key to HVC's marketing program.
- In two years, by July 2016, HVC will increase its sales of veterinary services by 30 percent.
- More generally, she hopes that within two years, in her market area, HVC will continue to be recognized as the *premier veterinary* clinic in the area—known for high-quality and compassionate care. This will primarily be recognized by the American Animal Hospital Association (AAHA), which conducts accreditation inspections every three years.

2.1.2 Screening Criteria

HVC, through past analysis of its own strengths and weaknesses, evaluation of the market, and its own goals and objectives, has developed criteria for the clinic to evaluate opportunities. The screening criteria help Dr. Hardy to evaluate and compare opportunities, and then decide which ones to pursue. These criteria are as follows:

- Investments in new equipment and services should break even within one year.
- Investments in marketing should contribute to the desired annual growth target of 14 percent.
- Marketing investments should earn a return on investment (ROI) of at least 25 percent before taxes.
- Our reputation for compassionate animal care remains our highest priority and no investments, new personnel, or strategy decisions should jeopardize that reputation.

2.1.3 Company Resources

The company resources include human resources, financial resources, and facility/equipment resources. The current status is briefly outlined below.

Human Resources HVC has a full-time staff of six people, including four veterinary technicians, one office manager (Karen), and one veterinarian. It should be noted that one of the vet techs—Rick—particularly enjoys interacting with people and has volunteered to do more outside activities. Dr. Hardy currently works about 60–70 hours per week, mostly providing veterinary services to customers. A local veterinary acupuncture specialist comes to the office to provide acupuncture services on an as-needed basis. The clinic has ready access to highly qualified personnel from the graduates and students at the nearby Colorado State University College of Veterinary Medicine.

In addition, students from out of state often move to Fort Collins to work for a couple of years before attending the College of Veterinary Medicine. This allows the applicant to gain state residency and earn money—these people often seek employment as veterinary technicians. These people have proven to be excellent employees.

In emergencies and for vacations, Dr. Hardy brings in a friend and former veterinarian who currently stays home with two young children. This woman has indicated an interest in some regular part-time work. This may be an opportunity to expand capacity—without the cost of adding a full-time vet.

Facility and Equipment Resources HVC's current building is located just off the highway in Wellington, which offers significant exposure. The building is large and recently built. HVC's location on Main Street makes awareness of the clinic very high among Wellington residents.

The clinic includes a variety of state-of-the art equipment—more than the average veterinary clinic. Equipment and facilities include:

- One digital radiograph machine to give in-house x-ray services
- Some in-house laboratory testing equipment
- Gas anesthesia (many veterinary practices use injection only)
- Complete anesthesia monitoring
  - ECG, pulse oximeter, Doppler blood pressure, respiratory monitor
  - Trained technicians
- IV infusion pump systems
- Recovery kennels—complete with blankets for ultimate comfort (many clinics just use newspaper)

Emergencies that cannot be handled in-house are referred to Colorado State University's Teaching Hospital or Animal Emergency Services (another local clinic).

2.1.4 Marketing Plans (Marketing Program)

Hillside Veterinary Clinic has two marketing plans that are currently being implemented or refined. Its two marketing plans are both *product development* strategies—which primarily focus on providing new products for present markets.

One marketing plan focuses on adding kennel services. That marketing plan calls for providing a higher level of service than competitors do. Animal pens will be larger than those of competitors and dog walking services will be standard fare.

The other marketing plan calls for HVC to offer pet supplies to its customers through an attached retail store.

These additional services have been requested by customers, and the situation analysis conducted for these marketing plans provides support for both plans. Both plans are likely to build additional awareness of HVC and its traditional veterinary services.

2.1.5 Present Marketing Strategy

HVC's current marketing strategy for veterinary services involves the following elements:

Target Market The target market includes all families within a 10 mile radius of Wellington with small animals.

Product HVC currently offers a wide range of veterinary services including the following:

- Preventive Health Care
  - Vaccinations
  - Spay/Neuter (represents about 10–15 percent of the sales)
  - Parasite Control
  - Health Screens through diagnostic laboratory testing
  - Dentistry, including cleaning and oral surgery (noted as its most profitable service, currently utilized by only 5–10 percent of customers)

- Internal Medicine (includes dermatology—allergy and infections, neurology, orthopedics, pediatrics, endocrinology, ophthalmology, gastroenterology, infectious disease, and oncology-related services)
- General Surgery (orthopedics and soft tissue)
- Individualized Care
  - Each pet has its own nurse after surgery
- Acupuncture (offered by a part-time veterinarian who comes in on call)
- In-Depth Client Education (for disease diagnosis and treatment)
- Puppy or Kitten Package (customers pay a set price for all the services their pets need in their first year and receive a 20 percent discount. This helps retain customers and continue to bring them into the HVC clinic.)
- Behavioral Counseling
- Euthanasia
- Grief Support

From observation of the clinic and communication with the staff, the main thing that stands out is the high quality, personalized, and compassionate care each animal (and owner) receives. HVC takes a personalized approach in dealing with its clients' needs. Dr. Hardy spends extensive time with her clients explaining procedures and giving them options. A survey of current customers (details in the Customer section) suggest that customers view the clinic as a place that offers warm and compassionate care in a friendly and "homey" environment. Further, as is evidenced by the large amount of new clients based on referrals, HVC's customers are happy with the services they receive and recommend the clinic to their family and friends as a result. This appears to be a key distinguishing factor of the clinic.

Dr. Hardy is particularly interested in increasing spay and neutering services. These provide a great introduction to the clinic, and customers who contract for such are usually retained. They have a high lifetime value because the services are given to young pets. She also notes that dental services are highly profitable and underutilized by most pet owners. She feels there is a good opportunity to increase sales of these services.

Place   Services are primarily offered through the storefront location on the main street of Wellington. House calls are available upon request for additional charges on an as-available basis.

- Office hours:
  - 8:00 a.m. to 5:30 p.m. Monday, Wednesday, Thursday, and Friday
  - 8:00 a.m. to 7:00 p.m. Tuesday
  - 7:00 a.m. admissions are accepted any day if more convenient for the client
  - House calls are available (including euthanasia)

Promotion   The Hillside Veterinary Clinic currently utilizes a number of promotional techniques to acquire and retain customers. These include the following:

- One of the clinic's biggest strategies includes a large, lighted sign on the front of the building that can easily be seen on Main Street in Wellington.
- Over the years, the clinic has given out a variety of promotional items—refrigerator magnets, business cards, leashes, bandanas, and food bowls with the clinic name and phone number.
- The clinic recently participated, for the first time, in the Wellington Parade of Lights which occurs each December. This appears to be an effective and worthwhile venture. Because Wellington is a small town with small-town attitudes, many of its residents attend this parade.
- Last year, several pet-related companies—a groomer and a local general-goods retailer that sells pet supplies—and HVC participated in a *Pet Fair*. Participation involved vet techs answering questions and handing out promotional items.
- The clinic also has a small (1-inch) in-column advertisement located in the *Yellow Pages* telephone directory.

- The clinic tries to maintain regular contact with its current customer base. It keeps a database that includes owner names, addresses, e-mail addresses, pet names, and information about each pet. Christmas cards are sent to all customers, and in the spring each receives a reminder heartworm letter—most by e-mail. It also sends out a magazine, purchased from another company but customized with HVC's name and phone number, called *Healthy Pet*.
- HVC maintains an active social media presence where it publicizes events and promotions. It also uses social media to help return missing pets to their owners. At times, HVC's Facebook page features popular animal videos to help drive traffic to the page and create more "likes." Photos and news are shared through Instagram, Twitter, and Pinterest.
- HVC maintains a website that communicates services, hours, and prices to potential customers. There is extensive information about HVC's services. The website also provides biographies of staff members, who highlight their own contributions toward HVC's mission statement and HVC's focus on compassionate care.
- The following limitations are noted:
  - HVC has no pamphlet or web page listing the services they offer with price ranges.
  - HVC does not have optimal Search Engine Optimization (SEO) and their website is not always the first result for a search of "Wellington Vet Clinic."
  - HVC has a few negative reviews on Google and struggles to convince pleased clients to be as vocal as unhappy clients.

Price   As shown in the competitor analysis section of this plan, prices charged by HVC tend to be about 20 percent higher than those of competitors. The higher prices are not believed to be a threat to the business. Hardy believes the higher prices are justified by the company's use of the highest quality technology and assistance. If asked, the staff takes time and effort to inform their customers as to why their prices are higher than other clinics' prices. The staff does not believe that it loses many clients due to its higher prices. In general, the only price shopping they observe tends to be for spay/neuter services.

2.1.6 Marketing Collaborators—Current and Potential
HVC works closely with a few outside organizations that help it complete its marketing effort. There are also firms in related businesses that HVC could work with if it wanted to enhance its market offering.

Specialized Veterinary Service Providers   In order to expand its available services, HVC refers clients to various specialists when Dr. Hardy does not have the expertise or time to work with a particular patient. These amenities are used for critical care and specialty services such as internal medicine, neurology, oncology, critical care, complex soft tissue and orthopedic surgeries. Experts include Emergency Animal Service, The Eye Doctor for Animals, Colorado State University Veterinarians, Rocky Mountain Veterinary Specialists, and Peak Veterinary Imaging. Peak Veterinary Imaging is a highly valued source of radiological specialists. This company consists of two boarded veterinary radiologists who have a mobile practice and travel to the clinic to perform ultrasounds, echoes, and ultrasound-guided biopsies.

Diagnostic Service Center   HVC uses Heska Diagnostic Laboratory in Fort Collins to test routine samples.

Large-Animal Vet Clinics   These clinics are useful to HVC because of their association with animals. The clinics act as indirect competitors because they often fulfill basic small-animal health needs such as vaccinations and spay/neuters. Typically, these services are offered to pet owners who also have large animals—as a convenience to those customers. These clinics often refer customers to the HVC. Close ties between the HVC and large-animal clinics can be beneficial to both parties.

Dog Shows/Dog Trials   By being involved with dog trials and dog shows, HVC has acquired new customers and raised clinic awareness. Because these dog owners care about their pets a great deal, they are willing to invest time and money into their pets' health.

Pet Stores   Because of its plans to eventually offer pet supplies, HVC has not attempted to work closely with any pet stores. PetSmart and PetCo, two superstore chains, have locations in Fort Collins, and there are a number of smaller pet stores in the vicinity. PetSmart offers veterinary services and is unlikely to seek a relationship with a competitor—but PetCo does not offer veterinary services and may be open to working with HVC.

Animal Shelters   HVC does not currently have any relationship with Larimer County Humane Society or the Dumb Friends League. These organizations provide spay/neuter certificates—but the reimbursement on these is less than half of HVC's usual charges and at this time HVC does not honor them.

2.2 Customer Analysis

Practical limitations point to restricting initial customer analysis to a 20-mile radius from downtown Wellington, Colorado. While there are few vet clinics north of Wellington, the area is also sparsely populated—most residents have large animals if they live north of Wellington. It would also be difficult to target these groups. South of Wellington, there are many veterinary clinics in the Fort Collins area. Most customers value the convenience of a local clinic, so the focus is on Wellington.

2.2.1 Product-Market
The product-market for this marketing plan consists of the following elements:

- **Product type:** the veterinary services outlined in the company section under "Product."
- **Customer needs:** Customers need medical services and advice to care for their pets. They also need these services delivered in a caring and compassionate manner.
- **Customer types:** the final consumers are pet owners and caregivers.
- **Geographic area:** more than 90 percent of HVC's customers currently reside within a 10-mile radius of the city of Wellington.

2.2.2 Demographic Data on the Target Market
Customers are located in the geographic area of Wellington, which is situated 10 miles north of Fort Collins. The town's population is about 6,800. The town is growing rapidly because of its relatively affordable housing as compared to nearby Fort Collins. The population has grown 66 percent in the last five years—similar growth is projected for the next five years. Real estate professionals predict 800 new homes will be built in the next five years—160 new houses per year. Most of these homes are so-called "starter homes," often bought by young families. From past observation, the clinic's staff believes that many of these homeowners do not own pets when they move in, but often buy a new pet within the first year or two of home ownership. The median household income in Wellington is $66,411, up by $18,494 in the last ten years.

Pet ownership is an ongoing trend in the United States, with pet-owning households increasing by more than 1 million each year. Based on a Harris Interactive poll, the following was learned: more than three in five Americans (62 percent) have pets; among pet owners, seven in ten have dogs (69 percent), half have cats (51 percent), one in ten have fish (11 percent), and less than one in ten pet owners have birds (7 percent) or some other type of pet (8 percent).

From experience, the clinic staff believes that Wellington families tend to own dogs at a little higher rate and cats at a little lower rate than the national numbers.

The large majority of clients come from within a 10-mile radius of the city limits and will be our main focus for current and potential customers. HVC's current client base numbers 1,200. Each customer owns an average of two pets. Dogs make up 70 percent of vet visits, cats about 28 percent, and other small pets (e.g., rabbits, gerbils, hamsters) the final 2 percent. Clients' pets visited the HVC two times on average per year

2.2.3 Current Customers

To get a better understanding of current customers, HVC's office manager (Karen) and Dr. Hardy were interviewed, and 40 current customers completed a survey.

2.2.3.1 Database of Current Customers

According to HVC's office manager, current customers could be put into two broad categories—farmers/ranchers and town dwellers.

About a quarter of HVC's current customers are from the farming and ranching community—living outside the city limits. These customers tend to be more price sensitive and do not see much reason to spend money on preventive health care or dental services.

Town dwellers are the bulk of the business—and the fastest growing group. As more tract housing is built in Wellington, this will continue to be the growth market for HVC. These customers tend to be less price sensitive than the farmers and ranchers and view their pets as part of their family. They seem to value personalized care, attention from the doctor and vet techs. They are also more open to suggestions for preventive health care and dental services. Although, from experience, it usually takes them some time to embrace these ideas—it's not until after the second or third time preventive health and dental care are mentioned that customers proactively request for these services.

A review of the customer database showed 1,200 active pet owner customers who have made visits to the clinic within the last two years. The majority of its customers' own dogs and cats, which accounts for 1,306 dogs and 571 cats.

2.2.3.2 Survey of Current Customers

In order to get a better understanding of its current customers, a paper-and-pencil survey was designed and handed out to customers visiting the clinic over a two-week period. The purpose of the research was to learn a bit more about customers, to find out their attitudes toward their pets, to evaluate their receptivity to some potential new services, and to find out about their access to and use of the Internet.

The survey was completed by a convenience sample of 40 HVC customers who were asked to complete the survey while they waited during visits to the clinic in March. Almost all of those asked actually completed the survey. A copy of the survey and a tabulation of its results is shown in Appendix A. Some of the key findings include the following:

- 100 percent of these customers own dogs and 48 percent own cats.
- 93 percent of the customers considered their pets to be a "family member."
- Five factors were all found to be important to customers—but "Expertise of the vet staff," and "Friendly customer service" had the most listings as "very important."
- 88 percent indicated that having a "Location close to my home" was important or very important. And 83 percent lived within 10 miles of the clinic—suggesting a focus on customers in Wellington or a short drive away.
- Among possible new services, customers were most interested in seeing HVC add "Evening hours" (38 percent) and "Boarding" services (33 percent).
- 85 percent of respondents indicated the current hours are sufficient.
- Satisfaction level appears to be quite high, with only 5 percent indicating they had ever been dissatisfied with the clinic—and 90 percent indicating that HVC was the only vet clinic they used.
- 98 percent of customers had access to the Internet and only one of those did not have an e-mail address—so 95 percent of all these customers have an e-mail address.
- Social media usage varied considerably by platform—with 61 percent of current customers on Facebook, 19 percent on Pinterest, 14 percent on Instagram, and 12 percent using Twitter.

2.2.4 Customer Needs—Possible Segmenting Dimensions

Dr. Hardy asked her staff to generate a list of possible customer needs as they related to veterinary services. She understood that the clinic should not try to meet all customer needs, but wanted to know what the staff believed were customer needs.

The following list includes customer needs that were identified—but were not chosen as needs that HVC would try to address:

- Low costs/low prices
  - Although this might appeal to a limited set of customers, the clinic's traditional emphasis on care and taking time with owners and pets makes it difficult to be profitable while also offering low prices. This option also is not consistent with current screening criteria.
- Mobile clinic—visiting pets at their owners' homes
  - Competitors provide this service.
  - Although this would fit with the clinic's goal of compassionate, personal care, it would sacrifice the ability to provide good care to more customers at the clinic.
- Add services for large animals
  - Another vet could be hired to provide these services (Dr. Hardy does not have this specialty), but most of current customers do not have these needs, and the current facility does not fit well with providing good service to large animals.
- Convenient location
  - Moving to a new location in the short run is not practical. A new location is being planned for and will be in the same general area so that it remains convenient to most customers.
  - Other options—such as adding a satellite office—were considered too costly.
  - The current location is convenient to the vast majority of current customers and allows some to fit in some shopping on the same trip.
- Treatment of exotic animals
  - Some veterinarians specialize in the treatment of exotic animals. This requires additional training, which Dr. Hardy does not currently have.
  - The local market has very limited call for this need—given the small size of the market, the clinic chose not to address these needs directly but to make referrals to clinics that could provide these services.

HVC feels that it can deliver on the following customer needs—and that these needs are consistent with its current screening criteria:

- Compassionate treatment of animals
  - This is part of the current approach to the market and consistent with Dr. Hardy's personal values.
  - Although this is a customer need, customers only learn that HVC delivers on this need after visiting the clinic. Marketing communications do not emphasize this benefit of HVC's services.
- Compassionate treatment of owners
  - This is part of the current approach to the market and consistent with Dr. Hardy's personal values.
  - Although this is a customer need, customers only learn that HVC delivers on this need after visiting the clinic. Marketing communications do not emphasize this benefit of HVC's services.
- High-quality medical care
  - This also fits with the current approach and facilities. Over the last few years the clinic has invested in state-of-the-art diagnostic and treatment equipment.
  - Although this is a customer need, customers only learn that HVC delivers on this need after visiting the clinic. Marketing communications do not emphasize this benefit of HVC's services.
- Treatment of small animals
  - This is the current focus of the clinic and is consistent with the clinic's expertise and facilities.

2.2.5 Identification of Qualifying Dimensions and Determining Dimensions

HVC believes the following market segments could be combined and approached with a similar marketing strategy:

- Qualifying dimension: owners of cats, dogs, and other small animals
- Qualifying dimension: living within 20 miles of Wellington, Colorado
- Determining dimension: pet owners that value high-quality care that is compassionate and personalized.
- Determining dimension: currently a client of HVC or not

HVC believes that different marketing strategies are needed for customers who already utilize HVC's services and pet owners who use another veterinarian, are new to the area, or who obtain a new pet.

2.2.6 Identification of Target Market(s) (One or More Specific Segments)

Therefore, HVC's marketing strategy may have to be adapted to these two target markets:

1. Pet owners with small animals living within 10 miles of Wellington, Colorado, who *are not currently* customers of HVC.
2. Pet owners with small animals living within 10 miles of Wellington, Colorado, who *are currently* customers of HVC.

2.3 Competitor Analysis

The northern Colorado market can be pretty competitive for veterinary services. Each year more than a hundred new veterinarians graduate from the Colorado State University College of Veterinary Medicine in nearby Fort Collins. Many of these graduates want to stay in the local area—so they open a practice or join a local clinic, often for below-market wages.

As noted in the customer section, most customers make an initial screening of veterinarians based on location—choosing a vet that is located relatively close to their homes. We identified four veterinary practices that seemed to target the same geography and addressed similar customer needs. Key information about each of the major competitors—and similar information about Hillside Veterinary Clinic—is shown in the competitor matrix in Appendix B. Competitive information was gathered by reviewing each competitor's website and *Yellow Pages* ad, and by contacting each by phone and asking questions about prices and services offered. Each clinic was asked for spay and neuter prices because the services are widely used, relatively comparable from clinic to clinic, and these represent important services that help a clinic acquire new customers.

Comparing HVC to its primary competitors, the matrix in Appendix B points out competitive advantages and competitive disadvantages. These are outlined below.

Competitive disadvantages for HVC:

- When these competitors were compared to the HVC, some disadvantages for HVC are the hours of operation and the price of the neutering and spaying operations. HVC is not open on the weekends, and East Side Animal Hospital and Flatiron Veterinary Clinic are open on the weekends.
- The cost for the spaying and neutering operations was higher for HVC than for the other clinics—although this does not take into account the discounted puppy/kitten package of bundled services. HVC tests blood work before surgery using its in-house lab facility. The other reason the price is higher is because of the more expensive type of anesthesia that is used. Dr. Hardy feels it is the best and safest type to use.

Competitive advantages for HVC include:

- HVC is the only clinic that would schedule appointments at seven in the morning.
- HVC utilizes the services of an acupuncture specialist—this is offered by only one other competitor.
- HVC gives individualized care (holds animal when it comes out of surgery).

- HVC offers more services (grief support, dentistry, in-house laboratory testing, and IV infusion pump system).
- HVC's social media presence and the information on its website are superior to all competitors in quantity and quality.

2.4 Analysis of the Market Context— External Market Environment

2.4.1 Economic Environment

Regional and local economies continue to show strength, following a severe decline during the recession of 2008 to 2011. Pet care has been known to be robust to economic conditions—considered recession resistant. On the other hand, a poor economy can make it more difficult to sell customers on preventive health care products.

2.4.2 Technological Environment

The technological environment is changing rapidly in a variety of ways that may affect HVC's business:

- Veterinary medicine relies to a much greater extent on technology as new diagnostic equipment becomes available. Lower prices for this equipment make it easier for veterinary clinics to provide more services in-house. This may be a greater advantage for larger clinics, which can utilize the equipment more often, and therefore more easily cost-justify highly advanced/expensive equipment. An example of this advanced technology is the laser technology that de-claws animals. It is a faster and easier procedure and is less painful for pets. This will eventually become a common piece of equipment for vets to have.
- The growth of the Internet continues to impact how customers shop and how business can interact with potential and current customers.
- There are a growing number of affordable off-the-shelf software products that allow small service firms to develop customer relationship management databases. Some of these are customized for veterinary clinics.

2.4.3 Political and Legal Environment

State and local laws regulate some of the care that must be given to pets. For example, dogs and cats are required to obtain rabies vaccinations at 4 months and then 2 months later at 6 months of age. Regulations also specify that the owner must obtain a license within 14 days of obtaining the animal.

Currently, there are no limitations on the number of animals a person may own. However, there are specific regulations enforced with regard to the care of animals. One such regulation specifies that a person should only have animals that they can properly care for in healthy conditions, and these animals should not be bothersome to the neighbors. These rules emphasize the importance of the community and animals living together in a safe and healthy environment.

Recently, an animal cruelty law was passed that made it a felony for any animal abuse. It is now much easier to prosecute pet owners who abuse animals. Therefore, there will be more pressure on pet owners to care, feed, and treat their animals with respect. It will also be crucial for pet owners to get the necessary vaccines and vet treatments for their pets.

2.4.4 Cultural and Social Environment

HVC reflects many of Wellington's small-town values. HVC customers value that the staff greets them by name when they come into the clinic. The friendliness of the staff keeps the customers happy, feeling valued and welcomed. Many customers walk to the clinic; they enjoy the fact that they don't have to drive to the vet's office. Some clients have been with the HVC since the start of the clinic, and have enjoyed going to the same location for years and watching it grow and change.

There is some risk that growth and an eventual move to a larger location will make it more difficult to maintain the small-town values. It may become more difficult for the staff to remember customer names and pet names. As the facility expands, an additional vet may need to be hired. Which means some current customers will have to see a veterinarian other than Dr. Hardy—which may jeopardize established relationships. Pets and their owners get attached to their vet and it can be difficult for people to change.

Pet health care expenditures spiked immediately following the terrorist attacks in 2001. It was suggested that this was a side effect of the "cocooning" that followed these attacks—with more people staying close to home and perhaps bonding more with their pets. According to a recent Harris poll, 91 percent of respondents considered their pets to be members of their families.

A recent story of animal abuse brought animal care to the local headlines. A woman was charged with cruelty to animals when she was found to be running a puppy mill with 60 puppies crammed into 10 cages.

2.5 S.W.O.T.

This situation analysis gives insights about the company, customers, competitors, and external marketing environment in which Hillside Veterinary Clinic operates. In reviewing this information, the data can be summarized in a SWOT analysis that highlights Hillside's **S**trengths and **W**eaknesses—and the **O**pportunities and **T**hreats in its current market. These are summarized in the following sections.

2.5.1 HVC's Strengths

HVC's strengths include the following:

- Location on Wellington's main street creates high awareness
- Staff is extremely informed, highly trained, has great people and communication skills
- About 70 percent of customers come from referrals
- Good reputation in the local community
- Wide range of services offered
- Strong ethical principles
- Emphasis on quality care and customized attention
- Quality and technologically-advanced equipment
- High standards for staff and services
- The clinic's atmosphere—comfortable and homey, not intimidating (for example, pictures of patients posted on wall)
- Excellent "bedside manner"
- Differentiation comes from service level offered, including
  - One nurse assigned to each patient
  - Safer type of anesthesia used
  - Fluid support given while animal recovers
  - Outpatient care has pets' and owners' best interests at heart (for example, they use plastic kennels rather than metal and give blankets instead of newspaper)
- Willingness to increase marketing budget if justified

2.5.2 HVC's Weaknesses

HVC's weaknesses include the following:

- Small facility—not enough exam rooms for amount of business performed
- In the short-term, "smallish" facility and veterinarian availability (Dr. Hardy is the only vet) constrain growth options—adding an additional vet alone will not help, because there are limited examination rooms
- Lack of parking availability

- Higher-than-average pricing
- Understaffed—people have to work very hard to offer the level of service they strive to give
- Lack of business knowledge
- Lack of attention focused on marketing/promotional strategies

2.5.3 HVC's Opportunities

Opportunities for HVC include the following:

- Direct competitors in Wellington and surrounding areas are few
- Fast growing community—particularly in nearby new housing developments
- Many cross-selling opportunities—customers do not seem to buy other preventive health services for their pets
- First mover advantage—they are the first clinic in town
- Competitor entry barriers are high because HVC has established itself as a clinic that has high standards for staff and services
- Some local customers use other vet clinics—there are opportunities to attract new customers from the local market
- Constant advances in technology open doors for HVC to distinguish itself with the latest and greatest equipment
- Staff is comfortable using web-based marketing strategies to access young home-buyers in the area

2.5.4 HVC's Threats

Threats for HVC include the following:

- As Wellington grows, it is increasingly likely to attract more competitors—particularly with Colorado State University graduating so many vets each year
- A Fort Collins–based clinic could set up a satellite branch or a new clinic may open in this area
- The relatively lackluster local economy—rising interest rates threaten the housing boom that has fueled Wellington's growth
- The slowing economy could reduce discretionary income and cause pet owners to become more price sensitive and to reduce spending on preventive health care for their pets
- Potential loss of small-town ambiance
- Potential loss of existing clients (if facility moves to a new location)

3. Marketing Plan Objectives

This marketing plan focuses specifically on the primary veterinary services offered by Hillside Veterinary Clinic. After reviewing the situation analysis, HVC believes that two opportunities stand out as the best options to grow the clinic. First, it hopes to take advantage of the population growth in Wellington and attract customers who move to the area. Once customers come to HVC, they tend to be very loyal to the clinic—so it is important that anyone new to the area choose HVC for vet services. To maintain that loyalty, the clinic must make sure that it continues to provide the high-quality customer service, compassionate treatment, and veterinary services that create this loyalty.

Second, HVC believes that current customers do not utilize enough of the clinic's preventive health care services. Dr. Hardy feels most pets would have a better quality of life and live longer if owners took advantage of some of these services. She particularly believes that two services are under-utilized: 1) dental services (annual teeth cleaning) for dogs and cats, and 2) health test screenings, which are now used almost exclusively when an animal is sick, but could be used as part of an annual check-up. The clinic will attempt to grow these services.

Taking advantage of these opportunities, HVC sets the following objectives for their marketing plan:

- Within two years, the number of customers (currently 1,200) will increase by 15 percent, or by180 (to 1,380).
  - Most of this new growth will come from new homeowners in the area. But additional growth will occur by converting local customers to HVC through promotional efforts.
- The retention rate of current customers will remain at 95 percent (not counting those who leave the area).
  - This is an estimate of the current customer retention rate.
- Within two years, 30 percent of customers will have annual dental examinations and teeth cleanings done on their dogs (up from 5–10 percent today).
- Within two years, 30 percent of customers (up from 7 percent today) will have had a well-pet health test screening on their dogs or cats—and this screening will be repeated at least every two years.

4. Differentiation and Positioning

An evaluation of Hillside Veterinary Clinics' strengths and weaknesses, their competitors, and their customers provides insights into opportunities for differentiation and positioning. This review suggests that HVC can be differentiated from the competition by its high level of customer service, compassionate health care, and location in Wellington. These points of differentiation lead to the following statement that best describes HVC's desired positioning:

> *For all small-pet owners within a 10-mile radius of Wellington, Colorado, Hillside Veterinary Clinic provides the most* compassionate *and* personalized *care of all local veterinary clinics, because its staff loves animals and provides excellent customer service for both pets and pet owners.*

This positioning and differentiation will help drive the marketing strategy decisions that follow.

5. Marketing Strategy

Because two different, but related, target markets are identified for HVC's veterinary services, two strategies are proposed. The first target market includes noncustomers and involves a marketing strategy to attract these customers to try Hillside Veterinary Clinic. The second target market focuses on current customers—and objectives focus on increasing their use of health screening and dental services. HVC also wants to continue to have high retention of its current customers. Some of the elements of the marketing strategy directed at one target market will also serve the other target market—those situations are noted.

5.1 Target Market #1— Noncustomers

The first target market for HVC will be pet owners with small animals living within 10 miles of Wellington, Colorado, who are not currently customers of HVC.

A quick summary of the marketing tactics directed toward this target market is followed by a more detailed explanation of each tactic:

- Product—Bundled Service Package for Puppies and Kittens
- Promotion—Logo and Slogan
- Promotion—Participation in Community Events
- Promotion—Create a Large Vinyl Sign
- Promotion—*Yellow Pages* Advertising

- Promotion—Search Engine Optimization
- Place—Extended Clinic Hours
- Place—Long Term (New Facility)
- Price—Prices to Be Adjusted for Inflation

5.1.1 Product—Bundled Service Package for Puppies and Kittens

HVC currently offers a bundled service package for puppies and kittens. Because this program targets young pets, the lifetime customer value will rise per patient if this program is a success. Success can be defined as retaining those clients for the life of the animal—assuming the person continues to live in the local area. The primary goal for this program will be to acquire new customers for the clinic. Many of the families buying a new home in Wellington follow that purchase by getting a pet—typically a puppy or kitten. The cost savings will provide an incentive for them to come to the clinic and experience first-hand the high-quality care from HVC. This should be the first step in creating a lifelong relationship between the clinic and the pet owner.

This package includes spay or neuter, all vaccinations, a book on puppy or cat care and training, and coupons for grooming services. The package also includes a free one-year-old check-up. Each package will continue to be priced at $129, a 10 percent discount on the services and goods if ordered separately.

5.1.2 Promotion—Logo and Slogan

Hillside Veterinary Clinic does not currently have a logo or slogan. HVC will work with a local design firm to develop a logo that reinforces the positioning themes of compassionate and personalized care offered by its staff. HVC has used the phrase "we treat pets like family" in the past because of its simple, direct message. This slogan captures its positioning and will become its official slogan. A designer will be hired to develop the new logo—and to design other elements of this plan including brochures, refrigerator magnets, bandanas, letterhead, business cards, and signage.

5.1.3 Promotion—Participation in Community Events

Events in the community of Wellington are a way for HVC to enhance their reputation and create more awareness of their business. Residents of Wellington appreciate the small town and tend to want to support local businesses that also support the town.

Previously HVC participated in the *Parade of Lights* and *Pet Fair*. These have been very positive experiences—creating a positive image in the community and introducing new customers to the clinic. The community events program will be expanded and formalized in the coming year, and HVC will participate in the following events:

- Community *Easter Egg Hunt*, held annually on Easter weekend
- *Wellington Town Garage Sale*, held annually in May
- *Family Fun Fest*, held annually on July 4th
- *Wellington Pet Fair*, October
- *Parade of Lights*, held annually during the Christmas season

When involved in these events, HVC must not only interact with the public but also proactively sell itself through various tactics. One of these tactics would be to use banners to generate customer awareness or serve as a reminder. The banners would be displayed somewhere visible to people passing by such as wrapped around the front of a table at the *Wellington Pet Fair*. The banners would encourage people to stop by the conveniently located clinic. Business cards, as well as color brochures, would be available or handed out to people. The clinic's dogs could also be present wearing the HVC bandanas—the dogs can help create a face for HVC, support the "we treat pets as family" slogan, and serve as conversation "ice breakers" with passersby. When it is possible to have some sort of table or booth at events, the clinic could also have brochures and swag (e.g., bandanas and refrigerator magnets).

These activities will help to remind current customers (the second target market) and demonstrate HVC's commitment to the community.

5.1.4 Create a Large Vinyl Sign

HVC will purchase two large (3 foot × 5 foot) vinyl signs. The sign will include the name of the clinic, the company's slogan, and its new logo. This size sign can be placed on the front of a table and/or around any special events where HVC participates.

5.1.5 Promotion—*Yellow Pages* Advertising

New residents to an area are known to use the *Yellow Pages* to find goods and services in their new community. HVC knows that about 10 percent of current customers learn about the clinic from these ads. HVC's ad is undersized in comparison with many of the other small-animal veterinary clinics. East Side Small Animal Hospital has a full-page color ad with a lot of description, whereas HVC only has a 1 inch in-column black-and-white ad with limited information.

Therefore, in the next edition of the *Yellow Pages*, the ad will be a 3 inch in-column ad, adding color and emphasizing the Wellington location, listing of key services new clients would most likely be interested in using (spay/neuter and vaccination), and bundled services (see section 5.2.2 below for more details). Further, the new ad will include its new logo and slogan, which conveys their caring quality.

Current customers may also look in the *Yellow Pages* to find HVC's phone number, so the ad will also serve this second target market.

5.1.6 Promotion—Search Engine Optimization

Many of the younger residents of Wellington are less likely to utilize the *Yellow Pages* and would rather use search engines such as Google or Bing to find veterinary service providers. HVC will work with a web-marketing specialist to ensure its dominance in the search results when locals are looking for veterinary clinics.

5.1.7 Place—Extended Clinic Hours

HVC operates its current facility at near capacity. There is no way to expand the current facility—there are occupied buildings on either side, and ordinances prevent building out the back. Without the new facility, which is not certain or anticipated for at least two more years, the only way to increase capacity will be to offer longer hours. This change also addresses something that some customers indicated they wanted to see when they filled out the survey.

Therefore, the clinic will increase the hours it is open from the current 49 hours per week to 57.5 hours per week. The new hours will be Monday–Thursday, 8:00 a.m. to 7:00 p.m.; Friday, 8:00 a.m. to 5:30 p.m.; and Saturday, 8:00 a.m. to 12:00 p.m.

New staff will be needed to implement this element of the plan. It will require additional hours from another veterinarian, as Dr. Hardy will be unable to work all these hours. At least for the first few months, vet techs could have their schedules adjusted, but additional hours will not be needed. A part-time receptionist will also be hired.

- Clinic hours will not be extended until September—to save money and in time for the busier fall season (summer tends to be a slower time of year). Promotion of the expanded clinic hours will occur in the first year with signs inside the clinic.
- Dr. Hardy believes that a veterinarian friend who currently comes in occasionally— to fill in for vacations or in other emergencies—will want to have more stable and regular part-time hours.
- A part-time receptionist will be hired in August.

This element of the marketing strategy will also appeal to current customers, some of whom have indicated a desire for evening and weekend hours.

5.1.8 Place—Long Term (New Facility)

HVC intends to build a new facility in about two years. While this marketing plan anticipates the new facility, it does not directly address those plans. The new facility will attract new customers and help retain customers as well.

5.1.9 Price—Prices to Be Adjusted for Inflation

HVC believes that it is important to raise prices every one to two years—so that prices do not become so low that large increases must be mandated to catch up with inflation. HVC does not want to compete on a price basis, and current prices are higher than the competition. Further, higher prices are necessary for the staffing required to deliver the caring and compassionate service that HVC strives to maintain. Higher prices can also carry higher quality expectations from customers—many of whom are willing to pay higher prices for the convenience, service, and quality that HVC is known to deliver. Finally, current prices are already about 20 percent above the local competition.

Prices were raised about 5 percent about six months ago—so price increases will not be implemented until the end of the coming year. Based on inflation, price increases are anticipated to be about 5 percent.

This element of the marketing strategy also addresses the current customers target market.

5.2 Target Market #2—Current Customers

The second target market in this marketing plan involves retaining and growing current customers.

- Product—Compassionate and Personalized Care
- Product/Price—Bundled Service Packages for Dental Services and Geriatric Pet Care
- Promotion—In-Store Signage and Point-of-Purchase Materials
- Promotion—Website Design
- Promotion—Customer Database Enhancement
- Promotion—Brochures to Describe Clinic and Key Special Services
- Promotion—Swag
- Promotion—Social Media

Some of the elements of the marketing strategy that primarily target customer acquisition will have the additional benefit of helping retain and grow business with current customers. These elements are described in detail in Section 5.1:

- Promotion—Logo and Slogan
- Promotion—Participation in Community Events
- Promotion—Create a Large Vinyl Sign
- Promotion—*Yellow Pages* Advertising
- Place—Extended Clinic Hours
- Price—Prices to Be Adjusted for Inflation

5.2.1 Product—Compassionate and Personalized Care

HVC delivers compassionate and personalized care. As HVC grows and hires additional staff, it is important that all employees continue to deliver on the high standards initially set by Dr. Hardy. This will be achieved by carefully hiring employees who share HVC's core values.

5.2.2 Product—Bundled Service Packages for Dental Care and Geriatric Pet Care

Bundled service packages create value for HVC, customers, and their pets. The bundled packages will be offered at price discounts as compared to the purchases of individual services. This creates value for the customer. The package encourages pet owners to focus more on their pets' health, and increases the revenue received by HVC. Best of all, the pets receive better quality care.

With only limited promotion, HVC has had success with its Puppy and Kitten Bundles.

Similar packages will be introduced for dental services—and later, one targeting older pets with specialized geriatric pet services. The specifics on these future packages are described below:

Dental Service Package   Dental services provide significant health benefits for cats and dogs—and provide a good profit margin for HVC. The dental package includes the following:

- Standard medical examination
- Health screen six and CBC (complete blood count)
- Dental radiographs (x-rays)
- Teeth cleaning from Dr. Hardy or the vet tech trained in this area
- A short training session on teeth brushing for the dog/cat owner
- Dental Kit by Pet Dentist (a kit that includes toothbrush, toothpaste, and breath mints designed especially for dogs/cats)
- Sample package of Greenies Dog/Cat Treats, which are designed to clean teeth and freshen breath

The total cost of these bundled goods and services is $189. If purchased separately, they would amount to $215. The package provides higher perceived value to customers and helps them get more actively involved in their pets' health care. Once customers get into the habit of this service, there will be less veterinary work required at the time of the annual check-up.

The Dental Service Package will be introduced in the next two months. A promotional brochure and point-of-purchase signs that describe the benefits will be created to support this product. The vet techs and Dr. Hardy will make efforts to mention the service to customers who are in for other reasons.

Geriatric Health Care Package for Dogs and Cats   This package is designed for dogs and cats six years of age or older. The package would be targeted at pet owners with aging animals and consists of the following services:

- Standard medical examination
- Health screen six and CBC (complete blood count)
- Urinalysis
- ERD Screen (kidney screen)

Customers will receive these services, a $165 value (if purchased separately), for $139. This gives customers cost savings, encourages purchasing more services for their pets, and enhances their pets' quality of life.

This product will be introduced about one year from now. Adaptations to the product or promotion will be made based on experiences with the dental services package.

A promotional brochure and point-of-purchase sign describing the benefits and procedures will be created to support this product.

5.2.3 Promotion—In-Store Signage and Point-of-Purchase Materials

Currently, HVC has no signage or point-of-purchase materials. The store's large counter top—where customers check in and check out—is currently bare. Small 8.5" × 5" laminated stand-up signs (which work like picture frames) will be placed on the counter tops. Four signs will be purchased, one each promoting the three bundled packages (puppy/kitten, dental services, and geriatric pet care), and one promoting the clinic. The signs will be rotated—keeping two on the counter at any one time.

A shelf will be created to hold the clinic's new brochures (see 5.2.6). The shelf will be placed next to the countertop at check out and will hold four different brochures.

5.2.4 Promotion—Website Design

A newly revised website will include existing features and some additions for current customers:

- A home page will give basic information about the clinic—phone number, office hours, e-mail address, logo, slogan, and so on.
- The home page would include links to social media as well.
- Separate pages will show photos of staff members and their pets—to help personalize the people and clinic
- Photos and descriptions of the clinic mascots—Dr. Hardy's two dogs and three cats.
- A customer photo page—which allows for photos of customers and/or their pets.
- A page will list the main services offered by the clinic and provide links to detailed descriptions of each service. This allows for customer education about the services, demonstration of the high-quality and state-of-the-art equipment the clinic utilizes, and to emphasize the extra efforts the clinic uses to provide compassionate and individualized care for pets and their owners.

This plan results in approximately 25 web pages. The larger site can be expanded to meet customer needs.

The website will also help to attract new customers—the other target market in this plan.

5.2.5 Promotion—Customer Database Enhancement

The initial cost of development and investment in a customer relationship management (CRM) program is beyond HVC's available time and financial resources at this time. On the other hand, it is anticipated that such a program will be cost justified in a few years. The company currently has a very simple customer database that tends to include only limited information for each customer. In the next couple of years, HVC must make sure that the data on each customer is complete in anticipation of migrating data to a sophisticated CRM package. Specific data to be collected on each customer:

- Name, address, phone, and e-mail
- Detailed information about each pet
  - Name
  - Breed
  - Vaccination records
  - Prescription/medication records
  - Services purchased by pet
  - Food—brand/type
  - Other pertinent information

At some point in the future, this information may be included into a yet more sophisticated program that allows for scheduling reminders and mailing of customized promotions. This remains an opportunity that has yet to be funded.

5.2.6 Promotion—Brochures to Describe the Clinic and Key Special Services

The clinic will create three different 8.5 × 11 inch, tri-fold brochures—two black-and-white brochures will promote the puppy/kitten services and dental health services, and a full-color brochure will be used to promote the clinic in general. The brochures will be designed by the same designer hired to create the logo and other promotional materials. The brochure should include contact information, various services, benefits to the pet and the owner, and possibly testimonials.

Brochures will be made available at the front counter of the clinic so customers can easily grab one to take and read. They will also be provided at any type of community/promotional event HVC attends. Brochures can be placed on the tables or other areas where they are clearly accessible for people to take.

Three different brochures will be created:

- Overview of HVC (services and staff)
  - Available in the clinic
  - Handed out at community events

- Distributed in the new residence packet—this is a packet given to each new resident.
  - Puppy/Kitten Service Bundle (description and prices)
    - Available in the clinic
    - Mailed to customers upon request
    - Distributed at the local Humane Society and by interested breeders in the area who currently use HVC
  - Dental Health Care Service Bundle (description and prices)
    - Available in the clinic
    - Handed out to interested customers following a discussion of the importance of regular dental care for dogs and cats

5.2.7 Promotion—Swag

HVC will use two different types of swag—free promotional materials—as giveaways at the clinic and when appearing at various community events. The items will include:

- Refrigerator magnets. Business card–sized refrigerator magnets with the HVC name, logo, phone number, and website address.
- Bandanas. Bandanas with the HVC name and logo—many local dog owners like to put bandanas around their dog's necks.

5.2.8 Promotion—Social Media

HVC will utilize slow periods in the workday to generate more online content for the website and social media pages. This initiative will include promotional pricing, community events, public service announcements (e.g., lost pets), national reminders (i.e., World Rabies Day), and fun and light-hearted pictures or videos of pets from the clinic and around the world. Animal-related videos have a strong following on the Internet and would likely move web traffic toward HVC's social media sites.

HVC's online presence currently includes:

- Website—a modern clinic website that is simple and attractive while providing all the necessary information.
- Facebook—this is how HVC keeps in touch with it's clientele on a day-to-day basis. Also, through its connected Instagram account, HVC posts humorous but appropriate content and veterinary tips and information.
- Twitter—HVC maintains an active Twitter feed to provide short news clips and to focus spreading the word about lost pets.
- Pinterest—although a less important part of the social media presence, vet tech Rick Woo enjoys photography and takes many excellent photos of the clinic's patients for sharing on Instagram and Pinterest.

Although there was some discussion of pulling back on Pinterest and Twitter (where followers are fewer), the additional cost of these social media tools is relatively modest. They are mostly updated during the receptionist's downtime.

6. Implementation and Control

This section on implementation and control outlines key details related to implementing the marketing plan.

- Special Implementation Problems to Overcome
- Control
- Budget, Sales Forecasts, and Estimates
  - Budget for Total Marketing Plan
  - Monthly Expenses for Total Marketing Plan
  - Pro Forma Income Statement
- Timing of Implementation Activities
- Contingency Plans

6.1 Special Implementation Problems to Overcome

The marketing plan will require the hiring of two additional part-time employees. These employees are necessary to staff extended office hours. One new employee would be a part-time veterinarian who has already been identified. This person would work about 15 hours per week. Annual cost for this additional person would be about $1,250 per month.

It would also be necessary to hire a receptionist to work the extra hours. Currently the office manager also works as a receptionist. The new receptionist would work about 20 hours per week. Incremental cost would be about $750 per month for the new receptionist.

6.2 Control

The objectives for this marketing plan outline specific targets for increased sales of some products, overall sales, and number of additional customers. These goals will be monitored on a monthly basis with a report developed by the office manager (Karen) for Dr. Hardy.

HVC also wants to be sure that it continues to deliver compassionate and individualized care to its customers. This important aspect of the clinic will be monitored through customer feedback. Beginning in January, HVC will give each customer a post card addressed to HVC following each visit. The post card will have three questions on the back:

- Would you recommend Hillside Veterinary Clinic to a friend? Yes/No
- On this visit to Hillside Veterinary Clinic, did you receive compassionate and individualized care for your pet? Yes definitely/Yes somewhat/No
- Do you have any comments for Hillside Veterinary Clinic? [create a box for comments]

HVC will monitor this information on a monthly basis to assure that sales targets and customer service delivery maintain high standards.

Control will also be done with routine monitoring and management of the company's owned media—in particular its website and social media pages. Weekly reports will be prepared to determine which pages get the most hits, the longest visits, and which social media gets liked, favorite, and forwarded.

6.3 Budget, Sales Forecasts, and Estimates

6.3.1 Budget for Total Marketing Plan

Marketing Tactic	Cost
Customer satisfaction survey post cards	$ 100
Brochure for Puppy/Kitten bundle (500)	125
Brochure for all clinic services (1,000)	500
Brochure for dental services bundle (500)	125
Design services for logo and various promotional materials	500
Website maintenance and updating (including purchase of URL and one-year maintenance)	750
Participation in five community events (costs for planning/attendance)	750
Vinyl signs and point-of-purchase signs	175
Costs for running ad and training new personnel	250
Yellow Pages advertisement	2,520
Personnel needed for extended clinic hours (4 months)	8,332
Refrigerator magnets (1,000)	224
Bandanas (600)	455
Maintaining and monitoring social media*	0
Total costs for implementing marketing plan	$14,806

* Lab tech Robert really enjoys social media and photography. He feels that in 1–2 hours per week he will be able to maintain a good social media presence for HVC.

6.3.2 Monthly Expenses for Total Marketing Plan

For cash flow planning purposes, the anticipated expenses are shown on a monthly basis.

Month	Major Expenses*	Cost
January	Customer satisfaction surveys, design services	$ 810
February	Brochures	960
March	Signs, magnets, bandanas	1,064
April	Community event	360
May	Community event	360
June	Website update and maintenance—annual contract due	585
July	Website design, community event	735
August	Ad and training for part-time receptionist	460
September	Personnel for longer hours	2,293
October	Personnel for longer hours, community event	2,443
November	Personnel for longer hours	2,293
December	Personnel for longer hours, community event	2,443
Monthly	Regular posting to website and social media—done on as needed basis by everyone	0

* *Yellow Pages* ads bill monthly at $210

6.3.3 Pro Forma Income Statement

	2016	2017	2018
Sales revenue	$375,000	$430,000	$485,000
Expenses			
Labor costs	250,000	285,000	320,000
Operating expenses	75,000	77,500	80,000
Marketing expenses	3,174	6,000	7,500
Depreciation	7,300	7,500	8,000
Net income	$ 39,526	$ 54,000	$ 69,500

Notes:

- Sales revenue growth assumes the marketing plan objectives outlined in this plan are achieved.
    - 15 percent growth in total customers over two years will increase revenues by an estimated $60,000
    - More aggressive promotion of dental services package and geriatric dog care package will result in an additional $30,000 in sales growth over two years.
    - Price increases of 5 percent over that time will yield about $20,000
- Routine operating expenses include various fixed costs like lease payments and loan payments on equipment and insurance.
- The costs of additional personnel, their hiring expenses and training, are included in operating costs—even though earlier analysis notes these costs are part of implementing the marketing plan.

6.4 Timing of Implementation Activities

The implementation of many of the marketing activities will be done by Karen (office manager) who already orders other supplies. In addition, Rick is the vet tech who most enjoys getting out among people—so he will coordinate and attend all event activities with Karen.

Date	Activity	Responsibility	Vendor
November	Sign *Yellow Pages* ad	• Karen	Qwest – Yellow Pages
Weekly	Manage social media: daily post on Facebook, four times a week Instagram	• Karen	
Monthly	Review and update website	• Dr. Hardy & Karen	Jay's Website Design Service
January	Training of receptionist to ensure complete understanding of office culture and procedures	• Dr. Hardy & Karen (Receptionist)	
January	Contract for logo and brochure design • Design new logo • Design two brochures • Design refrigerator magnets • Design bandanas • Design signs • Design letterhead • Design business cards	• Dr. Hardy will coordinate with Lisa (our designer)	Specialisa Design Service
February	Print brochures • Puppy/kitten package • Dental services package • Clinic list of services	• Karen	Kinko's Wellington
March	Order new business cards	• Karen	
March	Order refrigerator magnets	• Karen	Magnets.com
March	Order bandanas	• Karen	BandanaMan
March	Order vinyl signs and point-of-purchase signs to promote dental services	• Karen	FasterSigns Fort Collins
March	Develop plan for Easter Egg Hunt (April) and Town-Wide Garage Sale (May)	• ~ 2 hours Rick and Karen	
April	Attend Easter Egg Hunt event	• Rick and Karen (maybe Dr. Hardy)	
May	Attend Wellington Town-Wide Garage Sale event	• Rick and Karen (maybe Dr. Hardy)	
June	Plan for Family Fun Fest event (July)	• Rick and Karen (maybe Dr. Hardy)	
June	Talk to part-time vet to determine interest; if needed, run ads	• Dr. Hardy	
July	Attend Family Fun Fest event	• Rick and Karen (maybe Dr. Hardy)	
July	Develop and run ad for part-time receptionist; inform staff to spread word of mouth for opening	• Karen	Coloradoan newspaper ad
September	Start extended office hours	• New hires will be key to starting • Dr. Hardy and Karen to work later to help transition	
September	Plan for Annual Pet Fair	• Rick and Karen	
October	Attend Family Fun Fest event	• Rick, Karen, and Dr. Hardy	
November	Plan for Parade of Lights	• Rick and Karen	
December	Attend Parade of Lights	• Rick, Karen, and Dr. Hardy	
	Extended clinic hours	• $1,250/month (vet) • $833/month (receptionist)	Mid-year

6.5 Contingency Plans

If market conditions change, it may be necessary to re-evaluate elements of this plan or to develop an alternative plan. Potential environmental changes and the plans for addressing them follow:

- Difficulty hiring a part-time veterinarian. Although we anticipate our current part-time veterinarian will desire more stable and regular hours, this may not happen. We would then need to look on the open job market where it may not be possible to find a suitable vet.
  - If that is the case, the extended clinic hours program may be delayed.
- Slowdown in housing growth. Growth projections are largely based on continuing growth in the local housing market—which will bring new families and pets to the local area. If this slows down,
  - Delay the extended clinic hours proposal.
  - Delay the new building, currently planned for about two years out.
- Economic slowdown. Customers are less likely to be interested in health care prevention services—so this aspect of the marketing plan will be toned down.
- Faster growth in the housing market. Although a housing slowdown may come suddenly, the long lead time for new housing makes faster growth something we can more easily foresee. But if growth appears to be picking up:
  - We will speed up plans for the new building.
- New competitor enters the market. The fast growth of the town of Wellington and having CSU's local College of Veterinary Medicine, may result in a new competitor coming into the Wellington market.
  - Extended hours will be instituted earlier—to try to attract more customers.
  - Carefully re-evaluate the entire plan depending upon the nature of the new competitor—work hard to gather reliable information.
  - Consider more aggressive acquisition activities.

7 Appendices

7.1 Appendix A: Survey of Current Customers

To gather additional information in advance of the development of the marketing plan, a survey of current customers was conducted during March 2015. A convenience sample of 40 current customers completed the survey during visits to the clinic. The complete survey and percentage responding to each question are included below. Because some questions allowed respondents to circle more than one answer or due to rounding, percentages may not always total 100 percent.

Hillside Veterinary Clinic Customer Survey
This survey has been designed to give us more information about your needs. Please fill out this survey to the best of your ability.
Sincerely…Dr. Kelly Hardy, Hillside Veterinary Clinic

1. How many pets do you bring to Hillside Veterinary Clinic? (Circle one)

1 (38%)	2 (35%)	3 (10%)	4 (8%)	5+ (15%)

2. What type of pet(s) do you have? (Circle all that apply)

Dog	Cat	Bird	Hamster/ Guinea Pig	Ferret	Other
100%	48%	0%	0%	0%	5% (rabbit, chameleon)

3. Please list your pet's type, name, and age.
   Type: Name: Age:

   _____
   _____
   _____

4. Which of the following best describe how you view your pet(s)? (circle all the apply)

Family Member	Companion	Work Animal	Show Animal	Breeding
93%	15%	8%	3%	3%

Other __ 5% (rescue dog, hunting companion)

5. How many times in the last 12 months have you visited Hillside Veterinary Clinic? (circle one)

1–2	3–4	5–6	7+
38%	23%	23%	18%

6. About how much do you spend each year on your pet(s)? (circle one)

$0–60	$61–150	$151–300	$301+	No Reply
3%	10%	28%	53%	8%

7. How important are each of the following to you? (please rank)

	Not at all Important	Not very Important	Somewhat Important	Important	Very Important
Location close to my home	1 (0%)	2 (5%)	3 (8%)	4 (35%)	5 (53%)
Convenient hours	1 (0%)	2 (5%)	3 (10%)	4 (50%)	5 (35%)
Expertise of vet staff	1 (5%)	2 (5%)	3 (0%)	4 (13%)	5 (78%)
Quality of equipment	1 (8%)	2 (0%)	3 (10%)	4 (28%)	5 (55%)
Friendly customer service	1 (5%)	2 (0%)	3 (3%)	4 (30%)	5 (63%)

8. What services do you use at Hillside Veterinary Clinic? (circle all that apply)

House Calls	5%	Whelping	0%	Dermatology	13%
Vaccinations	80%	Tick/Flea Control	15%	General Surgery	25%
Spay/Neuter	40%	X-Rays	28%	Behavioral Counseling	3%
Parasite Control	35%	Heartworm	53%	Grief Support	5%
Health Screens	68%	Dentistry	10%	Hip Certifications	5%

9. What additional services would you like to see at Hillside Veterinary Clinic? (circle all that apply)

Boarding	33%	Daycare	10%
Weekend hours	20%	Training	3%
Acupuncture	10%	Other _____	5% (ultrasound, emergency hours)
Evening hours	38%		

10. About how many miles do you travel to get to Hillside Veterinary Clinic? (circle one)

0–5 **(70%)**   6–10 **(13%)**   11–15 **(5%)**   16–20 **(10%)**   21–25 **(0%)**   26+ **(3%)**

11. If Hillside Veterinary Clinic were to expand their facility in the general area, how would this effect your decision to do business with them? (circle one)

Would Not Switch Clinics	90%
Would Consider Switching Clinics	5%
Would Probably Switch Clinics	0%
Would Definitely Switch Clinics	0%
No Reply	3%

12. Are the hours of the clinic sufficient for you? (circle one)

Yes **(88%)**   No **(12%)**

If No, what hours would best serve you? (circle all that apply)

Mornings **(3%)**	Days **(3%)**	Evenings **(38%)**	Saturdays **(18%)**	Sundays **(0%)**

13. Have you ever been dissatisfied with the Hillside Veterinary Clinic? (circle one)

Yes **(5%)**   No **(95%)**

If Yes, explain briefly, _____ **("personal—do not want to explain," "poor treatment from an employee who is no longer working here")**

14. Is the Hillside Veterinary Clinic the only clinic you take your pet to? (circle one)

Yes **(90%)**   No **(10%)**

If No, What other clinic(s) do you use? **CSU Vet Clinic (2), East Side (2)**
If No, why? **(specialized services at CSU, I like East Side, convenience, hours)**

15. How did you hear about Hillside Veterinary Clinic? (circle all that apply)

Word of mouth (e.g., friend, neighbor, relative)	**35%**		
Referral from other clinic	**5%**	Pet Fair	**0%**
Magazine	**0%**	Sign	**40%**
Parade of Lights	**3%**	Yellow Pages	**10%**
Other _____		**8% newspaper article (2), Heska (1)**	

16. Have you recommended the Hillside Veterinary Clinic to anyone? (circle one)

Yes **(88%)**   No **(12%)**

17. Where do you purchase your pet food and/or supplies? (please circle all that apply)

Grocery Store	**20%**
Pet Specialty Store	**68%**
Discount Store (e.g., Walmart)	**35%**

18. Do you have access to the Internet? (circle one)

Yes	No
98%	**3%**

If Yes, do you have an email address?

Yes **(95%)**   No **(3%)**   No reply **(3%)**

19. Which of the following social media platforms do you currently use? (check all that apply)

Facebook **(61%)**	Twitter **(12%)**
Instagram **(14%)**	Pinterest **(19%)**
I don't use any social media platforms **(38%)**	

7.2 Appendix B: Competitor Matrix

	Hillside Veterinary Clinic	East Side Small Animal Hospital	Baker & Reid Veterinary Clinic	Flatirons Veterinary Clinic	Fossil Creek Veterinary Services
Nature of practice	• Small animals, birds and exotics	• Small animals only	• Equine and small animals	• Small animals only	• Dogs, cats, and some large animals
Location	• Downtown Wellington	• 10 miles southwest of HVC in Fort Collins	• One mile west of HVC	• 8 miles south of HVC in Fort Collins	• Mobile service for Wellington and outlying areas
# of Doctors	• One	• Five	• Two	• One	• One
Extra Services	• House calls • Acupuncture	• Emergency services • Acupuncture	• Ambulatory services, equine reproduction, and equine embryo transfer	• Grooming, 24-hour emergency care, specialize in dentistry	• Mobile—they only make housecalls
Gas or Anesthesia	• Anesthesia	• Both—depends on animal weight	• Anesthesia	• Gas	• Gas
Boarding	• No	• No	• No	• Yes	• No
Hours of operation	• MWThF 8-5:30; Tu 8-7	• M-Th 7:30-8 • F 7:30-6 • Sat 9-1 • Sun 1-3	• Services by appointment only	• M-F 8-5:30 • Sa 9-12 noon	• By appointment only
Prices spay dog/cat*	• $200/$150	• $136-210/$78	• $125/$90	• $110/$85	• Unknown
Advertising	• One inch in-column Y/P ad	• Full page Y/P ad, occasional direct mail, about 3–4/year	• One inch in- text Y/P ad • 2–3 /year in Val-Pak mailer	• One inch in-text Y/P ad	• Single line in Y/P
Website	• Extensive site	• Extensive site	• Modest site	• Extensive site	• Basic site
Social media	• Facebook page with 602 likes and daily posts • Instagram posts images 3–5 times per week • Twitter 3–5 tweets/week • Pinterest growing	• Facebook page with 698 likes—post 1–2 times per day • Twitter feed with 107 likes • Instagram occasional post • YouTube channel	• Facebook with 240 likes weekly posts • Big Instagram page with mostly large animal photos	• Facebook page with 187 likes and weekly posts • Pinterest page that appears dormant	• No Facebook page • Blog page with weekly posts
Positioning	• Try to emphasize compassionate and caring atmosphere	• Emphasize "in area since 1961" • Focus on per safety/comfort • Photo of large staff, 5 vets—promote size	• Personalized business • Emphasize equine health—small animals as convenience to horse customers	• "I treat your pet like my own." • Emphasize small town nature	• Promote convenience of mobile—we come to you. • Difficult to infer

* All respondents indicated that the size of the animal made pricing somewhat variable.

BONUS CHAPTERS

Now available to all adopters of *Essentials of Marketing 15e* are two chapters that previously resided only in our hard cover book *Basic Marketing*. These are available through Connect and SmartBook and can be bound in a printed version of the text through McGraw-Hill's Create custom publishing. We are calling them "Bonus Chapters" because they are something extra and optional for instructors seeking this extended coverage. You will be able to access these optional chapters online within the Connect/SmartBook platform. Once you're logged into Connect, access your Smart-Book and click on the Bonus Chapters Tab to access these additional chapters.

Bonus Chapter 1: Implementing and Controlling Marketing Plans: Evolution and Revolution

Previously chapter 18 in *Basic Marketing 19e*, this chapter builds on implementation and control, two concepts introduced in Chapter 2. This chapter goes into more depth on these concepts and offers how-to approaches for making implementation and control more effective. The chapter discusses how new information technology tools facilitate these practices and demonstrates how firms use sales analysis, performance analysis, and cost analysis to control marketing strategies and plans.

LEARNING OBJECTIVES

When you finish this chapter you should be able to:

1. Understand how information technology speeds up feedback for better implementation and control.

2. Know why effective implementation is critical to customer satisfaction and profits.

3. Understand how sales analysis can aid marketing strategy planning.

4. Understand the differences in sales analysis, performance analysis, and performance analysis using performance indexes.

5. Understand the difference between the full-cost approach and the contribution-margin approach.

6. Understand how planning and control can be combined to improve the marketing management process.

7. Understand what a marketing audit is and when and where it should be used.

8. Understand the important new terms (shown in red).

Brief chapter outline

- Good plans set the framework for implementation and control
- Speed up information for better implementation and control
- Effective implementation means that plans work as intended
- Control provides feedback to improve plans and implementation
- Sales analysis shows what's happening
- Performance analysis looks for differences
- Performance indexes simplify human analysis
- A series of performance analyses may find the real problem
- Marketing cost analysis—controlling costs too
- Planning and control combined
- The marketing audit

Bonus Chapter 2: Managing Marketing's Link with Other Functional Areas

Previously Chapter 19 in *Basic Marketing 19e*, this revised chapter covers some of the important ways that marketing links to other functional areas. The emphasis is not on the technical details of these other functional areas, but rather on the most important ways that cross-functional links impact your ability to develop marketing strategies and plans that really work. The chapter includes separate sections that describe how finance, production and operations, accounting, information systems, and human resources interact with marketing to create and implement successful marketing plans.

LEARNING OBJECTIVES

When you finish this chapter you should be able to:

1. Understand why turning a marketing plan into a profitable business requires money, information, people, and a way to get or produce goods and services.

2. Understand the ways that marketing strategy decisions need to be adjusted in light of available financing.

3. Understand how a firm can implement and expand a marketing plan using internally generated cash flow.

4. Understand how different aspects of production capacity, flexibility, and the cost and location of production affect marketing strategy planning.

5. Describe how marketing managers and accountants work together to analyze the costs and profitability of specific products and customers.

6. Understand how information systems enable marketing strategy.

7. Know some of the human resource issues that a marketer should consider when planning a strategy and implementing a plan.

8. Understand the important new terms (shown in red).

Chapter outline

- Marketing in the broader context
- The finance function: money to implement marketing plans
- Production must be coordinated with the marketing plan
- Accounting data can help in understanding costs and profits
- Enabling marketing strategy with information technology
- People put plans into action
- *Conclusion*
- *Key terms*
- *Questions and problems*
- *Marketing planning for hillside veterinary clinic*
- *Suggested cases*

Video Cases

Essentials of Marketing includes two different types of marketing cases: the 8 special video cases in this section and the 36 traditional cases in the next section. All of the cases offer you the opportunity to evaluate marketing concepts at work in a variety of real-world situations. However, the video cases add a multimedia dimension because we have produced a special video to accompany each of the following written cases. The videos are available to professors who adopt *Essentials of Marketing* for use in their courses. (These case-based videos are in addition to the teaching videos we have custom produced and made available to instructors for possible use with other parts of the text.)

The videos bring to life many of the issues considered in each case. However, you can read and analyze the written case descriptions even if there is no time or opportunity to view the video. Either way, you'll find the cases interesting and closely tied to the important concepts you've studied in the text.

The set of questions at the end of each case will get you started in thinking about the marketing issues in the case. Further, we provide instructors with a number of suggestions on using the video cases—both for group discussion in class or individual assignments. Thus, as is also true with the traditional cases in the next section, the video cases can be used in many different ways and sequences. You can analyze all of the cases, or only a subset. In fact, the same case can be analyzed several times for different purposes. As your understanding of marketing deepens throughout the course, you'll "see" many more of the marketing issues considered in each case.

1. Chick-fil-A: "Eat Mor Chikin" (Except on Sunday)*

There aren't many companies like Chick-fil-A. Most U.S. companies struggle to balance ambitious financial objectives with the desire to be ethical in business dealings and demonstrate a social conscience. Chick-fil-A easily surpasses industry norms for financial performance and eagerly embraces and protects a corporate culture rich with religious values and charity. The contrast is striking to most observers. Yet the Chick-fil-A phenomenon is easily understood when you study its entrepreneurial heritage.

S. Truett Cathy, founder, chairman, and CEO of Chick-fil-A, started his restaurant career in 1946 when he and his brother Ben opened a restaurant in Atlanta called the Dwarf Grill (renamed the Dwarf House two years later). It was not until 1967 that Cathy opened the first Chick-fil-A restaurant in Atlanta's Greenbriar Shopping Center. He is credited with introducing the original boneless breast of chicken sandwich and pioneering the placement of fast-food restaurants in shopping malls. Today, Chick-fil-A is the second-largest quick-service chicken restaurant chain in the United States, based on sales ($1.975 billion in 2005). It operates more than 1,250 restaurants in 37 states and Washington, D.C.

Chick-fil-A's unique corporate culture derives from Cathy's Christian background and his desire to inspire and influence people. The company's official statement of corporate purpose is "to glorify God by being a faithful steward of all that is entrusted to us and to have a positive influence on all who come in contact with Chick-fil-A." This level of commitment to religious values is reflected in a number of ways. For example, all Chick-fil-A locations, in a mall or stand-alone, are closed on Sundays. Cathy has been quoted on numerous occasions as saying, "Our decision to close on Sunday (starting in 1946) was our way of honoring God and directing our attention to things more important than our business. If it took seven days to make a living with a restaurant, then we needed to be in some other line of work. Through the years, I have never wavered from that position."

Chick-fil-A also has an extensive corporate giving program. The company has helped thousands of restaurant employees, foster children, and other young people through the WinShape Foundation that Cathy established in 1984 to help "shape winners." The foundation sponsors WinShape Homes, which currently operates 14 homes in Georgia, Tennessee, Alabama, and Brazil. The WinShape College Program at Berry College in Rome, Georgia, is a co-op program offering joint four-year scholarship funding to incoming freshmen of up to $32,000. In addition to the WinShape scholarships, Chick-fil-A offers $1,000 college scholarships to its restaurant team members. Camp WinShape is a summer camp for boys and girls. WinShape Marriage provides development, education, and encouragement for married couples on the campus of WinShape Retreat, a multiuse conference and retreat facility located on the Mountain Campus of Berry College.

Chick-fil-A's unique corporate culture is matched by its equally unique marketing efforts, especially in the advertising and promotion areas. Its "Eat Mor Chikin" campaign is one of the longest-running advertising campaigns in the United States. Started in June 1995 when the first Chick-fil-A billboard was erected in Atlanta, the Eat Mor Chikin cows have become cult figures, convincing diners to stray from the herd of beef-burger eateries and to "eat mor chikin"—particularly in Chick-fil-A restaurants. In focus groups, respondents rate the cows as one of the three things they like best about the Chick-fil-A brand—the other two being the food and the company's policy of being closed on Sundays.

The Eat Mor Chikin theme, created by Dallas-based ad agency the Richards Group, was first introduced in 1995 as a three-dimensional billboard concept depicting a black-and-white cow sitting atop the back of another cow painting the words "Eat-Mor-Chikin" on the billboard. Since then, the theme has been used as the basis of an integrated marketing campaign, which encompasses billboards, in-store point-of-purchase materials, promotions, radio and TV advertising, clothing and merchandise (e.g., plush cows, bobble-head cows), and calendars. Introduced in 1998, Chick-fil-A's cow calendars have been a marketer's dream come true. The calendar is produced annually by the Richards Group. Sales have sharply increased—from 337,000 for the first printed calendar to 1.5 million for the 2006 renaissance-themed calendar entitled "Cows in Shining Armor," featuring "famous" medieval cows named Angus Kahn, Charbroilemagne, Boldhoof, Lady Guineveal, and Moolius Caesar. The calendars sell for $5 and contain Chick-fil-A food and beverage coupon offers.

Sponsorship of collegiate sports such as the Chick-fil-A Peach Bowl (renamed the Chick-fil-A Bowl in 2006) are another way in which Chick-fil-A builds its brand. A local promotion emphasis at the market and restaurant level completes Chick-fil-A's integrated marketing approach.

In 1998, the Eat Mor Chikin campaign won a national silver EFFIE award in the Fast Food/Restaurants category for creativity and effectiveness in advertising. The outdoor Advertising Association of America recognized Chick-fil-A and its renegade cows with the organization's OBIE Hall of Fame Award in 2006.

Chick-fil-A is growing rapidly through store openings and menu additions. Menu additions include Chick-fil-A Chick-n Strips in 1995, Chick-fil-A Cool Wraps in 2001, Chick-fil-A Southwest char-grilled salad in 2003, fruit cup in 2004, and a breakfast menu featuring Chick-fil-A Chick-n Minis, a chicken or sausage breakfast burrito, and a chicken, egg, and cheese bagel in 2004. The chain introduced the industry's first premium two-blend coffee line in 2005 with Café Blends and the complementary Cinnamon Cluster. Hand-Spun milkshakes were launched in 2006.

The company had sales of $1.975 billion in 2005 and forecasts sales of $3 billion by 2010. Also by 2010, the company looks to double its current size in terms of new locations, primarily through stand-alone restaurants and

---

*This case was prepared by Dr. J. B. Wilkinson, professor emeritus, Youngstown State University.

aggressive expansion into the western United States. Chick-fil-A also has licensed restaurants in nontraditional locations such as airports, corporate offices, hospitals, and college campuses.

Dan Cathy, the son of S. Truett Cathy and Chick-fil-A's current president and COO, takes restaurant openings seriously. The openings are not simple ribbon-cuttings. Cathy holds a dedication dinner during which he and other company leaders wait on newly hired employees. He also "camps out" the night before a store opening with Chick-fil-A raving fans and customers. Beginning in 2003, Chick-fil-A offered the first 100 customers in line at its new stores a free combo meal each week for a year. People lined up hours in advance, setting up tents and lawn chairs overnight in the parking lot to ensure a place in line. Observing this, Cathy decided to join them and since then, camping out with Chick-fil-A fans and customers at store openings has become a tradition for him.

Dan Cathy fills his leadership role through interactions with customers and employees. He frequently visits Chick-fil-A restaurants and often pitches in to help. Like his father, Dan Cathy is on a mission to meet customers, franchisees, and employees face to face and spread the Chick-fil-A business philosophy of "Second Mile" (making every extra effort) customer service, great food, and influencing others.

1. *What types of marketing strategies is Chick-fil-A following?*
2. *How would you describe Chick-fil-A's positioning strategy?*
3. *Is Sunday closing a competitive advantage for Chick-fil-A? Explain.*
4. *Should other retailers consider closing on Sunday? Why? Why not?*

2. Bass Pro Shops (Outdoor World)*

Have you ever seen an elk, an antelope, or a buffalo? What about a largemouth bass? Don't fret—you don't have to go to Montana to see what wildlife looks like! You can visit your nearest Bass Pro Shops Outdoor World and experience merchandising at its best, participate in workshops that teach outdoor skills (e.g., safe boating and hunting, beginning fishing, outdoor cooking, fly tying, nature photography, and GPS navigation), and take advantage of in-store amusements like an indoor trout stream, shooting arcades, or a live mermaid show (in the Las Vegas store). Better yet, you can visit the original Outdoor World store referred to as the "Grand Daddy," located in Springfield, Missouri, and spend your vacation at the largest hunting, boating, camping, and fishing outlet in the country—330,000 square feet of experiential retailing!

Bass Pro Shops are part of a larger trend in retailing called "destination development"—a trend in retail development that blends goods and services with theater and entertainment. Destination retailers offer shoppers more than just merchandise; each offers a unique environment in which customers enjoy a quality personal experience. The idea that a store is more than just a "big box filled with merchandise" has spawned a number of destination developments that function as open-air centers with exciting landscapes and architecture. Each store within the development operates as a stage for fresh and engaging experiences for shoppers (e.g., the Bass Pro Shops stock-car-racing simulations, snowboarding, or natural rock-climbing walls) and with unusual attractions, activities, learning opportunities, theme restaurants, and entertainment. These types of developments act as "tourism districts," attracting visitors from 200 to 300 miles away.

Bass Pro Shops have successfully implemented the concept of destination development. Operating about 50 large retail stores in the United States and one in Canada, Bass Pro Shops has become the nation's leading retailer of outdoor gear. Its stores rank among the top tourist destinations in their respective states. More than 100 million people visit its stores annually and spend an estimated $1.9 billion to experience one of the most exciting store environments in retailing today!

Industry analysts agree that Bass Pro stores are unlike any other in terms of customer service, awesome displays and visual imagery, exciting activities, and deep merchandise assortments in fishing, boating, hunting, outdoor gear, and camping. All stores have several common features including: taxidermy mounts, indoor water displays that showcase fish species, Outdoor Skills Workshops, artwork, and activity areas (e.g., archery and firing ranges, fishing tournaments). In addition, each store is uniquely designed to pick up the local flavor of the area's outdoor heritage and to include historical pictures, indigenous wildlife exhibits, and artifacts from local hunters and fishers. Several stores are spectacular in this regard. For example, the Denham Springs, Louisiana, store (near Baton Rouge) opened to crowds of shoppers (65,000 in the first four days). The store features an artistic replication of a Louisiana swamp complete with towering cypress trees draped in Spanish moss. Another example is the Bass Pro Shops Sportsman's Center in Miami, Florida. It is designed to make visitors feel like they are walking through a sunken ship, complete with barnacle-encrusted trusses. Suspended ceiling dioramas portray underwater scenes, and colorful fish appear to swim overhead. The Bass Pro Shops store located along the western shore of Lake Ray Hubbard (in Dallas, Texas) has a panoramic view of the lake through floor-to-ceiling windows that extend the entire Eastern exposure of the building. As shoppers progress toward this enticing feature, they have an equally panoramic view of a vast

*This case was prepared by Dr. J. B. Wilkinson, professor emeritus, Youngstown State University.

indoor boat showroom that can be reached by descending twin staircases that circle past waterfalls and around a swimming pool–size aquarium. The store also features a 365-seat World Famous Islamorada Fish Company Restaurant overlooking the lake. The recently opened Independence, Missouri, store features an indoor mill with a working wheel plus a 30-acre park complete with a lake stocked with bass and bluegill where customers can try out their new purchases.

Bass Pro stores have been difficult for competitors to emulate. They are large, expensive, and labor intensive. For example, the new 150,000-square-foot store in Rossford, Ohio (near Toledo) will employ 250 to 300 associates, many of whom are highly skilled in outdoor activities such as fly-fishing, boating, and hunting. To make each Bass Pro store look different, an in-house group located in Nixa, Missouri, designs the interior and exterior of stores. An eclectic group of artisans and craftspeople—blacksmiths, metalworkers, welders, woodcarvers, and fabricators—handmake the chandeliers, lights, lanterns, wood carvings, ironwork, murals, mounted animals, displays, and special features that go into the stores. About 30 percent of each store's retail space is devoted to aquariums, waterfalls, murals, metalwork, museum-quality dioramas, and fireplaces. Bass Pro Shops' philosophy on merchandising also ups the ante. In-store displays aren't just fixtures—they are marketing tools designed to reflect local traditions and attract customers. For example, in the Lake Ray Hubbard store, canoes serve as shelving for apparel. In-store digital networks entertain and educate shoppers (how-to spots, technical features, PSAs for fishing, hunting, and conservation) and provide targeted advertising at the point of sale (vendor-sponsored ads and in-store promotions). The programming also includes vivid scenes of the outdoors and highlights of its NASCAR team. Six to seven 42-inch plasma-screen displays are located in key departments of each Bass Pro store. Some of the programming content is common across all stores, and some of it is customized to fit an individual store (targeted marketing). In addition, the level of customer service has become legendary. Bass Pro Shops has been recognized many times for its conservation efforts and outdoor education programs. The company supports a wide range of environmental, habitat conservation, and youth education programs through philanthropic efforts.

Bass Pro Shops can trace its roots to a small fishing department started by founder John Morris in 1972 to sell homemade bait and worms. Located in the back of his dad's liquor store in Springfield, Missouri (on the road to Table Rock Lake and Branson), the business was popular enough that Morris launched a catalog in 1974 to sell homemade bait. Soon, it became the world's largest mail-order sporting goods store. The flagship Springfield store has been improved over the years to become the tourist mecca that it is today. Along the way, other businesses were added: American Rod and Gun in 1975 (a wholesaling entity serving independently owned retailers), Tracker Marine in 1978 (a producer of recreational boats for Tracker dealerships and independent marine dealers under various brands, including Tracker Boats), Big Cedar Lodge in 1988 (a resort on Table Rock Lake), and the Islamorada Fish Company Restaurant chain. Other endeavors include Bass Pro Shops Outdoor World Television (on the Outdoor Channel), Bass Pro Shops Outdoor World Radio, Outdoor World Tips (written for newspapers and magazines), and Bass Pro Shops NASCAR participation. Beginning in 1995, the company began adding stores, beginning with the Bass Pro Shops Sportsman's Warehouse in Atlanta, Georgia. Since then, more than 48 stores have been added to the chain. Bass Pro Shops is regarded as the nation's leading retailer of outdoor gear, selling through massive stores, catalogs, and a website (www.basspro.com).

However, industry analysts have posed the question, "Are there limits to growth in the sporting and outdoor goods retail category?" Competition is intense. Competitors include large-format sporting goods stores, traditional and specialty sporting goods stores, mass-merchandisers, and catalog and Internet-based retailers. The most direct competitor to Bass Pro Shops is Cabela's—a chain of retail stores that has similar but less distinctive décor and merchandise. Other important competitors include Sports Authority, Dick's Sporting Goods, Academy Sports and Outdoors, Gander Mountain, Sportsman's Warehouse, and Walmart. All are growing rapidly despite the fact that the industry is declining in terms of active participants in outdoor activities such as hunting, fishing, and camping. Some markets such as Denver, Kansas City, Dallas, and Milwaukee seem "overstuffed" with outdoor chains. But some experts are predicting renewed growth in outdoor sales as consumers experience Bass Pro's destination stores. They point to Home Depot's ability to "grow its customer base" (increasing the number of "do-it-yourself" consumers) through how-to clinics and quality construction materials and tools. In addition, U.S. demographics favor increased sales of outdoor goods as the baby-boom generation retires and takes up more leisure-time activities.

Pessimists argue that large-format stores are risky in economic downturns. To build a Bass Pro Shop Outdoor World requires a big initial investment. Once open, high overhead and low inventory turnover are common in some merchandise categories. As a consequence, break-even sales must draw customers from a large trading area. Recessions and adverse weather conditions may also hurt sales, especially in overstocked markets.

Despite concerns by industry experts, recent Bass Pro store openings have attracted hordes of customers. It's been estimated that the average customer travels two hours to reach the store and shops for more than three hours! Shoppers also seem blind to pricing differences for identical products between Bass Pro stores and discounters like Walmart. All of this suggests that destination retailing works and that the marriage between retailing and entertainment is here to stay!

1. *Prepare a S.W.O.T. analysis for Bass Pro Shops. What types of strategies do you recommend based on your analysis?*
2. *Can you think of retailers in other categories that might successfully emulate the format and execution of Bass Pro Shops?*

3. Toyota Prius: The Power of Excellence in Product Innovation and Marketing*

Prius (Latin for "to go before") was introduced to the Japanese market in 1997 amid much publicity and extravaganza. It was the world's first mass-produced car powered by a combination of gasoline and electricity. For the Toyota Motor Corporation, the Prius product launch represented a major strategic commitment and a long-term financial gamble.

The Prius story begins in the early 1990s when Toyota released its first Earth Charter, setting the goal of minimizing its overall environmental impact. In September 1993, the company began to plan for the development of a car for the next century. Called Globe 21st Century, or G21, the plan was to produce a car with better fuel economy and lower emissions than existing automobiles.

Alternative ideas were considered before deciding to press ahead with a gas-electric hybrid system; these included direct-injection diesel engines, electric motors, hydrogen-powered fuel cells, and solar-powered vehicles. Mass production of gasoline-electric hybrids was not possible until recently. Improved technology with respect to batteries and powerful control electronics to coordinate the two propulsion systems made the idea more attractive.

GM (as well as Ford, Honda, and Toyota) failed to successfully market electric cars in the 1990s. Although GM's EV1 was a technical triumph, consumers were scared off by its limited battery life. All three American carmakers developed diesel-electric hybrid cars in the 1990s, but none were deemed acceptable to the market. A diesel engine is more expensive than a gasoline engine, so a diesel hybrid required a higher price premium. Development of a hydrogen-powered fuel cell vehicle was simply not technically feasible within the time frame that Toyota had set for its goal.

The hybrid technology chosen to power the Prius combines a gasoline engine with an integrated electric-drive system. Like conventional cars and trucks, the hybrid system relies on a gasoline-fueled engine to generate power; the electric motor system provides a second power channel. These two complementary systems work together to create a more efficient powertrain.

At start-up, only the electric motor is used, and it powers the vehicle at low- to mid-range speeds. Under normal driving conditions, the gas engine is engaged and power is allocated between the two engines to maximize efficiency during operations such as acceleration, deceleration, coasting, and stopping. In the city, with its stop-and-go traffic, the Prius relies more on the electric engine, whereas for highway driving, the gas engine is the primary power producer. The benefits of this powertrain combination are greater fuel efficiency and low exhaust emissions. Compared to electric cars, the hybrid system offers a high level of convenience because the battery is recharged from surplus engine power.

The Prius development effort took four years. The biggest challenges Toyota engineers faced were handling the powerful

*This case was prepared by Dr. J. B. Wilkinson, professor emeritus, Youngstown State University.

voltage between the battery and the electric motor and determining how to fit the gas engine, the electric motor, and a jumbo battery into a compact car frame. Solving these problems involved adapting the heavy-duty transistors used in Japan's bullet trains and shrinking the parts through computer modeling. A prototype car was shown to the public in 1995 and in December 1997, the first production car rolled out of Toyota's Takaoka factory in Toyota City near Nagoya. For the next two years, Toyota sold Prius only in Japan. First-year sales were around 12,000 units due to limited production capability. Toyota elected to defer capital investment in manufacturing facilities and to produce the Prius on existing assembly lines: a "hedging" strategy in case the hybrid "flopped." The initial price was just $16,929, which industry analysts say was below the estimated cost of building a Prius. However, even at that price, buyers paid a premium of several thousand dollars for a Prius compared to similar-size conventional cars. Industry analysts speculated that Toyota would have to sell around 250,000 Priuses a year to make a profit.

Prius was introduced to the U.S. market in 2000. The Honda Insight, a two-seater gas-electric hybrid, had been in the U.S. market for a year with first-year sales of about 3,500. Toyota limited U.S. sales of the Prius to 17,000 units during the introductory year. Base price for the Prius was $19,995 (roughly the same as for a Honda Insight). Both the Prius and the Insight were priced below cost but several thousand dollars higher than similar-sized conventional cars. However, the higher price was partially offset by better gasoline mileage (52 m.p.g. in city driving for the first-generation Prius).

The advertising campaign that launched the Prius into the U.S. market used "Prius Genius" as its tagline and courted leading-edge buyers of the technological generation. Celebrity buyers like Cameron Diaz heightened Toyota's publicity efforts, which included an "Engine of Change" tour—a 15-city circuit where the Prius was shown to leaders in government, media, and environmental groups. In addition, the Prius was seen by millions of Academy Award viewers as an "alternative limo" used by environmentally friendly Hollywood celebrities.

Toyota enjoyed a dramatic jump in Prius sales after its U.S. debut. Sales were so strong that demand outstripped production capability. It was not uncommon for buyers to wait up to six months to receive their new Prius. By 2004, global sales totaled 250,000, and Toyota was earning a modest profit per vehicle. The second-generation Prius (Prius II) hit U.S. showrooms in October 2003. As other car manufacturers (Ford, GM) entered the market with hybrid vehicles and Honda increased its number of hybrid models (Civic), Toyota changed its marketing strategy to emphasize its Hybrid Synergy Drive in Prius II as the powertrain of choice—a classic selective demand-building strategy, suitable for the growth stage in a product's life cycle. The objective of this strategy was to differentiate Toyota's hybrid technology from other hybrid systems emerging in the market. Unlike competitive systems on the market in 2004, the new high-voltage/high-power Hybrid Synergy Drive powertrain was capable of operating in either gas or electric modes, as well as a mode in which both the gas engine and electric motor are in operation. Compared to the original Toyota Hybrid System (THS) in Prius I, the new Hybrid Synergy Drive system delivered significantly more power and performance, best-in-class fuel economy, and best-in-market emissions performance. Toyota also worked to reduce the cost of its hybrids. Because gasoline-electric hybrids employ two motors under the hood, hybrids are more expensive to produce than conventional gas-powered vehicles (about $3,000 more). Cost reductions would lead to price reductions, making Toyota's hybrid cars more affordable.

The 2004 second-generation Prius was designed to appeal to a broader market. It was larger, more powerful, with numerous technical improvements and aerodynamic styling (plus a four-door, lift-back configuration), and loaded with high-tech options like the Smart Entry/Smart Start, which allows the driver to open and start the vehicle without inserting a key. Other options included a hands-free cell phone system and a navigation system. Base price was held at $19,995, the same as the first Prius cost during its introductory year in the United States. This second-generation car won some of the industry's most prestigious awards and was named European Car of the Year 2005.

The success of the Prius has provided Toyota with numerous product opportunities, including hybrid technology extension and licensing strategies. Toyota introduced a hybrid Lexus RX400h (2004) and Highlander (2005). A hybrid Camry and Lexus GS sedan were planned for 2006. Toyota expects that a quarter of its unit sales in the United States will use gasoline-electric technology by 2010. To achieve that goal, virtually all Toyota vehicles including trucks will offer hybrid power systems.

1. In what stage of the product life cycle is the Toyota Prius? Explain.
2. Describe the marketing strategies being followed by Toyota for the Prius.
3. Do you think Toyota should convert all of its cars to hybrids? Why? Why not?

4. Potbelly Sandwich Works Grows through "Quirky" Marketing*

Want an inexpensive gourmet sandwich served in a fun and funky place by friendly young people? Lots of people do, including celebrities Will Ferrell, Sandra Bullock, and Keanu Reaves. In fact, Potbelly Sandwich Works was ranked as one of the top fastest-growing chains in the restaurant industry.[1]

Chances are you have never eaten at a Potbelly, but you probably will in the near future. Under the leadership of Bryant Keil, chairman and CEO, Chicago-based Potbelly Sandwich Works is expanding rapidly (see Table 1). Keil bought the original Potbelly in 1996. Prior to that, it was a very successful neighborhood sandwich shop run by a couple who had originally started the business as an antique store in 1977. They added homemade sandwiches and desserts to bolster the business and soon the food became more popular than the antiques. As time went on, booths were added along with ovens for toasting the sandwiches and the antiques became "décor" rather than merchandise for sale. A prominently placed antique potbelly stove provided inspiration for the sandwich shop's name.

Although Potbelly has many sandwich shop rivals in the fierce quick-serve segment of the restaurant industry, Potbelly has more than held its own. Billed as "a unique and quirky sandwich joint," it has a unique appeal. Potbelly's core strategy elements include *product, place, promotion,* and *price.*

PRODUCT

According to Keil, "Anyone can sell a sandwich. You need to sell an experience." Industry observers point to several aspects of the Potbelly experience that make it the first choice for young professionals on a quick lunch break. First is the menu, which features made-to-order toasted sandwiches, soups, homemade desserts, malts, shakes, and yogurt smoothies. Toasting is part of what makes Potbelly's sandwiches distinctive. Quality ingredients, including a freshly baked Italian sub roll and freshly sliced meats and cheese also contribute to superior value. Friendly service and an upbeat atmosphere, live music, antique fixtures, real books for customers to read or borrow, and vintage memorabilia create a homey environment for customers. The idea behind Potbelly is simple: superior value, fun-filled atmosphere, warm, comfy décor, and quick, friendly service.

PLACE

Potbelly stores average 2,200 square feet but can top 4,000 square feet. Most units have indoor seating for more than 50 and outdoor seating during warmer months. Geographic locations are selected carefully. Keil looks for cities that are not saturated with sandwich chains and have an urban/suburban density of core customers—young professionals younger than 35 years old. Locations must be convenient for them because Potbelly stores rely on high repeat business. All units are corporate owned and operated.

PROMOTION

Historically, Potbelly Sandwich Works has not had an ad budget. Promotions are keyed to events like store openings and National Sandwich Day. For example, on National Sandwich Day, Potbelly hosts a "Belly Buster" sandwich-eating contest at Potbelly stores. Prizes are awarded to winners and runners-up. Diners randomly receive free meals. Other event promotions raise money for local charities such as food banks and community-based reading and music appreciation programs.

---

*This case was prepared by Dr. J. B. Wilkinson, professor emeritus, Youngstown State University.

[1]"Way to Grow: A Tight Real Estate Market Doesn't Deter Top Chains' Expansion Plans," *Restaurants and Institutions,* July 2005, p. 121.

Table 1 Potbelly Store Openings by Year and City, 1997–2005

Market	1997	1998	1999	2000	2001	2002	2003	2004	2005	Total
Chicago	1	1	1	2	3	8	11	9	11	48*
Washington, D.C.						8	3	4	3	18
Michigan							4	2	1	7
Minnesota							1	3	2	6
Wisconsin							2		2	4
Indiana								1	1	2
Texas								3	8	11
Ohio									6	6
Total	1	1	1	2	3	16	21	22	34	102

*Includes the original Potbelly opened in 1977 and bought by Keil in 1996.

PRICE

Potbelly sandwiches sell for $3.79. Sheila's Dream Bar, made of oatmeal, caramel, and chocolate, is $1.29, while homemade chocolate chip or sugar cookies go for only 99 cents. Checks average about $6.50. Pricing is an integral part of the value Potbelly offers customers and can be summed up as, "Just good food at good prices!"

Considered separately, any one of Potbelly's marketing strategy elements may not seem overly powerful as a competitive weapon, but combined and implemented with zeal, they are a significant competitive threat to national, regional, and local competitors. Brands such as Subway, Quiznos, Cosi, Panera, Jimmy John's, and Schlotzsky's Deli are wary that Potbelly will become a major national competitor. The Potbelly experience appears to be difficult to duplicate. For example, Quiznos may have similar food quality but not similar atmosphere; Cosi may have the hangout ambience down but not the

food! Subway is especially vulnerable because it has neither the food nor the warm and comfy store environment.

Yet Potbelly has a tough road ahead. It requires management to maintain the superior performance of current units while creating new Potbelly units in new markets. Each Potbelly is special in terms of location, décor, and staff. The unit must be tailored to its neighborhood and community. Attentive, enthusiastic workers must be found. Food quality and a fun atmosphere must become an integral part of the store culture. Not an easy task!

1. Identify and describe Potbelly's strategy in terms of product (present or new) and market (present or new).
2. How would you describe Potbelly's positioning strategy?
3. What types of environmental opportunities and threats do you see in Potbelly's external environment? How might they affect Potbelly's current strategy?

5. Suburban Regional Shopping Malls: Can the Magic Be Restored?*

The suburban regional shopping mall is regarded by many as the "crown jewel" of shopping experiences. In a single location, shoppers can visit more than a hundred stores, go to a movie, eat, walk, and lounge for an entire day in a secure, pleasant atmosphere sheltered from undesirable weather and the demands of everyday life. Most Americans at one time or another have escaped for the day to such a mall and felt "uplifted" in spirit by the experience. So pervasive is the suburban regional shopping mall that William Kowinski in the *The Malling of America* (1985) claims that in the United States

alone there are more enclosed malls than cities, four-year colleges, or television stations! Indeed, few of us can remember a time when shopping was a trip to "downtown," or the central business district (CBD) of a large city.

Many suburban regional shopping malls are more than one million square feet in size, contain more than a hundred stores, and offer shoppers free parking, restaurants, play facilities, lounge facilities, restrooms, and movie theaters. Some centers even provide amusement rides and other entertainment opportunities. One of the dominant features of these large shopping complexes is the presence of multiple department stores that "anchor" the extreme points of the mall's layout and "pull" shoppers to the mall from surrounding suburban areas. Department stores also encourage shoppers to walk through the mall. In fact, department stores were the driving force behind the

---

*This case and the script for the accompanying video were prepared by Dr. J. B. Wilkinson, professor emeritus, Youngstown State University, and Dr. David J. Burns, Xavier University.

original development of suburban regional shopping malls and have played a critical role in their continuing success.

The movement of traditional department stores from CBD locations to the suburbs, complete with large "full-line" departments, contributed greatly to the explosive growth of suburban regional shopping malls during the post–World War II era. At its inception, the suburban regional shopping mall was designed to be a substitute, or even a replacement, for a city's CBD, but without the usual congestion or parking difficulties. This strategy was particularly attractive after the opening of Southdale Center in suburban Minneapolis in 1956 (www.southdale.com), which demonstrated the viability of a regional shopping mall with multiple anchors.

In 2002 there were a total of 46,336 shopping centers in the United States, of which about 1,200 could be considered regional or superregional malls (www.icsc.org). In addition to regional and superregional malls, numerous types of shopping centers have evolved since the 1950s. The International Council of Shopping Centers has defined eight principal shopping center types: neighborhood, community, regional, superregional, fashion/specialty, power, theme/festival, and outlet.

The suburban regional shopping malls and their department store anchors enjoyed great success for almost 50 years and seemed virtually invincible to threats until the final decade of the twentieth century. During that era, several chinks developed in the competitive armor of this type of retail institution, and the problems seem to be getting worse. Shopper activity is declining: the number of tenant vacancies is increasing; and the delinquency rate on mall mortgages is disturbing. Increasingly larger percentages of consumer discretionary income are being spent elsewhere. To make matters worse, many of the older malls need renovating to remain attractive to shoppers. Renovation of an older mall can cost tens of millions of dollars.

Changes in consumers' wants and needs appear to be the major factor that underlies the woes of suburban regional shopping malls. Because the first multi-anchor center opened in 1956, the lifestyles of American families have changed significantly. In 1950, for instance, only 24 percent of wives worked outside the home; today, that percentage exceeds 60 percent. Women between the ages of 18 and 45, the mainstay of mall shoppers, simply do not have the time to shop like they once had. As a result, shopping has become much more purpose-driven. Shopping statistics bear this out. Shoppers are visiting suburban regional shopping malls less frequently, visiting fewer stores when they do shop, and also spending less time at the mall when they shop. Mall visitors, however, are more likely to make a purchase when they shop. Yet the typical suburban regional shopping mall was designed for a "shop-all-day" or a "shop-'til-you drop" philosophy.

Another consumer trend that spells trouble for suburban regional shopping malls is increased shopper price sensitivity. A wider selection of shopping alternatives from which to choose and the desire to make the family income go further (which, in essence, is equal to a pay increase) have proven to be strong forces pushing shoppers to comparison shop between retail establishments—something that most malls are not designed to facilitate. Despite the large number of stores contained within a regional suburban shopping mall, comparison shopping between stores is not an easy task. Most malls are laid out to cater to a leisure-oriented shopper. Similar stores are located in different wings of the shopping mall to encourage shoppers to walk through the entire center. Shoppers may walk upwards to a quarter-mile in their quest to compare products! This is not consistent with the desire for shopping convenience and efficiency on the part of most consumers.

Competition also has played a role in the problems that plague suburban regional shopping malls. High levels of competition characterize most mature industries, and the shopping center industry is no exception. Regional malls have both direct and indirect competitors. Direct competitors are nearby shopping centers with either similar or dissimilar formats. Indirect competitors comprise other types of retail store sites like freestanding or clustered sites and nonstore retailing sites. Nonstore retailing includes online shopping, catalog shopping, home TV shopping, telemarketing, and other forms of direct marketing, all of which have made considerable inroads into retail store sales. Suburban regional shopping malls have been especially vulnerable to both forms of competition.

Many of the more successful retailers (e.g., Kohl's, Home Depot) are located on freestanding sites or in large open-air centers—locations that have greater appeal to time-pressed, purpose-driven shoppers than mall locations. Similarly, many outlet malls, which cater to price-sensitive shoppers, are typically open-air centers to facilitate store access. In addition, some of the newer small shopping centers cater to a focused lifestyle (teen or professional woman) or have an organizing theme (home decor, hobby) that satisfies the specific needs of a market niche by offering a more focused product assortment than what can be found in a suburban regional shopping mall.

Oversupply of retail space has posed considerable problems to all shopping centers. The United States has 20 square feet for every man, woman, and child, compared to 1.4 square feet per person in Great Britain. Sales per square foot of retail space is declining in the United States. In fact, revenue from retail sales is contracting. It grew an average of 2.5 percent in the 1970s; 1.3 percent in the 1980s; and only 0.8 percent in the 1990s, adjusted for inflation. The result has been retail consolidation, store closings, and bankruptcies, leaving shopping centers fighting for a shrinking base of retail tenants.

Finally, department stores, the primary traffic generators for suburban regional shopping malls, are experiencing serious competitive problems. Over the past two decades, department stores have lost half of their market share to discounters and specialty stores. They also have suffered a significant sales revenue decline, causing store closings and consolidation. Given the role department stores have played as traffic generators for shopping malls, the problems of department stores have added to the problems of suburban regional shopping malls. Quite simply, fewer department store shoppers have meant fewer shoppers in the mall. To make matters worse, an empty department store space in a mall gives shoppers less reason to visit that portion of the mall and often leads to the closure of nearby stores. Besides being unproductive, the resulting empty retail space is unsightly, projecting the same image that empty storefronts in the CBDs of cities do—decay and decline.

The predictable outcome of all these changes is that construction of new suburban regional shopping malls has virtually come to a halt. Furthermore, a significant number of existing centers are being "decommissioned"—converted into alternative uses such as office space, learning centers, and telemarketing call centers, or torn down to be replaced by other forms of retail centers. Moret than 300 malls have been decommissioned since the mid-1990s, a trend which is expected to continue.

The dim outlook for suburban regional shopping malls has stimulated much creative thought about turnaround strategies for those still in operation. One turnaround strategy that has been suggested deals with the way suburban regional shopping malls are traditionally configured and involves changing the way stores in the center are arranged with respect to one another. The traditional layout locates similar stores in different wings or corridors of the center to encourage shoppers to travel through the entire center in their quest to locate and compare products. This type of layout maximizes customer interchange between stores but does not address shopping efficiency. Zonal merchandising represents a different approach to a center's layout. Under zonal merchandising, similar tenants are located in close proximity to one another. This reduces shopping time for shoppers who come to the mall to purchase a specific product. It also creates opportunities for differentiating mall areas in terms of decor, music, amenities, and special events to suit the tastes of shoppers who are most likely to be visiting stores in those areas.

Zonal merchandising has been used most commonly for fast food. Called "food courts," these clusters of fast-food providers have been very successful. Food court tenants have experienced higher levels of sales than under traditional layouts. Food courts also have shown that they are able to draw shoppers from other locations in the mall, similar to the traffic-generating role of a traditional anchor store.

Based on the success of the food court, several attempts to implement zonal merchandising on a wider scale have been made. Beginning with Bridgewater Commons in New Jersey (www.bridgewatercommons.com), several new projects have incorporated zonal merchandising principles, including Rivertown Crossings in Grand Rapids, Michigan (www.rivertown-crossings.com), which has grouped some categories of stores by product line carried, and Park Meadows in Denver, Colorado (www.parkmeadows.com), which has grouped stores by customer lifestyle. The results of these endeavors have been promising, and General Growth (www.generalgrowth.com), the developer of Rivertown Crossings, plans to implement some form of clustering at all of its future projects. Attempts to reconfigure existing centers around zonal merchandising ideas, such as the changes at Glendale Galleria in Glendale, California (www.glendalegalleria.com), seem to be successful as well.

An alternative strategy, which has been proposed for turning around traditional suburban regional shopping malls, is the incorporation of entertainment within the center. The idea behind this strategy is quite simple: Add value to the shopper's visit to a mall and give shoppers additional reasons to shop in the mall rather than at home. Entertainment can run the gamut from simple play areas or a carousel for children to video arcades and virtual golf courses to a full-scale amusement park, such as the Mall of America (www.mallofamerica.com). However, adding entertainment offerings to suburban regional shopping malls does not guarantee success. The entertainment must be something that will attract shoppers and keep their interest for a lengthy period of time—not something which shoppers tire of easily. Also the effect of the entertainment activities on a center's retailing activities must be considered. Entertainment centers in suburban regional malls often attract people with social goals instead of shopping goals, which does not benefit a center's merchandise-based stores.

Some industry analysts suggest that the key to revitalizing the suburban regional shopping mall is to make the shopping experience itself more exciting. Even at Mall of America, the home of the largest mall-based entertainment facility in the United States, the primary attraction of the center is the entertainment and excitement provided by the shopping experience itself; shoppers find stores and products which they cannot find elsewhere in the region.

Most suburban regional shopping malls are unexciting. They offer shoppers a relatively nondescript homogeneous shopping experience. They look alike, possess the same stores, and sell the same products. What has been forgotten by mall managers is that entertainment, in a mall sense, is not necessarily what activities can be added to the center, but what entertainment is provided by the shopping experience. Shoppers are searching for shopping experiences that are fresh, different, and fun. To provide this experience, suburban regional shopping malls need to attract stores and sell products that are unique, interesting, and ever-changing. The recent addition of the Build-a-Bear Workshop to several suburban regional shopping malls is one such example. The Build-a-Bear Workshop (www.buildabear.com) is a novel retail concept that provides a playful, creative environment. The challenge for mall managers is to find new and exciting retailing concepts like Build-a-Bear Workshop on a continual basis.

The Easton Town Center in Columbus, Ohio (www.eastontowncenter.com) is an example of a suburban regional shopping center that was explicitly designed to provide shoppers with a fun, exciting, entertaining place to shop. Easton Town Center was designed as an open-air center that mimics small-town America over 50 years ago. The center possesses an entertainment-oriented product mix with numerous restaurants, 30 movie theaters, spas, a comedy club, a cabaret, specialty stores, and Nordstrom and Lazarus as anchor department stores. The center has a "town square" and special event areas. It is considered to be one of the most successful retail centers in the region.

The challenge to mall developers and managers is clear. Since the opening of Southdale Center in 1956, changes in competition, retailing, and consumer shopping behavior have resulted in significant threats and opportunities. If suburban regional shopping malls are to enjoy continued success, they must creatively adapt to the new industry and shopping environment. Managers and owners of suburban regional shopping malls must determine the change strategy that is best for them. A number of considerations should guide their thinking—the competition, the needs of shoppers in their area, the opportunities available, and the center's resources. Just as one size does not fit all, the same turnaround strategy will not suit all suburban regional shopping malls.

1. *Imagine yourself as the manager of a struggling local suburban regional shopping mall. What do you think the mall should do to improve its performance?*

2. *What shopping trends do you foresee over the next 10 years? How might these trends affect suburban regional shopping malls?*

3. *What new retail concepts can you identify? How might you learn about more? What strategies do you suggest for learning about new retail concepts?*

6. Strategic Marketing Planning in Big Brothers Big Sisters of America*

For more than a century Big Brothers and Big Sisters of America (BBBSA) has helped children reach their potential through professionally supported one-on-one mentoring. With a network of about 400 agencies in all 50 states, BBBSA serves approximately 260,000 children between the ages of 6 and 18. A sister organization, BBBS International, has a global scope with agencies in 12 countries and similar plans to expand and improve international programs.

PROGRAMS

BBBSA has two core programs:

1. **Community-based mentoring** that requires a mentor ("big") to meet with a child ("little") at least one hour each week to engage in community activities.
2. **School-based mentoring** that encourages "bigs" to meet with their "littles" in schools, libraries, and community centers at least once a week to talk and play.

BBBSA "matches" between children ("littles") and mentors ("bigs") are carefully administered and supported by rigorous standards and trained personnel. Professional staff ensure that matches are safe and well-suited to the individuals involved. Each potential mentor ("big") is evaluated and trained before a match takes place. With each match, the intent is to provide a satisfying experience for both parties and to help the child develop positive outcomes.

BBBSA attempts to meet the needs of the most vulnerable children in a community. Because the demographics of these vulnerable children vary from community to community, BBBSA has developed different programs that consider these racial, ethnic, and social demographics. Each local affiliate launches a specific program that meets the needs of its community. The targets of these programs include:

1. **African American mentoring.** BBBSA recognizes that African American boys constitute one of the most at-risk populations in the United States. So it makes a concerted effort to recruit male African American "bigs" to serve this population by partnering with the Alpha Phi Alpha fraternity and United Methodist Men.
2. **Hispanic mentoring.** Given the huge increases in the Hispanic population, BBBSA also recognizes the many needs of Hispanic children in the United States. It actively recruits Latino "bigs" by building collaborations within Hispanic communities.
3. **Native American mentoring.** With more than 4 million Native Americans and Alaskan Natives living in the United States and more than a quarter of them living at or below poverty, BBBSA began a recruitment initiative in 2007 in Native American communities. The BBBSA program is run under the guidance of both formal and informal elders, members of Native American community programs, and American Indian/Alaska Native board members with 30 agencies participating in 16 states.
4. **Amachi Program (Mentoring Children of Promise).** BBBSA developed this program to serve children who have a parent in prison. Amachi is a Nigerian word of hope— "who knows but what God has brought us through this child." BBBSA focuses on recruiting "bigs" from local congregations.
5. **Military Children.** BBBSA established a partnership with the T. Boone Pickens Foundation to serve children with a parent in the military and to provide civic engagement for military personnel returning from deployment. A BBBSA Military Community Advisory Council has been set up for this program.

ORGANIZATION

Like most national nonprofit organizations, BBBSA has two levels of operation. The national office in Philadelphia has an executive staff and national board of directors that provide strategic direction and support to local agencies across the United States. Each local agency has an executive director, board of directors, and program staff who address the specific needs of children within its community. Each agency must operate under an affiliation agreement with BBBSA, which gives it the rights to:

1. Operate an organization using the BBBSA name.
2. Receive a designated service community area which is a specific geographical area in the United States. The local agency is restricted to recruitment and fund-raising within that geographical area.
3. Associate with BBBSA long term, unless the affiliation is terminated by the local board or by the national office.
4. Collaborate with BBBSA and other member agencies.

Membership fees are paid quarterly and are based on the total expenditures of the agency. Four deductions are allowed: fees paid to BBBSA, capital purchases, depreciation, and fund-raising expenses. The fee is then calculated by taking 3.8 percent of the first $100,000; 2.25 percent of the next $100,000; 1 percent of the next $300,000; and 0.5 percent of the remaining expenditures. The affiliation fee is directly related to the size of the agency, with larger agencies paying more for the national affiliation than smaller agencies. Agencies are also given discounts if they pay their entire affiliation fee up front: 5 percent discount if paid by January 31, 4.5 percent discount if paid by February 28, or 4 percent discount if paid by March 31. Otherwise, affiliation fees are due on March 31, June 30, September 30, and December 31. In order to better manage its own annual budget, the national office encourages early payments from the affiliated agencies.

---

*This case was prepared by Dr. Jane S. Reid, Youngstown State University.

Local agencies benefit from their national affiliation with BBBSA. First and foremost, the national office provides strategic direction to local agencies. Second, BBBSA sets standards that local agencies must follow in order to use the BBBSA brand, but through networking, local agencies are able to share "best practices." Local agencies also have access to research that the national office conducts. In addition, the national office provides a management information system (MIS) which allows local agencies to process information about volunteers, children, families, and donors. Further, the MIS helps local agencies manage their efforts and measure outcomes. Last, and probably the most important from a marketing standpoint, local agencies benefit from a nationally recognized brand with high credibility, which helps them in recruiting "bigs" and "littles" and attracting donors. This is especially important during economic downturns when funding from foundations, the public sector, and individual donors decline. Agencies with proven programs and high brand recognition and credibility are more likely to survive. Moreover, BBBSA has a competitive advantage compared to other nonprofit organizations that provide programs for youth. It is the only national organization that focuses on one-on-one mentoring.

STRATEGIC PLANNING INITIATIVES

In 2000, BBBSA launched its strategic-planning initiative by hiring Bridgespan Consulting (www.bridgespan.org). The Bridgespan Group helps nonprofit and philanthropic leaders to develop strategic plans and build organizations that inspire and accelerate social change. The use of a professional consulting service to develop a strategic planning process was made possible by the generous support of the Edna McConnell Clark Foundation (www.emcf.org), a foundation that seeks to improve the lives of people in poverty, especially low-income youth in the United States.

The first step was to establish a steering committee to work with the consulting firm. The steering committee consisted of four local agency leaders, one BBBSA board member who also served on a local BBBSA board, and five BBBSA leaders. One of the first activities of the committee was to collect information about the problems, practices, opinions, and attitudes of local agencies. The committee surveyed more than 160 local agencies and received input from leaders at more than 70 agencies, representing all of the different regions, sizes, and types of communities served by BBBSA.

As part of the process, Bridgespan Consulting guided BBBSA through a S.W.O.T. analysis that included examining its mission statement: "To help children reach their potential through professionally supported, one-to-one relationships with measurable impact." As a result of the analysis, the vision statement became: "Successful mentoring relationships for all children who need and want them, contributing to better schools, brighter futures, and stronger communities for all."[2] BBBSA also included a promise statement as part of its guiding principles, which commits BBBSA to a culture of diversity and inclusion, partnership and collaboration, continuous learning, people development, and high performance.

In setting its organizational goals, BBBSA built on its past strengths of accountability for outcomes in three areas: (1) the number of children served; (2) how well those children are served; and (3) which children are served, with a focus on children who are most in need and most likely to benefit from BBBSA programs. From there, BBBSA developed four goals with specific outcomes:

1. Quality growth—to serve more than 300,000 children by 2010 (a 25 percent increase over its 2006 level).
2. Positive outcomes for a higher percentage of children served—increasing the average match length from 10 to 13 months and increasing the six-month retention rate from 80 percent to 85 percent. The overall intent of this goal is to increase the strength of the relationship between "bigs" and "littles." During this planning period, BBBSA also committed to lead the development of new real-time outcome measures for local affiliates.
3. Increased intentionality about which children are served. Although each local agency serves a unique population, the overriding national goals would be

    a. Increase the percentage of boys served and the percentage of male volunteers (from 38 percent to 41 percent of all volunteers). The focus on males is to counteract the recent increase in the number of female matches and to better serve the large number of boys on the waiting lists.
    b. Increase the percentage of Hispanic youth served from 17 to 22 percent of all matches.
    c. Increase the percentage of African American and Hispanic youth served by same-ethnicity volunteers to at least 57 percent by increasing African American volunteers from 15 to 18 percent of all volunteers and by increasing Hispanic volunteers from 7 to 13 percent of all volunteers.
    d. Establish clear baseline data for measuring the percent of "littles" who are in moderate-to-high need.

4. Strengthen local agencies' capacity for sustainable, quality growth. The specific goals for making that happen include

    a. 10 percent annual total revenue growth to $385 million by 2010.
    b. 10 percent revenue growth by 50 percent of local agencies (up from 35 percent).
    c. 3 months' cash reserves by 65 percent of local agencies (up from 49 percent).
    d. $1 million in revenues by 80 percent of large market agencies (up from 67 percent).
    e. $500,000 in revenues by 40 percent of regional and smaller market agencies (up from 20 percent).
    f. Board and leadership development plans in 60 percent of agencies. In addition, each agency with $500,000 or more in revenue should have four key leadership positions: CEO, VP Program, Chief Development Officer, and VP Partnership/Recruitment.

The goals outlined above are detailed, measurable, and a "stretch" for both the local agencies and the national office. However, BBBSA outlined specific implications and expectations for the national office and agencies.

AGENCIES

- Sustained, quality growth should be at the core of each agency's effort.
- Each agency should work toward maximizing its impact and community support by being intentional about whom it serves.
- Both the Community-Based Mentoring and School-Based Mentoring programs should be strong and robust in terms of quality and growth.
- Resource development (funds and volunteer recruitment) should be a central leadership focus for all agencies.
- Agencies should ensure that their talent and organizational structures are strong enough to support the complex challenges of sustained quality growth.

NATIONAL OFFICE

- Leadership on the definition of success (agreement on "what is achieved" versus "what is done").
- Increased direct support to agencies through financial grants.
- Maintenance of current level of support to agencies with a focus on technology, outcome data, and best practices sharing.
- Enhanced capacity in key central functions including marketing, corporate partnerships, and human resources.
- Emphasis on talent and leadership in the five key roles—board, executive director, vice president of program, chief development officer, and vice president of partnerships.

Research plays an important role within BBBSA. Its MIS is designed to measure the effectiveness of its programs. In a nationwide study, BBBSA found that "littles" were

- 46 percent less likely to begin using illegal drugs.
- 27 percent less likely to begin using alcohol.
- 52 percent less likely to skip school.
- 37 percent less likely to skip a class.

BBBSA has encouraged and supported similar strategic planning efforts in local agencies. Local agencies are encouraged to identify appropriate targets within their communities and to adapt national programs and strategies with measurable objectives. One example of how the national organization supports the marketing efforts of local agencies is public service announcements (PSAs). BBBSA has produced several PSAs that address the specific goals of recruiting male "bigs" and "littles" of both Hispanic and African American ethnicities. However, local agencies must decide which PSAs to use and then get local broadcast stations to run them—perhaps to coincide with major fund-raising events like Bowl for Kids' Sake. Local agencies also develop collateral material such as posters, flyers, and brochures.

CURRENT AND FUTURE STRATEGIC INITIATIVES

BBBSA has committed to reviews of its strategic plan on a three-year cycle because it believes the key to an organization's survival is recognizing opportunities and threats and adjusting to them.

BBBSA has already begun its second planning cycle and it faces some specific challenges. The first is to achieve greater consistency in its brand image. Although local agencies are autonomous, BBBSA needs to have a consistent image across all communication efforts: ads, PSAs, events, web pages, and so on.

Another key concern (identified in focus group research) is that BBBSA is now viewed as a "volunteer agency"—not an agency to which people would consider donating money. Consequently, this perception needs to be modified so that, when people think of BBBSA, they think of becoming donors as well as volunteers.

BBBSA recruitment is (and will continue to be) constrained by economic concerns and family demands. These constraints make it hard to attract not only volunteers, but also active and talented people to serve on boards of local agencies or to hire competent staff at modest salaries.

To address some of these concerns, BBBSA has initiated a repositioning campaign (Project: BigChange$) at the national level. It is working with Publicis Groupe on a pro-bono basis to redefine mentoring in a more powerful way and to establish itself as a donor-supported, as well as volunteer-supported, organization. To coordinate the campaign, the national office has provided local agencies with specific strategies for communicating to potential donors and volunteers. Some key points are

- Emphasizing BBBSA's commitment to measurable outcomes.
- Connecting donors to its program similar to the connection that volunteers feel.
- Describing services as donor-funded and not "free."
- Ensuring that each staff member understands his/her position is funded by a donor.
- Explaining to each potential "big" that donors make matches possible.
- Using adult "littles" (alumni) to demonstrate successes.
- Focusing on stewardship—the impact that the agency and the donors have on the community.

BBBSA is a strong nonprofit organization. It prides itself on being accountable to its stakeholders by providing meaningful and effective programs to children. Under a new president and CEO, BBBSA seems poised to be a significant influence during the next decade. It's focusing on its strengths and addressing its problems through strategic planning.

1. *Compare strategic planning by BBBSA with planning by for-profit organizations. What are the similarities? What are the differences?*

2. *Using Exhibit 2-9 on the marketing strategy planning process in Chapter 2, identify the components of BBBSA's strategic planning process from the information presented in this case. Who are BBBSA's customers and competitors? How has BBBSA chosen to segment its market? Describe BBBSA's target markets. How does BBBSA differentiate itself from the "competition"? How would you describe the 4Ps of BBBSA's marketing strategy?*

3. *What are the benefits of a local nonprofit organization affiliating with a national nonprofit organization? Can you identify any disadvantages?*

4. *Refer to the BBBSA website (www.bbbs.org). What changes have occurred in the mission, vision, goals, and strategies? Has BBBSA successfully met the goals stated in this case? Has the organization successfully overcome the challenges of brand image and recruitment of volunteers?*

7. Invacare Says, "Yes, You Can!" to Customers Worldwide*

"On this vote the yeas are two hundred and nineteen, the nays are two hundred and twelve. The motion to concur in the Senate amendment is adopted." As he watched the U.S. House of Representatives pass Health Care Reform on March 23, 2010, Invacare Chairman and CEO Malachi "Mal" Mixon contemplated the impact of this landmark legislation on his company.

COMPANY AND INDUSTRY HISTORY

Modern devices that provide mobility where it is needed can trace their history to the Fay Manufacturing Company in Elyria, Ohio, in the 1880s. Originally a bicycle and tricycle manufacturer, the company changed directions when Winslow Fay recognized the need for mobility among wounded veterans and children. He redesigned his tricycles to enable people considered "crippled" at that time to move about. After achieving nationwide distribution of these products, Fay sold out to the Worthington Manufacturing Company in the early 1890s. After a series of mergers and acquisitions, the company became Invacare and, in 1979, an entrepreneurial group led by Mal Mixon and J. B. Richey purchased the company.

Changes in the company paralleled changes in the wheelchair industry. Although wheelchair-like devices were used in ancient times, something akin to modern wheelchairs were not developed until the 16th century. However, because chronically ill or disabled people had short life spans, the need for wheelchairs was not perceived to be important. By the late 19th century, survival rates were higher, but most people needing a wheelchair were considered to be invalids—best kept at home or in an institution. Two world wars and a polio pandemic in the first half of the 20th century greatly increased the number of people with limited mobility, but attitudes about their care had not changed much.

When Franklin Delano Roosevelt, President of the United States from 1933 to 1945, became a victim of polio at the age of 39, perceptions started to change.[3] Determined to lead an active life, Roosevelt developed his own wheelchair—a lightweight chair on rollers that could pass through normal-sized doors.

In the 1970s, the Vietnam War produced large numbers of young wounded soldiers who wanted normal civilian lives. At the same time, there was greater awareness of the need to break down socioeconomic boundaries between groups, including the disabled. Heavy, bulky chairs were not suitable for people who wanted to work, participate in sports, dance, and travel with family and friends.

Other changes in the 1970s helped the medical devices industry grow and evolve. Up until that time, Everest & Jennings, then the major supplier of wheelchairs, set the standards for the rest of the industry through its contractual arrangements with the U.S. government. These government contracts determined styles and materials for the products that would be purchased directly—and indirectly influenced what would be acceptable for reimbursement under many insurance programs. This type of market power enabled Everest & Jennings to command a dominant market share without the necessity of adapting to the rapidly changing needs and wants of its target market.

The Medical Devices Act of 1976 changed the dynamics of the industry. The Bureau of Medical Devices was created within the Food and Drug Administration to oversee production of a vast array of devices from catheters to wheelchairs to MRI machines. This new agency took a fresh look at the needs and wants of individual users, as well as the needs of physicians and insurers. Change did not come immediately, but Invacare began to see new market opportunities.

Under its new leadership of Mixon and Richey, Invacare reexamined its strategy and found itself deficient in many areas. Product quality and delivery were poor; no new products were under development; production costs were high; competition from new producers in Asia was growing; and Invacare had done little to penetrate foreign markets. Moreover, the company had no real strategic plan.

Mixon addressed these issues by first working through the distributor network to improve product design, quality, and delivery times. Distributors were offered better financing support to offset high interest rates which were a problem at the time. New products, new product lines, and the acquisition of related companies followed. Invacare became a major player in the design, construction, and sale of therapeutic beds and oxygen concentrators, in addition to its traditional product lines. Invacare also entered the "prescription wheelchair" business. Prescription chairs are custom products, designed for individual users. Today, Invacare is known for its customized wheelchair products.

In a related change of strategy, Invacare brought new vitality to the self-powered wheelchair in 1981 with the introduction of a lighter, more capable model. The Rolls IV, as it was known, provided users with a much improved sense of independence and mobility. Wheelchair users began to recognize and communicate their needs and wants to distributors who conveyed this market information to Invacare's sales force. In turn, company engineers added desirable features and attributes, which improved products and increased customer satisfaction.

As a result, Invacare pioneered the idea of "One Stop Shopping" for medical devices. "One Stop Shopping" continues to define the company's product and distribution strategies to this day.

CURRENT STRATEGIES AND CHALLENGES

Today, Invacare is the world's leading manufacturer and distributor for medical equipment used in the home: power and manual wheelchairs, personal mobility, seating and positioning products, home care bed systems, and home oxygen systems. Vertical integration, Statistical Process Control, and total quality management (TQM) have all contributed to the success of

---

*This case was prepared by Dr. Douglas Hausknecht, The University of Akron. Using iron braces on his hips and legs, he also taught himself to walk a short distance by swiveling his torso while supporting himself with a cane. He funded and developed a hydrotherapy center for the treatment of polio patients in Warm Springs, Georgia, and after becoming president, helped to found the National Foundation for Infantile Paralysis (now known as the March of Dimes).

Invacare's multiple product lines. In its modern manufacturing facilities in Ohio, Mexico, and elsewhere, the company produces and assembles many of the components for its products—whether standard or customized. Invacare also supplies the components necessary for service and repair of chairs, beds, oxygen concentrators, and other products. Its new-product development process includes representatives from marketing, quality, manufacturing, purchasing, finance, and design.

Because cost has become increasingly important in the medical devices industry, Invacare actively pursues a cost-containment strategy. While the need for specialized products has increased, the availability of insurance or government programs to pay for them has not. Prior to WWII, the cost of medical devices typically was borne by the family or community contributions. As medical insurance developed and evolved into an employee benefit, some of the costs were covered that way. Beginning in 1972, the federal government covered costs for the permanently disabled through Medicare, but because products were intended to be affordable, design took a back seat. Changes in government regulation, most notably the 1990 Americans with Disabilities Act (ADA), encouraged improvements in product design and extensions of existing product lines. Medicare policies were slow to change, however, and even in the 1980s insureds were only reimbursed for equipment necessary to "perform the activities of daily living within the four walls of the home." Customers were not permitted to upgrade from basic models unless they paid the entire cost themselves. Medicare rules at the time did not permit augmenting the basic cost with private funds.

Currently, a greater range of options in government support, insurance, and flexible spending plans—as well as private and foundation money—help to fund purchases of customized equipment. Invacare's domestic revenues are equally dependent on private insurance and Medicare: together contributing about 80 percent of its income. However, cost-containment language in the 2010 Health Care Reform Act may once again limit the availability of funds for high-end equipment.

Invacare sells its products to more than 25,000 home health care and medical equipment providers, distributors, and government locations in the United States, Australia, Canada, Europe, New Zealand, and Asia through its sales force, telesales associates, and various independent agent distributors. Distributors in individual markets work with medical care facilities, doctors, rehabilitation clinics, and retailers to identify potential new customers and current users. Invacare's sales force works with distributors to monitor and meet demand. Awareness of the available range of products is enhanced through a variety of means. Invacare has sponsored individual wheelchair races, a wheelchair racing circuit, and the Wounded Warrior Project. Team Invacare competes in racing, basketball, handcycling, and tennis. Special-purpose chairs encourage participation in sports as demanding as rugby—even to the extent of having specially-designed chairs for offense and defense. These sponsorships and participation in special events heighten awareness of customized equipment among potential customers and with the general public. Rather than featuring the attributes of specific pieces of equipment, Invacare's advertisements and promotional materials emphasize people enjoying life with its products.

As Mal Mixon considered Invacare's past strategies, he wondered about the future. How might the new environment for health care affect Invacare and its competitors? Everest & Jennings' sturdy and utilitarian chairs are still being manufactured under the umbrella of GF Health Products. They look the same as they always have. But other competitors have carved out positions in all-terrain accessibility (e.g., Permobil), lightweight portability (e.g., Lifecare Medical), niche uses (e.g., Colours in Motion), and increasingly low price (imports). Dean Kamen, inventor of the Segway, developed the IBOT—a pricey wheelchair that can climb stairs. Would future price pressures and regulatory changes allow all of these competitors to coexist?

Invacare is also a leader in the oxygen concentrator market. The HomeFill combines the efficiency of stationary oxygen concentrators with the convenience of pre-filled bottles to enable a greater range of travel for those who are dependent on supplementary oxygen. Will new regulations favor less costly "standard" products, such as those offered also by DeVilbiss and Respironics? Will pricing pressures allow for further innovation?

The Health Care Reform Act that was passed in 2010 broadly refers to changes in the managed care medical insurance system in the United States. It is expected to affect all Americans in some way and will impact all companies in the medical equipment, services, and insurance industries. In general, it requires all Americans to be covered by health insurance. Insurers are no longer allowed to deny coverage to individuals with pre-existing conditions, and young adults will be able to stay on their parents' plans until the age of 26. These changes are expected to be very costly, and some critics predict a shortage of primary care physicians. In addition, implementation of the bill will require cost reductions and savings that are likely to affect the availability of health care services and payments. However, some aspects of the act remain in flux. A sales tax on home medical devices was delayed. A provision that would reduce the ability to sell directly to the customer in favor of leasing arrangements has not been implemented. So the overall impact of the Health Care Reform Bill on Invacare is unknown. Will the promise of greater access to health care and life-improving treatment and devices create a larger domestic market, or will greater restrictions on prices and product design reverse decades of product innovation and improvements?

Markets outside the United States are a concern as well. As of 2010, Invacare produces components or complete products in several countries. It also distributes products in 80 countries worldwide (a range of coverage difficult for a company that prides itself on meeting the needs of its customers), but not all of the company's product lines are available in all markets. In addition, many of its products sold in foreign markets are still based in part on designs from acquired companies. So while quality, reliability, and service are emphasized throughout the global corporation, design has been allowed to fluctuate. This "globalization" of the company's strategy has led to nonstandard components and problems with "cataloging" the product line worldwide.

Further, in the global marketplace, cultural factors account for some differences in local markets. Take China, for example. Basic health care is provided by the government in China, but private health care and individual personal benefits (not available to everyone) are viewed negatively. In recent years, some of these attitudes have changed, but only slowly. Still, income and a willingness to spend on personal items is increasing among the middle-to-upper classes. At the same time, care of the elderly is becoming less reliant on immediate family. In addition, the "one child per household" policy and the preference for male children will continue to strain the ability of earning generations to support their parents. Invacare's competitors in China include the Jiangsu Yuyue Company with product lines very similar to its own. Invacare has some manufacturing and distribution in China now and is contemplating future strategy in light of the culture and competition.

Brazil is another example. It is a large emerging market, but the problems Invacare faces there are somewhat different from the ones in China. Brazil has a history of being a very protectionist economy. High tariffs and duties restrict the ability to import finished goods of many types, and there is a strong preference for locally manufactured products. Nevertheless, the country's abundant natural resources permit global corporations to compete through direct foreign investment in manufacturing and distribution. The downside is that direct investment requires duplication of production facilities and other corporate resources within the country. But Brazil is a major exporter to other South American markets and that could make it an attractive market for Invacare.

Mal Mixon believes in his company and its future. He thinks it has the resources and energy to grow and to serve a customer base that needs and appreciates its products. Invacare's motto of, "Yes, you can!" truly conveys the positive corporate attitude that underlies its mission: to remove real and perceived barriers that may restrict the lives of its customers. But Mal wonders how the company can best meet the challenges both within the United States and in foreign markets. How will the company grow and prosper in the next decade?

1. *How might the anticipated changes in U.S. health care coverage affect Invacare's current marketing strategies and demand for its products?*
2. *Conduct a S.W.O.T. analysis for Invacare. What types of opportunities and threats do you see? What types of marketing strategies are suggested by your S.W.O.T. analysis?*
3. *What have been the "keys to success" for Invacare in the past? Are these likely to change in the future?*
4. *What do you think will be necessary for Invacare to conduct operations successfully in Brazil? What about China? Which of these two countries is a better "fit" for Invacare's business model?*

8. Segway Finds Niche Markets for Its Human Transporter Technology*

Amid heavy media coverage and much speculation, "Ginger" made its debut on ABC's *Good Morning America* on December 3, 2001. It thrilled some and disappointed others, but the technology was breathtaking to all.

Now known as the Segway Human Transporter (HT), Ginger was the brainchild of inventor and entrepreneur Dean Kamen, who is best known for his inventions in the medical field. While in college, Kamen invented the first wearable drug-infusion pump. In the following years, he invented the first portable insulin pump, the first portable dialysis machine, and an array of heart stents. This string of successes established Kamen's reputation and turned DEKA Research and Development Corp., the R&D lab he founded, into a premier company for medical-device design.

The inspiration for Ginger occurred during the development of the IBOT wheelchair at DEKA. Developed for and funded by Johnson & Johnson, the IBOT wheelchair is a gyro-stabilized, microprocessor-controlled wheelchair that gives disabled people the same kind of mobility the rest of us take for granted. Officially called the Independence IBOT mobility system, this six-wheel machine can go up and down curbs, cruise effortlessly through sand or gravel, climb stairs, and rise up on its wheels to lift its occupant to eye level while maintaining balance and maneuverability with such stability that it can't be knocked over. The IBOT wheelchair has been likened to a sophisticated robot.

As Kamen and his team at DEKA were working on the IBOT, it dawned on them that they could build a device using similar technology for pedestrians—one that could go farther, move more quickly, and carry more. The IBOT was also the source of the "Ginger" code name for the Segway HT during its development stage. Watching the IBOT "dance up the stairs," Kamen's team likened it to Fred Astaire—hence the name Ginger for its smaller partner with only two wheels!

Segway's breakthrough technology is based on dynamic stabilization. A self-balancing, electric-powered transport device, the Segway HT contains gyroscopes and sensors that monitor a user's center of gravity and respond to subtle shifts in weight. Lean forward, go forward; lean back, go back; lean back a bit more and you go in reverse; turn by twisting your wrist; arch your back a tad and you slow to a halt. Exactly how the Segway achieves this is difficult to explain, but in every Segway, there are gyroscopes that act like your inner ear, a computer that acts like your brain, motors that act like your muscles, and wheels that act like your feet. You step aboard and it "oscillates" for a few seconds, getting the feel of you, and then it's fully cruiseable at 6 mph in "learning mode," and 12.5 miles per hour "flat-out." It has a range of about 17 to 25 miles per battery charge and can support package weights of 80 pounds. It has no brakes, no engine, no throttle, no gearshift, no steering wheel, and gives off no emissions. It is much cleaner than a car and faster than a bike. It is more pedestrian-friendly than bikes or scooters and safer than a skateboard.

The commercial potential for Segway is enormous. For this reason, Kamen decided to move development and manufacturing of the Segway HT to a new company with the vision to

---

*This case was prepared by Dr. J. B. Wilkinson, professor emeritus, Youngstown State University.

develop highly efficient, zero-emission transportation solutions using dynamic stabilization technology. The new company, Segway LLC (changed to Segway, Inc., in 2005) is headquartered in Bedford, New Hampshire, and construction of a manufacturing and assembly plant was completed in 2001.

Kamen has openly stated that the Segway "will be to the car what the car was to the horse and buggy!" He imagines them everywhere: in parks, on battlefields, on factory floors, zipping around distribution centers, and especially on downtown sidewalks. But market acceptance and penetration has been slow for this engineering marvel.

The Segway HT was initially marketed to major corporations and government agencies. Kamen personally demonstrated the Segway to the postmaster general who was keen to put letter carriers on Segways and to the head of the National Park Service who wanted to do the same with park rangers. Both were among Segway's first customers. The Pentagon's research agency, DARPA, bought Segways to give to robotics labs. The objective was to use Segway bases in the development of robots to do menial tasks (cleaning, picking crops), specialized jobs (nurses aids), and dangerous missions (bomb removal or rescue work in earthquake debris). Amazon.com, GE Plastics, and Delphi Automotive Systems purchased Segways for use in warehouses and manufacturing plants. Police departments, cities, and airports bought Segways for use by foot patrols, security personnel, and meter readers. Customer studies by these early buyers showed double-digit productivity gains and reduced reliance on motorized transport. For postal workers, the Segway has increased their carrying capacity and delivery speed. Test studies with police officers and security personnel have shown faster response times and better sightlines from being higher in the air than pedestrians.

In 2002, Segways went on sale to the public for the first time on Amazon.com at a price of around $5,000. In 2003, the retail store Brookstone became the first retailer to sell the Segway HT. By January 2004, it was estimated by industry observers that about 6,000 Segways had been sold. Given Kamen's stated ambition of replacing automobiles and other forms of personal transport alternatives, initial consumer sales were disappointing.

However, the Segway HT is still in the early stages of its product life cycle. According to product life-cycle theories and related empirical studies on diffusion of innovations, products move through their life cycles in different ways and the length of any particular stage varies according to many factors. In general, the speed with which a product moves through its introduction and growth stages varies according to product characteristics, market characteristics, competition, and environmental factors. The initial marketing strategy for a product will also affect market acceptance (adoption). A product will move quickly through the introduction and growth stages when it has high relative advantage—cost and benefits—compared to alternative products and is highly compatible with a buyer's current attitudes, lifestyle, and usage situation. The more complex a product is to understand and use, the slower will be its rate of adoption. In addition, if the product can be tried in small amounts, potential buyers perceive less risk associated with initial trial and this will speed adoption. Communication of the new product will affect market acceptance because buyers must first learn about a new product before the buying process can be initiated. Thus, a company's communication strategies and the degree to which favorable word-of-mouth opinion occurs will

impact sales. Finally, new products will have higher rates of market acceptance if market conditions, competition, and environmental trends are favorable.

Industrial and government applications for the Segway HT continue to be positive. It's ideally suited for use in large-scale manufacturing plants and warehousing operations, for use by the police and security personnel in certain types of situations, for meter reading, for corporate and university campus transportation, and for package and mail delivery. And it has found a number of new niches in recent years. For example, tour groups are using Segways to move tourists between attractions in cities where tour buses and cars have operational difficulties. For example, Bill and Emily Neuenschwander's tours use Segways equipped with a radio on the handlebars that provide a running commentary to guide customers through tours of the Minneapolis, Minnesota, riverfront and surrounding historic landmarks. Visitors to theme parks, museums, and islands (e.g., Amelia Island Plantation Resort) use them. Some lawyers use them between offices and courtrooms. Some medics use them to reach injured people faster.

However, in the consumer market, the Segway HT is still an unsought product for many people. Industry observers believe that the automobile is a preferred alternative for a number of reasons, including the infrastructure of cities, commuting distances, weather, and the American family lifestyle. Most people agree that the use of a Segway HT on highways and busy streets is dangerous. Also, many commuters live more than 5 miles from work. The need to recharge Segways raises the question of public sources of electricity. Issues related to public safety also have slowed consumer sales. Although the Segway HT is approved in most states for use on sidewalks, restrictions have been placed on speed, helmet use, minimum operating age, and use on streets and highways. At the local level, additional regulations apply. For example, San Francisco banned their use on city sidewalks, and they are outlawed in subways in Washington, D.C. Many see the mix of pedestrians, bicycles, skateboards, roller skates, ATVs, scooters, and Segways as a dangerous mix on sidewalks, hiking trails, and other public areas.

On the other hand, the Segway HT has obvious advantages to walking and other types of personal transport in situations where people need to get from one place to another rapidly and efficiently using a clean, quiet, and environment-friendly transport device. The market potential for the product has barely been tapped. Early consumer buyers were mostly "techies" who like to own new, high-tech products, and they have played an important role in communicating the benefits and fun of owning a Segway HT. They have established local clubs across America and have started a number of websites devoted to Segway. In 2003, owners and enthusiasts held the first SegwayFest to celebrate all things Segway. The Fest has been held every year since.

In 2004, Segway launched a repositioning campaign to change the image of the Segway HT from "staid," "high-tech," and "serious" to "fun, smart transportation." The new and more traditional marketing campaign included new customer materials, dealer displays, and cable TV advertising with the tagline "Get Moving." Segway also has been increasing the number of dealerships and distributors worldwide. The new distribution strategy allows potential buyers to see the different models and to try them out before buying. The dealer network increases the visibility of the product and lowers buyers' perceived risk associated with servicing. Publicity, media appearances, and product placement on television shows such as *Frasier, Arrested Development,* and *The Simpsons* continue to provide important market exposure.

The new positioning strategy emphasizes the leisure aspect of the Segway HT. New models aimed at the recreation market have been introduced. For example, the Segway GT is geared toward golf enthusiasts and includes a golf bag carrier. The Segway XT is the company's off-road vehicle which can perform well in a variety of environments. The Centaur is a four-wheeled ATV-like vehicle that can pick up its wheels to climb over obstacles or simply glide on two wheels at 25 mph.

To further develop the market for the Segway technology, the company has started to market Segway Smart Motion Technology through licensing and partnering with third parties to codevelop new products. Under this program, any number of specialized products could emerge.

The future for Segway is unlimited. America's commitment to end its dependence on petroleum and reduce harmful emissions is not likely to change. Segway 's technology supports this commitment. The consumer market for Segway has developed slowly, but the future is assured. For this "new-to-the-world" product, the life cycle will be long and classically configured. Its impact on all sectors of the economy will be profound. How we work, play, and get around will radically change in the 21st century. From the company's perspective, this is just dandy! Its ultimate goal is to "be to the car what the car was to the horse and buggy!"

1. *How might Segway, Inc., further develop the market for Segway technology? Hint: What types of marketing strategies are associated with sales growth?*
2. *What would be some advantages and disadvantages of using a Segway HT to get around on campus?*
3. *What types of applications and usage situations are there for Segway HTs in your area?*
4. *What kinds of problems would the use of Segway HTs create in your area? What are some possible solutions for these problems? Explain.*

Cases

Guide to the Use of These Cases

Cases can be used in many ways. And the same case can be analyzed several times for different purposes.

"Suggested cases" are listed at the end of most chapters, but these cases can also be used later in the text. The main criterion for the order of these cases is the amount of technical vocabulary—or text principles—that are needed to read the case meaningfully. The first cases are "easiest" in this regard. This is why an early case can easily be used two or three times—with different emphasis. Some early cases might require some consideration of Product and Price, for example, and might be used twice, perhaps regarding product planning and later pricing. In contrast, later cases, which focus more on Price, might be treated more effectively *after* the Price chapters are covered.

In some of the cases, we have disguised certain information—such as names or proprietary financial data—at the request of the people or firms involved in the case. However, such changes do not alter the basic substantive problems you will be analyzing in a case.

1. McDonald's "Seniors" Restaurant

Lisa Aham manages a McDonald's restaurant in a city with many "seniors." She has noticed that some senior citizens have become not just regular patrons, but patrons who come for breakfast and stay on until about 3 p.m. Many of these older customers were attracted initially by a monthly breakfast special for people aged 55 and older. The meal costs $1.99, and refills of coffee are free. Every fourth Monday, between 100 and 150 seniors jam Lisa's McDonald's for the special offer. But now almost as many of them are coming every day—turning the fast-food restaurant into a meeting place. They sit for hours with a cup of coffee, chatting with friends. On most days, as many as 100 will stay from one to four hours.

Lisa's employees have been very friendly to the seniors, calling them by their first names and visiting with them each day. In fact, Lisa's McDonald's is a happy place—with her employees developing close relationships with the seniors. Some employees have even visited customers who have been hospitalized. "You know," Lisa says, "I really get attached to the customers. They're like my family. I really care about these people." They are all "friends," and it is part of McDonald's corporate philosophy (as reflected in its website, www.mcdonalds.com) to be friendly with its customers and to give back to the communities it serves.

These older customers are an orderly group and very friendly to anyone who comes in. Further, they are neater than most customers and carefully clean up their tables before they leave. Nevertheless, Lisa is beginning to wonder if anything should be done about her growing "non-fast-food" clientele. There's no crowding problem yet, during the time when the seniors like to come. But if the size of the senior citizen group continues to grow, crowding could become a problem. Further, Lisa is concerned that her restaurant might come to be known as an "old people's" restaurant—which might discourage some younger customers. And if customers felt the restaurant was crowded, some might feel that they wouldn't get fast service. On the other hand, a place that seems busy might be seen as a "good place to go" and a "friendly place."

Lisa also worries about the image she is projecting. McDonald's is a fast-food restaurant (there are more than 35,000 of them serving more than 65 million people in more than 119 countries every day), and normally customers are expected to eat and run. Will allowing people to stay and visit change the whole concept? In the extreme, Lisa's McDonald's might become more like a European-style restaurant where the customers are never rushed and feel very comfortable about lingering over coffee for an hour or two! Lisa knows that the amount her senior customers spend is similar to the average customer's purchase—but the seniors do use the facilities for a much longer time. However, in actuality, most of the older customers leave McDonald's by 11:30, before the noon crowd comes in.

Lisa is concerned about another possibility. If catering to seniors is OK, then should she do even more with this age group? In particular, she is considering offering bingo games during the slow morning hours—9 a.m. to 11 a.m. Bingo is popular with some seniors, and this could be a new revenue source—beyond the extra food and drink purchases that probably would result. She figures she could charge $5 per person for the two-hour period and run it with two underutilized employees. The prizes would be coupons for purchases at her store (to keep it legal) and would amount to about two-thirds of the bingo receipts (at retail prices). The party room area of her McDonald's would be perfect for this use and could hold up to 150 persons.

Evaluate Lisa Aham's current strategy regarding senior citizens. Does this strategy improve this McDonald's image? What should she do about the senior citizen market—that is, should she encourage, ignore, or discourage her seniors? What should she do about the bingo idea? Explain.

2. Nature's Way Foods, Inc.

It is 2015, and Neal Middleton, newly elected president of Nature's Way Foods, Inc., faces a severe decline in profits. Nature's Way Foods, Inc., is a 127-year-old California-based food processor. Its multiproduct lines are widely accepted under the Nature's Way Foods brand. The company and its subsidiaries prepare, package, and sell canned and frozen foods, including fruits, vegetables, pickles, and condiments. Nature's Way Foods, which operates more than 30 processing plants in the United States, is one of the larger U.S. food processors—with annual sales of about $650 million.

Until 2015, Nature's Way Foods was a subsidiary of a major Midwestern food processor, and many of the present managers came from the parent company. Nature's Way Foods' last president recently said:

> The influence of our old parent company is still with us. As long as new products look like they will increase the company's sales volume, they are introduced. Traditionally, there has been little, if any, attention paid to margins. We are well aware that profits will come through good products produced in large volume.

Alex May, a 25-year employee and now production manager, agrees with the multiproduct-line policy. As he puts it, "Volume comes from satisfying needs. We will can or freeze any vegetable or fruit we think consumers might want." May also admits that much of the expansion in product lines was encouraged by economics. The typical plants in the industry are not fully used. By adding new products to use this excess capacity, costs are spread over greater volume. So the production department is always looking for new ways to make more effective use of its present facilities.

Nature's Way Foods has a line-forcing policy, requiring any store that wants to carry its brand name to carry most of the 65 items in the Nature's Way Foods line. This policy, coupled with its wide expansion of product lines, has resulted in 88 percent of the firm's sales coming from major supermarket chain stores, such as Safeway, Kroger, and Winn Dixie.

Smaller stores are generally not willing to accept the Nature's Way Foods policy. May explains, "We know that only large stores can afford to stock all our products. But the large stores are the volume! We give consumers the choice of any Nature's Way Foods product they want, and the result is maximum sales." Many small retailers have complained about Nature's Way Foods' policy, but they have been ignored because they are considered too small in potential sales volume per store to be of any significance.

In late 2015, a stockholders' revolt over low profits (in 2015, profits were only $500,000) resulted in Nature's Way Foods' president and two of its five directors being removed. Neal Middleton (introduced earlier), an accountant from the company's outside auditing firm, was brought in as president. One of the first things he focused on was the variable and low levels of profits in the past several years. A comparison of Nature's Way Foods' results with similar operations of some large competitors supported his concern. In the past 13 years, Nature's Way Foods' closest competitors had an average profit return on shareholders' investment of 5 to 9 percent, whereas Nature's Way Foods averaged only 1.5 percent. Further, Nature's Way Foods' sales volume has not increased much from the 2001 level (after adjusting for inflation)—while operating costs have soared upward. Profits for the firm were about $8 million in 2001. The closest Nature's Way Foods has come since then is about $6 million—in 2004. The outgoing president blamed his failure on an inefficient sales department. He said, "Our sales department has deteriorated. I can't exactly put my finger on it, but the overall quality of salespeople has dropped, and morale is bad. The team just didn't perform." When Middleton e-mailed Shelley Walton, the vice president of sales, with this charge, her reply was:

It's not our fault. I think the company made a key mistake in the late '80s. It expanded horizontally—by increasing its number of product offerings—while major competitors were expanding vertically, growing their own raw materials and making all of their packing materials. They can control quality and make profits in manufacturing that can be used in promotion. I lost some of my best people from frustration. We just aren't competitive enough to reach the market the way we should with a comparable product and price.

In a lengthy e-mail from Shelley Walton, Middleton learned more about the characteristics of Nature's Way Foods' market. Although all the firms in the food-processing industry advertise heavily, the size of the market for most processed foods hasn't grown much for many years. Further, most consumers are pressed for time and aren't very selective. If they can't find the brand of food they are looking for, they'll pick up another brand rather than go to some other store. No company in the industry has much effect on the price at which its products are sold. Chain store buyers are very knowledgeable about prices and special promotions available from all the competing suppliers, and they are quick to play one supplier against another to keep the price low. Basically, they have a price they are willing to pay—and they won't exceed it. Then the chains will charge any price they wish on a given brand sold at retail. That is, a 48-can case of beans might be purchased from any supplier for $23.10, no matter whose product it is. Generally, the shelf price for each is no more than a few pennies different, but chain stores occasionally attract customers by placing a well-known brand on sale.

Besides insisting that processors meet price points, like for the canned beans, some chains require price allowances if special locations or displays are desired. They also carry non-advertised brands and/or their own brands at a lower price—to offer better value to their customers. And most willingly accept producers' cents-off coupons, which are offered by Nature's Way Foods as well as most of the other major producers of full lines.

At this point, Neal Middleton is trying to decide why Nature's Way Foods, Inc., isn't as profitable as it once was. And he is puzzled about why some competitors are putting products on the market with low potential sales volume. (For example, one major competitor recently introduced a line of exotic foreign vegetables with gourmet sauces.) And others have been offering frozen dinners or entrees with vegetables for several years. Apparently, Nature's Way Foods' managers considered trying such products several years ago but decided against it because of the small potential sales volumes and the likely high costs of new-product development and promotion.

Evaluate Nature's Way Foods' present situation. What would you advise Neal Middleton to do to improve Nature's Way Foods' profits? Explain why.

3. Real NOCO Soccer Academy

Wesley Diekens came to the United States from the U.K. in 2005 on a soccer scholarship. Wesley grew up playing soccer on many competitive teams through high school and had a brief professional career in England. When St. Albans College recruited him to play soccer, he thought it would open his life to a grand adventure. That adventure changed his life.

While at St. Albans, Diekens met his future wife, Alyce Bilski, who also played soccer there. She graduated a year ahead of him and went to Fort Collins, Colorado, where she played on the semiprofessional Fort Collins Force women's soccer team. When Diekens finished college, he followed Bilski to northern Colorado. Bilski was captain of the Force and worked for the sports marketing company that owned the team.

Diekens got a job at a local meat packing plant, but soccer was his passion. He made the practice squad for the Colorado Rapids Major League Soccer team, but injuries cut his professional career short. Teaching soccer to kids became a new passion for Diekens. He has a natural talent for coaching. Diekens is charismatic, kids enjoy his easygoing demeanor and British accent, and he really knows soccer and how to teach the game to youngsters.

In 2009, Diekens founded the Real NOCO Soccer Academy (NOCO standing for NOrthern COlorado). At first he trained small groups of young players aged 7 to 14. He grouped them by age, gender, and skill and conducted training sessions for small groups of five to seven at a local park. The first kids he attracted came by word-of-mouth as they quickly told friends and teammates about "this British guy who teaches soccer and makes it fun." His small after-school camps quickly grew to include more than 50 kids. Word continued to get around, and by the following summer Diekens conducted 10 different camps—and quit his job at the meat packing plant. He also trained 11 different Real NOCO 3v3 soccer teams that competed in tournaments across the state and nation during the summer. All of his players had bright blue jerseys with the Real NOCO name across the front, and the success of these teams made the jerseys a great promotion vehicle. In 2012, four of his teams competed in the national 3v3 soccer tournament, with one winning a national championship.

To keep up with the rapid growth, Diekens brought a few friends over from England to assist with training. Will Bowman moved to the United States to become Diekens' assistant director of coaching. Diekens and Bowman planned to work year-round as trainers and hire a couple of local coaches to help them conduct training sessions. During the summer he added a couple of local college soccer players and a few former teammates from England. The summer season works well for his British mates, because that is the off-season for those still playing professionally. Diekens is confident he can hire and train more coaches if he needs them to handle future growth.

Youth soccer is big in Colorado and across much of the United States. It is the largest participation sport for kids. Fort Collins is a soccer hotbed, and this has helped Diekens' business grow. He now trains about 600 kids per year. But he has even greater ambitions. For example, he would like to build a training facility; the space he currently rents is not always well-suited to soccer. However, he figures he would need to double his business to justify the cost of the soccer complex he wants to build. So he is now wondering how to grow his business.

About 90 percent of his current customers live in Fort Collins, which has a population of about 150,000 people. Diekens believes awareness of his program is close to 100 percent among competitive soccer players ages 11 to 14—and is probably at about 40 percent among families with soccer-playing kids ages 6 to 10. Most of his customers are 10 to 13 years old and enroll in two to three Real NOCO programs per year. He has also run a few camps in Boulder and

Northglenn—both are about 50 miles from Fort Collins. These have been successful but are currently limited.

There are several small cities within 25 miles of Fort Collins. Loveland, a city of about 70,000, borders Fort Collins on the south. Greeley and Longmont, each with about 90,000 to 100,000 people, are about 25 miles away by interstate highway. These areas have very limited soccer training programs except for their competitive teams, and awareness of Real NOCO is not very high. Those who have heard of his academy are often not familiar with its philosophy and programs. Diekens is not sure if parents in these communities would be willing to drive their kids to Fort Collins for training. If not, he would have to run his programs there.

Diekens knows that he wants to grow his business, but wonders how he can accomplish his goal. He currently sees a few options:

1. His current customer retention rate is pretty high: about 80 percent. However, when the kids reach 14 or 15 years old, other high school sports and activities make them less interested in extra soccer training. One option is to try to increase retention by developing programs targeted at kids older than 14.
2. Another option is to develop a marketing strategy that would encourage his current customers to buy more. He wonders if they have other needs that he might be able to serve.
3. Diekens could try to grow the business by entering new markets and acquiring new customers. His market penetration with kids 6 to 9 years old is still quite modest. He might develop new programs to better meet this group's needs.
4. Another new market option would be to serve more kids from Loveland, Longmont, and Greeley.

Evaluate Diekens' different options for growing Real NOCO's customer equity. Develop a set of marketing strategy ideas for each of the options. What market research could Diekens perform to better assess his options?

4. Computer Xperts

Claire Kelly is getting desperate about her new business. She's not sure she can make a go of it—and she really wants to stay in her hometown of Petoskey, Michigan, a beautiful summer resort area along the eastern shore of Lake Michigan. The area's permanent population of 10,000 more than triples in the summer months and doubles at times during the winter skiing and snowmobiling season.

Claire spent four years in the Navy after college graduation, returning home in June 2015. When she couldn't find a good job in the Petoskey area, she decided to go into business for herself and set up Computer Xperts. Claire's plan was to work by herself and basically serve as a "for hire" computer consultant and troubleshooter for her customers. She knew that many of the upscale summer residents relied on home computers to keep in touch with business dealings and friends at home, and it seemed that someone was always asking her for computer advice. She was optimistic that she could keep busy with a

variety of on-site services—setting up a customer's new computer, repairing hardware problems, installing software or upgrades, creating a wireless network, correcting problems created by viruses, and the like.

Claire thought that her savings would allow her to start the business without borrowing any money. Her estimates of required expenditures were $7,000 for a used SUV; $1,125 for tools, diagnostic equipment, and reference books; $1,700 for a laptop computer, software, and accessories; $350 for an initial supply of fittings and cables; and $500 for insurance and other incidental expenses. This total of $10,675 still left Claire with about $5,000 in savings to cover living expenses while getting started.

Claire chose the technology services business because of her previous work experience. She worked at a computer "help desk" in college and spent her last year in the Navy troubleshooting computer network problems. In addition, from the time Claire was 16 years old until she finished college, she had also worked during the summer for Eric Steele. Eric operates the only successful computer services company in Petoskey. (There was one other local computer store that also did some on-location service work when the customer bought equipment at the store, but that store recently went out of business.)

Eric prides himself on quality work and has been able to build up a good business with repeat customers. Specializing in services to residential, small business, and professional offices, Eric has built a strong customer franchise. For 20 years, Eric's major source of new business has been satisfied customers who tell friends or coworkers about his quality service. He is highly regarded as a capable person who always treats clients fairly and honestly. For example, seasonal residents often give Eric the keys to their vacation homes so that he can do upgrades or maintenance while they are away for months at a time. Eric's customers are so loyal, in fact, that Fix-A-Bug—a national computer service franchise—found it impossible to compete with him. Even price-cutting was not an effective weapon against Eric.

From having worked with Eric, Claire thought that she knew the computer service business as well as he did; in fact, she had sometimes been able to solve technical problems that left him stumped. Claire was anxious to reach her $70,000-per-year sales objective because she thought this would provide her with a comfortable living in Petoskey. While aware of opportunities to do computer consulting for larger businesses, Claire felt that the sales opportunities for her services were limited because many firms had their own computer specialists or even IT departments. As Claire saw it, her only attractive opportunity was direct competition with Eric.

To get started, Claire spent $1,400 to advertise her business in the local newspaper and on an Internet website. With this money she bought two large announcement ads and 52 weeks of daily ads in the classified section, listed under "Miscellaneous Residential and Business Services." The website simply listed businesses in the Petoskey area and gave a telephone number, e-mail address, and brief description. She also listed her business under "Computer Services" at Craigslist for Northern Michigan—updating this notice and information once a month. Further, she built a small website with just a basic home page, a page with her picture and experience, and a third page that lists services she offers. She thought about creating a Facebook page and blog, but hasn't done that yet. She put magnetic sign boards on her SUV and has waited for business to take off.

At the end of three months, Claire had a few customers, but much of the time she wasn't busy and she was able to gross only about $300 a week. Of course, she had expected much more. Many of the people who did call were regular Eric customers who had some sort of crisis when he was already busy. While these people agreed that Claire's work was of the same quality as Eric's, they preferred Eric's "quality-care" image and they liked the fact that they had an ongoing relationship with him.

On occasion, Claire did get more work than she could handle. This happened during April and May, when seasonal businesses were preparing for summer openings and owners of summer homes and condos were ready to "open the cottage." The same rush occurred in September and October, as many of these places were being closed for the winter; those customers often wanted help backing up computer files or packing up computer equipment so they could take it with them. During these months, Claire was able to gross about $150 to $200 a day.

Toward the end of her discouraging first year in business, Claire Kelly is thinking about quitting. While she hates to think about leaving Petoskey, she can't see any way of making a living there with her independent technology services business. Eric seems to dominate the market, except in the rush seasons and for people who need emergency help. And the resort market is not growing very rapidly, so there is little hope of a big influx of new businesses and homeowners to spur demand.

Evaluate Claire Kelly's strategy planning for her new business. Why isn't she able to reach her objective of $70,000? What should Claire do now? Explain.

5. Polymer Dynamics

Paige Chen, a chemist in Polymer Dynamics' resins laboratory, is trying to decide how hard to fight for the new product she has developed. Chen's job is to find new, more profitable applications for the company's present resin products—and her current efforts are running into unexpected problems.

During the last four years, Chen has been under heavy pressure from her managers to come up with an idea that will open up new markets for the company's foamed polystyrene.

Two years ago, Chen developed the "foamed-dome concept"—a method of using foamed polystyrene to make dome-shaped roofs and other structures. She described the procedure for making domes as follows: The construction of a foamed dome involves the use of a specially designed machine that bends, places, and bonds pieces of plastic foam together into a predetermined dome shape. In forming a dome, the machine head is mounted on a boom, which swings around a pivot like the hands of a clock, laying and bonding layer upon layer of foam board in a rising spherical form.

According to Chen, polystyrene foamed boards have several advantages, such as:

1. Foam board is stiff—but can be formed or bonded to itself by heat alone.
2. Foam board is extremely lightweight and easy to handle. It has good structural rigidity.
3. Foam board has excellent and permanent insulating characteristics. (In fact, the major use for foam board is as an insulator.)
4. Foam board provides an excellent base on which to apply a variety of surface finishes, such as a readily available concrete-based stucco that is durable and inexpensive.

Using her good selling abilities, Chen easily convinced her managers that her idea had potential.

According to a preliminary study by the marketing research department, the following were areas of construction that could be served by the domes:

1. Bulk storage
2. Cold storage
3. Educational construction
4. Covers for industrial tanks

5. Light commercial construction
6. Planetariums
7. Recreational construction (such as a golf-course starter house)

The marketing research study focused on uses for existing dome structures. Most of the existing domes are made of cement-based materials. The study showed that large savings would result from using foam boards, due to the reduction of construction time.

Because of the new technology involved, the company decided to do its own contracting (at least for the first four to five years). Chen thought this was necessary to make sure that no mistakes were made by inexperienced contractor crews. (For example, if not applied properly, the plastic may burn.)

After building a few domes in the United States to demonstrate the concept, Chen contacted some leading U.S. architects. Reactions were as follows:

"It's very interesting, but we're not sure the fire marshal of Chicago would ever give his OK."

"Your tests show that foamed domes can be protected against fires, but there are no good tests for unconventional building materials as far as I am concerned."

"I like the idea, but foam board does not have the impact resistance of cement."

"We design a lot of recreational facilities, and kids will find a way to poke holes in the foam."

"Building codes in our area are written for wood and cement structures. Maybe we'd be interested if the codes change."

After this unexpected reaction, management didn't know what to do. Chen still thinks they should go ahead with the project. She wants to build several more demonstration projects in the United States and at least three each in Europe and Japan to expose the concept in the global market. She thinks an interactive website and online video will also help spread the idea. She thinks architects outside the United States may be more receptive to really new ideas. Further, she says, it takes time for potential users to "see" and accept new ideas. She is sure that more exposure to more people will speed acceptance. And she is convinced that a few reports of well-constructed domes in leading trade papers and magazines will go a long way toward selling the idea. She is working on getting such reports right now. But her managers aren't sure they want to OK spending more money on "her" project. Her immediate boss is supportive, but the rest of the review board is less sure about more demonstration projects or going ahead at all—just in the United States or in global markets.

Evaluate how Polymer Dynamics got into the present situation. What should Paige Chen do? What should Chen's managers do? Explain.

6. Steel Solutions

Steel Solutions is one of two major producers of wide-flange beams in the United States. The other producer is USX. A number of small firms also compete, but they tend to compete mainly on price in nearby markets where they can keep transport costs low. Typically, all interested competitors charge the same delivered price, which varies some depending on how far the customer is from either of the two major producers. In other words, local prices are higher in more remote geographic markets.

Wide-flange beams are one of the principal steel products used in construction. They are the modern version of what are commonly known as I-beams. USX rolls a full range of wide flanges from 6 to 36 inches. Steel Solutions entered the field about 30 years ago, when it converted an existing mill to produce this product. Steel Solutions' mill is limited to flanges up to 24 inches, however. At the time of the conversion, Steel Solutions felt that customer usage of sizes over 24 inches was likely to be small. In recent years, however, there has been a definite trend toward the larger and heavier sections.

The beams produced by the various competitors are almost identical—because customers buy according to standard dimensional and physical-property specifications. In the smaller size range, there are a number of competitors. But above 14 inches, only USX and Steel Solutions compete. Above 24 inches, USX has no competition.

All the steel companies sell these beams through their own sales forces. The customer for these beams is called a structural fabricator. This fabricator typically buys unshaped beams and other steel products from the mills and shapes them according to the specifications of each customer. The fabricator sells to the contractor or owner of the structure being built.

The structural fabricator usually must sell on a competitive-bid basis. The bidding is done on the plans and specifications prepared by an architectural or structural engineering firm and forwarded to the fabricator by the contractor who wants the bid. Although thousands of structural fabricators compete in the United States, relatively few account for the majority of wide-flange tonnage in the various geographical regions. Because the price is the same from all producers, they typically buy beams on the basis of availability (i.e., availability to meet production schedules) and performance (i.e., reliability in meeting the promised delivery schedule).

Several years ago, Steel Solutions' production schedulers saw that they were going to have an excess of hot-rolled plate capacity in the near future. At the same time, development of a new production technology allowed Steel Solutions to weld three plates together into a section with the same dimensional and physical properties and almost the same cross section as a rolled wide-flange beam. This development appeared to offer two key advantages to Steel Solutions: (1) it would enable Steel Solutions to use some of the excess plate capacity, and (2) larger sizes of wide-flange beams could be offered. Cost analysts showed that by using a fully depreciated plate mill and the new welding process, it would be possible to produce and sell larger wide-flange beams at competitive prices—that is, at the same price charged by USX.

Steel Solutions' managers were excited about the possibilities because customers usually appreciate having a second source of supply. Also, the new approach would allow the production of up to a 60-inch flange. With a little imagination, these larger sizes might offer a significant breakthrough for the construction industry.

Steel Solutions decided to go ahead with the new project. As the production capacity was converted, the salespeople were kept well informed of the progress. They, in turn, promoted this new capability to their customers, emphasizing that soon they would be able to offer a full range of beam products. Steel Solutions sent several general information letters to a broad mailing list but did not advertise. The market development section of the sales department was very busy explaining the new possibilities of the process to fabricators at engineering trade associations and shows.

When the new production line was finally ready to go, the market reaction was disappointing. No orders came in and none were expected. In general, customers were wary of the new product. The structural fabricators felt they couldn't use it without the approval of their customers, because it would involve deviating from the specified rolled sections. And as long as they could still get the rolled section, why make the extra effort for something unfamiliar, especially with no price advantage. The salespeople were also bothered with a very common question: How can you take plate that you sell for about $460 per ton and make a product that you can sell for $470 per ton? This question came up frequently and tended to divert the whole discussion to the cost of production rather than to the way the new product might be used or its value in the construction process.

Evaluate Steel Solutions' situation. What should Steel Solutions do?

7. Waimate Springs Lodge

Nestled in the high country of New Zealand's South Island is a getaway adventure playground aimed unashamedly at the world's very wealthy. Presidents, movie stars, and other such globe-trotters are the prime targets of this fledgling tourism business developed by Waimate Springs Lodge. The lodge offers this exclusive niche the opportunity of a secluded holiday in a little-known paradise. Guests, commonly under public scrutiny in their everyday lives, can escape such pressures at a hunting retreat designed specifically with their needs in mind.

A chance meeting between a New Zealand Department of Conservation investigator and the son of the former Indonesian president marked the beginning of this specialty tourist operation. Recognizing that "filthy rich" public figures are constantly surrounded by security and seldom have the luxury of going anywhere incognito, the New Zealander, Peter Slater, suggested that he and his new friend purchase a high-country station and hunting-guide company that was for sale. Slater believed that the facilities, and their secluded and peaceful environment, would make an ideal holiday haven for this elite group. His Indonesian partner concurred.

Slater, who was by now the company's managing director, developed a carefully tailored package of goods and services for the property. Architecturally designed accommodations, including a game trophy room and eight guest rooms, were constructed using high-quality South Island furniture and fittings, to create the ambiance necessary to attract and satisfy the demands of their special clientele.

Although New Zealand has an international reputation for being sparsely populated and green, Slater knew that rich travelers frequently complained that local accommodations were below overseas standards. Because the price (NZ$700 a night) was not a significant variable for this target market, sumptuous guest facilities were built. These were designed to be twice the normal size of most hotel rooms, with double-glazed windows that revealed breathtaking views. Ten full-time staff and two seasonal guides were recruited to ensure that visitors received superior customized service, in fitting with the restrained opulence of the lodge.

The 28,000 hectares of original farmland that made up the retreat and backed onto the South Island's Mount Cook National Park were converted into a big-game reserve. All merino sheep on the land were sold, and deer, elk, chamois, and wapiti were brought in and released. This was a carefully considered plan. Slater, the former conservationist, believed that financially and environmentally this was the correct decision. Not only do tourists, each staying for one week and taking part in safari shooting, inject as much cash into the business as the station's annual wool clip used to fetch, but the game does less harm to the environment than sheep. Cattle, however, once part of the original station, were left to graze on lower river-flat areas.

For those high-flying customers seeking less bloodthirsty leisure activities, Waimate Springs developed photographic "safaris" and other product-line extensions. Horse-trekking, golfing on a nearby rural course (with no need for hordes of security forces), helicopter trips around nearby Lake Tekapo, nature walks, and other such activities formed part of the exclusive package.

While still in the early stages of operation, this retreat has already attracted a steady stream of visitors. To date, the manager has relied solely on positive word-of-mouth, publicity, and public relations to draw in new customers. Given the social and business circles in which his potential target market moves, Slater considers these to be the most appropriate forms of marketing communication. The only real concern for Waimate Springs Lodge has been the criticism of at least one New Zealand lobby group that the company is yet another example of local land passing into "foreign" hands, and that New Zealanders are prevented from using the retreat and excluded from its financial returns. However, this unwelcome attention has been fairly short-lived.

Identify the likely characteristics of the market segment being targeted by the company. Why are most target customers likely to be foreigners rather than New Zealanders? Suggest what expectations target customers are likely to have regarding the quality, reliability, and range of services. What are the implications for Waimate Springs Lodge? How difficult is it for Waimate Springs Lodge to undertake market research? Elaborate.

8. Salvaggio's Trattoria

Rita Salvaggio, the owner and manager of Salvaggio's Trattoria, is reviewing the slow growth of her restaurant. She's also thinking about the future and wondering if she should change her strategy. In particular, she is wondering if she should join a fast-food or family restaurant franchise chain. Several are located near her, but there are many franchisors without local restaurants. After doing some research on the Internet, she has learned that with help from the franchisors, some of these places gross $500,000 to $1 million a year. Of course, she would have to follow someone else's strategy and thereby lose her independence, which she doesn't like to think about. But those sales figures do sound good, and she has also heard that the return to the owner-manager (including salary) can be more than $150,000 per year. She has also considered creating a Facebook page for Salvaggio's Trattoria but is not sure how that will help. She knows people go to Salvaggio's web page for directions and to see the menu—but why might she need Facebook or some other social media?

Salvaggio's Trattoria is a fairly large restaurant—about 3,000 square feet—located in the center of a small shopping center completed early in 2013. Salvaggio's sells mainly full-course "home-cooked" Italian-style dinners (no bar) at moderate prices. In addition to Salvaggio's Trattoria, other businesses in the shopping center include a supermarket, a hair salon, a liquor store, a computer repair business, and a vacant space that used to be a hardware store. The hardware store failed when a Home Depot located nearby. Rita has learned that a pizzeria is considering locating there soon. She wonders how that competition will affect her. Ample parking space is available at the shopping center, which is located in a residential section of a growing suburb to the east, along a heavily traveled major traffic route.

Rita graduated from a local high school and a nearby university and has lived in this town with her husband and two children for many years. She has been self-employed in the restaurant business since her graduation from college in 1998. Her most recent venture before opening Salvaggio's was a large restaurant that she operated successfully with her brother from 2004 to 2010. In 2010, Rita sold out her share because of illness. Following her recovery, she was anxious for something to do and opened the present restaurant in April 2014. Rita feels her plans for the business and her opening were well thought out. When she was ready to start her new restaurant, she looked at several possible locations before finally deciding on the present one. Rita explained, "I looked everywhere, but here I particularly noticed the heavy traffic when I first looked at it. This is the crossroads for three major interstate highways. So obviously the potential is here."

Having decided on the location, Rita signed a 10-year lease with the option to renew for 10 more years, and then eagerly attacked the problem of outfitting the almost empty store space in the newly constructed building. She tiled the floor, put in walls of surfwood, installed plumbing and electrical fixtures, added an extra washroom, and purchased the necessary restaurant equipment. All this cost $240,000—which came from her own cash savings. She then spent an additional $3,000 for glassware, $4,000 for an initial food stock, and $4,250 to advertise the opening of Salvaggio's Trattoria in the local newspaper. The paper serves the whole metro area, so the $4,250 bought only three quarter-page ads. These expenditures also came from her personal savings. Next she hired five waitresses at $550 a week and one chef at $1,100 a week. Then, with a $48,000 cash reserve for the business, she was ready to open. Reflecting her sound business sense, Rita knew she would need a substantial cash reserve to fall back on until the business got on its feet. She expected this to take about one year. She had no expectations of getting rich overnight. (Her husband, a high school teacher, was willing to support the family until the restaurant caught on.)

The restaurant opened in April and by August had a weekly gross revenue of only $4,800. Rita was a little discouraged with this, but she was still able to meet all her operating expenses without investing any new money in the business. She also got a few good customer reviews on Yelp. By September business was still slow, and Rita had to invest an additional $6,000 in the business just to survive.

Business had not improved by November, so Rita stepped up her advertising—hoping this would help. In December, she spent $2,400 of her cash reserve for radio advertising—10 late-evening spots on a news program at a station that aims at middle-income America. Rita also spent $1,600 more during the next several weeks for some Google Local advertising.

By April 2014, the situation had begun to improve, and by June her weekly gross was up to between $6,100 and $6,600. By March 2015, the weekly gross had risen to about $8,400. Rita increased the working hours of her staff six to seven hours a week and added another cook to handle the increasing number of customers. Rita was more optimistic for the future because she was finally doing a little better than breaking even. Her full-time involvement seemed to be paying off. She had not put any new money into the business since summer 2014 and expected business to continue to rise. She had not yet taken any salary for herself, even though she had built up a small surplus of about $18,000. Instead, she planned to put in a bigger air-conditioning system at a cost of $10,000 and was also planning to use what salary she might have taken for herself to hire two new waitresses to handle the growing volume of business. And she saw that if business increased much more she would have to add another cook.

Evaluate Rita's past and present marketing strategy. What should she do now? Should she seriously consider joining some franchise chain?

9. Restful Night Motel

Tristan Knaus is trying to decide whether he should make some minor changes in the way he operates his Restful Night Motel or if he should join either the Days Inn or Holiday Inn motel chains. Some decision must be made soon because his present operation is losing money. But joining either of the chains will require fairly substantial changes, including new capital investment if he goes with Holiday Inn.

Tristan bought the recently completed 60-room motel two years ago after leaving a successful career as a production manager for a large producer of industrial machinery. He was looking for an interesting opportunity that would be less demanding than the production manager job. The Restful Night Motel is located at the edge of a very small town near a rapidly expanding resort area and about one-half mile off an interstate highway. It is 10 miles from the tourist area, with several nationally franchised full-service resort motels suitable for "destination" vacations. There is a Best Western, a Ramada Inn, and a Hilton Inn, as well as many mom-and-pop and limited-service, lower-priced motels—and some quaint bed-and-breakfast facilities—in the tourist area. The interstate highway near the Restful Night Motel carries a great deal of traffic, because the resort area is between several major metropolitan areas. No development has taken place around the turnoff from the interstate highway. The only promotion for the tourist area along the interstate highway is two large signs near the turnoffs. They show the popular name for the area and that the area is only 10 miles to the west. These signs are maintained by the tourist area's Tourist Bureau. In addition, the state transportation department maintains several small signs showing (by symbols) that near this turnoff one can find gas, food, and lodging. Tristan does not have any signs advertising Restful Night Motel except the two on his property. He has been relying on people finding his motel as they go toward the resort area.

Initially, Tristan was very pleased with his purchase. He had traveled a lot himself and stayed in many different hotels and motels—so he had some definite ideas about what travelers wanted. He felt that a relatively plain but modern room with a comfortable bed, standard bath facilities, and free cable TV would appeal to most customers. Further, Tristan thought a swimming pool or any other nonrevenue-producing additions were not necessary. And he felt a restaurant would be a greater management problem than the benefits it would offer. However, after many customers commented about the lack of convenient breakfast facilities, Tristan served a free continental breakfast of coffee, juice, and rolls in a room next to the registration desk.

Day-to-day operations went fairly smoothly in the first two years, in part because Tristan and his wife handled registration and office duties as well as general management. During the first year of operation, occupancy began to stabilize around 55 percent of capacity. But according to industry figures, this was far below the average of 68 percent for his classification—motels without restaurants.

After two years of operation, Tristan was concerned because his occupancy rates continued to be below average. He decided to look for ways to increase both occupancy rate and profitability and still maintain his independence.

Tristan wanted to avoid direct competition with the full-service resort motels. He stressed a price appeal in his signs and brochures and was quite proud of the fact that he had been able to avoid all the "unnecessary expenses" of the full-service resort motels. As a result, Tristan was able to offer lodging at a very modest price—about 40 percent below the full-service hotels and comparable to the lowest-priced resort area motels. The customers who stayed at Restful Night Motel said they found it quite acceptable. The hotels' online reviews at sites such as TripAdvisor and Hotels.com, although not numerous, were generally pretty positive. But he was troubled by what seemed to be a large number of people driving into his parking lot, looking around, and not coming in to register.

Tristan was particularly interested in the results of a recent study by the regional tourist bureau. This study revealed the following information about area vacationers:

1. 68 percent of the visitors to the area are young couples and older couples without children
2. 40 percent of the visitors plan their vacations and reserve rooms more than 60 days in advance
3. 66 percent of the visitors stay more than three days in the area and at the same location
4. 78 percent of the visitors indicated that recreational facilities were important in their choice of accommodations
5. 13 percent of the visitors had family incomes of less than $27,000 per year
6. 38 percent of the visitors indicated that it was their first visit to the area

After much thought, Tristan began to seriously consider affiliating with a national motel chain in hopes of attracting more customers and maybe protecting his motel from the increasing competition. There were constant rumors that more motels were being planned for the area. After some investigating, he focused on two national chain possibilities: Days Inn and Holiday Inn. Neither had affiliates in the area even though they each have about 2,000 units nationwide.

Days Inn of America, Inc., is an Atlanta-based chain of economy lodgings. It has been growing rapidly and is willing to take on new franchisees. A major advantage of Days Inn is that it would not require a major capital investment by Tristan. The firm is targeting people interested in lower-priced motels, in particular, senior citizens, the military, school sports teams, educators, and business travelers. In contrast, Holiday Inn would probably require Tristan to upgrade some of his facilities, including adding a swimming pool. The total new capital investment would be between $300,000 and $500,000, depending on how fancy he got. But then Tristan would be able to charge higher prices, perhaps $75 per day on the average rather than the $45 per day he's charging now.

The major advantages of going with either of these national chains would be their central reservation systems and their national names. Both companies offer nationwide, toll-free reservation lines, which produce about 40 percent of all bookings in affiliated motels. Both companies also offer websites (www.daysinn.com and www.holiday-inn.com) that help find a specific hotel by destination, rate, amenities, quality rating, and availability.

A major difference between the two national chains is their method of promotion. Days Inn uses little TV advertising and less print advertising than Holiday Inn. Instead, Days Inn emphasizes sales promotions. In one campaign, for example, Blue Bonnet margarine users could exchange proof-of-purchase seals for a free night at a Days Inn. This tie-in led to the Days Inn system selling an additional 10,000 rooms. Further, Days Inn operates a September Days Club for travelers 50 and older who receive such benefits as discount rates and a quarterly travel magazine.

Days Inn also has other membership programs, including its InnCentives loyalty club for frequent business and leisure travelers. Other programs targeted to business travelers include two Corporate Rate programs and its new Days Business Place hotels. Not to be outdone, Holiday Inn has a membership program called Priority Club Worldwide. Both firms charge 8 percent of gross room revenues for belonging to their chain—to cover the costs of the reservation service and national promotion. This amount is payable monthly. In addition, franchise members must agree to maintain their facilities and make repairs and improvements as required. Failure to maintain facilities can result in losing the franchise. Periodic inspections are conducted as part of supervising the whole chain and helping the members operate more effectively.

Evaluate Tristan Knaus's present strategy. What should he do? Explain.

10. Sampson's Ice Center

Mark Sampson, the manager of Sampson's Ice Center, is trying to decide what strategies to use to increase profits.

Sampson's Ice Center is an ice-skating rink with a conventional hockey rink surface (85 feet × 200 feet). It is the only indoor ice rink in a northern U.S. city of about 450,000. The city's recreation department operates some outdoor rinks in the winter, but they don't offer regular ice skating programs because of weather variability.

Mark runs a successful hockey program that is more than breaking even—but this is about all he can expect if he offers only hockey. To try to increase his profits, Mark is trying to expand and improve his public skating program. With such a program, he could have as many as 700 people in a public session at one time, instead of limiting the use of the ice to 12 to 24 hockey players per hour. While the receipts from hockey can be as high as $200 an hour (plus concession sales), the receipts from a two-hour public skating session—charging $5 per person—could yield up to $3,500 for a two-hour period (plus much higher concession sales). The potential revenue from such large public skating sessions could make Sampson's Ice Center a really profitable operation. But, unfortunately, just scheduling public sessions doesn't mean that a large number will come. In fact, only a few prime times seem likely: Friday and Saturday evenings and Saturday and Sunday afternoons.

Mark has included 14 public skating sessions in his ice schedule, but so far they haven't attracted as many people as he hoped. In total, they generate only a little more revenue than if the times were sold for hockey use. Offsetting this extra revenue are extra costs. More staff people are needed to handle a public skating session—guards, a ticket seller, skate rental, and more concession help. So the net revenue from either use is about the same. He could cancel some of the less attractive public sessions—like the noon-time daily sessions, which have very low attendance—and make the average attendance figures look a lot better. But he feels that if he is going to offer public skating he must have a reasonable selection of times. He does recognize, however, that the different public skating sessions do seem to attract different people and *really* different kinds of people.

The Saturday and Sunday afternoon public skating sessions have been the most successful, with an average of 200 people attending during the winter season. Typically, this is a "kid-sitting" session. More than half of the patrons are young children who have been dropped off by their parents for several hours, but there are also some family groups.

In general, the kids and the families have a good time—and a fairly loyal group comes every Saturday and/or Sunday during the winter season. In the spring and fall, however, attendance drops by about half, depending on how nice the weather is. (Mark schedules no public sessions in the summer, focusing instead on hockey clinics and figure skating.)

The Friday and Saturday evening public sessions are a big disappointment. The sessions run from 8 until 10, a time when he had hoped to attract teenagers and young adult couples. At $5 per person, plus $1.50 for skate rental, this would be an economical date. In fact, Mark has seen quite a few young couples—and some keep coming back. But he also sees a surprising number of 8- to 14-year-olds who have been dropped off by their parents. The younger kids tend to race around the rink playing tag. This affects the whole atmosphere, making it less appealing for dating couples and older patrons.

Mark has been hoping to develop a teenage and young-adult market for a "social activity," adapting the format used by roller-skating rinks. Their public skating sessions feature a variety of couples-only and group games as well as individual skating to dance music. Turning ice-skating sessions into such social activities is not common, however, although industry newsletters suggest that a few ice-rink operators have had success with the roller-skating format. Seemingly, the ice-skating sessions are viewed as active recreation, offering exercise or a sports experience.

Mark installed some soft lights to try to change the evening atmosphere. The music was selected to encourage people to skate to the beat and couples to skate together. Some people complained about the "old" music, but it was "danceable," and some skaters really liked it. For a few sessions, Mark even tried to have some couples-only skates. The couples liked it, but this format was strongly resisted by the young boys who felt that they had paid their money and there was no reason why they should be kicked off the ice. Mark also tried to attract more young people and especially couples by bringing in a local rock radio station disc jockey to broadcast from Sampson's Ice Center—playing music and advertising the Friday and Saturday evening public sessions. Sampson's son even set up Facebook and MySpace pages for Sampson's, but only a few people joined the groups. All of this appeared to have no effect on attendance, which varies from 50 to 100 per two-hour session during the winter.

Mark seriously considered the possibility of limiting the Friday and Saturday evening sessions to people age 14 and older—to try to change the environment. He knew it would take time to change people's attitudes. But when he counted the customers, he realized this would be risky. More than a quarter of his customers on an average weekend night appear to be 13 or younger. This meant that he would have to make a serious commitment to building the teen and young-adult market. And, so far, his efforts haven't been successful. He had already invested more than $3,000 in lighting changes and more than $9,000 promoting the sessions over the rock music radio station, with very disappointing results. Although the station's sales rep said the station reached teenagers all over town, an on-air offer for a free skating session did not get a single response! Friends suggest he start a Facebook page—but he doesn't even know what he would put on the page.

Some days, Mark feels it's hopeless. Maybe he should accept that most public ice-skating sessions are a mixed bag. Or maybe he should just sell the time to hockey groups. Still he keeps hoping that something can be done to improve weekend evening public skating attendance, because the upside potential is so good. And the Saturday and Sunday afternoon sessions are pretty good money-makers.

Evaluate Sampson's Ice Center's situation. What should Mark Sampson do? Why?

11. Run Free

Carla Gomez is the owner of Run Free—a retail store that sells shoes and accessories to runners. Carla is trying to decide what she should do with her retail business and how committed she should be to her current target market.

Carla is 42 years old; she started her Run Free retail store in 1994 when she was only 24 years old. At that time, she was a nationally ranked runner and felt that the growing interest in jogging offered real potential for a store that provided serious runners with the shoes and advice they needed. The jogging boom quickly turned Run Free into a profitable business selling high-end running shoes—and Carla made a very good return on her investment for the first 10 years. From 1998 until 2008, Carla emphasized Nike shoes, which were well accepted and seen as top quality. Nike's aggressive promotion and quality shoes resulted in a positive image that made it possible to get a $5 to $7 per pair premium for Nike shoes. Good volume and good margins resulted in attractive profits for Carla.

Committing so heavily to Nike seemed like a good idea when its marketing and engineering was the best available. In addition to running shoes, Nike had other athletic shoes Carla could sell. So even though they were not her primary focus, Carla did stock other Nike shoes, including walking shoes, shoes for aerobic exercise, basketball shoes, tennis shoes, and cross-trainers. She also added more sportswear to her store and put more emphasis on fashion rather than just function.

Even with this broadened product line, Carla's sales flattened out—and she wasn't sure what to do to get her business back in growth mode. She realized that she was growing older and so were many of her longer-term customers. Many of them were finding that jogging isn't just hard work—it's hard on the body, especially the knees. Some were not running as often—and buying shoes less often. Other of her previously loyal runner-customers were switching to other, less demanding exercise programs. However, when she tried to orient her store and product line more toward these people, she wasn't as effective in serving the needs of serious runners—still an important source of sales for the store.

She was also facing more competition on all fronts. Many consumers who don't really do any serious exercise buy running shoes as their day-to-day casual shoes. As a result, many department stores, discount stores, and regular shoe stores have put more and more emphasis on athletic shoes in their product assortment. Many customers were growing more comfortable buying shoes online. When Carla added other brands and put more emphasis on fashion, she found that she was in direct competition with a number of other stores, which put more pressure on her to lower prices and cut her profit margins. For example, in Carla's area there are a number of local retail chains offering lower-cost and lower-quality versions of similar shoes as well as related fashion apparel. Walmart also expanded its assortment of athletic shoes—and it offers rock-bottom prices. Other chains, such as Foot Locker, have focused their promotion and product lines on specific target markets. Still, all of them (including Carla's Run Free, the local chains, Walmart, and Foot Locker) are scrambling to catch up with rival category killers whose selections are immense.

In the spring of 2014 Carla tried an experiment. She took on a line of high-performance athletic shoes that were made to order. The distinctive feature of these shoes was that the sole was molded to precisely fit the customer's foot. A pair of these custom-made shoes cost about $170, so the market was not large. Further, Carla didn't put much promotional emphasis on this line. However, when a customer came in the store with a serious interest in high-performance shoes, Carla's sales clerks would tell them about the custom shoe alternative and show a sample. When a customer was interested, a mold of the customer's bare foot was made at the store, using an innovative material that hardened in just a few minutes without leaving a sticky mess. Carla sent the mold off to the manufacturer by UPS, and about two weeks later the finished shoes arrived. Customers who tried these shoes were delighted with the result. However, the company that offered them ran into financial trouble and went out of business.

Carla recently learned about another company that is offering a very similar custom shoe program. However, that company requires more promotion investment by retailers and in return provides exclusive sales territories. Another requirement is that the store establish a website promoting the shoes and providing more detail on how the order process works. Run Free had a pretty basic website, so Carla knew she would have to spend some money to make this happen. In addition, all of a retailer's salesclerks are also required to go through a special two-day training program so that they know how to present the benefits of the shoe and do the best job creating the molds. The training program is free, but Carla would have to pay travel, hotel, and food expenses for her salespeople. So before even getting started, the new program would cost her several thousand dollars.

Carla is uncertain about what to do. Although sales have dropped, she is still making a reasonable profit and has a relatively good base of repeat customers, with the serious runners still more than half of her sales and profits. She thinks that the custom shoe alternative is a way to differentiate her store from the mass-merchandisers and to sharpen her focus on the target market of serious runners. On the other hand, that doesn't really solve the problem that the "runners" market seems to be shrinking. It also doesn't address the question of how best to keep a lot of the aging customers she already serves who seem to be shifting away from an emphasis on running. She also worries that she'll lose the loyalty of her repeat customers if she shifts the store further away from her running niche and more toward fashionable athletic shoes or fashionable casual wear. Yet athletic wear—women's, in particular—has come a long way in recent years. Designers such as Donna Karan, Calvin Klein, Georgio Armani, and Ralph Lauren are part of the fast-growing women's athletic wear business.

So Carla is trying to decide if there is anything else she can do to better promote her current store and product line, or if she should think about changing her strategy in a more dramatic way. Any change from her current focus would involve retraining her current salespeople and perhaps hiring new salespeople. Adding and maintaining a website isn't an insurmountable challenge, but it is not an area where she has either previous experience or skill.

Clearly, a real shift in emphasis would require that Carla make some hard decisions about her target market and her whole marketing mix. She's got some flexibility—it's not like she's a manufacturer of shoes with a big investment in a factory that can't be changed. On the other hand, she's not certain she's ready for a big change, especially a change that would mean starting over again from scratch. She started Run Free because she was interested in running and felt she had something special to offer. Now she worries that she's just grasping at straws without a real focus or any obvious competitive advantage. She also knows that she is already much more successful than she ever dreamed when she started her business—and in her heart she wonders if she wasn't just spoiled by growth that came fast and easy at the start.

Evaluate Carla Gomez's present strategy. Evaluate the alternative strategies she is considering. Is her primary problem her emphasis on running shoes, her emphasis on trying to hang on to her current customers, or is it something else? What should she do? Why?

12. DrV.com—Custom Vitamins

Dr. Victoria van der Walt has to decide how to handle a complaint letter from a customer. When she received the letter, she passed it along to Paul Zimbalist, the firm's customer service manager, to get his recommendation. Now van der Walt has a reply from Zimbalist, and she must decide how to respond to the customer and determine if changes are needed in her company's customer service operations.

Dr. van der Walt has a reputation as a health and nutrition guru. Her fame grew after she published two books—both of which were very popular and received a lot of attention in the press. Five years ago, Internet entrepreneur Tania Cox approached her with the idea of creating a website to sell custom vitamins under Dr. Victoria's name.

van der Walt and Cox became partners, and the business enjoyed success in its first four years of operation. Cox handles the website technology, inventory, production, and shipping. Dr. van der Walt is the health expert, creates content provided on the website, and is in charge of marketing and customer service. The complaint letter and reply from Zimbalist follow:

Dear Dr. van der Walt,

I am a longtime fan of your books and like to visit your website for health tips. As a new grandmother, my health is even more important to me. I want to see my grandchildren graduate from high school, go to college, and have kids of their own.

You have made me a bit of a guru as well. I work out every day. People always ask me how I stay so fit and healthy. Having read both your books, I tell them they should exercise regularly and take vitamins and supplements for long-term health. I always recommend your DrV.com website and especially the section on your custom vitamins. That is my favorite part of your website. I really like that you take information about me and my medical history—and then recommend custom vitamins and supplements. I also like how you send me packages that each contain a daily dose.

But after my recent experiences, my loyalty to you and your company is now in jeopardy. Here is my story.

Six months ago, I went to the website to reorder my vitamins and supplements. The home page announced a new and improved health survey and custom health program. So I went through the survey and filled out all the details—it would have been nice if you had saved some of them from my previous survey. At the end of the survey the website offered me a 90-day supply of a custom set of vitamins and supplements selected for my specific needs. The $212 price was about $50 more than my previous 90-day supply, but I trusted your advice so I placed the order.

About two-and-a-half months later, I phoned your 800 number for DrV.com to place a refill order. The person on the phone was very nice and asked if I wanted to set up automatic refills. I said no because I hate those automatic programs. They remind me of those book clubs that automatically send you books you don't want if you do not reply fast enough. About a week later my order arrived—then two days later another identical order arrived. I did not understand this, but I figured I would eventually use them up and I kept everything (and I was billed for both orders—$424 on my credit card). I should mention there was no e-mail explaining this mystery delivery. I was a little annoyed and sent an e-mail to customer service seeking an explanation. I received an automated response, "Thank you for your inquiry; someone will get back to you within 24 hours." No one ever replied, but I forgot about it.

Then two weeks ago I received an e-mail from DrV.com telling me my refill order had been shipped and would arrive in a few days. But I did not place a refill order! I did not even need more vitamins because I was still working off the two 90-day supplies that I received three months ago. So I replied by e-mail that I did not want the order and to cancel it. A reply e-mail (from Sally) told me that I had signed up for automatic refill six months ago. I replied that I certainly had not and that I would not pay for the order that was being sent.

A few days later I received a call from Paul Zimbalist, your director of customer service. He told me that I had originally signed up for automatic refill and that was why I received vitamins. I told him that was impossible, and he told me that unless I checked some box on my original order that this was done automatically, "for my convenience." He said there were also several warnings and that I must have missed those. *Basically, I think he told me this was my fault. I did not like that one bit!!!*

Mr. Zimbalist told me the vitamins were on their way, but I could refuse delivery of them. He offered to let me have them for 20 percent off if I simply kept them. Unfortunately, the vitamins were on my doorstep when I arrived home that day. I had to take the vitamins to UPS to get them shipped back to you.

You guys are no longer very good at your business. You might have a great product, but I am now seeing other vitamin companies offering the same products. I have no doubt these other companies offer better customer service. If you want me back as a customer, I would expect a formal apology from Mr. Zimbalist and a free 90-day supply. Otherwise, I figure my business will be welcomed at one of your competitors. I will be sure all my friends know about my experience at DrV.com, and I intend to post a bad review at resellerratings.com, too.

Sincerely,
Maxine Slezak

Next is the reply that Paul Zimbalist sent to Dr. van der Walt concerning Maxine Slezak's letter.

Dear Victoria,

As per your request, I reviewed Mrs. Slezak's order history. Yes, she is a very good customer who spent almost $800 with us last year. And she is a member of our referral program—and we can count at least seven new customers she has directed to us in the last 18 months. But I want to clarify some of this particular situation.

- You might recall that our automatic refill program has been a big success. Since we instituted the program a year ago, our customer retention rate has jumped by 10 percent. There are occasional complaints, but given the large number of customers we serve, the complaints are really just a "drop in the bucket."
- When Mrs. Slezak placed her order six months ago, there were at least two different warnings about the automatic refill program—customers have to check a box at the bottom of the screen to "opt out" of the program. We all agreed that it was better to make them part of the program automatically, but to give them two chances to remove themselves from automatic delivery.
- I do not know if we replied to her e-mail asking for customer service help.
- I did not tell Mrs. Slezak that this was her fault, but I did tell her that when she signed up there were two chances for her to choose to not be part of the automatic refill program.
- Mrs. Slezak did not get an e-mail notifying her of the first refill order because that system was not yet in place. But this has now been fixed, and the e-mail notifying her when we ship shows that this works.
- I offered her 20 percent off, as is our standard policy when we make a mistake. Considering this was her mistake, I thought this was generous.
- If Mrs. Slezak had called and asked, I could have had UPS come out and pick up the package for return to us.

I do not recommend giving her a free 90-day supply. This may simply encourage her to complain again in the future. Besides, this was not our mistake. We may be better off without certain customers—and I think Mrs. Slezak falls into this category.

Feel free to call me if you have any more questions.

Paul

Assess the customer service operations at DrV.com. What should van der Walt do about Mrs. Slezak? What changes, if any, should van der Walt make to customer service and ordering operations?

13. AAA Office World (AAA)*

Stasia Acosta, marketing manager for AAA Office World, must decide whether she should permit her largest customer to buy some of AAA's commonly used file folders under the customer's brand rather than AAA's own FILEX brand. She is afraid that if she refuses, this customer—Business Center, Inc.—will go to another file folder producer and AAA will lose this business.

Business Center, Inc., is a major distributor of office supplies and has already managed to put its own brand on more than 45 high-sales-volume office supply products. It distributes these products—as well as the branded products of many manufacturers—through its nationwide distribution network, which includes 150 retail stores. Now Lance Richardson, vice president of marketing for Business Center, is seeking a line of file folders similar in quality to AAA's FILEX brand, which now has more than 60 percent of the market.

This is not the first time that Business Center has asked AAA to produce a file folder line for Business Center. On both previous occasions, Stasia turned down the requests and Business Center continued to buy. In fact, Business Center not only continued to buy the file folders but also the rest of AAA's product lines. And total sales continued to grow as Business Center built new stores. Business Center accounts

---

* Adapted from a case by Professor Hardy, University of Western Ontario.

for about 30 percent of Stasia Acosta's business. And FILEX brand file folders account for about 35 percent of this volume.

In the past, AAA consistently refused such dealer-branding requests as a matter of corporate policy. This policy was set some years ago because of a desire (1) to avoid excessive dependence on any one customer and (2) to sell its own brands so that its success is dependent on the quality of its products rather than just a low price. The policy developed from a concern that if it started making products under other customers' brands, those customers could shop around for a low price and the business would be very fickle. At the time the policy was set, Stasia realized that it might cost AAA some business. But it felt wise, nevertheless, to be better able to control the firm's future.

AAA has been in business 28 years and now has a sales volume of $40 million. Its primary products are file folders, file markers and labels, and a variety of indexing systems. AAA offers such a wide range of size, color, and type that no competitor can match it in its part of the market. About 40 percent of AAA's file folder business is in specialized lines such as files for oversized blueprint and engineer drawings; see-through files for medical markets; and greaseproof and waterproof files for marine, oil field, and other hazardous environmental markets. AAA's competitors are mostly small paper converters. But excess capacity in the industry is substantial, and these converters are always hungry for orders and willing to cut prices. Further, the raw materials for the FILEX line of file folders are readily available.

AAA's distribution system consists of 10 regional stationery suppliers (40 percent of total sales), Business Center, Inc. (30 percent), and more than 40 local stationers who have wholesale and retail operations (30 percent). The 10 regional stationers each have about six branches, while the local stationers each have one wholesale and three or four retail locations. The regional suppliers sell directly to large corporations and to some retailers. In contrast, Business Center's main volume comes from sales to local businesses and walk-in customers at its 150 retail stores.

Stasia has a real concern about the future of the local stationers' business. Some are seriously discussing the formation of buying groups to obtain volume discounts from vendors and thus compete more effectively with Business Center's 150 retail stores, the large regionals, and the superstore chains, which are spreading rapidly. These chains—for example, Staples, Office Max, and Office Depot—operate stores of 16,000 to 20,000 square feet (i.e., large stores compared to the usual office supply stores) and let customers wheel through high-stacked shelves to supermarket-like checkout counters. These chains stress convenience, wide selection, and much lower prices than the typical office supply retailers. They buy directly from manufacturers, such as AAA, bypassing wholesalers like Business Center. It is likely that the growing pressure from these chains is causing Business Center to renew its proposal to buy a file line with its own name. For example, Staples offers its own dealer brand of files and many other types of products.

None of Stasia's other accounts is nearly as effective in retailing as Business Center, which has developed a good reputation in every major city in the country. Business Center's profits have been the highest in the industry. Further, its brands are almost as well-known as those of some key producers—and its expansion plans are aggressive. And now, these plans are being pressured by the fast-growing superstores, which are already knocking out many local stationers.

Stasia is sure that AAA's brands are well entrenched in the market, despite the fact that most available money has been devoted to new-product development rather than promotion of existing brands. But Stasia is concerned that if Business Center brands its own file folders, it will sell them at a discount and may even bring the whole market price level down. Across all the lines of file folders, Stasia is averaging a 35 percent gross margin, but the commonly used file folders sought by Business Center are averaging only a 20 percent gross margin. And cutting this margin further does not look very attractive to Stasia.

Stasia is not sure whether Business Center will continue to sell AAA's FILEX brand of folders along with Business Center's own file folders if Business Center is able to find a source of supply. Business Center's history has been to sell its own brand and a major brand side by side, especially if the major brand offers high quality and has strong brand recognition.

Stasia is having a really hard time deciding what to do about the existing branding policy. AAA has excess capacity and could easily handle the Business Center business. And she fears that if she turns down this business, Business Center will just go elsewhere and its own brand will cut into AAA's existing sales at Business Center stores. Further, what makes Business Center's offer especially attractive is that AAA's variable manufacturing costs would be quite low in relation to any price charged to Business Center—that is, there are substantial economies of scale, so the extra business could be very profitable—if Stasia doesn't consider the possible impact on the FILEX line. This Business Center business will be easy to get, but it will require a major change in policy, which Stasia will have to sell to Ramon Torres, AAA's president. This may not be easy. Ramon is primarily interested in developing new and better products so the company can avoid the "commodity end of the business."

Evaluate AAA's current strategy. What should Stasia Acosta do about Business Center's offer? Explain.

14. Schrock & Oh Design

Kevin Schrock and Katie Oh met while studying architecture in college. They became good friends and after graduating decided to start a modern architecture firm in Los Angeles. Schrock & Oh Design opened in 2011, specializing in contemporary residential and commercial projects.

Starting an architecture business in the midst of a recession was not easy. The business struggled in those first few years. But they loved what they did, scrimped and saved, and took whatever work they could get. The economy gradually improved. They soon built a modest business based mostly on word-of-mouth; Kevin noted that their only marketing investment was business cards and a small five-page website. They did not have the money to invest in much more. They survived and eventually built a bit of a reputation for their work.

Reputation and word-of-mouth were carrying Schrock and Oh Design only so far. They wanted to move their business to the next level. They started by advertising on Yahoo and Google. Although this lead to some initial inquiries, very few panned out into actual work. People seemed most interested in just asking questions, seeing photographs of their work, and learning more; they were just gathering ideas. These customers were early in the buying process. Kevin and Katie spent lots of time talking to customers but not much time designing and billing out. "It feels like we spend so much time educating these customers that in the end, we hardly make any money even if they do work with us on a design project," noted Kevin.

Their next foray was to start blogging. Katie was a pretty good writer and started a blog on the SchrockOhDesign.com website. She blogged about the industry—"Development Fact of the Day—China," which discussed a magazine article she read about architecture in *Metropolis Magazine* and "Is Prefab the Future," which described issues around the modern prefabricated home.

Prefab homes were one of their competitors. Although low in cost, they are not easily customized to a customer's specific needs. Some of her posts generated traffic to the website, but few turned into leads for the design firm. When they looked at clickstream data, they found that most customers read the blog and then left the company's website.

They were stumped about where to go next. "We tried all the marketing we knew. We started with advertising, which did not seem to work. So we went to this new 'owned media' approach but that isn't getting us any business either," claimed Katie. "It doesn't seem like a Facebook page or Twitter feed is our best route either. Our goal is to attract qualified leads. We would like to attract customers who already know they want to build a contemporary home or commercial building—and then we can use our time with them to discuss what our design firm can do."

Evaluate Schrock & Oh Design's strategy so far. What would you recommend to help the architecture firm attract more qualified leads?

15. The Olentangy Group

Theresa Campana owns The Olentangy Group (named after a local river)—a manufacturer's rep agency. The Olentangy Group sells similar products for noncompeting producers in the technology industry. She is deciding whether to add a new product line—serving another producer. She is very concerned because, although she wants more lines, she feels that something is wrong with her latest candidate.

Theresa graduated from a large Midwestern university in 2006 with a B.S. in business. She worked selling cell phones for a year. Then Theresa decided to go into business for herself and formed The Olentangy Group. Looking for opportunities, Theresa placed several ads in her local newspaper in Columbus, Ohio, announcing that she was interested in becoming a sales representative in the area. She was quite pleased to receive a number of responses. Eventually, she became the sales representative in the Columbus area for three local computer software producers: Accto Company, which produces accounting-related software; Saleco, Inc., a producer of sales management software; and Invo, Inc., a producer of inventory control software. All of these companies were relatively small and were represented in other areas by other sales representatives like Theresa. The companies often sent her leads when customers from her area expressed interest at a trade show or through the company's website.

Theresa's main job was to call on possible customers. Once she made a sale, she would fax the signed license agreement to the respective producer, who would then UPS the programs directly to the customer or, more often, provide a key code for a website download. The producer would bill the customer, and Theresa would receive a commission varying from 5 to 10 percent of the dollar value of the sale. Theresa was expected to pay her own expenses. And the producers would handle any user questions, either by using 800 numbers for out-of-town calls or by e-mail queries to a technical support group.

Theresa called on anyone in the Columbus area who might use the products she sold. At first, her job was relatively easy, and sales came quickly because she had little competition.

Many national companies offer similar products, but at that time they were not well represented in the Columbus area. Most small businesses needed someone to demonstrate what the software could do.

In 2008, Theresa sold $250,000 worth of Accto software, earning a 10 percent commission; $100,000 worth of Saleco software, also earning a 10 percent commission; and $200,000 worth of Invo software, earning a 7 percent commission. She was encouraged with her progress and looked forward to expanding sales in the future. She was especially optimistic because she had achieved these sales volumes without overtaxing herself. In fact, she felt she was operating at about 60 percent of her capacity and could easily take on new lines. So she began looking for other products she could sell in the Columbus area.

A local software company has recently approached Theresa about selling its newly developed software, which is basically a network security product. It is designed to secretly track all of the keystrokes and mouse clicks of each employee as he or she uses the computer—so that an employer can identify inappropriate uses of its computers or confidential data. Theresa isn't too enthusiastic about this offer because the commission is only 2 percent on potential annual sales of about $150,000—and she also doesn't like the idea of selling a product that might undermine the privacy of employees who are not doing anything wrong.

Now Theresa is faced with another decision. The owner of the MetalCoat Company, also in Columbus, has made what looks like an attractive offer. She called on MetalCoat to see if the firm might be interested in buying her accounting software. The owner didn't want the software, but he was very impressed with Theresa. After two long discussions, he asked if she would like to help MetalCoat solve its current problem. MetalCoat is having trouble with marketing, and the owner would like Theresa to take over the whole marketing effort.

MetalCoat produces solvents used to make coatings for metal products. It sells mainly to industrial customers in the mid-Ohio area and faces many competitors selling essentially the same products and charging the same low prices.

MetalCoat is a small manufacturer. Last year's sales were $500,000. It could handle at least four times this sales volume with ease and is willing to expand to increase sales—its main objective in the short run. MetalCoat's owner is offering Theresa a 12 percent commission on all sales if she will take charge of its pricing, advertising, and sales efforts. Theresa is flattered by the offer, but she is a little worried because it is a different type of product and she would have to learn a lot

about it. The job also might require a great deal more traveling than she is doing now. For one thing, she would have to call on new potential customers in mid-Ohio, and she might have to travel up to 200 miles around Columbus to expand the solvent business. Further, she realizes that she is being asked to do more than just sell. But she did have marketing courses in college and thinks the new opportunity might be challenging.

Evaluate Theresa Campana's current strategy and how the proposed solvent line fits in with what she is doing now. What should she do? Why?

16. Tall Timber Lumber Supply

Joe Hanratty, owner of Tall Timber Lumber Supply, feels his business is threatened by a tough new competitor. And now Joe must decide quickly about an offer that may save his business.

Joe has been a sales rep for lumber mills for about 20 years. He started selling in a clothing store but gave it up after two years to work in a lumberyard because the future looked much better in the building materials industry. After drifting from one job to another, Joe finally settled down and worked his way up to manager of a large wholesale building materials distribution warehouse in Richmond, Virginia. In 2000, he formed Tall Timber Lumber Supply and went into business for himself, selling carload lots of lumber to lumberyards in southeastern Virginia.

Joe works with five large lumber mills on the West Coast. They notify him when a carload of lumber is available to be shipped, specifying the grade, condition, and number of each size board in the shipment. Joe isn't the only person selling for these mills—but he is the only one in his area. He isn't required to take any particular number of carloads per month—but once he tells a mill he wants a particular shipment, title passes to him and he has to sell it to someone. Joe's main function is to find a buyer, buy the lumber from the mill as it's being shipped, and have the railroad divert the car to the buyer.

Having been in this business for 20 years, Joe knows all of the lumberyard buyers in his area very well and is on good working terms with them. He does most of his business over the telephone or by e-mail from his small office, but he tries to see each of the buyers about once a month. He has been marking up the lumber between 4 and 6 percent—the standard markup, depending on the grades and mix in each carload—and has been able to make a good living for himself and his family. The going prices are widely publicized in trade publications and are listed on the Internet, so the buyers can easily check to be sure Joe's prices are competitive.

In the last few years, a number of Joe's lumberyard customers have gone out of business—and others have lost sales. The main problem is competition from several national home improvement chains that have moved into Joe's market area. These chains buy lumber in large quantities direct from a mill, and their low prices, available inventory, and one-stop shopping are taking some customers away from the traditional lumberyards. Some customers think the quality of the lumber is not quite as good at the big chains, and some contractors stick with the lumberyards out of loyalty or because they get better service, including rush deliveries when they're needed. Then

came the mortgage crisis, and the residential housing market really slowed down, though not as bad in Richmond as in other parts of the country. Fortunately for Joe, the commercial market remained pretty strong and he had good relationships there—or Joe's profits would have taken an even bigger hit.

Six months ago, though, things got even worse. An aggressive young salesman set up in the same business, covering about the same area but representing different lumber mills. This new salesman charges about the same prices as Joe but undersells him once or twice a week in order to get the sale. On several occasions he even set up what was basically an e-mail-based auction to quickly sell excess wood that was not moving fast enough. Many lumber buyers—feeling the price competition from the big chains and realizing that they are dealing with a homogeneous product—seem to be willing to buy from the lowest-cost source. This has hurt Joe financially and personally—because even some of his old friends are willing to buy from the new competitor if the price is lower. The near-term outlook seems dark, because Joe doubts that there is enough business to support two firms like his, especially if the markup gets shaved any closer. Now they seem to be splitting the shrinking business about equally, as the newcomer keeps shaving his markup.

A week ago, Joe was called on by Amy Balderas of Arbor Door and Window Co., a large manufacturer of windows, raised-panel doors, and accessories. Arbor doesn't sell to the big chains and instead distributes its quality line only through independent lumberyards. Amy knows that Joe is well acquainted with the local lumberyards and wants him to become Arbor's exclusive distributor (sales rep) of residential windows and accessories in his area. Amy gave Joe several brochures on Arbor's product lines. She also explained Arbor's new support program, which will help train and support Joe and interested lumberyards on how to sell the higher markup accessories. Later, in a lengthy e-mail, Amy explained how this program will help Joe and interested lumberyards differentiate themselves in this very competitive market.

Most residential windows of specified grades are basically "commodities" that are sold on the basis of price and availability, although some premium and very low-end windows are sold also. The national home-improvement chains usually stock and sell only the standard sizes. Most independent lumberyards do not stock windows because there are so many possible sizes. Instead, the lumberyards custom order from the stock sizes each factory offers. Stock sizes are not set by industry standards; they vary from factory to factory, and some offer more sizes. Most factories can deliver these custom orders in two to six weeks, which is usually adequate to satisfy contractors who buy and install them according to architectural plans. This part of the residential window business is well established, and most lumberyards buy from several different window manufacturers—to ensure sources of supply in case of strikes, plant fires, and so on. How the business is split depends on price and the personality and persuasiveness of the sales reps. And given that prices are usually similar, the sales rep–customer relationship can be quite important.

Arbor gives more choice than just about any other supplier. It offers many variations in 1/8-inch increments—to cater to remodelers who must adjust to many situations. Arbor has even set up a special system on an Internet website. The lumberyard can connect to the website, enter the specs for a window online, and within seconds get a price quote and estimated delivery time.

One reason Amy has approached Joe is because of Joe's many years in the business. But the other reason is that Arbor is aggressively trying to expand—relying on its made-to-order windows, a full line of accessories, and a newly developed factory support system to help differentiate it from the many other window manufacturers. To give Joe a quick big picture of the opportunity she is offering, Amy explained the window market as follows:

1. For commercial construction, the usual building code ventilation requirements are satisfied with mechanical ventilation. So the windows do not have to operate to permit natural ventilation. They are usually made with heavy-grade aluminum framing. Typically, a distributor furnishes and installs the windows. As part of its service, the distributor provides considerable technical support, including engineered drawings and diagrams to the owners, architects, and/or contractors.

2. For residential construction, on the other hand, windows must be operable to provide ventilation. Residential windows are usually made of wood, frequently with light-gauge aluminum or vinyl on the exterior. The national chains get some volume with standard-size windows, but lumberyards are the most common source of supply for contractors in Joe's area. These lumberyards do not provide any technical support or engineered drawings. A few residential window manufacturers do have their own sales centers in selected geographic areas, which provide a full range of support and engineering services, but none are anywhere near Joe's area.

Arbor feels a big opportunity exists in the commercial building repair and rehabilitation market (sometimes called the retrofit market) for a crossover of residential windows to commercial applications—and it has designed some accessories and a factory support program to help lumberyards get this "commercial" business. For applications such as nursing homes and dormitories (which must meet commercial codes), the wood interior of a residential window is desired, but the owners and architects are accustomed to commercial grades and building systems. And in some older facilities, the windows may have to provide supplemental ventilation for a deficient mechanical system. So what is needed is a combination of the residential *operable* window with a heavy-gauge commercial exterior frame that is easy to specify and install. And this is what Arbor is offering with a combination of its basic windows and easily adjustable accessory frames. Two other residential window manufacturers offer a similar solution, but neither has pushed its products aggressively and neither offers technical support to lumberyards or trains sales reps like Joe to do the necessary job. Amy feels this could be a unique opportunity for Joe.

The sales commission on residential windows would be about 5 percent of sales. Arbor would do the billing and collecting. By getting just 20 to 30 percent of his lumberyards' residential window business, Joe could earn about a third of his current income. But the real upside would come in the long term by increasing his residential window share. Joe is confident that the housing market will turn around soon, and when it does he will be well-positioned for growth. To do this, he will have to help the lumberyards get a lot more (and more profitable) business by invading the commercial market with residential windows and the bigger markup accessories needed for this market. Joe will also earn a 20 percent commission on the accessories, adding to his profit potential.

Joe is somewhat excited about the opportunity because the retrofit market is growing. And owners and architects are seeking ways of reducing costs (which Arbor's approach does—over usual commercial approaches). He also likes the idea of developing a new line to offset the slow-growing market for new construction housing. But he is concerned that a lot of sales effort will be needed to introduce this new idea. He is not afraid of work, but he is concerned about his financial survival.

Joe thinks he has three choices:

1. Take Amy's offer and sell both window and lumber products.
2. Take the offer and drop lumber sales.
3. Stay strictly with lumber and forget the offer.

Amy is expecting an answer within one week, so Joe has to decide soon.

Evaluate Joe Hanratty's current strategy and how the present offer fits in. What should he do now? Why?

17. Simply Pure H₂O4U, Inc.

Morton Rinke established his company, Simply Pure H$_2$O$_4$U, Inc., to market a product designed to purify drinking water. The product, branded as the PURITY II Naturalizer Water Unit, is produced by Environmental Control, Inc., a corporation that focuses primarily on water purification and filtering products for industrial markets.

Simply Pure H$_2$O$_4$U is a small but growing business. Morton started the business with an initial capital of only $20,000, which came from his savings and loans from several relatives. Morton manages the company himself. He has a secretary and six full-time salespeople. In addition, he employs two college students part-time; they make telephone calls to prospect for customers and set up appointments for a salesperson to demonstrate the unit in the consumer's home. He has built a small website that primarily provides detailed information and allows customers to request a call from a salesperson. By holding spending to a minimum, Morton has kept the firm's monthly operating budget at only $4,500—and most of that goes for rent, his secretary's salary, and other necessities such as computer supplies and telephone bills.

The PURITY II system uses a reverse osmosis purification process. Reverse osmosis is the most effective technology known for improving drinking water. The device is certified by the Environmental Protection Agency to reduce levels of most foreign substances, including fluoride, mercury, rust, sediment, arsenic, lead, phosphate, bacteria, and most insecticides.

Each PURITY II unit consists of a high-quality 1-micron sediment removal cartridge, a carbon filter, a sediment filter, a housing, a faucet, and mounting hardware. The compact system fits under a kitchen sink or a wet bar sink. An H_2O_4U salesperson can typically install the PURITY II in about a half hour. Installation involves attaching the unit to the cold water supply line, drilling a hole in the sink, and fastening the special faucet. It works equally well with water from a municipal system or well water, and it can purify up to 15 gallons daily. H_2O_4U sells the PURITY II to consumers for $395, which includes installation.

The system has no movable parts or electrical connections, and it has no internal metal parts that will corrode or rust. However, the system does use a set of filters that must be replaced after about two years. H_2O_4U sells the replacement filters for $80. Taking into consideration the cost of the filters, the system provides drinking water at a cost of approximately $0.05 per gallon for the average family.

There are two major benefits from using the PURITY II system. First, water treated by this system tastes better. Blind taste tests confirm that most consumers can tell the difference between water treated with the PURITY II and ordinary tap water. Consequently, the unit improves the taste of coffee, tea, frozen juices, ice cubes, mixed drinks, soup, and vegetables cooked in water. Perhaps more important, the PURITY II's ability to remove potentially harmful foreign matter makes the product of special interest to the growing number of people who are concerned about health and the safety of the water they consume. For example, there is growing controversy surrounding public fluoridation of drinking water—and many consumers are looking for filters that remove fluoride.

The number of people with health and safety concerns is growing. In spite of increased efforts to protect the environment and water supplies, there are still many problems. Hundreds of new chemical compounds—ranging from insecticides to industrial chemicals to commercial cleaning agents—are put into use each year. Some of the residue from chemicals and toxic waste eventually enters water supply sources. Further, floods and hurricanes have damaged or completely shut down water treatment facilities in some cities. Problems like these have led to rumors of possible epidemics of such dread diseases as cholera and typhoid—and more than one city has recently experienced near-panic buying of bottled water.

Given these problems and the need for pure water, Morton believes that the market potential for the PURITY II system is very large. Residences, both single-family homes and apartments, are one obvious target. The unit is also suitable for use in boats and recreational vehicles; in fact, the PURITY II is standard equipment on several upscale RVs. And it can be used in taverns and restaurants, in institutions such as schools and hospitals, and in commercial and industrial buildings.

There are several competing ways for customers to solve the problem of getting pure water. Some purchase bottled water. Companies such as Ozarka deliver water monthly for an average price of $0.60 per gallon. The best type of bottled water is distilled water; it is absolutely pure because it is produced by the process of evaporation. However, it may be *too pure*. The distilling process removes needed elements such as calcium and phosphate—and there is some evidence that removing these trace elements contributes to heart disease. In fact, some health-action groups recommend that consumers not drink distilled water.

A second way to obtain pure water is to use some system to treat tap water. PURITY II is one such system. Another system uses an ion exchange process that replaces ions of harmful substances such as iron and mercury with ions that are not harmful. Ion exchange is somewhat less expensive than the PURITY II process, but it is not well suited for residential use because bacteria can build up before the water is used. In addition, there are a number of other filtering and softening systems. In general, these are less expensive and less reliable than the PURITY II. For example, water softeners remove minerals but do not remove bacteria or germs.

Morton's first year with his young company has gone quite well. Customers who have purchased the system like it, and there appear to be several ways to expand the business and increase profits. For example, so far he has had little time to make sales calls on potential commercial and institutional users or residential builders. He also sees other possibilities such as expanding his promotion effort or targeting consumers in a broader geographic area.

At present, H_2O_4U distributes the PURITY II in the 13-county Gulf Coast region of Texas. Because of the Robinson-Patman Act, the manufacturer cannot grant an exclusive distributorship. However, H_2O_4U is currently the only PURITY II distributor in this region. In addition, H_2O_4U has the right of first refusal to set up distributorships in other areas of Texas. The manufacturer has indicated that it might even give H_2O_4U distribution rights in a large section of northern Mexico.

The agreement with the manufacturer allows H_2O_4U to distribute the product to retailers, including hardware stores and plumbing supply dealers. Morton has not yet pursued this channel, but a PURITY II distributor in Florida reported some limited success selling the system to retailers at a wholesale price of $275. Retailers for this type of product typically expect a markup of about 33 percent of their selling price.

Environmental Control, Inc., ships the PURITY II units directly from its warehouse to the H_2O_4U office via UPS. The manufacturer's $200 per unit selling price includes the cost of shipping. H_2O_4U needs to keep only a few units on hand because the manufacturer accepts faxed orders and then ships immediately—so delivery never takes more than a few days. Further, the units are small enough to inventory in the back room of the H_2O_4U sales office. Several of the easy-to-handle units will fit in the trunk of a salesperson's car.

Morton is thinking about recruiting additional salespeople. Finding capable people has not been a problem so far. However, there has already been some turnover, and one of the current salespeople is complaining that the compensation is not high enough. Morton pays salespeople on a straight commission basis. A salesperson who develops his or her own prospects gets $100 per sale; the commission is $80 per unit on sales leads generated by the company's telemarketing people. For most salespeople, the mix of sales is about half and half. H_2O_4U pays the students who make the telephone contacts $4 per appointment set up and $10 per unit sold from an appointment. A growing number of leads are coming from the company's website, largely due to search ads placed on Google and Yahoo!

An average H_2O_4U salesperson easily sells 30 units per month. However, Morton believes that a really effective and well-prepared salesperson can sell much more, perhaps 50 units per month.

H_2O_4U and its salespeople get good promotion support from Environmental Control, Inc. For example, Environmental Control supplies sales training manuals and sales presentation flip charts. The materials are also well done, in part because Environmental Control's promotion manager previously worked for Electrolux vacuum cleaners, which are sold in a similar way. The company also supplies print copy for magazine and newspaper advertising and tapes of commercials for radio and television. Thus, all H_2O_4U has to do is buy media space or time. In addition, Environmental Control furnishes each salesperson with a portable demonstration unit, and the company recently gave H_2O_4U three units to be placed in models of condominium apartments.

Morton has worked long hours to get his company going, but he realizes that he has to find time to think about how his strategy is working and to plan for the future.

Evaluate Morton Rinke's current marketing strategy for Simply Pure H_2O_4U. How do you think he's doing so far, and what should he do next? Why?

18. West Tarrytown Volunteer Fire Department (WTVFD)

Cheyne Morgan raced out the front door of the Target store where he worked as soon as his beeper sounded. In his pickup truck, he heard the call on his special radio scanner: "Highway 18 Fire Department, there is a grass fire at the old McCullough place. That's a mile down the old dirt road just past the Wilson house." The directions might appear cryptic to someone who had not grown up around West Tarrytown, but it was all Cheyne needed to know. Upon arriving at the fire, Cheyne quickly pulled on his fire-retardant bunker pants and boots. He left his Nomex hood, helmet, and fire pants in the back of his truck—he would not need them for this fire.

Less than 10 minutes from the time the call was placed, Cheyne and 20 other members of the West Tarrytown Volunteer Fire Department (WTVFD) had arrived at the old McCullough place. They were able to put out the fire in less than half an hour, but not before a football-field-size patch of grass was scorched. Their quick response saved the neighbor's barn and kept the fire from spreading to a nearby forest. A third straight year of drought has the crew on high alert.

Cheyne threw his gear in the back of his truck and headed back to finish his shift at Target. He had worked there as a department manager for two years, ever since he graduated from the local state college with a marketing degree. As he drove, Cheyne thought about what WTVFD Chief Fran Holland recently asked him to do. Over the last few years, the fire department had more to do but fewer people to do it with. So Chief Holland asked Cheyne to draw up a marketing plan to recruit new volunteers.

Cheyne had already started to gather information for the marketing plan. From an online search he found that WTVFD was one of an estimated 30,000 volunteer fire departments in the United States and that these departments had almost a million volunteers. Cheyne was surprised that more than 75 percent of all U.S. firefighters were volunteers. West Tarrytown, a small city of just over 100,000 and hours from a big city, had only volunteer firefighters.

There are 48 firefighters currently in the WTVFD—down from 55 five years ago. Although there was a surge of interest in the year following the terrorist attacks in 2001, only a few of those volunteers remain. Over time, WTVFD has found that about half of new recruits quit before their three-year anniversary. Those who remain usually stay with the department until they can't keep up with the job's physical demands. Fran Holland has been chief for the last three years. She replaced long-time chief, Ken Reeb, who retired after being with WTVFD for more than 40 years—the last 10 as chief.

The current volunteers include 44 men and 4 women; more than half of the force is older than 40 years old, and Cheyne is one of only five volunteers younger than 30. Almost all of them started volunteering while still in their 20s or early 30s. The crew represents all walks of life, and their ranks include a lawyer, a real estate salesperson, a college professor, a carpenter, a stay-at-home mom, and a few guys from the local factory. Many entered firefighting for the thrill of it or because they hoped the experience might help them land a paid firefighting job in a bigger city. But most of the crew stay with it because they feel good about giving back to their community, view it as a hobby, and enjoy the camaraderie with the other firefighters.

Being a volunteer firefighter is much different than Cheyne thought it would be when he started. Last year he counted 238 hours volunteering for WTVFD, but less than a third of that was actually responding to emergencies. And fewer than half of the emergencies were actual fires. He spent about a quarter of this time in required training and drills. He had to be trained for the many different possible calls, including car accidents, hazardous chemical spills, and terrorist attacks. Another 20 percent of his time was spent in meetings and a similar amount helping with fund-raising. Depending upon financial needs, WTVFD holds at least four fund-raising events a year—some years six or eight. These include annual activities such as a chili cook-off, pancake breakfast, and booth at the county fair—and as-needed events such as pie auctions, turkey shoots, and basketball tournaments.

The biggest requirement to be a volunteer firefighter is the willingness to make the time commitment. Cheyne's time commitment and allocation of hours is typical of all the firefighters at WTVFD. Volunteers have to be able to attend at least 80 percent of the twice-monthly drills—scheduled on the second and fourth Tuesdays of every month. Firefighters also have to live or work near the town of West Tarrytown so they can quickly respond to emergencies. They also have to be at least 18 years old and have a valid driver's license. There is a physical ability test to make sure that firefighters can stand the rigors of the job. Although one doesn't have to be a weight-lifter, the job requires volunteers to be in good physical shape.

WTVFD has never really had a marketing strategy or any formal promotion efforts. Most of Cheyne's fellow volunteers heard about WTVFD through word-of-mouth. People are always curious when a volunteer firefighter runs out the door from work or suddenly leaves a party. These occasions give volunteers a chance to tell others about what they do. Sometimes those questions bring someone out to see drills and to apply to become a volunteer. One of Cheyne's high school friends was a volunteer and he encouraged Cheyne to join up while Cheyne was in his junior year of college. But still, awareness of volunteer firefighting in the West Tarrytown area is very low. When Cheyne tells friends about his volunteer work,

most are surprised and think the town has full-time paid staff fighting fires.

Cheyne thinks his marketing strategy should focus mostly on promotion. From his studies he remembers the AIDA model and integrated marketing communications. WTVFD does not really have an advertising budget and right now only a one-page informational website. He is pretty sure he could get some money to build a more robust website—especially because one of the recent recruits would do the work for free. Cheyne also wonders if his plan should focus only on gaining new recruits or if current volunteers might also be the target of new promotion. Cheyne also considers how and what he should communicate to his target market. He knows he will have limited funding for his efforts. Should he consider starting a Facebook page or blog? Maybe a website would be better—but what kind of information would be on the website? What about advertising or information sessions? Who should be his target market?

What are the promotion objectives Cheyne Morgan should include in his plan? What promotion methods should he use to achieve those objectives?

19. UltimateWedding.com

Sterling Bassett is happy with her life but disappointed that the idea she had for starting her own business hasn't taken off as expected. Within a few weeks, she either has to renew the contract for her Internet website or decide not to put any more time and money into her idea. She knows that it doesn't make sense to renew the contract if she can't come up with a plan to make her website-based business profitable—and she doesn't like to plan. She's a "doer," not a planner.

Sterling's business, UltimateWedding.com, started as an idea 18 months ago as she was planning her own wedding. She attended a bridal fair at the convention center in Raleigh, North Carolina, to get ideas for a wedding dress, check out catering companies and florists, and in general learn more about the various services available to newlyweds. While there, she and her fiancé went from one retailer's booth to another to sign up for their wedding gift registries. Almost every major retailer in the city—ranging from the Home Depot warehouse to the Belk department store to the specialty shops that handle imported crystal glassware—offered a gift registry. Some had computers set up to provide access to their online registries. Being listed in all of the registries improved the odds that her wedding gifts would be items she wanted and could use—and it saved time and hassle for gift-givers. On the way back from the fair, Sterling and her fiancé discussed the idea that it would be a lot easier to register gift preferences once on a central Internet site than to provide lots of different stores with bits and pieces of information. A list at a website would also make it easier for gift-givers, at least those who were computer users.

When Sterling got home, she did an Internet search and found several sites that focused on weddings. The biggest seemed to be www.theknot.com. It had features for couples who were getting married, including a national gift registry. The site featured products from a number of companies, especially large national retail chains; however, there was a search feature to locate people who provide wedding-related services

in a local ZIP code area. Sterling thought that the sites she found looked quite good, but that they were not as helpful as a site could be with a more local focus.

The more Sterling and her fiancé discussed the idea of a website offering local wedding-related services, the more it looked like an interesting opportunity. Except for the annual bridal fair, there was no other obvious local place for consumers to get information about planning a wedding and buying wedding-related services. And for local retailers, florists, catering companies, insurance agents, home builders, and many other types of firms, there was no other central place to target promotion to newlyweds. Further, the amount of money spent on weddings and wedding gifts is substantial, and right before and after getting married many young couples make many important purchase decisions for everything from life insurance to pots and pans. Spending on the wedding alone can easily exceed the cost of a year of college.

Sterling was no stranger to the Internet. She worked as a website designer for a small firm whose only client was IBM. That IBM was the only client was intentional rather than accidental. A year earlier IBM had decided that it wanted to outsource certain aspects of its website development work and have it handled by an outside contractor. After negotiating a three-year contract to do IBM's work, several IBM employees quit their jobs and started the business. IBM was a good client, and all indications were that IBM could give the firm as much work as it could handle as it hired new people and prospected for additional accounts over the next few years. Sterling especially liked the creative aspects of designing the "look" of a website, and technical specialists handled a lot of the subtle details.

Before joining this new company, Sterling had several marketing-related jobs—but none had been the glamorous ad agency job she dreamed of in college as an advertising major. Her first job as a college graduate was with an ad agency, but she was in a backroom operation handling a lot of the arrangements for printing and mailing large-scale direct-mail promotions. In spite of promises that it was a path to other jobs at the agency, the pay was bad, the work was always pressured, and every aspect of what she had to do was boring. After six punishing months, she quit and went looking for something else.

When a number of job applications didn't turn up something quickly, she took a part-time job doing telemarketing calls for a mortgage refinance company. Sterling's boss told her that she was doing a great job reeling in prospects—but she hated disturbing people at night and just didn't like making sales pitches. Fortunately for her, that pain didn't last long. A neighbor in Sterling's apartment complex got Sterling an interview for a receptionist position at an ad agency. That, at least, got her foot in the door. Her job description wasn't very interesting, but in a small agency she had the opportunity to learn a lot about all aspects of the business—ranging from working on client proposals and media plans to creative sessions for new campaigns. In fact, it was from a technician at that agency that she learned to work with the graphics software used to create ad layouts and website pages. When the website design job came open at the new firm, her boss gave her a glowing recommendation, and in two days she was off on her new career.

Although Sterling's jobs had not been high-profile positions, they did give her some experience in sales promotion, personal selling, and advertising. Those skills were complemented by the technical computer skills of her fiancé (now husband), who made a living as a database programmer for a large software consulting firm. Taking everything as a whole, they thought that they could get a wedding-related website up and running and make it profitable.

There were several different facets to the original plan for UltimateWedding.com. One focused on recruiting local advertisers and "sponsors" who would pay to be listed at the website and be allocated a web page (which Sterling would design) describing their services, giving contact information, and links to their own websites. Another focused on services for people who were planning to be married. In addition to an online wedding gift registry, sections of the website provided information about typical wedding costs, planning checklists, details about how to get a required marriage license, and other helpful information (including a discussion forum with comments about the strengths and weaknesses of various local suppliers). Sterling also started a blog that helped foster more feedback from customers. A man and woman could sign up for the service online and could pay the modest $20 "membership" fee for a year by credit card. Friends, family, and invited guests could visit the website at no charge and get information about wedding preferences, local hotels, discounts on local car rentals, and even printable maps to all of the churches and synagogues in the area.

When Sterling told friends about her plan, they all thought it sounded like a great idea. In fact, each time she discussed it, someone came up with another idea for a locally oriented feature to add to the website. Several friends said that they had tried national websites but that the information was often too general. But generating more new ideas was not the problem. The problem was generating revenue. Sterling had already contracted for space from an Internet service provider and created some of the initial content for the website, but she only had four paying sponsors, two of whom happened to be family friends.

Sterling started by creating a colorful flyer describing the website and sent it to most of the firms that had participated in the bridal fair. When no one sent back the reply coupon for more information, Sterling started to make calls (mainly during her lunch hour at her full-time job). Some stores seemed intrigued by the concept, but no one seemed ready to sign up. One reason was that they all seemed surprised at the cost to participate and get ad space at the website—$2,400 a year (about the same as a 1/16-page display ad in the Raleigh *Yellow Pages*). Another problem was that no one wanted to be the first to sign up. As one florist shop owner put it, "If you pull this off and other florists sign up, then come back and I will too."

Getting couples to sign up went slowly too. At first, Sterling paid for four display ads in local Sunday newspapers in the society section, sent information sheets about the website to clergy in the area, listed the website with about 25 Internet search engines, and sent carefully crafted press releases announcing the service to almost every publication in the area. One article that resulted from a press release got some attention, and for a few weeks there was a flurry of e-mail inquiries about her web page. But after that it slowed to a trickle again. More recently, she tried to use Google AdWords, which places ads next to Google search results when someone from the greater Raleigh area searches on the keyword *wedding*. She got a few more hits from this and wondered if she should increase the number of keywords—and wondered what the best keywords could be. She thought about creating a Facebook page but wondered how it would help. She knows that many brides are on Pinterest and wasn't sure if she should start her own page there.

Sterling's diagnosis of the problem was simple. Most people thought it was a great idea, but few couples knew where to look on the Internet for such a service. Similarly, potential advertisers—many of them small local businesses—were not accustomed to the idea of paying for Internet advertising. They didn't know if the cost was reasonable or if her site would be effective in generating business.

Sterling's life as a married person was going great and her job as a web page designer kept her very busy. Her free time outside of work was always in short supply because the young crowd at her office always had some scheme for how to keep entertained. So she wasn't about to quit her job to devote full time to her business idea. Further, she thought that once it got rolling she would only have to devote 10 hours a week to it to earn an extra $30,000 a year. She didn't have delusions of becoming a "dot-com millionaire." She just wanted a good locally oriented business.

However, it still wasn't clear how to get it rolling. After a year of trying on and off, she only had four paying ad sponsors, and one of them had already notified her that he didn't plan to sign up again because it wasn't clear that the website had generated any direct leads or sales. Further, it looked like anything she could do to attract more "members" would end up being expensive and inefficient.

Her parents offered her $10,000 to keep the idea alive. Sterling believes that proper promotion is the key. Now the question is how to budget this latest investment. She was thinking about doing some search advertising—that can be narrowly targeted to local people searching under "wedding," "wedding planning," and other keywords. She was also thinking about building up her owned media content on the site. While Sterling could create the pages at no cost, she felt she would need help creating content. She wondered about maybe going with some user-generated content. Social media was another possibility—Twitter? Facebook? So many choices, and time was Sterling's scarcest resources (oh yeah, money is scarce, too).

Sterling thinks the idea has real potential, and she's willing to do the work. But she's not certain if she can make it pay off. She doesn't want to lose her parents' money.

What is Sterling's strategy? What should she do? If she were to move forward, what strategy would you recommend? Does her financial goal seem realistic? Why?

20. Minnehaha Marine & Camp

Rusty Steuben, owner of Minnehaha Marine & Camp, is worried about his business' future. He has tried various strategies for two years now, and he's still barely breaking even.

Two years ago, Rusty bought the inventory, supplies, equipment, and business of Minnehaha Marine & Camp, located on the edge of Minneapolis, Minnesota. The business is in an older building along a major highway leading out of town, several miles from any body of water. The previous owner had sales of about $500,000 a year but was just breaking even. For this reason—plus the desire to retire to Arizona—the owner sold to Rusty for roughly the value of the inventory.

Minnehaha Marine & Camp had been selling two well-known brands of small pleasure boats, a leading outboard motor, two brands of snowmobiles and jet skis, and a line of trailer and pickup-truck campers. The total inventory was valued at $250,000—and Rusty used all of his own savings and borrowed some from two friends to buy the inventory and the business. At the same time, he took over the lease on the building—so he was able to begin operations immediately. Rusty had never operated a business of his own before, but he was sure that he would be able to do well. He had worked in a variety of jobs—as a used-car salesman, an auto repairman, and a jack-of-all-trades in the maintenance departments of several local businesses.

Soon after starting his business, Rusty hired his friend, Ginny Wooten. She had worked with Rusty selling cars and had experience as a receptionist and in customer service. Together, they handle all selling and setup work on new sales and do maintenance work as needed. Sometimes the two are extremely busy—at the peaks of each sport season. Then both sales and maintenance keep them going up to 16 hours a day. At these times it's difficult to have both new and repaired equipment available as soon as customers want it. At other times, however, Rusty and Ginny have almost nothing to do.

Rusty usually charges the prices suggested by the various manufacturers, except at the end of a weather season when he is willing to make deals to clear the inventory. He is annoyed that some of his competitors sell mainly on a price basis—offering 10 to 30 percent off a manufacturer's suggested list prices—even at the beginning of a season! Rusty doesn't want to get into that kind of business, however. He hopes to build a loyal following based on friendship and personal service. Further, he doesn't think he really has to cut prices because all of his lines are exclusive to his store. No stores within a five-mile radius carry any of his brands, although nearby retailers offer many brands of similar products. Right now, the Internet does not provide much competition, but he fears future price competition from online boat shows.

To try to build a favorable image for his company, Rusty occasionally places ads in local papers and buys some radio spots. The basic theme of this advertising is that Minnehaha Marine & Camp is a friendly, service-oriented place to buy the equipment needed for the current season. Sometimes he mentions the brand names he carries, but generally Rusty tries to build an image for concerned, friendly service—both in new sales and repairs—stressing, "We do it right the first time." He chose this approach because, although he has exclusives on the brands he carries, there generally are 10 to 15 different manufacturers' products being sold in the area in each product category—and most of the products are quite similar. Rusty feels that this similarity among competing products almost forces him to try to differentiate himself on the basis of his own store's services.

The first year's operation wasn't profitable. In fact, after paying minimal salaries to Ginny and himself, the business just about broke even. Rusty made no return on his $250,000 investment.

In hopes of improving profitability, Rusty jumped at a chance to add a line of lawn mowers, tractors, and trimmers as he was starting into his second year of business. This line was offered by a well-known equipment manufacturer that wanted to expand into the Minneapolis area. The equipment is similar to that offered by other lawn equipment manufacturers. The manufacturer's willingness to do some local advertising and to provide some point-of-purchase displays appealed to Rusty. And he also liked the idea that customers probably would want this equipment sometime earlier than boats and other summer items. So he thought he could handle this business without interfering with his other peak selling seasons.

It's been two years since Rusty bought Minnehaha Marine & Camp—and he's still only breaking even. Sales have increased a little, but costs have gone up too because he had to hire some part-time help. The lawn equipment helped to expand sales—as he had expected—unfortunately, it did not increase profits as he had hoped. Rusty needed part-time helpers to handle this business—in part because the manufacturer's advertising had generated a lot of sales inquiries. Relatively few inquiries resulted in sales, however, because many people seemed to be shopping for deals. So Rusty may have even lost money handling the new line. But he hesitates to give it up because he doesn't want to lose that sales volume, and the manufacturer's sales rep has been most encouraging, assuring Rusty that things will get better and that his company will be glad to continue its promotion support during the coming year.

Rusty is now considering the offer of a mountain bike producer that has not been represented in the area. The bikes have become very popular with students and serious bikers in the last several years. The manufacturer's sales rep says industry sales are still growing (but not as fast as in the past) and probably will grow for many more years. The sales rep has praised

Rusty's service orientation and says this could help him sell lots of bikes because many mountain bikers are serious about buying a quality bike and then keeping it serviced. He says Rusty's business approach would be a natural fit with bike customers' needs and attitudes. As a special inducement to get Rusty to take on the line, the sales rep says Rusty will not have to pay for the initial inventory of bikes, accessories, and repair parts for 90 days. And, of course, the company will supply the usual promotion aids and a special advertising allowance of $10,000 to help introduce the line to Minneapolis.

Rusty likes the idea of carrying mountain bikes because he has one himself and knows that they do require some service year-round. But he also knows that the proposed bikes are very similar in price and quality to the ones now being offered by the bike shops in town. These bike shops are service- rather than price-oriented, and Rusty feels that they are doing a good job on service; consequently, he is concerned with how he can be "different."

Evaluate Rusty Steuben's overall strategy(ies) and the mountain bike proposal. What should he do now?

21. Geonovo Chemical, Inc. (GCI)

Geonovo Chemical, Inc., (GCI) is a multinational producer of various chemicals and plastics with plants in the United States, England, France, and Germany. Its headquarters are in New Jersey.

Kenneth Shibata is marketing manager of GCI's plastics business. Kenneth is reconsidering his promotion approach. He is evaluating what kind of promotion—and how much—should be directed to car producers and to other major plastics customers worldwide. Currently, Kenneth has one salesperson dedicated to the automobile industry. This man is based in the Detroit area and focuses on GM, Ford, and Chrysler—as well as the various firms that mold plastics to produce parts to supply the car industry. This approach worked well when relatively little plastic was used in each car and the auto producers did all of the designing themselves and then sent out specifications for very price-oriented competitive bidding. But now the whole product planning and buying system is changing—and of course foreign producers with facilities in the United States are much more threatening as competitors.

How the present system works can be illustrated in terms of the team approach Ford used on its project to design the Flex, the full-size crossover introduced as a 2009 model. For the Flex, representatives from all the various functions—planning, design, engineering, purchasing, marketing, and manufacturing—worked together. In fact, representatives from key suppliers were involved from the outset. The whole team takes final responsibility for a car. Because all of the departments are involved from the start, problems are resolved as the project moves on—before they cause a crisis. Manufacturing, for example, can suggest changes in design that will result in higher productivity or better quality, which is especially important at a time when Ford's initial quality ratings are beating those of Honda and Toyota.

The old approach was different. It involved a five-year process of creating a new vehicle in sequential steps. Under the old system, product planners would come up with a general concept and then expect the design team to give it artistic form. Next, engineering would develop the specifications and pass them on to manufacturing and suppliers. There was little communication between the groups and no overall project responsibility.

In the Flex project, Ford engineers followed the Japanese lead and did some reverse engineering of their own. They dismantled several competitors' cars, piece by piece, looking for ideas they could copy or improve. This helped them learn how the parts were assembled and how they were designed. Eventually, Ford incorporated or modified some of the best features into its design of the Flex. For example, the Flex uses a new design to seal the doors and eliminate wind noise.

In addition to reverse engineering, Ford researchers conducted a series of market studies. This led to positioning the Flex as an "anti-minivan." That positioning resulted in a decision to eliminate the sliding side doors and instead to use traditional hinged doors. That cut costs, but the savings were used for dress-up features, such as 19-inch aluminum wheels and a special new seat design that reduces movement in the seat and gives the car an even smoother drive. The Flex's optional refrigerator/freezer is another example of a feature that did well in concept tests.

Ford also asked assembly-line workers for suggestions before the car was redesigned and then incorporated their ideas into the new car. Most bolts have the same-size head, for example, so workers don't have to switch from one wrench to another.

Finally, Ford included its best suppliers as part of the planning effort. Instead of turning to a supplier after the car's design was completed, Ford invited them to participate in product planning. For example, Microsoft's Sync system provides the Flex with voice control of the entertainment system.

Most other vehicles are now developed with an approach similar to this. GM, for example, used a very similar team approach to redesign its new Malibu. And major firms in many other industries are using similar approaches. A major outgrowth of this effort has been a trend by these producers to develop closer working relationships with a smaller number of suppliers. To some extent, this is a direct outgrowth of the decision to try to reduce unnecessary costs by using the same components for different vehicles. For example, the powertrain for the Flex is the same as the one used in Ford's Edge.

Many of the suppliers selected for the Flex project had not only the facilities, but also the technical and professional managerial staff who could understand—and become part of—the program management approach. Ford expected these major suppliers to join in its total quality management push and to be able to provide just-in-time delivery systems. Ford dropped suppliers whose primary sales technique was to entertain buyers and then submit bids on standard specifications.

Because many firms have moved to these team-oriented approaches and developed closer working relationships with a subset of their previous suppliers, Kenneth is trying to determine if GCI's present effort is still appropriate. Kenneth's strategy has focused primarily on responding to inquiries and bringing in GCI's technical people as the situation seems to require. Potential customers with technical questions are sometimes referred to other noncompeting customers already using the materials or to a GCI plant—to be sure that all questions are answered. But basically, all producer-customers are treated more or less alike. The sales reps make calls and try to find good business wherever they can.

Each GCI sales rep usually has a geographic area. If an area like Detroit needs more than one rep, each may specialize in one or several similar industries. But GCI uses the same basic approach—call on present users of plastic products and try to find opportunities for getting a share (or bigger share) of existing purchases or new applications. The sales reps are supposed to be primarily order getters rather than technical specialists. Technical help can be brought in when the customer wants it, or sometimes the sales rep simply sets up a conference call between GCI's technical experts, the buyer, and the users at the buyer's facility.

Kenneth sees that some of his major competitors are becoming more aggressive. They are seeking to affect specifications and product design from the start rather than after a product design is completed. This takes a lot more effort and resources, but Kenneth thinks it may get better results. A major problem he sees, however, is that he may have to drastically change the nature of GCI's promotion. Instead of focusing primarily on buyers and responding to questions, it may be necessary to try to contact *all* the multiple buying influences and not only answer their questions but help them understand what

questions to raise—to find solutions. Such a process may even require more technically trained sales reps. In fact, it may require that people from GCI's other departments—engineering, design, manufacturing, R&D, and distribution—get actively involved in discussions with their counterparts in customer firms. Further, use of e-mail and a website might make ongoing contacts faster and easier.

While Kenneth doesn't want to miss the boat if changes are needed, he also doesn't want to go off the deep end. After all, many of the firm's customers don't seem to want GCI to do anything very different from what it's been doing. In fact, some say that they're very satisfied with their current supply arrangements and really have no interest in investing in a close relationship with a single supplier. Even with the Flex project, Ford wasn't 100 percent dedicated to the team approach. For example, when Ford's research showed that the target market viewed quiet and comfortable seats as an especially important factor in purchases, Ford didn't turn to a supplier for help but rather assigned a team of its own design engineers to develop and test them in-house. Now some of what was learned on the Flex project is going to be used in redesigning other models.

Contrast Ford's previous approach of designing and producing cars to Flex's program management approach, especially as it might affect suppliers' promotion efforts. Given that many other major producers have moved in the program management direction, what promotion effort should Kenneth Shibata develop for Geonovo Chemical? Should every producer in every geographic area be treated alike, regardless of size? Explain.

22. Bright Light Innovations: The Starlight Stove*

The top management team of Bright Light Innovations is preparing to meet and review its market situation. The team is a combination of students and faculty from Colorado State University's (CSU) Colleges of Business and Engineering: Dr. Bryan Wilson, Paul Hudnut, Ajay Jha, Sachin Joshi, Katie Lucchesi, Dan Mastbergen, Ryan Palmer, and Chaun Sims. They are excited about the Starlight Stove product they have developed—and passionate about the opportunity that it provides to improve the quality of life for some of the world's poorest people. They know they have a great technology, but they need a marketing plan to bring this product to market.

Every day, more than 2.4 billion people—more than one-third of the world's population—burn solid biomass fuel (wood, charcoal, dung, and coal) for cooking and heating. These fuel sources are usually burned indoors in open pits or traditional cook stoves. About two-thirds of the people using biomass fuel also have no electricity, so the open fires often burn into the night to provide light. These fires create indoor air pollution, which is a leading contributor to respiratory diseases. U.N. Secretary General Kofi Annan has called for

greater energy efficiency and noted that "indoor air pollution has become one of the top 10 causes of mortality and premature death." It is estimated that this source of pollution contributes each year to the deaths of 1 million children younger than the age of 5, and it is a leading cause of miscarriage and women's health problems.

Hoping to address these consumers' needs for safe cooking and electricity, CSU's Engines and Energy Conversion Laboratory developed the Starlight Stove. The Starlight Stove's improved technology requires 50 to 70 percent less biomass fuel than traditional stoves. It also has a thermoelectric generator that converts heat from the stove into electricity that can power a small lightbulb or be stored in a rechargeable battery for later use. The technology has been refined, and the team believes it is ready to go to market.

There are other competing enclosed cookstoves, but none produce electricity. Solar panels can provide electricity, but they are expensive—costing $360 each. Micro-hydropower allows households to convert the power from streams and rivers into electricity, but homes must be close to a river, and water flow in many areas of the country is seasonal. These technologies—solar panels and hydropower—are understood by many consumers and are already in use in some areas. The Starlight Stove, on the other hand, offers a new technology, and that may slow its adoption.

---

*This case is based on a business plan written by Ajay Jha, Sachin Joshi, Katie Lucchesi, Dan Mastbergen, Ryan Palmer, and Chaun Sims.

The management team decided on Nepal as the initial target market for the Starlight Stove. Several factors made this market particularly attractive. The climate is relatively cold, and only 11 percent of the households have access to electricity, so the heat and electricity production of the stove are particularly beneficial. Eighty-eight percent of the population uses firewood as their main source of energy. In addition, deforestation creates environmental problems in Nepal because it contributes to erosion and flooding. So the social benefits of the Starlight Stove will be particularly appealing to the Nepalese government and aid organizations.

There are approximately 9.2 million households in Nepal, but the gross national income per capita is only about $400, with most adults making between $1 and $3 per day. Nepal is largely rural, with only 17 percent of the population living in urban areas. The country is divided into 75 districts. Each district is further divided into about 60 village development committees (a sort of local government) consisting of about 450 households. The similar characteristics of northern India—immediately south of Nepal—make it a logical follow-up market.

The Starlight Stove offers several benefits to this population. For example, the longer hours with light—thanks to the electricity—and less time required to collect wood or other fuel could allow families to earn money by weaving, farming, or producing other crafts. Family productivity could increase 20 percent or more per day. Or the added hours with light might allow children to gain an education. If the product were manufactured locally, it could provide jobs for the population and help them learn the benefits of technology.

With obvious benefits for such a large number of people, the Bright Light Innovations team could look to donations to subsidize the Starlight Stove for the Nepalese people. But the team has concerns about this traditional form of aid. Financing in the form of grants, government relief, or donations is unreliable. If it is not renewed, projects wallow or die. Further, grants often fail to teach disadvantaged people skills and responsibility. So the team wants to create a sustainable venture that provides benefits for all—and has set up Bright Light Innovations as a for-profit business.

The management team has to make a number of marketing decisions. For example, it has to decide how to price the Starlight Stove. It estimates that the stove will cost about $60 to manufacture after setting up a plant in Nepal and expects that microfinancing organizations will provide loans for families. If units are sold for $80, the loan can be financed at 20 percent interest for three years with payments of $0.68 per week (microfinancing institutions typically collect on a weekly, or sometimes daily, basis). The team thinks that it will be easy to find a microfinancing institution to provide these loans. But the team is still unsure about whether this price will provide adequate margins for distributors.

The team also has to decide how to promote the stove to a population where less than half the adults can read. However, the team does have contacts with some business leaders, government officials, and nongovernmental organizations that may be able to provide advice and help.

What should be the marketing strategy of the Bright Light Innovations team for the Starlight Stove? Why?

23. Schmidt Furniture

Rosann Schmidt, owner of Schmidt Furniture, is discouraged with her salespeople and is even thinking about hiring some new blood. Schmidt has been running Schmidt Furniture for 10 years and has slowly built the sales to $3.5 million a year. Her store is located on the outskirts of a growing city of 275,000 people. This is basically a factory city, and she has deliberately selected blue-collar workers as her target market. She carries some higher-priced furniture lines but emphasizes budget combinations and easy credit terms.

Schmidt is concerned that she may have reached the limit of her sales growth—her sales have not been increasing during the last two years even though total furniture sales have been increasing in the city as new people move in. Her local cable TV spots, newspaper advertising, and some ads on the local newspaper website seem to attract her target market, but many of these people come in, shop around, and leave. Some of them come back—but most do not. She thinks her product selections are very suitable for her target market and is concerned that her salespeople don't close more sales with potential customers. Several times, she has discussed this matter with her 10 salespeople. Her staff feels they should treat customers the way they personally want to be treated. They argue that their role is to answer questions and be helpful when asked—not to make suggestions or help customers make decisions. They think this would be too "hard sell."

Schmidt says their behavior is interpreted as indifference by the customers attracted to the store by her advertising. She has tried to convince her salespeople that customers must be treated on an individual basis and that some customers need more help in looking and deciding than others. Moreover, Schmidt is convinced that some customers would appreciate more help and suggestions than the salespeople themselves might want. To support her views, she showed her staff the data from a study of furniture store customers (see Tables 1 and 2) that she found on the Internet website for a furniture trade association. She tried to explain the differences in demographic groups and pointed out that her store was definitely trying to aim at specific people. She argued that they (the salespeople) should cater to the needs and attitudes of their customers and think less about how they would like to be treated themselves. Further, Schmidt announced that she is considering changing the sales compensation plan or hiring new blood if the present employees can't do a better job. Currently, the sales reps are paid $26,000 per year plus a 5 percent commission on sales.

Contrast Renee Carson's strategy and thoughts about her salespeople with their apparent view of her strategy and especially their role in it. What should she do now? Explain.

Table 1 Shopping Behavior by Demographic Group

In Shopping for Furniture I Found (Find) That	Demographic Groups			
	Group A	**Group B**	**Group C**	**Group D**
I looked at furniture in many stores before I made a purchase.	78%	72%	52%	50%
I went (am going) to only one store and bought (will buy) what I found (find) there.	2	5	10	11
To make my purchase I went (am going) back to one of the stores I shopped in previously.	63	59	27	20
I looked (am looking) at furniture in no more than three stores and made (will make) my purchase in one of these.	20	25	40	45
I like a lot of help in selecting the right furniture.	27	33	62	69
I like a very friendly salesperson.	23	28	69	67

Table 2 The Demographic Status

Demographic Status
Upper class (Group A); 13 percent of sample
This group consists of managers, proprietors, or executives of large businesses; professionals, including doctors, lawyers, engineers, college professors, and school administrators; and research personnel and sales personnel, including managers, executives, and upper-income salespeople above level of clerks. *Family income is more than $80,000.*
Middle class (Group B); 37 percent of sample
Group B consists of white-collar workers, including clerical, secretarial, salesclerks, bookkeepers, and so on. It also includes school teachers, social workers, semiprofessionals, proprietors or managers of small businesses, industrial foremen, and other supervisory personnel. *Family income is between $45,000 and $80,000.*
Lower middle class (Group C); 36 percent of sample
Skilled workers and semiskilled technicians are in this category, along with custodians, elevator operators, telephone linemen, factory operatives, construction workers, and some domestic and personal service employees. *Family income is between $30,000 and $45,000. No one in this group has above a high school education.*
Lower class (Group D); 14 percent of sample
Nonskilled employees, day laborers. It also includes some factory operatives and domestic and service people.. *Family income is less than $30,000.* *None one has completed high school; some have only grade-school education.*

24. WireX

Wendy Keating, marketing manager of consumer products for WireX, is trying to set a price for her most promising new product: a space-saving shoe rack suitable for small homes or apartments.

WireX—located in Ft. Worth, Texas—is a custom producer of industrial wire products. The company has a lot of experience bending wire into many shapes and also can chrome- or gold-plate finished products. The company was started 16 years ago and has slowly built its sales volume to $3.6 million a year. Just one year ago, Keating was appointed marketing manager of the consumer products division. It is her responsibility to develop this division as a producer and marketer of the company's own branded products—as distinguished from custom orders, which the industrial division produces for others.

Keating has been working on a number of different product ideas for almost a year now and has developed several designs for DVD holders, racks for soft-drink cans, plate holders, doll stands, collapsible book ends, laptop stands, and other such products. Her most promising product is a shoe rack for crowded homes and apartments. The wire rack attaches to the inside of a closet door and holds eight pairs of shoes.

The shoe rack is very similar to one the industrial division produced for a number of years for another company. That company sold the shoe rack and hundreds of other related items out of its "products for organizing and storing" mail-order catalog. Managers at WireX were surprised by the high sales volume the catalog company achieved with the rack. In fact, that is what interested WireX in the consumer market and led to the development of the separate consumer products division.

Keating has sold hundreds of the shoe racks to various local hardware, grocery and general merchandise stores, and wholesalers on a trial basis, but each time she has negotiated a price—and no firm policy has been set. Now she must determine what price to set on the shoe rack, which she plans to push aggressively wherever she can. Actually, she hasn't decided on exactly which channels of distribution to use. But trials in the local area have been encouraging, and as noted earlier, the experience in the industrial division suggests that there is a large market for this type of product. Further, she has noticed that a Walmart store in her local area is selling a similar rack made of plastic. When she talked casually about her product with the store manager, he suggested that she contact the chain's houseware buyers in the home office in Arkansas.

The manufacturing cost of her rack—when made in reasonable quantities—is approximately $2.80 if it is painted black and $3.60 if it is chromed. Similar products have been selling at retail in the $9.95 to $19.95 range. The sales and administrative overhead to be charged to the division will amount to $95,000 a year. This will include Keating's salary and some travel and office expenses. She expects that a number of other products will be developed in the near future. But for the coming year, she hopes the shoe rack will account for about half the consumer products division's sales volume.

Evaluate Wendy Keating's strategy planning so far. What should she do now? What price should she set for the shoe rack?

25. Whittier Plastics

Simon Howe, the marketing manager of Whittier Plastics, wants to increase sales by adding sales reps rather than "playing with price." That's how Simon describes what Judy Howe, his mother and Whittier Plastics' president, is suggesting. Judy is not sure what to do, either. But she does want to increase sales, so something new is needed.

Whittier Plastics—of Whittier, California—is a leading producer in the plastic forming machinery industry. It has patents covering more than 200 variations, but Whittier Plastics' customers seldom buy more than 30 different types in a year. The machines are sold to plastic forming manufacturers to increase production capacity or replace old equipment.

Established in 1970, the company has enjoyed a steady growth to its present position with annual sales of $50 million. Judy took over as president 15 years ago, after her husband, Charles, the founder of the company, died of a sudden heart attack. The first few years were tough, but Judy emerged as a strong executive who has steered the company well. She is well respected in the industry.

Twelve U.S. firms compete in the U.S. plastic forming machinery market. Several Japanese, German, and Swedish firms compete in the global market, but the Howes have not seen much of them on the West Coast. Apparently the foreign firms rely on manufacturers' agents who have not provided an ongoing presence. They are not good about following up on inquiries, and their record for service on the few sales they have made on the East Coast is not satisfactory. So the Howes are not worried about them right now.

Each of the 12 U.S. competitors is about the same size and manufactures similar machinery. Each has tended to specialize in its own geographic region. Six of the competitors are located in the East, four in the Midwest, and two—including Whittier Plastics—on the West Coast. The other West Coast firm is in Tacoma, Washington. All of the competitors offer similar prices and sell F.O.B. from their factories. Demand has been fairly strong in recent years. As a result, all of the competitors have been satisfied to sell in their geographic areas and avoid price-cutting. In fact, price-cutting is not a popular idea in this industry. About 15 years ago, one firm tried to win more business and found that others immediately met the price cut—but industry sales (in units) did not increase at all. Within a few years, prices returned to their earlier level, and since then competition has tended to focus on promotion and avoid price.

Whittier Plastics' promotion depends mainly on six company sales reps, who cover the West Coast. In total, these reps cost about $880,000 per year including salary, bonuses, supervision, travel, and entertaining. When the sales reps are close to making a sale, they are supported by two sales engineers—at a cost of about $130,000 per year per engineer. Whittier Plastics does some advertising in trade journals—less than $100,000—and occasionally uses direct mailings and trade show exhibits. It also has a simple website on the Internet—the main content on the site consists of PDF files of all the company's sales brochures. But the main promotion emphasis is on personal selling. Any personal contact outside the West Coast market is handled by manufacturers' agents who are paid 4 percent on sales—but sales are very infrequent.

Judy is not satisfied with the present situation. Industry sales have leveled off and so have Whittier Plastics' sales—although the firm continues to hold its share of the market. Judy would like to find a way to compete more effectively in the other regions because she sees great potential outside the West Coast.

Competitors and buyers agree that Whittier Plastics is the top-quality producer in the industry. Its machines have generally been somewhat superior to others in terms of reliability, durability, and production capacity. The difference, however, usually has not been great enough to justify a higher price—because the others are able to do the necessary job—unless a Whittier Plastics sales rep convinces the customer that the extra quality will improve the customer's product and lead to fewer production line breakdowns. The sales rep also tries to sell the advantages of Whittier Plastics' better sales engineers and technical service people—and sometimes is successful.

But if a buyer is mainly interested in comparing delivered prices for basic machines—the usual case—Whittier Plastics' price must be competitive to get the business. In short, if such a buyer has a choice between Whittier Plastics' and another machine *at the same price,* Whittier Plastics will usually win the business in its part of the West Coast market. But it's clear that Whittier Plastics' price has to be at least competitive in such cases.

The average plastic forming machine sells for about $220,000, F.O.B. shipping point. Shipping costs within any of the three major regions average about $4,000—but another $3,000 must be added on shipments between the West Coast and the Midwest (either way) and another $3,000 between the Midwest and the East.

Judy is thinking about expanding sales by absorbing the extra $3,000 to $6,000 in freight cost that occurs if a midwestern or eastern customer buys from her West Coast location. By doing this, she would not actually be cutting price in those markets but rather reducing her net return. She thinks that her competitors would not see this as price competition and therefore would not resort to cutting prices themselves.

Simon disagrees. Simon thinks that the proposed freight absorption plan would stimulate price competition in the Midwest and East and perhaps on the West Coast. He proposes instead that Whittier Plastics hire some sales reps to work the Midwest and Eastern regions—selling quality—rather than relying on the manufacturers' agents. He argues that two additional sales reps in each of these regions would not increase costs too much and might greatly increase the sales from these markets over that brought in by the agents. With this plan, there would be no need to absorb the freight and risk disrupting the status quo. Adding more of Whittier Plastics' own sales reps is especially important, he argues, because competition in the Midwest and East is somewhat hotter than on the West Coast—due to the number of competitors (including foreign competitors) in those regions. A lot of expensive entertaining, for example, seems to be required just to be considered as a potential supplier. In contrast, the situation has been rather quiet in the West—because only two firms are sharing this market and each is working harder near its home base. The eastern and midwestern competitors don't send any sales reps to the West Coast—and if they have any manufacturers' agents, they haven't gotten any business in recent years.

Judy agrees that her son has a point, but industry sales are leveling off and Judy wants to increase sales. Further, she thinks the competitive situation may change drastically in the near future as global competitors get more aggressive and some possible new production methods and machines become more competitive with existing ones. She would rather be a leader in anything that is likely to happen than a follower. But she is impressed with Simon's comments about the greater competitiveness in the other markets and therefore is unsure about what to do.

Evaluate Whittier Plastics' current strategies. Given Judy Howe's sales objective, what should Whittier Plastics do? Explain.

26. Abundant Harvest

Chelsea Skye-Rice, president of Abundant Harvest, is not sure what she should propose to the board of directors. Her recent strategy change isn't working. And Don Bartley, Abundant Harvest's only sales rep (and a board member), is so frustrated that he refuses to continue his discouraging sales efforts. Don wants Chelsea to hire a sales force or do *something.*

Abundant Harvest is a long-time processor in the highly seasonal vegetable canning industry. Abundant Harvest packs and sells canned beans, peas, carrots, corn, peas and carrots mixed, and kidney beans. It sells mainly through food brokers to merchant wholesalers, supermarket chains (such as Kroger, Safeway, A&P, and Jewel), cooperatives, and other outlets, mostly in the Midwest. Of less importance, by volume, are sales to local institutions, grocery stores, and supermarkets—and sales of dented canned goods at low prices to walk-in customers.

Abundant Harvest is located in Wisconsin's beautiful Devil's Valley. The company has more than $28 million in sales annually (exact sales data are not published by the closely held corporation). Plants are located in strategic places along the valley, with main offices in the valley also. The Abundant Harvest brand is used only on canned goods sold in the local market. Most of the goods are sold and shipped under a retailer's label or a broker's/wholesaler's label.

Abundant Harvest is well known for the consistent quality of its product offerings. And it's always willing to offer competitive prices. Strong channel relations were built by Robert Skye, Abundant Harvest's former chairman of the board and chief executive officer. Robert—who still owns controlling interest in the firm—worked the Chicago area as the company's sales rep in its earlier years, before he took over from his father as president in 1974. Robert was an ambitious and hardworking top manager—the firm prospered under his direction. He became well known within the canned food processing industry for technical/product innovations.

During the off-canning season, Robert traveled widely. In the course of his travels, he arranged several important business deals. His 1990 and 2001 trips resulted in the following two events: (1) inexpensive pineapple was imported from Taiwan and sold by Abundant Harvest, primarily to expand the product line, and (2) a technically advanced continuous process cooker (65 feet high) was imported from England and installed at one of Abundant Harvest's plants. It was the first of its kind in the United States and cut processing time sharply while improving quality.

Robert retired in 2010 and named his daughter, 35-year-old Chelsea Skye-Rice, as his successor. Chelsea is intelligent and hardworking. She has been concerned primarily with the company's financial matters and only recently with marketing problems. During her seven years as financial director, the firm received its highest credit rating and was able to borrow working capital ($5 million to meet seasonal can and wage requirements) at the lowest rate ever.

The fact that the firm isn't unionized allows some competitive advantage. However, changes in minimum wage laws have increased costs. And these and other rising costs have squeezed profit margins. This led to the recent closing of two plants as they became less efficient to operate. Abundant Harvest expanded capacity of the remaining two plants (especially warehouse facilities) so they could operate more profitably with maximum use of existing processing equipment.

Shortly after Robert's retirement, Chelsea reviewed the company's situation with her managers. She pointed to narrowing profit margins, debts contracted for new plants and equipment, and an increasingly competitive environment. Even considering the temporary labor-saving competitive advantage of the new cooker system, there seemed to be no way to improve the status quo unless the firm could sell direct—as it does in the local market—thereby eliminating the food brokers' 5 percent commission on sales. This was the chosen plan, and Don Bartley was given the new sales job. An inside salesperson was retained to handle incoming orders and do some telemarketing to smaller accounts.

Don, the only full-time outside sales rep for the firm, lives in Devil's Valley. Other top managers do some selling but not much. Being a nephew of Robert, Don is also a member of the board of directors. He is well qualified in technical matters and has a college degree in food chemistry. Although Don formerly did call on some important customers with the brokers' sales reps, he is not well known in the industry or even by Abundant Harvest's usual customers.

It is now five months later. Don is not doing very well. He has made several selling trips, placed hundreds of telephone calls, and maintained constant e-mail contacts with prospective customers—all with discouraging results. He is unwilling to continue sales efforts on his own. There seem to be too many potential customers for one person to reach. And much negotiating and wining-and-dining seems to be needed—certainly more than he can or wants to do.

Don insists that Abundant Harvest hire a sales force to continue the present way of operating. Sales are down in comparison both to expectations and to the previous year's results. Some regular supermarket chain customers have stopped buying—though basic consumer demand has not changed. Further, buyers for some supermarket chains that might be potential new customers have demanded quantity guarantees much larger than Abundant Harvest can supply. Expanding supply would be difficult in the short run—because the firm typically must contract with growers to ensure supplies of the type and quality it normally offers.

Robert, still the controlling stockholder, has asked for a special meeting of the board in two weeks to discuss the present situation.

Evaluate Abundant Harvest's past and current strategy planning. What should Chelsea Skye-Rice tell Robert Skye? What should Abundant Harvest do now?

27. Advanced Molding, Inc.

Anya Winrow is trying to decide whether to leave her present job to buy into another business and be part of top management.

Anya is now a sales rep for a plastics components manufacturer. She calls mostly on large industrial accounts—such as refrigerator manufacturers—who might need large quantities of custom-made products like door liners. She is on a straight salary of $55,000 per year, plus expenses and a company car. She expects some salary increases but doesn't see much long-run opportunity with this company.

As a result, she is seriously considering changing jobs and investing $60,000 in Advanced Molding, Inc., an established Chicago, Illinois, thermoplastic molder (manufacturer). Gary Beal, the present owner, is nearing retirement and has not trained anyone to take over the business. He has agreed to sell the business to Joseph O'Sullivan, a lawyer, who has invited Anya to invest and become the sales manager. Joseph has agreed to match Anya's current salary plus expenses, plus a bonus of 2 percent of profits. However, she must invest to become part of the new company. She will get a 5 percent interest in the business for the necessary $60,000 investment—all of her savings.

Advanced Molding, Inc., is well established and last year had sales of $3.2 million—but zero profits (after paying Gary a salary of $90,000). In terms of sales, cost of materials was 46 percent; direct labor, 13 percent; indirect factory labor, 15 percent; factory overhead, 13 percent; and sales overhead and general expenses, 13 percent. The company has not been making any profit for several years—but it has been continually adding new computer-controlled machines to replace those made obsolete by technological developments. The machinery is well maintained and modern, but most of it is similar to that used by its many competitors. Most of the machines in the industry are standard. Special products are made by using specially made dies with these machines.

Sales have been split: about two-thirds custom-molded products (that is, made to the specifications of other producers or merchandising concerns) and the balance, proprietary items (such as housewares and game items, such as poker chips).

The housewares are copies of items developed by others and indicate neither originality nor style. Gary is in charge of selling the proprietary items, which are distributed through any available wholesale channels. The custom-molded products are sold through two full-time sales reps—who receive a 10 percent commission on individual orders up to $30,000 and then 3 percent above that level—and also by three manufacturers' reps who get the same commissions.

The company seems to be in fairly good financial condition, at least as far as book value is concerned. The $60,000 investment will buy almost $88,000 in assets—and ongoing operations should pay off the seven-year note (see Table 1). Joseph thinks that with new management the company has a good chance to make big profits. He expects to make some economies in the production process—because he feels most production operations can be improved. He plans to keep custom-molding sales at approximately the present $2 million level. His new strategy will try to increase the proprietary sales volume from $1.2 million to $3 million a year. Anya is expected to be a big help here because of her sales experience. This will bring the firm up to about capacity level—but it will

Table 1 Advanced Molding, Inc., Statement of Financial Conditions, December 31, 2010

Assets			Liabilities and Net Worth	
Cash		$ 19,500	Liabilities:	
Accounts receivable		82,500	Accounts payable	$ 105,000
Building	$337,500		Notes payable—7 years (machinery)	291,000
Less: depreciation	112,500			
		225,000		
Machinery	2,100,000		Net worth:	
Less: depreciation	675,000		Capital stock	1,350,000
		1,425,000	Retained earnings	6,000
Total assets		$1,752,000	Total liabilities and net worth	$1,752,000

mean adding additional employees and costs. The major advantage of expanding sales will be spreading overhead.

Some of the new products proposed by Joseph for expanding proprietary sales are listed below.

> Safety helmets for cyclists
> Water bottles for cyclists
> Waterproof cases for digital cameras
> Toolboxes
> Closet organizer/storage boxes for toys
> Short legs for furniture
> Step-on garbage cans without liners
> Exterior house shutters and siding
> Importing and distributing foreign housewares

Advanced Molding faces heavy competition from many other similar companies, including firms that have outsourced production to China and Eastern Europe where labor costs are much lower. Further, most retailers expect a wide margin, sometimes 50 to 60 percent of the retail selling price. Even so, manufacturing costs are low enough that Advanced Molding can spend some money for promotion while still keeping the price competitive. Apparently, many customers are willing to pay for novel new products—if they see them in stores. And Anya isn't worried too much by tough competition. She sees plenty of that in her present job. And she does like the idea of being an "owner and sales manager."

Evaluate Advanced Molding's situation and Joseph O'Sullivan's strategy. What should Anya Winrow do? Why?

28. AAT Tools (AAT)

Pedro Gomez, president and marketing manager of AAT Tools, is deciding what strategy, or strategies, to pursue.

AAT Tools (AAT) is a manufacturer of industrial cutting tools. These tools include such items as lathe blades, drill press bits, and various other cutting edges used in the operation of large metal cutting, boring, or stamping machines. Pedro takes great pride in the fact that his company—whose $5.7 million sales in 2010 is small by industry standards—is recognized as a producer of a top-quality line of cutting tools.

Competition in the cutting-tool industry is intense. AAT competes not only with the original machine manufacturers, but also with many other larger domestic and foreign manufacturers offering cutting tools as one of their many different product lines. This has had the effect, over the years, of standardizing the price, specifications, and, in turn, the quality of the competing products of all manufacturers. It has also led to fairly low prices on standard items.

About a year ago, Pedro was tiring of the financial pressure of competing with larger companies enjoying economies of scale. At the same time, he noted that more and more potential cutting-tool customers were turning to small tool-and-die shops that used computer-controlled equipment to meet specialized needs that could not be met by the mass production firms. Pedro thought perhaps he should consider some basic strategy changes. Although he was unwilling to become strictly a custom producer, he thought that the recent trend toward buying customized cutting edges suggested new markets might be developing—markets too small for the large, multi-product line companies to serve profitably but large enough to earn a good profit for a flexible company of AAT's size.

Pedro hired a marketing research company, MResearchPro, to study the feasibility of serving these markets. The initial results were encouraging. It was estimated that AAT might increase sales by 65 percent and profits by 90 percent by serving the emerging markets. The research showed that there are many large users of standard cutting tools who buy directly from large cutting-tool manufacturers (domestic or foreign) or wholesalers who represent these manufacturers. This is the bulk of the cutting-tool business (in terms of units sold and sales dollars). But there are also many smaller users all over the United States who buy in small but regular quantities. And some of these needs are becoming more specialized. That is, a special cutting tool may make a machine and/or worker much more productive, perhaps eliminating several steps with time-consuming setups. This is the area that the research company sees as potentially attractive.

The next strategy change made by Pedro was to have the sales manager hire two technically oriented market researchers (at a total cost of $85,000 each per year, including travel expenses) to maintain continuous contact with potential cutting-tool customers. The researchers were supposed to identify any present or future needs that might exist in enough cases to make it possible to profitably produce a specialized product. The researchers were not to take orders or sell AAT's products to the potential customers. Pedro felt that only through this policy could these researchers talk to the right people.

The initial feedback from the market researchers was most encouraging. Many firms (large and small) had special needs—although it often was necessary to talk to the shop foreman or individual machine operators to find these needs. Most operators were making do with the tools available. Either they didn't know customizing was possible or doubted that their supervisors would do anything about it if they suggested that a more specialized tool could increase productivity. But these operators were encouraging because they said that it would be easier to persuade supervisors to order specialized tools if the tools were already produced and in stock than if they had to be custom made. So Pedro decided to continually add high-quality products to meet the ever-changing, specialized needs of users of cutting tools and edges.

AAT's potential customers for specialized tools are located all over the United States. The average sale per customer is likely to be less than $500, but the sale will be repeated several times within a year. Because of the widespread market and the small order size, Pedro doesn't think that selling direct—as is done by small custom shops—is practical. At the present time, AAT sells 90 percent of its regular output through a large industrial wholesaler—Superior Mill Supply—which serves the area east of the Mississippi River and carries a very complete line of industrial supplies (to "meet every industrial need"). Superior carries more than 10,000 items. Some sales come from customers who know exactly what they want and just place orders directly by fax or at the firm's website. But most of the selling is by Superior's sales reps, who work from an electronic catalog on a laptop computer. Superior, although very large and well known, is having trouble moving cutting tools. It's losing sales of cutting tools in some cities to newer wholesalers specializing in the cutting tool industry. The new wholesalers are able to give more technical help to potential customers and therefore better service. Superior's president is convinced that the newer, less-experienced concerns will either realize that a substantial profit margin can't be maintained along with their aggressive strategies, or they will eventually go broke trying to overspecialize.

From Pedro's standpoint, the present wholesaler has a good reputation and has served AAT well in the past. Superior has been of great help in holding down Pedro's inventory costs—by increasing the inventory in Superior's 35 branch locations. Although Pedro has received several complaints about the lack of technical assistance given by Superior's sales reps—as well as their lack of knowledge about AAT's new special products—he feels that the present wholesaler is providing the best service it can. All its sales reps have been told about the new products at a special training session, and new pages have been added to the electronic catalog on their laptops. So regarding the complaints, Pedro says, "The usual things you hear when you're in business."

Pedro thinks there are more urgent problems than a few complaints. Profits are declining, and sales of the new cutting tools are not nearly as high as forecast—even though all research reports indicate that the company's new products meet the intended markets' needs perfectly. The high costs involved in producing small quantities of special products and in adding the market research team—together with lower than expected sales—have significantly reduced AAT's profits. Pedro is wondering whether it is wise to continue to try to cater to the needs of many specific target markets when the results are this discouraging. He also is considering increasing advertising expenditures, including some search engine advertising, in the hope that customers will pull the new products through the channel.

Evaluate AAT's situation and Pedro Gomez's present strategy. What should he do now?

29. Quality Iron Castings, Inc.

Mallory Rizocki, marketing manager for Quality Iron Castings, Inc., is trying to figure out how to explain to her boss why a proposed new product line doesn't make sense for them. Mallory is sure it's wrong for Quality Iron Castings, but isn't able to explain why.

Quality Iron Castings, Inc., is a producer of malleable iron castings for automobile and aircraft manufacturers and a variety of other users of castings. Last year's sales of castings amounted to more than $70 million.

Quality Iron Castings also produces about 30 percent of all the original equipment bumper jacks installed in new U.S.-made automobiles each year. This is a very price-competitive business, but Quality Iron Castings has been able to obtain a large market share with frequent personal contact between the company's executives and its customers—supported by very close cooperation between the company's engineering department and its customers' buyers. This has been extremely important because the wide variety of models and model changes frequently requires alterations in the specifications of the bumper jacks. All of Quality Iron Castings' bumper jacks are sold directly to automobile manufacturers. No attempt has been made to sell bumper jacks to final consumers through hardware and automotive channels—although they are available through the manufacturers' automobile dealers.

Tim Kingston, Quality Iron Castings' production manager, now wants to begin producing hydraulic garage jacks for sale through auto-parts wholesalers to auto-parts retailers. Tim saw a variety of hydraulic garage jacks at a recent automotive show and knew immediately that his plant could produce these products. This especially interested him because of the possibility of using excess capacity. Further, he says "jacks are jacks," and the company would merely be broadening its product line by introducing hydraulic garage jacks. (Note: Hydraulic garage jacks are larger than bumper jacks and are intended for use in or around a garage. They are too big to carry in a car's trunk.)

As Tim became more enthusiastic about the idea, he found that Quality Iron Castings' engineering department already had a patented design that appeared to be at least comparable to the products now offered on the market. Further, Tim says that the company would be able to produce a product that is better made than the competitive products (i.e., smoother castings)—although he agrees that most customers probably wouldn't notice the difference. The production department estimates that the cost of producing a hydraulic garage jack comparable to those currently offered by competitors would be about $48 per unit.

Mallory has just received an e-mail from Jesse Zachary, the company president, explaining the production department's enthusiasm for broadening Quality Iron Castings' present jack line into hydraulic jacks. Jesse seems enthusiastic about the idea too, noting that it would be a way to make fuller use of the company's resources and increase its sales. Jesse's e-mail asks for Mallory's reaction, but Jesse already seems sold on the idea.

Given Jesse's enthusiasm, Mallory isn't sure how to respond. She's trying to develop a good explanation of why she isn't excited about the proposal. The firm's six sales reps are already overworked with their current accounts. And Mallory couldn't possibly promote this new line herself—she's already helping other reps make calls and serving as sales manager. So it would be necessary to hire someone to promote the line. And

this sales manager would probably have to recruit manufacturers' agents (who probably will want 10 to 15 percent commission on sales) to sell to automotive wholesalers who would stock the jack and sell to the auto-parts retailers. The wholesalers will probably expect trade discounts of about 20 percent, trade show exhibits, some national advertising, and sales promotion help (catalog sheets, mailers, and point-of-purchase displays). Further, Mallory sees that Quality Iron Castings' billing and collection system will have to be expanded because many more customers will be involved. It will also be necessary to keep track of agent commissions and accounts receivable.

Auto-parts retailers are currently selling similar hydraulic garage jacks for about $99. Mallory has learned that such retailers typically expect a trade discount of about 35 percent off of the suggested list price for their auto parts.

All things considered, Mallory feels that the proposed hydraulic jack line is not very closely related to the company's present emphasis. She has already indicated her lack of enthusiasm to Tim, but this made little difference in Tim's thinking. Now it's clear that Mallory will have to convince the president or she will soon be responsible for selling hydraulic jacks.

Contrast Quality Iron Castings, Inc.'s current strategy and the proposed strategy. What should Mallory Rizocki say to Jesse Zachary to persuade him to change his mind? Or should she just plan to sell hydraulic jacks? Explain.

30. Walker-Winkle Mills, Ltd.*

Valerie Boudreau, marketing manager of Walker-Winkle Mills, Ltd.—a Canadian company—is being urged to approve the creation of a separate marketing plan for Quebec. This would be a major policy change because Walker-Winkle Mills' international parent is trying to move toward a global strategy for the whole firm, and Boudreau has been supporting Canada-wide planning.

Boudreau has been the marketing manager of Walker-Winkle Mills, Ltd., for the last four years—since she arrived from international headquarters in Minneapolis. Walker-Winkle Mills, Ltd., headquartered in Toronto, is a subsidiary of a large U.S.-based consumer packaged food company with worldwide sales of more than $2.8 billion in 2007. Its Canadian sales are more than $450 million, with the Quebec and Ontario markets accounting for 69 percent of the company's Canadian sales.

The company's product line includes such items as cake mixes, puddings, pie fillings, pancakes, prepared foods, and frozen dinners. The company has successfully introduced at least six new products every year for the last five years. Products from Walker-Winkle Mills are known for their high quality and enjoy much brand preference throughout Canada, including the Province of Quebec.

The company's sales have risen every year since Boudreau took over as marketing manager. In fact, the company's market share has increased steadily in each of the product categories in which it competes. The Quebec market has closely followed

the national trend except that, in the past two years, total sales growth in that market began to lag.

According to Boudreau, a big advantage of Walker-Winkle Mills over its competitors is the ability to coordinate all phases of the food business from Toronto. For this reason, Boudreau meets at least once a month with her product managers—to discuss developments in local markets that might affect marketing plans. Although each manager is free to make suggestions and even to suggest major changes, Boudreau has the responsibility of giving final approval for all plans.

One of the product managers, Jackie Provence, expressed great concern at the last monthly meeting about the poor performance of some of the company's products in the Quebec market. Although a broad range of possible reasons—ranging from inflation and the threat of job losses to politics—were reviewed to try to explain the situation, Provence insisted that it was due to a basic lack of understanding of that market. She felt not enough managerial time and money had been spent on the Quebec market—in part because of the current emphasis on developing all-Canada plans on the way to having one global strategy.

Provence felt the current marketing approach to the Quebec market should be reevaluated because an inappropriate marketing plan may be responsible for the sales slowdown. After all, she said, "80 percent of the market is French-speaking. It's in the best interest of the company to treat that market as being separate and distinct from the rest of Canada."

Provence supported her position by showing that Quebec's per capita consumption of many product categories in which the firm competes is above the national average (see Table 1). Research projects conducted by Walker-Winkle Mills also

---
* This case was adapted from one written by Professor Roberta Tamilia, University of Windsor, Canada.

Table 1 Per Capita Consumption Index, Province of Quebec (Canada = 100)*

Cake mixes	107	Soft drinks	126
Pancakes	87	Pie fillings	118
Puddings	114	Frozen dinners	79
Salad dressings	85	Prepared packaged foods	83
Molasses	132	Cookies	123

*An index shows the relative consumption as compared to a standard. In this table, the standard is all of Canada. The data show that per capita consumption of cake mixes is 7% higher in Quebec and pancake consumption 13% lower compared to all of Canada.

support the "separate and distinct" argument. Over the years, the firm has found many French–English differences in brand attitudes, lifestyles, usage rates, and so on.

Provence argued that the company should develop a unique Quebec marketing plan for some or all of its brands. She specifically suggested that the French-language advertising plan for a particular brand be developed independently of the plan for English Canada.

Currently, the Toronto agency assigned to the brand just translates its English-language ads for the French market. Boudreau pointed out that the present advertising approach assured Walker-Winkle Mills of a uniform brand image across Canada. Provence said she knew what the agency is doing, and that straight translation into Canadian-French may not communicate the same brand image. The discussion that followed suggested that a different brand image might be needed in the French market if the company wanted to stop the brand's decline in sales.

The managers also discussed the food distribution system in Quebec. The major supermarket chains have their lowest market share in that province. Independents are strongest there—the mom-and-pop food stores fast disappearing outside Quebec remain alive and well in the province. Traditionally, these stores have stocked a higher proportion (than supermarkets) of their shelf space with national brands, an advantage for Walker-Winkle Mills.

Finally, various issues related to discount policies, pricing structure, sales promotion, and cooperative advertising were discussed. All of these suggested that things were different in Quebec and that future marketing plans should reflect these differences to a greater extent than they do now. After the meeting, Boudreau stayed in her office to think about the situation. Although she agreed with the basic idea that the Quebec market was in many ways different, she wasn't sure how far the company should go in recognizing this fact. She knew that regional differences in food tastes and brand purchases existed not only in Quebec but in other parts of Canada as well. But people are people, after all, with far more similarities than differences, so a Canadian and, eventually, a global strategy makes some sense too.

Boudreau was afraid that giving special status to one region might conflict with top management's objective of achieving standardization whenever possible—one national strategy for Canada, on the way to one worldwide global strategy. She was also worried about the long-term effect of such a policy change on costs, organizational structure, and brand image. Still, enough product managers had expressed their concern over the years about the Quebec market to make her wonder if she shouldn't modify the current approach. Perhaps they could experiment with a few brands—and just in Quebec. She could cite the language difference as the reason for trying Quebec rather than any of the other provinces. But Boudreau realizes that any change of policy could be seen as the beginning of more change, and what would Minneapolis think? Could she explain it successfully there?

Evaluate Walker-Winkle Mills, Ltd.'s present strategy. What should Valerie Boudreau do now? Explain.

31. Bowman Home Health Services (BHHS)

Chelsea Bowman, executive director of Bowman Home Health Services, is trying to clarify her strategies. She's sure some changes are needed, but she's less sure about how *much* change is needed and/or whether it can be handled by her people.

Bowman Home Health Services (BHHS) is a nonprofit organization that has been operating—with varying degrees of success—for 25 years, offering nursing services in clients' homes. Some of its funding comes from the local United Way—to provide emergency nursing services for those who can't afford to pay. The balance of the revenues—about 90 percent of the $2.2 million annual budget—comes from charges made directly to the client or to third-party payers, including insurance companies, health maintenance organizations (HMOs), and the federal government, for Medicare or Medicaid services.

Chelsea has been executive director of BHHS for two years. She has developed a well-functioning organization able to meet most requests for service that come from local doctors and from the discharge officers at local hospitals. Some business also comes by self-referral—the client finds the BHHS name in the yellow pages of the local phone directory.

The last two years have been a rebuilding time—because the previous director had personnel problems. This led to a weakening of the agency's image with the local referring agencies. Now their image is more positive. But Chelsea is not completely satisfied with the situation. By definition, Bowman Home Health Services is a nonprofit organization. Yet it still must cover all its costs: payroll, rent payments, phone expenses, and so on, including Chelsea's own salary. She can see that although BHHS is growing slightly and is now breaking even, it doesn't have much of a cash cushion to fall back on if (1) the demand for BHHS nursing services declines, (2) the government changes its rules about paying for BHHS's kind of nursing services, either cutting back what it will pay for or reducing the amount it will pay for specific services, or (3) new competitors enter the market. In fact, the last possibility concerns Chelsea greatly. Some hospitals, squeezed for revenue, are expanding into home health care—especially nursing services—as patients are being released earlier from hospitals because of payment limits set by government guidelines. For-profit organizations (e.g., Kelly Home Care Services) are expanding around the country to provide a complete line of home health care services, including nursing services of the kind offered by BHHS. These for-profit organizations appear to be efficiently run, offering good service at competitive and sometimes even lower prices than some nonprofit organizations. And they seem to be doing this at a profit, which suggests that it would be possible for these for-profit companies to lower their prices if nonprofit organizations try to compete on price.

Chelsea is considering whether she should ask her board of directors to let her offer a complete line of home health care services—that is, move beyond just nursing services into what she calls "care and comfort" services.

Currently, BHHS is primarily concerned with providing professional nursing care in the home. But BHHS nurses are much too expensive for routine home health care activities—helping fix meals, bathing and dressing patients, and other care and comfort activities. The full cost of a nurse to BHHS, including benefits and overhead, is about $65 per hour. But a registered nurse is not needed for care and comfort services. All that is required is someone who is honest, can get along with all kinds of people, and is willing to do this kind of work. Generally, any mature person can be trained fairly quickly to do the job—following the instructions and under the general supervision of a physician, a nurse, or family members. The full cost of aides is $9 to $16 per hour for short visits and as low as $75 per 24 hours for a live-in aide who has room and board supplied by the client.

The demand for all kinds of home health care services seems to be growing. With more dual-career families and more single-parent households, there isn't anyone in the family to take over home health care when the need arises—due to emergencies or long-term disabilities. Further, hospitals send patients home earlier than in the past. And with people living longer, there are more single-survivor family situations where there is no one nearby to take care of the needs of these older people. But often some family members—or third-party payers such as the government or insurers—are willing to pay for some home health care services. Chelsea now occasionally recommends other agencies or suggests one or another of three women who have been doing care and comfort work on their own, part-time. But with growing demand, Chelsea wonders if BHHS should get into this business, hiring aides as needed.

Chelsea is concerned that a new, full-service home health care organization may come into her market and be a single source for both nursing services *and* less-skilled home care and comfort services. This has happened already in two nearby but somewhat larger cities. Chelsea fears that this might be more appealing than BHHS to the local hospitals and other referrers. In other words, she can see the possibility of losing nursing service business if BHHS does not begin to offer a complete home health care service. This would cause real problems for BHHS—because overhead costs are more or less fixed. A loss in revenue of as little as 10 percent would require some cutbacks—perhaps laying off some nurses or secretaries, giving up part of the office, and so on.

Another reason for expanding beyond nursing services—using paraprofessionals and relatively unskilled personnel—is to offer a better service to present customers *and* make more effective use of the computer systems and organization structure that she has developed over the last two years. Chelsea estimates that the administrative and office capabilities could handle twice as many clients without straining the system. It would be necessary to add some clerical help if the expansion were quite large. But this increase in overhead would be minor compared to the present proportion of total revenue that goes to covering overhead. In other words, additional clients or more work for some current clients could increase revenue and ensure the survival of BHHS, provide a cushion to cover the normal fluctuations in demand, and ensure more job security for the administrative personnel.

Further, Chelsea thinks that if BHHS were successful in expanding its services—and therefore could generate some surplus—it could extend services to those who aren't now able to pay. Chelsea says one of the worst parts of her job is refusing service to clients whose third-party benefits have run out or for whatever reason can no longer afford to pay. She is uncomfortable about having to cut off service, but she must schedule her nurses to provide revenue-producing services if she's going to meet the payroll every two weeks. By expanding to provide more services, she might be able to keep serving more of these nonpaying clients. This possibility excites Chelsea because her nurse's training has instilled a deep desire to serve people in need, whether they can pay or not. This continual pressure to cut off service because people can't pay has been at the root of many disagreements and even arguments between the nurses serving the clients and Chelsea, as executive director and representative of the board of directors.

Chelsea knows that expanding into care and comfort services won't be easy. Some decisions would be needed about relative pay levels for nurses, paraprofessionals, and aides. BHHS would also have to set prices for these different services and tell current customers and referral agencies about the expanded services.

These problems aren't bothering Chelsea too much, however—she thinks she can handle them. She is sure that care and comfort services are in demand and could be supplied at competitive prices.

Her primary concern is whether this is the right thing for Bowman Home Health Services—basically a nursing organization—to do. BHHS's whole history has been oriented to supplying *nurses' services*. Nurses are dedicated professionals who bring high standards to any job they undertake. The question is whether BHHS should offer less-professional services. Inevitably, some of the aides will not be as dedicated as the nurses might like them to be. And this could reflect unfavorably on the nurse image. At a minimum, she would need to set up some sort of training program for the aides. As Chelsea worries about the future of BHHS, and her own future, it seems that there are no easy answers.

Evaluate BHHS's present strategy. What should Chelsea Bowman do? Explain.

32. Lever, Ltd.*

Sung Wu is product manager for Guard Deodorant Soap. He was just transferred to Lever, Ltd., a Canadian subsidiary of Lever Group, Inc., from world headquarters in New York. Sung is anxious to make a good impression because he is hoping to transfer to Lever's London office. He is working on developing and securing management approval of next year's marketing plan for Guard. His first job is submitting a draft marketing plan to Sierra King, his recently appointed group product manager, who is responsible for several such plans from product managers like Sung.

Sung's marketing plan is the single most important document he will produce on this assignment. This annual marketing plan does three main things:

1. It reviews the brand's performance in the past year, assesses the competitive situation, and highlights problems and opportunities for the brand.
2. It spells out marketing strategies and the plan for the coming year.
3. Finally, and most importantly, the marketing plan sets out the brand's sales objectives and advertising/promotion budget requirements.

In preparing this marketing plan, Sung gathered the information in Table 1.

*Adapted from a case prepared by Daniel Aronchick, who at the time of its preparation was marketing manager at Thomas J. Lipton, Limited.

Sung was somewhat surprised at the significant regional differences in the bar soap market:

1. The underdevelopment of the deodorant bar segment in Quebec, with a corresponding overdevelopment of the beauty bar segment. But some past research suggested that this is due to cultural factors—English-speaking people have been more interested than others in cleaning, deodorizing, and disinfecting. A similar pattern is seen in most European countries, where the adoption of deodorant soaps has been slower than in North America. For similar reasons, the perfumed soap share is highest in French-speaking Quebec.
2. The overdevelopment of synthetic bars (Zest, Dial) in the Prairies (Manitoba/Saskatchewan and Alberta). These bars, primarily in the deodorant segment, lather better in the hard water of the Prairies. Nonsynthetic bars lather very poorly in hard-water areas and leave a soap film.
3. The overdevelopment of the "all-other" segment in Quebec. This segment, consisting of smaller brands, fares better in Quebec, where 43 percent of the grocery trade is done by independent stores. Conversely, large chain grocery stores dominate in Ontario and the Prairies.

Sung's brand, Guard, is a highly perfumed deodorant bar. His business is relatively weak in the key Ontario market. To confirm this share data, Sung calculated consumption of Guard per thousand people in each region (see Table 2).

Table 1 Past 12-Month Share of Bar Soap Market (percent)

	Maritimes	Quebec	Ontario	Manitoba/Saskatchewan	Alberta	British Columbia
Deodorant segment						
Zest	21.3%	14.2%	24.5%	31.2%	30.4%	25.5%
Dial	10.4	5.1	12.8	16.1	17.2	14.3
Lifebuoy	4.2	3.1	1.2	6.4	5.8	4.2
Guard	2.1	5.6	1.0	4.2	4.2	2.1
Beauty bar segment						
Camay	6.2	12.3	7.0	4.1	4.0	5.1
Lux	6.1	11.2	7.7	5.0	6.9	5.0
Dove	5.5	8.0	6.6	6.3	6.2	4.2
Lower-priced bars						
Ivory	11.2	6.5	12.4	5.3	5.2	9.0
Sunlight	6.1	3.2	8.2	4.2	4.1	8.0
All others (including stores' own brands)	26.9	30.8	18.6	17.2	16.0	22.6
Total bar soap market	100.0%	100.0%	100.0%	100.0%	100.0%	100.0%

Table 2 Standard Cases of 3-Ounce Bars Consumed per 1,000 People in 12 Months

	Maritimes	Quebec	Ontario	Manitoba/ Saskatchewan	Alberta	British Columbia
Guard	4.1	10.9	1.9	8.1	4.1	6.2
Sales index	66	175	31	131	131	100

These differences are especially interesting since per capita sales of all bar soap products are roughly equal in all provinces.

A consumer attitude and usage research study was conducted approximately a year ago. This study revealed that consumer "top-of-mind" awareness of the Guard brand differed greatly across Canada. This was true despite the even—by population—expenditure of advertising funds in past years. Also, trial of Guard was low in the Maritimes, Ontario, and British Columbia (see Table 3).

The attitude portion of the research revealed that consumers who had heard of Guard were aware that its deodorant protection came mainly from a high fragrance level. This was the main selling point in the copy, and it was well communicated by Guard's advertising. The other important finding was that consumers who had tried Guard were satisfied with the product. About 70 percent of those trying Guard had repurchased the product at least twice.

Sung has also discovered that bar soap competition is especially intense in Ontario. It is Canada's largest market, and many competitors want a share of it. The chain stores are also quite aggressive in promotion and pricing—offering specials, in-store coupons, and so on. They want to move goods. And because of this, two key Ontario chains have put Guard on their pending delisting sheets. These chains, which control about half the grocery volume in Ontario, are dissatisfied with how slowly Guard is moving off the shelves.

Now Sung feels he is ready to set a key part of the brand's marketing plan for next year: how to allocate the advertising/sales promotion budget by region.

Guard's present advertising/sales promotion budget is 20 percent of sales. With forecast sales of $4 million, this would amount to an $800,000 expenditure. Traditionally such funds have been allocated in proportion to population (see Table 4).

Sung feels he should spend more heavily in Ontario where the grocery chain delisting problem exists. Last year, 36 percent of Guard's budget was allocated to Ontario, which accounted for only 12 percent of Guard's sales. Sung wants to increase Ontario spending to 48 percent of the total budget by taking funds evenly from all other areas. Sung expects this will increase business in the key Ontario market, which has more than a third of Canada's population, because it is a big increase and will help Guard "outshout" the many other competitors who are promoting heavily.

Sung presented this idea to King, his newly appointed group product manager. King strongly disagrees. She has also been reviewing Guard's business and feels that promotion funds have historically been misallocated. It is her strong belief that, to use her words, "A brand should spend where its business is." King believes that the first priority in allocating funds regionally is to support the areas of strength. She suggested to Sung that there may be more business to be had in the brand's strong areas, Quebec and the Prairies, than in chasing sales in Ontario. The needs and attitudes toward Guard, as well as competitive pressures, may vary a lot among the provinces. Therefore, King suggested that spending for Guard in the coming year be proportional to the brand's sales by region rather than to regional population.

Sung is convinced this is wrong, particularly in light of the Ontario situation. He asked King how the Ontario market should be handled. She said that the conservative way to build business in Ontario is to invest incremental promotion funds. However, before these incremental funds are invested, a test of this Ontario investment proposition should be conducted. King recommended that some of the Ontario money should be used to conduct an investment-spending market test in a small area or town in Ontario for 12 months. This will enable Sung to see if the incremental spending results in higher sales and profits—profits large enough to justify higher spending. In other words, an investment payout should be assured before spending any extra money in Ontario. Similarly, King would do the same kind of test in Quebec—to see if more money should go there.

After several e-mails back and forth, Sung feels this approach would be a waste of time and unduly cautious, given the importance of the Ontario market and the likely delistings in two key chains.

Evaluate the present strategy for Guard and Sung's and King's proposed strategies. How should the promotion money be allocated? Should investment-spending market tests be run first? Why? Explain.

Table 3 Usage Results (in percent)

	Maritimes	Quebec	Ontario	Manitoba/ Saskatchewan	Alberta	British Columbia
Respondents aware of Guard	20%	58%	28%	30%	32%	16%
Respondents ever trying Guard	3	18	2	8	6	4

Table 4 Allocation of Advertising/Sales Promotion Budget, by Population

	Maritimes	Quebec	Ontario	Manitoba/ Saskatchewan	Alberta	British Columbia	Canada
Percent of population	10%	27%	36%	8%	8%	11%	100%
Possible allocation of budget based on population (in 000s)	$80	$216	$288	$64	$64	$88	$800
Percent of Guard business at present	7%	51%	12%	11%	11%	8%	100%

33. Kennedy & Gaffney (K&G)

The partners of Kennedy & Gaffney are having a serious discussion about what the firm should do in the near future.

Kennedy & Gaffney (K&G) is a medium-size regional certified public accounting firm based in Grand Rapids, Michigan, with branch offices in Lansing and Detroit. Kennedy & Gaffney has nine partners and a professional staff of approximately 105 accountants. Gross service billings for the fiscal year ending June 30, 2010, were $6.9 million. See Table 1, which presents financial data for 2010, 2009, and 2008.

K&G's professional services include auditing, tax preparation, bookkeeping, and some general management consulting. Its client base includes municipal governments (cities, villages, and townships), manufacturing companies, professional organizations (attorneys, doctors, and dentists), and various other small businesses. A good share of revenue comes from the firm's municipal practice. Table 1 details K&G's gross revenue by service area and client industry for 2010, 2009, and 2008.

At the monthly partners' meeting held in July 2010, Robert Kennedy, the firm's managing partner (CEO), expressed concern about the future of the firm's municipal practice. Robert's presentation to his partners follows:

Although our firm is considered to be a leader in municipal auditing in our geographic area, I am concerned that as

municipals attempt to cut their operating costs, they will solicit competitive bids from other public accounting firms to perform their annual audits. Three of the four largest accounting firms in the world have local offices in our area. Because they concentrate their practice in the manufacturing industry—which typically has December 31 fiscal year-ends—they have "available" staff during the summer months.

Therefore, they can afford to low-ball competitive bids to keep their staffs busy and benefit from on-the-job training provided by municipal clientele. I am concerned that we may begin to lose clients in our most established and profitable practice area.*

Sherry Gaffney, a senior partner in the firm and the partner in charge of the firm's municipal practice, was the first to respond to Robert's concern.

Robert, we all recognize the potential threat of being underbid for our municipal work by our large accounting competitors. However, K&G is a leader in municipal auditing in Michigan, and we have much more local experience than our

---

*Organizations with December fiscal year-ends require audit work to be performed during the fall and in January and February. Those with June 30 fiscal year-ends require auditing during the summer months.

Table 1 Fiscal Year Ending June 30

	2010	2009	2008
Gross billings	$6,900,000	$6,400,000	$5,800,000
Gross billings by service area:			
Auditing	3,100,000	3,200,000	2,750,000
Tax preparation	1,990,000	1,830,000	1,780,000
Bookkeeping	1,090,000	745,000	660,000
Other	720,000	625,000	610,000
Gross billings by client industry:			
Municipal	3,214,000	3,300,000	2,908,000
Manufacturing	2,089,000	1,880,000	1,706,000
Professional	1,355,000	1,140,000	1,108,000
Other	242,000	80,000	78,000

competitors. Furthermore, it is a fact that we offer a superior level of service to our clients—which goes beyond the services normally expected during an audit to include consulting on financial and other operating issues. Many of our less sophisticated clients depend on our nonaudit consulting assistance. Therefore, I believe, we have been successful in differentiating our services from our competitors. In many recent situations, K&G was selected over a field of as many as 10 competitors even though our proposed prices were much higher than those of our competitors.

The partners at the meeting agreed with Sherry's comments. Yet even though K&G had many success stories regarding their ability to retain their municipal clients—despite being underbid—they had lost three large municipal clients during the past year. Sherry was asked to comment on the loss of those clients. She explained that the lost clients are larger municipalities with a lot of in-house financial expertise and therefore less dependent on K&G's consulting assistance. As a result, K&G's service differentiation went largely unnoticed. Sherry explained that the larger, more sophisticated municipals regard audits as a necessary evil and usually select the low-cost reputable bidder.

Robert then requested ideas and discussion from the other partners at the meeting. One partner, Rosa Basilio, suggested that K&G should protect itself by diversifying. Specifically, she felt a substantial practice development effort should be directed toward manufacturing. She reasoned that because manufacturing work would occur during K&G's off-season, K&G could afford to price very low to gain new manufacturing clients. This strategy would also help to counter (and possibly discourage) low-ball pricing for municipals by the three large accounting firms mentioned earlier.

Another partner, Wade Huntoon, suggested that "if we have consulting skills, we ought to promote them more, instead of hoping that the clients will notice and come to appreciate us. Further, maybe we ought to be more aggressive in calling on smaller potential clients."

Another partner, Stan Walsh, agreed with Wade, but wanted to go further. He suggested that they recognize that there are at least two types of municipal customers and that two (at least) different strategies be implemented, including lower prices for auditing only for larger municipal customers and/or higher prices for smaller customers who are buying consulting too. This caused a big uproar from some who said this would lead to price cutting of professional services, and K&G didn't want to be price cutters: "One price for all is the professional way."

However, another partner, Isabel Ventura, agreed with Stan and suggested they go even further—pricing consulting services separately. In fact, she suggested that the partners consider setting up a separate department for consulting—like the large accounting firms have done: "This can be a very profitable business. But it is a different kind of business and eventually may require different kinds of people and a different organization. For now, however, it may be desirable to appoint a manager for consulting services—with a budget—to be sure it gets proper attention." This suggestion too caused serious disagreement. Partners pointed out that having a separate consulting arm had led to major conflicts, especially in some larger accounting firms. The initial problems were internal. The consultants often brought in more profit than the auditors, but the auditors controlled the partnership, and the successful consultants didn't always feel that they got their share of the rewards. There had also been serious external problems and charges of unethical behavior based on the concern that big accounting firms had a conflict of interest when they did audits on publicly traded companies that they in turn relied on for consulting income. Because of problems in this area, the Securities and Exchange Commission created new guidelines that have changed how the big four accounting firms handle consulting. On the other hand, several partners argued that this was really an opportunity for K&G because their firm handled very few companies listed with the SEC, and the conflict of interest issues didn't even apply with municipal clients.

Robert thanked everyone for their comments and encouraged them to debate these issues in smaller groups and to share ideas by e-mail before coming to a one-day retreat (in two weeks) to continue this discussion and come to some conclusions.

Evaluate K&G's situation. What strategy(ies) should the partners select? Why?

34. Chess Aluminum Worldwide (CAW)*

Mickey Zhang, newly hired VP of marketing for Chess Aluminum Worldwide (CAW), is reviewing the firm's international distribution arrangements because they don't seem to be very well thought out. He is not sure if anything is wrong, but he feels that the company should follow a global strategy rather than continuing its current policies.

CAW is based in Atlanta, Georgia, and produces finished aluminum products, such as aluminum ladders, umbrella-type clothes racks, scaffolding, and patio tables and chairs that fold flat. Sales in 2014 reached $25 million, primarily to U.S. customers.

In 2010, CAW decided to try selling in select foreign markets. The sales manager, Jacqueline Windsor, believed the growing affluence of European workers would help the company's products gain market acceptance quickly.

Jacqueline's first step in investigating foreign markets was to join a trade mission to Europe, a tour organized by the U.S. Department of Commerce. This trade mission visited Italy, Germany, Denmark, Holland, France, and England. During this trip, Jacqueline was officially introduced to leading buyers for department store chains, import houses, wholesalers, and buying groups. The two-week trip convinced Jacqueline that there was ample buying power to make exporting a profitable opportunity.

On her return to Atlanta, Jacqueline's next step was to obtain credit references for the firms she considered potential distributors. To those who were judged creditworthy, she sent letters expressing interest and samples, brochures, prices, and other relevant information.

*Adapted from a case written by Professor Hardy, University of Western Ontario, Canada.

The first orders were from a French wholesaler. Sales in this market totaled $70,000 in 2011. Similar success was achieved in Germany and England. Italy, on the other hand, did not produce any sales. Jacqueline felt the semi-luxury nature of the company's products and the lower incomes in Italy encouraged a "making do" attitude rather than purchase of goods and services that would make life easier.

In the United States, CAW distributes through fairly aggressive and well-organized merchant hardware distributors and buying groups, such as cooperative and voluntary hardware chains, which have taken over much of the strategy planning for cooperating producers and retailers. In its foreign markets, however, there is no recognizable pattern. Channel systems vary from country to country. To avoid channel conflict, CAW has only one account in each country. The chosen distributor is the exclusive distributor.

In France, CAW distributes through a wholesaler based in Paris. This wholesaler has five salespeople covering the country. The firm specializes in small housewares and has contacts with leading buying groups, wholesalers, and department stores. Jacqueline is impressed with the firm's aggressiveness and knowledge of merchandising techniques.

In Germany, CAW sells to a Hamburg-based buying group for hardware wholesalers throughout the country. Jacqueline felt this group would provide excellent coverage of the market because of its extensive distribution network.

In Denmark, CAW's line is sold to a buying group representing a chain of hardware retailers. This group recently expanded to include retailers in Sweden, Finland, and Norway. Together this group purchases goods for about 500 hardware retailers. The buying power of Scandinavians is quite high, and it is expected that CAW's products will prove very successful there.

In the United Kingdom, CAW uses an importer-distributor, who both buys on his own account and acts as a sales agent. The distributor approached CAW after finding the company from an online search. This firm sells to department stores and hardware wholesalers. This firm has not done very well overall, but it has done very well with CAW's line of patio tables and chairs.

Australia is handled by an importer that operates a chain of discount houses. It heard about CAW from a UK contact. After extensive e-mailing, this firm discovered it could land aluminum patio furniture in Melbourne at prices competitive with Chinese imports. So it started ordering because it wanted to cut prices in a high-priced garden furniture market.

The Argentina market is handled by an American who lives in Buenos Aires but came to the United States in search of new lines. CAW attributes success in Argentina to the efforts of this aggressive and capable agent. He has built a sizable trade in aluminum ladders.

In Trinidad and Jamaica, CAW's products are handled by traders who carry such diversified lines as insurance, apples, plums, and fish. They have been successful in selling aluminum ladders. This business grew out of inquiries sent to the U.S. Department of Commerce and in researching its website (www.commerce.gov), which Jacqueline followed up by phone.

Jacqueline's export policies for CAW are as follows:

1. *Product:* No product modifications will be made in selling to foreign customers. This may be considered later after a substantial sales volume develops.

2. *Place:* New distributors will be contacted through foreign trade shows. Jacqueline considers large distributors desirable. She feels, however, that they are not as receptive as smaller distributors to a new, unestablished product line. Therefore, she prefers to appoint small distributors. Larger distributors may be appointed after the company has gained a strong consumer franchise in a country.

3. *Promotion:* The firm does no advertising in foreign markets. Brochures and sales literature already being used in the United States are supplied to foreign distributors, who are encouraged to adapt them or create new materials as required. CAW will continue to promote its products by participating in overseas trade shows. These are handled by the sales manager. All inquiries are forwarded to the firm's distributor in that country.

4. *Price:* The company does not publish suggested list prices. Distributors add their own markup to their landed costs. Supply prices will be kept as low as possible. This is accomplished by (a) removing advertising expenses and other strictly domestic overhead charges from price calculations, (b) finding the most economical packages for shipping (smallest volume per unit), and (c) bargaining with carriers to obtain the lowest shipping rates possible.

5. *Financing:* CAW sees no need to provide financial help to distributors. The company views its major contribution as providing good products at the lowest possible prices.

6. *Marketing and planning assistance:* Jacqueline feels that foreign distributors know their own markets best. Therefore, they are best equipped to plan for themselves.

7. *Selection of foreign markets:* The evaluation of foreign market opportunities for the company's products is based primarily on disposable income and lifestyle patterns. For example, Jacqueline fails to see any market in North Africa for CAW's products, which she thinks are of a semi-luxury nature. She thinks that cheaper products such as wood ladders (often homemade) are preferred to prefabricated aluminum ladders in regions such as North Africa and Southern Europe. Argentina, on the other hand, she thinks is a more highly industrialized market with luxury tastes. Thus, Jacqueline sees CAW's products as better suited for more highly industrialized and affluent societies.

Evaluate CAW's present foreign markets strategies. Should it develop a global strategy? What strategy or strategies should Mickey Zhang (the new VP of marketing) develop? Explain.

35. Skipper's Pizza Pies

Cassidy Newman, manager of the Skipper's Pizza Pies store in Flint, Michigan, is trying to develop a plan for the "sick" store she just took over.

Skipper's Pizza Pies is an owner-managed pizza take-out and delivery business with three stores located in Ann Arbor, Southfield, and Flint, Michigan. Skipper's business comes from telephone, fax, or walk-in orders. Each Skipper's store prepares its own pizzas. In addition to pizzas, Skipper's also sells and delivers a limited selection of soft drinks.

Skipper's Ann Arbor store has been very successful. Much of the store's success may be due to being close to the University of Michigan campus. Most of these students live within 5 miles of Skipper's Ann Arbor store.

The Southfield store has been moderately successful. It serves mostly residential customers in the Southfield area, a largely residential suburb of Detroit. Recently, the store advertised—using direct-mail flyers—to several office buildings within 3 miles of the store. The flyers described Skipper's willingness and ability to cater large orders for office parties, business luncheons, and so on. The promotion was quite successful. With this new program and Skipper's solid residential base of customers in Southfield, improved profitability at the Southfield location seems assured.

Skipper's Flint location has had mixed results during the last three years. The Flint store has been obtaining only about half of its orders from residential delivery requests. Cassidy, the Flint store's new manager, believes the problem with residential pizza delivery in Flint is due to the location of residential neighborhoods in the area. Flint has several large industrial plants (mostly auto industry related) located throughout the city. Small, mostly factory-worker neighborhoods are distributed in between the various plant sites. As a result, Skipper's store location can serve only two or three of these neighborhoods on one delivery run. Competition is also relevant. Skipper's has several aggressive competitors who advertise heavily, distribute cents-off coupons, and offer 2-for-1 deals. This aggressive competition is probably why Skipper's residential sales leveled off in the last year or so. And this competitive pressure seems likely to continue as some of this competition comes from aggressive national chains that are fighting for market share and squeezing little firms like Skipper's. For now, anyway, Cassidy feels she knows how to meet this competition and hold on to the present residential sales level.

Most of the Flint store's upside potential seems to be in serving the large industrial plants. Many of these plants work two or three shifts, five days a week. During each work shift, workers are allowed one half-hour lunch break—which usually occurs at 11 a.m., 8 p.m., or 2:30 a.m., depending on the shift.

Customers can order by phone, fax, e-mail, or at the Skipper's website. About 30 minutes before a scheduled lunch break Skipper's can expect an order for several (5 to 10) pizzas for a work group. Skipper's may receive many orders of this size from the same plant (i.e., from different groups of workers). The plant business is very profitable for several reasons. First, a large number of pizzas can be delivered at the same time to the same location, saving transportation costs.

Second, plant orders usually involve many different toppings (double cheese, pepperoni, mushrooms, hamburger) on each pizza. This results in $11 to $14 revenue per pizza. The delivery drivers also like delivering plant orders because the tips are usually $1 to $2 per pizza.

Despite the profitability of the plant orders, several factors make it difficult to serve the plant market. Skipper's store is located 5 to 8 minutes from most of the plant sites, so Skipper's staff must prepare the orders within 20 to 25 minutes after it receives the telephone order. Often, inadequate staff and/or oven capacity means it is impossible to get all the orders heated at the same time.

Generally, plant workers will wait as long as 10 minutes past the start of their lunch break before ordering from various vending trucks that arrive at the plant sites during lunch breaks. (Currently, no other pizza delivery stores are in good positions to serve the plant locations and have chosen not to compete.) But there have been a few instances when workers refused to pay for pizzas that were only five minutes late! Worse yet, if the same work group gets a couple of late orders, they are lost as future customers. Cassidy believes that the inconsistent profitability of the Flint store is partly the result of such lost customers.

Table 1 Practical Capacities and Sales Potential of Current Equipment and Personnel

	11 A.M. Break	8 P.M. Break	2:30 A.M. Break	Daily Totals
Current capacity (pizzas)	48	48	48	144
Average selling price per unit	$ 12.50	$ 12.50	$ 12.50	$ 12.50
Sales potential	$600	$600	$600	$1,800
Variable cost (approximately 40 percent of selling price)*	240	240	240	720
Contribution margin of pizzas	360	360	360	1,080
Beverage sales (2 medium-sized beverages per pizza ordered at 75¢ a piece)'	72	72	72	216
Cost of beverages (30 percent per beverage)	22	22	22	66
Contribution margin of beverages	50	50	50	150
Total contribution of pizza and beverages	$ 410	$ 410	$ 410	$1,230

*The variable cost estimate of 40 percent of sales includes variable costs of delivery to plant locations.

'Amounts shown are not physical capacities (there is almost unlimited physical capacity), but potential sales volume is constrained by number of pizzas that can be sold.

Table 2 Capacity and Demand for Plant Customer Market

	Estimated Daily Demand	Current Daily Capacity	Proposed Daily Capacity
Pizza units (1 pizza)	320	144	300

In an effort to rebuild the plant delivery business, Cassidy is considering various methods to ensure prompt customer delivery. She thinks that potential demand during lunch breaks is significantly above Skipper's present capacity. Cassidy also knows that if she tries to satisfy all phone or fax orders on some peak days, she won't be able to provide prompt service and may lose more plant customers.

Cassidy has outlined three alternatives that may win back some of the plant business for the Flint store. She has developed these alternatives to discuss with Skipper's owner. Each alternative is briefly described below:

Alternative 1: Determine practical capacities during peak volume periods using existing equipment and personnel. Accept orders only up to that capacity and politely decline orders beyond. This approach will ensure prompt customer service and high product quality. It will also minimize losses resulting from customers' rejection of late deliveries. Financial analysis of this alternative—shown in Table 1—indicates that a potential daily contribution to profit of $1,230 could result if this alternative is implemented successfully. This would be profit before promotion costs, overhead, and net profit (or loss). *Note:* Any alternative will require several thousand dollars to reinform potential plant customers that Skipper's has improved its service and "wants your business."

Alternative 2: Buy additional equipment (one oven and one delivery car) and hire additional staff to handle peak loads. This approach would ensure timely customer delivery and high product quality as well as provide additional capacity to handle unmet demand. Table 2 is a conservative estimate of potential daily demand for plant orders compared to current capacity and proposed increased capacity. Table 3 gives the cost of acquiring the additional equipment and relevant information related to depreciation and fixed costs.

Using this alternative, the following additional pizza delivery and preparation personnel costs would be required:

	Hours Required	Cost per Hour	Total Additional Daily Cost
Delivery personnel	6	6	$36.00
Preparation personnel	8	6	48.00
			$84.00

The addition of even more equipment and personnel to handle all unmet demand was not considered in this alternative because the current store is not large enough.

Alternative 3: Add additional equipment and personnel as described in alternative 2, but move to a new location that would reduce delivery lead times to 2 to 5 minutes. This move would probably allow Skipper's to handle all unmet demand—because the reduction in delivery time will provide for additional oven time. In fact, Skipper's might have excess capacity using this approach.

A suitable store is available near about the same number of residential customers (including many of the store's current residential customers). The available store is slightly larger than needed. And the rent is higher. Relevant cost information on the proposed store follows:

Additional rental expense of proposed store over current store	$1,600 per year
Cost of moving to new store (one-time cost)	$16,000

Cassidy presented the three alternatives to Skipper's owner, Skipper Kipnis. Skipper was pleased that Cassidy had done her homework. He decided that Cassidy should make the final decision on what to do (in part because she had a profit-sharing agreement with Skipper) and offered the following comments and concerns:

1. Skipper agreed that the plant market was extremely sensitive to delivery timing. Product quality and pricing, although important, were of less importance.

Table 3 Cost of Required Additional Assets

	Cost	Estimated Useful Life	Salvage Value	Annual Depreciation*	Daily Depreciation[†]
Delivery car (equipped with pizza warmer)	$11,000	5 years	$1,000	$2,000	$5.71
Pizza oven	$20,000	8 years	$2,000	$2,250	$6.43

*Annual depreciation is calculated on a straight-line basis.

[†]Daily depreciation assumes a 350-day (plant production) year. All variable expenses related to each piece of equipment (e.g., utilities, gas, oil) are included in the variable cost of a pizza.

2. He agreed that plant demand estimates were conservative. "In fact, they may be 10 to 30 percent low."

3. Skipper expressed concern that under alternative 2, and especially under alternative 3, much of the store's capacity would go unused more than 80 percent of the time.

4. He was also concerned that Skipper's store had a bad reputation with plant customers because the prior store manager was not sensitive to timely plant delivery. So Skipper suggested that Cassidy develop a promotion plan to improve Skipper's reputation in the plants and be sure that everyone knows that Skipper's has improved its delivery service.

Evaluate Cassidy's possible strategies for the Flint store's plant market. What should Cassidy do? Why? Suggest possible promotion plans for your preferred strategy.

36. Silverglade Homes*

Brian Silverglade, who seven years ago founded Silverglade Homes in Asheville, North Carolina, is excited that he'll complete his first LEED-certified "green" home this month. The LEED (Leadership in Energy and Environmental Design) rating means that the home uses 30 percent less energy and 20 percent less water than a conventional house; it also means that construction waste going into landfills must also be reduced. The house will be the model home to showcase Brian's new development, which includes four more homes that he hopes to complete in the next six months.

Although Brian is excited, he is also nervous. Rising interest rates and an uncertain economy have reduced demand in the local housing market. People who do buy homes are more price-sensitive. That's a problem because building a green house usually increases construction costs—but customers are not always aware of the benefits that come with the higher price tag. So Brian has to figure out how to find home buyers who are willing to pay a premium for his "green" homes.

Prior to building this home, Brian tried to make environmentally responsible building choices that didn't increase his costs. However, two years ago while at the National Association of Home Builders' convention in Orlando, Florida, Brian visited a booth that described LEED Certification, and it appealed to him. He also met a number of new suppliers who were offering sustainable building materials. When Brian returned from the convention in Orlando, Silverglade Homes salesperson Karen Toller told him that more home buyers were asking about environmental and energy-saving features. Brian thought the time was right to commit to building at least a few homes that met higher environmental standards.

Brian kept his eye out for a good piece of property for his project. Before long he found a 3-acre parcel of land about 15 minutes from downtown Asheville. The land had a nice mix of hardwood trees and a small stream, but lacked the panoramic mountain views expected by high-end home buyers in the area. Nevertheless, Brian thought the property would be ideal for a small neighborhood of moderate-size green homes. He purchased the land—and his first green project was under way.

Brian worked closely with a local architect, Katie Kelly, who had won several awards from the Green Building Council for her innovative designs. Katie proposed that each home follow a theme based on a classic Appalachian farmhouse design that would blend well with the rural surroundings and fit the concept of clustered development. Clustered development allows a builder to increase the number of home sites allowed if

land is set aside for open space. For example, regulations usually required at least one acre for a rural home site. However, in a clustered development, the county would allow Brian to build five homes on 1.5 acres of his land if he dedicated the remaining 1.5 acres as open space controlled by a conservation easement.

Initially, Brian thought the additional two home sites and preservation of open space would be a huge benefit for his project. However, to get the development permit, he had to provide the county with a special land survey and biological inventory of the site. This extra survey work cost Brian $25,000 more than was normal.

Brian is behind schedule with construction because working with new types of materials has slowed him down. In some cases, his workers even had to be trained by factory representatives on the proper installation of materials. In addition, many of the materials in a LEED home—such as low-E windows, blown foam insulation, a high-efficiency furnace and water heater, and Energy Star appliances—have premium prices. As a result, Brian's LEED-certified homes cost about 10 percent more than conventionally built homes of the same size.

However, LEED homes do offer buyers a number of benefits. Toxin-free building materials help combat indoor air pollution—and green homes are less likely to have problems with mold or mildew. Energy and water savings for the homes Brian is building should be $2,000 to $3,000 per year. Plus, buyers can feel good that their homes produce fewer greenhouse gases, reduce dependence on fossil fuels, and send less construction waste to the local landfill.

Brian priced the five homes he is building at $250,000 to $300,000—about 10 percent more than similar non-LEED certified homes in the area. So far, the homes are getting a few looks, but none have sold and he hasn't had an offer. The feedback that Karen Toller hears is that people like the homes, but think that the price seems to be high; they like the general idea of owning a green home and saving money on energy, but they don't focus on the benefits. Perhaps that is because real estate agents in the area have little experience with green building and are used to talking about value in terms of "cost per square foot."

Karen Toller works full-time as a real estate agent—and Silverglade Homes is one of her clients. She receives a 1 percent sales commission for every Silverglade home that is sold. She typically writes the listing that all real estate agents can read on the Multiple Listing Service (MLS) website and also handles the contract to complete a sale. With no movement on Brian's new houses and with prime spring selling season coming up fast, Brian has asked Karen to meet with him to discuss ways to spark

---

*Erik Hardy did the research for an earlier version of this case.

more interest in his development. Brian wants a plan that will bring people out to see his new homes and development—and a way to ensure that they are aware of the benefits he is offering.

Brian wonders what needs to be done to tell customers about the benefits of green building. Some other builders are advertising in local media and developing brochures to leave in a rack outside of their homes—but Brian has not needed to do that before. He wonders if he might be able to generate some inexpensive publicity by working with the local newspaper; it has run several feature stories about the environment but none about green building. He also thinks he needs to do more to convince real estate agents about the benefits of green housing. One idea is to ask someone at the Green Building Council or possibly his architect to put on a seminar, but Brian doesn't know if real estate agents will show up. He also wonders if putting signs in his model home to point out the environmental benefits might be helpful.

When Brian started his project, he thought his green homes would sell themselves, but now he wonders if he isn't ahead of his time.

What do you think of Brian Silverglade's marketing strategy so far? What promotion objectives should Brian set for his marketing strategy? What are the advantages and disadvantages of targeting communications at consumers as compared to real estate agents? What would you recommend as a promotion blend?

37. Mallory's Lemonade Stand (A)

Eleven-year-old Mallory is a budding entrepreneur. She is always coming up with new business ideas. In early summer 2014, her latest venture is a lemonade stand. Mallory is focused on making a high level of profits—she is saving for a new bike. Mallory is trying to to develop a marketing strategy to help her achieve this goal.

Last year, Mallory helped a friend with a lemonade stand. This year she wants to run her own business. Her parents expect her to pay for almost everything related to her business. Her dad built her a small lemonade stand—and although he donated his time, he did ask for the $12 in materials needed to build the stand. Mallory had to purchase other supplies as well. She bought a nice one-gallon pitcher for $5, and cups cost her $0.10. She figured out that sugar and lemons were costing her $0.30 for each 12-ounce cup she sold. Her parents let her use ice from the freezer—no cost there. Mallory initially planned to charge $0.75 per cup for her lemonade. Oh, and Mallory has a secret weapon. Her grandma had a little spice combination she put into lemonade that people just love—she knows from experience that once customers taste *her* lemonade they will be coming back for more.

Mallory is looking for help with some of her calculations, especially the final determination of an appropriate price. Answer the following questions:

1. Which of Mallory's costs are **fixed costs**? These are the costs that will not change whether Mallory sells few or many cups of lemonade.
2. What are the **variable costs**? These are costs that change directly with Mallory's sales. They go up proportionately to Mallory's increased number of sales.
3. What is Mallory's **fixed-cost contribution per unit** *(assumed selling price minus the variable cost per unit)?*

4. *How many cups of lemonade does Mallory need to sell to* **break-even (BEP)**? *Recall that the break-even point (in units) = (total fixed costs)/(fixed cost contribution per unit).*
5. *After conferring with her sister (a marketing major in college), Mallory considered four marketing strategies in addition to her original plan. Calculate the break-even point (in cups) for each (assume for the moment that each is an independent alternative):*
   a) *Mallory's family lives on a cul-de-sac and her parents said she has to sell from her driveway. This means her street gets limited traffic. She thinks creating two signs and placing them at the entrance of the cul-de-sac would make more people aware of her stand. The materials to make the signs cost $5. With this change what is her BEP?*
   b) *Mallory saw some fancier plastic cups that she thought might make her lemonade look nicer. The larger cups would go for $0.15 each, and because they were a little larger, costs for lemons and sugar would rise $0.05 per cup. With this change what is her BEP?*
   c) *Her sister said she was charging too much for a cup of lemonade. So Mallory considered charging $0.50 per cup instead of the planned $0.75. With this change what is her BEP?*
   d) *She also wanted to consider a higher price of $1 per cup instead of the planned $0.75. With this change what is her BEP?*
6. *What other information would be helpful to know before you make your final recommendation?*
7. *What else could Mallory do to deliver more value to her customers?*

38. Mallory's Lemonade Stand (B)

It is March 2016 and Mallory has come a long way since last summer. Her lemonade was a hit—everyone raved about her secret formula (she added some special spices suggested by her grandmother). When Damien Cuban (billionaire investor) happened to drive through the neighborhood, he had a cup of Mallory's lemonade and offered to invest in the company. So Mallory's Lemonade Stand Lemonade will soon be found in a limited number of local Whole Foods Stores. Mallory had to figure out pricing once again. She started with the knowledge that retailers would want to sell her 20 oz. bottles for $2.00 at retail.

Mallory figured her costs as follows:

- $10,000 in fixed costs for various costs including some local advertising to support the Whole Foods launch.
- A co-packer (company that manufactures food products to specifications) will charge $0.50 for each 20 oz. bottle—including bottles, packages, and delivery.
- Mallory assumes she can sell 30,000 bottles.
- Mallory plans to charge Whole Foods $1.00 each for the bottles. Whole Foods will charge $2.00.
- Using average cost pricing, she is counting on a $5,000 profit.

1. *Assuming the numbers shown here, what is Whole Foods* **markup percent** *on each bottle of Mallory's Lemonade Stand Lemonade?*
2. *Using Mallory's projected sales of 30,000 bottles, calculate Mallory's: a)* **average fixed cost**, *b)* **average variable cost**, *c) margin in dollars per bottle, and d) total profit.*
3. *What is Mallory's profit if sales turn out to be only 15,000 bottles?*

When MLS Lemonade failed to meet sales targets, Whole Foods quietly dropped the line. But all was not lost. Damien Cuban was able to help her obtain a presence in a convenience store chain. Cuban suggested that Mallory use **marginal analysis** (which focuses on the changes in total revenue and total cost from selling one more unit to find the most profitable price and quantity). This approach recognized that price and quantity sold change together. Cuban called in a favor from a friend who is an expert in the beverage market. This woman was able to provide a well-informed estimate of how much Mallory could sell during her test at different prices. Fill out the table and suggest an appropriate price. Because the convenience store manager knew it would have a 50 percent markup, the first column is actually the store's purchase price and Mallory's selling price.

Mallory has partially filled out a spreadsheet with the numbers (see below). Finish this spreadsheet based on the following questions.

4. *Assuming the expert's estimates are accurate, what price maximizes revenue? What is that revenue?*
5. *Assuming the expert's estimates are accurate, what price maximizes profit? What is that profit?*
6. *What would help Mallory reduce the price sensitivity some customers may have for her lemonade?*

Price (P)	Quantity	Revenue (P*Q)	Total VC	Total FC	Total Cost	Profit (Rev – Cost)
$3.00	0	$0	$0	$10,000	$10,000	−$10,000
$1.75	10,000	$17,500	$5,000		$15,000	$2,500
$1.40	15,000	$21,000			$17,500	$3,500
$1.20	20,000	$24,000	$10,000			
$1.00	30,000	$30,000	$15,000			
$0.85	45,000	$38,250				
$0.77	51,000	$39,270				
$0.70	55,000				$37,500	$1,000

Glossary

2/10, net 30 Allows a 2 percent discount off the face value of the invoice if the invoice is paid within 10 days.

Accessories Short-lived capital items—tools and equipment used in production or office activities.

Accumulating Collecting products from many small producers.

Administered channel systems Various channel members informally agree to cooperate with one another.

Administered prices Consciously set prices aimed at reaching the firm's objectives.

Adoption curve Shows when different groups accept ideas.

Adoption process The steps individuals go through on the way to accepting or rejecting a new idea.

Advertising Any *paid* form of nonpersonal presentation of ideas, goods, or services by an identified sponsor.

Advertising agencies Specialists in planning and handling mass-selling details for advertisers.

Advertising allowances Price reductions to firms in the channel to encourage them to advertise or otherwise promote the firm's products locally.

Advertising managers Managers of their company's mass-selling effort in television, newspapers, magazines, and other media.

Advertising media The various means by which a message is communicated to its target market.

Agent wholesalers Wholesalers who do not own (take title to) the products they sell.

AIDA model Consists of four promotion jobs: (1) to get *Attention,* (2) to hold *Interest,* (3) to arouse *Desire,* and (4) to obtain *Action.*

Allowance (accounting term) Occurs when a customer is not satisfied with a purchase for some reason and the seller gives a price reduction on the original invoice (bill), but the customer keeps the goods or services.

Allowances Reductions in price given to final consumers, customers, or channel members for doing something or accepting less of something.

Assorting Putting together a variety of products to give a target market what it wants.

Attitude A person's point of view toward something.

Auction companies Agent wholesalers that provide a place where buyers and sellers can come together and complete a transaction.

Automatic vending Selling and delivering products through vending machines.

Average cost (per unit) The total cost divided by the related quantity.

Average-cost pricing Adding a reasonable markup to the average cost of a product.

Average fixed cost (per unit) The total fixed cost divided by the related quantity.

Average variable cost (per unit) The total variable cost divided by the related quantity.

Baby boomers People born between 1946 and 1964.

Bait pricing Setting some very low prices to attract customers but trying to sell more expensive models or brands once the customer is in the store.

Balance sheet An accounting statement that shows a company's assets, liabilities, and net worth.

Basic list prices The prices that final customers or users are normally asked to pay for products.

Basic sales tasks *Order-getting, order-taking,* and *supporting.*

Battle of the brands The competition between dealer brands and manufacturer brands.

Belief A person's opinion about something.

Bid pricing Offering a specific price for each possible job rather than setting a price that applies for all customers.

Big data Data sets too large and complex to work with typical database management tools.

Blog A regularly updated website, usually managed by one person or a small group and written in an informal, conversational style

Brand community A group of customers joined around a particular brand or common set of shared interests.

Brand equity The value of a brand's overall strength in the market.

Brand familiarity How well customers recognize and accept a company's brand.

Brand insistence Customers insist on a firm's branded product and are willing to search for it.

Brand managers Manage specific products, often taking over the jobs formerly handled by an advertising manager—sometimes called *product managers.*

Brand name A word, letter, or a group of words or letters.

Brand nonrecognition Final customers don't recognize a brand at all—even though intermediaries may use the brand name for identification and inventory control.

Brand preference Target customers usually choose the brand over other brands, perhaps because of habit or favorable past experience.

Brand recognition Customers remember the brand.

Brand rejection Potential customers won't buy a brand—unless its image is changed.

Branded apps Sponsored software applications that benefit customers by providing entertainment, solving a problem, and/or saving time.

Branded services Valued services a brand provides that are not directly connected to a core product offering.

Branding The use of a name, term, symbol, or design—or a combination of these—to identify a product.

Break-even analysis An approach to determine whether the firm will be able to break even—that is, cover all its costs—with a particular price.

Break-even point (BEP) The sales quantity where the firm's total cost will just equal its total revenue.

Breakthrough opportunities Opportunities that help innovators develop hard-to-copy marketing strategies that will be very profitable for a long time.

Brokers Agent wholesalers who specialize in bringing buyers and sellers together.

Bulk-breaking Dividing larger quantities into smaller quantities as products get closer to the final market.

Business and organizational customers Any buyers who buy for resale or to produce other goods and services.

Business products Products meant for use in producing other products.

Buying center All the people who participate in or influence a purchase.

Buying function Looking for and evaluating goods and services.

Capital The money invested in a firm.

Capital item A long-lasting product that can be used and depreciated for many years.

Case studies Success stories about how a company helped another customer.

Cash discounts Reductions in the price to encourage buyers to pay their bills quickly.

Cash flow statement A financial report that forecasts how much cash will be available after paying expenses.

Cash-and-carry wholesalers Like service wholesalers, except that the customer must pay cash.

Catalog wholesalers Sell out of catalogs that may be distributed widely to smaller industrial customers or retailers that might not be called on by other wholesalers.

Channel captain A manager who helps direct the activities of a whole channel and tries to avoid, or solve, channel conflicts.

Channel of distribution Any series of firms or individuals who participate in the flow of products from producer to final user or consumer.

Close The salesperson's request for an order.

Clustering techniques Approaches used to try to find similar patterns within sets of data.

Collaborators Firms that provide one or more of the marketing functions other than buying.

Combination export manager A blend of manufacturers' agent and selling agent—handling the entire export function for several producers of similar but noncompeting lines.

Combined target market approach Combining two or more submarkets into one larger target market as a basis for one strategy.

Combiners Firms that try to increase the size of their target markets by combining two or more segments.

Command economy Government officials decide what and how much is to be produced and distributed by whom, when, to whom, and why.

Communication process A source trying to reach a receiver with a message.

Comparative advertising Advertising that makes specific brand comparisons using actual product names.

Competitive advantage A firm has a marketing mix that the target market sees as better than a competitor's mix.

Competitive advertising Advertising that tries to develop selective demand for a specific brand rather than a product category.

Competitive bids Terms of sale offered by different suppliers in response to the buyer's purchase specifications.

Competitive environment The number and types of competitors the marketing manager must face and how they may behave.

Competitive rivals A firm's closest competitors.

Competitor analysis An organized approach for evaluating the strengths and weaknesses of current or potential competitors' marketing strategies.

Competitor matrix A table depicting the results of a competitor analysis.

Complementary product pricing Setting prices on several related products as a group.

Components Processed expense items that become part of a finished product.

Concept testing Getting reactions from customers about how well a new-product idea fits their needs.

Confidence intervals The range on either side of an estimate from a sample that is likely to contain the true value for the whole population.

Consultative selling approach A type of sales presentation in which the salesperson develops a good understanding of the individual customer's needs before trying to close the sale.

Consumer panel A group of consumers who provide information on a continuing basis.

Consumer Product Safety Act A 1972 law that set up the Consumer Product Safety Commission to encourage more awareness of safety in product design and better quality control.

Consumer products Products meant for the final consumer.

Consumer surplus The difference to consumers between the value of a purchase and the price they pay.

Containerization Grouping individual items into an economical shipping quantity and sealing them in protective containers for transit to the final destination.

Continuous improvement A commitment to constantly make things better one step at a time.

Contractual channel systems Various channel members agree by contract to cooperate with one another.

Contribution-margin approach A cost analysis approach in which all costs are not allocated in *all* situations.

Control The feedback process that helps the marketing manager learn (1) how ongoing plans and implementation are working and (2) how to plan for the future.

Convenience (food) stores A convenience-oriented variation of the conventional limited-line food stores.

Convenience products Products a consumer needs but isn't willing to spend much time or effort shopping for.

Cooperative advertising Producers sharing in the cost of ads with wholesalers or retailers.

Copy thrust What the words and illustrations of an ad should communicate.

Corporate chain A firm that owns and manages more than one store—and often it's many.

Corporate channel systems Corporate ownership all along the channel.

Corrective advertising Ads to correct deceptive advertising.

Cost of sales Total value (at cost) of the sales during the period.

Cues Products, signs, ads, and other stimuli in the environment.

Cultural and social environment Affects how and why people live and behave as they do.

Culture The whole set of beliefs, attitudes, and ways of doing things of a reasonably homogeneous set of people.

Cumulative quantity discounts Reductions in price for larger purchases over a given period, such as a year.

Customer equity The expected earnings stream (profitability) of a firm's current and prospective customers over some period of time.

Customer lifetime value Total stream of purchases that a customer could contribute to the company over the length of the relationship.

Customer relationship management (CRM) An approach where the seller fine-tunes the marketing effort with information from a detailed customer database.

Customer satisfaction The extent to which a firm fulfills a consumer's needs, desires, and expectations.

Customer service A personal communication between a seller and a customer who wants the seller to resolve a problem with a purchase; often the key to building repeat business.

Customer service level How rapidly and dependably a firm can deliver what customers want.

Customer service reps Supporting salespeople who work with customers to resolve problems that arise with a purchase, usually after the purchase has been made.

Customer value The difference between the benefits a customer sees from a market offering and the costs of obtaining those benefits.

Data warehouse A place where databases are stored so that they are available when needed.

Dealer brands Brands created by intermediaries—sometimes referred to as *private brands*.

Debt financing Borrowing money based on a promise to repay the loan, usually within a fixed time period and with a specific interest charge.

Decision support system (DSS) A computer program that makes it easy for marketing managers to get and use information *as they are making decisions.*

Decoding The receiver in the communication process translating the message.

Demand curve A graph of the relationship between price and quantity demanded in a market, assuming all other things stay the same.

Demand-backward pricing Setting an acceptable final consumer price and working backward to what a producer can charge.

Department stores Larger stores that are organized into many separate departments and offer many product lines.

Derived demand Demand for business products derives from the demand for final consumer products.

Determining dimensions The dimensions that actually affect the customer's purchase of a *specific* product or brand in a product-market.

Differentiation The marketing mix is distinct from and better than what's available from a competitor.

Direct competitive advertising Competitive advertising that aims for immediate buying action.

Direct investment A parent firm has a division (or owns a separate subsidiary firm) in a foreign market.

Direct marketing Direct communication between a seller and an individual customer using a promotion method other than face-to-face personal selling.

Discount houses Stores that sell hard goods (cameras, TVs, appliances) at substantial price cuts to customers who go to discounter's low-rent store, pay cash, and take care of any service or repair problems themselves.

Discounts Reductions from list price given by a seller to buyers, who either give up some marketing function or provide the function themselves.

Discrepancy of assortment The difference between the lines a typical producer makes and the assortment final consumers or users want.

Discrepancy of quantity The difference between the quantity of products it is economical for a producer to make and the quantity final users or consumers normally want.

Discretionary income What is left of disposable income after paying for necessities.

Dissonance Tension caused by uncertainty about the rightness of a decision.

Distribution center A special kind of warehouse designed to speed the flow of goods and avoid unnecessary storing costs.

Diversification Moving into totally different lines of business—perhaps entirely unfamiliar products, markets, or even levels in the production-marketing system.

Door-to-door selling Going directly to the consumer's home.

Drive A strong stimulus that encourages action to reduce a need.

Drop-shippers Wholesalers that own (take title to) the products they sell but do not actually handle, stock, or deliver them.

Dumping Pricing a product sold in a foreign market below the cost of producing it or at a price lower than in its domestic market.

E-commerce Exchanges between individuals or organizations—and activities that facilitate those exchanges—based on applications of information technology.

Early adopters The second group in the adoption curve to adopt a new product; these people are usually well respected by their peers and often are opinion leaders.

Early majority A group in the adoption curve that avoids risk and waits to consider a new idea until many early adopters try it and like it.

Earned media Promotional messages *not* directly generated by the company or brand, but rather by third parties such as journalists or customers.

Economic buyers People who know all the facts and logically compare choices to get the greatest satisfaction from spending their time and money.

Economic environment Refers to macro-economic factors including national income, economic growth, and inflation that affect patterns of consumer and business spending.

Economic needs Needs concerned with making the best use of a consumer's time and money—as the consumer judges it.

Economic system The way an economy organizes to use scarce resources to produce goods and services and distribute them for consumption by various people and groups in the society.

Economies of scale As a company produces larger numbers of a particular product, the cost of each unit of the product goes down.

Elastic demand If prices are dropped, the quantity demanded will stretch enough to increase total revenue.

Elastic supply The quantity supplied does stretch more if the price is raised.

Electronic data interchange (EDI) An approach that puts information in a standardized format easily shared between different computer systems.

Emergency products Products that are purchased immediately when the need is great.

Empowerment Giving employees the authority to correct a problem without first checking with management.

Empty nesters People whose children are grown and who are now able to spend their money in other ways.

Encoding The source in the communication process deciding what it wants to say and translating it into words or symbols that will have the same meaning to the receiver.

Equilibrium point The quantity and the price sellers are willing to offer are equal to the quantity and price that buyers are willing to accept.

Everyday low pricing Setting a low list price rather than relying on frequent sales, discounts, or allowances.

Exclusive distribution Selling through only one intermediary in a particular geographic area.

Expectation An outcome or event that a person anticipates or looks forward to.

Expense item A product whose total cost is treated as a business expense in the period it's purchased.

Expenses All the remaining costs that are subtracted from the gross margin to get the net profit.

Experimental method A research approach in which researchers compare the responses of two or more groups that are similar except on the characteristic being tested.

Export agents Manufacturers' agents who specialize in export trade.

Export brokers Brokers who specialize in bringing together buyers and sellers from different countries.

Exporting Selling some of what the firm produces to foreign markets.

Extensive problem solving when consumers put much effort into deciding how to satisfy a need.

F.O.B. A transportation term meaning free on board some vehicle at some point.

Facebook An online social networking website that allows registered users to create profiles, upload photos and video, and send messages to friends, family, and colleagues

Factor A variable that shows the relation of some other variable to the item being forecast.

Factor method An approach to forecast sales by finding a relation between the company's sales and some other factor (or factors).

Fad An idea that is fashionable only to certain groups who are enthusiastic about it—but these groups are so fickle that a fad is even more short-lived than a regular fashion.

Family brand A brand name that is used for several products.

Farm products Products grown by farmers, such as oranges, sugar cane, and cattle.

Fashion Currently accepted or popular style.

Federal Fair Packaging and Labeling Act A 1966 law requiring that consumer goods be clearly labeled in easy-to-understand terms.

Federal Trade Commission (FTC) Federal government agency that polices antimonopoly laws.

Financing Provides the necessary cash and credit to produce, transport, store, promote, sell, and buy products.

Fixed-cost (FC) contribution per unit The selling price per unit minus the variable cost per unit.

Flexible-price policy Offering the same product and quantities to different customers at different prices.

Focus group interview An interview of 6 to 10 people in an informal group setting.

Foreign Corrupt Practices Act A law passed by the U.S. Congress in 1977 that prohibits U.S. firms from paying bribes to foreign officials.

Franchise operation A franchisor develops a good marketing strategy, and the retail franchise holders carry out the strategy in their own units.

Free trade Refers to agreements between countries to not restrict imports and exports.

Freight-absorption pricing Absorbing freight cost so that a firm's delivered price meets the nearest competitor's.

Full-cost approach All costs are allocated to products, customers, or other categories.

Full-line pricing Setting prices for a whole line of products.

Functional accounts The categories to which various costs are charged to show the *purpose* for which expenditures are made.

General merchandise wholesalers Service wholesalers that carry a wide variety of nonperishable items such as hardware, electrical supplies, furniture, drugs, cosmetics, and automobile equipment.

General stores Early retailers who carried anything they could sell in reasonable volume.

Generation X (Gen X) People born between 1965 and 1977.

Generation Y (Gen Y) People born between 1978 and 1994. Also called Millennials.

Generation Z People born since 1995.

Generic market A market with *broadly* similar needs—and sellers offering various and *often diverse* ways of satisfying those needs.

Generic products Products that have no brand at all other than identification of their contents and the manufacturer or intermediary.

Gross domestic product (GDP) The total market value of all goods and services provided in a country's economy in a year by both residents and nonresidents of that country.

Gross margin (gross profit) The money left to cover the expenses of selling the products and operating the business.

Gross national income (GNI) A measure that is similar to GDP, but GNI does not include income earned by foreigners who own resources in that nation.

Gross sales The total amount charged to all customers during some time period.

Heterogeneous shopping products Shopping products the customer sees as different and wants to inspect for quality and suitability.

Homogeneous shopping products Shopping products the customer sees as basically the same and wants at the lowest price.

Hypermarkets Very large stores that try to carry not only food and drug items but all goods and services that the consumer purchases *routinely* (also called *supercenters*).

Hypotheses Educated guesses about the relationships between things or about what will happen in the future.

Iceberg principle Much good information is hidden in summary data.

Ideal market exposure When a product is available widely enough to satisfy target customers' needs but not exceed them.

Implementation Putting marketing plans into operation.

Import agents Manufacturers' agents who specialize in import trade.

Import brokers Brokers who specialize in bringing together buyers and sellers from different countries.

Impulse products Products that are bought quickly as *unplanned* purchases because of a strongly felt need.

Indirect competitive advertising Competitive advertising that points out product advantages—to affect future buying decisions.

Individual brands Separate brand names used for each product.

Individual product A particular product within a product line.

Inelastic demand Although the quantity demanded increases if the price is decreased, the quantity demanded will not stretch enough to avoid a decrease in total revenue.

Inelastic supply The quantity supplied does not stretch much (if at all) if the price is raised.

Infographic A visual image such as a chart or diagram used to represent information or data.

Innovation The development and spread of new ideas, goods, and services.

Innovators The first group to adopt new products.

Instagram A free online photo and video sharing service geared to mobile phones.

Installations Important capital items such as buildings, land rights, and major equipment.

Institutional advertising Advertising that tries to promote an organization's image, reputation, or ideas rather than a specific product.

Integrated marketing communications The intentional coordination of every communication from a firm to a target customer to convey a consistent and complete message.

Intensive distribution Selling a product through all responsible and suitable wholesalers or retailers who will stock or sell the product.

Intermediary Someone who specializes in trade rather than production.

Intranet A system for linking computers within a company.

Introductory price dealing Temporary price cuts to speed new products into a market and get customers to try them.

Inventory The amount of goods being stored.

ISO 9000 A way for a supplier to document its quality procedures according to internationally recognized standards.

Job description A written statement of what a salesperson is expected to do.

Joint venture In international marketing, a domestic firm entering into a partnership with a foreign firm.

Jury of executive opinion Forecasting by combining the opinions of experienced executives, perhaps from marketing, production, finance, purchasing, and top management.

Just-in-time delivery Reliably getting products there *just* before the customer needs them.

Laggards Prefer to do things the way they have been done in the past and are very suspicious of new ideas; sometimes called *nonadopters*—see *adoption curve*.

Landing page A customized web page that logically follows from clicking on an organic search result, online advertisement, or other link

Lanham Act A 1946 law that spells out what kinds of marks (including brand names) can be protected and the exact method of protecting them.

Late majority A group of adopters who are cautious about new ideas—see *adoption curve*.

Law of diminishing demand If the price of a product is raised, a smaller quantity will be demanded—and if the price of a product is lowered, a greater quantity will be demanded.

Leader pricing Setting some very low prices—real bargains—to get customers into retail stores.

Learning A change in a person's thought processes caused by prior experience.

Licensed brand A well-known brand that sellers pay a fee to use.

Licensing Selling the right to use some process, trademark, patent, or other right for a fee or royalty.

Lifestyle analysis The analysis of a person's day-to-day pattern of living as expressed in that person's *Activities*, *Interests*, and *Opinions*—sometimes referred to as *AIOs* or *psychographics*.

Limited problem solving When a consumer is willing to put *some* effort into deciding the best way to satisfy a need.

Limited-function wholesalers Merchant wholesalers that provide only *some* wholesaling functions.

Limited-line stores Stores that specialize in certain lines of related products rather than a wide assortment—sometimes called *single-line stores*.

LinkedIn A social networking website for businesspeople who create personal or company profiles

Logistics The transporting, storing, and handling of goods in ways that match target customers' needs with a firm's marketing mix—both within individual firms and along a channel of distribution (i.e., another name for *physical distribution*).

Low-involvement purchases Purchases that have little importance or relevance for the customer.

Macro-marketing A social process that directs an economy's flow of goods and services from producers to consumers in a way that effectively matches supply and demand and accomplishes the objectives of society.

Magnuson-Moss Act A 1975 law requiring that producers provide a clearly written warranty if they choose to offer any warranty.

Major accounts sales force Salespeople who sell directly to large accounts such as major retail chain stores.

Management contracting The seller provides only management skills—others own the production and distribution facilities.

Manufacturer brands Brands created by producers.

Manufacturers' agents Agent wholesalers who sell similar products for several noncompeting producers for a commission on what is actually sold.

Manufacturers' sales branches Separate warehouses that producers set up away from their factories.

Marginal analysis Evaluating the change in total revenue and total cost from selling one more unit to find the most profitable price and quantity.

Markdown A retail price reduction that is required because customers won't buy some item at the originally marked-up price.

Markdown ratio A tool used by many retailers to measure the efficiency of various departments and their whole business.

Market A group of potential customers with similar needs who are willing to exchange something of value with sellers offering various goods or services—that is, ways of satisfying those needs.

Market development Trying to increase sales by selling present products in new markets.

Market-directed economy The individual decisions of the many producers and consumers make the macro-level decisions for the whole economy.

Market growth A stage of the product life cycle when industry sales grow fast—but industry profits rise and then start falling.

Market information function The collection, analysis, and distribution of all the information needed to plan, carry out, and control marketing activities.

Market introduction A stage of the product life cycle when sales are low as a new idea is first introduced to a market.

Market maturity A stage of the product life cycle when industry sales level off and competition gets tougher.

Market penetration Trying to increase sales of a firm's present products in its present markets—probably through a more aggressive marketing mix.

Market potential What a whole market segment might buy.

Market research online community (MROC) An online group of participants who are joined together by a common interest, and who participate in ongoing research.

Market segment A relatively homogeneous group of customers who will respond to a marketing mix in a similar way.

Market segmentation A two-step process of (1) *naming* broad product-markets and (2) *segmenting* these broad product-markets in order to select target markets and develop suitable marketing mixes.

Marketing The performance of activities that seek to accomplish an organization's objectives by anticipating customer or client needs and directing a flow of need-satisfying goods and services from producer to customer or client.

Marketing audit A systematic, critical, and unbiased review and appraisal of the basic objectives and policies of the marketing function and of the organization, methods, procedures, and people employed to implement the policies.

Marketing automation software Software that tracks individual customer's behavior and triggers actions in response to specific customer actions.

Marketing company era A time when, in addition to short-run marketing planning, marketing people develop long-range plans—sometimes five or more years ahead—and the whole company effort is guided by the marketing concept.

Marketing concept The idea that an organization should aim *all* its efforts at satisfying its *customers*—at a *profit*.

Marketing dashboard Displaying up-to-the-minute marketing data in an easy-to-read format.

Marketing department era A time when all marketing activities are brought under the control of one department to improve short-run policy planning and to try to integrate the firm's activities.

Marketing ethics The moral standards that guide marketing decisions and actions.

Marketing information system (MIS) An organized way of continually gathering, accessing, and analyzing information that marketing managers need to make ongoing decisions.

Marketing management process The process of (1) *planning* marketing activities, (2) directing the *implementation* of the plans, and (3) *controlling* these plans.

Marketing mix The controllable variables that the company puts together to satisfy a target group.

Marketing model A statement of relationships among marketing variables.

Marketing orientation Trying to carry out the marketing concept.

Marketing plan A written statement of a marketing strategy *and* the time-related details for carrying out the strategy.

Marketing program Blends all of the firm's marketing plans into one big plan.

Marketing research Procedures to develop and analyze new information to help marketing managers make decisions.

Marketing research process A five-step application of the scientific method that includes (1) defining the problem, (2) analyzing the situation, (3) getting problem-specific data, (4) interpreting the data, and (5) solving the problem.

Marketing strategy Specifies a target market and a related marketing mix.

Markup A dollar amount added to the cost of products to get the selling price.

Markup (percent) The percentage of selling price that is added to the cost to get the selling price.

Markup chain The sequence of markups firms use at different levels in a channel—determining the price structure in the whole channel.

Mass customization Tailoring the principles of mass production to meet the unique needs of individual customers.

Mass marketing The typical production-oriented approach that vaguely aims at everyone with the same marketing mix.

Mass selling Communicating with large numbers of potential customers at the same time.

Mass-merchandisers Large, self-service stores with many departments that emphasize soft goods (housewares, clothing, and fabrics) and staples (like health and beauty aids) and selling on lower margins to get faster turnover.

Mass-merchandising concept The idea that retailers should offer low prices to get faster turnover and greater sales volume by appealing to larger numbers.

Merchant wholesalers Wholesalers who own (take title to) the products they sell.

Message channel The carrier of the message.

Micro-macro dilemma What is good for some producers and consumers may not be good for society as a whole.

Mission statement Sets out the organization's basic purpose for being.

Missionary salespeople Supporting salespeople who work for producers by calling on intermediaries and their customers.

Modified rebuy The in-between process where some review of the buying situation is done—though not as much as in new-task buying or as little as in straight rebuys.

Monopolistic competition A market situation that develops when a market has (1) different (heterogeneous) products and (2) sellers who feel they do have some competition in this market.

Multichannel distribution When a producer uses several competing channels to reach the same target market—perhaps using several intermediaries in addition to selling directly.

Multichannel shoppers Shoppers who use different retailers as they move through the purchase process.

Multiple buying influence Several people share in making a purchase decision—perhaps even top management.

Multiple target market approach Segmenting the market and choosing two or more segments, then treating each as a separate target market needing a different marketing mix.

Nationalism An emphasis on a country's interests before everything else.

Natural accounts The categories to which various costs are charged in the normal financial accounting cycle.

Natural products Products that occur in nature—such as timber, iron ore, oil, and coal.

Needs The basic forces that motivate a person to do something.

Negotiated contract buying Agreeing to a contract that allows for changes in the purchase arrangements.

Negotiated price A price that is set based on bargaining between the buyer and seller.

Net An invoice term meaning that payment for the face value of the invoice is due immediately—also see *cash discounts*.

Net profit What the company earns from its operations during a particular period.

Net sales The actual sales dollars the company receives.

New product A product that is new *in any way* for the company concerned.

New unsought products Products offering really new ideas that potential customers don't know about yet.

New-task buying When an organization has a new need and the buyer wants a great deal of information.

Noise Any distraction that reduces the effectiveness of the communication process.

Nonadopters Prefer to do things the way they have been done in the past and are very suspicious of new ideas; sometimes called *laggards*—see *adoption curve*.

Noncumulative quantity discounts Reductions in price when a customer purchases a larger quantity on an *individual order*.

Nonprice competition Aggressive action on one or more of the Ps other than Price.

North American Industry Classification System (NAICS) codes Codes used to identify groups of firms in similar lines of business.

Odd-even pricing Setting prices that end in certain numbers.

Oligopoly A special market situation that develops when a market has (1) essentially homogeneous products, (2) relatively few sellers, and (3) fairly inelastic industry demand curves.

Omnichannel A multichannel selling approach where a single retailer provides a seamless customer shopping experience from desktop computer, mobile device, telephone, or brick-and-mortar store.

One-price policy Offering the same price to all customers who purchase products under essentially the same conditions and in the same quantities.

Operating ratios Ratios of items on the operating statement to net sales.

Operating statement A simple summary of the financial results of a company's operations over a specified period of time.

Operational decisions Short-run decisions to help implement strategies.

Opinion leader A person who influences others.

Order getters Salespeople concerned with establishing relationships with new customers and developing new business.

Order takers Salespeople who sell to regular or established customers, complete most sales transactions, and maintain relationships with their customers.

Order-getting Seeking possible buyers with a well-organized sales presentation designed to sell a good, service, or idea.

Order-taking The routine completion of sales made regularly to target customers.

Outsource When the buying organization chooses to contract with an outside firm to produce goods or services rather than producing them internally.

Owned media Promotional messages generated by a brand (or company or nonprofit organization) communicated through a message channel the brand directly controls

Packaging Promoting, protecting, and enhancing the product.

Paid media Messages generated by a brand (or company or nonprofit organization) and communicated through a message channel the brand pays to access

Pass-along When one customer makes a recommendation for (or against) a specific brand to another customer.

Patent Grants the inventor the ability to "exclude others from making, using, offering for sales, or selling the invention."

Pay-per-click an advertiser pays media costs only when a customer clicks on the ad that leads to the advertiser's website

Penetration pricing policy Trying to sell the whole market at one low price.

Perception How we gather and interpret information from the world around us.

Performance analysis Analysis that looks for exceptions or variations from planned performance.

Performance index A number that shows the relation of one value to another.

Personal needs An individual's need for personal satisfaction unrelated to what others think or do.

Personal selling Direct spoken communication between sellers and potential customers, usually in person but sometimes over the telephone or even via a video conference over the Internet.

Phony list prices Misleading prices that customers are shown to suggest that the price they are to pay has been discounted from list.

Physical distribution (PD) The transporting, storing, and handling of goods in ways that match target customers' needs with a firm's marketing mix—both within individual firms and along a channel of distribution (i.e., another name for *logistics*).

Physical distribution (PD) concept All transporting, storing, and product-handling activities of a business and a whole channel system should be coordinated as one system that seeks to minimize the cost of distribution for a given customer service level.

Physiological needs Biological needs such as the need for food, drink, rest, and sex.

Piggyback service Loading truck trailers or flatbed trailers carrying containers on railcars to provide both speed and flexibility.

Pinterest A website that allows registered users to share ideas and images they find online with fellow users.

Pioneering advertising Advertising that tries to develop primary demand for a product category rather than demand for a specific brand.

Place Making goods and services available in the right quantities and locations—when customers want them.

Population In marketing research, the total group you are interested in.

Positioning An approach that refers to how customers think about proposed or present brands in a market.

Positioning statement A positioning statement concisely identifies the firm's desired target market, product type, primary benefit or point of differentiation, and the main reasons a buyer should believe the firm's claims.

Prepared sales presentation A memorized presentation that is not adapted to each individual customer.

Prestige pricing Setting a rather high price to suggest high quality or high status.

Price The amount of money that is charged for "something" of value.

Price discrimination Injuring competition by selling the same products to different buyers at different prices.

Price fixing Competitors illegally getting together to raise, lower, or stabilize prices.

Price lining Setting a few price levels for a product line and then marking all items at these prices.

Primary data Information specifically collected to solve a current problem.

Primary demand Demand for the general product idea, not just the company's own brand.

Private brands Brands created by intermediaries—sometimes referred to as *dealer brands*.

Private warehouses Storing facilities owned or leased by companies for their own use.

Product The need-satisfying offering of a firm.

Product advertising Advertising that tries to sell a specific product.

Product assortment The set of all product lines and individual products that a firm sells.

Product development Offering new or improved products for present markets.

Product liability The legal obligation of sellers to pay damages to individuals who are injured by defective or unsafe products.

Product life cycle The stages a new-product idea goes through from beginning to end.

Product line A set of individual products that are closely related.

Product managers Manage specific products, often taking over the jobs formerly handled by an advertising manager—sometimes called *brand managers*.

Product-bundle pricing Setting one price for a set of products.

Product-market A market with *very* similar needs—and sellers offering various *close substitute* ways of satisfying those needs.

Production Actually *making* goods or *performing* services.

Production capacity The ability to produce a certain quantity and quality of specific goods or services.

Production era A time when a company focuses on production of a few specific products—perhaps because few of these products are available in the market.

Production orientation Making whatever products are easy to produce and *then* trying to sell them.

Professional services Specialized services that support a firm's operations.

Profit maximization objective An objective to get as much profit as possible.

Promotion Communicating information between seller and potential buyer or others in the channel to influence attitudes and behavior.

Prospecting Following all the leads in the target market to identify potential customers.

Prototype An early sample or model built to test a concept.

Psychographics The analysis of a person's day-to-day pattern of living as expressed in that person's *A*ctivities, *I*nterests, and *O*pinions—sometimes referred to as *AIOs* or *lifestyle analysis*.

Psychological pricing Setting prices that have special appeal to target customers.

Public relations Communication with noncustomers—including labor, public interest groups, stockholders, and the government.

Public warehouses Independent storing facilities.

Publicity Any *unpaid* form of nonpersonal presentation of ideas, goods, or services.

Pulling Using promotion to get consumers to ask intermediaries for the product.

Purchase discount A reduction of the original invoice amount for some business reason.

Purchase situation Takes into account the purpose, time available, and location where a purchase is made.

Purchasing managers Buying specialists for their employers.

Purchasing specifications A written (or electronic) description of what the firm wants to buy.

Pure competition A market situation that develops when a market has (1) homogeneous (similar) products, (2) many buyers and sellers who have full knowledge of the market, and (3) ease of entry for buyers and sellers.

Pure subsistence economy Each family unit produces everything it consumes.

Push money (or prize money) allowances Allowances (sometimes called *PMs* or *spiffs*) given to retailers by manufacturers or wholesalers to pass on to the retailers' salesclerks for aggressively selling certain items.

Pushing Using normal promotion effort—personal selling, advertising, and sales promotion—to help sell the whole marketing mix to possible channel members.

Qualifying dimensions The dimensions that are relevant to including a customer type in a product-market.

Qualitative research Seeks in-depth, open-ended responses, not yes or no answers.

Quality A product's ability to satisfy a customer's needs or requirements.

Quantitative research Seeks structured responses that can be summarized in numbers—such as percentages, averages, or other statistics.

Quantity discounts Discounts offered to encourage customers to buy in larger amounts.

Rack jobbers Merchant wholesalers that specialize in hard-to-handle assortments of products that a retailer doesn't want to manage—and they often display the products on their own wire racks.

Raw materials Unprocessed expense items—such as logs, iron ore, and wheat—that are moved to the next production process with little handling.

Rebates Refunds to consumers after a purchase.

Receiver The target of a message in the communication process, usually a potential customer.

Reference group The people to whom an individual looks when forming attitudes about a particular topic.

Reference price The price a consumer expects to pay.

referral program offers a current customer an incentive for recommending a new customer to a business.

Regrouping activities Adjusting the quantities or assortments of products handled at each level in a channel of distribution.

Regularly unsought products Products that stay unsought but not unbought forever.

Reinforcement Occurs in the learning process when the consumer's response is followed by satisfaction—that is, reduction in the drive.

Reminder advertising Advertising to keep the product's name before the public.

Requisition A request to buy something.

Research proposal A plan that specifies what marketing research information will be obtained and how.

Response An effort to satisfy a drive.

Response rate The percent of people contacted in a research sample who complete the questionnaire.

Retailing All of the activities involved in the sale of products to final consumers.

Retargeting (or behavioral retargeting) displays ads to a web user based on sites they ave previously visited

Return When a customer sends back purchased products.

Return on assets (ROA) The ratio of net profit (after taxes) to the assets used to make the net profit—multiplied by 100 to get rid of decimals.

Return on investment (ROI) Ratio of net profit (after taxes) to the investment used to make the net profit—multiplied by 100 to get rid of decimals.

Reverse channels Channels used to retrieve products that customers no longer want.

Risk taking Bearing the uncertainties that are part of the marketing process.

Robinson-Patman Act A 1936 law that makes illegal any price discrimination if it injures competition.

Routinized response behavior When consumers regularly select a particular way of satisfying a need when it occurs.

S.W.O.T. analysis Identifies and lists the firm's strengths and weaknesses and its opportunities and threats.

Safety needs Needs concerned with protection and physical well-being.

Sale price A temporary discount from the list price.

Sales analysis A detailed breakdown of a company's sales records.

Sales decline A stage of the product life cycle when new products replace the old.

Sales era A time when a company emphasizes selling because of increased competition.

Sales forecast An estimate of how much an industry or firm hopes to sell to a market segment.

Sales managers Managers concerned with managing personal selling.

Sales presentation A salesperson's effort to make a sale or address a customer's problem.

Sales promotion Those promotion activities—other than advertising, publicity, and personal selling—that stimulate interest, trial, or purchase by final customers or others in the channel.

Sales promotion managers Managers of their company's sales promotion effort.

Sales quota The specific sales or profit objective a salesperson is expected to achieve.

Sales territory A geographic area that is the responsibility of one salesperson or several working together.

Sales-oriented objective An objective to get some level of unit sales, dollar sales, or share of market—without referring to profit.

Sample A part of the relevant population.

Scientific method A decision-making approach that focuses on being objective and orderly in *testing* ideas before accepting them.

Scrambled merchandising Retailers carrying any product lines that they think they can sell profitably.

Search engine optimization (SEO) The process of designing a website so that it ranks high in a search engine's unpaid results.

Seasonal discounts Discounts offered to encourage buyers to buy earlier than present demand requires.

Secondary data Information that has been collected or published already.

Segmenters Aim at one or more homogeneous segments and try to develop a different marketing mix for each segment.

Segmenting An aggregating process that clusters people with similar needs into a market segment.

Selective demand Demand for a company's own brand rather than a product category.

Selective distribution Selling through only those intermediaries who will give the product special attention.

Selective exposure Our eyes and minds seek out and notice only information that interests us.

Selective perception People screen out or modify ideas, messages, and information that conflict with previously learned attitudes and beliefs.

Selective retention People remember only what they want to remember.

Selling agents Agent wholesalers who take over the whole marketing job of producers, not just the selling function.

Selling formula approach A sales presentation that starts with a prepared presentation outline—much like the prepared approach—and leads the customer through some logical steps to a final close.

Selling function Promoting the product.

Senior citizens People older than 65.

Service An intangible offering involving a deed, performance, or effort.

Service mark Those words, symbols, or marks that are legally registered for use by a single company to refer to a service offering.

Service wholesalers Merchant wholesalers that provide all the wholesaling functions.

Shopping products Products that a customer feels are worth the time and effort to compare with competing products.

Simple trade era A time when families traded or sold their surplus output to local distributors.

Single target market approach Segmenting the market and picking one of the homogeneous segments as the firm's target market.

Single-line (or general-line) wholesalers Service wholesalers that carry a narrower line of merchandise than general merchandise wholesalers.

Single-line stores Stores that specialize in certain lines of related products rather than a wide assortment—sometimes called *limited-line stores*.

Situation analysis An informal study of what information is already available in the problem area.

Skimming price policy Trying to sell the top of the market—the top of the demand curve—at a high price before aiming at more price-sensitive customers.

Social class A group of people who have approximately equal social position as viewed by others in the society.

Social media Websites or software applications that allow users to create and share ideas, information, photos and videos, and interact in a social network.

Social needs Needs concerned with love, friendship, status, and esteem—things that involve a person's interaction with others.

Social responsibility A firm's obligation to improve its positive effects on society and reduce its negative effects.

Sorting Separating products into grades and qualities desired by different target markets.

Source The sender of a message.

Specialty products Consumer products that the customer really wants and makes a special effort to find.

Specialty shop A type of conventional limited-line store—usually small and with a distinct personality.

Specialty wholesalers Service wholesalers that carry a very narrow range of products and offer more information and service than other service wholesalers.

Standardization and grading Sorting products according to size and quality.

Staples Products that are bought often, routinely, and without much thought.

Statistical packages Easy-to-use computer programs that analyze data.

Status quo objectives "Don't-rock-the-*pricing*-boat" objectives.

Stock A share in the ownership of a company.

Stocking allowances Allowances given to wholesalers or retailers to get shelf space for a product—sometimes called *slotting allowances*.

Stockturn rate The number of times the average inventory is sold during a year.

Storing The marketing function of holding goods.

Storing function Holding goods until customers need them.

Straight rebuy A routine repurchase that may have been made many times before.

Strategic (management) planning The managerial process of developing and maintaining a match between an organization's resources and its market opportunities.

Substitutes Products that offer the buyer a choice.

Supercenters (hypermarkets) Very large stores that try to carry not only food and drug items, but all goods and services that the consumer purchases routinely (also called *hypermarkets*).

Supermarkets Large stores specializing in groceries—with self-service and wide assortments.

Supplies Expense items that do not become part of a finished product.

Supply chain The complete set of firms and facilities and logistics activities that are involved in procuring materials, transforming them into intermediate and finished products, and distributing them to customers.

Supply curve The quantity of products that will be supplied at various possible prices.

Supporting salespeople Salespeople who help the order-oriented salespeople but don't try to get orders themselves.

Sustainability The idea that it's important to meet present needs without compromising the ability of future generations to meet their own needs.

Sustainable competitive advantage A marketing mix that customers see as better than a competitor's mix and cannot be quickly or easily copied.

Target market A fairly homogeneous (similar) group of customers to whom a company wishes to appeal.

Target marketing A marketing mix is tailored to fit some specific target customers.

Target return objective A specific level of profit as an objective.

Task method An approach to developing a budget—basing the budget on the job to be done.

Task transfer Using telecommunications to move service operations to places where there are pools of skilled workers.

Team selling Different sales reps working together on a specific account.

Technical specialists Supporting salespeople who provide technical assistance to order-oriented salespeople.

Technology The application of science to convert an economy's resources to output.

Telemarketing Using the telephone to call on customers or prospects.

Total cost The sum of total fixed and total variable costs.

Total cost approach Evaluating each possible PD system and identifying all of the costs of each alternative.

Total fixed cost The sum of those costs that are fixed in total—no matter how much is produced.

Total quality management (TQM) The philosophy that everyone in the organization is concerned about quality, throughout all of the firm's activities, to better serve customer needs.

Total variable cost The sum of those changing expenses that are closely related to output—such as expenses for parts, wages, packaging materials, outgoing freight, and sales commissions.

Trade (functional) discount A list price reduction given to channel members for the job they are going to do.

Trade-in allowance A price reduction given for used products when similar new products are bought.

Trademark Those words, symbols, or marks that are legally registered for use by a single company.

Traditional channel systems A channel in which the various channel members make little or no effort to cooperate with one another.

Transporting The marketing function of moving goods.

Transporting function The movement of goods from one place to another.

Trend extension Extends past experience to predict the future.

Triple bottom line A measure of long-term success that includes an organization's economic, social, and environmental outcomes.

Truck wholesalers Wholesalers that specialize in delivering products that they stock in their own trucks.

Trust The confidence a person has in the promises or actions of another person, brand, or company.

Twitter A social networking microblogging service that allows registered users to send out short (140 characters or less) messages called "tweets."

Unfair trade practice acts Put a lower limit on prices, especially at the wholesale and retail levels.

Uniform delivered pricing Making an average freight charge to all buyers.

Universal functions of marketing Buying, selling, transporting, storing, standardizing and grading, financing, risk taking, and market information.

Unsought products Products that potential customers don't yet want or know they can buy.

User-generated content Any type of communication created by customers for other customers. User-generated content can take many forms

Validity The extent to which data measure what they are intended to measure.

Value in use pricing Setting prices that will capture some of what customers will save by substituting the firm's product for the one currently being used.

Value pricing Setting a fair price level for a marketing mix that really gives the target market superior customer value.

Vendor analysis Formal rating of suppliers on all relevant areas of performance.

Vertical integration Acquiring firms at different levels of channel activity.

Vertical marketing systems Channel systems in which the whole channel focuses on the same target market at the end of the channel.

Virtual corporation The firm is primarily a coordinator-with a good marketing concept-instead of a producer.

Wants Needs that are learned during a person's life.

Warranty What the seller promises about its product.

Wheel of retailing theory New types of retailers enter the market as low-status, low-margin, low-price operators and then, if successful, evolve into more conventional retailers offering more services with higher operating costs and higher prices.

Wheeler Lea Amendment Law that bans unfair or deceptive acts in commerce.

White paper An authoritative report or guide that addresses important issues in an industry and offers solutions.

Wholesalers Firms whose main function is providing *wholesaling activities*.

Wholesaling The *activities* of those persons or establishments that sell to retailers and other merchants, or to industrial, institutional, and commercial users, but who do not sell in large amounts to final consumers.

Working capital Money to pay for short-term expenses such as employee salaries, advertising, marketing research, inventory storing costs, and what the firm owes suppliers.

Zone pricing Making an average freight charge to all buyers within specific geographic areas.

Notes

CHAPTER 1

1. See www.nike.com; "Nike's New Marketing Mojo," *Fortune,* February 13, 2012; "Is Nike's Flyknit the Swoosh of the Future?" *Bloomberg Businessweek,* March 15, 2012; "In China, Nike Sets Out to Alter Sports Mindset," *Wall Street Journal,* October 12, 2011; "Nike's Sustainablility Report Takes Top Ceres-ACCA Award," *GreenBiz.com,* May 11, 2011; "How Nike Rules the World," *Fortune,* February 3, 2011; "Adidas' Brand Ambitions," *Portland Business Journal,* December 10, 2010; "Nike Releases Apparel Sustainability Software," *Waste and Recycling News,* December 6, 2010; "Nike, Inc.," *Datamonitor,* December 1, 2010; "Nike, Adidas Readjust Marketing Strategy," *China Daily,* August 30, 2010; "Despite Its Way with Women, Underdog Reebok Fixates on Nike," *AdAge.com,* July 12, 2010; "Letter to Shareholders," July 1, 2010; "Nike Women's Biz Gets Pounded as Toning Footwear Kicks Butt," *AdAge.com,* June 7, 2010; "Nike Looks Beyond 'Swoosh' for Growth," *Wall Street Journal,* May 20, 2010; "Nike Launches GreenXchange for Corporate Idea-Sharing," *Fast Company,* February 2, 2010; "Li Ning and Ziba Design Want to Build China's First Truly Global Brand," *Fast Company,* October 1, 2009; "Best in Show: Nike's Scrappy Trash Talk Shoes," *Bloomberg Businessweek,* July 29, 2009; "Cool Runnings," *Time,* October 4, 2007; "Nike's Big Gay-Marketing Coup," *Bloomberg Businessweek,* April 12, 2013; "Nike CEO Mark Parker on His Company's Digital Future: Body-Controlled Music, Color-Coded Heart Rates," *Fast Company,* February 12, 2013; "The World's Most Valuable Brands, 2015," *Forbes,* http://www.forbes.com/powerful-brands/list/#tab:rank.

2. See http://www.learnthe4ps.com/category/personal-marketing-plan/ for articles related to developing your own personal marketing plan.

3. Gregory D. Upah and Richard E. Wokutch, "Assessing Social Impacts of New Products: An Attempt to Operationalize the Macromarketing Concept," *Journal of Public Policy and Marketing,* 4 (1985).

4. An American Marketing Association committee recently defined marketing as "the activity, set of institutions, and processes for creating, communicating, delivering, and exchanging offerings that have value for customers, clients, partners, and society at large." The definition of marketing can be a source of debate; see "AMA's Definition of Marketing Stirs Debate," *B to B,* February 11, 2008; see also David Glen Mick, "The End(s) of Marketing and the Neglect of Moral Responsibility by the American Marketing Association," *Journal of Public Policy & Marketing,* Fall 2007; Debra Jones Ringold and Barton Weitz, "The American Marketing Association Definition of Marketing: Moving from Lagging to Leading Indicator," *Journal of Public Policy & Marketing,* Fall 2007; George M. Zinkhan and Brian C. Williams, "The New American Marketing Association Definition of Marketing: An Alternative Assessment," *Journal of Public Policy & Marketing,* Fall 2007; Gregory T. Gundlach, "The American Marketing Association's 2004 Definition of Marketing: Perspectives on Its Implications for Scholarship and the Role and Responsibility of Marketing in Society," *Journal of Public Policy & Marketing,* Fall 2007; Jagdish N. Sheth and Can Uslay, "Implications of the Revised Definition of Marketing: From Exchange to Value Creation," *Journal of Public Policy & Marketing,* Fall 2007; William L. Wilkie and Elizabeth S. Moore, "What Does the Definition of Marketing Tell Us About Ourselves?" *Journal of Public Policy & Marketing,* Fall 2007.

5. "Nielsen Breakthrough Innovation Report," *European Edition,* September 2014.

6. Based on William McInnes, "A Conceptual Approach to Marketing," Theory in Marketing, second series, ed. Reavis Cox, Wroe Alderson, and Stanley J. Shapiro (Homewood, IL: Richard D. Irwin, 1964).

7. B. J. Calder, E. C. Malthouse, and U. Schaedel, "An Experimental Study of the Relationship between Online Engagement and Advertising Effectiveness," *Journal of Interactive Marketing* 23, #4, 2009; P. Gupta, M. S. Yadav, and R. Varadarajan, "How Task-Facilitative Interactive Tools Foster Buyers' Trust in Online Retailers: A Process View of Trust Development in the Electronic Marketplace," *Journal of Retailing* 85, #2, 2009; Roderick J. Brodie, Heidi Winklhofer, Nicole E. Coviello, and Wesley J. Johnston, "Is E-Marketing Coming of Age? An Examination of the Penetration of E-Marketing and Firm Performance," *Journal of Interactive Marketing,* Spring 2007.

8. Graham Hooley, Tony Cox, John Fahy, David Shipley et al., "Market Orientation in the Transition Economies of Central Europe: Tests of the Narver and Slater Market Orientation Scales," *Journal of Business Research,* December 2000; Saeed Samiee, "Globalization, Privatization, and Free Market Economy," *Journal of the Academy of Marketing Science,* Summer 2001.

9. "Rustic Wisdom: Unilever to Take Project Shakti Global," *Economic Times,* January 19, 2009; "Strategic Innovation: Hindustan Lever Ltd.," *Fast Company,* December 19, 2007; "Shakti—Changing Lives in Rural India," http://hll.com/-citizen_lever/project_shakti.asp; P. Indu, Komal Chary, and Vivek Gupta, "Reviving Hindustan Lever Limited," ICFAI Center for Management Research, Case Study #306-410-1, 2006; V. Kasturi Rangan and Rhithari Rajan, "Unilever in India: Hindustan Lever's Project Shakti—Marketing FMCG to the Rural Consumer," Harvard Business School, Case #9-505-056; C. K. Prahalad, *The Fortune at the Bottom of the Pyramid* (Philadelphia: Wharton School Publishing, 2005).

10. Kevin D. Bradford, Gregory T. Gundlach, and William L. Wilkie, "Countermarketing in the Courts: The Case of Marketing Channels and Firearms Diversion," *Journal of Public Policy & Marketing,* Fall 2005; Marian Friestad and Peter Wright, "The Next Generation: Research for Twenty-First-Century Public Policy on Children and Advertising," *Journal of Public Policy & Marketing,* Fall 2005; Kathleen Seiders and Ross D. Petty, "Taming the Obesity Beast: Children, Marketing, and Public Policy Considerations," *Journal of Public Policy & Marketing,* Fall 2007; James M. Carman and Robert G. Harris, "Public Regulation of Marketing Activity, Part III: A Typology of Regulatory Failures and Implications for Marketing and Public Policy," *Journal of Macromarketing,* Spring 1986.

11. John Elkington, *Cannibals with Forks: The Triple Bottom Line of 21st Century Business* (New York: Wiley, 1997); "Triple Bottom Line," *The Economist,* November 17, 2009.

12. "Can Firms Aim to Do Good If It Hurts Profits?" *Wall Street Journal,* April 10, 2013.

13. Angulo-Ruiz, Fernando, Naveen Donthu, Diego Prior, and Josep Rialp. "The Financial Contribution of Customer-oriented Marketing Capability." *Journal of the Academy of Marketing Science* 42.4 (2014): 380–99. A. Grinstein, "The Effect of Market Orientation and Its Components on Innovation Consequences: A Meta-Analysis," *Journal of the Academy of Marketing Science,* 2 (2008); Ahmet H. Kirca, Satish Jayachandran, and William O. Bearden, "Market Orientation: A Meta-Analytic Review and Assessment of Its Antecedents and Impact on Performance," *Journal of Marketing,* April 2005; Jagdish N. Sheth, Rajendra S. Sisodia, and Arun Sharma, "The Antecedents and Consequences of Customer-Centric Marketing," *Journal of the Academy of Marketing Science,* Winter 2000; Stanley F. Slater and John C. Narver, "Market Orientation and the Learning Organization," *Journal of Marketing,* July 1995; R. W. Ruekert, "Developing a Market Orientation: An Organizational Strategy Perspective," *International Journal of Research in Marketing,* August

1992; Bernard J. Jaworski and Ajay K. Kohli, "Market Orientation: Antecedents and Consequences," *Journal of Marketing,* July 1993; Neil Morgan, "Marketing and Business Performance," *Journal of the Academy of Marketing Science,* January 2012; Son K. Lam, Florian Kraus, and Michael Ahearne, "The Diffusion of Market Orientation Throughout the Organization: A Social Learning Theory Perspective," *Journal of Marketing* 74 (September 2012); V. Kumar, Eli Jones, Rajkumar Venkatesan, and Robert P. Leone, "Is Market Orientation a Source of Sustainable Competitive Advantage or Simply the Cost of Competing?" *Journal of Marketing* 75 (January 2010); Christopher P. Blocker, Daniel J. Flint, Matthew B. Myers, and Stanley F. Slater, "Proactive Customer Orientation and Its Role for Creating Customer Value in Global Markets," *Journal of the Academy of Marketing Science,* 2011.

14. A. F. Payne, K. Storbacka, and P. Frow, "Managing the Co-Creation of Value," *Journal of the Academy of Marketing Science* 36, #1 (2008); "Companies Strive Harder to Please Customers," *Wall Street Journal,* July 27, 2009; "Would You Recommend Us?" *BusinessWeek,* January 30, 2006; "Get Creative! How to Build Innovative Companies," *BusinessWeek,* August 1, 2005; Xie Chunyan, Richard P. Bagozzi, and Sigurd V. Troye, "Trying to Prosume: Toward a Theory of Consumers as Co-creators of Value," *Journal of the Academy of Marketing Science,* Spring 2008; Min Soonhong, John T. Mentzer, and Robert T. Ladd, "A Market Orientation in Supply Chain Management," *Journal of the Academy of Marketing Science,* Winter 2007; Wolfgang Ulaga and Andreas Eggert, "Value-Based Differentiation in Business Relationships: Gaining and Sustaining Key Supplier Status," *Journal of Marketing,* January 2006; Roger Baxter, Sheelagh Matear, James C. Anderson, James A. Narus, and Wouter van Rossum, "Customer Value Propositions in Business Markets," *Harvard Business Review,* March 2006; Ronald L. Hess, Jr., Shankar Ganesan, and Noreen M. Klein, "Service Failure and Recovery: The Impact of Relationship Factors on Customer Satisfaction," *Journal of the Academy of Marketing Science,* Spring 2003; Stanley F. Slater and John C. Narver, "Market Orientation, Customer Value, and Superior Performance," *Business Horizons,* March–April 1994; Sharon E. Beatty, "Keeping Customers," *Journal of Marketing,* April 1994.

15. See www.chipotle.com; "Fast Casual Nation," *Time,* April 23, 2012; "Chipotle Aims to Buck Fast-food Convention—While It Still Can," *Advertising Age,* March 3, 2012; "For Exploding All the Rules of Fast Food," *Fast Company,* June 2012; "Chipotle's Rise," *Fortune,* October 18, 2010; "The Great Casual Dining Upheaval," *Bloomberg Businessweek,* August 29–September 4, 2012; "Chipotle CMO Wants the Whole Enchilada," *Brandweek,* February 16, 2009; "Burrito Buzz—And So Few Ads," *BusinessWeek,* March 12, 2007; "Marketing Is Dead, and Loyalty Killed It" *Harvard Business Review,* February 2015; "Chipotle: The Definitive Oral History," *Bloomberg Business,* February 2, 2015.

16. "Nonprofits Tell Story on Social Networks," *Investor's Business Daily,* February 8, 2010; Stacy Landreth Grau and Judith Anne Garreson Folse, "Cause-Related Marketing (CRM)," *Journal of Advertising,* Winter 2007; "Uncle Sam Wants You in the Worst Way," *BusinessWeek,* August 11, 2005; "Modern Marketing Helps Sell Life as a Nun," *Wall Street Journal,* May 11, 1999; Glenn B. Voss and Zannie Giraud Voss, "Strategic Orientation and Firm Performance in an Artistic Environment," *Journal of Marketing,* January 2000; Dennis B. Arnett, Steve D. German, and Shelby D. Hunt, "The Identity Salience Model of Relationship Marketing Success: The Case of Nonprofit Marketing," *Journal of Marketing,* April 2003.

17. "NYC Promotes Free Water," *Brandweek,* July 9, 2007.

18. "Debate Club: Is Fracking a Good Idea," *US News & World Report,* http://www.usnews.com/debate-club/is-fracking-a-good-idea; "Fracking: Gas Drilling's Environmental Threat," *Pro Publica,* http://www.propublica.org/series/fracking; "Fracking: Pro and Con," *Tufts Now,* December 11, 2012; See also Korschun, Daniel, C. B. Bhattacharya, and Scott D. Swain. "Corporate Social Responsibility, Customer Orientation, and the Job Performance of Frontline Employees." *Journal of Marketing* 78.3 (2014): 20-37; Homburg, Christian, Marcel Stierl, and Torsten Bornemann. "Corporate Social Responsibility in Business-to-Business Markets: How Organizational Customers Account for Supplier Corporate Social Responsibility Engagement." *Journal of Marketing* 77.6 (2013): 54-72; Chernev, Alexander, and Sean Blair. "Doing Well by Doing Good: The Benevolent Halo of Corporate Social Responsibility." *Journal of Consumer Research* 41.6 (2015): 1412-425.

Xuerning Luo and C. B. Bhattacharya, "Corporate Social Responsibility, Customer Satisfaction, and Market Value," *Journal of Marketing,* October 2006; Alan R. Andreasen, "Social Marketing: Its Definition and Domain," *Journal of Public Policy & Marketing,* Spring 1994.

19. "Coke to Curb Ads to Kids, Push Diet Drinks," *Wall Street Journal,* May 8, 2013.

20. Carlos J., Torelli, Alokparna Basu Monga, and Andrew M. Kaikati, "Doing Poorly by Doing Good: Corporate Social Responsibility and Brand Concepts," *Journal of Consumer Research,* 2012; William Wilkie and Elizabeth Moore, "Expanding Our Understanding of Marketing in Society," *Journal of the Academy of Marketing Science,* January 2012; C. B. Bhattacharya and Sankar Sen, "Doing Better at Doing Good: When, Why, and How Customers Respond to Corporate Social Initiatives," *California Management Review,* Fall 2004.

21. Kelly Martin, Jean Johnson, and Joseph French, "Institutional Pressures and Marketing Ethics Initiatives: The Focal Role of Organizational Identity," *Journal of the Academy of Marketing Science,* July 2011; Nidhi Agrawal and Adam Duhachek, "Emotional Compatibility and the Effectiveness of Antidrinking Messages: A Defensive Processing Perspective on Shame and Guilt," *Journal of Marketing Research,* April 2010; Andrew V. Abela and Patrick E. Murphy, "Marketing with Integrity: Ethics and the Service-Dominant Logic for Marketing," *Journal of the Academy of Marketing Science,* Spring 2008; Lawrence B. Chonko and Shelby D. Hunt, "Ethics and Marketing Management: A Retrospective and Prospective Commentary," *Journal of Business Research,* December 2000; Jeffrey G. Blodgett, Long-Chuan Lu, Gregory M. Rose, and Scott J. Vitell, "Ethical Sensitivity to Stakeholder Interests: A Cross-Cultural Comparison," *Journal of the Academy of Marketing Science,* Spring 2001; George G. Brenkert, "Ethical Challenges of Social Marketing," *Journal of Public Policy & Marketing,* Spring 2002.

22. Ferrell, O. C., John Fraedrich, and Linda Ferrell, *Business Ethics: Ethical Decision Making & Cases,* South-Western Publishing; C. B. Bhattacharya and Daniel Korschun, "Stakeholder Marketing: Beyond the Four Ps and the Customer," *Journal of Public Policy & Marketing,* Spring 2008.

23. Bhattacharya, C. B. and Sankar Sen, *Leveraging Corporate Social Responsibility: The Stakeholder Route to Maximizing Business and Social Value,* Cambridge University Press, 2011; Ferrell, O. C., John Fraedrich, and Linda Ferrell, *Business Ethics: Ethical Decision Making & Cases,* South-Western Publishing 2015;

CHAPTER 2

1. See www.cirquedusoleil.com; "Cirque du Soleil Shows Big Brands How to Be Remarkable—And Magical," *Forbes,* February 27, 2012; "Viva Viva Elvis!" *Time,* February 22, 2010; "Cirque's Midlife Crisis," *Canadian Business,* May 10, 2010; "U.S. Casinos' Bet on Macau Pays Off," *USA Today,* January 12, 2010; "Stanley Ho's Last Laugh in Macao," *BusinessWeek,* May 11, 2009; "Big Top to Burlesque: A Circus Sampler," *Wall Street Journal,* January 24, 2008; "Talent Scouts for Cirque du Soleil Walk a Tightrope," *Wall Street Journal,* September 8, 2007; "CMO Strategy: Unleash Emotions for Business Growth," *Advertising Age,* March 12, 2007; "Super Pregame Show," *MiamiHerald.com,* January 10, 2007; "Cirque du Success," *U.S. News and World Report,* November 20, 2006; "The Onliness of Strong Brands," *BusinessWeek,* November 16, 2006; "Crazy for

'Delirium,'" *Billboard*, July 15, 2006; "The Disney of the New Age," *Maclean's*, June 26, 2006; "Cirque du Balancing Act," *Fortune*, June 12, 2006; "How Cirque du Soleil Uses Email to Sell Out Shows at Local Cities," *Marketing Sherpa*, June 1, 2006; W. Chan Kim and Renée Mauborgne, *Blue Ocean Strategy* (Boston: Harvard Business School Press, 2005); "Join the Circus," *Fast Company*, July 1, 2005; "Lord of the Rings," *Economist*, February 5, 2005; "Best Launch: Zumanity," *Marketing Magazine*, November 11, 2004; "Big Top Television," *Marketing Magazine*, August 9–16, 2004; "Mario D'Amico—Cirque du Soleil," *Reveries*, July 2002; "Michael Jackson's New Vegas Show 'One' Will Double the Fun," *Forbes.com*, February 22, 2013; "Cirque's Dramatic Road Work," *Billboard*, March 16, 2013; "Cirque du Soleil's Next Act: Rebalancing the Business," *Wall Street Journal*, December 1, 2014.

2. Rajan Varadarajan, "Strategic Marketing and Marketing Strategy: Domain, Definition, Fundamental Issues and Foundational Premises," *Journal of the Academy of Marketing Science*, March 2012; J. Burnett, "Hidden in Plain Sight: How to Find and Execute Your Company's Next Big Growth Strategy," *Journal of Advertising Research* 48, #1 (2008); George S. Day, "Is It Real? Can We Win? Is It Worth Doing?" *Harvard Business Review*, December 2007; John G. Singer, "What Strategy Is Not," *Sloan Management Review*, Winter 2008; Rebecca J. Slotegraaf and Peter R. Dickson, "The Paradox of a Marketing Planning Capability," *Journal of the Academy of Marketing Science*, Fall 2004; Kwaku Atuahene-Gima and Janet Y. Murray, "Antecedents and Outcomes of Marketing Strategy Comprehensiveness," *Journal of Marketing*, October 2004; Gail J. McGovern, David Court, John A. Quelch, and Blair Crawford, "Bringing Customers into the Boardroom," *Harvard Business Review*, November 2004; George S. Day, "Marketing's Contribution to the Strategy Dialogue," *Journal of the Academy of Marketing Science*, Fall 1992; P. Rajan Varadarajan and Terry Clark, "Delineating the Scope of Corporate, Business, and Marketing Strategy," *Journal of Business Research*, October–November 1994.

3. See www.herbalessences.com/us/default.jsp; "The Issue: How P&G Brought Back Herbal Essences," *BusinessWeek*, June 17, 2008; "Herbal Essence Snags 2007 ReBrand 100 Global Award," *Marketing Daily*, July 11, 2007; "Nature Boy," *Brandweek*, September 7, 2008; Ram Charan and A. G. Lafley, *The Game Changer* (New York: Crown Business).

4. For information on Silverman's new business, see www.preschoolians.com. For more on Toddler University see "Genesco Names New Executive of Children's Footwear Division," Press Release, Genesco, July 15, 1994; "Toddler University Ends Up in Westport," *Westport News*, March 8, 1991; "Whiz Kid," *Connecticut*, August 1989; "The Young and the Restless," *Children's Business*, May 1989; "Welcome to the Programmable World," *Wired*, May 2013.

5. Orville C. Walker, Jr., and Robert W. Ruekert, "Marketing's Role in the Implementation of Business Strategies: A Critical Review and Conceptual Framework," *Journal of Marketing*, July 1987; Thomas V. Bonoma, "A Model of Marketing Implementation," 1984 *AMA Educators' Proceedings*, Chicago: American Marketing Association, 1984.

6. Richard A. D'Aveni, "Mapping Your Competitive Position," *Harvard Business Review*, February 2008; George S. Day and Robin Wensley, "Assessing Advantage: A Framework for Diagnosing Competitive Superiority," *Journal of Marketing*, April 1988; Michael E. Porter, *Competitive Advantage—Creating and Sustaining Superior Performance* (New York: Free Press, MacMillan, 1986); Mark B. Houston, "Competing for the Future: Breakthrough Strategies for Seizing Control of Your Industry and Creating the Markets of Tomorrow," *Journal of the Academy of Marketing Science*, Winter 1996; Kevin P. Coyne, "Sustainable Competitive Advantage—What It Is, What It Isn't," *Business Horizons*, January–February 1986.

7. www.ikea.com; www.jetblue.com; www.in-n-out.com; Youngme Moon, *Different: Escaping the Competitive Herd* (New York: Crown Business, 2010); "Manland: Ikea's Day-care for Husbands," *The Week*, September 16, 2011.

8. Ruth N. Bolton, Katherine N. Lemon, and Peter C. Verhoef, "Expanding Business-to-Business Customer Relationships: Modeling the Customer's Upgrade Decision," *Journal of Marketing*, January 2008; Douglas W. Vorhies and Neil A. Morgan, "A Configuration Theory Assessment of Marketing Organization Fit with Business Strategy and Its Relationship with Marketing Performance," *Journal of Marketing*, January 2003.

9. For more on Coleman, see www.coleman.com; "The Grill of Their Dreams," *Business 2.0*, February 2002; "Growing to Match Its Brand Name," *Fortune*, June 13, 1994. See also Youjae Yi and Hoseong Jeon, "Effects of Loyalty Programs on Value Perception, Program Loyalty, and Brand Loyalty," *Journal of the Academy of Marketing Science*, Summer 2003.

10. For more on E-Z-Go, see www.ezgo.com; "Wanna Drag? Now Golf Carts Are in the Race," *Wall Street Journal*, March 6, 2007; "Off-Roading, Golf-Cart Style," *Wall Street Journal*, June 14, 2001. See also Michael S. Garver, "Best Practices in Identifying Customer-Driven Improvement Opportunities," *Industrial Marketing Management*, August 2003; John H. Roberts, "Developing New Rules for New Markets," *Journal of the Academy of Marketing Science*, Winter 2000.

11. "Body Cameras for All: One Way to Avert Lawsuits," *Wall Street Journal*, January 5, 2015.

12. For more on Campbell, see www.campbellsoup.com; "Campbell Soup Boosts Outlook as Net Rises," *Wall Street Journal*, November 24, 2009; "Campbell's: Not About to Let the Soup Cool," *BusinessWeek*, September 28, 2009; "Campbell's Lowering Sodium in Almost 50 Soups," *USA Today*, February 18, 2008. For more on ski resorts, see "Seeking Growth, Ski Areas Target Minorities," *Wall Street Journal*, December 22, 2004. See also Sarah J. Marsh and Gregory N. Stock, "Building Dynamic Capabilities in New Product Development Through Intertemporal Integration," *Journal of Product Innovation Management*, March 2003; George C. Kingston and Beebe Nelson, "Leading Product Innovation: Accelerating Growth in a Product-Based Business," *Journal of Product Innovation Management*, November 2001.

13. For more on McDonald's and its hotel diversification effort, see "Would You Like a Bed with Your Burger?" *Ad Age Global*, February 2001; "The Golden Arches: Burgers, Fries and 4-Star Rooms," *Wall Street Journal*, November 17, 2000; "Welcome to the Programmable World," *Wired*, May 2013.

14. For more on JLG, see www.jlg.com; "JLG Industries Acquisition Gives a Big Lift to Oshkosh Truck Sales," *Investor's Business Daily*, October 31, 2007; "The Secret of U.S. Exports: Great Products," *Fortune*, January 10, 2000.

15. For more on international marketing, see "Novelty of Mexican Food in India Is a Hit for Yum," *Wall Street Journal*, March 30, 2010; "Yum Brands Bet on India's Young for Growth," *Wall Street Journal*, December 17, 2009; "McDonald's Creates Asian-Inspired Versions of Food as Part of Olympics Blitz," *Wall Street Journal*, July 1, 2008; "In Vietnam, Fast Food Acts Global, Tastes Local," *Wall Street Journal*, March 12, 2008; "Foreign Distribution? Just Ask Mom (& Pop)," *Brandweek*, November 19, 2007; "Scrambling to Bring Crest to the Masses," *BusinessWeek*, June 25, 2007; Naresh K. Malhotra, Francis M. Ulgado, and James Agarwal, "Internationalization and Entry Modes: A Multitheoretical Framework and Research Propositions," *Journal of International Marketing*, 2003; Shaoming Zou and S. Tamer Cavusgil, "The GMS: A Broad Conceptualization of Global Marketing Strategy and Its Effect on Firm Performance," *Journal of Marketing*, October 2002; Susan P. Douglas, "Exploring New Worlds: The Challenge of Global Marketing," *Journal of Marketing*, January 2001.

CHAPTER 3

1. See www.amazon.com; *Amazon.com: The Hidden Empire*, FABERNOVEL, May 2011; "No Holiday Cheer for Amazon.com," *Chicago Tribune*, November 27, 2011; "Amazon Pressured on Sales Tax," *New York Times*, March 13, 2011; "Retailers Struggle in

Amazon's Jungle," *Wall Street Journal,* February 22, 2011; "Price Check for iPhone," *Wired,* November 23, 2010; "What's in Amazon's Box? Instant Gratification," *Bloomberg Businessweek,* November 23, 2010; "Wal-Mart Fires Shot in Toy War," *Wall Street Journal,* November 8, 2010; "Study: Amazon.com Is Most Trusted Brand in U.S," *CNET News,* February 22, 2010; "Now, It's Google vs. . . . Amazon.com?" *Investor's Business Daily,* November 19, 2009; "Walmart Making Push Online, Where It's a Pygmy vs. Amazon," *Investor's Business Daily,* October 20, 2009; "Walmart Strafes Amazon in Book War," *Wall Street Journal,* October 16, 2009; "Amazon Packages Green Site," *Investor's Business Daily,* February 25, 2009; "Amazon.com's Third-Party Sales Balloon," *Investor's Business Daily,* April 8, 2009; "When Service Means Survival: How Amazon Aims to Keep You Clicking," *BusinessWeek,* March 2, 2009; "The World's Most Innovative Companies," *Fast Company,* March 2009. For more on Kindle, see "Hachette Enters the E-Book Fray, Saying It, Too, Wants New Pricing," *Wall Street Journal,* February 5, 2010; "Trying to Avert a Digital Horror Story," *BusinessWeek,* January 11, 2010; "Sony E-Reader Opens New Chapters in Kindle Rivalry," *Wall Street Journal,* January 14, 2010; "More Makers Jump into the E-Reader Fray," *Wall Street Journal,* January 8, 2010; "Publishers Aren't Happy with Amazon's Pricing," *USA Today,* December 11, 2009; "IPod Touch, iPhone Join Kindle's Book Club," *USA Today,* March 4, 2009; "Amazon's Kindle 2 Improves the Good, Leaves Out the Bad," *Wall Street Journal,* February 26, 2009; "Kindle's New, but Price Is Old," *USA Today,* February 10, 2009; "As the Kindle Turns Five, Amazon Girds for a New Fight," *Bloomberg Businessweek,* November 26, 2012; "Amazon's (Not So Secret) War on Taxes," *Fortune,* May 23, 2013; "Amazon Bets On Web Groceries, Expands AmazonFresh to L.A." *TechCrunch,* June 10, 2013; "Once Refined, Same-Day Delivery Will Be Commonplace," *Wired,* May 2013; "Amazon Preps Faster Deliveries by Bike and by Drone," *Wall Street Journal,* December 8, 2014; "Amazon's First Staffed College Campus Store Should Have Retailers Worried," TechCrunch, February 3, 2015; "Amazon Makes a Push on College Campuses," *Wall Street Journal,* February 1, 2015. Jeff Bezos, "Can Amazon's Jeff Bezos Save Planet Earth?" NPR. January 08, 2014

2. "Till death us do part: What's your one piece of social media advice?" *Conferenz,* June 5, 2012.

3. www.redcross.org; Lance Leuthesser and Chiranjeev Kohli, "Corporate Identity: The Role of Mission Statements," *Business Horizons,* May–June 1997; Christopher K. Bart, "Sex, Lies, and Mission Statements," *Business Horizons,* November–December 1997. Red Cross mission statement from "Mission & Principles" of the American Red Cross. Copyright © by the American Red Cross. All rights reserved. Used with permission. For more general discussions of marketing strategy, see Peter F. Drucker, *Management: Tasks, Responsibilities, Practices, and Plans* (New York: Harper & Row, 1973); Sev K. Keil, "The Impact of Business Objectives and the Time Horizon of Performance Evaluation on Pricing Behavior," *International Journal of Research in Marketing,* June 2001; George S. Day and Christine Moorman, *Strategy from the Outside In* (McGraw-Hill, 2010).

4. www.usaa.com; "USAA's Battle Plan," *BusinessWeek,* February 18, 2010; "Customer Service Champs," *BusinessWeek,* March 5, 2007; "USAA Soldiering on in Insurance," *BusinessWeek,* March 5, 2007.

5. For more on Starbucks, see www.starbucks.com; "Starbucks Plans Big Expansion in China," *Wall Street Journal,* April 14, 2010; "Mature Coffee Brewer Finds New Ways to Stir Earnings Growth," *Investor's Business Daily,* January 6, 2010; "Starbucks Says Demand Perking Up," *Wall Street Journal,* November 6, 2009; "Starbucks Takes New Road with Instant Coffee," *Wall Street Journal,* September 29, 2009; "Howard Schultz versus Howard Schultz," *BusinessWeek,* August 17, 2009; "Starbucks Plays Common Joe," *Wall Street Journal,* February 9, 2009; "Starbucks' Dismal Quarter Leads to 'Value' Offerings," *Advertising Age,* January 28, 2009; "Starbucks' Surprise Success: Oatmeal," *Advertising Age,* October 13, 2008; "New Starbucks Brew Attracts Customers, Flak," *Wall Street Journal,* July 1, 2008.

6. For more on competition, see Timothy B. Heath, Gangseog Ryu, Subimal Chatterjee, Michael S. McCarthy, "Asymmetric Competition in Choice and the Leveraging of Competitive Disadvantages," *Journal of Consumer Research,* December 2000; Kao, (Cambridge, MA: Harvard Business School Press, 1984); Bruce R. Klemz, "Managerial Assessment of Potential Entrants: Processes and Pitfalls," *International Journal of Research in Marketing,* June 2001. For more on P&G's diaper competition in United States see "Value Positioning Becomes a Priority," *Advertising Age,* February 23, 2004; "Rivals Take P&G to Court to Challenge Ads," *Wall Street Journal,* June 17, 2003; "Dueling Diapers," Fortune, February 17, 2003.

7. For more on corporate spying and competitive intelligence, see "Cybercrooks Stalk Small Businesses," *USA Today,* December 31, 2009; "Hounding the Hackers," *BusinessWeek,* September 14, 2009; "How Team of Geeks Cracked Spy Trade," *Wall Street Journal,* September 4, 2009; "Accusations of Snooping in Ink-Cartridge Dispute," *Wall Street Journal,* August 11, 2009; "Today's Spies Find Secrets in Plain Sight," *USA Today,* August 1, 2008; "Snooping on a Shoestring," *Business 2.0,* May 2003. See also Shaker A. Zahra, "Unethical Practices in Competitive Analysis: Patterns, Causes and Effects," *Journal of Business Ethics,* January 1994.

8. For more on economic environment, see Rajdeep Grewal, "Building Organizational Capabilities for Managing Economic Crisis: The Role of Market Orientation and Strategic Flexibility," *Journal of Marketing,* April 2001.

9. See the boy's hand in action at http://youtube/kB53-D N8Uc; "Doctors Save Life Of Kaiba Gionfriddo, Ohio Boy, By 3-D 'Printing' Him an Airway Tube," *Huffington Post,* May 22, 2013; "Baby's Life Saved with 3D Printing," *Live Science,* May 22, 2013; "3-D Printer Brings Dexterity to Children with No Fingers," *Morning Edition, NPR.org,* June 18, 2013; "What Is 3D Printing? An Overview," *3D Printer.net,* 2013; "Ten Principles of 3D Printing," *Big Think,* March 2, 2013; "In Tomorrow's Wars, Battles Will Be Fought with a 3-D Printer," *Wired.com,* May 17, 2013; "10 Industries 3D Printing Will Disrupt or Decimate," *TechRepublic,* February 12, 2014; "Our Future With 3D Printers: 7 Disrupted Industries," *Forbes,* October 29, 2013.

10. "The driverless road ahead," *The Economist,* October 20, 2012; "Baby, You Can Program My Car," *Freakonomics.com,* May 29, 2013.

11. For more on technological environment, see Brian T. Ratchford, Debabrata Talukdar, and L. E. E. Myung-Soo, "The Impact of the Internet on Consumers' Use of Information Sources for Automobiles: A Re-Inquiry," *Journal of Consumer Research,* June 2007; Anand V. Bodapati, "Recommendation Systems with Purchase Data," *Journal of Marketing Research,* February 2008. For more on privacy, see Chapter 19.

12. "Chrysler's 'Imported from Detroit' Super Bowl Ad Inspires Political Debate," *CBSNews,* February 7, 2011; for other examples of nationalism, see "Coming Home: Appliance Maker Drops China to Produce in Texas," *Wall Street Journal,* August 24, 2009; "Buy American Clause Stirs Up Controversy," *USA Today,* February 4, 2009; "Which Is More American?" *USA Today,* March 22, 2007. See also Durairaj Maheswaran and Cathy Yi Chen, "Nation Equity: Incidental Emotions in Country-of-Origin Effects," *Journal of Consumer Research,* October 2006; George Balabanis and Adamantios Diamantopoulos, "Domestic Country Bias, Country-of-Origin Effects, and Consumer Ethnocentrism: A Multidimensional Unfolding Approach," *Journal of the Academy of Marketing Science,* Winter 2004; Zeynep Gurhan-Canli and Durairaj Maheswaran, "Determinants of Country-of-Origin Evaluations," *Journal of Consumer Research,* June 2000.

13. For more on NAFTA, see www.nafta.org; "Central American Free Trade Agreement Faces Obstacles," *USA Today,* May 12, 2005; "Refighting NAFTA," *BusinessWeek,* March 31, 2008; "10 Years Ago, NAFTA Was Born," *USA Today,* December 31, 2003; "Was NAFTA Worth It? A Tale of What Free Trade Can and Cannot Do," *BusinessWeek,* December 22, 2003.

14. For other examples, see "German Shoppers May Get Sale Freedom," *Wall Street Journal,* January 23, 2002; "Border Crossings," *Wall Street Journal,* November 22, 1999. For another example, see "Corn Flakes Clash Shows the Glitches in European Union," *Wall Street Journal,* November 1, 2005. For more on EU, see "Euro Zone Debt Crisis Intensifies on Summit Eve," *Reuters,* March 10, 2011; "Hopes Raised, Punches Pulled," *The Economist,* February 10, 2011; "Squeezed by the Euro," *BusinessWeek,* June 6, 2005. See also Andrew Paddison, "Retailing in the European Union: Structures, Competition and Performance," *International Journal of Retail & Distribution Management,* 6 (2003).

15. For more on Beech-Nut, see "What Led Beech-Nut Down the Road to Disgrace," *BusinessWeek,* February 22, 1988. See also Kersi D. Antia, Mark E. Bergen, Shantanu Dutta, and Robert J. Fisher, "How Does Enforcement Deter Gray Market Incidence?" *Journal of Marketing,* January 2006; Debra M. Desrochers, Gregory T. Gundlach, and Albert A. Foer, "Analysis of Antitrust Challenges to Category Captain Arrangements," *Journal of Public Policy & Marketing,* Fall 2003; "Europe: A Different Take on Antitrust," *BusinessWeek,* June 25, 2001; "In ArcherDaniels Saga, Now the Executives Face Trial," *Wall Street Journal,* July 9, 1998. See also Mary W. Sullivan, "The Role of Marketing in Antitrust," *Journal of Public Policy & Marketing,* Fall 2002; Jeff Langenderfer and Steven W. Kopp, "Which Way to the Revolution? The Consequences of Database Protection as a New Form of Intellectual Property," *Journal of Public Policy & Marketing,* Spring 2003. See also Louis W. Stern and Thomas L. Eovaldi, *Legal Aspects of Marketing Strategy: Antitrust and Consumer Protection Issues* (Englewood Cliffs, NJ: Prentice-Hall, 1984).

16. "Ford vs. Firestone: A Corporate Whodunit," *Businessweek,* June 10, 2001. For more on auto safety, see "States Go After Texting Drivers: Safety Concerns Fuel New Legislation," *USA Today,* January 25, 2010; "The Number of Small-Car Owners Is Growing Even Though More Drivers Die in Small Cars," *USA Today,* August 20, 2007. For more on CPSC, see "More Paper Tiger than Watchdog?" *BusinessWeek,* September 3, 2007, p. 45; "Product-Safety Cops Handcuffed," *Wall Street Journal,* December 18, 2007. For an overview of the toy, food, and pet product recalls of 2007, see "The New China Price," *Fortune,* November 12, 2007; "Spate of Recalls Boosts Potency of User Reviews," *Advertising Age,* October 29, 2007.

17. "Tesla Clashes with Car Dealers," *Wall Street Journal,* June 18, 2013; "Judge Rules Airbnb Illegal in New York City," *CNNMoney,* May 21, 2013.

18. "Time to Rethink Your Message: Now the Cart Belongs to Daddy," *Advertising Age,* January 17, 2011. For more on the changing role of women, see "The Rise of the Real Mom," *Advertising Age,* White Paper, November 16, 2009; "Daisy Rock Amps Up Girl Power: Specially Designed Guitars Fit a Woman Just Right," *USA Today,* December 15, 2009; "Videogame Firms Make a Play for Women," *Wall Street Journal,* October 13, 2009; "Verizon Targets Women with Hub Phone," *Advertising Age,* March 9, 2009; "Pretty in Pink," *CNN.com,* October 5, 2007; "Meet Jane Geek," *BusinessWeek,* November 28, 2005.

19. Based on U.S. Census data including Statistical Abstract of the United States 2010 (Washington, DC: U.S. Government Printing Office, October 2009), Table 1296, pp. 818–20, available online at www.census.gov/statab; U.S. Census Bureau "International Data Base" available online at www.census.gov/ipc/www/idb/; Population Reference Bureau data, including 2009 World Pop. Data Sheet, available online at www.prb.org/Publications/Datasheets/2009; World Bank data, available online at http://web.worldbank.org/WBSITE/EXTERNAL/DATASTATISTICS; CIA data, including CIA Factbook 2010, available online at https://www.cia.gov/library/publications/the-world-factbook; ICT Statistics Database, Mobile Cellular Subscriptions Per 100 People, 2008, International Telecommunications Union, available online at www.itu.int/ITU-D/icteye/Indicators/Indicators.aspx; and Internet World Stats, 2010, available online at www.internetworldstats.com/stats.htm; GlobalEDGE data from Michigan State University at http://globaledge.msu.edu. See also

"Baby Bundle: Japan's Cash Incentive for Parenthood," *Wall Street Journal,* October 8, 2009; "China Inc. Looks Homeward as U.S. Shoppers Turn Frugal," *Wall Street Journal,* September 29, 2009; "Can Greed Save Africa?" *BusinessWeek,* December 10, 2007; "China's Grappling with One Helluva Problem," *USA Today,* September 18, 2007; "India Rising," *Newsweek,* March 6, 2006; "The Battle for the Face of China," *Fortune,* December 12, 2005; "The Rise of Central Europe," *Business-Week,* December 12, 2005; "India's Bumpy Ride," *Fortune,* October 31, 2005; "China & India," *BusinessWeek* (special issue), August 22, 2005; "Global Aging: Now, the Geezer Glut," *BusinessWeek,* January 31, 2005; "Tamer S. Cavusgil, "Measuring the Potential of Emerging Markets: An Indexing Approach," *Business Horizons,* January–February 1997. See also C. Riegner, "Wired China: The Power of the World's Largest Internet Population," *Journal of Advertising Research* 48, #4 (2008).

20. Based on World Bank GNI and GDP data and available online at http://web.worldbank.org/WBSITE/EXTERNAL/DATASTATISTICS; Data source World Bank, except for projected population where source is U.S. Census Bureau International Data Base and literacy data from the CIA World Book.

21. Based on CIA data, including CIA Factbook 2010, available online at https://www.cia.gov/library/publications/the-world-factbook. See also Madhubalan Viswanathan, Jose Antonio Rosa, and James Edwin Harris, "Decision Making and Coping of Functionally Illiterate Consumers and Some Implications for Marketing Management," *Journal of Marketing,* January 2005; Natalie Ross Adkins, Julie L. Ozanne, Dawn Iacobucci, and Eric Arnould, "The Low Literate Consumer," *Journal of Consumer Research,* June 2005.

22. "In Kerala, Cell Phones Go Fishing," *Liberation,* October 2, 2006; "ITC eChoupal Initiative," Harvard Business School Case #604016, 2003.

23. A. M. Chircu and V. Mahajan, "Perspective: Revisiting the Digital Divide: An Analysis of Mobile Technology Depth and Service Breadth in the BRIC Countries," *Journal of Product Innovation Management* 26, #4 (2009).

24. Based on U.S. Census data including Statistical Abstract of the United States 2010, pp. 18 and 20, and available at www.census.gov/statab; "2010 America: What the 2010 Census Means for Marketing and Advertising," *Advertising Age,* White Paper, October 12, 2009; "No More Joe Consumer in America," *Advertising Age,* October 12, 2009. See also "For Florida, 'the End of an Era' of Growth," *USA Today,* September 1, 2009; "Is Florida Over?" *Wall Street Journal,* September 29, 2007; "The Coming Crunch," *Wall Street Journal,* October 13, 2006; "Fastest Growth Found in Red States," Also based on data from Population Reference Bureau at www.prb.org>www.prb.org.

25. Based on U.S. Census data including Statistical Abstract of the United States 2010, pp. 11–12, and available online at www.census.gov/statab. See also "Boomer$," *CNBC,* March 4, 2010; "The 15 Biggest Baby Boomer Brands," *Advertising Age,* March 1, 2010; "Clothing Stores Rediscover Boomers," *USA Today,* September 12, 2008; "Love Those Boomers," *BusinessWeek,* October 24, 2005; K. G. Gronbach, *The Age Curve: How to Profit from the Coming Demographic Storm* (2008); Charlene Li and Josh Bernoff, *Groundswell: Winning in a World Transformed by Social Technologies* (Cambridge: Harvard Business School Press, 2008).

26. "'iGeneration' Has No Off Switch," *USA Today,* February 10, 2010; Kit Yarrow and Jayne O'Donnell, *Gen BuY: How Tweens, Teens, and Twenty-Somethings Are Revolutionizing Retail* (Jossey-Bass, 2009); "Why 'Millennials' Are Impulse Shoppers," *Brandweek,* November 12, 2009; "Generation Y Forces Retailers to Keep Up with Technology, New Stuff," *Wall Street Journal,* September 14, 2009; "Trying to Connect with Generation Y," *Wall Street Journal,* October 13, 2005; "Target Revamps Groceries for Millennials," *Wall Street Journal,* March 2, 2015; "MIllennials – Breaking the Myths," *The Nielsen Company,* 2014.

27. Frank N. Magid Associates, "The First Generation of the Twenty First Century," April 30, 2012; "Generation Z: Rebels with a Cause," *Forbes,* May 28, 2013.

28. Frank R. Bacon, Jr., and Thomas W. Butler, Jr., *Planned Innovation,* rev. ed. (Ann Arbor: Institute of Science and Technology, University of Michigan, 1980).

29. "Ahead of the Pack," *Wall Street Journal,* March 24, 2008; "50 Ways to Green Your Business," *Fast Company,* December 19, 2007; www.greenbiz.com/news/. For some academic research on sustainability see Gershoff, Andrew D., and Judy K. Frels. "What Makes It Green? The Role of Centrality of Green Attributes in Evaluations of the Greenness of Products." *Journal of Marketing* 79.1 (2015): 97–110; Barnhart, Michelle, and Lisa Peñaloza. "Who Are You Calling Old? Negotiating Old Age Identity in the Elderly Consumption Ensemble." *Journal of Consumer Research* 39.6 (2013): 1133–153; Xie, Chunyan, Richard Bagozzi, and Kjell Grønhaug. "The Role of Moral Emotions and Individual Differences in Consumer Responses to Corporate Green and Non-green Actions." *Journal of the Academy of Marketing Science* 43.3 (2015): 333–56; Olson, Erik. "It's Not Easy Being Green: The Effects of Attribute Tradeoffs on Green Product Preference and Choice." *Journal of the Academy of Marketing Science* 41.2 (2013): 171–84; Olsen, Mitchell C., Rebecca J. Slotegraaf, and Sandeep R. Chandukala. "Green Claims and Message Frames: How Green New Products Change Brand Attitude." *Journal of Marketing* 78.5 (2014): 119–37; Newman, George E., Margarita Gorlin, and Ravi Dhar. "When Going Green Backfires: How Firm Intentions Shape the Evaluation of Socially Beneficial Product Enhancements." *Journal of Consumer Research* 41.3 (2014): 823–39; Haws, Kelly L., Karen Page Winterich, and Rebecca Walker Naylor. "Seeing the World through GREEN-tinted Glasses: Green Consumption Values and Responses to Environmentally Friendly Products." *Journal of Consumer Psychology,* 24.3 (2014): 336–54.

30. Paul F. Anderson, "Marketing, Strategic Planning and the Theory of the Firm," *Journal of Marketing,* Spring 1982; Ronnie Silverblatt and Pradeep Korgaonkar, "Strategic Market Planning in a Turbulent Business Environment," *Journal of Business Research,* August 1987.

31. Keith B. Murray and Edward T. Popper, "Competing under Regulatory Uncertainty: A U.S. Perspective on Advertising in the Emerging European Market," *Journal of Macromarketing,* Fall 1992; "Inside Russia—Business Most Unusual," *UPS International Update,* Spring 1994; "Freighted with Difficulties," *Wall Street Journal,* December 10, 1993; "Russia Snickers after Mars Invades," *Wall Street Journal,* July 13, 1993.

32. "Sensitive Export: Seeking New Markets for Tampons, P&G Faces Cultural Barriers," *Wall Street Journal,* December 8, 2000; "Pizza Queen of Japan Turns Web Auctioneer," *Wall Street Journal,* March 6, 2000; Kamran Kashani, "Beware the Pitfalls of Global Marketing," *Harvard Business Review,* September–October 1989.

CHAPTER 4

1. www.lego.com; "Innovation Almost Bankrupted LEGO—Until It Rebuilt with a Better Blueprint," *Knowledge@Wharton,* July 18, 2012; *The Brick* (Annual Magazine), 2010; *Company Profile: An Introduction to the LEGO Group, 2009;* "Toymaker Grows by Listening to Customers," *Advertising Age,* November 9, 2009; "Innovating a Turnaround at LEGO," *Harvard Business Review,* September 2009; "LEGO Proves Itself a Blockbuster Once Again," *The Times,* February 24, 2009; Charlene Li and Josh Bernoff, *Groundswell* (Harvard Business School Press: Boston, 2008); "Innovation at the LEGO Group (A) and (B)" (case series), International Institute for Management Development, 2008; "Please Don't Touch Daddy's LEGO," *Maclean's,* October 6, 2008; "Lego Introduces WeDo Package for Education," *Macworld,* June 30, 2008; "LEGO® Education WeDo™ Unveiled at 2008 National Educational Computing Conference," at Lego.com; "LEGO Learns a Lesson," *Change Agent,* June, 2008; "Geeks in Toyland," *Wired,* February 2006; Majken Schultz and Mary Jo Hatch, "The Cycles of Corporate Branding: The Case of LEGO Company," *California Management Review,* Fall 2003. See also H. J.

Schau, A. M. Muniz, and E. J. Arnould, "How Brand Community Practices Create Value," *Journal of Marketing* 73, #5 (2009); "Lego Builds New Billionaires as Toymaker Topples Mattel," *Bloomberg,* March 13, 2013; Annual Report 2012, The LEGO Group; "Lego Has Become the World's Largest Toy Brand by Constructing a Highly Lucrative TV and Film Model," *Adweek,* April 15, 2013; "For Lego, Pink Is the New Black," *Bloomberg Businessweek,* February 22, 2013; Jensen, Morten Berg, Christoph Hienerth, and Christopher Lettl (2014), "Forecasting the Commercial Attractiveness of User-Generated Designs Using the LEGO User Community," *Journal of Product Innovation Management, December,* 31, 75–93; "How Lego Became The Apple of Toys," *Fast Company,* February 2015; "LEGO's VP of Marketing on Listening to Customers, Movies, and 360 Marketing," *Marketing Week,* March 23, 2015; "Lego Bucks Industry Trend with Profit Growth."

2. See www.hallmark.com; 2011 Annual Report, Hallmark; "Hallmark Rethinks Approach to Greeting Cards," *Chain Drug Review,* March 16, 2015; "Writing Mother's Day Cards at Hallmark: An Inside Look," *Bloomberg.com,* May 1, 2014.

3. Glen L. Urban and John R. Hauser, "Listening In to Find and Explore New Combinations of Customer Needs," *Journal of Marketing,* April 2004; Terri C. Albert, "Need-Based Segmentation and Customized Communication Strategies in a Complex-Commodity Industry: A Supply Chain Study," *Industrial Marketing Management,* May 2003; Rajendra K. Srivastava, Mark I. Alpert, and Allan D. Shocker, "A Customer-Oriented Approach for Determining Market Structures," *Journal of Marketing,* Spring 1984.

4. "Life Stage: Its Impact on the Future of Traditional and Emerging Media," *e-Poll Market Research,* February 2010.

5. For more on Herman Miller, see www.hermanmiller.com; 2011 Annual Report, Herman Miller; "Herman Miller Is Sitting Pretty," *Fortune,* November 27, 2006; "A Cult Chair Gets a Makeover," *Wall Street Journal,* September 17, 2002.

6. Sally Dibb and Lyndon Simkin, "Market Segmentation: Diagnosing and Treating the Barriers," *Industrial Marketing Management,* November 2001; Terry Elrod and Russell S. Winer, "An Empirical Evaluation of Aggregation Approaches for Developing Market Segments," *Journal of Marketing,* Fall 1982; Frederick W. Winter, "A Cost-Benefit Approach to Market Segmentation," *Journal of Marketing,* Fall 1979.

7. See www.kaepa.com; "Tapping into Cheerleading," *Adweek's Marketing Week,* March 2, 1992.

8. Frank, Björn, Takao Enkawa, and Shane Schvaneveldt. "How Do the Success Factors Driving Repurchase Intent Differ between Male and Female Customers?" *Journal of the Academy of Marketing Science* 42.2 (2014): 171–85; 04 Haenlein, Michael, and Barak Libai. "Targeting Revenue Leaders for a New Product." *Journal of Marketing* 77.3 (2013): 65–80; Paharia, Neeru, Jill Avery, and Anat Keinan. Thomas Reutterer, Andreas Mild, Martin Natter, and Alfred Taudes, "A Dynamic Segmentation Approach for Targeting and Customizing Direct Marketing Campaigns," *Journal of Interactive Marketing,* Summer 2006; S. Tamer Cavusgil, Tunga Kiyak, and Sengun Yeniyurt, "Complementary Approaches to Preliminary Foreign Market Opportunity Assessment: Country Clustering and Country Ranking," *Industrial Marketing Management,* October 2004; Malaika Brengman, Maggie Geuens, Bert Weijters, Scott M. Smith, and William R. Swinyard, "Segmenting Internet Shoppers Based on Their Web-Usage-Related Lifestyle: A Cross-Cultural Validation," *Journal of Business Research,* January 2005; Ruth N. Bolton and Matthew B. Myers, "Price-Based Global Market Segmentation for Services," *Journal of Marketing,* July 2003; Philip A. Dover, "Segmentation and Positioning for Strategic Marketing Decisions," *Journal of the Academy of Marketing Science,* Summer 2000.

9. "Ford Offers Free Driver's Ed in Vietnam," *USA Today,* August 5, 2010.

10. For more on buyer personas see: "The Beginner's Guide to Segmentation and Buyer Personas," *HubSpot Academy Blog,* March 19, 2014; http://blog.hubspot.com/customers/getting-started-with-segmentation; "Buyer Personas and Segmentation: One Is Not Like the Other," *ClickZ*, March 25, 2015.

11. This ethics question was inspired by the following article that might provide the instructor with useful background reading: "Apps for Kids Are Data Magnets; FTC Rules to Kick In," *Wall Street Journal*, June 27, 2013.

12. Stephen D. Ross, "Segmenting Sports Fans Using Brand Associations: A Cluster Analysis," *Sports Marketing Quarterly*, 1 (2007); Rajan Sambandam, "Cluster Analysis Gets Complicated," *Marketing Research*, Spring 2003; "Girish Punj and David W. Stewart, "Cluster Analysis in Marketing Research: Review and Suggestions for Application," *Journal of Marketing Research*, May 1983.

13. Timothy Bohling, Douglas Bowman, Steve Lavalle, Vikas Mittal, Das Narayandas, Girish Ramani, and Rajan Varadarajan, "CRM Implementation: Effectiveness Issues and Insights," *Journal of Service Research*, May 2006; H. Wilson, M. Clark, and B. Smith, "Justifying CRM Projects in a Business-to-Business Context: The Potential of the Benefits Dependency Network," *Industrial Marketing Management*, June 2007; Katherine N. Lemon, Tiffany Barnett White, and Russell S. Winer, "Dynamic Customer Relationship Management: Incorporating Future Considerations into the Service Retention Decision," *Journal of Marketing*, January 2002; "How Big Data Is Changing the Whole Equation for Business," *Wall Street Journal*, March 8, 2013.

14. Mobile Marketing That Works, Advertising Age Special Report, June 30, 2014; "Audi attracts feminine consumers with geotargeted banner ad," Luxury Daily, January 30, 2015

15. "How Companies Learn Your Secrets," *New York Times*, February 16, 2012; Charles Duhigg, *The Power of Habit* (New York: Random House, 2012); "Data Mining and Predictive Analytics," *Abbott Analytics*, February 18, 2012; "How Target Knew a High School Girl Was Pregnant Before Her Parents Did," *Time*, February 17, 2012.

16. "Positioning Brands Against Large Competitors to Increase Sales." *Journal of Marketing Research (JMR)* 51.6 (2014): 647–56; Garrett Sonnier and Andrew Ainslie, "Estimating the Value of Brand-Image Associations: The Role of General and Specific Brand Image," *Journal of Marketing Research*, June 2011; V. Kumar and Denish Shah, "Uncovering Implicit Consumer Needs for Determining Explicit Product Positioning: Growing Prudential Annuities' Variable Annuity Sales," *Marketing Science*, 4 (2011); Ji Kyung Park and Deborah Roedder John, "Got to Get You into My Life: Do Brand Personalities Rub off on Consumers?" *Journal of Consumer Research*, August 2010; Charles Blankson, Stavros P. Kalafatis, Julian Ming-Sung Cheng, and Costas Hadjicharalambous, "Impact of Positioning Strategies on Corporate Performance," *Journal of Advertising Research*, March 2008; Girish Punj and Junyean Moon, "Positioning Options for Achieving Brand Association: A Psychological Categorization Framework," *Journal of Business Research*, April 2002; Kalpesh Kaushik Desai and S. Ratneshwar, "Consumer Perceptions of Product Variants Positioned on Atypical Attributes," *Journal of the Academy of Marketing Science*, Winter 2003; David A. Aaker and J. Gary Shansby, "Positioning Your Product," *Business Horizons*, May/June 1982; Al Ries and Jack Trout, *Positioning: The Battle for Your Mind* (New York: McGraw-Hill, 1981).

17. "At Hyundai, Branding Is Job 2," *Bloomberg Businessweek*, May 20, 2007; "Hyundai Gains in Measure of Brand Loyalty," *Los Angeles Times*, July 18, 2011.

18. Douglas B. Holt, *How Brands Become Icons* (Cambridge, MA: Harvard Business Press, 2004), quote slightly modified p. 63.

CHAPTER 5

1. "How Tim Cook Is Changing Apple," *Fortune*, June 11, 2012; "How Long Can Apple Sustain Its Torrid Growth in China," *Advertising Age*, June 11, 2012; "Apple Navigates China Maze," *Wall Street Journal*, January 14, 2012; "Apple Macs Land on More Corporate Desks," *Wall Street Journal*, January 18, 2012; "Apple's Lower Prices Are All Part of the Plan," *New York Times*, October 24, 2011; "Secrets from Apple's Genius Bar: Full Loyalty, No Negativity," *Wall Street Journal*, June 15, 2011; Walter Isaacson, *Steve Jobs* (New York: Simon and Schuster); "iPad 2: Thin, Not Picture Perfect," *Wall Street Journal*, March 16, 2011; "iPad Storybook Apps and the Kids Who Love Them," *NPR.org*, February 7, 2011; "For iPad, Lines but No Shortage," *Wall Street Journal*, April 4, 2010; "Laptop Killer? Pretty Close: iPad Is a Game Changer," *Wall Street Journal*, April 1, 2010; "App Developers Pump Up for iPad: It's a Winner," *USA Today*, April 1, 2010; "The iPad Changes Everything," *Fortune*, March 22, 2010; "Turning an iPad into an iMust-Have," *BusinessWeek*, February 15, 2010; "Apple Takes Big Gamble on New iPad," January 28, 2010; "AT&T Looks beyond the iPhone," *Wall Street Journal*, April 22, 2010; "Sales of iPhone Keep on Sizzling," *USA Today*, April 21, 2010; "Apple vs. Google," *BusinessWeek*, January 25, 2010; "Apple Adds Second iPhone Seller in U.K.," *Wall Street Journal*, September 29, 2009; "The Next iPod Generation," *BusinessWeek*, August 10, 2009; "Apple's iPhone 3G S Offers Speed, Life; Old Model Now $99," *Investor's Business Daily*, June 9, 2009; "iPhone's Asian Disconnect," *BusinessWeek*, April 13, 2009; "New iPhone also Brings New Way of Mobile Marketing," *Advertising Age*, June 16, 2008; "All Eyes on Apple," *Fast Company*, December 2007; "Steve Jobs Offers Rare Apology, Credit for iPhone," *Wall Street Journal*, September 7, 2007; "From the Start, iPhone Is iFun," *USA Today*, June 27, 2007; "iPhone Mania Nears Fever Pitch," *USA Today*, June 20, 2007; "Apple Buffs Marketing Savvy to a High Shine," *USA Today*, March 9, 2007; "Has Apple Lost Its Cool to Samsung?" *Wall Street Journal*, January 28, 2013; "5 Truths That Explain Our Love-Hate Affair With Apple," *Fast Company*, April 2013; "Can Apple Win Over China?" *Fortune*, October 11, 2012; "Apple Watch Review: The Smartwatch Finally Makes Sense," *Wall Street Journal*, April 8, 2015; "What Exactly is Apple Watch For?" *Wall Street Journal*, February 16, 2015; "Apple: Luxury Brand or Mass Marketer," *Harvard Business Review Blog*, October 2, 2014; "Why China loves Apple Best," *Campaign*, February 26, 2015.

2. US Census Bureau. (n.d.). Percentage distribution of household income in the United States in 2013. In Statista–The Statistics Portal. Retrieved June 09, 2015, from http://www.statista.com/statistics/203183/percentage-distribution-of-household-income-in-the-us/. US Census Bureau. (n.d.). Median household income in the United States from 1990 to 2013 (in U.S. dollars). In Statista—The Statistics Portal. Retrieved June 09, 2015, from http://www.statista.com/statistics/200838/median-household-income-in-the-united-states/.

3. For more on economic factors and consumer behavior see Gordon, Brett R., Avi Goldfarb, and Yang Li. "Does Price Elasticity Vary with Economic Growth? A Cross-Category Analysis." *Journal of Marketing Research (JMR)* 50.1 (2013): 4–23; Kamakura, Wagner A., and Rex Yuxing Du. "How Economic Contractions and Expansions Affect Expenditure Patterns." *Journal of Consumer Research* (2013): S92–110; Soster, Robin L., Andrew D. Gershoff, and William O. Bearden. "The Bottom Dollar Effect: The Influence of Spending to Zero on Pain of Payment and Satisfaction." *Journal of Consumer Research* 41.3 (2014): 656–77; Tully, Stephanie M., Hal E. Hershfield, and Tom Meyvis. "Seeking Lasting Enjoyment with Limited Money: Financial Constraints Increase Preference for Material Goods over Experiences." *Journal of Consumer Research* 42.1 (2015): 59–75; Jeffrey S. Larson and Ryan Hamilton, "When Budgeting Backfires: How Self-Imposed Price Restraints Can Increase Spending," *Journal of Marketing Research*, April 2012; R. Y. Du and W. A. Kamakura, "Where Did All That Money Go? Understanding How Consumers Allocate Their Consumption Budget," *Journal of Marketing*, 6 (2008); R. Saini and A. Monga, "How I Decide Depends on What I Spend: Use of Heuristics Is Greater for Time than for Money," *Journal of Consumer Research*, 6 (2008); Ravindra Chitturi, Rajagopal Raghunathan, and Vijay Mahajan, "Delight by Design: The Role of Hedonic versus Utilitarian Benefits," *Journal of Marketing*, June 2008.

4. Kristina D. Frankenberger, "Consumer Psychology for Marketing," *Journal of the Academy of Marketing Science,* Summer 1996; A. H. Maslow, *Motivation and Personality* (New York: Harper & Row, 1970); for academic research on psychological influences see Escalas, Jennifer, Katherine White, Jennifer J. Argo, Jaideep Sengupta, Claudia Townsend, Sanjay Sood, Morgan K. Ward, Susan M. Broniarczyk, Cindy Chan, Jonah Berger, Leaf Van Boven, Keri L. Kettle, Gerald Häubl, Kathryn R. Mercurio, and Mark R. Forehand. "Self-Identity and Consumer Behavior." *Journal of Consumer Research* 39.5 (2013): xv–xviii; Ferraro, Rosellina, Amna Kirmani, and Ted Matherly. "Look at Me! Look at Me! Conspicuous Brand Usage, Self-Brand Connection, and Dilution." *Journal of Marketing Research (JMR)* 50.4 (2013): 477–88; Hsee, Christopher K., Yang Yang, Xingshan Zheng, and Hanwei Wang. "Lay Rationalism: Individual Differences in Using Reason Versus Feelings to Guide Decisions." *Journal of Marketing Research (JMR)* 52.1 (2015): 134–46; Janiszewski, Chris, Andrew Kuo, and Nader T. Tavassoli. "The Influence of Selective Attention and Inattention to Products on Subsequent Choice." *Journal of Consumer Research* 39.6 (2013): 1258–274; Liu-Thompkins, Yuping, and Leona Tam. "Not All Repeat Customers Are the Same: Designing Effective Cross-Selling Promotion on the Basis of Attitudinal Loyalty and Habit." *Journal of Marketing* 77.5 (2013): 21–36; Williams, Patti. "Emotions and Consumer Behavior." *Journal of Consumer Research* (2014): S268–269;

5. Bob Gilbreath, *The Next Evolution of Marketing* (New York: McGraw-Hill, 2010).

6. See Darron Billeter, Ajay Kalra, and George Loewenstein, "Underpredicting Learning after Initial Experience with a Product," *Journal of Consumer Research,* October 2011; Xavier Drèze and Joseph C. Nunes, "Recurring Goals and Learning: The Impact of Successful Reward Attainment on Purchase Behavior," *Journal of Marketing Research,* April 2011; Marcus Cunha, Jr., Chris Janiszewski, and Juliano Laran, "Protection of Prior Learning in Complex Consumer Learning Environments," *Journal of Consumer Research,* April 2008; Les Carlson, Russell N. Laczniak, and Ann Walsh, "Socializing Children about Television: An Intergenerational Study," *Journal of the Academy of Marketing Science,* Summer 2001; Elizabeth S. Moore and Richard J. Lutz, "Children, Advertising, and Product Experiences: A Multimethod Inquiry," *Journal of Consumer Research,* June 2000; Thomas W. Gruen, Talai Osmonbekov, and Andrew J. Czaplewski, "eWOM: The Impact of Customer-to-Customer Online Know-How Exchange on Customer Value and Loyalty," *Journal of Business Research,* April 2006; C. A. de Matos and C. A. V. Rossi, "Word-of-Mouth Communications in Marketing: A Meta-Analytic Review of the Antecedents and Moderators," *Journal of the Academy of Marketing Science,* 4 (2008).

7. Charles Duhigg, *The Power of Habit* (2012); Anna S. Mattila and Jochen Wirtz, "Congruency of Scent and Music as a Driver of In-Store Evaluations and Behavior," *Journal of Retailing,* Summer 2001.

8. Kirkpatrick, Jerry (2008) *In Defense of Advertising: Arguments from Reason, Ethical Egoism, and Laissez-Faire Capitalism,* TLJ Books.

9. "Sweet Success," *Brandweek,* May 12, 2003.

10. "Nike Makes Shoes from Trash, Nokia Envisions Remade Cell Phones," *Greenbiz,* February 15, 2008; "Nothing but Green Skies," *Inc.,* November 2007; "UPS: Getting Big Brown Machines to Go Green," *Investor's Business Daily,* November 26, 2007; "Subway's Diet: Less Oil, More Recycling," *Wall Street Journal,* November 21, 2007.

11. For examples, see "Will the British Warm Up to Iced Tea? Some Big Marketers Are Counting on It," *Wall Street Journal,* August 22, 1994, and "Starbucks Hits a Humorous Note in Pitching Iced Coffee to Brits," *Wall Street Journal,* September 1, 1999.

12. For more on wrinkle-free clothing, see "Botox for Broadcloth," *Wall Street Journal,* October 7, 2002; "'Wrinkle-Free' Shirts Don't Live Up to the Name," *Wall Street Journal,* May 11, 1994. For more on service quality, see Chapter 8. For more on service

expectations, see "Can I Get a Smile with My Burger and Fries?" *Wall Street Journal,* September 23, 2003. See also Chezy Ofir and Itamar Simonson, "The Effect of Stating Expectations on Customer Satisfaction and Shopping Experience," *Journal of Marketing Research,* February 2007.

13. Janet Schwartz, Mary Frances Luce, and Dan Ariely, "Are Consumers Too Trusting? The Effects of Relationships with Expert Advisers," *Journal of Marketing Research,* 2011; K. Grayson, D. Johnson, and D. F. R. Chen, "Is Firm Trust Essential in a Trusted Environment? How Trust in the Business Context Influences Customers," *Journal of Marketing Research,* 2 (2008); P. Gupta, M. S. Yadav, and R. Varadarajan, "How Task-Facilitative Interactive Tools Foster Buyers' Trust in Online Retailers: A Process View of Trust Development in the Electronic Marketplace," *Journal of Retailing,* 2 (2009).

14. "It's Mind Vending . . . in the World of Psychographics," *Time,* October 2003; "Lifestyles Help Shape Innovation," *DSN Retailing Today,* August 4, 2003; "Generation Next," *Advertising Age,* January 15, 2001; "Head Trips," *American Demographics,* October 2000; "Join the Club," *Brandweek,* February 15, 1999; "The Frontier of Psychographics," *American Demographics,* July 1996; W. D. Wells, "Psychographics: A Critical Review," *Journal of Marketing Research,* May 1975.

15. "My Days as a Zipster: It's Easy—and It Works," *Automotive News,* December 20, 2010; "Renting Cars by the Hour Is Becoming Big Business," *Economist,* September 4, 2010; "Car Sharing Grows," *Wall Street Journal,* March 24, 2010; "Zipcar Campus Car-Sharing Program Booms," *Design News,* December 2009; "Zipcar," *Advertising Age,* November 16, 2009; "An iPhone Gets Zipcar Drivers on Their Way," *USA Today,* September 30, 2009; "The Best New Idea in Business." *Fortune,* September 14, 2009; "Temporary Plates," *Brandweek,* July 12, 2007; "The Rise of Collaborative Consumption and the Experience Economy," *The Guardian,* January 3, 2014; "Why Don't Young Americans Buy Cars," *The Atlantic,* March 25, 2012; Botsman, Rachel and Roo Rogers (2010), *What's Mine is Yours: The Rise of Collaborative Consumption,* HarperBusiness; "What that Car Really Costs to Own," *Consumer Reports,* August 2012; "RelayRides Reinvents the Rental-Car Relationship," *The Denver Post,* March 18, 2015; "RelayRides Revs up Car-Sharing, Fueled by $52M in Financing to Date," *Tnooz,* January 12, 2015; "Why Uber Isn't the Only Future For the Business of Other People's Cars," *Wired,* December 2014.

16. Patrick E. Murphy and William A. Staples, "A Modernized Family Life Cycle," *Journal of Consumer Research,* June 1979.

17. Based on U.S. Census data and "The American Consumer 2006," *Advertising Age,* January 2, 2006; "The State of Our Unions," *USA Today,* February 26, 2004; "Do Us Part," *American Demographics,* September 2002; "The Ex-Files," *American Demographics,* February 2001. See also James A. Roberts, Chris Manolis, and John F. Tanner, Jr., "Family Structure, Materialism, and Compulsive Buying: A Reinquiry and Extension," *Journal of the Academy of Marketing Science,* Summer 2003.

18. Based on U.S. Census data and "Borders Aims to Capitalize on Teens with New Shops," *Wall Street Journal,* July 21, 2009; "It's Cooler than Ever to Be a Tween," *USA Today,* February 4, 2009; "American Express Tries to Find Its Place with a Younger Crowd," *Wall Street Journal,* September 22, 2005.

19. Based on U.S. Census data and "The Older Audience Is Looking Better than Ever," *New York Times,* April 20, 2009; "Why Grown Kids Come Home," *USA Today,* January 11, 2005.

20. For more on kids' influence in purchase decisions, see A. M. Epp and L. L. Price, "Family Identity: A Framework of Identity Interplay in Consumption Practices," *Journal of Consumer Research,* 1 (2008); L. A. Flurry and Alvin C. Burns, "Children's Influence in Purchase Decisions: A Social Power Theory Approach," *Journal of Business Research,* May 2005; "Kiddies' *Wired* Wish Lists," *Wall Street Journal,* December 19, 2007; "Inconvenient Youths," *Wall Street Journal,* September 29, 2007; "This Is the Car We Want, Mommy," *Wall Street Journal,* November 9, 2006. See also Sharon E. Beatty and

Salil Talpade, "Adolescent Influence in Family Decision Making: A Replication with Extension," *Journal of Consumer Research,* September 1994; Marketingvox, "Rand Youth Poll, Seventeen," Packaged Facts, September 8, 2012.

21. "Consumers Enjoy Lap of Luxury," *Investor's Business Daily,* October 27, 2003; "Downsized Luxury," *Wall Street Journal,* October 14, 2003. See also W. Amaldoss and S. Jain, "Trading Up: A Strategic Analysis of Reference Group Effects," *Marketing Science,* 5 (2008); Lan Nguyen Chaplin and Deborah Roedder John, "Growing Up in a Material World: Age Differences in Materialism in Children and Adolescents," *Journal of Consumer Research,* December 2007; Tamara F. Mangleburg, Patricia M. Doney, and Terry Bristol, "Shopping with Friends and Teens' Susceptibility to Peer Influence," *Journal of Retailing,* Summer 2004; Cornelia Pechmann and Susan J. Knight, "An Experimental Investigation of the Joint Effects of Advertising and Peers on Adolescents' Beliefs and Intentions about Cigarette Consumption," *Journal of Consumer Research,* June 2002; David B. Wooten and Americus Reed II, "Playing It Safe: Susceptibility to Normative Influence and Protective Self-Presentation," *Journal of Consumer Research,* December 2004.

22. For more on opinion leaders and word-of-mouth publicity, see Chapter 16. See also "Beware Social Media Snake Oil," *Business-Week,* December 3, 2009; "Why Brands Love Mommy Bloggers," *Adweek,* March 30, 2009. See also Dee T. Allsop, Bryce R. Bassett, and James A. Hoskins, "Word-of-Mouth Research: Principles and Applications," *Journal of Advertising Research,* December 2007; Ed Keller, "Unleashing the Power of Word of Mouth: Creating Brand Advocacy to Drive Growth," *Journal of Advertising Research,* December 2007; Girish N. Punj and Robert Moore, "Smart versus Knowledgeable Online Recommendation Agents," *Journal of Interactive Marketing,* Fall 2007; Judith A. Chevalier and Dina Mayzlin, "The Effect of Word of Mouth on Sales: Online Book Reviews," *Journal of Marketing Research,* August 2006; Thomas W. Gruen, Talai Osmonbekov, and Andrew J. Czaplewski, "Customer-to-Customer Exchange: Its MOA Antecedents and Its Impact on Value Creation and Loyalty," *Journal of the Academy of Marketing Science,* Winter 2007; for more research on social influence on consumer behavior see Scott, Maura L., Martin Mende, and Lisa E. Bolton. "Judging the Book by Its Cover? How Consumers Decode Conspicuous Consumption Cues in Buyer-Seller Relationships." *Journal of Marketing Research (JMR)* 50.3 (2013): 334–47; Warren, Caleb, and Margaret C. Campbell, "What Makes Things Cool? How Autonomy Influences Perceived Coolness." *Journal of Consumer Research* 41.2 (2014): 543–63.

23. "Art of Noise," *Brandweek,* November 1, 1999.

24. "Hola: P&G Seeks Latino Shoppers," *Wall Street Journal,* September 11, 2011.

25. Statistics in this and previous section based on "2010 America," *Advertising Age* (White Paper), October 12, 2009; U.S. Census data including Current Population Survey 2009 Annual Social and Economic Supplement, "Table FINC-01. Selected Characteristics of Families by Total Money Income in 2008" and "Table FINC-02. Age of Reference Person, by Total Money Income in 2008, Type of Family, Race and Hispanic Origin of Reference Person" (see parts 1, 4, 6, 8, and 9 of both tables) and available online at www.census.gov/hhes/www/cpstables/032009/faminc; Current Population Reports, P60–236, *Income, Poverty, and Health Insurance Coverage in the United States: 2008;* Statistical Abstract of the United States 2010, pp. 16 and 51; and "The Multicultural Economy 2004, America's Minority Buying Power," Selig Center for Economic Growth, University of Georgia. For an overview of ethnic populations in the United States, see "Brands Prepare for a More Diverse 'General Market,'" *Advertising Age,* November 30, 2009; "U.S. Allots $145 Million to Reach Out to Minorities," *Advertising Age,* October 26, 2009; "In Step with American Indians," *Investor's Business Daily,* February 6, 2008. For more on the African-American market, see U.S. Census data, including "The Black Population in the United States: April 2003" at www.census.gov/population/www/socdemo/race; "Blacks Push for 'Unified'

Census Tally," *USA Today,* January 12, 2010; "Report Shows a Shifting African-American Population," *Brandweek,* January 11, 2010; "Are Mattel's New Dolls Black Enough?" *Wall Street Journal,* December 3, 2009. For more on the Hispanic market, see U.S. Census data, including "The Hispanic Population in the United States," www.census.gov/population/www/socdemo/race; Nitish Singh, Arun Pereira, Daniel W. Baack, and Donald Baack, "Culturally Customizing Websites for U.S. Hispanic Online Consumers," *Journal of Advertising Research* 48, #2 (2008); R. Villarreal and R. A. Peterson, "Hispanic Ethnicity and Media Behavior," *Journal of Advertising Research* 48, #2 (2008); "The Hispanic Market Is Set to Soar," *Adweek,* November 2, 2009; "Latin Flavor," *Next* (Supplement to *Brandweek*), November 2, 2009; "The Payoff from Targeting Hispanics," *Business-Week,* April 20, 2009; "Home Depot's New Website Opens Door to Hispanics," *Wall Street Journal,* November 17, 2008. For more on the Asian-American market, see U.S. Census data, including "The Asian and PI Population in the United States: March 2002" at www.census.gov/population/www/socdemo/race; "The Invisible Market," *Brandweek,* January 30, 2006; Sonya A. Grier, Anne M. Brumbaugh, and Corliss G. Thornton, "Crossover Dreams: Consumer Responses to Ethnic-Oriented Products," *Journal of Marketing,* April 2006; David Luna and Laura A. Peracchio, "Advertising to Bilingual Consumers: The Impact of Code Switching on Persuasion," *Journal of Consumer Research,* March 2005; Shi Zhang and Bernd H. Schmitt, "Activating Sound and Meaning: The Role of Language Proficiency in Bilingual Consumer Environments," *Journal of Consumer Research,* June 2004; Ainsworth Anthony Bailey, "A Year in the Life of the African-American Male in Advertising: A Content Analysis," *Journal of Advertising,* Spring 2006; D. Anthony Platha and Thomas H. Stevenson, "Financial Services Consumption Behavior across Hispanic American Consumers," *Journal of Business Research,* August 2005.

26. "Women in Italy Like to Clean but Shun the Quick and Easy," *Wall Street Journal,* April 25, 2006. See also Tuba Üstuner and Douglas B. Holt, "Toward a Theory of Status Consumption in Less Industrialized Countries," *Journal of Consumer Research,* February 2010; Eric J. Arnould and Craig J. Thompson, "Consumer Culture Theory (CCT): Twenty Years of Research," *Journal of Consumer Research,* March 2005; John L. Graham, "How Culture Works," *Journal of Marketing,* April 1996; Grant McCracken, "Culture and Consumption: A Theoretical Account of the Structure and Movement of the Cultural Meaning of Consumer Goods," *Journal of Consumer Research,* June 1986.

27. For more research on cultural influences on consumer behavior see Briley, Donnel, Robert S. Wyer Jr., and En Li. "A Dynamic View of Cultural Influence: A Review." *Journal of Consumer Psychology,* 24.4 (2014): 557–71; Cross, Samantha N., and Mary C. Gilly. "Cultural Competence and Cultural Compensatory Mechanisms in Binational Households." *Journal of Marketing* 78.3 (2014): 121–39; Üstuner, Tuba, and Douglas B. Holt. "Toward a Theory of Status Consumption in Less Industrialized Countries." *Journal of Consumer Research* (2014): S248–267; "Fuel and Freebies," *Wall Street Journal,* June 10, 2002; Madhu Viswanathan, José Antonio Rosa, and Julie A Ruth, "Exchanges in Marketing Systems: The Case of Subsistence Consumer–Merchants in Chennai, India," *Journal of Marketing,* May 2010; Kelly D. Martin and Ronald Paul Hill, "Life Satisfaction, Self-Determination, and Consumption Adequacy at the Bottom of the Pyramid," *Journal of Consumer Research,* December 2011.

28. For research on situational factors influencing consumer behavior see Baskin, Ernest, Cheryl J. Wakslak, Yaacov Trope, and Nathan Novemsky. "Why Feasibility Matters More to Gift Receivers than to Givers: A Construal-Level Approach to Gift Giving." *Journal of Consumer Research* 41.1 (2014): 169–82; Etkin, Jordan, Ioannis Evangelidis, and Jennifer Aaker. "Pressed for Time? Goal Conflict Shapes How Time Is Perceived, Spent, and Valued." *Journal of Marketing Research (JMR)* 52.3 (2015): 394–406; Gilbride, Timothy J., J. Jeffrey Inman, and Karen Melville Stilley, "The Role of Within-Trip Dynamics in Unplanned Versus Planned Purchase Behavior." *Journal* of Marketing 79.3 (2015): 57–73; Lee, Leonard, Michelle P. Lee, Marco Bertini, Gal Zauberman, and Dan Ariely. "Money, Time, and the Stability of Consumer Preferences." Journal of Marketing Research (JMR) 52.2 (2015): 184–99; Paolacci, Gabriele, Laura M. Straeter, and Ilona E. De Hooge. "Give Me Your Self: Gifts Are Liked More When They Match the Giver's Characteristics." Journal of Consumer Psychology, 25.3 (2015): 487–94; Ward, Morgan K., and Susan M. Broniarczyk. "It's Not Me, It's You: How Gift Giving Creates Giver Identity Threat as a Function of Social Closeness." Journal of Consumer Research (2013): S270-287; Woermann, Niklas, and Joonas Rokka. "Timeflow: How Consumption Practices Shape Consumers' Temporal Experiences." Journal of Consumer Research 41.6 (2015): 1486-508; Steffel, Mary, and Robyn A. Le Boeug. "Overindividuation in Gift Giving: Shopping for Multiple Recipients Leads Givers to Choose Unique but Less Preferred Gifts." Journal of Consumer Research 40.6 (2014): 1167–180; Su, Lei, and Leilei Gao. "Strategy Compatibility: The Time versus Money Effect on Product Evaluation Strategies." Journal of Consumer Psychology, 24.4 (2014): 549–56; Tu, Yanping, and Dilip Soman. "The Categorization of Time and Its Impact on Task Initiation." Journal of Consumer Research 41.3 (2014): 810–22; Michelle F. Weinberger and Melanie Wallendorf, "Intracommunity Gifting at the Intersection of Contemporary Moral and Market Economies," Journal of Consumer Research, January 2012; C. Page Moreau, Leff Bonney, and Kelly B Herd, "It's the Thought (and the Effort) That Counts: How Customizing for Others Differs from Customizing for Oneself," Journal of Marketing, September 2011; "Markus Giesler, "Consumer Gift Systems," Journal of Consumer Research, August 2006; Jennifer Chang Coupland, Dawn Iacobucci, and Eric Arnould, "Invisible Brands: An Ethnography of Households and the Brands in Their Kitchen Pantries," Journal of Consumer Research, June 2005; S. Christian Wheeler, Richard E. Petty, and George Y. Bizer, "Self-Schema Matching and Attitude Change: Situational and Dispositional Determinants of Message Elaboration," Journal of Consumer Research, March 2005; Russell W. Belk, "Situational Variables and Consumer Behavior," Journal of Consumer Research, 2 (1975); John F. Sherry, Jr., "Gift Giving in Anthropological Perspective," Journal of Consumer Research, September 1983.

29. Adapted and updated from James H. Myers and William H. Reynolds, Consumer Behavior and Marketing Management (Boston: Houghton Mifflin, 1967). See also Raquel Castaño, Mita Sujan, Manish Kacker, and Harish Sujan, "Managing Consumer Uncertainty in the Adoption of New Products: Temporal Distance and Mental Simulation," Journal of Marketing Research, 3 (2008); Anna Lund Jepsen, "Factors Affecting Consumer Use of the Internet for Information Search," Journal of Interactive Marketing, Summer 2007; Kineta H. Hung and Stella Yiyan Li, "The Influence of eWOM on Virtual Consumer Communities: Social Capital, Consumer Learning, and Behavioral Outcomes," Journal of Advertising Research, December 2007; "How and What Do Consumers Maximize?" Psychology & Marketing, September 2003; Ronald E. Goldsmith, "A Theory of Shopping," Journal of the Academy of Marketing Science, Fall 2000; Judith Lynne Zaichkowsky, "Consumer Behavior: Yesterday, Today, and Tomorrow," Business Horizons, May–June 1991; James R. Bettman, An Information Processing Theory of Consumer Choice (Reading, MA: Addison-Wesley Publishing, 1979); Richard W. Olshavsky and Donald H. Granbois, "Consumer Decision Making: Fact or Fiction?" Journal of Consumer Research, September 1979; Craig J. Thompson, "Consumer Risk Perceptions in a Community of Reflexive Doubt," Journal of Consumer Research, September 2005; Alice M. Tybout, Brian Sternthal, Prashant Malaviya, Georgios A. Bakamitsos, Se-Bum Park, Dawn Iacobucci, and Frank Kardes, "Information Accessibility as a Moderator of Judgments: The Role of Content versus Retrieval Ease," Journal of Consumer Research, June 2005; Laura L. Pingol and Anthony D. Miyazaki, "Information Source Usage and Purchase Satisfaction: Implications for Product-Focused Print Media," Journal of Advertising Research, March 2005; Stijn M. J. Van Osselaer, Joseph W. Alba, and Puneet Manchanda, "Irrelevant Information and Mediated

Intertemporal Choice," Journal of Consumer Psychology, 2004; Judi Strebel, Tulin Erdem, and Joffre Swait, "Consumer Search in High Technology Markets: Exploring the Use of Traditional Information Channels," Journal of Consumer Psychology, 1 (2004); Ram D. Gopal, Bhavik Pathak, Arvind K. Tripathi, and Fang Yin, "From Fatwallet to eBay: An Investigation of Online Deal-Forums and Sales Promotions," Journal of Retailing, June 2006; Raj Arora, "Consumer Involvement—What It Offers to Advertising Strategy," International Journal of Advertising 4, #2 (1985); J. Brock Smith and Julia M. Bristor, "Uncertainty Orientation: Explaining Differences in Purchase Involvement and External Search," Psychology & Marketing, November/December 1994.

30. For research on the consumer decision process see Block, Lauren, Nilufer Z. Aydinoglu, Aradhna Krishna, Koert Van Ittersum, Brian Wansink, Stacey R. Finkelstein, Ayelet Fishbach, Caglar Irmak, Beth Vallen, Stefanie Rosen Robinson, Brent Mcferran, Darren W. Dahl, Gavan J. Fitzsimons, and Andrea C. Morales. "Food Decision Making." Journal of Consumer Research 39.5 (2013): iv–vi; Hsee, Christopher K., Jiao Zhang, Liangyan Wang, and Shirley Zhang. "Magnitude, Time, and Risk Differ Similarly between Joint and Single Evaluations." Journal of Consumer Research 40.1 (2013): 172–84; Yang, Liu (Cathy), Olivier Toubia, and Martijn G. De Jong. "A Bounded Rationality Model of Information Search and Choice in Preference Measurement." Journal of Marketing Research (JMR) 52.2 (2015): 166–83; Jeffrey V. Rayport, "Demand-Side Innovation: Where IT Meets Marketing," InformationWeek, February 1, 2007; "Web Stores Tap Product Reviews," Wall Street Journal, September 11, 2007; David R. Bell, Daniel Corsten, and George Knox, "From Point of Purchase to Path to Purchase: How Preshopping Factors Drive Unplanned Buying," Journal of Marketing, January 2011; Wendy Attaya Boland, Merrie Brucks, and Jesper H. Nielsen, "The Attribute Carryover Effect: What the 'Runner-Up' Option Tells Us about Consumer Choice Processes," Journal of Consumer Research, October 2012; Uzma Khan, Meng Zhu, and Ajay Kalra, "When Trade-offs Matter: The Effect of Choice Construal on Context Effects," Journal of Marketing Research, February 2011.

31. J. Jeffrey Inman and Marcel Zeelenberg, "Regret in Repeat Purchase versus Switching Decisions: The Attenuating Role of Decision Justifiability," Journal of Consumer Research, June 2002; Michael Tsiros and Vikas Mittal, "Regret: A Model of its Antecedents and Consequences in Consumer Decision Making," Journal of Consumer Research, March 2000; Thomas A. Burnham, Judy K. Frels, and Vijay Mahajan, "Consumer Switching Costs: A Typology, Antecedents, and Consequences," Journal of the Academy of Marketing Science, Spring 2003; Ziv Carmon, Klaus Wertenbroch, and Marcel Zeelenberg, "Option Attachment: When Deliberating Makes Choosing Feel Like Losing," Journal of Consumer Research, June 2003; Alan D. J. Cooke, Tom Meyvis, and Alan Schwartz, "Avoiding Future Regret in Purchase-Timing Decisions," Journal of Consumer Research, March 2001; Anna S. Mattila, "The Impact of Cognitive Inertia on Postconsumption Evaluation Processes," Journal of the Academy of Marketing Science, Summer 2003; William Cunnings and Mark Venkatesan, "Cognitive Dissonance and Consumer Behavior: A Review of the Evidence," Journal of Marketing Research, August 1976.

32. C. Aaron, E. Edwards, and X. Lanier, "Turning Blogs and User-Generated Content into Search Engine Results." SES, May 2009.

33. Adapted from E. M. Rogers, Diffusion of Innovation (New York: Free Press, 2003). See also Claudy, Marius, Rosanna Garcia, and Aidan O'Driscoll. "Consumer Resistance to Innovation-A Behavioral Reasoning Perspective." Journal of the Academy of Marketing Science 43.4 (2015): 528–44; Rex Yuxing Du and Wagner A. Kamakura, "Measuring Contagion in the Diffusion of Consumer Packaged Goods," Journal of Marketing Research, February 2011; Donald Lehmann and Mercedes Esteban-Bravo, "When Giving Some Away Makes Sense to Jump-start the Diffusion Process," Marketing Letters, October 2006; Stephen J. Hoch, "Product Experience Is Seductive," Journal of Consumer Research, December 2002.

CHAPTER 6

1. See www.deere.com and www.metokote.com, *2015 Annual Report,* Deere & Company; "Deere Hurt by Weak Farm-Equipment Demand," *The Wall Street Journal,* February 20, 2015; "Brazil Raises Ag Equipment Funding, Deere Benefits?" *Barron's Emering Markets Daily* blog, June 4, 2015; "Deere Should Reap Harvest in Due Time," *The Wall Street Journal,* February 19, 2015; "Deere's Big Green Profit Machine," *Bloomberg Businessweek,* July 5, 2012; "Farmer's Prepare for the Data Harvest," *Wall Street Journal,* June 14, 2012; "Teaching Drones to Farm," *Wall Street Journal,* September 20, 2011; "American Farmers Venture into New Field: Social Media," *Technorati,* September 7, 2010; "John Deere India Introduces Two New Tractor Models," *Economic Times,* August 13, 2010; "Global Innovation: John Deere's Farm Team," *Fortune,* April 14, 2008; "John Deere's Big-Wheel Rally," *Investor's Business Daily,* September 24, 2007; "Why Deere Is Weeding Out Dealers Even as Farms Boom," *Wall Street Journal,* August 14, 2007; "Deere's Revolution on Wheels," *BusinessWeek,* July 2, 2007; "Deere," *Fortune,* April 30, 2007; "John Deere Cultivates Its Image," *Advertising Age,* July 25, 2005; "Metokote Develops Customized Systems for Applying High Tech Coatings; More than Just Painting a Part," *Diesel Progress,* April 2003.

2. "Takata's Future Clipped by Steep Recall Costs," *The Wall Street Journal,* May 20, 2015.

3. "New Research: What Motivates Buyers to Receive and Engage with Vendor Email?" *Marketing Sherpa,* February 10, 2010.

4. "J&J Is Acccused of Kickbacks to Omnicare on Drug Sales," *Wall Street Journal,* January 16, 2010; "J&J Penalty May Total $2.2 Billion," *Wall Street Journal,* July 19, 2012; Richard F. Beltramini, "Exploring the Effectiveness of Business Gifts: Replication and Extension," *Journal of Advertising,* Summer 2000; Jeanette J. Arbuthnot, "Identifying Ethical Problems Confronting Small Retail Buyers During the Merchandise Buying Process," *Journal of Business Ethics,* May 1997; Gail K. McCracken and Thomas J. Callahan, "Is There Such a Thing as a Free Lunch?" *International Journal of Purchasing & Materials Management,* Winter 1996; Robert W. Cooper, Garry L. Frank, and Robert A. Kemp, "The Ethical Environment Facing the Profession of Purchasing and Materials Management," *International Journal of Purchasing & Materials Management,* Spring 1997; I. Fredrick Trawick, John E. Swan, Gail W. McGee, and David R. Rink, "Influence of Buyer Ethics and Salesperson Behavior on Intention to Choose a Supplier," *Journal of the Academy of Marketing Science,* Winter 1991; J. A. Badenhorst, "Unethical Behaviour in Procurement: A Perspective on Causes and Solutions," *Journal of Business Ethics,* September 1994.

5. M. D. Steward, F. N. Morgan, L. A. Crosby, and A. Kumar, "Exploring Cross-National Differences in Organizational Buyers' Normative Expectations of Supplier Performance," *Journal of International Marketing,* 1 (2010); Kelly Hewett, R. Bruce Money, and Subhash Sharma, "An Exploration of the Moderating Role of Buyer Corporate Culture in Industrial Buyer-Seller Relationships," *Journal of the Academy of Marketing Science,* Summer 2002; Jae-Eun Chung, Brenda Sternquist, and Zhengyi Chen, "Retailer-Buyer Supplier Relationships: The Japanese Difference," *Journal of Retailing,* December 2006; Masaaki Kotabe and Janet Y. Murray, "Global Sourcing Strategy and Sustainable Competitive Advantage," *Industrial Marketing Management,* January 2004.

6. Gregory T. Gundlach and Joseph P. Cannon, "Trust but Verify"? The Performance Implications of Verification Strategies in Trusting Relationships," *Journal of the Academy of Marketing Science,* July 2010; E. Fang, R. Palmatier, L. K. Scheer, and N. Li, "Trust at Different Organizational Levels," *Journal of Marketing,* 2 (2008); Jeffrey E. Lewin and Naveen Donthu, "The Influence of Purchase Situation on Buying Center Structure and Involvement: A Select Meta-Analysis of Organizational Buying Behavior Research," *Journal of Business Research,* October 2005; Jae H. Pae, Namwoon Kim, Jim K. Han, and Leslie Yip, "Managing Intraorganizational Diffusion of Innovations: Impact of Buying Center Dynamics and Environments," *Industrial Marketing Management,* November 2002; R. Venkatesh, Ajay K. Kohli, and Gerald Zaltman, "Influence Strategies in Buying Centers," *Journal of Marketing,* October 1995; "Major Sales: Who Really Does the Buying?" *Harvard Business Review,* May–June 1982.

7. Patrick J. Robinson, Charles W. Faris, and Yoram Wind, *Industrial Buying Behavior and Creative Marketing,* 1967.

8. "Detroit to Suppliers: Quality or Else," *Fortune,* September 30, 1996. See also Thomas H. Stevenson and Frank C. Barnes, "What Industrial Marketers Need to Know Now about ISO 9000 Certification: A Review, Update, and Integration with Marketing," *Industrial Marketing Management,* November 2002; Roger Calantone and Gary Knight, "The Critical Role of Product Quality in the International Performance of Industrial Firms," *Industrial Marketing Management,* November 2000; Sime Curkovic and Robert Handfield, "Use of ISO 9000 and Baldrige Award Criteria in Supplier Quality Evaluation," *International Journal of Purchasing & Materials Management,* Spring 1996.

9. Jessica J. Hoppner and David A. Griffith, "The Role of Reciprocity in Clarifying the Performance Payoff of Relational Behavior," *Journal of Marketing Research,* October 2011; Jason Shachat and Wei Lijia, "Procuring Commodities: First-Price Sealed-Bid or English Auctions?" *Marketing Science,* 2 (2012); S. Khan and B. Schroder, "Use of Rules in Decision-Making in Government Outsourcing," *Industrial Marketing Management,* 4 (2009); Neeraj Bharadwaj, "Investigating the Decision Criteria Used in Electronic Components Procurement," *Industrial Marketing Management,* May 2004; Jacques Verville and Alannah Halingten, "A Six-Stage Model of the Buying Process for ERP Software," *Industrial Marketing Management,* October 2003; Carol C. Bienstock, "Understanding Buyer Information Acquisition for the Purchase of Logistics Services," *International Journal of Physical Distribution & Logistics Management,* 8 (2002); David Tucker and Laurie Jones, "Leveraging the Power of the Internet for Optimal Supplier Sourcing," *International Journal of Physical Distribution & Logistics Management,* 3 (2000); H. L. Brossard, "Information Sources Used by an Organization During a Complex Decision Process: An Exploratory Study," *Industrial Marketing Management,* January 1998; Michele D. Bunn, "Taxonomy of Buying Decision Approaches," *Journal of Marketing,* January 1993; Mark A. Farrell and Bill Schroder, "Influence Strategies in Organizational Buying Decisions," *Industrial Marketing Management,* July 1996; Edward F. Fern and James R. Brown, "The Industrial/Consumer Marketing Dichotomy: A Case of Insufficient Justification," *Journal of Marketing,* Spring 1984.

10. Chakravarty, Anindita, Alok Kumar, and Rajdeep Grewal. "Customer Orientation Structure for Internet-Based Business-to-Business Platform Firms." *Journal of Marketing* 78.5 (2014): 1–23; Hada, Mahima, Rajdeep Grewal, and Gary L. Lilien. "Supplier-Selected Referrals." *Journal of Marketing* 78.2 (2014): 34–51; Werner Delfmann, Sascha Albers, and Martin Gehring, "The Impact of Electronic Commerce on Logistics Service Providers," *International Journal of Physical Distribution & Logistics Management,* 3 (2002); Daniel Knudsen, "Aligning Corporate Strategy and E-procurement Tools," *International Journal of Physical Distribution & Logistics Management,* 8 (2003).

11. "The Role of Search in Business to Business Buying Decisions," *Enquiro Search Solutions,* October 27, 2004. See also "10 Great Websites," *B2B,* September 10, 2007; "Usability Problems Plague B-to-B Sites," *BtoBonline.com,* April 23, 2007; Goutam Chakraborty, Prashant Srivastava, and David L. Warren, "Understanding Corporate B2B Websites' Effectiveness from North American and European Perspective," *Industrial Marketing Management,* July 2005; Samir Gupta, Jack Cadeaux, and Arch Woodside, "Mapping Network Champion Behavior in B2B Electronic Venturing," *Industrial Marketing Management,* July 2005; Cindy Claycomb, Karthik Iyer, and Richard Germain, "Predicting the Level of B2B E-Commerce in Industrial

Organizations," *Industrial Marketing Management,* April 2005; D. Eric Boyd and Robert E. Spekman, "Internet Usage within B2B Relationships and Its Impact on Value Creation: A Conceptual Model and Research Propositions," *Journal of Business-to-Business Marketing,* 1 (2004); B. Mahadevan, "Making Sense of Emerging Market Structures in B2B E-Commerce," *California Management Review,* Fall 2003.

12. See www.spiceworks.com; "Reaching Folks on Their Turf," *New York Times,* March 5, 2009.

13. Haruvy, Ernan, and Sandy D. Jap, "Differentiated Bidders and Bidding Behavior in Procurement Auctions," *Journal of Marketing Research (JMR)* 50.2 (2013): 241–58; Daniel J. Flint, Robert B. Woodruff, and Sarah Fisher Gardial, "Exploring the Phenomenon of Customers' Desired Value Change in a Busines-to-Business Context," *Journal of Marketing,* October 2002.

14. "Proterra, an Electric Bus Maker, Aims to Follow the Tesla Model," *Bloomberg Businessweek,* June 18, 2014; "Green PC Push by Feds May Seed Wider Adoption," *Computerworld,* January 14, 2008; "Working with the Enemy," *Fast Company,* September 2007; "Eco Walmart Costs Marketers Green," *Advertising Age,* October 1, 2007; "Guide to the Business Case & Benefits of Sustainability Purchasing," Sustainability Purchasing Network, March 2007; "The Mayor's Green Procurement Code," *Local Economy,* February 2007; "Innovation Wednesday: Walmart Surpasses Goal to Sell 100 Million Fluorescent Light Bulbs Three Months Early, "*Fast Company,* October 3, 2007; "Home Depot to Display an Environmental Label," *New York Times,* April 17, 2007.

15. "The New Golden Rule of Business," *Fortune,* February 21, 1994; Janet L. Hartley and Thomas Y. Choi, "Supplier Development: Customers as a Catalyst of Process Change," *Business Horizons,* July–August 1996.

16. "Ford Seeks Big Savings by Overhauling Supply System," *Wall Street Journal,* September 29, 2005; "Turning Vendors into Partners," *Inc.,* August 2005; "A 'China Price' for Toyota," *Business-Week,* February 21, 2005; "Ford to Suppliers: Let's Get Cozier," *BusinessWeek,* September 20, 2004; "How Would You Like Your Ford?" *BusinessWeek,* August 9, 2004; "Walmart's Low-Price Obsession Puts Suppliers through Wringer," *Investor's Business Daily,* January 30, 2004; "Push from Above," *Wall Street Journal,* May 23, 1996; Jan B. Heide, "Plural Governance in Industrial Purchasing," *Journal of Marketing,* October 2003; Shibin Sheng, James R. Brown, Carolyn Y. Nicholson, and Laura Poppo, "Do Exchange Hazards Always Foster Relational Governance? An Empirical Test of the Role of Communication," *International Journal of Research in Marketing,* March 2006; Erin Anderson and Sandy D. Jap, "The Dark Side of Close Relationships," *Sloan Management Review,* Spring 2005.

17. Much of the discussion in this section is based on research reported in Joseph P. Cannon and William D. Perreault, Jr., "Buyer-Seller Relationships in Business Markets," *Journal of Marketing Research,* November 1999. See also Samaha, Stephen A., Joshua T. Beck, and Robert W. Palmatier. "The Role of Culture in International Relationship Marketing." *Journal of Marketing* 78.5 (2014): 78–98; Luo, Anita, and V. Kumar. "Recovering Hidden Buyer-Seller Relationship States to Measure the Return on Marketing Investment in Business-to-Business Markets." *Journal of Marketing Research (JMR)* 50.1 (2013): 143–60; Palmatier, Robert W., Mark B. Houston, Rajiv P. Dant, and Dhruv Grewal. "Relationship Velocity: Toward A Theory of Relationship Dynamics." *Journal of Marketing* 77.1 (2013): 13–30; Wang, Qiong, Julie Li, William Ross, and Christopher Craighead. "The Interplay of Drivers and Deterrents of Opportunism in Buyer-supplier Relationships." *Journal of the Academy of Marketing Science* 41.1 (2013): 111–31; Christopher P. Blocker, Mark B. Houston, and Daniel J. Flint, "Unpacking What a 'Relationship' Means to Commercial Buyers: How the Relationship Metaphor Creates Tension and Obscures Experience," *Journal of Consumer Research,* 38 (October 2012); Shankar Ganesan, Steven P. Brown, Babu John Mariadoss, and Hillbun (Dixon) Ho, "Buffering and Amplifying Effects of Relationship Commitment in Business-to-Business Relationships," *Journal of Marketing Research,* April 2010; Alok Kumar, Jan B. Heide, and Kenneth H. Wathne, "Performance Implications of Mismatched Governance Regimes Across External and Internal Relationships." *Journal of Marketing,* March 2011; Kapil R. Tuli, Sundar G. Bharadwaj, and Ajay K. Kohli, "Ties That Bind: The Impact of Multiple Types of Ties with a Customer on Sales Growth and Sales Volatility," *Journal of Marketing Research,* February 2010; Rajdeep Grewal, Anindita Chakravarty, and Amit Saini, "Governance Mechanisms in Business-to-Business Electronic Markets," *Journal of Marketing,* July 2010; R. W. Palmatier, "Interfirm Relational Drivers of Customer Value," *Journal of Marketing,* 4 (2008); R. W. Palmatier, L. K. Scheer, K. R. Evans, and T. J. Arnold, "Achieving Relationship Marketing Effectiveness in Business-to-Business Exchanges," *Journal of the Academy of Marketing Science,* 2 (2008); R. N. Bolton, K. N. Lemon, and P. C. Verhoef, "Expanding Business-to-Business Customer Relationships: Modeling the Customer's Upgrade Decision," *Journal of Marketing,* 1 (2008); Jan B. Heide and Kenneth H. Wathne, "Friends, Businesspeople, and Relationship Roles: A Conceptual Framework and a Research Agenda," *Journal of Marketing,* July 2006; Robert W. Palmatier, Rajiv P. Dant, Dhruv Grewal, and Kenneth R. Evans, "Factors Influencing the Effectiveness of Relationship Marketing: A Meta-Analysis," *Journal of Marketing,* October 2006; Kapil R. Tuli, Ajay K. Kohli, and Sundar G. Bharadwaj, "Rethinking Customer Solutions: From Product Bundles to Relational Processes," *Journal of Marketing,* July 2007; Joseph P. Cannon and Christian Homburg, "Buyer-Supplier Relationships and Customer Firm Costs," *Journal of Marketing,* January 2001; Das Narayandas and V. Kasturi Rangan, "Building and Sustaining Buyer-Seller Relationships in Mature Industrial Markets," *Journal of Marketing,* July 2004.

18. "Purchasing's New Muscle," *Fortune,* February 20, 1995.

19. "Early Warnings in the Supply Chain," *Financial Times,* March 24, 2009; "United They'll Stand," *Wall Street Journal,* March 23, 2009.

20. For more on outsourcing, see "Big Three's Outsourcing Plan: Make Parts Suppliers Do It," *Wall Street Journal,* June 10, 2004; See also M. Ahearne and P. Kothandaraman, "Impact of Outsourcing on Business-to-Business Marketing: An Agenda for Inquiry," *Industrial Marketing Management,* 4 (2009); "HP Will Direct More U.S. Customers to U.S. Call Centers," *Investor's Business Daily,* February 28, 2008; "The Future of Outsourcing," *BusinessWeek,* January 30, 2006; "Pulling the Plug," *Fortune,* August 8, 2005, pp. 96B–D; "Outsourcing with a Twist," *Wall Street Journal,* January 18, 2005.

21. "H-P Wields Its Clout to Undercut PC Rivals," *Wall Street Journal,* September 25, 2009. For other examples of big/small partnerships, see "A Fruitful Relationship," *BusinessWeek,* November 20, 2000, pp. EB94–EB96; "Automating an Automaker," *Inc.* Tech 2000, #4.

22. "Thai Floods Jolt PC Supply Chain," *Wall Street Journal,* October 18, 2011.

23. Jeffrey K. Liker and Thomas Y. Choi, "Building Deep Supplier Relationships," *Harvard Business Review,* December 2004; see also G. L. Frazier, E. Maltz, K. D. Antia, and A. Rindfleisch, "Distributor Sharing of Strategic Information with Suppliers," *Journal of Marketing,* #4 (2009).

24. See U.S. Census data including "Industry Statistics for Subsectors and Industries by Employment Size: 2007," from *2007 Economic Census—Manufacturing, Summary Series, General Summary* (Washington, DC: U.S. Government Printing Office, 2010) and available online at www.census.gov. See also "Radical Shifts Take Hold in U.S. Manufacturing." *Wall Street Journal,* February 3, 2010; "Manufacturing Index Hits 5-Year High," *Investor's Business Daily,* February 2, 2010; "Growth Hits 6-Year High," *Wall Street Journal,* January 30, 2010; "Lean Manufacturing Helps Companies Survive," *USA Today,* November 2, 2009; "Can the Future Be Built in America?" *BusinessWeek,* September 21, 2009; "Not Every Nation Can Export

Its Way to Recovery," *USA Today,* September 3, 2009; "Are We Engineering Ourselves Out of Manufacturing Jobs?" Federal Reserve Bank of Cleveland, January 1, 2006; "If You Can Make It Here," *New York Times,* September 4, 2005.

25. See www.naiccs.com. See also "Classified Information," *American Demographics,* July 1999; "SIC: The System Explained," *Sales and Marketing Management,* April 22, 1985; "Enhancement of SIC System Being Developed," *Marketing News,* Collegiate Edition, May 1988.

26. "The Long Road to Walmart," *Wall Street Journal,* September 19, 2005. See also Peter Kaufman, Satish Jayachandran, and Randall L. Rose, "The Role of Relational Embeddedness in Retail Buyers' Selection of New Products," *Journal of Marketing Research,* November 2006.

27. Based on U.S. Census data and "Eyes Wide Open," *Fortune,* September 19, 2005, pp. 316B–D; "How Bikers' Water Backpack Became Soldiers' Essential," *Wall Street Journal,* July 19, 2005; "Targeting the DHS," *Inc.,* May 2005; "Heavy Load Now Lighter with Bleex," *Investor's Business Daily,* December 29, 2004; "Pentagon Sales Give Powerful Jolt to Ultralife's Business," *Investor's Business Daily,* April 6, 2004; "Uncle Sam Is a Tough Customer," *Investor's Business Daily,* October 20, 2003; "Super Soldiers," *BusinessWeek,* July 28, 2003.

28. "Not just Wal-Mart: Dozens of U.S. Companies Face Bribery Suspicions," *Fortune,* April 26, 2012. For a detailed discussion of business ethics in a number of countries, see *Journal of Business Ethics,* October 1997. See also John B. Ford, Michael S. LaTour, and Tony L. Henthorne, "Cognitive Moral Development and Japanese Procurement Executives: Implications for Industrial Marketers," *Industrial Marketing Management,* November 2000; "U.S., Other Nations Step Up Bribery Battle," *Wall Street Journal,* September 12, 2008; "How Can a U.S. Company Go International, Avoid the Economic Disaster of a Thai Baht . . . and Pay No Bribes?" *USA Today,* November 17, 1997; Larry R. Smeltzer and Marianne M. Jennings, "Why an International Code of Business Ethics Would Be Good for Business," *Journal of Business Ethics,* January 1998.

CHAPTER 7

1. See www.dunkinvip.com; telldunkin.com; dunkindonuts.com; "Dunkin' CIO to Lead Corporate Strategy," *The Wall Street Journal,* March 25, 2015; "Dunkin' Blends Big Data with Intuition," *Data Informed,* March 31, 2014; "Retailers Tap Software to Pick Best Locations for New Stores," *The Boston Globe,* August 29, 2013; "When It Comes to Ads in Games, These Guys Aren't Playing Around," *Adweek,* June 19, 2012; "Marketing Case Studies: Dunkin' Donuts," *Copernicus Marketing;* "Brand Transformation: Dunkin' Donuts," *Ivy Cohen, Marketing Coach;* "High Five! Dunkin' Donuts Is Number One in Customer Loyalty," press release, Dunkin' Donuts, February 16, 2011; "The Cold Hard Facts: New Dunkin' Donuts Survey Shows Popularity of Iced Coffee in the Winter Is Heating Up," press release, Dunkin' Donuts, January 18, 2011; "Singular Pursuit: Dunkin' Donuts Tests Expansion in Home Market," *Boston.com,* October 9, 2010; "CareerBuilder and Dunkin' Donuts Survey Finds Which Professions Need Coffee the Most," press release, Dunkin' Donuts, September 27, 2010; "Getting a Grip," *Marketing Management,* Spring 2010; "Dunkin' Donuts Tests Facebook," *Social Media Optimization,* March 16, 2009; "Facebook Fans and Dunkin' Donuts," *eMarketer,* February 27, 2009; "It's Not About the Doughnuts," *Fast Company,* December 19, 2007; "Takeout-Breakfast War Reheats," *Wall Street Journal,* September 5, 2007; "Dunkin' Donuts Going Zero Grams Trans Fat," *MSNBC.com,* August 27, 2007; "Dunkin' Donuts Whips Up a Recipe for Expansion," *Wall Street Journal,* May 3, 2007; "Dunkin' Donuts Uses Business Intelligence in War Against Starbucks," *Information Week,* April 16, 2007; "Brand New Buzz," *Time,* March 9, 2007; "Dunkin' Begins New Push into China," *Wall Street Journal,* January 17, 2007; "Dunkin' Donuts Cheap Chic," *BusinessWeek,* April 12, 2006; "Dunkin' Donuts Tries to Go Upscale, but Not Too Far," *Wall*

Street Journal, April 8, 2006; *Time to Make the Donuts,* William Rosenberg, 2001.

2. For more on big data, see "Big Data: The Next Frontier for Innovation, Competition, and Productivity," *McKinsey Global Institute,* May 2011; "Data Analytics: Crunching the Future," *Bloomberg Businessweek,* September 8, 2011; "Clouds, Big Data, and Smart Assets: Ten Tech-Enabled Business Trends to Watch," *McKinsey Quarterly,* August 2012; "Unlocking Hidden Profits with Big Data Analytics,"*Forbes,* September 27, 2012; "Seizing the Potential of 'Big Data,'"*McKinsey Quarterly,* 4 (2011); "Are You Ready for the Era of 'Big Data'?" *McKinsey Quarterly,* 4 (2011); "How Intuit Uses Big Data for the Little Guy," *Forbes,* April 26, 2012; "Big Data Requires Complex Analysis, but Don't Be Scared Off," *Advertising Age,* May 8, 2012; Daria Dzyabura and John R. Hauser, "Active Machine Learning for Consideration Heuristics," *Marketing Science,* 5 (2011); "Big Data Broadens Its Range," *Wall Street Journal,* March 13, 2013.

3. "The Technology that Unmasks Your Hidden Emotions," *The Wall Street Journal,* January 28, 2015; "Phone Firms Sell Data on Customers," *The Wall Street Journal,* May 21, 2013; "Smile! Marketing Firms Are Mining Your Selfies," *The Wall Street Journal,* October 9, 2014.

4. "Age of Big Data," *New York Times,* February 12, 2012; "What Is Big Data?" *O'Reilly.com,* January 11, 2012; "Big Bets on Big Data," *Forbes,* June 22, 2012; "Big Data and Its Myths," *Forbes,* June 21, 2012.

5. Gene Gellinger, Durval Castro, and Anthony Mills, "Data, Information Knowledge and Wisdom," 2004, http://www.systems-thinking.org/dikw/dikw.htm; Jennifer Rowley, "The Wisdom Hierarchy: Representations of the DIKW Hierarchy," *Journal of Information Science,* 2 (2007).

6. Oded Netzer, Ronen Feldman, Jacob Goldenberg, and Moshe Fresko, "Mine Your Own Business: Market-Structure Surveillance Through Text Mining," *Marketing Science,* 3 (2012); M. Reimann, O. Schilke, and J. S. Thomas, "Customer Relationship Management and Firm Performance: The Mediating Role of Business Strategy," *Journal of the Academy of Marketing Science,* 3 (2010); Venkatesh Shankar and Russell S. Winer, "When Customer Relationship Management Meets Data Mining," *Journal of Interactive Marketing,* Summer 2006; Amy Miller and Jennifer Cioffi, "Measuring Marketing Effectiveness and Value: The Unisys Marketing Dashboard," *Journal of Advertising Research,* September 2004; "Making Marketing Measure Up," *BusinessWeek,* December 13, 2004; "How Verizon Flies by Wire," *CIO Magazine,* November 1, 2004; Martin Reimann, Oliver Schilke, and Jacquelyn Thomas, "Customer Relationship Management and Firm Performance: The Mediating Role of Business Strategy," *Journal of the Academy of Marketing Science,* May 2010.

7. "Most Innovative Companies 2015, Next Big Sound" *Fast Company,* March 2015; "Moneyball For Music: The Rise of Next Big Sound," *Forbes,* March 3, 2013; "The Shazam Effect," *The Atlantic,* December 2014; "The Scientific Formula for Predicting a Hit," *Gizmag,* December 27, 2011; "Rock Music's Latest New Heroes: Lady Gaga and … Big Data?" *CNBC.com,* October 11, 2013; "Predicting What You Want To Hear: Music And Data Get It On," *Billboard,* March 25, 2014; "How Shazam Uses Big Data to Predict Music's Next Big Artists," *The Guardian,* December 10, 2013.

8. Gary L. Lilien, Arvind Rangaswamy, Gerrit H. van Bruggen, and Berend Wierenga, "Bridging the Marketing Theory-Practice Gap with Marketing Engineering," *Journal of Business Research,* February 2002; "Virtual Management," *BusinessWeek,* September 21, 1998; John T. Mentzer and Nimish Gandhi, "Expert Systems in Marketing: Guidelines for Development," *Journal of the Academy of Marketing Science,* Winter 1992; William D. Perreault, Jr., "The Shifting Paradigm in Marketing Research," *Journal of the Academy of Marketing Science,* Fall 1992.

9. "Big Data Broadens Its Range," *Wall Street Journal,* March 13, 2013.

10. J. Rubinson, "The New Marketing Research Imperative: It's about Learning," *Journal of Advertising Research,* 1 (2009); Larry Selden and Ian C. MacMillan, "Manage Customer-Centric Innovation Systematically," *Harvard Business Review,* April 2006; Bruce H. Clark, "Business Intelligence Using Smart Techniques," *Journal of the Academy of Marketing Science,* Fall 2003; Mark Peyrot, Nancy Childs, Doris Van Doren, and Kathleen Allen, "An Empirically Based Model of Competitor Intelligence Use," *Journal of Business Research,* September 2002; Stanley F. Slater and John C. Narver, "Intelligence Generation and Superior Customer Value," *Journal of the Academy of Marketing Science,* Winter 2000; Jim Bessen, "Riding the Marketing Information Wave," *Harvard Business Review,* September–October 1993; Lawrence B. Chonko, John F. Tanner, Jr., and Ellen Reid Smith, "The Sales Force's Role in International Marketing Research and Marketing Information Systems," *Journal of Personal Selling and Sales Management,* Winter 1991; William Boulding, Richard Staelin, Michael Ehret, and Wesley J. Johnston, "A Customer Relationship Management Roadmap: What Is Known, Potential Pitfalls, and Where to Go," *Journal of Marketing,* October 2005; Satish Jayachandran, Subhash Sharma, Peter Kaufman, and Pushkala Raman, "The Role of Relational Information Processes and Technology Use in Customer Relationship Management," *Journal of Marketing,* October 2005; Yong Cao and Thomas S. Gruca, "Reducing Adverse Selection Through Customer Relationship Management," *Journal of Marketing,* October 2005; Darrell K. Rigby and Dianne Ledingham, "CRM Done Right," *Harvard Business Review,* November 2004; Peter M. Chisnall, "The Effective Use of Market Research: A Guide for Management to Grow the Business," *International Journal of Market Research,* 42, #2 (Summer 2000); Seymour Sudman and Edward Blair, *Marketing Research: A Problem Solving Approach* (Burr Ridge, IL: Irwin/McGraw-Hill, 1998). See also Christine Moorman, Rohit Deshpande, and Gerald Zaltman, "Factors Affecting Trust in Market Research Relationships," *Journal of Marketing,* January 1993.

11. See www.kiwicare.com; "Kiwi Goes beyond Shine in Effort to Step up Sales," *Wall Street Journal,* December 20, 2007.

12. Charlene Li and Josh Bernoff, *Groundswell* (Boston: Harvard Business Press, 2008).

13. For more on focus groups, see "Mucus to Maxi Pads: Marketing's Dirtiest Jobs," *Advertising Age,* February 16, 2009; "Hypnosis Brings Groups into Focus," *Brandweek,* March 24, 2008; "The Perils of Packaging: Nestlé Aims for Easier Openings," *Wall Street Journal,* November 17, 2005; "Puppet's Got a Brand-New Bag," *Business 2.0,* October 2005; "Focus Groups Should Be Abolished," *Advertising Age,* August 8, 2005; "Web Enhances Market Research," *Advertising Age,* June 18, 2001. See also William J. McDonald, "Focus Group Research Dynamics and Reporting: An Examination of Research Objectives and Moderator Influences," *Journal of the Academy of Marketing Science,* Spring 1993; Thomas Kiely, "Wired Focus Groups," *Harvard Business Review,* January–February 1998; see also James R. Stengel, Andrea L. Dixon, and Chris T. Allen, "Listening Begins at Home," *Harvard Business Review,* November 2003; Salini Bahl and George R. Milne, "Talking to Ourselves: A Dialogical Exploration of Consumption Experiences," *Journal of Consumer Research,* February 2010; "How to Run an Online Focus Group to Discover What Business Prospects Really Want (Tips on Launching an E-Commerce Website)," *Marketing Sherpa,* September 28, 2005; "The New Focus Groups: Online Networks," *Wall Street Journal,* January 14, 2008; "Expand Your Brand Community Online," *Advertising Age,* January 7, 2008; "Design It before You Buy It," *Wall Street Journal,* August 2, 2007; "P&G Plunges into Social Networking," *Wall Street Journal,* January 8, 2007; "It Takes a Web Village," *BusinessWeek,* September 4, 2006; "Shoot the Focus Group," *BusinessWeek Online,* November 14, 2005,

14. Hair, Joseph, Jr., Mary Wolfinbarger, Robert Bush, and David Ortinau (2013), *Essentials of Marketing Research, 3rd edition,* Burr Ridge: McGraw-Hill; "Take Your Market Research Online," *Fortune Small Business,* May 29, 2005.

15. "'Dear Airline, Here's the Problem...'" *The Wall Street Journal,* April 3, 2013.

16. "Selling Sibelius Isn't Easy," *American Demographics,* The 1994 Directory; "Symphony Strikes a Note for Research as It Prepares to Launch a New Season," *Marketing News,* August 29, 1988. For more on surveys, see "Forget Phone and Mail: Online's the Best Place to Administer Surveys," *Advertising Age,* July 17, 2006; "Electrolux Cleans Up," *BusinessWeek,* February 27, 2006; "Chrysler's Made-Up Customers Get Real Living Space at Agency," *Wall Street Journal,* January 4, 2006; "VW's American Road Trip," *Wall Street Journal,* January 4, 2006; "The Only Question That Matters," *Business 2.0,* September 2005. See also Pierre Chandon, Vicki G. Morwitz, and Werner J. Reinartz, "Do Intentions Really Predict Behavior? Self-Generated Validity Effects in Survey Research," *Journal of Marketing,* April 2005; Stanley E. Griffis, Thomas J. Goldsby, and Martha Cooper, "Web-Based and Mail Surveys: A Comparison of Response, Data, and Cost," *Journal of Business Logistics,* 2 (2003); Terry L. Childers and Steven J. Skinner, "Toward a Conceptualization of Mail Survey Response Behavior," *Psychology & Marketing,* March 1996; J. B. E. M. Steenkamp, M. G. De Jong, and H. Baumgartner, "Socially Desirable Response Tendencies in Survey Research," *Journal of Marketing Research,* 2 (2010).

17. "'Quantilitative' Research & Beyond: New Platforms for Customer Insights," *Marketing News,* March 1, 2008; "Communispace and Charles Schwab Win Social Technologies Award for Generation X Online Customer Community," *Business Wire,* October 12, 2007; "Build Community to Build Brand and Business," *EContent,* November 2008; "Qual Research by the Numbers," *Marketing News,* September 1, 2008; Pete Comley, "Online Research Communities: A User Guide," *International Journal of Market Research* 50, #5; "Customer-Centric Approach Earns CDW Corporation a Prestigious Social Media Award," *Business Wire,* October 28, 2009; "Expand Your Brand Community Online," *Advertising Age,* January 7, 2008; S. A. Thompson and R. K. Sinha, "Brand Communities and New Product Adoption: The Influence and Limits of Oppositional Loyalty," *Journal of Marketing,* 6 (2008).

18. "Old Ketchup Packet Heads for Trash," *Wall Street Journal,* September 19, 2011.

19. Paco Underhill, *Why We Buy* (New York: Simon and Shuster, 1999); see also N. Diamond, J. F. Sherry, A. M. Muniz, M. A. McGrath, R. V. Kozinets, and S. Borghini, "American Girl and the Brand Gestalt: Closing the Loop on Sociocultural Branding Research," *Journal of Marketing,* 3 (2009); Stephen R. Rosenthal and Mark Capper, "Ethnographies in the Front End: Designing for Enhanced Customer Experiences," *Journal of Product Innovation Management,* May 2006; Pierre Berthon, James Mac Hulbert, and Leyland Pitt, "Consuming Technology: Why Marketers Sometimes Get It Wrong," *California Management Review,* Fall 2005. See also "Why Are Tech Gizmos So Hard to Figure Out?" *USA Today,* November 2, 2005; "Poll: Many Like Tech Gizmos but Are Frustrated," *USA Today,* October 31, 2005; "The Fine Art of Usability Testing," *Dev Source,* March 2005.

20. "Seeing Store Shelves through Senior Eyes," *Wall Street Journal,* September 14, 2009; "They Feel Your Pain," *Brandweek,* June 16, 2008; see also "Architects Live in Senior Spaces to Help Elderly," *USA Today,* August 21, 2014;

21. For more on Nielsen's people meters, see "Made to Measure," *Fortune,* March 3, 2008; "Couch to Supermarket: Connecting Dots," *Wall Street Journal,* February 11, 2008; "TNS Aims to Take Bite Out of Nielsen," *Wall Street Journal,* January 31, 2008; "Where's the Ratings, Dude?" *Wall Street Journal,* March 7, 2005; "Confessions of a Nielsen Household," *American Demographics,* May 2001. See also Peter J. Danaher and Terence W. Beed, "A Coincidental Survey of People Meter Panelists: Comparing What People Say with What They Do," *Journal of Advertising Research,* January–February 1993; "Are Retailers Going Too Far Tracking Our Web Habits?" *USA Today,* October 26, 2009; "The Web Knows What You Want," *BusinessWeek,*

July 27, 2009; "Connect the Thoughts: The Analysis of Social Networking Data . . . ," *AdweekMedia*, June 29, 2009; "The Next: Companies May Soon Know Where Customers Are Likely to Be Every Minute . . . ," *BusinessWeek*, March 9, 2009; "Feel Like Someone's Watching You?" *USA Today*, February 9, 2009; "We Know Where You Are," *Wall Street Journal*, September 29, 2008; "Websites Want You to Stick Around," *Wall Street Journal*, April 15, 2008.

22. "Will Your Web Business Work? Take It for a Test Drive," *Ecompany*, May 2001; "Ads Awaken to Fathers' New Role in Family Life," *Advertising Age*, January 10, 1994; "AT&T's Secret MultiMedia Trials Offer Clues to Capturing Interactive Audiences," *Wall Street Journal*, July 28, 1993; "Experimenting in the U.K.: Phone, Cable Deals Let U.S. Test Future," *USA Today*, June 28, 1993. See also Raymond R. Burke, "Virtual Shopping: Breakthrough in Marketing Research," *Harvard Business Review*, March–April 1996; Glen L. Urban, Bruce D. Weinberg, and John R. Hauser, "Premarket Forecasting of Really-New Products," *Journal of Marketing*, January 1996.

23. For more on types of observation, see "How to Get People to Change," *Inc.*, February 2010; "At CBS Television City, Tube-Watching Is a Science," *Advertising Age*, January 18, 2010; "Meet Melissa, Your Recessionary Consumer," *Advertising Age*, September 7, 2009; "A Virtual View of the Store Aisle," *Wall Street Journal*, October 3, 2007; "Marketers Zooming In on Your Daily Routines," *USA Today*, April 30, 2007; "Seeing Through Buyers' Eyes," *Wall Street Journal*, January 29, 2007. See also Stephen J. Grove and Raymond P. Fisk, "Observational Data Collection Methods for Services Marketing: An Overview," *Journal of the Academy of Marketing Science*, Summer 1992; Thomas Y. Lee and Eric T. Bradlow, "Automated Marketing Research Using Online Customer Reviews," *Journal of Marketing Research*, October 2011.

24. "Pen Proving to Be Mighty for Brands, Consumers," *Brandweek*, May 7, 2007; "More than Squeaking By: WD-40 CEO Garry Ridge Repackages a Core Product," *Wall Street Journal*, May 23, 2006; "WD-40 Is Well-Oiled for Growth," *BusinessWeek*, April 18, 2006; "P&G Provides Product Launchpad, a Buzz Network of Moms," *Advertising Age*, March 20, 2006; "Loosening the Wheels of Innovation," *Quirk's Marketing Research Review*, March 2006.

25. "Marketing Research on a Shoestring," *Fortune*, May 29, 2005; "Listen Up: Your Customers Are Talking About You Online," *MarketingProfs.com*, May 24, 2005; "Why Market Research Matters," *Fortune*, August 31, 2004; "On Target," *Entrepreneur*, August 2004; "Borrowing from the Big Boys," *MarketingProfs.com*, June 17, 2003.

26. For more detail on data analysis techniques, see Joe Hair, Rolph Anderson, Ron Tatham, and William Black, *Multivariate Data Analysis* (New York: Prentice-Hall, 2005), or other marketing research texts. See also "Ice Cream Shop Gets Scoop on Locales," *Investor's Business Daily*, February 17, 2006; "Is Your Business in the Right Spot?" *Business 2.0*, May 2004; Michael D. Johnson and Elania J. Hudson, "On the Perceived Usefulness of Scaling Techniques in Market Analysis," *Psychology & Marketing*, October 1996; Milton D. Rosenau, "Graphing Statistics and Data: Creating Better Charts," *Journal of Product Innovation Management*, March 1997.

27. "Careful What You Ask For," *American Demographics*, July 1998. See also John G. Keane, "Questionable Statistics," *American Demographics*, June 1985. Detailed treatment of confidence intervals is beyond the scope of this text, but it is covered in most marketing research texts, such as Donald R. Lehmann and Russ Winer, *Analysis for Marketing Planning* (Burr Ridge, IL: Irwin/McGraw-Hill, 2005).

28. For a discussion of ethical issues in marketing research, see "What Makes Tesco, Kroger More than Just Rivals?" *Wall Street Journal*, December 24, 2007; "Intimate Shopping: Should Everyone Know What You Bought Today?" *New York Times*, December 23, 2007; "Ma Bell, the Web's New Gatekeeper?" *BusinessWeek*, November 19, 2007; "Firm Mines Offline Data to Target Online Ads," *Wall Street Journal*, October 17, 2007; "How 'Tactical Research' Muddied Diaper Debate: A Case," *Wall Street Journal*, May 17, 1994. See also Rita Marie Cain, "Supreme Court Expands Federal Power to Regulate

the Availability and Use of Data," *Journal of the Academy of Marketing Science*, Fall 2001; Malcolm Kirkup and Marylyn Carrigan, "Video Surveillance Research in Retailing: Ethical Issues," *International Journal of Retail & Distribution Management*, 11 (2000); Eve M. Caudill and Patrick E. Murphy, "Consumer Online Privacy: Legal and Ethical Issues," *Journal of Public Policy & Marketing*, Spring 2000; John R. Sparks and Shelby D. Hunt, "Marketing Researcher Ethical Sensitivity: Conceptualization, Measurement, and Exploratory Investigation," *Journal of Marketing*, April 1998; Naresh K. Malhotra and Gina L. Miller, "An Integrated Model for Ethical Decisions in Marketing Research," *Journal of Business Ethics*, February 1998.

29. "China Market Research Strategies," *China Business Review*, May–June 2004.

30. "More Companies Are Offshoring R&D," *Investor's Business Daily*, November 21, 2005; "Chinese Puzzle: Spotty Consumer Data," *Wall Street Journal*, October 15, 2003. See also Thomas Tsu Wee Tan and Tan Jee Lui, "Globalization and Trends in International Marketing Research in Asia," *Journal of Business Research*, October 2002; Masaaki Kotabe, "Using Euromonitor Database in International Marketing Research," *Journal of the Academy of Marketing Science*, Spring 2002.

CHAPTER 8

1. See www.underarmour.com; Aaker, David (2015), "Under Armour Wills Itself to Success," *Marketing News*, April, 26–27; "Why Under Armour Is Making a Costly Bet on Connected Fitness," *Fortune*, April 21, 2015; "Ad Age's 2014 Marketer of the Year: Under Armour," *Advertising Age*, December 8, 2014; "Under Armour to Exploit 'Quiet Shift' for Women Wearing Athletic Product Outside the Gym," *Marketing Week*, September 5, 2014; "Under Armour's Founder on Learning to Leverage Celebrity Endorsements," *Harvard Business Review*, May 2012; "Under Armour Scores $1 Billion In Sales Through Laser Focus On Athletes," *Womens Wear Daily*, December 1, 2011; "Tough Mudder Brings In $25 Million, Signs Under Armour," *CNBC*, December 5, 2011; "Under Armour Gets Serious," *Fortune*, November 7, 2011; "Under Armour's Best Idea: A Shirt That Measures Heart Rate and G-Force," *The Atlantic*, November 10, 2011; "Under Armour Signs Groundbreaking Deal with Tough Mudder," *Forbes*, December 8, 2011; "Under Armour Expands Fitness Line Overseas," *Business Insider*, March 16, 2011; "Under Armour's Kevin Plank: Creating 'the Biggest, Baddest Brand on the Planet,'" *Knowledge@Wharton*, January 5, 2011; "Under Armour's Daring Half-Court Shot," *Bloomberg Businessweek*, November 1, 2010; "Under Armour Can't Live Up to Own Hype," *Advertising Age*, November 2, 2009; "Under Armour Reboots," *Fortune*, February 2, 2009; "Under Armour Enters the Running Shoe Race," *CNBC.com*, February 1, 2009; "Under Armour Hopes to Outrun Nike," *Advertising Age*, April 28, 2008; "Do These Clothes Help You Work Out?" *BusinessWeek*, March 24, 2008; "True Confessions of a Super Bowl Ad Virgin," *Advertising Age*, February 4, 2008; "Nike Seeks to Undercut New Under Armour Line," *Brandweek*, January 28, 2008; "Even Rookie Advertisers Feel Big-Game Pressure," *Wall Street Journal*, January 15, 2008; "No Sugar and Spice Here," *Advertising Age*, June 18, 2007; "Under Armour May Be Overstretched," *BusinessWeek*, April 30, 2007; "Under Armour: Thrown for a Loss," *BusinessWeek*, February 1, 2007; "Under Armour," *Apparel Magazine*, February 2007; "Perspiration Inspiration," *BusinessWeek*, June 5, 2006; "Rag Trade Rivalry," *Forbes*, June 5, 2006; "Under Armour, a Brawny Tee House? No Sweat," *BusinessWeek* Online, May 25, 2006; "Hot and Cool," *Government Executive*, October 15, 2005; "Protect This House," *Fast Company*, August 2005; "Under Armour Shows Feminine Side," *Women's Wear Daily*, February 24, 2005; "Under Armour's Apparel Appeal," *Brandweek*, February 21, 2005; *2009 Annual Report*, Under Armour; *2009 Annual Report*, Army and Air Force Exchange Service; "Kevin Plank," *Brandweek*, April 12, 2004; Under Armour Finds Feminine Side to Go Beyond $2 Billion,"

Bloomberg Businessweek, February 15, 2013; "Moving Beyond Shrink It & Pink It," *Marketing News*, February 2013; "No More 'Shrinking It and Pinking It' at Under Armour," *Advertising Age*, September 24, 2012.

2. Lukas, Bryan A., Gregory J. Whitwell, and Jan B. Heide. "Why Do Customers Get More Than They Need? How Organizational Culture Shapes Product Capability Decisions." *Journal of Marketing* 77.1 (2013): 1-12; Peter N. Golder, Debanjan Mitra, and Christine Moorman, "What Is Quality? An Integrative Framework of Processes and States," *Journal of Marketing*, July 2012; Marco Bertini, Luc Wathieu, and Sheena S. Iyengar, "The Discriminating Consumer: Product Proliferation and Willingness to Pay for Quality," *Journal of Marketing Research*, February 2012; T. Erdem, M. P. Keane, and B. Sun, "A Dynamic Model of Brand Choice When Price and Advertising Signal Product Quality," *Marketing Science*, 6 (2008); Neil A. Morgan and Douglas W. Vorhies, "Product Quality Alignment and Business Unit Performance," *The Journal of Product Innovation Management*, November 2001.

3. This example was inspired by other case studies: Robert Solomon and Kathleen Higgins, Case Study: Cement for Sale, Center for the Study of Ethics, Utah Valley State College; C. B. Fledderman, Denver Runway Concrete, Engineering Ethics (Prentice Hall, 1999).

4. For academic literature on products and product lines, see Carter, Robert, and David Curry. "Perceptions versus Performance When Managing Extensions: New Evidence about the Role of Fit between a Parent Brand and an Extension." *Journal of the Academy of Marketing Science* 41.2 (2013): 253-69; Sinapuelas, Ian, Hui-Ming Wang, and Jonathan Bohlmann. "The Interplay of Innovation, Brand, and Marketing Mix Variables in Line Extensions." *Journal of the Academy of Marketing Science* 43.5 (2015): 558–73.

5. For more on service quality, see "The Payoff for Trying Harder," *Business 2.0*, July 2002; "Avis to Try Even Harder with Ads Touting High Quality of Service," *Wall Street Journal*, February 18, 2000. For more on air service, see "Paved Paradise: The New Airport Parking Lots," *Wall Street Journal*, November 12, 2003; "Flat-Out Winners," *BusinessWeek*, October 27, 2003. See also Wolfgang Ulaga and Werner J. Reinartz, "Hybrid Offerings: How Manufacturing Firms Combine Goods and Services Successfully," *Journal of Marketing*, November 2011; Narayan Janakiraman, Robert J. Meyer, and Stephen J. Hoch, "The Psychology of Decisions to Abandon Waits for Service," *Journal of Marketing Research*, November 2011; Jaihak Chung and Vithala R. Rao, "A General Consumer Preference Model for Experience Products: Application to Internet Recommendation Services," *Journal of Marketing Research*, June 2012; Michael K. Brady, Clay M. Voorhees, and Michael J. Brusco, "Service Sweethearting: Its Antecedents and Customer Consequences," *Journal of Marketing*, March 2012; Elisabeth C. Brüggen, Bram Foubert, and Dwayne D. Gremler, "Extreme Makeover: Short- and Long-Term Effects of a Remodeled Servicescape," *Journal of Marketing*, September 2011; Roland T. Rust and Chung Tuck Siong, "Marketing Models of Service and Relationships," *Marketing Science*, November–December 2006; Frances X. Frei, "The Four Things a Service Business Must Get Right," *Harvard Business Review*, April 2008; Paul P. Maglio and Jim Spohrer, "Fundamentals of Service Science," *Journal of the Academy of Marketing Science*, Spring 2008; James C. Anderson and James A. Narus, "Capturing the Value of Supplementary Services," *Harvard Business Review*, January–February 1995; Matthew L. Meuter, Mary Jo Bitner, Amy L. Ostrom, and Stephen W. Brown, "Choosing Among Alternative Service Delivery Modes: An Investigation of Customer Trial of Self-Service Technologies," *Journal of Marketing*, April 2005; D. Todd Donavan, Tom J. Brown, and John C. Mowen, "Internal Benefits of Service-Worker Customer Orientation: Job Satisfaction, Commitment, and Organizational Citizenship Behaviors," *Journal of Marketing*, January 2004; Stephen L. Vargo and Robert F. Lusch, "Evolving to a New Dominant Logic for Marketing," *Journal of Marketing*, January 2004; Ruth N. Bolton, George S. Day, John Deighton, Das Narayandas, Evert Gummesson, Shelby D. Hunt, C. K.

Prahalad, Roland T. Rust, and Steven M. Shugan, "Invited Commentaries on 'Evolving to a New Dominant Logic for Marketing,'" *Journal of Marketing*, January 2004; Leonard L. Berry, Venkatesh Shankar, Janet Turner Parish, Susan Cadwallader, and Thomas Dotzel, "Creating New Markets Through Service Innovation," *Sloan Management Review*, Winter 2006; P. C. Verhoef, K. N. Lemon, A. Parasuraman, A. Roggeveen, M. Tsiros, L. A. Schlesinger, "Customer Experience Creation: Determinants, Dynamics and Management Strategies," *Journal of Retailing*, 1 (2009); Allen, Alexis, Michael Brady, Stacey Robinson, and Clay Voorhees. "One Firm's Loss Is Another's Gain: Capitalizing on Other Firms' Service Failures." *Journal of the Academy of Marketing Science* 43.5 (2015): 648-62; Gallan, Andrew, Cheryl Jarvis, Stephen Brown, and Mary Bitner. "Customer Positivity and Participation in Services: An Empirical Test in a Health Care Context." *Journal of the Academy of Marketing Science* 41.3 (2013): 338–56; Sirianni, Nancy J., Mary Jo Bitner, Stephen W. Brown, and Naomi Mandel. "Branded Service Encounters: Strategically Aligning Employee Behavior with the Brand Positioning." *Journal of Marketing* 77.6 (2013): 108–23.

6. For research on logos see, Cian, Luca, Aradhna Krishna, and Ryan S. Elder. "This Logo Moves Me: Dynamic Imagery from Static Images." *Journal of Marketing Research (JMR)* 51.2 (2014): 184–97.

7. "The Coming Era of 'On-Demand' Marketing," *McKinsey Quarterly*, April 2013; "The Futurists's Cheat Sheet: Internet of Things," *ReadWrite.com*, August 31, 2012; *Disruptive Technologies: Advances That Will Transform Life, Business, and the Global Economy*, McKinsey & Company, May 2013; "Sensing the Future Before It Occurs," *MIT Sloan Management Review*, December 20, 2012; "Welcome to the Programmed World," *Wired*, May 2013; "The Internet of Things and the Future of Manufacturing," *McKinsey.com*, June 2013; "GE Tries to Make Its Machines Cool and Connected," *Bloomberg Businessweek*, December 6, 2012.

8. For more on Listerine PocketPaks, see "The Strip Club," *Business 2.0*, June 2003; "Marketer of the Year: PocketPaks, a Breath of Minty Fresh Air," *Brandweek*, October 14, 2002, pp. M42–M46. For more on brand extensions, see "A Little Less Salt, a Lot More Sales: Campbell's Line Extension," *Advertising Age*, March 10, 2008; "Like Our Sunglasses? Try Our Vodka!" *Wall Street Journal*, November 8, 2007; "P&G Rekindles an Old Flame: New Febreze Candles," *Wall Street Journal*, June 5, 2007; Academic treatment of branding includes Baumeister, Christoph, Anne Scherer, and Florian Wangenheim. "Branding Access Offers: The Importance of Product Brands, Ownership Status, and Spillover Effects to Parent Brands." *Journal of the Academy of Marketing Science* 43.5 (2015): 574-88. Epp, Amber M., Hope Jensen Schau, and Linda L. Price. "The Role of Brands and Mediating Technologies in Assembling Long-Distance Family Practices." *Journal of Marketing* 78.3 (2014): 81-101; Fournier, Susan, and Claudio Alvarez. "Relating Badly to Brands." *Journal of Consumer Psychology*, 23.2 (2013): 253-64; Jayachandran, Satish, Peter Kaufman, V. Kumar, and Kelly Hewett, "Brand Licensing: What Drives Royalty Rates?" *Journal of Marketing* 77.5 (2013): 108-22; Newman, George E., and Ravi Dhar. "Authenticity Is Contagious: Brand Essence and the Original Source of Production." *Journal of Marketing Research (JMR)* 51.3 (2014): 371-86; Yang, Linyun W., Keisha M. Cutright, Tanya L. Chartrand, and Gavan J. Fitzsimons. "Distinctively Different: Exposure to Multiple Brands in Low-Elaboration Settings." *Journal of Consumer Research* 40.5 (2014): 973-92. Sanjay Sood and Kevin Lane Keller, "The Effects of Brand Name Structure on Brand Extension Evaluations and Parent Brand Dilution," *Journal of Marketing Research*, June 2012; Ryan Hamilton and Alexander Chernev. "The Impact of Product Line Extensions and Consumer Goals on the Formation of Price Image," *Journal of Marketing Research*, February 2010; Tom Meyvis, Kelly Goldsmith, and Ravi Dhar, "The Importance of the Context in Brand Extension: How Pictures and Comparisons Shift Consumers' Focus from Fit to Quality," *Journal of Marketing Research*, April 2012; Franziska Völckner and Henrik Sattler, "Drivers of Brand Extension Success," *Journal of*

Marketing, April 2006; Chris Pullig, Carolyn J. Simmons, and Richard G. Netemeyer, "Brand Dilution: When Do New Brands Hurt Existing Brands?" *Journal of Marketing,* April 2006; Thomas J. Madden, Frank Fehle, and Susan Fournier, "Brands Matter: An Empirical Demonstration of the Creation of Shareholder Value Through Branding," *Journal of the Academy of Marketing Science,* Spring 2006; Thomas J. Reynolds and Carol B. Phillips, "In Search of True Brand Equity Metrics: All Market Share Ain't Created Equal," *Journal of Advertising Research,* June 2005. For more on brand equity and brand value, see Florian Stahl, Mark Heitmann, Donald R. Lehmann, and Scott A. Neslin, "The Impact of Brand Equity on Customer Acquisition, Retention, and Profit Margin," *Journal of Marketing,* July 2012; Marc Fischer, Franziska Völckner, and Henrik Sattler, "How Important Are Brands? A Cross-Category, Cross-Country Study," *Journal of Marketing Research,* October 2010; Rajeev Batra, Aaron Ahuvia, and Richard P. Bagozzi, "Brand Love," *Journal of Marketing,* March 2010; J. J. Brakus, B. H. Schmitt, and L. Zarantonello, "Brand Experience: What Is It? How Is It Measured? Does It Affect Loyalty?" *Journal of Marketing,* 3 (2009); D. E. Boyd and K. D. Bahn, "When Do Large Product Assortments Benefit Consumers? An Information-Processing Perspective," *Journal of Retailing,* 3 (2009); R. J. Slotegraaf and K. Pauwels, "The Impact of Brand Equity and Innovation on the Long-Term Effectiveness of Promotions," *Journal of Marketing Research,* 3 (2008); "Built for the Long Haul," *BusinessWeek,* January 30, 2006; "Ranking Corporate Reputations," *Wall Street Journal,* December 6, 2005; "Hershey's Trumps Donald, McDonald's, and Martha," *Brandweek,* November 28, 2005; "High Tech High Loyalty," *Brandweek,* October 31, 2005, pp. 22–24; "Welch's Juices Equity with Fresh-Fruit Line," *Brandweek,* August 22, 2005; "Tech Sector Ponders: What's in a Name?" *Advertising Age,* May 9, 2005; "The New Science of Naming," *Business 2.0,* December 2004. See also Arjun Chaudhuri and Morris B. Holbrook, "The Chain of Effects from Brand Trust and Brand Affect to Brand Performance: The Role of Brand Loyalty," *Journal of Marketing,* April 2001; Russell Casey, "Designing Brand Identity: A Complete Guide to Creating, Building, and Maintaining Strong Brands," *Journal of the Academy of Marketing Science,* Winter 2004; Subramanian Balachander and Sanjoy Ghose, "Reciprocal Spillover Effects: A Strategic Benefit of Brand Extensions," *Journal of Marketing,* January 2003; Elizabeth S. Moore, William L. Wilkie, and Richard J. Lutz, "Passing the Torch: Intergenerational Influences as a Source of Brand Equity," *Journal of Marketing,* April 2002.

9. "What's New with the Chinese Consumer," *McKinsey Quarterly,* October 2008; R. Ahluwalia, "How Far Can a Brand Stretch? Understanding the Role of Self-Construal," *Journal of Marketing Research* 3 (2008).

10. "Rocking the Most Hated Brand in America," *Fast Company,* July/August 2011.

11. "Fueling Growth Through Word of Mouth," *BCG Perspectives,* December 2013.

12. "He Really Rolls in the Dough," *Investor's Business Daily,* January 26, 2010; "Rising Dough," *Fast Company,* October 2009; "Slicing the Bread but Not the Prices," *Wall Street Journal,* August 18, 2009; "Panera Bakes a Recipe for Success," *USA Today,* July 23, 2009.

13. Jennifer J. Argo, Monica Popa, and Malcolm C. Smith, "The Sound of Brands," *Journal of Marketing,* 74, #4; "IKEA's Products Make Shoppers Blush in Thailand," *Wall Street Journal,* June 5, 2012; "Lost in Translation," *Business 2.0,* August 2004; "Global Products Require Name-Finders," *Wall Street Journal,* April 11, 1996; Martin S. Roth, "Effects of Global Market Conditions on Brand Image Customization and Brand Performance," *Journal of Advertising,* Winter 1995.

14. Samuel M. McClure, Jian Li, Damon Tomlin, Kim S. Cypert, Latané M. Montague, and P. Read Montague, "Neural Correlates of Behavioral Preference for Culturally Familiar Drinks," *Neuron* 44, #2 (2004); "BrandZ Top 100 Most Valuable Global Brands, 2015," Millward Brown, April 2015.

15. "The In-N-Out Effect: Trademark Mistakes You Need to Avoid," *Business.com,* March 16, 2015; "McCurry Wins Big McAttack in Malaysia," *Wall Street Journal,* September 9, 2009; "Hey, That Nutrasweet Looks Like Splenda," *Advertising Age,* May 19, 2008; "TiVo's Time Ticks Away, DirecTV Programs Attack," *Brandweek,* October 10, 2005; "Road to Foreign Franchises Is Paved with New Problems," *Wall Street Journal,* May 14, 2001; "Tiger Fight Sees Kellogg, ExxonMobil Clash in Court," *Ad Age Global,* November 2000; "Wrestling, Wildlife Fund Battle over WWF Site," *USA Today,* October 25, 2000; "More Firms Flash New Badge," *USA Today,* October 4, 2000; "Name Lawsuit Prompts AppleSoup to Become Flycode," *USA Today,* September 11, 2000. See also Karen Gantt, "Revisiting the Scope of Lanham Act Protection," *Journal of the Academy of Marketing Science,* Winter 2004; Maureen Morrin and Jacob Jacoby, "Trademark Dilution: Empirical Measures for an Elusive Concept," *Journal of Public Policy & Marketing,* Fall 2000; F. C. Hong, Anthony Pecotich, and Clifford J. Schultz II, "Brand Name Translation: Language Constraints, Product Attributes, and Consumer Perceptions in East and Southeast Asia," *Journal of International Marketing,* 2 (2002); Lee B. Burgunder, "Trademark Protection of Product Characteristics: A Predictive Model," *Journal of Public Policy & Marketing,* Fall 1997.

16. For more on piracy, see "Episode 125: Duplitecture," *99% Invisible,* July 29, 2014; "Raids Crack Down on Fake Goods," *USA Today,* December 18, 2009; "HP Declares War on Counterfeiters," *BusinessWeek,* June 8, 2009; "EBay Fined over Selling Counterfeits," *Wall Street Journal,* July 1, 2008; "The Economic Effect of Counterfeiting and Piracy," *Executive Summary,* Organization for Economic Co-Operation and Development, 2007; Ashutosh Prasad and Vijay Mahajan, "How Many Pirates Should a Software Firm Tolerate? An Analysis of Piracy Protection on the Diffusion of Software," *International Journal of Research in Marketing,* December 2003. See also K. H. Wilcox, M. Kim, and S. Sen, "Why Do Consumers Buy Counterfeit Luxury Brands?" *Journal of Marketing Research,* 2 (2009); Laurence Jacobs, A. Coskun Samli, and Tom Jedlik, "The Nightmare of International Product Piracy: Exploring Defensive Strategies," *Industrial Marketing Management,* August 2001; Janeen E. Olsen and Kent L. Granzin, "Using Channels Constructs to Explain Dealers' Willingness to Help Manufacturers Combat Counterfeiting," *Journal of Business Research,* June 1993.

17. For more on licensing, see "The Final Frontier for Licensors," *Brandweek,* June 9, 2008; "The Power Behind J. D. Power," *Investor's Business Daily,* July 17, 2007; "Licensing Life," *Brandweek,* June 11, 2007; "Food Marketers Hope Veggies Look Fun to Kids," *USA Today,* July 15, 2005; "Testing Limits of Licensing: SpongeBob-Motif Holiday Inn," *Wall Street Journal,* October 9, 2003; "Making Tracks beyond Tires," *Brandweek,* September 15, 2003; "Candy Cosmetics: Licensing's Sweet Spot," *DSN Retailing Today,* August 4, 2003; "The Creative License," *Brandweek,* June 9, 2003; "Procter & Gamble Deals License Several Brand Names," *USA Today,* April 18, 2003.

18. For more on branding organic products, see "When Buying Organic Makes Sense—and When It Doesn't," *Wall Street Journal,* January 26, 2006; "The Organic Myth," *BusinessWeek,* October 16, 2006; "Private Food Labels also Seeking Organic Growth," *Brandweek,* November 7, 2005; "Soap Can Proudly Display Certified 'Organic' Label," *USA Today,* August 25, 2005; "Health-Food Maker Hain Faces Rivals," *Wall Street Journal,* August 13, 2003; "Big Brand Logos Pop Up in Organic Aisle," *Wall Street Journal,* July 29, 2003; "USDA Enters Debate on Organic Label Law," *New York Times,* February 26, 2003; "Food Industry Gags at Proposed Label Rule for Trans Fat," *Wall Street Journal,* December 27, 2002; "Curbs Are Eased on Food Makers' Health Claims," *Wall Street Journal,* December 19, 2002; "In Natural Foods, a Big Name's No Big Help," *Wall Street Journal,* June 7, 2002. See also Amitabh Mungale, "Managing Product Families," *Journal of Product Innovation Management,* January 1998; Gloria Barczak, "Product Management," *Journal of Product Innovation Management,* September 1997.

19. S. Chan Choi and Anne T. Coughlan, "Private Label Positioning: Quality versus Feature Differentiation from the National Brand," *Journal of Retailing,* June 2006; David E. Sprott and Terence A. Shimp, "Using Product Sampling to Augment the Perceived Quality of Store Brands," *Journal of Retailing,* Winter 2004.

20. "The State of Private Label Around the World," Nielsen, November 2014.

21. "Store Brands Step Up Their Game, and Prices," *Wall Street Journal,* January 31, 2012; "Why Grocers Are Boosting Private Labels," *Bloomberg Businessweek,* November 23, 2011; "Consumers Praise Store Brands," *Brandweek,* April 8, 2010; "Safeway Cultivates Its Private Labels as Brands to Be Sold by Other Chains," *Wall Street Journal,* May 7, 2009; "P&G, Colgate Hit by Consumer Thrift," *Wall Street Journal,* May 1, 2009; "How P&G Plans to Clean Up," *BusinessWeek,* April 13, 2009; "Store Brands Squeeze Major Food Makers," *Wall Street Journal,* March 27, 2009; "Private Label Winning Battle of Brands," *Advertising Age,* February 23, 2009; "P&G, Others Are Confident Higher Prices Will Stick," *Wall Street Journal,* February 20, 2009; "Brand-Name Food Makers, Private Labels Share Stage," *Wall Street Journal,* February 18, 2009; "Store Brands Lift Grocers in Troubled Times," *New York Times,* December 13, 2008; "Rise of Private-Label Products Gives Retailers Clout," *Wall Street Journal,* December 3, 2008. See also Inge Geyskens, Katrijn Gielens, and Els Gijsbrechts, "Proliferating Private-Label Portfolios: How Introducing Economy and Premium Private Labels Influences Brand Choice," *Journal of Marketing Research,* October 2010; Jack (Xinlei) Chen, Om Narasimhan, George John, and Tirtha Dhar, "An Empirical Investigation of Private Label Supply by National Label Producers," *Marketing Science,* 4 (2010); Tülin Erdem, and Sue Chang, "A Cross-Category and Cross-Country Analysis of Umbrella Branding for National and Store Brands," *Journal of the Academy of Marketing Science,* January 2012; Jan-Benedict E. M. Steenkamp, Harald J. Van Heerde, and Inge Geyskens, "What Makes Consumers Willing to Pay a Price Premium for National Brands over Private Labels?" *Journal of Marketing Research,* December 2010; Maureen Morrin, Jonathan Lee, and Greg M. Allenby, "Determinants of Trademark Dilution," *Journal of Consumer Research,* August 2006; Bart J. Bronnenberg, Sanjay K. Dhar, and Jean-Pierre Dub, "Consumer Packaged Goods in the United States: National Brands, Local Branding," *Journal of Marketing Research,* February 2007; Donna F. Davis, Susan L. Golicic, and Adam J. Marquardt, "Branding a B2B Service: Does a Brand Differentiate a Logistics Service Provider?" *Industrial Marketing Management,* February 2008.

22. "Coke, Pepsi, A-B Attracted to Metal," *Brandweek,* December 17, 2007; "Can Wine in a Sippy Box Lure Back French Drinkers?" *Wall Street Journal,* August 24, 2007; "As Costs Rise, Whirlpool Makes a Dent in Dings," *Wall Street Journal,* July 30, 2007. See also Deng, Xiaoyan, and Raji Srinivasan. "When Do Transparent Packages Increase (or Decrease) Food Consumption?" *Journal of Marketing* 77.4 (2013): 104-17; Ordabayeva, Nailya, and Pierre Chandon. "Predicting and Managing Consumers' Package Size Impressions." *Journal of Marketing* 77.5 (2013): 123-37. Brian Wansink and Koert van Ittersum, "Bottoms Up! The Influence of Elongation on Pouring and Consumption Volume," *Journal of Consumer Research,* December 2003; U. R. Orth and K. Malkewitz, "Holistic Package Design and Consumer Brand Impressions," *Journal of Marketing,* 3 (2008).

23. "Green Packaging: Waste Not, Want Not," *Inbound Logistics,* July 2008.

24. For more on food labeling, see "Honest: New ingredient in food labels," *USA Today,* June 12, 2014; "The Whole Truth about Whole Grain," *Wall Street Journal,* February 16, 2006; "Major Changes Set for Food Labels," *Wall Street Journal,* December 28, 2005; "FDA Says Food Labels Can Tout Tomatoes' Benefits on Cancer," *Wall Street Journal,* November 10, 2005; "Read It and Weep? Big Mac Wrapper to Show Fat, Calories," *Wall Street Journal,* October 26, 2005; "FDA Re-examines 'Serving Sizes,' May Change Misleading Labels," *Wall Street Journal,* November 20, 2003; "A 'Fat-Free' Product That's 100% Fat: How Food Labels Legally Mislead," *Wall Street Journal,* July 15, 2003. See also Shah, Avni M., James R. Bettman, Peter A. Ubel, Punam Anand Keller, and Julie A. Edell, "Surcharges Plus Unhealthy Labels Reduce Demand for Unhealthy Menu Items," *Journal of Marketing Research (JMR)* 51.6 (2014): 773-89; Lauren G. Block and Laura A. Peracchio, "The Calcium Quandary: How Consumers Use Nutrition Labels," *Journal of Public Policy & Marketing,* Fall 2006; Siva K. Balasubramanian and Catherine Cole, "Consumers' Search and Use of Nutrition Information: The Challenge and Promise of the Nutrition Labeling and Education Act," *Journal of Marketing,* July 2002; Bruce A. Silverglade, "The Nutrition Labeling and Education Act—Progress to Date and Challenges for the Future," *Journal of Public Policy & Marketing,* Spring 1996; Sandra J. Burke, Sandra J. Milberg, and Wendy W. Moe, "Displaying Common but Previously Neglected Health Claims on Product Labels: Understanding Competitive Advantages, Deception, and Education," *Journal of Public Policy & Marketing,* Fall 1997; Christine Moorman, "A Quasi Experiment to Assess the Consumer and Informational Determinants of Nutrition Information Processing Activities: The Case of the Nutrition Labeling and Education Act," *Journal of Public Policy & Marketing,* Spring 1996.

25. For more on package volume, see "Products Shrink but Prices Don't," *USA Today,* June 12, 2008; "Pay the Same, Get Less as Package Volume Falls," *USA Today,* March 17, 2003; "Taking the Value Out of Value-Sized," *Wall Street Journal,* August 14, 2002; "Critics Call Cuts in Package Size Deceptive Move," *Wall Street Journal,* February 5, 1991. For more on food claims, see R. Brennan, B. Czarnecka, S. Dahl, L. Eagle, and O. Mourouti, "Regulation of Nutrition and Health Claims in Advertising," *Journal of Advertising Research,* 1 (2008); Paula Fitzgerald, Bone Corey, and Robert J. Corey, "Ethical Dilemmas in Packaging: Beliefs of Packaging Professionals," *Journal of Macromarketing,* Spring 1992.

26. For more on warranties and service guarantees, see "17 American Companies that Offer Great Guarantees," *ConsumerReports.org,* September 23, 2014; Junhong Chu and Pradeep K. Chintagunta, "An Empirical Test of Warranty Theories in the U.S. Computer Server and Automobile Markets," *Journal of Marketing,* March 2011; "Little Tikes Proves Durable with Low-Tech Plastic Toys," *USA Today,* December 15, 2005. See also Monika Kukar-Kinney, Rockney G. Walters, and Scott B. MacKenzie, "Consumer Responses to Characteristics of Price-Matching Guarantees: The Moderating Role of Price Consciousness," *Journal of Retailing,* June 2007; Jennifer Hamilton and Ross D. Petty, "The European Union's Consumer Guarantees Directive," *Journal of Public Policy & Marketing,* Fall 2001; X. L. Chen, G. John, J. M. Hays, A.V. Hill, and S. E. Geurs, "Learning from a Service Guarantee Quasi Experiment," *Journal of Marketing Research,* 5 (2009).

27. Edward M. Tauber, "Why Do People Shop?" *Journal of Marketing,* October 1972; Christopher H. Lovelock, "Classifying Services to Gain Strategic Marketing Insights," *Journal of Marketing,* Summer 1983; Tom Boyt and Michael Harvey, "Classification of Industrial Services," *Industrial Marketing Management,* July 1997.

28. Dennis W. Rook, "The Buying Impulse," *Journal of Consumer Research,* September 1987; Cathy J. Cobb and Wayne D. Hoyer, "Planned versus Impulse Purchase Behavior," *Journal of Retailing,* Winter 1986.

29. For example, see "Russian Maneuvers Are Making Palladium Ever More Precious," *Wall Street Journal,* March 6, 2000. See also William S. Bishop, John L. Graham, and Michael H. Jones, "Volatility of Derived Demand in Industrial Markets and Its Management Implications," *Journal of Marketing,* Fall 1984.

30. William B. Wagner and Patricia K. Hall, "Equipment Lease Accounting in Industrial Marketing Strategy," *Industrial Marketing Management,* 20, #4 (1991); Robert S. Eckley, "Caterpillar's Ordeal: Foreign Competition in Capital Goods," *Business Horizons,* March–April 1989; M. Manley, "To Buy or Not to Buy," *Inc.,* November 1987.

31. P. Matthyssens and W. Faes, "OEM Buying Process for New Components: Purchasing and Marketing Implications," *Industrial Marketing Management*, August 1985; Paul A. Herbig and Frederick Palumbo, "Serving the Aftermarket in Japan and the United States," *Industrial Marketing Management*, November 1993.

32. Ruth H. Krieger and Jack R. Meredith, "Emergency and Routine MRO Part Buying," *Industrial Marketing Management*, November 1985; Warren A. French, et al., "MRO Parts Service in the Machine Tool Industry," *Industrial Marketing Management*, November 1985. See also "The Web's New Plumbers," *Ecompany*, March 2001.

CHAPTER 9

1. See www.irobot.com; "Robots Lead the Way for Investigations," *Claims Magazines*, June 2015; IRobot Introduces System to Help Machines Think for Themselves," *The Wall Street Journal*, October 9, 2014; "For iRobot the Future Is Getting Closer," *New York Times*, March 3, 2012; "In the Afgan War, a Little Robot Can Be a Soldier's Best Friend," *Wall Street Journal*, June 13, 2012; "Exploring the Oceans: Fleets of Robot Submarines Will Change Oceanography," *Economist*, June 9, 2012; "Where Humans Fear to Tread," *Wall Street Journal*, April 18, 2011; "Service Robots: The Rise of Machines (Again)," March 3, 2011; "The Future Is Automated," *Canadian Business*, March 14, 2011; "The *Wired* Interview: iRobot CEO Colin Angle," *Wired.com*, October 23, 2010; "TR50 2010: The World's Most Innovative Companies," *Technology Review*, February 10, 2010; "The Robot Revolution May Finally Be Here," *US News & World Report*, April 9, 2008; "2008 CRM Service Awards: Elite—iRobot," *CRM Magazine*, April 2008; "IRobot," *Fast Company*, March 2008; "IRobot Boots Up 2 New Models," *Investor's Business Daily*, September 28, 2007; "IRobot's Military Business on a Roll," *Investor's Business Daily*, August 22, 2007; "Maker Eyes Mainstream with Its Cleanup Robot," *Investor's Business Daily*, August 22, 2007; "Cleaning Up with Customer Evangelists," *BtoB*, August 13, 2007; "Keep Up with the Jetsons: iRobot's New Scooba," *Fortune*, February 20, 2006; "Robotic Orb Can Scrubba, Dub, Dub," *Raleigh News and Observer*, December 25, 2005; "What Can Scooba Do? Wash the Floor for You," *USA Today*, December 8, 2005; "A Robot That Could Hit the Wall," *BusinessWeek* Online, September 5, 2005; "Death to Cool . . . iRobot," *Inc.*, July 2005; "How the Roomba Was Realized," *BusinessWeek*, October 6, 2003; "Telepresence Robots Invade Hospitals—Doctors Can Be Anywhere, Anytime," *Singularity Hub*, December 4, 2012; "Robots with Your Face Want to Invade Workplaces and Hospitals," *Forbes*, June 10, 2013; "iRobot's RP-Vita Telepresence Robots Start Work at Seven Hospitals," *Singularity Hub*, May 18, 2013.

2. "Nielsen Breakthrough Innovation Report," *The Nielsen Company*, June 2014, U.S. Edition.

3. Raquel Castaño, Mita Sujan, Manish Kacker, and Harish Sujan, "Managing Consumer Uncertainty in the Adoption of New Products: Temporal Distance and Mental Simulation," *Journal of Marketing Research*, 3 (2008); Rosanna Garcia, Fleura Bardhi, and Colette Friedrich, "Overcoming Consumer Resistance to Innovation," *Sloan Management Review*, Summer 2007; Shih Chuan-Fong and Alladi Venkatesh, "Beyond Adoption: Development and Application of a Use-Diffusion Model," *Journal of Marketing*, January 2004; Youngme Moon, "Break Free from the Product Life Cycle," *Harvard Business Review*, May 2005; Alina B. Sorescu, Rajesh K. Chandy, and Jaideep C. Prabhu, "Sources and Financial Consequences of Radical Innovation: Insights from Pharmaceuticals," *Journal of Marketing*, October 2003; Christopher M. McDermott and Gina Colarelli O'Connor, "Managing Radical Innovation: An Overview of Emergent Strategy Issues," *Journal of Product Innovation Management*, November 2002; Ronald W. Niedrich and Scott D. Swain, "The Influence of Pioneer Status and Experience Order on Consumer Brand Preference: A Mediated-Effects Model," *Journal of the Academy of Marketing Science*, Fall 2003; Rajesh K. Chandy and Gerard J. Tellis, "The Incumbent's Curse? Incumbency, Size, and Radical Product Innovation," *Journal of Marketing*, July 2000; George Day, "The Product Life Cycle: Analysis and Applications Issues," *Journal of Marketing*, Fall 1981; Igal Ayal, "International Product Life Cycle: A Reassessment and Product Policy Implications," *Journal of Marketing*, Fall 1981.

4. "Soft Drink War Rages in Kenya—But Not Over Cola," *Wall Street Journal*, June 4, 2009.

5. See Jorge Alberto Sousa De Vasconcellos, "Key Success Factors in Marketing Mature Products," *Industrial Marketing Management* 20, #4 (1991); Paul C. N. Michell, Peter Quinn, and Edward Percival, "Marketing Strategies for Mature Industrial Products," *Industrial Marketing Management* 20, #3 (1991); Peter N. Golder and Gerard J. Tellis, "Pioneer Advantage: Marketing Logic or Marketing Legend?" *Journal of Marketing Research*, May 1993.

6 "Milk Industry's Pitch in Asia: Try the Ginger or Rose Flavor," *Wall Street Journal*, August 9, 2005.

7. McGowan, Heather, "Everything Is Accelerated (5 Pictures, 500 Words)," *LinkedIn*, March 25, 2015.

8. "Video Slips as DVD Market Matures," *USA Today*, January 4, 2006; "DVD's Success Steals the Show," *USA Today*, January 8, 2004; "DVD: It Pays to Spend a Little More," *USA Today*, December 3, 2003; "Backseat Movies: Car DVD Entertainment Systems . . . ," *BusinessWeek*, May 26, 2003; "High-Definition Discs Aim to Outshine DVDs," *Investor's Business Daily*, May 6, 2003.

9. For another example involving the portable digital music market, see "An iPod Casualty: The Rio Digital-Music Player," *Wall Street Journal*, September 1, 2005; "When Being First Doesn't Make You #1," *Wall Street Journal*, August 12, 2004. See also Sungwook Min, Manohar U. Kalwani, and William T. Robinson, "Market Pioneer and Early Follower Survival Risks: A Contingency Analysis of Really New versus Incrementally New Product-Markets," *Journal of Marketing*, January 2006; W. Boulding and M. Christen, "Disentangling Pioneering Cost Advantages and Disadvantages," *Marketing Science*, 4 (2008). See also footnotes 4 and 9 from this chapter.

10. "The Problem with Being a Trendsetter," *Wall Street Journal*, April 29, 2010; "Forget Fleece? Wool Makes a Comeback," *Wall Street Journal*, November 28, 2009; "Cheap and Trendy Gains as Luxury Fades in Japan," *Wall Street Journal*, November 10, 2009; "Life after Lasik: A Clear-Eyed Urge to Wear Glasses, Specs Are Looking Hot on Runway Models," *Wall Street Journal*, April 26, 2008; "Put a Patent on That Pleat," *BusinessWeek*, March 31, 2008; "Runway to Rack: Finding Looks That Will Sell," *Wall Street Journal*, March 6, 2008; "Work Wear: Designers Who Get It," *Wall Street Journal*, February 14, 2008; "How Fashion Makes Its Way from the Runway to the Rack," *Wall Street Journal*, February 8, 2007; "Men Say Bling It On," *Wall Street Journal*, November 30, 2005. See also Craig J. Thompson and Diana L. Haytko, "Speaking of Fashion: Consumers' Uses of Fashion Discourses and the Appropriation of Countervailing Cultural Meanings," *Journal of Consumer Research*, June 1997.

11. *2010 Annual Report*, RJR Nabisco; "Oreo, Ritz Join Nabisco's Low-Fat Feast," *Advertising Age*, April 4, 1994; "They're Not Crying in Their Crackers at Nabisco," *BusinessWeek*, August 30, 1993; "Nabisco Unleashes a New Batch of Teddies," *Adweek*'s *Marketing Week*, September 24, 1990.

12. "Going Global by Going Green," *Wall Street Journal*, February 26, 2008.

13. "With Bottle-Fillers in Mind, the Water Fountain Evolves," *Wall Street Journal*, March 24, 2013.

14. "Philly Cream Cheese's Spreading Appeal," *Bloomberg Businessweek*, December 8, 2011.

15. There is an extensive academic literature on new product planning and new product development. For some insights, see Barone, Michael J., and Robert D. Jewell. "The Innovator's License: A Latitude to Deviate from Category Norms." *Journal of Marketing* 77.1 (2013): 120-34; Wu, Qingsheng, Xueming Luo, Rebecca Slotegraaf, and Jaakko Aspara. "Sleeping with Competitors: The Impact of NPD Phases on Stock Market Reactions to Horizontal Collaboration." *Journal of the Academy of Marketing Science* 43.4 (2015): 490-511; Zhao, Min, Darren W. Dahl, and Steve Hoeffler. "Optimal

Visualization Aids and Temporal Framing for New Products." *Journal of Consumer Research* 41.4 (2014): 1137-151; Brexendorf, Tim, Barry Bayus, and Kevin Keller. "Understanding the Interplay between Brand and Innovation Management: Findings and Future Research Directions." *Journal of the Academy of Marketing Science* 43.5 (2015): 548-57; Fang, Eric (Er), Jongkuk Lee, and Zhi Yang. "The Timing of Codevelopment Alliances in New Product Development Processes: Returns for Upstream and Downstream Partners." *Journal of Marketing* 79.1 (2015): 64-82; Stock, Ruth, and Ines Reiferscheid. "Who Should Be in Power to Encourage Product Program Innovativeness, R&D or Marketing?" *Journal of the Academy of Marketing Science* 42.3 (2014): 264-76; Dotzel, Thomas, Venkatesh Shankar, and Leonard L. Berry. "Service Innovativeness and Firm Value." *Journal of Marketing Research (JMR)* 50.2 (2013): 259-76; Homburg, Christian, Martin Schwemmle, and Christina Kuehnl. "New Product Design: Concept, Measurement, and Consequences." *Journal of Marketing* 79.3 (2015): 41-56; Ma, Zhenfeng, Zhiyong Yang, and Mehdi Mourali. "Consumer Adoption of New Products: Independent Versus Interdependent Self-Perspectives." *Journal of Marketing* 78.2 (2014): 101-17.

16. C. Christenson, *The Innovator's Dilemma,* 1997, Cambridge: Harvard Business School Press; C. Christenson and M. Overdorf, "Meeting the Challenge of Disruptive Change," *Harvard Business Review,* March–April 2000; S. D. Anthony, M. W. Johnson, J. V Sinfield, and E. J. Altman, *Innovator's Guide to Growth—Putting Disruptive Innovation to Work,* 2008, Boston: Harvard Business School Press; "Ten for '10: New Gadgets for Home and Away," *Wall Street Journal,* January 7, 2010; "The World's Most Inventive Companies," *BusinessWeek,* December 23, 2009; "Book of Tens," *Advertising Age,* December 14, 2009. For more on ChotuKool, see "Clarifying Innovation for Success," *Bloomberg Businessweek,* October 6, 2010; "How Can You Enter an Emerging Market—And Improve the Lives of Millions?" *Innosight.com;* "Cool Products for Small Towns," *The Times of Bangalore,* June 1, 2010; "India's New Retailers," *OutlookBusiness,* July 11, 2009.

17. For more on new-product definition, see "Electronic Code of Federal Regulations: Title 16 (Commercial Practices), Part 502 (Introductory Offers)" at http://ecfr.gpoaccess.gov/. For more about types of new products, see G. A. Athaide and R. R. Klink, "Managing Seller-Buyer Relationships During New Product Development," *Journal of Product Innovation Management,* 5 (2009); K. Aboulnasr, O. Narashimhan, E. Blair, and R. Chandy, "Competitive Response to Radical Product Innovations," *Journal of Marketing,* 3 (2008); D. L. Alexander, J. G. Lynch, and Q. Wang, "As Time Goes By: Do Cold Feet Follow Warm Intentions for Really New versus Incrementally New Products?" *Journal of Marketing Research,* 3 (2008).

18. Definition of a patent from the United States Patent and Trademark Office, online Glossary, http://www.uspto.gov/main/glossary/#p. For more on Apple v. Samsung see "Apple v. Samsung Patent Trial Recap: How It All Turned Out (FAQ)," *CNET.com,* May 7, 2014.

19. Boldrin, Michele and David K. Levine (2013), "The Case Against Patents," *Journal of Economic Perspectives,* Winter, 3–22.

20. "Reposition: Simplifying the Customer's Brandscape," *Brandweek,* October 2, 2000; "Consumers to GM: You Talking to Me?" *BusinessWeek,* June 19, 2000; "How Growth Destroys Differentiation," *Brandweek,* April 24, 2000; "P&G, Seeing Shoppers Were Being Confused, Overhauls Marketing," *Wall Street Journal,* January 15, 1997.

21. "Ignore the Consumer," *Point,* September 2005; "Too Many Choices," *Wall Street Journal,* April 20, 2001; "New Products," *Ad Age International,* April 13, 1998; "The Ghastliest Product Launches," *Fortune,* March 16, 1998; "Flops: Too Many New Products Fail; Here's Why—and How to Do Better," *BusinessWeek,* August 16, 1993; Brian D. Ottum and William L. Moore, "The Role of Market Information in New Product Success/Failure," *Journal of Product Innovation Management,* July 1997; E. Ofek and O. Turut, "To Inno-

vate or Imitate? Entry Strategy and the Role of Market Research," *Journal of Marketing Research,* 5 (2008).

22. "Flavor Experiment for KitKat Leaves Nestle with a Bad Taste," *Wall Street Journal,* July 6, 2006; "Makers of Chicken Tonight Find Many Cooks Say, 'Not Tonight,'" *Wall Street Journal,* May 17, 1994; "Failure of Its Oven Lovin' Cookie Dough Shows Pillsbury Pitfalls of New Products," *Wall Street Journal,* June 17, 1993; Sharad Sarin and Gour M. Kapur, "Lessons from New Product Failures: Five Case Studies," *Industrial Marketing Management,* November 1990.

23. "Agility in Action: How Four Brands Are Using Agile Marketing," *CMO.com,* May 20, 2013.

24. Martin Schreier and Reinhard Prugl, "Extending Lead-User Theory: Antecedents and Consequences of Consumers' Lead Userness," *Journal of Product Innovation Management,* July 2008; Lance A. Bettencourt and Anthony W. Ulwick, "The Customer-Centered Innovation Map," *Harvard Business Review,* May 2008; "Mosh Pits of Creativity." *BusinessWeek,* November 7, 2005; "Employers See Gold Mining Employees for Ideas," *Brandweek,* October 10, 2005; "It Was a Hit in Buenos Aires—So Why Not Boise?" *BusinessWeek,* September 7, 1998. See also Rudy K. Moenaert, Filip Caeldries, Annouk Lievens, and Elke Wauters, "Communication Flows in International Product Innovation Teams," *Journal of Product Innovation Management,* September 2000; Vittorio Chiesa, "Global R&D Project Management and Organization: A Taxonomy," *Journal of Product Innovation Management,* September 2000; John J. Cristiano, Jeffrey K. Liker, and Chelsea C. White III, "Customer-Driven Product Development Through Quality Function Deployment in the U.S. and Japan," *Journal of Product Innovation Management,* July 2000; Lisa C. Troy, David M. Szymanskis, and P. Rajan Varadarajan, "Generating New Product Ideas: An Initial Investigation of the Role of Market Information and Organizational Characteristics," *Journal of the Academy of Marketing Science,* Winter 2001; X. M. Song and Mitzi M. Montoya-Weiss, "Critical Development Activities for Really New versus Incremental Products." *Journal of Product Innovation Management,* March 1998.

25. P. N. Bloom, G. T. Gundlach, and J. P. Cannon, "Slotting Allowances and Fees: Schools of Thought and the Views of Practicing Managers," *Journal of Marketing,* April 2000; "Shielding the Shield Makers," *Wall Street Journal,* November 26, 2003; "Gun Makers to Push Use of Gun Locks," *Wall Street Journal,* May 9, 2001; Jennifer J. Argo and Kelley J. Main, "MetaAnalyses of the Effectiveness of Warning Labels," *Journal of Public Policy & Marketing,* Fall 2004.

26. This box was inspired by a TEDxBozeman talk by Professor Jakki Mohr, "Biomimicry: Business Innovations Inspired by Nature"; "Biomimicry," *Wikipedia,* accessed July 2012; "15 Coolest Cases of Biomimicry," *Brainz.* For more on other forms of idea generation, see: "Pipe Up, People! Rounding Up Staff Ideas," *Inc.,* February 2010; "Twitter Serves Up New Ideas from Its Followers," *New York Times,* October 25, 2009; "Where Do the Best Ideas Come From? The Unlikeliest Sources," *Advertising Age,* July 14, 2008; "The Customer Is the Company: Threadless," *Inc.,* June 2008; "Breakthrough Thinking from Inside the Box," *Harvard Business Review,* December 2007; "Let Consumers Control More than Just Ads," *Advertising Age,* April 9, 2007; "Turn Customer Input into Innovation," *Harvard Business Review,* January 2002; Judy A. Siguaw, Penny M. Simpson, and Cathy A. Enz, "Conceptualizing Innovation Orientation: A Framework for Study and Integration of Innovation Research," *Journal of Product Innovation Management,* November 2006; V. Blazevic and A. Lievens, "Managing Innovation through Customer Coproduced Knowledge in Electronic Services: An Exploratory Study," *Journal of the Academy of Marketing Science,* 1 (2008).

27. "Test-Marketing a Modern Princess" *Wall Street Journal,* April 9, 2013.

28. Susumu Ogawa and Frank T. Piller, "Reducing the Risks of New Product Development," *Sloan Management Review,* Winter 2006; Joseph M. Bonner, Robert W. Ruekert, and Orville C. Walker, Jr., "Upper Management Control of New Product Development

Projects and Project Performance," *Journal of Product Innovation Management,* May 2002; Sundar Bharadwaj and Anil Menon, "Making Innovations Happen in Organizations: Individual Creativity Mechanisms, Organizational Creativity Mechanisms or Both?" *Journal of Product Innovation Management,* November 2000; Paul S. Adler, Avi Mandelbaum, Vien Nguyen, and Elizabeth Schwerer, "Getting the Most Out of Your Product Development Process," *Harvard Business Review,* March–April 1996.

29. C. K. Chua, K. F. Leong, and C. S. Lim, *Rapid Prototyping: Principles and Applications,* 2010, World Scientific Publishing Company; Jeanne Liedtka, "Learning to Use Design Thinking Tools for Successful Innovation," *Strategy & Leadership,* 5 (2011); T. Brown, "Design Thinking," *Harvard Business Review,* June 2008; T. Brown, *Change by Design: How Design Thinking Transforms Organizations and Inspires Innovation,* 2009, HarperBusiness; see also www.ideo.com.

30. "Torture Testing," *Fortune,* October 2, 2000; "Industry's Amazing New Instant Prototypes," *Fortune,* January 12, 1998; "Secrets of Product Testing," *Fortune,* November 28, 1994; "A Smarter Way to Manufacture," *BusinessWeek,* April 30, 1990.

31. "Oops! Marketers Blunder Their Way Through the 'Herb Decade,'" *Advertising Age,* February 13, 1989.

32. James E. Burroughs, Darren W. Dahl, C. Page Moreau, Amitava Chattopadhyay, and Gerald J. Gorn, "Facilitating and Rewarding Creativity During New Product Development," *Journal of Marketing,* November 2011; Donna L. Hoffman, Praveen K. Kopalle, and Thomas P. Novak, "The 'Right' Consumers for Better Concepts: Identifying Consumers High in Emergent Nature to Develop New Product Concepts," *Journal of Marketing Research,* October 2010; Kimmy Wa Chan, Chi Kin (Bennett) Yim, and Simon S. K. Lam, "Is Customer Participation in Value Creation a Double-Edged Sword? Evidence from Professional Financial Services Across Cultures," *Journal of Marketing,* May 2010; Ashwin W. Joshi, "Salesperson Influence on Product Development: Insights from a Study of Small Manufacturing Organizations," *Journal of Marketing* 74, #1, pp. 94–107; Rebecca J. Slotegraaf and Kwaku Atuahene-Gima, "Product Development Team Stability and New Product Advantage: The Role of Decision-Making Processes," *Journal of Marketing,* January 2011; Rajesh Sethi, Zafar Iqbal, and Anju Sethi, "Developing New-to-the-Firm Products: The Role of Micropolitical Strategies," *Journal of Marketing,* March 2012; Ji Hoon Jhang, Susan Jung Grant, and Margaret C. Campbell, "Get It?? Got It. Good! Enhancing New Product Acceptance by Facilitating Resolution of Extreme Incongruity," *Journal of Marketing Research,* April 2012; L. C. Troy, T. Hirunyawipada, and A. K. Paswan, "Cross-Functional Integration and New Product Success: An Empirical Investigation of the Findings," *Journal of Marketing,* 6 (2008); Albert L. Page and Gary R. Schirr, "Growth and Development of a Body of Knowledge: 16 Years of New Product Development Research, 1989–2004," *Journal of Product Innovation Management,* May 2008; Gloria Barczak, Kenneth B. Kahn, and Roberta Moss, "An Exploratory Investigation of NPD Practices in Nonprofit Organizations," *Journal of Product Innovation Management,* November 2006; Kwaku Atuahene-Gima and Janet Y. Murray, "Exploratory and Exploitative Learning in New Product Development: A Social Capital Perspective on New Technology Ventures in China," *Journal of International Marketing,* 2 (2007); Khaled Aboulnasr, Om Narasimhan, Edward Blair, and Rajesh Chandy, "Competitive Response to Radical Product Innovations," *Journal of Marketing,* May 2008; Stephen J. Carson, "When to Give Up Control of Outsourced New Product Development," *Journal of Marketing,* January 2007; Subin Im and John P. Workman, Jr., "Market Orientation, Creativity, and New Product Performance in High-Technology Firms," *Journal of Marketing,* April 2004; Steven C. Michael and Tracy Pun Palandjian, "Organizational Learning and New Product Introductions," *Journal of Product Innovation Management,* July 2004; John P. Workman, Jr., "Marketing's Limited Role in New Product Development in One Computer Systems Firm," *Journal of Marketing Research,* November 1993.

33. *Innovation Leadership Study,* Capgemini Consulting and IESE Business School, 2014.

34. "Care, Feeding, and Building of a Billion-Dollar Brand," *Advertising Age,* February 23, 2004; "Brands at Work," *Brandweek,* April 13, 1998; "Auto Marketing & Brand Management," *Advertising Age,* April 6, 1998; "P&G Redefines the Brand Manager," *Advertising Age,* October 13, 1997. See also Sanjay K. Dhar, Stephen J. Hoch, and Nanda Kumar, "Effective Category Management Depends on the Role of the Category," *Journal of Retailing,* Summer 2001; Don Frey, "Learning the Ropes: My Life as a Product Champion," *Harvard Business Review,* September–October 1991; Stephen K. Markham, "New Products Management," *Journal of Product Innovation Management,* July 1997; Ertimur, Burçak, and Gokcen Coskuner-Balli. "Navigating the Institutional Logics of Markets: Implications for Strategic Brand Management." *Journal of Marketing* 79.2 (2015): 40-61.

35. "Soy Sauce Flavored Kit Kats? In Japan, They're #1," *AdAge. com,* March 4, 2010; "Flavor Experiment for KitKat Leaves Nestlé with a Bad Taste," *Wall Street Journal,* July 6, 2006.

36. See "Hotels Train Employees to Think Fast," *USA Today,* November 29, 2006; "Takin' Off the Ritz—a Tad," *Wall Street Journal,* June 23, 2006; "Hotels Take 'Know Your Customer' to New Level," *Wall Street Journal,* February 7, 2006; "Listener Runner-up: W Hotels," *Fast Company,* October 2005; "Companies Give Front-Line Employees More Power," *USA Today,* June 27, 2005; "Thinking Outside the Cereal Box," *BusinessWeek,* July 28, 2003; "Pentair Fixes Its Own Mess," *Fortune,* September 30, 2002; "Glass Act: How a Window Maker Rebuilt Itself," *Fortune,* November 13, 2000. See also Douglas W. Vorhies and Neil A. Morgan, "Benchmarking Marketing Capabilities for Sustainable Competitive Advantage," *Journal of Marketing,* January 2005; Roland T. Rust, Tim Ambler, Gregory S. Carpenter, V. Kumar, and Rajendra K. Srivastava, "Measuring Marketing Productivity: Current Knowledge and Future Directions," *Journal of Marketing,* October 2004; Roland T. Rust, Anthony J. Zahorik, and Timothy L. Keiningham, *Return on Quality* (Chicago: Probus, 1994); J. J. Cronin and Steven A. Taylor, "SERVPERF versus SERVQUAL: Reconciling Performance-Based and Perceptions-Minus-Expectations Measurement of Service Quality," *Journal of Marketing,* January 1994; Shirley Taylor, "Waiting for Service: The Relationship Between Delays and Evaluations of Service," *Journal of Marketing,* April 1994; Mary J. Bitner, Bernard H. Booms, and Lois A. Mohr, "Critical Service Encounters: The Employee's Viewpoint," *Journal of Marketing,* October 1994.

37. For more on quality management and control, see Roland T. Rust, Anthony J. Zahorik, and Timothy L. Keiningham, "Return on Quality (ROQ): Making Service Quality Financially Accountable," *Journal of Marketing,* April 1995. See also Mark R. Colgate and Peter J. Danaher, "Implementing a Customer Relationship Strategy: The Asymetric Impact of Poor versus Excellent Execution," *Journal of the Academy of Marketing Science,* Summer 2000; Simon J. Bell and Bulent Menguc, "The Employee-Organization Relationship, Organizational Citizenship Behaviors, and Superior Service Quality," *Journal of Retailing,* Summer 2002; Pratibha A. Dabholkar, C. David Shepherd, and Dayle I. Thorpe, "A Comprehensive Framework for Service Quality: An Investigation of Critical Conceptual and Measurement Issues Through a Longitudinal Study," *Journal of Retailing,* Summer 2000; Sivakumar, K., Mei Li, and Beibei Dong. "Service Quality: The Impact of Frequency, Timing, Proximity, and Sequence of Failures and Delights." *Journal of Marketing* 78.1 (2014): 41-58; Heijden, Gielis, Jeroen Schepers, Edwin Nijssen, and Andrea Ordanini, "Don't Just Fix It, Make It Better! Using Frontline Service Employees to Improve Recovery Performance," *Journal of the Academy of Marketing Science* 41.5 (2013): 515-30.

CHAPTER 10

1. See www.dell.com; www.lenovo.com; "Lenovo, the Treasure Hunter of Tech," *Bloomberg Businessweek,* May 8, 2014; "How a Chinese Company Became a Global PC Powerhouse," *Time,* May 4, 2015; "Lenovo's Mobile Chief Steps Down Amid Slowdown in Chinese Smartphone Market," *FierceWireless*, June 2, 2015; "Lenovo Fine-Tunes Partner Strategy as Sales Continue to Defy Gravity," *Channel Partners*, May 22, 2014; "Lenovo: A Chinese Dragon in the Global Village," *Ivey Case #W13085*, 2013; "Personal Computer Business – Lenovo Leading the Pack," *Amity Research Centers, Case Study # 313-302-1*, 2013; "Lenovo: Challenger to Leader," *IBS Center for Management Research #314-094-1*, 2014; "China's Competitiveness, Myth Reality, and Lessons for the United States and Japan, Case Study: Lenovo," *Center for Strategic & International Studies*, January 2013; "Dell's Reinvention Efforts Hold Promise," *Wall Street Journal*, February 21, 2012; "Dell Outlook Cloudy," *Wall Street Journal*, November 16, 2011; "PC Makers Ready iPad Rivals," *Wall Street Journal*, February 18, 2011; "Dell's Faith in Business Sales Pays Off," *Wall Street Journal*, February 16, 2011; "Dell Spurs Sales by Lending to Hard-Hit Small Businesses," *Wall Street Journal*, March 30, 2010; "Discounting Continues to Haunt Dell as Its Turnaround Struggles," *Wall Street Journal*, February 19, 2010; "Direct Seller Dell Now Offers the Full Middleman Route," *Investor's Business Daily*, April 15, 2009; "Dell to Lift Its Data-Center Game," *Wall Street Journal*, March 25, 2009; "New Dell Notebook Fashion-Model Thin, Unfashionable Price," *Investor's Business Daily*, March 18, 2009; "Former Direct-Only Seller Dell Adds Best Buy," *Investor's Business Daily*, December 7, 2007; "Dell's U.S. Sales Fall, Profits Disappear," *USA Today*, November 30, 2007; "Where Dell Sells with Brick and Mortar," *BusinessWeek*, October 8, 2007; "Direct-Selling PC Specialist Dell Hooks Up with Retailer in China," *Investor's Business Daily*, September 25, 2007; "Dell Pushes Reset Button on Its Image," *Wall Street Journal*, July 10, 2007; "Hmm, Hell Can Freeze Over—Dell to Sell PCs at Retail," *Investor's Business Daily*, May 25, 2007; "Where Dell Went Wrong," *BusinessWeek*, February 19, 2007; "Grudge Match in China," *BusinessWeek*, April 2, 2007; "Can Dell Succeed in an Encore?" *Wall Street Journal*, February 5, 2007; "Consumer Demand and Growth in Laptops Leave Dell Behind," *Wall Street Journal*, August 30, 2006; "Dell May Have to Reboot in China," *BusinessWeek*, November 7, 2005; "What You Don't Know about Dell," *BusinessWeek*, November 3, 2003.

2. S. Chan Choi, "Expanding to Direct Channel: Market Coverages as Entry Barrier," *Journal of Interactive Marketing*, Winter 2003; David Shipley, Colin Egan, and Scott Edgett, "Meeting Source Selection Criteria: Direct versus Distributor Channels," *Industrial Marketing Management* 20, #4 (1991); R. E. Bucklin, S. Siddarth, and J. M. Silva-Risso, "Distribution Intensity and New Car Choice," *Journal of Marketing Research*, 4 (2008).

3. For more on Glacéau, see "Are Sodas Losing Their Fizz?" *Investor's Business Daily*, November 19, 2007; "Coke Unit Adds Some Muscle to Water Line," *USA Today*, October 31, 2007; "Coke Plan Riles Glacéau's Old Network," *Wall Street Journal*, September 14, 2007; "Move Over, Coke: How a Small Beverage Maker Managed to Win Shelf Space . . . ," *Wall Street Journal Reports*, January 30, 2006; "Pepsi Picks Water Fight with Surging Glaceau," *Advertising Age*, October 17, 2005.

4. For more on Avon, see "Direct Sellers Happy to Toe the Party Line," *Advertising Age*, November 3, 2008; "Lean Times Swell Avon's Sales Force," *Wall Street Journal*, October 15, 2008; "Avon's Calling, but China Opens Door Only a Crack," *Wall Street Journal*, February 26, 2007; "China's New Rules Open Door to Amway, Avon, Others," *USA Today*, December 1, 2005. For other examples of direct channels, see "Amway: Shining Up a Tarnished Name," *BusinessWeek*, August 11, 2008; "Party Time: Home Events See Sales," *USA Today*, October 5, 2005; "Catwalk to Coffee Table," *Wall Street Journal*, November 7, 2003; "India's Retailing Makeover," *Wall Street Journal*, October 28, 2003. See also Ruud T. Frambach, Henk C. A. Roest, and Trichy V. Krishnan, "The Impact of Consumer Internet Experience on Channel Preference and Usage Intentions across the Different Stages of the Buying Process," *Journal of Interactive Marketing*, Spring 2007.

5. Bob Stone and Ron Jacobs, *Successful Direct Marketing Methods* (New York: McGraw-Hill, 2008).

6. For an example of Levi Strauss's new indirect channels via discount stores, see "Levi's Signature Spreads Its Wings," *DSN Retailing Today*, April 25, 2005; "In Bow to Retailers' New Clout, Levi Strauss Makes Alterations," *Wall Street Journal*, June 17, 2004. For two examples of unsuccessful attempts at indirect channels, see "Ovens Are Cooling at Krispy Kreme as Woes Multiply," *Wall Street Journal*, September 3, 2004; "A Deal with Target Put Lid on Revival at Tupperware," *Wall Street Journal*, February 14, 2004.

7. For a classic discussion of the discrepancy concepts, see Wroe Alderson, "Factors Governing the Development of Marketing Channels," in *Marketing Channels for Manufactured Goods*, ed. Richard M. Clewett (Homewood, IL: Richard D. Irwin, 1954).

8. See hulu.com; "The Future of TV," *Advertising Age*, November 30, 2009. "Searching for Life on Hulu," *AdweekMedia*, May 25, 2009; "Hulu," *Fast Company*, March 2009.

9. For some examples of how channels change to adjust discrepancies, see "Selling Literature like Dog Food Gives Club Buyer Real Bite," *Wall Street Journal*, April 10, 2002. See also Robert Tamilia, Sylvain Senecal, and Gilles Corriveau, "Conventional Channels of Distribution and Electronic Intermediaries: A Functional Analysis," *Journal of Marketing Channels* 3, #4 (2002); Robert A. Mittelstaedt and Robert E. Stassen, "Structural Changes in the Phonograph Record Industry and Its Channels of Distribution, 1946–1966," *Journal of Macromarketing*, Spring 1994; Arun Sharma and Luis V. Dominguez, "Channel Evolution: A Framework for Analysis," *Journal of the Academy of Marketing Science*, Winter 1992; A. Ansari, C. F. Mela, and S. A. Neslin, "Customer Channel Migration," *Journal of Marketing Research*, 1 (2008).

10. Arne Nygaard and Robert Dahlstrom, "Role Stress and Effectiveness in Horizontal Alliances," *Journal of Marketing*, April 2002; M. B. Sarkar, Raj Echambadi, S. Tamer Cavusgil, and Preet S. Aulakh, "The Influence of Complementarity, Compatibility, and Relationship Capital on Alliance Performance," *Journal of the Academy of Marketing Science*, Fall 2001; Jakki J. Mohr, Robert J. Fisher, and John R. Nevin, "Collaborative Communication in Interfirm Relationships: Moderating Effects of Integration and Control," *Journal of Marketing*, July 1996; S. Ganesan, M. George, S. Jap, R. W. Palmatier, and B. Weitz, "Supply Chain Management and Retailer Performance: Emerging Trends, Issues, and Implications for Research and Practice," *Journal of Retailing*, 1 (2009).

11. "Gamers Applaud Used Games and Trade-Ins: Paying Less for Their Habit," *Investor's Business Daily*, April 20, 2009; "Ode to Joystick: Downloading Titles without Leaving the Sofa," *Wall Street Journal*, February 17, 2009; "Used Games Score Big for GameStop," *Wall Street Journal*, January 21, 2009.

12. "Fender's Move to Sell Instruments Directly to Musicians Upsets Dealers," *LA Times*, January 20, 2015.

13. Nirmalya Kumar, "Living with Channel Conflict," *CMO*, October 2004. See also Antia, Kersi D., Xu (Vivian) Zheng, and Gary L. Frazier. "Conflict Management and Outcomes in Franchise Relationships: The Role of Regulation." *Journal of Marketing Research (JMR)* 50.5 (2013): 577-89; Wang, Danny T., Flora F. Gu, and Maggie Chuoyan Dong. "Observer Effects of Punishment in a Distribution Network." *Journal of Marketing Research (JMR)* 50.5 (2013): 627-43; Gregory M. Rose and Aviv Shoham, "Interorganizational Task and Emotional Conflict with International Channels of Distribution," *Journal of Business Research*, September 2004.

14. "Get Great Results from Salespeople by Finding What Really Moves Them," *Investor's Business Daily*, July 2, 2001.

15. Shailendra Gajanan, Suman Basuroy, and Srinath Beldona, "Category Management, Product Assortment, and Consumer Welfare," *Marketing Letters*, July 2007; Kenneth H. Wathne and Jan B. Heide, "Relationship Governance in a Supply Chain Network," *Journal of Marketing*, January 2004; David I. Gilliland, "Designing Channel Incentives to Overcome Reseller Rejection," *Industrial Marketing Management*, February 2004; James R. Brown, Anthony T. Cobb, and Robert F. Lusch, "The Roles Played by Interorganizational

Contracts and Justice in Marketing Channel Relationships," *Journal of Business Research,* February 2006; Keysuk Kim and Changho Oh, "On Distributor Commitment in Marketing Channels for Industrial Products: Contrast Between the United States and Japan," *Journal of International Marketing,* 1 (2002).

16. For research on control in channels of distribution see Crosno, Jody, and James Brown. "A Meta-analytic Review of the Effects of Organizational Control in Marketing Exchange Relationships." *Journal of the Academy of Marketing Science* 43.3 (2015): 297-314; Gilliland, David, and Stephen Kim. "When Do Incentives Work in Channels of Distribution?" *Journal of the Academy of Marketing Science* 42.4 (2014): 361-79;

17. For some examples of vertical integration, see "Moving On Up: Agricultural Firms Are Looking for New Growth Model . . . Vertical Integration," *Wall Street Journal Reports,* October 25, 2004.

18. Flora F. Gu, Namwoon Kim, David K. Tse, and Danny T. Wang, "Managing Distributors' Changing Motivations over the Course of a Joint Sales Program,"*Journal of Marketing,* September 2010; David I. Gilliland, Daniel C. Bello, and Gregory T. Gundlach, "Control-based Channel Governance and Relative Dependence,"*Journal of the Academy of Marketing Science,* July 2010; Vishal Kashyap, Kersi D. Antia, and Gary L. Frazier, "Contracts, Extracontractual Incentives, and Ex Post Behavior in Franchise Channel Relationships,"*Journal of Marketing Research,* April 2012; Stephen K. Kim, Richard G. McFarland, Soongi Kwon, Sanggi Son, and David A. Griffith, "Understanding Governance Decisions in a Partially Integrated Channel: A Contingent Alignment Framework,"*Journal of Marketing Research,* May 2011; Kevin L. Webb, "Managing Channels of Distribution in the Age of Electronic Commerce," *Industrial Marketing Management,* February 2002; Charles A. Ingene and Mark E. Parry, "Is Channel Coordination All It Is Cracked Up to Be?" *Journal of Retailing,* Winter 2000; Kenneth H. Wathne and Jan B. Heide, "Opportunism in Interfirm Relationships: Forms, Outcomes, and Solutions," *Journal of Marketing,* October 2000; Kersi D. Antia and Gary L. Frazier, "The Severity of Contract Enforcement in Interfirm Channel Relationships," *Journal of Marketing,* October 2001; Aric Rindfleisch and Jan B. Heide, "Transaction Cost Analysis: Past, Present, and Future Applications," *Journal of Marketing,* October 1997.

19. "A Talk with the Man Who Got Rayovac All Charged Up," *BusinessWeek,* February 21, 2000.

20. "Antitrust Issues and Marketing Channel Strategy" and "Case 1—Continental T.V., Inc. et al. v. GTE Sylvania, Inc.," in Louis W. Stern and Thomas L. Eovaldi, *Legal Aspects of Marketing Strategy* (Englewood Cliffs, NJ: Prentice Hall, 1984). See also Debra M. Desrochers, Gregory T. Gundlach, and Albert A. Foer, "Analysis of Antitrust Challenges to Category Captain Arrangements," *Journal of Public Policy & Marketing,* Fall 2003. For some examples of exclusive deals, see "Blue Nile: Online Jewelry Seller Looks to Be a Cut Above the Competition," *Investor's Business Daily,* December 15, 2005; "When Exclusivity Means Illegality," *Wall Street Journal,* January 6, 2005; "Bringing Chic to Sheets," *Wall Street Journal,* September 8, 2004.

21. For more on Reebok, see *2010 Annual Report* and www.reebok.com, Reebok; "Reebok's Direct Sales Spark a Retail Revolt," *Adweek*'s *Marketing Week,* December 2, 1991. For more on multichannel distribution, see Kushwaha, Tarun, and Venkatesh Shankar. "Are Multichannel Customers Really More Valuable? The Moderating Role of Product Category Characteristics." *Journal of Marketing* 77.4 (2013): 67-85; Li, Hongshuang (Alice), and P. K. Kannan. "Attributing Conversions in a Multichannel Online Marketing Environment: An Empirical Model and a Field Experiment." *Journal of Marketing Research (JMR)* 51.1 (2014): 40-56; Lund, Donald J., and Detelina Marinova. "Managing Revenue Across Retail Channels: The Interplay of Service Performance and Direct Marketing." *Journal of Marketing* 78.5 (2014): 99-118. Andrea Godfrey, Kathleen Seiders, and Glenn B. Voss, "Enough Is Enough! The Fine Line in Executing Multichannel Relational Communication,"*Journal of Marketing,* July 2011; U. Konus,

P. C. Verhoef, and S. A. Neslin, "Multichannel Shopper Segments and Their Covariates," *Journal of Retailing,* 4 (2008); Rajkumar Venkatesan, V. Kumar, and Nalini Ravishanker, "Multichannel Shopping: Causes and Consequences," *Journal of Marketing,* April 2007; Scott A. Neslin, Dhruv Grewal, Robert Leghorn, Venkatesh Shankar, Marije L. Teerling, Jacquelyn S. Thomas, and Peter C. Verhoef, "Challenges and Opportunities in Multichannel Customer Management," *Journal of Service Research,* May 2006; Sertan Kabadayi, Nermin Eyuboglu, and Gloria P. Thomas, "The Performance Implications of Designing Multiple Channels to Fit with Strategy and Environment," *Journal of Marketing,* October 2007; Arun Sharma and Anuj Mehrotra, "Choosing an Optimal Channel Mix in Multichannel Environments," *Industrial Marketing Management,* January 2007; Bert Rosenbloom, "Multi-channel Strategy in Business-to-Business Markets: Prospects and Problems," *Industrial Marketing Management,* January 2007; Asim Ansari, Carl F. Mela, and Scott A. Neslin, "Customer Channel Migration," *Journal of Marketing Research,* February 2008; Jule B. Gassenheimer, Gary L. Hunter, and Judy A. Siguaw, "An Evolving Theory of Hybrid Distribution: Taming a Hostile Supply Network," *Industrial Marketing Management,* May 2007; Peter C. Verhoef, Scott A. Neslin, and Björn Vroomen, "Multichannel Customer Management: Understanding the Research-Shopper Phenomenon," *International Journal of Research in Marketing,* June 2007; Jacquelyn S. Thomas and Ursula Y. Sullivan, "Managing Marketing Communications with Multichannel Customers," *Journal of Marketing,* October 2005.

22. Gregory T. Gundlach and Patrick E. Murphy, "Ethical and Legal Foundations of Relational Marketing Exchanges," *Journal of Marketing,* October 1993; Craig B. Barkacs, "Multilevel Marketing and Antifraud Statutes: Legal Enterprises or Pyramid Schemes?" *Journal of the Academy of Marketing Science,* Spring 1997; Robert A. Robicheaux and James E. Coleman, "The Structure of Marketing Channel Relationships," *Journal of the Academy of Marketing Science,* Winter 1994; Brett A. Boyle and F. Robert Dwyer, "Power, Bureaucracy, Influence and Performance: Their Relationships in Industrial Distribution Channels," *Journal of Business Research,* March 1995.

23. Elie Ofek, Zsolt Katona, and Miklos Sarvary, "Bricks and Clicks: The Impact of Product Returns on the Strategies of Multichannel Retailers,"*Marketing Science,* 1 (2011); Jeffrey D. Shulman, Anne T. Coughlan, and R. Canan Savaskan, "Optimal Reverse Channel Structure for Consumer Product Returns,"*Marketing Science,* 6 (2010); J. A. Petersen and V. Kumar, "Are Product Returns a Necessary Evil? Antecedents and Consequences," *Journal of Marketing,* 3 (2009); R. Glenn Richey, Haozhe Chen, Stefan E. Genchev, and Patricia J. Daugherty, "Developing Effective Reverse Logistics Programs," *Industrial Marketing Management,* November 2005; Joseph D. Blackburn, V. Daniel, R. Guide, Jr., Gilvan C. Souza, and Luk N. Van Wassenhove, "Reverse Supply Chains for Commercial Returns," *California Management Review,* Winter 2004.

24. "Hyper-Green Products Go Cradle to Cradle," *MSNBC.com,* October 12, 2007; "Can One Green Deliver the Other," *Harvard Business Review,* 2005; "HP Wants Your Old PCs Back," *BusinessWeek.com,* April 10, 2006.

25. See Rene B. M. de Koster, Marisa P. de Brito, and Masja A. van de Vendel, "Return Handling: An Exploratory Study with Nine Retailer Warehouses," *International Journal of Retail & Distribution Management,* 8 (2002); Chad W. Autry, Patricia J. Daugherty, and R. Glenn Richey, "The Challenge of Reverse Logistics in Catalog Retailing," *International Journal of Physical Distribution & Logistics Management,* 1 (2001); Dale S. Rogers and Ronald Tibben Lembke, "An Examination of Reverse Logistics Practices," *Journal of Business Logistics,* 2 (2001).

26. "Small Business: The Cost of Expanding Overseas," *The Wall Street Journal,* February 26, 2014.

27. "Year of the Grease Monkey in China," *Denver Post,* April 26, 2009; "Danone Pulls Out of Disputed China Venture," *Wall Street Journal,* October 1, 2009; "Special Report: Gone Global, How to Get Ahead in China," *Inc.,* May 2008; For academic research on this topic, see Grewal, Rajdeep, Alok Kumar, Girish Mallapragada, and Amit Saini, "Marketing Channels in Foreign Markets: Control Mechanisms and the Moderating Role of Multinational Corporation Headquarters-Subsidiary Relationship," *Journal of Marketing Research (JMR)* 50.3 (2013): 378-98; Joseph Johnson and Gerard J. Tellis, "Drivers of Success for Market Entry into China and India," *Journal of Marketing,* May 2008; Neil Morgan, Constantine Katsikeas, and Douglas Vorhies, "Export Marketing Strategy Implementation, Export Marketing Capabilities, and Export Venture Performance," *Journal of the Academy of Marketing Science,* March 2012.

CHAPTER 11

1. "The Guy Who Invented The Segway Is Working With Coca-Cola To Bring His Water Distilling Invention To Third-World Countries," *Business Insider,* June 19, 2014; "Drink Dispenser Analytics: Coca-Cola Goes Freestyle, with Help from SAP BI," *Business Analytics,* June 19, 2009; "What Do You Call a Soda Dispenser with Onboard Data Analytics," *Spotfire, Trends and Outliers,* October 7, 2010; "Africa: Coke's Last Frontier," *Bloomberg Businessweek,* October 28, 2010; "Eliminating Inefficiencies through Automation," *Beverage Industry,* January 2010; "Coca-Cola Expands Hybrid Electric Fleet in Canada," *Beverage Industry,* January 2010; "Coca-Cola Deal Is U.S. Strategy Shift," *Wall Street Journal,* February 26, 2010; "Coke Takes Juice Lead from Pepsi," *Advertising Age,* February 1, 2010; "Masters of Design," *Fast Company,* October 2009; "Coke: Buy 1 Rival, Get Our Brand Free," *Advertising Age,* March 9, 2009; "Sustainability and a Smile," *Advertising Age,* February 25, 2008; "Iran's Cola War," *Fortune,* February 6, 2008; "Coke Tries to Pop Back in Vital Japan Market," *Wall Street Journal,* July 11, 2006; "Coke Gets a Jolt," *Fortune,* May 15, 2006; "Thirsting for More Variety," *Investor's Business Daily,* April 24, 2006; "In the Newest Snack Packs, Less Is More," *USA Today,* April 13, 2006; "Afghan Coke a Taste of Things to Come," *Financial Times,* December 6, 2005; "EU Limits Coke's Sales Tactics in Settlement of Antitrust Case," *Wall Street Journal,* June 23, 2005; "To Pitch New Soda, Coke Wants the World to Sing—Again," *Wall Street Journal,* June 13, 2005; "How a Global Web of Activists Gives Coke Problems in India," *Wall Street Journal,* June 7, 2005; "The Soda with Buzz," *Forbes,* March 28, 2005; "Into the Fryer: How Coke Officials Beefed Up Results of Marketing Tests," *Wall Street Journal,* August 20, 2003; "Mooove Over, Milkman," *Wall Street Journal,* June 9, 2003; "Fountain Dispenses Problems," *USA Today,* May 28, 2003.

2. "U.S. Logistics Costs Drop for First Time in Six Years, Benchmark Report Says," *Supply Chain Management Review,* June 18, 2009; "2009 Annual Report on State of Logistics: Collaboration Time," *Logistics Management,* 2009; "Latin America: Addressing High Logistics Costs and Poor Infrastructure for Merchandise Transportation and Trade Facilitation," working paper, The World Bank, August 2007; "The Cost of Being Landlocked: Logistics Costs and Supply Chain Reliability," Policy Research working paper, The World Bank, June 1, 2007.

3. "Compaq Stumbles as PCs Weather New Blow," *Wall Street Journal,* March 9, 1998; See also Alexander E. Ellinger, Scott B. Keller, and John D. Hansen, "Bridging the Divide Between Logistics and Marketing: Facilitating Collaborative Behavior," *Journal of Business Logistics,* 2 (2006); Kofi Q. Dadzie, Cristian Chelariu, and Evelyn Winston, "Customer Service in the Internet-Enabled Logistics Supply Chain: Website Design Antecedents and Loyalty Effects," *Journal of Business Logistics,* January 2005; Elliot Rabinovich and Philip T. Evers, "Product Fulfillment in Supply Chains Supporting Internet-Retailing Operations," *Journal of Business Logistics,* January 2003; Daniel Corsten and Thomas Gruen, "Stock-Outs Cause Walkouts," *Harvard Business Review,* May 2004; William D. Perreault, Jr., and Frederick A. Russ, "Physical Distribution Service in Industrial Purchase Decisions," *Journal of Marketing,* April 1976; "Walmart Faces the Cost of Cost-Cutting: Empty Shelves," *Bloomberg Businessweek,* March 28, 2013.

4. "H-P Wields Its Clout to Undercut PC Rivals," *Wall Street Journal,* September 24, 2009; "Walmart's H-P Elves," *Wall Street Journal,* December 15, 2005; "A More Profitable Harvest," *Business 2.0,* May 2005; "Costs Too High? Bring in the Logistics Experts," *Fortune,* November 10, 1997. See also G. Tomas M. Hult, Kenneth K. Boyer, and David J. Ketchen, Jr., "Quality, Operational Logistics Strategy, and Repurchase Intentions: A Profile Deviation Analysis," *Journal of Business Logistics,* 2 (2007); Thierry Sauvage, "The Relationship Between Technology and Logistics Third Party Providers," *International Journal of Physical Distribution & Logistics Management,* 3 (2003); Donald J. Bowersox, David J. Closs, and Theodore P. Stank, "Ten Mega-Trends That Will Revolutionize Supply Chain Logistics," *Journal of Business Logistics,* 2 (2000); James R. Stock, "Marketing Myopia Revisited: Lessons for Logistics," *International Journal of Physical Distribution & Logistics Management,* 1 (2002); Mark Goh and Charlene Ling, "Logistics Development in China," *International Journal of Physical Distribution & Logistics Management,* 9 (2003); James H. Bookbinder and Chris S. Tan, "Comparison of Asian and European Logistics Systems," *International Journal of Physical Distribution & Logistics Management,* 1 (2003).

5. www.Amazon.com; www.walmart.com; "Walmart Expands 'To Go' Test As Competition Heats Up For Online Grocery Sales," *Forbes,* January 30, 2014. See also Forrest E. Harding, "Logistics Service Provider Quality: Private Measurement, Evaluation, and Improvement," *Journal of Business Logistics,* 1998; Carol C. Bienstock, John T. Mentzer, and Monroe M. Bird, "Measuring Physical Distribution Service Quality," *Journal of the Academy of Marketing Science,* Winter 1997.

6. "More Green from Green Beans," *Business 2.0,* August 2004. See also Mikko Karkkainen, Timo Ala-Risku, and Jan Holmstrom, "Increasing Customer Value and Decreasing Distribution Costs with Merge-In-Transit," *International Journal of Physical Distribution & Logistics Management,* 1 (2003); Marc J. Schniederjans and Qing Cao, "An Alternative Analysis of Inventory Costs of JIT and EOQ Purchasing," *International Journal of Physical Distribution & Logistics Management,* 2 (2001).

7. For more on JIT, see "Retailers Rely More on Fast Deliveries," *Wall Street Journal,* January 14, 2004; "Uncertain Economy Hinders Highly Precise Supply System," *New York Times,* March 15, 2003; "Port Tie-Up Shows Vulnerability," *USA Today,* October 9, 2002; "Deadline Scramble: A New Hazard for Recovery, Last-Minute Pace of Orders," *Wall Street Journal,* June 25, 2002; "Parts Shortages Hamper Electronics Makers," *Wall Street Journal,* July 7, 2000. See also Richard E. White and John N. Pearson, "JIT, System Integration and Customer Service," *International Journal of Physical Distribution & Logistics Management,* 5 (2001).

8. "How Technology Is Changing Disaster Relief," *BBC News,* September 24, 2014; For more on Haiti, see "Sharing in the USA: Social Websites, 'Apps' among Latest Conduits," *USA Today* (Special Report), April 13, 2010; "Aid Frustration: We're Racing against the Clock," *USA Today,* January 18, 2010; "Haitian Rescue Stymied Amid Chaos," *Wall Street Journal,* January 15, 2010; "Quake Severely Strains Telecom Services," *USA Today,* January 15, 2010; "Companies Efficiently Pour Out $16M to Help Haiti," *USA Today,* January 15, 2010. See also Ozlem Ergun, Pinar Keskiocak, and Julie Swann, "Humanitarian Relief Logistics," *OR/MS Today,* December 2007. For more on Katrina, see "Good Logistics Offer Better Relief," *Financial Times,* December 16, 2005; "Disasters Demand Supply Chain Software, Research Shows," *eWeek,* October 5, 2005; "The Only Lifeline Was the Walmart," *Fortune,* October 3, 2005; "For FedEx, It Was Time to Deliver," *Fortune,* October 3, 2005; "They Don't Teach This in B-School," *BusinessWeek,* September 19, 2005, pp. 46–48; "At Walmart, Emergency Plan Has Big Payoff," *Wall Street Journal,* September 12, 2005; "Walmart Praised for Hurricane Katrina Response Efforts," *NewsMax.com,* September 6, 2005; "Logistics and the Effective Delivery of Humanitarian Relief," The Fritz Institute,

2005; "Emergency Relief Logistics—A Faster Way across the Global Divide," *Logistics Quarterly,* Summer 2001; Anisya Thomas and Lynn Fritz, "Disaster Relief, Inc," *Harvard Business Review,* November 2006; "Wal-Mart Japan: A Shift into Crisis Mode," *Wall Street Journal,* March 25, 2011.

9. "A New Industrial Revolution," *Wall Street Journal,* April 28, 2008; "Global Scramble for Goods Gives Corporate Buyers a Lift," *Wall Street Journal,* October 2, 2007.

10. See "Clarity Is Missing Link in Supply Chain," *Wall Street Journal,* May 18, 2009; Martin Christopher and John Gattorna, "Supply Chain Cost Management and Value-Based Pricing," *Industrial Marketing Management,* February 2005; G. Tomas M. Hult, "Global Supply Chain Management: An Integration of Scholarly Thoughts," *Industrial Marketing Management,* January 2004; Daniel J. Flint, "Strategic Marketing in Global Supply Chains: Four Challenges," *Industrial Marketing Management,* January 2004; Daniel C. Bello, Ritu Lohtia, and Vinita Sangtani, "An Institutional Analysis of Supply Chain Innovations in Global Marketing Channels," *Industrial Marketing Management,* January 2004; Brian J. Gibson, John T. Mentzer, and Robert L. Cook, "Supply Chain Management: the Pursuit of a Consensus Definition," *Journal of Business Logistics,* 2005; Theodore P. Stank, Beth R. Davis, and Brian S. Fugate, "A Strategic Framework for Supply Chain Oriented Logistics," *Journal of Business Logistics,* 2005; Terry L. Esper, Thomas D. Jensen, Fernanda L. Turnipseed, and Scot Burton, "The Last Mile: An Examination of Effects of Online Retail Delivery Strategies on Consumers," *Journal of Business Logistics,* 2003; Christopher R. Moberg and Thomas W. Speh, "Evaluating the Relationship Between Questionable Business Practices and the Strength of Supply Chain Relationships," *Journal of Business Logistics,* 2 (2003); Subroto Roy, K. Sivakumar, and Ian F. Wilkinson, "Innovation Generation in Supply Chain Relationships: A Conceptual Model and Research Propositions," *Journal of the Academy of Marketing Science,* Winter 2004; Rakesh Niraj, "Customer Profitability in a Supply Chain," *Journal of Marketing,* July 2001.

11. For an excellent example of EDI, see "To Sell Goods to WalMart, Get on the Net," *Wall Street Journal,* November 21, 2003. See also Cornelia Droge and Richard Germain, "The Relationship of Electronic Data Interchange with Inventory and Financial Performance," *Journal of Business Logistics,* 2 (2000).

12. "A Smart Cookie at Pepperidge," *Fortune,* December 22, 1986.

13. "A New Push Against Sweatshops," *Time,* October 7, 2005; "Cops of the Global Village," *Fortune,* June 27, 2005; "Stamping Out Sweatshops," *BusinessWeek* Online, May 23, 2005; "Nike Opens Its Books on Sweatshop Audits," *BusinessWeek Online,* April 27, 2000; "Nike Names Names," *BusinessWeek Online,* April 13, 2005; "Corporate Social Responsibility—Companies in the News Nike," see www.mallenbaker.net/csr/CSRfiles/nike.html.

14. David Grant, Douglas Lambert, James R. Stock, and Lisa M. Ellram, *Fundamentals of Logistics* (Burr Ridge, IL: Irwin/ McGraw-Hill, 2005).

15. For more on transportation security, see "Calif. Port Goes Tech in Security," *Investor's Business Daily,* February 11, 2009; "Technology Roots Out Cargo Risks," *Investor's Business Daily,* October 4, 2005; "Keeping Cargo Safe from Terror," *Wall Street Journal,* July 29, 2005; "Protecting America's Ports," *Fortune,* November 10, 2003.

16. For a more detailed comparison of mode characteristics, see Robert Dahlstrom, Kevin M. McNeilly, and Thomas W. Speh, "Buyer-Seller Relationships in the Procurement of Logistical Services," *Journal of the Academy of Marketing Science,* Spring 1996.

17. "Rail Renaissance," *BusinessWeek,* November 3, 2008; "New Rail-Building Era Dawns," *Wall Street Journal,* February 13, 2008; "Next Stop: The 21st Century," *Business 2.0,* September 2003; "Back on Track: Left for Dead, Railroads Revive by Watching Clock," *Wall Street Journal,* July 25, 2003; "Trains: Industry Report," *Investor's Business Daily,* May 7, 2001.

18. "Truckers Question Traffic-Relief Efforts," *USA Today,* December 27, 2007; "Shipping Hubs Spring Up Inland," *USA Today,* December 17, 2007; "Waterways Could Be Key to Freeing Up Freeways," *USA Today,* October 11, 2007; "Costs of Trucking Seen Rising under New Safety Rules," *Wall Street Journal,* November 12, 2003; "Trucker Rewards Customers for Good Behavior," *Wall Street Journal,* September 9, 2003; "Trucking: Rig and Roll," *Wall Street Journal,* October 23, 2000; "Trucking Gets Sophisticated," *Fortune,* July 24, 2000.

19. For more on overnight carriers, see "UPS Battles Traffic Jams to Gain Ground in India," *Wall Street Journal,* January 25, 2008; "Why FedEx Is Gaining Ground," *Business 2.0,* October 2003; "FedEx Recasts Itself on the Ground," *Wall Street Journal,* September 4, 2003; "UPS, FedEx Wage Handheld Combat," *Investor's Business Daily,* May 19, 2003.

20. "Amazon's Drones Exiled to Canada," *The Wall Street Journal,* April 5, 2015; "Deutsche Post DHL to Deliver Medicine via Drone," *The Wall Street Journal,* September 25, 2014; "Swiss Postal Service Will Start Using Delivery Drones in Pilot Program This Summer," *Slate,* April 23, 2015.

21. "Foldable Shipping Containers Try to Stack Up," *Wall Street Journal,* April 12, 2010; "The Mega Containers Invade," *Wall Street Journal,* January 26, 2009; K. Raguraman and Claire Chan, "The Development of SeaAir Intermodal Transportation: An Assessment of Global Trends," *Logistics and Transportation Review,* December 1994; "Yule Log Jam," *Fortune,* December 13, 2004; "Monsters of the High Seas," *BusinessWeek,* October 13, 2003.

22. "Western Grocer Modernizes Passage to Indian Markets," *Wall Street Journal,* November 28, 2007; "Widening Aisles for Indian Shoppers," *BusinessWeek,* April 30, 2007.

23. "DHL Completes More Eco-Friendly Ship Voyage as Industry Comes under Fire," *GreenBiz.com,* February 15, 2008; State of Green Business 2008; Greener World Media, 2008; GreenBiz.com. See also *2009 Annual Report,* Du Pont; *2009 Annual Report,* Matlack; *2009 Annual Report,* Shell; *2009 Annual Report,* FedEx; *2009 Annual Report,* UPS.

24. "Data Analytics: Crunching the Future," *Bloomberg Businessweek,* September 8, 2011.

25. "Hospital Cost Cutters Push Use of Scanners to Track Inventories," *Wall Street Journal,* June 10, 1997. See also Charu Chandra and Sameer Kumar, "Taxonomy of Inventory Policies for Supply-Chain Effectiveness," *International Journal of Retail & Distribution Management,* 4 (2001); Matthew B. Myers, Patricia J. Daugherty, and Chad W. Autry, "The Effectiveness of Automatic Inventory Replenishment in Supply Chain Operations: Antecedents and Outcomes," *Journal of Retailing,* Winter 2000.

26. "The Supersizing of Warehouses," *New York Times,* February 4, 2004; "New Warehouses Take On a Luxe Look," *Wall Street Journal,* June 18, 2003; Chad W. Autry, Stanley E. Griffis, Thomas J. Goldsby, and L. Michelle Bobbitt, "Warehouse Management-Systems: Resource Commitment, Capabilities, and Organizational Performance," *Journal of Business Logistics,* 2005.

27. "Veggie Tales," *Fortune,* June 8, 2009; "Sysco Hustles to Keep Restaurants Cooking," *BusinessWeek,* May 18, 2009; "Sysco Website Helps Its Customers Build Business," *Nation's Restaurant News,* May 18, 2009; "Sysco Corporation: Company Profile," *Datamonitor,* June 10, 2008.

28. "Frito-Lay," Short Cases from the CSCMP Toolbox, 2005.

29. "Whirlpool Cleans Up Its Delivery Act," *Wall Street Journal,* September 24, 2009; "Walmart's Need for Speed," *Wall Street Journal,* September 26, 2005.

CHAPTER 12

1. See Macys.com, Macy's *Annual Report, 2014;* "The World's Top 10 Most Innovative Companies in Retail," *Fast Company,* February 10, 2014; "Is E-commerce Helping Macy's 'Age Gracefully'?"

Forbes, May 15, 2014; "Macy's Regroups in Warehouse Wars," *Wall Street Journal,* May 14, 2012; "When CMOs Learn to Love Data, They'll Be VIPs in the C-Suite," *AdAge,* February 13, 2012; "Luring Online Shoppers Offline," *New York Times,* July 4, 2012; "The Goal: A Perfect First Time Fit," *Wall Street Journal,* March 23, 2012; "Macy's in China Internet Push," *Women's Wear Daily,* May 24, 2012; "Macy's Sets Tech Push to Propel Growth," *Women's Wear Daily,* May 21, 2012; "Supply Chain in Action," *Apparel Magazine,* April 2012; "Macy's Sets Strategy for Gen-Y Shoppers," *Women's Wear Daily,* March 22, 2012; "Macy's Expands Fashion Incubator Program," *Women's Wear Daily,* March 27, 2012; "Macy's 2.0 Strategy Puts the Pedal to the Metal," *Forbes,* May 21, 2012; "A Holiday to Remember for Prestige Retailers," *Women's Wear Daily,* January 6, 2012; "Retailers Are Striving to Combine the Advantages of Physical Shops with the Benefits of Online Selling," *Economist,* February 5, 2012; "Macy's Plan: Boots, Bieber," *Wall Street Journal,* November 26, 2011; "How Department Stores Came Back into Fashion," *BloombergBusinessweek,* March 21, 2011; "At Macy's Big Brother Is Watching You," *Wall Street Journal,* March 18, 2011; "Macy's Transformation," *DM News,* April 1, 2012; "How Macy's Latest Moves Are Paying Off," *Business Courier,* November 25, 2011; "Dunnhumby-USA, Macy's Forge Exclusive Client Agreement," August 13, 2008; "Dowdy Department Stores Start Looking Cool Again," *Wall Street Journal,* August 4, 2011; "For the New Macy's All Marketing Is Local," *Adweek,* June 7, 2010; "Going on Impulse: Macy's Plots Push in Contemporary with Exclusives," *Womens Wear Daily,* January 27, 2011; "Retailers on Quest to Rekindle the Personal Touch of a Bygone Era," *Advertising Age,* February 14, 2011; "Atlanta Hats? Seattle Socks? Macy's Goes Local," *New York Times,* October 1, 2010; "Macy's Looks to Broaden Appeal," *Womens Wear Daily,* May 14, 2013; "RFID the Macy's Way," *Modern Materials Management,* June 2013; "Game On, Amazon! eBay Rolls Out One-Hour Delivery, Targeting the Web and Wal-Mart," *Forbes.com,* May 7, 2013; "Macy's Millennial Push," *WWD: Women's Wear Daily*, October 18, 2012.

2. See U.S. Census data including "Summary Statistics by Employment Size of Establishments for the U.S.: 2007" from *2007 Economic Census—Retail Trade, Subject Series, Establishment and Firm Size* (Washington, DC: U.S. Government Printing Office, 2010) and available online at www.census.gov. See also Kusum L. Ailawadi, "The Retail Power Performance Conundrum: What Have We Learned?" *Journal of Retailing,* Fall 2001; Dale D. Achabal, John M. Heineke, and Shelby H. McIntyre, "Issues and Perspectives on Retail Productivity," *Journal of Retailing,* Fall 1984; Charles A. Ingene, "Scale Economies in American Retailing: A Cross-Industry Comparison," *Journal of Macromarketing* 4, #2 (1984).

3. For an excellent example of AutoZone as successful chain, see "*Fortune* 500: In the Zone," *Fortune,* April 13, 2009; "AutoZone Smashes Views as Aging Cars Need Parts," *Investor's Business Daily,* March 4, 2009; "Rallying the Troops to Get Back in the Profit Zone," *DSN Retailing Today,* September 6, 2004. See also Gary K. Rhoads, William R. Swinyard, Michael D. Geurts, and William D. Price, "Retailing as a Career: A Comparative Study of Marketers," *Journal of Retailing,* Spring 2002.

4. "The Top 10 Franchises of 2015" *Entrepreneur,* January 2015 ; "Burger King Franchisees Can't Have It Their Way," *Inc.,* January 21, 2010; "Do You Have What It Takes?" *Wall Street Journal Reports,* September 19, 2005; "How to Grow a Chain That's Already Everywhere," *Business 2.0,* March 2005; "When Franchisees Lose Part of Their Independence," *New York Times,* February 3, 2005. See also Surinder Tikoo, "Franchiser Influence Strategy Use and Franchisee Experience and Dependence," *Journal of Retailing,* Fall 2002; Patrick J. Kaufmann and Rajiv P. Dant, "The Pricing of Franchise Rights," *Journal of Retailing,* Winter 2001; Madhav Pappu and David Strutton, "Toward an Understanding of Strategic Inter-Organizational Relationships in Franchise Channels," *Journal of Marketing Channels,* 1, 2 (2001); Rajiv P. Dant and Patrick J. Kaufmann, "Structural and Strategic Dynamics in Franchising," *Journal of Retailing,* 2 (2003); A. K.

Paswan and C. M. Wittmann, "Knowledge Management and Franchise Systems," *Industrial Marketing Management,* 2 (2009).

5. Data on failure rate found at: Entrepreneur Weekly, Small Business Development Center, Bradley University; found at *Statistic Brain Research Institute,* http://www.statisticbrain.com/startup-failure-by-industry/: "5 Ways Small Retailers Can Compete (& Win)," *Inc.,* January 8, 2013.]

6. See www.census.gov/retail/mrts/www/benchmark/2009/html/annrev09.html; U.S. Census Bureau, *Statistical Abstract of the United States 2010* (Washington, DC: U.S. Government Printing Office, 2009); *2007 Economic Census—Retail Trade, Subject Series, Establishment and Firm Size* (Washington, DC: U.S. Government Printing Office, 2010); "Pop-Up Stores Fill Retail Space as Vacancies Hit Decade Highs," *Investor's Business Daily,* November 12, 2009; "Retailers Embrace Pop-Ups," *USA Today,* October 30, 2009; "The Hard Sell: How Retailers Are Fighting for the Hearts and Minds of the New Consumer," *BusinessWeek,* October 15, 2009; "Retail 2.0," *Brandweek,* December 17, 2007; Preyas S. Desai, Oded Koenigsberg, and Devavrat Purohit, "Forward Buying by Retailers," *Journal of Marketing Research,* February 2010; Kristin Diehl and Cait Poynor, "Great Expectations?! Assortment Size, Expectations, and Satisfaction," *Journal of Marketing Research,* April 2010; Kinshuk Jerath and Z. John Zhang, "Store within a Store," *Journal of Marketing Research,* August 2010; Hai Che, Xinlei (Jack) Chen, and Yuxin Chen, "Investigating Effects of Out-of-Stock on Consumer Stockkeeping Unit Choice," *Journal of Marketing Research,* August 2012; Simon J. Bell, Bülent Mengüç, and Robert E. Widing II, "Salesperson Learning, Organizational Learning, and Retail Store Performance," *Journal of the Academy of Marketing Science,* March 2010; Douglas E. Hughes and Michael Ahearne, "Energizing the Reseller's Sales Force: The Power of Brand Identification," *Journal of Marketing,* July 2010; Velitchka D. Kaltcheva and Barton A. Weitz, "When Should a Retailer Create an Exciting Store Environment?" *Journal of Marketing,* January 2006; Kathleen Seiders, Glenn B. Voss, Dhruv Grewal, and Andrea L. Godfrey, "Do Satisfied Customers Buy More? Examining Moderating Influences in a Retailing Context," *Journal of Marketing,* October 2005; Ruth N. Bolton and Venkatesh Shankar, "An Empirically Derived Taxonomy of Retailer Pricing and Promotion Strategies," *Journal of Retailing,* Winter 2003; Katherine B. Hartman and Rosann L. Spiro, "Recapturing Store Image in Customer-Based Store Equity: A Construct Conceptualization," *Journal of Business Research,* August 2005; Mark J. Arnold, Kristy E. Reynolds, Nicole Ponder, and Jason E. Lueg, "Customer Delight in a Retail Context: Investigating Delightful and Terrible Shopping Experiences," *Journal of Business Research,* August 2005.

7. "Payless ShoeSource, Inc. Company Profile," *Datamonitor,* November 2, 2009; "Payless ShoeSource: Putting Its Best Foot Forward," *The Journal of Commerce,* May 29, 2006.

8. "Zappos.com: Developing a Supply Chain to Deliver WOW!" Stanford Graduate School of Business Case #GS 65, February 13, 2009; "Tireless Employees Get Their Tribute, Even If It's in Felt and Polyester," *New York Times,* March 4, 2010; "Why Everybody Loves Zappos," *Inc.,* May 2009; "Zappos CEO: How to Build a Brand without Spending Big on Ads," *Brandweek,* December 22, 2008; "Zappos Touts More than Just Shoes," *Adweek,* February 23, 2009. For more on retailer marketing strategies, see Brocato, E., Julie Baker, and Clay Voorhees. "Creating Consumer Attachment to Retail Service Firms through Sense of Place." *Journal of the Academy of Marketing Science* 43.2 (2015): 200-20; Castro, Iana A., Andrea C. Morales, and Stephen M. Nowlis. "The Influence of Disorganized Shelf Displays and Limited Product Quantity on Consumer Purchase." *Journal of Marketing* 77.4 (2013): 118-33; Dagger, Tracey S., and Peter J. Danaher. "Comparing the Effect of Store Remodeling on New and Existing Customers." *Journal of Marketing* 78.3 (2014): 62-80; Danziger, Shai, Liat Hadar, and Vicki G. Morwitz. "Retailer Pricing Strategy and Consumer Choice under Price Uncertainty." *Journal of Consumer Research* 41.3 (2014): 751-74; Hamilton, Ryan, and Alexander Chernev. "Low Prices

Are Just the Beginning: Price Image in Retail Management." *Journal of Marketing* 77.6 (2013): 1-20; Van Lin, Arjen, and Els Gijsbrechts. "Shopper Loyalty to Whom? Chain Versus Outlet Loyalty in the Context of Store Acquisitions." *Journal of Marketing Research (JMR)* 51.3 (2014): 352-70; Vroegrijk, Mark, Els Gijsbrechts, and Katia Campo. "Close Encounter with the Hard Discounter: A Multiple-Store Shopping Perspective on the Impact of Local Hard-Discounter Entry." *Journal of Marketing Research (JMR)* 50.5 (2013): 606-26; Ward, Morgan K., and Darren W. Dahl. "Should the Devil Sell Prada? Retail Rejection Increases Aspiring Consumers' Desire for the Brand." *Journal of Consumer Research* 41.3 (2014): 590-609.

9. "Small Toy Shops Play Up the Perks," *The Wall Street Journal*, December 3, 2014; "Malls Race to Stay Relevant in Downturn," *Wall Street Journal,* February 26, 2009; Sharon E. Beatty, Morris Mayer, James E. Coleman, Kristy E. Reynolds, and Jungki Lee, "Customer-Sales Associate Retail Relationships," *Journal of Retailing,* Fall 1996.

10. See www.census.gov; U.S. Census Bureau, *2007 Economic Census*—Retail Trade, Subject Series, Establishment and Firm Size. For more on department stores, see "Big Retailers Seek Teens (and Parents)," *USA Today,* April 14, 2008; "The Department Store Rises Again," *Business 2.0,* August 2004.

11. David Appel, "The Supermarket: Early Development of an Institutional Innovation," *Journal of Retailing,* Spring 1972.

12. See www.census.gov and www.fmi.org/facts_figs/; "Do-It-Yourself Supermarket Checkout," *Wall Street Journal,* April 5, 2007. See also R. A. Briesch, P. K. Chintagunta, and E. J. Fox, "How Does Assortment Affect Grocery/Store Choice?" *Journal of Marketing Research,* 2 (2009).

13. For more on supercenters, see Kusum L. Ailawadi, Jie Zhang, Aradhna Krishna, and Michael W. Kruger, "When Wal-Mart Enters: How Incumbent Retailers React and How This Affects Their Sales Outcomes,"*Journal of Marketing Research*, August 2010; "Retailers Cut Back on Variety, Once the Spice of Marketing," *Wall Street Journal,* June 26, 2009; "Walmart, the Category King," *DSN Retailing Today,* June 9, 2003; "Price War in Aisle 3," *Wall Street Journal,* May 27, 2003.

14. For more on warehouse clubs, see "Club Stores Accepting Coupons," *Wall Street Journal,* August 20, 2009; "Sam's Club Tests the Big-Box Bodega," *Wall Street Journal,* August 10, 2009; "Thinking Outside the Big Box: Costco," *Fast Company,* November 2008; "Costco's Artful Discounts," *BusinessWeek,* October 20, 2008; "Costco's Well-Off Customers Still Shopping," *Investor's Business Daily,* April 8, 2008; "Why Costco Is So Damn Addictive," *Fortune,* October 30, 2006.

15. For more on category killers, see "Newcomers Challenge Office-Supply Stalwarts," *Wall Street Journal,* April 29, 2009; "Big Boxes Aim to Speed Up Shopping," *Wall Street Journal,* June 27, 2007.

16. For more on 7-Eleven, see "Know What Customers Want," *Inc.,* August 2005; "Can 7-Eleven Win over Hong Kong Foodies?" *Time,* October 1, 2009; "Convenience Stores Score in Japan," *Wall Street Journal,* August 19, 2008.

17. For more on vending and wireless, see "Vending Machines Get Smart to Accommodate the Cashless," *Bloomberg Businessweek*, August 29, 2013; "Soda? iPod? Vending Machines Diversity," *USA Today,* September 4, 2007; "Self-Serve Movie Rental Kiosks a Surprise Hit with Consumers," *Investor's Business Daily,* May 31, 2007.

18. "In Digital Era, Marketers Still Prefer a Paper Trail," *Wall Street Journal,* October 16, 2009; "Cutting the Stack of Catalogs," *BusinessWeek,* December 31, 2007; "This Isn't the Holiday Catalog You Remember," *Advertising Age,* October 29, 2007.

19. "The Future of Shopping," *Harvard Business Review*, December 2011.

20. Lal, Rajiv, José B. Alvarez, and Dan Greenberg, "The Scale of the Ecommerce Threat," *HBS Working Knowledge,* March 2, 2015.

21. "Same-Day Delivery's Second Act," *Inc.*, March 2014; "Using Selfies to Lower Online Clothing Returns," *Bloomberg Businessweek,* September 4, 2014.

22. For more information on showrooming, webrooming, and multichannel shopping, see: "Customer Desires vs. Retailer Capabilities: Minding the Omni-Channel Gap," *Forrester Consulting,* January 2014; "The New Digital Divide," *Deloitte Digital,* 2014; "Omnichannel Retail," *L2 Intelligence Report,* July 30, 2014; "Seamless Retailing Research Study 2014," *Accenture,* 2014.

23. "5 Excellent Examples of Omnichannel Retailing Done Right," *Multichannel Merchant,* May 14, 2014; see also previous endnote.

24. Chip E. Miller, "The Effects of Competition on Retail Structure: An Examination of Intratype, Intertype, and Intercategory Competition," *Journal of Marketing,* October 1999; "Aspirin, Q-Tips and a New You: Drug-stores Try to Sell Glamour, Offering Cosmetic Boutiques, Facials, Eyebrow Bars," *Wall Street Journal,* March 25, 2010; "Root Canal? Try Aisle Five," *BusinessWeek,* October 13, 2008; "Doing Whatever Gets Them in the Door," *BusinessWeek,* June 30, 2008; "New Options for Saving at the Pump," *Wall Street Journal,* August 16, 2005; Ronald Savitt, "The 'Wheel of Retailing' and Retail Product Management," *European Journal of Marketing* 18, #6/7 (1984).

25. "Tracking Technology Sheds Light on Shopper Habits," *The Wall Street Journal*, December 9, 2013; "Personalization: Show Me You Know Me," *Path to Purchase Institute,* July 22, 2013; "Designer Rebecca Minkoff's New Stores Have Touch Screens for an Online Shopping Experience," *The Wall Street Journal,* November 11, 2014; "Retailers Wage War Against Long Lines," *The Wall Street Journal,* May 1, 2013; "The End of the Coffee Line," *Bloomberg Businessweek,* December 1, 2014. "Big Brother Is Watching You Shop," *BloombergBusinessweek,* December 15, 2011; "Check Out the Future of Shopping," *Wall Street Journal,* May 18, 2011. For more generally on the effects of technology on retail, see "Retailers Reach Out on Cellphones," *Wall Street Journal,* April 21, 2010; "The Hard Sell," *BusinessWeek,* October 26, 2009; "Ring Up E-Commerce Gains with a True Multichannel Strategy," *Advertising Age,* March 10, 2008; "Retailing: What's Working Online," *The McKinsey Quarterly,* 3 (2005); Jill Avery, Thomas J. Steenburgh, John Deighton, and Mary Caravella, "Adding Bricks to Clicks: Predicting the Patterns of Cross-Channel Elasticities over Time,"*Journal of Marketing*, May 2012; Xiaoqing Jing and Michael Lewis, "Stockouts in Online Retailing,"*Journal of Marketing Research,* April 2011; J. Ganesh, K. E. Reynolds, M. Luckett, and N. Pomirleanu, "Online Shopper Motivations, and E-Store Attributes: An Examination of Online Patronage Behavior and Shopper Typologies," *Journal of Retailing,* 1 (2010); P. Gupta, M. S. Yadav, and R. Varadarajan, "How Task-Facilitative Interactive Tools Foster Buyers' Trust in Online Retailers: A Process View of Trust Development in the Electronic Marketplace," *Journal of Retailing,* 2 (2009); W. S. Kwon, and S. J. Lennon, "Reciprocal Effects between Multichannel Retailers' Offline and Online Brand Images," *Journal of Retailing,* 3 (2009); Joel E. Collier and Carol C. Bienstock, "How Do Customers Judge Quality in an E-tailer?" *Sloan Management Review,* Fall 2006; A. E. Schlosser, T. B. White, and S. M. Lloyd, "Converting Website Visitors into Buyers: How Website Investment Increases Consumer Trusting Beliefs and Online Purchase Intentions," *Journal of Marketing,* April 2006; Yakov Bart, Venkatesh Shankar, Fareena Sultan, and Glen L. Urban, "Are the Drivers and Role of Online Trust the Same for All Websites and Consumers? A Large-Scale Exploratory Empirical Study," *Journal of Marketing,* October 2005; S. A. Neslin and V. Shankar, "Key Issues in Multichannel Customer Management: Current Knowledge and Future Directions," *Journal of Interactive Marketing,* 1 (2009).

26. "Most Consumers Reject In-Store Mobile Tracking—Or Do They?" *Marketing Land,* July 23, 2014; See also John Paul Fraedrich, "The Ethical Behavior of Retail Managers," *Journal of Business Ethics,* March 1993.

27. "What Price Virtue? At Some Retailers, 'Fair Trade' Carries a Very High Cost," *Wall Street Journal,* June 8, 2004.

28. "A Dollar Store's Rich Allure in India," *Wall Street Journal,* January 23, 2007; "Retailers Still Expanding in China: Walmart, Carrefour, Tesco," *Wall Street Journal,* January 22, 2009; "Walmart:

Looking Overseas for Growth," *CNNMoney.com,* October 24, 2007; "Walmart: Struggling in Germany," *BusinessWeek,* April 11, 2005; "Japan Isn't Buying The Walmart Idea," *BusinessWeek,* February 28, 2005.

29. "Understanding Online Shoppers in Europe," *McKinsey Quarterly,* May 2009; "Forrester Forecast: Online Retail Sales Will Grow to $250 Billion by 2014," *TechCrunch,* March 8, 2010; "Forester Forecast: Double-Digit Growth for Online Retail in the US and Western Europe," *Tekrati,* March 9, 2010.

30. See www.friedas.com; "How Lower-Tech Gear Beat Web 'Exchanges' at Their Own Game," *Wall Street Journal,* March 16, 2001; "Family Firms Confront Calamities of Transfer," *USA Today,* August 29, 2000; "Business, Too Close to Home," *Time,* July 17, 2000; "The Kiwi to My Success," *Hemispheres,* July 1999; "Searching for the Next Kiwi: Frieda's Branded Produce," *Brandweek,* May 2, 1994; "Strange Fruits," *Inc.,* November 1989; "The Produce Marketer," *Savvy,* June 1988.

31. See U.S. Census data including "Summary Statistics for the U.S.: 2007" from *2007 Economic Census—Wholesale Trade, Geographic Area Series, United States* (Washington, DC: U.S. Government Printing Office, 2010) and available online at www.census.gov.

32. See www.fastenal.com; "The *BusinessWeek* 50: Fastenal," *BusinessWeek,* April 6, 2009; "Fastenal: Need to Fix Up a Building? This Firm's Got Your One-Stop Shop," *Investor's Business Daily,* November 28, 2005; "Fastenal: In This Sluggish Market, You Gotta Have Faith," *Investor's Business Daily,* August 13, 2001.

33. "Revolution in Japanese Retailing," *Fortune,* February 7, 1994; Arieh Goldman, "Evaluating the Performance of the Japanese Distribution System," *Journal of Retailing,* Spring 1992; "Japan Begins to Open the Door to Foreigners, a Little," *Brandweek,* August 2, 1993.

34. See www.rell.com; "Richardson Electronics Ltd.: Maker of Ancient Tech Finds a Way to Prosper," *Investor's Business Daily,* June 27, 2000; *2009 Annual Report,* Richardson Electronics.

35. See www.inmac.com and www.grainger.com.

36. For more on manufacturers' agents being squeezed, see "Philips to End Long Relations with North American Reps—Will Build Internal Sales Force Instead," *EBN,* November 10, 2003. See also Daniel C. Bello and Ritu Lohtia, "The Export Channel Design: The Use of Foreign Distributors and Agents," *Journal of the Academy of Marketing Science,* Spring 1995.

CHAPTER 13

1. See www.geico.com; "Cost Efficiency Helps Geico Keep Prices Down, Get Big Bang For Its '15-Minute Message'," *Advertising Age,* September 2, 2013; "Muscling Past Mayhem: Geico Rides Giant Ad Budget Past Allstate," *Advertising Age,* July 8, 2013; "GEICO, In Numbers," *Guru Focus,* November 25, 2014; "GEICO Advertising Soars to $1 Billion," *Media Post,* June 26, 2012; "Big Blue Makes Big Moves in Big Data," *Forbes,* May 8, 2012; "Customer Service Playing a Bigger Role as a Marketing Tool," *Advertising Age,* November 7, 2011; "GEICO Launches Social Media Platform for Military Personnel," *InsuranceTech,* July 5, 2011; "Consumers: Who's Who?" *Advertising Age,* February 21, 2011; "How the Insurance Industry Got into a $4 Billion Ad Brawl," *Advertising Age,* February 21, 2011; "Umbrella Coverage for Preventing Your Ruin," *New York Times,* March 18, 2008; "Clan of the Caveman," *Fast Company,* December 19, 2007; "Geico," *Advertising Age,* October 15, 2007; "Leapin' Lizards," *Brandweek,* October 8, 2007; "Cavemen (TV Series)," *Wikipedia,* April 21, 2007; "Will the Cavemen's Evolution Boost Geico?" *Fortune,* April 2, 2007; "The Caveman: Evolution of a Character," *Adweek,* March 12, 2007; "Trio of TV Ad Campaigns Succeeds in Wooing Different Target Audience," *Television Week,* March 12, 2007; "How a Gecko Shook Up Insurance Ads," *Wall Street Journal,* January 2, 2007; "When Geckos Aren't Enough," *BusinessWeek,* October 16, 2006; "10 Breakaway Brands," *Fortune,* September 8,

2006; "Loving the Lizard," *Adweek,* October 24, 2005; "Buffet Wants to Know: Do Geico Ads Get Job Done?" *USA Today,* January 24, 2005; "Meet America's 25 Biggest Advertisers," *Advertising Age,* July 8, 2013; "How Big Data Spawned the Geico Gecko," *Advertising Age,* March 18, 2013; "Muscling Past Mayhem: Why Geico's Marketing Works," *Advertising Age,* July 8, 2013.

2. P. J. Kitchen, I. Kim, and D. E. Schultz, "Integrated Marketing Communication: Practice Leads Theory," *Journal of Advertising Research,* 4 (2008); Kim Bartel Sheehan and Caitlin Doherty, "Re-Weaving the Web: Integrating Print and Online Communications," *Journal of Interactive Marketing,* Spring 2001.

3. https://www.slugger.com/our-history; Quesenberry, Keith A. and Michael K. Coolsen (2014) "What Makes a Super Bowl Ad Super? Five-Act Dramatic Form Affects Consumer Super Bowl Advertising Ratings," *Journal of Marketing Theory and Practice,* 22, 4. 437–454; "How Great Marketers Tell Stories," *Fortune,* April 18, 2014; Godin, Seth (2005) *All Marketers Are Liars,* Portfolio Hardcover; "Ode: How to Tell a Great Story," *Seth's Blog,* April 27, 2006; "Lifebucy Reduces Diarrhea from 36% to 5% in Thesgora," Hindustan Lever Limited Press Release, March 19, 2014.

4. "In a Shift, Marketers Beef Up Ad Spending Inside Stores," *Wall Street Journal,* September 21, 2005.

5. Barbara B. Stern, "A Revised Communication Model for Advertising: Multiple Dimensions of the Source, the Message, and the Recipient," *Journal of Advertising,* June 1994; George S. Low and Jakki J. Mohr, "Factors Affecting the Use of Information in the Evaluation of Marketing Communications Productivity," *Journal of the Academy of Marketing Science,* Winter 2001; David I. Gilliland and Wesley J. Johnston, "Toward a Model of Business-to-Business Marketing Communications Effects," *Industrial Marketing Management,* January 1997.

6. "Don't Let Your Brand Get Lost in Translation," *Brandweek,* February 8, 2010; "Capturing a Piece of the Global Market," *Brandweek,* June 20, 2005; "Global Branding: Same, But Different," *Brandweek,* April 9, 2001; "Hey, #!@*% Amigo, Can You Translate the Word 'Gaffe'?" *Wall Street Journal,* July 8, 1996; "Lost in Translation: How to 'Empower Women' in Chinese," *Wall Street Journal,* September 13, 1994.

7. "18 of the Best Email Subject Lines You've Ever Read" *HubSpot Marketing blog,* February 13, 2015.

8. "Brands as Publishers: The Changing Rules of SEO," *Search Engine Watch,* July 11, 2012.

9. We cover word of mouth later in this chapter.

10. As an example of cooperation between direct and indirect communication channels, see Berend Wierenga and Han Soethoudt, "Sales Promotions and Channel Coordination," *Journal of the Academy of Marketing Science,* May 2010.

11. "The New B-to-B Fundamentals," *Target Marketing,* October 2003, at www.targetonline.com; "The Changing Face of B-to-B Sales & Marketing," October 20, 2003, http://news.thomasnet.com/IMT/archives/; G. Martin-Herran, S. P. Sigue, and G. Zaccour, "The Dilemma of Pull- and Push-Price Promotions," *Journal of Retailing,* 1 (2010). For more on advertising and sales, see Hughes, Douglas. "This Ad's for You: The Indirect Effect of Advertising Perceptions on Salesperson Effort and Performance." *Journal of the Academy of Marketing Science* 41.1 (2013): 1-18.

12. For more on diffusion of innovation, see the classic work of Everett M. Rogers and F. Floyd Shoemaker, *Communication of Innovations: A Cross-Cultural Approach* (New York: Free Press, 1971). See also Hokey Min and William P. Galle, "E-Purchasing: Profiles of Adopters and Nonadopters," *Industrial Marketing Management,* April 2003; Yikuan Lee and Gina Colarelli O'Connor, "The Impact of Communication Strategy on Launching New Products: The Moderating Role of Product Innovativeness," *Journal of Product Innovation Management,* January 2003; Subin Im, Barry L. Bayus, and Charlotte H. Mason, "An Empirical Study of Innate Consumer Innovativeness, Personal Characteristics, and New-Product Adoption Behavior,"

Journal of the Academy of Marketing Science, Winter 2003; Robert J. Fisher and Linda L. Price, "An Investigation into the Social Context of Early Adoption Behavior," *Journal of Consumer Research,* December 1992. See also Petersen, J. Andrew, Tarun Kushwaha, and V. Kumar. "Marketing Communication Strategies and Consumer Financial Decision Making: The Role of National Culture." *Journal of Marketing* 79.1 (2015): 44-63; Risselada, Hans, Peter C. Verhoef, and Tammo H. A. Bijmolt. "Dynamic Effects of Social Influence and Direct Marketing on the Adoption of High-Technology Products." *Journal of Marketing* 78.2 (2014): 52-68.

13. "All-in-One Dinner Kits Gain Popularity," *Food Retailing Today,* May 5, 2003; "Marketers of the Year: This One's a Stove Topper," *Brandweek,* October 14, 2002.

14. Kusum L. Ailawadi, Paul W. Farris, and Mark E. Parry, "Share and Growth Are Not Good Predictors of the Advertising and Promotion/Sales Ratio," *Journal of Marketing,* January 1994.

15. Ashwin Aravindakshan, Kay Peters, and Prasad A Naik, "Spatiotemporal Allocation of Advertising Budgets," *Journal of Marketing Research,* February 2012; Kissan Joseph and Vernon J. Richardson, "Free Cash Flow, Agency Costs, and the Affordability Method of Advertising Budgeting," *Journal of Marketing,* January 2002; Kim P. Corfman and Donald R. Lehmann, "The Prisoner's Dilemma and the Role of Information in Setting Advertising Budgets," *Journal of Advertising,* June 1994; C. L. Hung and Douglas West, "Advertising Budgeting Methods in Canada, the UK and the USA," *International Journal of Advertising* 10, #3 (1991); Pierre Filiatrault and Jean-Charles Chebat, "How Service Firms Set Their Marketing Budgets," *Industrial Marketing Management,* February 1990.

CHAPTER 14

1. Based on author interviews with Ferguson salespeople and management. See also www.ferguson.com; *2011 Annual Report and Accounts,* Wolseley; "Customer Focused," *US Business Review,* May 2005; "Customer Loyalty Pays Off," *T1D,* February 2011; "PP-R Piping Shaves Six Figures at Florida Football Stadium," *Contractor,* February 2012; Wolseley plc, *Datamonitor Report,* February 16, 2012; Wolseley Faces the Future," *bmj,* December 2011.

2. Cron, William, Artur Baldauf, Thomas Leigh, and Samuel Grossenbacher. "The Strategic Role of the Sales Force: Perceptions of Senior Sales Executives." *Journal of the Academy of Marketing Science* 42.5 (2014): 471-89; Kumar, V., Sarang Sunder, and Robert P. Leone. "Measuring and Managing a Salesperson's Future Value to the Firm." *Journal of Marketing Research (JMR)* 51.5 (2014): 591-608; "Expanding Abroad? Avoid Cultural Gaffes," *Wall Street Journal,* January 19, 2010; "Cultural Training Has Global Appeal," *USA Today,* December 22, 2009; "Where Yellow's a Faux Pas and White Is Death," *Wall Street Journal,* December 6, 2007; "Doing Business Abroad? Simple Faux Pas Can Sink You," *USA Today,* August 24, 2007; "Why the Chinese Hate to Use Voice Mail," *Wall Street Journal,* December 1, 2005; "Mind Your Manners," *Inc.,* September 2005; Paul A. Herbig and Hugh E. Kramer, "Do's and Don'ts of Cross-Cultural Negotiations," *Industrial Marketing Management,* November 1992; Alan J. Dubinsky et al., "Differences in Motivational Perceptions among U.S., Japanese, and Korean Sales Personnel," *Journal of Business Research,* June 1994; Carl R. Ruthstrom and Ken Matejka, "The Meanings of 'YES' in the Far East," *Industrial Marketing Management,* August 1990.

3. Daniel Pink, 2013, *To Sell Is Human: The Surprising Truth About Moving Others,* Riverhead Books.

4. "Shhh!" *Forbes,* November 24, 2003; "Deliver More Value to Earn Loyalty," *Selling,* May 2003; "Hush: Improving NVH through Improved Material," *Automotive Design and Production,* July 2003.

5. C. R. Plouffe, J. Hulland, and T. Wachner, "Customer-Directed Selling Behaviors and Performance: A Comparison of Existing Perspectives," *Journal of the Academy of Marketing Science,* 4 (2009); Andris A. Zoltners, Prabhakant Sinha, and Sally E. Lorimer, "Match Your Sales Force Structure to Your Business Life Cycle," *Harvard Business Review,* July–August 2006; George R. Franke and Jeong-Eun Park, "Salesperson Adaptive Selling Behavior and Customer Orientation: A Meta-Analysis," *Journal of Marketing Research,* November 2006; Diane Coutu, "Leveraging the Psychology of the Salesperson," *Harvard Business Review,* July–August 2006; David Mayer and Herbert M. Greenberg, "What Makes a Good Salesman," *Harvard Business Review,* July–August 2006; Christian Pfeil, Thorsten Posselt, and Nils Maschke, "Incentives for Sales Agents after the Advent of the Internet," *Marketing Letters,* January 2008; Dawn R. Deeter-Schmelz, Daniel J. Goebel, and Karen Norman, "What Are the Characteristics of an Effective Sales Manager? An Exploratory Study Comparing Salesperson and Sales Manager Perspectives," *Journal of Personal Selling & Sales Management,* Winter 2008; Jerome A. Colletti and Mary S. Fiss, "The Ultimately Accountable Job: Leading Today's Sales Organization," *Harvard Business Review,* July–August 2006; Robert W. Palmatier, Lisa K. Scheer, and Jan-Benedict E. M. Steenkamp, "Customer Loyalty to Whom? Managing the Benefits and Risks of Salesperson-Owned Loyalty," *Journal of Marketing Research,* May 2007; Judy A. Siguaw, Sheryl E. Kimes, and Jule B. Gassenheimer, "B2B Sales Force Productivity: Applications of Revenue Management Strategies to Sales Management," *Industrial Marketing Management,* October 2003; William C. Moncrief, Greg W. Marshall, and Felicia G. Lassk, "A Contemporary Taxonomy of Sales Positions," *Journal of Personal Selling & Sales Management,* Winter 2006; Eli Jones, Steven P. Brown, Andris A. Zoltners, and Barton A. Weitz, "The Changing Environment of Selling and Sales Management," *Journal of Personal Selling & Sales Management,* Spring 2005.

6. "Delta Brings Back Red Coats," *USA Today,* June 25, 2009; "Bank of (Middle) America," *Fast Company,* March 2003; "A French Bank Hits the Road," *BusinessWeek,* November 17, 2003; "NationsBank Asks Tellers to Branch Out," *Raleigh News & Observer,* September 12, 1993. For more on frontline sales, see Alex R. Zablah, George R. Franke, Tom J. Brown, and Darrell E. Bartholomew, "How and When Does Customer Orientation Influence Frontline Employee Job Outcomes? A Meta-Analytic Evaluation," *Journal of Marketing,* May 2012; Vishag Badrinarayanan and Debra A. Laverie, "Brand Advocacy and Sales Effort by Retail Salespeople: Antecedents and Influence of Identification with Manufacturers' Brands," *Journal of Personal Selling & Sales Management,* Spring 2011; Susan Cadwallader, Cheryl Burke Jarvis, Mary Jo Bitner, and Amy L. Ostrom, "Frontline Employee Motivation to Participate in Service Innovation Implementation," *Journal of the Academy of Marketing Science,* March 2010.

7. "A Twitterati Calls Out Whirlpool." *Forbes,* September 2, 2009; "The Customer Strikes Back," *Brandweek,* April 26, 2008; "Hello, Houston . . . We Have a Customer Service Problem," *Investor's Business Daily,* March 31, 2008; "Customer Service Champs," *BusinessWeek,* March 3, 2008; "Consumer Vigilantes," *BusinessWeek,* February 21, 2008; "Comcast Takes Its Whacks on Service," *USA Today,* December 3, 2007; "Comcast Must Die," *Advertising Age,* November 19, 2007, p. 1; "One Tough Customer," *Brandweek,* March 19, 2007, pp. 18–24; "Customer Service Champs," *BusinessWeek,* March 5, 2007, pp. 52–64; "Price Points: Good Customer Service Costs Money," *Wall Street Journal,* October 30, 2006, p. R7; "The Customer Vigilante Files," *Church of the Customer Blog,* November 25, 2003.

8. For some recent research on team selling and sales force structure see Menguc, Bulent, Seigyoung Auh, and Aypar Uslu. "Customer Knowledge Creation Capability and Performance in Sales Teams." *Journal of the Academy of Marketing Science* 41.1 (2013): 19-39; Schmitz, Christian, and Shankar Ganesan. "Managing Customer and Organizational Complexity in Sales Organizations." *Journal of Marketing* 78.6 (2014): 59-77; Schmitz, Christian, You-Cheong Lee, and Gary L. Lilien. "Cross-Selling Performance in Complex Selling Contexts: An Examination of Supervisory- and Compensation-Based Controls." *Journal of Marketing* 78.3 (2014): 1-19; Schmitz, Christian. "Group Influences of Selling Teams on Industrial Salespeople's

Cross-selling Behavior." *Journal of the Academy of Marketing Science* 41.1 (2013): 55-72.

9. For more about major account selling see Christopher P. Blocker, Joseph P. Cannon, Nikolaos G. Panagopoulos, and Jeffrey K. Sager, "The Role of the Sales Force in Value Creation and Appropriation: New Directions for Research,"*Journal of Personal Selling & Sales Management,* Winter 2011; Kevin D. Bradford, Goutam N. Challagalla, Gary K. Hunter, and William C. Moncrief, "Strategic Account Management: Conceptualizing, Integrating, and Extending the Domain from Fluid to Dedicated Accounts,"*Journal of Personal Selling & Sales Management,* Winter 2012; Michelle Steward, Beth Walker, Michael Hutt, and Ajith Kumar, "The Coordination Strategies of High-Performing Salespeople: Internal Working Relationships That Drive Success,"*Journal of the Academy of Marketing Science,* September 2010; Michael Ahearne, Scott B. MacKenzie, Philip M. Podsakoff, John E. Mathieu, and Son K. Lam, "The Role of Consensus in Sales Team Performance,"*Journal of Marketing Research,* June 2010; Michael Ahearne, Son K. Lam, John E. Mathieu, and Willy Bolander, "Why Are Some Salespeople Better at Adapting to Organizational Change?"*Journal of Marketing,* May 2010; George S. Yip and Audrey J. M. Bink, "Managing Global Accounts," *Harvard Business Review,* September 2007; Paolo Guenzi, Catherine Pardo, and Laurent Georges, "Relational Selling Strategy and Key Account Managers' Relational Behaviors: An Exploratory Study," *Industrial Marketing Management,* January 2007; Eli Jones, Andrea L. Dixon, Lawrence B. Chonko, and Joseph P. Cannon, "Key Accounts and Team Selling: A Review, Framework, and Research Agenda," *Journal of Personal Selling & Sales Management,* Spring 2005; Michael G. Harvey, Milorad M. Novicevic, Thomas Hench, and Matthew Myers, "Global Account Management: A Supply-Side Managerial View," *Industrial Marketing Management,* October 2003; Sanjit Sengupta, Robert E. Krapfel, and Michael A. Pusateri, "An Empirical Investigation of Key Account Salesperson Effectiveness," *Journal of Personal Selling & Sales Management,* Fall 2000; Mark A. Moon and Susan F. Gupta, "Examining the Formation of Selling Centers: A Conceptual Framework," *Journal of Personal Selling & Sales Management,* Spring 1997.

10. "Matchmaking with Math: How Analytics Beats Intuition to Win Customers," *MIT Sloan Management Review,* Winter 2011.

11. "How to Remake Your Sales Force," *Fortune,* May 4, 1992; "Apparel Makers Play Bigger Part on Sales Floor," *Wall Street Journal,* March 2, 1988.

12. Charlene Li and Josh Bernoff, *Groundswell* (Boston: Harvard Business Press, 2008).

13. "Cloud's Fast Rise Even Surprised Salesforce's CEO," *Investor's Business Daily,* January 13, 2010; "Pfizer Adds New Type of Tablet to Sales Calls," *Wall Street Journal,* December 15, 2009; "Videoconferencing Eyes Growth Spurt," *USA Today,* June 23, 2009; "Salesforce Hits Its Stride," *Fortune,* March 2, 2009; "An Early Adopter's New Idea," *Wall Street Journal,* January 22, 2008; Scott M. Widmier, Donald W. Jackson, Jr., and Deborah Brown McCabe, "Infusing Technology into Personal Selling," *Journal of Personal Selling & Sales Management,* November 2002.

14. For research on these topics see Giebelhausen, Michael, Stacey G. Robinson, Nancy J. Sirianni, and Michael K. Brady. "Touch Versus Tech: When Technology Functions as a Barrier or a Benefit to Service Encounters." *Journal of Marketing* 78.4 (2014): 113-24; S. Albers, M. Krafft, and M. Mantrala, "Special Section on Enhancing Sales Force Productivity," *International Journal of Research in Marketing,* 1 (2010); L. Ferrell, T. Gonzalez-Padron, and O. C. Ferrell, "An Assessment of the Use of Technology in the Direct Selling Industry," *Journal of Personal Selling & Sales Management,* 2 (2010); S. Sarin, T. Sego, A. Kohli, and G. Challagalla, "Characteristics That Enhance Training and Effectiveness in Implementing Technological Change in Sales Strategy: A Field-Based Exploratory Study," *Journal of Personal Selling & Sales Management,* 2 (2010); G. Wright, K. Fletcher, B. Donaldson, and J. H. Lee, "Sales Force Automation Systems: An Analysis of Factors Underpinning the Sophistication of Deployed Systems in the UK Financial Services Industry," *Industrial Marketing Management,* 8 (2008); V. Crittenden, R. Peterson, and G. Albaum. "Technology and Business-to-Consumer Selling: Contemplating Research and Practice," *Journal of Personal Selling & Sales Management,* 2 (2010); Michael Ahearne and Adam Rapp, "The Role of Technology at the Interface between Salespeople and Consumers," *Journal of Personal Selling & Sales Management,* 2 (2010); Gary K. Hunter and William D. Perreault, "Making Sales Technology Effective," *Journal of Marketing,* January 2007; Michael Ahearne, Douglas E. Hughes, and Niels Schillewaert, "Why Sales Reps Should Welcome Information Technology: Measuring the Impact of CRM-Based IT on Sales Effectiveness," *International Journal of Research in Marketing,* December 2007; Earl D. Honeycutt, Jr., Tanya Thelen, Shawn T. Thelen, and Sharon K. Hodge, "Impediments to Sales Force Automation," *Industrial Marketing Management,* May 2005; Alan J. Bush, Jarvis B. Moore, and Rich Rocco, "Understanding Sales Force Automation Outcomes: A Managerial Perspective," *Industrial Marketing Management,* May 2005; Richard E. Buehrer, Sylvain Senecal, and Ellen Bolman Pullins, "Sales Force Technology Usage—Reasons, Barriers, and Support: An Exploratory Investigation," *Industrial Marketing Management,* May 2005; Leroy Robinson, Jr., Greg W. Marshall, and Miriam B. Stamps, "An Empirical Investigation of Technology Acceptance in a Field Sales Force Setting," *Industrial Marketing Management,* May 2005; Devon S. Johnson and Sundar Bharadwaj, "Digitization of Selling Activity and Sales Force Performance: An Empirical Investigation," *Journal of the Academy of Marketing Science,* Winter 2005; Thomas G. Brashear, Danny N. Bellenger, James S. Boles, and Hiram C. Barksdale, Jr., "An Exploratory Study of the Relative Effectiveness of Different Types of Sales Force Mentors," *Journal of Personal Selling & Sales Management,* Winter 2006; Gary L. Hunter, "Information Overload: Guidance for Identifying When Information Becomes Detrimental to Sales Force Performance," *Journal of Personal Selling & Sales Management,* Spring 2004; Cheri Speier and Viswanath Venkatesh, "The Hidden Minefields in the Adoption of Sales Force Automation Technologies," *Journal of Marketing,* July 2002.

15. "Selling Salesmanship," *Business 2.0,* December 2002; "The Art of the Sale," *Wall Street Journal,* January 11, 2001.

16. See Boichuk, Jeffrey P., Willy Bolander, Zachary R. Hall, Michael Ahearne, William J. Zahn, and Melissa Nieves. "Learned Helplessness Among Newly Hired Salespeople and the Influence of Leadership." *Journal of Marketing* 78.1 (2014): 95-111; Shannahan, Kirby, Alan Bush, and Rachelle Shannahan. "Are Your Salespeople Coachable? How Salesperson Coachability, Trait Competitiveness, and Transformational Leadership Enhance Sales Performance." *Journal of the Academy of Marketing Science* 41.1 (2013): 40-54; Thomas L. Powers, Thomas E. DeCarlo, and Gouri Gupte, "An Update on the Status of Sales Management Training,"*Journal of Personal Selling & Sales Management,* Fall 2010; Felicia G. Lassk, Thomas N. Ingram, Florian Kraus, and Rita Di Mascio, "The Future of Sales Training: Challenges and Related Research Questions,"*Journal of Personal Selling & Sales Management,* Winter 2012; M. Asri Jantan, Earl D. Honeycutt, Shawn T. Thelen, and Ashraf M. Atria, "Managerial Perceptions of Sales Training and Performance," *Industrial Marketing Management,* October 2004; Karen E. Flaherty and James M. Pappas, "Job Selection Among Salespeople: A Bounded Rationality Perspective," *Industrial Marketing Management,* May 2004; Anand Krishnamoorthy, Sanjog Misra, and Ashutosh Prasad, "Scheduling Sales Force Training: Theory and Evidence," *International Journal of Research in Marketing,* December 2005; William L. Cron, Greg W. Marshall, Jagdip Singh, Rosann L. Spiro, and Harish Sujan, "Salesperson Selection, Training, and Development: Trends, Implications, and Research Opportunities," *Journal of Personal Selling & Sales Management,* Spring 2005; Brian P. Matthews and Tom Redman, "Recruiting the Wrong Salespeople: Are the Job Ads to Blame?" *Industrial Marketing Management,* October 2001.

17 William H. Murphy, Peter A. Dacin, and Neil M. Ford, "Sales Contest Effectiveness: An Examination of Sales Contest Design Preferences of Field Sales Forces," *Journal of the Academy of Marketing Science,* Spring 2004; Steven P. Brown, Kenneth R. Evans, Murali K. Mantrala, and Goutam Challagalla, "Adapting Motivation, Control, and Compensation Research to a New Environment," *Journal of Personal Selling & Sales Management,* Spring 2005; Charles H. Schwepker, Jr., and David J. Good, "Marketing Control and Sales Force Customer Orientation," *Journal of Personal Selling & Sales Management,* Summer 2004; Jeong Eun Park and George D. Deitz, "The Effect of Working Relationship Quality on Salesperson Performance and Job Satisfaction: Adaptive Selling Behavior in Korean Automobile Sales Representatives," *Journal of Business Research,* February 2006; J. K. Sager, H. D. Strutton, and D. A. Johnson, "Core Self-Evaluations and Salespeople," *Psychology & Marketing,* February 2006; Joseph O. Rentz, C. David Shepherd, Armen Tashchian, Pratibha A. Dabholkar, and Robert T. Ladd, "A Measure of Selling Skill: Scale Development and Validation," *Journal of Personal Selling & Sales Management,* Winter 2002.

18. Kishore, Sunil, Raghunath Singh Rao, Om Narasimhan, and George John. "Bonuses Versus Commissions: A Field Study." *Journal of Marketing Research (JMR)* 50.3 (2013): 317-33; Lim, Noah, and Hua Chen. "When Do Group Incentives for Salespeople Work?" *Journal of Marketing Research (JMR)* 51.3 (2014): 320-34; Miao, C., and Kenneth Evans. "The Interactive Effects of Sales Control Systems on Salesperson Performance: A Job Demands-resources Perspective." *Journal of the Academy of Marketing Science* 41.1 (2013): 73-90; Manfred Krafft, Thomas E. DeCarlo, F. Juliet Poujol, and John F. Tanner, "Compensation and Control Systems: A New Application of Vertical Dyad Linkage Theory,"*Journal of Personal Selling & Sales Management,* Winter 2012; Michael Ahearne, Adam Rapp, Douglas E. Hughes, and Rupinder Jindal, "Managing Sales Force Product Perceptions and Control Systems in the Success of New Product Introductions,"*Journal of Marketing Research,* August 2010; Jason Garrett and Srinath Gopalakrishna, "Customer Value Impact of Sales Contests," *Journal of the Academy of Marketing Science,* November 2010; Desmond (Ho-Fu) Lo, Mrinal Ghosh, and Francine Lafontaine, "The Incentive and Selection Roles of Sales Force Compensation Contracts,"*Journal of Marketing Research,* August 2011; René Y. Darmon and Xavier C. Martin, "A New Conceptual Framework of Salesforce Control Systems,"*Journal of Personal Selling & Sales Management,* Summer 2011; Frank Q. Fu, Keith A. Richards, Douglas E. Hughes, and Eli Jones, "Motivating Salespeople to Sell New Products: The Relative Influence of Attitudes, Subjective Norms, and Self-Efficacy,"*Journal of Marketing,* November 2010; Sridhar N. Ramaswami and Jagdip Singh, "Antecedents and Consequences of Merit Pay Fairness for Industrial Salespeople," *Journal of Marketing,* October 2003.

19. "New Software's Payoff? Happier Salespeople," *Investor's Business Daily,* May 23, 2000.

20. Eric G. Harris, John C. Mowen, and Tom J. Brown, "Re-examining Salesperson Goal Orientations: Personal Influencers, Customer Orientation, and Work Satisfaction," *Journal of the Academy of Marketing Science,* Winter 2005; Dominique Rouziès, Erin Anderson, Ajay K. Kohli, Ronald E. Michaels, Barton A. Weitz, and Andris A. Zoltners, "Sales and Marketing Integration: A Proposed Framework," *Journal of Personal Selling & Sales Management,* Spring 2005; Eric Fang, Kenneth R. Evans, and Shaoming Zou, "The Moderating Effect of Goal-Setting Characteristics on the Sales Control Systems Job Performance Relationship," *Journal of Business Research,* September 2005; Kenneth B. Kahn, Richard C. Reizenstein, and Joseph O. Rentz, "Sales-Distribution Interfunctional Climate and Relationship Effectiveness," *Journal of Business Research,* October 2004; Rolph E. Anderson and Wen-yeh Huang, "Empowering Salespeople: Personal, Managerial, and Organizational Perspectives," *Psychology & Marketing,* February 2006; Thomas G. Brashear, James S. Boles, Danny N. Bellenger, and Charles M. Brooks, "An Empirical Test of Trust-Building

Processes and Outcomes in Sales Manager–Salesperson Relationships," *Journal of the Academy of Marketing Science,* Spring 2003; Andrea L. Dixon, Rosann L. Spiro, and Lukas P. Forbes, "Attributions and Behavioral Intentions of Inexperienced Salespersons to Failure: An Empirical Investigation," *Journal of the Academy of Marketing Science,* Fall 2003; Douglas N. Behrman and William D. Perreault, Jr., "A Role Stress Model of the Performance and Satisfaction of Industrial Salespersons," *Journal of Marketing,* Fall 1984.

21. Gonzalez, Gabriel R., Danny P. Claro, and Robert W. Palmatier. "Synergistic Effects of Relationship Managers' Social Networks on Sales Performance." *Journal of Marketing* 78.1 (2014): 76-94; Hall, Zachary R., Michael Ahearne, and Harish Sujan. "The Importance of Starting Right: The Influence of Accurate Intuition on Performance in Salesperson--Customer Interactions." *Journal of Marketing* 79.3 (2015): 91-109; Hughes, Douglas, Joël Bon, and Adam Rapp. "Gaining and Leveraging Customer-based Competitive Intelligence: The Pivotal Role of Social Capital and Salesperson Adaptive Selling Skills." *Journal of the Academy of Marketing Science* 41.1 (2013): 91-110; Mullins, Ryan R., Michael Ahearne, Son K. Lam, Zachary R. Hall, and Jeffrey P. Boichuk. "Know Your Customer: How Salesperson Perceptions of Customer Relationship Quality Form and Influence Account Profitability." *Journal of Marketing* 78.6 (2014): 38-58; "Chief Executives Are Increasingly Chief Salesmen," *Wall Street Journal,* August 6, 1991; Joe F. Alexander, Patrick L. Schul, and Emin Babakus, "Analyzing Interpersonal Communications in Industrial Marketing Negotiations," *Journal of the Academy of Marketing Science,* Spring 1991.

22. "Managing Technology: Selling Software," *Wall Street Journal,* March 19, 2007. For more on lead management, see Sabnis, Gaurav, Sharmila C. Chatterjee, Rajdeep Grewal, and Gary L. Lilien. "The Sales Lead Black Hole: On Sales Reps' Follow-Up of Marketing Leads." *Journal of Marketing* 77.1 (2013): 52-67.

23. Christian Homburg, Michael Müller, and Martin Klarmann, "When Should the Customer Really Be King? On the Optimum Level of Salesperson Customer Orientation in Sales Encounters,"*Journal of Marketing,* March 2011; Gabriel R. Gonzalez, K. Douglas Hoffman, Thomas N. Ingram, and Raymond W. LaForge, "Sales Organization Recovery Management and Relationship Selling: A Conceptual Model and Empirical Test," *Journal of Personal Selling & Sales Management,* Summer 2010; Dennis B. Arnett, Barry A. Macy, and James B. Wilcox, "The Role of Core Selling Teams in Supplier-Buyer Relationships," *Journal of Personal Selling & Sales Management,* Winter 2005; Kirk Smith, Eli Jones, and Edward Blair, "Managing Salesperson Motivation in a Territory Realignment," *Journal of Personal Selling & Sales Management,* Fall 2000; Andris A. Zoltners, "Sales Territory Alignment: An Overlooked Productivity Tool," *Journal of Personal Selling & Sales Management,* Summer 2000; Ken Grant, "The Role of Satisfaction with Territory Design on the Motivation, Attitudes, and Work Outcomes of Salespeople," *Journal of the Academy of Marketing Science,* Spring 2001.

24. "How to Get Your Company Where You Want It," *American Salesman,* December 2003; "When Should I Give Up on a Sales Prospect?" *Inc.,* May 1998. See also Sean Dwyer, John Hill, and Warren Martin, "An Empirical Investigation of Critical Success Factors in the Personal Selling Process for Homogenous Goods," *Journal of Personal Selling & Sales Management,* Summer 2000; Doris C. Van Doren and Thomas A. Stickney, "How to Develop a Database for Sales Leads," *Industrial Marketing Management,* August 1990.

25. "Novartis' Marketing Doctor," *BusinessWeek,* March 5, 2001.

26. "Consultative Selling—We See Great Examples Everywhere," *Partners in Excellence Blog,* July 24, 2012.

27. For more on sales presentation approaches, see "Three Strategies to Get Customers to Say Yes," *Wall Street Journal,* May 29, 2009; Richard G. McFarland, Goutam N. Challagalla, and Tasadduq A. Shervani, "Influence Tactics for Effective Adaptive Selling," *Journal of Marketing,* October 2006; "The 60-Second Sales Pitch," *Inc.,* October 1994. See also Daniel M. Eveleth and Linda Morris, "Adaptive

Selling in a Call Center Environment: A Qualitative Investigation," *Journal of Interactive Marketing,* Winter 2002; Thomas W. Leigh and John O. Summers, "An Initial Evaluation of Industrial Buyers' Impressions of Salespersons' Nonverbal Cues," *Journal of Personal Selling & Sales Management,* Winter 2002; Kalyani Menon and Laurette Dube, "Ensuring Greater Satisfaction by Engineering Salesperson Response to Customer Emotions," *Journal of Retailing,* Fall 2000; Susan K. DelVecchio, James E. Zemanek, Roger P. McIntyre, and Reid P. Claxton, "Buyers' Perceptions of Salesperson Tactical Approaches," *Journal of Personal Selling & Sales Management,* Winter 2002–2003; Alfred M. Pelham, "An Exploratory Model and Initial Test of the Influence of Firm Level Consulting-Oriented Sales Force Programs on Sales Force Performance," *Journal of Personal Selling & Sales Management,* Spring 2002; Thomas E. DeCarlo, "The Effects of Sales Message and Suspicion of Ulterior Motives on Salesperson Evaluation," *Journal of Consumer Psychology,* 2005; Amy Sallee and Karen Flaherty, "Enhancing Salesperson Trust: An Examination of Managerial Values, Empowerment, and the Moderating Influence of SBU Strategy," *Journal of Personal Selling & Sales Management,* Fall 2003.

28. J. Hansen and R. Riggle, "Ethical Salesperson Behavior in Sales Relationships," *Journal of Personal Selling & Sales Management,* 2 (2009); Thomas N. Ingram, Raymond W. LaForge, and Charles H. Schwepker, Jr., "Salesperson Ethical Decision Making: The Impact of Sales Leadership and Sales Management Control Strategy," *Journal of Personal Selling & Sales Management,* Fall 2007; Jay Prakash Mulki, Fernando Jaramillo, and William B. Locander, "Effects of Ethical Climate and Supervisory Trust on Salespersons' Job Attitudes and Intentions to Quit," *Journal of Personal Selling & Sales Management,* Winter 2006; Lawrence B. Chonko, Thomas R. Wotruba, and Terry W. Loe, "Direct Selling Ethics at the Top: An Industry Audit and Status Report," *Journal of Personal Selling & Sales Management,* Spring 2002.

CHAPTER 15

1. See www.subway.com; "Explore Our World," Subway.com. Retrieved June 27, 2015; "10 Top Chain Restaurants Get the Grade From 'Eat This, Not That,'" Press Release, June 16, 2015; "Latest Subway Ad Campaign Highlights Vegetables," *Nation's Restaurant News,* August 4, 2014; "Subway Touts Healthful Sandwiches for Fall," *Nations Restaurant News,* September 3, 2014; "Facebook's Video Ads Risk Alienating Users," *The Wall Street Journal,* December 17, 2013; "How to Get More Out of Facebook Ads," *Social Media Examiner,* October 21, 2014; www.facebook.com/subway; "Subway Mixes Video into Summer Campaign to Up Mobile Advertising Strategy," *Mobile Marketer,* June 5, 2012; "Subway Runs Past McDonald's Chain," *Wall Street Journal,* March 8, 2011; "How Subway Built a $4B Brand, Five Bucks at a Time," *Brandweek,* September 27, 2010; "Celeb Dieters: What Happens When the Pounds Creep Back?" *Advertising Age,* February 15, 2010; "The Accidental Hero," *BusinessWeek,* November 16, 2009; "Subway's $5 Foot-Long Becomes Yardstick for Fast-Food Meal Deals," *Advertising Age,* June 8, 2009; "Subway Seeks to Slice Domino's, Pizza Hut Pie," *Brandweek,* April 9, 2007; "Friday's, Subway Tailor Meals for Health-Conscious," *USA Today,* March 1, 2007; "Finding Just Enough of That Sticky Stuff," *Brandweek,* January 29, 2007; "Subway Corporate Grabs for Advertising Control: Franchisees Wary of Power Play," *AdAge.com,* April 24, 2006; "Subway Announces 3-Year Little League Baseball and Softball Sponsorship, Reflects Chain's Dual Focus on Good Nutrition and Physical Activity," *PR Newswire US,* August 20, 2005; "Subway Targets Teen Appetites," *Connecticut Post,* May 17, 2005; "Subway to Sell Kids Pak Meal That Focuses on Health," *USA Today,* September 26, 2003; "Subway Orders Weightier Campaign," *Wall Street Journal,* August 21, 2003; "Marketers of the Year: Subway, in Search of Fresh Ideas," *Brandweek,* October 15, 2001; "Chick-fil-A, Starbucks, and Subway Are CX Leaders in Fast Food," *Customer Experience Matters,* February 29, 2012; "Subway Targets

Families to Broaden Brand Appeal," *Marketing Week,* June 17, 2013; "The Sandwich That Ate the World," *Inc.,* May 2013.

2. For insights on advertising effectiveness, see "What Do We Know About Advertising Effectiveness?", *Marketing Science Institute,* May 21, 2013; Lodish, Leonard M., Magid Abraham, Stuart Kalmenson, Jeanne Livelsberger, Beth Lubetkin, Bruce Richardson, and Mary Ellen Stevens (1995), "How T.V. Advertising Works: A Meta-Analysis of 389 Real World Split Cable T.V. Experiments." *Journal of Marketing Research* 32 (2), 125–39; Vakratsas, Demetrios, and Prasad Naik (2007), "Essentials of Planning Media Schedules." In *Handbook of Advertising,* eds. Gerard J. Tellis and Tim Ambler, 333–48. Los Angeles. Calif.: Sage Publications; Danaher, Peter J., André Bonfrer, and Sanjay Dhar (2008), "The Effect of Competitive Advertising on Sales for Packaged Goods." *Journal of Marketing Research* 45 (2), 211–25; Vakratsas, Demetrios, Fred M. Feinberg, Frank M. Bass, and Gurumurthy Kalyanaram (2004), "The Shape of Advertising Response Functions Revisited: A Model of Dynamic Probabilistic Thresholds." *Marketing Science* 23 (1), 109–19; Sethuraman, Raj, and Gerard J. Tellis (1991), "An Analysis of the Tradeoff Between Advertising and Price Discounting." *Journal of Marketing Research* 28 (2), 160–74; Vakratsas, Demetrios, and Tim Ambler (1999), "How Advertising Works: What Do We Really Know?" *Journal of Marketing* 63 (1), 26–43.

3. See "Total US Ad Spending to See Largest Increase Since 2004," *eMarketer,* July 2, 2014.

4. For more on advertising to sales ratios, see AdAge datacenter, "Advertising to Sales Ratios by Industry." For some striking data, see "Marketing Spend: Facts and Stats," *CMO Council,* https://www.cmo-council.org/facts_stats.php.

5. Exact data on this industry are elusive, but see U.S. Census Bureau, *Statistical Abstract of the United States 2010* (Washington, DC: U.S. Government Printing Office, 2009), p. 403. For some striking data, see "Marketing Spend: Facts and Stats," *CMO Council,* https://www.cmocouncil.org/facts_stats.php;

6. Yan Ruiliang, "Cooperative Advertising, Pricing Strategy and Firm Performance in the E-Marketing Age,"*Journal of the Academy of Marketing Science,* July 2012; Steffen Jorgensen, Simon Pierre Sigue, and Georges Zaccour, "Dynamic Cooperative Advertising in a Channel," *Journal of Retailing,* Spring 2000.

7. For more information on the various kinds of advertising, see "So Sue Me: Why Big Brands Are Taking Claims to Court," *Advertising Age,* January 4, 2010; "AT&T Sues Verizon over 'There's a Map for That' Ads," *Engadget.com,* November 3, 2009; "Comparative Disadvantage," *AdweekMedia,* June 15, 2009; "Feature: Cause Marketing," *Advertising Age,* June 13, 2005; "The Selling of Breast Cancer," *Business 2.0,* February 2003. See also Peter J. Danaher, André Bonfrer, and Sanjay Dhar, "The Effect of Competitive Advertising Interference on Sales for Packaged Goods," *Journal of Marketing Research,* May 2008; Debora Viana Thompson and Rebecca W. Hamilton, "The Effects of Information Processing Mode on Consumers' Responses to Comparative Advertising," *Journal of Consumer Research,* March 2006; Robert D. Jewell, H. Rao Unnava, David Glen Mick, and Merrie L. Brucks, "When Competitive Interference Can Be Beneficial," *Journal of Consumer Research,* September 2003; Diana L. Haytko, "Great Advertising Campaigns: Goals and Accomplishments," *Journal of Marketing,* April 1995; Michael J. Barone, Anthony D. Miyazaki, and Kimberly A. Taylor, "The Influence of Cause-Related Marketing on Consumer Choice: Does One Good Turn Deserve Another?" *Journal of the Academy of Marketing Science,* Spring 2000; Minette E. Drumwright, "Company Advertising with a Social Dimension: The Role of Noneconomic Criteria," *Journal of Marketing,* October 1996; Wilfred Amaldoss, and Chuan He, "Product Variety, Informative Advertising, and Price Competition," *Journal of Marketing Research,* February 2010.

8. Data in Exhibit 15–5 for advertising spending differs depending on the source, but the overall ratios and trends are similar. For another source, see IAB Internet advertising revenue report, 2014 full year results, April 2015, an industry survey conducted by PwC and sponsored by the Interactive Advertising Bureau. These data come from: "Total US Ad Spending to See Largest Increase Since 2004," *eMarketer*, July 2, 2014

9. For more on various media, see Comparing the Relative Effectiveness of Advertising Channels: A Case Study of a Multimedia Blitz Campaign. 50 *Journal of Marketing Research* (JMR) 517-34; D. W. Baack, R. T. Wilson, and B. D. Till, "Creativity and Memory Effects Recall, Recognition, and an Exploration of Nontraditional Media," *Journal of Advertising*, 4 (2008); J. Rubinson, "Marketing in the Era of Long-Tail Media," *Journal of Advertising Research*, 3 (2008); "TV Commercials: Who Needs Them?" *BusinessWeek*, May 25, 2009; "Days Growing Darker for Media," *Advertising Age*, November 3, 2008; "Phone Giants Roll Out 'Three Screen' Strategy," *Wall Street Journal*, June 26, 2008; "Lend Me Your Ears: Advertisers Begin to Target Podcasts," *Investor's Business Daily*, June 23, 2008; "Attention-Deficit Advertising," *BusinessWeek*, May 5, 2008; "The Results Issue," *Brandweek*, July 23, 2007; "Brands in the 'Hood,'" *Point*, December 2005; "TV's New Parallel Universe," *BusinessWeek*, November 14, 2005. For more on videogame medium, see V. Cauberghe and P. De Pelsmacker, "Advergames: The Impact of Brand Prominence and Game Repetition on Brand Responses," *Journal of Advertising*, 1 (2010); Victoria Mallinckrodt and Dick Mizerski, "The Effects of Playing an Advergame on Young Children's Perceptions, Preferences, and Requests," *Journal of Advertising*, Summer 2007; Mira Lee and Ronald J. Faber, "Effects of Product Placement in On-Line Games on Brand Memory," *Journal of Advertising*, Winter 2007. For more on cell phone medium, see V. Shankar and S. Balasubramanian, "Mobile Marketing: A Synthesis and Prognosis," *Journal of Interactive Marketing*, 2 (2009); R. Friedrich, F. Grone, K. Holbling, and M. Petersen, "The March of Mobile Marketing: New Chances for Consumer Companies, New Opportunities for Mobile Operators," *Journal of Advertising Research*, 1 (2009); Shintaro Okazaki, Akihiro Katsukura, and Mamoru Nishiyama, "How Mobile Advertising Works: The Role of Trust in Improving Attitudes and Recall," *Journal of Advertising Research*, June 2007; Mark Ferris, "Insights on Mobile Advertising, Promotion, and Research," *Journal of Advertising Research*, March 2007. For more on in-store medium, see "In a Shift, Marketers Beef Up Ad Spending Inside Stores," *Wall Street Journal*, September 21, 2005; P. Chandon, J. W. Hutchinson, E. T. Bradlow, and S. H. Young, "Does In-Store Marketing Work? Effects of the Number and Position of Shelf Facings on Brand Attention and Evaluation at the Point of Purchase," *Journal of Marketing*, 6 (2009). For more on the outdoor medium, see "Celebrating the Renaissance of Out-of-Home Advertising," *Advertising Age* (special report), June 22, 2009; "Neighbors Hope to Pull Plug on Signs," *USA Today*, September 5, 2007; "In Billboard War, Digital Signs Spark a Truce," *Wall Street Journal*, February 3, 2007. See also Charles R. Taylor, George R. Franke, and Bang Hae-Kyong, "Use and Effectiveness of Billboards," *Journal of Advertising*, Winter 2006; Charles R. Taylor and John C. Taylor, "Regulatory Issues in Outdoor Advertising: A Content Analysis of Billboards," *Journal of Public Policy & Marketing*, Spring 1994. For more on the radio medium, see "The New Radio Revolution: From Satellite to Podcasts . . . ," *BusinessWeek*, March 14, 2005; Daniel M. Haygood, "A Status Report on Podcast Advertising," *Journal of Advertising Research*, December 2007. For more on the newspaper medium, see "Major Detroit Newspaper Takes Cues from Advertisers," *Wall Street Journal*, November 2, 2009; "Extra! Extra! Are Newspapers Dying?" *USA Today*, March 18, 2009. For more on the magazine medium, see "Mags Grow Online but Still Dwarfed by Web Bigs," *Advertising Age*, March 3, 2008. For more on the television and cable medium, see Y. Hu, L. M. Lodish, A. M. Krieger, and B. Hayati, "An Update of Real-World TV Advertising Tests," *Journal of Advertising Research*, 2 (2009); Kenneth C. Wilbur, "How the Digital Video Recorder (DVR) Changes Traditional Television Advertising," *Journal of Advertising*, Spring 2008; Ye Hu, Leonard M. Lodish, and Abba M. Krieger, "An Analysis of Real World TV Advertising Tests: A 15-Year Update," *Journal of Advertising*

Research, September 2007; S. A. Brasel and J. Gips, "Breaking through Fast-Forwarding: Brand Information and Visual Attention," *Journal of Marketing*, 6 (2008).

10. "Underwear Ads Caught in Bind over Sex Appeal," *Advertising Age*, July 8, 1996.

11. "Looking for Mr. Plumber," *MediaWeek*, June 27, 1994; "Those Really Big Shows Are Often Disappointing to Those Who Advertise," *Wall Street Journal*, June 14, 1994.

12. "TV's Next Wave: Tuning In to You," *Wall Street Journal*, March 6, 2011.

13. "Media Plan of the Year," *Adweek*, July 23, 2012.

14. "Coming Soon to Your Desktop at Work: Ads," *Bloomberg Businessweek*, April 19, 2012.

15. Data from "The Nine Slides That Matter From Mary Meeker's State of the Internet," *Bloomberg Business*, May 27, 2015. See also Fang, Eric (ER), Xiaoling Li, Minxue Huang, and Robert W. Palmatier. "Direct and Indirect Effects of Buyers and Sellers on Search Advertising Revenues in Business-to-Business Electronic Platforms." *Journal of Marketing Research (JMR)* 52.3 (2015): 407-22; Hu, Ye, Rex Yuxing Du, and Sina Damangir. "Decomposing the Impact of Advertising: Augmenting Sales with Online Search Data." *Journal of Marketing Research (JMR)* 51.3 (2014): 300-19; Dinner, Isaac M., Harald J. Van Heerde, and Scott A. Neslin. "Driving Online and Offline Sales: The Cross-Channel Effects of Traditional, Online Display, and Paid Search Advertising." *Journal of Marketing Research (JMR)* 51.5 (2014): 527-45; Draganska, Michaela, Wesley R. Hartmann, and Gena Stanglein. "Internet Versus Television Advertising: A Brand-Building Comparison." *Journal of Marketing Research (JMR)* 51.5 (2014): 578-90; Goldstein, Daniel G., Siddharth Suri, R. Preston Mcafee, Matthew Ekstrand-Abueg, and Fernando Diaz. "The Economic and Cognitive Costs of Annoying Display Advertisements." *Journal of Marketing Research (JMR)* 51.6 (2014): 742-52; Hoban, Paul R., and Randolph E. Bucklin. "Effects of Internet Display Advertising in the Purchase Funnel: Model-Based Insights from a Randomized Field Experiment." *Journal of Marketing Research (JMR)* 52.3 (2015): 375-93; Lambrecht, Anja, and Catherine Tucker. "When Does Retargeting Work? Information Specificity in Online Advertising." *Journal of Marketing Research (JMR)* 50.5 (2013): 561-76; Schumann, Jan H., Florian Von Wangenheim, and Nicole Groene. "Targeted Online Advertising: Using Reciprocity Appeals to Increase Acceptance Among Users of Free Web Services." *Journal of Marketing* 78.1 (2014): 59-75. "Video Consumer Mapping Study," *The Council for Research Excellence*, March 2009; "Google's Latest Bid to Boost Revenue: Interest-Based Ads," *Investor's Business Daily*, March 12, 2009; "Online Ads: Beyond Counting Clicks," *BusinessWeek*, March 9, 2009. See also Ashish Agarwal, Kartik Hosanagar, and Michael D Smith, "Location, Location, Location: An Analysis of Profitability of Position in Online Advertising Markets," *Journal of Marketing Research*, December 2011; Avi Goldfarb and Catherine Tucker, "Implications of Online Display Advertising: Targeting and Obtrusiveness," *Marketing Science*, 3 (2011); Tat Y. Chan, Chunhua Wu, and Ying Xie, "Measuring the Lifetime Value of Customers Acquired from Google Search Advertising," *Marketing Science*, 5 (2011); Oliver J. Rutz, Michael Trusov, and Randolph E. Bucklin, "Modeling Indirect Effects of Paid Search Advertising: Which Keywords Lead to More Future Visits?" *Marketing Science*, 4 (2011); G. M. Fulgoni and M. P. Morn, "Whither the Click? How Online Advertising Works," *Journal of Advertising Research*, 2 (2009); B. J. Calder, E. C. Malthouse, and U. Schaedel, "An Experimental Study of the Relationship between On-line Engagement and Advertising Effectiveness," *Journal of Interactive Marketing*, 4 (2009); J. Q. Chen, D. Liu, and A. B. Whinston, Auctioning Keywords in Online Search," *Journal of Marketing*, 4 (2009); Juran Kim and Sally J. McMillan, "Evaluation of Internet Advertising Research," *Journal of Advertising*, Spring 2008.

16. "SmartMoney Finds Using Fewer Ads Can Boost Click-Through," *Advertising Age*, March 2, 2009; "Average Search CPC Data by Category for March 2008," *Search Engine Watch*, April 7,

2008. See also "So Many Ads, So Few Clicks," *BusinessWeek,* November 12, 2007; "Competing for Clients, and Paying by the Click," *New York Times,* October 15, 2007; "The New Benefits of Web-Search Queries," *Wall Street Journal,* February 6, 2007; "Web Numbers: What's Real?" *BusinessWeek,* October 23, 2006. See also "Click Fraud: The Dark Side of Online Advertising," *BusinessWeek,* October 2, 2006.

17. Larson, Jeff and Stuart Draper, *Internet Marketing Essentials,* 2015, Stukent, Inc.; "How Advertisers Use Internet Cookies to Track You," *Teach the 4 Ps,* August 8, 2010; "Help! A Web Ad Is Stalking Me," *PCWorld,* June 20, 2011; "Are Retailers Going Too Far Tracking Our Web Habits?" *USA Today,* October 26, 2009; "The Web Knows What You Want," *BusinessWeek,* July 27, 2009; "Connect the Thoughts: The Analysis of Social Networking Data . . . ," *AdweekMedia,* June 29, 2009; "The Next: Companies May Soon Know Where Customers Are Likely to Be Every Minute . . . ," *BusinessWeek,* March 9, 2009; "Feel Like Someone's Watching You?" *USA Today,* February 9, 2009; "We Know Where You Are," *Wall Street Journal,* September 29, 2008; "Agencies Know the Score on Web Tracking," *Wall Street Journal,* April 21, 2008; "Internet Firms Get Better at Targeting Ads," *Investor's Business Daily,* December 3, 2007; "Behavioral Targeting: The New Killer App for Research," *Advertising Age,* January 22, 2007; "Technology: Analyze This," *BusinessWeek,* Winter 2006.

18. Exhibit 15–6 and related discussion draws on the following sources: Xu, Jun, *Managing Digital Enterprise: Ten Essential Topics,* Springer, 2014; Turban, E., King, D., Lee, J. K., Liang, T. P., and Turban, D. (2012). *Electronic Commerce 2012: A Managerial and Social Networks Perspective,* Upper Saddle River, NJ: Prentice Hall; Rayport, J. F. (2013). "Advertising's New Medium: Human Experience," *Harvard Business Review,* March, 77–84; Kirby, J. (2013). "Creative that Cracks the Code," *Harvard Business Review,* March, 86–89; IAB Internet advertising revenue report, 2014 full year results, April 2015, an industry survey conducted by PwC and sponsored by the Interactive Advertising Bureau; "Total US Ad Spending to See Largest Increase Since 2004," *eMarketer,* July 2, 2014; "Advantages and Disadvantages of Various Advertising Mediums," *PowerHomeBiz.com*; Stephen, Andrew, Yakov Bart, and Miklos Sarvary (2013) "Making Mobile Ads That Work," *Harvard Business Review,* December.

19. "US, Europe, and Worldwide Display Ad Clickthrough Rates Statistics Summary," *Smart Insights,* April 21, 2015.

20. "Mobile Advertising Begins to Take Off," *The Wall Street Journal,* October 9, 2013; "Top 10 Mobile Advertising Campaigns of Q2," *Mobile Marketer,* June 5, 2012; "Cell Phone Ads That Consumers Love," *Harvard Business School Working Knowledge,* February 28, 2005; Rama Yelkur, Chuck Tomkovick, and Patty Traczyk, "Super Bowl Advertising Effectiveness: Hollywood Finds the Games Golden," *Journal of Advertising Research,* March 2004. For information on apps and shopping, see "Yes, There's an App for That, Too: How Mobile Is Changing Shopping," *Advertising Age,* March 1, 2010; "Brands Get a Boost by Opening Up APIs to Outside Developers," *Advertising Age,* November 30, 2009. See also Bart, Yakov, Andrew T. Stephen, and Miklos Sarvary. "Which Products Are Best Suited to Mobile Advertising? A Field Study of Mobile Display Advertising Effects on Consumer Attitudes and Intentions." *Journal of Marketing Research (JMR)* 51.3 (2014): 270-85.

21. "Using Google's Data to Reach Consumers," *New York Times,* December 22, 2011.

22. "Ads Tied to Web Searches Criticized as Deceptive," *The Wall Street Journal,* October 13, 2014.

23. "More Than Half of the Ads That Google Sells Are Never Seen," *Atlantic,* December 8, 2014; "Click Fraud," *Bloomberg Businessweek,* October 1, 2006.

24. All examples are real. For more thoughts on this topic see "Media Plan of the Year," *Adweek,* July 23, 2012; "The Cost of Paying Attention," *New York Times,* March 7, 2015; "Dominated by Advertising: #Mydunkin Story," *Huffington Post,* March 24, 2015.

25. "The Cookies You Can't Crumble," *Bloomberg Businessweek,* August 21, 2014; "Everybody Hates Mobile Advertising," *Business Insider,* July 1, 2014; see also Tucker, Catherine E. "Social Networks, Personalized Advertising, and Privacy Controls." *Journal of Marketing Research (JMR)* 51.5 (2014): 546-62; Connell, Paul M., Merrie Brucks, and Jesper H. Nielsen. "How Childhood Advertising Exposure Can Create Biased Product Evaluations That Persist into Adulthood." *Journal of Consumer Research* 41.1 (2014): 119-34.

26. For academic research on this topic see Aydınoğlu, Nilüfer Z., and Luca Cian. "Show Me the Product, Show Me the Model: Effect of Picture Type on Attitudes toward Advertising." *Journal of Consumer Psychology,* 24.4 (2014): 506-19; Barone, Michael, and Robert Jewell. "How Brand Innovativeness Creates Advertising Flexibility," *Journal of the Academy of Marketing Science* 42.3 (2014): 309-21.

27. For more examples of creative campaigns, see "Edgy Advertising in a Tenuous Time," *BusinessWeek,* January 12, 2009; "Hey, No Whopper on the Menu?" *Wall Street Journal,* February 8, 2008; "Did Telling a Whopper Sell the Whopper?" *Advertising Age,* January 14, 2008; "From Admirable to Addlebrained," *USA Today,* December 31, 2007; "Marketers Get More Creative with TV Ads," *USA Today,* November 12, 2007. For some creative and controversial ads, see "Burger Joints Pull Out Oldest Ad Trick in Book: Sex," *USA Today,* December 21, 2009; "Taste Strips Give Ads a New Flavor," *Advertising Age,* June 2, 2008. See also M. R. Brown, R. K. Bhadury, and N. K. L. Pope, "The Impact of Comedic Violence on Viral Advertising Effectiveness," *Journal of Advertising,* 1 (2010); Josephine L. C. M., Woltman Elpers, Ashesh Mukherjee, and Wayne D. Hoyer, "Humor in Television Advertising: A Moment-to-Moment Analysis," *Journal of Consumer Research,* December 2004; Edward F. McQuarrie and Barbara J. Phillips, "Indirect Persuasion in Advertising," *Journal of Advertising,* Summer 2005; Ryan S. Elder and Aradhna Krishna, "The 'Visual Depiction Effect' in Advertising: Facilitating Embodied Mental Simulation through Product Orientation,"*Journal of Consumer Research,* 6 (2012); Theodore J. Noseworthy, June Cotte, and Seung Hwan (Mark) Lee, "The Effects of Ad Context and Gender on the Identification of Visually Incongruent Products," *Journal of Consumer Research,* 2 (2011).

28. "Quiz: Is This Story an Ad?" *Marketplace,* December 3, 2013; "Here's What Else Is Wrong With Native Advertising," *Advertising Age,* September 2, 2014; "BuzzFeed – The Promise of Native Advertising," *Harvard Business School case study 9-0714-512,* August 15, 2014.

29. Ibid, see previous endnotes offering some insights about native advertising. For a send-up of the practice see *Last Week Tonight with John Oliver: Native Advertising,* on YouTube at https://youtu.be/E_F5GxCwizc.

30. See "Agency Report," *Advertising Age* (Special Report), April 26, 2010. See also "Madison Ave. Lights Up," *Fortune,* December 12, 2005; "Ending Advertising's Spiral," *Business 2.0,* September 2005; "Agencies Are from Mars, Clients Are from Venus," *Point,* July 2005; "The Fall of a Madison Avenue Icon," *Adweek,* July 25, 2005.

31. "Auto Companies Struggle to Get Green Message Right," *Brandweek,* November 19, 2007; "Domino's Has No Problem Sharing an Agency with Burger King," *Advertising Age,* September 24, 2007. See also M. E. Drumwright and P. E. Murphy, "The Current State of Advertising Ethics: Industry and Academic Perspectives," *Journal of Advertising,* 1 (2009).

32. "Paying for Viewers Who Pay Attention," *BusinessWeek,* May 18, 2009; "Guess Which Medium Is as Effective as Ever: TV," *Advertising Age,* February 23, 2009; "Web vs. TV: Research Aims to Gauge Ads," *Wall Street Journal,* March 19, 2008.

33. For more on international differences see, "P&G's Crest Fined Almost $1 Million Over Chinese Ad," *Advertising Age,* March 10, 2015, "Beauty Riskier than Booze on Spanish TV," *Advertising Age,* January 25, 2010; "Catching the Eye of China's Elite," *BusinessWeek,* February 11, 2008; "In Korea, Ads Become Must-See TV," *Wall Street Journal,* December 13, 2007; "For Reality Shows in China, Rules Have Never Been Tighter," *Advertising Age,* October 8,

2007. See also Young Sook Moon and George R. Franke, "Cultural Influences on Agency Practitioners' Ethical Perceptions: A Comparison of Korea and the U.S.," *Journal of Advertising,* Spring 2000.

34. "What Bayer Campaign Means for Pharma Ads," *Advertising Age,* February 16, 2009.

35. "FTC Cracks Down on Weight-Loss Product Marketers," *The Wall Street Journal,* January 7, 2014; "Skechers Settles Deceptive Ad Case with FTC for $40M," *Adweek,* May 16, 2012. For more on KFC, see "Hey, Fast Food: We Love You Just the Way You Are," *Brandweek,* November 24, 2003; "FTC Examines Health Claims in KFC's Ads," *Wall Street Journal,* November 19, 2003; "Garfield's Ad Review: KFC Serves Big, Fat Bucket of Nonsense in 'Healthy' Spots," *Advertising Age,* November 3, 2003. See also "The Plug Stops Here," *Next,* November 2, 2009; "Cheerios First in FDA Firing Line. Who's Next?" *Advertising Age,* May 18, 2009; "Health Claims for Cheerios Break Rules, FDA Warns," *Wall Street Journal,* May 13, 2009; "FDA Makes Viagra Feel Blue about Online Ads," *Brandweek,* September 15, 2008.

36. For more on deceptive advertising, see Adam W. Craig, Yuliya Komarova Loureiro, Stacy Wood, and Jennifer M.C. Vendemia, "Suspicious Minds: Exploring Neural Processes During Exposure to Deceptive Advertising," *Journal of Marketing Research,* June 2012; Alison Jing Xu and Robert S. Wyer, Jr., "Puffery in Advertisements: The Effects of Media Context, Communication Norms, and Consumer Knowledge," *Journal of Consumer Research,* 2 (2010). For more on advertising to kids, see Chapter 19; G. R. Milne, A. Rohm, and S. Bahl, "If It's Legal, Is It Acceptable? Consumer Reactions to Online Covert Marketing," *Journal of Advertising,* 4 (2009); Kathy R. Fitzpatrick, "The Legal Challenge of Integrated Marketing Communication (IMC)," *Journal of Advertising,* Winter 2005.

37. "The Goody-Bag Game," *Wall Street Journal,* December 7, 2005; "High Noon in Aisle Five," *Inc.,* January 2004; "P&G Breaks Out of Its Slump," *USA Today,* October 14, 2003; "Ads: Mmm, Junk Mail," *Newsweek,* August 18, 2003; "Road Shows Take Brands to the People," *Wall Street Journal,* May 14, 2003; "Offbeat Marketing Sells," *Investor's Business Daily,* March 27, 2002. For academic research on sales promotion, see Laporte, Sandra, and Gilles Laurent. "More Prizes Are Not Always More Attractive: Factors Increasing Prospective Sweepstakes Participants' Sensitivity to the Number of Prizes." *Journal of the Academy of Marketing Science* 43.3 (2015): 395-410; Pappu, Ravi, and T. Cornwell. "Corporate Sponsorship as an Image Platform: Understanding the Roles of Relationship Fit and Sponsor-sponsee Similarity." *Journal of the Academy of Marketing Science* 42.5 (2014): 490-510; G. Martin-Herran, S. P. Sigue, and G. Zaccour, "The Dilemma of Pull- and Push-Price Promotions," *Journal of Retailing,* 1 (2010); K. L. Ailawadi, J. P. Beauchamp, N. Donthu, D. K. Gauri, and V. Shankar, "Communication and Promotion Decisions in Retailing: A Review and Directions for Future Research," *Journal of Retailing,* 1 (2009); M. Tsiros and D. M. Hardesty, "Ending a Price Promotion: Retracting It in One Step or Phasing It Out Gradually," *Journal of Marketing,* 1 (2010); S. P. Sigue, "Consumer and Retailer Promotions: Who Is Better Off?" *Journal of Retailing,* 4 (2008); R. J. Slotegraaf and K. Pauwels, "The Impact of Brand Equity and Innovation on the Long-Term Effectiveness of Promotions," *Journal of Marketing Research,* 3 (2008); Page Moreau, Aradhna Krishna, and Bari Harlam, "The Manufacturer-Retailer-Consumer Triad: Differing Perceptions Regarding Price Promotions," *Journal of Retailing,* Winter 2001; Devon DelVecchio, David H. Henard, and Traci H. Freling, "The Effect of Sales Promotion on Post-Promotion Brand Preference: A Meta-Analysis," *Journal of Retailing,* September 2006; Kusum L. Ailawadi, Bari A. Harlam, Jacques César, and David Trounce, "Promotion Profitability for a Retailer: The Role of Promotion, Brand, Category, and Store Characteristics," *Journal of Marketing Research,* November 2006; Kusum L. Ailawadi, Karen Gedenk, Christian Lutzky, and Scott A. Neslin, "Decomposition of the Sales Impact of Promotion-Induced Stockpiling," *Journal of Marketing Research,* August 2007.

38. For more on Pampers example, see "P&G Promotion Is Too Successful, Angering Buyers," *Wall Street Journal,* April 2, 2002. For another example, see "Shopper Turns Lots of Pudding into Free Miles," *Wall Street Journal,* January 24, 2000; "The Pudding Guy Flies Again (and Again) over Latin America," *Wall Street Journal,* March 16, 2000.

39. George E. Belch and Michael E. Belch, *Advertising and Promotion: An Integrated Marketing Communication Perspective* (Burr Ridge, IL: McGraw-Hill, 2012); Priya Raghubir, J. Jeffrey Inman, and Hans Grande, "The Three Faces of Consumer Promotions," *California Management Review,* Summer 2004.

40. "BtoB's Best 2009 Marketers & Creative," *BtoB* (Special Issue), Fall 2009; "CEBA Awards," *Brandweek* (Special Section), October 12, 2009; "The Show Goes On: Online Trade Shows," *Wall Street Journal Reports,* April 28, 2003; "The Cyber-Show Must Go On," *Trade Media,* May 7, 2001; "Getting the Most from a Trade Show Booth," *Investor's Business Daily,* April 25, 2000. See also Li Ling-Yee, "Relationship Learning at Trade Shows: Its Antecedents and Consequences," *Industrial Marketing Management,* February 2006; Timothy M. Smith, Srinath Gopalakrishna, and Paul M. Smith, "The Complementary Effect of Trade Shows on Personal Selling," *International Journal of Research in Marketing,* March 2004; Marnik G. Dekimpe, Pierre Francois, Srinath Gopalakrishna, Gary L. Lilien, and Christophe Van den Bulte, "Generalizing about Trade Show Effectiveness: A Cross-National Comparison," *Journal of Marketing,* October 1997; Scott Barlass, "How to Get the Most out of Trade Shows," *Journal of Product Innovation Management,* September 1997; Srinath Gopalakrishna, Gary L. Lilien, Jerome D. Williams, and Ian K. Sequeira, "Do Trade Shows Pay Off?" *Journal of Marketing,* July 1995; "Trade Promotion Rises," *Advertising Age,* April 3, 2000.

41. "Creating Incentives Down in Ranks: Marriott Ties Pay to Guest Replies," *Investor's Business Daily,* July 6, 2001; "Get Great Results from Salespeople by Finding What Really Moves Them," *Investor's Business Daily,* July 2, 2001.

CHAPTER 16

1. Hubspot.com; Martinez-Jerez, F. Asis, Thomas Steenburgh, Jill Avery, and Lisa Brem (2013) "HubSpot: Lower Churn through Greater CHI," Harvard Business School Case Study 9-110–052; Halligan, Brian and Dharmesh Shah (2010) *Inbound Marketing,* John Wiley & Sons, Inc.; Scott, David Meerman (2013), *The New Rules of Marketing and PR,* Wiley; Steenburgh, Thomas, Jill Avery, and Naseem Dahod (2011) "HubSpot: Inbound Marketing and Web 2.0," Harvard Business School Case Study 9-509-049; "Repeat after Me: The Customer Is Always Human," *Inc.,* November 2013; "HubSpot: Inbound Marketing and Web 2.0 (2011)" (2014) Harvard Business School Case Study Flash Forward #6064, November; "HubSpot IPO Taps Into Social Media Advertising Trends," *Investor's Business Daily,* October 9, 2014.

2. Thompson, Debora V., and Prashant Malaviya. "Consumer-Generated Ads: Does Awareness of Advertising Co-Creation Help or Hurt Persuasion?" *Journal of Marketing* 77.3 (2013): 33–47.

3. *Global Trust in Advertising and Brand Messages,* September 2013; The Nielsen Company, this report includes information about cross-country differences in trust. For example, regional differences were observed for trust in various forms of advertising; 75 percent of Latin Americans trust television ads as compared to just 46 percent of Europeans (and 61 percent of North Americans). Latin Americans (58%) are also more likely to trust display ads on mobile phones as compared to only 28 percent of Europeans (and just 35 percent of North Americans). Cross-region differences were less pronounced for sources of earned media.

4. Scott, David Meerman (2015), *The New Rules of Marketing & PR,* New York: Wiley; Scott, David Meerman (2014) *The New Rules of Sales and Service,* New York: Wiley; Handley, Ann (2014) *Everybody Writes: Your Guide to Creating Ridiculously Good Content,* New York: Wiley; Halligan, Brian and Dharmesh Shah (2014) *Inbound Marketing, Revised and Updated,* New York: Wiley.

5. Stephen, Andrew T., and Jeff Galak. "The effects of traditional and social earned media on sales: A study of a microlending marketplace." *Journal of Marketing Research* 49.5 (2012): 624–639. There is a growing body of academic research on word of mouth. See Alexandrov, Aliosha, Bryan Lilly, and Emin Babakus. "The Effects of Social- and Self-motives on the Intentions to Share Positive and Negative Word of Mouth." *Journal of the Academy of Marketing Science* 41.5 (2013): 531–46; Barasch, Alixandra, and Jonah Berger. "Broadcasting and Narrowcasting: How Audience Size Affects What People Share." *Journal of Marketing Research (JMR)* 51.3 (2014): 286–99; Berger, Jonah, and Raghuram Iyengar. "Communication Channels and Word of Mouth: How the Medium Shapes the Message." *Journal of Consumer Research* 40.3 (2013): 567–79; Berger, Jonah. "Word of Mouth and Interpersonal Communication: A Review and Directions for Future Research." *Journal of Consumer Psychology,* 24.4 (2014): 586–607; Chen, Zoey, and Jonah Berger. "When, Why, and How Controversy Causes Conversation." *Journal of Consumer Research* 40.3 (2013): 580–93; Chen, Zoey, and Nicholas H. Lurie. "Temporal Contiguity and Negativity Bias in the Impact of Online Word of Mouth." *Journal of Marketing Research (JMR)* 50.4 (2013): 463–76; He, Stephen X., and Samuel D. Bond. "Why Is the Crowd Divided? Attribution for Dispersion in Online Word of Mouth." *Journal of Consumer Research* 41.6 (2015): 1509–527; He, Stephen X., and Samuel D. Bond. "Word-of-mouth and the Forecasting of Consumption Enjoyment." *Journal of Consumer Psychology,* 23.4 (2013): 464–82; Hennig-Thurau, Thorsten, Caroline Wiertz, and Fabian Feldhaus. "Does Twitter Matter? The Impact of Microblogging Word of Mouth on Consumers' Adoption of New Movies." *Journal of the Academy of Marketing Science* 43.3 (2015): 375–94; Ho-Dac, Nga N., Stephen J. Carson, and William L. Moore. "The Effects of Positive and Negative Online Customer Reviews: Do Brand Strength and Category Maturity Matter?" *Journal of Marketing* 77.6 (2013): 37–53; Libai, Barak, Eitan Muller, and Renana Peres. "Decomposing the Value of Word-of-Mouth Seeding Programs: Acceleration Versus Expansion."*Journal of Marketing Research (JMR)* 50.2 (2013): 161–76; Lovett, Mitchell J., Renana Peres, and Ron Shachar. "On Brands and Word of Mouth." *Journal of Marketing Research (JMR)* 50.4 (2013): 427–44; You, Ya, Gautham G. Vadakkepatt, and Amit M. Joshi. "A Meta-Analysis of Electronic Word-of-Mouth Elasticity." *Journal of Marketing* 79.2 (2015): 19–39; Zhang, Yinlong, Lawrence Feick, and Vikas Mittal. "How Males and Females Differ in Their Likelihood of Transmitting Negative Word of Mouth." *Journal of Consumer Research* 40.6 (2014): 1097–108. There is also research on reviews, for example Anderson, Eric T., and Duncan I. Simester. "Reviews Without a Purchase: Low Ratings, Loyal Customers, and Deception." *Journal of Marketing Research (JMR)* 51.3 (2014): 249–69.

6. Jerath, Kinshuk, Liye Ma, and Young-Hoon Park. "Consumer Click Behavior at a Search Engine: The Role of Keyword Popularity." *Journal of Marketing Research (JMR)* 51.4 (2014): 480–86.

7. Berger, Johan (2013) *Contagious: Why Things Go Viral*, Simon and Shuster; see also Schulze, Christian, Lisa Schöler, and Bernd Skiera. "Not All Fun and Games: Viral Marketing for Utilitarian Products." *Journal of Marketing* 78.1 (2014): 1–19.

8. For more on black hat SEO, see "What is black hat SEO?" *About.com,* http://websearch.about.com/od/seononos/a/spamseo.htm; "Search Engine Optimization," *Wikipedia.com,* https://en.wikipedia.org/wiki/Search_engine_optimization

9. Bob Gilbreath, *The Next Evolution of Marketing*, New York: McGraw-Hill, 2010; "Samsung Mobile Installs 77 Charging Stations at 18 U.S. Colleges and Universities during 2010 Spring Semester to Help Students and Faculty Stay Connected for Free," *Business Wire,* April 17, 2010.

10. Scott, David Meerman (2015), *The New Rules of Marketing & PR*, New York: Wiley; Scott, David Meerman (2014), *The New Rules of Sales and Service*, New York: Wiley; Handley, Ann (2014), *Everybody Writes: Your Guide to Creating Ridiculously Good Content*, New York: Wiley; Halligan, Brian and Dharmesh Shah (2014), *Inbound Marketing, Revised and Updated*, New York: Wiley.

11. Scott, David Meerman (2014) *The New Rules of Sales and Service*, New York: Wiley.

12. Scott, David Meerman (2014) *The New Rules of Sales and Service*, New York: Wiley.

13. Lankow, Jason and Josh Ritchie (2012), *Infographics: The Power of Visual Storytelling*, New York: Wiley.

14. Muniz Jr, Albert M., and Thomas C. O'guinn (2001), "Brand community." *Journal of Consumer Research*; Fournier, S., & Lee, L. (2009), "Getting brand communities right," *Harvard Business Review;* Gruner, Richard, Christian Homburg, and Bryan Lukas. "Firm-hosted Online Brand Communities and New Product Success." *Journal of the Academy of Marketing Science* 42.1 (2014): 29–48; Tian, Kelly, Pookie Sautter, Derek Fisher, Sarah Fischbach, Cuauhtemoc Luna-Nevarez, Kevin Boberg, Jim Kroger, and Richard Vann. "Transforming Health Care: Empowering Therapeutic Communities through Technology-Enhanced Narratives." *Journal of Consumer Research* 41.2 (2014): 237–60.

15. Brodie, Ian (2013) *Email Persuasion*, Fairfax, VA: Rainmaker Publishing; White, Chad (2014), *Email Marketing Rules*, CreateSpace Independent Publishing Platform.

16. "How Southwest Airlines Sold $1.5 Million in Tickets by Posting Four Press Releases Online," Marketing Sherpa, October 27, 2004.

17. "How Marketers Use Online Influencers to Boost Branding Efforts," *Advertising Age*, December 21, 2009; "Big Diaper Makers Square Off," Wall Street Journal, April 13, 2009; Scott, David Meerman (2015), *The New Rules of Marketing & PR*, New York: Wiley.

18. "Wal-Mart's Jim and Laura: The Real Story," *Bloomberg Businessweek*, October 9, 2006.

19. For more on opinion leaders, word-of-mouth publicity, and buzz marketing, see Chapter 5 and: Berger, Jonah, and Eric M Schwartz, "What Drives Immediate and Ongoing Word of Mouth?," *Journal of Marketing Research*, October 2011; Moore, Sarah G, "Some Things Are Better Left Unsaid: How Word-of-Mouth Influences the Storyteller," *Journal of Consumer Research*, #6, 2012; Chen, Yubo, Qi Wang, and Jinhong Xie, "Online Social Interactions: A Natural Experiment on Word of Mouth Versus Observational Learning," *Journal of Marketing Research*, April 2011; Cheema, Amar, and Andrew M Kaikati, "The Effect of Need for Uniqueness on Word of Mouth," *Journal of Marketing Research*, June 2010; Bruce, Norris I, Natasha Zhang Foutz, and Ceren Kolsarici, "Dynamic Effectiveness of Advertising and Word of Mouth in Sequential Distribution of New Products," *Journal of Marketing Research*, August 2012; Trusov, Michael, Anand V Bodapati, and Randolph E Bucklin, "Determining Influential Users in Internet Social Networks," *Journal of Marketing Research*, August 2010; M. Trusov, R. E. Bucklin, and K. Pauwels, "Effects of Word-of-Mouth Versus Traditional Marketing: Findings from an Internet Social Networking Site," *Journal of Marketing*, #5, 2009; C. A. de Matos and C. A. V. Rossi, "Word-of-Mouth Communications in Marketing: A Meta-Analytic Review of the Antecedents and Moderators," *Journal of the Academy of Marketing Science*, #4, 2008; G. Ryu and J. K. Han, "Word-of-Mouth Transmission in Settings with Multiple Opinions: The Impact of Other Opinions on WOM Likelihood and Valence," *Journal of Consumer Psychology*, #3, 2009; D. Godes and D. Mayzlin, "Firm-Created Word-of-Mouth Communication: Evidence from a Field Test," *Marketing Science*, #4, 2009; De Liu, Xianjun Geng, and Andrew B. Whinston, "Optimal Design of Consumer Contests," *Journal of Marketing*, October 2007; Kelly D. Martin and N. Craig Smith, "Commercializing Social Interaction: The Ethics of Stealth Marketing," *Journal of Public Policy & Marketing*, Spring 2008; George R. Milne, Shalini Bahl, and Andrew Rohm, "Toward a Framework for Assessing Covert Marketing Practices," *Journal of Public Policy & Marketing*, Spring 2008; Aviv Shoham and Ayalla Ruvio, "Opinion Leaders and Followers: A Replication and Extension," *Psychology & Marketing*, March 2008.

20. Retail Customer Dissatisfaction Study—2006, Verde Group—Baker Retail Initiative at Wharton, 2006.

21. For more on BzzAgent, see "BzzAgent Seeks to Turn Word of Mouth into a Saleable Medium," *Advertising Age*, February 13, 2006; "Small Firms Turn to Marketing Buzz Agents," *Wall Street Journal*, December 27, 2005.

22. "The selfish truth about word of mouth (why referrals don't happen)" *Seth's Blog*, April 2, 2015.

23. For more on referral programs, see Schmitt, P., Skiera, B., & Van den Bulte, C. (2011). Referral programs and customer value. *Journal of Marketing*, 75(1), 46–59; Garnefeld, Ina, Andreas Eggert, Sabrina V. Helm, and Stephen S. Tax. "Growing Existing Customers' Revenue Streams Through Customer Referral Programs." *Journal of Marketing* 77.4 (2013): 17–32.

24. Clemens F. Köhler, Andrew J. Rohm, Ko de Ruyter, and Martin Wetzels, "Return on Interactivity: The Impact of Online Agents on Newcomer Adjustment," *Journal of Marketing,* March 2011; Feng Zhu and Xiaoquan Zhang, "Impact of Online Consumer Reviews on Sales: The Moderating Role of Product and Consumer Characteristics," *Journal of Marketing,* 2 (2010); James C. Ward and Amy L. Ostrom, "Complaining to the Masses: The Role of Protest Framing in Customer-Created Complaint Websites," *Journal of Consumer Research,* August 2006; Shahana Sen and Dawn Lerman, "Why Are You Telling Me This? An Examination into Negative Consumer Reviews on the Web," *Journal of Interactive Marketing,* Fall 2007; V. Kumar, J. Andrew Petersen, and Robert P. Leone, "How Valuable Is Word of Mouth?" *Harvard Business Review,* October 2007; J. Goldenberg, S. Han, D. R. Lehmann, and J. W. Hong, "The Role of Hubs in the Adoption Process," *Journal of Marketing,* 2 (2009); P. Huang, N. H. Lurie, and S. Mitra, "Searching for Experience on the Web: An Empirical Examination of Consumer Behavior for Search and Experience Goods," *Journal of Marketing,* 2 (2009); sor (see EM14, C15, note 39). For academic research on reviews, see A. M. Weiss, N. H. Lurie, and D. J. Macinnis, "Listening to Strangers: Whose Responses Are Valuable, How Valuable Are They, and Why?" *Journal of Marketing Research,* 4 (2008); V. Dhar and E. A. Chang, "Does Chatter Matter? The Impact of User-Generated Content on Music Sales," *Journal of Interactive Marketing,* 4 (2009); A. Finn, L. M. Wang, and T. Frank, "Attribute Perceptions, Customer Satisfaction and Intention to Recommend E-Services," *Journal of Interactive Marketing,* 3 (2009); E. Keller and B. Fay, "The Role of Advertising in Word of Mouth," *Journal of Advertising Research,* 2 (2009).

25. "How Amazon Is Turning Opinions into Gold," *Business-Week,* October 26, 2009; "What Do You Think?" *Wall Street Journal,* October 12, 2009; "Global Advertising: Consumers Trust Real Friends and Virtual Strangers the Most," *Nielsenwire ,* July 7, 2009;

26. This entire section influenced by Larson, Jeff and Stuart Draper (2015), *Internet Marketing Essentials*, Stukent, Inc. Data in this section from *Social Media Update 2014*, Pew Research Center, January 9, 2015. Research on social media is emerging, for example see Wilcox, Keith, and Andrew T. Stephen. "Are Close Friends the Enemy? Online Social Networks, Self-Esteem, and Self-Control." *Journal of Consumer Research* (2014): S63–76; Yadav, Manjit S., and Paul A. Pavlou. "Marketing in Computer-Mediated Environments: Research Synthesis and New Directions." *Journal of Marketing* 78.1 (2014): 20–40; Schweidel, David A., and Wendy W. Moe. "Listening In on Social Media: A Joint Model of Sentiment and Venue Format Choice." *Journal of Marketing Research (JMR)* 51.4 (2014): 387–402.

27. Data in this section draws largely from *Social Media Update 2014*, Pew Research Center, January 9, 2015.

28. See www.faceook.com, definition drawn from http://whatis.techtarget.com/definition/Facebook.

29. See www.twitter.com, definition draws fromhttp://whatis.techtarget.com/definition/Twitter.

30. see instragram.com.

31. see www.pinterest.com.

32. see www.linkedin.com.

33. see www.hootsuite.com.

34. "31 Cart Abandonment Statistics," *Baymard Institute*, http://goo.gl/gyK8S [May 8, 2015]

35. See "8 Tips for Social Business" at https://hootsuite.com/resources/white-paper/8-tips-for-social-business.

CHAPTER 17

1. www.methodhome.com; *Method Company Booklet,* 2012; "Method Products: Sustainability Innovation as Entrepreneurial Strategy," *Darden Business Publishing*, Case # UVA-ENT-0159; "Method Sold to European Green-Cleaning Rival Ecover," *Advertising Age*, September 4, 2012; "The Seven Obsessions Behind Method," *TriplePundit.com*, October 10, 2011; "Designing Consumer Products for Home: A Case Study," *Padosa*, March 5, 2009; "Home as Corporate Strategy," *Investor Environmental Health Network Case Studies*; "Design Star Method Takes Cue from BK," *Advertising Age*, November 8, 2004; "Rolling Through the Legs of Goliath," *Forbes*, February 2006; "Is Innovation Killing the Soap Business?" *Wall Street Journal*, April 3, 2013; "For the Dishwasher's Sake, Go Easy on the Detergent," *New York Times*, March 12, 2010; "Method Products, Inc.," *Hoover's Company Records*, July 24, 2013; "Eco-friendly Works for Cleaning-Products Firm," *The Washington Post*, March 31, 2013; "Mates Find a Method to Clean Up, Adam Lowry and Eric Ryan Have Combined the Environment, Design, and Great Products," *The Sunday Times (London)*, November 20, 2011; "A Soap Maker Sought Compabability in a Merger Partner," *New York Times*, January 16, 2013.

2. "Car Makers Cut Free Maintenance," *Wall Street Journal,* July 7, 2005; "Detroit's Latest Offer: Pay More, Get Less," *Wall Street Journal,* July 24, 2002; "Sticker Shock: Detroit's Hidden Price Hikes," *Wall Street Journal,* April 10, 2002. For another example involving the car rental industry, see "Car-Rental Agencies Talk of Realistic Total Pricing," *New York Times,* February 10, 2004. See also Srabana Dasgupta, S. Siddarth, and Jorge Silva-Risso, "To Lease or to Buy? A Structural Model of a Consumer's Vehicle and Contract Choice Decisions," *Journal of Marketing Research,* August 2007.

3. David M. Szymanski, Sundar G. Bharadwaj, and P. Rajan Varadarajan, "An Analysis of the Market Share-Profitability Relationship," *Journal of Marketing,* July 1993.

4. "Decision on Lipitor Sets Express Scripts Apart from Its Field," *Investor's Business Daily,* November 7, 2005; "EU Court Backs Resale of Drugs," *Wall Street Journal,* April 2, 2004; "The Telecom Follies," *Wall Street Journal,* March 26, 2004; "It's Time to Look at Rx Pricing," *Modern Healthcare,* March 15, 2004; "The New Drug War," *Fortune,* March 8, 2004; "Rethinking Restructuring," *Public Utilities Fortnightly,* February 2004; "The Economy: Steel Prices Jump, Spurring Protests from Customers," *Wall Street Journal,* January 23, 2004.

5. "Aluminum Firms Offer Wider Discounts but Price Cuts Stop at Some Distributors," *Wall Street Journal,* November 16, 1984. For another example of administered pricing, see "Why a Grand Plan to Cut CD Prices Went off the Track," *Wall Street Journal,* June 4, 2004.

6. Moritz Fleischmann, Joseph M. Hall, and David F. Pyke, "Smart Pricing," *Sloan Management Review,* Winter 2004; ManMohan S. Sodhi and Navdeep S. Sodhi, "Six Sigma Pricing," *Harvard Business Review,* May 2005; Eric Anderson and Duncan Simester, "Mind Your Pricing Cues," *Harvard Business Review,* September 2003; Kissan Joseph, "On the Optimality of Delegating Pricing Authority to the Sales Force," *Journal of Marketing,* January 2001; Michael V. Marn and Robert L. Rosiello, "Managing Price, Gaining Profit," *Harvard Business Review,* September–October 1992; Peter R. Dickson and Joel E. Urbany, "Retailer Reactions to Competitive Price Changes," *Journal of Retailing,* Spring 1994.

7. "Dynamic Pricing: The Future of Ticket Pricing in Sports," *Forbes,* January 6, 2012; "How Dynamic Pricing Is Changing Sports Ticketing," *CNBC,* July 18, 2012; "Pricing Baseball Tickets Like

Airline Seats," *Bloomberg Businessweek,* May 20, 2010. See also Sucharita Chandran and Vicki G. Morwitz, "Effects of Participative Pricing on Consumers' Cognitions and Actions: A Goal Theoretic Perspective," *Journal of Consumer Research,* September 2005; B. T. Ratchford, "Online Pricing: Review and Directions for Research," *Journal of Interactive Marketing,* 1 (2009); Weisstein, Fei, Kent Monroe, and Monika Kukar-Kinney, "Effects of Price Framing on Consumers' Perceptions of Online Dynamic Pricing Practices," *Journal of the Academy of Marketing Science* 41.5 (2013): 501–14.

8. For more on pricing in business markets, see Markus Voeth and Uta Herbst, "Supply-Chain Pricing: A New Perspective on Pricing in Industrial Markets," *Industrial Marketing Management,* January 2006; Howard Forman and James M. Hunt, "Managing the Influence of Internal and External Determinants on International Industrial Pricing Strategies," *Industrial Marketing Management,* February 2005; Eric Matson, "Customizing Prices," *Harvard Business Review,* November–December 1995; Michael H. Morris, "Separate Prices as a Marketing Tool," *Industrial Marketing Management,* May 1987; P. Ronald Stephenson, William L. Cron, and Gary L. Frazier, "Delegating Pricing Authority to the Sales Force: The Effects on Sales and Profit Performance," *Journal of Marketing,* Spring 1979.

9. "Hagglers Thrive in New Economy," *USA Today,* March 16, 2009; "Haggling Starts to Go the Way of the Tail Fin," *BusinessWeek,* October 29, 2007; "Online Stores Charge Different Prices Based on Shoppers' Surfing Habits," *USA Today,* June 2, 2005. For more on Amazon offering different prices to different customers, see "Price? For You, $2; For the Rich Guy, $5," *Investor's Business Daily,* September 29, 2000.

10. "What's a Fair Price for Drugs?" *BusinessWeek,* April 30, 2001; "AIDS Gaffes in Africa Come Back to Haunt Drug Industry at Home," *Wall Street Journal,* April 23, 2001; "Vaccine's Price Drives a Debate about Its Use," *Wall Street Journal,* February 16, 2000. See also Richard A. Spinello, "Ethics, Pricing and the Pharmaceutical Industry," *Journal of Business Ethics,* August 1992; Nicholas H. Lurie and Joydeep Srivastava, "Price-Matching Guarantees and Consumer Evaluations of Price Information," *Journal of Consumer Psychology,* 2005; Bruce McWilliams and Eitan Gerstner, "Offering Low Price Guarantees to Improve Customer Retention," *Journal of Retailing,* June 2006; Sujay Dutta and Abhijit Biswas, "Effects of Low Price Guarantees on Consumer Post-Purchase Search Intention: The Moderating Roles of Value Consciousness and Penalty Level," *Journal of Retailing,* 4 (2005).

11. For information about pricing in the early years of cell phones, see "Mobile Warfare," *Time,* May 26, 1997; "Motorola Goes for the Hard Cell," *BusinessWeek,* September 23, 1996; "Why Motorola Has Nonworking Numbers," *BusinessWeek,* July 22, 1996; "Cell-Phone Service May Be Getting Cheaper," *Wall Street Journal,* January 11, 1996. See also Hongju Liu, "Dynamics of Pricing in the Video Game Console Market: Skimming or Penetration?" *Journal of Marketing Research,* June 2010.

12. "New Features Coming for Blu-ray Format," *USA Today,* March 19, 2008; "Sony's PS3 Gets Boost from Its Blu-ray Drive," *Wall Street Journal,* March 12, 2008; "Getting Back into the Game," *Investor's Business Daily,* December 18, 2006.

13. Check out foreign exchange rates at www.imf.org and www.federalreserve.gov and www.x-rates.com. See also "Small U.S. Firms Make Big Global Sales," *USA Today,* April 7, 2008; "Trade Winds," *Inc.,* November 2003.

14. "Selling Solar Panels on the Installment Plan," *Bloomberg Businessweek,* May 30, 2013.

15. "New Rules Place Barriers between Students, Credit Card Issuers," *U.S. News & World Report,* February 19, 2010; "More Consumers Just Say No to Credit Cards," *USA Today,* February 8, 2010; "The Latest Credit-Card Tricks," *BusinessWeek,* December 28, 2009; "Anger at Overdraft Fees Gets Hotter, Bigger, and Louder," *USA Today,* September 29, 2009. See also Keith Wilcox, Lauren G. Block, and Eric M. Eisenstein, "Leave Home without It? The Effects of Credit Card Debt and Available Credit on Spending," *Journal of Marketing Research;* Promothesh Chatterjee and Randall L. Rose, "Do Payment Mechanisms Change the Way Consumers Perceive Products?" *Journal of Consumer Research,* 6 (2012).

16. "Sale Sale Sale, Today, Everyone Wants a Deal," *USA Today,* April 21, 2010. For more on P&G's everyday low pricing, see "P&G, Others Try New Uses for Coupon-Heavy Media," *Advertising Age,* September 22, 1997; "Move to Drop Coupons Puts Procter & Gamble in Sticky PR Situation," *Wall Street Journal,* April 17, 1997. See also Biswas, Abhijit, Sandeep Bhowmick, Abhijit Guha, and Dhruv Grewal. "Consumer Evaluations of Sale Prices: Role of the Subtraction Principle." *Journal of Marketing* 77.4 (2013): 49–66. Alavi, Sascha, Torsten Bornemann, and Jan Wieseke. "Gambled Price Discounts: A Remedy to the Negative Side Effects of Regular Price Discounts." *Journal of Marketing* 79.2 (2015): 62–78. Andrews, Michelle, Xueming Luo, Zheng Fang, and Jaakko Aspara. "Cause Marketing Effectiveness and the Moderating Role of Price Discounts." *Journal of Marketing* 78.6 (2014): 120–42. Aydinli, Aylin, Marco Bertini, and Anja Lambrecht. "Price Promotion for Emotional Impact." *Journal of Marketing* 78.4 (2014): 80-96. Coulter, Keith S., and Anne L. Roggeveen. "Price Number Relationships and Deal Processing Fluency: The Effects of Approximation Sequences and Number Multiples." *Journal of Marketing Research (JMR)* 51.1 (2014): 69–82. Lee, Leonard, and Claire I. Tsai. "How Price Promotions Influence Postpurchase Consumption Experience over Time." *Journal of Consumer Research* 40.5 (2014): 943–59. Kusum L. Ailawadi, Donald R. Lehmann, and Scott A. Neslin, "Market Response to a Major Policy Change in the Marketing Mix: Learning from Procter & Gamble's Value Pricing Strategy," *Journal of Marketing,* January 2001; Monika Kukar-Kinney and Rockney G. Walters, "Consumer Perceptions of Refund Depth and Competitive Scope in Price-Matching Guarantees: Effects on Store Patronage," *Journal of Retailing,* Fall 2003; P. B. Ellickson and S. Misra, "Supermarket Pricing Strategies," *Marketing Science,* 5 (2008); J. W. Henke, S. Yeniyurt, and C. Zhang, "Supplier Price Concessions: A Longitudinal Empirical Study," *Marketing Letters,* 1 (2009); Ashok K. Lalwani and Kent B. Monroe, "A Reexamination of Frequency Depth Effects in Consumer Price Judgments," *Journal of Consumer Research,* December 2005; Chris Janiszewski and Marcus Cunha Jr., "The Influence of Price Discount Framing on the Evaluation of a Product Bundle," *Journal of Consumer Research,* March 2004; V. Kumar, Vibhas Madan, and Srini S. Srinivasan, "Price Discounts or Coupon Promotions: Does It Matter?" *Journal of Business Research,* September 2004; David Smagalla, "Does Promotional Pricing Grow Future Business?" *Sloan Management Review,* Summer 2004; Priya Raghubir and Joydeep Srivastava, "Effect of Face Value on Product Valuation in Foreign Currencies," *Journal of Consumer Research,* December 2002.

17. For more on slotting fees, see "Kraft Speeds New Product Launch Times," *Advertising Age,* November 18, 2002; "The Hidden Cost of Shelf Space," *BusinessWeek,* April 15, 2002. See also Ramarao Desiraju, "New Product Introductions, Slotting Allowances, and Retailer Discretion," *Journal of Retailing,* Fall 2001; David Balto, "Recent Legal and Regulatory Developments in Slotting Allowances and Category Management," *Journal of Public Policy & Marketing,* Fall 2002; William L. Wilkie, Debra M. Desrochers, and Gregory T. Gundlach, "Marketing Research and Public Policy: The Case of Slotting Fees," *Journal of Public Policy & Marketing,* Fall 2002.

18. For more on coupons, see "Sign In with Pals, Get Better Coupons," *USA Today,* May 14, 2010; "Safeway Delivers Facebook Users Exclusive Coupons," *SN Supermarket News,* October 9, 2009; "A Clip-and-Save Renaissance," *New York Times,* September 24, 2009; "Coupons Are Hot, Clipping Is Not," *Wall Street Journal,* February 25, 2009.

19. "The Real Problem with Rebates," *Primedia,* January 11, 2006; "The Great Rebate Runaround," *BusinessWeek,* December 5, 2005; "Would You Like Some E-Mail with That Pizza? Papa John's,

Blackberry Tie-in," *Advertising Age,* July 11, 2005; "Many Consumers Never Cash in Rebates," *Newsday,* January 23, 2005. See also Luo, Xueming, Michelle Andrews, Yiping Song, and Jaakko Aspara. "Group-Buying Deal Popularity." *Journal of Marketing* 78.2 (2014): 20–33.

20. "Yes, You Can Raise Prices," *Fortune,* March 2, 2009; "Sweetening a Sour Economy: Americans Reach for Small Luxuries . . . ," *USA Today,* February 24, 2009; "Marketers Try to Promote Value without Cheapening Image," *USA Today,* November 17, 2008.

21. "In Cancer Care, Cost Matters," *New York Times,* October 14, 2012; "How Much Would You Pay For A Year Of Life?" *Radiolab,* December 22, 2104; Experts in Chronic Myeloid Leukemia (2013), "Price of drugs for chronic myeloid leukemia (CML), reflection of the unsustainable prices of cancer drugs: perspective of CML experts," *Blood,* May 30, 121, 22; "The Cost of Living," *New York Magazine,* October 20, 2013; "Incredible Prices for Cancer Drugs," *New York Times,* November 12, 2012; "Doctors Blast Ethics of $100,000 Cancer Drugs," *CNN Money,* April 26, 2013; "Pharma Execs Don't Know Why Anyone Is Upset by a $94,500 Miracle Cure," *Bloomberg Businessweek,* June 3, 2015;

22. "Freeze-Dried Berries Heat Up Cereal Duel," *Wall Street Journal,* May 15, 2003; "Garfield's Ad Review: A Few Spoons of Truth Tossed into Special K Red Berries Spot," *Advertising Age,* May 12, 2003.

23. For more on price-quality see Gneezy, Ayelet, Uri Gneezy, and Dominique Olie Lauga. "A Reference-Dependent Model of the Price-Quality Heuristic." *Journal of Marketing Research (JMR)* 51.2 (2014): 153–64. Lalwani, Ashok K., and Sharon Shavitt. "You Get What You Pay For? Self-Construal Influences Price-Quality Judgments." *Journal of Consumer Research* 40.2 (2013): 255–67. For more on free trials see Datta, Hannes, Bram Foubert, and Harald J. Van Heerde. "The Challenge of Retaining Customers Acquired with Free Trials." *Journal of Marketing Research (JMR)* 52.2 (2015): 217–34; Palmeira, Mauricio M., and Joydeep Srivastava. "Free Offer # Cheap Product: A Selective Accessibility Account on the Valuation of Free Offers." *Journal of Consumer Research* 40.4 (2013): 644–56.

24. "Intel Fine Jolts Tech Sector," *Wall Street Journal,* May 14, 2009. See also "Europe Inc. Takes Aim at Price-Fixers," *Business-Week,* November 2, 2009. For an excellent discussion of laws related to pricing, see Louis W. Stern and Thomas L. Eovaldi, *Legal Aspects of Marketing Strategy: Antitrust and Consumer Protection Issues* (Englewood Cliffs, NJ: Prentice-Hall, 1984). See also Joseph P. Guiltinan and Gregory T. Gundlach, "Aggressive and Predatory Pricing: A Framework for Analysis," *Journal of Marketing,* July 1996. For more general research on price fairness see Jin, Liyin, Yanqun He, and Ying Zhang. "How Power States Influence Consumers' Perceptions of Price Unfairness." *Journal of Consumer Research* 40.5 (2014): 818–33. Kan, Christina, Donald R. Lichtenstein, Susan Jung Grant, and Chris Janiszewski. "Strengthening the Influence of Advertised Reference Prices through Information Priming." *Journal of Consumer Research* 40.6 (2014): 1078–096. Rusetski, Alexander, Jonlee Andrews, and Daniel Smith. "Unjustified Prices: Environmental Drivers of Managers' Propensity to Overprice." *Journal of the Academy of Marketing Science* 42.4 (2014): 452–69.

25. Patrick J. Kaufmann, N. Craig Smith, and Gwendolyn K. Ortmeyer, "Deception in Retailer High-Low Pricing: A 'Rule of Reason' Approach," *Journal of Retailing,* Summer 1994.

26. Charlayne Hunter-Gault, "ADM: Who's Next?" *MacNeil/Lehrer Newshour (PBS) (online),* October 15, 1996. Retrieved October 17, 2007.

27. "Century-Old Ban Lifted on Minimum Retail Pricing," *New York Times,* June 29, 2007.

28. Richard L. Pinkerton and Deborah J. Kemp, "The Industrial Buyer and the Robinson-Patman Act," *International Journal of Purchasing & Materials Management,* Winter 1996.

29. "Firms Must Prove Injury from Price Bias to Qualify for Damages, High Court Says," *Wall Street Journal,* May 19, 1981.

30. "Booksellers Say Five Publishers Play Favorites," *Wall Street Journal,* May 27, 1994; Joseph P. Vaccaro and Derek W. F. Coward, "Managerial and Legal Implications of Price Haggling: A Sales Manager's Dilemma," *Journal of Personal Selling & Sales Management,* Summer 1993; John R. Davidson, "FTC, Robinson-Patman and Cooperative Promotion Activities," *Journal of Marketing,* January 1968; L. X. Tarpey, Sr., "Buyer Liability under the Robinson-Patman Act: A Current Appraisal," *Journal of Marketing,* January 1972.

CHAPTER 18

1. http://www.samsung.com/us/video/tvs; "Is now the time to buy a 4K TV?" *CNET,* November 12, 2014; "TVs," *Consumer Reports,* June 2015; "Seoul Fines Six LCD Manufacturers in Price-Fixing Case," *Wall Street Journal,* October 31, 2011; "How Faulty Marketing Has Stalled TV Sales," *Bloomberg Businessweek,* January 20, 2011; "Sony TV Unit Seeks Path to Profitability," *Wall Street Journal,* November 26, 2010; "Sony Pledges to Corral Inventory," *Wall Street Journal,* November 2, 2010; "Samsung Edges Out TV Rivals," *Wall Street Journal,* February 17, 2010; "Sony Swings Back to the Black," *Wall Street Journal,* February 5, 2010; "Sony Bravia Internet Video Brings Social Media to Your 3D TV," *Media Mentalism,* January 15, 2010; "Sony Pins Future on a 3-D-Revival," *Wall Street Journal,* January 7, 2010; "Sony's 3D TV Plans Become Clearer," *PC World,* November 29, 2009; "U.S. Upstart Takes on TV Giants in Price War," *Wall Street Journal,* April 15, 2008; "Sony Teams with Sharp in Flat-Panel LCD Plant," *Investor's Business Daily,* February 27, 2008; "TV Makers Aren't Turned Off by Slump," *Wall Street Journal,* January 29, 2008; "The Picture Gets Fuzzy for TV Deals," *Wall Street Journal,* December 6, 2007; "How Walmart's TV Prices Crushed Rivals," *BusinessWeek,* April 23, 2007; "Flat Panels, Thin Margins," *BusinessWeek,* February 26, 2007; "Hefty Discounting of Flat-Panel TVs Pinches Retailers," *Wall Street Journal,* December 12, 2006; "As Flat-Panel TV Sales Soar, Unlikely Retailers Step In," *Wall Street Journal,* September 21, 2006; "Cheaper Flat-Panel TVs—from PC Makers," *Wall Street Journal,* December 23, 2004; "Texas Instruments Inside?" *BusinessWeek,* December 6, 2004; "Flat TV Prices Are Falling, but . . . Not Low Enough . . . Blame Retailers' Margins," *Wall Street Journal,* November 3, 2004; "Selling TVs at Full Price," *Wall Street Journal,* May 23, 2012; "Low Prices Hurt the Core of Samsung," *International Herald Tribune,* April 15, 2006; "Outlook Brighter for LCDs," *International Herald Tribune,* April 6, 2007; "To Change Its Image and Attract Customers, Samsung Electronics Is Putting On a Show," *New York Times,* September 20, 2004; "Samsung Speeds Up Corporate Dynamism," *Korea Times,* June 7, 2004; "The Samsung Way," *BusinessWeek,* June 16, 2003; "Samsung Electronics: Innovation and Design Strategy," *Asian Case Research Centre,* 2009; "The Paradox of Samsung's Rise," *Harvard Business Review,* July–August 2011.

2. For more on margins see Kusum L. Ailawadi and Bari Harlam, "An Empirical Analysis of the Determinants of Retail Margins: The Role of Store-Brand Share," *Journal of Marketing,* January 2004; Ritu Lohtia, Ramesh Subramaniam, and Rati Lohtia, "Are Pricing Practices in Japanese Channels of Distribution Finally Changing?" *Journal of Marketing Channels,* 1, 2 (2001); Marvin A. Jolson, "A Diagrammatic Model for Merchandising Calculations," *Journal of Retailing,* Summer 1975; C. Davis Fogg and Kent H. Kohnken, "Price-Cost Planning," *Journal of Marketing,* April 1978.

3. Douglas G. Brooks, "Cost Oriented Pricing: A Realistic Solution to a Complicated Problem," *Journal of Marketing,* April 1975; Stephen M. Shugan, "Retail Product-Line Pricing Strategy When Costs and Products Change," *Journal of Retailing,* Spring 2001.

4. For more on break-even analysis, see G. Dean Kortge, "Inverted Breakeven Analysis for Profitable Marketing Decisions," *Industrial Marketing Management,* October 1984; Thomas L. Powers, "Break-even Analysis with Semifixed Costs," *Industrial Marketing Management,* February 1987.

5. Approaches for estimating price-quantity relationships are reviewed in Kent B. Monroe, *Pricing: Making Profitable Decisions* (New York: McGraw-Hill, 2003). See also Michael F. Smith and Indrajit Sinha, "The Impact of Price and Extra Product Promotions on Store Preference," *International Journal of Retail & Distribution Management,* 2 (2000); Michael H. Morris and Mary L. Joyce, "How Marketers Evaluate Price Sensitivity," *Industrial Marketing Management,* May 1988; David E. Griffith and Roland T. Rust, "The Price of Competitiveness in Competitive Pricing," *Journal of the Academy of Marketing Science,* Spring 1997; Robert J. Dolan, "How Do You Know When the Price Is Right?" *Harvard Business Review,* September–October 1995.

6. Robert Carter and David Curry, "Transparent Pricing: Theory, Tests, and Implications for Marketing Practice," *Journal of the Academy of Marketing Science,* November 2010; E. T. Anderson and D. I. Simester, "Does Demand Fall When Customers Perceive that Prices Are Unfair? The Case of Premium Pricing for Large Sizes," *Marketing Science,* 3 (2008); F. Volckner, "The Dual Role of Price: Decomposing Consumers' Reactions to Price," *Journal of the Academy of Marketing Science,* 3 (2008); J. H. Chu, P. Chintagunta, and J. Cebollada, "A Comparison of Within-Household Price Sensitivity across Online and Offline Channels," *Marketing Science,* 2 (2008); Lisa E. Bolton, Hean Tat Keh, and Joseph W. Alba, "How Do Price Fairness Perceptions Differ Across Culture?" *Journal of Marketing Research,* June 2010; Lisa E. Bolton and Joseph W. Alba, "Price Fairness: Good and Service Differences and the Role of Vendor Costs," *Journal of Consumer Research,* August 2006; Lan Xia, Kent B. Monroe, and Jennifer L. Cox, "The Price Is Unfair! A Conceptual Framework of Price Fairness Perceptions," *Journal of Marketing,* October 2004; Narayan Janakiraman, Robert J. Meyer, and Andrea C. Morales, "Spillover Effects: How Consumers Respond to Unexpected Changes in Price and Quality," *Journal of Consumer Research,* October 2006; Shuba Srinivasan, Koen Pauwels, and Vincent Nijs, "Demand-Based Pricing versus Past-Price Dependence: A Cost-Benefit Analysis," *Journal of Marketing,* March 2008; Marc Vanhuele, Gilles Laurent, and Xavier Drèze, "Consumers' Immediate Memory for Prices," *Journal of Consumer Research,* August 2006; Manoj Thomas and Geeta Menon, "When Internal Reference Prices and Price Expectations Diverge: The Role of Confidence," *Journal of Marketing Research,* August 2007; Kirk L. Wakefield and J. Jeffrey Inman, "Situational Price Sensitivity: The Role of Consumption Occasion, Social Context and Income," *Journal of Retailing,* Winter 2003. For the ethics exercise see D. Talukdar, "Cost of Being Poor: Retail Price and Consumer Price Search Differences across Inner-City and Suburban Neighborhoods," *Journal of Consumer Research,* 3 (2008); for more on price sensitivity, see Shane Frederick, "Overestimating Others' Willingness to Pay," *Journal of Consumer Research* 39, #1 (2012), pp. 1–21; Klaus M. Miller, Reto Hofstetter, Harley Krohmer, and Z. John Zhang, "How Should Consumers' Willingness to Pay Be Measured? An Empirical Comparison of State-of-the-Art Approaches," *Journal of Marketing Research,* February 2011; Hong Yuan and Song Han, "The Effects of Consumers' Price Expectations on Sellers' Dynamic Pricing Strategies," *Journal of Marketing Research,* February 2011; Rashmi Adaval and Robert S. Wyer, "Conscious and Nonconscious Comparisons with Price Anchors: Effects on Willingness to Pay for Related and Unrelated Products," *Journal of Marketing Research,* April 2011; Marcus Cunha, Jr., and Jeffrey D. Shulman, "Assimilation and Contrast in Price Evaluations," *Journal of Consumer Research,* 5 (2011); Joanna Phillips Melancon, Stephanie M. Noble, and Charles H. Noble, "Managing Rewards to Enhance Relational Worth," *Journal of the Academy of Marketing Science,* May 2011.

7. "Seeking Perfect Prices, CEO Tears Up the Rules," *Wall Street Journal,* March 27, 2007.

8. Thomas T. Nagle and Reed R. Holder, *The Strategy and Tactics of Pricing* (Englewood Cliffs, NJ: Prentice-Hall, 2002); Andreas Hinterhuber, "Towards Value-Based Pricing—An Integrative Framework for Decision Making," *Industrial Marketing Management,* November 2004; Benson P. Shapiro and Barbara P. Jackson, "Industrial Pricing to Meet Customer Needs," *Harvard Business Review,* November–December 1978; "The Race to the $10 Light Bulb," *BusinessWeek,* May 19, 1980. See also Michael H. Morris and Donald A. Fuller, "Pricing an Industrial Service," *Industrial Marketing Management,* May 1989.

9. For more on auctions, see "Copart: Auctioneer's Web Move Puts It in Fast Lane," *Investor's Business Daily,* June 16, 2004; "Renaissance in Cyberspace," *Wall Street Journal,* November 20, 2003; "Sold! To Save the Farm," *Wall Street Journal,* August 29, 2003. See also Larry R. Smeltzer and Amelia S. Carr, "Electronic Reverse Auctions: Promises, Risks and Conditions for Success," *Industrial Marketing Management,* August 2003; Sandy D. Jap, "An Exploratory Study of the Introduction of Online Reverse Auctions," *Journal of Marketing,* July 2003.

10. "The Price Is Really Right," *BusinessWeek,* March 31, 2003; "New Software Manages Price Cuts," *Investor's Business Daily,* March 31, 2003; "The Power of Optimal Pricing," *Business 2.0,* September 2002; "Priced to Move: Retailers Try to Get Leg Up on Markdowns with New Software," *Wall Street Journal,* August 7, 2001; "The Price Is Right," *Inc.,* July 2001. See also Ashutosh Dixit, Thomas W. Whipple, George M. Zinkhan, and Edward Gailey, "A Taxonomy of Information Technology-Enhanced Pricing Strategies," *Journal of Business Research,* April 2008; Devon DelVecchio, H. Shanker Krishnan, and Daniel C. Smith, "Cents or Percent? The Effects of Promotion Framing on Price Expectations and Choice," *Journal of Marketing,* July 2007; Kelly L. Haws and William O. Bearden, "Dynamic Pricing and Consumer Fairness Perceptions," *Journal of Consumer Research,* October 2006; Tridib Mazumdar, S. P. Raj, and Indrajit Sinha, "Reference Price Research: Review and Propositions," *Journal of Marketing,* October 2005; Michael J. Barone, Kenneth C. Manning, and Paul W. Miniard, "Consumer Response to Retailers' Use of Partially Comparative Pricing," *Journal of Marketing,* July 2004; Chezy Ofir, "Reexamining Latitude of Price Acceptability and Price Thresholds: Predicting Basic Consumer Reaction to Price," *Journal of Consumer Research,* March 2004; Aradhna Krishna, Mary Wagner, Carolyn Yoon, and Rashmi Adaval, "Effects of Extreme-Priced Products on Consumer Reservation Prices," *Journal of Consumer Psychology,* 2006; Sangkil Moon, Gary J. Russell, and Sri Devi Duvvuri, "Profiling the Reference Price Consumer," *Journal of Retailing,* March 2006; John T. Gourville and Youngme Moon, "Managing Price Expectations Through Product Overlap," *Journal of Retailing,* Spring 2004; Marc Vanhuele and Xavier Dreze, "Measuring the Price Knowledge Shoppers Bring to the Store," *Journal of Marketing,* October 2002; Rashmi Adaval and Kent B. Monroe, "Automatic Construction and Use of Contextual Information for Product and Price Evaluations," *Journal of Consumer Research,* March 2002; Joel E. Urbany, Peter R. Dickson, and Alan G. Sawyer, "Insights into Cross- and Within-Store Price Search: Retailer Estimates vs. Consumer Self-Reports," *Journal of Retailing,* Summer 2000; Ronald W. Niedrich, Subhash Sharma, and Douglas H. Wedell, "Reference Price and Price Perceptions: A Comparison of Alternative Models," *Journal of Consumer Research,* December 2001; Erica Mina Okada, "Trade-Ins, Mental Accounting, and Product Replacement Decisions," *Journal of Consumer Research,* March 2001; Aradhna Krishna, Richard Briesch, Donald R. Lehmann, and Hong Yuan, "A Meta-Analysis of the Impact of Price Presentation on Perceived Savings," *Journal of Retailing,* Summer 2002; Valerie A. Taylor and William O. Bearden, "The Effects of Price on Brand Extension Evaluations: The Moderating Role of Extension Similarity," *Journal of the Academy of Marketing Science,* Spring 2002.

11. For a classic example applied to a high-price item, see "Sale of Mink Coats Strays a Fur Piece from the Expected," *Wall Street Journal,* March 21, 1980.

12. "The High Cost of Free," *Fast Company,* October 2009; "The Economics of Giving It Away," *Wall Street Journal,* January

31, 2009; "Would You Pay Money to See Your Favorite Site Ad-Free?" *Advertising Age,* December 8, 2008; "Free! Why $0.00 Is the Future of Business," *Wired Magazine,* March 2008; "Free Love," *Trendwatching.com,* March 2008; "Danger of Free," *ReadWriteWeb,* January 16, 2008. See also J. Y. Kim, M. Natter, and M. Spann, "Pay What You Want: A New Participative Pricing Mechanism," *Journal of Marketing,* 1 (2009); K. Pauwels and A. Weiss, "Moving from Free to Fee: How Online Firms Market to Change Their Business Model Successfully," *Journal of Marketing,* 3 (2008); Dominik Papies, Felix Eggers, and Nils Wlömert, "Music for Free? How Free Ad-Funded Downloads Affect Consumer Choice," *Journal of the Academy of Marketing Science,* September 2012.

13. Franziska Völckner and Julian Hofmann, "The Price-Perceived Quality Relationship: A Meta-Analytic Review and Assessment of Its Determinants," *Marketing Letters,* October 2007; K. Douglas Hoffman, L. W. Turley, and Scott W. Kelley, "Pricing Retail Services," *Journal of Business Research,* December 2002; Steven M. Shugan and Ramarao Desiraju, "Retail Product Line Pricing Strategy When Costs and Products Change," *Journal of Retailing,* Spring 2001; Tung-Zong Chang and Albert R. Wildt, "Impact of Product Information on the Use of Price as a Quality Cue," *Psychology & Marketing,* January 1996; B. P. Shapiro, "The Psychology of Pricing," *Harvard Business Review,* July–August 1968; Lutz Hildebrandt, "The Analysis of Price Competition between Corporate Brands," *International Journal of Research in Marketing,* June 2001.

14. Kenneth C. Manning and David E. Sprott, "Price Endings, Left-Digit Effects, and Choice," *Journal of Consumer Research,* 2 (2009); Keith S. Coulter and Robin A. Coulter, "Distortion of Price Discount Perceptions: The Right Digit Effect," *Journal of Consumer Research,* August 2007; Lee C. Simmons and Robert M. Schindler, "Cultural Superstitions and the Price Endings Used in Chinese Advertising," *Journal of International Marketing,* 2 (2003); Robert M. Schindler and Thomas M. Kibarian, "Image Communicated by the Use of 99 Endings in Advertised Prices," *Journal of Advertising,* Winter 2001; Robert M. Schindler and Patrick N. Kirby, "Patterns of Rightmost Digits Used in Advertised Prices: Implications for Nine-Ending Effects," *Journal of Consumer Research,* September 1997.

15. "P&G's Global Target: Shelves of Tiny Stores," *Wall Street Journal,* July 16, 2007.

16. For examples, see "For Landlords, Jewelry Stores Are Big Gems," *Wall Street Journal,* May 20, 2005; "Diamond Store in the Rough: Opening of De Beers Boutique . . . ," *Wall Street Journal,* May 20, 2005; "Reaching Out to Younger Crowd Works for Tiffany," *USA Today,* February 26, 2004; "Tiffany & Co. Branches Out under an Alias," *Wall Street Journal,* July 23, 2003; "The Cocoon Cracks Open," *Brandweek,* April 28, 2003; "Goodbye, Mr. Goodbar: Chocolate Gets Snob Appeal," *Wall Street Journal,* February 13, 2003. See also Xing Pan, Brian T. Ratchford, and Venkatesh Shankar, "Can Price Dispersion in Online Markets Be Explained by Differences in E-Tailer Service Quality?" *Journal of the Academy of Marketing Science,* Fall 2002; G. Dean Kortge and Patrick A. Okonkwo, "Perceived Value Approach to Pricing," *Industrial Marketing Management,* May 1993.

17. For more on Gillette's complementary pricing, see "Will Frugal Shoppers Still Pay $25 for Razor Blades?" *Wall Street Journal,* October 6, 2008; "How Many Blades Is Enough?" *Fortune,* October 31, 2005; "Gillette's Smooth Bet: Men Will Pay More for Five-Blade Razor," *Wall Street Journal,* September 15, 2005; "Can Gillette Regain Its Edge?" *BusinessWeek,* January 26, 2004.

18. For more on bundling, see "Google, Sun Agree to Bundle Programs," *Investor's Business Daily,* October 5, 2005; "Adobe Turns Page with New Software Line," *Investor's Business Daily,* November 13, 2003; "The Allure of Bundling," *Wall Street Journal,* October 7, 2003; "Dining Out at 32,000 Feet," *Wall Street Journal,* June 3, 2003; "Food Flights," *USA Today,* January 17, 2003. See also Subramanian Balachander, Bikram Ghosh, and Axel Stock, "Why Bundle Discounts Can Be a Profitable Alternative to Competing on Price Promotions," *Marketing Science,* 4 (2010); Haipeng (Allan) Chen, Howard Marmorstein, Michael Tsiros, and Akshay R Rao, "When More Is Less: The Impact of Base Value Neglect on Consumer Preferences for Bonus Packs over Price Discounts," *Journal of Marketing,* July 2012; Uzma Khan and Ravi Dhar, "Price-Framing Effects on the Purchase of Hedonic and Utilitarian Bundles," *Journal of Marketing Research,* December 2010. See also Michael J. Barone and Tirthankar Roy, "Does Exclusivity Always Pay Off? Exclusive Price Promotions and Consumer Response," *Journal of Marketing,* March 2010; Alexander Chernev, "Differentiation and Parity in Assortment Pricing," *Journal of Consumer Research,* August 2006; Bram Foubert and Els Gijsbrechts, "Shopper Response to Bundle Promotions for Packaged Goods," *Journal of Marketing Research,* November 2007; R. Venkatesh and RabikarChatterjee, "Bundling, Unbundling, and Pricing of Multiform Products: The Case of Magazine Content," *Journal of Interactive Marketing,* Spring 2006; Andrea Ovans, "Make a Bundle Bundling," *Harvard Business Review,* November–December 1997; Manjit S. Yadav and Kent B. Monroe, "How Buyers Perceive Savings in a Bundle Price: An Examination of a Bundle's Transaction Value," *Journal of Marketing Research,* August 1993; Dorothy Paun, "When to Bundle or Unbundle Products," *Industrial Marketing Management,* February 1993; "Flying Spirit's 'Dollar Store in the Sky' to Profit," *Wall Street Journal,* November 20, 2012.

19. Mary Anne Raymond, John F. Tanner, Jr., and Jonghoon Kim, "Cost Complexity of Pricing Decisions for Exporters in Developing and Emerging Markets," *Journal of International Marketing,* 3 (2001); Peter E. Connor and Robert K. Hopkins, "Cost Plus What? The Importance of Accurate Profit Calculations in Cost-Plus Agreements," *International Journal of Purchasing & Materials Management,* Spring 1997; Daniel T. Ostas. "Ethics of Contract Pricing," *Journal of Business Ethics,* February 1992.

CHAPTER 19

1. For more on global cell phone adoption, see "Wireless Carriers Facing Hurdles in India, Brazil," *Investor's Business Daily,* February 24, 2010. For more on consumer choice, see Ross D. Petty, "Limiting Product Choice: Innovation, Market Evolution, and Antitrust," *Journal of Public Policy & Marketing,* Fall 2002; Terry Clark, "Moving Mountains to Market: Reflections on Restructuring the Russian Economy," *Business Horizons,* March–April 1994. For more on Tesco, see "Grocery Home Delivery in the UK: Big and Getting Bigger. Why Not the U.S.? *Food Logistics,* April 15, 2014; "Tesco Tries to Catch a U.S. Curveball," *Wall Street Journal,* March 2, 2009; "Tesco Broadens Discount Line as Retailers Fight for Shoppers," *Wall Street Journal,* February 13, 2009; "British Invasion Hits Grocery Stores," *USA Today,* April 7, 2008; "British Supermarket Giant Cooks Up Plans to Go Global," *Wall Street Journal,* July 5, 2001. For more on obesity concerns, see C. L. Ogden, M. D. Carroll, L. R. Curtin, M. M. Lamb, and K. M. Flegal, "Prevalence of High Body Mass Index in U.S. Children and Adolescents, 2007–2008," *Journal of the American Medical Association,* 303, #3 (2010); National Center for Health Statistics, *Health, United States, 2010: With Special Features on Death and Dying* (Hyattsville, MD: U.S. Department of Health and Human Services, 2011); Gina S. Mohr, Donald R. Lichtenstein, and Chris Janiszewski, "The Effect of Marketer-Suggested Serving Size on Consumer Responses: The Unintended Consequences of Consumer Attention to Calorie Information," *Journal of Marketing,* January 2012; Sekar Raju, Priyali Rajagopal, and Timothy J Gilbride, "Marketing Healthful Eating to Children: The Effectiveness of Incentives, Pledges, and Competitions," *Journal of Marketing,* May 2010; Koert Van Ittersum and Brian Wansink, "Plate Size and Color Suggestibility: The Delboeuf Illusion's Bias on Serving and Eating Behavior," *Journal of Consumer Research,* #2 (2012); Tirtha Dhar and Kathy Baylis, "Fast-Food Consumption and the Ban on Advertising Targeting Children: The Quebec Experience," *Journal of Marketing Research,* October 2011; Jennifer J. Argo and Katherine White, "When Do Consumers Eat More? The Role of Appearance Self-Esteem and Food

Packaging Cues," *Journal of Marketing*, March 2012; Caglar Irmak, Beth Vallen, and Stefanie Rosen Robinson. "The Impact of Product Name on Dieters' and Nondieters' Food Evaluations and Consumption," *Journal of Consumer Research*, 2 (2011); Margaret C. Campbell and Gina S. Mohr, "Seeing Is Eating: How and When Activation of a Negative Stereotype Increases Stereotype-Conductive Behavior," *Journal of Consumer Research*, 3 (2011); "Pepsi Brings in the Health Police," *BusinessWeek*, January 25, 2010; "A Revolution in School Lunches Takes Hold," *USA Today*, December 2, 2009; "Taxing the Rich—Foods, That Is," *BusinessWeek*, February 23, 2009; "Obesity of China's Kids Stuns Officials," *USA Today*, January 9, 2007; Debra M. Desrochers and Debra J. Holt, "Children's Exposure to Television Advertising: Implications for Childhood Obesity," *Journal of Public Policy & Marketing*, Fall 2007; Elizabeth S. Moore and Victoria J. Rideout, "The Online Marketing of Food to Children: Is It Just Fun and Games?" *Journal of Public Policy & Marketing*, Fall 2007; Kathleen Seiders and Leonard L. Berry, "Should Business Care About Obesity?" *Sloan Management Review*, Winter 2007; Jaideep Sengupta and Rongrong Zhou, "Understanding Impulsive Eaters' Choice Behaviors: The Motivational Influences of Regulatory Focus," *Journal of Marketing Research*, May 2007; Kelly Geyskens, Mario Pandelaere, Siegfried Dewitte, and Luk Warlop, "The Backdoor to Overconsumption: The Effect of Associating 'Low-Fat' Food with Health References," *Journal of Public Policy & Marketing*, Spring 2007; Pierre Chandon and Brian Wansink, "Is Obesity Caused by Calorie Underestimation? A Psychophysical Model of Meal Size Estimation," *Journal of Marketing Research*, February 2007; Melissa Grills Robinson, Paul N. Bloom, and Nicholas H. Lurie, "Combating Obesity in the Courts: Will Lawsuits Against McDonald's Work?" *Journal of Public Policy & Marketing*, Fall 2005; Kathleen Seiders and Ross D. Petty, "Obesity and the Role of Food Marketing: A Policy Analysis of Issues and Remedies," *Journal of Public Policy & Marketing*, Fall 2004; Brian Wansink and Mike Huckabee, "De-Marketing Obesity," *California Management Review*, Summer 2005. Martin, Kelly D., and Ronald Paul Hill. "Life Satisfaction, Self-Determination, and Consumption Adequacy at the Bottom of the Pyramid." *Journal of Consumer Research* (2013): S78–91. Ordabayeva, Nailya, and Pierre Chandon. "Getting Ahead of the Joneses: When Equality Increases Conspicuous Consumption among Bottom-Tier Consumers." *Journal of Consumer Research* (2014): S48-62. For recent research in marketing on food consumption, see Kidwell, Blair, Jonathan Hasford, and David M. Hardesty. "Emotional Ability Training and Mindful Eating." *Journal of Marketing Research (JMR)* 52.1 (2015): 105–19. Irmak, Caglar, Beth Vallen, and Stefanie Rosen Robinson. "The Impact of Product Name on Dieters' and Nondieters' Food Evaluations and Consumption." *Journal of Consumer Research* (2013): S45–60. Ma, Yu, Kusum L. Ailawadi, and Dhruv Grewal. "Soda Versus Cereal and Sugar Versus Fat: Drivers of Healthful Food Intake and the Impact of Diabetes Diagnosis." *Journal of Marketing* 77.3 (2013): 101-20. Haws, Kelly L., and Karen Page Winterich. "When Value Trumps Health in a Supersized World." *Journal of Marketing* 77.3 (2013): 48–64. Briers, Barbara, and Sandra Laporte. "A Wallet Full of Calories: The Effect of Financial Dissatisfaction on the Desire for Food Energy." *Journal of Marketing Research (JMR)* 50.6 (2013): 767–81. Parker, Jeffrey R., and Donald R. Lehmann. "How and When Grouping Low-Calorie Options Reduces the Benefits of Providing Dish-Specific Calorie Information." *Journal of Consumer Research* 41.1 (2014): 213–35. Pham, Michel Tuan. "Using Consumer Psychology to Fight Obesity." *Journal of Consumer Psychology*, July 2014: 411–12. Wansink, Brian, and Pierre Chandon. "Slim by Design: Redirecting the Accidental Drivers of Mindless Overeating." *Journal of Consumer Psychology*, 24.3 (2014): 413–31.

2. The American Customer Satisfaction Index, www.theacsi.org; "Now Are You Satisfied? The 1998 American Customer Satisfaction Index," *Fortune*, February 16, 1998. See also "Would You Recommend Us?" *BusinessWeek*, January 30, 2006; X. M. Luo and C. Homburg, "Satisfaction, Complaint, and the Stock Value Gap," *Journal of Marketing*, 4 (2008); L. Aksoy, B. Cooil, C. Groening, T. L. Keiningham, and A. Yalcin, "The Long-Term Stock Market Valuation of Customer Satisfaction," *Journal of Marketing*, 4 (2008). Knox, George, and Rutger Van Oest. "Customer Complaints and Recovery Effectiveness: A Customer Base Approach." *Journal of Marketing* 78.5 (2014): 42–57. Rego, Lopo L., Neil A. Morgan, and Claes Fornell. "Reexamining the Market Share—Customer Satisfaction Relationship." *Journal of Marketing* 77.5 (2013): 1–20.

3. Chiara Orsingher, Sara Valentini, and Matteo de Angelis, "A Meta-Analysis of Satisfaction with Complaint Handling in Services," *Journal of the Academy of Marketing Science*, March 2010; Judy Strauss and Donna J. Hill, "Consumer Complaints by E-Mail: An Exploratory Investigation of Corporate Responses and Customer Reactions," *Journal of Interactive Marketing*, Winter 2001; James G. Maxham III and Richard G. Netemeyer, "Modeling Customer Perceptions of Complaint Handling over Time: The Effects of Perceived Justice on Satisfaction and Intent," *Journal of Retailing*, Winter 2002; James G. Maxham III and Richard G. Netemeyer, "A Longitudinal Study of Complaining Customers' Evaluations of Multiple Service Failures and Recovery Efforts," *Journal of Marketing*, October 2002; James G. Maxham III and Richard G. Netemyer, "Firms Reap What They Sow: The Effects of Shared Values and Perceived Organizational Justice on Customers' Evaluations of Complaint Handling," *Journal of Marketing*, January 2003; Michael Brady, "Improving Your Measurement of Customer Satisfaction: A Guide to Creating, Conducting, Analyzing, and Reporting Customer Satisfaction Measurement Programs," *Journal of the Academy of Marketing Science*, Spring 2000; David M. Szymanski, "Customer Satisfaction: A Meta-Analysis of the Empirical Evidence," *Journal of the Academy of Marketing Science*, Winter 2001; Thorsten Hennig-Thurau and Alexander Klee, "The Impact of Customer Satisfaction and Relationship Quality on Customer Retention: A Critical Reassessment and Model Development," *Psychology & Marketing*, December 1997; Scott W. Hansen, Thomas L. Powers, and John E. Swan, "Modeling Industrial Buyer Complaints: Implications for Satisfying and Saving Customers," *Journal of Marketing Theory & Practice*, Fall 1997.

4. Xueming Luo, Christian Homburg, and Jan Wieseke, "Customer Satisfaction, Analyst Stock Recommendations, and Firm Value," *Journal of Marketing Research*, December 2010; Casse Mogilner, Jennifer Aaker, and Sepandar D. Kamvar, "How Happiness Affects Choice," *Journal of Consumer Research*, 2 (2012); Forrest V. Morgeson III, Sunil Mithas, Timothy L. Keiningham, and Lerzan Aksoy, "An Investigation of the Cross-National Determinants of Customer Satisfaction," *Journal of the Academy of Marketing Science*, March 2011; Paul-Valentin Ngobo, Jean-François Casta, and Olivier Ramond, "Is Customer Satisfaction a Relevant Metric for Financial Analysts?" *Journal of the Academy of Marketing Science;* May 2012; Claes Fornell, Roland T. Rust, and Marnik G. Dekimpe, "The Effect of Customer Satisfaction on Consumer Spending Growth," *Journal of Marketing Research*, February 2010; Claes Fornell, Sunil Mithas, Forrest V. Morgeson III, and M. S. Krishnan, "Customer Satisfaction and Stock Prices: High Returns, Low Risk," *Journal of Marketing*, January 2006; Neil A. Morgan, Eugene W. Anderson, and Vikas Mittal, "Understanding Firms' Customer Satisfaction Information Usage," *Journal of Marketing*, July 2005; Eugene W. Anderson, Claes Fornell, and Sanal K. Mazvancheryl, "Customer Satisfaction and Shareholder Value," *Journal of Marketing*, October 2004; Michael Tsirod, Vikas Mittal, and William T. Ross, Jr., "The Role of Attributions in Customer Satisfaction: A Reexamination," *Journal of Consumer Research*, September 2004. For a classic discussion of the problem and mechanics of measuring the efficiency of marketing, see Reavis Cox, *Distribution in a High-Level Economy* (Englewood Cliffs, NJ: Prentice-Hall, 1965).

5. For more on criticisms of advertising, see David C. Vladeck, "Truth and Consequences: The Perils of Half-Truths and Unsubstantiated Health Claims for Dietary Supplements," *Journal of Public Policy & Marketing*, Spring 2000; Barbara J. Phillips, "In Defense of

Advertising: A Social Perspective," *Journal of Business Ethics,* February 1997; Charles Trappey, "A Meta-Analysis of Consumer Choice and Subliminal Advertising," *Psychology & Marketing,* August 1996; Karl A. Boedecker, Fred W. Morgan, and Linda B. Wright, "The Evolution of First Amendment Protection for Commercial Speech," *Journal of Marketing,* January 1995; Thomas C. O'Guinn and L. J. Shrum, "The Role of Television in the Construction of Consumer Reality," *Journal of Consumer Research,* March 1997. See also Robert B. Archibald, Clyde A. Haulman, and Carlisle E. Moody, Jr., "Quality, Price, Advertising, and Published Quality Ratings," *Journal of Consumer Research,* March 1983; M. L. Capella, C. R. Taylor, and C. Webster, "The Effect of Cigarette Advertising Bans on Consumption—A Meta-Analysis," *Journal of Advertising,* 2 (2008).

6. Thomas O. Jones and W. E. Sasser, "Why Satisfied Customers Defect," *Harvard Business Review,* November–December 1995; "The Satisfaction Trap," *Harvard Business Review,* March–April 1996.

7. "Retouching Ruckus Leaves Dove Flailing," *Advertising Age,* May 12, 2008; "For Unilever, P&G, No Good Deed Is Going Unpunished," *Advertising Age,* May 5, 2008; James E. Burroughs and Aric Rindfleisch, "Materialism and Well-Being: A Conflicting Values Perspective," *Journal of Consumer Research,* December 2002; John Watson, Steven Lysonski, Tamara Gillan, and Leslie Raymore, "Cultural Values and Important Processions: A Cross-Cultural Analysis," *Journal of Business Research,* November 2002; Roy F. Baumeister, "Yielding to Temptation: Self-Control Failure, Impulsive Purchasing, and Consumer Behavior," *Journal of Consumer Research,* March 2002; Donald F. Dixon, "The Economics of Conspicuous Consumption: Theory and Thought Since 1700," *Journal of Macromarketing,* 21, #1 (June 2001). See also Michael J. Barone, Randall L. Rose, Kenneth C. Manning, and Paul W. Miniard, "Another Look at the Impact of Reference Information on Consumer Impressions of Nutrition Information," *Journal of Public Policy & Marketing,* Spring 1996; Arnold J. Toynbee, *America and World Revolution* (New York: Oxford University Press, 1966); John Kenneth Galbraith, *Economics and the Public Purpose* (Boston: Houghton Mifflin, 1973). Challagalla, Goutam, Brian R. Murtha, and Bernard Jaworski. "Marketing Doctrine: A Principles-Based Approach to Guiding Marketing Decision Making in Firms." *Journal of Marketing* 78.4 (2014): 4–20.

8. Peter R. Dickson, Paul W. Farris, and Willem J. M. I. Verbeke, "Dynamic Strategic Thinking," *Journal of the Academy of Marketing Science,* Summer 2001; Gloria Barczak, "Analysis for Marketing Planning," *Journal of Product Innovation Management,* September 1997; William A. Sahlman, "How to Write a Great Business Plan," *Harvard Business Review,* July–August 1997; Rita G. McGrath and Ian C. MacMillan, "Discovery-Driven Planning," *Harvard Business Review,* July–August 1995; Jeffrey Elton and Justin Roe, "Bringing Discipline to Project Management," *Harvard Business Review,* March–April 1998; Andrew Campbell and Marcus Alexander, "What's Wrong with Strategy?" *Harvard Business Review,* November–December 1997.

9. "Why Chick-fil-A and Other Brands Aren't Being Bullied," *Bloomberg BusinessWeek,* August 1, 2012.

10. For more on corporate social responsibility, see Chapter 1. See also C. B. Bhattacharya, Sankar Sen, and Daneil Korschun, *Leveraging Corporate Responsibility* (Cambridge: Cambridge University Press); "Tuning In," *Wall Street Journal Magazine,* May 2010; "Smaller, Smarter," *Wall Street Journal,* February 11, 2008; "Her Signal Is Loud and Clear," *Investor's Business Daily,* December 26, 2007; "Behind One Effort to Tap into India's Water Market," *Wall Street Journal,* August 14, 2007; J. Craig Andrews, Richard G. Netemeyer, Scot Burton, D. Paul Moberg, and Ann Christiansen, "Understanding Adolescent Intentions to Smoke: An Examination of Relationships Among Social Influence, Prior Trial Behavior, and Antitobacco Campaign Advertising," *Journal of Marketing,* July 2004; Jill Gabrielle Klein, N. Craig Smith, and Andrew John, "Why We Boycott: Consumer Motivations for Boycott Participation," *Journal of Marketing,* July 2004; Robert V. Kozinets and Jay M.

Handelman, "Adversaries of Consumption: Consumer Movements, Activism, and Ideology," *Journal of Consumer Research,* December 2004; Eric J. Arnould and Jakki J. Mohr, "Dynamic Transformations for Base-of-the-Pyramid Market Clusters," *Journal of the Academy of Marketing Science,* Summer 2005; Jagdip Singh, Jean E. Kilgore, Rama K. Jayanti, Kokil Agarwal, and Ramadesikan R. Gandarvakottai, "What Goes Around Comes Around: Understanding Trust—Value Dilemmas of Market Relationships," *Journal of Public Policy & Marketing,* Spring 2005; Julie M. Donohue and Ernst R. Berndt, "Effects of Direct-to-Consumer Advertising on Medication Choice: The Case of Antidepressants," *Journal of Public Policy & Marketing,* Fall 2004; Ajit M. Menon, Aparna D. Deshpande, Matthew Perri III, and George M. Zinkhan, "Consumers' Attention to the Brief Summary in Print Direct-to-Consumer Advertisements: Perceived Usefulness in Patient–Physician Discussions," *Journal of Public Policy & Marketing,* Fall 2003; Donald A. Fuller and Jacquelyn A. Ottman, "Moderating Unintended Pollution: The Role of Sustainable Product Design," *Journal of Business Research,* November 2004; Marie-Louise Fry and Michael Jay Polonsky, "Examining the Unintended Consequences of Marketing," *Journal of Business Research,* November 2004; Joann Peck and Barbara Loken, "When Will Larger-Sized Female Models in Advertisements Be Viewed Positively? The Moderating Effects of Instructional Frame, Gender, and Need for Cognition," *Psychology & Marketing,* June 2004; Renato J. Orsato, "Competitive Environmental Strategies: When Does It Pay to Be Green?" *California Management Review,* Winter 2006; Jill Meredith Ginsberg and Paul N. Bloom, "Choosing the Right Green Marketing Strategy," *Sloan Management Review,* Fall 2004.

11. "Green Goods, Red Flags," *Wall Street Journal,* April 24, 2010; "Going Truly Green Might Require Detective Work," *USA Today,* April 22, 2010; "Milestones in Green Consuming," *Wall Street Journal,* April 17, 2010; "False 'Green' Ads Draw Global Scrutiny," *Wall Street Journal,* January 30, 2008; TerraChoice Environmental Marketing, www.terrachoice.com; "The Six Sins of Greenwashing," *Inc.,* November 2007; "Most Americans and Canadians Say 'Green' Labeling Just a Marketing Tactic," *GreenBiz.com,* October 2, 2007; Gregory C. Unruh, "The Biosphere Rules," *Harvard Business Review,* February 2008. Catlin, Jesse R., and Yitong Wang. "Recycling Gone Bad: When the Option to Recycle Increases Resource Consumption." *Journal of Consumer Psychology,* 23.1 (2013): 122-27. Leonidou, Constantinos, Constantine Katsikeas, and Neil Morgan. "'Greening' the Marketing Mix: Do Firms Do It and Does It Pay Off?" *Journal of the Academy of Marketing Science* 41.2 (2013): 151-70. Trudel, Remi, and Jennifer J. Argo. "The Effect of Product Size and Form Distortion on Consumer Recycling Behavior." *Journal of Consumer Research* 40.4 (2013): 632-43. White, Katherine, and Bonnie Simpson. "When Do (and Don't) Normative Appeals Influence Sustainable Consumer Behaviors?" *Journal of Marketing* 77.2 (2013): 78-95.

12. For other environmental issues, see "PepsiCo in Recycling Push," *Wall Street Journal,* April 22, 2010; "Best Buy Wants Your Junk," *Fortune,* December 7, 2009; "War on the Water Front," *Time,* December 19, 2005; "Whole Fuels," *Business 2.0,* December 2005; "Is It Too Easy Being Green?" *Wall Street Journal,* October 19, 2005; "Turning Waste into Watts," *Business 2.0,* October 2005; "Getting More Miles to the Gallon—Fast," *BusinessWeek,* September 26, 2005; "It's Easier Being Green," *BusinessWeek,* September 19, 2005; "Automakers Jack Up MPG PDG," *USA Today,* September 16, 2005; "New Incentives for Being Green," *Wall Street Journal,* August 4, 2005; "The Great Windfall," *Business 2.0,* August 2005; "China: Wasteful Ways," *BusinessWeek,* April 11, 2005; "Eco Trends," *BusinessWeek,* March 21, 2005; Anil Menon and Ajay Menon, "Enviropreneurial Marketing Strategy: The Emergence of Corporate Environmentalism as Market Strategy," *Journal of Marketing,* January 1997; William E. Kilbourne, "Green Advertising: Salvation or Oxymoron?" *Journal of Advertising,* Summer 1995.

13. For more on privacy, see "Facebook Draws Protests on Privacy Issue," *USA Today,* May 14, 2010; "Facebook Wants to Know More than Just Who Your Friends Are," *Wall Street Journal,* April 22, 2010; "Friends No More? For Some, Social Networking Has Become Too Much of a Good Thing," *USA Today,* February 10, 2010; "Rogue Marketers Can Mine Your Info on Facebook," *Wired,* January 2010; "Why Facebook Wants Your ID," *BusinessWeek,* December 28, 2009; "Cracking the Code," *USA Today,* April 23, 2009; "Anti-Virus Software Isn't Only Online Security Tool," *USA Today,* April 9, 2008.

14. While the scenarios described are fictional and the brands listed are not necessarily involved in these practices, the activities described are real. Joseph Turow, *The Daily You* (New Haven: Yale University Press, 2011); Lori Andrews, *I Know Who You Are and I Saw What You Did* (New York: Free Press, 2012); Nicolas Negroponte, *Being Digital* (New York: Knopf, 1995).

15. For more on socially responsible and ethical behavior, see www.consumerist.com; "Ordering Ethics Rx for Bedeviled Execs," *Investor's Business Daily,* September 21, 2009; "FTC Criticizes College-Themed Cans in Anheuser-Busch Marketing Efforts," *Wall Street Journal,* August 25, 2009; "Team-Color Bud Cans Leave Colleges Flat," *Wall Street Journal,* August 21, 2009; "To Catch a Corporate Thief," *BusinessWeek,* February 16, 2009; "Consumers Have Allies on the Web," *New York Times,* February 3, 2007; "Alcohol Makers Tread Tricky Path in Marketing to College Students," *USA Today,* November 17, 2005; "The Debate over Doing Good," *BusinessWeek,* August 15, 2005; "Cops of the Global Village," *Fortune,* June 27, 2005; "At Some Retailers, 'Fair Trade' Carries a Very High Cost," *Wall Street Journal,* June 8, 2004; "Drug Ills? Follow the Money," *Brandweek,* February 7, 2005, pp. 24–28; "Car Seats for Eight- Year-Olds," *Wall Street Journal,* January 27, 2005; "Money and Morals at GE," *Fortune,* November 15, 2004; "Nestlé Markets Baby Formula to Hispanic Mothers in U.S.," *Wall Street Journal,* March 4, 2004; "Teaching the Wrong Lesson," *Business 2.0,* November 2003. See also John C. Kozup, Elizabeth H. Creyer, and Scot Burton, "Making Healthful Food Choices: The Influence of Health Claims and Nutrition Information on Consumers' Evaluations of Packaged Food Products and Restaurant Menu Items," *Journal of Marketing,* April 2003; Sankar Sen, Zeynep Gurhan-Canli, and Vicki Morwitz, "Withholding Consumption: A Social Dilemma Perspective on Consumer Boycotts," *Journal of Consumer Research,* December 2001; Steve Hoeffler and Kevin Lane Keller, "Building Brand Equity through Corporate Societal Marketing," *Journal of Public Policy & Marketing,* Spring 2002; Dwane Hal Dean, "Associating the Corporation with a Charitable Event through Sponsorship: Measuring the Effects on Corporate Community Relations," *Journal of Advertising,* Winter 2002; Paul N. Bloom, George R. Milne, and Robert Adler, "Avoiding Misuse of New Information Technologies: Legal and Societal Considerations," *Journal of Marketing,* January 1994; James A. Muncy and Scott J. Vitell, "Consumer Ethics: An Investigation of the Ethical Beliefs of the Final Consumer," *Journal of Business Research,* June 1992; Gene R. Laczniak and Patrick E. Murphy, "Fostering Ethical Marketing Decisions," *Journal of Business Ethics,* April 1991. Korschun, Daniel, C. B. Bhattacharya, and Scott D. Swain. "Corporate Social Responsibility, Customer Orientation, and the Job Performance of Frontline Employees." *Journal of Marketing* 78.3 (2014): 20-37; Homburg, Christian, Marcel Stierl, and Torsten Bornemann. "Corporate Social Responsibility in Business-to-Business Markets: How Organizational Customers Account for Supplier Corporate Social Responsibility Engagement." *Journal of Marketing* 77.6 (2013): 54-72; Chernev, Alexander, and Sean Blair. "Doing Well by Doing Good: The Benevolent Halo of Corporate Social Responsibility." *Journal of Consumer Research* 41.6 (2015): 1412-425. Andrews, J. Craig, Richard G. Netemeyer, Jeremy Kees, and Scot Burton. "How Graphic Visual Health Warnings Affect Young Smokers' Thoughts of Quitting." *Journal of Marketing Research (JMR)* 51.2 (2014): 165-83. Devezer, Berna, David E. Sprott, Eric R. Spangenberg, and Sandor Czellar. "Consumer Well-Being: Effects of Subgoal Failures and Goal Importance." *Journal of Marketing* 78.2 (2014): 118-34. Giesler, Markus, and Ela Veresiu. "Creating the Responsible Consumer: Moralistic Governance Regimes and Consumer Subjectivity." *Journal of Consumer Research* 41.3 (2014): 840-57.

APPENDIX D

1. Revised June, 2015. Hillside Veterinary Clinic Marketing Plan case has been developed as a tool to facilitate student learning and class discussion. The plan is based on a real veterinary clinic, but the names, locations, financial data, and other information used in the plan have been altered to preserve confidentiality. This plan is not intended to serve as a source of primary data or to illustrate effective or ineffective planning. This plan draws on ideas from many former student marketing plans, especially marketing plans created for a real veterinary clinic by Patrick Akers, Kristin Arnal, Betsy Arneil, Sarah Bigum, JennaRae Hall, Ryan Hilgers, Dhania Iman, Heather Jewett, Brad Kaufman, Tim Montano, Robert Mozer, Chantal Pearson, Anna Prendergast, Teresa Rodriguez, Angela Sackett, Bobbi Thorson, and Doan Winkel.

VIDEOCASES

1. "Way to Grow: A Tight Real Estate Market Doesn't Deter Top Chains' Expansion Plans," *Restaurants and Institutions,* July 2005, p. 121.

2. Copyright © by Big Brothers Big Sisters of America. All rights reserved. Used with permission.

Author Index

Company Index

Subject Index